IEEE Standards documents are developed within the Technical Committees of the IEEE Societies and the Standards Coordinating Committees of the IEEE Standards Board. Members of the committees serve voluntarily and without compensation. They are not necessarily members of the Institute. The standards developed within IEEE represent a consensus of the broad expertise on the subject within the Institute as well as those activities outside of IEEE that have expressed an interest in participating in the development of the standard.

Use of an IEEE Standard is wholly voluntary. The existence of an IEEE Standard does not imply that there are no other ways to produce, test, measure, purchase, market, or provide other goods and services related to the scope of the IEEE Standard. Furthermore, the viewpoint expressed at the time a standard is approved and issued is subject to change brought about through developments in the state of the art and comments received from users of the standard. Every IEEE Standard is subjected to review at least every five years for revision or reaffirmation. When a document is more than five years old and has not been reaffirmed, it is reasonable to conclude that its contents, although still of some value, do not wholly reflect the present state of the art. Users are cautioned to check to determine that they have the latest edition of any IEEE Standard.

Comments for revision of IEEE Standards are welcome from any interested party, regardless of membership affiliation with IEEE. Suggestions for changes in documents should be in the form of a proposed change of text, together with appropriate supporting comments.

Interpretations: Occasionally questions may arise regarding the meaning of portions of standards as they relate to specific applications. When the need for interpretations is brought to the attention of IEEE, the Institute will initiate action to prepare appropriate responses. Since IEEE Standards represent a consensus of all concerned interests, it is important to ensure that any interpretation has also received the concurrence of a balance of interests. For this reason IEEE and the members of its technical committees are not able to provide an instant response to interpretation requests except in those cases where the matter has previously received formal consideration.

Comments on standards and requests for interpretations should be addressed to:

Secretary, IEEE Standards Board
445 Hoes Lane
P.O. Box 1331
Piscataway, NJ 08855-1331
USA

IEEE Standards documents are adopted by the Institute of Electrical and Electronics Engineers without regard to whether their adoption may involve patents on articles, materials, or processes. Such adoption does not assume any liability to any patent owner, nor does it assume any obligation whatever to parties adopting the standards documents.

IEEE Software Engineering Standards Collection 1993 Edition

Introduction by
Leonard L. Tripp

For nearly the last 100 years, the Institute of Electrical and Electronics Engineers, Inc. (IEEE) has been involved in the generation and promulgation of standards. IEEE standards represent the formalization of current norms of professional practice through the process of obtaining the consensus of concerned, practicing professionals in the given field. Today, the IEEE Computer Society is the fastest growing area of IEEE standardization efforts.

Software engineering has emerged as a specific engineering field in recent years, and those involved have increasingly recognized the need for standards. As a result, the Computer Society of the IEEE formed a committee to codify these norms of professional software engineering practices into standards. This volume presents 22 software engineering standards approved by the consensus process. Six standards have been added to the collection. They are IEEE Std 1045, IEEE Std 1061, IEEE Std 1074, IEEE Std 1209, IEEE Std 1219, and IEEE Std 1298. IEEE Std 1074 and IEEE Std 1298 provides a basic framework for the software development process from both a development organization and a buyer-developer point of view. IEEE Std 1045 and IEEE Std 1061 address software measurement. IEEE Std 1209 focuses on tools used for software development. IEEE Std 1219 provides a framework for the software maintenance process.

(1) IEEE Std 610.12-1990, Glossary of Software Engineering Terminology
(2) IEEE Std 730-1989, Standard for Software Quality Assurance Plans
(3) IEEE Std 828-1990, Standard for Software Configuration Management Plans
(4) IEEE Std 829-1983, Standard for Software Test Documentation
(5) IEEE Std 830-1984, Guide for Software Requirements Specifications
(6) IEEE Std 982.1-1988, Standard Dictionary of Measures to Produce Reliable Software
(7) IEEE Std 982.2-1988, Guide for the Use of Standard Dictionary of Measures to Produce Reliable Software
(8) IEEE Std 990-1987 (Reaff 1992), Recommended Practice for Ada as a Program Design Language
(9) IEEE Std 1002-1987 (Reaff 1992) Standard Taxonomy for Software Engineering Standards
(10) IEEE Std 1008-1987, Standard for Software Unit Testing
(11) IEEE Std 1012-1987 (Reaff 1992) Standard for Software Verification and Validation
(12) IEEE Std 1016-1987, Recommended Practice for Software Design Descriptions
(13) IEEE Std 1028-1988, Standard for Software Reviews and Audits
(14) IEEE Std 1042-1987, Guide to Software Configuration Management
(15) IEEE Std 1045-1992, Standard for Software Productivity Metrics
(16) IEEE Std 1058.1-1987, Standard for Software Project Management Plans
(17) Draft IEEE Std 1061-1992, Standard for a Software Quality Metrics Methodology
(18) IEEE Std 1063-1987, Standard for Software User Documentation
(19) IEEE Std 1074-1991, Standard for Developing Software Life Cycle Processes
(20) Draft IEEE Std 1209-1992, Recommended Practice for the Evaluation and Selection of CASE Tools
(21) Draft IEEE Std 1219-1992, Standard for Software Maintenance
(22) IEEE Std 1298-1992, (AS 3563.1-1991), Software Quality Management System, Part 1: Requirements

Each IEEE software engineering standard is prepared with two goals in mind:

— The standard shall conform with all other IEEE software engineering; that is, it shall be compatible with and not contradict any of the other existing standards.
— The standard shall be capable of being used without the need to refer to other IEEE standards. Since all IEEE standards are voluntary use in nature, the compliance with one software engineering standard does not require or imply compliance with any other.

Historical Perspective

In 1976, a subgroup under the auspices of the IEEE was formed to develop a software quality assurance standard. The result of the subgroup was IEEE Std 730, Standard for Software Quality Assurance Plans. The standard was first published as a trial-use standard in 1980. It was approved as a full-use standard in 1981. The document was organized around the plan outline:

a) Purpose
b) Reference documents
c) Management
d) Documentation
e) Standards, practice, and conventions
f) Reviews and audits
g) Configuration management
h) Problem reporting and corrective action
i) Tools, techniques, and methodologies
j) Code control
k) Media control
l) Supplier control
m) Records collection, maintenance, and retention

In 1982, IEEE Std 729, Standard Terminology for Software Engineering, (redesignated to IEEE Std 610.12) and IEEE Std 829, Standard for Software Test Documentation were approved. In 1983, IEEE Std 828, Standard for Software Configuration Management Plans and IEEE Std 830, Guide for Software Requirements Specifications were approved. The above foundation has been extended by the completion of IEEE Std 1074, Standard for Developing Software Life Cycle Processes, and IEEE Std 1298, Software Quality Management System, Part 1: Requirements.

Additional standards efforts are underway to build on this foundation. The two principal directions are to:

a) Provide additional tutorial material on existing standards
b) Augment product standards with the associated process standards and associated measurements

Throughout all of this work there have been two themes, the first of which has been consensus. These standards have been averaging a ballot return of over 85%, and over 90% of the returned ballots have been approvals.

The second theme has been timeliness. The best standards in the world will not help if they are not provided in a timely manner. The time from project approval to the resulting standard is slightly over three years. This reflects the efforts to attain the consensus of concerned practicing professionals in the fields.

Synopses of the Standards

The main motivation behind the creation of these IEEE Standards has been to provide recommendations reflecting the state-of-practice in development and maintenance of software. For those who are new to software engineering, these standards are an invaluable source of carefully considered advice, brewed in the cauldron of a consensus process of professional discussion and debate. For those who are on the cutting edge of the field, these standards serve as a baseline against which advances can be communicated and evaluated.

The following are synopses of the standards included in this volume:

IEEE Std 610.12. IEEE Std 610.12 is a revision and redesignation of IEEE Std 729. This standard contains definitions for more than 1000 terms, establishing the basic vocabulary of software engineering. Building on a foundation of American National Standards Institute (ANSI) and International Organization for Standardization (ISO) terms, it promotes clarity and consistency in the vocabulary of software engineering and associated fields.

IEEE Std 730. This standard has legal liability as its basic rationale. It is directed toward the development and maintenance of critical software, that is, where failure could impact safety or cause large financial or social losses. The orientation is toward delineating all of the planned and systematic actions on a particular project that would provide adequate confidence that the software product conforms to established technical requirement.
The standard establishes a required format and a set of minimum contents for software quality assurance plans.

IEEE Std 828. This standard is similar in format to IEEE Std 730, but deals with the more limited subject of software configuration management. The standard identifies requirements for configuration identification, configuration control, configuration status accounting and reporting, and configuration audits and reviews. The implementation of those requirements provides a means by which the evolution of the software product items are recorded, communicated, and controlled. This provides assurance of the integrity and continuity of the software product items as they evolve through the software development and maintenance life cycle.

IEEE Std 829. This standard defines the content and format of eight documents that cover the entire testing process. The test plan prescribes the scope, approach, resources, and schedule of the testing activities. It identifies the items to be tested, the testing tasks to be performed, the personnel responsible for each task, and the risks associated with the plan. Test specification is covered by three document types, while test reporting is covered by four document types. The standard shows the relationships of these documents to one another as they are developed, and to the test process they document.

IEEE Std 830. This guide describes alternate approaches to good practice in the specification of software requirements. To enable the reader to make knowledgeable choices, extensive tutorial material is provided. This guide covers the attributes of a good software requirements specification, as well as specification methodologies and associated formats.

IEEE Std 982.1. This standard provides definitions of selected measures. The measures are intended for use throughout the software development life cycle in order to produce reliable software. The standard does not specify or require the use of any of the measures. Its intent is to describe the individual measures and their use.

IEEE Std 982.2. IEEE Std 982.2 is a companion to IEEE Std 982.1 and provides guidance in the use of the measures in IEEE Std 982.1. It provides information needed by industry to make the best use of IEEE Std 982.1.

IEEE Std 990. This recommended practice provides recommendations reflecting state-of-the-art and alternate approaches to good practice for characteristics of Program Design Languages (PDLs) based on the syntax and semantics of the Ada Programming Language. In this document, these are referred to as Ada PDLs.

IEEE Std 1002. This standard describes the form and content of a software engineering standards taxonomy. It explains the various types of software engineering standards, their functional and external relationships, and the role of various functions participating in the software life cycle. The taxonomy may be used as a method for planning the development or evaluation of standards for an organization. It could also serve as a basis for classifying a set of standards or for organizing a standards manual.

IEEE Std 1008. Software unit testing is a process that includes the performance of test planning, the development of a test set, and the measurement of a test unit against its requirement. Measuring entails the use of sample data to exercise the unit and the comparison of the unit's actual behavior with its required behavior as specified in the units's requirement documentation.
This standard defines an integrated approach to systematic and documented unit testing. The approach uses unit design and unit implementation information, in addition to unit requirements, to determine the completeness of the testing. The standard describes a testing process composed of a hierarchy of phases, activities, and tasks. Further, it defines a minimum set of tasks for each activity, although additional tasks may be added to any activity.

IEEE Std 1012. This standard has a threefold purpose:

a) To provide, for both critical and noncritical software, uniform and minimum requirements for the format and content of Software Verification and Validation Plans (SVVPs).
b) To define, for critical software, specific minimum Verification and Validation (V&V) tasks and their required inputs and outputs that shall be included in SVVPs.
c) To suggest optional V&V tasks to be used to tailor SVVPs as appropriate for the particular V&V effort.

IEEE Std 1016. A software design description is a representation of a software system. It is used as a medium for communicating software design information. This recommended practice describes that documentation of software designs. It specifies the necessary information content and the recommended organization for a software design description.

IEEE Std 1028. Software reviews and audits are a basic part of the ongoing evaluation of software products as they pass along the software development life cycle. This standard provides direction to the reviewer or auditor on the conduct of evaluations. Included are processes applicable to both critical and noncritical software and the procedures required for the execution of reviews and audits.

IEEE Std 1042. The purpose of this guide is to provide guidance in planning Software Configuration Management (SCM) practices that are compatible with IEEE Std 828. The guide focuses on the process of SCM planning and provides a broad perspective for the understanding of software configuration management.

IEEE Std 1045. This standard defines a framework for measuring and reporting productivity of the software process. It focuses on definitions of how to measure software process productivity and what to report when giving productivity results. It is meant for those who want to measure the productivity of the software process for creating code and documentation products.

IEEE Std 1058.1. This standard specifies the format and contents of software project management plans. It does not specify the procedures or techniques to be used in the development of project management plans, nor does it provide examples of project management plans, instead the standard sets a foundation for an organization to build its own set of practices and procedures for developing project management plans.

Draft IEEE Std 1061. This standard provides a methodology for establishing quality requirements and identifying, implementing, analyzing, and validating the process and product of software quality metrics. This standard does not prescribe specific metrics. It does includes examples of metrics together with a complete example of the standard's use.

IEEE Std 1063. This standard provides minimum requirements on the structure and information content of user documentation. It applies primarily to technical substance rather than to style. Users of this standard may develop their own style manual for use within their organizations to implement the requirements of this standard.

IEEE Std 1074. This standard defines the set of activities that constitute the processes that are mandatory for the development and maintenance of software. The management and support processes that continue throughout the entire life cycle, as well as all aspects of the software life cycle from concept exploration through retirement, are covered. Associated input and output information is also provided. Utilization of the processes and their component activities maximizes the benefits to the user when the use of this standard is initiated early in the software life cycle. This standard requires definition of a user's software life cycle and shows its mapping into typical software life cycles. It is not intended to define or imply a software life cycle of its own.

Draft IEEE Std 1209. This recommended practice provides individuals and organizations a process for the evaluation and selection of computer-aided software engineering (CASE) tools. The recommended practice addresses the evaluation and selection of tools supporting software engineering processes including project management processes, development processes, and integral processes.

Draft IEEE Std 1219. This standard defines the process for performing the maintenance of software. It prescribes requirements for process, control, and management of the planning, execution, and documentation of the software maintenance activities.

IEEE Std 1298. This is Australian Standard AS 3563.1-1991. This standard establishes requirements for a software developer's quality management system. It identifies each of the elements of a quality management system to be designed, developed, and maintained by the developer with the objective of ensuring that the software will meet the requirements of a contract, purchase order, or other agreement.

Summary

The evolution of software engineering as a recognized scientific discipline has been rapid, and not always without conflict. The work represented in this volume is an outgrowth of this evolution and represents, in many cases, the resolution of some of the evolutionary conflicts. By seeking the consensus of concerned, practicing professionals in the field, the most up-to-date statements of current norms of professional practice are developed.

Additional software engineering standards and the 22 IEEE standards contained herein will themselves be revisited, no less often than every five years, to ensure their continued applicability. In this way, through timely, consensus-based standards, the IEEE will continue to foster and support the evolution of the software engineering discipline.

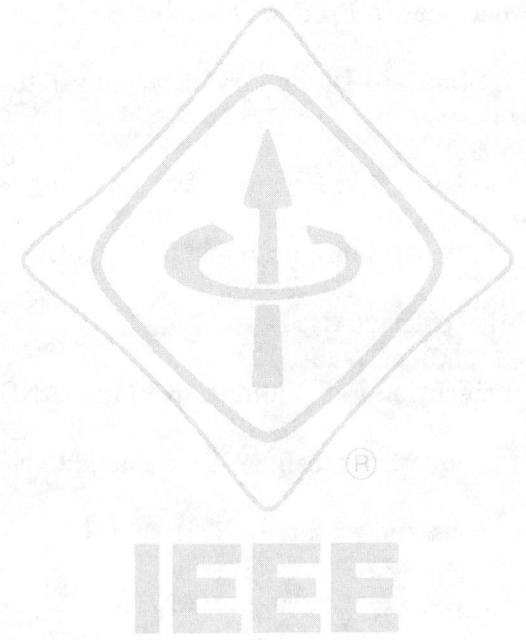

Contents

*Ada is a Registered trademark of the US Government (Ada Joint Program Office).

Recognized as an
American National Standard (ANSI)

IEEE
Std 610.12-1990
(Revision and redesignation of IEEE Std 729-1983)

IEEE Standard Glossary of Software Engineering Terminology

Sponsor

Standards Coordinating Committee of the IEEE Computer Society

Approved September 28, 1990

IEEE Standards Board

Approved February 15, 1991

American National Standards Institute

Abstract: IEEE Std 610.12-1990, *IEEE Standard Glossary of Software Engineering Terminology*, identifies terms currently in use in the field of Software Engineering. Standard definitions for those terms are established.
Keywords: Software engineering; glossary; terminology; definitions; dictionary

Corrected Edition
February, 1991

The Institute of Electrical and Electronics Engineers, Inc.
345 East 47th Street, New York, NY 10017-2394, USA

ISBN 1-55937-067-X

IEEE Standards documents are developed within the Technical Committees of the IEEE Societies and the Standards Coordinating Committees of the IEEE Standards Board. Members of the committees serve voluntarily and without compensation. They are not necessarily members of the Institute. The standards developed within IEEE represent a consensus of the broad expertise on the subject within the Institute as well as those activities outside of IEEE which have expressed an interest in participating in the development of the standard.

Use of an IEEE Standard is wholly voluntary. The existence of an IEEE Standard does not imply that there are no other ways to produce, test, measure, purchase, market, or provide other goods and services related to the scope of the IEEE Standard. Furthermore, the viewpoint expressed at the time a standard is approved and issued is subject to change brought about through developments in the state of the art and comments received from users of the standard. Every IEEE Standard is subjected to review at least once every five years for revision or reaffirmation. When a document is more than five years old, and has not been reaffirmed, it is reasonable to conclude that its contents, although still of some value, do not wholly reflect the present state of the art. Users are cautioned to check to determine that they have the latest edition of any IEEE Standard.

Comments for revision of IEEE Standards are welcome from any interested party, regardless of membership affiliation with IEEE. Suggestions for changes in documents should be in the form of a proposed change of text, together with appropriate supporting comments.

Interpretations: Occasionally questions may arise regarding the meaning of portions of standards as they relate to specific applications. When the need for interpretations is brought to the attention of IEEE, the Institute will initiate action to prepare appropriate responses. Since IEEE Standards represent a consensus of all concerned interests, it is important to ensure that any interpretation has also received the concurrence of a balance of interests. For this reason IEEE and the members of its technical committees are not able to provide an instant response to interpretation requests except in those cases where the matter has previously received formal consideration.

Comments on standards and requests for interpretations should be addressed to:

Secretary, IEEE Standards Board
345 East 47th Street
New York, NY 10017
USA

Foreword

(This Foreword is not a part of IEEE Std 610.12-1990, IEEE Standard Glossary of Software Engineering Terminology.)

The computer field is continuing to expand. New terms are being generated and new meanings are being adopted for existing terms. The IEEE Computer Dictionary project was undertaken to document this vocabulary. Its purpose is to identify terms currently in use in the computer field and to establish standard definitions for these terms. The dictionary is intended to serve as a useful reference for those in the computer field and for those who come into contact with computers either through their work or in their everyday lives.

The dictionary is being developed as a set of subject-area glossaries covering Computer Architecture, Computer Processors, Computer Storage, Software Engineering, Mathematics of Computing, Theory of Computation, Computer Applications, Artificial Intelligence, Data Management, Image Processing and Pattern Recognition, Modeling and Simulation, Computer Graphics, Computer Networking, Computer Languages, and Computer Security and Privacy. This glossary contains the terms related to Software Engineering. It updates IEEE Std 729-1983, IEEE Standard Glossary of Software Engineering Terminology (ANSI).

Every effort has been made to use definitions from established standards in this dictionary. When existing standards were found to be incomplete, unclear, or inconsistent with other entries in the dictionary, however, new, revised, or composite definitions have been developed.

At the time this glossary was approved, the following people formed the steering committee of the Computer Dictionary working group:

Jane Radatz, Chairperson, *Software Engineering Glossary*

Other subgroup leaders:

Anne Geraci
Freny Katki
Dr. John Lane
Louise McMonegal
Bennett Meyer
Dr. Hugh Porteous
Dr. Fredrick Springsteel
Paul Wilson
Mary Yee
John Young

Other working group members who contributed to this glossary were as follows:

Russell J. Abbott
A. Frank Ackerman
Roger R. Baldwin
H. Ronald Berlack
J. David Bezek
James H. Bradley
Kathleen L.Briggs
Homer C. Carney
Susann Chonoles
Taz Daughtrey
Frank J. Douglas
William P. Dupras
John D. Earls
Mary Forcht-Tucker
David Gelperin
Al Gillen
Shirley A. Gloss-Soler
John A. Goetz
David A. Gustafson
Virl Haas
James Ingram
Gary S. Lindsay
Robert McBeth
Alicia McCurdy
Dr. José Muñoz
Geraldine Neidhart
Mary Rasmussen
Max Schindler
Paul Schmid
Leonard W. Seagren
Sonja Peterson Shields
Kevin Smith
Wayne Smith
Paul U. Thompson
Andrew H. Weigel
W. Martin Wong

Special representatives to the Computer Dictionary working group were as follows:

Frank Jay, *Advisor, IEEE Standards Office*

Rollin Mayer, *Liaison, Accredited Standards Committee X3K5*

The following organizations supported employee participation in the development of this standard:

Applied Information Development
Atlantic Consultants
Babcock and Wilcox
Burroughs Wellcome
Carney Associates
Computer Sciences Corporation
Datapoint Corporation
Dutchess Engineering Company
Edinboro University of Pennsylvania
Electronics Design Magazine
Eyring Research Institute
General Electric Company
Harris Corporation
Information Spectrum, Inc.
Institute for Zero Defect Software
International Bureau of Software Test
Kansas State University
Lockheed
Logicon
Marine Midland Bank
The MITRE Corporation
Perkin-Elmer Corporation
Quality Assurance Institute
Rabbitt Software Corporation
RCA
Sanders Associates
SILOGIC
Softran
Teledyne Brown Engineering
University of Wisconsin, Madison
U.S. Naval Facilities
U.S. Dept. of HUD
Wyse Technology

The IEEE 610 working group wishes to acknowledge the contribution of those who developed IEEE Std 729-1983, IEEE Standard Glossary of Software Engineering Terminology (ANSI), which formed the basis for this glossary. The steering committee of this group had the following members:

Shirley A. Gloss-Soler, *Chair*

Russell J. Abbott
Joan P. Bateman
Stephen R. Beason
Milton E. Boyd, Jr.
Kurt F. Fischer
John M. Ives
John J. McKissick, Jr.
Albrecht J. Neumann
John N. Postak
Jane W. Radatz
Marilyn J. Stewart
Alan N. Sukert
Donald A. Woodmancy
David Yablon

The sponsor for the Computer Dictionary project is the IEEE Computer Society Standards Coordinating Committee, which at the time of publication had the following membership:

Harrison Beasley
H. Ronald Berlack
William Billowitch
Richard Boberg
John Boebinger
Paul L. Borrill
Terry Bowen
Elliott Brebner
J. Reese Brown, Jr.
Lin Brown
Fletcher Buckley
Randy Bush
Clyde Camp
Steve Carter
Alan Cobb
Paul Cook
Bill Corwin
Alan Davis
Steven Deller
Bulent Dervisoglu
Bob Donnan
Paul Eastman
D. Vera Edelstein
Tim Elsmore
Dick Evans
Richard Fairley
Wayne Fischer
Kester Fong
David Gelperin
Anne Geraci
Al Gilman
John Graham
Steve Grout
Dave Gustavson
Al Hankinson
Fred Harrison
Chris Haynes
Rick Henderson
Ken Hobday
Scott Hopkinson
John Horch
Russell Housley
Charles Hudson
Marlyn Huckeby
Mike Humphrey
John Hyde
James Isaak
David James
Hal Jespersen
Richard Kalish
Matt Kaltenbach
Hans Karlsson
Freni Katki
Guy Kelley
Kim Kirkpatrick
Bob Knighten
Stanley Krolikoski
John B. Lane
Ron Leckie
Kevin Lewis
William Lidinsky
Donald C. Loughry
Al Lowenstein
Bill Maciejewski
Roger Martin
Philip Marriott
Colin Maunder
John McGrory
Louise McMonegal
Sunil Mehta
Paul Menchini
Jerry Mersky
Bennett Meyer
Louis Miller
James Mollenauer
Jim Mooney
Gary A. Nelson
Tom Pittman
Robert M. Poston
Shlomo Pri-Tal
Jane Radatz
Michael Raynham
Gordon Robinson
Larry Saunders
Richard Schmidt
Norman Schneidewind
Rudolph Schubert
David Schultz
Karen Sheaffer
Basil Sherlund
Sava Sherr
Fred Springsteel
John Starkweather
Dennis Steinauer
Robert Sulgrove
Oryal Tanir
Michael D. Teener
Donn Terry
Pat Thaler
Joseph Toy
Leonard Tripp
Margaret Updike
Eike Waltz
John W. Walz
Camille White-Partain
Les Wibberley
Cynthia Wright
John Young
Jason Zions

The following persons were on the balloting committee that approved this document for submission to the IEEE Standards Board:

Michael Bame
J. P. Barbera
Boris Beizer
Mordechai Ben-Menachem
H. Ronald Berlack
Robert Both
Kathleen L. Briggs
Winsor A. Brown
F. Buckley
Lorie J. Call
T. S. Chow
Won L. Chung
François Coallier
Michael A. Daniels
Taz Daughtrey
Daniel L. Deluna
Claudia Dencker
Bostjan K. Derganc
Merlin Dorfman
William P. Dupras
Robert E. Dwyer
Dr. L. G. Egan
Monte D. Egeland
Steven R. Eisen
John W. Fendrich
Glenn S. Fields
Jarrellann Filsinger
A. M. Foley
Thomas J. Fouser
Anne K. Geraci
Yair Gershkovitch
Edward L. Gibbs
Arthur Gittleman
Shirley A. Gloss-Soler
John A. Goetz
Julio Gonzalez Sanz
Clark Hay
Andrej Grebeno
William E. Hefley
Charles P. Hollocker
Grace M. Hopper
L. Arnold Johnson
Richard M. Karcich
Dr. Ron Kenett
Judy Kerner
R. A. Kessler
Capt. Peter P. Klopfeustein
Tom Kurihara
Lak Ming Lam
John B. Lane
Robert A. C. Lane
Gregory N. Larsen
Burton S. Liebesman
F. C. Lim
Bertil Lindberg
Harold Mains
Henry A. Malec
Philip C. Marriott
Roger J. Martin
Tomoo Matsubara
Ivano Mazzo
Glen A. Meldrum
Gene T. Morun
Hironobu Nagano
Saied Najafi
Geraldine Neidhart
Dennis E. Nickle
S. R. Norman
Tom Parrish
Michael T. Perkins
Ron Pfaff
John W. Young
Charles Plinta
John D. Pope
John N. Postak
I. C. Pyle
Jane Radatz
Gordon T. Ray
Meir Razy
John Reddon
Samuel T. Redwine
R. Waldo Roth
Steven M. Rowan
Frances Ruhlman
Dr. Stephen R. Schach
Hans Schaefer
Max Schindler
Dr. Norman Schneidewind
Wolf A. Schnoege
Greg Schumacher
R. J. Scott-Kerr
Leonard W. Seagren
Robert W. Shillato
David M. Siefert
Harry M. Sneed
Barbara J. Taute Bina
Richard H. Thayer
Terrence L. Tillmanns
Mark-Rene Uchida
Roger van Scoy
Udo Voges
Ralph Wachter
Dolores R. Wallace
John P. Walter
Andrew H. Weigel
Paul Wolfgang
Natalie C. Yopconka
Peter F. Zoll

When the IEEE Standards Board approved this standard on September 28, 1990, it had the following membership:

Contents

IEEE Standard Glossary of Software Engineering Terminology

1. Scope

This glossary defines terms in the field of Software Engineering. Topics covered include addressing; assembling, compiling, linking, loading; computer performance evaluation; configuration management; data types; errors, faults, and failures; evaluation techniques; instruction types; language types; libraries; microprogramming; operating systems; quality attributes; software documentation; software and system testing; software architecture; software development process; software development techniques; and software tools.

Every effort has been made to include all terms that meet these criteria. Terms were excluded if they were considered to be parochial to one group or organization; company proprietary or trademarked; multi-word terms whose meaning could be inferred from the definitions of the component words; or terms whose meaning in the computer field could be directly inferred from their standard English meaning.

This glossary is an update and expansion of IEEE Std 729-1983, IEEE Standard Glossary of Software Engineering Terminology (ANSI) [3].[1] It increases the number of terms from approximately 500 to 1300, and updates or refines the definitions of many terms included in the initial glossary. A few terms that were included in the initial glossary have been moved to other glossaries in the 610 series. Some definitions have been recast in a system, rather than software, context. Every effort has been made to preserve the fine work that went into the initial glossary.

2. Glossary Structure

Entries in the glossary are arranged alphabetically. An entry may consist of a single word, such as "software," a phrase, such as "test case," or an acronym, such as "CM." Phrases are given in their natural order (test plan) rather than in reversed order (plan, test).

Blanks precede all other characters in alphabetizing. Hyphens and slashes are treated as blanks. Alternative spellings are shown in parentheses.

If a term has more than one definition, the definitions are numbered. In most cases, noun definitions are given first, followed by verb and adjective definitions as applicable. Examples, notes, and illustrations have been added to clarify selected definitions.

The following cross-references are used to show a term's relationship to other terms in the dictionary:

- *Contrast with* refers to a term with an opposite or substantially different meaning.
- *Syn* refers to a synonymous term.
- *See also* refers to a related term.
- *See* refers to a preferred term or to a term where the desired definition can be found.

The word "deprecated" indicates a term or definition whose use is discouraged because such use is obsolete, misleading, or ambiguous. "DoD" refers to usage by the U.S. Department of Defense.

3. Definitions for Software Engineering Terms

1GL. Acronym for **first generation language.** *See:* **machine language.**

2GL. Acronym for **second generation language.** *See:* **assembly language.**

3GL. Acronym for **third generation language.** *See:* **high order language.**

4GL. Acronym for **fourth generation language.**

5GL. Acronym for **fifth generation language.**

[1]Numbers in brackets correspond to those in the Bibliography in Section 4.

abend. Abbreviation for **abnormal end.**

abnormal end (abend). Termination of a process prior to completion. *See also:* **abort; exception.**

abort. To terminate a process prior to completion. *See also:* **abend; exception.**

absolute address. An address that is permanently assigned to a device or storage location and that identifies the device or location without the need for translation or calculation. *Syn:* **explicit address; specific address.** *Contrast with:* **relative address; relocatable address; symbolic address.** *See also:* **absolute assembler; absolute code; absolute instruction; absolute loader.**

absolute assembler. An assembler that produces absolute code. *Contrast with:* **relocating assembler.**

absolute code. Code in which all addresses are absolute addresses. *Syn:* **specific code.** *Contrast with:* **relocatable code.**

absolute instruction. A computer instruction in which all addresses are absolute addresses. *See also:* **direct instruction; effective instruction; immediate instruction; indirect instruction.**

absolute loader. A loader that reads absolute machine code into main memory, beginning at the initial address assigned to the code by the assembler or compiler, and performs no address adjustments on the code. *Contrast with:* **relocating loader.**

abstract data type. A data type for which only the properties of the data and the operations to be performed on the data are specified, without concern for how the data will be represented or how the operations will be implemented.

abstraction. (1) A view of an object that focuses on the information relevant to a particular purpose and ignores the remainder of the information. *See also:* **data abstraction.**
(2) The process of formulating a view as in (1).

acceptance criteria. The criteria that a system or component must satisfy in order to be accepted by a user, customer, or other authorized entity. *See also:* **requirement; test criteria.**

acceptance testing. (1) (IEEE Std 1012-1986 [12]) Formal testing conducted to determine whether or not a system satisfies its acceptance criteria and to enable the customer to determine whether or not to accept the system.
(2) Formal testing conducted to enable a user, customer, or other authorized entity to determine whether to accept a system or component.
Contrast with: **development testing.** *See also:* **operational testing; qualification testing.**

accuracy. (1) A qualitative assessment of correctness, or freedom from error.
(2) A quantitative measure of the magnitude of error.
Contrast with: **precision.**

active redundancy. In fault tolerance, the use of redundant elements operating simultaneously to prevent, or permit recovery from, failures. *Contrast with:* **standby redundancy.**

actual instruction.* *See:* **effective instruction.**
* Deprecated.

actual parameter. *See:* **argument (3).**

Ada. *Note:* Ada and other specific computer languages are defined in P610.13 [17].

adaptability. *See:* **flexibility.**

adaptation data. Data used to adapt a program to a given installation site or to given conditions in its operational environment.

adaptation parameter. A variable that is given a specific value to adapt a program to a given installation site or to given conditions in its operational environment; for example, the variable Installation_Site_Latitude.

adaptive maintenance. Software maintenance performed to make a computer program usable in a changed environment.

Contrast with: **corrective maintenance; perfective maintenance.**

address. (1) A number, character, or group of characters that identifies a given device or storage location.
(2) To refer to a device or storage location by an identifying number, character, or group of characters.
See also: **absolute address; effective address; implied addressing; indirect address; relative address; relocatable address; symbolic address; virtual address.**

address field. Any of the fields of a computer instruction that contain addresses, information necessary to derive addresses, or values of operands. *Syn:* **address part.** *Contrast with:* **operation field.**

address format. (1) The number and arrangement of address fields in a computer instruction. *See also:* ***n*-address instruction; *n*-plus-one address instruction.**
(2) The number and arrangement of elements within an address, such as the elements needed to identify a particular channel, device, disk sector, and record in magnetic disk storage.

address modification. Any arithmetic, logical, or syntactic operation performed on an address. *See also:* **effective address; indexed address; relative address; relocatable address.**

address part. *See:* **address field.**

address space. (1) The addresses that a computer program can access. *Note:* In some systems, this may be the set of physical storage locations that a program can access, disjoint from other programs, together with the set of virtual addresses referring to those storage locations, which may be accessible by other programs.
(2) The number of memory locations that a central processing unit can address.

addressing exception. An exception that occurs when a program calculates an address outside the bounds of the storage available to it. *See also:* **data exception; operation exception; overflow exception; protection exception; underflow exception.**

afferent. Pertaining to a flow of data or control from a subordinate module to a superordinate module in a software system. *Contrast with:* **efferent.**

algebraic language. A programming language that permits the construction of statements resembling algebraic expressions, such as $Y = X + 5$. For example, FORTRAN. *See also:* **algorithmic language; list processing language; logic programming language.**

algorithm. (1) A finite set of well-defined rules for the solution of a problem in a finite number of steps; for example, a complete specification of a sequence of arithmetic operations for evaluating sine x to a given precision.
(2) Any sequence of operations for performing a specific task.

algorithmic language. A programming language designed for expressing algorithms; for example, ALGOL. *See also:* **algebraic language; list processing language; logic programming language.**

allocated baseline. In configuration management, the initial approved specifications governing the development of configuration items that are part of a higher level configuration item. *Contrast with:* **developmental configuration; functional baseline; product baseline.** *See also:* **allocated configuration identification.**

allocated configuration identification. In configuration management, the current approved specifications governing the development of configuration items that are part of a higher level configuration item. Each specification defines the functional characteristics that are allocated from those of the higher level configuration item, establishes the tests required to demonstrate achievement of its allocated functional characteristics, delineates necessary interface requirements with other associated configuration items, and establishes design constraints, if any. *Contrast with:* **func-**

tional configuration identification; product configuration identification. *See also:* **allocated baseline.**

allocation. (1) The process of distributing requirements, resources, or other entities among the components of a system or program.
(2) The result of the distribution in (1).

anomaly. (IEEE Std 1012-1986 [12]) Anything observed in the documentation or operation of software that deviates from expectations based on previously verified software products or reference documents.

anticipatory buffering. A buffering technique in which data are stored in a buffer in anticipation of a need for the data. *See also:* **dynamic buffering; simple buffering.**

anticipatory paging. A storage allocation technique in which pages are transferred from auxiliary storage to main storage in anticipation of a need for those pages. *Contrast with:* **demand paging.**

application generator. A code generator that produces programs to solve one or more problems in a particular application area; for example, a payroll generator.

application-oriented language. A computer language with facilities or notations applicable primarily to a single application area; for example, a language for computer-assisted instruction or hardware design. *See also:* **authoring language; specification language; query language.**

application software. Software designed to fulfill specific needs of a user; for example, software for navigation, payroll, or process control. *Contrast with:* **support software; system software.**

architectural design. (1) The process of defining a collection of hardware and software components and their interfaces to establish the framework for the development of a computer system. *See also:* **functional design.**
(2) The result of the process in (1).

architecture. The organizational structure of a system or component. *See also:* **component; module; subprogram; routine.**

argument. (1) An independent variable; for example, the variable *m* in the equation $E = mc^2$.
(2) A specific value of an independent variable; for example, the value $m = 24$ kg.
(3) A constant, variable, or expression used in a call to a software module to specify data or program elements to be passed to that module. *Syn:* **actual parameter.** *Contrast with:* **formal parameter.**

array. An *n*-dimensional ordered set of data items identified by a single name and one or more indices, so that each element of the set is individually addressable. For example, a matrix, table, or vector.

artificial intelligence. *Note:* P610.8 [15] defines terminology pertaining to artificial intelligence.

artificial language. *See:* **formal language.**

assemble. To translate a computer program expressed in an assembly language into its machine language equivalent. *Contrast with:* **compile; disassemble; interpret.**

assemble-and-go. An operating technique in which there are no stops between the assembling, linking, loading, and execution of a computer program.

assembled origin. The address of the initial storage location assigned to a computer program by an assembler, a compiler, or a linkage editor. *Contrast with:* **loaded origin.** *See also:* **offset (1); starting address.**

assembler. A computer program that translates programs expressed in assembly language into their machine language equivalents. *See also:* **absolute assembler; cross-assembler; relocating assembler.** *Contrast with:* **compiler; interpreter.**

assembler code. *See:* **assembly code.**

assembler language. *See:* **assembly language.**

assembly code. Computer instructions and data definitions expressed in a form that can be recognized and processed by an assembler. *Syn:* **assembler code.** *Contrast with:* **compiler code; interpretive code; machine code.**

assembly language. A programming language that corresponds closely to the instruction set of a given computer, allows symbolic naming of operations and addresses, and usually results in a one-to-one translation of program instructions into machine instructions. *Syn:* **assembler language; low level language; second generation language.** *Contrast with:* **fifth generation language; fourth generation language; high order language; machine language.** *Note:* Specific languages are defined in P610.13 [17].

assertion. A logical expression specifying a program state that must exist or a set of conditions that program variables must satisfy at a particular point during program execution. Types include input assertion, loop assertion, output assertion. *See also:* **invariant; proof of correctness.**

assignment statement. A computer program statement that assigns a value to a variable; for example, $Y := X - 5$. *Contrast with:* **control statement; declaration.** *See also:* **clear; initialize; reset.**

atomic type. A data type, each of whose members consists of a single, nondecomposable data item. *Syn:* **primitive type.** *Contrast with:* **composite type.**

attribute. A characteristic of an item; for example, the item's color, size, or type. *See also:* **quality attribute.**

audit. An independent examination of a work product or set of work products to assess compliance with specifications, standards, contractual agreements, or other criteria. *See also:* **functional configuration audit; physical configuration audit.**

authoring language. A high level programming language used to develop courseware for computer-assisted instruction. *See also:* **authoring system.**

authoring system. A programming system that incorporates an authoring language.

automated verification system. (1) A software tool that accepts as input a computer program and a representation of its specification and produces, possibly with human help, a proof or disproof of the correctness of the program.
(2) Any software tool that automates part or all of the verification process.

availability. The degree to which a system or component is operational and accessible when required for use. Often expressed as a probability. *See also:* **error tolerance; fault tolerance; robustness.**

back-to-back testing. Testing in which two or more variants of a program are executed with the same inputs, the outputs are compared, and errors are analyzed in case of discrepancies. *See also:* **mutation testing.**

background. In job scheduling, the computing environment in which low-priority processes or those not requiring user interaction are executed. *Contrast with:* **foreground.** *See also:* **background processing.**

background processing. The execution of a low-priority process while higher priority processes are not using computer resources, or the execution of processes that do not require user interaction. *Contrast with:* **foreground processing.**

backup. (1) A system, component, file, procedure, or person available to replace or help restore a primary item in the event of a failure or externally caused disaster.
(2) To create or designate a system, component, file, procedure, or person as in (1).

backup programmer. The assistant leader of a chief programmer team; responsibilities include contributing significant portions of the software being developed by the team, aiding the chief programmer in reviewing the work of other team members, substituting for the chief programmer when necessary, and having an overall technical understanding of the software being developed. *See also:* **chief programmer.**

backward execution. *See:* **reversible execution.**

backward recovery. (1) The reconstruction of a file to a given state by reversing all changes made to the file since it was in that state.
(2) A type of recovery in which a system, program, database, or other system resource is restored to a previous state in which it can perform required functions.
Contrast with: **forward recovery.**

base address. An address used as a reference point to which a relative address is added to determine the address of the storage location to be accessed. *See also:* **indexed address; relative address; self-relative address.**

baseline. (1) A specification or product that has been formally reviewed and agreed upon, that thereafter serves as the basis for further development, and that can be changed only through formal change control procedures.
(2) A document or a set of such documents formally designated and fixed at a specific time during the life cycle of a configuration item. *Note:* Baselines, plus approved changes from those baselines, constitute the current configuration identification. *See also:* **allocated baseline; developmental configuration; functional baseline; product baseline.**
(3) Any agreement or result designated and fixed at a given time, from which changes require justification and approval.

baseline management. In configuration management, the application of technical and administrative direction to designate the documents and changes to those documents that formally identify and establish baselines at specific times during the life cycle of a configuration item.

batch. Pertaining to a system or mode of operation in which inputs are collected and processed all at one time, rather than being processed as they arrive, and a job, once started, proceeds to completion without additional input or user interaction. *Contrast with:* **conversational; interactive; on-line; real time.**

bathtub curve. A graph of the number of failures in a system or component as a function of time. The name is derived from the usual shape of the graph: a period of decreasing failures (the early-failure period), followed by a relatively steady period (the constant-failure period), followed by a period of increasing failures (the wearout-failure period).

benchmark. (1) A standard against which measurements or comparisons can be made.
(2) A procedure, problem, or test that can be used to compare systems or components to each other or to a standard as in (1).
(3) A recovery file.

big-bang testing. A type of integration testing in which software elements, hardware elements, or both are combined all at once into an overall system, rather than in stages.

binary digit (bit). (1) A unit of information that can be represented by either a zero or a one.
(2) An element of computer storage that can hold a unit of information as in (1).
(3) A numeral used to represent one of the two digits in the binary numeration system; zero (0) or one (1).
See also: **byte; word.**

bind. To assign a value to an identifier. For example, to assign a value to a parameter or to assign an absolute address to a symbolic address in a computer program. *See also:* **dynamic binding; static binding.**

bit. Acronym for **binary digit.**

bit steering. A microprogramming technique in which the meaning of a field in a microinstruction is dependent on the value of another field in the microinstruction. *Syn:* **immediate control.** *Contrast with:* **residual control.** *See also:* **two-level encoding.**

black box. (1) A system or component whose inputs, outputs, and general function are

known but whose contents or implementation are unknown or irrelevant. *Contrast with:* **glass box.**
(2) Pertaining to an approach that treats a system or component as in (1). *See also:* **encapsulation.**

black-box testing. *See:* **functional testing (1).**

block. (1) A group of contiguous storage locations, computer program statements, records, words, characters, or bits that are treated as a unit. *See also:* **block-structured language; delimiter.**
(2) To form a group as in (1). *Contrast with:* **deblock.**

block allocation. *See:* **paging (1).**

block diagram. A diagram of a system, computer, or device in which the principal parts are represented by suitably annotated geometrical figures to show both the functions of the parts and their functional relationships. *Syn:* **configuration diagram; system resources chart.** *See also:* **box diagram; bubble chart; flowchart; graph; input-process-output chart; structure chart.**

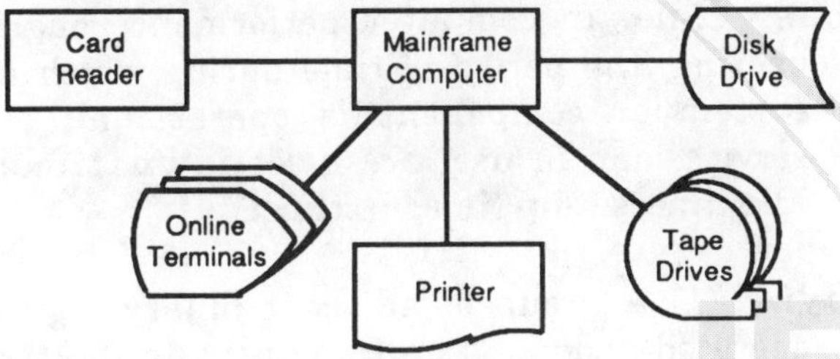

Fig 1
Block Diagram

block-structured language. A design or programming language in which sequences of statements, called blocks, are defined, usually with begin and end delimiters, and variables or labels defined in one block are not recognized outside that block. Examples include **Ada, ALGOL, PL/I.** *See also:* **structured programming language.**

blocking factor. The number of records, words, characters, or bits in a block.

boot. To initialize a computer system by clearing memory and reloading the operating system. Derived from **bootstrap.**

bootstrap. (1) A short computer program that is permanently resident or easily loaded into a computer and whose execution brings a larger program, such as an operating system or its loader, into memory.
(2) To use a program as in (1). *Syn:* **initial program load.**

bootstrap loader. A short computer program used to load a bootstrap.

bottom-up. Pertaining to an activity that starts with the lowest-level components of a hierarchy and proceeds through progressively higher levels; for example, bottom-up design; bottom-up testing. *Contrast with:* **top-down.** *See also:* **critical piece first.**

boundary value. A data value that corresponds to a minimum or maximum input, internal, or output value specified for a system or component. *See also:* **stress testing.**

box diagram. A control flow diagram consisting of a rectangle that is subdivided to show sequential steps, if-then-else conditions, repetition, and case conditions. *Syn:* **Chapin chart; Nassi-Shneiderman chart; program structure diagram.** *See also:* **block diagram; bubble chart; flowchart; graph; input-process-output chart; program structure diagram; structure chart.**

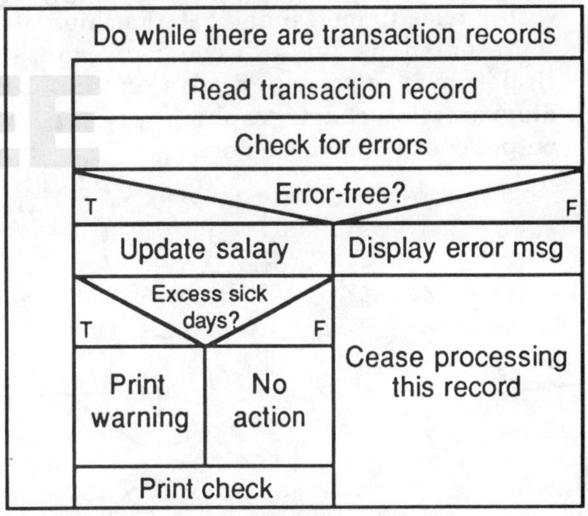

Fig 2
Box Diagram

branch. (1) A computer program construct in which one of two or more alternative sets of

program statements is selected for execution. *See also:* **case; jump; go to; if-then-else.**
(2) A point in a computer program at which one of two or more alternative sets of program statements is selected for execution. *Syn:* **branchpoint.**
(3) Any of the alternative sets of program statements in (1).
(4) To perform the selection in (1).

branch testing. Testing designed to execute each outcome of each decision point in a computer program. *Contrast with:* **path testing; statement testing.**

branchpoint. *See:* **branch (2).**

breakpoint. A point in a computer program at which execution can be suspended to permit manual or automated monitoring of program performance or results. Types include code breakpoint, data breakpoint, dynamic breakpoint, epilog breakpoint, programmable breakpoint, prolog breakpoint, static breakpoint. *Note:* A breakpoint is said to be set when both a point in the program and an event that will cause suspension of execution at that point are defined; it is said to be initiated when program execution is suspended.

bubble chart. A data flow, data structure, or other diagram in which entities are depicted with circles (bubbles) and relationships are represented by links drawn between the circles. *See also:* **block diagram; box diagram; flowchart; graph; input-process-output chart; structure chart.**

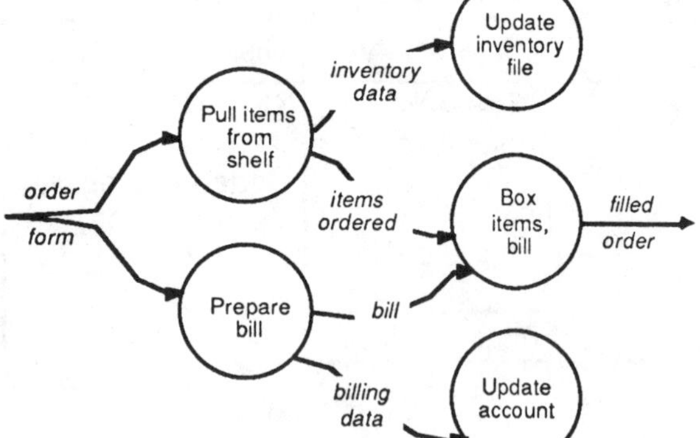

Fig 3
Bubble Chart

buffer. (1) A device or storage area used to store data temporarily to compensate for differences in rates of data flow, time of occurrence of events, or amounts of data that can be handled by the devices or processes involved in the transfer or use of the data.
(2) A routine that accomplishes the objectives in (1).
(3) To allocate, schedule, or use devices or storage areas as in (1). *See also:* **anticipatory buffering; dynamic buffering; simple buffering.**

bug. *See:* **error; fault.**

bug seeding. *See:* **error seeding.**

build. An operational version of a system or component that incorporates a specified subset of the capabilities that the final product will provide.

burn-in period. *See:* **early-failure period.**

busy. Pertaining to a system or component that is operational, in service, and in use. *See also:* **down; idle; up.**

busy time. In computer performance engineering, the period of time during which a system or component is operational, in service, and in use. *See also:* **down time; idle time; set-up time; up time.**

byte. (1) A group of adjacent binary digits operated upon as a unit and usually shorter than a computer word (frequently connotes a group of eight bits).
(2) An element of computer storage that can hold a group of bits as in (1).
See also: **bit; word.**

call. (1) A transfer of control from one software module to another, usually with the implication that control will be returned to the calling module. *Contrast with:* **go to.**
(2) A computer instruction that transfers control from one software module to another as in (1) and, often, specifies the parameters to be passed to and from the module.
(3) To transfer control from one software module to another as in (1) and, often, to pass

parameters to the other module. *Syn:* **cue.**
See also: **call by name; call by reference; call by value; call list; calling sequence.**

call by address. *See:* **call by reference.**

call by location. *See:* **call by reference.**

call by name. A method for passing parameters, in which the calling module provides to the called module a symbolic expression representing the parameter to be passed, and a service routine evaluates the expression and provides the resulting value to the called module. *Note:* Because the expression is evaluated each time its corresponding formal parameter is used in the called module, the value of the parameter may change during the execution of the called module. *Contrast with:* **call by reference; call by value.**

call by reference. A method for passing parameters, in which the calling module provides to the called module the address of the parameter to be passed. *Note:* With this method, the called module has the ability to change the value of the parameter stored by the calling module. *Syn:* **call by address; call by location.** *Contrast with:* **call by name; call by value.**

call by value. A method of passing parameters, in which the calling module provides to the called module the actual value of the parameter to be passed. *Note:* With this method, the called module cannot change the value of the parameter as stored by the calling module. *Contrast with:* **call by name; call by reference.**

call graph. A diagram that identifies the modules in a system or computer program and shows which modules call one another. *Note:* The result is not necessarily the same as that shown in a structure chart. *Syn:* **call tree; tier chart.** *Contrast with:* **structure chart.** *See also:* **control flow diagram; data flow diagram; data structure diagram; state diagram.**

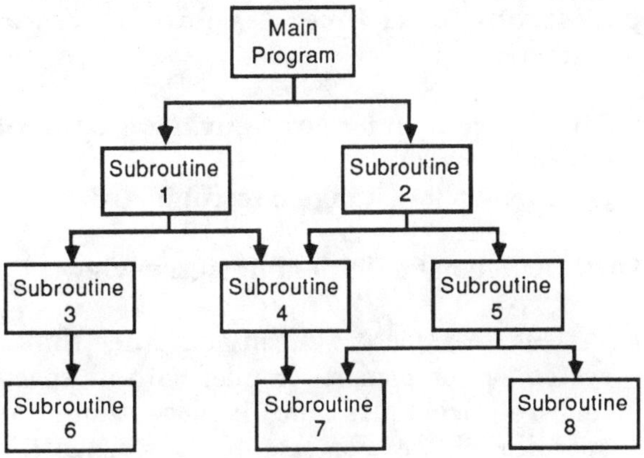

Fig 4
Call Graph

call list. The ordered list of arguments used in a call to a software module.

call trace. *See:* **subroutine trace.**

call tree. *See:* **call graph.**

calling sequence. A sequence of computer instructions and, possibly, data necessary to perform a call to another module.

CASE. Acronym for **computer-aided software engineering.**

case. A single-entry, single-exit multiple-way branch that defines a control expression, specifies the processing to be performed for each value of the control expression, and returns control in all instances to the statement immediately following the overall construct. *Syn:* **multiple exclusive selective construct.** *Contrast with:* **go to; jump; if-then-else.** *See also:* **multiple inclusive selective construct.**

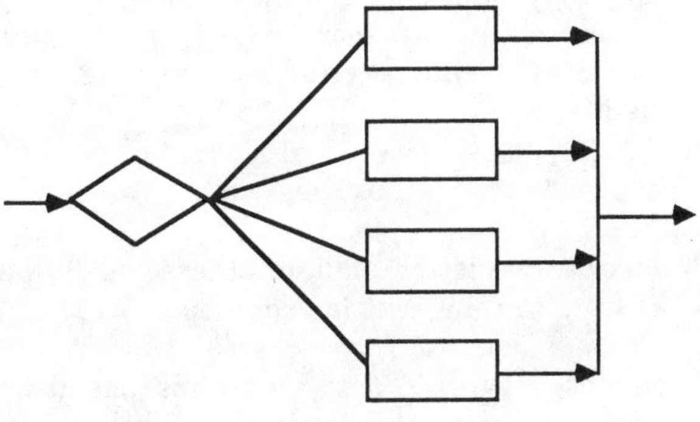

Fig 5
Case Construct

catastrophic failure. A failure of critical software.

CCB. (1) Acronym for **configuration control board.**
(2) Acronym for **change control board.**

CDR. Acronym for **critical design review.**

certification. (1) A written guarantee that a system or component complies with its specified requirements and is acceptable for operational use. For example, a written authorization that a computer system is secure and is permitted to operate in a defined environment.
(2) A formal demonstration that a system or component complies with its specified requirements and is acceptable for operational use.
(3) The process of confirming that a system or component complies with its specified requirements and is acceptable for operational use.

change control. *See:* **configuration control.**

change control board. *See:* **configuration control board.**

change dump. A selective dump of those storage locations whose contents have changed since some specified time or event. *Syn:* **differential dump.** *See also:* **dynamic dump; memory dump; postmortem dump; selective dump; snapshot dump; static dump.**

channel capacity. The maximum amount of information that can be transferred on a given channel per unit of time; usually measured in bits per second or in baud. *See also:* **memory capacity; storage capacity.**

Chapin chart. *See:* **box diagram.**

character. A letter, digit, or other symbol that is used to represent information.

character type. A data type whose members can assume the values of specified characters and can be operated on by character operators, such as concatenation. *Contrast with:* **enumeration type; integer type; logical type; real type.**

characteristic. (IEEE Std 1008-1987 [10]) *See:* **data characteristic; software characteristic.**

checkout. Testing conducted in the operational or support environment to ensure that a software product performs as required after installation.

checkpoint. A point in a computer program at which program state, status, or results are checked or recorded.

chief programmer. The leader of a chief programmer team; a senior-level programmer whose responsibilities include producing key portions of the software assigned to the team, coordinating the activities of the team, reviewing the work of the other team members, and having an overall technical understanding of the software being developed. *See also:* **backup programmer; chief programmer team.**

chief programmer team. A software development group that consists of a chief programmer, a backup programmer, a secretary/librarian, and additional programmers and specialists as needed, and that employs procedures designed to enhance group communication and to make optimum use of each member's skills. *See also:* **backup programmer; chief programmer; egoless programming.**

CI. Acronym for **configuration item.**

clear. To set a variable, register, or other storage location to zero, blank, or other null value. *See also:* **initialize; reset.**

closed loop. A loop that has no exit and whose execution can be interrupted only by intervention from outside the computer program or procedure in which the loop is located. *Contrast with:* **UNTIL; WHILE.**

closed subroutine. A subroutine that is stored at one given location rather than being copied into a computer program at each place that it is called. *Contrast with:* **open subroutine.**

CM. Acronym for **configuration management.**

code. (1) In software engineering, computer instructions and data definitions expressed in a programming language or in a form output by an assembler, compiler, or other translator. *See also:* **source code; object code; machine code; microcode.**
(2) To express a computer program in a programming language.
(3) A character or bit pattern that is assigned a particular meaning; for example, a status code.

code breakpoint. A breakpoint that is initiated upon execution of a given computer instruction. *Syn:* **control breakpoint.** *Contrast with:* **data breakpoint.** *See also:* **dynamic breakpoint; epilog breakpoint; programmable breakpoint; prolog breakpoint; static breakpoint.**

code generator. (1) A routine, often part of a compiler, that transforms a computer program from some intermediate level of representation (often the output of a root compiler or parser) into a form that is closer to the language of the machine on which the program will execute.
(2) A software tool that accepts as input the requirements or design for a computer program and produces source code that implements the requirements or design. *Syn:* **source code generator.** *See also:* **application generator.**

code inspection. *See:* **inspection.**

code of ethics standard. (IEEE Std 1002-1987 [9]) A standard that describes the characteristics of a set of moral principles dealing with accepted standards of conduct by, within, and among professionals.

code review. A meeting at which software code is presented to project personnel, managers, users, customers, or other interested parties for comment or approval. *Contrast with:* **design review; formal qualification review; requirements review; test readiness review.**

code trace. *See:* **execution trace.**

coding. (1) In software engineering, the process of expressing a computer program in a programming language.
(2) (IEEE Std 1002-1987 [9]) The transforming of logic and data from design specifications (design descriptions) into a programming language.
See also: **software development process.**

cohesion. The manner and degree to which the tasks performed by a single software module are related to one another. Types include coincidental, communicational, functional, logical, procedural, sequential, and temporal. *Syn:* **module strength.** *Contrast with:* **coupling.**

coincidental cohesion. A type of cohesion in which the tasks performed by a software module have no functional relationship to one another. *Contrast with:* **communicational cohesion; functional cohesion; logical cohesion; procedural cohesion; sequential cohesion; temporal cohesion.**

command. An expression that can be input to a computer system to initiate an action or affect the execution of a computer program; for example, the "log on" command to initiate a computer session.

command-driven. Pertaining to a system or mode of operation in which the user directs the system through commands. *Contrast with:* **menu-driven.**

command language. A language used to express commands to a computer system. *See also:* **command-driven.**

comment. Information embedded within a computer program, job control statements, or a set of data, that provides clarification to human readers but does not affect machine interpretation.

common. *See:* **common storage.**

common area. *See:* **common storage.**

common block. *See:* **common storage.**

common coupling. *See:* **common-environment coupling.**

common data. *See:* **global data.**

common-environment coupling. A type of coupling in which two software modules access a common data area. *Syn:* **common coupling.** *Contrast with:* **content coupling; control coupling; data coupling; hybrid coupling; pathological coupling.**

common storage. A portion of main storage that can be accessed by two or more modules in a software system. *Syn:* **common area; common block.** *See also:* **global data.**

communicational cohesion. A type of cohesion in which the tasks performed by a software module use the same input data or contribute to producing the same output data. *Contrast with:* **coincidental cohesion; functional cohesion; logical cohesion; procedural cohesion; sequential cohesion; temporal cohesion.**

compaction. In microprogramming, the process of converting a microprogram into a functionally equivalent microprogram that is faster or shorter than the original. *See also:* **local compaction; global compaction.**

comparator. A software tool that compares two computer programs, files, or sets of data to identify commonalities or differences. Typical objects of comparison are similar versions of source code, object code, database files, or test results.

compatibility. (1) The ability of two or more systems or components to perform their required functions while sharing the same hardware or software environment.
(2) The ability of two or more systems or components to exchange information.
See also: **interoperability.**

compile. To translate a computer program expressed in a high order language into its machine language equivalent. *Contrast with:* **assemble; decompile; interpret.**

compile-and-go. An operating technique in which there are no stops between the compiling, linking, loading, and execution of a computer program.

compiler. A computer program that translates programs expressed in a high order language into their machine language equivalents. *Contrast with:* **assembler; interpreter.** *See also:* **cross-compiler; incremental compiler; root compiler.**

compiler code. Computer instructions and data definitions expressed in a form that can be recognized and processed by a compiler. *Contrast with:* **assembly code; interpretive code; machine code.**

compiler compiler. *See:* **compiler generator.**

compiler generator. A translator or interpreter used to construct part or all of a compiler. *Syn:* **compiler compiler; metacompiler.**

completion code. A code communicated to a job stream processor by a batch program to influence the execution of succeeding steps in the input stream.

complexity. (1) The degree to which a system or component has a design or implementation that is difficult to understand and verify. *Contrast with:* **simplicity.**
(2) Pertaining to any of a set of structure-based metrics that measure the attribute in (1).

component. One of the parts that make up a system. A component may be hardware or software and may be subdivided into other components. *Note:* The terms "module," "component," and "unit" are often used interchangeably or defined to be subelements of one another in different ways depending upon the context. The relationship of these terms is not yet standardized.

component standard. (IEEE Std 1002-1987 [9]) A standard that describes the characteristics of data or program components.

component testing. Testing of individual hardware or software components or groups of related components. *Syn:* **module testing.** *See also:* **integration testing; interface testing; system testing; unit testing.**

composite type. A data type each of whose members is composed of multiple data items. For example, a data type called PAIRS whose members are ordered pairs (*x,y*). *Contrast with:* **atomic type.**

computer-aided software engineering (CASE). The use of computers to aid in the software engineering process. May include the application of software tools to software design, requirements tracing, code production, testing, document generation, and other software engineering activities.

computer instruction. (1) A statement in a programming language, specifying an operation to be performed by a computer and the addresses or values of the associated operands; for example, Move A to B. *See also:* **instruction format; instruction set.**
(2) Loosely, any executable statement in a computer program.

computer language. A language designed to enable humans to communicate with computers. *See also:* **design language; query language; programming language.** *Note:* P610.13 [17] defines specific computer languages.

computer performance evaluation. An engineering discipline that measures the performance of computer systems and investigates methods by which that performance can be improved. *See also:* **system profile; throughput; utilization; workload model.**

computer program. A combination of computer instructions and data definitions that enable computer hardware to perform computational or control functions. *See also:* **software.**

computer program abstract. A brief description of a computer program that provides sufficient information for potential users to determine the appropriateness of the program to their needs and resources.

computer program component (CPC).* *See:* **computer software component.**
*Deprecated.

computer program configuration item (CPCI).* *See:* **computer software configuration item.**
*Deprecated.

computer resource allocation. The assignment of computer resources to current and waiting jobs; for example, the assignment of main memory, input/output devices, and auxiliary storage to jobs executing concurrently in a computer system. *See also:* **dynamic resource allocation; storage allocation.**

computer resources. The computer equipment, programs, documentation, services, facilities, supplies, and personnel available for a given purpose. *See also:* **computer resource allocation.**

computer security. *Note:* P610.9 [16] defines terminology pertaining to computer security.

computer software component (CSC). A functionally or logically distinct part of a computer software configuration item, typically an aggregate of two or more software units.

computer software configuration item (CSCI). An aggregation of software that is designated for configuration management and treated as a single entity in the configuration management process. *Contrast with:* **hardware configuration item.** *See also:* **configuration item.**

computer system. A system containing one or more computers and associated software.

computer word. *See:* **word.**

computing center. A facility designed to provide computer services to a variety of users through the operation of computers and auxiliary hardware and through services provided by the facility's staff.

concept phase. (1) (IEEE Std 1002-1987 [9]) The period of time in the software development cycle during which the user needs are described and evaluated through documentation (for example, statement of needs,

advance planning report, project initiation memo, feasibility studies, system definition, documentation, regulations, procedures, or policies relevant to the project).
(2) (IEEE Std 1012-1986 [12]) The initial phase of a software development project, in which the user needs are described and evaluated through documentation (for example, statement of needs, advance planning report, project initiation memo, feasibility studies, system definition, documentation, regulations, procedures, or policies relevant to the project).

concurrent. Pertaining to the occurrence of two or more activities within the same interval of time, achieved either by interleaving the activities or by simultaneous execution. *Syn:* **parallel (2).** *Contrast with:* **simultaneous.**

condition code. *See:* **status code.**

conditional branch.* *See:* **conditional jump.**
*Deprecated.

conditional jump. A jump that takes place only when specified conditions are met. *Contrast with:* **unconditional jump.**

configuration. (1) The arrangement of a computer system or component as defined by the number, nature, and interconnections of its constituent parts.
(2) In configuration management, the functional and physical characteristics of hardware or software as set forth in technical documentation or achieved in a product. *See also:* **configuration item; form, fit, and function; version.**

configuration audit. *See:* **functional configuration audit; physical configuration audit.**

configuration control. An element of configuration management, consisting of the evaluation, coordination, approval or disapproval, and implementation of changes to configuration items after formal establishment of their configuration identification. *Syn:* **change control.** *Contrast with:* **configuration identification; configuration status accounting.** *See also:* **configuration control board; deviation; engineering change; interface control; notice of revision; specification change notice; waiver.**

configuration control board (CCB). A group of people responsible for evaluating and approving or disapproving proposed changes to configuration items, and for ensuring implementation of approved changes. *Syn:* **change control board.** *See also:* **configuration control.**

configuration diagram. *See:* **block diagram.**

configuration identification. (1) An element of configuration management, consisting of selecting the configuration items for a system and recording their functional and physical characteristics in technical documentation. *Contrast with:* **configuration control; configuration status accounting.**
(2) The current approved technical documentation for a configuration item as set forth in specifications, drawings, associated lists, and documents referenced therein. *See also:* **allocated configuration identification; functional configuration identification; product configuration identification; baseline.**

configuration index. A document used in configuration management, providing an accounting of the configuration items that make up a product. *See also:* **configuration item development record; configuration status accounting.**

configuration item (CI). An aggregation of hardware, software, or both, that is designated for configuration management and treated as a single entity in the configuration management process. *See also:* **hardware configuration item; computer software configuration item; configuration identification; critical item.**

configuration item development record. A document used in configuration management, describing the development status of a configuration item based on the results of configuration audits and design reviews. *See also:* **configuration index; configuration status accounting.**

configuration management (CM). A discipline applying technical and administrative direction and surveillance to: identify and document the functional and physical characteristics of a configuration item, control changes to those characteristics, record and report change processing and implementation status, and verify compliance with specified requirements. *See also:* **baseline; configuration identification; configuration control; configuration status accounting; configuration audit.**

configuration status accounting. An element of configuration management, consisting of the recording and reporting of information needed to manage a configuration effectively. This information includes a listing of the approved configuration identification, the status of proposed changes to the configuration, and the implementation status of approved changes. *Contrast with:* **configuration control; configuration identification.** *See also:* **configuration index; configuration item development record.**

consecutive. Pertaining to the occurrence of two sequential events or items without the intervention of any other event or item; that is, one immediately after the other.

consistency. The degree of uniformity, standardization, and freedom from contradiction among the documents or parts of a system or component. *See also:* **traceability.**

constant. A quantity or data item whose value cannot change; for example, the data item FIVE, with an unchanging value of 5. *Contrast with:* **variable.** *See also:* **figurative constant; literal.**

constant-failure period. The period of time in the life cycle of a system or component during which hardware failures occur at an approximately uniform rate. *Contrast with:* **early-failure period; wearout-failure period.** *See also:* **bathtub curve.**

content coupling. A type of coupling in which some or all of the contents of one software module are included in the contents of another module. *Contrast with:* **common-environment coupling; control coupling; data coupling; hybrid coupling; pathological coupling.**

contiguous allocation. A storage allocation technique in which programs or data to be stored are allocated a block of storage of equal or greater size, so that logically contiguous programs and data are assigned physically contiguous storage locations. *Contrast with:* **paging (1).**

continuous iteration. A loop that has no exit.

control breakpoint. *See:* **code breakpoint.**

control coupling. A type of coupling in which one software module communicates information to another module for the explicit purpose of influencing the latter module's execution. *Contrast with:* **common-environment coupling; content coupling; data coupling; hybrid coupling; pathological coupling.**

control data. Data that select an operating mode, direct the sequential flow of a program, or otherwise directly influence the operation of software; for example, a loop control variable.

control flow. The sequence in which operations are performed during the execution of a computer program. *Syn:* **flow of control.** *Contrast with:* **data flow.**

control flow diagram. A diagram that depicts the set of all possible sequences in which operations may be performed during the execution of a system or program. Types include box diagram, flowchart, input-process-output chart, state diagram. *Contrast with:* **data flow diagram.** *See also:* **call graph; structure chart.**

control flow trace. *See:* **execution trace.**

control language. *See:* **job control language.**

control program. *See:* **supervisory program.**

control statement. A program statement that selects among alternative sets of program statements or affects the order in which operations are performed. For example, if-then-else, case. *Contrast with:* **assignment statement; declaration.**

control store. In a microprogrammed computer, the computer memory in which microprograms reside. *See also:* **microword; nanostore.**

control variable. *See:* **loop-control variable.**

conventions. (IEEE Std 983-1986 [7]) Requirements employed to prescribe a disciplined uniform approach to providing consistency in a software product, that is, uniform patterns or forms for arranging data. *See also:* **practices; standards.**

conversational. Pertaining to an interactive system or mode of operation in which the interaction between the user and the system resembles a human dialog. *Contrast with:* **batch.** *See also:* **interactive; on-line; real time.**

conversational compiler. *See:* **incremental compiler.**

conversion. Modification of existing software to enable it to operate with similar functional capability in a different environment; for example, converting a program from FORTRAN to Ada, converting a program that runs on one computer to run on another.

copy. (1) To read data from a source, leaving the source data unchanged, and to write the same data elsewhere in a physical form that may differ from that of the source. For example, to copy data from a magnetic disk onto a magnetic tape. *Contrast with:* **move.**
(2) The result of a copy process as in (1). For example, a copy of a data file.

core dump.* *See:* **memory dump.**
*Deprecated.

coroutine. A routine that begins execution at the point at which operation was last suspended, and that is not required to return control to the program or subprogram that called it. *Contrast with:* **subroutine.**

corrective maintenance. Maintenance performed to correct faults in hardware or software. *Contrast with:* **adaptive maintenance; perfective maintenance.**

correctness. (1) The degree to which a system or component is free from faults in its specification, design, and implementation.
(2) The degree to which software, documentation, or other items meet specified requirements.
(3) The degree to which software, documentation, or other items meet user needs and expectations, whether specified or not.

correctness proof. *See:* **proof of correctness.**

counter. A variable used to record the number of occurrences of a given event during the execution of a computer program; for example, a variable that records the number of times a loop is executed.

coupling. The manner and degree of interdependence between software modules. Types include common-environment coupling, content coupling, control coupling, data coupling, hybrid coupling, and pathological coupling. *Contrast with:* **cohesion.**

CPC. Acronym for **computer program component.** *See:* **computer software component.**

CPCI. Acronym for **computer program configuration item.** *See:* **computer software configuration item.**

crash. The sudden and complete failure of a computer system or component. *See also:* **hard failure.**

critical design review (CDR). (1) A review conducted to verify that the detailed design of one or more configuration items satisfy specified requirements; to establish the compatibility among the configuration items and other items of equipment, facilities, software, and personnel; to assess risk areas for each configuration item; and, as applicable, to assess the results of producibility analyses, review preliminary hardware product specifications, evaluate preliminary test planning, and evaluate the adequacy of preliminary operation and support documents. *See also:* **preliminary design review; system design review.**
(2) A review as in (1) of any hardware or software component.

critical item. In configuration management, an item within a configuration item that, because of special engineering or logistic considerations, requires an approved specification to establish technical or inventory control at the component level.

critical piece first. A system development approach in which the most critical aspects of a system are implemented first. The critical piece may be defined in terms of services provided, degree of risk, difficulty, or other criteria. *See also:* **bottom-up; top-down.**

critical software. (IEEE Std 1012-1986 [12]) Software whose failure could have an impact on safety, or could cause large financial or social loss.

criticality. The degree of impact that a requirement, module, error, fault, failure, or other item has on the development or operation of a system. *Syn:* **severity.**

cross-assembler. An assembler that executes on one computer but generates machine code for a different computer.

cross-compiler. A compiler that executes on one computer but generates machine code for a different computer.

cross-reference generator. A software tool that accepts as input the source code of a computer program and produces as output a listing that identifies each of the program's variables, labels, and other identifiers and indicates which statements in the program define, set, or use each one. *Syn:* **cross-referencer.**

cross-reference list. A list that identifies each of the variables, labels, and other identifiers in a computer program and indicates which statements in the program define, set, or use each one.

cross-referencer. *See:* **cross-reference generator.**

CSC. Acronym for **computer software component.**

CSCI. Acronym for **computer software configuration item.**

cue. *See:* **call (3).**

curriculum standard. (IEEE Std 1002-1987 [9]) A standard that describes the characteristics of a course of study on a body of knowledge that is offered by an educational institution.

cycle. (1) A period of time during which a set of events is completed. *See also:* **software development cycle; software life cycle.**
(2) A set of operations that is repeated regularly in the same sequence, possibly with variations in each repetition; for example, a computer's read cycle. *See also:* **pass.**

cycle stealing. The process of suspending the operation of a central processing unit for one or more cycles to permit the occurrence of other operations, such as transferring data from main memory in response to an output request from an input/output controller.

cyclic search. A storage allocation technique in which each search for a suitable block of storage begins with the block following the one last allocated.

data. (1) A representation of facts, concepts, or instructions in a manner suitable for communication, interpretation, or processing by humans or by automatic means. *See also:* **data type.** *Note:* IEEE Std 610.5-1990 [2] defines terminology pertaining to data management.
(2) Sometimes used as a synonym for documentation.

data abstraction. (1) The process of extracting the essential characteristics of data by defining data types and their associated functional characteristics and disregarding representation details. *See also:* **encapsulation; information hiding.**
(2) The result of the process in (1).

data breakpoint. A breakpoint that is initiated when a specified data item is accessed. *Syn:* **storage breakpoint.** *Contrast with:* **code breakpoint.** *See also:* **dynamic breakpoint; epilog breakpoint; programmable breakpoint; prolog breakpoint; static breakpoint.**

data characteristic. (IEEE Std 1008-1987 [10]) An inherent, possibly accidental, trait, quality, or property of data (for example, arrival rates, formats, value ranges, or relationships between field values).

data coupling. A type of coupling in which output from one software module serves as input to another module. *Syn:* **input-output coupling.** *Contrast with:* **common-environment coupling; content coupling; control coupling; hybrid coupling; pathological coupling.**

data definition. *Note:* This term is defined in IEEE Std 610.5-1990 [2].

data exception. An exception that occurs when a program attempts to use or access data incorrectly. *See also:* **addressing exception; operation exception; overflow exception; protection exception; underflow exception.**

data flow. The sequence in which data transfer, use, and transformation are performed during the execution of a computer program. *Contrast with:* **control flow.**

data flow diagram (DFD). A diagram that depicts data sources, data sinks, data storage, and processes performed on data as nodes, and logical flow of data as links between the nodes. *Syn:* **data flowchart; data flow graph.** *Contrast with:* **control flow diagram; data structure diagram.**

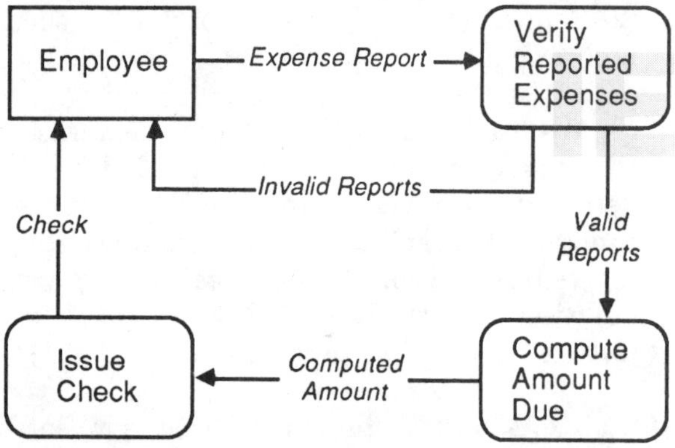

Fig 6
Data Flow Diagram

data flow graph. *See:* **data flow diagram.**

data flow trace. *See:* **variable trace.**

data flowchart (flow chart). *See:* **data flow diagram.**

data input sheet. User documentation that describes, in a worksheet format, the required and optional input data for a system or component. *See also:* **user manual.**

data-sensitive fault. A fault that causes a failure in response to some particular pattern of data. *Syn:* **pattern-sensitive fault.** *Contrast with:* **program-sensitive fault.**

data structure. A physical or logical relationship among data elements, designed to support specific data manipulation functions. *Note:* IEEE Std 610.5-1990 [2] defines specific data structures.

data structure-centered design. A software design technique in which the architecture of a system is derived from analysis of the structure of the data sets with which the system must deal. *See also:* **input-process-output; modular decomposition; object-oriented design; rapid prototyping; stepwise refinement; structure clash; structured design; transaction analysis; transform analysis.**

data structure diagram. A diagram that depicts a set of data elements, their attributes, and the logical relationships among them. *Contrast with:* **data flow diagram.** *See also:* **entity-relationship diagram.**

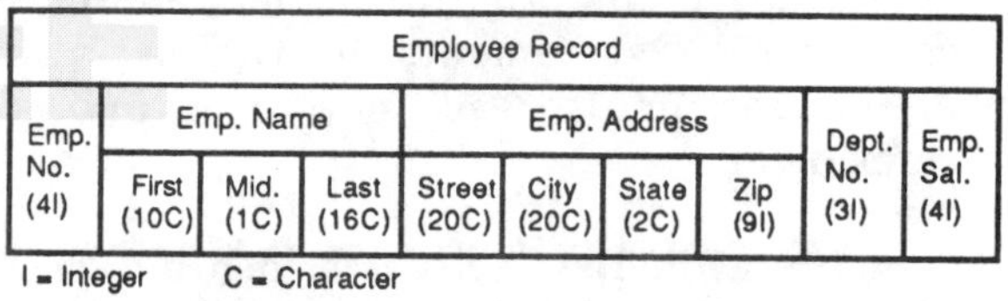
Employee Record
Emp. No. (4I)
Emp. Name
First (10C)
Mid. (1C)
Last (16C)
Emp. Address
Street (20C)
City (20C)
State (2C)
Zip (9I)
Dept. No. (3I)
Emp. Sal. (4I)
I = Integer
C = Character

Fig 7
Data Structure Diagram

data trace. *See:* **variable trace.**

data type. A class of data, characterized by the members of the class and the operations that can be applied to them. For example, character type, enumeration type, integer type, logical type, real type. *See also:* **strong typing.**

database. A collection of interrelated data stored together in one or more computerized files. *Note:* IEEE Std 610.5-1990 [2] defines terminology pertaining to databases.

datum. Singular for **data.**

deadlock. A situation in which computer processing is suspended because two or more devices or processes are each awaiting resources assigned to the others. *See also:* **lockout.**

deassembler.* *See:* **disassembler.**
* Deprecated.

deblock. To separate the parts of a block. *Contrast with:* **block (2).**

debug. To detect, locate, and correct faults in a computer program. Techniques include use of breakpoints, desk checking, dumps, inspection, reversible execution, single-step operation, and traces.

decision table. A table used to show sets of conditions and the actions resulting from them.

declaration. A non-executable program statement that affects the assembler or compiler's interpretation of other statements in the program. For example, a statement that identifies a name, specifies what the name represents, and, possibly, assigns it an initial value. *Contrast with:* **assignment statement; control statement.** *See also:* **pseudo instruction.**

declarative language. A nonprocedural language that permits the user to declare a set of facts and to express queries or problems that use these facts. *See also:* **interactive language; rule-based language.**

decompile. To translate a compiled computer program from its machine language version into a form that resembles, but may not be identical to, the original high order language program. *Contrast with:* **compile.**

decompiler. A software tool that decompiles computer programs.

decoupling. The process of making software modules more independent of one another to decrease the impact of changes to, and errors in, the individual modules. *See also:* **coupling.**

delimiter. A character or set of characters used to denote the beginning or end of a group of related bits, characters, words, or statements.

delivery. Release of a system or component to its customer or intended user. *See also:* **software life cycle; system life cycle.**

demand paging. A storage allocation technique in which pages are transferred from auxiliary storage to main storage only when those pages are needed. *Contrast with:* **anticipatory paging.**

demodularization. In software design, the process of combining related software modules, usually to optimize system performance. *See also:* **downward compression; lateral compression; upward compression.**

demonstration. A dynamic analysis technique that relies on observation of system or component behavior during execution, without need for post-execution analysis, to detect errors, violations of development standards, and other problems. *See also:* **testing.**

derived type. A data type whose members and operations are taken from those of another data type according to some specified rule. *See also:* **subtype.**

description standard. (IEEE Std 1002-1987 [9]) A standard that describes the characteristics of product information or procedures provided to help understand, test, install, operate, or maintain the product.

design. (1) The process of defining the architecture, components, interfaces, and other characteristics of a system or component. *See also:* **architectural design; preliminary design; detailed design.**
(2) The result of the process in (1).

design description. A document that describes the design of a system or component.

Typical contents include system or component architecture, control logic, data structures, input/output formats, interface descriptions, and algorithms. *Syn:* **design document; design specification.** *See also:* **product specification.** *Contrast with:* **requirements specification.**

design document. *See:* **design description.**

design element. (IEEE Std 990-1987 [8]) A basic component or building block in a design.

design entity. (IEEE Std 1016-1987 [13]) An element (component) of a design that is structurally and functionally distinct from other elements and that is separately named and referenced.

design inspection. *See:* **inspection.**

design language. A specification language with special constructs and, sometimes, verification protocols, used to develop, analyze, and document a hardware or software design. Types include hardware design language, program design language. *See also:* **requirements specification language.**

design level. (IEEE Std 829-1983 [5]) The design decomposition of the software item (for example, system, subsystem, program, or module).

design phase. The period of time in the software life cycle during which the designs for architecture, software components, interfaces, and data are created, documented, and verified to satisfy requirements. *See also:* **detailed design; preliminary design.**

design requirement. A requirement that specifies or constrains the design of a system or system component. *Contrast with:* **functional requirement; implementation requirement; interface requirement; performance requirement; physical requirement.**

design review. A process or meeting during which a system, hardware, or software design is presented to project personnel, managers, users, customers, or other interested parties for comment or approval. Types include critical design review, preliminary design review, system design review. *Contrast with:* **code review; formal qualification review; requirements review; test readiness review.**

design specification. *See:* **design description.**

design standard. (IEEE Std 1002-1987 [9]) A standard that describes the characteristics of a design or a design description of data or program components.

design unit. (IEEE Std 990-1987 [8]) A logically related collection of design elements. In an Ada PDL, a design unit is represented by an Ada compilation unit.

design view. (IEEE Std 1016-1987 [13]) A subset of design entity attribute information that is specifically suited to the needs of a software project activity.

desk checking. A static analysis technique in which code listings, test results, or other documentation are visually examined, usually by the person who generated them, to identify errors, violations of development standards, or other problems. *See also:* **inspection; walk-through.**

destination address. The address of the device or storage location to which data is to be transferred. *Contrast with:* **source address.**

destructive read. A read operation that alters the data in the accessed location. *Contrast with:* **nondestructive read.**

detailed design. (1) The process of refining and expanding the preliminary design of a system or component to the extent that the design is sufficiently complete to be implemented. *See also:* **software development process.**
(2) The result of the process in (1).

development cycle. *See:* **software development cycle.**

development life cycle. *See:* **software development cycle.**

development specification. *See:* **requirements specification.**

development testing. Formal or informal testing conducted during the development of a system or component, usually in the development environment by the developer. *Contrast with:* **acceptance testing; operational testing.** *See also:* **qualification testing.**

developmental baseline.* *See:* **developmental configuration.**
*Deprecated.

developmental configuration. In configuration management, the software and associated technical documentation that define the evolving configuration of a computer software configuration item during development. *Note:* The developmental configuration is under the developer's control, and therefore is not called a baseline. *Contrast with:* **allocated baseline; functional baseline; product baseline.**

deviation. (1) A departure from a specified requirement.
(2) A written authorization, granted prior to the manufacture of an item, to depart from a particular performance or design requirement for a specific number of units or a specific period of time. *Note:* Unlike an engineering change, a deviation does not require revision of the documentation defining the affected item. *See also:* **configuration control.** *Contrast with:* **engineering change; waiver.**

device. A mechanism or piece of equipment designed to serve a purpose or perform a function.

DFD. Acronym for **data flow diagram.**

diagnostic. Pertaining to the detection and isolation of faults or failures; for example, a diagnostic message, a diagnostic manual.

diagnostic manual. A document that presents the information necessary to execute diagnostic procedures for a system or component, identify malfunctions, and remedy those malfunctions. Typically described are the diagnostic features of the system or component and the diagnostic tools available for its support. *See also:* **installation manual; operator manual; programmer manual; support manual; user manual.**

diagonal microinstruction. A microinstruction capable of specifying a limited number of simultaneous operations needed to carry out a machine language instruction. *Note:* Diagonal microinstructions fall, in size and functionality, between horizontal microinstructions and vertical microinstructions. The designation "diagonal" refers to this compromise rather than to any physical characteristic of the microinstruction. *Contrast with:* **horizontal microinstruction; vertical microinstruction.**

differential dump. *See:* **change dump.**

digraph. *See:* **directed graph.**

direct address. An address that identifies the storage location of an operand. *Syn:* **one-level address.** *Contrast with:* **immediate data; indirect address; *n*-level address.** *See also:* **direct instruction.**

direct insert subroutine. *See:* **open subroutine.**

direct instruction. A computer instruction that contains the direct addresses of its operands. *Contrast with:* **immediate instruction; indirect instruction.** *See also:* **absolute instruction; effective instruction.**

directed graph. A graph (sense 2) in which direction is implied in the internode connections. *Syn:* **digraph.** *Contrast with:* **undirected graph.**

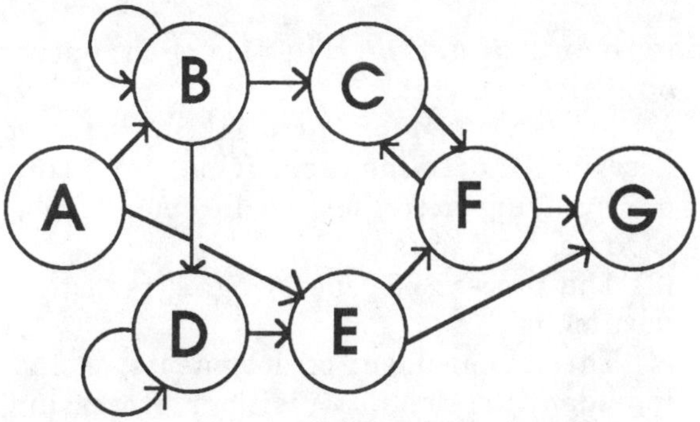

Fig 8
Directed Graph

directory. A list of data items and information about those data items. *Note:* IEEE Std 610.5-1990 [2] defines Data Management terms.

disassemble. To translate an assembled computer program from its machine language version into a form that resembles, but may not be identical to, the original assembly language program. *Contrast with:* **assemble.**

disassembler. A software tool that disassembles computer programs. *Syn:* **deassembler.**

discrete type. A data type whose members can assume any of a set of distinct values. A discrete type may be an enumeration type or an integer type.

diverse redundancy. *See:* **diversity.**

diversity. In fault tolerance, realization of the same function by different means. For example, use of different processors, storage media, programming languages, algorithms, or development teams. *See also:* **software diversity.**

do-nothing operation. *See:* **no-operation.**

document. (1) A medium, and the information recorded on it, that generally has permanence and can be read by a person or a machine. Examples in software engineering include project plans, specifications, test plans, user manuals.
(2) To create a document as in (1).
(3) To add comments to a computer program.

documentation. (1) A collection of documents on a given subject.
(2) Any written or pictorial information describing, defining, specifying, reporting, or certifying activities, requirements, procedures, or results.
(3) The process of generating or revising a document.
(4) The management of documents, including identification, acquisition, processing, storage, and dissemination.

documentation tree. A diagram that depicts all of the documents for a given system and shows their relationships to one another. *See also:* **specification tree.**

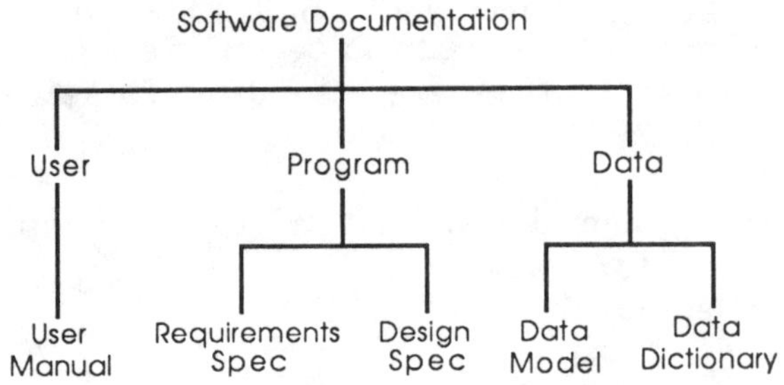

Fig 9
Documentation Tree

double-operand instruction. *See:* **two-address instruction.**

down. Pertaining to a system or component that is not operational or has been taken out of service. *Contrast with:* **up.** *See also:* **busy; crash; idle.**

down time. The period of time during which a system or component is not operational or has been taken out of service. *Contrast with:* **up time.** *See also:* **busy time; idle time; mean time to repair; set-up time.**

downward compatible. Pertaining to hardware or software that is compatible with an earlier or less complex version of itself; for example, a program that handles files created by an earlier version of itself. *Contrast with:* **upward compatible.**

downward compression. In software design, a form of demodularization in which a superordinate module is copied into the body of a subordinate module. *Contrast with:* **lateral compression; upward compression.**

driver. (1) A software module that invokes and, perhaps, controls and monitors the execution of one or more other software modules. *See also:* **test driver.**
(2) A computer program that controls a peripheral device and, sometimes, reformats data for transfer to and from the device.

dual coding. *See:* **software diversity.**

dump. (1) A display of some aspect of a computer program's execution state, usually the contents of internal storage or registers. Types include change dump, dynamic dump, memory dump, postmortem dump, selective dump, snapshot dump, static dump.
(2) A display of the contents of a file or device.
(3) To copy the contents of internal storage to an external medium.
(4) To produce a display or copy as in (1), (2), or (3).
Contrast with: **static dump.** *See also:* **change dump; memory dump; postmortem dump; selective dump; snapshot dump.**

dyadic selective construct. An if-then-else construct in which processing is specified for both outcomes of the branch. *Contrast with:* **monadic selective construct.**

dynamic. Pertaining to an event or process that occurs during computer program execution; for example, dynamic analysis, dynamic binding. *Contrast with:* **static.**

dynamic allocation. *See:* **dynamic resource allocation.**

dynamic analysis. The process of evaluating a system or component based on its behavior during execution. *Contrast with:* **static analysis.** *See also:* **demonstration; testing.**

dynamic binding. Binding performed during the execution of a computer program. *Contrast with:* **static binding.**

dynamic breakpoint. A breakpoint whose predefined initiation event is a runtime characteristic of the program, such as the execution of any twenty source statements. *Contrast with:* **static breakpoint.** *See also:* **code breakpoint; data breakpoint; epilog breakpoint; programmable breakpoint; prolog breakpoint.**

dynamic buffering. A buffering technique in which the buffer allocated to a computer program varies during program execution, based on current need. *Contrast with:* **simple buffering.**

dynamic dump. A dump that is produced during the execution of a computer program. *Contrast with:* **static dump.** *See also:* **change dump; memory dump; postmortem dump; selective dump; snapshot dump.**

dynamic error. An error that is dependent on the time-varying nature of an input. *Contrast with:* **static error.**

dynamic relocation. Relocation of a computer program during its execution.

dynamic resource allocation. A computer resource allocation technique in which the resources assigned to a program vary during program execution, based on current need.

dynamic restructuring. The process of restructuring a database, data structure, computer program, or set of system components during program execution.

dynamic storage allocation. A storage allocation technique in which the storage assigned to a computer program varies during program execution, based on the current needs of the program and of other executing programs.

E-R diagram. Acronym for **entity-relationship diagram.**

early-failure period. The period of time in the life cycle of a system or component during which hardware failures occur at a decreasing rate as problems are detected and repaired. *Syn:* **burn-in period.** *Contrast with:* **constant-failure period; wearout-failure period.** *See also:* **bathtub curve.**

echo. (1) To return a transmitted signal to its source, often with a delay to indicate that the signal is a reflection rather than the original.
(2) A returned signal, as in (1).

ECP. Acronym for **engineering change proposal.**

edit. To modify the form or format of computer code, data, or documentation; for example, to insert, rearrange, or delete characters.

editor. (1) *See:* **text editor.**
(2) *See:* **linkage editor.**

effective address. The address that results from performing any required indexing, indirect addressing, or other address modification on a specified address. *Note:* If the specified address requires no modification, it is also the effective address. *See also:* **generated address; indirect address; relative address.**

effective instruction. The computer instruction that results from performing any required indexing, indirect addressing, or other modification on the addresses in a specified computer instruction. *Note:* If the specified instruction requires no modification, it is also the effective instruction. *See also:* **absolute instruction; direct instruction; immediate instruction; indirect instruction.**

efferent. Pertaining to a flow of data or control from a superordinate module to a subordinate module in a software system. *Contrast with:* **afferent.**

efficiency. The degree to which a system or component performs its designated functions with minimum consumption of resources. *See also:* **execution efficiency; storage efficiency.**

egoless programming. A software development technique based on the concept of team, rather than individual, responsibility for program development. Its purpose is to prevent individual programmers from identifying so closely with their work that objective evaluation is impaired.

embedded computer system. A computer system that is part of a larger system and performs some of the requirements of that system; for example, a computer system used in an aircraft or rapid transit system.

embedded software. Software that is part of a larger system and performs some of the requirements of that system; for example, software used in an aircraft or rapid transit system.

emulation. (1) A model that accepts the same inputs and produces the same outputs as a given system. *See also:* **simulation.**

(2) The process of developing or using a model as in (1).

emulator. A device, computer program, or system that accepts the same inputs and produces the same outputs as a given system. *See also:* **simulator.**

encapsulation. A software development technique that consists of isolating a system function or a set of data and operations on those data within a module and providing precise specifications for the module. *See also:* **data abstraction; information hiding.**

engineering. The application of a systematic, disciplined, quantifiable approach to structures, machines, products, systems, or processes.

engineering change. In configuration management, an alteration in the configuration of a configuration item or other designated item after formal establishment of its configuration identification. *See also:* **configuration control; engineering change proposal.** *Contrast with:* **deviation; waiver.**

engineering change proposal (ECP). In configuration management, a proposed engineering change and the documentation by which the change is described and suggested. *See also:* **configuration control.**

entity. In computer programming, any item that can be named or denoted in a program. For example, a data item, program statement, or subprogram.

entity attribute. (IEEE Std 1016-1987 [13]) A named characteristic or property of a design entity. It provides a statement of fact about the entity.

entity-relationship (E-R) diagram. A diagram that depicts a set of real-world entities and the logical relationships among them. *Syn:* **entity-relationship map.** *See also:* **data structure diagram.**

entity-relationship (E-R) map. *See:* **entity-relationship diagram.**

entrance. *See:* **entry point.**

entry. *See:* **entry point.**

entry point. A point in a software module at which execution of the module can begin. *Syn:* **entrance; entry.** *Contrast with:* **exit.** *See also:* **reentry point.**

enumeration type. A discrete data type whose members can assume values that are explicitly defined by the programmer. For example, a data type called COLORS with possible values RED, BLUE, and YELLOW. *Contrast with:* **character type; integer type; logical type; real type.**

epilog breakpoint. A breakpoint that is initiated upon exit from a given program or routine. *Syn:* **postamble breakpoint.** *Contrast with:* **prolog breakpoint.** *See also:* **code breakpoint; data breakpoint; dynamic breakpoint; programmable breakpoint; static breakpoint.**

equivalent faults. Two or more faults that result in the same failure mode.

error. (1) The difference between a computed, observed, or measured value or condition and the true, specified, or theoretically correct value or condition. For example, a difference of 30 meters between a computed result and the correct result.
(2) An incorrect step, process, or data definition. For example, an incorrect instruction in a computer program.
(3) An incorrect result. For example, a computed result of 12 when the correct result is 10.
(4) A human action that produces an incorrect result. For example, an incorrect action on the part of a programmer or operator.
Note: While all four definitions are commonly used, one distinction assigns definition 1 to the word "error," definition 2 to the word "fault," definition 3 to the word "failure," and definition 4 to the word "mistake." *See also:* **dynamic error; fatal error; indigenous error; semantic error; syntactic error; static error; transient error.**

error model. In software evaluation, a model used to estimate or predict the number of remaining faults, required test time, and similar characteristics of a system. *Syn:* **error prediction model.**

error prediction. A quantitative statement about the expected number or nature of faults in a system or component. *See also:* **error model; error seeding.**

error prediction model. *See:* **error model.**

error seeding. The process of intentionally adding known faults to those already in a computer program for the purpose of monitoring the rate of detection and removal, and estimating the number of faults remaining in the program. *Syn:* **bug seeding; fault seeding.** *See also:* **indigenous error.**

error tolerance. The ability of a system or component to continue normal operation despite the presence of erroneous inputs. *See also:* **fault tolerance; robustness.**

exception. An event that causes suspension of normal program execution. Types include addressing exception, data exception, operation exception, overflow exception, protection exception, underflow exception.

execute. To carry out an instruction, process, or computer program.

execution efficiency. The degree to which a system or component performs its designated functions with minimum consumption of time. *See also:* **execution time; storage efficiency.**

execution monitor. *See:* **monitor (1).**

execution time. The amount of elapsed time or processor time used in executing a computer program. *Note:* Processor time is usually less than elapsed time because the processor may be idle (for example, awaiting needed computer resources) or employed on other tasks during the execution of a program. *Syn:* **run time (3); running time.** *See also:* **overhead time.**

execution trace. A record of the sequence of instructions executed during the execution of a computer program. Often takes the form of a list of code labels encountered as the program executes. *Syn:* **code trace; control-flow trace.** *See also:* **retrospective trace; subroutine trace; symbolic trace; variable trace.**

executive. *See:* **supervisory program.**

executive program. *See:* **supervisory program.**

executive state. *See:* **supervisor state.**

exit. A point in a software module at which execution of the module can terminate. *Contrast with:* **entry point.** *See also:* **return.**

exit routine. A routine that receives control when a specified event, such as an error, occurs.

expandability. *See:* **extendability.**

explicit address. *See:* **absolute address.**

extendability. The ease with which a system or component can be modified to increase its storage or functional capacity. *Syn:* **expandability; extensibility.** *See also:* **flexibility; maintainability.**

extensibility. *See:* **extendability.**

factoring. (1) The process of decomposing a system into a hierarchy of modules. *See also:* **modular decomposition.**
(2) The process of removing a function from a module and placing it into a module of its own.

fail safe. Pertaining to a system or component that automatically places itself in a safe operating mode in the event of a failure; for example, a traffic light that reverts to blinking red in all directions when normal operation fails. *Contrast with:* **fail soft.** *See also:* **fault secure; fault tolerance.**

fail soft. Pertaining to a system or component that continues to provide partial operational capability in the event of certain failures; for example, a traffic light that continues to alternate between red and green if the yellow light fails. *Contrast with:* **fail safe.** *See also:* **fault secure; fault tolerance.**

failure. The inability of a system or component to perform its required functions within specified performance requirements. *Note:* The fault tolerance discipline distinguishes between a human action (a mistake), its manifestation (a hardware or software fault), the result of the fault (a failure), and the amount by which the result is incorrect (the error). *See also:* **crash; exception; failure mode; failure rate; hard failure; incipient failure; random failure; soft failure.**

failure mode. The physical or functional manifestation of a failure. For example, a system in failure mode may be characterized by slow operation, incorrect outputs, or complete termination of execution.

failure rate. The ratio of the number of failures of a given category to a given unit of measure; for example, failures per unit of time, failures per number of transactions, failures per number of computer runs. *Syn:* **failure ratio.**

failure ratio. *See:* **failure rate.**

fatal error. An error that results in the complete inability of a system or component to function.

fault. (1) A defect in a hardware device or component; for example, a short circuit or broken wire.
(2) An incorrect step, process, or data definition in a computer program. *Note:* This definition is used primarily by the fault tolerance discipline. In common usage, the terms "error" and "bug" are used to express this meaning. *See also:* **data-sensitive fault; program-sensitive fault; equivalent faults; fault masking; intermittent fault.**

fault dictionary. A list of faults in a system or component, and the tests that have been designed to detect them.

fault masking. A condition in which one fault prevents the detection of another.

fault secure. Pertaining to a system or component in which no failures are produced from a prescribed set of faults. *See also:* **fault tolerance; fail safe; fail soft.**

fault seeding. *See:* **error seeding.**

fault tolerance. (1) The ability of a system or component to continue normal operation despite the presence of hardware or software faults. *See also:* **error tolerance; fail safe; fail soft; fault secure; robustness.**
(2) The number of faults a system or component can withstand before normal operation is impaired.
(3) Pertaining to the study of errors, faults, and failures, and of methods for enabling systems to continue normal operation in the presence of faults. *See also:* **recovery; redundancy; restart.**

fault tolerant. Pertaining to a system or component that is able to continue normal operation despite the presence of faults.

FCA. Acronym for **functional configuration audit.**

feasibility. The degree to which the requirements, design, or plans for a system or component can be implemented under existing constraints.

feature. (IEEE Std 1008-1987 [10]) *See:* **software feature.**

fetch. To locate and load computer instructions or data from storage. *See also:* **move; store.**

fifth generation language (5GL). A computer language that incorporates the concepts of knowledge-based systems, expert systems, inference engines, and natural language processing. *Contrast with:* **assembly language; fourth generation language; high order language; machine language.** *Note:* Specific languages are defined in P610.13 [17].

figurative constant. A data name that is reserved for a specific constant in a programming language. For example, the data name THREE may be reserved to represent the value 3. *See also:* **literal.**

file. A set of related records treated as a unit. For example, in stock control, a file could consist of a set of invoice records.

finite state machine. A computational model consisting of a finite number of states and transitions between those states, possibly with accompanying actions.

firmware. The combination of a hardware device and computer instructions and data that reside as read-only software on that device. *Notes:* (1) This term is sometimes used to refer only to the hardware device or only to the computer instructions or data, but these meanings are deprecated.
(2) The confusion surrounding this term has led some to suggest that it be avoided altogether.

first generation language (1GL). *See:* **machine language.**

flag. A variable that is set to a prescribed state, often "true" or "false," based on the results of a process or the occurrence of a specified condition. *See also*: **indicator; semaphore.**

flexibility. The ease with which a system or component can be modified for use in applications or environments other than those for which it was specifically designed. *Syn:* **adaptability.** *See also:* **extendability; maintainability.**

flow diagram. *See:* **flowchart.**

flow of control. *See:* **control flow.**

flowchart (flow chart). A control flow diagram in which suitably annotated geometrical figures are used to represent operations, data, or equipment, and arrows are used to indicate the sequential flow from one to another. *Syn:* **flow diagram.** *See also:* **block diagram; box diagram; bubble chart; graph; input-process-output chart; structure chart.**

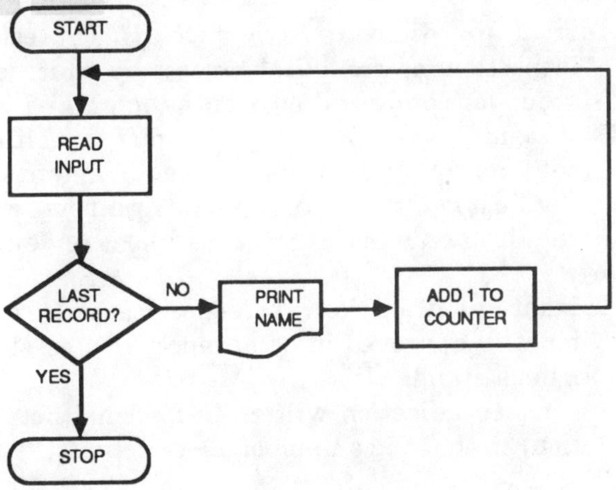

Fig 10
Flowchart

flowcharter. A software tool that accepts as input a design or code representation of a program and produces as output a flowchart of the program.

foreground. In job scheduling, the computing environment in which high-priority processes or those requiring user interaction are executed. *Contrast with:* **background.** *See also:* **foreground processing.**

foreground processing. The execution of a high-priority process while lower priority processes await the availability of computer resources, or the execution of processes that require user interaction. *Contrast with:* **background processing.**

form, fit, and function. In configuration management, that configuration comprising the physical and functional characteristics of an item as an entity, but not including any characteristics of the elements making up the item. *See also:* **configuration identification.**

formal language. A language whose rules are explicitly established prior to its use. Examples include programming languages and mathematical languages. *Contrast with:* **natural language.**

formal parameter. A variable used in a software module to represent data or program elements that are to be passed to the module by a calling module. *Contrast with:* **argument (3).**

formal qualification review (FQR). The test, inspection, or analytical process by which a group of configuration items comprising a system is verified to have met specific contractual performance requirements. *Contrast with:* **code review; design review; requirements review; test readiness review.**

formal specification. (1) A specification written and approved in accordance with established standards.
(2) A specification written in a formal notation, often for use in proof of correctness.

formal testing. Testing conducted in accordance with test plans and procedures that have been reviewed and approved by a customer, user, or designated level of management. *Contrast with:* **informal testing.**

forward recovery. (1) The reconstruction of a file to a given state by updating an earlier version, using data recorded in a chronological record of changes made to the file.
(2) A type of recovery in which a system, program, database, or other system resource is restored to a new, not previously occupied state in which it can perform required functions.
Contrast with: **backward recovery.**

four-address instruction. A computer instruction that contains four address fields. For example, an instruction to add the contents of locations A, B, and C, and place the result in location D. *Contrast with:* **one-address instruction; two-address instruction; three-address instruction; zero-address instruction.**

four-plus-one address instruction. A computer instruction that contains five address fields, the fifth containing the address of the instruction to be executed next. For example, an instruction to add the contents of locations A, B, and C, place the results in location D, then execute the instruction at location E. *Contrast with:* **one-plus-one address instruction; two-plus-one address instruction; three-plus-one address instruction.**

fourth generation language (4GL). A computer language designed to improve the productivity achieved by high order (third generation) languages and, often, to make computing power available to non-programmers. Features typically include an integrated database management system, query language, report generator, and screen definition facility. Additional features may include a graphics generator, decision support function, financial modeling, spreadsheet capability, and statistical analysis functions. *Contrast with:* **machine language; assembly language; high order language; fifth generation language.** *Note:* Specific languages are defined in P610.13 [17].

FQR. Acronym for **formal qualification review.**

function. (1) A defined objective or characteristic action of a system or component. For example, a system may have inventory control as its primary function. *See also:* **functional requirement; functional specification; functional testing.**
(2) A software module that performs a specific action, is invoked by the appearance of its name in an expression, may receive input values, and returns a single value. *See also:* **subroutine.**

function field. *See:* **operation field.**

functional baseline. In configuration management, the initial approved technical documentation for a configuration item. *Contrast with:* **allocated baseline; developmental configuration; product baseline.**

functional cohesion. A type of cohesion in which the tasks performed by a software module all contribute to the performance of a single function. *Contrast with:* **coincidental cohesion; communicational cohesion; logical cohesion; procedural cohesion; sequential cohesion; temporal cohesion.**

functional configuration audit (FCA). An audit conducted to verify that the development of a configuration item has been completed satisfactorily, that the item has achieved the performance and functional characteristics specified in the functional or allocated configuration identification, and that its operational and support documents are complete and satisfactory. *See also:* **configuration management; physical configuration audit.**

functional configuration identification. In configuration management, the current approved technical documentation for a configuration item. It prescribes all necessary functional characteristics, the tests required to demonstrate achievement of specified functional characteristics, the necessary interface characteristics with associated configuration items, the configuration item's key functional characteristics and its key lower level configuration items, if any, and design constraints. *Contrast with:* **allocated configuration identification; product configuration identification.** *See also:* **functional baseline.**

functional decomposition. A type of modular decomposition in which a system is broken down into components that correspond to system functions and subfunctions. *See also:* **hierarchical decomposition; stepwise refinement.**

functional design. (1) The process of defining the working relationships among the components of a system. *See also:* **architectural design.**
(2) The result of the process in (1).

functional language. A programming language used to express programs as a sequence of functions and function calls. Examples include LISP.

functional requirement. A requirement that specifies a function that a system or system component must be able to perform. *Contrast with:* **design requirement; implementation requirement; interface requirement; performance requirement; physical requirement.**

functional specification. A document that specifies the functions that a system or component must perform. Often part of a requirements specification.

functional testing. (1) Testing that ignores the internal mechanism of a system or component and focuses solely on the outputs generated in response to selected inputs and execution conditions. *Syn:* **black-box testing.** *Contrast with:* **structural testing.**
(2) Testing conducted to evaluate the compliance of a system or component with specified functional requirements. *See also:* **performance testing.**

garbage collection. In computer resource management, a synonym for **memory compaction (1).**

generality. The degree to which a system or component performs a broad range of functions. *See also:* **reusability.**

generated address. An address that has been calculated during the execution of a computer program. *Syn:* **synthetic address.** *See also:* **absolute address; effective address; relative address; indirect address.**

generic program unit. A software module that is defined in a general manner and that requires substitution of specific data, instructions, or both, in order to be used in a computer program. *See also*: **instantiation.**

glass box. (1) A system or component whose internal contents or implementation are known. *Syn:* **white box.** *Contrast with:* **black box.**
(2) Pertaining to an approach that treats a system or component as in (1).

glass-box testing. *See:* **structural testing.**

global compaction. In microprogramming, compaction in which microoperations may be moved beyond the boundaries of the single-entry, single-exit sequential blocks in which they occur. *Contrast with:* **local compaction.**

global data. Data that can be accessed by two or more non-nested modules of computer program without being explicitly passed as parameters between the modules. *Syn:* **common data.** *Contrast with:* **local data.**

global variable. A variable that can be accessed by two or more non-nested modules of a computer program without being explicitly passed as a parameter between the modules. *Contrast with:* **local variable.**

go to. A computer program statement that causes a jump. *Contrast with:* **call; case; if-then-else.** *See also:* **branch.**

graph. (1) A diagram that represents the variation of a variable in comparison with that of one or more other variables; for example, a graph showing a bathtub curve.

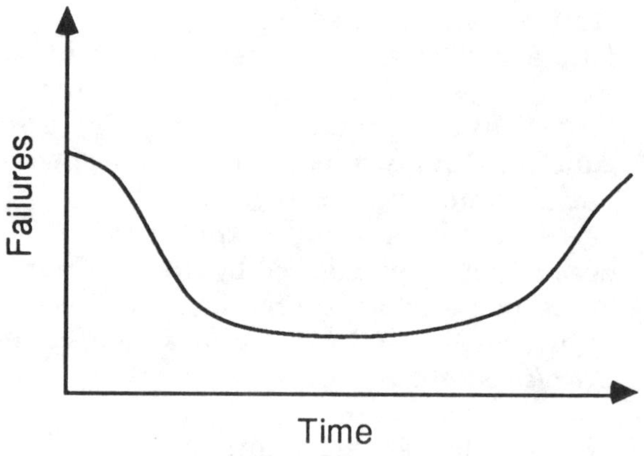

Fig 11
Graph (1)

(2) A diagram or other representation consisting of a finite set of nodes and internode connections called edges or arcs. *See also:* **block diagram; box diagram; bubble chart; directed graph; flowchart; input-process-output chart; structure chart.**

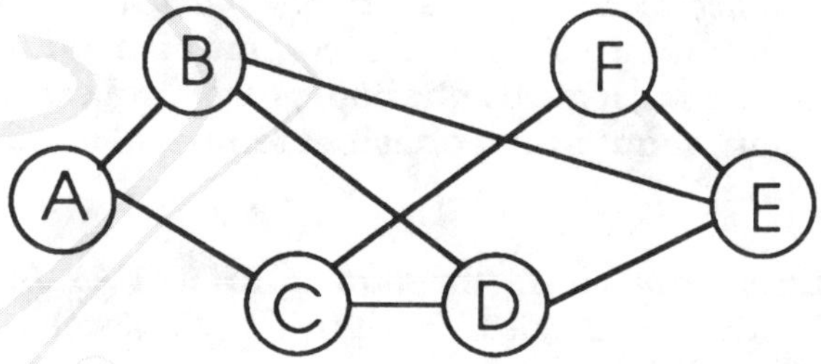

Fig 12
Graph (2)

Grosch's law. A guideline formulated by H. R. J. Grosch, stating that the computing power of a computer increases proportionally to the square of the cost of the computer. *See also:* **computer performance evaluation.**

halt. (1) Most commonly, a synonym for **stop.**
(2) Less commonly, a synonym for **pause.**

hard failure. A failure that results in complete shutdown of a system. *Contrast with:* **soft failure.**

hardware. Physical equipment used to process, store, or transmit computer programs or data. *Contrast with:* **software.**

hardware configuration item (HWCI). An aggregation of hardware that is designated for configuration management and treated as a single entity in the configuration management process. *Contrast with:* **computer software configuration item.** *See also:* **configuration item.**

hardware design language (HDL). A language with special constructs and, sometimes, verification protocols, used to develop, analyze, and document a hardware design. *See also:* **program design language.**

hardware monitor. (1) A device that measures or records specified events or characteristics of a computer system; for example, a device that counts the occurrences of various electrical events or measures the time between such events.
(2) A software tool that records or analyzes hardware events during the execution of a computer program.
See also: **monitor; software monitor.**

HDL. Acronym for **hardware design language.** *See:* **design language.**

header. (1) A block of comments placed at the beginning of a computer program or routine.
(2) Identification or control information placed at the beginning of a file or message.
Contrast with: **trailer.**

hierarchical decomposition. A type of modular decomposition in which a system is broken down into a hierarchy of components through a series of top-down refinements. *See also:* **functional decomposition; stepwise refinement.**

hierarchical input-process-output (HIPO). *See:* **input-process-output.**

hierarchical modeling. A technique used in computer performance evaluation, in which a computer system is represented as a hierarchy of subsystems, the subsystems are analyzed to determine their performance characteristics, and the results are used to evaluate the performance of the overall system.

hierarchy. A structure in which components are ranked into levels of subordination; each component has zero, one, or more subordinates; and no component has more than one superordinate component. *See also:* **hierarchical decomposition; hierarchical modeling.**

hierarchy chart. *See:* **structure chart.**

high level language. *See:* **high order language.**

high order language (HOL). A programming language that requires little knowledge of the computer on which a program will run, can be translated into several different machine languages, allows symbolic naming of operations and addresses, provides features designed to facilitate expression of data structures and program logic, and usually results in several machine instructions for each program statement. Examples include Ada, COBOL, FORTRAN, ALGOL, PASCAL. *Syn:* **high level language; higher order language; third generation language.** *Contrast with:* **assembly language; fifth generation language; fourth generation language; machine language.** *Note:* Specific languages are defined in P610.13 [17].

higher order language. *See:* **high order language.**

HLL. Acronym for **high level language.** *See:* **high order language.**

HMI. Acronym for **human-machine interface.** *See:* **user interface.**

HOL. Acronym for **high order language.**

homogeneous redundancy. In fault tolerance, realization of the same function with identical means, for example, use of two identical processors. *Contrast with:* **diversity.**

horizontal microinstruction. A microinstruction that specifies a set of simultaneous operations needed to carry out a given machine language instruction. *Note:* Horizontal microinstructions are relatively long, often 64 bits or more, and are called "horizontal" because the set of simultaneous operations that they specify are written on a single line, rather than being listed sequentially down the page. *Contrast with:* **diagonal microinstruction; vertical microinstruction.**

host machine. (1) A computer used to develop software intended for another computer. *Contrast with:* **target machine (1).**
(2) A computer used to emulate another computer. *Contrast with:* **target machine (2).**
(3) The computer on which a program or file is installed.
(4) In a computer network, a computer that provides processing capabilities to users of the network.

housekeeping operation. A computer operation that establishes or reestablishes a set of initial conditions to facilitate the execution of a computer program; for example, initializing storage areas, clearing flags, rewinding tapes, opening and closing files. *Syn:* **overhead operation.**

human-machine interface (HMI). *See:* **user interface.**

HWCI. Acronym for **hardware configuration item.**

hybrid coupling. A type of coupling in which different subsets of the range of values that a data item can assume are used for different and unrelated purposes in different software modules. *Contrast with:* **common-environment coupling; content coupling; control coupling; data coupling; pathological coupling.**

identifier. The name, address, label, or distinguishing index of an object in a computer program.

idle. Pertaining to a system or component that is operational and in service, but not in use. *See also:* **busy; down; up.**

idle time. The period of time during which a system or component is operational and in service, but not in use. *Syn:* **standby time.** *See also:* **busy time; down time; set-up time; up time.**

if-then-else. A single-entry, single-exit two-way branch that defines a condition, specifies the processing to be performed if the condition is met and, optionally, if it is not, and returns control in both instances to the statement immediately following the overall construct. *Contrast with:* **case; jump; go to.** *See also:* **dyadic selective construct; monadic selective construct.**

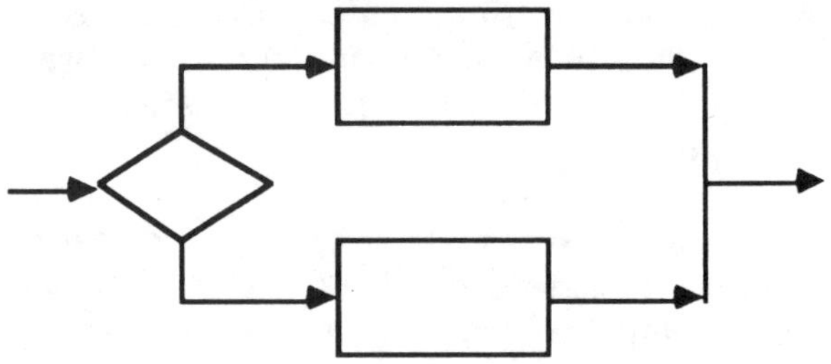

Fig 13
If-Then-Else Construct

immediate address.* *See:* **immediate data.**
* Deprecated.

immediate control. *See:* **bit steering.**

immediate data. Data contained in the address field of a computer instruction. *Contrast with:* **direct address; indirect address; *n*-level address.** *See also:* **immediate instruction.**

immediate instruction. A computer instruction whose address fields contain the values of the operands rather than the operands' addresses. *Contrast with:* **direct instruction; indirect instruction.** *See also:* **absolute instruction; effective instruction; immediate data.**

imperative construct. A sequence of one or more steps not involving branching or iteration.

imperative statement. *See:* **instruction.**

implementation. (1) The process of translating a design into hardware components, software components, or both. *See also:* **coding.**
(2) The result of the process in (1).

implementation phase. The period of time in the software life cycle during which a software product is created from design documentation and debugged.

implementation requirement. A requirement that specifies or constrains the coding or construction of a system or system component. *Contrast with:* **design requirement; functional requirement; interface requirement; performance requirement; physical requirement.**

implied addressing. A method of addressing in which the operation field of a computer instruction implies the address of the operands. For example, if a computer has only one accumulator, an instruction that refers to the accumulator needs no address information describing it. Types include one-ahead addressing, repetitive addressing. *See also:* **direct address; indirect address; relative address.**

incident. (IEEE Std 1008-1987 [10]) *See:* **software test incident.**

incipient failure. A failure that is about to occur.

incremental compiler. A compiler that completes as much of the translation of each source statement as possible during the input or scanning of the source statement. Typically used for on-line computer program development and checkout. *Syn:* **conversational compiler; interactive compiler; on-line compiler.**

incremental development. A software development technique in which requirements definition, design, implementation, and testing occur in an overlapping, iterative (rather than sequential) manner, resulting in incremental completion of the overall software product. *Contrast with:* **waterfall model.** *See also:* **data structure-centered design; input-process-output; modular decomposition; object-oriented design; rapid prototyping; spiral model; stepwise refinement; structured design; transaction analysis; transform analysis.**

independent verification and validation (IV&V). Verification and validation performed by an organization that is technically, managerially, and financially independent of the development organization.

indexed address. An address that must be added to the contents of an index register to obtain the address of the storage location to be accessed. *See also:* **offset (2); relative address; self-relative address.**

indicator. A device or variable that can be set to a prescribed state based on the results of a process or the occurrence of a specified condition. For example, a flag or semaphore.

indigenous error. A computer program error that has not been purposely inserted as part of an error-seeding process.

indirect address. An address that identifies the storage location of another address. The designated storage location may contain the address of the desired operand or another indirect address; the chain of addresses eventually leads to the operand. *Syn:* **multilevel address.** *Contrast with:* **direct address; immediate data.** *See also:* **indirect instruction; *n*-level address.**

indirect instruction. A computer instruction that contains indirect addresses for its operands. *Contrast with:* **direct instruction; immediate instruction.** *See also:* **absolute instruction; effective instruction.**

inductive assertion method. A proof of correctness technique in which assertions are written describing program inputs, outputs, and intermediate conditions, a set of theorems is developed relating satisfaction of the input assertions to satisfaction of the output assertions, and the theorems are proved or disproved using proof by induction.

infant mortality. The set of failures that occur during the early-failure period of a system or component.

informal testing. Testing conducted in accordance with test plans and procedures that have not been reviewed and approved by a customer, user, or designated level of management. *Contrast with:* **formal testing.**

information hiding. A software development technique in which each module's interfaces reveal as little as possible about the module's inner workings and other modules are prevented from using information about the module that is not in the module's interface specification. *See also:* **encapsulation.**

inherited error. An error carried forward from a previous step in a sequential process.

initial program load. *See:* **bootstrap.**

initial program loader. A bootstrap loader used to load that part of an operating system needed to load the remainder of the operating system.

initialize. To set a variable, register, or other storage location to a starting value. *See also:* **clear; reset.**

inline code. A sequence of computer instructions that is physically contiguous with the instructions that logically precede and follow it.

input. (1) Pertaining to data received from an external source.
(2) Pertaining to a device, process, or channel involved in receiving data from an external source.
(3) To receive data from an external source.
(4) To provide data from an external source.
(5) Loosely, input data.
Contrast with: **output.**

input assertion. A logical expression specifying one or more conditions that program inputs must satisfy in order to be valid. *Contrast with:* **loop assertion; output assertion.** *See also:* **inductive assertion method.**

input-output coupling. *See:* **data coupling.**

input-process-output. A software design technique that consists of identifying the steps involved in each process to be performed and identifying the inputs to and outputs from each step. *Note:* A refinement called hierarchical input-process-output identifies the steps, inputs, and outputs at both general and detailed levels of detail. *See also:* **data structure-centered design; input-process-output chart; modular decomposition; object-oriented design; rapid prototyping; stepwise refinement; structured design; transaction analysis; transform analysis.**

input-process-output (IPO) chart. A diagram of a software system or module, consisting of a rectangle on the left listing inputs, a rectangle in the center listing processing steps, a rectangle on the right listing outputs, and arrows connecting inputs to processing steps and processing steps to outputs. *See also:* **block diagram; box diagram; bubble chart; flowchart; graph; structure chart.**

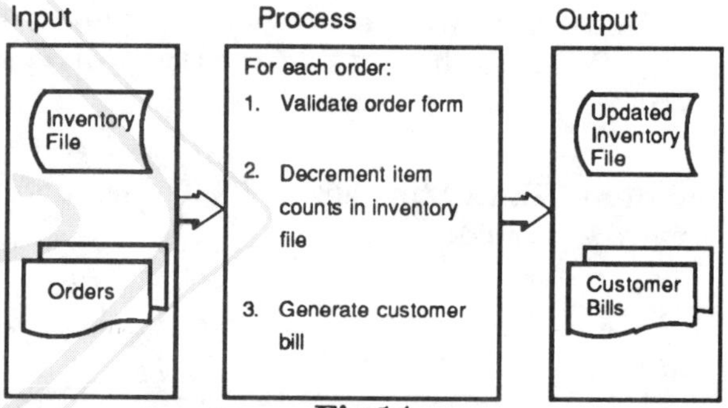

Fig 14
Input-Process-Output Chart

inspection. A static analysis technique that relies on visual examination of development products to detect errors, violations of development standards, and other problems. Types include code inspection; design inspection.

installation and checkout phase. The period of time in the software life cycle during which a software product is integrated into its operational environment and tested in this environment to ensure that it performs as required.

installation manual. A document that provides the information necessary to install a system or component, set initial parameters, and prepare the system or component for operational use. *See also:* **diagnostic manual; operator manual;**

programmer manual; support manual; user manual.

instantiation. The process of substituting specific data, instructions, or both into a generic program unit to make it usable in a computer program.

instruction. *See:* **computer instruction.**

instruction counter. A register that indicates the location of the next computer instruction to be executed. *Syn:* **program counter.**

instruction cycle. The process of fetching a computer instruction from memory and executing it. *See also:* **instruction time.**

instruction format. The number and arrangement of fields in a computer instruction. *See also:* **address field; address format; operation field.**

instruction length. The number of words, bytes, or bits needed to store a computer instruction. *See also:* **instruction format.**

instruction modifier. A word or part of a word used to alter a computer instruction.

instruction repertoire. *See:* **instruction set.**

instruction set. The complete set of instructions recognized by a given computer or provided by a given programming language. *Syn:* **instruction repertoire.**

instruction time. The time it takes a computer to fetch an instruction from memory and execute it. *See also:* **instruction cycle.**

instrument. In software and system testing, to install or insert devices or instructions into hardware or software to monitor the operation of a system or component.

instrumentation. Devices or instructions installed or inserted into hardware or software to monitor the operation of a system or component.

integer type. A data type whose members can assume only integer values and can be operated on only by integer arithmetic operations, such as addition, subtraction, and multiplication. *Contrast with:* **character type; enumeration type; logical type; real type.**

integrated programming support environment (IPSE). *See:* **programming support environment.**

integration. The process of combining software components, hardware components, or both into an overall system.

integration testing. Testing in which software components, hardware components, or both are combined and tested to evaluate the interaction between them. *See also:* **component testing; interface testing; system testing; unit testing.**

integrity. The degree to which a system or component prevents unauthorized access to, or modification of, computer programs or data.

interactive. Pertaining to a system or mode of operation in which each user entry causes a response from or action by the system. *Contrast with:* **batch.** *See also:* **conversational; on-line; real time.**

interactive compiler. *See:* **incremental compiler.**

interactive language. A nonprocedural language in which a program is created as a result of interactive dialog between the user and the computer system. The system provides questions, forms, and so on, to aid the user in expressing the results to be achieved. *See also:* **declarative language; rule-based language.**

interface. (1) A shared boundary across which information is passed.
(2) A hardware or software component that connects two or more other components for the purpose of passing information from one to the other.
(3) To connect two or more components for the purpose of passing information from one to the other.
(4) To serve as a connecting or connected component as in (2).

interface control. (1) (IEEE Std 828-1983 [4]) In configuration management, the process of: (a) identifying all functional and physical

characteristics relevant to the interfacing of two or more configuration items provided by one or more organizations, and (b) ensuring that proposed changes to these characteristics are evaluated and approved prior to implementation.
(2) (DoD usage) In configuration management, the administrative and technical procedures and documentation necessary to identify functional and physical characteristics between and within configuration items provided by different developers, and to resolve problems concerning the specified interfaces. *See also:* **configuration control.**

interface requirement. A requirement that specifies an external item with which a system or system component must interact, or that sets forth constraints on formats, timing, or other factors caused by such an interaction. *Contrast with:* **design requirement; functional requirement; implementation requirement; performance requirement; physical requirement.**

interface specification. A document that specifies the interface characteristics of an existing or planned system or component.

interface testing. Testing conducted to evaluate whether systems or components pass data and control correctly to one another. *See also:* **component testing; integration testing; system testing; unit testing.**

interleave. To alternate the elements of one sequence with the elements of one or more other sequences so that each sequence retains its identity; for example, to alternately perform the steps of two different tasks in order to achieve concurrent operation of the tasks.

intermittent fault. A temporary or unpredictable fault in a component. *See also:* **random failure; transient error.**

interoperability. The ability of two or more systems or components to exchange information and to use the information that has been exchanged. *See also:* **compatibility.**

interpret. To translate and execute each statement or construct of a computer program before translating and executing the next. *Contrast with:* **assemble; compile.**

interpreter. A computer program that translates and executes each statement or construct of a computer program before translating and executing the next. *Contrast with:* **assembler; compiler.**

interpretive code. Computer instructions and data definitions expressed in a form that can be recognized and processed by an interpreter. *Contrast with:* **assembly code; compiler code; machine code.**

interrupt. (1) The suspension of a process to handle an event external to the process. *Syn:* **interruption.** *See also:* **interrupt latency; interrupt mask; interrupt priority; interrupt service routine; priority interrupt.**
(2) To cause the suspension of a process.
(3) Loosely, an interrupt request.

interrupt latency. The delay between a computer system's receipt of an interrupt request and its handling of the request. *See also:* **interrupt priority.**

interrupt mask. A mask used to enable or disable interrupts by retaining or suppressing bits that represent interrupt requests.

interrupt priority. The importance assigned to a given interrupt request. This importance determines whether the request will cause suspension of the current process and, if there are several outstanding interrupt requests, which will be handled first.

interrupt request. A signal or other input requesting that the currently executing process be suspended to permit performance of another process.

interrupt service routine. A routine that responds to interrupt requests by storing the contents of critical registers, performing the processing required by the interrupt request, restoring the register contents, and restarting the interrupted process.

interruption. *See:* **interrupt.**

invariant. An assertion that should always be true for a specified segment or at a specified point of a computer program.

IPO chart. Acronym for **input-process-output chart.**

IPSE. Acronym for **integrated programming support environment.** *See:* **programming support environment.**

iteration. (1) The process of performing a sequence of steps repeatedly. *See also:* **loop; recursion.**
(2) A single execution of the sequence of steps in (1).

iterative construct. *See:* **loop.**

IV&V. Acronym for **independent verification and validation.**

JCL. Acronym for **job control language.**

job. A user-defined unit of work that is to be accomplished by a computer. For example, the compilation, loading, and execution of a computer program. *See also:* **job control language; job step; job stream.**

job control language (JCL). A language used to identify a sequence of jobs, describe their requirements to an operating system, and control their execution.

job function. (IEEE Std 1002-1987 [9]) A group of engineering processes that is identified as a unit for the purposes of work organization, assignment, or evaluation. Examples are design, testing, or configuration management.

job step. A user-defined portion of a job, explicitly identified by a job control statement. A job consists of one or more job steps.

job stream. A sequence of programs or jobs set up so that a computer can proceed from one to the next without the need for operator intervention. *Syn:* **run stream.**

jump. (1) To depart from the implicit or declared order in which computer program statements are being executed. *Syn:* **transfer.**
(2) A program statement that causes a departure as in (1). *Contrast with:* **case; if-then-else.** *See also:* **branch; go to.**
(3) The departure described in (1). *See also:* **conditional jump; unconditional jump.**

kernel. (1) That portion of an operating system that is kept in main memory at all times. *Syn:* **nucleus; resident control program.**
(2) A software module that encapsulates an elementary function or functions of a system. *See also:* **security kernel.**

KOPS. Acronym for kilo-operations per second; that is, thousands of operations per second. A measure of computer processing speed. *See also:* **MFLOPS; MIPS.**

label. (1) A name or identifier assigned to a computer program statement to enable other statements to refer to that statement.
(2) One or more characters, within or attached to a set of data, that identify or describe the data.

language. (1) A systematic means of communicating ideas by the use of conventionalized signs, sounds, gestures, or marks and rules for the formation of admissible expressions.
(2) (IEEE Std 830-1984 [6]) A means of communication, with syntax and semantics, consisting of a set of representations, conventions, and associated rules used to convey information.
See also: **computer language.**

language processor. A computer program that translates, interprets, or performs other tasks required to process statements expressed in a given language. *See also:* **assembler; compiler; interpreter; translator.**

language standard. (IEEE Std 1002-1987 [9]) A standard that describes the characteristics of a language used to describe a requirements specification, a design, or test data.

latency. The time interval between the instant at which an instruction control unit issues a call for data and the instant at which the transfer of data is started.

lateral compression. In software design, a form of demodularization in which two or more modules that execute one after the other are combined into a single module. *Contrast with:* **downward compression; upward compression.**

leading decision. A loop control that is executed before the loop body. *Contrast with:* **trailing decision.** *See also:* **WHILE.**

library. *See:* **software library.**

licensing standard. (IEEE Std 1002-1987 [9]) A standard that describes the characteristics of an authorization given by an official or a legal authority to an individual or organization to do or own a specific thing.

life cycle. *See:* **software life cycle; system life cycle.**

link. (1) To create a load module from two or more independently translated object modules or load modules by resolving cross-references among them. *See also:* **linkage editor.**
(2) A part of a computer program, often a single instruction or address, that passes control and parameters between separate modules of the program. *Syn:* **linkage.**
(3) To provide a link as in (2).

linkage. *See:* **link (2).**

linkage editor. A computer program that creates a single load module from two or more independently translated object modules or load modules by resolving cross-references among the modules and, possibly, by relocating elements. May be part of a loader. *Syn:* **linker.** *See also:* **linking loader.**

linker. *See:* **linkage editor.**

linking loader. A computer program that reads one or more object modules into main memory in preparation for execution, creates a single load module by resolving cross-references among the separate modules, and, in some cases, adjusts the addresses to reflect the storage locations into which the code has been loaded. *See also:* **absolute loader; relocating loader; linkage editor.**

list. (1) A set of data items, each of which has the same data definition.
(2) To print or otherwise display a set of data items.
Note: IEEE Std 610.5-1990 [2] defines Data Management terms.

list processing language. A programming language designed to facilitate the manipulation of data expressed in the form of lists. Examples are LISP and IPL. *See also:* **algebraic language; algorithmic language; logic programming language.**

listing. An ordered display or printout of data items, program statements, or other information.

literal. In a source program, an explicit representation of the value of an item; for example, the word FAIL in the instruction: If $x = 0$ then print "FAIL". *See also:* **immediate data; figurative constant.**

load. (1) To read machine code into main memory in preparation for execution and, in some cases, to perform address adjustment and linking of modules. *See also:* **loader.**
(2) To copy computer instructions or data from external storage to internal storage or from internal storage to registers. *Contrast with:* **store (2).** *See also:* **fetch; move.**

load-and-go. An operating technique in which there are no stops between the loading and execution phases of a computer program.

load map. A computer-generated list that identifies the location or size of all or selected parts of memory-resident code or data.

load module. A computer program or subprogram in a form suitable for loading into main storage for execution by a computer; usually the output of a linkage editor. *See also:* **object module.**

loaded origin. The address of the initial storage location of a computer program at the time the program is loaded into main memory. *Contrast with:* **assembled origin.** *See also:* **offset (1); starting address.**

loader. (1) A computer program that reads machine code into main memory in preparation for execution and, in some cases, adjusts the addresses and links the modules. Types include absolute loader, linking loader, relocating loader. *See also:* **bootstrap; linkage editor.**
(2) Any program that reads programs or data into main memory.

local compaction. In microprogramming, compaction in which microoperations are not moved beyond the boundaries of the single-entry, single-exit sequential blocks in which they occur. *Contrast with:* **global compaction.**

local data. Data that can be accessed by only one module or set of nested modules in a computer program. *Contrast with:* **global data.**

local variable. A variable that can be accessed by only one module or set of nested modules in a computer program. *Contrast with:* **global variable.**

lockout. A computer resource allocation technique in which shared resources (especially data) are protected by permitting access by only one device or process at a time. *See also:* **deadlock; semaphore.**

logic programming language. A programming language used to express programs in terms of control constructs and a restricted predicate calculus; for example, PROLOG. *See also:* **algebraic language; algorithmic language; list processing language.**

logical cohesion. A type of cohesion in which the tasks performed by a software module perform logically similar functions; for example, processing of different types of input data. *Contrast with:* **coincidental cohesion; communicational cohesion; functional cohesion; procedural cohesion; sequential cohesion; temporal cohesion.**

logical trace. An execution trace that records only branch or jump instructions. *See also:* **execution trace; retrospective trace; subroutine trace; symbolic trace; variable trace.**

logical type. A data type whose members can assume only logical values (usually TRUE and FALSE) and can be operated on only by logical operators, such as AND, OR, and NOT. *Contrast with:* **character type; enumeration type; integer type; real type.**

loop. (1) A sequence of computer program statements that is executed repeatedly until a given condition is met or while a given condition is true. *Syn:* **iterative construct.** *See also:* **loop body; loop control; UNTIL; WHILE.**
(2) To execute a sequence of computer program statements as in (1).

loop assertion. A logical expression specifying one or more conditions that must be met each time a particular point in a program loop is executed. *Syn:* **loop invariant.** *Contrast with:* **input assertion; output assertion.** *See also:* **inductive assertion method.**

loop body. The part of a loop that accomplishes the loop's primary purpose. *Contrast with:* **loop control.**

loop control. The part of a loop that determines whether to exit from the loop. *Contrast with:* **loop body.** *See also:* **leading decision; trailing decision.**

loop-control variable. A program variable used to determine whether to exit from a loop.

loop invariant. *See:* **loop assertion.**

loopback testing. Testing in which signals or data from a test device are input to a system or component, and results are returned to the test device for measurement or comparison.

low level language. *See:* **assembly language.**

machine address.* *See:* **absolute address.**
*Deprecated.

machine code. Computer instructions and data definitions expressed in a form that can be recognized by the processing unit of a computer. *Contrast with:* **assembly code; compiler code; interpretive code.**

machine dependent. Pertaining to software that relies on features unique to a particular type of computer and therefore executes only on computers of that type. *Contrast with:* **machine independent.**

machine independent. Pertaining to software that does not rely on features unique to a particular type of computer, and therefore executes on computers of more than one type. *Contrast with:* **machine dependent.** *See also:* **portability.**

machine language. A language that can be recognized by the processing unit of a computer. Such a language usually consists of patterns of 1s and 0s, with no symbolic naming of operations or addresses. *Syn:* **first generation language; machine-oriented language.** *Contrast with:* **assembly language; fifth generation language; fourth generation language; high order language; symbolic language.**

machine-oriented language. *See:* **machine language.**

machine readable. Pertaining to data in a form that can be automatically input to a computer; for example, data encoded on a diskette.

macro. In software engineering, a predefined sequence of computer instructions that is inserted into a program, usually during assembly or compilation, at each place that its corresponding macroinstruction appears in the program. *Syn:* **macro definition.** *See also:* **macroinstruction; macrogenerator; open subroutine.**

macro definition. *See:* **macro.**

macro generating program. *See:* **macrogenerator.**

macro library. A collection of macros available for use by a macrogenerator. *See also:* **system library.**

macroassembler. An assembler that includes, or performs the functions of, a macrogenerator.

macrogenerator. A routine, often part of an assembler or compiler, that replaces each macroinstruction in a source program with the predefined sequence of instructions that the macroinstruction represents. *Syn:* **macro generating program.**

macroinstruction. A source code instruction that is replaced by a predefined sequence of source instructions, usually in the same language as the rest of the program and usually during assembly or compilation. *See also:* **macro; macrogenerator.**

macroprocessor. A routine or set of routines provided in some assemblers and compilers to support the definition and use of macros.

macroprogramming. Computer programming using macros and macroinstructions.

main program. A software component that is called by the operating system of a computer and that usually calls other software components. *See also:* **routine; subprogram.**

maintainability. (1) The ease with which a software system or component can be modified to correct faults, improve performance or other attributes, or adapt to a changed environment. *See also:* **extendability; flexibility.**
(2) The ease with which a hardware system or component can be retained in, or restored to, a state in which it can perform its required functions.

maintenance. (1) The process of modifying a software system or component after delivery to correct faults, improve performance or other attributes, or adapt to a changed environment. *Syn:* **software maintenance.** *See also:* **adaptive maintenance; corrective maintenance; perfective maintenance.**
(2) The process of retaining a hardware system or component in, or restoring it to, a state in which it can perform its required functions. *See also:* **preventive maintenance.**

maintenance manual. *See:* **support manual.**

man-machine interface (MMI). *See:* **user interface.**

manufacture. In software engineering, the process of copying software to disks, chips, or other devices for distribution to customers or users.

manufacturing phase. (IEEE Std 1002-1987 [9]) The period of time in the software life cycle during which the basic version of a software product is adapted to a specified set of operational environments and is distributed to a customer base.

map program. A software tool, often part of a compiler or assembler, that generates a load map.

mask. A pattern of bits or characters designed to be logically combined with an unknown data item to retain or suppress portions of the data item; for example, the bit string "00000011" when logically ANDed with an eight-bit data item, gives a result that retains the last two bits of the data item and has zero in all the other bit positions. *See also:* **interrupt mask.**

master library. A software library containing master copies of software and documentation from which working copies can be made for distribution and use. *Contrast with:* **production library; software development library; software repository; system library.**

master state. *See:* **supervisor state.**

mean time between failures (MTBF). The expected or observed time between consecutive failures in a system or component. *See also:* **up time.**

mean time to repair (MTTR). The expected or observed time required to repair a system or component and return it to normal operations. *See also:* **down time.**

measurement standard. (IEEE Std 1002-1987 [9]) A standard that describes the characteristics of evaluating a process or product.

memory capacity. The maximum number of items that can be held in a given computer memory; usually measured in words or bytes. *See also:* **channel capacity; storage capacity.**

memory compaction. (1) A storage allocation technique in which the contents of all allocated storage areas are moved to the beginning of the storage space and the remaining storage blocks are combined into a single block. *Syn:* **garbage collection.**
(2) A storage allocation technique in which contiguous blocks of nonallocated storage are combined to form single blocks.

memory dump. A display of the contents of all or part of a computer's internal storage, usually in binary, octal, or hexadecimal form. *See also:* **change dump; dynamic dump; postmortem dump; selective dump; snapshot dump; static dump.**

memory map. A diagram that shows where programs and data are stored in a computer's memory.

menu by-pass. In a menu-driven system, a feature that permits advanced users to perform functions in a command-driven mode without selecting options from the menus.

menu-driven. Pertaining to a system or mode of operation in which the user directs the system through menu selections. *See also:* **menu by-pass.** *Contrast with:* **command-driven.**

metacompiler. *See:* **compiler generator.**

metalanguage. A language used to specify some or all aspects of a language; for example, Backus-Naur form. *See also:* **stratified language; unstratified language.**

method standard. (IEEE Std 1002-1987 [9]) A standard that describes the characteristics of the orderly process or procedure used in the engineering of a product or performing a service.

metric. A quantitative measure of the degree to which a system, component, or process possesses a given attribute. *See also:* **quality metric.**

MFLOPS. Acronym for millions of floating point operations per second. A measure of computer processing speed. *See also:* **KOPS; MIPS.**

microarchitecture. The microword definition, data flow, timing constraints, and precedence constraints that characterize a given microprogrammed computer.

microcode. A collection of microinstructions, comprising part of, all of, or a set of microprograms.

microcode assembler. A computer program that translates microprograms from symbolic form to binary form.

microinstruction. In microprogramming, an instruction that specifies one or more of the basic operations needed to carry out a machine language instruction. Types include diagonal microinstruction, horizontal microinstruction, vertical microinstruction. *See also:* **microcode; microoperation; microprogram.**

microoperation. In microprogramming, one of the basic operations needed to carry out a machine language instruction. *See also:* **microinstruction.**

microprogram. A sequence of instructions, called microinstructions, specifying the basic operations needed to carry out a machine language instruction.

microprogrammable computer. A microprogrammed computer in which microprograms can be created or altered by the user.

microprogrammed computer. A computer in which machine language instructions are implemented by microprograms rather than by hard-wired logic. *Note:* A microprogrammed computer may or may not be a microcomputer; the concepts are not related despite the similarity of the terms. *See also:* **microarchitecture; microprogrammable computer.**

microprogramming. The process of designing and implementing the control logic of a computer by identifying the basic operations needed to carry out each machine language instruction and representing these operations as sequences of instructions in a special memory called control store. This method is an alternative to hard wiring the control signals necessary to carry out each machine language instruction. Techniques include bit steering, compaction, residual control, single-level encoding, two-level encoding. *See also:* **microcode; microinstruction; microprogram.**

microword. An addressable element in the control store of a microprogrammed computer.

minimum delay programming. A programming technique in which storage locations for computer instructions and data are chosen so that access time is minimized.

MIPS. Acronym for million instructions per second. A measure of computer processing speed. *See also:* **KOPS; MFLOPS.**

mistake. A human action that produces an incorrect result. *Note:* The fault tolerance discipline distinguishes between the human action (a mistake), its manifestation (a hardware or software fault), the result of the fault (a failure), and the amount by which the result is incorrect (the error).

mixed mode. Pertaining to an expression that contains two or more different data types. For example, $Y := X + N$, where X and Y are floating point variables and N is an integer variable. *Syn:* **mixed type.**

mixed type. *See:* **mixed mode.**

MMI. Acronym for **man-machine interface.** *See:* **user interface.**

modular. Composed of discrete parts. *See also:* **modular decomposition; modular programming.**

modular decomposition. The process of breaking a system into components to facilitate design and development; an element of modular programming. *Syn:* **modularization.** *See also:* **cohesion; coupling; demodularization; factoring; functional decomposition; hierarchical decomposition; packaging.**

modular programming. A software development technique in which software is developed as a collection of modules. *See also:* **data structure-centered design; input-process-output; modular decomposition; object-oriented design; rapid prototyping; stepwise refinement; structured design; transaction analysis; transform analysis.**

modularity. The degree to which a system or computer program is composed of discrete components such that a change to one component has minimal impact on other components. *See also:* **cohesion; coupling.**

modularization. *See:* **modular decomposition.**

module. (1) A program unit that is discrete and identifiable with respect to compiling, combining with other units, and loading; for example, the input to, or output from, an assembler, compiler, linkage editor, or executive routine.
(2) A logically separable part of a program. *Note:* The terms "module," "component," and "unit" are often used interchangeably or defined to be sub-elements of one another in different ways depending upon the context. The relationship of these terms is not yet standardized.

module strength. *See:* **cohesion.**

module testing. *See:* **component testing.**

monadic selective construct. An if-then-else construct in which processing is specified for only one outcome of the branch, the other outcome resulting in skipping this processing. *Contrast with:* **dyadic selective construct.**

monitor. A software tool or hardware device that operates concurrently with a system or component and supervises, records, analyzes, or verifies the operation of the system or component. *Syn:* **execution monitor.** *See also:* **hardware monitor; software monitor.**

move. (1) To read data from a source, altering the contents of the source location, and to write the same data elsewhere in a physical form that may differ from that of the source. For example, to move data from one file to another. *Contrast with:* **copy.**
(2) Sometimes, a synonym for **copy.**
See also: **fetch; load; store.**

MTBF. Acronym for **mean time between failures.**

MTTR. Acronym for **mean time to repair.**

multiaddress instruction. A computer instruction that contains more than one address field. *Syn:* **multiple-address instruction.** *Contrast with:* **one-address instruction.**

multilevel address. *See:* **indirect address.**

multilevel storage. *See:* **virtual storage.**

multiple-address instruction. *See:* **multiaddress instruction.**

multiple exclusive selective construct. *See:* **case.**

multiple inclusive selective construct. A special instance of the case construct in which two or more different values of the control expression result in the same processing. For example, values 1 and 2 cause one branch, 3 and 4 cause another, and so on.

multiprocessing. A mode of operation in which two or more processes are executed concurrently by separate processing units that have access (usually) to a common main storage. *Contrast with:* **multiprogramming.** *See also:* **multitasking; time sharing.**

multiprogramming. A mode of operation in which two or more computer programs are executed in an interleaved manner by a single processing unit. *Contrast with:* **multiprocessing.** *See also:* **multitasking; time sharing.**

multitasking. A mode of operation in which two or more tasks are executed in an interleaved manner. *See also:* **multiprocessing; multiprogramming; time sharing.**

mutation. *See:* **program mutation.**

mutation testing. A testing methodology in which two or more program mutations are executed using the same test cases to evaluate the ability of the test cases to detect differences in the mutations.

***n*-address instruction.** A computer instruction that contains *n* address fields, where *n* may be any non-negative integer. *See also:* **one-address instruction; two-address instruction; etc.** *Contrast with:* ***n*-plus-one address instruction.**

***n*-level address.** An indirect address that specifies the first of a chain of *n* storage locations, the first *n*-1 of which contains the address of the next location in the chain and the last of which contains the desired operand. For example, a two-level address. *Contrast with:* **direct address; immediate data.**

***n*-plus-one address instruction.** A computer instruction that contains *n*+1 address fields, the last containing the address of the instruction to be executed next. *See also:* **one-plus-one address instruction; two-plus-one address instruction; etc.** *Contrast with:* ***n*-address instruction.**

nanocode. A collection of nanoinstructions.

nanoinstruction. In a two-level implementation of microprogramming, an instruction that specifies one or more of the basic operations needed to carry out a microinstruction.

nanostore. In a two-level implementation of microprogramming, a secondary control store in which nanoinstructions reside.

Nassi-Shneiderman chart. *See:* **box diagram.**

natural language. A language whose rules are based on usage rather than being pre-established prior to the language's use. Examples include German and English. *Contrast with:* **formal language.**

nest. To incorporate a computer program construct into another construct of the same kind. For example, to nest one subroutine, block, or loop within another; to nest one data structure within another.

no-op. Abbreviation for **no-operation.**

no-operation. A computer operation whose execution has no effect except to advance the instruction counter to the next instruction. Used to reserve space in a program or, if executed repeatedly, to wait for a given event. Often abbreviated **no-op.** *Syn:* **do-nothing operation.**

node. (1) In a diagram, a point, circle, or other geometric figure used to represent a state, event, or other item of interest. *See also:* **graph (2).**
(2) *Note:* The meaning of this term in the context of computer networks is covered in P610.7 [14].

nomenclature standard. (IEEE Std 1002-1987 [9]) A standard that describes the characteristics of a system or set of names, or designations, or symbols.

nondestructive read. A read operation that does not erase the data in the accessed location. *Contrast with:* **destructive read.**

nonprocedural language. A language in which the user states what is to be achieved without having to state specific instructions that the computer must execute in a given sequence. *Contrast with:* **procedural language.** *See also:* **declarative language; interactive language; rule-based language.**

NOR. (1) In configuration management, an acronym for **notice of revision.**
(2) *Note:* The meaning of this term as a logical operator is given in IEEE Std 610.1/1084-1986 [1, 11].

notation standard. (IEEE Std 1002-1987 [9]) A standard that describes the characteristics of formal interfaces within a profession.

notice of revision (NOR). A form used in configuration management to propose revisions to a drawing or list, and, after approval, to notify users that the drawing or list has been, or will be, revised accordingly. *See also:* **configuration control; engineering change; specification change notice.**

nucleus. *See:* **kernel (1).**

object. (1) Pertaining to the outcome of an assembly or compilation process. *See also:* **object code; object module; object program.**
(2) A program constant or variable.
(3) An encapsulation of data and services that manipulate that data. *See also:* **object-oriented design.**

object code. Computer instructions and data definitions in a form output by an assembler or compiler. An object program is made up of object code. *Contrast with:* **source code.**

object language. *See:* **target language.**

object module. A computer program or subprogram that is the output of an assembler or compiler. *See also:* **load module; object program.**

object-oriented design. A software development technique in which a system or component is expressed in terms of objects and connections between those objects. *See also:* **data structure-centered design; input-process-output; modular decomposition; rapid prototyping; stepwise refinement; structured design; transaction analysis; transform analysis.**

object-oriented language. A programming language that allows the user to express a program in terms of objects and messages between those objects. Examples include Smalltalk and LOGO.

object program. A computer program that is the output of an assembler or compiler. *Syn:* **target program.** *Contrast with:* **source program.** *See also:* **object module.**

occupational title standard. (IEEE Std 1002-1987 [9]) A standard that describes the characteristics of the general areas of work or profession.

off-line. Pertaining to a device or process that is not under the direct control of the central processing unit of a computer. *Contrast with:* **on-line (2).**

offset. (1) The difference between the loaded origin and the assembled origin of a computer program. *Syn:* **relocation factor.**
(2) A number that must be added to a relative address to determine the address of the storage location to be accessed. This number may be the difference defined in (1) or another number defined in the program. *See also:* **base address; indexed address; relative address; self-relative address.**

on-line. (1) Pertaining to a system or mode of operation in which input data enter the computer directly from the point of origin or output data are transmitted directly to the point where they are used. For example, an airline reservation system. *Contrast with:* **batch.** *See also:* **conversational; interactive; real time.**
(2) Pertaining to a device or process that is under the direct control of the central processing unit of a computer.
Contrast with: **off-line.**

on-line compiler. *See:* **incremental compiler.**

one-address instruction. A computer instruction that contains one address field. For example, an instruction to load the contents of location A. *Syn:* **single-address instruction; single-operand instruction.** *Contrast with:* **multiaddress instruction; two-address instruction; three-address instruction; four-address instruction; zero-address instruction.**

one-ahead addressing. A method of implied addressing in which the operands for a computer instruction are understood to be in the storage locations following the locations of the operands used for the last instruction executed. *Contrast with:* **repetitive addressing.**

one-level address. *See:* **direct address.**

one-plus-one address instruction. A computer instruction that contains two address fields, the second containing the address of the instruction to be executed next. For example, an instruction to load the contents of location A, then execute the instruction at location B. *Contrast with:* **two-plus-one address instruction; three-plus-one address instruction; four-plus-one address instruction.**

op code (opcode). *See:* **operation code.**

open subroutine. A subroutine that is copied into a computer program at each place that it is called. *Syn:* **direct insert subroutine.** *Contrast with:* **closed subroutine.** *See also:* **inline code; macro.**

operand. A variable, constant, or function upon which an operation is to be performed. For example, in the expression $A = B + 3$, B and 3 are the operands.

operating system. A collection of software, firmware, and hardware elements that controls the execution of computer programs and provides such services as computer resource allocation, job control, input/output control, and file management in a computer system.

operation. (1) In computer mathematics, the action specified by an operator on one or more operands. For example, in the expression $A = B + 3$, the process of adding B to 3 to obtain A.
(2) In programming, a defined action that can be performed by a computer system; for example, addition, comparison, branching. *Note:* Unlike the mathematical meaning, such an operation may not involve an operator or operands; for example, the operation Halt.
(3) The process of running a computer system in its intended environment to perform its intended functions.

operation and maintenance phase. The period of time in the software life cycle during which a software product is employed in its operational environment, monitored for satisfactory performance, and modified as necessary to correct problems or to respond to changing requirements.

operation code. A character or set of characters that specifies a computer operation; for example, the code BNZ to designate the operation "branch if not zero." *Syn:* **op code.**

operation exception. An exception that occurs when a program encounters an invalid operation code. *See also:* **addressing exception; data exception; overflow exception; protection exception; underflow exception.**

operation field. The field of a computer instruction that specifies the operation to be performed. *Syn:* **function field; operation part.** *Contrast with:* **address field.**

operation part. *See:* **operation field.**

operational. (1) Pertaining to a system or component that is ready for use in its intended environment.
(2) Pertaining to a system or component that is installed in its intended environment.
(3) Pertaining to the environment in which a system or component is intended to be used.

operational testing. Testing conducted to evaluate a system or component in its operational environment. *Contrast with:* **development testing.** *See also:* **acceptance testing; qualification testing.**

operator. (1) A mathematical or logical symbol that represents an action to be performed in an operation. For example, in the expression $A = B + 3$, $+$ is the operator, representing addition.
(2) A person who operates a computer system.

operator field. *See:* **operation field.**

operator manual. A document that provides the information necessary to initiate and operate a system or component. Typically described are procedures for preparation, operation, monitoring, and recovery. *Note:* An operator manual is distinguished from a user manual when a distinction is made between those who operate a computer system (mounting tapes, etc.) and those who use the system for its intended purpose. *See also:* **diagnostic manual; installation manual; programmer manual; support manual; user manual.**

order clash. In software design, a type of structure clash in which a program must deal with two or more data sets that have been sorted in different orders. *See also:* **data structure-centered design.**

origin. The address of the initial storage location assigned to a computer program in main memory. *See also:* **assembled origin; loaded origin.** *Contrast with:* **starting address.**

output. (1) Pertaining to data transmitted to an external destination.
(2) Pertaining to a device, process, or channel involved in transmitting data to an external destination.
(3) To transmit data to an external destination.
(4) Loosely, output data.
Contrast with: **input.**

output assertion. A logical expression specifying one or more conditions that program outputs must satisfy in order for the program to be correct. *Contrast with:* **input assertion; loop assertion.** *See also:* **inductive assertion method.**

overflow exception. An exception that occurs when the result of an arithmetic operation exceeds the size of the storage location designated to receive it. *See also:* **addressing exception; data exception; operation exception; protection exception; underflow exception.**

overhead operation. *See:* **housekeeping operation.**

overhead time. The amount of time a computer system spends performing tasks that do not contribute directly to the progress of any user task; for example, time spent tabulating computer resource usage for billing purposes.

overlay. (1) A storage allocation technique in which computer program segments are loaded from auxiliary storage to main storage when needed, overwriting other segments not currently in use.
(2) A computer program segment that is maintained in auxiliary storage and loaded into main storage when needed, overwriting other segments not currently in use.
(3) To load a computer program segment from auxiliary storage to main storage in such a way that other segments of the program are overwritten.

overlay supervisor. A routine that controls the sequencing and positioning of overlays.

overload. To assign an operator, identifier, or literal more than one meaning, depending upon the data types associated with it at any given time during program execution.

pack. To store data in a compact form in a storage medium, using known characteristics of the data and medium in such a way as to permit recovery of the data. *Contrast with:* **unpack.**

package. A separately compilable software component consisting of related data types, data objects, and subprograms. *See also:* **data abstraction; encapsulation; information hiding.**

packaging. In software development, the assignment of modules to segments to be handled as distinct physical units for execution by a computer.

padding. (1) The technique of filling out a fixed-length block of data with dummy characters, words, or records.
(2) Dummy characters, words, or records used to fill out a fixed-length block of data.

page. (1) A fixed-length segment of data or of a computer program treated as a unit in storage allocation. *See also:* **paging.**
(2) In a virtual storage system, a fixed-length segment of data or of a computer program that has a virtual address and is transferred as a unit between main and auxiliary storage.
(3) A screenful of information on a video display terminal.

page breakage. A portion of main storage that is unused when the last page of data or of a computer program does not fill the entire block of storage allocated to it. *See also:* **paging.**

page frame. A block of main storage having the size of, and used to hold, a page. *See also:* **paging.**

page swapping. The exchange of pages between main storage and auxiliary storage. *See also:* **paging.**

page table. A table that identifies the location of pages in storage and gives significant attributes of those pages. *See also:* **paging.**

page turning. *See:* **paging (3).**

page zero. In the paging method of storage allocation, the first page in a series of pages.

pager. A routine that initiates and controls the transfer of pages between main and auxiliary storage. *See also:* **paging.**

paging. (1) A storage allocation technique in which programs or data are divided into fixed-length blocks called pages, main storage is divided into blocks of the same length called page frames, and pages are stored in page frames, not necessarily contiguously or in logical order. *Syn:* **block allocation.** *Contrast with:* **contiguous allocation.**
(2) A storage allocation technique in which programs or data are divided into fixed-length blocks called pages, main storage is divided into blocks of the same length called page frames, and pages are transferred between main and auxiliary storage as needed. *See also:* **anticipatory paging; demand paging; virtual storage.**
(3) The transfer of pages as in (2). *Syn:* **page turning.**
See also: **page; page breakage; page frame; page swapping; page table; page zero; pager; working set.**

parallel. (1) Pertaining to the simultaneous transfer, occurrence, or processing of the individual parts of a whole, such as the bits of a character, using separate facilities for the various parts. *Contrast with:* **serial (1).**
(2) *See:* **concurrent.**

parallel construct. A program construct consisting of two or more procedures that can occur simultaneously.

parameter. (1) A variable that is given a constant value for a specified application. *See also:* **adaptation parameter.**
(2) A constant, variable, or expression that is used to pass values between software modules. *See also:* **argument; formal parameter.**

parse. To determine the syntactic structure of a language unit by decomposing it into more elementary subunits and establishing the relationships among the subunits. For example, to decompose blocks into statements, statements into expressions, expressions into operators and operands.

parser. A software tool that parses computer programs or other text, often as the first step of assembly, compilation, interpretation, or analysis.

partial correctness. In proof of correctness, a designation indicating that a program's output assertions follow logically from its input assertions and processing steps. *Contrast with:* **total correctness.**

partitioning. (IEEE Std 830-1984 [6]) Decomposition; the separation of the whole into its parts.

pass. A single cycle in the processing of a set of data, usually performing part of an overall process. For example, a pass of an assembler through a source program; a pass of a sort program through a set of data.

pass/fail criteria. (IEEE Std 829-1983 [5]) Decision rules used to determine whether a software item or a software feature passes or fails a test. *See also:* **test criteria.**

patch. (1) A modification made directly to an object program without reassembling or recompiling from the source program.
(2) A modification made to a source program as a last-minute fix or afterthought.
(3) Any modification to a source or object program.
(4) To perform a modification as in (1), (2), or (3).

path. (1) In software engineering, a sequence of instructions that may be performed in the

execution of a computer program.
(2) In file access, a hierarchical sequence of directory and subdirectory names specifying the storage location of a file.

path analysis. Analysis of a computer program to identify all possible paths through the program, to detect incomplete paths, or to discover portions of the program that are not on any path.

path condition. A set of conditions that must be met in order for a particular program path to be executed.

path expression. A logical expression indicating the input conditions that must be met in order for a particular program path to be executed.

path testing. Testing designed to execute all or selected paths through a computer program. *Contrast with:* **branch testing; statement testing.**

pathological coupling. A type of coupling in which one software module affects or depends upon the internal implementation of another. *Contrast with:* **common-environment coupling; content coupling; control coupling; data coupling; hybrid coupling.**

pattern-sensitive fault. *See:* **data-sensitive fault.**

pause. To suspend the execution of a computer program. *Syn:* **halt (2).** *Contrast with:* **stop.**

PCA. Acronym for **physical configuration audit.**

PDL. Acronym for **program design language.**

PDR. Acronym for **preliminary design review.**

perfective maintenance. Software maintenance performed to improve the performance, maintainability, or other attributes of a computer program. *Contrast with:* **adaptive maintenance; corrective maintenance.**

performance. The degree to which a system or component accomplishes its designated functions within given constraints, such as speed, accuracy, or memory usage.

performance requirement. A requirement that imposes conditions on a functional requirement; for example, a requirement that specifies the speed, accuracy, or memory usage with which a given function must be performed. *Contrast with:* **design requirement; functional requirement; implementation requirement; interface requirement; physical requirement.**

performance specification. A document that specifies the performance characteristics that a system or component must possess. These characteristics typically include speed, accuracy, and memory usage. Often part of a requirements specification.

performance testing. Testing conducted to evaluate the compliance of a system or component with specified performance requirements. *See also:* **functional testing.**

Petri net. An abstract, formal model of information flow, showing static and dynamic properties of a system. A Petri net is usually represented as a graph having two types of nodes (called places and transitions) connected by arcs, and markings (called tokens) indicating dynamic properties.

physical configuration audit (PCA). An audit conducted to verify that a configuration item, as built, conforms to the technical documentation that defines it. *See also:* **functional configuration audit.**

physical requirement. A requirement that specifies a physical characteristic that a system or system component must possess; for example, material, shape, size, weight. *Contrast with:* **design requirement; functional requirement; implementation requirement; interface requirement; performance requirement.**

pipeline. A software or hardware design technique in which the output of one process serves as input to a second, the output of the second process serves as input to a third, and so on, often with simultaneity within a single cycle time.

plan standard. (IEEE Std 1002-1987 [9]) A standard that describes the characteristics of a scheme for accomplishing defined objectives or work within specified resources.

playback. *See:* **reversible execution.**

pointer. A data item that specifies the location of another data item; for example, a data item that specifies the address of the next employee record to be processed.

port-to-port time. The elapsed time between the application of a stimulus to an input interface and the appearance of the response at an output interface. *See also:* **response time; think time; turnaround time.**

portability. The ease with which a system or component can be transferred from one hardware or software environment to another. *Syn:* **transportability.** *See also:* **machine independent.**

post-tested iteration. *See:* **UNTIL.**

postamble breakpoint. *See:* **epilog breakpoint.**

postmortem dump. A dump that is produced upon abnormal termination of a computer program. *See also:* **change dump; dynamic dump; memory dump; selective dump; snapshot dump; static dump.**

postprocessor. A computer program or routine that carries out some final processing step after the completion of the primary process; for example, a routine that reformats data for output. *Contrast with:* **preprocessor.**

practices. (IEEE Std 983-1986 [7]) Requirements employed to prescribe a disciplined uniform approach to the software development process. *See also:* **conventions; standards.**

pragma. *See:* **pseudo-instruction.**

pre-tested iteration. *See:* **WHILE.**

preamble breakpoint. *See:* **prolog breakpoint.**

precision. The degree of exactness or discrimination with which a quantity is stated; for example, a precision of 2 decimal places versus a precision of 5 decimal places. *Contrast with:* **accuracy.**

precompiler. A computer program or routine that processes source code and generates equivalent code that is acceptable to a compiler. For example, a routine that converts structured FORTRAN to ANSI-standard FORTRAN. *See also:* **preprocessor.**

preliminary design. (1) The process of analyzing design alternatives and defining the architecture, components, interfaces, and timing and sizing estimates for a system or component. *See also:* **detailed design.**
(2) The result of the process in (1).

preliminary design review (PDR). (1) A review conducted to evaluate the progress, technical adequacy, and risk resolution of the selected design approach for one or more configuration items; to determine each design's compatibility with the requirements for the configuration item; to evaluate the degree of definition and assess the technical risk associated with the selected manufacturing methods and processes; to establish the existence and compatibility of the physical and functional interfaces among the configuration items and other items of equipment, facilities, software and personnel; and, as applicable, to evaluate the preliminary operational and support documents. *See also:* **critical design review; system design review.**
(2) A review as in (1) of any hardware or software component.

preprocessor. A computer program or routine that carries out some processing step prior to the primary process; for example, a precompiler or other routine that reformats code or data for processing. *Contrast with:* **postprocessor.**

prestore. To store data that are required by a computer program or routine before the program or routine is entered.

prettyprinting. The use of indentation, blank lines, and other visual cues to show the logical structure of a program.

preventive maintenance. Maintenance performed for the purpose of preventing problems before they occur.

primitive type. *See:* **atomic type.**

priority. The level of importance assigned to an item.

priority interrupt. An interrupt performed to permit execution of a process that has a higher priority than the process currently executing.

private type. A data type whose structure and possible values are defined but are not revealed to the user of the type. *See also:* **information hiding.**

privileged instruction. A computer instruction that can be executed only by a supervisory program.

privileged state. *See:* **supervisor state.**

problem-oriented language. A programming language designed for the solution of a given class of problems. Examples are list processing languages, information retrieval languages, simulation languages.

problem state. In the operation of a computer system, a state in which programs other than the supervisory program can execute. *Syn:* **slave state; user state.** *Contrast with:* **supervisor state.**

procedural cohesion. A type of cohesion in which the tasks performed by a software module all contribute to a given program procedure, such as an iteration or decision process. *Contrast with:* **coincidental cohesion; communicational cohesion; functional cohesion; logical cohesion; sequential cohesion; temporal cohesion.**

procedural language. A programming language in which the user states a specific set of instructions that the computer must perform in a given sequence. All widely-used programming languages are of this type. *Syn:* **procedure-oriented language.** *Contrast with:* **nonprocedural language.** *See also:* **algebraic language; algorithmic language; list processing language; logic programming language.**

procedure. (1) A course of action to be taken to perform a given task.
(2) A written description of a course of action as in (1); for example, a documented test procedure.
(3) A portion of a computer program that is named and that performs a specific action.

procedure-oriented language. *See:* **procedural language.**

process. (1) A sequence of steps performed for a given purpose; for example, the software development process.
(2) An executable unit managed by an operating system scheduler. *See also:* **task; job.**
(3) To perform operations on data.

process management. (IEEE Std 1002-1987 [9]) The direction, control, and coordination of work performed to develop a product or perform a service. Example is quality assurance.

process standard. (IEEE Std 1002-1987 [9]) A standard that deals with the series of actions or operations used in making or achieving a product.

product analysis. (IEEE Std 1002-1987 [9]) The process of evaluating a product by manual or automated means to determine if the product has certain characteristics.

product baseline. In configuration management, the initial approved technical documentation (including, for software, the source code listing) defining a configuration item during the production, operation, maintenance, and logistic support of its life cycle. *Contrast with:* **allocated baseline; developmental configuration; functional baseline.** *See also:* **product configuration identification.**

product configuration identification. The current approved or conditionally approved technical documentation defining a configuration item during the production, operation, maintenance, and logistic support phases of its life cycle. It prescribes all necessary physical or form, fit, and function characteristics of a configuration item, the selected functional characteristics designated for production acceptance testing, and the production acceptance tests. *Contrast with:* **allocated configuration identification; functional configuration identification.** *See also:* **product baseline.**

product engineering. (IEEE Std 1002-1987 [9]) The technical processes to define, design, and construct or assemble a product.

product management. (IEEE Std 1002-1987 [9]) The definition, coordination, and control of the characteristics of a product during its development cycle. Example is configuration management.

product specification. (1) A document that specifies the design that production copies of a system or component must implement. *Note:* For software, this document describes the as-built version of the software. *See also:* **design description.**
(2) A document that describes the characteristics of a planned or existing product for consideration by potential customers or users.

product standard. (IEEE Std 1002-1987 [9]) A standard that defines what constitutes completeness and acceptability of items that are used or produced, formally or informally, during the software engineering process.

product support. (IEEE Std 1002-1987 [9]) The providing of information, assistance, and training to install and make software operational in its intended environment and to distribute improved capabilities to users.

production library. A software library containing software approved for current operational use. *Contrast with:* **master library; software development library; software repository; system library.**

professional standard. (IEEE Std 1002-1987 [9]) A standard that identifies a profession as a discipline and distinguishes it from other professions.

program. (1) *See:* **computer program.**
(2) To write a computer program.

program counter. *See:* **instruction counter.**

program definition language. *See:* **program design language.**

program design language (PDL). A specification language with special constructs and, sometimes, verification protocols, used to develop, analyze, and document a program design. *See also:* **hardware design language; pseudo code.**

program flowchart (flow chart). *See:* **flowchart.**

program instruction. A computer instruction in a source program. *Note:* A program instruction is distinguished from a computer instruction that results from assembly, compilation, or other interpretation process.

program library. *See:* **software library.**

program listing. A printout or other human readable display of the source and, sometimes, object statements that make up a computer program.

program mutation. (1) A computer program that has been purposely altered from the intended version to evaluate the ability of test cases to detect the alteration. *See also:* **mutation testing.**
(2) The process of creating an altered program as in (1).

program network chart. A diagram that shows the relationship between two or more computer programs.

program-sensitive fault. A fault that causes a failure when some particular sequence of program steps is executed. *Contrast with:* **data-sensitive fault.**

program status word (PSW). (1) A computer word that contains information specifying the current status of a computer program. The information may include error indicators, the address of the next instruction to be executed, currently enabled interrupts,

and so on.
(2) A special-purpose register that contains a program status word as in (1).
Syn: **status word.**

program structure diagram. *See:* **structure chart.**

program support library. *See:* **software development library.**

program synthesis. The use of software tools to aid in the transformation of a program specification into a program that realizes that specification.

programmable breakpoint. A breakpoint that automatically invokes a previously specified debugging process when initiated. *See also:* **code breakpoint; data breakpoint; dynamic breakpoint; epilog breakpoint; prolog breakpoint; static breakpoint.**

programmer manual. A document that provides the information necessary to develop or modify software for a given computer system. Typically described are the equipment configuration, operational characteristics, programming features, input/output features, and compilation or assembly features of the computer system. *See also:* **diagnostic manual; installation manual; operator manual; support manual; user manual.**

programming language. A language used to express computer programs. *See also:* **assembly language; high order language; machine language.** *Contrast with:* **query language; specification language.**

programming support environment. An integrated collection of software tools accessed via a single command language to provide programming support capabilities throughout the software life cycle. The environment typically includes tools for specifying, designing, editing, compiling, loading, testing, configuration management, and project management. Sometimes called integrated programming support environment. *See also:* **scaffolding.**

programming system. A set of programming languages and the support software (editors, compilers, linkers, etc.) necessary for using these languages with a given computer system.

project file. A central repository of material pertinent to a project. Contents typically include memos, plans, technical reports, and related items. *Syn:* **project notebook.**

project library. *See:* **software development library.**

project notebook. *See:* **project file.**

project plan. A document that describes the technical and management approach to be followed for a project. The plan typically describes the work to be done, the resources required, the methods to be used, the procedures to be followed, the schedules to be met, and the way that the project will be organized. For example, a software development plan.

prolog breakpoint. A breakpoint that is initiated upon entry into a program or routine. *Syn:* **preamble breakpoint.** *Contrast with:* **epilog breakpoint.** *See also:* **code breakpoint; data breakpoint; dynamic breakpoint; programmable breakpoint; static breakpoint.**

prompt. (1) A symbol or message displayed by a computer system, requesting input from the user of the system.
(2) To display a symbol or message as in (1).

proof of correctness. (1) A formal technique used to prove mathematically that a computer program satisfies its specified requirements. *See also:* **assertion; formal specification; inductive assertion method; partial correctness; total correctness.**
(2) A proof that results from applying the technique in (1).

protection exception. An exception that occurs when a program attempts to write into a protected area in storage. *See also:* **addressing exception; data exception; operation exception; overflow exception; underflow exception.**

protocol. A set of conventions that govern the interaction of processes, devices, and other components within a system.

prototype. A preliminary type, form, or instance of a system that serves as a model for later stages or for the final, complete version of the system.

prototyping. A hardware and software development technique in which a preliminary version of part or all of the hardware or software is developed to permit user feedback, determine feasibility, or investigate timing or other issues in support of the development process. *See also:* **rapid prototyping.**

pseudo code (pseudocode). A combination of programming language constructs and natural language used to express a computer program design. For example:

```
IF the data arrives faster than expected,
  THEN reject every third input.
  ELSE process all data received.
ENDIF
```

pseudo instruction. A source language instruction that provides information or direction to the assembler or compiler and is not translated into a target language instruction. For example, an instruction specifying the desired format of source code listings. *Syn:* **pragma; pseudo-op; pseudo operation.**

pseudo operation. *See:* **pseudo instruction.**

pseudo-op. *See:* **pseudo instruction.**

PSW. Acronym for **program status word.**

QA. Acronym for **quality assurance.**

QC. Acronym for **quality control.**

qualification. The process of determining whether a system or component is suitable for operational use.

qualification testing. Testing conducted to determine whether a system or component is suitable for operational use. *See also:* **acceptance testing; development testing; operational testing.**

quality. (1) The degree to which a system, component, or process meets specified requirements.
(2) The degree to which a system, component, or process meets customer or user needs or expectations.

quality assurance (QA). (1) A planned and systematic pattern of all actions necessary to provide adequate confidence that an item or product conforms to established technical requirements.
(2) A set of activities designed to evaluate the process by which products are developed or manufactured. *Contrast with:* **quality control (1).**

quality attribute. A feature or characteristic that affects an item's quality. *Syn:* **quality factor.** *Note:* In a hierarchy of quality attributes, higher level attributes may be called quality factors, lower level attributes called quality attributes.

quality control (QC). *Note:* This term has no standardized meaning in software engineering at this time. Candidate definitions are: (1) A set of activities designed to evaluate the quality of developed or manufactured products. *Contrast with:* **quality assurance (2).**
(2) The process of verifying one's own work or that of a co-worker.
(3) Synonym for **quality assurance.**

quality factor. *See:* **quality attribute.** *Note:* In a hierarchy of quality attributes, higher level attributes may be called quality factors, lower level attributes called quality attributes.

quality metric. (1) A quantitative measure of the degree to which an item possesses a given quality attribute.
(2) A function whose inputs are software data and whose output is a single numerical value that can be interpreted as the degree to which the software possesses a given quality attribute.

query language. A language used to access information stored in a database. *Contrast with:* **programming language; specification language.**

queue. A list in which items are appended to the last position of the list and retrieved from the first position of the list. *Note:* IEEE Std 610.5-1990 [2] defines Data Management terms.

quiescing. The process of bringing a device or system to a halt by rejecting new requests for work.

random failure. A failure whose occurrence is unpredictable except in a probabilistic or statistical sense. *See also:* **intermittent fault; transient error.**

rapid prototyping. A type of prototyping in which emphasis is placed on developing prototypes early in the development process to permit early feedback and analysis in support of the development process. *Contrast with:* **waterfall model.** *See also:* **data structure-centered design; incremental development; input-process-output; modular decomposition; object-oriented design; spiral model; stepwise refinement; structured design; transaction analysis; transform analysis.**

read. To access data from a storage device or data medium. *See also:* **destructive read; nondestructive read.** *Contrast with:* **write.**

real address. The address of a storage location in the main storage part of a virtual storage system. *Contrast with:* **virtual address.**

real storage. The main storage portion of a virtual storage system. *Contrast with:* **virtual storage.**

real time. Pertaining to a system or mode of operation in which computation is performed during the actual time that an external process occurs, in order that the computation results can be used to control, monitor, or respond in a timely manner to the external process. *Contrast with:* **batch.** *See also:* **conversational; interactive; interrupt; on-line.**

real type. A data type whose members can assume real numbers as values and can be operated on by real number arithmetic operations, such as addition, subtraction, multiplication, division, and square root. *Contrast with:* **character type; enumeration type; integer type; logical type.**

record. A set of related data items treated as a unit. For example, in stock control, the data for each invoice could constitute one record.

recovery. The restoration of a system, program, database, or other system resource to a state in which it can perform required functions. *See also:* **backward recovery; checkpoint; forward recovery.**

recursion. (1) A process in which a software module calls itself. *See also:* **simultaneous recursion.**
(2) The process of defining or generating a process or data structure in terms of itself.

recursive. (1) Pertaining to a software module that calls itself.
(2) Pertaining to a process or data structure that is defined or generated in terms of itself.

redundancy. In fault tolerance, the presence of auxiliary components in a system to perform the same or similar functions as other elements for the purpose of preventing or recovering from failures. *See also:* **active redundancy; diversity; homogeneous redundancy; standby redundancy.**

reenterable. *See:* **reentrant.**

reentrant. Pertaining to a software module that can be entered as part of one process while also in execution as part of another process and still achieve the desired results. *Syn:* **reenterable.**

reentry point. The place in a software module at which the module is reentered following a call to another module.

regression testing. Selective retesting of a system or component to verify that modifications have not caused unintended effects and that the system or component still complies with its specified requirements.

relative address. An address that must be adjusted by the addition of an offset to determine the address of the storage location to be accessed. *Contrast with:* **absolute address.** *See also:* **base address; indexed address; self-relative address.**

relative loader. *See:* **relocating loader.**

reliability. The ability of a system or component to perform its required functions under stated conditions for a specified period of time. *See also:* **availability; MTBF.**

reliability growth. The improvement in reliability that results from correction of faults.

relocatable. Pertaining to code that can be loaded into any part of main memory. The starting address is established by the loader, which then adjusts the addresses in the code to reflect the storage locations into which the code has been loaded. *See also:* **relocating loader.**

relocatable address. An address that is to be adjusted by the loader when the computer program containing the address is loaded into memory. *Contrast with:* **absolute address.**

relocatable code. Code containing addresses that are to be adjusted by the loader to reflect the storage locations into which the code is loaded. *Contrast with:* **absolute code.**

relocate. To move machine code from one portion of main memory to another and to adjust the addresses so that the code can be executed in its new location.

relocating assembler. An assembler that produces relocatable code. *Contrast with:* **absolute assembler.**

relocating loader. A loader that reads relocatable code into main memory and adjusts the addresses in the code to reflect the storage locations into which the code has been loaded. *Syn:* **relative loader.** *Contrast with:* **absolute loader.**

relocation dictionary. The part of an object module or load module that identifies the addresses that must be adjusted when a relocation occurs.

relocation factor. *See:* **offset (1).**

remote batch entry. *See:* **remote job entry.**

remote job entry (RJE). Submission of jobs through a remote input device connected to a computer through a data link. *Syn:* **remote batch entry.**

repeatability. *See:* **test repeatability.**

repetitive addressing. A method of implied addressing in which the operation field of a computer instruction is understood to address the operands of the last instruction executed. *Contrast with:* **one-ahead addressing.**

replay. *See:* **reversible execution.**

report standard. (IEEE Std 1002-1987 [9]) A standard that describes the characteristics of describing results of engineering and management activities.

representation standard. (IEEE Std 1002-1987 [9]) A standard that describes the characteristics of portraying aspects of an engineering or management product.

requirement. (1) A condition or capability needed by a user to solve a problem or achieve an objective.
(2) A condition or capability that must be met or possessed by a system or system component to satisfy a contract, standard, specification, or other formally imposed documents.
(3) A documented representation of a condition or capability as in (1) or (2).
See also: **design requirement; functional requirement; implementation requirement; interface requirement; performance requirement; physical requirement.**

requirement standard. (IEEE Std 1002-1987 [9]) A standard that describes the characteristics of a requirements specification.

requirements analysis. (1) The process of studying user needs to arrive at a definition of system, hardware, or software requirements.
(2) The process of studying and refining

system, hardware, or software requirements.

requirements phase. The period of time in the software life cycle during which the requirements for a software product are defined and documented.

requirements review. A process or meeting during which the requirements for a system, hardware item, or software item are presented to project personnel, managers, users, customers, or other interested parties for comment or approval. Types include system requirements review, software requirements review. *Contrast with:* **code review; design review; formal qualification review; test readiness review.**

requirements specification. A document that specifies the requirements for a system or component. Typically included are functional requirements, performance requirements, interface requirements, design requirements, and development standards. *Contrast with:* **design description.** *See also:* **functional specification; performance specification.**

requirements specification language. A specification language with special constructs and, sometimes, verification protocols, used to develop, analyze, and document hardware or software requirements. *See also:* **design language.**

rescue point. *See:* **restart point.**

reserved word. A word in a programming language whose meaning is fixed by the rules of that language and which, in certain or all contexts, cannot be used by the programmer for any purpose other than its intended one. Examples include IF, THEN, WHILE.

reset. To set a variable, register, or other storage location back to a prescribed state. *See also:* **clear; initialize.**

resident control program. *See:* **kernel (1).**

residual control. A microprogramming technique in which the meaning of a field in a microinstruction depends on the value in an auxiliary register. *Contrast with:* **bit steering.** *See also:* **two-level encoding.**

resource allocation. *See:* **computer resource allocation.**

resource management. (IEEE Std 1002-1987 [9]) The identification, estimation, allocation, and monitoring of the means used to develop a product or perform a service. Example is estimating.

response time. The elapsed time between the end of an inquiry or command to an interactive computer system and the beginning of the system's response. *See also:* **port-to-port time; think time; turnaround time.**

restart. To cause a computer program to resume execution after a failure, using status and results recorded at a checkpoint.

restart point. A point in a computer program at which execution can be restarted following a failure. *Syn:* **rescue point.**

retirement. (1) Permanent removal of a system or component from its operational environment.
(2) Removal of support from an operational system or component.
See also: **software life cycle; system life cycle.**

retirement phase. The period of time in the software life cycle during which support for a software product is terminated.

retrospective trace. A trace produced from historical data recorded during the execution of a computer program. *Note:* This differs from an ordinary trace, which is produced cumulatively during program execution. *See also:* **execution trace; subroutine trace; symbolic trace; variable trace.**

return. (1) To transfer control from a software module to the module that called it. *See also:* **return code.**
(2) To assign a value to a parameter that is accessible by a calling module; for example, to assign the value 25 to parameter AGE for use by a calling module. *See also:* **return value.**

(3) A computer instruction or process that performs the transfer in (1).

return code. A code used to influence the execution of a calling module following a return from a called module.

return value. A value assigned to a parameter by a called module for access by the calling module.

reusability. The degree to which a software module or other work product can be used in more than one computer program or software system. *See also:* **generality.**

reusable. Pertaining to a software module or other work product that can be used in more than one computer program or software system.

reverse execution. *See:* **reversible execution.**

reversible execution. A debugging technique in which a history of program execution is recorded and then replayed under the user's control, in either the forward or backward direction. *Syn:* **backward execution; playback; replay; reverse execution.**

review. A process or meeting during which a work product, or set of work products, is presented to project personnel, managers, users, customers, or other interested parties for comment or approval. Types include code review, design review, formal qualification review, requirements review, test readiness review.

RJE. Acronym for **remote job entry.**

robustness. The degree to which a system or component can function correctly in the presence of invalid inputs or stressful environmental conditions. *See also:* **error tolerance; fault tolerance.**

roll in. To transfer data or computer program segments from auxiliary storage to main storage. *Contrast with:* **roll out.** *See also:* **swap.**

roll out. To transfer data or computer program segments from main storage to auxiliary storage for the purpose of freeing main storage for other uses. *Contrast with:* **roll in.** *See also:* **swap.**

root compiler. A compiler whose output is a machine independent, intermediate-level representation of a program. A root compiler, when combined with a code generator, comprises a full compiler.

routine. A subprogram that is called by other programs and subprograms. *Note:* The terms "routine," "subprogram," and "subroutine" are defined and used differently in different programming languages; the preceding definition is advanced as a proposed standard. *See also:* **coroutine; subroutine.**

rule-based language. A nonprocedural language that permits the user to state a set of rules and to express queries or problems that use these rules. *See also:* **declarative language; interactive language.**

run. (1) In software engineering, a single, usually continuous, execution of a computer program. *See also:* **run time.**
(2) To execute a computer program.

run stream. *See:* **job stream.**

run time. (1) The instant at which a computer program begins to execute.
(2) The period of time during which a computer program is executing.
(3) *See:* **execution time.**

running time. *See:* **execution time.**

scaffolding. Computer programs and data files built to support software development and testing, but not intended to be included in the final product. For example, dummy routines or files, test case generators, software monitors, stubs. *See also:* **programming support environment.**

scheduler. A computer program, usually part of an operating system, that schedules, initiates, and terminates jobs.

SCN. Acronym for **specification change notice.**

SDD. (1) Acronym for **software design description.**
(2) (DoD) Acronym for software design document.

SDP. Acronym for **software development plan.**

SDR. Acronym for **system design review.**

second generation language (2GL). *See:* **assembly language.**

security kernel. A small, self-contained collection of key security-related statements that works as a privileged part of an operating system, specifying and enforcing criteria that must be met for programs and data to be accessed.

segment. (1) One of the subsystems or combinations of subsystems that make up an overall system; for example, the accounts payable segment of a financial system.
(2) In storage allocation, a self-contained portion of a computer program that can be executed without maintaining the entire program in main storage. *See also:* **page.**
(3) A collection of data that is stored or transferred as a unit.
(4) In path analysis, a sequence of computer program statements between two consecutive branch points.
(5) To divide a system, computer program, or data file into segments as in (1), (2), or (3).

selective choice construct. *See:* **branch.**

selective dump. A dump of designated storage location areas only. *See also:* **change dump; dynamic dump; memory dump; postmortem dump; snapshot dump; static dump.**

selective trace. A variable trace that involves only selected variables. *See also:* **execution trace; retrospective trace; subroutine trace; symbolic trace; variable trace.**

self-descriptiveness. The degree to which a system or component contains enough information to explain its objectives and properties. *See also:* **maintainability; testability; usability.**

self-documented. Pertaining to source code that contains comments explaining its objectives, operation, and other information useful in understanding and maintaining the code.

self-relative address. An address that must be added to the address of the instruction in which it appears to obtain the address of the storage location to be accessed. *See also:* **base address; indexed address; offset; relative address.**

semantic error. An error resulting from a misunderstanding of the relationship of symbols or groups of symbols to their meanings in a given language. *Contrast with:* **syntactic error.**

semantics. The relationships of symbols or groups of symbols to their meanings in a given language. *Contrast with:* **syntax.**

semaphore. A shared variable used to synchronize concurrent processes by indicating whether an action has been completed or an event has occurred. *See also:* **flag; indicator.**

sequential. Pertaining to the occurrence of two or more events or activities in such a manner that one must finish before the next begins. *Syn:* **serial (2).** *See also:* **consecutive.**

sequential cohesion. A type of cohesion in which the output of one task performed by a software module serves as input to another task performed by the module. *Contrast with:* **coincidental cohesion; communicational cohesion; functional cohesion; logical cohesion; procedural cohesion; temporal cohesion.**

sequential construct. *See:* **serial construct.**

serial. (1) Pertaining to the sequential transfer, occurrence, or processing of the individual parts of a whole, such as the bits of a character, using the same facilities for successive parts. *Contrast with:* **parallel (1).**
(2) *See:* **sequential.**

serial construct. A program construct consisting of a sequence of steps not involving a decision or loop. *Syn:* **sequential construct.**

set-up time. The period of time during which a system or component is being prepared for a specific operation. *See also:* **busy time; down time; idle time; up time.**

severity. *See:* **criticality.**

shell. A computer program or routine that provides an interface between the user and a computer system or program.

simple buffering. A buffering technique in which a buffer is allocated to a computer program for the duration of the program's execution. *Contrast with:* **dynamic buffering.**

simplicity. The degree to which a system or component has a design and implementation that is straightforward and easy to understand. *Contrast with:* **complexity.**

simulation. (1) A model that behaves or operates like a given system when provided a set of controlled inputs. *See also:* **emulation.**
(2) The process of developing or using a model as in (1).

simulator. A device, computer program, or system that behaves or operates like a given system when provided a set of controlled inputs. *See also:* **emulator.**

simultaneous. Pertaining to the occurrence of two or more events at the same instant of time. *Contrast with:* **concurrent.**

simultaneous recursion. A situation in which two software modules call each other.

single-address instruction. *See:* **one-address instruction.**

single-level encoding. A microprogramming technique in which different microoperations are encoded as different values in the same field of a microinstruction. *Contrast with:* **two-level encoding.**

single-operand instruction. *See:* **one-address instruction.**

single-step execution. *See:* **single-step operation.**

single-step operation. A debugging technique in which a single computer instruction, or part of an instruction, is executed in response to an external signal. *Syn:* **single-step execution; step-by-step operation.**

sizing. The process of estimating the amount of computer storage or the number of source lines required for a software system or component. *Contrast with:* **timing.**

slave state. *See:* **problem state.**

snapshot dump. A dynamic dump of the contents of one or more specified storage areas. *See also:* **change dump; dynamic dump; memory dump; postmortem dump; selective dump; static dump.**

soft error.* *See:* **transient error.**
* Deprecated.

soft failure. A failure that permits continued operation of a system with partial operational capability. *Contrast with:* **hard failure.**

software. Computer programs, procedures, and possibly associated documentation and data pertaining to the operation of a computer system. *See also:* **application software; support software; system software.** *Contrast with:* **hardware.**

software characteristic. (IEEE Std 1008-1987 [10]) An inherent, possibly accidental, trait, quality, or property of software (for example, functionality, performance, attributes, design constraints, number of states, lines or branches).

software configuration management. *See:* **configuration management.**

software design description (SDD). (1) (IEEE Std 1012-1986 [12]) A representation of software created to facilitate analysis, planning, implementation, and decision making. The software design description is used as a medium for communicating software design information, and may be

thought of as a blueprint or model of the system.
(2) (IEEE Std 1016-1987 [13]) A representation of a software system created to facilitate analysis, planning, implementation, and decision making. A blueprint or model of the software system. The SDD is used as the primary medium for communicating software design information.

software development cycle. The period of time that begins with the decision to develop a software product and ends when the software is delivered. This cycle typically includes a requirements phase, design phase, implementation phase, test phase, and sometimes, installation and checkout phase. *Contrast with:* **software life cycle.**
Notes: (1) The phases listed above may overlap or be performed iteratively, depending upon the software development approach used.
(2) This term is sometimes used to mean a longer period of time, either the period that ends when the software is no longer being enhanced by the developer, or the entire software life cycle.

software development file (SDF). A collection of material pertinent to the development of a given software unit or set of related units. Contents typically include the requirements, design, technical reports, code listings, test plans, test results, problem reports, schedules, and notes for the units. *Syn:* **software development folder; software development notebook; unit development folder.**

software development folder. *See:* **software development file.**

software development library. A software library containing computer readable and human readable information relevant to a software development effort. *Syn:* **project library; program support library.** *Contrast with:* **master library; production library; software repository; system library.**

software development notebook. *See:* **software development file.**

software development plan (SDP). A project plan for a software development project.

software development process. The process by which user needs are translated into a software product. The process involves translating user needs into software requirements, transforming the software requirements into design, implementing the design in code, testing the code, and sometimes, installing and checking out the software for operational use. *Note:* These activities may overlap or be performed iteratively. *See also:* **incremental development; rapid prototyping; spiral model; waterfall model.**

software diversity. A software development technique in which two or more functionally identical variants of a program are developed from the same specification by different programmers or programming teams with the intent of providing error detection, increased reliability, additional documentation, or reduced probability that programming or compiler errors will influence the end results. *See also:* **diversity.**

software engineering. (1) The application of a systematic, disciplined, quantifiable approach to the development, operation, and maintenance of software; that is, the application of engineering to software.
(2) The study of approaches as in (1).

software engineering environment. The hardware, software, and firmware used to perform a software engineering effort. Typical elements include computer equipment, compilers, assemblers, operating systems, debuggers, simulators, emulators, test tools, documentation tools, and database management systems.

software feature. (1) (IEEE Std 829-1983 [5]) A distinguishing characteristic of a software item (for example, performance, portability, or functionality).
(2) (IEEE Std 1008-1987 [10]) A software characteristic specified or implied by requirements documentation (for example, functionality, performance, attributes, or design constraints).

software item. (IEEE Std 829-1983 [5]) Source code, object code, job control code, control data, or a collection of these items.

software library. A controlled collection of software and related documentation designed to aid in software development, use, or maintenance. Types include master library, production library, software development library, software repository, system library. *Syn:* **program library.**

software life cycle. The period of time that begins when a software product is conceived and ends when the software is no longer available for use. The software life cycle typically includes a concept phase, requirements phase, design phase, implementation phase, test phase, installation and checkout phase, operation and maintenance phase, and, sometimes, retirement phase. *Note:* These phases may overlap or be performed iteratively. *Contrast with:* **software development cycle.**

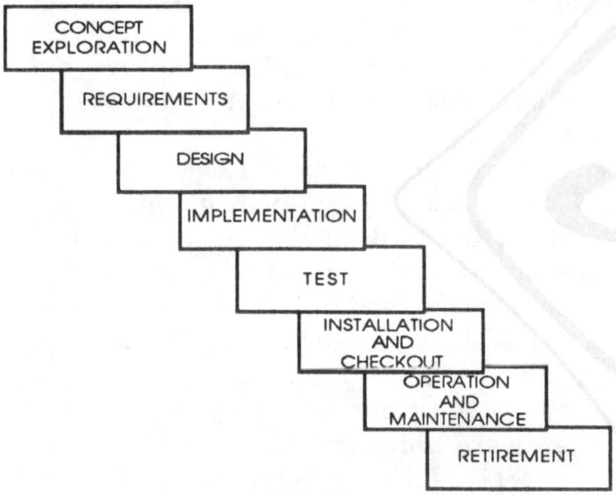

Fig 15
Sample Software Life Cycle

software maintenance. *See:* **maintenance (1).**

software monitor. A software tool that executes concurrently with another program and provides detailed information about the execution of the other program. *See also:* **hardware monitor; monitor.**

software product. (1) The complete set of computer programs, procedures, and possibly associated documentation and data designated for delivery to a user.
(2) Any of the individual items in (1).

software quality assurance. *See:* **quality assurance.**

software quality metric. *See:* **quality metric.**

software repository. A software library providing permanent, archival storage for software and related documentation. *Contrast with:* **master library; production library; software development library; system library.**

software requirements review (SRR). (1) A review of the requirements specified for one or more software configuration items to evaluate their responsiveness to and interpretation of the system requirements and to determine whether they form a satisfactory basis for proceeding into preliminary design of the configuration items. *See also:* **system requirements review.** *Note:* This review is called software specification review by the U.S. Department of Defense.
(2) A review as in (1) for any software component.

software requirements specification (SRS). (IEEE Std 1012-1986 [12]) Documentation of the essential requirements (functions, performance, design constraints, and attributes) of the software and its external interfaces.

software specification review (SSR). *See:* **software requirements review.**

software test incident. (IEEE Std 1008-1987 [10]) Any event occurring during the execution of a software test that requires investigation.

software tool. A computer program used in the development, testing, analysis, or maintenance of a program or its documentation. Examples include comparator, cross-reference generator, decompiler, driver, editor, flowcharter, monitor, test case generator, timing analyzer.

source address. The address of a device or storage location from which data is to be transferred. *Contrast with:* **destination address.**

source code. Computer instructions and data definitions expressed in a form suitable for input to an assembler, compiler, or other translator. *Note:* A source program is made up of source code. *Contrast with:* **object code.**

source code generator. *See:* **code generator (2).**

source language. The language in which the input to a machine-aided translation process is represented. For example, the language used to write a computer program. *Contrast with:* **target language.**

source program. A computer program that must be compiled, assembled, or otherwise translated in order to be executed by a computer. *Contrast with:* **object program.**

specific address. *See:* **absolute address.**

specific code. *See:* **absolute code.**

specification. A document that specifies, in a complete, precise, verifiable manner, the requirements, design, behavior, or other characteristics of a system or component, and, often, the procedures for determining whether these provisions have been satisfied. *See also:* **formal specification; product specification; requirements specification.**

specification change notice (SCN). A document used in configuration management to propose, transmit, and record changes to a specification. *See also:* **configuration control; engineering change; notice of revision.**

specification language. A language, often a machine-processible combination of natural and formal language, used to express the requirements, design, behavior, or other characteristics of a system or component. For example, a design language or requirements specification language. *Contrast with:* **programming language; query language.**

specification tree. A diagram that depicts all of the specifications for a given system and shows their relationships to one another. *See also:* **documentation tree.**

spiral model. A model of the software development process in which the constituent activities, typically requirements analysis, preliminary and detailed design, coding, integration, and testing, are performed iteratively until the software is complete. *Contrast with:* **waterfall model.** *See also:* **incremental development; rapid prototyping.**

spool. To read input data, or write output data, to auxiliary or main storage for later processing or output, in order to permit input/output devices to operate concurrently with job execution. Derived from the acronym SPOOL for Simultaneous Peripheral Output On Line.

spooler. A program that initiates and controls spooling.

SRR. (1) Acronym for **software requirements review.**
(2) (DoD) Acronym for system requirements review.

SRS. Acronym for **software requirements specification.**

SSR. Acronym for **software specification review.** *See:* **software requirements review.**

stand-alone. Pertaining to hardware or software that is capable of performing its function without being connected to other components; for example, a stand-alone word processing system.

standards. (IEEE Std 983-1986 [7]) Mandatory requirements employed and enforced to prescribe a disciplined uniform approach to software development, that is, mandatory conventions and practices are in fact standards. *See also:* **practices.**

standby redundancy. In fault tolerance, the use of redundant elements that are left inoperative until a failure occurs in a primary element. *Contrast with:* **active redundancy.**

standby time. *See:* **idle time.**

starting address. The address of the first instruction of a computer program in main storage. *Note:* This address may or may not be the same as the program's origin, depending upon whether there are data preceding the first instruction. *Contrast with:* **origin.** *See also:* **assembled origin; loaded origin.**

state. (1) A condition or mode of existence that a system, component, or simulation may be in; for example, the pre-flight state of an aircraft navigation program or the input state of given channel.
(2) The values assumed at a given instant by the variables that define the characteristics of a system, component, or simulation.

state data. (IEEE Std 1008-1987 [10]) Data that defines an internal state of the test unit and is used to establish that state or compare with existing states.

state diagram. A diagram that depicts the states that a system or component can assume, and shows the events or circumstances that cause or result from a change from one state to another.

state transition diagram. *See:* **state diagram.**

statement. In a programming language, a meaningful expression that defines data, specifies program actions, or directs the assembler or compiler. *See also:* **assignment statement; control statement; declaration.**

statement testing. Testing designed to execute each statement of a computer program. *Contrast with:* **branch testing; path testing.**

static. Pertaining to an event or process that occurs without computer program execution; for example, static analysis, static binding. *Contrast with:* **dynamic.**

static analysis. The process of evaluating a system or component based on its form, structure, content, or documentation. *Contrast with:* **dynamic analysis.** *See also:* **inspection; walk-through.**

static binding. Binding performed prior to the execution of a computer program and not subject to change during program execution. *Contrast with:* **dynamic binding.**

static breakpoint. A breakpoint that can be set at compile time, such as entry into a given routine. *Contrast with:* **dynamic breakpoint.** *See also:* **code breakpoint; data breakpoint; epilog breakpoint; programmable breakpoint; prolog breakpoint.**

static dump. A dump that is produced before or after the execution of a computer program. *Contrast with:* **dynamic dump.** *See also:* **change dump; memory dump; postmortem dump; selective dump; snapshot dump.**

static error. An error that is independent of the time-varying nature of an input. *Contrast with:* **dynamic error.**

status code. A code used to indicate the results of a computer program operation. For example, a code indicating a carry, an overflow, or a parity error. *Syn:* **condition code.**

step-by-step operation. *See:* **single-step operation.**

stepwise refinement. A software development technique in which data and processing steps are defined broadly at first and then further defined with increasing detail. *See also:* **data structure-centered design; input-process-output; modular decomposition; object-oriented design; rapid prototyping; structured design; transaction analysis; transform analysis.**

stop. To terminate the execution of a computer program. *Syn:* **halt (1).** *Contrast with:* **pause.**

storage allocation. An element of computer resource allocation, consisting of assigning storage areas to specific jobs and performing related procedures, such as transfer of data between main and auxiliary storage, to support the assignments made. *See also:* **buffer; contiguous allocation; cyclic search; memory compaction; overlay; paging; virtual storage.**

storage breakpoint. *See:* **data breakpoint.**

storage capacity. The maximum number of items that can be held in a given storage device; usually measured in words or bytes. *See also:* **channel capacity; memory capacity.**

storage efficiency. The degree to which a system or component performs its designated functions with minimum consumption of available storage. *See also:* **execution efficiency.**

store. (1) To place or retain data in a storage device.
(2) To copy computer instructions or data from a register to internal storage or from internal storage to external storage. *Contrast with:* **load (2).** *See also:* **fetch; move.**

straight-line code. A sequence of computer instructions in which there are no loops.

straight-line coding. A programming technique in which loops are avoided by stating explicitly and in full all of the instructions that would be involved in the execution of each loop. *See also:* **unwind.**

stratified language. A language that cannot be used as its own metalanguage. Examples include FORTRAN, COBOL. *Contrast with:* **unstratified language.**

stress testing. Testing conducted to evaluate a system or component at or beyond the limits of its specified requirements. *See also:* **boundary value.**

strong typing. A feature of some programming languages that requires the type of each data item to be declared, precludes the application of operators to inappropriate data types, and prevents the interaction of data items of incompatible types.

structural testing. Testing that takes into account the internal mechanism of a system or component. Types include branch testing, path testing, statement testing. *Syn:* **glass-box testing; white-box testing.** *Contrast with:* **functional testing (1).**

structure chart. A diagram that identifies modules, activities, or other entities in a system or computer program and shows how larger or more general entities break down into smaller, more specific entities. *Note:* The result is not necessarily the same as that shown in a call graph. *Syn:* **hierarchy chart; program structure chart.** *Contrast with:* **call graph.**

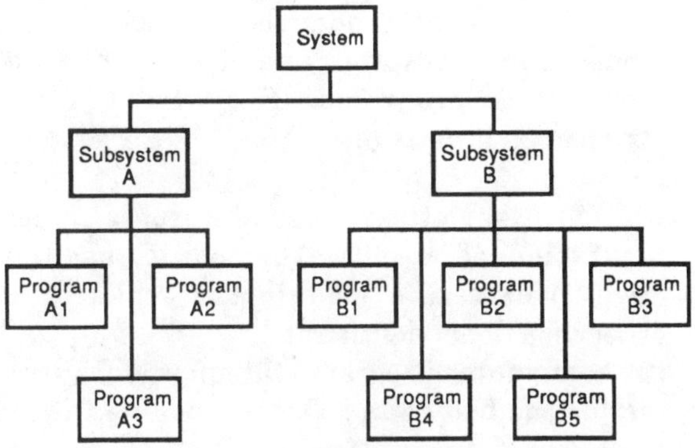

Fig 16
Structure Chart

structure clash. In software design, a situation in which a module must deal with two or more data sets that have incompatible data structures. *See also:* **data structure-centered design; order clash.**

structured design. (1) Any disciplined approach to software design that adheres to specified rules based on principles such as modularity, top-down design, and stepwise refinement of data, system structures, and processing steps. *See also:* **data structure-centered design; input-process-output; modular decomposition; object-oriented design; rapid prototyping; stepwise refinement; transaction analysis; transform analysis.**
(2) The result of applying the approach in (1).

structured program. A computer program constructed of a basic set of control structures, each having one entry and one exit. The set of control structures typically includes: sequence of two or more instructions, conditional selection of one of two or more sequences of instructions, and repetition of a sequence of instructions. *See also:* **structured design.**

structured programming. Any software development technique that includes structured design and results in the development of structured programs.

structured programming language. A programming language that provides the structured program constructs, namely, single-entry-single-exit sequences, branches, and loops, and facilitates the development of structured programs. *See also:* **block-structured language.**

stub. (1) A skeletal or special-purpose implementation of a software module, used to develop or test a module that calls or is otherwise dependent on it.
(2) A computer program statement substituting for the body of a software module that is or will be defined elsewhere.

subprogram. A separately compilable, executable component of a computer program. *Note:* The terms "routine," "subprogram," and "subroutine" are defined and used differently in different programming languages; the preceding definition is advanced as a proposed standard. *See also:* **coroutine; main program; routine; subroutine.**

subroutine. A routine that returns control to the program or subprogram that called it. *Note:* The terms "routine," "subprogram," and "subroutine" are defined and used differently in different programming languages; the preceding definition is advanced as a proposed standard. *Contrast with:* **coroutine.** *See also:* **closed subroutine; open subroutine.**

subroutine trace. A record of all or selected subroutines or function calls performed during the execution of a computer program and, optionally, the values of parameters passed to and returned by each subroutine or function. *Syn:* **call trace.** *See also:* **execution trace; retrospective trace; subroutine trace; symbolic trace; variable trace.**

subsystem. A secondary or subordinate system within a larger system.

subtype. A subset of a data type, obtained by constraining the set of possible values of the data type. *Note:* The operations applicable to the subtype are the same as those of the original data type. *See also:* **derived type.**

supervisor. *See:* **supervisory program.**

supervisor state. In the operation of a computer system, a state in which the supervisory program is executing. This state usually has higher priority than, and precludes the execution of, application programs. *Syn:* **executive state; master state; privileged state.** *Contrast with:* **problem state.**

supervisory program. A computer program, usually part of an operating system, that controls the execution of other computer programs and regulates the flow of work in a computer system. *Syn:* **control program; executive; executive program; supervisor.** *See also:* **supervisor state.**

support. The set of activities necessary to ensure that an operational system or component fulfills its original requirements and any subsequent modifications to those requirements. For example, software or hardware maintenance, user training. *See also:* **software life cycle; system life cycle.**

support manual. A document that provides the information necessary to service and maintain an operational system or component throughout its life cycle. Typically described are the hardware and software that make up the system or component and procedures for servicing, repairing, or reprogramming it. *Syn:* **maintenance manual.** *See also:* **diagnostic manual; installation manual; operator manual; programmer manual; user manual.**

support software. Software that aids in the development or maintenance of other software; for example, compilers, loaders, and other utilities. *Contrast with:* **application software.** *See also:* **system software.**

swap. (1) An exchange of the contents of two storage areas, usually an area of main storage with an area of auxiliary storage. *See also:* **roll in; roll out.**
(2) To perform an exchange as in (1).

symbol table. A table that presents program symbols and their corresponding addresses, values, and other attributes.

symbolic address. An address expressed as a name or label that must be translated to the absolute address of the device or storage location to be accessed. *Contrast with:* **absolute address.**

symbolic execution. A software analysis technique in which program execution is simulated using symbols, such as variable names, rather than actual values for input data, and program outputs are expressed as logical or mathematical expressions involving these symbols.

symbolic language. A programming language that expresses operations and addresses in symbols convenient to humans rather than in machine language. Examples are assembly language, high order language. *Contrast with:* **machine language.**

symbolic trace. A record of the source statements and branch outcomes that are encountered when a computer program is executed using symbolic, rather than actual, values for input data. *See also:* **execution trace; retrospective trace; subroutine trace; variable trace.**

syntactic error. A violation of the structural or grammatical rules defined for a language; for example, using the statement $B + C = A$ in FORTRAN, rather than the correct $A = B + C$. *Syn:* **syntax error.** *Contrast with:* **semantic error.**

syntax. The structural or grammatical rules that define how the symbols in a language are to be combined to form words, phrases, expressions, and other allowable constructs. *Contrast with:* **semantics.**

syntax error. *See:* **syntactic error.**

synthetic address. *See:* **generated address.**

system. A collection of components organized to accomplish a specific function or set of functions.

system design review (SDR). A review conducted to evaluate the manner in which the requirements for a system have been allocated to configuration items, the system engineering process that produced the allocation, the engineering planning for the next phase of the effort, manufacturing considerations, and the planning for production engineering. *See also:* **critical design review; preliminary design review.**

system development cycle. The period of time that begins with the decision to develop a system and ends when the system is delivered to its end user. *Note:* This term is sometimes used to mean a longer period of time, either the period that ends when the system is no longer being enhanced, or the entire system life cycle. *Contrast with:* **system life cycle.** *See also:* **software development cycle.**

system flowchart (flow chart). *See:* **flowchart.**

system library. A software library containing system-resident software that can be accessed for use or incorporated into other programs by reference; for example, a macro library. *Contrast with:* **master library; production library; software development library; software repository.**

system life cycle. The period of time that begins when a system is conceived and ends when the system is no longer available for use. *See also:* **system development cycle; software life cycle.**

system model. In computer performance evaluation, a representation of a system depicting the relationships between workloads and performance measures in the system. *See also:* **workload model.**

system profile. A set of measurements used in computer performance evaluation, describing the proportion of time each of the major resources in a computer system is busy, divided by the time that resource is available.

system requirements review (SRR). A review conducted to evaluate the completeness and adequacy of the requirements defined for a system; to evaluate the system engineering process that produced those requirements; to assess the results of system engineering studies; and to evaluate system engineering plans. *See also:* **software requirements review.**

system resources chart. *See:* **block diagram.**

system software. Software designed to facilitate the operation and maintenance of a computer system and its associated programs; for example, operating systems, assemblers, utilities. *Contrast with:* **application software.** *See also:* **support software.**

system testing. Testing conducted on a complete, integrated system to evaluate the system's compliance with its specified requirements. *See also:* **component testing; integration testing; interface testing; unit testing.**

target language. The language in which the output from a machine-aided translation process is represented. For example, the language output by an assembler or compiler. *Syn:* **object language.** *Contrast with:* **source language.**

target machine. (1) The computer on which a program is intended to execute. *Contrast with:* **host machine (1).**
(2) A computer being emulated by another computer. *Contrast with:* **host machine (2).**

target program. *See:* **object program.**

task. (1) A sequence of instructions treated as a basic unit of work by the supervisory program of an operating system.
(2) In software design, a software component that can operate in parallel with other software components.

taxonomy. (IEEE Std 1002-1987 [9]) A scheme that partitions a body of knowledge and defines the relationships among the pieces. It is used for classifying and understanding the body of knowledge.

technical management. (IEEE Std 1002-1987 [9]) The application of technical and administrative resources to plan, organize, and control engineering functions.

technical standard. (IEEE Std 1002-1987 [9]) A standard that describes the characteristics of applying accumulated technical or management skills and methods in the creation of a product or performing a service.

techniques. (IEEE Std 983-1986 [7]) Technical and managerial procedures that aid in the evaluation and improvement of the software development process.

temporal cohesion. A type of cohesion in which the tasks performed by a software module are all required at a particular phase of program execution; for example, a module containing all of a program's initialization tasks. *Contrast with:* **coincidental cohesion; communicational cohesion; functional cohesion; logical cohesion; procedural cohesion; sequential cohesion.**

termination construct. A program construct that results in a halt or exit.

test. (1) An activity in which a system or component is executed under specified conditions, the results are observed or recorded, and an evaluation is made of some aspect of the system or component.
(2) To conduct an activity as in (1).
(3) (IEEE Std 829-1983 [5]) A set of one or more test cases.
(4) (IEEE Std 829-1983 [5]) A set of one or more test procedures.
(5) (IEEE Std 829-1983 [5]) A set of one or more test cases and procedures.

test bed. An environment containing the hardware, instrumentation, simulators, software tools, and other support elements needed to conduct a test.

test case. (1) A set of test inputs, execution conditions, and expected results developed for a particular objective, such as to exercise a particular program path or to verify compliance with a specific requirement.
(2) (IEEE Std 829-1983 [5]) Documentation specifying inputs, predicted results, and a set of execution conditions for a test item.

See also: **test case generator; test case specification.**

test case generator. A software tool that accepts as input source code, test criteria, specifications, or data structure definitions; uses these inputs to generate test input data; and, sometimes, determines expected results. *Syn:* **test data generator; test generator.**

test case specification. A document that specifies the test inputs, execution conditions, and predicted results for an item to be tested. *Syn:* **test description; test specification.** *See also:* **test incident report; test item transmittal report; test log; test plan; test procedure; test report.**

test coverage. The degree to which a given test or set of tests addresses all specified requirements for a given system or component.

test criteria. The criteria that a system or component must meet in order to pass a given test. *See also:* **acceptance criteria; pass-fail criteria.**

test data generator. *See:* **test case generator.**

test description. *See:* **test case specification.**

test design. (IEEE Std 829-1983 [5]) Documentation specifying the details of the test approach for a software feature or combination of software features and identifying the associated tests.

test documentation. Documentation describing plans for, or results of, the testing of a system or component. Types include test case specification, test incident report, test log, test plan, test procedure, test report.

test driver. A software module used to invoke a module under test and, often, provide test inputs, control and monitor execution, and report test results. *Syn:* **test harness.**

test generator. *See:* **test case generator.**

test harness. *See:* **test driver.**

test incident report. A document that describes an event that occurred during testing which requires further investigation. *See also:* **test case specification; test item transmittal report; test log; test plan; test procedure; test report.**

test item. (IEEE Std 829-1983 [5]) A software item which is an object of testing.

test item transmittal report. (IEEE Std 829-1983 [5]) A document that identifies one or more items submitted for testing. It contains current status and location information. *See also:* **test case specification; test incident report; test log; test plan; test procedure; test report.**

test log. A chronological record of all relevant details about the execution of a test. *See also:* **test case specification; test incident report; test item transmittal report; test plan; test procedure; test report.**

test objective. (IEEE Std 1008-1987 [10]) An identified set of software features to be measured under specified conditions by comparing actual behavior with the required behavior described in the software documentation.

test phase. The period of time in the software life cycle during which the components of a software product are evaluated and integrated, and the software product is evaluated to determine whether or not requirements have been satisfied.

test plan. (1) (IEEE Std 829-1983 [5]) A document describing the scope, approach, resources, and schedule of intended test activities. It identifies test items, the features to be tested, the testing tasks, who will do each task, and any risks requiring contingency planning.
(2) A document that describes the technical and management approach to be followed for testing a system or component. Typical contents identify the items to be tested, tasks to be performed, responsibilities, schedules, and required resources for the testing activity. *See also:* **test case specification; test incident report; test item transmittal report; test log; test procedure; test report.**

test procedure. (1) Detailed instructions for the set-up, execution, and evaluation of results for a given test case.
(2) A document containing a set of associated instructions as in (1).
(3) (IEEE Std 829-1983 [5]) Documentation specifying a sequence of actions for the execution of a test.
Syn: **test procedure specification; test script.**
See also: **test case specification; test incident report; test item transmittal report; test log; test plan; test report.**

test procedure specification. *See:* **test procedure.**

test readiness review (TRR). (1) A review conducted to evaluate preliminary test results for one or more configuration items; to verify that the test procedures for each configuration item are complete, comply with test plans and descriptions, and satisfy test requirements; and to verify that a project is prepared to proceed to formal testing of the configuration items.
(2) A review as in (1) for any hardware or software component.
Contrast with: **code review; formal qualification review; design review; requirements review.**

test repeatability. An attribute of a test, indicating that the same results are produced each time the test is conducted.

test report. A document that describes the conduct and results of the testing carried out for a system or component. *Syn:* **test summary report.** *See also:* **test case specification; test incident report; test item transmittal report; test log; test plan; test procedure.**

test script. *See*: **test procedure.**

test set architecture. (IEEE Std 1008-1987 [10]) The nested relationships between sets of test cases that directly reflect the hierarchic decomposition of the test objectives.

test specification. *See:* **test case specification.**

test summary report. (IEEE Std 829-1983 [5]) A document summarizing testing activities and results. It also contains an evaluation of the corresponding test items. *See also:* **test case specification; test incident report; test item transmittal report; test log; test plan; test procedure; test report.**

test unit. (IEEE Std 1008-1987 [10]) A set of one or more computer program modules together with associated control data (for example, tables), usage procedures, and operating procedures that satisfy the following conditions: (a) All modules are from a single computer program; (b) At least one of the new or changed modules in the set has not completed the unit test; (c) The set of modules together with its associated data and procedures are the sole object of a testing process.

testability. (1) The degree to which a system or component facilitates the establishment of test criteria and the performance of tests to determine whether those criteria have been met.
(2) The degree to which a requirement is stated in terms that permit establishment of test criteria and performance of tests to determine whether those criteria have been met.

testing. (1) The process of operating a system or component under specified conditions, observing or recording the results, and making an evaluation of some aspect of the system or component.
(2) (IEEE Std 829-1983 [5]) The process of analyzing a software item to detect the differences between existing and required conditions (that is, bugs) and to evaluate the features of the software items.
See also: **acceptance testing; benchmark; checkout; component testing; development testing; dynamic analysis; formal testing; functional testing; informal testing; integration testing; interface testing; loopback testing; mutation testing; operational testing; performance testing; qualification testing; regression testing; stress testing; structural testing; system testing; unit testing.**

text editor. A computer program, often part of a word processing system, that allows a user to enter, alter, and view text. *Syn:* **editor.**

think time. The elapsed time between the end of a prompt or message generated by an interactive system and the beginning of a human user's response. *See also:* **port-to-port time; response time; turnaround time.**

third generation language (3GL). *See:* **high order language.**

thrashing. A state in which a computer system is expending most or all of its resources on overhead operations, such as swapping data between main and auxiliary storage, rather than on intended computing functions.

three-address instruction. A computer instruction that contains three address fields. For example, an instruction to add the contents of locations A and B, and place the results in location C. *Contrast with:* **one-address instruction; two-address instruction; four-address instruction; zero-address instruction.**

three-plus-one address instruction. A computer instruction that contains four address fields, the fourth containing the address of the instruction to be executed next. For example, an instruction to add the contents of locations A and B, place the results in location C, then execute the instruction at location D. *Contrast with:* **one-plus-one address instruction; two-plus-one address instruction; four-plus-one address instruction.**

throughput. The amount of work that can be performed by a computer system or component in a given period of time; for example, number of jobs per day. *See also:* **turnaround time; workload model.**

tier chart. *See:* **call graph.**

time out. (1) A condition that occurs when a predetermined amount of time elapses without the occurrence of an expected event. For example, the condition that causes termination of an on-line process if no user input is received within a specified period of time.
(2) To experience the condition in (1).

time sharing. A mode of operation that permits two or more users to execute computer programs concurrently on the same computer system by interleaving the execution of their program. *Note:* Time sharing may be implemented by time slicing, priority-based interrupts, or other scheduling methods.

time slicing. A mode of operation in which two or more processes are each assigned a small, fixed amount of continuous processing time on the same processor, and the processes execute in a round-robin manner, each for its allotted time, until all are completed.

timing. The process of estimating or measuring the amount of execution time required for a software system or component. *Contrast with:* **sizing.**

timing analyzer. A software tool that estimates or measures the execution time of a computer program or portion of a computer program, either by summing the execution times of the instructions along specified paths or by inserting probes at specified points in the program and measuring the execution time between probes.

top-down. Pertaining to an activity that starts with the highest level component of a hierarchy and proceeds through progressively lower levels; for example, top-down design; top-down testing. *Contrast with:* **bottom-up.** *See also:* **critical piece first.**

total correctness. In proof of correctness, a designation indicating that a program's output assertions follow logically from its input assertions and processing steps, and that, in addition, the program terminates under all specified input conditions. *Contrast with:* **partial correctness.**

trace. (1) A record of the execution of a computer program, showing the sequence of instructions executed, the names and values of variables, or both. Types include execution trace, retrospective trace, subroutine trace, symbolic trace, variable trace.
(2) To produce a record as in (1).
(3) To establish a relationship between two or more products of the development process; for example, to establish the relationship between a given requirement and the design element that implements that requirement.

traceability. (1) The degree to which a relationship can be established between two or more products of the development process, especially products having a predecessor-successor or master-subordinate relationship to one another; for example, the degree to which the requirements and design of a given software component match. *See also:* **consistency.**
(2) The degree to which each element in a software development product establishes its reason for existing; for example, the degree to which each element in a bubble chart references the requirement that it satisfies.

traceability matrix. A matrix that records the relationship between two or more products of the development process; for example, a matrix that records the relationship between the requirements and the design of a given software component.

trailer. Identification or control information placed at the end of a file or message. *Contrast with:* **header (2).**

trailing decision. A loop control that is executed after the loop body. *Contrast with:* **leading decision.** *See also:* **UNTIL.**

transaction. In software engineering, a data element, control element, signal, event, or change of state that causes, triggers, or initiates an action or sequence of actions.

transaction analysis. A software development technique in which the structure of a system is derived from analyzing the transactions that the system is required to process. *Syn:* **transaction-centered design.** *See also:* **data structure-centered design; input-process-output; modular decomposition; object-oriented design; rapid prototyping; stepwise refinement; structured design; transform analysis.**

transaction-centered design. *See:* **transaction analysis.**

transaction matrix. A matrix that identifies possible requests for database access and relates each request to information categories or elements in the database.

transfer. (1) To send data from one place and receive it at another.
(2) To relinquish control by one process and assume it at another, either with expectation of return (*see* **call**) or without such expectation (*see* **jump**).

transform analysis. A software development technique in which the structure of a system is derived from analyzing the flow of data through the system and the transformations that must be performed on the data. *Syn:* **transformation analysis; transform-centered design.** *See also:* **data structure-centered design; input-process-output; modular decomposition; object-oriented design; rapid prototyping; stepwise refinement; structured design; transaction analysis.**

transform-centered design. *See:* **transform analysis.**

transformation analysis. *See:* **transform analysis.**

transient error. An error that occurs once, or at unpredictable intervals. *See also:* **intermittent fault; random failure.**

translator. A computer program that transforms a sequence of statements expressed in one language into an equivalent sequence of statements expressed in another language. *See also:* **assembler; compiler.**

transportability. *See:* **portability.**

trap. (1) A conditional jump to an exception or interrupt handling routine, often automatically activated by hardware, with the location from which the jump occurred recorded.
(2) To perform the operation in (1).

TRR. Acronym for **test readiness review.**

turnaround time. The elapsed time between the submission of a job to a batch processing system and the return of completed output. *See also:* **port-to-port time; response time; think time.**

turnkey. Pertaining to a hardware or software system delivered in a complete, operational state.

two-address instruction. A computer instruction that contains two address fields. For example, an instruction to add the contents of A to the contents of B. *Syn:* **double-operand instruction.** *Contrast with:* **one-address instruction; three-address instruction; four-address instruction; zero-address instruction.**

two-level address. An indirect address that specifies the storage location containing the address of the desired operand. *See also:* ***n*-level address.**

two-level encoding. A microprogramming technique in which different microoperations may be encoded identically into the same field of a microinstruction, and the one that is executed depends upon the value in another field internal or external to the microinstruction. *See also:* **bit steering; residual control.** *Contrast with:* **single-level encoding.**

two-plus-one address instruction. A computer instruction that contains three address fields, the third containing the address of the instruction to be executed next. For example, an instruction to add the contents of A to the contents of B, then execute the instruction at location C. *Contrast with:* **one-plus-one address instruction; three-plus-one address instruction; four-plus-one address instruction.**

type. *See:* **data type.**

UDF. Acronym for **unit development folder.** *See:* **software development file.**

unconditional branch.* *See:* **unconditional jump.**
*Deprecated.

unconditional jump. A jump that takes place regardless of execution conditions. *Contrast with:* **conditional jump.**

underflow exception. An exception that occurs when the result of an arithmetic operation is too small a fraction to be represented by the storage location designated to receive it. *See also:* **addressing exception; data exception; operation exception; overflow exception; protection exception.**

undirected graph. A graph (sense 2) in which no direction is implied in the internode connections. *Contrast with:* **directed graph.**

unit. (1) A separately testable element specified in the design of a computer software component.
(2) A logically separable part of a computer program.
(3) A software component that is not subdivided into other components.
(4) (IEEE Std 1008-1987 [10]) *See:* **test unit.**
Note: The terms "module," "component," and "unit" are often used interchangeably or defined to be sub-elements of one another in different ways depending upon the context. The relationship of these terms is not yet standardized.

unit development folder (UDF). *See:* **software development file.**

unit requirements documentation. (IEEE Std 1008-1987 [10]) Documentation that sets forth the functional, interface, performance, and design constraint requirements for a test unit.

unit testing. Testing of individual hardware or software units or groups of related units. *See also:* **component testing; integration testing; interface testing; system testing.**

unpack. To recover the original form of one or more data items from packed data. *Contrast with:* **pack.**

unstratified language. A language that can be used as its own metalanguage; for example, English, German. *Contrast with:* **stratified language.**

UNTIL. A single-entry, single-exit loop, in which the loop control is executed after the loop body. *Syn:* **post-tested iteration.** *Contrast with:* **closed loop; WHILE.** *See also:* **trailing decision.**

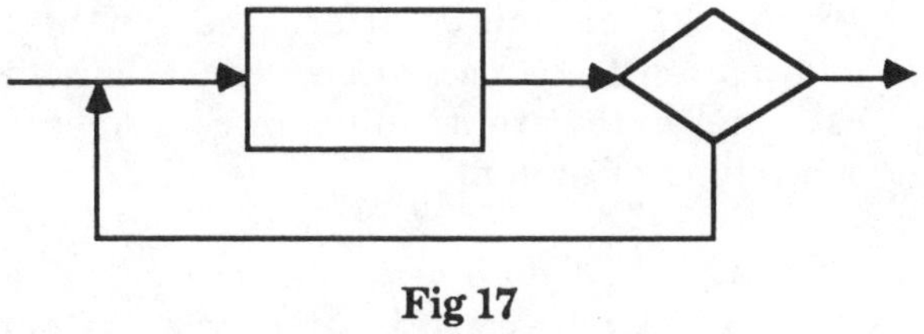

Fig 17
UNTIL Construct

unwind. In programming, to state explicitly and in full all of the instructions involved in multiple executions of a loop. *See also:* **straightline coding.**

up. Pertaining to a system or component that is operational and in service. Such a system is either busy or idle. *Contrast with:* **down.** *See also:* **busy; idle.**

up time. The period of time during which a system or component is operational and in service; that is, the sum of busy time and idle time. *Contrast with:* **down time.** *See also:* **busy time; idle time; mean time between failures; set-up time.**

upward compatible. Pertaining to hardware or software that is compatible with a later or more complex version of itself; for example, a program that handles files created by a later version of itself. *Contrast with:* **downward compatible.**

upward compression. In software design, a form of demodularization in which a subordinate module is copied in-line into the body of a superordinate module. *Contrast with:* **lateral compression; downward compression.**

usability. The ease with which a user can learn to operate, prepare inputs for, and interpret outputs of a system or component.

user documentation. Documentation describing the way in which a system or component is to be used to obtain desired results. *See also:* **data input sheet; user manual.**

user friendly. Pertaining to a computer system, device, program, or document designed with ease of use as a primary objective.

user guide. *See:* **user manual.**

user interface. An interface that enables information to be passed between a human user and hardware or software components of a computer system.

user manual. A document that presents the information necessary to employ a system or component to obtain desired results. Typically described are system or component capabilities, limitations, options, permitted inputs, expected outputs, possible error messages, and special instructions. *Note:* A user manual is distinguished from an operator manual when a distinction is made between those who operate a computer system (mounting tapes, etc.) and those who use the system for its intended purpose. *Syn:* **user guide.** *See also:* **data input sheet; diagnostic manual; installation manual; operator manual; programmer manual; support manual.**

user state. *See:* **problem state.**

utility. A software tool designed to perform some frequently used support function. For example, a program to copy magnetic tapes.

utilization. In computer performance evaluation, a ratio representing the amount of time a system or component is busy divided by the time it is available. *See also:* **busy time; idle time; up time.**

V&V. Acronym for **verification and validation.**

validation. The process of evaluating a system or component during or at the end of the development process to determine whether it satisfies specified requirements. *Contrast with:* **verification.**

value trace. *See:* **variable trace.**

variable. A quantity or data item whose value can change; for example, the variable Current_time. *Contrast with:* **constant.** *See also:* **global variable; local variable.**

variable trace. A record of the name and values of variables accessed or changed during the execution of a computer program. *Syn:* **data-flow trace; data trace; value trace.** *See also:* **execution trace; retrospective trace; subroutine trace; symbolic trace.**

variant. In fault tolerance, a version of a program resulting from the application of software diversity.

VDD. Acronym for **version description document.**

verification. (1) The process of evaluating a system or component to determine whether the products of a given development phase satisfy the conditions imposed at the start of that phase. *Contrast with:* **validation.**
(2) Formal proof of program correctness. *See:* **proof of correctness.**

verification and validation (V&V). The process of determining whether the requirements for a system or component are complete and correct, the products of each development phase fulfill the requirements or conditions imposed by the previous phase, and the final system or component complies with specified requirements. *See also:* **independent verification and validation.**

version. (1) An initial release or re-release of a computer software configuration item, associated with a complete compilation or recompilation of the computer software configuration item.
(2) An initial release or complete re-release of a document, as opposed to a revision resulting from issuing change pages to a previous release.
See also: **configuration control; version description document.**

version description document (VDD). A document that accompanies and identifies a given version of a system or component. Typical contents include an inventory of system or component parts, identification of changes incorporated into this version, and installation and operating information unique to the version described.

vertical microinstruction. A microinstruction that specifies one of a sequence of operations needed to carry out a machine language instruction. *Note:* Vertical microinstructions are relatively short, 12 to 24 bits, and are called "vertical" because a sequence of such instruction, normally listed vertically on a page, is required to carry out a single machine language instruction. *Contrast with:* **diagonal microinstruction; horizontal microinstruction.**

virtual address. In a virtual storage system, the address assigned to an auxiliary storage location to allow that location to be accessed as though it were part of main storage. *Contrast with:* **real address.**

virtual memory. *See:* **virtual storage.**

virtual storage. A storage allocation technique in which auxiliary storage can be addressed as though it were part of main storage. Portions of a user's program and data are placed in auxiliary storage, and the operating system automatically swaps them in and out of main storage as needed. *Syn:* **multilevel storage, virtual memory.** *Contrast with:* **real storage.** *See also:* **virtual address; paging (2).**

waiver. A written authorization to accept a configuration item or other designated item which, during production or after having been submitted for inspection, is found to depart from specified requirements, but is nevertheless considered suitable for use as is or after rework by an approved method. *See also:* **configuration control.** *Contrast with:* **deviation; engineering change.**

walk-through. A static analysis technique in which a designer or programmer leads members of the development team and other interested parties through a segment of documentation or code, and the participants ask questions and make comments about possible errors, violation of development standards, and other problems.

waterfall model. A model of the software development process in which the constituent activities, typically a concept phase, requirements phase, design phase, implementation phase, test phase, and installation and checkout phase, are performed in that order, possibly with overlap but with little or no iteration. *Contrast with:* **incremental development; rapid prototyping; spiral model.**

wearout-failure period. The period in the life cycle of a system or component during which hardware failures occur at an increasing rate due to deterioration. *Contrast with:* **constant-failure period; early-failure period.** *See also:* **bathtub curve.**

WHILE. A single-entry, single-exit loop in which the loop control is executed before the loop body. *Syn:* **pre-tested iteration.** *Contrast with:* **closed loop; UNTIL.** *See also:* **leading decision.**

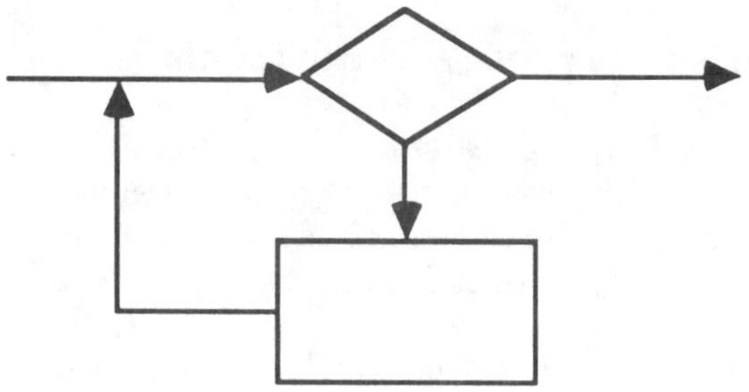

Fig 18
WHILE Construct

white box. *See:* **glass box.**

white-box testing. *See:* **structural testing.**

word. (1) A sequence of bits or characters that is stored, addressed, transmitted, and operated on as a unit within a given computer. *Syn:* **computer word.**
(2) An element of computer storage that can hold a sequence of bits or characters as in (1).
(3) A sequence of bits or characters that has meaning and is considered an entity in some language; for example, a reserved word in a computer language.
See also: **bit; byte.**

working area. *See:* **working space.**

working set. In the paging method of storage allocation, the set of pages that are most likely to be resident in main storage at any given point of a program's execution.

working space. That portion of main storage that is assigned to a computer program for temporary storage of data. *Syn:* **working area, working storage.**

working storage. *See:* **working space.**

workload. The mix of tasks typically run on a given computer system. Major characteristics include input/output requirements, amount and kinds of computation, and computer resources required. *See also:* **workload model.**

workload model. A model used in computer performance evaluation, depicting resource utilization and performance measures for anticipated or actual workloads in a computer system. *See also:* **system model.**

write. To record data in a storage device or on a data medium. *Contrast with:* **read.**

zero-address instruction. A computer instruction that contains no address fields. *Contrast with:* **one-address instruction; two-address instruction; three-address instruction; four-address instruction.**

4. Bibliography

[1] IEEE Std 610.1—see IEEE Std 1084-1986, IEEE Standard Glossary of Mathematics of Computing Terminology (ANSI) [11].[2]

[2] IEEE Std 610.5-1990, IEEE Standard Glossary of Data Management Terminology.

[3] IEEE Std 729-1983, IEEE Standard Glossary of Software Engineering Terminology (ANSI).[3]

[4] IEEE Std 828-1983, IEEE Standard for Software Configuration Management Plans (ANSI).[3]

[5] IEEE Std 829-1983, IEEE Standard for Software Test Documentation (ANSI).

[6] IEEE Std 830-1984, IEEE Guide for Software Requirements Specifications (ANSI).

[7] IEEE Std 983-1986, IEEE Guide for Software Quality Assurance Planning (ANSI).

[8] IEEE Std 990-1987, IEEE Recommended Practice for Ada as a Program Design Language (ANSI).

[2]IEEE publications are available from the IEEE Service Center, Institute of Electrical and Electronics Engineers, 445 Hoes Lane, P.O. Box 1331, Piscataway, NJ 08855-1331.

[3]IEEE Stds 729-1983 and 828-1983 have been superseded by this document and 828-1990, but archival copies are available from the Standards Department at the above address.

[9] IEEE Std 1002-1987, IEEE Standard Taxonomy for Software Engineering Standards (ANSI).

[10] IEEE Std 1008-1987, IEEE Standard for Software Unit Testing (ANSI).

[11] IEEE Std 1084-1986, IEEE Standard Glossary of Mathematics of Computing Terminology (ANSI).

[12] IEEE Std 1012-1986, IEEE Standard for Software Verification and Validation Plans (ANSI).

[13] IEEE Std 1016-1987, IEEE Recommended Practice for Software Design Descriptions (ANSI).

When the following documents are completed, approved, and published by IEEE, they will become a part of the Bibliography of this standard:

[14] P610.7, Draft Standard Glossary of Computer Networking Terminology.

[15] P610.8, Draft Standard Glossary of Artificial Intelligence Terminology.

[16] P610.9, Draft Standard Glossary of Computer Security and Privacy Terminology.

[17] P610.13, Draft Standard Glossary of Computer Languages Terminology.

IEEE

Recognized as an
American National Standard (ANSI)

IEEE 730-1989
(Revision of IEEE Std 730-1984 and Redesignation of IEEE 730.1-1989)

IEEE Standard for Software Quality Assurance Plans

Sponsor

Technical Committee on Software Engineering of the IEEE Computer Society

Approved August 17, 1989

IEEE Standards Board

Approved January 22, 1990

American National Standards Institute

The Institute of Electrical and Electronics Engineers, Inc
345 East 47th Street, New York, NY 10017, USA

Foreword

(This Foreword is not a part of IEEE Std 730.1-1989, IEEE Standard for Software Quality Assurance Plans.)

This standard assists in the preparation and content of Software Quality Assurance Plans and provides a standard against which such plans can be prepared and assessed. It is directed toward the development and maintenance of critical software—that is, where failure could impact safety or cause large financial or social losses.

The readers of this document are referred to ANSI/IEEE Std 983-1986, IEEE Guide for Software Quality Assurance Planning, for recommended approaches to good software quality assurance practices in support of this standard. While ANSI/IEEE Std 983-1986 specifically refers to ANSI/IEEE Std 730-1984, almost all of its content applies directly to this revision.

In this standard, firmware is considered to be software and is to be treated as such.

Footnotes are not part of the standard.

There are three groups to whom this standard applies: the user, the developer, and the public.

(1) The user, who may be another element of the same organization developing the software, has a need for the product. Further, the user needs the product to meet the requirements identified in the specification. The user thus cannot afford a "hands-off" attitude toward the developer and rely solely on a test to be executed at the end of the software development time period. If the product should fail, not only does the same need still exist, but also a portion of the development time has been lost. Therefore, the user needs to obtain a reasonable degree of confidence that the product is in the process of acquiring required attributes during software development.

(2) The developer needs an established standard against which to plan and to be measured. It is unreasonable to expect a complete reorientation from project to project. Not only is it not cost effective, but, unless there exists a stable framework on which to base changes, improvement cannot be made.

(3) The public may be affected by the users' use of the product. These users include, for example, depositors at a bank or passengers using a reservation system. Users have requirements, such as legal rights, which preclude haphazard development of software. At some later date, the user and the developer may be required to show that they acted in a reasonable and prudent professional manner to ensure that required software attributes were acquired.

This standard was prepared by the Software Engineering Standards Subcommittee of the Software Engineering Technical Committee of the IEEE Computer Society. It was initially approved by the IEEE Standards Board for "trial use" in December of 1979, with a subsequent "full use" approval in September of 1981, and a revision approved on June 14, 1984.

The Working Group consisted of the following members:

F. Buckley, *Chairperson* **C. White-Partain,** *Vice-Chairperson*

Executive Committee:

S. Ali
W. Barret
R. Braun
W. Eventoff
R. Fordham
M. Hein
R. Kosinski
E. Maginnius
L. Marquis
C. Modell
S. Norman
S. Trauth
A. Tegtmeier

Members:

J. Agrawal
M. Ben-Menachem
J. Case
J. Chihorek
M. Dewalt
D. Doty
R. Euler
R. Evans
J. Ewin
M. Fitch
M. Ghiassi
J. Gilmore
B. Gundaker
J. Horch
R. Ivy
S. Jones
H. Kaplan
M. Karasik
R. Kenneavy
T. Kurihara
B. Livson
A. Miller
R. Martin
P. Pfister
R. Poston
F. Rienstra
J. Roberts
F. Rose
W. Schultzer
W. Schunk
C. Seddin
A. Serna, Jr.
R. Shillato
T. Smith
R. Stanton
R. Stenglein
A. Sullivan
O. Tanir
E. Testa
L. To
G. Tucker
H. van Doornum
C. Von Schantz
D. Wallace
P. Willis
P. Wolfgang

Special Representatives to the Software Engineering Standards Subcommittee for this action were as follows:

Nuclear Power Engineering Committee/Power Engineering Society: N. Farr

Quality Assurance Management Committee of the IEEE Communications Society: R. Mosher

Canadian Standards Association: B. Dyczkowsky

Data Processing Manufacturers' Association: W. Perry

At the time that the IEEE Standards Board approved this revision, the Software Engineering Standards Subcommittee, which was the balloting committee that approved this document for submission to the IEEE Standards Board, had the following membership:

John Horch, *Chairman*

W. Arfvidson
C. Arnold
R. Aurbach
E. Baker
B. Banerjee
B. Beizer
M. Ben-Menachem
R. Berlack
B. Bina
M. Blackledge
R. Blasewitz
R. Both
K. Briggs
A. Brown
W. Bryan
F. Buckley
C. Carpenter
J. Case
T. Chow
W. Chung
F. Coallier
G. Copeland
P. Daggett
M. Daniels
T. Daughtrey
K. DeJong
D. Deluna
C. Dencker
P. Denny
B. Derganc
A. Dolinsky
R. Dwyer
L. Egan
M. Egeland
S. Eisen
R. Erickson
R. Euler
C. Evans
J. Fendrich
A. Foley
R. Fordham
J. Forman
J. Franklin
I. Fuentes
A. Geraci
Y. Gershkovitch
D. Geyer
E. Gibbs
J. Gilmore
S. Gloss-Soler
J. Glynn
J. Gonzalez-Sanz
V. Guarnera
D. Gustafson
J. Guttman
B. Harbort
C. Hay
J. Hillawi
J. Horch
P. Hung
D. Johnson III
J. Kalasky
L. Kaleda
M. Karasik
R. Karcich
O. Kato
P. Klopfenstein
S. Koenig
R. Kosinski
T. Kurihara
L. Lam
J. Lane
R. Lane
G. Larsen
F. Lim
K. Linberg
B. Lindberg
B. Livson
H. Mains
H. Malec
J. Malsbury
L. Marquis
P. Marriott
R. Martin
T. Matsubara
I. Mazza
J. Mersky
C. Modell
H. Nagano
S. Najafi
G. Neidhart
D. Nickle
J. O'Day
M. Olson
W. Osbourne
T. Parrish
M. Perkins
P. Peterson
J. Phippen
J. Pope
R. Poston
I. Pyle
G. Ray
M. Razy
J. Reddan
S. Redwine
J. Roberts
R. Roman
R. Roth
F. Ruhlman
S. Schach
H. Schaefer
N. Schneidewind
W. Schnoege
H. Schock
D. Schultz
G. Schumacher
L. Seagren
L. Shafer
R. Shillato
D. Siefert
I. Sjors
A. Sorkowitz
T. Stalhane
N. Stewart
W. Strigel
R. Thayer
P. Thompson
G. Tice
T. Tillmanns
E. Tomlin
S. Trauth
L. Tripp
M. Uchida
D. Ulery
H. Verne
C. Von Schantz
D. Wallace
J. Walter
R. Weger
P. Willis
P. Wolfgang
T. Worthington
N. Yopconka
P. Zoll

Contents

IEEE Standard for Software Quality Assurance Plans

1. Scope and References

1.1 Scope. The purpose of this standard is to provide uniform, minimum acceptable requirements for preparation and content of Software Quality Assurance Plans (SQAPs).

In considering adoption of this standard, regulatory bodies should be aware that specific application of this standard may already be covered by one or more IEEE or ANSI standards documents relating to quality assurance, definitions, or other matters. It is not the purpose of this document to supersede, revise or amend existing standards directed to specific industries or applications.

This standard applies to the development and maintenance of critical software. For non-critical software, or for software already developed, a subset of the requirements of this standard may be applied.

The existence of this standard should not be construed to prohibit additional content in a SQAP. An assessment should be made for the specific software item to assure adequacy of coverage. Where this standard is invoked for an organization or project engaged in producing several software items, the applicability of the standard should be specified for each of the software items.

1.2 References. The standards listed below should be used for further information. In using these references, the latest revisions should be obtained. Compliance with this standard does not require nor imply compliance with any of those listed.

[1] ANSI/ASME NQA-1-1983, Quality Assurance Program Requirements for Nuclear Facilities.[1]

[2] ANSI/IEEE Std 603-1980, IEEE Standard Criteria for Safety Systems for Nuclear Power Generating Stations.

[3] ANSI/IEEE Std 729-1983, IEEE Standard Glossary of Software Engineering Terminology.[2]

[4] ANSI/IEEE Std 828-1983, IEEE Standard for Software Configuration Management Plans.

[5] ANSI/IEEE Std 829-1983, IEEE Standard for Software Test Documentation.

[6] ANSI/IEEE Std 830-1984, IEEE Guide for Software Requirements Specifications.

[7] IEEE Std 982.1-1988, IEEE Standard Dictionary of Measures to Produce Reliable Software.

[8] IEEE Std 982.2-1988, IEEE Guide for the Use of IEEE Standard Dictionary of Measures to Produce Reliable Software.

[9] ANSI/IEEE Std 983-1986, IEEE Guide for Software Quality Assurance Planning. (This is being redesignated to 730.2.)

[10] ANSI/IEEE Std 990-1987, IEEE Recommended Practice for Ada as a Program Design Language.

[11] ANSI/IEEE Std 1002-1987, IEEE Standard Taxonomy of Software Engineering Standards.

[12] ANSI/IEEE Std 1008-1987, IEEE Standard for Software Unit Testing.

---

[1]ANSI/ASME publications are available from the Sales Department, American National Standards Institute, 1430 Broadway, New York, NY 10018 or from the ASME Order Department, 22 Law Drive, P.O. Box 2300, Fairfield, NJ 07007-2300.

[2]ANSI/IEEE publications may be obtained from the IEEE Service Center, 445 Hoes Lane, P.O. Box 1331, Piscataway, NJ 08855-1331 or from the Sales Department, American National Standards Institute, 1430 Broadway, New York, NY 10018.

[13] ANSI/IEEE Std 1012-1986, IEEE Standard for Software Verification and Validation Plans.

[14] ANSI/IEEE Std 1016-1987, IEEE Recommended Practice for Software Design Descriptions.

[15] IEEE Std 1028-1988, IEEE Standard for Software Reviews and Audits.

[16] ANSI/IEEE Std 1033-1985, IEEE Recommended Practice for Application of IEEE Std 828 to Nuclear Power Generating Stations.

[17] ANSI/IEEE Std 1042-1987, IEEE Guide to Software Configuration Management.

[18] ANSI/IEEE Std 1058.1-1988, IEEE Standard for Software Project Management Plans.

[19] ANSI/IEEE Std 1063-1987, IEEE Standard for Software User Documentation.

[20] ANSI/IEEE/ANS 7-4.3.2-1982, Application Criteria for Programmable Digital Computer Systems in Safety Systems of Nuclear Power Generating Stations.

2. Definitions and Acronyms

2.1 Definitions. The definitions listed below establish meaning in the context of this standard. Other definitions can be found in ANSI/IEEE Std 729-1983, IEEE Standard Glossary of Software Engineering Terminology, or latest revision thereof [3].[3] For the purpose of this standard, the term "software" includes firmware, documentation, data, and execution control statements (eg, command files, job control language, etc).

branch metric. The result of dividing the total number of modules in which every branch has been executed at least once by the total number of modules.[4]

critical software. Software whose failure would impact safety or cause large financial or social losses.

decision point metric. The result of dividing the total number of modules in which every decision point has had (1) all valid conditions, and (2) at least one invalid condition, correctly processed, divided by the total number of modules.[5]

domain metric. The result of dividing the total number of modules in which one valid sample and one invalid sample of every class of input data items (external messages, operator inputs, and local data) have been correctly processed, by the total number of modules.[6]

error message metric. The result of dividing the total number of error messages that have been formally demonstrated, by the total number of error messages.

quality assurance. A planned and systematic pattern of all actions necessary to provide adequate confidence that the item or product conforms to established technical requirements.

requirements demonstration metric. The result of dividing the total number of separately-identified requirements in the software requirements specification (SRS) that have been successfully demonstrated by the total number of separately-identified requirements in the SRS.

2.2 Acronyms. The following alphabetical contractions appear within the text of this standard:

CDR—critical design review
PDR—preliminary design review
SCMP—software configuration management plan
SCMPR—software configuration management plan review
SDD—software design description
SQA—software quality assurance
SQAP—software quality assurance plan
SRR—software requirements review
SRS—software requirements specification
SVVP—software verification and validation plan
SVVPR—software verification and validation plan review
SVVR—software verification and validation report
UDR—user documentation review

[3] The numbers in brackets correspond to those of the references listed in 1.2.

[4] This definition assumes that the modules are essentially the same size.

[5] See footnote 4.

[6] See footnote 4.

3. Software Quality Assurance Plan

The Software Quality Assurance Plan shall include the sections listed below to be in compliance with this standard. The sections should be ordered in the described sequence. If the sections are not ordered in the described sequence, then a table shall be provided at the end of the SQAP that provides a cross-reference from the lowest numbered subsection of this standard to that portion of the SQAP where that material is provided. If there is no information pertinent to a section, the following shall appear below the section heading, "This section is not applicable to this plan," together with the appropriate reasons for the exclusion.

(1) Purpose
(2) Reference documents
(3) Management
(4) Documentation
(5) Standards, practices, conventions, and metrics
(6) Reviews and audits
(7) Test
(8) Problem reporting and corrective action
(9) Tools, techniques, and methodologies
(10) Code control
(11) Media control
(12) Supplier control
(13) Records collection, maintenance, and retention
(14) Training
(15) Risk management

Additional sections may be added as required.

Some of the material may appear in other documents. If so, then reference to these documents should be made in the body of the SQAP. In any case, the contents of each section of the plan shall be specified either directly or by reference to another document.

The SQAP shall be approved by the chief operating officer of each unit of the organization having responsibilities defined within this SQAP or their designated representatives.

Details for each section of the SQAP are described in 3.1 through 3.15 of this standard.[7]

[7]Guidance in the use of this standard can be found in ANSI/IEEE Std 983-1986 [9]. For an expansion of the quality and equipment qualification requirements of IEEE Std 603-1980, IEEE Standard Criteria for Safety Systems for Nuclear Power Generating Stations [2]; to encompass software design, software implementation, and computer systems validation, see ANSI/IEEE/ANS 7-4.3.2-1982 [20].

3.1 Purpose (Section 1 of the SQAP). This section shall delineate the specific purpose and scope of the particular SQAP. It shall list the name(s) of the software items covered by the SQAP and the intended use of the software. It shall state the portion of the software life cycle covered by the SQAP for each software item specified.

3.2 Reference Documents (Section 2 of the SQAP). This section shall provide a complete list of documents referenced elsewhere in the text of the SQAP.

3.3 Management (Section 3 of the SQAP). This section shall describe organization, tasks, and responsibilities.[8]

3.3.1 Organization. This paragraph shall depict the organizational structure that influences and controls the quality of the software. This shall include a description of each major element of the organization together with the delegated responsibilities. Organizational dependence or independence of the elements responsible for SQA from those responsible for software development and use shall be clearly described or depicted.

3.3.2 Tasks. This paragraph shall describe (a) that portion of the software life cycle covered by the SQAP, (b) the tasks to be performed with special emphasis on software quality assurance activities, and (c) the relationships between these tasks and the planned major check-points. The sequence of the tasks shall be indicated.

3.3.3 Responsibilities. This paragraph shall identify the specific organizational elements responsible for each task.

3.4 Documentation (Section 4 of the SQAP)

3.4.1 Purpose. This section shall perform the following functions:

(1) Identify the documentation governing the development, verification and validation, use, and maintenance of the software.
(2) State how the documents are to be checked for adequacy. This shall include the criteria and the identification of the review or audit by which the adequacy of each document shall be confirmed, with reference to Section 6 of the SQAP.

[8]See ANSI/IEEE Std 1002-1987 [11] and ANSI/IEEE Std 1058.1-1988 [18].

3.4.2 Minimum Documentation Requirements. To ensure that the implementation of the software satisfies requirements, the following documentation is required as a minimum:

3.4.2.1 Software Requirements Specification (SRS). The SRS shall clearly and precisely describe each of the essential requirements (functions, performances, design constraints, and attributes) of the software and the external interfaces. Each requirement shall be defined such that its achievement is capable of being objectively verified and validated by a prescribed method; for example, inspection, analysis, demonstration, or test.[9]

3.4.2.2 Software Design Description (SDD). The SDD shall depict how the software will be structured to satisfy the requirements in the SRS. The SDD shall describe the components and subcomponents of the software design, including data bases and internal interfaces. The SDD shall be prepared first as the Preliminary SDD (also referred to as the Top-Level SDD) and shall be subsequently expanded to produce the Detailed SDD.[10]

3.4.2.3 Software Verification and Validation Plan (SVVP). The SVVP shall identify and describe the methods (for example, inspection, analysis, demonstration, or test) to be used:[11]

(1) To verify that (a) the requirements in the SRS have been approved by an appropriate authority, (b) the requirements in the SRS are implemented in the design expressed in the SDD; and (c) the design expressed in the SDD is implemented in the code.

(2) To validate that the code, when executed, complies with the requirements expressed in the SRS.

3.4.2.4 Software Verification and Validation Report (SVVR). The SVVR shall describe the results of the execution of the SVVP.

3.4.2.5 User Documentation. User documentation (eg, manual, guide, etc) shall specify and describe the required data and control inputs, input sequences, options, program limitations, and other activities or items necessary for successful execution of the software. All error messages shall be identified and corrective actions described. A method of describing user-identified errors or problems to the developer or the owner of the software shall be described. (Embedded software that has no direct user interaction has no need for user documentation and is therefore exempted from this requirement.)[12]

3.4.2.6 Software Configuration Management Plan (SCMP). The SCMP shall document methods to be used for identifying software items, controlling and implementing changes, and recording and reporting change implementation status.[13]

3.4.3 Other. Other documentation may include the following:

(1) Software Development Plan
(2) Standards and Procedures Manual
(3) Software Project Management Plan
(4) Software Maintenance Manual.

3.5 Standards, Practices, Conventions and Metrics (Section 5 of the SQAP)

3.5.1 Purpose. This section shall:

(1) Identify the standards, practices, conventions and metrics to be applied.
(2) State how compliance with these items is to be monitored and assured.

3.5.2 Content. The subjects covered shall include the basic technical, design, and programming activities involved, such as documentation, variable and module naming, programming, inspection, and testing. As a minimum, the following information shall be provided:[14]

(1) Documentation standards
(2) Logic structure standards
(3) Coding standards
(4) Commentary standards
(5) Testing standards and practices
(6) Selected software quality assurance product and process metrics such as:
    (a) Branch metric
    (b) Decision point metric
    (c) Domain metric
    (d) Error message metric
    (e) Requirements demonstration metric

[9]See ANSI/IEEE Std 830-1984 [6].

[10]See ANSI/IEEE Std 1016-1987 [14].

[11]See ANSI/IEEE Std 829-1983 [5], ANSI/IEEE Std 1008-1987 [12], and ANSI/IEEE Std 1012-1986 [13].

[12]See ANSI/IEEE Std 1063-1988 [19].

[13]See ANSI/IEEE Std 828-1983 [4] and ANSI/IEEE Std 1042-1987 [17]. See also ANSI/IEEE Std 1033-1985 [16].

[14]See ANSI/IEEE Std 990-1987 [10], ANSI/IEEE Std 982.1-1988 [7] and ANSI/IEEE Std 982.2-1988 [8].

3.6 Reviews and Audits (Section 6 of the SQAP)

3.6.1 Purpose. This section shall:[15]

(1) Define the technical and managerial reviews and audits to be conducted.
(2) State how the reviews and audits are to be accomplished.
(3) State what further actions are required and how they are to be implemented and verified.

3.6.2 Minimum Requirements. As a minimum, the following reviews and audits shall be conducted:

3.6.2.1 Software Requirements Review (SRR). The SRR is held to ensure the adequacy of the requirements stated in the SRS.

3.6.2.2 Preliminary Design Review (PDR). The PDR (also known as top-level design review) is held to evaluate the technical adequacy of the preliminary design (also known as top-level design) of the software as depicted in the preliminary software design description.

3.6.2.3 Critical Design Review (CDR). The CDR (also known as detailed design review) is held to determine the acceptability of the detailed software designs as depicted in the detailed software design description in satisfying the requirements of the SRS.

3.6.2.4 Software Verification and Validation Plan Review (SVVPR). The SVVPR is held to evaluate the adequacy and completeness of the verification and validation methods defined in the SVVP.

3.6.2.5 Functional Audit. This audit is held prior to the software delivery to verify that all requirements specified in the SRS have been met.

3.6.2.6 Physical Audit. This audit is held to verify that the software and its documentation are internally consistent and are ready for delivery.

3.6.2.7 In-Process Audits. In-process audits of a sample of the design are held to verify consistency of the design, including:

(1) Code versus design documentation
(2) Interface specifications (hardware and software)
(3) Design implementations versus functional requirements
(4) Functional requirements versus test descriptions

3.6.2.8 Managerial Reviews. Managerial reviews are held periodically to assess the execution of all of the actions and the items identified in the SQAP. These reviews shall be held by an organizational element independent of the unit being reviewed, or by a qualified third party. This review may require additional changes in the SQAP itself.

3.6.2.9 Software Configuration Management Plan Review (SCMPR). The SCMPR is held to evaluate the adequacy and completeness of the configuration management methods defined in the SCMP.

3.6.2.10 Post Mortem Review. This review is held at the conclusion of the project to assess the development activities implemented on that project and to provide recommendations for appropriate actions.

3.6.3 Other. Other reviews and audits may include the user documentation review (UDR). This review is held to evaluate the adequacy (eg, completeness, clarity, correctness, and usability) of user documentation.

3.7 Test (Section 7 of the SQAP). This section shall identify all the tests not included in the SVVP for the software covered by the SQAP and shall state the methods to be used.[16]

3.8 Problem Reporting and Corrective Action (Section 8 of the SQAP). This section shall:

(1) Describe the practices and procedures to be followed for reporting, tracking, and resolving problems identified in both software items and the software development and maintenance process.
(2) State the specific organizational responsibilities concerned with their implementation.

3.9 Tools, Techniques, and Methodologies (Section 9 of the SQAP). This section shall identify the special software tools, techniques, and methodologies that support SQA, state their purposes, and describe their use.

3.10 Code Control (Section 10 of the SQAP). This section shall define the methods and facilities used to maintain, store, secure and document controlled versions of the identified software during all phases of the software life cycle. This may be implemented in conjunction with a computer program library. This may be provided as a part of the SCMP.

[15]See IEEE Std 1028-1988 [15].

[16]See ANSI/IEEE Std 829-1983 [5] and ANSI/IEEE Std 1008-1987 [12].

If so, an appropriate reference shall be made thereto.

3.11 Media Control (Section 11 of the SQAP). This section shall state the methods and facilities to be used to (a) identify the media for each computer product and the documentation required to store the media, including the copy and restore process, and (b) protect computer program physical media from unauthorized access or inadvertent damage or degradation during all phases of the software life cycle. This may be provided as a part of the SCMP. If so, an appropriate reference shall be made thereto.

3.12 Supplier Control (Section 12 of the SQAP). This section shall state the provisions for assuring that software provided by suppliers meets established requirements. In addition, this section shall state the methods that will be used to assure that the software supplier receives adequate and complete requirements. For previously-developed software, this section shall state the methods to be used to assure the suitability of the product for use with the software items covered by the SQAP. For software that is to be developed, the supplier shall be required to prepare and implement a SQAP in accordance with this standard. This section shall also state the methods to be employed to assure that the developers comply with the requirements of this standard.

3.13 Records Collection, Maintenance, and Retention (Section 13 of the SQAP). This section shall identify the SQA documentation to be retained, shall state the methods and facilities to be used to assemble, safeguard, and maintain this documentation, and shall designate the retention period.

3.14 Training (Section 14 of the SQAP). This section shall identify the training activities necessary to meet the needs of the SQAP.

3.15 Risk Management (Section 15 of the SQAP). This section shall specify the methods and procedures employed to identify, assess, monitor, and control areas of risk arising during the portion of the software life cycle covered by the SQAP.

Recognized as an
American National Standard (ANSI)

IEEE
Std 828-1990
(Revision of IEEE Std 828-1983)

IEEE Standard for Software Configuration Management Plans

Sponsor

Software Engineering Standards Subcommittee of the Technical Committee on Software Engineering of the IEEE Computer Society

Approved September 28, 1990

IEEE Standards Board

Approved February 15, 1991

American National Standards Institute

Abstract: IEEE Std 828-1990, *IEEE Standard for Software Configuration Management Plans,* establishes the minimum required contents of a Software Configuration Management Plan and defines the specific activities to be addressed and their requirements for any portion of a software product's life cycle.
Keywords: configuration control board, configuration items, software configuration management, software configuration management activities.

ISBN 1-55937-064-5

IEEE Standards documents are developed within the Technical Committees of the IEEE Societies and the Standards Coordinating Committees of the IEEE Standards Board. Members of the committees serve voluntarily and without compensation. They are not necessarily members of the Institute. The standards developed within IEEE represent a consensus of the broad expertise on the subject within the Institute as well as those activities outside of IEEE which have expressed an interest in participating in the development of the standard.

Use of an IEEE Standard is wholly voluntary. The existence of an IEEE Standard does not imply that there are no other ways to produce, test, measure, purchase, market, or provide other goods and services related to the scope of the IEEE Standard. Furthermore, the viewpoint expressed at the time a standard is approved and issued is subject to change brought about through developments in the state of the art and comments received from users of the standard. Every IEEE Standard is subjected to review at least once every five years for revision or reaffirmation. When a document is more than five years old, and has not been reaffirmed, it is reasonable to conclude that its contents, although still of some value, do not wholly reflect the present state of the art. Users are cautioned to check to determine that they have the latest edition of any IEEE Standard.

Comments for revision of IEEE Standards are welcome from any interested party, regardless of membership affiliation with IEEE. Suggestions for changes in documents should be in the form of a proposed change of text, together with appropriate supporting comments.

Interpretations: Occasionally questions may arise regarding the meaning of portions of standards as they relate to specific applications. When the need for interpretations is brought to the attention of IEEE, the Institute will initiate action to prepare appropriate responses. Since IEEE Standards represent a consensus of all concerned interests, it is important to ensure that any interpretation has also received the concurrence of a balance of interests. For this reason IEEE and the members of its technical committees are not able to provide an instant response to interpretation requests except in those cases where the matter has previously received formal consideration.

Comments on standards and requests for interpretations should be addressed to:

Secretary, IEEE Standards Board
445 Hoes Lane
P.O. Box 1331
Piscataway, NJ 08855-1331
USA

Foreword

(This Foreword is not part of IEEE Std 828-1990, IEEE Standard for Software Configuration Management Plans.)

This standard is concerned with the activity of planning for software configuration management (SCM). SCM activities, whether planned or not, are performed on all software development projects; planning makes these activities more effective. Good planning results in a document that captures the planning information, makes the information the property of the project, communicates to all who are affected, and provides a basis for ongoing planning.

SCM is a formal engineering discipline that, as part of overall system configuration management, provides the methods and tools to identify and control the software throughout its development and use. SCM activities include the identification and establishment of baselines; the review, approval, and control of changes; the tracking and reporting of such changes; the audits and reviews of the evolving software product; and the control of interface documentation and project supplier SCM.

SCM is the means through which the integrity and traceability of the software system are recorded, communicated, and controlled during both development and maintenance. SCM also supports reduction of overall software life cycle cost by providing a foundation for product and project measurement.

SCM constitutes good engineering practice for all software projects, whether phased development, rapid prototyping, or ongoing maintenance. It enhances the reliability and quality of software by

- Providing a structure for identifying and controlling documentation, code, interfaces, and databases to support all life cycle phases
- Supporting a chosen development/maintenance methodology that fits the requirements, standards, policies, organization, and management philosophy
- Producing management and product information concerning the status of baselines, change control, tests, releases, audits, etc.

IEEE Std 828-1983 was originally prepared by a Working Group of the Software Engineering Standards Subcommittee of the Technical Committee on Software Engineering of the IEEE Computer Society and approved in June, 1983, by the IEEE Standards Board. This current standard is the first revision and has been completely rewritten to

- Update the standard to recognize current software engineering practices
- Be consistent with IEEE Std 1042-1987, IEEE Guide to Software Configuration Management, which is anticipated to be reviewed and revised as Std 828.1 to maintain this consistency
- Be more flexible and easier to use for all levels of expertise

The following individuals contributed to IEEE Std 828-1990 by attendance at two or more working sessions or substantial written commentary or both:

H. R. Berlack, *Co-Chair* **M. Updike-Rumley,** *Co-Chair*

Editorial Committee

R. Frederick
D. L. Knirk
L. Roy

Working Group

B. Banerjee
F. J. Buckley
B. Conger
M. A. Daniels
N. P. Ginex
A. Hartman
R. Horner
W. M. Osborne
B. F. Rospide
D. P. Schwartz
E. Showalter
L. Siwiec
M. Swain
L. Tran
R. L. Van Tilburg
A. M. Vaughan

At the time that the IEEE Standards Board approved this revision, the Software Engineering Standards Subcommittee, which was the balloting committee that approved this document for submission to the IEEE Standards Board, included the following members:

John W. Horch, *Chairman*

K. A. Alley
R. L. Aurbach
M. Azuma
B. Banerjee
L. Beltracchi
M. Ben-Menachem
H. R. Berlack
W. J. Boll, Jr.
G. Bracon
K. L. Briggs
W. L. Bryan
F. J. Buckley
H. Carl
E. Chikofsky
F. A. Chimenti
S. V. Chiyyarata
T. S. Chow
P. H. Christensen
W. L. Chung
R. T. Close
F. Coallier
P. W. Daggett
M. A. Daniels
T. Daughtrey
P. I. Davis
P. A. Denny
B. Derganc
P. R. DeWeese
H. Dhama
K. Diggins
J. H. Dobbins
D. C. Doty
E. Dunaye
R. E. Dwyer
M. L. Eads
R. S. Euler
R. L. Evans
R. Fairley
J. Fendrich
A. M. Foley
J. J. Forman
J. Forster
M. Galinier
A. K. Geraci
Y. Gershkovitch
E. L. Gibbs
J. A. Gilmore
N. P. Ginex
S. Gloss-Soler
M. Goldberg
J. Gonzalez-Sanz
J. K. Grau
D. A. Gustafson
U. Hartmann
C. M. Hay
C. P. Hollocker
R. S. Hurst
L. Ihlenfeldt
F. Jay
D. Johnson III
M. S. Karasik
R. H. Karpinski
A. N. Kasad
R. A. Kessler
P. P. Klopfenstein
D. M. Knepper, Sr.
D. L. Knirk
S. Koenig
R. Kosinski
J. Krupinski
T. Kurihara
R. A. Lane
G. N. Larsen
F. C. Lim
B. Livson
I. S. Ludin
A. J. Maher
K. C. Majumdar
H. A. Malec
P. C. Marriott
R. J. Martin
T. Matsubara
I. Mazza
J. P. McArdle
M. C. McElvany
P. E. McKenney
G. A. Meldrum
J. Mersky
C. H. Modell
R. E. Monahan
R. C. Natale
G. Neidhart
D. E. Nickle
W. M. Osborne
D. E. Peercy
W. E. Perry
D. J. Pfeiffer
R. M. Poston
I. C. Pyle
J. Rault
M. Razy
S. T. Redwine, Jr.
B. F. Rospide
F. A. Ruhlman
D. A. Rutherford
S. R. Schach
W. A. Schnoege
R. G. Schueppert
D. J. Schultz
G. Schumacher
D. P. Schwartz
L. W. Seagren
T. Sgarlatti
G. P. Shabe
R. W. Shillato
E. Showalter
D. M. Siefert
M. W. Smith
R. Staunton
R. N. Sulgrove
W. G. Sutcliffe
C. Swain
B. J. Taute
P. U. Thompson
S. Trauth
D. L. Ulery
M. Updike-Rumley
R. L. Van Tilburg
A. M. Vaughan
H. E. Verne
D. R. Wallace
J. W. Walz
A. H. Weigel
A. T. Williams
A. F. Wilson
T. J. Wojcik
P. A. T. Wolfgang
D. L. Wood
A. W. Yonda
N. C. Yopconka
P. F. Zoll

When the IEEE Standards Board approved this standard on September 28, 1990, it had the following membership:

Marco W. Migliaro, *Chairman* **James M. Daly,** *Vice Chairman*

Andrew G. Salem, *Secretary*

Dennis Bodson
Paul L. Borrill
Fletcher J. Buckley
Allen L. Clapp
Stephen R. Dillon
Donald C. Fleckenstein
Jay Forster*
Thomas L. Hannan
Kenneth D. Hendrix
John W. Horch
Joseph L. Koepfinger*
Irving Kolodny
Michael A. Lawler
Donald J. Loughry
John E. May, Jr.
Lawrence V. McCall
L. Bruce McClung
Donald T. Michael*
Stig Nilsson
Roy T. Oishi
Gary S. Robinson
Terrance R. Whittemore
Donald W. Zipse

*Member Emeritus

Contents

IEEE Standard for Software Configuration Management Plans

1. Introduction to the Standard

1.1 Scope. IEEE Std 828-1990 establishes the minimum required contents of a Software Configuration Management (SCM) Plan (the Plan). It is supplemented by IEEE Std 1042-1987 [4][1], which provides approaches to good software configuration management planning. This standard applies to the entire life cycle of critical software; for example, where failure could impact safety or cause large financial or social losses. It also applies to noncritical software and to software already developed. The application of this standard is not restricted to any form, class, or type of software.

The Plan documents what SCM activities are to be done, how they are to be done, who is responsible for doing specific activities, when they are to happen, and what resources are required. It can address SCM activities over any portion of a software product's life cycle.

The content of the Plan is identified in Section 2 of this standard. The required information is indicated by the words "shall" and "required." Additional optional information is also identified as appropriate. The user of this standard, however, is expected to expand and supplement the minimum requirements as necessary for the development environment, specific industry, organization, and project. Tailoring of a plan in conformance with this standard is described in Section 3.

The primary users of this standard are assumed to be those planning SCM activities or performing SCM audits.

In considering adoption of this standard, regulatory bodies should be aware that specific application of this standard may already be covered by one or more IEEE Standards documents relating to quality assurance, definitions, or other matters (see [2]). It is not the purpose of IEEE Std 828-1990 to supersede, revise, or amend existing standards directed to specific industries or applications.

1.2 References. This standard may be used in conjunction with the following IEEE Software Engineering Standards:

[1] IEEE Std 610.12-1990, IEEE Standard Glossary of Software Engineering Terminology.[2]

[2] IEEE Std 730.1-1989, IEEE Standard for Software Quality Assurance Plans (ANSI).

[3] IEEE Std 1042-1987, IEEE Guide to Software Configuration Management (ANSI).

[1]The numbers in brackets correspond to those of the references listed in 1.2.

[2]IEEE publications may be obtained from the IEEE Service Center, 445 Hoes Lane, P.O. Box 1331, Piscataway, NJ 08855-1331.

Table 1
SCM Classes of Information

Class of Information	Description	Section in Standard	Section in Plan
Introduction	Describes the Plan's purpose, scope of application, key terms, and references	2.1	1
SCM Management	*(Who?)* Identifies the responsibilities and authorities for accomplishing the planned activities	2.2	2
SCM Activities	*(What?)* Identifies all activities to be performed in applying to the project	2.3	3
SCM Schedules	*(When?)* Identifies the required coordination of SCM activities with the other activities in the project	2.4	4
SCM Resources	*(How?)* Identifies tools and physical and human resources required for execution of the Plan	2.5	5
SCM Plan Maintenance	Identifies how the Plan will be kept current while in effect	2.6	6

1.3 Definitions and Acronyms. The definitions below describe specific terms as used within the context of this standard.

control point (project control point). A project agreed on point in time or times when specified agreements or controls are applied to the software configuration items being developed, e.g., an approved baseline or release of a specified document/code.

release. The formal notification and distribution of an approved version.

Additional terms that are relevant are defined in IEEE Std 610.12-1990 [1], and are as follows: baseline, component, configuration, configuration audit, configuration control, configuration control board, configuration identification, configuration item, configuration management, configuration status accounting, interface, interface control, software, software library, software life cycle, unit, version.

The following acronyms appear within the text of this standard:

CCB	Configuration Control Board
CI	Configuration Item
SCM	Software Configuration Management

The term "the Plan" is used throughout this standard to refer to the Software Configuration Management Plan.

2. The Software Configuration Management Plan

SCM planning information shall be partitioned into the six classes described in Table 1. The referenced sections of the standard provide the reader with detailed requirements for each class of information.

SCM planning information may be presented in any format, sequence, or location that is meaningful to the intended users of the Plan with the following restrictions:

(1) A document with the title "Software Configuration Management Plan" shall exist either in stand-alone form or embedded in another project document.

(2) This document shall contain all SCM planning information either by inclusion or by reference to other locations, such as other documents or automated systems.

(3) A format for this document shall be defined.

The writer of the Plan shall use the sequence of sections specified in Table 1 unless a different format has been defined in the Introduction of the Plan (see 2.1).

2.1 Introduction. Introduction information provides a simplified overview of the SCM activities so that those approving, those performing, and those interacting with SCM can obtain a clear understanding of the Plan. The

Introduction shall include four topics: the purpose of the Plan, the scope, the definition of key terms, and references.

The purpose shall briefly address why the Plan exists and who the intended audience is.

The scope shall address SCM applicability, limitations, and assumptions on which the Plan is based. The following items shall be included:

(1) Overview description of the software development project
(2) Identification of the software CI(s) to which SCM will be applied
(3) Identification of other software to be included as part of the Plan (e.g., support or test software)
(4) Relationship of SCM to the hardware or system configuration management activities for the project
(5) The degree of formality, depth of control, and portion of the software life cycle for applying SCM on this project
(6) Limitations, such as time constraints, that apply to the Plan
(7) Assumptions that might have an impact on the cost, schedule, or ability to perform defined SCM activities (e.g., assumptions of the degree of customer participation in SCM activities or the availability of automated aids)

Key terms shall be defined as they apply to the Plan in order to establish a common terminology among all users of the Plan.

All references in the Plan to policies, directives, procedures, standards, terminology, and related documents shall be uniquely identified to enable retrieval by users of the Plan.

2.2 SCM Management. SCM management information describes the allocation of responsibilities and authorities for SCM activities to organizations and individuals within the project structure.

SCM management information shall include three topics: the project organization(s) within which SCM is to apply; the SCM responsibilities of these organizations; and references to the SCM policies and directives that apply to this project.

2.2.1 Organization. The organizational context, both technical and managerial, within which the planned SCM activities are to be implemented shall be described. The Plan shall identify the following:

(1) All organizational units that participate in or are responsible for any SCM activity on the project
(2) The functional roles of these organizational units within the project structure
(3) Relationships between organizational units

Organizational units may consist of a vendor and customer, a prime contractor and subcontractors, or different groups within one organization. Organization charts, supplemented by statements of function and relationships, can be an effective way of presenting this information.

2.2.2 SCM Responsibilities. The allocation of SCM activities to organizational units shall be specified. For each activity listed within SCM activities (see 2.3), the name of the organizational unit or job title to perform this activity shall be provided. A matrix that relates the organizations defined above to the SCM functions, activities, and tasks can be useful for documenting the SCM responsibilities.

For any review board or special organization established for performing SCM activities on this project, the Plan shall describe its

(1) Purpose and objectives
(2) Membership and affiliations
(3) Period of effectivity
(4) Scope of authority
(5) Operational procedures

2.2.3 Applicable Policies, Directives, and Procedures. Any external constraints placed on the Plan by other policies, directives, and procedures shall be identified. For each, its impact and effect on the Plan shall be stated.

2.3 SCM Activities. SCM activities information identifies all functions and tasks required to manage the configuration of the software system as specified in the scope of the Plan. Both technical and managerial SCM activities shall be identified. General project activities that have SCM implications shall be described from the SCM perspective.

SCM activities are traditionally grouped into four functions: configuration identification, configuration control, status accounting, and configuration audits and reviews. The information requirements for each function are identified in 2.3.1 through 2.3.4.

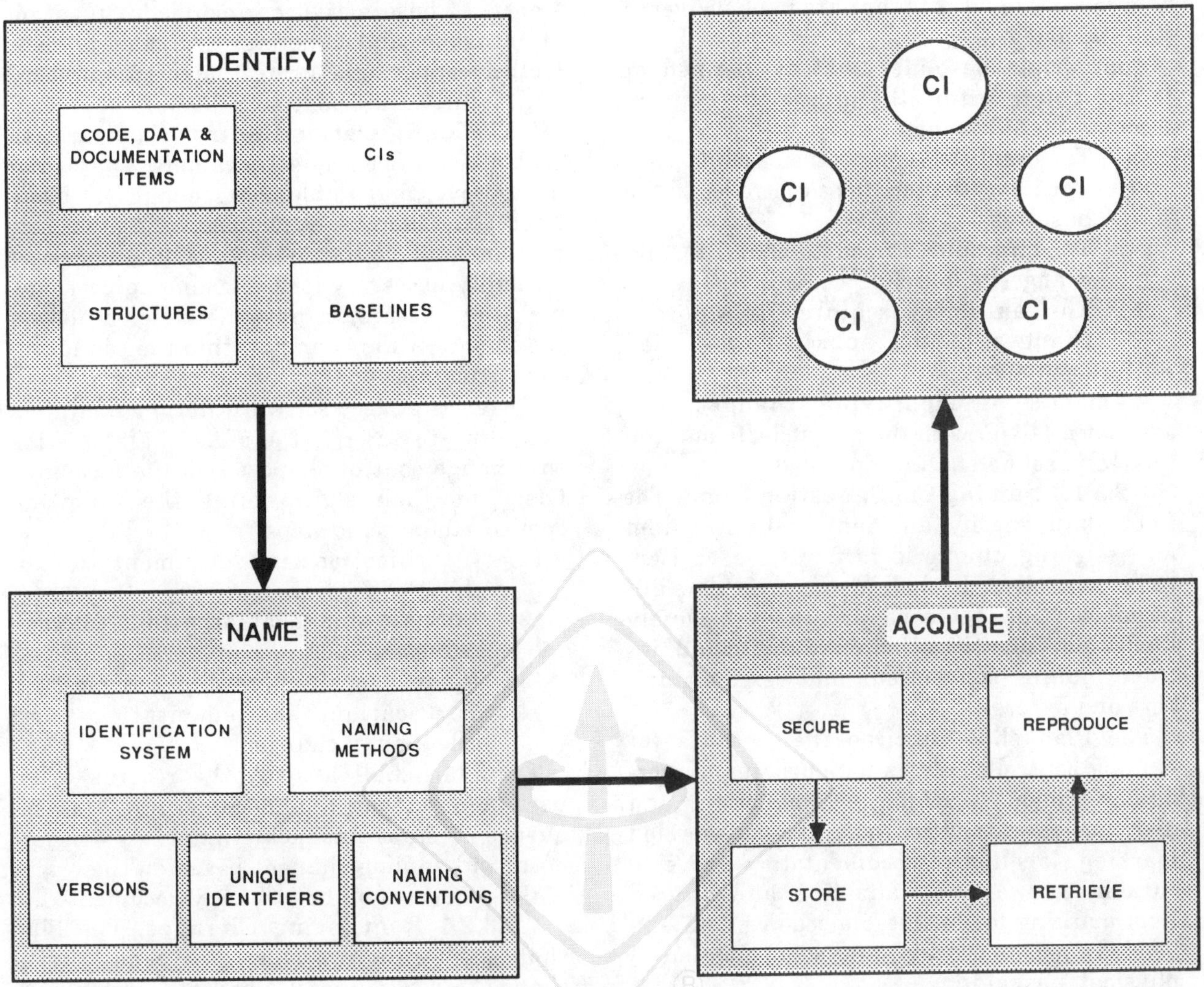

Fig 1
Configuration Identification Processes

Due to their high risk nature, the requirements for interface control and subcontractor/vendor control activities are identified separately in 2.3.5 and 2.3.6.

2.3.1 Configuration Identification. Configuration identification activities shall identify, name, and describe the documented physical and functional characteristics of the code, specifications, design, and data elements to be controlled for the project. The documents are acquired for configuration control. Controlled items may be intermediate and final outputs (such as executable code, source code, user documentation, program listings, data bases, test cases, test plans, specifications, and management plans) and elements of the support environment (such as compilers, operating systems, programming tools, and test beds).

The Plan shall identify the project configuration items (CI) and their structures at each project control point. The Plan states how each CI and its versions are to be uniquely named and describes the activities performed to define, track, store, and retrieve CIs. The following sections specify information required for configuration identification (see Fig 1).

2.3.1.1 Identifying Configuration Items. The Plan shall record the items to be controlled, the project CIs, and their definitions as they evolve or are selected. The Plan shall also describe how the list of items and the structures are to be maintained for the project.

As a minimum, all CIs that are to be delivered shall be listed.

Appropriate baselines shall be defined at control points within the project life cycle in terms of the following:

(1) The event that creates the baseline
(2) The items that are to be controlled in the baseline
(3) The procedures used to establish and change the baseline
(4) The authority required to approve changes to the approved baselined documents

A means of identifying changes and associating them with the affected CIs and the related baseline shall be specified.

2.3.1.2 Naming Configuration Items. The Plan shall specify an identification system for assigning unique identifiers to each item to be controlled. It shall also specify how different versions of each are to be uniquely identified. Identification methods could include naming conventions and version numbers and letters.

The Plan shall describe the methods for naming controlled items for purposes of storage, retrieval, tracking, reproduction, and distribution. Activities may include version marking, labeling of documentation and executable software, serialization and altered item marking for executable code or data embedded on a microchip, and identification of physical packaging.

Subcontracted software, vendor proprietary software, and support software may require special identification schemes and labeling.

2.3.1.3 Acquiring Configuration Items. The Plan shall identify the controlled software libraries for the project and describe how the code, documentation, and data of the identified baselines are to be physically placed under control in the appropriate library. For each library the format, location, documentation requirements, receiving and inspection requirements, and access control procedures shall be specified.

The Plan shall specify procedures for the actual storage of documents and magnetic media, including the physical marking and labeling of items. Data retention periods and disaster prevention and recovery procedures may also be described.

Procedures shall describe how to retrieve and reproduce controlled items from library storage. These activities include verification of marking and labeling, tracking of controlled copies, and protection of proprietary and security information.

2.3.2 Configuration Control. Configuration control activities request, evaluate, approve or disapprove, and implement changes to baselined CIs. Changes encompass both error correction and enhancement. The degree of formality necessary for the change process depends on the project baseline affected and on the impact of the change within the configuration structure.

For each project software library identified according to 2.3.1.3, the Plan shall describe the change controls imposed on the baselined CIs. The Plan shall define the following sequence of specific steps:

(1) Identification and documentation of the need for a change
(2) Analysis and evaluation of a change request
(3) Approval or disapproval of a request
(4) Verification, implementation, and release of a change

The Plan shall identify the records to be used for tracking and documenting this sequence of steps for each change. Any differences in handling changes based on the origin of the request shall be explicitly documented.

2.3.2.1 Requesting Changes. The Plan shall specify the procedures for requesting a change to a baselined CI and the information to be documented for the request. As a minimum, the information recorded for a proposed change shall contain the following:

(1) The name(s) and version(s) of the CIs where the problem appears
(2) Originator's name and organization
(3) Date of request
(4) Indication of urgency
(5) The need for the change
(6) Description of the requested change

Additional information, such as priority or classification, may be included to clarify the significance of the request and to assist in its analysis and evaluation. Other information, such as change request number, status, and disposition, may be recorded for change tracking.

2.3.2.2 Evaluating Changes. The Plan shall specify the analysis required to determine the impact of the proposed change and the procedures for reviewing the results of the analysis. Changes should be evaluated according to their effect on the deliverable and their impact on project resources.

2.3.2.3 Approving or Disapproving Changes. The Plan shall identify each configuration control board (CCB) and its level of authority for approving proposed changes. A CCB may be an individual or a group. Multiple levels of CCBs may be specified, depending upon the degree of system or project complexity and upon the project baseline involved. When multiple CCBs are used, the Plan shall specify how the proper level is determined for a change request, including any variations during the project life cycle.

For any CCB utilized, the Plan shall indicate its level of authority and its responsibilities as defined in 2.2.2.

2.3.2.4 Implementing Changes. The Plan shall specify the activities for verifying and implementing an approved change. The information recorded for the completion of a change shall contain the following as a minimum:

(1) The associated change request(s)
(2) The names and versions of the affected items
(3) Verification date and responsible party
(4) Release or installation date and responsible party
(5) The identifier of the new version

Additional information, such as software fault metrics or identification of the supporting software used to implement the change, may be included.

The Plan shall also specify activities for release planning and control, i.e., coordinating multiple changes, reconfiguring the CIs, and delivering a new baseline.

2.3.3 Configuration Status Accounting. Configuration status accounting activities record and report the status of project CIs.

The Plan shall include information on the following:

(1) What data elements are to be tracked and reported for baselines and changes
(2) What types of status accounting reports are to be generated and their frequency
(3) How information is to be collected, stored, processed, and reported
(4) How access to the status data is to be controlled

If an automated system is used for any status accounting activity, its function shall be described or referenced.

The following minimum data elements shall be tracked and reported for each CI: its initial approved version, the status of requested changes, and the implementation status of approved changes. The level of detail and specific data required may vary according to the information needs of the project and the customer.

2.3.4 Configuration Audits and Reviews. Configuration audits determine to what extent the actual CI reflects the required physical and functional characteristics. Configuration reviews are management tools for establishing a baseline.

The Plan shall identify the configuration audits and reviews to be held for the project. At a minimum, a configuration audit shall be performed on a CI prior to its release.

For each planned configuration audit or review, the Plan shall define the following:

(1) Its objective
(2) The CIs under audit or review
(3) The schedule of audit or review tasks
(4) The procedures for conducting the audit or review
(5) The participants by job title
(6) Documentation required to be available for review or to support the audit or review
(7) The procedure for recording any deficiencies and reporting corrective actions
(8) The approval criteria and the specific action(s) to occur upon approval

2.3.5 Interface Control. Interface control activities coordinate changes to the project CIs with changes to interfacing items outside the scope of the Plan. Hardware, system software and support software, as well as other projects and deliverables, should be examined for potential interfacing effects on the project.

The Plan shall identify the external items to which the project software interfaces. For each interface the Plan shall define the following:

(1) The nature of the interface
(2) The affected organizations
(3) How the interface code, documentation, and data are to be controlled
(4) How the interface control documents are approved and released into a specified baseline

For any CCB established to control interfaces, the Plan shall identify its responsibilities and procedures as specified in 2.2.2.

2.3.6 Subcontractor/Vendor Control. Subcontractor/vendor control activities incorporate items developed outside the project environment into the project CIs. Included are software developed by contract and software acquired in its finished form. Special attention should be directed to these SCM activities due to the added organizational and legal relationships.

For both subcontracted and acquired software, the Plan shall define the activities to incorporate the externally developed items into the project CIs and to coordinate changes to these items with their development organizations.

For subcontracted software, the Plan shall describe the following:

(1) What SCM requirements, including an SCM Plan, are to be part of the subcontractor's agreement
(2) How the subcontractor will be monitored for compliance
(3) What configuration audits and reviews of subcontractor items will be held
(4) How external code, documentation, and data will be tested, verified, accepted, and merged with the project software
(5) How proprietary items will be handled for security of information and traceability of ownership (e.g., copyright and royalties)
(6) How changes are to be processed, including the subcontractor's participation

For acquired software, the Plan shall describe how the software will be received, tested, and placed under SCM; how changes to the supplier's software are to be processed; and whether and how the supplier will participate in the project's change management process. Acquired software can come from a vendor, a subcontractor, a customer, another project, or other source.

2.4 SCM Schedules. SCM schedule information establishes the sequence and coordination for the identified SCM activities and for all events affecting the Plan's implementation.

The Plan shall state the sequence and dependencies among all SCM activities and the relationship of key SCM activities to project milestones or events. The schedule shall cover the duration of the Plan and contain all major milestones of the project related to SCM activities. SCM milestones shall include establishment of a configuration baseline, implementation of change control procedures, and the start and completion dates for a configuration audit.

Schedule information shall be expressed as absolute dates, as dates relative to either SCM or project milestones, or as a simple sequence of events. Graphic representation can be particularly appropriate for conveying this information.

2.5 SCM Resources. SCM resource information identifies the software tools, techniques, equipment, personnel, and training necessary for the implementation of the specified SCM activities.

SCM can be performed by a combination of software tools and manual procedures. Tools can be SCM-specific or embedded in general project aids; they can be standard organizational resources or ones specially acquired or built for this project. Tools can be applied to library structure and access control; documentation development and tracking; code control; baseline system generation; change processing, communication and authorization; change/problem tracking and status reporting; archiving, retention, and retrieval of controlled items; or the SCM planning process itself.

For each type of SCM activity identified, the Plan shall specify what tools, techniques, equipment, personnel, and training are required and how each resource will be provided or obtained.

For each software tool, whether developed within the project or brought in from outside the project, the Plan shall describe or reference its functions and shall identify the configuration controls to be placed on the tool.

2.6 SCM Plan Maintenance. SCM plan maintenance information identifies the activities and responsibilities necessary to ensure continued SCM planning during the life cycle of the project. The Plan shall state the following:

(1) Who is responsible for monitoring the Plan
(2) How frequently updates are to be performed
(3) How changes to the Plan are to be evaluated and approved
(4) How changes to the Plan are to be made and communicated

The Plan should be reviewed at the start of each project software phase, changed accordingly, and approved and distributed to the project team.

If the Plan has been constructed with detailed procedures documented elsewhere in appendixes or references, different maintenance mechanisms for those procedures may be appropriate.

3. Tailoring of the Plan

This standard permits significant flexibility in preparing an SCM Plan. A successful Plan reflects its project environment. It should be written in terms familiar to its users and should be consistent with the development and procurement processes of the project.

To conform to the requirements set forth in other applicable standards or to accommodate local practices, a Plan may be tailored upward, to add information, or tailored to use a specified format. The Plan may also be tailored downward, omitting information required by this standard, when specific standard requirements are identified as not applicable to this project.

3.1 Upward Tailoring. Some information requirements applicable to a particular project may not be stated in this standard due to its scope of establishing the minimum required contents of an SCM Plan. If additional requirements are applicable to the project, the Plan shall so state these additions as part of the Introduction and indicate the reason for their insertion. A cost-benefits analysis should be completed for each additional requirement. Requirements that are additional should be agreed on by all affected project functions and the parties responsible for approval of the plan.

3.2 Downward Tailoring. Some information requirements stated in this standard may not apply to a particular project due to the project's limited scope, low complexity, or unusual environment. If a requirement is not applicable to the project, the Plan shall so state this deletion as part of the Introduction and indicate the reason for removal. Requirements that are inapplicable should be agreed upon by all affected project functions and all parties responsible for approval of the Plan.

The Plan shall omit none of the six major classes of information. Detailed information may be omitted as indicated above but within the limits of the consistency criteria stated in Section 4.

If certain information has not been decided on or is unavailable at the time the Plan is initially approved, the Plan shall mark those areas or sections as "to be determined" and shall indicate, as part of Plan maintenance, information on how and when further information will be provided.

3.3 Format. The information may be presented in the Plan in any sequence or presentation style deemed suitable for the Plan's users. To achieve consistency and convenience within a single organization or industry segment, a standard format for SCM plans is desirable and appropriate. To customize this standard for a particular group of users, a supplement to the standard specifying Plan structure and standard terminology may be used.

4. Conformance to the Standard

An SCM Plan shall satisfy the following criteria in order to conform with this standard.

4.1 Minimum Information. The Plan shall include the six classes of SCM information identified in Section 2: Introduction, Management, Activities, Schedules, Resources, and Plan Maintenance. Within each class, all of the required information stated in Section 2 of this standard, as indicated by the words "shall" and "required," shall be documented within the Plan. If certain required information is not applicable, the reasons shall be so stated. If a sequence of information other than the sequence of this standard is used, an explicit cross reference between the Plan and the standard shall be provided.

4.2 Presentation Format. One document, section title, or such reference shall exist that is specifically labeled "Software Configuration Management Plan." Within this document, each of the six classes of information shall be included. While the information may be provided in a number of presentation styles, the requirement is to provide all Plan information and references in a single document.

4.3 Consistency Criteria. The documented information shall satisfy the following consistency criteria:

(1) All activities defined in the Plan (see 2.3.1 to 2.3.6) shall be assigned to an organizational unit (see 2.2.2).

(2) All activities defined shall have resources identified to accomplish the activities (see 2.5).

(3) All CIs identified in the Plan (see 2.3.1) shall have defined processes for baseline establishment and change control (see 2.3.2).

4.4 Conformance Declaration. If the preceding criteria are met, then the conformance of any SCM planning documentation with this standard may be stated accordingly: "This SCM Plan conforms with the requirements of IEEE Std 828-1990."

Appendix
Cross Reference to IEEE Std 1042-1987

(This Appendix is not part of IEEE Std 828-1990, IEEE Standard for Software Configuration Management Plans, but is included for information only.)

Section in IEEE Std 828-1990	Section in IEEE Std 1042-1987
1. Introduction to the Standard	1. Introduction 2. SCM Disciplines in Software Management
2. The SCM Plan	3. Software Configuration Management Plans
2.1 Introduction	3.1 Introduction
2.2 SCM Management	3.2 Management
2.3 SCM Activities	3.3 SCM Activities
2.3.1 Configuration Identification	3.3.1 Configuration Identification
2.3.2 Configuration Control	3.3.2 Configuration Control
2.3.3 Configuration Status Accounting	3.3.3 Configuration Status Accounting
2.3.4 Configuration Audits and Reviews	3.3.4 Audits and Reviews
2.3.5 Interface Control	3.2.3 Interface Control
2.3.6 Subcontractor/Vendor Control	3.5 Supplier Control
2.4 Schedules	3.2.4 SCM Plan Implementation
2.5 Resources	3.4 Tools, Techniques and Methodologies
2.6 SCM Plan Maintenance	2.5 The Planning of SCM
3. Tailoring of the Plan	2.5 The Planning of SCM
4. Conformance to the Standard	2.5 The Planning of SCM

Acknowledgments

The following organizations supported working group members in the development of this standard. This support does not constitute or imply approval or endorsement of this standard.

Babcock & Wilcox
Battelle Northwest Laboratories
BTG Inc.
Compass Corporation
CTA Inc.
DSC Communications
Eaton/AIL
General Electric–MSD
Jet Propulsion Laboratory
Lockheed Missiles & Space Company
Lockheed Sanders Inc.
MACTEC
McDonnell Douglas
Mitre Corporation
Motorola/Computer X
National Institute of Standards and Technology
Northrop Corporation
Programming Environments Inc.
Rockwell Telecommunications
Texas Instruments
Unisys Corporation

ANSI/IEEE
Std 829-1983

An American National Standard

IEEE Standard for Software Test Documentation

Sponsor

Software Engineering Standards Subcommittee of the Technical Committee on Software Engineering of the IEEE Computer Society

Approved December 3, 1982
Reaffirmed March 21, 1991

IEEE Standards Board

Approved August 19, 1983
Reaffirmed September 6, 1991

American National Standards Institute

The Institute of Electrical and Electronics Engineers, Inc
345 East 47th Street, New York, NY 10017, USA

IEEE Standards documents are developed within the Technical Committees of the IEEE Societies and the Standards Coordinating Committees of the IEEE Standards Board. Members of the committees serve voluntarily and without compensation. They are not necessarily members of the Institute. The standards developed within IEEE represent a consensus of the broad expertise on the subject within the Institute as well as those activities outside of IEEE which have expressed an interest in participating in the development of the standard.

Use of an IEEE Standard is wholly voluntary. The existence of an IEEE Standard does not imply that there are no other ways to produce, test, measure, purchase, market, or provide other goods and services related to the scope of the IEEE Standard. Furthermore, the viewpoint expressed at the time a standard is approved and issued is subject to change brought about through developments in the state of the art and comments received from users of the standard. Every IEEE Standard is subjected to review at least once every five years for revision or reaffirmation. When a document is more than five years old, and has not been reaffirmed, it is reasonable to conclude that its contents, although still of some value, do not wholly reflect the present state of the art. Users are cautioned to check to determine that they have the latest edition of any IEEE Standard.

Comments for revision of IEEE Standards are welcome from any interested party, regardless of membership affiliation with IEEE. Suggestions for changes in documents should be in the form of a proposed change of text, together with appropriate supporting comments.

Interpretations: Occasionally questions may arise regarding the meaning of portions of standards as they relate to specific applications. When the need for interpretations is brought to the attention of IEEE, the Institute will initiate action to prepare appropriate responses. Since IEEE Standards represent a consensus of all concerned interests, it is important to ensure that any interpretation has also received the concurrence of a balance of interests. For this reason IEEE and the members of its technical committees are not able to provide an instant response to interpretation requests except in those cases where the matter has previously received formal consideration.

Comments on standards and requests for interpretations should be addressed to:

Secretary, IEEE Standards Board
345 East 47th Street
New York, NY 10017
USA

Foreword

(This Foreword is not a part of ANSI/IEEE Std 829-1983, IEEE Standard for Software Test Documentation.)

Purpose

The purpose of this standard is to describe a set of basic software test documents. A standardized test document can facilitate communication by providing a common *frame of reference* (for example, a customer and a supplier have the same definition for a test plan). The content definition of a standardized test document can serve as a completeness checklist for the associated testing process. A standardized set can also provide a baseline for the evaluation of current test documentation practices. In many organizations, the use of these documents significantly increases the manageability of testing. Increased manageability results from the greatly increased visibility of each phase of the testing process.

This standard specifies the form and content of individual test documents. It does not specify the required set of test documents. It is assumed that the required set of test documents will be specified when the standard is applied. Appendix B contains an example of such a set specification.

Overview

The documents outlined in this standard cover test planning, test specification, and test reporting.

The test plan prescribes the scope, approach, resources, and schedule of the testing activities. It identifies the items to be tested, the features to be tested, the testing tasks to be performed, the personnel responsible for each task, and the risks associated with the plan.

Test specification is covered by three document types:

(1) A test-design specification refines the test approach and identifies the features to be covered by the design and its associated tests. It also identifies the test cases and test procedures, if any, required to accomplish the testing and specifies the feature pass/fail criteria.

(2) A test-case specification documents the actual values used for input along with the anticipated outputs. A test case also identifies any constraints on the test procedures resulting from use of that specific test case. Test cases are separated from test designs to allow for use in more than one design and to allow for reuse in other situations.

(3) A test procedure specification identifies all steps required to operate the system and exercise the specified test cases in order to implement the associated test design. Test procedures are separated from test-design specifications as they are intended to be followed step by step and should not have extraneous detail.

Test reporting is covered by four document types:

(1) A test item transmittal report identifies the test items being transmitted for testing in the event that separate development and test groups are involved or in the event that a formal beginning of test execution is desired.

(2) A test log is used by the test team to record what occurred during test execution.

(3) A test incident report describes any event that occurs during the test execution which requires further investigation.

(4) A test summary report summarizes the testing activities associated with one or more test-design specifications.

Figure 1 shows the relationships of these documents to one another as they are developed and to the testing process they document.

Terminology

The words *shall*, *must*, and the imperative form identify the mandatory material within this standard. The words *should* and *may* identify optional material.

Appendixes

The examples found in Appendix A are meant to clarify the intent of the document descriptions found in the standard. Some suggestions about implementing and using the standard are in Appendix B. Appendix C contains references to related test documentation standards. Appendix D contains references to testing-related documents of general interest which are not focused on test documentation.

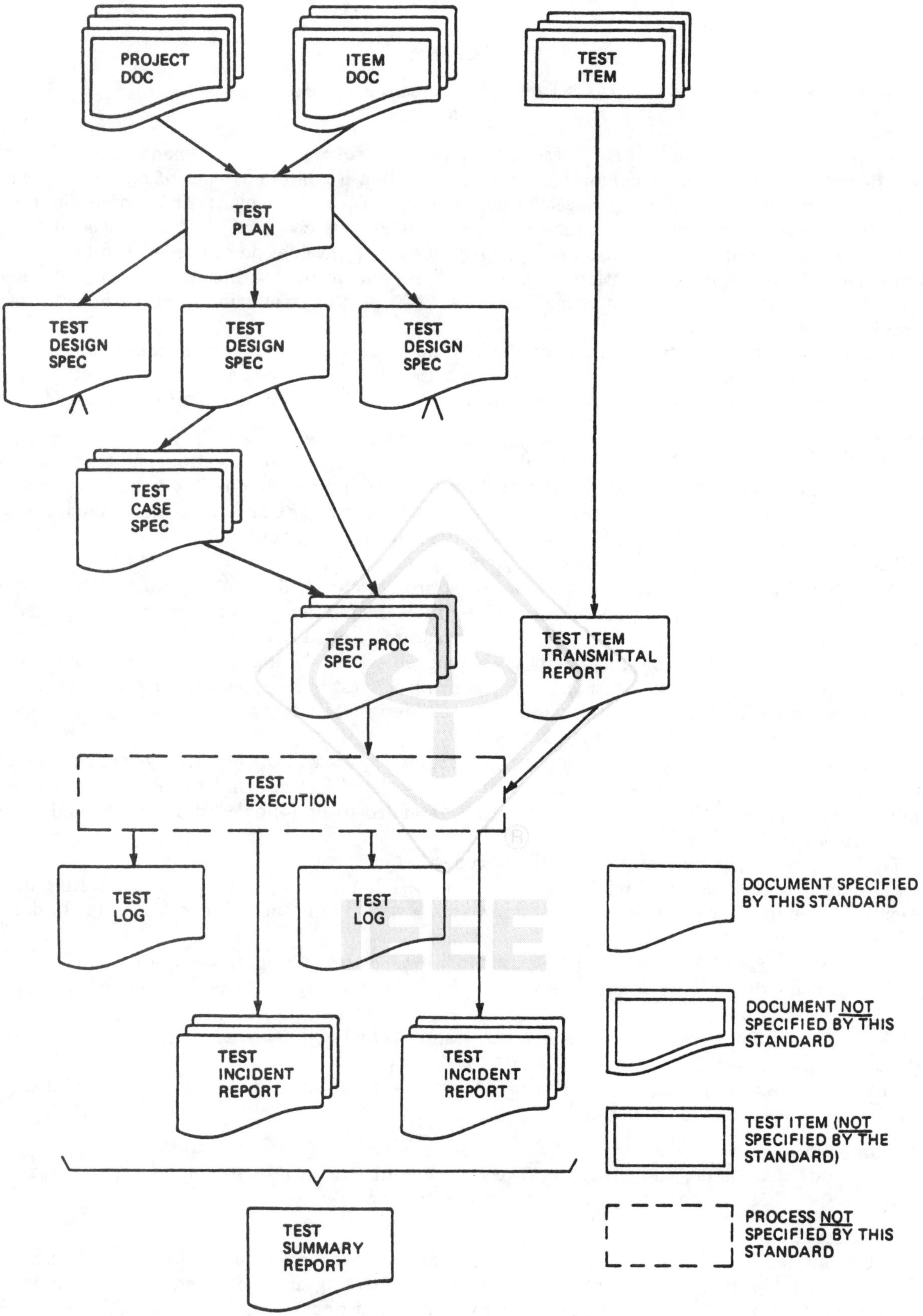

Fig 1
Relationship of Test Documents to Testing Process

Audience

The standard should be of interest to software users and software procurement personnel; to development, test, and maintenance personnel; to operations and acquisition support managers; to software quality assurance personnel and auditors; and to participants in the legal system.

History

The development of this standard began from discussions within the Software Engineering Standards Subcommittee in 1977. Some initial work was done by a group including Joan Bateman, Leonard Birns, Herb Hecht, and Bob Poston and resulted in an early draft outline. The project authorization request for this effort was approved by the IEEE Standards Board in May, 1980. Following authorization, a series of ten meetings which were held across the country from September, 1980 to May, 1982 produced the first draft submitted for balloting.

Suggestions for improvement of the standard will be welcome. They should be sent to:
Secretary
IEEE Standards Board
Institute of Electrical and Electronics Engineers
345 East 47th Street
New York, NY 10017.

At the time this standard was approved on December 3, 1982, the IEEE Standards Board had the following membership:

Irvin N. Howell, *Chairman*

Edward Chelotti, *Vice Chairman*

Sava I. Sherr, *Secretary*

G. Y. R. Allen
J. J. Archambault
James H. Beall
John T. Boettger
J. V. Bonucchi
Edward J. Cohen
Len S. Corey
D. C. Fleckenstein
Jay Forster
Kurt Greene
Joseph L. Koepfinger
Irving Kolodny
John E. May
Donald T. Michael*
A. R. Parsons
J. P. Riganati
Frank L. Rose
Robert W. Seelbach
Jay A. Stewart
Clifford O. Swanson
Robert E. Weiler

*Member emeritus

This standard was completed by a working group with the following members:

David Gelperin, *Chairman*

Rick Adrion
Jules Aronson
Joan Bateman
Charlie Bates
A. Birnbaum
Leonard Birns
John Bowen
Martha Branstad
Fletcher Buckley
Douglas Burt
Ian Burton
John Cain
John Center
George Chapman
Santosh Chokhani
Bruce Clay
D. L. Cooper
Doc Craddock
James Cridge
Patricia Daggett
Bill Dupras
Mary Eads
Sharon Freid
Tom Frost
Tom Gilb
Loretta Guarino
John Hawthorne
Herb Hecht
Mike Hennell
Dan Hocking
Mark Holthouse
Ray Houghton
Paul Howley
John Kalasky
Jason Kazarian
Ed Kit
Denise Krauss
Joseph Krupinski
Tom Kurihara
Costa J. Labovites
Paula Levinton
Leo Lippman
Alex Long
Mable Love
Ben Manny
Albrecht Newmann
Bill Newsom
C. Donald Ostler
Varsha Pai
Art Pollari
Robert Poston
Sam Redwine
Charles Schult
David Schultz
Dennis Sharp
Jerry Smith
Wayne Smith
Joan Spalding
Bob Stewart
S. L. Stewart
Sarah Swales
Barbara Taute
J. R. Taylor
Rudolf Van Megen
David Vatsaas
John Walter
Andrew Weigel
Jonathon Wexler
Paul White
Bruce Wilkins
Harry Wilkinson
F. T. Woodall
Fred Yonda

The standard was approved by the Software Engineering Standards Subcommittee of the IEEE Computer Society. At the time it approved this standard, the subcommittee had the following membership:

Fletcher J. Buckley, *Chairman*

Russell J. Abbott
A. Frank Ackerman
Leo Beltracchi
Richard L. Bernstein
Nestore G. Biasi
Dennis W. Bragg
Douglas W. Burt
Homer C. Carney
John Center
Won L. Chung
Anonio M. Cicu
Lori A. Clarke
Gilmore G. Cooke
A. J. Cote, Jr
Patricia W. Daggett
George Darling
B. Dasarathy
Noah S. Davids
James A. Dobbins
Mary L. Eads
John D. Earls
Leo G. Egan, Jr
John W. Fendrich
Dennis W. Fife
Joel J. Forman
M. Galinier
Forrest Karl Gardner
David Gelperin
Gary Gladden
Shirley A. Gloss-Soler
John J.Greene
Jack W. Grigsby
Robert M. Gross
David A. Gustafson
Russell T. Gustin
Thomas L. Hannan
Herbert Hecht
Leslie R. Heselton, III
Sam Horvitz
Paul Howley
Shuenn-Chang Hwang
Jim H. Ingram
John P. Kalasky
Laurel V. Kaleda
Thomas M. Kurihara
Domenic V. La-Rosa
Robert A. C. Lane
Gregory N. Larsen
Geoffrey R. Lewis
A. Lip Lim
G. S. Lindsay
Myron Lipow
William M. Lively
Marvin Lubofsky
Don Lundquist
Alan Cheuk-Wai Ma
Andy K. Mahindru
Philip C. Marriott
Mike McCollough
Belden Menkus
Edward F. Miller, Jr
G. Scott Morris
Gene T. Morun
Walter G. Murch
Jack Nebb
Geraldine Rajcula Neidhart
Michael A. Neighbors
Leon Osterweil
Donald J. Ostrom
William E. Perry
Donald J. Pfeiffer
Robert M. Poston
Patricia B. Powell
Farzad Raji
Jean Claude Rault
Samuel T. Redwine
T. L. Regulinski
William E. Riddle
Clarence W. Rutter, III
Norman F. Schneidewind
Antonia D. Schuman
Leonard W. Seagren
Wayne Smith
Harry M. Sneed
Lee Sprague
Edward A. Straker
Kou Chung Tai
Barbara J. Taute
George D. Tice, Jr
Terrence L. Tillmanns
William S. Turner, III
Edwin A. Ulbrich, Jr
Udo Voges
John P. Walter
Andrew H. Weigel
N. P. Wilburn
Martin Wong
David C. Wood
Ted Workman
Alfred W. Yonda
Peter F. Zoll

Special representatives to the Software Engineering Subcommittee were as follows:

William E. Perry, *DPMA*
Roy P. Pritchett, Jr, *EDP Auditors Association*
John Milandin, *ANSI Z1*

Contents

IEEE

An American National Standard

IEEE Standard for Software Test Documentation

1. Scope

This standard describes a set of basic test documents which are associated with the dynamic aspects of software testing (that is, the execution of procedures and code). The standard defines the purpose, outline, and content of each basic document. While the documents described in the standard focus on dynamic testing, several of them may be applicable to other testing activities (for example, the test plan and test incident report may be used for design and code reviews).

The standard may be applied to commercial, scientific, or military software which runs on any digitial computer. Applicability is not restricted by the size, complexity, or criticality of the software. However, the standard does *not* specify any class of software to which it must be applied. The standard addresses the documentation of both initial development testing and the testing of subsequent software releases. For a particular software release, it may be applied to all phases of testing from module testing through user acceptance. However, since all of the basic test documents may not be useful in each test phase, the particular documents to be used in a phase are *not* specified. Each organization using the standard will need to specify the classes of software to which it applies and the specific documents required for a particular test phase.

The standard does *not* call for specific testing methodologies, approaches, techniques, facilities, or tools, and does *not* specify the documentation of their use. Additional test documentation may be required (for example, code inspection checklists and reports). The standard also does *not* imply or impose specific methodologies for documentation control, configuration management, or quality assurance. Additional documentation (for example, a quality assurance plan) may be needed depending on the particular methodologies used.

Within each standard document, the content of each section (that is, the text which covers the designated topics) may be tailored to the particular application and the particular testing phase. In addition to tailoring content, additional documents may be added to the basic set, additional sections may be added to any document and additional content to any section. It may be useful to organize some of the sections into subsections. Some or all of the contents of a section may be contained in another document which is then referenced. Each organization using the standard should specify additional content requirements and conventions in order to reflect their own particular methodologies, approaches, facilities, and tools for testing, documentation control, configuration management, and quality assurance.

The standard applies to documentation on electronic media as well as paper. Paper must be used for documents requiring approval signatures, unless the electronic documentation system has a secure approval annotation mechanism and that mechanism is used.

2. Definitions

This section contains key terms as they are used in the standard.

design level. The design decomposition of the software item (for example, system, subsystem, program, or module).

pass/fail criteria. Decision rules used to determine whether a software item or a software feature passes or fails a test.

software feature. A distinguishing characteristic of a software item (for example, performance, portability, or functionality).

software item. Source code, object code, job control code, control data, or a collection of these items.

test. (1) A set of one or more test cases, or

(2) A set of one or more test procedures, or
(3) A set of one or more test cases and procedures.

test case specification. A document specifying inputs, predicted results, and a set of execution conditions for a test item.

test design specification. A document specifying the details of the test approach for a software feature or combination of software features and identifying the associated tests.

test incident report. A document reporting on any event that occurs during the testing process which requires investigation.

test item. A software item which is an object of testing.

test item transmittal report. A document identifying test items. It contains current status and location information.

test log. A chronological record of relevant details about the execution of tests.

test plan. A document describing the scope, approach, resources, and schedule of intended testing activities. It identifies test items, the features to be tested, the testing tasks, who will do each task, and any risks requiring contingency planning.

test procedure specification. A document specifying a sequence of actions for the execution of a test.

test summary report. A document summarizing testing activities and results. It also contains an evaluation of the corresponding test items.

testing. The process of analyzing a software item to detect the differences between existing and required conditions (that is, bugs) and to evaluate the features of the software item.

3. Test Plan

3.1 Purpose. To prescribe the scope, approach, resources, and schedule of the testing activities. To identify the items being tested, the features to be tested, the testing tasks to be performed, the personnel responsible for each task, and the risks associated with this plan.

3.2 Outline. A test plan shall have the following structure:

1. Test-plan identifier
2. Introduction
3. Test items
4. Features to be tested
5. Features not to be tested
6. Approach
7. Item pass/fail criteria
8. Suspension criteria and resumption requirements
9. Test deliverables
10. Testing tasks
11. Environmental needs
12. Responsibilities
13. Staffing and training needs
14. Schedule
15. Risks and contingencies
16. Approvals

The sections shall be ordered in the specified sequence. Additional sections may be included immediately prior to *Approvals.* If some or all of the content of a section is in another document, then a reference to that material may be listed in place of the corresponding content. The referenced material must be attached to the test plan or available to users of the plan.

Details on the content of each section are contained in the following sections.

3.2.1 Test-Plan Identifier. Specify the unique identifier assigned to this test plan.

3.2.2 Introduction. Summarize the software items and software features to be tested. The need for each item and its history may be included.

References to the following documents, when they exist, are required in the highest-level test plan:

Project authorization
Project plan
Quality assurance plan
Configuration management plan
Relevant policies
Relevant standards

In multilevel test plans, each lower-level plan must reference the next higher-level plan.

3.2.3 Test Items. Identify the test items including their version/revision level. Also specify characteristics of their transmittal media which impact hardware requirements or indicate the need for logical or physical transformations before testing can begin (for example, programs must be transferred from tape to disk).

Supply references to the following item documentation, if it exists:

Requirements specification
Design specification
Users guide
Operations guide
Installation guide

Reference any incident reports relating to the test items.

Items which are to be specifically excluded from testing may be identified.

3.2.4 Features to be Tested. Identify all software features and combinations of software features to be tested. Identify the test-design specification associated with each feature and each combination of features.

3.2.5 Features Not to be Tested. Identify all features and significant combinations of features which will not be tested and the reasons.

3.2.6 Approach. Describe the overall approach to testing. For each major group of features or feature combinations, specify the approach which will ensure that these feature groups are adequately tested. Specify the major activities, techniques, and tools which are used to test the designated groups of features.

The approach should be described in sufficient detail to permit identification of the major testing tasks and estimation of the time required to do each one.

Specify the minimum degree of comprehensiveness desired. Identify the techniques which will be used to judge the comprehensiveness of the testing effort (for example, determining which statements have been executed at least once). Specify any additional completion criteria (for example, error frequency). The techniques to be used to trace requirements should be specified.

Identify significant constraints on testing such as test-item availability, testing-resource availability, and deadlines.

3.2.7 Item Pass/Fail Criteria. Specify the criteria to be used to determine whether each test item has passed or failed testing.

3.2.8 Suspension Criteria and Resumption Requirements. Specify the criteria used to suspend all or a portion of the testing activity on the test items associated with this plan. Specify the testing activities which must be repeated, when testing is resumed.

3.2.9 Test Deliverables. Identify the deliverable documents. The following documents should be included:

Test plan
Test design specifications
Test case specifications
Test procedure specifications
Test item transmittal reports
Test logs
Test incident reports
Test summary reports

Test input data and test output data should be identified as deliverables.

Test tools (for example, module drivers and stubs) may also be included.

3.2.10 Testing Tasks. Identify the set of tasks necessary to prepare for and perform testing. Identify all intertask dependencies and any special skills required.

3.2.11 Environmental Needs. Specify both the necessary and desired properties of the test environment. This specification should contain: the physical characteristics of the facilities including the hardware, the communications and system software, the mode of usage (for example, stand-alone), and any other software or supplies needed to support the test. Also specify the level of security which must be provided for the test facilities, system software, and proprietary components such as software, data, and hardware.

Identify special test tools needed. Identify any other testing needs (for example, publications or office space). Identify the source for all needs which are not currently available to the test group.

3.2.12 Responsibilities. Identify the groups responsible for managing, designing, preparing, executing, witnessing, checking, and resolving. In addition, identify the groups responsible for providing the test items identified in 3.2.3 and the environmental needs identified in 3.2.11.

These groups may include the developers, testers, operations staff, user representatives, technical support staff, data administration staff, and quality support staff.

3.2.13 Staffing and Training Needs. Specify test staffing needs by skill level. Identify training options for providing necessary skills.

3.2.14 Schedule. Include test milestones identified in the Software Project Schedule as well as all item transmittal events.

Define any additional test milestones needed. Estimate the time required to do each testing task. Specify the schedule for each testing task and test milestone. For each testing resource (that is, facilities, tools, and staff), specify its periods of use.

3.2.15 Risks and Contingencies. Identify the high-risk assumptions of the test plan. Specify contingency plans for each (for example, delayed delivery of test items might require increased night shift scheduling to meet the delivery date).

3.2.16 Approvals. Specify the names and titles of all persons who must approve this plan. Provide space for the signatures and dates.

4. Test-Design Specification

4.1 Purpose. To specify refinements of the test approach and to identify the features to be tested by this design and its associated tests.

4.2 Outline. A test-design specification shall have the following structure:

(1) Test-design-specification identifier
(2) Features to be tested
(3) Approach refinements
(4) Test identification
(5) Feature pass/fail criteria

The sections shall be ordered in the specified sequence. Additional sections may be included at the end. If some or all of the content of a section is in another document, then a reference to that material may be listed in place of the corresponding content. The referenced material must be attached to the test-design specification or available to users of the design specification.

Details on the content of each section are contained in the following sections.

4.2.1 Test-Design-Specification Identifier. Specify the unique identifier assigned to this test-design specification. Supply a reference to the associated test plan, if it exists.

4.2.2 Features to be Tested. Identify the test items and describe the features and combinations of features which are the object of this design specification. Other features may be exercised, but need not be identified.

For each feature or feature combination, a reference to its associated requirements in the item requirement specification or design description should be included.

4.2.3 Approach Refinements. Specify refinements to the approach described in the test plan. Include specific test techniques to be used. The method of analyzing test results should be identified (for example, comparator programs or visual inspection).

Specify the results of any analysis which provides a rationale for test-case selection. For example, one might specify conditions which permit a determination of error tolerance (for example, those conditions which distinguish valid inputs from invalid inputs).

Summarize the common attributes of any test cases. This may include input constraints that must be true for every input in the set of associated test cases, any shared environmental needs, and any shared special procedural requirements, and any shared case dependencies.

4.2.4 Test Identification. List the identifier and a brief description of each test case associated with this design. A particular test case may be identified in more than one test design specification. List the identifier and a brief description of each procedure associated with this test-design specification.

4.2.5 Feature Pass/Fail Criteria. Specify the criteria to be used to determine whether the feature or feature combination has passed or failed.

5. Test-Case Specification

5.1 Purpose. To define a test case identified by a test-design specification.

5.2 Outline. A test-case specification shall have the following structure:

(1) Test-case-specification identifier
(2) Test items
(3) Input specifications
(4) Output specifications
(5) Environmental needs
(6) Special procedural requirements
(7) Intercase dependencies

The sections shall be ordered in the specified sequence. Additional sections may be included at the end. If some or all of the content of a section is in another document, then a reference to that material may be listed in place of the corresponding content. The referenced material must be attached to the test-case specification or available to users of the case specification.

Since a test case may be referenced by several test-design specifications used by different groups over a long time period, enough specific information must be included in the test-case specification to permit reuse.

Details on the content of each section are contained in the following sections.

5.2.1 Test-Case-Specification Identifier. Specify the unique identifier assigned to this test-case specification.

5.2.2 Test Items. Identify and briefly describe the items and features to be exercised by this test case.

For each item, consider supplying references to the following item documentation.

(1) Requirements specification
(2) Design specification
(3) Users guide
(4) Operations guide
(5) Installation guide

5.2.3 Input Specifications. Specify each input required to execute the test case. Some of the inputs will be specified by value (with tolerances where appropriate), while others, such as constant tables or transaction files, will be specified by name. Identify all appropriate data bases, files, terminal messages, memory resident areas, and values passed by the operating system.

Specify all required relationships between inputs (for example, timing).

5.2.4 Output Specifications. Specify all of the outputs and features (for example, response time) required of the test items. Provide the exact value (with tolerances where appropriate) for each required output or feature.

5.2.5 Environmental Needs.

5.2.5.1 Hardware. Specify the characteristics and configurations of the hardware required to execute this test case (for example, 132 character × 24 line CRT).

5.2.5.2 Software. Specify the system and application software required to execute this test case. This may include system software such as operating systems, compilers, simulators, and test tools. In addition, the test item may interact with application software.

5.2.5.3 Other. Specify any other requirements such as unique facility needs or specially trained personnel.

5.2.6 Special Procedural Requirements. Describe any special constraints on the test procedures which execute this test case. These constraints may involve special set up, operator intervention, output determination procedures, and special wrap up.

5.2.7 Intercase Dependencies. List the identifiers of test cases which must be executed prior to this test case. Summarize the nature of the dependencies.

6. Test-Procedure Specification

6.1 Purpose. To specify the steps for executing a set of test cases or, more generally, the steps used to analyze a software item in order to evaluate a set of features.

6.2 Outline. A test-procedure specification shall have the following structure:

(1) Test-procedure-specification identifier
(2) Purpose
(3) Special requirements
(4) Procedure steps

The sections shall be ordered in the specified sequence. Additional sections, if required, may be included at the end. If some or all of the content of a section is in another document, then a reference to that material may be listed in place of the corresponding content. The referenced material must be attached to the test-procedure specification or available to users of the procedure specification.

Details on the content of each section are contained in the following sections.

6.2.1 Test-Procedure-Specification Identifier. Specify the unique identifier assigned to this test-procedure specification. Supply a reference to the associated test-design specification.

6.2.2 Purpose. Describe the purpose of this procedure. If this procedure executes any test cases, provide a reference for each of them.

In addition, provide references to relevant sections of the test item documentation (for example, references to usage procedures).

6.2.3 Special Requirements. Identify any special requirements that are necessary for the execution of this procedure. These may include prerequisite procedures, special skills requirements, and special environmental requirements.

6.2.4 Procedure Steps. Include the following steps as applicable:

6.2.4.1 Log. Describe any special methods or formats for logging the results of test execution, the incidents observed, and any other events pertinent to the test (see Test Log, Section 8 and Test Incident Report, Section 9).

6.2.4.2 Set Up. Describe the sequence of actions necessary to prepare for execution of the procedure.

6.2.4.3 Start. Describe the actions necessary to begin execution of the procedure.

6.2.4.4 Proceed. Describe any actions necessary during execution of the procedure.

6.2.4.5 Measure. Describe how the test

measurements will be made (for example, describe how remote terminal response time is to be measured using a network simulator).

6.2.4.6 Shut Down. Describe the actions necessary to suspend testing, when unscheduled events dictate.

6.2.4.7 Restart. Identify any procedural restart points and describe the actions necessary to restart the procedure at each of these points.

6.2.4.8 Stop. Describe the actions necessary to bring execution to an orderly halt.

6.2.4.9 Wrap Up. Describe the actions necessary to restore the environment.

6.2.4.10 Contingencies. Describe the actions necessary to deal with anomolous events which may occur during execution.

7. Test-Item Transmittal Report

7.1 Purpose. To identify the test items being transmitted for testing. It includes the person responsible for each item, its physical location, and its status. Any variations from the current item requirements and designs are noted in this report.

7.2 Outline. A test-item transmittal report shall have the following structure:

(1) Transmittal-report identifier
(2) Transmitted items
(3) Location
(4) Status
(5) Approvals

The sections shall be ordered in the specified sequence. Additional sections may be included just prior to *Approvals.* If some or all of the content of a section is in another document, then a reference to that material may be listed in place of the corresponding content. The referenced material must be attached to the test-item transmittal report or available to users of the transmittal report.

Details on the content of each section are contained in the following sections.

7.2.1 Transmittal-Report Identifier. Specify the unique identifier assigned to this test-item transmittal report.

7.2.2 Transmitted Items. Identify the test items being transmitted, including their version/revision level. Supply references to the item documentation and the test plan relating to the transmitted items. Indicate the people responsible for the transmitted items.

7.2.3 Location. Identify the location of the transmitted items. Identify the media that contain the items being transmitted. When appropriate, indicate how specific media are labeled or identified.

7.2.4 Status. Describe the status of the test items being transmitted. Include deviations from the item documentation, from previous transmittals of these items, and from the test plan. List the incident reports which are expected to be resolved by the transmitted items. Indicate if there are pending modifications to item documentation which may affect the items listed in this transmittal report.

7.2.5 Approvals. Specify the names and titles of all persons who must approve this transmittal. Provide space for the signatures and dates.

8. Test Log

8.1 Purpose. To provide a chronological record of relevant details about the execution of tests.

8.2 Outline. A test log shall have the following structure:

(1) Test log identifier
(2) Description
(3) Activity and event entries

The sections shall be ordered in the specified sequence. Additional sections may be included at the end. If some or all of the content of a section is in another document, then a reference to that material may be listed in place of the corresponding content. The referenced material must be attached to the test log or available to users of the log.

Details on the content of each section are contained in the following sections.

8.2.1 Test-Log Identifier. Specify the unique identifier assigned to this test log.

8.2.2 Description. Information which applies to all entries in the log except as specifically noted in a log entry should be included here. The following information should be considered.

(1) Identify the items being tested including their version/revision levels. For each of these items, supply a reference to its transmittal report, if it exists.

(2) Identify the attributes of the environments in which the testing is conducted. Include facility identification, hardware being used (for example, amount of memory being

used, CPU model number, and number and model of tape drives, and/or mass storage devices), system software used, and resources available such as the amount of memory available.

8.2.3 Activity and Event Entries. For each event, including the beginning and end of activities, record the occurrence date and time along with the identity of the author.

The following information should be considered:

8.2.3.1 Execution Description. Record the identifier of the test procedure being executed and supply a reference to its specification. Record all personnel present during the execution including testers, operators, and observers. Also indicate the function of each individual.

8.2.3.2 Procedure Results. For each execution, record the visually observable results (for example, error messages generated, aborts, and requests for operator action). Also record the location of any output (for example, reel number). Record the successful or unsuccessful execution of the test.

8.2.3.3 Environmental Information. Record any environmental conditions specific to this entry (for example, hardware substitutions).

8.2.3.4 Anomalous Events. Record what happened before and after an unexpected event occurred (for example, *A summary display was requested and the correct screen displayed, but response seemed unusually long. A repetition produced the same prolonged response*). Record circumstances surrounding the inability to begin execution of a test procedure or failure to complete a test procedure (for example, a power failure or system software problem).

8.2.3.5 Incident-Report Identifiers. Record the identifier of each test-incident report, whenever one is generated.

9. Test-Incident Report

9.1 Purpose. To document any event that occurs during the testing process which requires investigation.

9.2 Outline. A test-incident report shall have the following structure:

(1) Test-incident-report identifier
(2) Summary
(3) Incident description
(4) Impact

The sections shall be ordered in the specified sequence. Additional sections may be included at the end. If some or all of the content of a section is in another document, then a reference to that material may be listed in place of the corresponding content. The referenced material must be attached to the test-incident report or available to users of the incident report.

Details on the content of each section are contained in the following sections.

9.2.1 Test-Incident-Report Identifier. Specify the unique identifier assigned to this test incident report.

9.2.2 Summary. Summarize the incident. Identify the test items involved indicating their version/revision level. References to the appropriate test-procedure specification, test-case specification, and test log should be supplied.

9.2.3 Incident Description. Provide a description of the incident. This description should include the following items:

Inputs
Expected results
Actual results
Anomalies
Date and time
Procedure step
Environment
Attempts to repeat
Testers
Observers

Related activities and observations that may help to isolate and correct the cause of the incident should be included. For example, describe any test-case executions that might have a bearing on this particular incident and any variations from the published test procedure.

9.2.4 Impact. If known, indicate what impact this incident will have on test plans, test-design specifications, test-procedure specifications, or test-case specifications.

10. Test-Summary Report

10.1 Purpose. To summarize the results of the designated testing activities and to provide evaluations based on these results.

10.2 Outline. A test-summary report shall have the following structure:

(1) Test-summary-report identifier
(2) Summary
(3) Variances
(4) Comprehensive assessment
(5) Summary of results
(6) Evaluation
(7) Summary of activities
(8) Approvals

The sections shall be ordered in the specified sequence. Additional sections may be included just prior to *Approvals.* If some or all of the content of a section is in another document, then a reference to that material may be listed in place of the corresponding content. The referenced material must be attached to the test-summary report or available to users of the summary report.

Details on the content of each section are contained in the following sections.

10.2.1 Test-Summary-Report Identifier. Specify the unique identifier assigned to this test-summary report.

10.2.2 Summary. Summarize the evaluation of the test items. Identify the items tested, indicating their version/revision level. Indicate the environment in which the testing activities took place.

For each test item, supply references to the following documents if they exist: test plan, test-design specifications, test-procedure specifications, test-item transmittal reports, test logs, and test-incident reports.

10.2.3 Variances. Report any variances of the test items from their design specifications. Indicate any variances from the test plan, test designs, or test procedures. Specify the reason for each variance.

10.2.4 Comprehensiveness Assessment. Evaluate the comprehensiveness of the testing process against the comprehensiveness criteria specified in the test plan (3.2.6) if the plan exists. Identify features or feature combinations which were not sufficiently tested and explain the reasons.

10.2.5 Summary of Results. Summarize the results of testing. Identify all resolved incidents and summarize their resolutions. Identify all unresolved incidents.

10.2.6 Evaluation. Provide an overall evaluation of each test item including its limitations. This evaluation must be based upon the test results and the item level pass/fail criteria. An estimate of failure risk may be included.

10.2.7 Summary of Activities. Summarize the major testing activities and events. Summarize resource consumption data, for example, total staffing level, total machine time, and total elapsed time used for each of the major testing activities.

10.2.8 Approvals. Specify the names and titles of all persons who must approve this report. Provide space for the signatures and dates.

Appendixes

(The following Appendixes are not a part of IEEE Std 829-1983, IEEE Standard for Software Test Documentation.)

A. Examples

The following examples are taken from commercial data processing. This should not imply any limitations on the applicability of the standard to other classes of software.

Contents

A1. Corporate Payroll-System Test Documentation

A1.1. Introduction

A1.1.1. Scope. The system test documentation example presented here is done in accordance with the IEEE Standard for Software Test Documentation. Each document is represented as it might be used for the system test of a payroll system.

The payroll system used in this example contains the following major functions:

(1) Maintain employee information

(2) Maintain payroll history information

(3) Prepare payroll checks

(4) Prepare payroll tax reports

(5) Prepare payroll history reports

A Phase 2.0 development plan exists for the payroll system which will be started at some future time. This phase covers, primarily, a personnel reporting system.

A1.1.2. Assumptions. The following assumptions were made when preparing this example:

(1) System testing activities assume that *module* and *integration* testing have been done. This implies that single program functionality has been comprehensively tested. System level testing, therefore, focuses on the testing of multiprogram functionality (for example, year-end processing) as well as external interfaces, security, recovery, and performance. In addition, operator and user procedures are tested.

(2) The payroll system will be system tested at only one site.

A1.1.3. Naming Conventions. The naming conventions which follow are used throughout the payroll-system example.

Corporate Payroll System

A P XX – YY ZZ

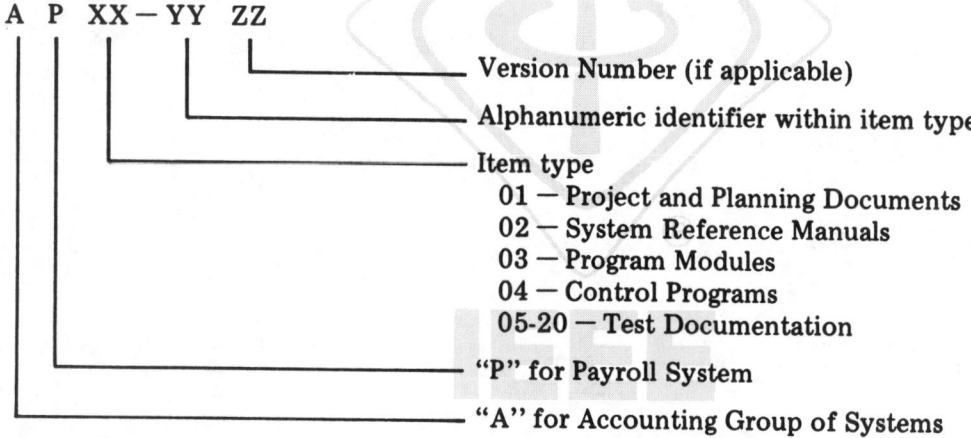

- ZZ — Version Number (if applicable)
- YY — Alphanumeric identifier within item type
- XX — Item type
  - 01 — Project and Planning Documents
  - 02 — System Reference Manuals
  - 03 — Program Modules
  - 04 — Control Programs
  - 05-20 — Test Documentation
- P — "P" for Payroll System
- A — "A" for Accounting Group of Systems

Project Planning Documents

AP01-01	Statement of Requirements
AP01-02	Preliminary Development Plan
AP01-03	Project Authorization
AP01-04	System Design Description
AP01-05	Business Plan
AP01-06	Final Development Plan
AP01-08	Quality Assurance Plan
AP01-09	Configuration Management Plan
AP01-12	Statement of Completion

System Reference Manuals

AP02-01	System Reference Manual
AP02-02	Operation Reference Manual

AP02-03	Module Reference Manual
AP02-04	User Transaction Reference Manual
Program Modules	
AP03-	Program Modules
Control Programs	
AP04-	Control Programs, Utilities, Sorts
Test Documentation	
AP05-YYZZ	Test Plan
AP06-YYZZ	Test Design Specification
AP07-YYZZ	Test Case Specification
AP08-YYZZ	Test Procedure Specification
AP09-YY	Test Log
AP10-00	Test Incident Report Log*
AP11-YY	Test Incident Report
AP12-YY	Test Summary Report
AP13-YY	Test Item Transmittal Report

*Note: This *test* document is not specified by this standard.

A.1.2

System Test Plan
for the
Corporate Payroll System

XYZ Corporation

AP05-0101

Prepared by
Manager, System Test Group
Manager, Corporate Payroll Department

January 21, 1982

System Test Plan
Corporate Payroll System

Contents

1. Test Plan Identifier

AP05-0103

2. Introduction

2.1 Objectives. A system test plan for the corporate payroll system should support the following objectives.

(1) To detail the activities required to prepare for and conduct the system test.

(2) To communicate to all responsible parties the tasks which they are to perform and the schedule to be followed in performing the tasks.

(3) To define the sources of the information used to prepare the plan.

(4) To define the test tools and environment needed to conduct the system test.

2.2 Background. Last year the XYZ Corporate Systems and Programming Department developed a new General Ledger System at the request of the Corporate Accounting Department. A request was made at the same time for a new corporate payroll system to be developed which would interface with the general ledger system.

The Management Systems Review Committee approved the request for the payroll system in September of 1981 and named a corporate payroll system advisory group to decide on the system requirements. The group finished a Statement of Requirements (AP01-01) and a Preliminary Development Plan (AP01-02) in December, 1981.

2.3 Scope. This test plan covers a full systems test of the corporate payroll system. This includes operator and user procedures, as well as programs and job control. In addition to comprehensively testing multiprogram functionality, external interfaces, security, recovery, and performance will also be evaluated.

2.4 References. The following documents were used as sources of information for the test plan.

Corporate Payroll System Preliminary Development Plan (AP01-02)
Corporate Payroll System Authorization (AP01-03)
Corporate Payroll System Final Development Plan (AP01-06)
Corporate Payroll System Quality Assurance Plan (AP01-08)
Corporate Payroll System Configuration Management Plan (AP01-09)
XYZ Corporate Systems Development Standards and Procedures (XYZ01-0100)
Corporate General Ledger System Design Description (AG01-04)
Corporate General Ledger System Test Plan (AG05-01)

3. Test Items

All items which make up the corporate payroll system will be tested during the system test. The versions to be tested will be placed in the appropriate libraries by the configuration administrator. The administrator will also control changes to the versions under test and notify the test group when new versions are available.

The following documents will provide the basis for defining correct operation.

Corporate Payroll System Statement of Requirements (AP01-01)
Corporate Payroll System Design Description (AP01-04)
Corporate Payroll System Reference Manual (AP02-01)
Corporate Payroll System Module Reference Manual (AP02-03)

The items to be tested are:

3.1 Program Modules. The program modules to be tested will be identified as follows:

Type	Library	Member Name
Source Code	SOURLIB1	AP0302
		AP0305

Executable Code	MACLIB1 SYSLIB1	AP0301 AP0302 AP0305

3.2 Job-Control Procedures. The control procedures for application programs, sorts, and utility programs will be identified as follows:

Type	Library	Member Name
Application Programs	PROCLIB1	AP0401
Sorts	PROCLIB1	AP0402
Utility Programs	PROCLIB1	AP0403

3.3 User Procedures. The online procedures specified in the Corporate Payroll Sytem User Transaction Reference Manual (AP02-04) will be tested.

3.4 Operator Procedures. The system test includes the procedures specified in the Corporate Payroll System Operation Reference Manual (AP02-02).

4. Features to be Tested

The following list describes the features that will be tested.

Test Design Specification Number	Description
AP06-01	Data base conversion
AP06-02	Complete payroll processing for salaried employees only
AP06-03	Complete payroll processing for hourly employees only
AP06-04	Complete payroll processing for all employees
AP06-05	Periodic reporting
AP06-06	General Ledger transaction building
AP06-07	Security
AP06-08	Recovery
AP06-09	Performance

5. Features not to be Tested

The following features will not be included in the system tests because they are not to be used when the system is initially installed.

Equal Employment Opportunity Commission Compliance Reports

Internal Training Schedule Reports

Salary/Performance Review Reports

The development Phase 2.0 documentation will contain a test plan for these features.

The test cases will not cover all possible combinations of options within the transaction or report being tested. Only combinations that are known to be required for current XYZ Corporate Payroll processing will be tested.

6. Approach

The test personnel will use the system documentation to prepare all test design, case, and procedure specifications. This approach will verify the accuracy and comprehensiveness of the information in the documentation in those areas covered by the tests.

Personnel from the Payroll and Corporate Accounting Departments will assist in developing the test designs and test cases. This will help ensure that the tests represent the production use of the system.

In order to ensure privacy, all test data extracted from production files will have privacy sensitive fields changed.

6.1 Conversion Testing. In addition to counting the input and output records, the validity of the converted data base will be verified in two ways. The first verification method involves the use of a *data base auditor* which must be built by the development group. When run against the converted data base, the data base auditor will check value ranges within a record and the required relationships between records.

The second verification method involves the random selection of a small subset of old records and than a direct comparison against a corresponding subset of the new records. The number of direct comparisons, c, and the number of old records, r, must be specified. A set of c random numbers will be generated from the range 1 to r. This set will be sorted and used during the conversion process to drive the selection of records for direct comparison.

NOTE: This same two-pronged verification approach should be used during the actual conversion.

6.2 Job Stream Testing. A comprehensive set of records of salaried employees, hourly employees, and a merged set of these two should be used to test payroll processing. The standard job stream testing approach should be used.

Run each of the periodic reporting job streams at least once.

6.3 Interface Testing. In order to test the interface between the payroll and general-ledger systems, the payroll system will build a comprehensive set of general-ledger transactions. These transactions will then be input to the general-ledger test system. The resulting general-ledger entries must be extracted, printed, and compared with a printout of the general-ledger transactions prepared by the payroll system.

6.4 Security Testing. Attempted access without a proper password to the online data entry and display transactions will be tested.

6.5 Recovery Testing. Recovery will be tested by halting the machine during stand alone time and then following the recovery procedures.

6.6 Performance Testing. Performance will be evaluated against the performance requirements (AP01-01) by measuring the run times of several jobs using production data volumes.

6.7 Regression. It is assumed that several iterations of the system test will be done in order to test program modifications made during the system test period. A regression test will be performed for each new version of the system to detect unexpected impact resulting from program modifications.

The regression test will be done by running all of the tests on a new version that were run on the previous version and then comparing the resulting files. The standard comparator program, UT08-0100, will be used to compare all system outputs.

6.8 Comprehensiveness. Each of the system features described in the Corporate Payroll System Reference Manual (AP02-01) will have at least one associated test-design specification. Each of the user procedures specified in the Corporate Payroll-System User Transaction Reference Manual (AP02-04) will be tested at least once. Each of the operating procedures specified in the Corporate Payroll-System Operation Reference Manual (AP02-02) also will be tested at least once. In addition, each job control procedure will be executed at least once.

A coverage matrix will be used to related test-design specifications to each of the areas described above.

6.9 Constraints. A final implementation date of August 31, 1982 has been planned for the Corporate Payroll System. It will be necessary to meet this date because the new ABC Division begins full operation on September 1, and they must have this payroll system to pay their employees.

7. Item Pass/Fail Criteria

The system must satisfy the standard requirements for system pass/fail stated in the XYZ Corporate Systems Development Standards and Procedures (XYZ01-0100).

The system must also satisfy the following requirements:

Memory requirements must not be greater than 64K of real storage

Consistency of user procedures with other accounting systems must satisfy the Payroll Supervisor

8. Suspension Criteria and Resumption Requirements

8.1 Suspension Criteria. Inability to convert the Employee Information Data Base will cause suspension of all testing activities.

8.2 Resumption Requirements. When a new version of the system is transmitted to the test group after a suspension of testing has occurred, a regression test as described in 6.7 will be run.

9. Test Deliverables

The following documents will be generated by the system test group and will be delivered to the configuration management group after test completion.

Test Documentation:

System Test Plan
System Test Design Specifications
System Test Case Specifications
System Test Procedure Specifications
System Test Logs
System Test Incident Report Log
System Test Incident Reports
System Test Summary Report

Test Data:

(1) Copies of all data entry and inquiry screens and the reply screens are to be attached to the related test case document.

(2) Copies of the input and output test files should be delivered to the configuration management group.

(3) Microfiche copies of the printed output from the final execution of each test procedure are to be delivered to the configuration management group along with the test documentation.

10. Testing Tasks

See Task List, Attachment A, page 28.

11. Environmental Needs

11.1 Hardware. The testing will be done on the XYZ hardware configuration.

Since most testing must be done during prime operating hours, 3 on-line terminals must be available to the test group during this period.

11.2 Software

11.2.1 Operating System. The production operating system will be used to execute these tests.

11.2.2 Communications Software. All on-line programs will be tested under the control of the test communication software.

11.3 Security. Security will be limited to existing controls.

11.4 Tools. The following test tools are required to develop and evaluate the system tests.

(1) Test Data Generator (UT09-0200). This program will be used to generate the majority of the test data. It is located in the standard system library, SYSLIBA.

(2) Comparator Program (UT08-0100). This program will be used to compare system results during the regression tests. It is located in the standard system library, SYSLIBA.

(3) Data Base Auditor. This program audits value ranges and interrecord relationships in the data base. It must be supplied by the development group.

11.5 Publications. The following documents are required to support systems testing.

Corporate Payroll System Statement of Requirements (AP01-01)
Corporate Payroll System Design Description (AP01-04)
Corporate Payroll System Reference Manual (AP02-01)
Corporate Payroll Operation Reference Manual (AP02-02)
Corporate Payroll System Module Reference Manual (AP02-03)
Corporate Payroll System User Transaction Reference Manual (AP02-04)

12. Responsibilities

The following groups have responsibility for segments of the testing.

12.1 System Test Group. This group provides the overall management of the testing and the technical testing expertise.

12.2 Corporate Payroll Department. This group is the end user of the Corporate Payroll System and will provide assistance to the test group in the following activities:

Reviewing the test-design specifications.
Executing the on-line tests.
Checking output screens and reports.

12.3 Development Project Group. This group transmits the system to be tested and responds to the System Test Incident Reports. This group does any program debugging that is required. It also supplies the data-base auditor.

13. Staffing and Training Needs

13.1 Staffing. The following staff is needed to carry out this testing project.

13.1.1 Test Group.

Test Manager	1
Senior Test Analyst	1
Test Analysts	2
Test Technician	1

13.1.2 Payroll Department.

Payroll Supervisor	1

13.2 Training. The Corporate Payroll Department personnel must be trained to do the data entry transactions. The User Transaction Reference Manual (AP02-04) will be the basis of this training.

14. Schedule

See attached Task List (Attachment A).

Hardware, software, and test tools will be used for testing during the period from June 1, 1982 through August 1, 1982.

15. Risks and Contingencies

If the testing schedule is significantly impacted by system failure, the development manager has agreed to assign a full-time person to the test group to do debugging.

If one payroll supervisor is not sufficiently available for testing, then the payroll manager has agreed to identify a second supervisor.

If hardware problems impact system availability during the day, then the test group will schedule their activities during the evening.

The first production runs of the Corporate Payroll System must be checked out in detail before the payroll checks are distributed, and any checks in error must be corrected manually.

16. Approvals

Test Manager	Date
Development Project Manager	Date
Quality Assurance Manager	Date

Attachment —A. Task List

Task		Predecessor Tasks	Special Skills	Responsibility	Effort	Finish Date
(1)	Prepare test plan.	Complete payroll system design description (AP01-04) and preliminary development plan (AP01-02)		Test manager Senior test analyst	4	01-21-82
(2)	Prepare test-design specifications.	Task 1	Knowledge of corporate payroll procedures	Senior test analyst	9	04-01-82
(3)	Prepare test-case specifcations.	Complete corresponding test designs (Task 2)		Test analyst	4	04-15-82
(4)	Prepare test-procedure specifications.	Complete corresponding test cases (Task 3)		Test analyst	6	05-15-82
(5)	Build the initial employee-information data base.	Task 4		Test analyst	6	06-01-82
(6)	Complete test-item transmittal and transmit the corporate payroll system to the test group.	Complete integration testing		Development project manager		06-01-82
(7)	Checkout all job-control procedures required to execute the system.	Task 6	Job control experience	Test technician	1	06-08-82
(8)	Assemble and link the corporate payroll system.	Task 6		Test technician	1	06-08-82
(9)	Execute data-entry test procedures.	Task 5 Task 8		Test analyst	1	06-22-82
(10)	Execute batch test procedures.	Task 5 Task 8		Test technician	3	06-30-82
(11)	Check out batch test results.	Task 10	Knowledge of payroll-report requirements	Test analyst	1	07-02-82
(12)	Resolve test-incident reports.	Task 9 Task 11		—Development group manager —System test-group manager —Corporate payroll department manager	2	07-16-82
(13)	Repeat tasks (6)—(12) until all test procedures have succeeded.	Task 12			2	07-30-82
(14)	Write the system test summary report.	Task 13		—System test-group manager —Corporate payroll-department manager	1	08-06-82
(15)	Transmit all test documentation and test data to the configuration management group.	Task 14		System test group	1	08-06-82

A1.3. Corporate Payroll System Test-Procedure Specification

1. Test-Procedure Specification Identifier

AP08-0101 March 5, 1982

2. Purpose

This procedure describes the steps necessary to perform the test specified in the test-design specification for data-base conversion (AP06-0101). The procedure describes the execution of the test case described in System Test-Case Specification AP07-0101. (NOTE: Neither the test-design specification nor test-case specification are included in this set of system test examples). This test will exercise the Employee Information Data Base Conversion Procedures specified in the Corporate Payroll System Reference Manual (AP02-01) and the conversion program (AP03-07) described in the Corporate Payroll System Module Reference Manual (AP02-03).

3. Special Requirements

In order to execute this procedure, the "random subset" program, the old data extract program, the new data extract program, and the data base auditor specified in AP06-0101 must be available.

4. Procedure Steps

4.1 Log. Record the execution of this procedure on a standard test log (AP09-YY).

4.2 Set Up

(1) Generate a test version of the old employee data base according to the test-case specification in AP07-0101 using the test data generator (UT09-0200).

(2) Execute the random subset program requesting 50 random numbers in the range 1 to 500.

(3) Sort the random number file into an increasing sequence.

(4) Execute the old data extract program with the test version of the old employee-information data base using the sorted random number file.

(5) Print the extracted records.

4.3 Proceed. Execute the conversion program with the test version of the old data base generating the new employee information data base.

4.4 Measure

(1) Execute the data-base auditor with the new employee information data base. Report violations in test-incident reports.

(2) Execute the new data extract program with the new data base using the sorted random-number file.

(3) Print the extracted records.

(4) Compare the extracted old records with the extracted new records. Report differences in test-incident reports.

4.5 Wrap Up. Delete both extracted files and the random number file.

A1.4. Corporate Payroll System Transmittal Report

1. Transmittal Report Identifier

AP13-03 June 24, 1982

2. Transmitted Items

A new version of the data conversion program (AP03-0702) is being transmitted.

The program is described in the Module Reference Manual (AP02-0305). The associated conversion procedures are specified in the System Reference Manual (AP02-0109). The transmitted program is associated with system test plan AP05-0103.

Communication about this program should be directed to the manager of the payroll system development project.

3. Location

The transmitted code is located as follows:

Source Code	SOURLIB1 (AP0307)
Object Code	SYSLIB1 (AP0307)

The system documentation and test plans are available in the documentation library.

4. Status

The conversion program has been fully retested at the unit and integration levels. The three incident reports (AP11-15, 16, and 17) generated by the June 10th execution of AP08-0101 are resolved by this new version.

The *invalid department code* messages (AP11-15) and the *blank home addresses* (AP11-16) resulted from insufficient logic in the conversion program. Additional logic was added. The *number of dependents* field processing problem (AP11-17) resulted from an imprecise program specification. The logic has been changed and comments have been added for clarity.

5. Approvals

Development Manager	Date
Test Manager	Date

A1.5 Corporate Payroll-System Test Log

1. Test Log Identifier

AP09-04 June 10, 1982

2. Description

The first version of the data conversion program (AP03-0701) is being tested. The program was transmitted (AP13-01) to the test group along with the entire payroll system.

This batch testing is being conducted using the standard corporate data-center facilities.

This log records the execution of the data conversion test procedure (AP08-0101). The tests are being submitted to background processing through a CRT by a senior test analyst.

3. Activities and Event Entries

June 10, 1982		Incidents
2:00 PM	Dick J. started testing.	
2:15 PM	Began to generate the old test data base.	
3:30 PM	Discovered a possible bug in the test data generator. Filled out an incident report and worked around the problem.	AP11-14
6:00 PM	Completed the old test data base generation. It is located on TEST1.	
6:15 PM	Dick J. stopped testing.	

June 11, 1982		Incidents
9:45 AM	Dick J. started testing.	
10:00 AM	Began to create the random number file.	
10:45 AM	Generated a sorted random number file.	
11:30 AM	Selected and printed a random subset of records from the old test data base.	
12:30 PM	Dick J. stopped testing.	
12:45 PM	Jane K. started testing.	
1:00 PM	Ran the conversion program against the old test data base. The new data base is on TEST2. The status report from the run contained 3 messages warning of invalid data in the department code field. The three records were checked and the values appeared valid. An incident report was generated.	AP11-15
3:30 PM	Ran the data-base auditor against the new data base. The auditor reported multiple instances of blank home addresses. A check found these addresses nonblank in the old data base. The incident was reported.	AP11-16
4:00 PM	Jane K. stopped testing.	

June 12, 1982		Incidents
8:15 AM	— Jane K. started testing.	
8:30 AM	— Selected and printed the random subset of records from the new data base. In one case, the *number of dependents* field was changed from three to zero (possibly because no names were present). The incident was reported.	AP11-17
11:30 AM	— The extract and random number files were deleted.	
11:45 AM	— Jane K. stopped testing.	

A1.6. Corporate Payroll System Test Incident Report

1. Report Identifier

AP11-17 June 12, 1982

2. Summary

Changes in the *number of dependents* field were found by comparing records from the new employee data base created by the conversion program (AP03-0701) with those from the old data base. Test log AP09-04 records this incident. The incident occurred during execution of test procedure AP08-0101.

3. Incident Description

June 12, 1982 8:30 AM Jane K.

A test version of the old employee data base was converted to its new format. The value in the *number of dependents* field was not expected to change during this process. This field value changed in the record indicated on the attached printouts.

Note that although the dependent count is three in the original record, none of the names appear. The number of names matches the count in all of the other records.

Perhaps the program is counting the names and forcing consistency.

4. Impact

Testing activity is suspended until this incident is resolved.

A2. Normalize Numeric Expression Module-Test Documentation

The following example describes the testing of a module which reformats a numeric expression entered on a CRT. The module removes all commas, the sign, and the decimal point. It also checks the validity of the input expression.

A2.1 Introduction

General Requirements. To provide user-friendly entry of numeric data on a CRT, a system permits the keying of numeric expressions containing optional non-numeric symbols such as commas, a decimal point, and a leading sign. Any of the following examples would be valid entries:

+0
1234.
-.012
12,345.6

To facilitate editing of such input, a routine is required to normalize the numeric expression to a decimal point aligned value and to describe it. An expression is described by various characteristics such as:

Includes sign
Includes commas
Includes decimal point
Number of fractional digits and
Number of integer digits

A return code should identify the specific nature of any edit error.
The routine will be accessed by COBOL programs.

Functional Design.
Input: A character string of length 25 called NUMERIC-EXPRESSION contains a numeric expression. The expression must contain at least 1 digit. It may contain no more than 14 integer digits and no more than 4 fractional digits. It may contain valid combinations of
Leading sign
Decimal point and
Grouping commas.
A valid entry field may have spaces on the left, the right, or both. Interior spaces are invalid.
Process: The input expression is edited and if invalid an error condition is recorded in the return code. If valid, any signs, decimal points, and commas are removed and the resulting numeric value is decimal-point aligned in a signed field. In addition, a set of input descriptors is calculated.
Output: A decimal-point aligned, signed numeric value in a PIC S9(14)V9(4) field called ALIGNED-NUMERIC-VALUE
A set of input descriptors

INTEGER-DIGIT-COUNT	(0 - 14)
FRACTIONAL-DIGIT-COUNT	(0 - 4)
WAS-SIGN-FOUND	(N-0, YES)
WERE-COMMAS-FOUND	(N-0, YES)
WAS-DECIMAL-POINT-FOUND	(N-0, YES)

A RETURN-CODE with the following values
- NORMALIZATION-OK
- INVALID-FIRST-CHAR

First character is other than a digit, period, or sign
- INVALID-NONFIRST-CHAR

Nonfirst character is other than a digit, period, or comma

· NO-DIGIT-FOUND
No numeric character was entered
· TOO-MANY-INTEGER-DIGITS
More than 14 consecutive digits without a decimal point
· TOO-MANY-FRACTIONAL-DIGITS
More than 4 digits to the right of a decimal point
· TOO-MANY-DECIMAL-POINTS
More than 1 decimal point
· COMMA-RIGHT-AFTER-SIGN
Comma immediately follows a sign
· INVALID-COMMA-INTERVAL
Less than 3 consecutive-digits following a comma
More than 3 consecutive digits preceding or following a comma
· COMMA-AFTER-POINT
Comma appears to the right of a decimal point

If the value of RETURN-CODE is *not* NORMALIZATION-OK, then the values of the other output fields are *undefined.*

TECHNICAL DESIGN.

LANGUAGE: COBOL

ACCESS: PERFORM of included sub-routine

HIERARCHY CHART: Normalize-Numeric-Exp
- Left-justify Expression
- Find Right-most Non-space
- Validate Expression
  - Initialize Descriptor Fields
  - Set Return OK
  - Do Validation Scan
  - Wrap Up Validation Scan
- Normalize Valid Expression
  - Save Digit
  - Delete Specials
  - Align Output Value
  - Establish Sign

NOTES:

Output Fields	Setting Procedures
Return Code (Error)	Do Validation Scan Wrap Up Validation Scan
Return Code (OK)	Set Return OK
Input Descriptors	Initialize Description Fields Do Validation Scan Wrap Up Validation Scan
ALIGNED-NUMERIC-VALUE	Align Output Value Establish Sign

Module Test Documentation for Normalize Numeric Expression

- Test Design Specification
- Test Case Specification
- Test Summary Report

Prepared by Module Developer
March 23, 1982

A2.2. Normalize Numeric Expression Module Test-Design Specification

1. Test-Design Specification Identifier

NNE.TD.01.05   15 March 1981

NOTE: No test plan is associated with this module, because its development was not associated with any particular application project (so there is no project level test plan) and because the special projects manager decided that a specific module test plan was unnecessary. The quality support manager concurred.

2. Features to be Tested

Individual Features
- 2.1 Digits Only Processing
- 2.2 Sign Processing
- 2.3 Decimal Point Processing
- 2.4 Commas Processing

Combinations
- 2.5 Sign and Decimal Point
- 2.6 Sign and Commas
- 2.7 Decimal Point and Commas
- 2.8 Sign, Decimal Point and Commas

All of these features are specified in the functional design description contained in the *common routines* section of the programmer's guide.

3. Approach Refinements

The individual processing features of the module will be tested first with valid and invalid input. All of the combinations will then be used.

A program will be written to drive the module. A file will be created with each record containing a single input value and fields to store the resulting values. The driver program will read a record, pass the corresponding input value to the module, store the resulting values in the record and rewrite it. The current version id of the module should be stored in each rewritten record.

Before testing begins, a test-case file will be generated in the same format as the driver file. The records will contain the input values along with the *predicted* resulting values. Following a test run, the driver file will be compared with the case file. The file comparison utility program will report any differences.

Since generation of all possible input values is impractical, test-set comprehensiveness will be evaluated based upon the following criteria:

(1) Requirements coverage — has each of the requirements been satisfied?

(2) Design coverage — has each of the functional design specifications been satisfied?

(3) Domain coverage — has each of the input constraints (for example, maximum of one decimal point) been tested? Have representative values been included? Have all error messages been generated?

(4) Branch coverage — has every branch been taken at least once?

(5) Statement coverage — has every statement been executed at least once?

Appropriate checklists will be generated to evaluate criteria 1-3. Existing code instrumentation tools will be used to evaluate 4 and 5.

The test set must satisfy each component of the five criteria specified above at least once.

Test Case Selection Rationale

Input constraints

(1) No more than 14 integer digits
(2) No more than 4 fractional digits
(3) No more than one decimal point
(4) Between 1 and 3 contiguous digits to the left of each comma
(5) Exactly 3 contiguous digits to the right of each comma
(6) No commas after the decimal point

There are no relevant internal or output constraints.

Common Test-Case Characteristics

All test cases require a module driver.

4. Test Identification

Cases

Digits Only	
Valid	
14 integer digits	NNE.TC.001
centered 6 integer digits	NNE.TC.002
left justified 1 integer digit	NNE.TC.003
Invalid	
15 integer digits	NNE.TC.010
digit string with imbedded space	NNE.TC.011
digit string with leading invalid character	NNE.TC.012
digit string with imbedded invalid character	NNE.TC.013
digit string with trailing invalid character	NNE.TC.014
Sign	
Valid	
right justified + signed 14 integers	NNE.TC.020
— signed integers	NNE.TC.021
Invalid	
imbedded sign	NNE.TC.030
trailing sign	NNE.TC.031
sign alone without digits	NNE.TC.032
2 leading signs	NNE.TC.033
2 separated signs	NNE.TC.034
Decimal Point	
Valid	
leading point with 4 fractional digits	NNE.TC.040
embedded point with 1 fractional digit	NNE.TC.041
trailing point with 14 integers	NNE.TC.042

Cases	
Invalid	
5 fractional digits	NNE.TC.050
2 points	NNE.TC.051
point without digits	NNE.TC.052
Commas	
Valid	
1 comma	NNE.TC.060
4 commas with 14 integer digits	NNE.TC.061
Invalid	
leading comma	NNE.TC.070
4 digits to left of a comma	NNE.TC.071
2 digits to right of a comma	NNE.TC.072
4 digits to right of a comma	NNE.TC.073
trailing comma	NNE.TC.074
comma without digits	NNE.TC.075
15 integer digits	NNE.TC.076
Sign and Decimal Point	
Valid	
sign and trailing point with 1 digit	NNE.TC.080
sign adjacent to point with 1 digit	NNE.TC.081
sign and point with 14 digits	NNE.TC.082
Invalid	
sign and point without digits	NNE.TC.090
Sign and Commas	
Valid	
sign and comma with 14 digits	NNE.TC.100
sign and comma with 4 digits	NNE.TC.101
Invalid	
sign adjacent to comma	NNE.TC.110
Decimal Point and Commas	
Valid	
comma with 14 integer digits and 4 fractional digits	NNE.TC.120
one comma with 4 digits and trailing point	NNE.TC.121
Invalid	
no digits between comma and point	NNE.TC.130
4 digits between comma and point	NNE.TC.131
comma following point	NNE.TC.132
Sign, Decimal Point and Commas	
Valid	
longest valid expression	NNE.TC.140
shortest valid expression	NNE.TC.141
representative valid expression	NNE.TC.142
Invalid	
15 integer and 4 fractional digits	NNE.TC.150
14 integer and 5 fractional digits	NNE.TC.151

Procedures. There are no *formal* test procedures associated with this design.

The procedure for using the module driver is in the *test tools* section of the programmer's guide.

5. Feature Pass/Fail Criteria

Each feature must pass all of its test cases in order to pass this test.

A2.3. Normalize Numeric Expression Module Test-Case Specification

1. Test Case Specification Identifier

NNE.TC.121.01 17 March 1981
One comma with 4 digits and trailing point.

2. Test Items

Normalized Numeric Expression Subroutine — This routine strips signs, commas, and decimal points from numeric expressions.

The requirements, functional design, and technical design specifications are contained in the *common routines* section of the programmer's guide.

3. Input Specifications

1,234. in NUMERIC-EXPRESSION

4. Output Specifications

+12340000 in ALIGNED-NUMERIC-VALUE
NORMALIZATION-OK in RETURN-CODE
4 in INTEGER-DIGIT-COUNT
0 in FRACTIONAL-DIGIT-COUNT
N-0 in WAS-SIGN-FOUND
YES in WERE-COMMAS-FOUND
YES in WAS-DECIMAL-POINT-FOUND

5. Environmental Needs

A module driver is required to execute this case.

6. Special Procedural Requirements

The procedure for using the module driver is in the *test tools* section of the programmer's guide.

7. Intercase Dependencies

None.

A2.4. Normalize Numeric Expression Module Test Summary Report

1. Test Summary Report Identifier

NNE.TS.01 23 March 1981

2. Summary

After correcting three faults, the Normalize Numeric Expression Module (Revision 5) passed all tests. The routine was tested using a module driver.

The following test documents are associated with this module.

(1) Module Test Design Specification
NNE.TD.01.05

(2) Module Test Case Specifications
NNE.TC.001 — .151

3. Variances

Conditions identified during testing resulted in enhancements to the set of invalid conditions described in the original functional design. This in turn resulted in the specification of eleven additional test cases. All of these changes are included in the current documentation.

4. Comprehensiveness Assessment

The attached (but not included with example) checklists and execution trace reports demonstrate that the minimum comprehensiveness requirements specified in the test design specification have been satisfied.

5. Summary of Results

Three of the test cases (071, 073, and 131) exposed faults involving insufficient logic. Additional logic was added, some new test cases were defined and the test set was rerun. All features passed their tests.

6. Evaluation

The module passed comprehensive testing with only three faults being detected. No more than one additional fault in the first six months of use is specified.

7. Summary of Activities

Begin Testing 03/12/82	Est	Actual
Test Design (including cases)	2.0 days	3.0 days
Module Driver Development	1.0 days	1.5 days
Test Execution	2.0 days	2.0 days
Module Revision	2.0 days	1.5 days
Test Reporting	0.5 days	0.5 days
End Testing 03/23/82	7.5 days	8.5 days

8. Approvals

____ Development Project Manager

____________________ Date

Appendix B
Implementation and Usage Guidelines

B1. Implementation Guidelines

When the standard is adopted by an organization, it is recommended that it be implemented in phases.

(1) Initial Phase. Begin by introducing the planning and reporting documents. The test plan will provide a foundation for the whole testing process. The reporting documents will encourage the testing organization to record the appropriate data in an organized manner.

Begin by implementing test documentation at the system level. The need for rigor and control during system testing is critical. System test documentation is a key element in meeting this need.

(2) Subsequent Phases. Introduce the balance of the documents in subsequent phases. Their sequence of introduction will depend upon the results of prior phases.

The test documentation eventually will form a document hierarchy corresponding to the design hierarchy, that is, system test documentation, subsystem test documentation, and module test documentation.

B2. Additional Test-Documentation Guidelines

Develop guidelines for the documentation of the specific testing techniques used in your organization (for example, code inspections or simulation). This documentation will supplement the basic documents of the standard.

B3. Usage Guidelines

(1) In the project plan or the organization's standards, identify which test documents are required during which testing activities. Provide guidelines for using these documents in your organization.

Figure B1 (below) is an example of a specification for the test documents required for various testing activities. The amount of documentation required will vary from organization to organization.

(2) Add sections and material within sections in order to tailor each document to a particular test item and a particular test environment.

(3) Consider documenting sets of modules at the module test level. For example, if might be useful to develop a module test design specification for a set of modules which generate reports. While different test cases would be required, a common test procedure specification might be appropriate.

Documents / Activities	Test Plan	Test Design Spec	Test Case Spec	Test Proc Spec	Test Item Trans Report	Test Log	Test Incident Report	Test Summary Report
Acceptance	X	X	X	X	X		X	X
Field	X	X			X		X	X
Installation	X	X	X	X	X		X	X
System	X	X	X	X	X	X	X	X
Subsystem		X	X	X	X	X	X	X
Program		X	X					X
Module		X	X					X

Fig B1
Example of a Required Test Documentation Specification

Appendix C
Related Documentation Standards

Several other standards which relate to test documentation are described below. Related testing standards can be found in Appendix D.

C1. National Standards

These references establish nationally recognized requirements for software documentation.

ANSI N413-1974, American National Standard Guidelines for the Documentation of Digital Computer Programs.[1]

ANSI/IEEE Std 100-1977, IEEE Standard Dictionary of Electrical and Electronics Terms.[2]

ANSI/IEEE Std 730-1981, Standard for Software Quality Assurance Plans.

IEEE Std 729-1983, IEEE Standard Glossary of Software Engineering Terminology.

Guide for Technical Documentation of Computer Projects, American National Standards Institute Technical Committee X3. Technical Report no 6, New York: June 1982.[3]

C2. Federal Standards

These references include standards and guidelines adopted for use by Federal agencies.

Guidelines for Documentation of Computer Programs and Automated Data Systems. Federal Information Processing Standards Pub 38. National Bureau of Standards, (FIPS PUB 38), February 1976.

C3. Military Standards

These references include standards and guidelines which may be invoked in Department of Defense contracts.

Automated Data Systems Documentation Standards, Standard 7935.1-S, Department of Defense, Sept 1977.

Tactical Digital Systems Documentation Standards SECNAVINST 3560.1, Department of the Navy, 1974.

WWMCCS CCTC Test Package Development Guidelines, Technical Memorandum TM 241-80, Defense Communications Agency, Nov 1980.

---

[1] ANSI standards are available from the Sales Department of American National Standards Institute, 1430 Broadway, New York, NY 10018.

[2] IEEE standards are available from the Institute of Electrical and Electronics Engineers, IEEE Service Center, 445 Hoes Lane, Piscataway, NJ 08854.

[3] This document is available from ANSI X3 Secretary, CBEMA, 311 1st Street NW, Suite 500, Washinton, DC 20001.

Appendix D
Annotated Bibliography

This bibliography contains two kinds of references. One set of references identifies a set of basic sources on software verification and testing. The objective is to identify a few basic references on testing for those who wish information on techniques and tools. The second set of references identifies some military testing standards which might serve as source material for those developing testing standards within their organization. These standards focus on testing rather than documentation.

D1 Basic Sources

ADRION, W.R., BRANSTAD, M.A. and CHERNIAVISKY, J.C. *Validation, Verification and Testing of Computer Software.* National Bureau of Standards: NBS Special Pub 500-75 1980.

This survey discusses testing and analysis techniques that can be used to validate software. Verification throughout the development process is stressed. Specific tools and techniques are described.

BARRY, M. *Airborne Systems Software Acquisition Engineering Guidebook for Software Testing and Evaluation.* TRW: 30323-6011-TU-00 1980.

This guidebook describes the planning and testing activities necessary to a successful software testing effort. It presents checklists and references to supplemental information in government documents and to summarized data from professional journals and books.

DEUTSCH, M.S. *Software Verification and Validation.* Prentice-Hall: 1982.

This book describes a testing methodology based upon techniques used at the Hughes Aircraft Company. It describes the application of automated verification systems and summarizes the verification activities used throughout the software life cycle. It provides insight into one effective approach to dealing with the verification of large software systems.

GLASS, R. *Software Reliability Guidebook.* Prentice-Hall: 1979.

This book defines reliability as the degree to which a software system both satisfies its requirements and delivers usable services. The book surveys many methodologies that are supposed to increase software reliability. These methodologies span the software life cycle requirements, design, implementation, checkout, and maintenance. The handbook rates each methodology as to its value, as a function of the degree of reliability required for the software program. The book is written for the practitioner but includes an annotated bibliography at the end of each chapter for readers desiring a more academic discussion of the topics. The section devoted to the checkout phase (testing) contains almost as much material as all the other life cycle sections combined. Test plans, procedures and reports are briefly described.

GUNTHER, R. *Management Methodology for Software Product Engineering.* John Wiley and Sons: Wiley-Interscience, 1978.

This book was selected for inclusion from the many management oriented books on software development because of its chapter devoted to managing the software product test. This chapter maps the product test groups activities into the traditional software life cycle phases. The chapter discusses software test documentation and even presents a table of contents for test plans and test logs. The author writes from his experience as a product planning manager for Amdahl Corporation.

HETZEL, W.C. Ed. *Program Test Methods.* Prentice-Hall: 1973.

This book is a collection of papers from a testing symposium held in 1972. It covers testing concepts, design of programs to facilitate testing, design of languages to facilitate testing, testing mathematical software, and testing large software systems. The book contains a comprehensive bibliography.

MILLER, E. and HOWDEN, W.E. *Tutorial: Software Testing and Validation Techniques (2nd Ed).* IEEE Computer Society Press: Catalog no EHO 180-0, 1981.

This IEEE Tutorial is a collection of papers that represent new developments in program structure analysis, test coverage, test results analysis, test project management techniques, and test tools. The publication also includes an extensive bibliography on testing.

MYERS, G. *The Art of Software Testing.* Wiley — Interscience, John Wiley and Sons: 1979.

This book is based upon material from Software Reliability: Principles and Practices by the same author. The book emphasizes testing as an activity which tries to find errors in a program, not an activity that attempts to show that a program works. The book expands this thesis into a set of testing principles. Testing techniques and methodology are covered along with a survey of existing tools. Test documentation is not addressed. The book does a good job of defining testing terms and classifying testing techniques.

PERRY, W. *Effective Methods of EDP Quality Assurance.* Wellesly Massachusetts: QED Systems, 1977.

This handbook contains the following four sections: The Quality Assurance Function, Planning The Quality Assurance Function, Quality Assurance Reviews, and Relationships and Other QA Tests. The appendix presents a sample software QA manual. Software testing is presented as one activity requiring a QA review. The handbook presents what points should be addressed by a detailed test plan as well as the test result report. The handbook's strength is its broad coverage of all the aspects of a well organized QA group. The book addresses software testing as an important activity in software development that should be reviewed by a QA function.

POWELL, P.B. Ed. *Planning for Software Validation, Verification and Testing.* National Bureau of Standards: NBS Special Pub 1982.

The document is for those who direct and those who implement computer projects. It explains the selection and use of validation, verification, and testing (VV and T) tools and techniques. It explains how to develop a plan to meet specific software VV and T goals.

POWELL, P.B. Ed. *Software Validation, Verification, and Testing Technique and Tool Reference Guide.* National Bureau of Standards: NBS Special Pub 1982.

Thirty techniques and tools for validation, verification, and testing (VV and T) are described. Each description includes the basic features of the technique or tool, the input, the output, an example, an assessment of the effectiveness and of the learning time and training, an estimate of the needed resources, and references.

WOOLRIDGE, S. *Systems and Programming Standards.* New York: Petrocelli/Charter, 1977.

The author's major purpose is to outline the contents of a programming standards manual. Chapter 8 addresses system testing and presents the table of contents for a system test plan as well as a checklist for system testing. The presentation differs from the other references because of the book's focus on standards and procedures as contrasted to testing philosophies and software QA techniques. The book shows that testing procedures can be integrated into general software development procedures.

YEH, R. *Current Trends in Programming Methodology.* vol II Program Validation. Prentice-Hall, 1977.

This book is a selection of papers published during the first half of the seventies. The collection of papers is indexed and the volume also includes an extensive annotated bibliography. Test documentation is not covered but the book provides a reference point to theoretical treatments of software testing.

D2. Military Testing Standards

Acquisition and Support Procedures for Computer Resources in Systems. AF Regulation 800-14, vol 2, Department of the Air Force, 1975.

The volume defines the Air Force procedures for the acquisition of computer programs used in military systems. It defines a software acquisition life cycle. In chapter four, it defines the required types, levels and phases of software testing and their relationship to this life cycle. It specifies policy for software testing at the following levels: informal testing, preliminary qualification testing, formal qualification testing, and system level testing. This volume identifies the required contents for test plans and procedures and it also discusses general methods for computer program verification and validation.

Testing of Computer Software Systems. Technical Bulletin, TB 18-104, Department of the Army, September 1981.

This technical bulletin defines the Army's computer software testing methodology. It identifies required tests and test documentation. It also identifies a variety of participants in the testing process and their responsibilities.

Weapon System Software Development. MIL-STD-1679. Department of the Navy, 1978.

This specification requires quality assurance procedures at each stage of development to validate accuracy, correctness, and performance of the product programs and to verify the accuracy and conformance of program documentation. In the area of software trouble reporting, the specification requires the development and implementation of procedures for handling and reporting software problems. Section 5.8 describes various testing requirements.

ANSI/IEEE
Std 830-1984

An American National Standard

IEEE Guide to Software Requirements Specifications

Sponsor

Software Engineering Standards Subcommittee of the Technical Committee on Software Engineering of the IEEE Computer Society

Approved September 30, 1983

IEEE Standards Board

Approved July 20, 1984

American National Standards Institute

The Institute of Electrical and Electronics Engineers, Inc
345 East 47th Street, New York, NY 10017, USA

IEEE Standards documents are developed within the Technical Committees of the IEEE Societies and the Standards Coordinating Committees of the IEEE Standards Board. Members of the committees serve voluntarily and without compensation. They are not necessarily members of the Institute. The standards developed within IEEE represent a consensus of the broad expertise on the subject within the Institute as well as those activities outside of IEEE which have expressed an interest in participating in the development of the standard.

Use of an IEEE Standard is wholly voluntary. The existence of an IEEE Standard does not imply that there are no other ways to produce, test, measure, purchase, market, or provide other goods and services related to the scope of the IEEE Standard. Furthermore, the viewpoint expressed at the time a standard is approved and issued is subject to change brought about through developments in the state of the art and comments received from users of the standard. Every IEEE Standard is subjected to review at least once every five years for revision or reaffirmation. When a document is more than five years old, and has not been reaffirmed, it is reasonable to conclude that its contents, although still of some value, do not wholly reflect the present state of the art. Users are cautioned to check to determine that they have the latest edition of any IEEE Standard.

Comments for revision of IEEE Standards are welcome from any interested party, regardless of membership affiliation with IEEE. Suggestions for changes in documents should be in the form of a proposed change of text, together with appropriate supporting comments.

Interpretations: Occasionally questions may arise regarding the meaning of portions of standards as they relate to specific applications. When the need for interpretations is brought to the attention of IEEE, the Institute will initiate action to prepare appropriate responses. Since IEEE Standards represent a consensus of all concerned interests, it is important to ensure that any interpretation has also received the concurrence of a balance of interests. For this reason IEEE and the members of its technical committees are not able to provide an instant response to interpretation requests except in those cases where the matter has previously received formal consideration.

Comments on standards and requests for interpretations should be addressed to:

Secretary, IEEE Standards Board
345 East 47th Street
New York, NY 10017
USA

Foreword

(This Foreword is not a part of IEEE Std 830-1984, IEEE Guide to Software Requirements Specifications.)

This guide describes alternate approaches to good practice in the specification of software requirements. The requirements may be explicitly stated by the user or they may be allocated to computer software (that is, programs) by the system requirements analysis process. This guide does not suggest that a hierarchy of software requirements specifications exists, of which each, in turn, defines a smaller subset of requirements.

As a guide, this document should help:

(1) Software customers to accurately describe what they wish to obtain.

(2) Software suppliers to understand exactly what the customer wants.

(3) Individuals to accomplish the following goals:

(a) Develop standard software requirements specifications (SRS) outline for their own organizations.

(b) Define the form and content of their specific software requirements specifications.

(c) Develop additional local supporting items such as an SRS quality checklist, or an SRS writer's handbook.

To the customers, suppliers and other individuals, a good SRS provides several specific benefits. It will accomplish the following goals:

(1) Establish the basis for agreement between the customers and the suppliers on what the software product is to do. The complete description of the functions to be performed by the software specified in the SRS will assist the potential user, to determine if the software specified meets their needs or how the software must be modified to meet their needs.

(2) Reduce the development effort. The preparation of the SRS forces the various concerned groups in the customer's organization to consider rigorously all of the requirements before design begins and reduces later redesign, recoding, and retesting. Careful review of the requirements in the SRS can reveal omissions, misunderstandings, and inconsistencies early in the development cycle when these problems are easier to correct.

(3) Provide a basis for estimating costs and schedules. The description of the product to be developed as given in the SRS is a realistic basis for estimating project costs and can be used to obtain approval for bids or price estimates. The SRS also provides a clear description of the required software and makes it easier to estimate and plan the necessary resources. The requirements which, together with a development plan, can be used to measure progress.

(4) Provide a baseline for validation and verification. Organizations can develop their validation and verification plans much more productively from a good SRS. As a part of the development contract, the SRS provides a baseline against which compliance can be measured. (However, that the converse is not true; a standard legal contract cannot be used as an SRS. Such documents rarely contain the detail required and are often incomplete.)

(5) Facilitate transfer. The SRS makes it easier to transfer the software product to new users or new machines. Customers thus find it easier to transfer the software to other parts of their organization, and suppliers find it easier to transfer it to new customers.

(6) Serves as a basis for enhancement. Because the SRS discusses the product but not the project that developed it, the SRS serves as a basis for later enhancement of the finished product. The SRS may need to be altered, but it does provide a solid foundation for continued production evolution.

This guide is based on a model in which the result of the software requirements specification process is an unambiguous and complete specification document. In principle, the SRS can be mechanically translated into the specified software program directly. As such, the resulting SRS document itself is the specified software, and the supplier's only duty (after completing the SRS) would be the mechanical compilation of the SRS into machine code for the target computer. The present state of the art does not support such a compiler with an optimizer of such efficiency to make it practical but this limitation need not, and should not, restrict the intermediate objective of an unambiguous SRS.

This guide is consistent with IEEE Std 729-1983, IEEE Standard Glossary of Software Engineering Terminology; ANSI/IEEE Std 730-1981, IEEE Standard for Software Quality Assurance Plans; and IEEE Std 829-1983, IEEE Standard for Software Test Documentation. This guide may be used in conjunction with those standards or separately.

This guide was prepared by the Software Requirements Working Group of the Software Engineering Standards Subcommittee of the Technical Committee on Software Engineering of the IEEE Computer Society.

At the time the guide was approved, the Software Requirements Working Group had the following membership:

At the time that it approved this guide, the Software Engineering Standards Subcommittee had the following membership:

Special representatives to the software engineering standards subcommittee were:

J. Milandin:	ANSI Z1
W. G. Perry:	Data Processing Manufacturers Association
R. Pritchett:	EDP Auditors Association
T. L. Regulinski:	IEEE Reliability Society
N. C. Farr:	Nuclear Power Engineering Committee, IEEE Power Engineering Society

Suggestions for improvement of this guide are welcome. They should be provided to:

The Secretary
IEEE Standards Board
345 East 47th St
New York, New York 10017

At the time the IEEE Standards Board approved this standard on September 20, 1983 it had the following members:

IEEE

Contents

FIGURES

TABLES

IEEE Guide to Software Requirements Specifications

1. Scope and Organization

1.1 Scope. This is a guide for writing software requirements specifications. It describes the necessary content and qualities of a good Software Requirements Specification (SRS) and presents a prototype SRS outline.

This guide does not specify industry-wide SRS standards nor state mandatory SRS requirements. This guide is written under the premise that the current state of the art does not warrant or support such a formal standards document.

This guide is applicable to in-house and commercial software products. Special care, however, should be used in its application because:

(1) This guide is aimed at specifying requirements of software to be developed. Application of this material to already-developed software is counter-productive.

(2) This guide does not cover the specification of requirements for software being developed using the techniques of rapid prototyping.

1.2 Organization. The remainder of this guide is organized as follows:

(1) Section 2 provides the references used throughout the guide.

(2) Section 3 provides definitions of specific terms used throughout the guide.

(3) Section 4 provides background information for writing a good SRS.

(4) Section 5 provides specific guidance for expressing software requirements.

(5) Section 6 discusses each of the essential parts of an SRS and provides alternate prototype outlines.

2. References

[1] ANSI/IEEE Std 100-1977, IEEE Standard Dictionary of Electrical and Electronics Terms.

[2] ANSI/IEEE Std 730-1981, IEEE Standard for Software Quality Assurance Plans.

[3] ANSI/IEEE Std 729-1983, IEEE Standard Glossary of Software Engineering Terminology.

[4] BRUSAW, C. T., ALRED, G. and OLIU, W., *Handbook of Technical Writing*, New York, St. Martin's Press, 1976.

[5] DASARATNY, B., *Timing Constraints of Real-Time Systems: Constructs for Expressing Them*, IEEE Real-Time Systems Symposium, Dec 1982.

[6] DAVIS, A., The Design of a Family of Applications-Oriented Requirements Languages, *IEEE Computer*, 15, 5 May 1982, pp 21–28.

[7] FREEDMAN, D. and WEINBERG, G., Handbook of Walkthroughs, *Inspections and Technical Reviews*, 3rd Ed, Little and Brown Publishers, New York.

[8] KAIN, R., Automata Theory: Machines and Languages, McGraw Hill, New York, 1972.

[9] KOHAVI, Z., Switching and Finite Automata Theory, McGraw Hill, New York, 1970.

[10] KRAMER, J., Editor, Application Oriented Specifications Glossary of Terms, *European Workshop on Industrial Computer Systems (EWICS)*, Imperial College, London, England, May 6, 1981.[1]

[1] Copies of this document are available from EWICS, c/o G. R. Koch, BIOMATIK Gmbh, Carl-Mez Str 81–83, D-7800 Freiburg, Federal Republic of Germany.

[11] MILLS, G., and WALTER, J., *Technical Writing*, New York, Holt, Rinehart and Winston, 4th Ed, 1978.

[12] PETERSON, J., *Petri Nets*, ACM Computing Surveys, 9, 4, Dec 1977, pp 223–252.

[13] RAMAMOORHY, C. and SO, H. H., *Software Requirements and Specifications: Status and Perspectives*, Tutorial: Software Methodology, RAMAMOORTHY, C. and YEH, R. T., Editors. IEEE Catalog no EHO 142-0, 1978, pp 43–164.

[14] TAGGART, W. M. Jr, and THARP, M. O., *A Survey of Information Requirements Analysis Techniques*, ACM Computing Surveys, 9, 4, Dec 1977, pp 273–290.

[15] TEICHROEW, D., *A Survey of Languages for Stating Requirements for Computer-Based Information Systems*, 1972 Fall Joint Computer Conference, 1972, pp 1203–1224.

3. Definitions

Except for the definitions listed below, the definitions of all terms used in this guide conform to the definitions provided in IEEE Std 729-1983 [3][2], for example, the terms requirement, requirements specification. If a term used in this guide does not appear in that Standard, then ANSI/IEEE Std 100-1977 [1], applies.

The terms listed in this section have been adopted from Section 2, [10].

contract. A legally binding document agreed upon by the customer and supplier. This includes the technical, organizational, cost and schedule requirements of a product.

customer. The person, or persons, who pay for the product and usually (but not necessarily) decides the requirements. In the context of this document the customer and the supplier may be members of the same organization.

language. A means of communication, with syntax and semantics, consisting of a set of representations, conventions and associated rules used to convey information.

partitioning. Decomposition; the separation of the whole into its parts.

supplier. The person, or persons, who produce a product for a customer. In the context of this document, the customer and the supplier may be members of the same organization.

user. The person, or persons, who operate or interact directly with the system. The user(s) and the customer(s) are often not the same person(s).

4. Background Information for Writing a Good SRS

This section provides background information necessary for writing an SRS. This includes:

(1) Examination of the nature of the SRS

(2) Environmental considerations surrounding the SRS

(3) Characteristics required for a good SRS

(4) Recommendations for joint preparation of an SRS

(5) Evolutionary aspects of the SRS

(6) The use of automated tools to develop an SRS

4.1 The SRS. The SRS is a specification for a particular software product, program, or set of programs that does certain things. See ANSI/IEEE Std 730-1981 [2], 3.4.2.1.

The description places two basic requirements on the SRS:

(1) It must say certain things. For example, software developed from an SRS that fails to specify that error messages will be provided, will probably fail to satisfy the customer.

(2) It must say those things in certain ways. For example, software developed from an SRS that fails to specify the format and content of error messages and instead is developed from a vague and non-quantifiable requirement such as *All error messages will be helpful*, will probably be unsatisfactory. What is *helpful* for one person can be a severe aggravation to another person.

For recommended contents of an SRS see Section 6.

4.2 Environment of the SRS. It is important to consider the part that the SRS plays in the total software project. The provisions in ANSI/IEEE Std 730-1981 [2], define the minimum required documents for a software project. See [2], 3.4.2.

ANSI/IEEE Std 730-1981 [2] also identifies the other useful documents. See [2], 3.4.3.

[2]Numbers in brackets correspond to those of the references in Section 2.

Since the SRS has a definite role to play in this documentation scheme, SRS writers should be careful not to go beyond the bounds of that role. This means the following requirements should be met:

(1) The SRS must correctly define all of the software requirements, but no more.

(2) The SRS should not describe any design, verification, or project management details, except for required design constraints.

Such a properly written SRS limits the range of valid solutions but does not specify any particular design and thus provides the supplier with maximum flexibility.

4.3 Characteristics of A Good SRS. The previous sections describe the types of information that should be contained in an SRS. The following concepts deal with particular characteristics. A good SRS is:

(1) Unambiguous
(2) Complete
(3) Verifiable
(4) Consistent
(5) Modifiable
(6) Traceable
(7) Usable during the Operation and Maintenance Phase

4.3.1 Unambiguous. An SRS is unambiguous if — and only if — every requirement stated therein has only one interpretation.

(1) As a minimum, this requires that each characteristic of the final product be described using a single unique term.

(2) In cases where a term used in a particular context could have multiple meanings, the term must be included in a glossary where its meaning is made more specific.

4.3.1.1 Natural Language Pitfalls. Requirements are often written in a natural language (for example, English). SRS writers who use a natural language must be especially careful to review their requirements for ambiguity. The following examples are taken from Section 2, [7].

(1) The specification *The data set will contain an end of file character*, might be read as:

(a) There will be one and only one end of file character

(b) Some character will be designated as an end of file character

(c) There will be at least one end of file character

(2) The specification *The control total is taken from the last record*, might be read as:

(a) The control total is taken from the record at the end of the file

(b) The control total is taken from the latest record

(c) The control total is taken from the previous record

(3) The specification *All customers have the same control field*, might be read as:

(a) All customers have the same value in their control field

(b) All customer control fields have the same format

(c) One control field is issued for all customers

(4) The specification *All files are controlled by a file control block*, might be read as:

(a) One control block controls the entire set of files

(b) Each file has its own block

(c) Each file is controlled by a control block, but one control block might control more than one file

4.3.1.2 Formal Requirements Specifications Languages. One way to avoid the ambiguity inherent in natural language is to write the SRS in a formal requirements specification language.[3]

(1) One major advantage in the use of such languages is the reduction of ambiguity. This occurs, in part, because the formal language processors automatically detect many lexical, syntactic, and semantic errors.

(2) One major disadvantage in the use of such languages is the length of time required to learn them.

4.3.2 Complete. An SRS is complete if it possesses the following qualities:

(1) Inclusion of all significant requirements, whether relating to functionality, performance, design constraints, attributes or external interfaces.

(2) Definition of the responses of the software to all realizable classes of input data in all realizable classes of situations. Note that it is important to specify the responses to valid and invalid input values.

(3) Conformity to any SRS standard that applies to it. If a particular section of the standard is not applicable, the SRS should

[3]For detailed discussion on this topic, suggested readings are [6], [13], [14], and [15].

include the section number and an explanation of why it is not applicable.

(4) Full labeling and referencing of all figures, tables, and diagrams in the SRS and definition of all terms and units of measure.

4.3.2.1 Use of TBDs. Any SRS that uses the phrase *to be determined* (TBD) is not a complete SRS.

(1) The TBD is, however, occasionally necessary and should be accompanied by:

(a) A description of the conditions causing the TBD (for example, why an answer is not known) so that the situation can be resolved.

(b) A description of what must be done to eliminate the TBD.

(2) Any project documents that are based on an SRS that contains TBDs, should:

(a) Identify the version or state the specific release number of the SRS associated with that particular document.

(b) Exclude any commitments dependent upon the sections of the SRS that are still identified as TBDs.

4.3.3 Verifiable. An SRS is verifiable if and only if every requirement stated therein is verifiable. A requirement is verifiable if and only if there exists some finite cost-effective process with which a person or machine can check that the software product meets the requirement.

(1) Examples of nonverifiable requirements include statements such as:

(a) *The product should work well*, or *The product should have a good human interface.* These requirements cannot be verified because it is impossible to define the terms *good* or *well.*

(b) *The program shall never enter an infinite loop.* This requirement is non-verifiable because the testing of this quality is theoretically impossible.

(c) *The output of the program shall usually be given within 10 s.* This requirement is non-verifiable because the term *usually* cannot be measured.

(2) An example of a verifiable statement is *The output of the program shall be given within 20 s of event* X, 60% *of the time; and shall be given within 30 s of event* X, 100% *of the time.* This statement can be verified because it uses concrete terms and measurable quantities.

(3) If a method cannot be devised to determine whether the software meets a particular requirement, then that requirement should be removed or revised.

(4) If a requirement is not expressible in verifiable terms at the time the SRS is prepared, then a point in the development cycle (review, test plan issue, etc) should be identified at which the requirement must be put into a verifiable form.

4.3.4 Consistent. An SRS is consistent if and only if no set of individual requirements described in it conflict. There are three types of likely conflicts in an SRS:

(1) Two or more requirements might describe the same real world object but use different terms for that object. For example, a program's request for a user input might be called a *prompt* in one requirement and a *cue* in another.

(2) The specified characteristics of real world objects might conflict. For example:

(a) The format of an output report might be described in one requirement as *tabular* but in another as *textual.*

(b) One requirement might state that all lights shall be green while another states that all lights shall be blue.

(3) There might be a logical or temporal conflict between two specified actions. For example:

(a) One requirement might specify that the program will add two inputs and another specify that the program will multiply them.

(b) One requirement might state that *A* must always follow *B*, while another requires that *A and B* occur simultaneously.

4.3.5 Modifiable. An SRS is modifiable if its structure and style are such that any necessary changes to the requirements can be made easily, completely, and consistently. Modifiability generally requires an SRS to:

(1) Have a coherent and easy-to-use organization, with a table of contents, an index, and explicit cross-referencing.

(2) Not be redundant; that is, the same requirement should not appear in more than one place in the SRS.

(a) Redundancy itself is not an error, but it can easily lead to errors. Redundancy can occasionally help to make an SRS more readable, but a problem can arise when the redundant document is updated. Assume, for instance, that a certain requirement is stated in two places. At some later time, it is determined that the requirement should be altered, but the change is made in only one of the two locations. The SRS then becomes inconsistent.

(b) Whenever redundancy is necessary, the SRS should include explicit cross-references to make it modifiable.

4.3.6 Traceable. An SRS is traceable if the origin of each of its requirements is clear and if it facilitates the referencing of each requirement in future development or enhancement documentation. Two types of traceability are recommended:

(1) Backward traceability (that is, to previous stages of development) depends upon each requirement explicitly referencing its source in previous documents.

(2) Forward traceability (that is, to all documents spawned by the SRS) depends upon each requirement in the SRS having a unique name or reference number.

When a requirement in the SRS represents an apportionment or a derivative of another requirement, both forward and backward traceability should be provided. Examples include:

4.3.6.1 The allocation of response time to a data base function from the overall user response time requirement.

4.3.6.2 The identification of a report format with certain functional and user interface requirements.

4.3.6.3 A software product that supports legislative or administrative needs (for example, tax computations, reporting of an overhead ratio). In this case, the exact legislative or administrative document that is being supported should be identified.

The forward traceability of the SRS is especially important when the software product enters the operation and maintenance phase. As code and design documents are modified, it is essential to be able to ascertain the complete set of requirements that may be affected by those modifications.

4.3.7 Usable During the Operation and Maintenance Phase. The SRS must address the needs of the operation and maintenance phase, including the eventual replacement of the software.

(1) Maintenance is frequently carried out by personnel not associated with the original development. Local changes (corrections) can be implemented by means of a well-commented code. For changes of wider scope, however, the design and requirements documentation is essential. This implies two actions

(a) The SRS should be modifiable as indicated in 4.3.5.

(b) The SRS should contain a record of all special provisions that apply to individual components such as:

(i) Their criticality (for example, where failure could impact safety or cause large financial or social losses).

(ii) Their relation to only temporary needs (for example, to support a display that may be retired soon).

(iii) Their origin (for example, function X is to be copied from an existing software product in its entirety).

(2) Knowledge of this type is taken for granted in the developing organization but is frequently missing in the maintenance organization. If the reason for or origin of a function is not understood, it is frequently impossible to perform adequate software maintenance on it.

4.4 Joint Preparation of the SRS. The software development process begins with supplier and customer agreement on what the completed software must do. This agreement, in the form of an SRS, should be jointly prepared. This is important because usually neither the customer nor the supplier is qualified to write a good SRS by himself.

(1) Customers usually do not understand the software design and development process well enough to write a usable SRS.

(2) Suppliers usually do not understand the customer's problem and field of endeavor well enough to specify requirements for a satisfactory system.

The customer and the supplier need to work together to produce a well written and completely understood SRS.[4]

4.5 SRS Evolution. The SRS may need to evolve as the development of the software product progresses.

(1) It may be impossible to specify some details at the time the project is initiated. For example, it may be impossible to define during the Requirements Phase, all of the screen formats for an interactive program in a manner that guarantees that they will not be altered later.

(2) Additional changes may ensue as deficien-

[4]This guide does not specifically discuss style, language usage, or techniques of good writing. It is quite important, however, that an SRS be well written; for guidance, please refer to general technical writing guides such as [1] and [11].

cies, shortcomings, and inaccuracies are discovered in the SRS, as the product evolves.

Two major considerations in this process are:

4.5.1 The requirements should be specified as completely and thoroughly as possible, even if evolutionary revisions can be forseen as inevitable. For example, the desired screen formats should be specified as well as possible in the SRS as a basis for later design.

4.5.2 A formal change process should be initiated to identify, control, track, and report projected changes, as soon as they are initially identified. Approved changes in requirements should be incorporated in the SRS in such a way as to:

(1) Provide an accurate and complete audit trail of changes.

(2) Permit the review of current and superseded portions of the SRS.

4.6 Tools for Developing an SRS. The most obvious way to create an SRS is to write it in a natural language (for example, English). But because natural languages are rich, although imprecise, a number of more formal methods have been devised to assist SRS writers.

4.6.1 Formal Specification Methodologies. The degree to which such formal methodologies may be useful in preparing an SRS depends upon a number of factors:

(1) The size and complexity of the program

(2) Whether a customer contract requires it

(3) Whether the SRS is a vehicle for contracts or merely an internal document

(4) Whether the SRS document will become the top level of the design document

(5) What computer facilities are available to support such a methodology

No attempt is made here to describe or endorse any particular tool.[5]

4.6.2 Production Tools. A computer-based word processor is a most useful production aid. Usually, an SRS will have several authors, will undergo several revisions, and will have several reorganizations. A word processor that manages the text as a computer file facilitates this process.

Almost all computer systems have a word processor and often a document preparation package is associated with it. This automates paragraphing and referencing, the printing of headings and subheadings, the compilation of tables of contents and indexes, etc, all of which help in the production of a more readable SRS.

4.6.3 Representation Tools. Some words in the SRS, especially nouns and verbs, refer specifically to entities and actions in the system. There are several advantages to identifying them as such.

(1) It is possible to verify that an entity or action always has the same name everywhere in the SRS. Thus *calculate trajectory* would not co-exist with *determine flight path*.

(2) It is possible to identify every place in the specification where a particular entity or action is described.

In addition, it may be desirable to formalize the English structure in some way to allow automated processing of the content of the SRS. With such constraints it becomes possible to:

4.6.3.1 Display the requirements in some tabular or graphical way.

4.6.3.2 Automatically check the SRS requirements in hierarchical layers of detail, where each layer is complete in itself but may also be expanded upon in a lower hierarchical layer or be a constituent of an upper hierarchical layer.

4.6.3.3 Automatically check that the SRS possesses some or all of the characteristics described in 4.3.

5. Software Requirements

Each software requirement in an SRS is a statement of some essential capability of the software to be developed. The following subsections describe:

(1) Methods used to express software requirements

(2) Annotation of the software requirements

(3) Common pitfalls encountered in the process

5.1 Methods Used To Express Software Requirements. Requirements can be expressed in a number of ways:

(1) Through input/output specifications

(2) By use of a set of representative examples

(3) By the specification of models

5.1.1 Input/Output Specifications. It is often effective to specify the required behavior of a software product as a sequence of inputs and outputs.

[5] For detailed discussion on this topic, see, for example, [6], [13], [14], and [15].

5.1.1.1 Approaches. There are at least three different approaches based on the nature of the software being specified:

(1) Some software products (such as reporting systems) are best specified by focusing on required outputs. In general, output-focused systems operate primarily on data files. User input usually serves to provide control information and trigger data file processing.

(2) Others are best specified by focusing on input/output behavior. Input/output-focused systems operate primarily on the current input. They are required to generate the *matching* output (as with data conversion routines or a package of mathematical functions).

(3) Some systems (such as process control systems) are required to remember their behavior so that they can respond to an input based on that input and past inputs; that is, behave like a finite state machine. In this case the focus is on both input/output pairs and sequences of such pairs.

5.1.1.2 Difficulties. Most software products can receive an infinite number of sequences as input. Thus, to completely specify the behavior of the product through input/output sequences would require that the SRS contain an infinitely long set of sequences of inputs and required outputs. With this approach, therefore, it may be impossible to completely specify every conceivable behavior that is required of the software.

5.1.2 Representative Examples. One alternative is to indicate what behavior is required by using representative examples of that behavior. Suppose, for example, that the system is required to respond with a "1" every time it receives a "0". Clearly, a list of all possible sequences of inputs and outputs would be impossible. However, by using representative sequences one might be able to fully understand the system's behavior. This system's behavior might be described by using this representative set of four dialogues:[6]

0101
010101010101
01
010101

These dialogues provide a good idea of the required inputs and outputs but they do not specify the system's behavior completely.

[6]Each of the four sample dialogues given here (one per line) represents a sequence of one-character user inputs and one-character system outputs.

5.1.3 Models. Another approach is to express the requirements in the form of a model.[7] This can be an accurate and efficient way to express complex requirements.

At least three generalized types of models are in common usage:

(1) Mathematical
(2) Functional
(3) Timing

Care should be taken to distinguish between the model for the application; that is, a linear programming model (with a set of linear inequalities and an objective function) and the model for the software which is required to implement the application model. See 5.1.3.5.

5.1.3.1 Mathematical Models. A mathematical model is a model that uses mathematical relations to describe the software's behavior. Mathematical models are especially useful for particular application areas, including navigation, linear programming, econometrics, signal processing and weather analysis.

A mathematical model might specify the response discussed in 5.1.2 like this:

(01)*

where * means that the parenthesized character string is repeated one or more times.

5.1.3.2 Functional Models. A functional model is a model that provides a mapping from inputs to outputs. Functional models, for example, finite state machines or Petri nets can help identify and define various features of the software or can demonstrate the intended operation of the system.

A functional model might specify the response, previously described by the mathematical model, in the form of a finite state machine as shown in Fig 1. In this figure, the incoming arrow points to the starting state. The double lined box represents the accepting state. The notation X/Y on the lines indicates that when X is accepted as an input, Y is produced as an output.

5.1.3.3 Timing Models. A timing model is a model that has been augmented with timing constraints. Timing models are quite useful for specifying the form and details of the software's behavior, particularly for real-time systems or for human factors of any system.

[7]For details on using modeling techniques, see [5], [8], [9], and [12].

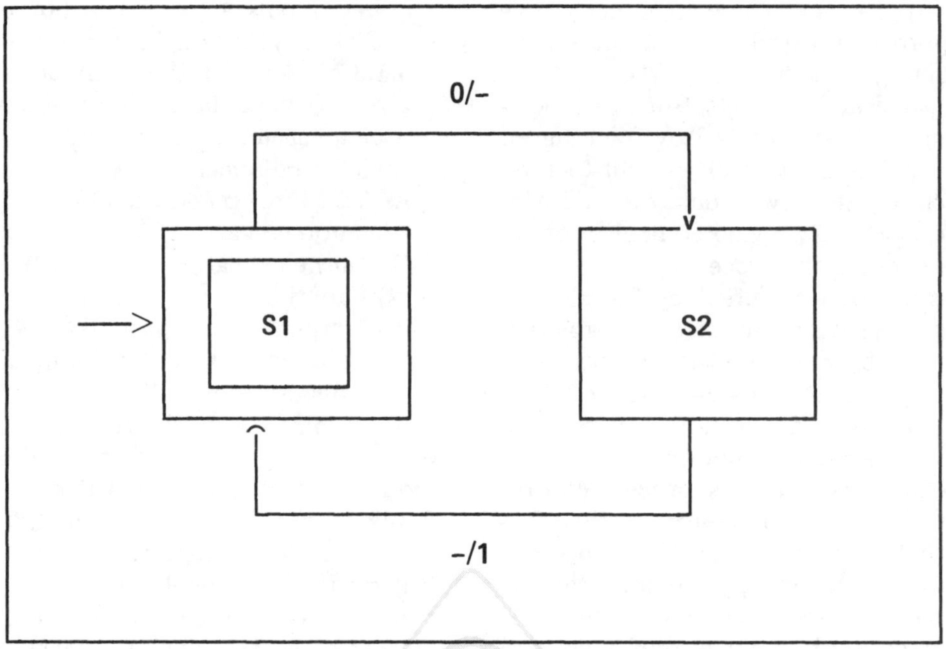

Fig 1
A Functional Model Specifying Any Sequence of Alternating 0s and 1s

A timing model might add these constraints to the model shown in Fig 1.

(1) The stimulus 0 will occur within 30 s of the arrival in state S1

(2) The response 1 will occur within 2 s of the arrival in state S2

5.1.3.4 Other Models. In addition to the aforementioned, specific applications have particularly helpful models. For example, a compiler specification might employ attribute grammars, or a payroll system might use tables. It is to be noted that the use of a formal requirements language for an SRS usually implies a need for the use of a particular model.

5.1.3.5 Cautions. Whatever type of model is used:

(1) It must be rigorously defined, either in the SRS or in a document referenced in the SRS. This definition should specify

(a) The required ranges of the model's parameters

(b) The values of constraints it uses

(c) The required accuracy of results

(d) The load capacity

(e) The required execution time

(f) Default or failure response

(2) Care must be taken to keep a model definition within the domain of requirements. Whenever an SRS uses a model:

(a) It means that the model provided an especially efficient and accurate way to specify the requirements

(b) It does not mean that the implementation of the software product must be based on that model.

A model that works effectively for explaining requirements in a written document may not be optimal for the actual software implementation.

5.2 Annotation of the Software Requirements. Typically, all of the requirements that relate to a software product are not equally important. Some requirements may be essential, especially for life-critical applications, while others may be just *nice to have.*

(1) Each requirement in the SRS should be annotated to make these differences in relative importance clear and explicit.

(2) Annotating the requirements in this manner, helps:

(a) Customers to give more careful consideration to each requirement, which often clarifies any hidden assumptions they may have.

(b) Developers to make correct design decisions and devote appropriate levels of effort to the different parts of the software product.

5.2.1 Stability. One method of annotating requirements uses the dimension of stability. A requirement may be considered *stable* when it is thought that the needs which it addresses will not change during the expected life of the software, or it may be considered *volatile* and subject to change.

5.2.2 Degree of Necessity. Another way to annotate is to distinguish classes of requirements as mandatory, desirable, and optional.

(1) Mandatory implies that the software will not be acceptable unless these requirements are provided in an agreed manner.

(2) Desirable implies that these are requirements that would enhance the software product, but would not make it unacceptable if they are absent.

(3) Optional implies a class of functions that may or may not be worthwhile, which gives the supplier the opportunity to propose something which exceeds the SRS.

5.2.3 Annotation Caution. Prior to annotating the requirements, a thorough understanding of the contractual implications of such annotations, should be obtained.

5.3 Common Pitfalls Encountered in Expressing Requirements. An essential point about the SRS is that it should specify the results that must be achieved by the software, not the means of obtaining those results.

(1) The basic issues that the requirements writer must address are these:

(a) *Functionality* — what the software is supposed to do

(b) *Performance* — the speed, availability, response time, recovery time of various software functions, etc

(c) *Design Constraints Imposed on an Implementation* —any required standards in effect, implementation language, policies for data base integrity, resource limits, operating environment(s), etc

(d) *Attributes* — considerations of portability, correctness, maintainability, security, etc

(e) *External Interfaces* — interactions with people, hardware, other software and other hardware

(2) The requirements writer should avoid placing either design or project requirements in the SRS. The requirements writer should clearly distinguish between identifying required design constraints and projecting a design.

5.3.1 Embedding Design in the SRS. Embedding design specifications in the SRS unduly constrains the software designs and artificially places potentially dangerous requirements in the SRS.

(1) The SRS must specify what functions are to be performed on what data to produce what results at what location for whom. The SRS should focus on the services to be performed. The SRS should not normally specify design items such as

(a) Partitioning the software into modules

(b) Allocating functions to the modules

(c) Describing the flow of information or control between modules

(d) Choosing data structures

(2) It is not always practical to consider the design as being completely isolated from the SRS. Security or safety considerations may impose requirements that reflect directly into design constraints; for example, the need to

(a) Keep certain functions in separate modules

(b) Permit only limited communication between some areas of the program

(c) Compute check sums for critical quantities

In general, it must be considered that the selection of an appropriate high-level design for the software may require vast amounts of resources (perhaps as much as 10% to 20% of the total product development cost). There are two alternatives:

(1) Ignore the warning in this guide and specify the design in the SRS. This will mean that either a potentially inadequate design is stated as a requirement (because insufficient time was spent in arriving at it), or an exorbitant amount of time is spent during the requirements phase (because an entire design analysis is performed before SRS completion).

(2) Use the advice in 5.1.3 of this guide. State the requirements using a *model* design used solely to assist in the description of the requirements and not intended to serve as the actual design.

5.3.2 Embedding Project Requirements in the SRS. The SRS should address the software product, not the process of producing the software product.

(1) Project requirements represent an understanding between a customer and a supplier about the contractual matters pertaining to the production of software (and thus should not be

included in the SRS). These normally include such items as:

(a) Cost
(b) Delivery schedules
(c) Reporting procedures
(d) Software development methods
(e) Quality assurance
(f) Validation and verification criteria
(g) Acceptance procedures

(2) Project requirements are specified in other documents, typically in a computer program development plan or a statement of work. The requirements for only the software product itself are given in the SRS.

6. An SRS Prototype Outline

This section discusses each of the essential parts of the SRS. These parts are arranged in Table 1 in an outline that can serve as a prototype for any SRS.

Software suppliers and customers should tailor the content requirements of this guide based on the particular package being specified, and individual companies might base their own SRS standards upon it. Remember that while an SRS does not have to follow this outline or use the names for its parts, any good SRS must include all of the information discussed here.

6.1 Introduction (Section 1 of the SRS). The following subsections of the SRS should provide an overview of the entire SRS.

Table 1
Prototype SRS Outline

Table of Contents
1. Introduction
    1.1 Purpose
    1.2 Scope
    1.3 Definitions, Acronyms, and Abbreviations
    1.4 References
    1.5 Overview
2. General Description
    2.1 Product Perspective
    2.2 Product Functions
    2.3 User Characteristics
    2.4 General Constraints
    2.5 Assumptions and Dependencies
3. Specific Requirements
    (See 6.3.2 of this guide for alternate organizations of this section of the SRS.)

Appendixes
Index

6.1.1 Purpose (1.1 of the SRS). This subsection should accomplish the following:

(1) Delineate the purpose of the particular SRS

(2) Specify the intended audience for the SRS

6.1.2 Scope (1.2 of the SRS). This subsection should:

(1) Identify the software product(s) to be produced by name; for example, Host DBMS, Report Generator, etc

(2) Explain what the software product(s) will, and, if necessary, will not do

(3) Describe the application of the software being specified. As a portion of this, it should:

(a) Describe all relevant benefits, objectives, and goals as precisely as possible. For example, to say that one goal is to provide *effective reporting capabilities* is not as good as saying *parameter-driven, user-definable reports with a 2 h turnaround and on-line entry of user parameters.*

(b) Be consistent with similar statements in higher-level specifications (for example, the System Requirement Specification), if they exist.

6.1.3 Definitions, Acronyms, and Abbreviations (1.3 of the SRS). This subsection should provide the definitions of all terms, acronyms, and abbreviations required to properly interpret the SRS. This information may be provided by reference to one or more appendixes in the SRS or by reference to other documents.

6.1.4 References (1.4 of the SRS). This subsection should:

(1) Provide a complete list of all documents referenced elsewhere in the SRS, or in a separate, specified document.

(2) Identify each document by title, report number — if applicable — date, and publishing organization.

(3) Specify the sources from which the references can be obtained.

This information may be provided by reference to an appendix or to another document.

6.1.5 Overview (1.5 of the SRS). This subsection should:

(1) Describe what the rest of the SRS contains

(2) Explain how the SRS is organized

6.2 The General Description (Section 2 of the SRS). This section of the SRS should describe the general factors that affect the product and its requirements.

This section usually consists of five subsections, as follows:

(1) Product Perspective
(2) Product Functions
(3) User Characteristics
(4) General Constraints
(5) Assumptions and Dependencies

It should be made clear that this section does not state specific requirements; it only makes those requirements easier to understand.

6.2.1 Product Perspective (2.1 of the SRS). This subsection of the SRS puts the product into perspective with other related products or projects.

(1) If the product is independent and totally self-contained, it should be stated here.

(2) If the SRS defines a product that is a component of a larger system or project — as frequently occurs — then this subsection should:

(a) Describe the functions of each component of the larger system or project, and identify interfaces

(b) Identify the principal external interfaces of this software product.

NOTE: This is not a detailed description of these interfaces; the detailed description is provided elsewhere in the SRS.

(c) Describe the computer hardware and peripheral equipment to be used.

NOTE: This is an overview description only.

A block diagram showing the major components of the larger system or project, interconnections, and external interfaces can be very helpful.

This subsection should not be used to impose a specific design solution or specific design constraints on the solution. This subsection should provide the reasons why certain design constraints are later specified as part of the Specific Requirements Section of the SRS.

6.2.2 Product Functions (2.2 of the SRS). This subsection of the SRS should provide a summary of the functions that the software will perform. For example, an SRS for an accounting program might use this part to address *customer account maintenance*, *customer statement and invoice preparation* without mentioning the vast amount of detail that each of those functions requires.

Sometimes the function summary that is necessary for this part can be taken directly from the section of the higher-level specification (if one exists) that allocates particular functions to the software product. Note that, for the sake of clarity:

(1) The functions should be organized in a way that makes the list of functions understandable to the customer or to anyone else reading the document for the first time.

(2) Block diagrams showing the different functions and their relationships can be helpful. Remember, however, that such a diagram is not a requirement on the design of a product itself; it is simply an effective explanatory tool.

This subsection should not be used to state specific requirements. This subsection should provide the reasons why certain specific requirements are later specified as part of the Specific Requirements Section(s) of the SRS.

6.2.3 User Characteristics (2.3 of the SRS). This subsection of the SRS should describe those general characteristics of the eventual users of the product that will affect the specific requirements.

Many people interact with a system during the operation and maintenance phase of the software life cycle. Some of these people are users, operators, and maintenance and systems personnel. Certain characteristics of these people, such as educational level, experience, and technical expertise impose important constraints on the system's operating environment.

If most users of the system are occasional users, a resulting specific requirement might be that the system contains reminders of how to perform essential functions rather than assuming that the user will remember these details from the last session or from reading the user's guide.

This subsection should not be used to state specific requirements or to impose specific design constraints on the solution. This subsection should provide the reasons why certain specific requirements or design constraints are later specified as part of the Specific Requirements Section(s) of the SRS.

6.2.4 General Constraints (2.4 of the SRS). This subsection of the SRS should provide a general description of any other items that will limit the developer's options for designing the system. These can include:

(1) Regulatory policies
(2) Hardware limitations; for example, signal timing requirements
(3) Interfaces to other applications
(4) Parallel operation
(5) Audit functions

(6) Control functions

(7) Higher-order language requirements

(8) Signal handshake protocols; for example, XON -XOFF, ACK - NACK.

(9) Criticality of the application

(10) Safety and security considerations

This subsection should not be used to impose specific requirements or specific design constraints on the solution. This subsection should provide the reasons why certain specific requirements or design constraints are later specified as part of the Specific Requirements Section of the SRS.

6.2.5 Assumptions and Dependencies (2.5 of the SRS). This subsection of the SRS should list each of the factors that affect the requirements stated in the SRS. These factors are not design constraints on the software but are, rather, any changes to them that can affect the requirements in the SRS. For example, an assumption might be that a specific operating system will be available on the hardware designated for the software product. If, in fact, the operating system is not available, the SRS would then have to change accordingly.

6.3 The Specific Requirements (Section 3 of the SRS). This section of the SRS should contain all the details the software developer needs to create a design. This is typically the largest and most important part of the SRS.

(1) The details within it should be defined as individual specific requirements, following the guidelines described in Section 3 of this guide (verifiable, unambiguous, etc)

(2) Background should be provided by cross-referencing each specific requirement to any related discussion in the Introduction, General Description, and Appendixes portions of the SRS, whenever possible.

(3) One way to classify the specific requirements is as follows:

(a) Functional Requirements

(b) Performance Requirements

(c) Design Constraints

(d) Attributes

(e) External Interface Requirements

The important points to be recognized are that:

(1) Specific requirements should be organized in a logical and readable fashion.

(2) Each requirement should be stated such that its achievement can be objectively verified by a prescribed method.

6.3.1 Information Required as Part of the Specific Requirements

6.3.1.1 Functional Requirements. This subsection of the SRS should specify how the inputs to the software product should be transformed into outputs. It describes the fundamental actions that must take place in the software.

For each class of function or sometimes for each individual function, it is necessary to specify requirements on inputs, processing, and outputs. These are usually organized with these four subparagraphs:

(1) Introduction. This subparagraph should provide a description of the purpose of the function and the approaches and techniques employed. It should contain any introductory or background material which might clarify the intent of the function.

(2) Inputs. This subparagraph should contain:

(a) A detailed description of all data input to this function to include:

(i) The sources of the inputs

(ii) Quantities

(iii) Units of measure

(iv) Timing

(v) The ranges of the valid inputs to include accuracies and tolerances.

(b) The details of operator control requirements should include names and descriptions of operator actions, and console or operator positions. For example, this might include required operator activities such as form alignment — when printing checks.

(c) References to interface specifications or interface control documents where appropriate.

(3) Processing. This subparagraph should define all of the operations to be performed on the input data and intermediate parameters to obtain the output. It includes specification of:

(a) Validity checks on the input data

(b) The exact sequence of operations to include timing of events

(c) Responses to *abnormal* situations, for example:

(i) Overflow

(ii) Communication failure

(iii) Error handling

(d) Parameters affected by the operations

(e) Requirements for degraded operation

(f) Any methods (for example, equations, mathematical algorithms, and logical operations) which must be used to transform the system inputs into corresponding outputs. For example, this might specify:

(i) The formula for computing the withholding tax in a payroll package

(ii) A least squares curve fitting technique for a plotting package

(iii) A meteorological model to be used for a weather forecasting package

(g) Validity checks on the output data

(4) Outputs. This subparagraph should contain:

(a) A detailed description of all data output from this function to include:

(i) Destinations of the outputs

(ii) Quantities

(iii) Units of measure

(iv) Timing

(v) The range of the valid outputs is to include accuracies and tolerances

(vi) Disposition of illegal values

(vii) Error messages

(b) References to interface specifications or interface control documents where appropriate

In addition, for those systems whose requirements focus on input/output behavior, the SRS should specify all of the significant input/output pairs and sequences of pairs. Sequences will be needed when a system is required to remember its behavior so that it can respond to an input based on that input and past behavior; that is, behave like a finite state machine.

6.3.1.2 Performance Requirements. This subsection should specify both the static and the dynamic numerical requirements placed on the software or on human interaction with the software, as a whole.

(1) Static numerical requirements may include:

(a) The number of terminals to be supported

(b) The number of simultaneous users to be supported

(c) Number of files and records to be handled

(d) Sizes of tables and files

Static numerical requirements are sometimes identified under a separate section entitled *capacity*.

(2) Dynamic numerical requirements may include, for example, the numbers of transactions and tasks and the amount of data to be processed within certain time periods for both normal and peak workload conditions.

All of these requirements should be stated in measurable terms, for example, *95% of the transactions shall be processed in less than 1 s*, rather than, *operator shall not have to wait for the transaction to complete.*

NOTE: Numerical limits applied to one specific function are normally specified as part of the processing subparagraph description of that function.

6.3.1.3 Design Constraints. Design constraints can be imposed by other standards, hardware limitations, etc.

6.3.1.3.1 Standards Compliance. This subsection should specify the requirements derived from existing standards or regulations. They might include:

(1) Report format

(2) Data naming

(3) Accounting procedures

(4) Audit Tracing. For example, this could specify the requirement for software to trace processing activity. Such traces are needed for some applications to meet minimum government or financial standards. An audit trace requirement might, for example, state that all changes to a payroll data base must be recorded in a trace file with before and after values.

6.3.1.3.2 Hardware Limitations. This subsection could include requirements for the software to operate inside various hardware constraints. For example, these could include:

(1) Hardware configuration characteristics (number of ports, instruction sets, etc)

(2) Limits on primary and secondary memory

6.3.1.4 Attributes. There are a number of attributes that can place specific requirements on the software. Some of these are indicated below. These should not be interpreted to be a complete list.

6.3.1.4.1 Availability. This could specify the factors required to guarantee a defined availability level for the entire system such as checkpoint, recovery and restart.

6.3.1.4.2 Security. This could specify the factors that would protect the software from accidental or malicious access, use, modification, destruction, or disclosure. Specific requirements in this area could include the need to:

(1) Utilize certain cryptographical techniques

(2) Keep specific log or history data sets

(3) Assign certain functions to different modules

(4) Restrict communications between some areas of a program

(5) Compute checksums for critical quantities

6.3.1.4.3 Maintainability. This could specify the requirements to ensure that the software could be maintained. For example, as a part of this,

(1) Specific coupling metrics for the software modules could be required

(2) Specific data/program partitioning requirements could be specified for micro-devices

6.3.1.4.4 Transferability/Conversion. This could specify the user procedures, user interface compatibility constraints (if any) etc, required to transport the software from one environment to another.

6.3.1.4.5 Caution. It is important that required attributes be specified so that their achievement can be objectively verified by a prescribed method.

6.3.1.5 External Interface Requirements

6.3.1.5.1 User Interfaces. This should specify:

(1) The characteristics that the software must support for each human interface to the software product. For example, if the user of the system operates through a display terminal, the following should be specified:

(a) Required screen formats

(b) Page layout and content of any reports or menus

(c) Relative timing of inputs and outputs

(d) Availability of some form of programmable function keys

(2) All the aspects of optimizing the interface with the person who must use the system. This may simply comprise a list of do's and don'ts on how the system will appear to the user. One example might be a requirement for the option of long or short error messages. Like all others, these requirements should be verifiable and for example, *a clerk typist grade 4 can do function X in Z min* after 1 h *of training* rather than *a typist can do function X.* (This might also be specified in the Attributes section under a section titled *Ease of Use.*)

6.3.1.5.2 Hardware Interfaces. This should specify the logical characteristics of each interface between the software product and the hardware components of the system. It also covers such matters as what devices are to be supported, how they are to be supported, and protocols. For example, terminal support might specify full screen support as opposed to line by line.

6.3.1.5.3 Software Interfaces. This should specify the use of other required software products (for example, a data management system, an operating system, or a mathematical package), and interfaces with other application systems (for example, the linkage between an accounts receivable system and a general ledger system).

For each required software product, the following should be provided:

(1) Name

(2) Mnemonic

(3) Specification number

(4) Version number

(5) Source

For each interface, this part should:

(1) Discuss the purpose of the interfacing software as related to this software product.

(2) Define the interface in terms of message content and format. It is not necessary to detail any well-documented interface, but a reference to the document defining the interface is required.

6.3.1.5.4 Communications Interfaces. This should specify the various interfaces to communications such as local network protocols, etc.

6.3.1.6 Other Requirements. Certain requirements may, due to the nature of the software, the user organization, etc, be placed in separate categories as indicated below.

6.3.1.6.1 Data Base. This could specify the requirements for any data base that is to be developed as part of the product. This might include:

(1) The types of information identified in 6.3.1.1

(2) Frequency of use

(3) Accessing capabilities

(4) Data element and file descriptors

(5) Relationship of data elements, records and files

(6) Static and dynamic organization

(7) Retention requirements for data

NOTE: If an existing data base package is to be used, this package should be named under *Interfaces to Software* and details of using it specified there.

6.3.1.6.2 Operations. This could specify the normal and special operations required by the user such as:

(1) The various modes of operations in the user organization; for example, user-initiated operations

(2) Periods of interactive operations and periods of unattended operations

(3) Data processing support functions

(4) Backup and recovery operations

NOTE: This is sometimes specified as part of the User Interfaces section.

6.3.1.6.3 Site Adaptation Requirements. This could:

(1) Define the requirements for any data or initialization sequences that are specific to a given site, mission, or operational mode, for example, grid values, safety limits, etc.

(2) Specify the site or mission-related features that should be modified to adapt the software to a particular installation.

6.3.2 Organizing The Specific Requirements. This subsection is often the largest and most complex of all the parts of the SRS.

(1) It may be necessary to organize this section into subdivisions according to the primary classes of functions to be performed by the software. For example, consider a large interactive accounting system. This may be broken down at the top level into operational software (which supports near-real-time transactions), support software (logging functions, disk back-up, loading tapes, etc), and diagnostic software (primarily hardware and communications support), and at the next level into accounts receivable, accounts payable, etc.

(2) It should be remembered, however, that the purpose of this subdivided organization is to improve the readability of the SRS, not to define the high level design of the software being specified.

The best organization for Section 3, Specific Requirements, in an SRS, depends on the application area and the nature of the software product being specified. Tables 2 through 4 show four possible organizations.

(1) In Prototype Outline 1 (Table 2), all the Functional Requirements are specified, then the four types of interface requirements are specified, and then the rest of the requirements are specified.

(2) Prototype Outline 2 (Table 3) shows the four classes of interface requirements applied to each individual Functional Requirement. This is followed by the specification of the rest of the requirements.

(3) In Prototype Outline 3 (Table 4), all of the issues addressed by the Functional Requirements are specified, then the other requirements that apply to them are specified. This pattern is then repeated for each of the External Interface Requirement Classifications.

Table 2
Prototype Outline 1 for SRS Section 3

3. Specific Requirements
  3.1 Functional Requirements
    3.1.1 Functional Requirement 1
      3.1.1.1 Introduction
      3.1.1.2 Inputs
      3.1.1.3 Processing
      3.1.1.4 Outputs
    3.1.2 Functional Requirement 2
    . . . .
    3.1.*n* Functional Requirement *n*
  3.2 External Interface Requirements
    3.2.1 User Interfaces
    3.2.2 Hardware Interfaces
    3.2.3 Software Interfaces
    3.2.4 Communications Interfaces
  3.3 Performance Requirements
  3.4 Design Constraints
    3.4.1 Standards Compliance
    3.4.2 Hardware Limitations
    . . . .
  3.5 Attributes
    3.5.1 Security
    3.5.2 Maintainability
    . . . .
  3.6 Other Requirements
    3.6.1 Data Base
    3.6.2 Operations
    3.6.3 Site Adaptation
    . . . .

Table 3
Prototype Outline 2 for SRS Section 3

3. Specific Requirements
  3.1 Functional Requirements
    3.1.1 Functional Requirement 1
      3.1.1.1 Specification
        3.1.1.1.1 Introduction
        3.1.1.1.2 Inputs
        3.1.1.1.3 Processing
        3.1.1.1.4 Outputs
      3.1.1.2 External Interfaces
        3.1.1.2.1 User Interfaces
        3.1.1.2.2 Hardware Interfaces
        3.1.1.2.3 Software Interfaces
        3.1.1.2.4 Communication Interfaces
    3.1.2 Functional Requirement 2
    . . . .
    3.1.*n* Functional Requirement *n*
  3.2 Performance Requirements
  3.3 Design Constraints
  3.4 Attributes
    3.4.1 Security
    3.4.2 Maintainability
    . . . .
  3.5 Other Requirements
    3.5.1 Data Base
    3.5.2 Operations
    3.5.3 Site Adaption
    . . . .

Table 4
Prototype Outline 3 for SRS Section 3

- 3. Specific Requirements
  - 3.1 Functional Requirements
    - 3.1.1 Functional Requirement 1
      - 3.1.1.1 Introduction
      - 3.1.1.2 Inputs
      - 3.1.1.3 Processing
      - 3.1.1.4 Outputs
      - 3.1.1.5 Performance Requirements
      - 3.1.1.6 Design Constraints
        - 3.1.1.4.1 Standards Compliance
        - 3.1.1.4.2 Hardware Limitations
        - . . . .
      - 3.1.1.7 Attributes
        - 3.1.1.7.1 Security
        - 3.1.1.7.2 Maintainability
        - . . . .
      - 3.1.1.8 Other Requirements
        - 3.1.1.8.1 Data Base
        - 3.1.1.8.2 Operations
        - 3.1.1.8.3 Site Adaption
        - . . . .
    - 3.1.2 Functional Requirement 2
    - . . . .
    - 3.1.*n* Functional Requirement *n*
  - 3.2 External Interface Requirements
    - 3.2.1 User Interfaces
      - 3.2.1.1 Performance Requirements
      - 3.2.1.2 Design Constraints
        - 3.2.1.2.1 Standards Compliance
        - 3.2.1.2.2 Hardware Limitations
        - . . . .
      - 3.2.1.3 Attributes
        - 3.2.1.3.1 Security
        - 3.2.1.3.2 Maintainability
        - . . . .
      - 3.2.1.4 Other Requirements
        - 3.2.1.4.1 Data Base
        - 3.2.1.4.2 Operations
        - 3.2.1.4.3 Site Adaption
        - . . . .
    - 3.2.2 Hardware Interfaces
    - 3.2.3 Software Interfaces
    - 3.2.4 Communications Interfaces

(4) In Prototype Outline 4 (Table 5), the interface requirements and the rest of the requirements are specified as they pertain to each Functional Requirement.

The organization of the Specific Requirements Section of the SRS should be chosen with the goal of properly specifying the requirements in the most readable manner.

6.4 Supporting Information. The supporting information; that is, the Table of Contents, the Appendixes, and the Index, make the SRS easier to use.

(1) The Table of Contents and Index are quite important and should follow the generally accepted rules for good documentation practices.[8]

(2) The Appendixes are not always considered part of the actual requirements specification and are not always necessary. They might include:

(a) Sample I/O formats, descriptions of cost analysis studies, or results of user surveys.

(b) Supporting or background information that can help the readers of the SRS.

(c) A description of the problems to be solved by the software.

(d) The history, background, experience and operational characteristics of the organization to be supported.

(e) A cross-reference list, arranged by milestone, of those incomplete software requirements that are to be completed by specified milestones. (See 4.3.2 and 4.3.3 (4).)

(f) Special packaging instructions for the code and the media to meet security, export, initial loading, or other requirements.

(3) When Appendixes are included, the SRS should explicitly state whether or not the Appendixes are to be considered part of the requirements.

Table 5
Prototype Outline 4 for SRS Section 3

- 3. Specific Requirements
  - 3.1 Functional Requirement 1
    - 3.1.1 Introduction
    - 3.1.2 Inputs
    - 3.1.3 Processing
    - 3.1.4 Outputs
    - 3.1.5 External Interfaces
      - 3.1.5.1 User Interfaces
      - 3.1.5.2 Hardware Interfaces
      - 3.1.5.3 Software Interfaces
      - 3.1.5.4 Communication Interfaces
    - 3.1.6 Performance Requirements
    - 3.1.7 Design Constraints
    - 3.1.8 Attributes
      - 3.1.8.1 Security
      - 3.1.8.2 Maintainability
      - . . . .
    - 3.1.9 Other Requirements
      - 3.1.9.1 Data Base
      - 3.1.9.2 Operations
      - 3.1.9.3 Site Adaption
      - . . . .
  - 3.2 Functional Requirement 2
  - . . . .
  - 3.*n* Functional Requirement *n*

[8]See, for example: [4] and [11].

Recognized as an
American National Standard (ANSI)

IEEE
Std 982.1-1988

IEEE Standard Dictionary of Measures to Produce Reliable Software

Sponsor

**Software Engineering Standards Subcommittee
of the
Technical Committee on Software Engineering
of the
IEEE Computer Society**

Approved June 9, 1988

IEEE Standards Board

Approved August 10, 1989

American National Standards Institute (ANSI)

Foreword

(This Foreword is not a part of IEEE Std 982.1-1988, IEEE Standard Dictionary of Measures to Produce Reliable Software.)

This standard provides a set of measures indicative of software reliability that can be applied to the software product as well as to the development and support processes. It was motivated by the need of software developers and users who are confronted with a plethora of models, techniques, and measures. There is a need for measures that can be applied early in the development process that may be indicators of the reliability of the delivered product. This standard provides a common, consistent definition of a set of measures that may meet those needs.

This standard is intended to serve as the foundation on which researchers and practitioners can build consistent methods. This document is designed to assist management in directing product development and support toward specific reliability goals. Its purpose is to provide a common set of definitions through which a meaningful exchange of data and evaluations can occur. Successful application of the measures is dependent upon their use as intended in the specific environments.

There is both a process goal and a product goal for this document:

(1) The process goal is to provide measures that may be applicable throughout the life cycle and may provide the means for continual self-assessment and reliability improvement.

(2) The product goal is to increase the reliability of the software in its actual use environment during the operations and support phases.

This standard is intended to be of interest to design, development, evaluation (for example, auditors, procuring agency) and maintenance personnel; software quality and software reliability personnel; and to operations and acquisition support managers. This document contains four sections:

Section 1: Scope, establishes the goals and boundaries of the standard.

Section 2: Definitions, serves as a central location for key terms used throughout the body of the document.

Section 3: Functional Classification of Measures, provides a taxonomy with respect to measure objectives.

Section 4: Measures for Reliable Software, presents the measures ordered in general by complexity.

The Software Reliability Measurement Working Group Steering Committee had the following membership:

James Dobbins, *Chairman*

Ray Leber, *Co-Chairman*

Ted Workman, *Co-Chairman*

Peter Bright	Laura Good	Frank Salvia
Antonio Cicu	Nancy Hall	David Siefert
Carlo Cucciati	Philip Marriott	Raghu Singh
Walter Ellis	Roger Martin	Vijaya Srivastava
William Farr	Walter Murch	Henry Trochesset
Stuart Glickman	Patricia Powell	William Wilson

The Software Reliability Measurement Working Group had the following membership:

B. Andrews
S. Beason
R. Berlack
M. Berry
N. Beser
J. Bieman
J. Blackman
J. Bowen
M. Bruyere
F. Buckley
N. Chu
G. Chisholm
G. Clow
J. Corrinne
W. Covington
W. Daney
B. Daniels
F. DeKalb
I. Doshay
E. Dunaye
F. Fisk
A. Florence
D. Frevert
D. Gacke
W. Goss
S. Gray
F. Gray
V. Haas
C. Harrison
S. Hartman
L. Hearn
H. Hecht
R. Hood
J. Horch
D. Hurst
N. Johnson, Jr
R. Kenett
R. Kessler
R. Kumar
M. Landes
R. Lane
J. Latimer
L. Lebowitz
M. Lipow
C. McPherson
A. Moseley
S. Nemecek
K. Nidiffer
K. Oar
R. Panchal
R. Pikul
E. Presson
R. Prudhomme
H. Richter
M. Richter
L. Sanders
R. Sandborgh
H. Schock
D. Simkins
O. Smith
R. Spear
E. Soistman
L. Sprague
A. Stone
D. Sudbeck
R. Sulgrove
D. Town
R. Wamser
J. Wang
D. Winterkorn
J. Wujek
B. Zamastil

The following persons were on the balloting committee that approved this document for submission to the IEEE Standards Board:

F. Ackerman
W. Boll
J. Bowen
P. Bright
F. Buckley
H. Carney
J. Chung
F. Coallier
P. Denny
J. Dobbins
D. Doty
R. Dwyer
W. Ellis
W. Farr
D. Favor
J. Fendrich
G. Fields
J. Forster
D. Gelperin
S. Glickman
S. Gloss-Sloer
L. Good
D. Gustavson
V. Haas
C. Hay
H. Hecht
L. Kaleda
T. Kurihara
G. Larsen
F. C. Lim
B. Lindberg
M. Lipow
B. Livson
P. Marriott
R. Martin
J. McCall
J. Mersky
W. Murch
J. Navlakha
D. Nickle
D. Peercy
W. Perry
P. Petersen
D. Pfeiffer
R. Poston
P. Powell
N. Schneidewind
W. Schnoege
R. Schueppert
R. Shillato
D. Siefert
D. Simkins
R. Singh
V. Srivastava
A. Sukert
K. Tai
R. Thibodeau
P. Thompson
D. Town
H. Trochesset
R. van Tilburg
P. Wolfgang
T. Workman
N. Yopconka

When the IEEE Standards Board approved this standard on June 9, 1988, it had the following membership:

Donald C. Fleckenstein, *Chairman*

Marco Migliaro, *Vice Chairman*

Andrew G. Salem, *Secretary*

Arthur A. Blaisdell
Fletcher J. Buckley
James M. Daly
Stephen R. Dillon
Eugene P. Fogarty
Jay Forster*
Thomas L. Hannan
Kenneth D. Hendrix
Theodore W. Hissey, Jr.
John W. Horch
Jack M. Kinn
Frank D. Kirschner
Frank C. Kitzantides
Joseph L. Koepfinger*
Irving Kolodny
Edward Lohse
John E. May, Jr.
Lawrence V. McCall
L. Bruce McClung
Donald T. Michael*
Richard E. Mosher
L. John Rankine
Gary S. Robinson
Frank L. Rose
Helen M. Wood
Karl H. Zaininger
Donald W. Zipse

*Member Emeritus

Contents

PAGE

FIGURES

TABLES

List of Symbols

Symbol	Meaning	Measures Used	Primitive/ Metric
A	(1) Number of arrivals during time period T (2) Reliability growth factor	37 26	P M
A_{existing}	Number of ambiguities in a program remaining to be eliminated	6	P
$A(t)$	System availability	39	M
A_{tot}	Total number of ambiguities identified	6	P
α	Test accuracy	36	M
AQ	Average queue length	37	M
AS	Average service time	37	P
B	Software science measure (number of errors)	14	M
B_1	Number of functions not satisfactorily defined	35	P
B_2	Number of functions	35	P
B_3	Number of data references not having an origin	35	P
B_4	Number of data references	35	P
B_5	Number of defined functions not used	35	P
B_6	Number of defined functions	35	P
B_7	Number of referenced functions not defined	35	P
B_8	Number of referenced functions	35	P
B_9	Number of decision points not using all conditions, options	35	P
B_{10}	Number of decision points	35	P
B_{11}	Number of condition options without processing	35	P
B_{12}	Number of condition options	35	P
B_{13}	Number of calling routines with parameters not agreeing with defined parameters	35	P
B_{14}	Number of calling routines	35	P
B_{15}	Number of condition options not set	35	P
B_{16}	Number of set condition options having no processing	35	P
B_{17}	Number of set condition options	35	P
B_{18}	Number of data references having no destination	35	P
β	Observed hardware failure rate	39	P
C	Complexity metric (static, dynamic, cyclomatic)	15, 16	M
c_i	Complexity for program invocation and return along each edge e_i as determined by the user	15	P
CE	Cause and effect measure	6	M
CM	Completeness measure	35	M
D	Software science measure (program difficulty)	14	M
d_k	Complexity for allocation of resource k as determined by the user	15	P

Symbol	Meaning	Measures Used	Primitive/ Metric
D_i	Total number of unique defects detected during the *i*th design or code inspection process or the *i*th life cycle phase	2, 8	P
DD	Defect density	2	M
DEs	Decomposition elements	23	P
DI	Defect index	8	M
DSM	Design structure metric	19	M
datain	Number of data structures from which the procedure retrieves data	25	P
dataout	Number of data structures that the procedure updates	25	P
E	(1) Number of edges (2) Software science measure (effort)	15, 16, 17 14	P M
e_i	Number of entry points for the *i*th module	13	P
F or F_i	Total number of unique faults found in a given time interval resulting in failures of a specified severity level	1	P
f or f_i	Total number of failures of a given severity level in a given time interval	3, 20, 21, 27, 31	P
F_d	Fault density	1	M
f_{ij}	Frequency execution of intermodule transfer from module *i* to *j*	38	P
F_a	Number of software functions (modules) in the current delivery that are additions in the current delivery	10	P
F_c	Number of software functions (modules) in the current delivery that include internal changes from a previous delivery	10	P
FD	Fault days metric	4	M
FD_i	Fault days for the *i*th fault	4	P
F_{del}	Number of software functions (modules) in the previous delivery that are deleted in the current delivery	10	P
FE	Number of the software functional (modular) requirements for which all test cases have been satisfactorily completed	5	P
F_{it}	Total number of faults detected to date in software integration testing	29	P
F_{pit}	Number of faults detected prior to software integration testing	29	P
FT	Total number of software functional (modular) test requirements	5	P
Γ	Average rate of jobs	37	M
ϒ	Observed hardware repair rate	39	P
I	Total number of inspections to date	2, 11	P
IFC	Information flow complexity	25	M
J	Total number of jobs completed	37	P
K	Number of resources	15	P

Symbol	Meaning	Measures Used	Primitive/ Metric
k	Number of runs for the specified period of time	18	P
KSLOC	Number of source lines of executable code and nonexecutable data declarations in thousands	1, 2, 8	P
KSLOD	Number of source lines of design statements in thousands that have been inspected to date	2, 8	P
L	Software science measure (observed program length)	14	M
l	Software science measure (program vocabulary)	14	M
Ll	Software science measure (program level)	14	M
$\lambda(t)$	Failure rate function	31	M
λ	Observed software failure rate	39	P
length	Number of source statements in a procedure	25	P
lfi	Local flows into a procedure	25	P
lfo	Local flows from a procedure	25	P
M	Manhours per major defect detected	11	M
M_i	Number of medium defects found	8	P
m_i	Number of entry and exit points for module i	13	M
MD	Number of modules	38	P
$ME(i)$	Measure effectiveness for the ith issue	34	P
M_{it}	Number of modules integrated	29	M
M_T	Number of software functions (modules) in the current delivery	10	M
M_{tot}	Total number of modules in final configuration	29	M
MTTF	Mean-time-to-failure	30	M
μi	Observed software fault correction rate with i faults in the software	39	P
N	Number of nodes	15, 16, 17	P
nc	Number of correct runs in a given test sample	18, 26	P
NF	Total number of faults within a program	29, 39	M
NF_{rem}	Total number of faults remaining within a program	22, 29	M
NF_{rem} (%)	Percentage of faults remaining within a program	36	M
n_F	Number of faults found that were not intentionally seeded	22	P
NR	Number of runs (or test cases) in a given test sample	18, 26	P
NS	Total number of stages	26	P
N_s	Number of seeded faults	22, 36	P
n_s	Number of seeded faults found	22	P
$N1$	Total number of occurrences of the operators in a program	14	P
$n1$	Number of distinct operators in a program	14	P

Symbol	Meaning	Measures Used	Primitive/ Metric
$N2$	Total number of occurrences of the operands in a program	14	P
$n2$	Number of distinct operands in a program	14	P
N_1	Number of errors detected using SVDs due to inconsistencies	23	P
N_2	Number of errors detected using SVDs due to incompleteness	23	P
N_3	Number of errors detected using SVDs due to misinterpretation	23	P
P	Probability measure over the sample space	18	P
p_n	Probability of repairing a hardware failure correctly	39	P
P_i	(1) Probability that the ith run is selected from the sample space	18, 38	P
	(2) Probability that the ith process that can be generated in a user environment is selected	39	P
P_s	Probability of correcting a software fault when detected	39	P
$P_{N,n}(t)$	System upstate probabilities	39	P
PI_i	Phase index metric for the ith life cycle phase	8	M
PL	Purity level	21	M
PS	Product size	8	P
$P1$	Total number of modules in the program	19	P
$P2$	Number of modules dependent on the input or output	19	P
$P3$	Number of modules dependent on prior processing	19	P
$P4$	Number of database elements	19	P
$P5$	Number of nonunique database elements	19	P
$P6$	Number of database segments (partition of the state)	19	P
$P7$	Number of modules not single entrance/single exit	19	P
Q	Queue length distribution	37	P
q_i	Probability that P_i will be generated in a user environment	38	P
R	(1) Total response time for each functional job	37	M
	(2) Reliability of the system	38	M
R_i	Reliability of the ith module	38	P
R_k	Run reliability at a specified stage	18, 26	M
$R(t)$	Reliability function	31	M
r_i	Flag to denote if the ith process generates the correct software system output	38	P
r_{ki}	Resource status array indicator flags	15	P
RG	Number of regions	16, 17	P
$RK(i)$	Risk factor for the ith measure	34	M
RT	Response time distribution	37	P
$R1$	Number of requirements met by the architecture	7	P

Symbol	Meaning	Measures Used	Primitive/ Metric
$R2$	Number of original requirements	7	P
S	Sample space of possible input patterns and states	18	P
S_i	Point from the sample space of possible inputs	18	P
s_i	Number of serious defects found	8, 11	P
SB	Total amount of time server is busy	37	P
SE	Server's efficiency	37	M
SN	Number of splitting nodes	16, 17	P
SMI	Software maturity index	10	M
ST	Service time distribution	37	P
T	(1) Time period over which measurements are made (2) Time	37 14	P M
T_i	Number of trivial defects found	8	P
t_i	Observed times between failures of a given severity level	20, 21, 27 28, 30, 31	P
TC	Test coverage	24	M
TM	Traceability measure	7	M
T_1	Time expended by the inspection team in preparation for design or code inspection meeting	11	P
T_2	Time expended by the inspection team in conduct of a design or code inspection meeting	11	P
U	Utilization	37	P
V	Software science measure (program volume)	14	M
VR	Number of requests per functional job for each server during time period T	37	P
W_i	Weighting distribution	8, 19, 34	P
WT	Waiting time distribution	37	P
X	Throughput	37	P
x_i	Number of exit points for the ith module	13	P

NOTE: P stands for primitive
M stands for derived metric

IEEE Standard Dictionary of Measures to Produce Reliable Software

1. Introduction

1.1 Scope. The objective of this standard is to provide the software community with defined measures currently used as indicators of reliability. The predictive nature of these measures is dependent on correct application of a valid model.

This standard presents a selection of applicable measures, the proper conditions for using each measure, the methods of computation, and the framework for a common language among users. It moreover provides the means for continual assessment of the process, as well as the products, at each phase of the life cycle. By emphasizing early reliability assessment, this standard supports methods through measurement to improve the product reliability. Successful application of the measures is dependent upon their use as intended in the specified environments.

Applicability is not restricted by the size, type, complexity, or criticality of the software. Typical life cycle phases based upon ANSI/IEEE Std 729-1983 [1],[1] are used to illustrate when each of the measures may be applied.

Errors, faults, and failures serve as primitive units for the majority of the measures.

1.2 References. The following publications shall be used in conjunction with this standard:

[1] ANSI/IEEE Std 729-1983, IEEE Standard Glossary of Software Engineering Terminology.[2]

[2] Software Maintainability — Evaluation Guide, AFOTEC Pamphlet 800-2, vol 3, Mar 1987.[3]

2. Definitions

Most of the definitions listed below can be found in ANSI/IEEE Std 729-1983 [1], IEEE Standard Glossary of Software Engineering Terminology. The definitions of the terms *concept phase*, *defect*, *measure*, *primitive*, and *software management* are not present in ANSI/IEEE Std 729-1983 [1], and establish meaning in the context of this standard. The acronym ISO (International Organization for Standardization) indicates that the definition is also accepted by ISO.

concept phase. The period of time in the software life cycle during which system concepts and objectives needed by the user are identified and documented. Precedes the requirements phase.

defect. A product anomaly. Examples include such things as (1) omissions and imperfections found during early life cycle phases and (2) faults contained in software sufficiently mature for test or operation. See also **fault**.

error. Human action that results in software containing a fault. Examples include omission or misinterpretation of user requirements in a software specification, incorrect translation, or omission of a requirement in the design specification (ANSI/IEEE Std 729-1983 [1]).

failure. (1) The termination of the ability of a functional unit to perform its required function (ISO; ANSI/IEEE Std 729-1983 [1]).

[1] The numbers in brackets correspond to those of the references listed in 1.2.

[2] ANSI/IEEE publications are available from the Sales Department, American National Standards Institute, 1430 Broadway, New York, NY 10018, or from the Institute of Electrical and Electronics Engineers, Service Center, 445 Hoes Lane, P.O. Box 1331, Piscataway, NJ 08854-1331.

[3] AFOTEC publications are available from the Air Force Operational Test and Evaluation Center (AFOTEC/DAP), Kirtland Air Force Base, NM 87117-7001.

(2) An event in which a system or system component does not perform a required function within specified limits. A failure may be produced when a fault is encountered (ANSI/IEEE Std 729-1983 [1]).

fault. (1) An accidental condition that causes a functional unit to fail to perform its required function (ISO; ANSI/IEEE Std 729-1983 [1]).

(2) A manifestation of an error in software. A fault, if encounterred, may cause a failure. Synonymous with **bug** (ANSI/IEEE Std 729-1983 [1]).

measure. A quantitative assessment of the degree to which a software product or process possesses a given attribute.

primitive. Data relating to the development or use of software that is used in developing measures or quantitative descriptions of software. Primitives are directly measurable or countable, or may be given a constant value or condition for a specific measure. Examples include: error, failure, fault, time, time interval, date, number of noncommentary source code statements, edges, and nodes.

software reliability. The probability that software will not cause the failure of a system for a specified time under specified conditions. The probability is a function of the inputs to and use of the system as well as a function of the existence of faults in the software. The inputs to the system determine whether existing faults, if any, are encountered (ANSI/IEEE Std 729-1983 [1]).

software reliability management. The process of optimizing the reliability of software through a program that emphasizes software error prevention, fault detection and removal, and the use of measurements ot maximize reliability in light of project constraints such as resources (cost), schedule, and performance.

3. Functional Classification of Measures

The measures can be divided into two functional categories: product and process (Table 3-1). Product measures are applied to the software objects produced and are divided into six subcategories. Process measures are applied to the activities of development, test, and maintenance. Process measures are divided into three subcategories.

3.1 Product Measures. The product measures address cause and effect of the static and dynamic aspects of both projected reliabilty prior to operation, and operational reliability. As an example, reliability may change radically during the maintenance effort, due to the complexity of the system design. These product measures cover more than the correctness aspect of reliability; they also address the system utility aspect of reliability. The following six product measure subcategories address these dimensions of reliability:

(1) Errors; Faults; Failures — Count of defects with respect to human cause, program bugs, observed system malfunctions.
(2) Mean-Time-to-Failure; Failure Rate — Derivative measures of defect occurrence and time.
(3) Reliability Growth and Projection — The assessment of change in failure-freeness of the product under testing and in operation.
(4) Remaining Product Faults — The assessment of fault-freeness of the product in development, test, or maintenance.
(5) Completeness and Consistency — The assessment of the presence and agreement of all necessary software system parts.
(6) Complexity — The assessment of complicating factors in a system.

3.2 Process Measures. The three process measure subcategories are directly related to process management:

(1) Management Control — The assessment of guidance of the development and maintenance processes.
(2) Coverage — The assessment of the presence of all necessary activities to develop or maintain the software product.
(3) Risk; Benefit; Cost Evaluation — The assessment of the process tradeoffs of cost, schedule, and performance.

The measure classification matrix (Table 3-1) is a cross index of the measures and functional categories and can be used to select measures applicable to each category.

4. Measures for Reliable Software

4.1 Fault Density

4.1.1 Application. This measure can be used to

(1) Predict remaining faults by comparison with expected fault density.

Table 3-1
Measure Classification Matrix

MEASURE CATEGORIES	PRODUCT MEASURES						PROCESS MEASURES		
Measures	Errors; Faults; Failures	Mean-Time-to-Failure; Failure Rate	Reliability Growth & Projection	Remaining Product Faults	Completeness & Consistency	Complexity	Management Control	Coverage	Risk Benefit; Cost Evaluation
1. Fault density	X								
2. Defect density	X								
3. Cumulative failure profile	X								
4. Fault - days number	X						X		
5. Functional test coverage					X			X	X
6. Cause and effect graphing					X			X	
7. Requirements traceability	X				X			X	
8. Defect indices	X						X		
9. Error distribution(s)							X		
10. Software maturity index			X						X
11. Man hours per major defect detected							X		X
12. Number of conflicting requirements	X				X			X	
13. Number of entries/exits per module						X			
14. Software science measures				X		X			X
15. Graph-theoretic complexity for architecture						X			
16. Cyclomatic complexity					X	X			
17. Minimal unit test case determination					X	X			
18. Run reliability			X						X
19. Design structure						X			X
20. Mean time to discover the next *K* faults							X		X
21. Software purity level			X						X
22. Estimated number of faults remaining (seeding)				X					
23. Requirements compliance	X				X			X	
24. Test coverage					X			X	
25. Data or information flow complexity						X			
26. Reliability growth function			X						
27. Residual fault count				X					X
28. Failure analysis using elapsed time			X	X					
29. Testing sufficiency			X					X	
30. Mean-time-to-failure		X	X						
31. Failure rate		X							X
32. Software documentation & source listings					X			X	
33. RELY (Required Software Reliability)								X	X
34. Software release readiness									X
35. Completeness					X			X	
36. Test accuracy				X	X			X	
37. System performance reliability			X						
38. Independent process **reliability**			X						
39. Combined HW/SW system operational availability			X						

(2) Determine if sufficient testing has been completed based on predetermined goals for severity class.
(3) Establish standard fault densities for comparison and prediction.

4.1.2 Primitives. Establish the severity levels for failure designation.

F = total number of unique faults found in a given time interval resulting in failures of a specified severity level

KSLOC = number of source lines of executable code and nonexecutable data declarations in thousands

4.1.3 Implementation. Establish severity, failure types, and fault types.

(1) Failure types might include I/O and user. Fault types might result from design, coding, documentation, and initialization.
(2) Observe and log each failure.
(3) Determine the program fault(s) that caused the failure. Classify the faults by type. Additional faults may be found resulting in total faults being greater than the number of failures observed. Or one fault may manifest itself by several failures. Thus, fault and failure density may both be measured.
(4) Determine total lines of executable and nonexecutable data declaration source code (KSLOC).
(5) Calculate the fault density for a given severity level as

$$F_d = F/K\text{SLOC}$$

4.2 Defect Density

4.2.1 Application. The defect density measure can be used after design and code inspections of new development or large block modifications. If the defect density is outside the norm after several inspections, it is an indication that the inspection process requires further scrutiny.

4.2.2 Primitives. Establish severity levels for defect designation.

D_i = total number of unique defects detected during the ith design or code inspection process

I = total number of inspections

KSLOD = in the design phase, the number of source lines of design statements in thousands

KSLOC = in the implementation phase, the number of source lines of executable code and nonexecutable data declarations in thousands

4.2.3 Implementation. Establish a classification scheme for severity and class of defect. For each inspection, record the product size, and the total number of unique defects. For example, in the design phase, calculate the ratio

$$DD = \frac{\sum_{i=1}^{I} D_i}{K\text{SLOD}}$$

This measure assumes that a structured design language is used. However, if some other design methodology is used, then some other unit of defect density has to be developed to conform to the methodology in which the design is expressed.

4.3 Cumulative Failure Profile

4.3.1 Applications. This is a graphical method used to

(1) Predict reliability through the use of failure profiles.
(2) Estimate additional testing time to reach an acceptability reliable system.
(3) Identify modules and subsystems that require additional testing.

4.3.2 Primitives. Establish the severity levels for failure designation.

f_i = total number of failures of a given severity level in a given time interval, i=1, ...

4.3.3 Implementation. Plot cumulative failures versus a suitable time base. The curve can be derived for the system as a whole, subsystems, or modules.

4.4 Fault-Days Number

4.4.1 Application. This measure represents the number of days that faults spend in the software system from their creation to their removal.

4.4.2 Primitives

(1) Phase when the fault was introduced in the system.
(2) Date when the fault was introduced in the system.
(3) Phase, date, and time when the fault is removed.

FD_i = fault days for the ith fault

NOTE: For more meaningful measures, the time unit can be made relative to test time or operational time.

4.4.3 Implementation. For each fault detected and removed, during any phase, the number of days from its creation to its removal is determined (fault-days).

The fault-days are then summed for all faults detected and removed, to get the fault-days number at system level, including all faults detected/removed up to the delivery date. In cases when the creation date for the fault is not known, the fault is assumed to have been created at the middle of the phase in which it was introduced.

In Fig 4.4.3-1 the fault-days for the design fault for module A can be accurately calculated because the design approval date for the detailed design of module A is known. The fault introduced during the requirements phase is assumed to have been created at the middle of the requirement phase because the exact knowledge of when the corresponding piece of requirement was specified, is not known.

The measure is calculated as shown in Fig 4.4.3-1.

4.5 Functional or Modular Test Coverage

4.5.1 Application. This measure is used to quantify a software test coverage index for a software delivery. The primitives counted may be either functions or modules. The operational user is most familiar with the system functional requirements and will report system problems in terms of functional requirements rather than module test requirements. It is the task of the evaluator to obtain or develop the functional requirements and associated module cross reference table.

4.5.2 Primitives

FE = number of the software functional (modular) requirements for which all test cases have been satisfactorily completed

FT = total number of software functional (modular) requirements

4.5.3 Implementation. The test coverage index is expressed as a ratio of the number of software functions (modules) tested to the total number of software functions (modules) that make up the users (developers) requirements. This ratio is expressed as

$$\text{FUNCTIONAL (MODULAR) TEST COVERAGE INDEX} = \frac{FE}{FT}$$

4.6 Cause and Effect Graphing

4.6.1 Application. Cause and effect graphing aids in identifying requirements that are incomplete and ambiguous. This measure explores the inputs and expected outputs of a program and identifies the ambiguities. Once these ambiguities are eliminated, the specifications are considered complete and consistent.

Cause and effect graphing can also be applied to generate test cases in any time of computing application where the specification is clearly stated (that is, no ambiguities) and combinations of input conditions can be identified. It is used in developing and designing test cases that have a

Fig 4.4.3-1
Calculation of Fault-Days

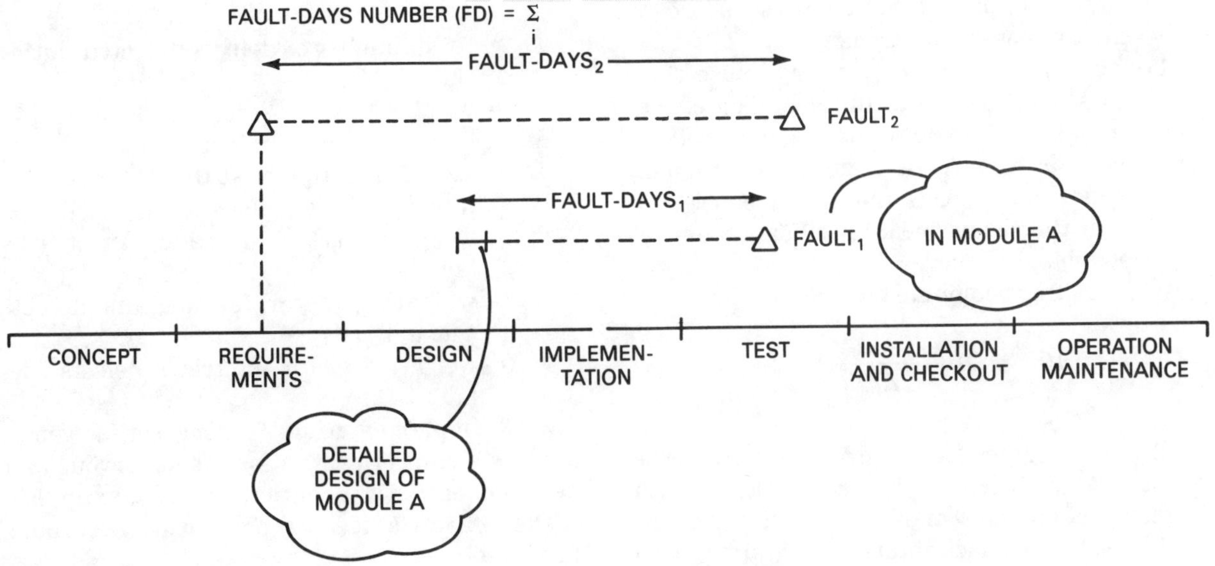

high probability of detecting faults that exist in programs. It is not concerned with the internal structure or behavior of the program.

4.6.2 Primitives

List of causes: distinct input conditions

List of effects: distinct output conditions or system transformation (effects are caused by changes in the state of the system)

$A_{existing}$ = number of ambiguities in a program remaining to be eliminated

A_{tot} = total number of ambiguities identified

4.6.3 Implementation. A cause and effect graph is a formal translation of a natural language specification into its input conditions and expected outputs. The graph depicts a combinatorial logic network.

To begin, identify all requirements of the system and divide them into separate identifiable entities. Carefully analyze the requirements to identify all the causes and effects in the specification. After the analysis is completed, assign each cause and effect a unique identifier. For example, E1 for effect one or I1 for input one.

To create the cause and effect graph:

(1) Represent each cause and each effect by a node identified by its unique number.

(2) Interconnect the cause and effect nodes by analyzing the semantic content of the specification and transforming it into a Boolean graph. Each cause and effect can be in one of two states: true or false. Using Boolean logic, set the possible states of the causes and determine under what conditions each effect will be present.

(3) Annotate the graph with constraints describing combinations of causes and effects that are impossible because of semantic or environmental constraints.

(4) Identify as an ambiguity any cause that does not result in a corresponding effect, any effect that does not originate with a cause as a source, and any combination of causes and effects that are inconsistent with the requirement specification or impossible to achieve.

The measure is computed as follows:

$$CE(\%) = 100 \times \left(1 - \frac{A_{existing}}{A_{tot}}\right)$$

To derive test cases for the program, convert the graph into a limited entry decision table with "effects" as columns and "causes" as rows. For each effect, trace back through the graph to find all combinations of causes that will set the effect to be TRUE. Each combination is represented as a column in the decision table. The state of all other effects should also be determined for each such combination. Each column in the table represents a test case.

4.7 Requirements Traceability

4.7.1 Application. This measure aids in identifying requirements that are either missing from, or in addition to, the original requirements.

4.7.2 Primitives

$R1$ = number of requirements met by the architecture

$R2$ = number of original requirements

4.7.3 Implementation. A set of mappings from the requirements in the software architecture to the original requirements is created. Count each requirement met by the architecture ($R1$) and count each of the original requirements ($R2$). Compute the traceability measure (TM):

$$TM = \frac{R1}{R2} \times 100\%$$

4.8 Defect Indices

4.8.1 Application. This measure provides a continuing, relative index of how correct the software is as it proceeds through the development cycle. This measure is a straightforward phase dependent, weighted, calculation that requires no knowledge of advanced mathematics or statistics. This measure may be applied as early in the life cycle as the user has products that can be evaluated.

4.8.2 Primitives. For each phase in the life cycle:

D_i = total number of defects detected during the ith phase

S_i = number of serious defects found

M_i = number of medium defects found

PS = size of the product at the ith phase

T_i = number of trivial defects found

W_1 = weighting factor for serious defects (default is 10)

W_2 = weighting factor for medium defects (default is 3)

W_3 = weighting factor for trivial defects (default is 1)

4.8.3 Implementation. The measure is generated as a sum of calculations taken throughout development. It is a continuing measure applied to the software as it proceeds from design through final tests.

At each phase of development, calculate the phase index (PI_i) associated with the number and severity of defects.

$$PI_i = W_1 \frac{S_i}{D_i} + W_2 \frac{M_i}{D_i} + W_3 \frac{T_i}{D_i}$$

The defect index (DI) is calculated at each phase by cumulatively adding the calculation for PI_i as the software proceeds through development:

$$DI = \sum_i (i * PI_i)/PS$$

$$= (PI_1 + 2PI_2 + 2PI_3 + \ldots + iPI_i + \ldots)/PS$$

where each phase is weighted such that the further into development the software has progressed, such as phase 2 or 3, the larger the weight (that is, 2 or 3, respectively) assigned.

The data collected in prior projects can be used as a baseline figure for comparison.

4.9 Error Distribution(s)

4.9.1 Application. The search for the causes of software faults and failures involves the analysis of the defect data collected during each phase of the software development. Distribution of the errors allows ranking of the predominant failure modes.

4.9.2 Primitives. Error description:

(1) Associated faults
(2) Types
(3) Severity
(4) Phase introduced
(5) Preventive measure
(6) Discovery mechanism, including reasons for earlier nondetection of associated faults

4.9.3 Implementation. The primitives for each error are recorded and the errors are counted according to the criteria adopted for each classification. The number of errors are then plotted for each class. Examples of such distribution plots are shown in Fig 4.9.3-1. In the three examples of Fig 4.9.3-1, the errors are classified and counted by phase, by the cause, and by the cause for deferred fault detection. Other similar classification could be used such as the type of steps suggested to prevent the reoccurrence of similar errors or the type of steps suggested for earlier detection of the corresponding faults.

4.10 Software Maturity Index

4.10.1 Application. This measure is used to quantify the readiness of a software product. Changes from a previous baseline to the current baseline are an indication of the current product stability. A baseline can be either an internal release or an external delivery.

4.10.2 Primitives

M_T = number of software functions (modules) in the current delivery

F_c = number of software functions (modules) in the current delivery that include internal changes from a previous delivery

F_a = number of software functions (modules) in the current delivery that are additions to the previous delivery

F_{del} = number of software functions (modules) in the previous delivery that are deleted in the current delivery

4.10.3 Implementation. The software maturity index (SMI) may be calculated in two different ways depending on the available data (primitives).

4.10.3.1 Implementation #1

(1) For the present (just delivered or modified) software baseline, count the number of functions (modules) that have been changed (F_c).
(2) For the present software baseline, count the number of functions (modules) that have been added (F_a) or deleted (F_{del}).
(3) For the present software baseline, count the number of functions (modules) that make up that baseline (M_T).

Calculate the maturity index:

$$\text{MATURITY INDEX} = \frac{\text{NUMBER OF CURRENT FUNCTIONS (MODULES)} - \left(\text{NUMBER OF CURRENT BASELINE FUNCTIONS (MODULES) THAT HAVE BEEN ADDED} + \text{NUMBER OF FUNCTIONS (MODULES) CHANGED} + \text{NUMBER OF CURRENT BASELINE FUNCTIONS (MODULES) THAT HAVE BEEN DELETED}\right)}{\text{NUMBER OF CURRENT FUNCTIONS (MODULES)}}$$

that is

$$SMI = \frac{M_T - (F_a + F_c + F_{del})}{M_T}$$

Notice that the total number of current functions (modules) equals the number of previous functions (modules) plus the number of current baseline functions (modules) that were added to the previous baseline minus the number of functions (modules) that were deleted from the previous baseline. In the software maturity index calculation, the deletion of a function (module) is treated the same as an addition of a function (module).

4.10.3.2 Implementation #2. The software maturity index may be estimated as

$$SMI = \frac{M_T - F_c}{M_T}$$

The change and addition of functions (modules) is tracked and the maturity index is calculated

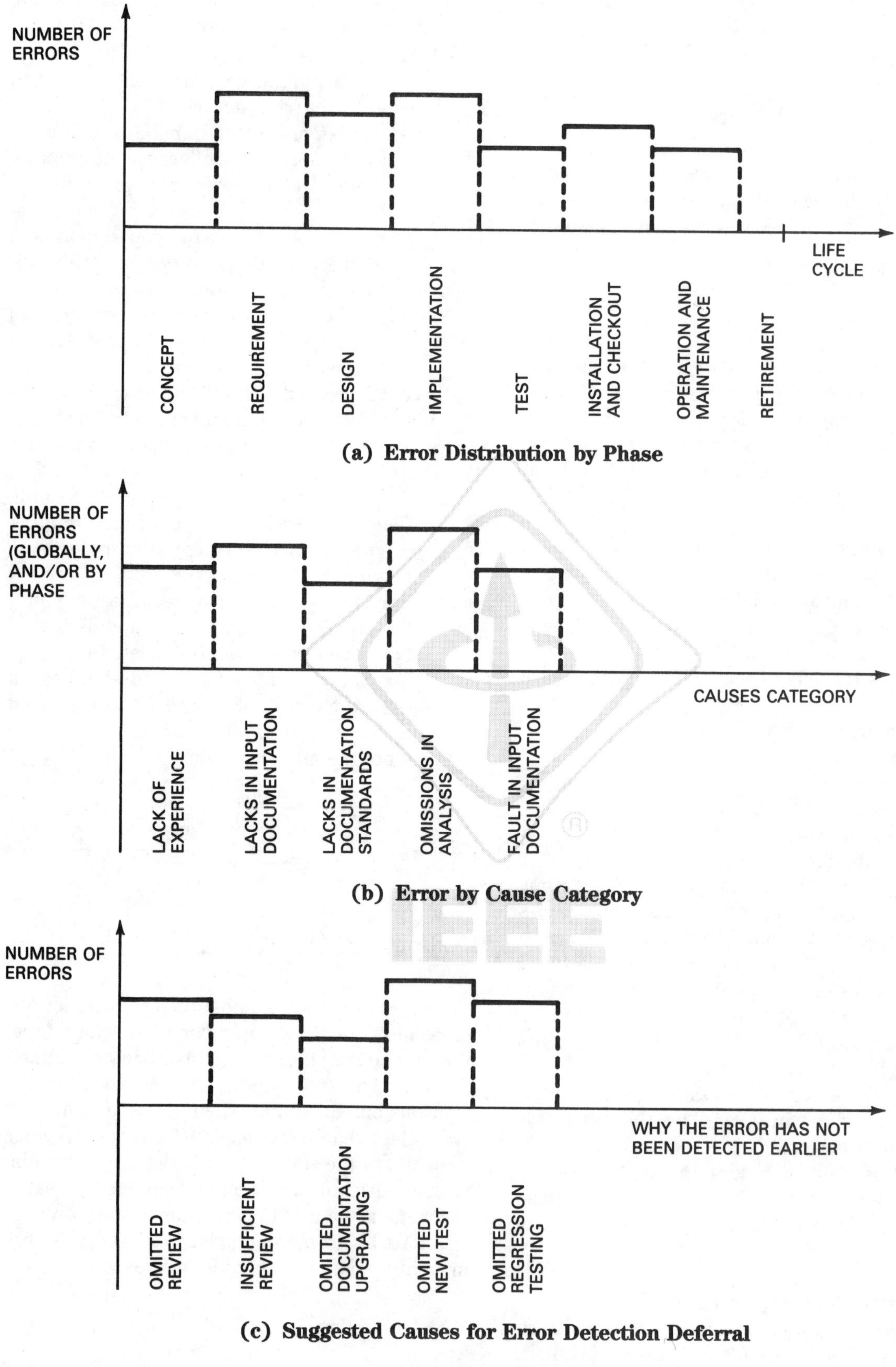

Fig 4.9.3-1
Error Analysis

for each baseline. Problem reports that would result in a software update subsequent to the tracking period are included in the maturity analysis by estimating the configuration of the subsequent baselines.

4.11 Manhours per Major Defect Detected

4.11.1 Application. The design and code inspection processes are two of the most effective defect removal processes available. The early removal of defects at the design and implementation phases, if done effectively and efficiently, significantly improves the reliability of the developed product and allows a more controlled test environment. This measure provides a quantitative figure that can be used to evaluate the efficiency of the design and code inspection processes.

4.11.2 Primitives

T_1 = time expended by the inspection team in preparation for design or code inspection meeting

T_2 = time expended by the inspection team in conduct of a design or code inspection meeting

S_i = number of major (nontrivial) defects detected during the ith inspection

I = total number of inspections to date

4.11.3 Implementation. At each inspection meeting, record the total preparation time expended by the inspection team. Also, record the total time expended in conducting the inspection meeting. All defects are recorded and grouped into major/minor categores. (A major defect is one which must be corrected for the product to function within specified requirements.)

The inspection times are summarized and the defects are cumulatively added. The computation should be performed during design and code. If the design is not written in a structural design language, then this measure can be only applied during the implementation phase.

The manhours per major defect detected is

$$M = \frac{\sum_{i=1}^{I} (T_1 + T_2)_i}{\sum_{i=1}^{I} S_i}$$

This computation should be initiated after approximately 8000 lines of detailed design or code have been inspected.

4.12 Number of Conflicting Requirements

4.12.1 Application. This measure is used to determine the reliability of a software system, resulting from the software architecture under consideration, as represented by a specification based on the entity-relationship-attribute model.

4.12.2 Primitives

(1) List of the inputs
(2) List of the outputs
(3) List of the functions performed by the program

4.12.3 Implementation. The mappings from the software architecture to the requirements are identified. Mappings from the same specification item to more than one differing requirement are examined for requirements inconsistency. Mappings from more than one specification item to a single requirement are examined for specification inconsistency.

4.13 Number of Entries and Exits per Module

4.13.1 Application. This measure is used to determine the difficulty of a software architecture, as represented by entry and exist points identified in a modular specification or design language.

4.13.2 Primitives

e_i = number of entry points for the ith module

x_i = number of exit points for the ith module

4.13.3 Implementation. The number of entry points and exit points for each module is

$$m_i = e_i + x_i$$

4.14 Software Science Measures

4.14.1 Application. These measures apply the Halstead Software Science to the properties and structure of computer programs. They provide measures of the complexity of existing software, predict the length of a program, and estimate the amount of time an average programmer can be expected to use to implement a given algorithm.

This measure computes the program length by counting "operators" and "operands." The measure suggests that the difficulty of a given program can be derived, based on the above counts.

4.14.2 Primitives

$n1$ = number of distinct operators in a program

$n2$ = number of distinct operands in a program

$N1$ = total number of occurrences of the operators in a program

$N2$ = total number of occurrences of the operands in a program

4.14.3 Implementation. Once the source code has been written, this measure can be applied to predict the program difficulty and other derived quantities using the following equations:

Program vocabulary: $l = n1 + n2$

Observed program length: $L = N1 + N2$

Estimated program length: $L = n1\,(\log_2 n1) + n2\,(\log_2 n2)$

Program volume: $V = L\,(\log_2 n)$

Program difficulty: $D = (n1/2)\,(N2/n2)$

Program level: $L1 = 1/D$

Effort: $E = \dfrac{V}{L1}$

Number of errors: $B = \dfrac{V}{3000} \simeq \dfrac{E^{2/3}}{3000}$

Time: $T = E/S$ (S = Stroud number; typical value is 18 elementary mental discriminations per second)

An alternate expression to estimate the program length is the factorial length estimator:

$$\hat{L} = \log_2((n1)!) + (\log_2((n2)!)$$

4.15 Graph-Theoretic Complexity for Architecture

4.15.1 Application. Complexity measures can be applied early in the product life cycle for development trade-offs as well as to assure system and module comprehensibility adequate for correct and efficient maintenance. Many system faults are introduced in the operational phase by modifications to systems that are reliable but difficult to understand. In time, a system's entropy increases making a fault insertion more likely with each new change. Through complexity measures the developer plans ahead for correct change by establishing initial order and thereby improves the continuing reliability of the system throughout its operational life.

There are three graph-theoretic complexity measures for software architecture:

(1) Static Complexity — A measure of software architecture, as represented by a network of modules, useful for design trade-off analyses. Network complexity is a function based on the countable properties of the modules (nodes) and intermodule connections (edges) in the network.

(2) Generalized Static Complexity — A measure of software architecture, as represented by a network of modules and the resources used. Since resources are acquired or released when programs are invoked in other modules, it is desirable to measure the complexity associated with allocation of those resources in addition to the basic (static) network complexity.

(3) Dynamic Complexity — A measure of software architecture, as represented by a network of modules during execution, rather than at rest, as is the case for the static measures. For example, modules may execute at different frequencies.

4.15.2 Primitives

K = number of resources, index by $K = 1, \ldots, K$

E = number of edges, indexed by $i = 1, \ldots, E$

N = number of nodes, indexed by $j = 1, \ldots, N$

c_i = complexity for program invocation and return along each edge e_i as determined by the user (such as operating system complexity)

Resource status array $R(K,E)$

$$r_{ki} = \begin{cases} 1 & \text{if } k\text{th resource is required for the } i\text{th edge } (e_i) \\ 0 & \text{otherwise} \end{cases}$$

d_k = complexity for allocation of resource k as determined by the user (for example, complexity associated with a procedure used to gain exclusive access to common data)

4.15.3 Implementation. Using nodes and edges, a strongly connected graph of the network is required. A strongly connected graph is one in which a node is reachable from any other node. This is accomplished by adding an edge between the exit node and the entry node. Each node represents a module that may or may not be executed concurrently with another module. Each edge represents program invocation and return between modules. In this case the edges are called single paths.

(1) Static Complexity — Once a strongly connected graph is constructed, with modules as nodes, and transfer of control as edges, the static complexity is calculated as

$$C = E - N + 1$$

(2) Generalized Static Complexity — Resources (storage, time, logic complexity, or other measurable factors) are allocated when programs are invoked in other modules. Given a network and resources to be controlled in the network, the generalized static complexity associated with allocation of these resources is

$$C = \sum_{i=1}^{E}\left(c_i + \sum_{k=1}^{K}(d_k * r_{ki})\right)$$

(3) Dynamic Complexity — A change in the number of edges may result from module interruption due to invocations and re-

turns. An average dynamic network complexity can be derived over a given time period to account for the execution of modules at different frequencies and also for module interruption during execution. Dynamic complexity is calculated using the formula for static complexity at various points in time. The behavior of the measure (ex. time average) is then used to indicate the evolution of the complexity of the software.

4.16 Cyclomatic Complexity

4.16.1 Application. This measure may be used to determine the structural complexity of a coded module. The use of this measure is designed to limit the complexity of a module, thereby promoting understandability of the module.

4.16.2 Primitives

N = number of nodes (sequential groups of program statements)

E = number of edges (program flows between nodes)

SN = number of splitting nodes (nodes with more than one edge emanating from it)

RG = number of regions (areas bounded by edges with no edges crossing)

4.16.3 Implementation. Using regions, or nodes and edges, a strongly connected graph of the module is required. A strongly connected graph is one in which a node is reachable from any other node: this is accomplished by adding an edge between the exit node and the entry node. Once the graph is constructed, the measure is computed as follows:

$$C - E - N + 1$$

The cyclomatic complexity is also equivalent to the number of regions (RG) or the number of splitting nodes plus one ($SN + 1$). If a program contains an N-way predicate, such as a CASE statement with N cases, the N-way predicate contributes $N-1$ to the count of SN.

4.17 Minimal Unit Test Case Determination

4.17.1 Application. This measure determines the number of independent paths through a module so that a minimal number of covering test cases can be generated for unit test. It is applied during unit testing.

4.17.2 Primitives

N = number of nodes; a sequential group of program statements

E = number of edges; program flow between nodes

SN = number of splitting nodes; a node with more than 1 edge emanating from it

RG = number of regions; in a graph with no edges crossing, an area bounded by edges

4.17.3 Implementation. The cyclomatic complexity is first computed using the cyclomatic complexity measure described in 4.16. The complexity of the module establishes the number of distinct paths. The user constructs test cases along each path so all edges of the graph are traversed. This set of test cases forms a minimal set of cases that covers all paths through the module.

4.18 Run Reliability. Run reliability (R_k) is the probability that k randomly selected runs (corresponding to a specified period of time) will produce correct results.

4.18.1 Application. The run reliability measure may be applied at any phase in the life cycle when the set of possible discrete input patterns and states can be identified. The sequence is randomly selected based on the probability assigned to selection of any one of them.

4.18.2 Primitives

NR = number of runs made in a given test sample

nc = number of correct runs in a given test sample

k = number of runs for the specified period of time

S = sample space of possible input patterns and states; $\{S_i, i = 1 \ldots\}$ are elements in the sample space (for each input pattern and state there is a unique output pattern and state; thus, S_i designates a given ((input, state), (output state)), which constitutes a run)

P = probability measure over the sample space

P_i = probability that the ith run is selected from the sample space

4.18.3 Implementation

4.18.3.1 Sample Space (S). The sample space is viewed as the set of possible inputs into the program. In the early phases of the life cycle, the sample space consists of operational scenarios. For instance, in the early requirements phase the inputs and states are the listed requirements for the program. In the later phases of the life cycle, the sample space consists of all detailed input and state conditions of the program. For a given life cycle phase, a single sample space (S) is determined and a probability measure (P) is assigned. Runs are then generated by randomly choosing input patterns and states from the sample space according to the assigned probability *P*.

4.18.3.2 Probability Measure (*P*). For each possible run i, a number p_i (between zero and one inclusive) must be assigned so that the sum of all the p_i's is 1. The simplest case is the assumption of a uniform probability distribution. However, in the operational environment some runs are more likely to occur than others and should be weighted appropriately.

4.18.3.3 Test *NR* Randomly Selected Runs. The accuracy of the measure R_k is determined by the number of runs *NR* used for estimation. The runs are randomly selected according to the probability distribution. The results of each run are examined for correctness. The number of correct runs is *nc*.

4.18.3.4 Probability of a Successful Run (P_r). The probability of a randomly selected run being correct (P_r) is estimated by the sum of the probabilities for the correct runs, divided by the sum of the probabilities for all runs. In the case of a uniform distribution $P_r = nc/NR$.

4.18.3.5 Run Reliability (R_k). Given k randomly selected runs during the specified period of time, the probability that all k runs give correct results is $R_k = P_r^k$.

4.19 Design Structure

4.19.1 Application. This measure is used to determine the simplicity of the detailed design of a software program. Also, the values determined for the associated primitives can be used to identify problem areas within the software design.

4.19.2 Primitives

$P1$ = total number of modules in the program
$P2$ = number of modules dependent on the input or output
$P3$ = number of modules dependent on prior processing (state)
$P4$ = number of database elements
$P5$ = number of nonunique database elements
$P6$ = number of database segments (partition of the state)
$P7$ = number of modules not single entrance/single exit

4.19.3 Implementation. The design structure measure is the weighted sum of six derivatives determined by using the primitives given above. The six derivatives are

$D1$ = design organized top down (Boolean)
$D2$ = module dependence ($P2/P1$)
$D3$ = module dependent on prior processing ($P3/P1$)
$D4$ = database size ($P5/P4$)
$D5$ = database compartmentalization ($P6/P4$)
$D6$ = module single entrance/single exit ($P7/P1$)

The design structure measure (*DSM*) can be expressed as

$$DSM = \sum_{i=1}^{6} W_i D_i$$

The weights (W_i) are assigned by the user based on the priority of each associated derivative. Each W_i has a value between 0 and 1 ($\Sigma W_i = 1.0$).

4.20 Mean Time to Discover the Next *K* Faults

4.20.1 Application. This measure can be used to project the average length of time until the next *K* faults are discovered. This can provide an indication of how much time would be required until a desired level of reliability is achieved.

4.20.2 Primitives

f = number of failures found from the beginning of testing to the present
t_i = observed time between the $(i-1)$st and ith failure for a given severity level, $i=1,\ldots$

4.20.3 Implementation. The mean-time-to-failure (see 4.30) should be used to estimate the mean time to discover the next *K* faults in the software. This estimate can then be expressed as

$$\text{mean time to discover the next } K \text{ faults} = \sum_{i=f}^{f+K-1} \widehat{\text{MTTF}}_i$$

where MTTF_i is an estimate of the mean-time-to-failure between the ith and $(i+1)$st failure.

The estimate of the mean-time-to-failure between the ith and $(i+1)$st failure can be calculated using any of the software models based upon time between failures. Suppose that estimate is

$$\text{MTTF}_i = \hat{E}\ \{\text{time between the } i\text{th and the } (i+1)\text{st failures}\}\ f \le i \le f+K-1$$

Notice that if $K=1$, then we simply have the estimate of the MTTF (see 4.30) between the fth and $(f+1)$st failure. Then the estimate is

$$\begin{pmatrix}\text{mean time to}\\ \text{discover the}\\ \text{next } K \text{ faults}\end{pmatrix} = \sum_{i=n}^{f+K-1} \hat{E} \begin{Bmatrix}\text{time between}\\ \text{the } i\text{th and the}\\ (i+1)\text{st failures}\end{Bmatrix}$$

By estimating the mean-time-to-failure, one can then estimate how much additional time will be required to discover all, or a subset, of the estimated remaining faults. One can judge how long it will take before the software achieves a desired level of reliability.

4.21 Software Purity Level

4.21.1 Application. The software purity level provides an estimate of the relative fault-freeness of a computer program at any specified point in time during the operational phase.

4.21.2 Primitives

t_i = observed times between failures (for example, execution time) for a given severity level

f = total number of failures in a given time interval

4.21.3 Implementation. Suppose f failures have occurred during the operational phase of the life cycle of the program. Suppose also the length of time in this phase when the fth failure is detected is t_f. Then the estimate of the purity level of the program at that point in time is

$$PL = \frac{\hat{Z}(t_0) - \hat{Z}(t_f)}{\hat{Z}(t_0)}$$

where t_0 is the start of the operations and maintenance phase and $\hat{Z}(t)$ is the estimated hazard (or failure) rate at time t. The hazard rate is defined as the conditional probability that a software failure happens in an interval of time $(t, t+\Delta t)$ given that the software has not failed up to time t. It is derived from any of the software reliability models that use time between failure data t_i. PL denotes the relative change in the hazard rate function from the beginning of the operations and maintenance phase to the time of the fth failure detection.

4.22 Estimated Number of Faults Remaining (by Seeding)

4.22.1 Application. The estimated number of faults remaining in a program is related to the reliability of the program. There are many sampling techniques that estimate this number. This section describes a simple form of seeding that assumes a homogeneous distribution of a representative class of faults.

This measure can be applied to any phase of the software life cycle. The search for faults continues for a determined period of time that may be less than that required to find all seeded faults. The measure is not computed unless some nonseeded faults are found.

4.22.2 Primitives

N_s = number of seeded faults

n_s = number of seeded faults found

n_F = number of faults found that were not intentionally seeded

4.22.3 Implementation. A monitor is responsible for error seeding. The monitor inserts (seeds) N_s faults representative of the expected indigenous faults. The test team reports to the monitor the faults found during a test period of predetermined length.

Before seeding, a fault analysis is needed to determine the types of faults and their relative frequency of occurrences expected under a particular set of software development conditions. Although an estimate of the number of faults remaining can be made on the basis of very few inserted faults, the accuracy of the estimate (and hence the confidence in it) increases as the number of seeded faults increases.

Faults should be inserted randomly throughout the software. Personnel inserting the faults should be different and independent of those persons later searching for the faults. The process of searching for the faults should be carried out without knowledge of the inserted faults. The search should be performed for a previously determined period of time (or effort) and each fault reported to the central monitor.

Each report fault should be reviewed to determine if it is in the class of faults being studied and, if so, if it is a seeded or an indigenous fault. The maximum likelihood estimate of the number of indigenous (unseeded) faults in the specified class is

$$\widehat{NF} = \frac{n_F N_s}{n_s}$$

where $\widehat{NF}$ is truncated to the integer value. The estimate of the remaining number of faults is then

$$\widehat{NF}_{\text{rem}} = \widehat{NF} - n_F$$

The probability of finding n_F of NF indigenous faults and n_F of N_s seeded faults, given that there are $(n_F + n_s)$ faults found in the program is $C(N_s, n_s)C(NF, n_F)/C(NF+N_s, n_F+n_s)$, where the function $C(x,y) = x!/(x-y)!y!$ is the combination of "x" things taken at "y" at a time. Using this relation one can calculate confidence intervals.

4.23 Requirements Compliance

4.23.1 Application. This analysis is used to verify requirements compliance by using system verification diagrams (*SVD*s), a logical interconnection of stimulus response elements (for example, stimulus and response), which detect inconsistencies, incompleteness, and misinterpretations.

4.23.2 Primitives

*DE*s = decomposition elements:

Stimulus — external input

Function — defined input/output process

Response — result of the function
Label — numerical *DE* identifier
Reference — specification paragraph number

Requirement errors detected using *SVDs*:

N_1 = number due to inconsistencies
N_2 = number due to incompleteness
N_3 = number due to misinterpretation

4.23.3 Implementation. The implementation of an *SVD* is composed of the following phases:

(1) The decomposition phase is initiated by mapping the system requirement specifications into stimulus/response elements (*DE*s). That is, all keywords, phrases, functional and/or performance requirements and expected outputs are documented on decomposition forms (see Fig 4.23.3-1).

(2) The graph phase uses the *DE*s from the decomposition phase and logically connects them to form the *SVD* graph.

(3) The analysis phase examines the *SVD* from the graph phase by using connectivity and reachability matrices. The various requirement error types are determined by examining the system verification diagram and identifying errors as follows:

(a) Inconsistencies — Decomposition elements that do not accurately reflect the system requirement specification.

(b) Incompleteness — Decomposition elements that do not completely reflect the system requirement specification.

(c) Misinterpretation — Decomposition elements that do not correctly reflect the system requirement specification. These errors may occur during translation of the requirements into decomposition elements, constructing the *SVD* graph, or interpreting the connectivity and reachability matrices.

An analysis is also made of the percentages for the various requirement error types for the respective categories: inconsistencies, incompleteness, and misinterpretation.

Inconsistencies (%) = $(N_1/(N_1+N_2+N_3)) \times 100$
Incompleteness (%) = $(N_2/(N_1+N_2+N_3)) \times 100$
Misinterpretation (%) = $(N_3/(N_1+N_2+N_3)) \times 100$

This analysis can aid also in future software development efforts.

Fig 4.23.3-1
Decomposition Form

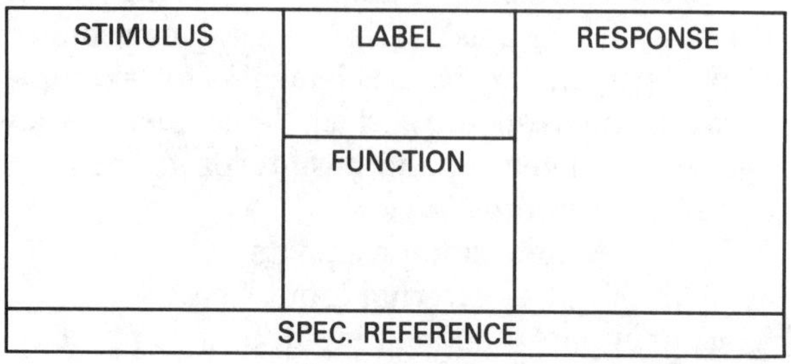

4.24 Test Coverage

4.24.1 Application. Test coverage is a measure of the completeness of the testing process from both a developer and a user perspective. The measure relates directly to the development, integration and operational test stages of product development, in particular, unit, functional, system and acceptance tests. Developers, using the program class of primitives, can apply the measure in unit test to obtain a measure of thoroughness of structural tests. System testers can apply the measure in two ways. First, by focusing on requirements primitives, the system tester can gain a user-view of the thoroughness of functional tests. Second, by focusing on the program class of primitives, the system tester can determine the amount of implementation in the operational environment.

4.24.2 Primitives. The primitives for test coverage are in two classes, program and requirements. For program, there are two types: functional and data. The program functional primitives are either modules, segments, statements, branches (nodes), or paths. Program data primitives are equivalence classes of data. Requirements primitives are either test cases or functional capabilities.

4.24.3 Implementation. Test coverage (*TC*) is the percentage of requirements primitives implemented times the percentage of primitives executed during a set of tests. A simple interpretation of test coverage can be expressed by the following formula:

$$TC(\%) = \frac{\text{(implemented capabilities)}}{\text{(required capabilities)}} \times \frac{\text{(program primitives tested)}}{\text{(total program primitives)}} \times 100$$

4.25 Data or Information Flow Complexity

4.25.1 Application. This is a structural complexity or procedural complexity measure that can be used to evaluate:

(1) The information flow structure of large scale systems

(2) The procedure and module information flow structure

(3) The complexity of the interconnections between modules

Moreover, this measure can also be used to indicate the degree of simplicity of relationships between subsystems and to correlate total observed failures and software reliability with data complexity.

4.25.2 Primitives

lfi = local flows into a procedure

datain = number of data structures from which the procedure retrieves data

lfo = local flows from a procedure

dataout = number of data structures that the procedure updates

length = number of source statements in a procedure (excludes comments in a procedure)

4.25.3 Implementation. Determine the flow of information between modules and/or subsystems by automated data flow techniques, HIPO charts, etc.

A local flow from module *A* to *B* exists if one of the following occurs:

(1) *A* calls *B*,

(2) *B* calls *A* and *A* returns a value to *B* that is passed by *B*, or

(3) Both *A* and *B* are called by another module that passes a value from *A* to *B*.

Values of primitives are obtained by counting the data flow paths directed into and out of the modules.

$$\text{fanin} = lfi + \text{datain}$$
$$\text{fanout} = lfo + \text{dataout}$$

The information flow complexity (*IFC*) is $IFC = (\text{fanin} \times \text{fanout})^2$.

$$\text{weighted } IFC = \text{length} \times (\text{fanin} \times \text{fanout})^2$$

4.26 Reliability Growth Function

4.26.1 Application. This measure provides an estimate (or prediction) of the time or stage of testing when a desired failure rate or fault density goal will be achieved. It is an indicator of the level of success of fault correction.

4.26.2 Primitives

NR_k = total number of test cases during the kth stage

NS = total number of stages

nc_k = total number of successful test cases during the kth stage

4.26.3 Implementation. Good record keeping of failure occurrences is needed to accurately document at which stage the failure occurred. Detailed failure analysis is required to determine if a fault was inserted by previous correction efforts. This will be used to calculate the reinsertion rate of faults (r), which is the ratio of the number of faults reinserted to the total number of faults found.

A test sequence of software is conducted in N stages (periods between changes to the software being tested). The reliability for the kth stage is

$$R(k) = R(u) - A/k \qquad \text{(Eq 4.26-1)}$$

where

$$R(u) = R(k) \text{ as } k \rightarrow \infty$$

The unknown parameter A represents the growth parameter of the model. An $A>0$ indicates the reliability is increasing as a function of the testing stage; an $A<0$ indicates it is decreasing. The estimation of $R(u)$ and A is done using least squares estimates. The two equations used to derive the estimates are

$$\sum_{k=1}^{NS} \left(\frac{nc_k}{NR_k} - R(u) + \frac{A}{k} \right) = 0 \qquad \text{(Eq 4.26-2)}$$

$$\sum_{k=1}^{NS} \left(\frac{nc_k}{NR_k} - R(u) + \frac{A}{k} \right) \frac{1}{k} = 0 \qquad \text{(Eq 4.26-3)}$$

The simultaneous solution of these two equations provides the estimates. If failure analysis was performed to determine a fault reinsertion rate (r), a third equation can be used in conjunction with Eq 4.26-2 and Eq 4.26-3 to estimate the fault insertion rate, r:

$$\sum_{k=1}^{NS} \left(\frac{nc_k}{NR_k} - R(u) + \frac{A}{k(1-r)} \right) \frac{1}{k(1-r)} = 0 \qquad \text{(Eq 4.26-4)}$$

4.27 Residual Fault Count

4.27.1 Application. This measure provides an indication of software integrity.

4.27.2 Primitives

t_i = observed time between the ith and $(i-1)$st failure of a given severity level

f_i = number of failures during the ith time interval of a given severity level

4.27.3 Implementation. The failure-rate class of models can be used to predict the remaining faults. This class of models is used to estimate the shape of a hypothesized hazard function from which an estimate of the number of remaining faults can be obtained.

4.28 Failure Analysis Using Elapsed Time

4.28.1 Application. This measure can be used to determine reliability growth based on the estimated number of remaining faults and software reliability. It can be used to

(1) Predict the total number of faults in the software
(2) Predict the software reliability
(3) Estimate required testing time for reliability goal
(4) Estimate required resource allocation

4.28.2 Primitives

t_i = observed time between failures of a given severity level (for example, execution time)

4.28.3 Implementation. Observed failures should be recorded and the associated faults identified. The time between failures (CPU or other unit that represents actual execution time of the software) should also be recorded.

Using the maximum likelihood estimation, the method of least squares, or the Newton-Raphson optimizing scheme, the parameters and normalizing constants of candidate models can be estimated. These can be interpreted as initial fault content (N_o), normalizing constants, and initial mean-time-to-failure (M_o) based on the model selected. Once a model has been successfully fitted to the data using any of the well-known statistical tests (for example, goodness-of-fit), then the model can be used to estimate the remaining faults (N), MTTF (M), and reliability (R).

4.29 Testing Sufficiency

4.29.1 Application. This measure assesses the sufficiency of software-to-software integration testing by comparing actual to predicted faults.

4.29.2 Primitives

$\hat{NF}$ = total number of faults predicted in the software

F_{it} = total number of faults detected to date in software integration testing

F_{pit} = number of faults detected prior to software integration testing

M_{it} = number of modules integrated

M_{tot} = total number of modules in final configuration

4.29.3 Implementation. The fault density (see 4.1) should be used to calculate the estimated total number of faults (NF) in the software. The number of faults remaining in the integrated portion of the software can then be estimated using

$$NF_{rem} = (NF - F_{pit})\, M_{it}/M_{tot}$$

Maximum and minimum tolerance coefficients (l_1 and l_2) should be established based on user experience. Values of 0.5 and 1.5 are suggested for use as the default values.

The guidelines shown in Table 4-1 assume that all scheduled integration tests have been run.

4.30 Mean-Time-to-Failure

4.30.1 Application. This measure is used for hypothesis testing a specified MTTF requirement.

4.30.2 Primitives. Mean-time-to-failure is the basic parameter required by most software reliability models. Computation is dependent on accurate recording of failure time (t_i), where t_i is the elapsed time between the ith and the $(i-1)$st failure. Time units used should be as precise as feasible. CPU execution time provides more resolution than wall-clock time. Thus CPU cycles would be more appropriate for a software development environment. For an operational environment that might require less resolution, an estimate based on wall-clock time could be used.

4.30.3 Implementation. Detailed record keeping of failure occurrences that accurately track the time (calendar or execution) at which the faults manifest themselves is essential. If weighting or organizing the failures by complexity, severity, or the reinsertion rate is desired, detailed

Table 4-1
Guidelines for Integration Testing Sufficiency

Measure Result	Interpretation	Recommended Action	Comments
$l_1 NF_{rem} < F_{it} < l_2 NF_{rem}$	Testing sufficiency is adequate	Proceed	—
$F_{it} > l_2 NF_{rem}$	Detected more faults than expected	Proceed, but apply fault density measure for each integrated module Recalculate F_p	Error-ridden modules may exist that should be replaced by a redesigned module
$F_{it} < l_1 NF_{rem}$	Detected less faults than expected	Apply test coverage measure (see 4.24) before proceeding	May not have designed adequate number or variety of tests

failure analysis must be performed to determine the severity and complexity. Prior failure experience or model fitting analysis (for example, goodness-of-fit test) can be used to select a model representative of a failure process, and to determine a reinsertion rate of faults.

4.31 Failure Rate

4.31.1 Application. This measure can be used to indicate the growth in the software reliability as a function of test time.

4.31.2 Primitives

t_i = observed times between failures (for example, execution time) for a given severity level, i=1, ...

f_i = number of failures of a given severity level in the ith time interval

4.31.3 Implementation. The failure rate $\lambda(t)$ at any point in time can be estimated from the reliability function, $R(t)$, which in turn can be obtained from the cumulative probability distribution, $F(t)$, of the time until the next failure using any of the software reliability growth models such as the nonhomogeneous Poisson process (NHPP) or a Bayesian type model. The failure rate is

$$\lambda(t) = -\frac{1}{R(t)}\left[\frac{dR(t)}{dt}\right]$$

where

$$R(t) = 1 - F(t)$$

4.32 Software Documentation and Source Listings

4.32.1 Application. The primary objective of this measure is to collect information to identify the parts of the software maintenance products that may be inadequate for use in a software maintenance environment. Two questionnaires are used to examine the format and content of the documentation and source code attributes from a maintainability perspective.

4.32.2 Primitive. The questionnaires examine the following primitive product characteristics:

(1) Modularity
(2) Descriptiveness
(3) Consistency
(4) Simplicity
(5) Expandability
(6) Testability

Subcharacteristics include format, interface, math models, and data/control.

4.32.3 Implementation. Two questionnaires, the Software Documentation Questionnaire and the Software Source Listing Questionnaire, are used to evaluate the software products in a desk audit. The questionnaires are contained in "Software Maintainability — Evaluation Guide [2]." The guide can be ordered from the Air Force Operational Test and Evaluation Center.

For the *software documentation evaluation*, the resource documents should include those that contain the program design specifications, program testing information and procedures, program maintenance information, and guidelines used in preparation of the documentation. These documents may have a variety of physical organizations depending upon the particular source, application, and documentation requirements. The documentation will in general consist of all documents that reveal the software design and implementation. A single evaluation of all the documents is done. Typical questions from the Software Documentation Questionnaire include the following:

(1) The documentation indicates that data storage locations are not used for more than one type of data structure.
(2) Parameter inputs and outputs for each module are explained in the documentation.
(3) Programming conventions for I/O processing have been established and followed.
(4) The documentation indicates the resource (storage, timing, tape drives, disks, consoles, etc) allocation is fixed throughout program execution.
(5) The documentation indicates that there is a reasonable time margin for each major time-critical program function (rate group, time slice, priority level, etc).
(6) The documentation indicates that the program has been designed to accommodate software test probes to aid in identifying processing performance.

For the *software source listings evaluation*, the program source code is evaluated. The source code may be either a high order language or assembler. Multiple evaluations using the questionnaire are conducted for the unit (module) level of the program. The units (modules) selected should represent a sample size of at least 10% of the total source code. Typical questions from the Source Listing Questionnaire include the following:

(1) Each function of this module is an easily recognizable block of code.
(2) The quantity of comments does not detract from the legibility of the source listings.

(3) Mathematical models as described/derived in the documentation correspond to the mathematical equations used in the module's source listing.

(4) Esoteric (clever) programming is avoided in this module.

(5) The size of any data structure that affects the processing logic of this module is parameterized.

(6) Intermediate results within this module can be selectively collected for display without code modification.

4.33 RELY (Required Software Reliability)

4.33.1 Application. RELY provides at the early planning phases of a project a measure that makes visible the trade-offs of cost and degree of reliability. It is recognized that reliability may vary relative to the system purpose. Man-rated software in space applications, for example, has higher reliability requirements than game software. The development processes for high reliability software especially integration and test should correspondingly be greater than that of average software.

4.33.2 Primitives. Required Reliability Rating:

Very low — The effect of a software failure is simply the inconvenience incumbent on the developers to fix the fault. Typical examples are a demonstration prototype of a voice typewriter or an early feasibility phase software simulation mode.[4]

Low — The effect of a software failure is a low level, easily-recoverable loss to users. Typical examples are a long range planning model or a climate forecasting model.[5]

Nominal — The effect of a software failure is a moderate loss to users, but a situation from which one can recover without extreme penalty. Typical examples are management information systems or inventory control systems.[6]

High — The effect of a software failure can be a major financial loss or a massive human inconvenience. Typical examples are banking systems and electric power distribution systems.[7]

Very high — The effect of a software failure can be the loss of human life. Examples are military command and control systems or nuclear reactor control systems.[8]

4.33.3 Implementation. Depending on the required reliability rating, the effort required for each phase of the development cycle can be adjusted to include the processes necessary to ensure that the product achieves the reliability goal. Figure 4.33.3-1[9] shows the effort factors relative to nominal required to achieve each of the required reliabililty ratings.

This technique can be used conversely to provide a reliability rating for a product through examination of the processes used to develop it (Fig 4.33.3-2).[10]

4.34 Software Release Readiness

4.34.1 Application. This measure is used to quantify the user and supporter (consumer) risk of ownership, based on either quantitative or subjective assessments of user and supporter issues. Given a number of issues, one can combine them to obtain a composite risk assessment. Although the primitives described here are designed for the Operational Test and Evaluation phases, the risk assessment method is applicable during any phase of the life cycle by the identification of appropriate issues and the selection or design of corresponding measures for assessment.

4.34.2 Primitives. The measurements of effectiveness, $ME(i)$, $i=1, \ldots, I$, for issues relating to software risk assessment. Example issues are

(1) Functional test coverage
(2) Software maturity
(3) Software source code listings quality factors
(4) Documentation quality factors
(5) Software operator-machine interface
(6) Software support resources assessments

4.34.3 Implementation. This measure assumes that I issues can be combined to assess the readiness of the software for release and the attendant consumer risk. For each issue i the measure $ME(i)$ is converted into an associated risk $RK(i)$ as it relates to the user and supporter. This risk is subjectively assigned by the evaluators and is defined to be in the range of 0 to 1.0, where zero denotes no risk and one denotes extreme risk. For the functional test coverage, maturity, and quality

[4] Definition of primitives and figures from Barry W. Boehm, *Software Engineering Economics*© 1981, pp 374-376. Reprinted by permission of Prentice-Hall, Inc., Englewood Cliffs, NJ.

[5] See footnote 4.

[6] See footnote 4.

[7] See footnote 4.

[8] See footnote 4.

[9] See footnote 4.

[10] See footnote 4.

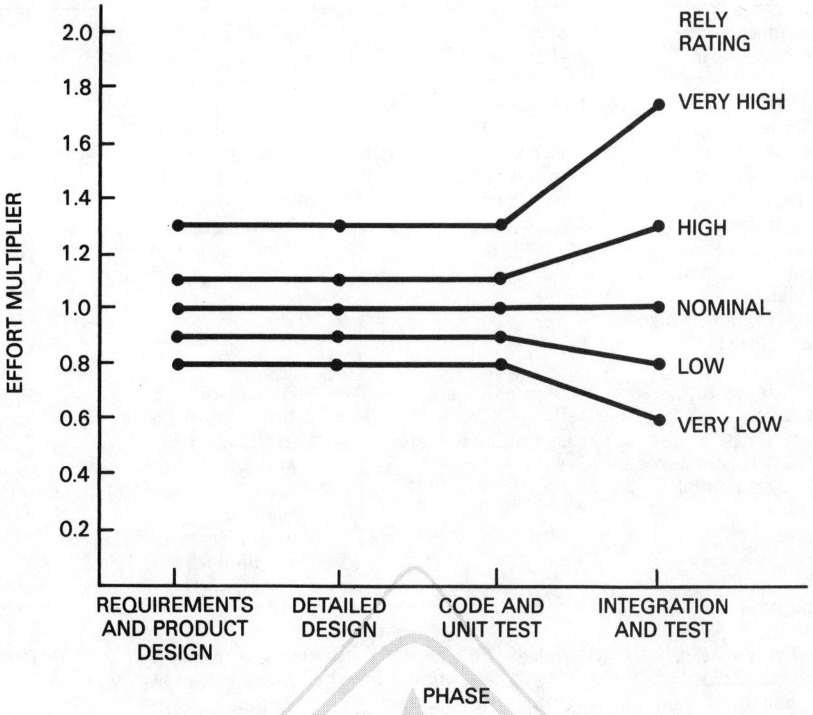

Fig 4.33.3-1
Effort Multipliers by Phase: Required Software Reliability
(Reprinted by permission of Prentice-Hall, Inc., Englewood Cliffs, NJ.)

factor primitives, the associated risk is determined by

$$RK(i) = 1.0 - ME(i)$$

Furthermore, each of the primitives $ME(i)$ is assigned a subjective, relative weight that represents its importance to the user (supporter). For each $ME(i)$ value, there is a corresponding $RK(i)$ risk and a $W(i)$ relative importance weight. All the relative weights $W(i)$ fo all user (supporter) measures sum to 1.0. Furthermore, there is an influence matrix $[S]$ that provides a modification factor to the risk $RK(i)$ when a measure $ME(i)$ is influenced by another measure $ME(j)$. For example, consider the influence between software maturity (the fraction of software modified and added during a test [see 4.10]) and functional test coverage (the fraction of code demonstrated during a test [see 4.5]). It is clear that incomplete testing would reduce the confidence in the resulting maturity score because of incomplete demonstration of the software functions. The influence matrix $S(i,j)$ coefficients are assigned values that are representative of the dependence between $ME(i)$ and $ME(j)$.

The following steps are used in calculating this measure:

(1) Evaluate each primitive $ME(i)$.

(2) Assign a risk value $RK(i)$ to the $ME(i)$ measure such that $RK(i)$ is between zero and one [for example, $RK(i) = 1.0 - ME(i)$]. Or for subjective assessments:

Low risk	=	0.0 to 0.33
Medium risk	=	0.34 to 0.66
High risk	=	0.67 to 1.0

(3) For each measure $ME(i)$, determine the weighting W(i) that reflects the importance of the measure to the total user (supporter). A suggested default value is $1/I$ giving equal weight to all issues.

(4) For each pair of measures $ME(i)$ and $ME(j)$, assign a value for the $S(i,j)$ influence coefficient that represents the subjective or quantified influence between the measures. The $S(i,j)$ coefficients vary between zero and one, where zero represents no influence (low correlation) and one represents high dependence (high correlation). Coefficient $S(i,j)$ is the measured or subjective value of measure $ME(i)$'s depen-

Rating	Requirements and Product Design	Detailed Design	Code and Unit Test	Integration and Test
Very high	Little detail Many TBDs Little Verification Minimal Quality Assurance (QA), Configuration Management (CM) draft user manual, test plans Minimal Program Design Review (PDR)	Basic design information Minimum QA, CM, draft user manual, test plans Informal design inspections	No test procedures Minimal path test, standards check Minimal QA, CM Minimal I/O and off-nominal tests Minimal user manual	No test procedures Many requirements untested Minimal QA, CM Minimal stress, off-nominal tests Minimal as-built documentation
Low	Basic information, verification Frequent TBDs Basic QA, CM, standards, draft user manual, test plans	Moderate detail Basic QA, CM, draft user manual, test plans	Minimal test procedures Partial path test, standards check Basic QA, CM, user manual Partial I/O and off-nominal tests	Minimal test procedures Frequent requirements untested Basic QA, CM, user manual Partial stress off-nominal tests
Nominal	Nominal project V & V			
High	Detailed verification, QA, CM, standards, PDR, documentation Detailed test plans, procedures	Detailed verification, QA, CM, standards, CDR, documentation Detailed test plans, procedures	Detailed test procedures, QA, CM, documentation Extensive off-nominal tests	Detailed test procedures, QA, CM, documentation Extensive stress, off-nominal tests
Very high	Detailed verification, QA, CM, standards, PDR, documentation IV & V interface Very detailed test plans, procedures	Detailed verification, QA, CM, standards, CDR, documentation Very thorough design inspections Very detailed test plans, procedures IV & V interface	Detailed test procedures, QA, CM, documentation Very thorough code inspections Very extensive off-nominal tests IV & V interface	Very detailed test procedures, QA, CM, documentation Very extensive stress, off-nominal tests IV & V interface

Fig 4.33.3-2
Projected Activity Differences Due to Required Software Reliability
(Reprinted by permission of Prentice-Hall, Inc., Englewood Cliffs, NJ.)

dence on measure $ME(j)$. Usually matrix $[S]$ is symmetric.

Let the apportioned risk $RK'(i)$ for measure i in relation to the other measures be:

$$RK'(i) = \frac{\sum_{j=1}^{I} RK(i) \times S(i,j)}{\sum_{j=1}^{I} S(i,j)}$$

Then combined user (supporter) risk is

$$R_{(\text{user/supporter})} = \sum_{i=1}^{I} RK'(i) \times W(i)$$

4.35 Completeness

4.35.1 Application. The purpose of this measure is to determine the completeness of the software specification during the requirements phase. Also, the values determined for the primitives associated with the completeness measure can be used to identify problem areas within the software specification.

4.35.2 Primitives. The completeness measure consists of the following primitives:

B_1 = number of functions not satisfactorily defined
B_2 = number of functions
B_3 = number of data references not having an origin
B_4 = number of data references
B_5 = number of defined functions not used
B_6 = number of defined functions
B_7 = number of referenced functions not defined
B_8 = number of referenced functions

B_9 = number of decision points not using all conditions, options
B_{10} = number of decision points
B_{11} = number of condition options without processing
B_{12} = number of condition options
B_{13} = number of calling routines with parameters not agreeing with defined parameters
B_{14} = number of calling routines
B_{15} = number of condition options not set
B_{16} = number of set condition options having no processing
B_{17} = number of set condition options
B_{18} = number of data references having no destination

4.35.3 Implementation. The completeness measure (CM) is the weighted sum of ten derivatives expressed as

$$CM = \sum_{i=1}^{10} w_i D_i$$

where for each i=1, ..., 10, each weight w_i has a value between 0 and 1, the sum of the weights is equal to 1, and each D_i is a derivative with a value between 1 and 0.

To calculate the completeness measure

(1) The definitions of the primitives for the particular application must be determined.
(2) The priority associated with the derivatives must also be determined. This prioritization would affect the weights used to calculate the completeness measure.

Each primitive value would then be determined by the number of occurrences related to the definition of the primitive.

Each derivative is determined as follows:

$D_1 = (B_2 - B_1)/B_2$ = functions satisfactorily defined
$D_2 = (B_4 - B_3)/B_4$ = data references having an origin
$D_3 = (B_6 - B_5)/B_6$ = defined functions used
$D_4 = (B_8 - B_7)/B_8$ = referenced functions defined
$D_5 = (B_{10} - B_9)/B_{10}$ = all condition options at decision points
$D_6 = (B_{12} - B_{11})/B_{12}$ = all condition options with processing at decision points are used
$D_7 = (B_{14} - B_{13})/B_{14}$ = calling routine parameters agree with the called routine's defined parameters
$D_8 = (B_{12} - B_{15})/B_{12}$ = all condition options that are set
$D_9 = (B_{17} - B_{16})/B_{17}$ = processing follows set condition options
$D_{10} = (B_4 - B_{18})/B_4$ = data references have a destination

4.36 Test Accuracy

4.36.1 Application. This measure can be used to determine the accuracy of the testing program in detecting faults. With a test coverage measure, it can be used to estimate the percentage of faults remaining.

4.36.2 Primitives

N_s = number of seeded faults
$\hat{N}_s$ = estimated number of detectable seeded faults

4.36.3 Implementation. The software to be tested is seeded with faults. The number of seeded faults detected in each testing time interval is recorded along with time to detect faults, and a mathematical model is selected to represent the cumulative seeded faults detected across the total testing period. The cumulative seeded faults detected at time infinity is then estimated and test accuracy is calculated:

$$\text{ALPHA} = \hat{N}_s/N_s$$

4.37 System Performance Reliability

4.37.1 Application. This measure assesses the system's performance reliability, the probability that the value of each performance requirement be less than or equal to a predefined threshold value. The specific performance requirements addressed in this measure are:

U = utilization
X = throughput
Q = queue length distribution
WT = waiting time distribution
SE = mean server's efficiency
RT = response time distribution
ST = service time distribution

The application of these derived measures will ensure that

(1) Reliability planning functions are done by all inter- and intra-organizations.
(2) Periodic reliability estimations during the software life cycle are done to track reliability development.
(3) Verification and validation are done on the system capacity.

4.37.2 Primitives. The following primitives quantify the basic performance attributes that are measured over a time period of length T.

A = number of arrivals (functional jobs) during the time period T

SB = total amount of time "server" is busy

J = number of jobs completed during T

VR = number of requests (visits) per functional job for each server during time period T

T = time period over which measurements are made

4.37.3 Implementation. These measures are applicable to operating systems and networks. Based upon the measured primitives the derived quantifiable measures are

Γ = A/T, average arrival rate of jobs

X = J/T, average throughput rate

U = SB/T, average utilization

AS = SB/J, average service time

WT = $f(\Gamma, U, AS, VR$, waiting time distribution (expressed as a function of arrival rate, utilization, service time, and visit rate)

SE = $A/(AS+W)$, server's efficiency of each job

R = $\sum_{i=1}^{k} (VR \times S)_i + \sum_{i=1}^{k} (VR \times W)_i$, total response time for each functional job over the k servers

AQ = $W \times \Gamma$, the average queue length

(Eq 4.37-1)

Using any of these measures, one can derive the corresponding probability distribution of the measure under the stated assumptions of the system. The distribution can then be used to calculate the probability that the measure will achieve a desired level.

The following step by step process can be followed to achieve this.

(1) Determine the infrastructure of the performance model. This involves identifying the critical system resources and the system's underpinning connections in the form of a Queueing Network Model (QNM). The basic idea of the model is that the "essential" part of the system's architecture is represented by a network of "servers" and queues that are connected by transition paths. Jobs circulate through the network, the flow being controlled by the transition probabilities.

(2) Define, qualify, and quantify the workload classes. This is to identify the resource demand characteristics of the different classes of jobs and their dynamic performance attribute matrix. This determines the apportionment of the utilization of each server by each work class.

(3) Measure the resource demands for each work class. The service time, arrival rate, visit ratios of each system resource are measured for each class of job.

(4) Solve the QNM. The approximation algorithms in analytic queueing theory and operations research techniques are used to solve the model.

(5) Perform the reliability evaluation. For example, suppose the response time R must meet the goal of $R \leq R_o$, where R is given by Eq 4.37-1. Calculate the system performance reilability as Reliability = Prob $\{R \leq R_o\}$ for stated assumptions during time period of length T. The system performance is not achieved if the desired reliability is not attained.

4.38 Independent Process Reliability

4.38.1 Application. This measure provides a direct method to compute reliability (R) of certain types of software systems such as telephone switching and business transaction systems in which the programs have no loops and no local dependencies exist. This is a measure of the reliability of service that a software system provides.

4.38.2 Primitives

f_{ij} = frequency of execution of intermodule transfer from module i to j

MD = number of modules

P_i = ith process, which can be generated in a user environment

q_i = probability that P_i will be generated in a user environment

r_i = random variable equal to 1 if the process P_i generates the correct software system output and zero otherwise

R_i = reliability of the ith module

4.38.3 Implementation. This measure assumes that a large program is composed of logically independent modules that can be designed, implemented, and tested independently.

Let L = set of processes P_i that can be generated by the software system corresponding to different input values. Then the reliability R of the software system can be computed from

$$R = \sum_{VP_i \epsilon L} q_i r_i$$

In large programs it is infeasible to evaluate r_i and q_i for each process P_i because L could be large. To circumvent this difficulty, a simple Markov model is developed with intermodule probabilities, (f_{ij}), as the user profiles. The reliability parameters of the program are expressed in terms of transitional probability parameters between states. The reliability R of the software system is defined as the probability of reaching the correct state [after module n] from the initial state [from module 1] of the Markov process, that is,

$$R = S(1, MD)\, R_n$$

where

$$S = [I-Q]^1$$

Q is the state transition matrix spanning the entire Markov graph program and I is the identity matrix.

Elements of the matrix, $f_{ij}R_i$ represent the probability that execution of module i produces the correct result and transfers control to module j. R_i is determined from experimentation as the ratio of the number of output sets generated by module i to the number of input sets when the software system is tested by samples of representative valid input.

4.39 Combined Hardware and Software (System) Operational Availability

4.39.1 Application. This measure provides a direct indication of system dependability, that is, if it is operating or operable when required by the user.

4.39.2 Primitives

λ = observed software failure rate
β = observed hardware failure rate
μ_i = observed software fault correction rate with i faults in the software
γ = observed hardware repair rate
NF = estimated number of remaining software faults
P_s = probability of correcting a software fault when detected $(0 \leq P_s \leq 1)$
P_h = probability of correctly repairing a hardware failure $(0 \leq P_h \leq 1)$

4.39.3 Implementation. Tha basic Markovian model is used for predicting combined hardware and software (system) availability as a function of operating time. System upstate probabilities $P_{NF,n}(t)$ with n remaining faults, given that there were NF software faults at the commissioning $(t=0)$ of the system, is computed for $n=0, 1, 2, \ldots, N$.

$$\text{System Availability } A(t) = \sum_{n=0}^{NF} P_{N,n}(t)$$

The expression for $P_{NF,n}(t)$, $n=1, \ldots, NF$ is derived as

$$P_{NF,n}(t) = G_{NF,n}(t) - \sum_{j=1}^{K} \frac{\prod_{i=n+1}^{K} (P_s\lambda_i\mu_i)(-x_jP_h\gamma)^{NF-n} A(-x_j)(1-e^{-x_jt}}{x_j \prod_{\substack{i=1\\ i\neq j}}^{K} (-x_j + x_i)}$$

where

$G_{NF,n}(t)$ = cumulative distribution function of the first passage time for operational state with NF faults to operational state with n faults and is expressed as

$$\sum_{j=1}^{K} \frac{\prod_{i=n+1}^{NF} (P_s\lambda_i\mu_i)(-x_j+P_h\gamma)^{NF-n}}{\prod_{\substack{i=1\\ i\neq j}}^{K} (-x_j+x_i)} \frac{1}{-x_j}(e^{-x_jt}-1)$$

$\lambda_i = i\lambda$
$\mu_i = i_\mu$
$K = 3\,(NF-n)$
$x_1 = x_{1,(n+1)}$
$x_2 = x_{2,(n+1)}$
$x_3 = x_{3,(n+1)}$
$x_4 = x_{1,(n+2)}$
$x_5 = x_{2,(n+2)}$
$x_6 = x_{3,(n+2)}$
.
.
.
$x_{1,(NF-n)} = x_{1,NF}$
$x_{2,(NF-n)} = x_{2,NF}$
$x_{3,(NF-n)} = x_{3,NF}$

$-x_{1,i}$, $-x_{2,i}$, and $-x_{3,i}$ $(i=n+1, \ldots, NF)$ are the roots of the polynomial:

$$S^3 + S^2(\lambda_i + \mu_i + \beta + P_h\gamma) + S(P_s\lambda_i\mu_i + \beta\mu_i + \lambda_iP_h\gamma) + \mu_iP_h\gamma) + P_sP_h\gamma\lambda_i\mu_i$$

Also

$$A(-x_j) = (-x_j\beta)(-x_j + \mu_n) + \lambda_n(-x_j + P_s\mu_n)(-x_j + P_h\gamma)$$

Acknowledgment

The following organizations supported the development of this standard:

Aerospace Corporation
Apple Computer, Inc.
Argonne National Laboratory
Bechtel Group, Inc.
Bell Canada
Boeing Aerospace
Computer Sciences Corp.
CTA, Inc.
Digital Equipment Corp.
Dynamics Research Corp.
EG&G
Federal Aviation Administration
General Dynamics
General Electric
Hewlett-Packard
Honeywell
Hughes Aircraft Co.
IBM
INTEL Corporation
International Bureau Software Test
ITT Telecom
Martin-Marietta
McDonnell Douglas
NASA
National Bureau of Standards
National Centre of Systems Reliability
NCR Corporation
Norden Systems
PRC
Product Assurances Consulting
RCA
Sanders Associates
Satellite Business Systems
SOFTECH Microsystems
SoHaR, Incorporated
Sperry
Stromberg Carlson
Tadiran, Ltd.
Tandem Computers
Teledyne Brown Engineering
Transport Canada
TRW
U.S. Air Force
U.S. Army
U.S. Navy
University of Southwestern Louisiana
Xerox Corporation

Recognized as an
American National Standard (ANSI)

IEEE
Std 982.2-1988

IEEE Guide for the Use of IEEE Standard Dictionary of Measures to Produce Reliable Software

Sponsor

Software Engineering Standards Subcommittee of the Technical Committee on Software Engineering of the IEEE Computer Society

Approved September 27, 1988

IEEE Standards Board

Approved August 10, 1989

American National Standards Institute

Corrected Edition
June 12, 1989

NOTE: A black bar has been placed in the margin next to each correction to aid in identifying the changes made to this printing.

Foreword

(This Foreword is not a part of IEEE Std 982.2-1988, IEEE Guide for the Use of IEEE Standard Dictionary of Measures to Produce Reliable Software.)

This guide provides the underlying concepts and motivation for establishing a measurement process for reliable software, utilizing IEEE Std 982.1-1988, IEEE Standard Dictionary of Measures to Produce Reliable Software. This guide contains information necessary for application of measures to a project. It includes guidance for the following:

(1) Applying product and process measures throughout the software life cycle, providing the means for continual self-assessment and reliability improvement;

(2) Optimizing the development of reliable software, beginning at the early development stages, with respect to constraints such as cost and schedule;

(3) Maximizing the reliability of software in its actual use environment during the operation and maintenance phases;

(4) Developing the means to manage reliability in the same manner that cost and schedule are managed.

The guide is intended for design, development, evaluation (eg, auditing or procuring agency) and maintenance personnel; software quality and software reliability personnel; and operations and acquisition support managers. It is organized to provide input to the planning process for reliability management.

This document contains six sections and one appendix.

Section 1, "Scope and References," establishes the goals and boundaries of the guide.

Section 2, "Definitions," serves as a central location for key terms used throughout the body of the document.

Section 3, "Measures to Produce Reliable Software," contains guidance for measure selection and application.

Section 4, "Measure Organization and Classification," provides both functional and software life cycle taxonomies of the measures.

Section 5, "Framework for Measures," refines the measurement process to nine stages for effective implementation.

Section 6, "Errors, Faults, and Failures Analysis for Reliability Improvement," provides further definition of the interrelationship of these concepts.

Appendix A, "Measures for Reliable Software," contains the standard set of measures.

The goal of IEEE Std 982.2-1988, IEEE Guide for the Use of Standard Dictionary of Measures to Produce Reliable Software is to generate a dialogue on the use and effectiveness of selected measures. This dialogue should result in the evolution of existing measures and the development of new measures that evaluate and promote software reliability. In this way, the body of knowledge of and experience with software reliability can be improved and expanded.

This is one of a series of integrated IEEE Software Engineering Standards. This guide is consistent with ANSI/IEEE Std 729-1983, Glossary of Software Engineering Terminology; ANSI/IEEE Std 730-1984, IEEE Standard for Software Quality Assurance Plans; ANSI/IEEE Std 828-1983, IEEE Standard for Software Configuration Management Plans; and ANSI/IEEE Std 1012-1986, IEEE Standard for Software Verification and Validation Plans. This guide may be applied either independently or in conjunction with those standards.

The following persons were on the balloting committee that approved this document for submission to the IEEE Standards Board:

F. Ackerman
W. Boll
J. Bowen
P. Bright
F. Buckley
H. Carney
J. Chung
F. Coallier
P. Denny
J. Dobbins
D. Doty
R. Dwyer
W. Ellis
W. Farr
D. Favor
J. Fendrich
G. Fields
J. Forster
D. Gelperin
S. Glickman
S. Gloss-Sloer
L. Good
D. Gustavson
V. Haas
C. Hay
H. Hecht
L. Kaleda
T. Kurihara
G. Larsen
F. C. Lim
B. Lindberg
M. Lipow
B. Livson
P. Marriott
R. Martin
J. MCCall
J. Mersky
W. Murch
J. Navlakha
D. Nickle
D. Peercy
W. Perry
P. Petersen
D. Pfeiffer
R. Poston
P. Powell
N. Schneidewind
W. Schnoege
R. Schueppert
R. Shillato
D. Siefert
D. Simkins
R. Singh
V. Srivastava
A. Sukert
K. Tai
R. Thibodeau
P. Thompson
D. Town
H. Trochesset
R. van Tilburg
P. Wolfgang
T. Workman
N. Yopconka

The Software Reliability Measurement Working Group had the following membership:

B. Andrews
S. Beason
R. Berlack
M. Berry
N. Beser
J. Bieman
J. Blackman
J. Bowen
M. Bruyere
F. Buckley
N. Chu
G. Chisholm
G. Clow
J. Corrinne
W. Covington
W. Daney
B. Daniels
F. DeKalb
I. Doshay
E. Dunaye
F. Fisk
A. Florence
D. Frevert
D. Gacke
W. Goss
S. Gray
F. Gray
V. Haas
C. Harrison
S. Hartman
L. Hearn
H. Hecht
R. Hood
J. Horch
D. Hurst
N. Johnson, Jr
R. Kenett
R. Kessler
R. Kumar
M. Landes
R. Lane
J. Latimer
L. Lebowitz
M. Lipow
C. McPherson
A. Moseley
S. Nemecek
K. Nidiffer
K. Oar
R. Panchal
R. Pikul
E. Presson
R. Prudhomme
H. Richter
M. Richter
L. Sanders
R. Sandborgh
H. Schock
D. Simkins
O. Smith
R. Spear
E. Soistman
L. Sprague
A. Stone
D. Sudbeck
R. Sulgrove
D. Town
R. Wamser
J. Wang
D. Winterkorn
J. Wujek
B. Zamastil

The Software Reliability Measurement Working Group Steering Committee had the following members:

James Dobbins, Chairman
Ray Leber, *Cochairman*
Ted Workman, *Cochairman*

P. Bright
A. Cicu
C. Cucciati
W. Ellis
W. Farr
S. Glickman
L. Good
N. Hall
P. Marriott
R. Martin
W. Murch
P. Powell
F. Salvia
D. Siefert
R. Singh
V. Srivastava
H. Trochesset
W. Wilson

Comments on this guide are welcome and should be addressed to:

James Dobbins
Director, Software Quality Engineering
AMS, Inc.
1525 Wilson Boulevard, 3rd Floor
Arlington, VA 22209

Contents

Figures

Tables

Appendix A
Measures for Reliable Software

APPENDIX FIGURES

APPENDIX TABLES PAGE

List of Symbols

Symbol	Meaning	Measures Used	Primitive/ Metric
A	(1) Number of arrivals during time period T (2) Reliability growth factor	37 26	P M
$A_{existing}$	Number of ambiguities in a program remaining to be eliminated	6	P
$A(t)$	System availability	39	M
A_{tot}	Total number of ambiguities identified	6	P
α	Test accuracy	36	M
AQ	Average queue length	37	M
AS	Average service time	37	P
B	Software science measure (number of errors)	14	M
B_1	Number of functions not satisfactorily defined	35	P
B_2	Number of functions	35	P
B_3	Number of data references not having an origin	35	P
B_4	Number of data references	35	P
B_5	Number of defined functions not used	35	P
B_6	Number of defined functions	35	P
B_7	Number of referenced functions not defined	35	P
B_8	Number of referenced functions	35	P
B_9	Number of decision points not using all conditions, options	35	P
B_{10}	Number of decision points	35	P
B_{11}	Number of condition options without processing	35	P
B_{12}	Number of condition options	35	P
B_{13}	Number of calling routines with parameters not agreeing with defined parameters	35	P
B_{14}	Number of calling routines	35	P
B_{15}	Number of condition options not set	35	P
B_{16}	Number of set condition options having no processing	35	P
B_{17}	Number of set condition options	35	P
B_{18}	Number of data references having no destination	35	P
β	Observed hardware failure rate	39	P
C	Complexity metric (static, dynamic, cyclomatic)	15, 16	M
C_i	Complexity for program invocation and return along each edge e_i as determined by the user	15	P
CE	Cause and effect measure	6	M
CM	Completeness measure	35	M
D	Software science measure (program difficulty)	14	M
d_k	Complexity for allocation of resource k as determined by the user	15	P

Symbol	Meaning	Measures Used	Primitive/ Metric
D_i	Total number of unique defects detected during the ith design or code inspection process or the ith life cycle phase	2, 8	P
DD	Defect density	2	M
DEs	Decomposition elements	23	P
DI	Defect index	8	M
DSM	Design structure metric	19	M
datain	Number of data structures from which the procedure retrieves data	25	P
dataout	Number of data structures that the procedure updates	25	P
E	(1) Number of edges (2) Software science measure (effort)	15, 16, 17 14	P M
e_i	Number of entry points for the ith module	13	P
F or F_i	Total number of unique faults found in a given time interval resulting in failures of a specified severity level	1	P
f or f_i	Total number of failures of a given severity level in a given time interval	3, 20, 21, 27, 31	P
F_d	Fault density	1	M
f_{ij}	Frequency execution of intermodule transfer from module i to j	38	P
F_a	Number of software functions (modules) in the current delivery that are additions in the current delivery	10	P
F_c	Number of software functions (modules) in the current delivery that include internal changes from a previous delivery	10	P
FD	Fault days metric	4	M
FD_i	Fault days for the ith fault	4	P
F_{del}	Number of software functions (modules) in the previous delivery that are deleted in the current delivery	10	P
FE	Number of the software functional (modular) requirements for which all test cases have been satisfactorily completed	5	P
F_{it}	Total number of faults detected to date in software integration testing	29	P
F_{pit}	Number of faults detected prior to software integration testing	29	P
FT	Total number of software functional test requirements (modular)	5	P
Γ	Average rate of jobs	37	M
Υ	Observed hardware repair rate	39	P
I	Total number of inspections to date	2, 11	P
IFC	Information flow complexity	25	M
J	Total number of jobs completed	37	P
K	Number of resources	15	P

Symbol	Meaning	Measures Used	Primitive/ Metric
k	Number of runs for the specified period of time	18	P
KSLOC	Number of source lines of executable code and nonexecutable data declarations in thousands	1, 2, 8	P
KSLOD	Number of source lines of design statements in thousands that have been inspected to date	2, 8	P
L	Software science measure (observed program length)	14	M
l	Software science measure (program vocabulary)	14	M
Ll	Software science measure (program level)	14	M
$\lambda(t)$	Failure rate function	31	M
λ	Observed software failure rate	39	P
length	Number of source statements in a procedure	25	P
lfi	Local flows into a procedure	25	P
lfo	Local flows from a procedure	25	P
M	Manhours per major defect detected	11	M
M_i	Number of medium defects found	8	P
m_i	Number of entry and exit points for module i	13	M
MD	Number of modules	38	P
$ME(i)$	Measure effectiveness for the ith issue	34	P
M_{it}	Number of modules integrated	29	M
M_T	Number of software functions (modules) in the current delivery	10	M
M_{tot}	Total number of modules in final configuration	29	M
MTTF	Mean-time-to-failure	30	M
μ_i	Observed software fault correction rate with i faults in the software	39	P
N	Number of nodes	15, 16, 17	P
nc	Number of correct runs in a given test sample	18, 26	P
NF	Total number of faults within a program	29, 39	M
NF_{rem}	Total number of faults remaining within a program	22, 29	M
NF_{rem} (%)	Percentage of faults remaining within a program	36	M
n_F	Number of faults found that were not intentionally seeded	22	P
NR	Number of runs (or test cases) in a given test sample	18, 26	P
NS	Total number of stages	26	P
N_s	Number of seeded faults	22, 36	P
n_s	Number of seeded faults found	22	P
$N1$	Total number of occurrences of the operators in a program	14	P
$n1$	Number of distinct operators in a program	14	P

Symbol	Meaning	Measures Used	Primitive/ Metric
$N2$	Total number of occurrences of the operands in a program	14	P
$n2$	Number of distinct operands in a program	14	P
N_1	Number of errors detected using SVDs due to inconsistencies	23	P
N_2	Number of errors detected using SVDs due to incompleteness	23	P
N_3	Number of errors detected using SVDs due to misinterpretation	23	P
P	Probability measure over the sample space	18	P
p_n	Probability of repairing a hardware failure correctly	39	P
P_i	(1) Probability that the ith run is selected from the sample space	18, 38	P
	(2) Probability that the ith process that can be generated in a user environment is selected	39	
P_s	Probability of correcting a software fault when detected	39	P
$P_{N,n}(t)$	System upstate probabilities	39	P
PI_i	Phase index metric for the ith life cycle phase	8	M
PL	Purity level	21	M
PS	Product size	8	P
$P1$	Total number of modules in the program	19	P
$P2$	Number of modules dependent on the input or output	19	P
$P3$	Number of modules dependent on prior processing	19	P
$P4$	Number of database elements	19	P
$P5$	Number of nonunique database elements	19	P
$P6$	Number of database segments (partition of the state)	19	P
$P7$	Number of modules not single entrance/single exit	19	P
Q	Queue length distribution	37	P
q_i	Probability that P_i will be generated in a user environment	38	P
R	(1) Total response time for each functional job	37	M
	(2) Reliability of the system	38	M
R_i	Reliability of the ith module	38	P
R_k	Run reliability at a specified stage	18, 26	M
$R(t)$	Reliability function	31	M
r_i	Flag to denote if the ith process generates the correct software system output	38	P
r_{ki}	Resource status array indicator flags	15	P
RG	Number of regions	16, 17	P
$RK(i)$	Risk factor for the ith measure	34	M
RT	Response time distribution	37	P
$R1$	Number of requirements met by the architecture	7	P

Symbol	Meaning	Measures Used	Primitive/ Metric
$R2$	Number of original requirements	7	P
S	Sample space of possible input patterns and states	18	P
S_i	Point from the sample space of possible inputs	18	P
s_i	Number of serious defects found	8, 11	P
SB	Total amount of time server is busy	37	P
SE	Server's efficiency	37	M
SN	Number of splitting nodes	16, 17	P
SMI	Software maturity index	10	M
ST	Service time distribution	37	P
T	(1) Time period over which measurements are made (2) Time	37 14	P M
T_i	Number of trivial defects found	8	P
t_i	Observed times between failures of a given severity level	20, 21, 27 28, 30, 31	P
TC	Test coverage	24	M
TM	Traceability measure	7	M
T_1	Time expended by the inspection team in preparation for design or code inspection meeting	11	P
T_2	Time expended by the inspection team in conduct of a design or code inspection meeting	11	P
U	Utilization	37	P
V	Software science measure (program volume)	14	M
VR	Number of requests per functional job for each server during time period T	37	P
W_i	Weighting distribution	8, 19, 34	P
WT	Waiting time distribution	37	P
X	Throughput	37	P
x_i	Number of exit points for the ith module	13	P

NOTE: P stands for primitive
M stands for derived metric

IEEE Guide for the Use of IEEE Standard Dictionary of Measures to Produce Reliable Software

1. Scope and References

1. Scope. This guide provides the conceptual insights, implementation considerations, and assessment suggestions for the application of IEEE Std 982.1-1988, IEEE Standard Dictionary of Measures to Produce Reliable Software [2].[1] The Dictionary, by its very nature, is limited in what it may contain. While this is necessary for standardization, abbreviation of detail might be detrimental to the most effective use of the Dictionary. This guide is written to provide a bridge between IEEE Std 982.1-1988 and the user, so that full benefit may be derived from the application of the standard to a software project.

1.2 References. This guide shall be used in conjunction with the following publications:

[1] ANSI/IEEE 729-1983, IEEE Standard Glossary of Software Engineering Terminology.[2]

[2] IEEE Std 982.1-1988, IEEE Standard Dictionary of Measures to Produce Reliable Software.[3]

2. Definitions

Most of the definitions listed below can be found in ANSI/IEEE Std 729-1983, IEEE Standard Glossary of Software Engineering Terminology [1]. The definitions of the terms "concept phase," "defect," "measure," "primitive," "software reliability management" are not present in ANSI/IEEE Std 729-1983, and establish meaning in the context of this guide. The acronym ISO (International Organization for Standardization) indicates that the definition is also accepted by ISO.

concept phase. The period of time in the software life cycle during which system concepts and objectives needed by the user are identified and documented. Precedes the requirements phase.

defect. A product anomaly. Examples include such things as (1) omissions and imperfections found during early life cycle phases and (2) faults contained in software sufficiently mature for test or operation. See also "fault."

error. Human action that results in software containing a fault. Examples include omission or misinterpretation of user requirements in a software specification, and incorrect translation or omission of a requirement in the design specification (see ANSI/IEEE Std 729-1983 [1]).

failure. (1) The termination of the ability of a functional unit to perform its required function. (ISO; ANSI/IEEE Std 729-1983 [1]). (2) An event in which a system or system component does not perform a required function within specified limits. A failure may be produced when a fault is encountered [1].

fault. (1) An accidental condition that causes a functional unit to fail to perform its required function. (ISO; ANSI/IEEE Std 729-1983 [1]). (2) A manifestation of an error in software. A fault, if encountered, may cause a failure. Synonymous with bug [1].

measure. A quantitative assessment of the degree to which a software product or process possesses a given attribute.

primitive. Data relating to the development or use of software that is used in developing measures or quantitative descriptions of software.

[1] The numbers in brackets correspond to those of the references in 1.2; numbers in brackets preceded by an "A" correspond to references in the Appendix.

[2] ANSI/IEEE publications are available from the Sales Department, American National Standards Institute, 1430 Broadway, New York, NY 10018, or from the IEEE Service Center, 445 Hoes Lane, P.O. Box 1331, Piscataway, NJ 08854-1331.

[3] IEEE publications are available from the IEEE Service Center, 445 Hoes Lane, P.O. Box 1331, Piscataway, NJ 08854-1331.

Primitives are directly measurable or countable, or may be given a constant value or condition for a specific measure. Examples include error, failure, fault, time, time interval, date, number of noncommentary source code statements, edges, nodes.

software reliability. The probability that software will not cause the failure of a system for a specified time under specified conditions. The probability is a function of the inputs to, and use of, the system as well as a function of the existence of faults in the software. The inputs to the system determine whether existing faults, if any, are encountered [1].

software reliability management. The process of optimizing the reliability of software through a program that emphasizes software error prevention, fault detection and removal, and the use of measurements to maximize reliability in light of project constraints such as resources (cost), schedule, and performance.

3. Measures to Produce Reliable Software

This guide addresses two major topics. The first is the rationale for the document IEEE Std 982.1-1988, IEEE Standard Dictionary of Measures to Produce Reliable Software. The guide presents the measure selection criteria. It address these questions: "To whom is the standard directed?" "When should the standard be applied?" and "Why was the standard created?"

The second topic is the application of these measures to product, project, and industry. For each measure the guide provides further definition, examples, interpretation, and references. The questions addressed include: "How can the standard be used effectively?" "How should results be interpreted?" and "How should objectives be set?"

The goal of the Dictionary is to support software developers, project managers, and system users in achieving optimum reliability levels in software products. It was designed to address the needs of software developers and customers who are confronted with a plethora of models, techniques, and measures in the literature, but who lack sufficient guidance to utilize them effectively. The standard addresses the need for a uniform interpretation of these and other indicators of reliability.

The Dictionary assumes an intimate relationship between the reliability of a product and the process used to develop that product. The reliable product provides confirmation of a successful process; the unreliable product provides a lesson for process change. It is in this general spirit that the measures selected give visibility to both process and product so that the essential facts necessary for process evaluation and change are available.

The measures were selected to provide information throughout the life cycle of a product. They can be used to make optimum operational reliability levels and to provide a *post factum* measurement of reliability levels achieved. The basic goal is to provide the elements of a measurement program that support a constructive approach for achieving optimum reliability of the end product.

The selected measures are related to various product and process factors that may have an impact on software reliability and that are observable throughout the entire life cycle. The Dictionary provides, even in the early life cycle phases, a means for continual assessment of the evolving product and the process. Through early reliability assessment, the Dictionary supports constructive optimization of reliability within given performance, resource, and schedule constraints.

The Dictionary focuses on measures of the potential causes of failure throughout the software life cycle, rather than just on measures of the effect of poor reliability of nearly completed products. The intent is to produce software that is reliable, rather than just an estimate of the failure-freeness of a nearly completed and possibly unreliable product. Both the traditional approach of measuring reliability and the constructive approach of building in reliability are placed in context in this document.

The primitives to be used and the method of computation are provided for each measure. The standard calibrates the rulers, the measurement tools, through the use of common units and a common language. It promotes the use of a common database in the industry. Through commonality the standard provides the justification for building effective tools for the measurement process itself.

The standard and this guide are intended to serve as the foundation on which researchers and practitioners can build consistent methods. These documents are designed to assist management in directing product development and support toward specific reliability goals. The purpose is to provide a common set of definitions through which a meaningful exchange of data and evaluations can occur. Successful application of the measures is dependent upon their use as intended in the specified environments.

The future study of extensive sets of basic data collected through the application of this standard will make it feasible to understand causal relationships, if any, between reliability indicators obtained during the process and operational reliability of a completed product. It will also promote the refinement of existing models and the development of new models based on this consistent data.

3.1 Constructive Approach to Reliable Software. An analysis of the relationship between the software development and maintenance processes and software reliability is provided. The purpose is to clarify the criteria used in the selection of measures.

Software reliability measurement is the determination of the probability that software will not cause the failure of a system for a specified time under specified conditions. The probability is a function of the inputs to, and use of, the system as well as a function of the existence of faults in the software. The inputs to the system determine whether existing faults, if any, are encountered [1].

3.1.1 Constructive Approach. Reliability is an estimation of system failure-freeness. System failures that are caused by software are a valid concern of the software community. A constructive approach to reliable software seeks to remove the root causes of this class of system failures (Fig 3.1.1-1) through software development and support processes that promote fault avoidance, early fault detection, appropriately prompt removal, and system-designed fault tolerance (Fig 3.1.1-2).

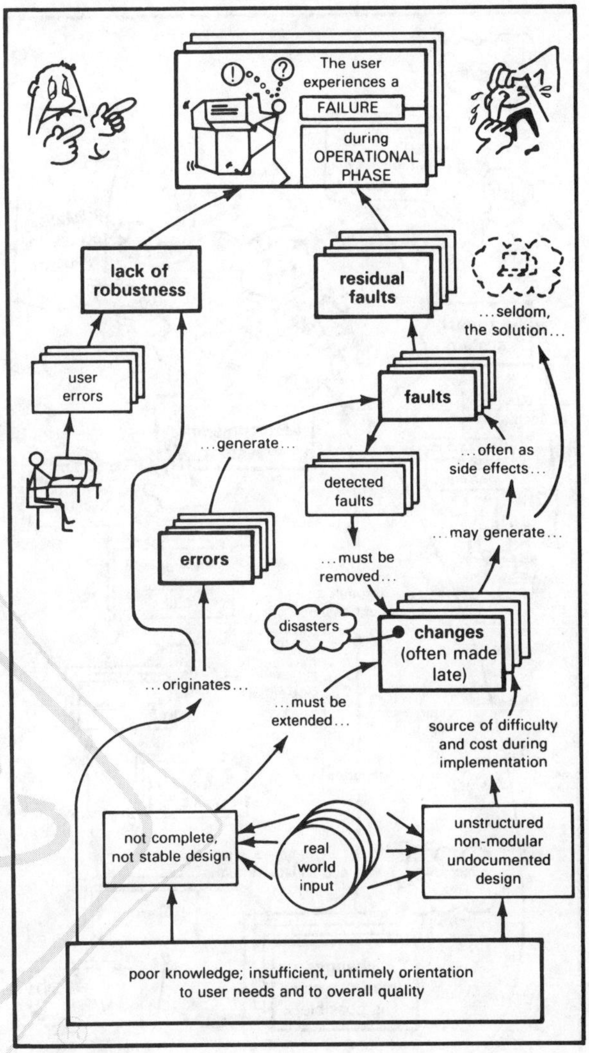

Fig 3.1.1-1
Causes of Failures

The analysis of the errors, faults, and failures from previous development and support processes can lead to improved future processes. While the exact functional relationships are not proven, it is through experience that the majority of failures are related to their origins. Examples include the following:

(1) Incompletely defined user needs and requirements
(2) Omissions in the design and coding process
(3) Improper usage of the system
(4) Excessive change activity

The error, fault, and failure analysis is detailed further in Section 6.

A process strategy to achieve reliable software includes activities, methods, tools, and measurements. Figure 3.1.1-3 shows the process strategy and the integrated role of measurements as the control window through which the quality of the product and of the process are monitored.

While Fig 3.1.1-3 is in large part self-explanatory, it is worthwhile to emphasize the major drivers for the process strategy. The strategy does not itself contain new techniques or new methodologies. It is a collection of known concepts, activities, and techniques, that can be used to drive a project toward better reliability.

The driving criteria of this constructive process strategy are as follows:

3.1.1.1 Do It Right the First Time. This approach stresses the use of all means necessary to define and build a product with no faults. "Doing it right the first time" must stress error prevention and fault avoidance through the following practices:

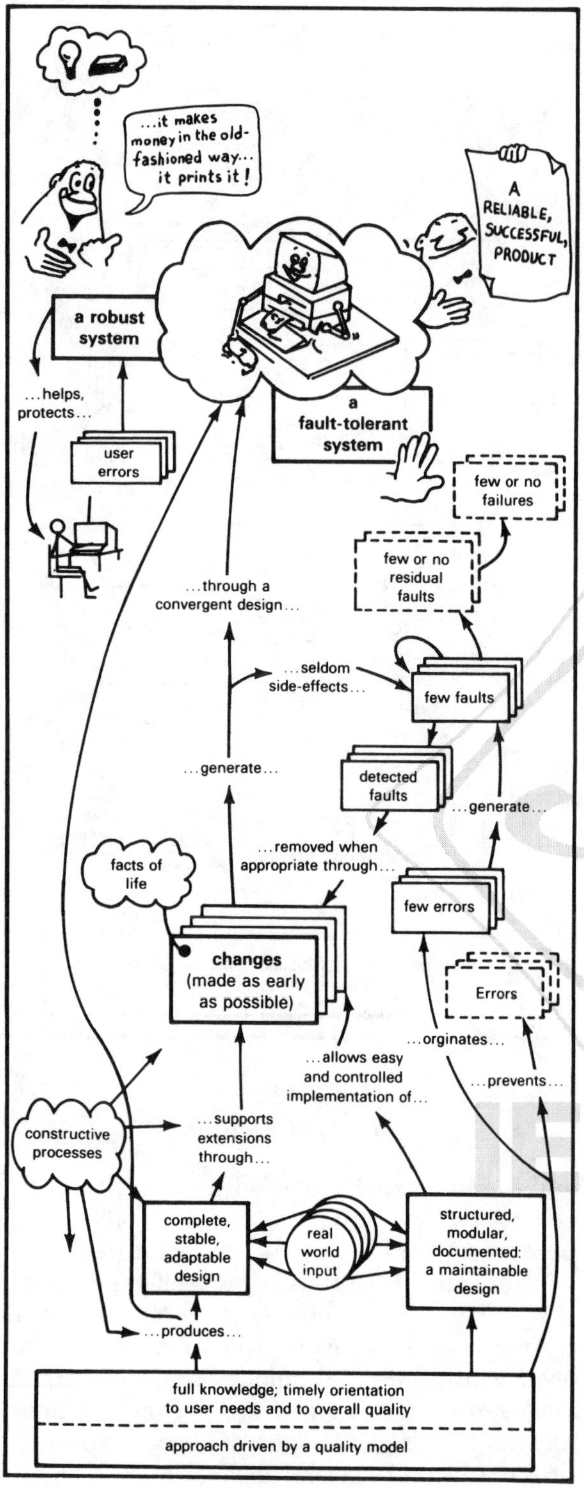

Fig 3.1.1-2
Constructors of a Reliable Product

(1) Employment of skilled, competent personnel is of foremost importance in building reliable products. It is important in all phases of development, especially the identification of user requirements and needs in the concept phase. The strategy stresses the necessity of intensely studying the stated and unstated needs of the user application, and of having sufficient experience in solving similar problems to apply to the present problem. For this reason, the concept phase is considered a major life cycle component toward a complete and stable definition of the objectives of a project. Quality work requires extensive knowledge of the application, which is often forgotten in the intermediate design phases, and remembered only when the user realizes some important features are missing during operation and maintenance.

(2) Early user involvement in the conception of the product through techniques such as prototyping must be stressed to ensure that usability matches failure-freeness in importance.

(3) Modern methods, languages and automated tools should be selected to promote productivity and quality in the activities of specification, design, coding and configuration management. The selected languages and tools must also support the verification activities through automation of requirements tracing, completeness and consistency analysis, performance simulation, complexity measurements, and configuration definition and control. Automation significantly reduces the risk of human errors.

3.1.1.2 Detect It Early; Fix It as Soon as Practicable. Detection and repair should be properly planned activities. Verification [1] is the process of determining whether or not the products of a given phase of the software development cycle fulfill the requirements established during the previous phase. Validation [1] is the process of evaluating software at the end of the software development process to ensure compliance with software requirements.

Early detection of faults throughout the life cycle through reviews, inspections, prototyping, simulation, or proof of correctness of the product will improve reliability. During the operations and maintenance phase, faults do not necessarily have to be fixed immediately. The severity of the problem, the frequency of occurrence of the problem, and the opportunity to manage and test the new configuration should weigh in the decision of when to fix a fault.

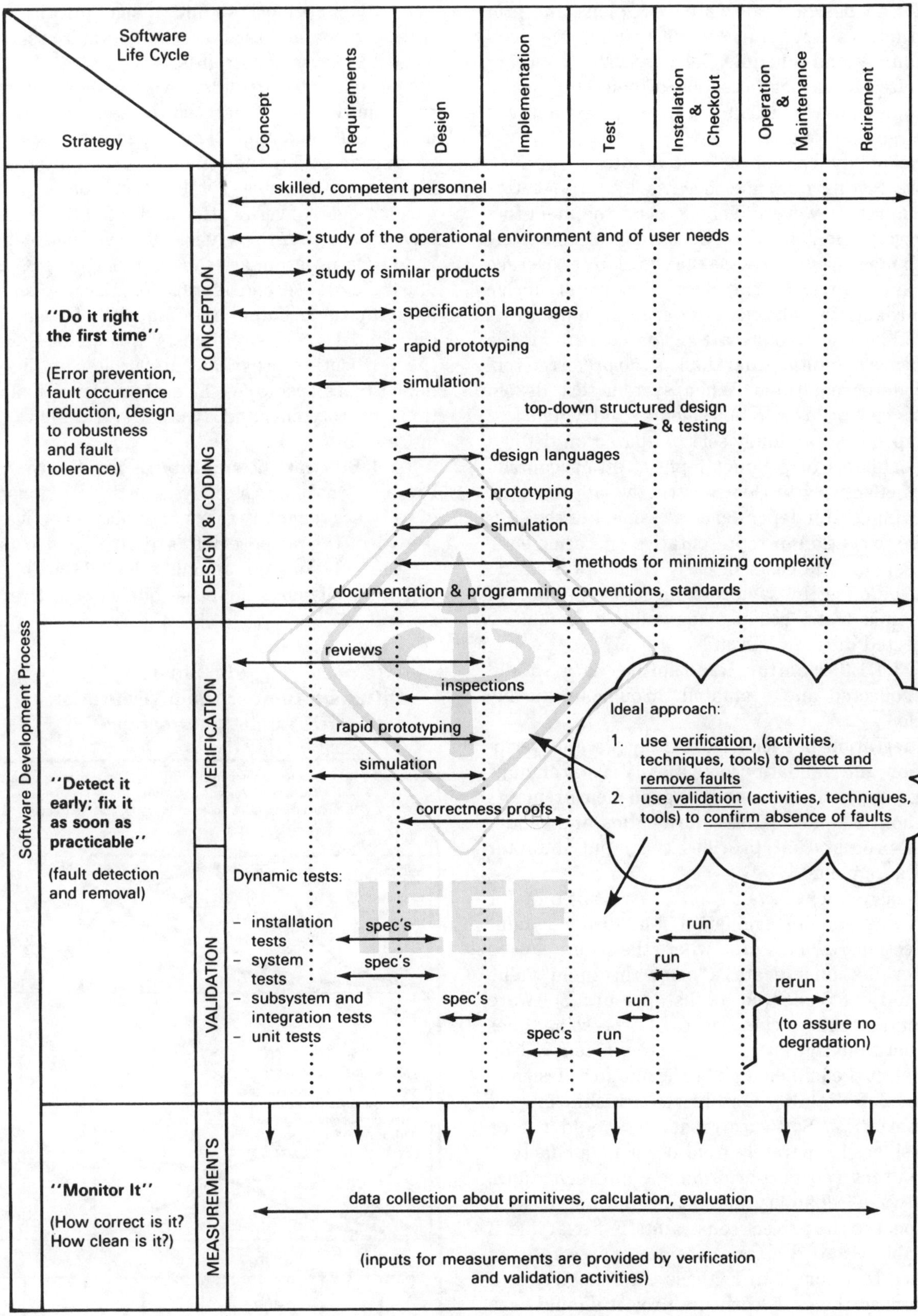

Fig. 3.1.1-3
Strategy of the Constructive Approach for Development of Reliable Software

Timely design of software tests, plans, and procedures is necessary to determine required resources and schedule. Early design of tests contributes to earlier detection of consistency and completeness faults, and ensures the testability of the requirements.

Reliability cannot be tested into a product. More testing does not necessarily mean better reliability. However, dynamic tests, the main tool for validation, have to be used cost-effectively with measures to provide the widest test coverage of a product. In the light of a constructive approach to reliable software, dynamic tests should be viewed as a tool for confirming the absence of faults rather than as the preferred tool for detecting them. When system test design is driven by user requirements, and when test samples are randomly selected based on defined probabilities of product inputs, testing contributes effectively to this constructive approach by providing an independent assessment of the software execution in representative operating environments. The costs of early verification efforts can be offset by savings from less repetition of dynamic tests, because most faults should be detected during verification.

3.1.1.3 Monitor It. Primitive data should be collected and evaluated throughout the life cycle.

Inegration between measurements and verification and validation activities is of paramount importance. There cannot be good measurements without a well-organized verification and validation process that provides the input data for measurements.

Measurements evaluation is used not only for software quality evaluation, but also for fault detection. Each instance where the criterion used for evaluation indicates a "below threshold" value should be considered an instance of a software fault. For example, measures of processing times higher than a given value may be sufficient reason to reject the implemented code and to redesign it.

3.1.2 Reliability Optimization within Project Constraints. Software reliability should not be considered separately from other major factors: resources (cost), performance, and schedules. Software reliability should be optimized with respect to the project constraints. For example, if reliability and cost are considered as a ratio in which to attempt to increase the reliability and minimize the cost, then the project should seek the more efficient fault detection and removal activities. If reliability and schedule are jointly considered, early fault detection should be emphasized. Each project should assign priorities to these project factors and seek to optimize reliability within these constraints.

The cost of fixing faults rises significantly from the time they are generated to the time they are detected. It is more efficient to dedicate resources to fault detection and removal as soon after fault insertion as possible. Total cost comparisons for various levels of verification and validation efforts have shown that the savings of a verification and validation program are substantial. Figure 3.1.2-1 illustrates these considerations. Cases A and B have an equal cumulative amount of costs but different distribution of costs in time. In Case B the verification program puts greater emphasis, hence more resources, in early reviews, inspections, prototyping, and dynamic test design than in Case A.

3.1.3 Software Reliability in the Context of Product Quality. An analysis of the relationship of software reliability to other quality objectives is provided. The purpose of this discussion is to clarify the relationship among selected measures, software reliability and other quality objectives in general.

Fig 3.1.2-1
Different Approaches in Verification and Validation Programs

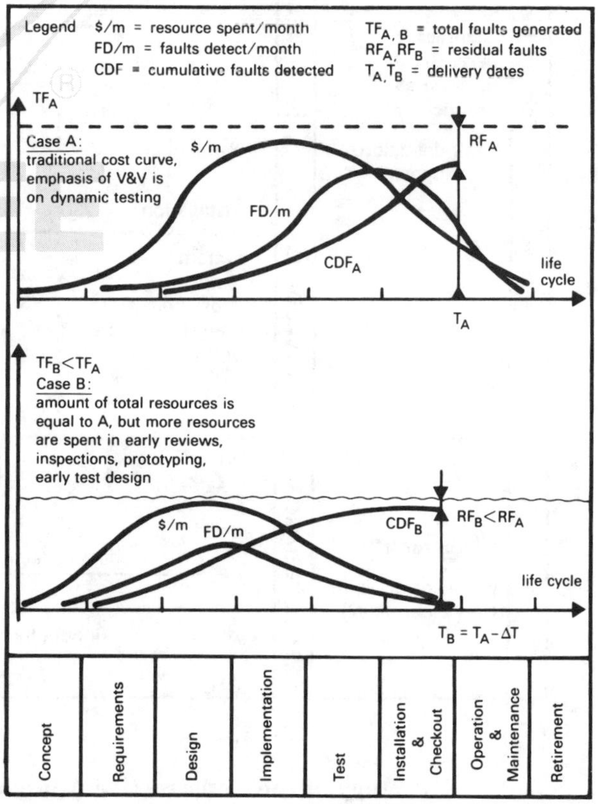

3.1.3.1 Quality Models for Adaptability and Reliability. Change, a fact of life for system developers and maintainers, is one of the major indirect causes of faults in a software system. Change can impact not only reliability but the other major project drivers — schedule and cost.

A program to construct reliable software must consider not only the initial correctness of the product, but also the plan for accommodating change. It is important to strive to minimize reasons for change during the life cycle. Design stability and product stability are extremely important. But it is a reality that unforeseen changes in requirements, market forces, and other factors may introduce change into the process.

Change most often occurs in response to unmet quality objectives (such as, ease-of-use, maintainability, or portability) that were not given proper attention during design. Therefore, there is a need for a quality model that defines user-oriented needs. This model must be evolved during the same time period as function and performance objectives (Fig 3.1.3.1-1). Such a quality model is the premise for both a complete and an adaptable design that can easily absorb changes due to unforeseen new requirements.

Software reliability is a major quality objective. Rarely is medium or low reliability acceptable. Software reliability is both an individual quality attribute and one that is interdependent on other user quality attributes. It is because of this duality that we must consider software reliability in context with other user quality objectives. It is for this reason that user quality objectives are within the scope of this guide.

3.1.3.2 User Quality Objectives and Reliability. User quality objectives should influence the system design and serve as criteria both for intermediate verification and for system validation and acceptance. The defined user quality objectives give the most direct means for fault search and detection. Examples of user quality objectives are ease-of-use for a word processor; ultra-high reliability for a telephone exchange plant; reliability and security for a banking application; safety and robustness for a nuclear power plant system.

User quality objectives are reached through intermediate software engineering objectives, which are achieved in the earlier phases of system development. Examples of intermediate software engineering objectives include complexity, traceability, modularity, topological coverage, defect index, and fault-days. These intermediate software engineering objectives are rarely of direct interest to the user. They constitute the tactics through which the software engineer achieves user quality objectives. Figure 3.1.3.2-1 gives a global, but not exhaustive, view of the mix of both user and software engineering objectives that have an impact on software reliability. The figure presents a schema for organizing quality objectives in each life cycle phase. Specific attention should be given to those intermediate quality objectives that directly affect project selected user quality objectives.

A software reliability management program requires the establishment of a balanced set of user quality objectives, and identification of intermediate quality objectives that will assist in achieving the user quality objectives. Resources should be spent commensurate with priority of objectives. Methods for measuring intermediate quality objectives related to reliability are identified in the Appendix of this guide.

A similar approach is applicable for the larger class of quality objectives in general and the maintenance activity specifically. Once software is delivered, the maintenance activity applied to that software has many of the same attributes that are associated with a new development effort. Thus, many of the same quality and reliability objectives are applicable.

A balanced quality program is both necessary and instrumental for a constructive approach to reliable software.

3.2 Measurement Environment. Measurement is the comparison of a property of an object to a similar property of a standard reference. Measurements are effective when they are used either to orient decisions, to define corrective actions, or to get a better understanding of causal relationships between intended expectations and observed facts. If there is no prestated objective on how the results will be used, there should be no measurements.

When measurements are used as process diagnostics, there must be a proper environment for data collection, analysis, and corrective action in a closed loop system. Measurement information must flow throughout the process, supporting integration of both technical and managerial activities (Fig 3.2-1).

The building blocks for deriving more complex measures from collected data are called primitives. Some primitives are derived directly from the product (specifications, source code, object code). Examples of these are statements, edges, nodes, branches, changes, capabilities, networks,

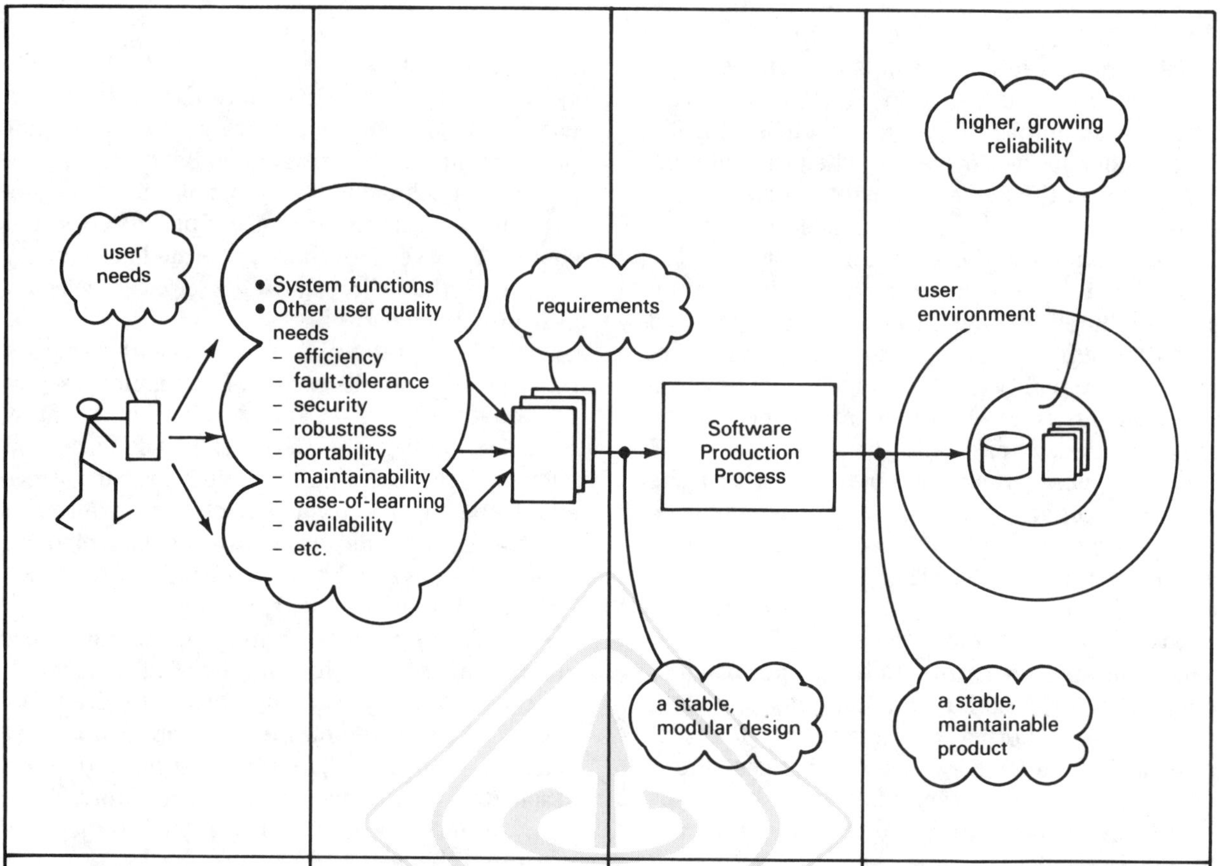

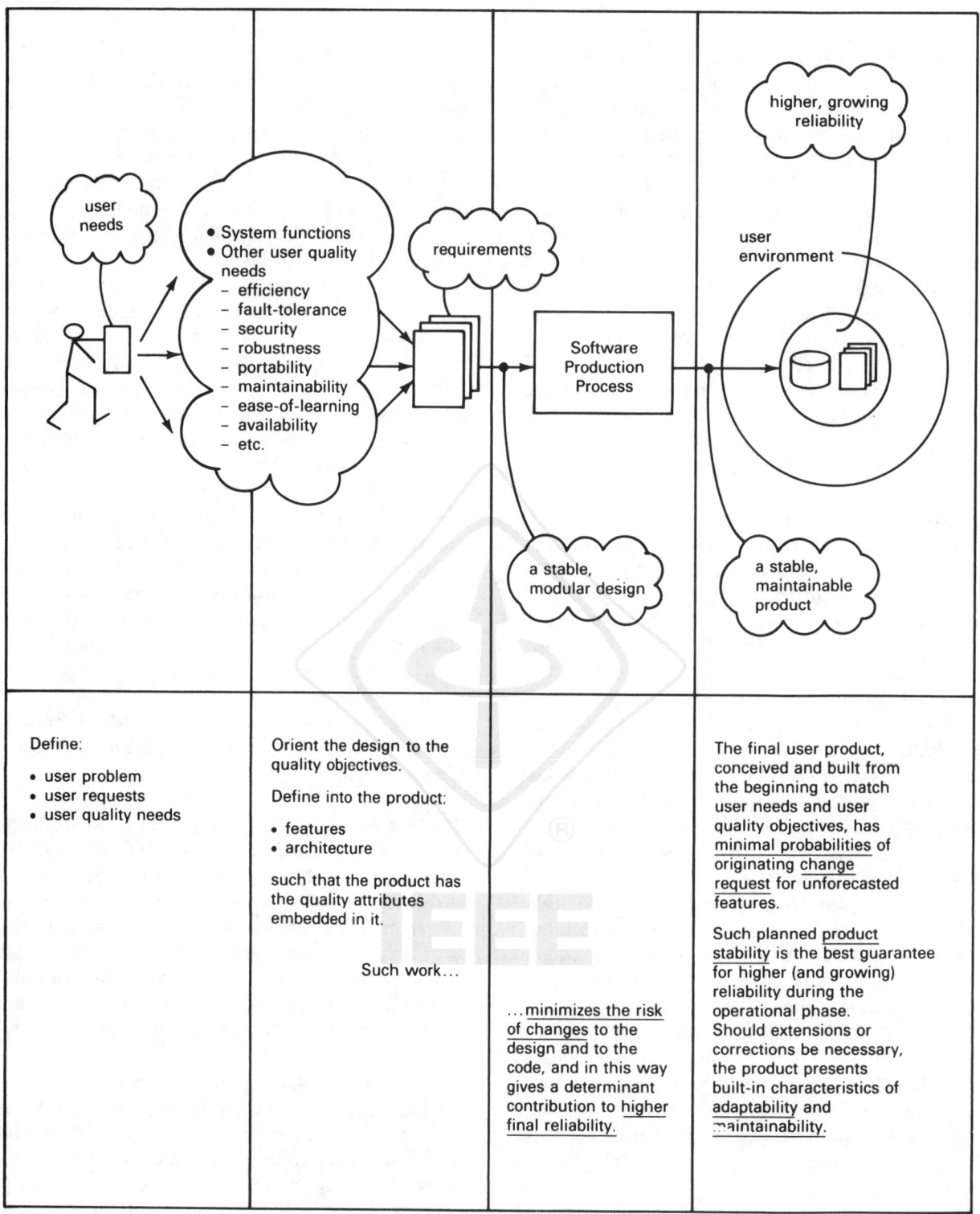

Define: • user problem • user requests • user quality needs	Orient the design to the quality objectives. Define into the product: • features • architecture such that the product has the quality attributes embedded in it. Such work...	...minimizes the risk of changes to the design and to the code, and in this way gives a determinant contribution to higher final reliability.	The final user product, conceived and built from the beginning to match user needs and user quality objectives, has minimal probabilities of originating change request for unforecasted features. Such planned product stability is the best guarantee for higher (and growing) reliability during the operational phase. Should extensions or corrections be necessary, the product presents built-in characteristics of adaptability and maintainability.

*During the operational phase, the quality model for software reliability is a function of product stability and adaptability.

Fig 3.1.3.1-1
Quality Model for Software Reliability

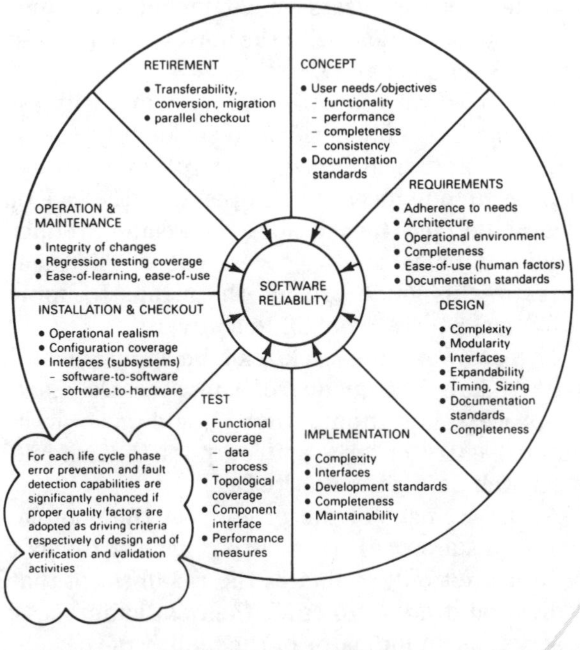

Fig 3.1.3.2-1
Quality Factors Impacting Software Reliability

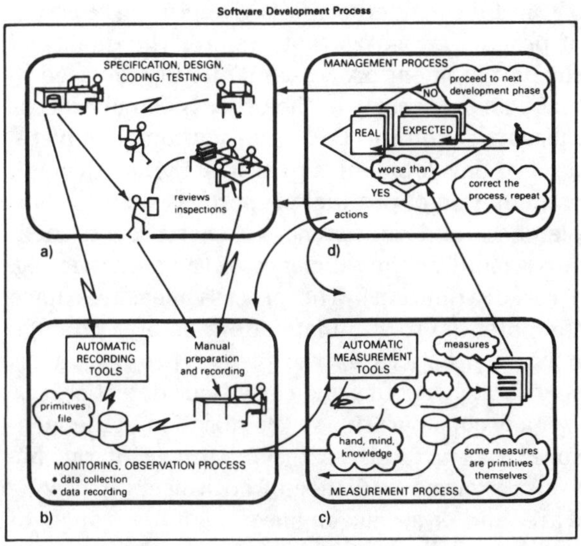

Fig 3.2-1
Measurement Information Flow: An Integral Part of Development Process

and goals. Other primitives, produced by verification and validation activities, include errors, faults and failures.

A two-step process is recommended to prepare for data collection:

(1) For each potential measure selected from IEEE Std 982.1-1988 [2], determine the data needed to perform the measurement from the list of primitives.

(2) Develop project practices for organizing data so information related to events during the development effort can be stored in a data base and retained for historical purposes and analysis. Automated tools integrated with the development environment should be considered.

Patient, accurate data collection and recording is the key to producing accurate measurements. If not well-organized, data collection can become very expensive. To contain these costs, the information gathering should be integrated with verification and validation activities. Appropriate mechanisms, such as forms or direct terminal entry, should be used to record the results of reviews. Use of automated tools for data retrieval and data entry can also reduce costs. Properly augmented configuration change control systems may furnish an ideal support environment for recording and evaluating most of the data for reliability assessment.

An important outgrowth of implementing a measurement effort is the ability to evaluate the results of collected data, develop measures, and apply analysis of the results to the end product. By tracking progress and evaluating the results, the measurement effort can be used to assess product reliability growth as well as the effectiveness of the development and support processes.

3.3 Measurement Selection Criteria. Current technology in software reliability is limited largely to the use of models that rely exclusively on test data applied to software at the end of development. The measures selected for the standard were extracted from available literature and from the collective experience of practitioners in the field. The primary emphasis was to identify a varied set of measures that cover the many aspects of the concept of reliability. This led to the inclusion of faults and failures as well as models for the traditional reliability calculations.

The constructive approach expanded the search to measures that promote reliability by minimizing residual faults through error prevention and early fault detection and removal. Therefore, the standard includes product measures to determine how carefully a product was verified (eg, completeness and traceability) and complexity measures to accommodate the possibility of change to the system.

Careful consideraton was given to the selection of process measures that monitor the quality of the development process and identify the need to make changes early in the process. Some process measures monitor the accuracy and completeness of development and test activities through examination of product properties (such as completeness and consistency). Other process measures monitor the efficiency of the activities (eg, error distribution). The process measures have the potential to stimulate adoption of good engineering practices at the proper project phase, specifically encouraging early fault detection.

A key consideration in the selection of the measures was to address the full range of the life cycle, a varied audience of both users and software and systems engineers, and a range of audience skills in reliability measurement.

The user class, which may include the owner, the operator and the recipient of the system capability, is more interested in measures related to system availability and operability, such as mean time to failure. The software engineer is more interested in software faults that cause excessive failure rates.

Reliability measures take on both aspects—system failures and software faults. The user can focus on system availability and capability; whereas the engineer can focus on the fault in the software product. Other measures, such as complexity, are of interest to managers and developers, assisting them to improve processes and control costs, schedules, personal productivity, and professional skills.

From the point of view of skill required, the measures are arranged in increasing order of difficulty. This allows individuals with little knowledge of computational methodologies to start making meaningful measurements. Subsequent measures depend upon increasing experience and sophistication with computational methodologies and automated assists.

4. Measure Organization and Classification

The measures in this guide are organized by the two basic objectives of reliability. The first objective is product maturity assessment—a certification of product readiness for operation (including an estimation of support necessary for corrective maintenance). The second objective of reliability is process maturity assessment—an ongoing evaluation of a software factory's capability to produce products of sufficient quality for user needs. Process maturity assessement includes product maturity assessment with the objective of process repair when necessary.

With hardware factories, process maturity assessment is usually performed through the technique of statistical process control. In software, this technique has been hampered by the lack of clearly defined measurables to relate product quality deficiencies to process cause. The measures in this guide provide the means to apply statistical process control to software.

The software life cycle can be modeled and refined into a sequence of subprocesses. Each subprocess has inputs that should meet well-defined entry criteria and outputs that should meet well-defined exit criteria.

An assessment of the product at the completion of a subprocess (the output against the exit criteria) not only evaluates the readiness of that individual product to enter the next subprocess, it serves as an indicator of the quality of the subprocess itself. It should be noted that failure of a product to pass the established exit criteria is a signal for further analysis. Either the subprocess could be defective or the criteria could be too stringent. Corrective action should be taken only after sufficient analysis (Fig 4-1).

For each measure the following topics are detailed in the Appendix: implementation, interpretation, considerations, training, an example, benefits, experience, and references.

Fig 4-1
Generalized Process Control

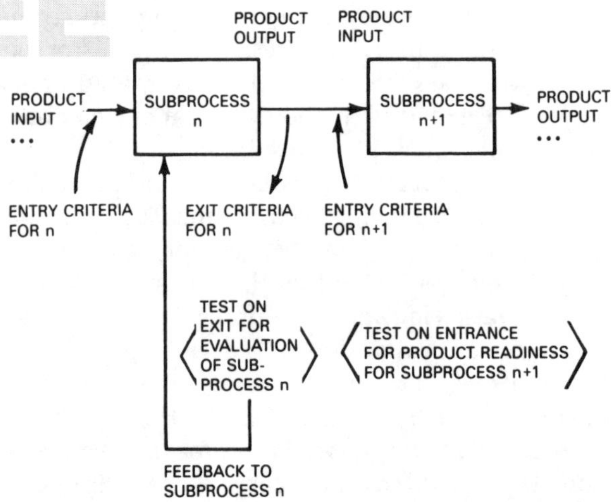

NOTE: Entry criteria n+1 might differ from exit criteria n since owners of subprocess n, entry criteria n, and exit criteria n could be separate organizations from those of n+1.

These measures can be divided into two functional categories: product and process. Product measures are applied to the software objects produced and are divided into six subcategories. Process measures are applied to the life cycle activities of development, test and maintenance and are divided into three subcategories.

The functional categories are as follows:

Product Measures

Errors, faults, and failures
Mean time to failure; failure rate
Reliability growth and projection
Remaining product faults
Completeness and consistency
Complexity

Process Measures

Management control
Coverage
Risk, benefit, cost evaluation

In addition to the functional classification, the measures are also classified by the software life cycle phases in which their use is appropriate. Typical software life cycle phases based upon IEEE Std 729-1983, IEEE Standard Glossary of Software Engineering Terminology [1] are used to illustrate when each of the measures may be applied. The life cycle phases are as follows:

Concepts
Requirements
Design
Implementation
Test
Installation and Checkout
Operation and Maintenance
Retirement

Finally, the measures can be classified as indicators or predictors.

4.1 Functional Classification. The measure classification matrix (Table 4.1-1) is a cross index of measures and functional categories. It can be used to select measures applicable to each category. For each functional category, a matrix is presented that cross-references the measures with the phases of the software life cycle in which they are applicable (Tables 4.2-1 through 4.2-9).

Table 4.1-1 includes an experience rating of 0, 1, 2, or 3. A "0" indicates that the measure has been formalized but has not been sufficiently validated to have operational experience. A "1" means that the measure has had limited use in the software community. This could be because the measure has been used only within an organization and has not had industry-wide exposure, or because the measure is not sufficiently well known to have been used on many projects. A "2" means that the measure has had moderate experience and a "3" means that it has had extensive experience. In no way does the experience rating imply that one measure is better than another.

Table 4-1
Category: Errors, Faults, Failures Counting

	Life Cycle Phase							
Measures	Concept	Requirements	Design	Implementation	Test	Installation & Checkout Installation	Operation & Maintenance	Retirement
1. Fault density	Δ	Δ	Δ	Δ	Δ	Δ	Δ	Δ
2. Defect density	Δ	Δ	Δ	Δ	Δ	Δ	Δ	Δ
3. Cumulative failure profile	Δ	Δ	Δ	Δ	Δ	Δ	Δ	Δ
4. Fault-days number	Δ	Δ	Δ	Δ	Δ	Δ	Δ	Δ
7. Requirements traceability		Δ	Δ				Δ	
8. Defect indices	Δ	Δ	Δ	Δ	Δ	Δ	Δ	Δ
12. Number of conflicting requirements		Δ					Δ	
23. Requirements compliance		Δ					Δ	

Table 4.1-1
Measure Classification Matrix

	Product Measures						Process Measures		
Measures (Experience)	Errors, Faults, Failures	Mean Time to Failure; Failure Rate	Reliability Growth & Projection	Remaining Product Faults	Completeness & Consistency	Complexity	Management Control	Coverage	Risk, Benefit, Cost Evaluation
1. Fault density (2)	X								
2. Defect density (3)	X								
3. Cumulative failure profile (1)	X								
4. Fault-days number (0)	X						X		
5. Functional or modular test coverage (1)					X			X	X
6. Cause and effect graphing (2)					X			X	
7. Requirements traceability (3)	X				X			X	
8. Defect indices (1)	X						X		
9. Error distribution(s) (1)							X		
10. Software maturity index (1)			X						X
11. Man hours per major defect detected (2)							X		X
12. Number of conflicting requirements (2)	X				X			X	
13. Number of entries/exits per module (1)					X	X			
14. Software science measures (3)				X		X			
15. Graph-theoretic complexity for architecture (1)						X			
16. Cyclomatic complexity (3)						X			
17. Minimal unit test case determination (2)					X	X			
18. Run reliability (2)			X		X	X			
19. Design structure (1)						X			
20. Mean time to discover the next *K* faults (3)									X
21. Software purity level (1)			X						
22. Estimated number of faults remaining (seeding) (2)				X					
23. Requirements compliance (1)	X				X			X	
24. Test coverage (2)					X			X	
25. Data or information flow complexity (1)						X			
26. Reliability growth function (2)			X						
27. Residual fault count (1)				X					
28. Failure analysis using elapsed time (3)			X	X					
29. Testing sufficiency (0)			X					X	
30. Mean-time-to-failure (3)		X	X						
31. Failure rate (3)		X							
32. Software documentation & source listings (2)					X				
33. RELY - (Required Software Reliability) (1)								X	X
34. Software release readiness (0)									X
35. Completeness (2)					X				
36. Test accuracy (1)				X	X			X	
37. System performance reliability (2)			X						
38. Independent process reliability (0)			X						
39. Combined HW/SW system operational availability (0)			X						

4.1.1 Product Measures. The product measures address cause and effect of the static/dynamic aspects of both projected reliability prior to operation, and operational reliability. As an example, reliability may change radically during the maintenance effort, due to the complexity of the system design. The six product measure subcategories address these dimensions of reliability.

(1) Errors, faults, failures — Count of defects with respect to human cause, program bugs, and observed system malfunctions.

(2) Mean-time-to-failure; failure rate — Derivative measures of defect occurrence and time.

(3) Reliability growth and projection — The assessment of change in failure-freeness of the product under testing and in operation.

(4) Remaining products faults — The assessment of fault-freeness of the product in development, test, or maintenance.

(5) Completeness and consistency — The assessment of the presence and agreement of all necessary software system parts.

(6) Complexity — The assessment of complicating factors in a system.

4.1.2 Process Measures. The process measures address cause and effect of both the static and dynamic aspects of the development and support management processes necessary for maximizing quality and productivity. The three process measure subcategories address the process dimension of reliability.

(1) Management control measures address the quantity and distribution of error and faults and the trend of cost necessary for defect removal.

(2) Coverage measures allow one to monitor the ability of developers and managers to guarantee the required completness in all the activities of the life-cycle and support the definition of corrective actions to carry the coverage indicators to the desired levels.

(3) Risks, benefits, and cost evaluation measures support delivery decisions based both on technical and cost criteria. Risk can be assessed based on residual faults present in the product at delivery and the cost associated with the resulting support activity.

Table 4.2-1
Life Cycle Classification Matrix: Errors, Faults, Failures Counting

	Life Cycle Phase							
Measures	Concept	Requirements	Design	Implementation	Test	Installation & Checkout Installation	Operation & Maintenance	Retirement
1. Fault density	Δ	Δ	Δ	Δ	Δ	Δ	Δ	Δ
2. Defect density	Δ	Δ	Δ	Δ	Δ	Δ	Δ	Δ
3. Cumulative failure profile	Δ	Δ	Δ	Δ	Δ	Δ	Δ	Δ
4. Fault-days number	Δ	Δ	Δ	Δ	Δ	Δ	Δ	Δ
7. Requirements traceability		Δ	Δ				Δ	
8. Defect indices	Δ	Δ	Δ	Δ	Δ	Δ	Δ	Δ
12. Number of conflicting requirements		Δ					Δ	
23. Requirements compliance		Δ					Δ	

Table 4.2-2
Life Cycle Classification Matrix: Mean-Time-to-Failure; Failure Rate

	Life Cycle Phase							
Measures	Concept	Requirements	Design	Implementation	Test	Installation & Checkout Installation	Operation & Maintenance	Retirement
30. Mean time to failure					Δ	Δ	Δ	
31. Failure rate					Δ	Δ	Δ	

Table 4.2-3
Life Cycle Classification Matrix: Reliability Growth and Projection

	Life Cycle Phase							
Measures	Concept	Requirements	Design	Implementation	Test	Installation & Checkout Installation	Operation & Maintenance	Retirement
10. Software maturity index	Δ	Δ	Δ			Δ	Δ	
18. Run reliability					Δ	Δ	Δ	
21. Software purity level					Δ	Δ	Δ	
26. Reliability growth function					Δ	Δ	Δ	
28. Failure analysis using elapsed time					Δ	Δ	Δ	
29. Testing sufficiency					Δ	Δ		
30. Mean time to failure					Δ	Δ	Δ	
37. System performance reliability		Δ	Δ	Δ	Δ	Δ	Δ	
38. Independent process reliability						Δ	Δ	
39. Combined HW/SW operational availability					Δ	Δ	Δ	

Table 4.2-4
Life Cycle Classification Matrix: Remaining Faults Estimation

	Life Cycle Phase							
Measures	Concept	Requirements	Design	Implementation	Test	Installation & Checkout Installation	Operation & Maintenance	Retirement
14. Software science measures				Δ			Δ*	
22. Estimated number of faults remaining (seeding)					Δ	Δ	Δ	
27. Residual fault count					Δ	Δ	Δ	
28. Failure analysis using elapsed time					Δ	Δ	Δ	
36. Test accuracy					Δ			

*If source code is changed

Table 4.2-5
Life Cycle Classification Matrix: Completeness, Consistency

	Life Cycle Phase							
Measures	Concept	Requirements	Design	Implementation	Test	Installation & Checkout Installation	Operation & Maintenance	Retirement
5. Functional or modular test coverage					Δ	Δ	Δ	
6. Cause and effect graphing		Δ	Δ	Δ	Δ		Δ	
7. Requirements traceability		Δ	Δ				Δ	
12. Number of conflicting requirements		Δ					Δ	
16. Cyclomatic complexity (testing phase)				Δ	Δ		Δ	
23. Requirements compliance		Δ					Δ	
24. Test coverage		Δ	Δ		Δ	Δ	Δ	
32. Software documentation and source listings				Δ	Δ	Δ	Δ	
35. Completeness		Δ	Δ				Δ	
36. Test accuracy					Δ			

Table 4.2-6
Life Cycle Classification Matrix: Complexity

	Life Cycle Phase							
Measures	Concept	Requirements	Design	Implementation	Test	Installation & Checkout Installation	Operation & Maintenance	Retirement
13. Number of entries/exits per module			Δ	Δ			Δ	
14. Software science measures				Δ			Δ	
15. Graph-theoretic complexity for architecture		Δ	Δ				Δ	
16. Cyclomatic complexity			Δ	Δ			Δ	
17. Minimal test case determination				Δ	Δ		Δ	
19. Design structure			Δ				Δ	
25. Data or information flow complexity			Δ	Δ			Δ	

Table 4.2-7
Life Cycle Classification Matrix: Management Control

	Life Cycle Phase							
Measures	Concept	Requirements	Design	Implementation	Test	Installation & Checkout Installation	Operation & Maintenance	Retirement
4. Fault-days number	Δ	Δ	Δ	Δ	Δ	Δ	Δ	
8. Defect indices		Δ	Δ	Δ	Δ	Δ	Δ	
9. Error distribution(s)		Δ	Δ	Δ	Δ	Δ	Δ	
11. Man-hours per major defect detected		Δ	Δ	Δ	Δ	Δ	Δ	
20. Mean time to discover next *K* faults					Δ	Δ	Δ	

Table 4.2-8
Life Cycle Classification Matrix: Coverage

Measures	Life Cycle Phase							
	Concept	Requirements	Design	Implementation	Test	Installation & Checkout Installation	Operation & Maintenance	Retirement
5. Functional or modular test coverage					Δ	Δ	Δ	
6. Cause and effect graphing		Δ	Δ	Δ	Δ		Δ	
7. Requirements traceability		Δ	Δ				Δ	
12. Number of conflicting requirements		Δ					Δ	
23. Requirements compliance		Δ					Δ	
24. Test coverage		Δ	Δ	Δ	Δ	Δ	Δ	
29. Testing sufficiency					Δ		Δ	
32. Software documentation & source listings				Δ	Δ	Δ	Δ	
33. RELY - Required Software Reliability	Δ	Δ	Δ	Δ	Δ	Δ	Δ	
35. Completeness		Δ	Δ				Δ	
36. Test accuracy					Δ			

Table 4.2-9
Life Cycle Classification Matrix: Risk, Benefit, and Cost Evaluation

Measures	Life Cycle Phase							
	Concept	Requirements	Design	Implementation	Test	Installation & Checkout Installation	Operation & Maintenance	Retirement
5. Functional or modular test coverage					Δ	Δ	Δ	
10. Software maturity index	Δ	Δ	Δ			Δ	Δ	
11. Man-hours per major defect detected		Δ	Δ	Δ	Δ	Δ	Δ	
14. Software science measures				Δ			Δ	
18. Run reliability					Δ	Δ	Δ	
19. Design structure			Δ					
20. Mean time to discover the next *K* faults					Δ	Δ	Δ	
21. Software purity level					Δ	Δ	Δ	
27. Residual fault count					Δ	Δ	Δ	
31. Failure rate					Δ	Δ	Δ	
33. RELY-Required Software Reliability	Δ	Δ	Δ	Δ	Δ	Δ	Δ	
34. Software release readiness					Δ	Δ		

4.2 Life Cycle Classification. To assist the user in more practical considerations, such as "When are the measures applied?" the life cycle classification (Fig 4.2-1) has been developed. The life cycle has been divided into early, middle, and late segments. In the early segment, the measures relate to the potential causes of system reliability. The middle segment measures relate to the reduction of process errors that can improve the efficiency of software development. The late segment measures relate to actual system performance reliability.

For each life cycle phase a set of possible measures that might be applied during the development effort should be identified. Selection need not be limited to one measure per development phase, but on the other hand, it is expected that overzealous selection of measures would not benefit a project.

4.2.1 Early Life Cycle Segment. The early segment — concepts, requirements, and design — is the period when many of the characteristics of the system, including potential reliability, are determined. Problems in these early phases tend to result from premature constraints on the system design that limit system solution alternatives and affect the real system objectives, which include reliability. Emphasis and focus of the measures in the early stages are on the goals and objectives of the system. The concrete feedback they provide aids in achieving completeness and consistency in the definition of user requirements as well as the design.

4.2.2 Middle Life Cycle Segment. The middle segment of the software life cycle includes implementation, test, installation and checkout. The software engineer's goal in this segment is to develop fault-free software efficiently. The objectives of reliability measurement in this segment include not only reliability projection, but also guidance of the process so that fault-free software is developed efficiently. For reliability projection, faults found in this segment can relate directly to operational failures, expecially when development activity is halted prematurely. These faults, in fact, can be used to determine software readiness. For the process evolution objective, these faults can be considered process errors and can be directly related to the effectiveness and efficiency of the previously applied processes. Cause-analysis can relate the fault to that point in the process where the error was made. Proper process-control techniques applied to these measures can indicate if and when action should be taken to change the process.

4.2.3 Late Life Cycle Segment. The late segment of the software life cycle — operation, maintenance, and retirement — is where system performance, as an expression of reliability and availability, can be directly measured using the traditional software reliability measures. Current software product performance can be used to project future performance. In addition, future development can be improved by relating the problems in the current software product to the steps in the development process that produced them.

In this segment there are two audiences for software reliability measures — the user and the software engineer. The users are the owner, the operator, and the recipient of the end product of the system capability. The software engineers include both the original developer and the subsequent maintainer. In most cases, the user is more interested in system availability and operability; the software engineer is more interested in the origins of software faults that cause failures. The user focuses on the capability of the system; the software engineer focuses on the faults in the restricted software domain.

Reliability measures should address both system failures and software faults to provide useful information to both user and software engineer. There are traditional measures of software performance that provide both a user and a software engineer view of system reliability. Many of these measures — for example, mean-time-to-failure (user) and software fault discovery rate (software engineer) — serve as primitives for reliability projections based on modeling techniques.

Fig 4.2-1
Life Cycle Classification

LIFE CYCLE SEGMENTS

EARLY
- CONCEPTS
- REQUIREMENTS
- DESIGN

MIDDLE
- IMPLEMENTATION
- TEST
- INSTALLATION AND CHECKOUT

LATE
- OPERATIONS AND MAINTENANCE
- RETIREMENT

4.3 Indicators and Predictors. Measures can also be organized with respect to their primary function as indicators or predictors. Indicator measures provide an assessment of reliability at the point in time the measurement is taken. Predictor measures project forecasted behavior as suggested by past behavior. Historical data based upon consistently applied indicator measures are the basic input for predictor measures. The higher the integrity and quantity of the historical record, the better results can be expected from the predictor measures. Note that some measures are both predictor and indicator in nature.

Indicator measures can be used to determine completion of activities throughout the life cycle. In this context, established goals are considered successfully achieved based on the value of the indicator measure. Using the history of indicator measurements, future behavior can be determined based upon predictor measures.

Table 4.3-1 provides a cross reference of measures — first, to the object or events that are subjects of measurement, and second, to the primary indicator or predictor nature of the measure.

Table 4.3-1
Indicator/Predictor Measure Classification

Object/Event	Measure
Requirements	
Indicator	4.6, 4.7, 4.12, 4.23, 4.33, 4.35
Predictor	—
Design	
Indicator	4.13, 4.15, 4.19, 4.25
Predictor	—
Source code	
Indicator	4.16, 4.17
Predictor	4.14
Test set	
Indicator	4.5, 4.24
Predictor	—
Any product	
Indicator	4.32
Predictor	—
Software faults	
Indicator	4.1, 4.2, 4.4, 4.8, 4.9, 4.11
Predictor	4.22, 4.29, 4.36
Software failures	
Indicator	4.3
Predictor	4.18, 4.20, 4.21, 4.26, 4.27, 4.28, 4.30, 4.31, 4.39
Release package	
Indicator	4.10, 4.34
Predictor	—
Performing object code	
Indicator	4.37
Predictor	—
Tested object modules	
Indicator	4.38
Predictor	—

5. Framework for Measures

Software reliability measurements take place in an environment that includes user needs and requirements, a process for developing products meeting those needs, and user environment within which the delivered software satisfies those needs. This measurement environment establishes a framework for determining and interpreting indicators of software reliability.

5.1 Measurement Process. In this section, a measurement process is detailed that can constructively affect the delivered reliability of software through the selection and interpretation of indicators of software reliability. This process formalizes the data collection practices in both development and support. It provides for product evaluation at major milestones in the life cycle. Furthermore, it relates measures from one life cycle phase to another. In summary, this process provides the basis for reliability measurement of a product.

5.2 Stages of a Measurement Process. The software reliability measurement process can be described in nine stages (Fig 5.2-1). These stages may overlap or occur in different sequences depending on organization needs. These stages provide a useful model for describing measurement process issues. Each of these stages in the measurement process influences the production of a delivered product with the potential for high reliability. Other factors influencing the measurement process include the following: a firm management commitment to continually assess product and process maturity, or stability, or both during the project; use of trained personnel in applying the measures to the project in a useful way; software support tools; and a clear understanding of the distinctions among errors, faults, and failures.

5.2.1 Stage 1: Plan Organizational Strategy. Initiate a planning process. Form a planning group and review reliability constraints and objectives, giving consideration to user needs and requirements. Identify the reliability characteristics of a software product necessary to achieve

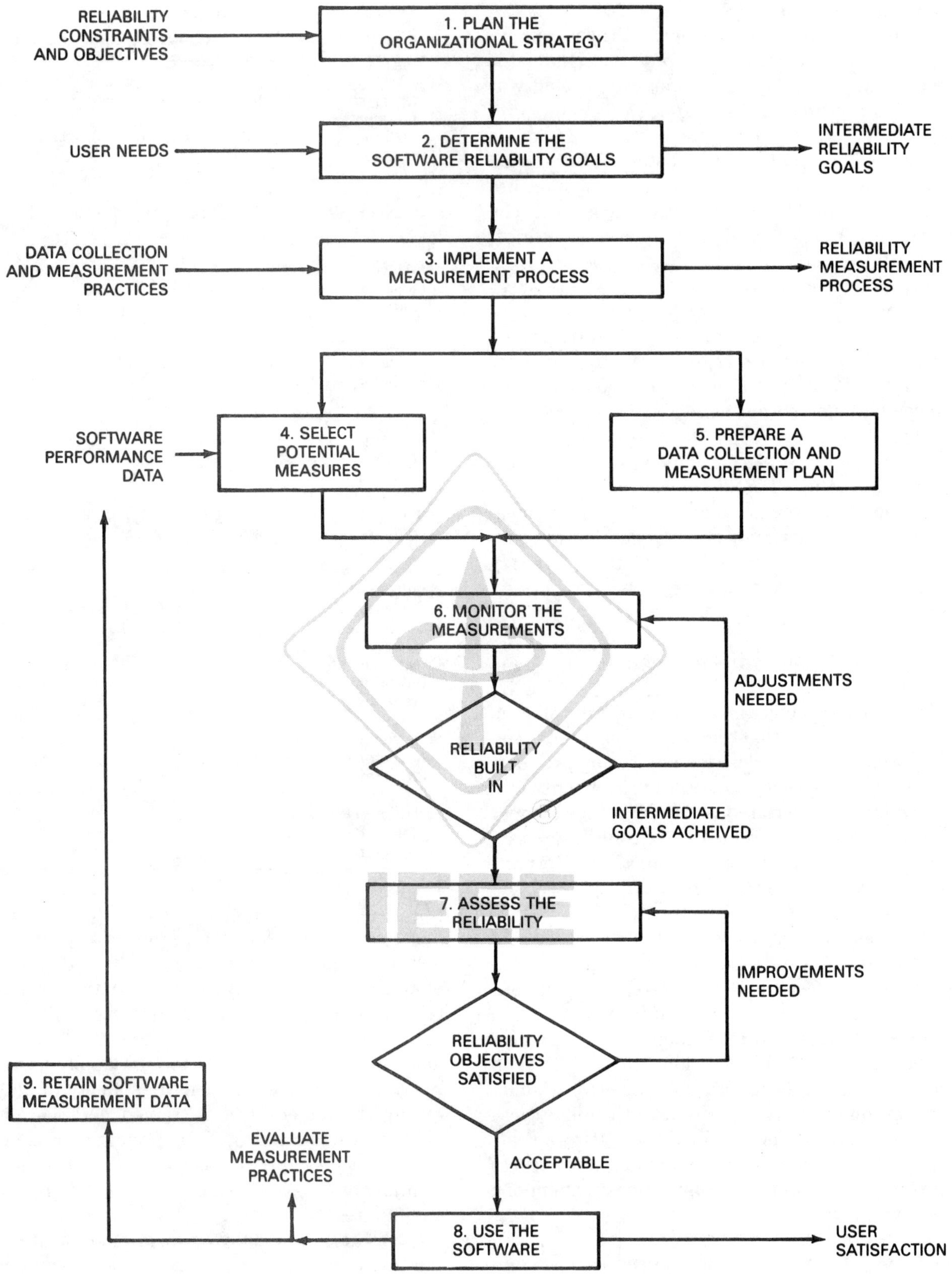

Fig 5.2-1
Reliability Measurement Process

these objectives. Establish a strategy for measuring and managing software reliability. Document practices for conducting measurements.

5.2.2 Stage 2: Determine Software Reliability Goals. Define the reliability goals for the software being developed in order to optimize reliability in light of realistic assessments of project constraints, including size, scope, cost, and schedule.

Review the requirements for the specific development effort, in order to determine the desired characteristics of the delivered software. For each characteristic, identify specific reliability goals that can be demonstrated by the software or measured against a particular value or condition. Establish an acceptable range of values. Consideration should be given to user needs and requirements, including user perception of software reliability and the system environment in which the software must interact.

Establish intermediate reliability goals at various points in the development effort to assist in achieving the reliability goals.

5.2.3 Stage 3: Implement Measurement Process. Establish a software reliability measurement process that best fits an organization's needs.

Review the process described in stages 4 through 8 and select those stages that best lead to optimum reliability. Add to or enhance these stages as needed to reflect the specific work environment. Consider the following suggestions when establishing the measurement process:

(1) Select appropriate data collection and measurement practices designed to optimize software reliability.
(2) Document the measures required, the intermediate and final milestones when measurements are taken, the data collection requirements, and the acceptable values for each measure.
(3) Assign responsibilities for performing and monitoring measurements, and provide necessary support for these activities from across the internal organization.
(4) Initiate a measure selection and evaluation process.
(5) Prepare educational materials for training personnel in concepts, principles, and practices of software reliability and reliability measures.

After selecting and establishing the steps of the measurement process, reduce it to an organization operation procedure. Maintain complete records of the measurement process to provide a historical perspective so that future reliability measurement programs may benefit.

5.2.4 Stage 4: Select Potential Measures. Identify potential measures that would be helpful in achieving the reliability goals established in Stage 2.

Once the organization software reliability goals are established, select the measures best suited to the development and support environments.

Use the classification scheme described in Section 4 to determine which category or categories of reliability measurements would be most useful to the project. When possible, measures should be chosen within a particular category to show a continuous relationship between early indicators and the final software reliability achieved at delivery.

Measures should be selected to span categories and development phases. Selection need not be limited to one measure per category or phase. However, overzealous selection of measures should be avoided.

The classification scheme assists in identifying and applying related measures across a development project (commonality) or in applying the same measure(s) to several projects (comparison).

5.2.5 Stage 5: Prepare Data Collection and Measurement Plan. Prepare a data collection and measurement plan for the development and support effort. For each potential measure, determine the primitives needed to perform the measurement. Data should be organized so that information related to events during the development effort can be properly recorded in a data base and retained for historical purposes.

For each intermediate reliability goal identified in Stage 2, identify the measures needed to achieve the goal. Identify the points during development when the measurements are to be taken. Establish acceptable values or a range of values to assess whether the intermediate reliability goals are achieved.

Include in the plan an approach for monitoring the measurement effort itself. The responsibility for collecting and reporting data, verifying its accuracy, computing measures, and interpreting the results should be described. Use historical data where possible.

5.2.6 Stage 6: Monitor Measurements. Once the data collection and reporting begins, monitor the measurements and the progress made during development, so as to manage the reliability and thereby achieve the goals for the delivered product. The measurements assist in determining whether the intermediate reliability goals are achieved and whether the final goal is achieveable. Analyze the measures and determine if the results are sufficient to satisfy the reliability goals. Decide whether a measure result assists in affirming the reliability of the product or process being measured. Take corrective action as necessary to improve the desired characteristics of the software being developed.

5.2.7 Stage 7: Assess Reliability. Analyze measurements to ensure that reliability of the delivered software satisfies the reliability objectives and that the reliability, as measured, is acceptable.

Identify assessment steps that are consistent with the reliability objectives documented in the data collection and measurement plan. Check the consistency of acceptance criteria and the sufficiency of tests to satisfactorily demonstrate that the reliability objectives have been achieved. Identify the organization responsible for determining final acceptance of the reliability of the software. Document the steps involved in assessing the reliability of the software.

Ensure that reliability improvements in the software have been made. Demonstrate satisfactory achievement of all reliability goals by reliability measurements and internal tests and by field reliability measurements during use.

5.2.8 Stage 8: Use Software. Assess the effectiveness of the measurement effort and perform necessary corrective action. Conduct a follow-up analysis of the measurement effort to evaluate reliability assessment and development practices, record lessons learned, and evaluate user satisfaction with the reliability of the software. Identify practices that are ineffective and requirements that indicate a need to develop and refine future measurement efforts.

5.2.9 Stage 9: Retain Software Measurement Data. Retain measurement data on the software throughout the development and operation phases for use by future projects. This data provides a baseline for reliability improvement and an opportunity to compare the same measures across completed projects. This information can assist in developing future guidelines and standards.

6. Errors, Faults, and Failures Analysis for Reliability Improvement

Reliability is a high-level indicator of the operational readiness of a system. Measurement for reliability need not be viewed as a passive score to be achieved, but rather as an active means of improving the processes used to build and maintain systems.

A key to reliability improvement is the maintenance of an accurate history of errors and faults associated with failure events. This section presents an introduction to the dynamics of errors, faults, and failures, with the goal of improving reliability by minimizing future failure events through error analysis and process control.

6.1 Dynamics of Errors, Faults, and Failures.

Errors, faults, and failures can be viewed as a series of cause and effect relationships (Fig 6.1-1). The source of errors is either developers or users. Those developer errors resulting in undetected faults in the product directly affect reliability. User errors, usually misunderstandings, can affect perceived reliability.

Failures may occur when a fault is encountered (for example, in the code or the user documentation), or when a how-to-use error is made by the user. Faults exist in the product due to errors made by the designer or programmer during the development process. How-to-use errors are originated by either human factor faults within the product, or by the user misunderstanding the product application.

Lacks within the product exist when a desired feature or characteristic is incomplete or missing from the software. These lacks or weaknesses are a subclass of faults.

While features due to how-to-use errors may be caused by the interaction of the product and user, or by the actions of the user alone, they are often perceived by the average user as a failure of the product.

These interactions must be clearly understood in order to measure and control the development and support processes.

6.2 Analysis of Error, Fault, Failure Events

6.2.1 Failure Analysis. The purpose of failure analysis is to acquire knowledge of the most important "failure modes" of the product in the user environment. It is important to distinguish between failure due to product faults and failure due to user error. Failures due to user error may be caused by the following:

- lack of clear, well-structured user documentation
- complex user interfaces
- lack of training
- lack of support
- insufficient user educational or systems background

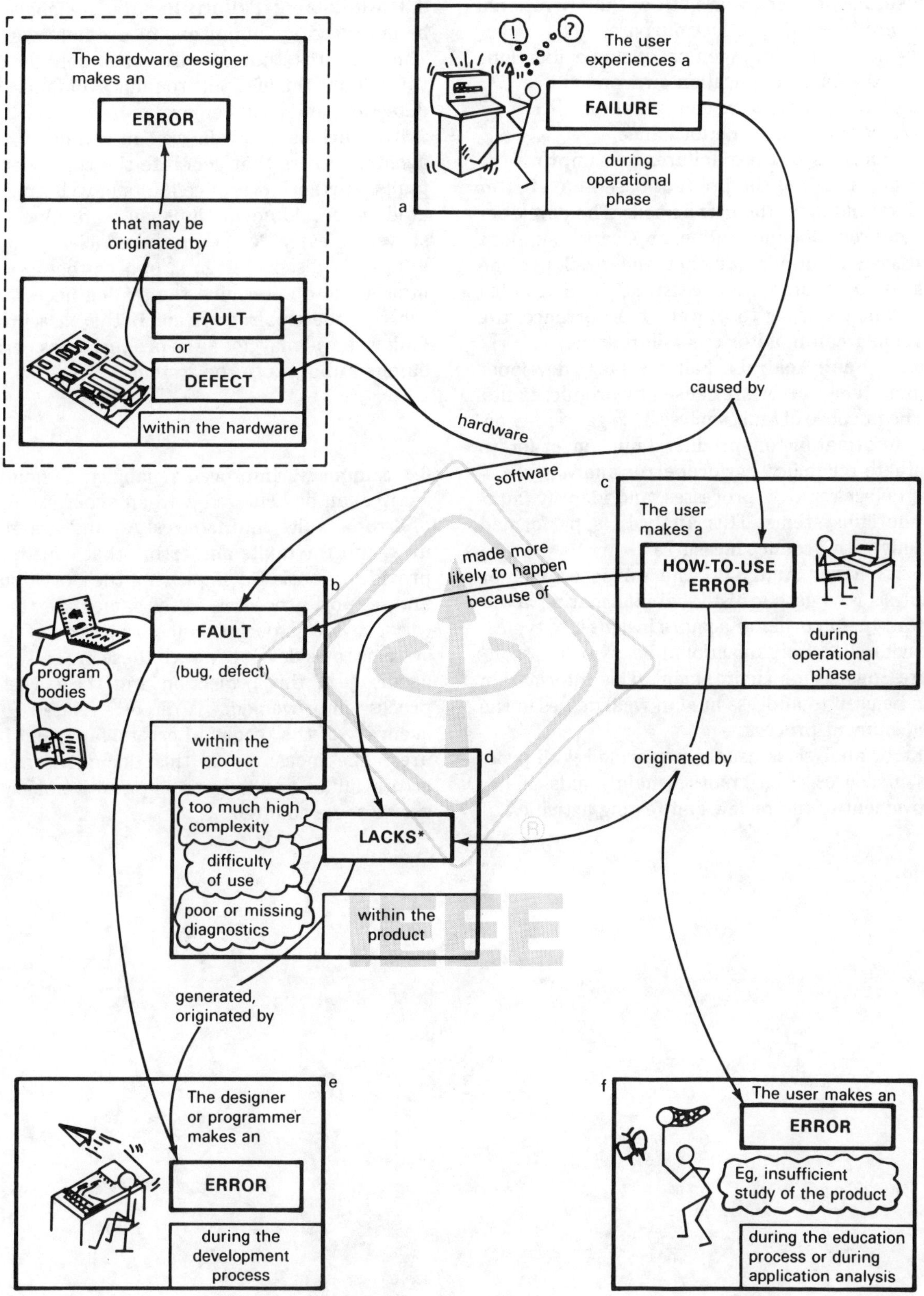

*Product lacks (or weaknesses) could also be seen as a subclass of faults.

Fig 6.1-1
The Error, Fault, Failure Chain

- insufficient user awareness of the operational environment or product purpose
- inconsistencies between product specifications and the user's application environment
- inadequate hardware configuration
- inadequate system performance.

An analysis of these failures can improve the human factors of the product based on a better understanding of the user's needs. The developer can improve documentation, application support, and system support. Further, the developer can suggest a tailored user assistance and training program. In order to prevent reoccurrence, the developer can monitor this failure type.

6.2.2 Fault Analysis. Failures due to developer or maintainer error are caused by product faults.

The purpose of fault analysis is to gather historical information on product faults in order to evaluate reliability, perform error analysis, sensitize defect removal processes, and identify fault-prone subsystems. This analysis is performed mainly with product measures.

6.2.3 Error Analysis. The purpose of error analysis is to gather historical information about error types in order to acquire insight into typical individual and organizational behavior in a software engineering environment. This information can be used to address human weaknesses in the development process.

Error analysis is usually performed with process measures. This analysis mainly aids in improvement of the review and testing activities.

6.3 Minimizing Failure Events. Reliability can be improved by minimizing future failure events. This requires that specific attention be given throughout the life cycle to fault avoidance, fault detection, and fault removal.

It is obvious that failures can be minimized by avoiding errors that generate the corresponding faults. Furthermore, once faults have been generated in development, it is more productive to strive for early detection and efficient removal. For faults discovered in support processes, it is important to determine the testing necessary to recertify the repaired system. In this case, prompt fault removal may not be as productive as periodic batched updates to the system.

6.4 Summary. Improved reliability, the end objective, can be achieved with an accurate history of errors, faults, and failures. An analysis of failures, and the faults and errors that cause them, provides a basis for improving the development and support processes. At the same time, this history provides a performance projection of future systems to be developed with these processes. The accuracy of this projection and the success of process improvements is directly related to the accuracy of the record of errors, faults, and failures. The measures in this document assume errors, faults, and failures as primitive objects or events to be counted.

Appendix

Measures for Reliable Software

(This Appendix is not a part of IEEE Std 982.2-1988, IEEE Guide for the Use of IEEE Standard Dictionary of Measures to Produce Reliable Software.)

A1. Fault Density

A1.1 Application. This measure can be used to perform the following functions:

(1) Predict remaining faults by comparison with expected fault density;

(2) Determine if sufficient testing has been completed, based on predetermined goals for severity class;

(3) Establish standard fault densities for comparison and prediction.

A1.2 Primitives. Establish the severity levels for failure designation.

F = Total number of unique faults found in a given time interval resulting in failures of a specified severity level

KSLOC = Number of source lines of executable code and non-executable data declarations in thousands

A1.3 Implementation. Establish severity, failure types and fault types.

(1) Failure types might include I/O (input, output, or both) and user. Fault types might result from design, coding, documentation, and initialization.

(2) Observe and log each failure.

(3) Determine the program fault(s) that caused the failure. Classify the faults by type. Additional faults may be found resulting in total faults being greater than the number of failures observed, or one fault may manifest itself by several failures. Thus, fault and failure density may both be measured.

(4) Determine total lines of executable and non-executable data declaration source code (KSLOC).

(5) Calculate the fault density for a given severity level as:

$$F_d = F/K\text{SLOC}$$

A1.4 Interpretation. Comparison of fault density measurements made on similar systems can give some indication of whether the current system has been sufficiently tested. Software reliability may be qualitatively assessed from this information. In earlier phases of the life cycle, when KSLOC is unavailable, some other normalizing factor (eg, thousands of words of prose) agreed upon for that life cycle phase could be used.

A1.5 Considerations

(1) Test results must be thoroughly analyzed to ensure that faults, not just failures, are identified. Test coverage must be comprehensive.

(2) KSLOC must be consistently calculated (executable code and data).

(3) It should be recognized when comparing products that expected fault densities and measured fault densities have class and severity.

A1.6 Training. Minimal training is required for the use of this measure. Previous software testing experience, however, is required to establish fault and failure classifications. Good record keeping techniques and a source counting tool are essential.

A1.7 Example

(1) Sample data collection form:

Failure/Fault Log Date: / /

Software Tested: ____ Version: ____ *K*SLOC: ____

Test Suite: ____ Recorder: ____

Hardware Configuration: ____

Software Configuration: ____

Failure #	Fault #	Date	Description	Severity
.	.	.	.	.
.	.	.	.	.
.	.	.	.	.

(2) Sample calculation:

Let the number of failures be 21, the number of unique faults from the 21 failures be F = 29, and the number of lines of source code be 6000. Then the fault density is

$F_d = F/K\text{SLOC} = 29/6 = 4.8$ faults/KSLOC.

A1.8 Benefits. This measure is simple to use and provides a first approximation for reliability estimates. Collected data can be used to calculate other measures.

A1.9 Experience. Many organizations are using this measure and have developed their own guidelines but have not published their results. See the references for published examples.

A1.10 References

[A1] BOWEN, J. B. A Survey of Standards and Proposed Metrics for Software Quality Metrics. *Computer*, 1979, 12 (8), pp 37-41.

[A2] SHOOMAN, M. L. *Software Engineering Design/Reliability/Management.* New York: McGraw Hill, 1983, pp 325-329.

A2. Defect Density

A2.1 Application. The defect density measure can be used after design and code inspections of new development or large block modifications. If the defect density is outside the norm after several inspections, it is an indication that the inspection process requires further scrutiny.

A2.2 Primitives. Establish severity levels for defect designation.

D_i = total number of unique defects detected during the ith design, or code inspection process, or the ith life cycle phase;

I = total number of inspections to date;

KSLOD = In the design phase, the number of source lines of design statements in thousands;

KSLOC = In the implementation phase, the number of source lines of executable code and non-executable data declarations in thousands.

A2.3 Implementation. Establish a classification scheme for severity and class of defect. For each inspection, record the product size and the total number of unique defects.

For example, in the design phase calculate the ratio

$$DD = \frac{\sum_{i=1}^{I} D_i}{K\text{SLOD}}$$

This measure assumes that a structured design language is used. However, if some other design methodology is used, then some other unit of defect density has to be developed to conform to the methodology in which the design is expressed.

A2.4 Interpretation. This measure has a degree of indeterminism. For example, a low value may indicate either a good process and a good product or it may indicate a bad process. If the value is low compared to similar past projects, the inspection process should be examined. If the inspection process is found to be adequate, it should then be concluded that the development process has resulted in a relatively defect-free product.

If the measurement value is too high compared to similar past projects, the development process should be examined to determine if poor programming practices have resulted in poor software products. In such a case, a breakdown of defects by type and severity should be made into defect categories such as design, logic, standards, interface, commentary, requirements, etc. The significance of the defect density can then be determined and management action taken. For example, if the defects are high due to requirements, it would be appropriate to halt development, at least in one area, until the requirements are corrected. If, on the other hand, the development process is judged to be adequate, then the inspection process is serving a valuable pretest function.

After significant experience with this measure, it may be appropriate to establish lower values as goals in order to ensure continued reliability growth of the software development process.

A2.5 Considerations. This measure assumes a knowledge of the design and code inspection process. It further assumes consistent and standard data collection and recording. The inspection process should prove effective if strongly committed to and supported by management. The earlier the inspection data can be derived and assessed, the greater the benefit.

A2.6 Training. Although little or no training is needed for calculation of the measure, training in the inspection process is required.

A2.7 Example. Suppose, in the design phase,

$I = 7$

$K\text{SLOD} = 8$

$$\sum_{i=1}^{7} D_i = 78 \text{ (total defects found)}$$

Then,

$$DD = \frac{78}{8} = 9.8 \text{ (estimated defect density)}$$

A2.8 Benefits. The measure is easy to compute and it serves as one of the parameters to evaluate the effectiveness of the inspection process. Deviations from the norm serve as an indicator that immediate management attention is required, and therefore gives the developer a chance to make whatever corrections are necessary to maintain significant product control, reliability, and correctness.

A2.9 Experience. The analysis of this measure in several studies [A3, A4] has shown the utilization of the inspection process and the measurement of the collected data to be a highly effective management tool for software development and defect removal. In addition, the results have been highly consistent and the impact on error profiles during test has been seen.

A2.10 References

[A3] DOBBINS, J., and BUCK, R. Software Quality in the 80's. *Trends and Applications Proceedings*, IEEE Computer Society, 1981.

[A4] DOBBINS, J., and BUCK, R. Software Quality Assurance. *Concepts, Journal of the Defense Systems Management College*, Autumn, 1982.

[A5] FAGAN, MICHAEL E. Design and Code Inspection to Reduce Errors in Program Development. *IBM Systems Journal*, vol 15, no 3, Jul 1976, pp 102-211.

A3. Cumulative Failure Profile

A3.1 Applications. This is a graphical method used to:

(1) Predict reliability through the use of failure profiles;

(2) Estimate additional testing time to reach an acceptably reliable system;

(3) Identify modules and subsystems that require additional testing.

A3.2 Primitives. Establish the severity levels for failure designation. f_i = total number of failures of a given severity level in a given time interval, i=1, ...

A3.3 Implementation. Plot cumulative failures versus a suitable time base. The curve can be derived for the system as a whole, subsystems, or modules.

A3.4 Interpretation. The shape of the cumulative failure curve can be used to project when testing will be complete, provided that test coverage is sufficiently comprehensive. The curve gives an assessment of software reliability. It can provide an indication of clustering of faults in modules, suggesting a further concentration of testing for those modules. The total failures for each testing phase may be estimated by the asymptotic nature of the curve. A non-asymptotic curve indicates the need for continued testing.

A3.5 Considerations. Failures must be observed and recorded, and must be distinct. The failure curve may be compared with open SPR curves (Software Problem Report) or other measures. Several shapes for curves are proposed in the literature [A6, A9]. Profiles may be organized on a system, subsystem, or module basis. Test coverage must be both comprehensive and random.

A3.6 Training. Previous software testing experience is required if classification of severity and of failures is to be established. Good recordkeeping techniques are essential. Knowledge of the modular structure of the program and how it correlates with the test base is required in order to assess if the testing has been comprehensive.

A3.7 Example

Fig A3.7-1
Failure Profile

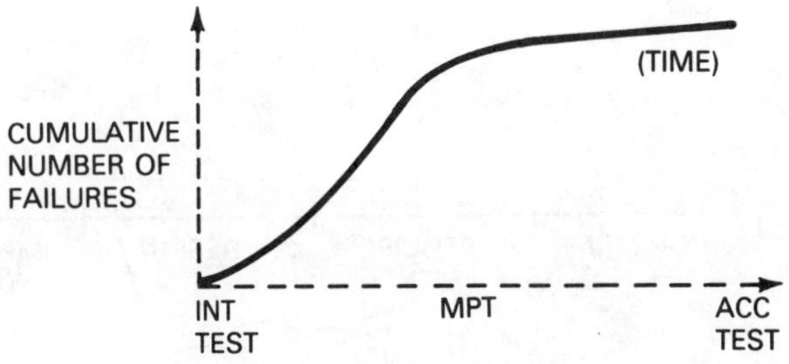

INT TEST = START OF INTEGRATION TEST.
MPT = MIDPOINT OF TESTING.
ACC TEST = START OF ACCEPTANCE TESTING.
SEE [A4, A6, A8, A9] FOR INTERPRETATIONS.

A3.8 Benefits. This measure is simple to use. Data can also be used as input to published reliability models.

A3.9 Experience. Many companies are using this measure and have developed their own guidelines but have not published their results [A8].

A3.10 References. See also Dobbins [A3, A4].

[A6] MENDIS, K. S. Quantifying Software Quality. *Quality Progress*, May 1982, pp 18-22.

[A7] MUSA, J. D., IANNINO, A., and OKUMOTO, K. *Software Reliability: Measurement, Prediction, Application.* New York: McGraw-Hill, 1987.

[A8] SHOOMAN, M. L. *Software Engineering Design/Reliability/Management.* New York: McGraw Hill, 1983, pp 329-335.

[A9] TRACHTENBERG, M. Discovering How to Ensure Software Reliability. *RCA Engineer*, vol 27, no 1, Jan/Feb 1982, pp 53-57.

A4. Fault-Days Number

A4.1 Application. This measure represents the number of days that faults spend in the software system from their creation to their removal.

A4.2 Primitives

(1) Phase when the fault was introduced in the system.

(2) Date when the fault was introduced in the system.

(3) Phase, date, and time when the fault is removed.

FD_i = Fault days for the ith fault

NOTE: For more meaningful measures, time units can be made relative to test time or operational time.

A4.3 Implementation. For each fault detected and removed, during any phase, the number of days from its creation to its removal is determined (fault-days).

The fault-days are then summed for all faults detected and removed, to get the fault-days number at system level, including all faults detected/removed up to the delivery date. In cases when the creation date for the fault is not known, the fault is assumed to have been created at the middle of the phase in which it was introduced.

In Fig A4.3-1 the fault-days for the design fault for module A can be accurately calculated because the design approval date for the detailed design of module A is known. The fault introduced during the requirements phase is assumed to have been created at the middle of the requirement phase because the exact time that the corresponding piece of requirement was specified is not known.

The measure is calculated as follows:

$$\text{Fault days number } (FD) = \sum_i FD_i$$

Fig A4.3-1
Calculation of Fault-Days

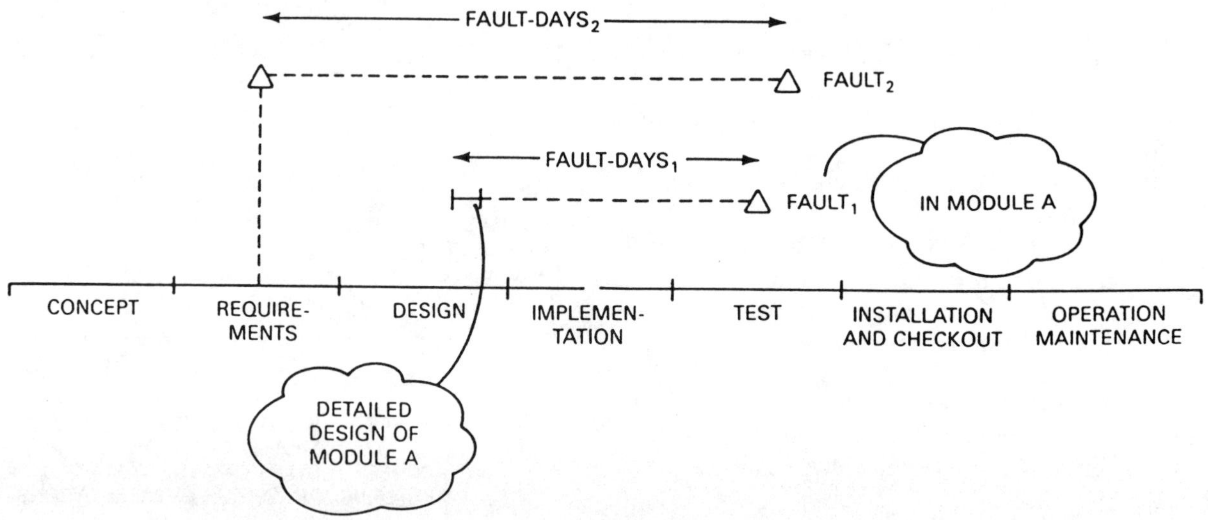

A4.4 Interpretation. The effectiveness of the software design and development process depends upon the timely removal of faults across the entire life cycle. This measure is an indicator of the quality of the software system design and of the development process. For instance, a high number of fault days indicates either many faults (probably due to poor design, indicative of product quality), or long-lived faults, or both (probably due to poor development effort, indicative of process quality).

A4.5 Considerations. Careful collection of primitive data is essential to the successful use of this measure.

A4.6 Training. In order to improve the effectiveness of the software design and development process and to lower development costs (by timely detection and removal of faults), it is essential for personnel to become aware of the importance of recording data that would be needed to generate fault-birth information for each phase across the entire software life cycle phase (for example, date of module creation, changes, deletions, integration, etc, during the design phase).

A4.7 Example. Table 4.7-1 (extracted from Mills [A10], gives fault day information for two systems (A and B). These systems were developed with the same specifications and acceptance conditions, and had the same number of known faults at delivery time. However, the two systems possess very different histories in terms of faults. In this case, the knowledge of fault-days would have helped in predicting their very different behavior in terms of faults detected during acceptance.

These systems, built with the same specifications and subjected to the same acceptance testing, are not the same even though each has no known faults.

A4.8 Benefits. This measure encourages timely inspections and testing and can also assist management in improving the design and development process.

A4.9 Experience. Although limited published experience is available, this measure can be used in a software reliability program to monitor the quality of process and product development effort.

A4.10 Reference

[A10] MILLS, HARLAN D. Software Development. *IEEE Transactions on Software Engineering*, vol SE-4, no 4, Dec 1976.

A5. Functional or Modular Test Coverage

A5.1 Application. This measure is used to quantify a software test coverage index for a software delivery. The primitives counted may be either functions or modules. The operational user is most familiar with system functional requirements and will report system problems in terms of functional requirements rather than module test requirements. It is the task of the evaluator to obtain or develop the functional requirements and associated module cross reference table.

A5.2 Primitives

FE = number of the software functional (modular) requirements for which all test cases have been satisfactorily completed.

FT = total number of software functional (modular) requirements.

Table A4.7-1
Fault Days

During Development	A	Fault Days	B	Fault Days
Lines of code	50 000		50 000	
Faults fixed				
day old	100	100	500	500
week old	10	50	50	250
month old	5	100	50	1000
year old	5	1250	20	5000
Known faults	0		0	
Fault-days (total)		1500		6750
During acceptance				
Faults fixed	10		50	
Known faults	0		0	

A5.3 Implementation. The test coverage index is expressed as a ratio of the number of software functions (modules) tested to the total number of software functions (modules) that make up user (developer) requirements. This ratio is expressed as:

$$\text{Functional (modular) test coverage index} = \frac{FE}{FT}$$

A5.4 Interpretation. The test coverage index can be compared with the status of planned testing and the impact that functional (modular) changes are having on schedule and resources.

A5.5 Considerations. Additional data required to support the test coverage index include:

(1) Software version identification and date of release.
(2) The functions (modules) delivered, changed, and added for each release.
(3) Test results treated as additional primitives.

A5.6 Training. Training is important in methods that identify functions and modules. Examples of such methods are given in Ceriani, Cicu, and Maiocchi [A11].

A5.7 Example. Table A5.7-1 depicts an example of the proposed test data and resulting test coverage index for a series of software releases.

A5.8 Benefit. The test coverage index provides a measure of the percentage of software tested at any time. For many applications programs, the function (modular) test coverage index might always be relatively low because of the system application (eg, automatic test equipment) and the restrictions of the test environment (eg, electronic warfare systems).

A5.9 Experience. Application references for the test coverage index are contained in Henderson [A12] and Maiocchi, Mazzetti, and Villa [A13].

A5.10 References

[A11] CERIANI, M., CICU, A., and MAIOCCHI, M. A Methodology for Accurate Software Test Specification and Auditing. *Computer Program Testing*, B. Chandrasekaran and S. Radicchi, eds, North Holland Publishing Company, 1981.

[A12] HENDERSON, JAMES B. Hierarchical Decomposition: Its Use in Testing. *Testing Techniques Newsletter*, vol 3, no 4, San Francisco: Software Research Associate, Nov 1980.

[A13] MAIOCCHI, M., MAZZETTI, A., and VILLA, M. TEFAX: An Automated Test Factory for Functional Quality Control of Software Projects. Colloque de Genie Logiciel #2, Nice, 1984.

[A14] MILLER, E. Coverage Measure Definition Reviewed. *Testing Techniques Newsletter*, vol 3, no 4, San Francisco: Software Research Associate, Nov 1980.

Table A5.7-1
Example of Software Test Coverage Index Evaluation

Release: Date:	1 3/82	2 5/82	3 8/82	4 12/82	5 2/83	6 5/83	7 Prod
Identification of deficiency corrected	n/a	n/a	#3	#15 #16	#17	#20	#25
Modules:	99	181	181	181	183	184	185
Changes:	13	6	2	36	23	Est(6)	Est(4)
Additions:	82	0	0	2	1	Est(1)	Est(0)
Deletions:	0	0	0	0	0	Est(0)	Est(0)
Module testing completed: (FE)	0	50	100	100	110	TBD	TBD
Module requirements: (FT)	181	181	181	183	184	Est(185)	Est(185)
Test coverage index	0	.28	.55	.55	.60	TBD	TBD

NOTE: This table uses modules as the counted quantities instead of user functions. A similar table would be generated for user functions as the quantities counted.

A6. Cause and Effect Graphing

A6.1 Application. Cause and effect graphing aids in identifying requirements that are incomplete and ambiguous. This measure explores the inputs and expected outputs of a program and identifies the ambiguities. Once these ambiguities are eliminated, the specifications are considered complete and consistent.

Cause and effect graphing can also be applied to generate test cases in any type of computing application where the specification is clearly stated (ie, no ambiguities) and combinations of input conditions can be identified. It is used in developing and designing test cases that have a high probability of detecting faults that exist in programs. It is not concerned with the internal structure or behavior of the program.

A6.2 Primitives

List of causes: distinct input conditions.

List of effects: distinct output conditions or system transformation (effects are caused by changes in the state of the system)

$A_{existing}$ = number of ambiguities in a program remaining to be eliminated

A_{tot} = total number of ambiguities identified

A6.3 Implementation. A cause and effect graph is a formal translation of a natural language specification into its input conditions and expected outputs. The graph depicts a combinatorial logic network.

To begin, identify all requirements of the system and divide them into separate identifiable entities. Carefully analyze the requirements to identify all the causes and effects in the specification. After the analysis is completed, assign each cause and effect a unique identifier. For example, $E1$ for effect one or $I1$ for input one.

To create the cause and effect graph, perform the following steps:

(1) Represent each cause and each effect by a node identified by its unique number.

(2) Interconnect the cause and effect nodes by analyzing the semantic content of the specification and transforming it into a Boolean graph. Each cause and effect can be in one of two states: true or false. Using Boolean logic, set the possible states of the causes and determine under what conditions each effect will be present.

(3) Annotate the graph with constraints describing combinations of causes and effects that are impossible because of semantic or environmental constraints.

(4) Identify as an ambiguity any cause that does not result in a corresponding effect, any effect that does not originate with a cause as a source, and any combination of causes and effects that are inconsistent with the requirement specification or impossible to achieve.

The measure is computed as follows:

$$CE(\%) = 100 \times \left(1 - \frac{A_{existing}}{A_{tot}}\right)$$

To derive test cases for the program, convert the graph into a limited entry decision table with "effects" as columns and "causes" as rows. For each effect, trace back through the graph to find all combinations of causes that will set the effect to be TRUE. Each such combination is represented as a column in the decision table. The state of all other effects should also be determined for each such combination. Each column in the table represents a test case.

A6.4 Interpretation. When all of the causes and effects are represented in the graph and no ambiguities exist, the measure is 100%. A measure of less than 100% indicates some ambiguities still exist that have not been eliminated. Some of these ambiguities may result from incomplete graphing of cause and effect relationships or from incomplete statements in the natural language specification. Such ambiguities should be examined and reconciled.

The columns in the limited entry decision table should be used to create a set of test cases. For each test case:

(1) Establish input values or conditions for each cause that sets the effect to be true;

(2) Determine the expected value or result that should be demonstrated when the effect is true;

(3) Consider boundary conditions, incorrect values, etc.

A6.5 Considerations. Cause and effect graphing is a technique used to identify incompleteness and ambiguities in program specifications. It works best with structured specifications. It has the added capability of producing a useful set of test cases. However, this technique does not produce all the useful test cases that might be identified. It also does not adequately explore boundary conditions. This technique should be supplemented by other test design techniques addressing these areas. The graph can be processed mechanically to provide test cases.

Manual application of this technique is a tedious, long, and moderately complex process. However, the technique could be applied to selected modules with complex conditional logic. The requirements specification must be complete.

A6.6 Training. The requirement specification of the system must be clearly understood in order to successfully apply the graphing techniques to eliminate ambiguities.

Cause and effect graphing is a mathematically based technique that requires some knowledge of Boolean logic.

A6.7 Example. A database management system requires that each file in the database has its name listed in a master index that identifies the location of each file. The index is divided into ten sections. A small system is being developed that will allow the user to interactively enter a command to display any section of the index at a terminal. Cause and effect graphing is used to identify ambiguities in the specifications and to develop a set of test cases for the system.

The requirements specification for this system is as follows: To display one of ten possible index sections, a command must be entered consisting of a letter and a digit. The first character entered must be a "D" (for display) or an "L" (for list) and it must be in column 1. The second character entered must be a digit (0-9) in column 2. If this command occurs, the index section identified by the digit is displayed on the terminal. If the first character is incorrect, error message A is printed. If the second character is incorrect, error message B is printed.

The error messages are:
A = INVALID COMMAND
B = INVALID INDEX NUMBER

The causes and effects are identified as follows (see Fig A6.7-1):

Causes
(1) Character in column 1 is a "D"
(2) Character in column 1 is an "L"
(3) Character in column 2 is a digit.

Effects
(50) Index section is displayed
(51) Error message A is displayed
(52) Error message B is displayed.

Figure A6.7-1 was constructed through analysis of the semantic content of the specification.

In Fig A6.7-1, node 20 is an intermediate node representing the Boolean state of node 1 or node 2. The state of node 50 is true if the state of nodes 20 and 3 are both true. The state of node 20 is true if the state of node 1 or node 2 is true. The state of node 51 is true if the state of node 20 is not true. The state of node 52 is true if the state of node 3 is not true. Nodes 1 and 2 are also annotated with a constraint that nodes 1 and 2 cannot be true simultaneously (the exclusive constraint).

An ambiguity in the requirements specification results from the statement that the index section is displayed on the terminal. The specification is not clear whether the index section is listed on the printer or displayed when a valid command (eg, L7) occurs. To eliminate this ambiguity, redefine effect 50 to be effect 50A (index section is displayed), and effect 50B (index section is listed).

To derive the test cases, the graph is converted into a decision table as shown in Table A6.7-1. For each test case, the bottom of the table indicates

Fig A6.7-1
Boolean Graph

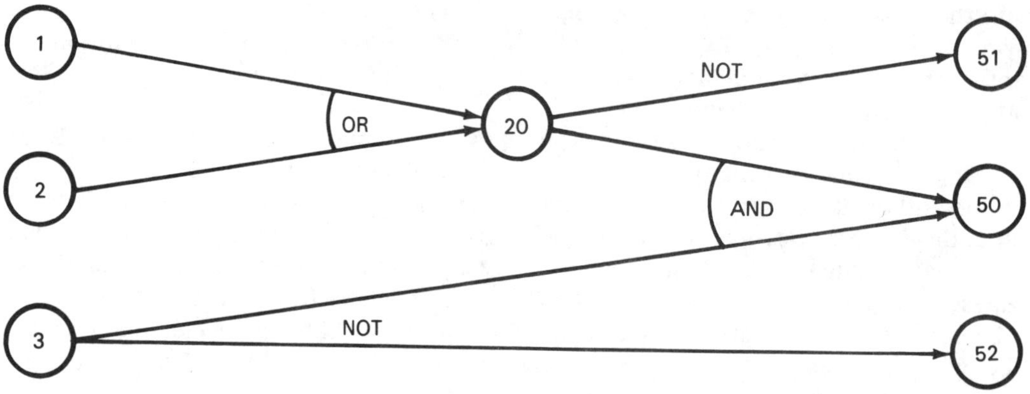

Table A6.7-1
Decision Table

	Effect						
Cause	20			50A	50B	51	52
1	1	1	0	1			
2	1	0	1		1		
20						0	
3				1	1		0
*Not allowed	*	1	1	1	1	1	1

Table A6.7-2
Test Cases

Test Case #	Inputs	Expected Results
1	*D*5	Index section 5 is displayed
2	*L*4	Index section 4 is listed
3	*B*2	Invalid command
4	*DA*	Invalid index number

which effect will be present (indicated by a 1). For each effect, all combinations of causes that will result in the presence of the effect is represented by the entries in the columns of the table. Blanks in the table mean that the state of the cause is irrelevant.

Last, each column in the decision table is converted into test cases. Table A6.7-2 gives one example of such an approach.

A6.8 Benefits. This measure provides thorough requirements analysis, elimination of ambiguities, and a good basis for test case development.

A6.9 Experience. This technique has a modest amount of experience.

A6.10 References

[A15] ELMENDORF, W. R. *Cause-Effect Graphs on Functional Testing.* Poughkeepsie: IBM Systems Development Division, TR-00.2487, 1973.

[A16] MYERS, GLENFORD J. *The Art of Software Testing.* New York: Wiley-Interscience, 1979.

[A17] POWELL, B. P., ed. *Validation, Verification, and Testing Technique and Tool Reference Guide.* National Bureau of Standards Special Publication 500-93, 1982.

A7. Requirements Traceability

A7.1 Application. This measure aids in identifying requirements that are either missing from, or in addition to, the original requirements.

A7.2 Primitives

$R1$ = number of requirements met by the architecture.

$R2$ = number of original requirements.

A7.3 Implementation. A set of mappings from the requirements in the software architecture to the original requirements is created. Count each requirement met by the architecture ($R1$) and count each of the original requirements ($R2$). Compute the traceability measure:

$$TM = \frac{R1}{R2} \times 100\%$$

A7.4 Interpretation. When all of the original software requirements are covered in the software architecture the traceability measure is 100%. A traceability measure of less than 100% indicates that some requirements are not included in the software architecture. The architecture may contain requirements beyond the original requirements. Some of these may result naturally from stepwise refinement. Others may result from new requirements being added to the architecture. Such cases should be examined and reconciled.

A7.5 Considerations. Stepwise refinement of the requirements into the architecture produces a natural set of mappings from which to derive the measure. For large systems, automation is desirable.

A7.6 Training. Training is needed to properly interpret the results, and to make suitable decisions about reconciling architectural issues.

A7.7 Example. Suppose there is a requirement to send an alert to the supervisor console, and to print a hard copy of the alert whenever high traffic mode is entered. The architecture for such a requirement might be as follows:

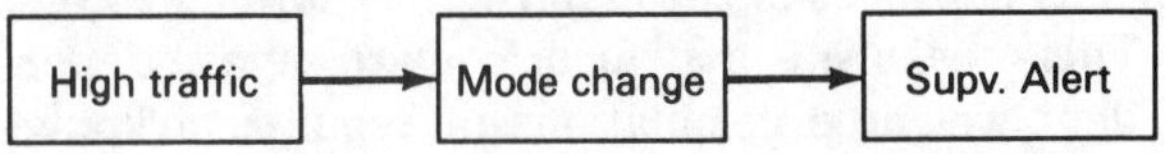

In this architecture, the hardcopy is not shown, so that complete traceability is not obtained, and the traceability will be less than 100%, with $R2 = R1 + 1$.

Alternatively, assume that there is a requirement to send an alert to the supervisor console whenever high traffic mode is entered. The architecture for this requirement might be as follows:

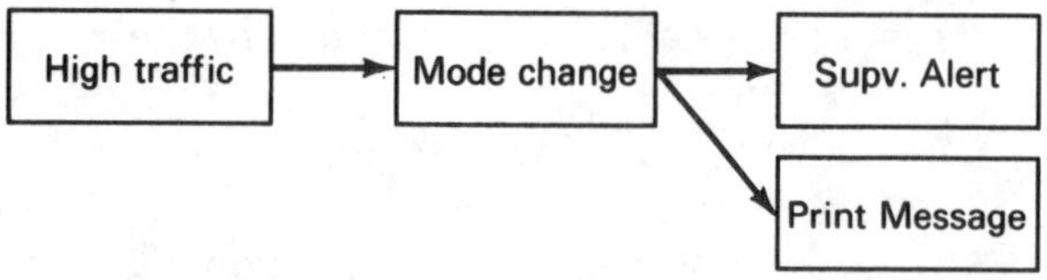

In this architecture, an additional requirement has been introduced that was not in the original requirements. This would result in a traceability error also, with traceability greater than 100%, and $R1 = R2 + 1$.

A7.8 Benefits. The requirements traceability measure applied to the software architecture phase can aid in identifying requirements that have not been accounted for in the architecture.

A7.9 Experience. This technique has been used extensively on large software projects [A18].

A7.10 References

[A18] HENNINGER, K. Specifying Software Requirements for Complex Systems, New Techniques and Their Application. *IEEE Transactions on Software Engineering*, vol SE-6, no 1, Jan 1980, pp 1-14.

[A19] PERRIENS, M. P. *Software Requirements Definition and Analysis with PSL and QBE.* IBM Technical Report FSD 80-0003, Bethesda: IBM Federal Systems Division, Oct 1980.

[A20] YEH, R., ZAVE, P., CONN, A., and COLE, G., Jr. *Software Requirements: A Report on the State of the Art.* Computer Science Technical Report Series TR-949, College Park, Maryland: University of Maryland, Oct 1980.

A8. Defect Indices

A8.1 Application. This measure provides a continuing, relative index of how correct the software is as it proceeds through the development cycle. This measure is a straightforward, phase dependent, weighted, calculation that requires no knowledge of advanced mathematics or statistics. This measure may be applied as early in the life cycle as the user has products that can be evaluated.

A8.2 Primitives. The following list applies to each phase in the life cycle:

D_i = Total number of defects detected during the ith phase.
S_i = Number of serious defects found.
M_i = Number of medium defects found.
PS = Size of the product at the ith phase.
T_i = Number of trivial defects found.
W_1 = Weighting factor for serious defects (default is 10).
W_2 = Weighting factor for medium defects (default is 3).
W_3 = Weighting factor for trivial defects (default is 1).

A8.3 Implementation. The measure is generated as a sum of calculations taken throughout development. It is a continuing measure applied to the software as it proceeds from design through final tests.

At each phase of development, calculate the phase index (PI_i) associated with the number and severity of defects.

$$PI_i = W_1 \frac{S_i}{D_i} + W_2 \frac{M_i}{D_i} + W_3 \frac{T_i}{D_i}$$

The defect index (DI) is calculated at each phase by cumulatively adding the calculation for PI_i as the software proceeds through development:

$$DI = \Sigma\,(i * PI_i)/PS$$
$$= (PI_1 + 2PI_2 + \ldots + iPI_i + \ldots)/PS$$

where each phase is weighted such that the further into development the software has progressed, such as phase 2 or 3, the larger the weight (ie, 2 or 3, respectively) assigned.

The data collected in prior projects can be used as a baseline figure for comparison.

A8.4 Interpretation. The interpretation is based on the magnitude of the defect index: the smaller the number, the better. Each organization or project should compute baseline numbers from past projects for each of the types of software produced. Then, each project should be tracked to assess the following:

(1) Whether performance has increased.
(2) Impact of programmer education programs.
(3) Impact of new programming practices.
(4) Impact of entering a new business area or performing new, unfamiliar tasks.
(5) Impact of mid-stream changes, such as major requirement changes.

This measure can be used as adjunct to either fault assessment or error cause analysis. Each user may determine a unique defect classification. For example, serious defects may be described as faults that keep the software from functioning. Medium defects may be described as faults that will cause the software to operate in a degraded mode. Trivial defects may be defined as those that will not affect functional performance, such as misspelled words on displays.

A8.5 Considerations. This measure is best applied when used with other measures because it gives an indication of what's happening, but not why. Error cause analysis in conjunction with defect index calculations can be quite enlightening.

A8.6 Training. Little or no measurement training is required.

A8.7 Example. For corresponding phases of development, calculated for three different projects, the results may be

$DI_1 = 15 \qquad DI_2 = 20 \qquad DI_3 = 205$

For these projects, the results show that project three has some significant problems as compared to measures of projects one and two taken at corresponding phases of development. It indicates that management action is clearly required in order to ascertain the difficulty.

A8.8 Benefits. This measure is both a process and a product measure.

As a process measure it provides an indication of whether the defect removal process employed at a given phase of development was employed in a sufficiently effective manner. It also affords the developer a means of assessing the effectiveness of phase related defect removal processes.

As a product measure, it allows the development management a means of assessing the degree of correctness of the software at a given phase, thereby providing an indication of the reliability growth as the product moves through the development phases toward final acceptance.

It is easy to use and interpret and is successively applicable across development phases. It can be done manually or automated. It can also be easily expanded to include sub-phases, with each sub-phase separately weighted. The index is weighted so that the more defects found early, the better the result. Use of the index thereafter encourages the application of early defect removal processes such as inspections.

If requirements are done in a structural requirements language, inspections can be started at the requirements level and this defect index (*DI*) measure can be adjusted to begin at the requirements phase.

A8.9 Experience. The experience base for this measure is small.

A8.10 Reference

[A21] SCHULMEYER, G., ed. Handbook for Software Quality Assurance. New York: Van Nostrand Publishing Company, 1985.

A.9 Error Distribution(s)

A9.1 Application. The search for the causes of software faults and failures involves the error analysis of the defect data collected during each phase of the software development. Distribution of the errors allows ranking of the predominant failure modes.

A9.2 Primitives. Error description notes the following points:

(1) Associated faults
(2) Types
(3) Severity
(4) Phase introduced
(5) Preventive measure
(6) Discovery mechanism including reasons for earlier non-detection of associated faults

A9.3 Implementation. The primitives for each error are recorded and the errors are counted according to the criteria adopted for each classification. The number of errors are then plotted for each class. Examples of such distribution plots are shown in Fig A9.3-1. In the three examples of Fig A9.3-1, the errors are classified and counted by phase, by the cause and by the cause for deferred fault detection. Other similar classifications could be used, such as the type of steps suggested to prevent the reoccurrence of similar errors or the type of steps suggested for earlier detection of the corresponding faults.

A9.4 Interpretation. Plots similar to Fig A9.3-1 could be analyzed by management to identify the phases that are most error prone, and to identify causes, risks, and recommend the nature and priority of corrective actions to improve error avoidance.

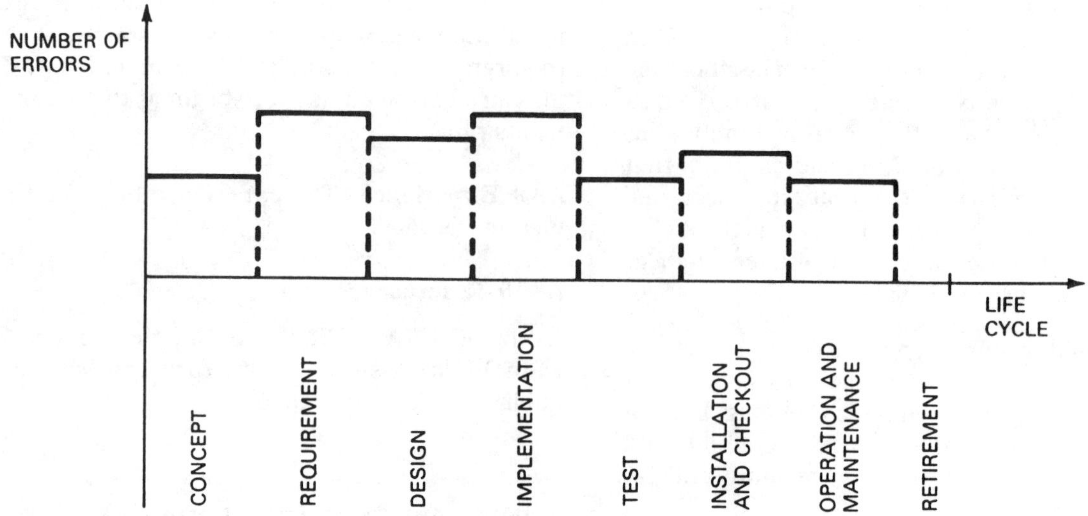

(a) Error Distribution by Phase

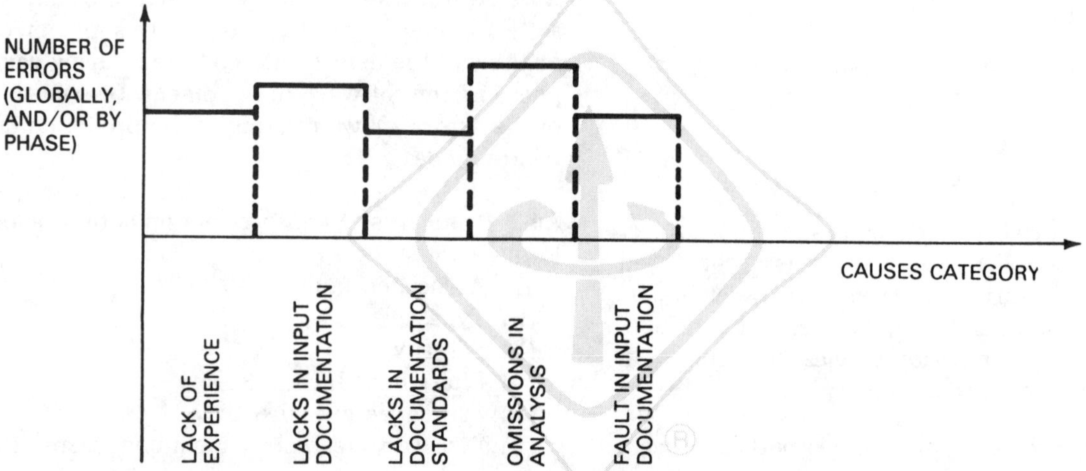

(b) Error by Cause Category

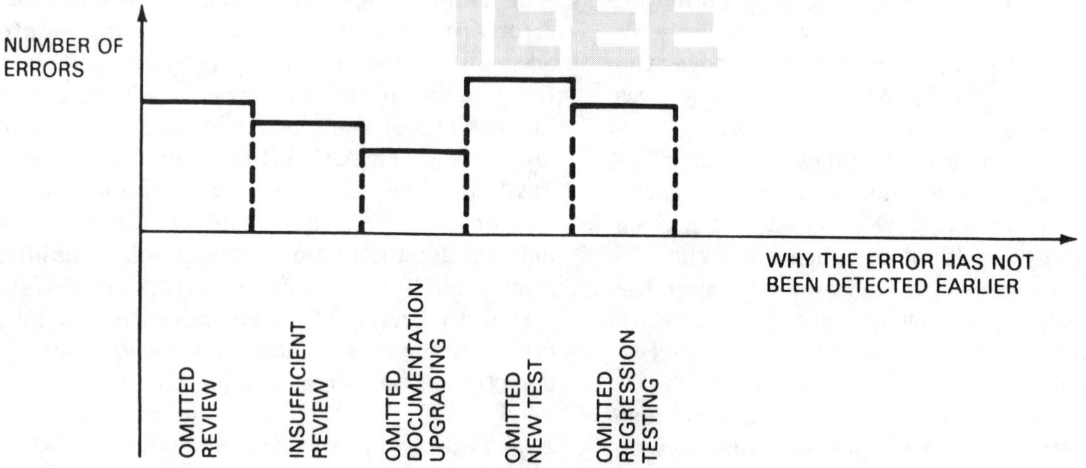

(c) Suggested Causes for Error Detection Deferral

Fig A9.3-1
Error Analysis

This measure is also useful to recommend steps to prevent the recurrence of similar errors, to eliminate known causes, and to detect faults earlier for purpose of reducing software life cycle costs.

A9.5 Considerations. Error analysis requires effective support and participation by management, because the errors usually have their origin in deficient procedures, methods, and techniques for design, inspection, and testing.

A9.6 Training. A global knowledge of the effective methodologies for the software development process for the entire life cycle phase is required to support effective error analysis and interpretation.

A9.7 Example. See Fig A9.3-1.

A9.8 Benefits. Error analysis by distributions is a key factor in understanding the areas where interventions or corrective actions or both are the most effective steps towards error and fault avoidance.

A9.9 Experience. Although there is little experience in the literature related to this measure, it is recommended as an important method for analyzing causes of errors and error prone areas.

A9.10 References

[A22] ANDRES, A. An Analysis of Errors and Their Causes in System Programs. *IEEE Transactions on Software Engineering*, Jun 1975 (reprinted in *Tutorial on Models and Metrics for Software Management and Engineering*). IEEE catalog no EHO-16-7, IEEE Computer Society, Sept 1980.

[A23] RZEVSKI, G. Identification of Factors which Cause Software Failures. Proceedings of Annual Reliability and Maintainability Symposium, Los Angeles, Jan 26-28, 1982.

A10. Software Maturity Index

A10.1 Application. This measure is used to quantify the readiness of a software product. Changes from a previous baseline to the current baseline are an indication of the current product stability. A baseline can be either an internal release or an external delivery.

A10.2 Primitives

M_T = Number of software functions (modules) in the current delivery

F_c = Number of software functions (modules) in the current delivery that include internal changes from a previous delivery

F_a = Number of software functions (modules) in the current delivery that are additions to the previous delivery

F_{del} = Number of software functions (modules) in the previous delivery that are deleted in the current delivery

A10.3 Implementation. The software maturity index (*SMI*) may be calculated in two different ways, depending on the available data (primitives).

A10.3.1 Implementation 1

(1) For the present (just delivered or modified) software baseline, count the number of functions (modules) that have been changed (F_c).

(2) For the present software baseline, count the number of functions (modules) that have been added (F_a) or deleted (F_{del}).

(3) For the present software baseline, count the number of functions (modules) that make up that release (M_T).

Calculate the maturity index using the following equation:

$$\text{Maturity Index} = \frac{\text{Number of current functions (modules)} - \left(\text{Number of current baseline functions (modules) that have been added} + \text{Number of functions (modules) changed} + \text{Number of current baseline functions (modules) that have been deleted}\right)}{\text{Number of current functions (modules)}}$$

$$\text{ie,} \quad SMI = \frac{M_T - (F_a + F_c + F_{del})}{M_T}$$

Notice that the total number of current functions (modules) equals the number of previous functions (modules) plus the number of current baseline functions (modules) that were added to the previous baseline minus the number of functions (modules) that were deleted from the previous baseline. In the software maturity index calculation, the deletion of a function (module) is treated the same as an addition of a function (module).

A10.3.2 Implementation 2. The software maturity index may be estimated as

$$SMI = \frac{M_T - F_c}{M_T}$$

The change and addition of functions (modules) is tracked and the maturity index is calculated for each baseline. Problem reports that would result in the software update subsequent to the tracking period are included in the maturity analysis by estimating the configuration of the subsequent releases.

A10.4 Interpretation. The maturity index for each software release can be tracked to determine the relative impact that changes and additions are having on the software configuration and whether the software is approaching a stable configuration.

A10.5 Considerations. Additional data that is required in conjunction with the maturity index measures are as follows:

(1) The impact software function (module) changes are having on previously completed testing (see A5, Functional or Modular Test Coverage).
(2) The software release identification and date of release.
(3) Identification of the customer (producer) problems that are corrected in the release.
(4) Estimate of the configuration changes that would be required to correct the remaining customer (producer) identified problems.

The maturity index is used as a primitive in software release readiness (see A34). The functional test coverage must also be calculated in conjunction with the maturity index (see A5).

A10.6 Training. The software training required would include identification of the user requirements and the associated software functions and modules that implement the requirements. The operational user must be familiar with the system functional requirements in order to report problems in terms of those requirements.

A10.7 Example. Table A10.7-1 depicts the data and resulting maturity index for a series of software releases. Keep in mind that a series of maturity index values determined throughout a test program will be misleading unless the corresponding functional test coverage index for each release is also determined.

A10.8 Benefits. The maturity index provides a measure of the relative impact that software changes and additions are making to the total software configuration. In addition, the maturity index provides an indication of the stability of the software throughout the period of user test and evaluation.

A10.9 Experience. See Ceriani, Cicu, and Maiocchi [A11] for related experience.

A11. Manhours per Major Defect Detected

A11.1 Application. The design and code inspection processes are two of the most effective defect removal processes available. The early removal of defects at the design and implementation phases, if done effectively and efficiently, significantly improves the reliability of the developed product and allows a more controlled test environment. This measure provides a quantitative figure that can be used to evaluate the efficiency of the design and code inspection processes.

A11.2 Primitives

T_1 = Time expended by the inspection team in preparation for design or code inspection meeting.

Table A10.7-1
Example Results of a Software Maturity Index Evaluation

Release:	1	2	3	4	5	6	7
Date:	3/82	5/82	8/82	12/82	2/83	5/83	Prod
Identification of deficiency corrected	n/a	n/a	#3	#15 #16	#17	#20	#25
Modules:	99	181	181	181	183	184	185
Changes:	13	6	2	36	23	Est(6)	Est(4)
Additions	82	0	0	2	1	Est(1)	Est(0)
Deletions	0	0	0	0	0	Est(0)	Est(0)
Maturity index	.475	.966	.99	.79	.868	(.96)	(.98)
	$\frac{181-95}{181}$	$\frac{181-6}{181}$	$\frac{179}{181}$	$\frac{181-38}{181}$	$\frac{183-24}{183}$	$\frac{184-6}{184}$	$\frac{181}{185}$

T_2 = Time expended by the inspection team in conduct of a design or code inspection meeting.

S_i = Number of major (non-trivial) defects detected during the ith inspection.

I = Total number of inspections to date.

A11.3 Implementation. At each inspection meeting, record the total preparation time expended by the inspection team. Also, record the total time expended in conducting the inspection meeting. All defects are recorded and grouped into major/minor categories. (A major defect is one that must be corrected for the product to function within specified requirements.)

The inspection times are summarized and the defects are cumulatively added. The computation should be performed during design and code. If the design is not written in a structural design language, then this measure can be only applied during the implementation phase.

The manhours per major defect detected is

$$M = \frac{\sum_{i=1}^{I} (T_1 + T_2)_i}{\sum_{i=1}^{I} S_i}$$

This computation should be initiated after approximately 8,000 lines of detailed design or code have been inspected.

A11.4 Interpretation. This measure is applied to new code development, not to modification of an old code, unless the modification is a large block change.

From empirical experience, the measure (M) for new code shall fall consistently between three and five. If significant deviation from this range is experienced, the matter should be investigated. If the measure is very low, the defect density may be too high and a major product examination may be in order. If the measure is very high, the inspection process is very likely not being properly implemented and, therefore, the anticipated impact on reliability improvement expected from the inspection will not be realized.

A11.5 Considerations. This measure assumes a knowledge of the design and code inspection process. It further assumes consistent, standard data collection and recording. Experience has shown that the inspection process is quite effective, if it is strongly committed to and supported by management. The earlier the inspection process can be applied, the greater the benefit derived. It is therefore recommended that program design languages be used.

A11.6 Training. Little or no training is required for calculation of the measure. Inspections require trained personnel.

A11.7 Example

$I = 2$

$$\left.\begin{aligned} T_1 &= 28 \\ T_2 &= 25 \\ S_1 &= 16 \end{aligned}\right\} i=1 \qquad \left.\begin{aligned} T_1 &= 40 \\ T_2 &= 50 \\ S_2 &= 4 \end{aligned}\right\} i=2$$

$$M = \frac{28 + 25 + 40 + 50}{16 + 4} = \frac{143}{20} = 7.15$$

A11.8 Benefits. This measure is easy to compute. It serves as one of the index parameters to evaluate the effectiveness and efficiency of the inspection process. Deviations from the norm serve as an indicator that immediate attention is required and, therefore, gives the developer a change to make whatever modifications are necessary to maintain sufficient product correctness and reliability during early development.

A11.9 Experience. Utilization of the inspection process has been found to be highly effective in defect removal and correction.

A11.10 References. See also Dobbins and Buck [A3, A4].

[A24] FAGAN, MICHAEL E. Design and Code Inspection to Reduce Errors in Program Development. *IBM Systems Journal*, vol 15, no 3, Jul 1976, pp 182-211.

A12. Number of Conflicting Requirements

A12.1 Application. This measure is used to determine the reliability of a software system, resulting from the software architecture under consideration, as represented by a specification based on the entity-relationship-attribute model [A19].

A12.2 Primitives

(1) List of the inputs
(2) List of the outputs
(3) List of the functions performed by the program

A12.3 Implementation. The mappings from the software architecture to the requirements are identified. Mappings from the same specification item to more than one differing requirement are examined for requirements inconsistency. Mappings from more than one specification item to a single requirement are examined for specification inconsistency.

A12.4 Interpretation. If the same specification item maps to two different requirements items, the requirements should be identical. Otherwise, the requirements are inconsistent. If more than one specification item maps to a single requirement, (this should result only from application of refinement techniques) the specification items should be checked for possible inconsistency.

A12.5 Considerations. Stepwise refinement or structured analysis of the requirements into the architecture produces the best results, since there is likely to be a natural set of mappings resulting from this process. For large systems, automation is desirable.

A12.6 Training. Training is needed to interpret the results, and make suitable decisions on the adequacy of the architecture and the requirements. Experience/training in requirements analysis, the entity-relationship-attribute model, and software specification techniques are needed [A20].

A12.7 Example. Consider an example taken from the air traffic control field. Suppose there are two distinct requirements for action to be taken in the event of high traffic. These requirements might be stated as:

(1) In the event of high traffic, send an operator alert to the supervisor console. If the supervisor console is busy, then send to the assistant.

(2) In the event of high traffic, send an operator alert to the assistant supervisor console.

In the architecture, this could be implemented as:

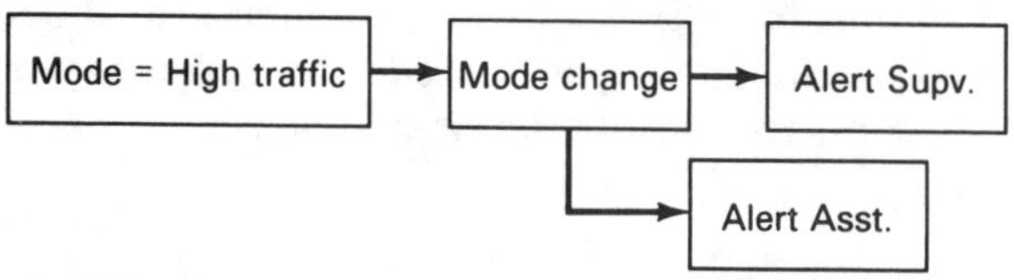

A PDL representation might be as follows:

If mode = high traffic
  Send operator alert to supervisor console
  Send operator alert to assistant console
Endif

This example represents a potential conflicting requirement between sending an alert to both the supervisor and the assistant. This would need to be examined and resolved.

A12.8 Benefits. Identification of conflicting requirements during the software architecture phase can avoid problems later in the life cycle.

A12.9 Experience. Many large software projects informally use these techniques for determining reliability [A18].

A13. Number of Entries and Exits per Module

A13.1 Application. This measure is used to determine the difficulty of a software architecture, as represented by entry/exit points identified in a modular specification/design language.

A13.2 Primitives

e_i = number of entry points for the ith module
x_i = number of exit points for the ith module

A13.3 Implementation. The number of entry points and exit points for each module is

$$m_i = e_i + x_i$$

A13.4 Interpretation. Each module should have one entry and one exit point for each major function. Additional exit points may be allowed for error handling. The number of functions per module should be limited. A suggested maximum number of functions per module is five.

A13.5 Considerations. Data encapsulation should be used to optimize the number of functions and entry/exit points. If data is properly encapsulated [A27], the number of entry and exit points for each module function will be small. For large systems, automation of the count of entries and exits is desirable, so the user does not need to manually examine each module.

A13.6 Training. In both the manual and automated situations, training is needed to interpret the results and make suitable trade-off decisions.

A13.7 Example. Given a module specification (Fig A13.7-1), this method can be used. This module has four entry points, and, since it is structured, four exit points.

```
mod idset
    def
        hash (id) = return an index value from 1 to max as a f(id)
        type item = rec
                        id: idtype
                        data: datatype
                    cer
ism
    input
        var in: item
        var searchid: idtype
    output
        var out:  item
        var status: (OK, full, notthere, alreadythere)
    state
        const max = [maximum size of set]
        var s: set of item [s ≤ max]
    init
        [s:=ϕ]
    trans
        entry add (in in, out status)
            [ (iεs) in.id=i.id → status: = alreadythere
              true → ( s <max → s, status: = s∪ (in),OK
                       true → status: = full)]
        entry delete (in Searchid, out status)
            [ (iεs) searchid = i.id → s,status: = s-(in),OK
              true → status: = notthere]
        entry has (in searchid, out status, out)
            [ (iεs) searchid = i.id → out, status: = i,OK
            true → status: = notthere]
        entry clear
            [s:=ϕ]
des
    (*to be added*)
dom
```

Fig A13.7-1
Program Design Language Module Specification

A13.8 Benefits. The entry/exit point measure applied to the software architecture phase can aid in identifying modules that do not exhibit proper data encapsulation, and are likely to result in high operating system overhead times (which occur when one module invokes another) and difficulty in testing.

A13.9 Experience. Minimizing the number of entry/exit points is a key feature of structured design and structured programming techniques that have been used in software architecture definition. Limited published experience is currently available.

A13.10 References

[A25] GUTTAG, J. Abstract Data Types and the Development of Data Structures. Conference on Data, Salt Lake City, 1976. *CACM*, vol 20, no 6, June 1977, pp 396-404.

[A26] LISKOV, B. H. and ZILLES, S. N. Specification Techniques for Data Abstractions. *IEEE Transactions on Software Engineering*, vol SE-2, no 1, Mar 1975, pp 7-19.

[A27] PARNAS, D. L. On the Criteria To Be Used in Decomposing Systems into Modules. *CACM*, vol 15, no 12, 1972, pp 1053-1058.

A14. Software Science Measures

A14.1 Application. These measures apply Halstead software science to the properties and structure of computer programs. They provide measures of the complexity of existing software, predict the length of a program, and estimate the amount of time an average programmer can be expected to use to implement a given algorithm.

This measure computes the program length by counting operators and operands. The measure suggests that the difficulty of a given program can be derived, based on the above counts.

A14.2 Primitives

n_1 = Number of distinct operators in a program

n_2 = Number of distinct operands in a program

N_1 = Total number of occurrences of the operators in a program

N_2 = Total number of occurrences of the operands in a program

A14.3 Implementation. Once the source code has been written, this measure can be applied to predict program difficulty and other derived quantities using the following equations (Halstead [A30]).

Program vocabulary: $l = n1 + n2$

Observed program length: $L = N1 + N2$

Estimated program length: $\hat{L} = n1\,(\log_2 n1) + n2\,(\log_2 n2)$

Program volume: $V = L\,(\log_2 l)$

Program difficulty: $D = (n1/2)\,(N2/n2)$

Program level: $L1 = 1/D$

Effort: $E = \dfrac{V}{L1}$

Number of errors: $B = \dfrac{V}{3000} \simeq \dfrac{E^{2/3}}{3000}$

Time: $T = E/S$ (S = Stroud number; typical value is eighteen elementary mental discriminations per second)

An alternate expression to estimate program length is the factorial length estimator (A32):

$$\hat{L} = \log_2((n1)!) + \log_2((n2)!)$$

A14.4 Interpretation. The interpretation of these measures is illustrated in the example (A14.7); for the average PL/I program, difficulty should be less than 115. Difficulty of greater than 160 indicates serious problems. Difficulty data is available for other languages as well [A29.5, A30, A35].

A14.5 Considerations. The technique is recommended only if automated support is available. The software needed to parse the programs and accumulate data is somewhat lengthy. However, there has been some experience in writing such software.

A14.6 Training. Training is needed in the definition of operators and operands and in the interpretation of the results. The results will differ depending on the language and applications. The user should examine results obtained in some of the reference material beforehand, and, if possible, contact other users.

A14.7 Example

Program fragment (written in *PL/I*):

```
/* x becomes the maximum of A and B*/
  if A > B
  then X = A;
  else X = B;
```

Software science basic parameters:

operators and their frequencies: $n1 = 4$ $N1 = 6$

if...then...else	1
>	1
=	2
;	2

operands and their frequencies: $n2 = 3$ $N2 = 6$

A	2
B	2
X	2

Software science measurements:

Program vocabulary: $l = n1 + n2 = 4 + 3 = 7$

Observed program length: $L = N1 + N2 = 6 + 6 = 12$

Estimated program length:

$$\hat{L} = n1\,(\log_2 n1) + n2\,(\log_2 n2) = 4(\log_2 4) + 3\,(\log_2 3) = 12.76$$

Estimated program length using the factorial length estimator is

$$\hat{L} = \log_2((4)!) + \log_2((3)!) = 7.17$$

Program volume: $V = L\,(\log_2 l) = 12\,(\log_2 7) = 33.68$

Program difficulty: $D = (n1/2)\,(N2/n2) = (4/2)\,(6/3) = 4.0$

Program level: $L1 = \dfrac{1}{D} = \dfrac{1}{4.0} = .25$

Effort: $E = V/L1 = 33.68/.25 = 134.72$

Number of errors: $B = V/3000 = 33.68/3000 = 0.01123$

Time: $T = E/S = 134.72/18 = 7.48$

A14.8 Benefit. Application of the software science measures to the implementation phase can aid in the identification of programs that are overly complex, and likely to result in excessive development effort.

A14.9 Experience. There has been considerable and notable experience reported concerning this measure.

A14.10 References

[A28] CONTE, S. D., DUNSMORE, H. E., and SHEN, V. Y. *Software Engineering Metrics and Models.* Menlo Park: Benjamin/Cummings Publishing Co, 1986.

[A29] COULTER, M. S. Software Science and Cognitive Psychology. *IEEE Transactions on Software Engineering*, vol SE-9, no 2, Mar 1983, pp 166-171.

[A29.5] FITZSIMMONS, A., and LOVE, T. A Review and Evaluation of Software Science. *ACM Computing Surveys*, vol 10, no 1, Mar 1978, pp 3-18.

[A30] HALSTEAD, M. H. *Elements of Software Science.* Operating and Programming Systems Series, P. J. Denning, ed, New York: Elsevier North Holland, 1977.

[A31] HALSTEAD, M. H., GORDON, R. D., and ELSHOFF, J. L. *On Software Physics and GM's PL/I Programs.* GM Research Publication GMR-2175, Warren, Michigan: GM Research Laboratories, Jun 1976.

[A32] JENSEN, H. J., and VAIRAVAN, K. An Experimental Study of Software Metrics for Real Time Software. *IEEE Transactions on Software Engineering*, vol SE-11, no 2, Feb 1985, pp 231-234.

[A33] LIND, R. K., and VAIRAVAN, K. *A Study of Software Metrics for Predicting Software Errors.* M.S. Thesis, University of Wisconsin, Milwaukee, Wisconsin, Dec 1986.

[A34] SCHNEIDER, V. Prediction of Software Effort and Project Duration. *SIGPLAN Notices*, vol 14, no 6, Jun 1978, pp 49-59.

[A35] SHEN, V. Y., CONTE, S. D., and DUNSMORE, H. E. Software Science Revisited: A Critical Analysis of the Theory and Its Empirical Support. *IEEE Transactions on Software Engineering*, vol SE-9, no 2, Mar 1983, pp 155-165.

A15. Graph-Theoretic Complexity for Architecture

A15.1 Application. Complexity measures can be applied early in the product life cycle for development trade-offs as well as to assure system and module comprehensibility adequate for correct and efficient maintenance. Many system faults are introduced in the operational phase by modifications to systems that are reliable but difficult to understand. In time, a system's entropy increases, making a fault insertion more likely with each new change. Through complexity measures the developer plans ahead for correct change by establishing initial order, and thereby improves the continuing reliability of the system throughout its operational life.

There are three graph-theoretic complexity measures for software architecture:

Static complexity is a measure of software architecture, as represented by a network of modules, useful for design tradeoff analyses. Network complexity is a function based on the countable properties of the modules (nodes) and inter-module connections (edges) in the network.

Generalized static complexity is a measure of software architecture, as represented by a network of modules and the resources used. Since resources are acquired or released when programs are invoked in other modules, it is desirable to measure the complexity associated with allocation of those resources in addition to the basic (static) network complexity.

Dynamic complexity is a measure of software architecture as represented by a network of modules during execution, rather than at rest, as is the case for the static measures. For example, modules may execute at different frequencies.

A15.2 Primitives

K = Number of resources, indexed by $k = 1, \ldots, K$

E = Number of edges, indexed by $i = 1, \ldots, E$

N = Number of nodes, indexed by $j = 1, \ldots, N$

c_i = complexity for program invocation and return along each edge e_i as determined by the user (such as operating system complexity).

Resource status array $R(K,E)$

$$r_{ki} = \begin{cases} 1 & \text{if } k^{th} \text{ resource is required for the } i\text{th edge } (e_i) \\ 0 & \text{otherwise} \end{cases}$$

d_k = complexity for allocation of resource k as determined by the user (eg, complexity associated with a procedure used to gain exclusive access to common data)

A15.3 Implementation. Using nodes and edges, a strongly connected graph of the network is required. A strongly connected graph is one in which a node is reachable from any other node. This is accomplished by adding an edge between the exit node and the entry node. Each node represents a module that may or may not be executed concurrently with another module. Each edge represents program invocation and return between modules. In this case the edges are called single paths.

A15.3.1 Static Complexity. Once a strongly connected graph is constructed, with modules as nodes, and transfer of control as edges, the static complexity is calculated as

$$C = E - N + 1$$

A15.3.2 Generalized Static Complexity. Resources (storage, time, logic complexity or other measurable factors) are allocated when programs are invoked in other modules. Given a network and resources to be controlled in the network, the generalized static complexity associated with allocation of these resources is

$$C = \sum_{i=1}^{E} \left(c_i + \sum_{k=1}^{K} (d_k * r_{ki}) \right)$$

A15.3.3 Dynamic Complexity. A change in the number of edges may result from module interruption due to invocations and returns. An average dynamic network complexity can be derived over a given time period to account for the execution of modules at different frequencies and also for module interruption during execution. Dynamic complexity is calculated using the formula for static complexity at various points in time. The behavior of the measure (except time average) is then used to indicate the evolution of the complexity of the software.

A15.4 Interpretation. For a typical subsystem, 10 represents the maximum ideal static complexity. A very complex system may be composed of a number of such subsystems. When the computed complexity is too large, one can consider more use of pipelining, fewer modules (if feasible), or more subsystems.

For a typical subsystem, $20E$ (E = number of edges) represents maximum ideal generalized static complexity, if the complexity of program invocation is 20 and no resources are needed.

The dynamic complexity is generally higher than the static complexity. Ideally, the dynamic complexity should be as close to the static complexity as possible. Addition or deletion of modules during execution affects the dynamic complexity. Minimization of the frequency of module interruption during execution reduces average dynamic network complexity. This results in an overall improvement in software reliability.

A15.5 Considerations. Pipeline architectures have lower static complexity value, since there is less overhead for transfer of control than for hierarchies. Decisions can be made on whether to implement services as distinct modules by combining the result obtained with this measure with the internal module complexity measures. For large systems, automation is desirable.

When the generalized static complexity is too large, one can consider more use of pipelining, fewer modules (if feasible), more subsystems, use of fewer resources, or less costly methods of resource acquisition.

When the dynamic network complexity is too large, one should consider reducing it by optimizing the dynamic creation and deletion of modules, or by minimizing task interruptions by timing adjustments, or both.

A15.6 Training. Training in graph theory is recommended for manual application of the measure. Training is also needed to interpret the results for suitable design trade-off decisions for software architecture design.

A15.7 Example. Static complexity measures for network hierarchies and pipelines are shown in Figs A15.7-1 and A15.7-2. Detailed examples for dynamic creation/deletion of modules, module interruption, modules in execution at different frequencies, and dynamic network complexity are illustrated in Halstead [A30].

A15.8 Benefits. These complexity measures, applied to the software architecture, can aid in identifying networks that are overly complex, and that are likely to result in high system overhead,

Fig A15.7-1
Hierarchy Network

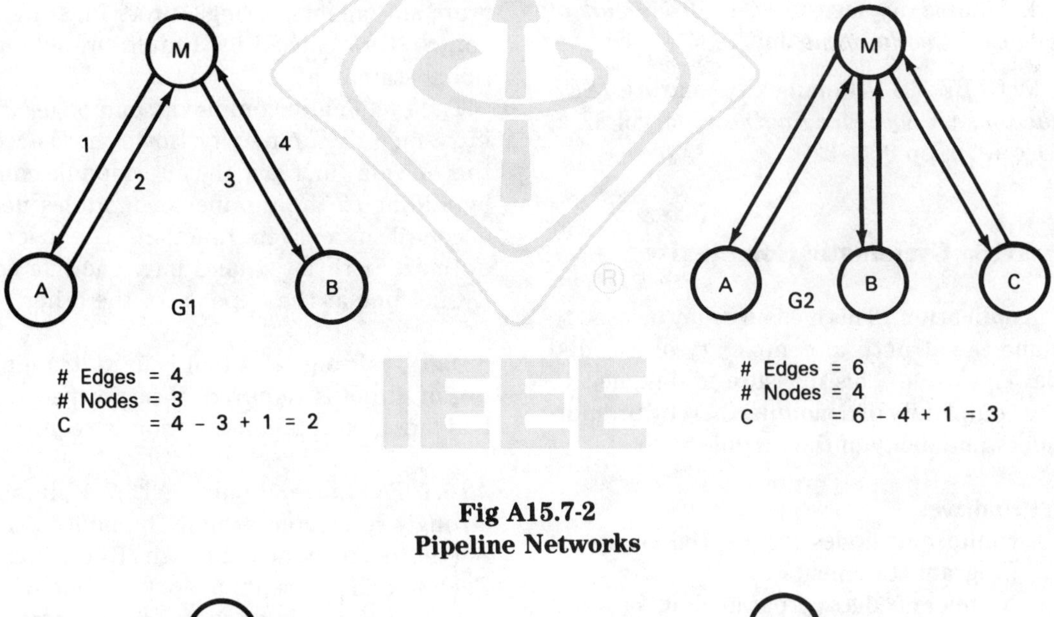

# Edges = 4
# Nodes = 3
C = 4 − 3 + 1 = 2

# Edges = 6
# Nodes = 4
C = 6 − 4 + 1 = 3

Fig A15.7-2
Pipeline Networks

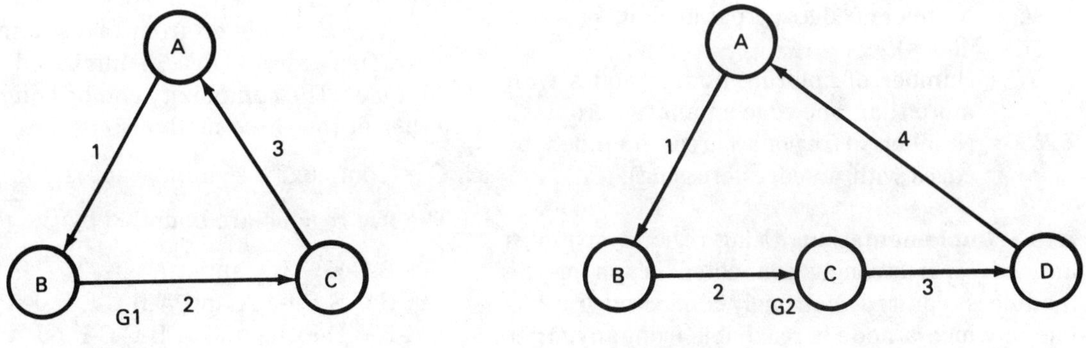

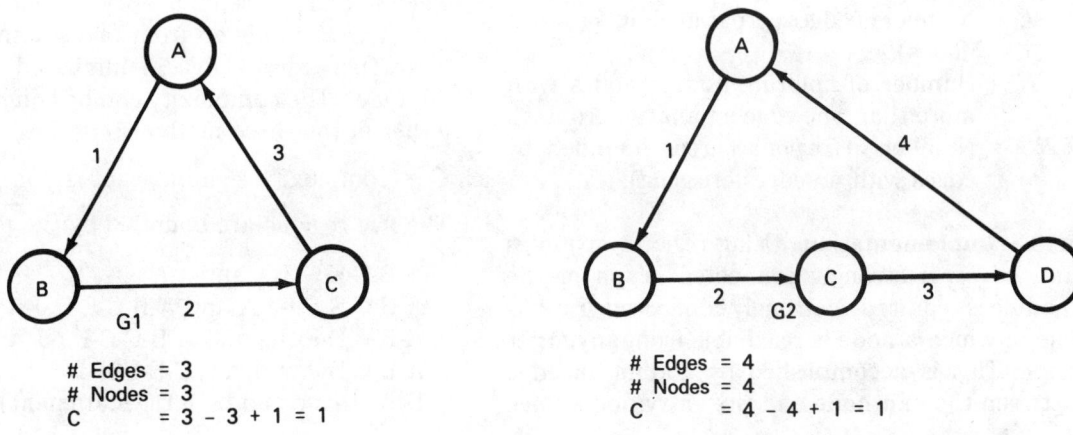

# Edges = 3
# Nodes = 3
C = 3 − 3 + 1 = 1

# Edges = 4
# Nodes = 4
C = 4 − 4 + 1 = 1

difficulty in testing, and difficulty in meeting performance requirements. They can also aid in identifying areas that make excessive use of resources, and areas in which resource acquisition overhead is high.

A15.9 Experience. The static complexity measure has been used extensively for design and code [A36]. Generalized static and dynamic complexity measures have been used in experiments, [A38], but not operationally.

A15.10 References. See also Conte, Dunsmore, and Shen [A28] and Halstead [A30].

[A36] HALL, N. R. *Complexity Measures for Systems Design.* Ph.D. Dissertation, Polytechnic Institute of New York, Brooklyn, Jun 1983.

[A37] HALL, N. R. and PREISER, S. Dynamic Complexity Measures for Software Design. *Proceedings of Total Systems Reliability Symposium,* IEEE Computer Society, Dec 1983.

[A38] HALL, N. R. and PREISER, S. Combined Network Complexity Measures. *IBM Journal of Research and Development,* Jan 1984.

[A39] McCABE, T. J. A Complexity Measure. *IEEE Transactions on Software Engineering,* vol SE-2, no 4, Dec 1976, pp 308-320.

A16. Cyclomatic Complexity

A16.1 Application. This measure may be used to determine the structural complexity of a coded module. The use of this measure is designed to limit the complexity of a module, thereby promoting understandability of the module.

A16.2 Primitives

- N = Number of nodes (sequential groups of program statements).
- E = Number of edges (program flows between nodes).
- SN = Number of splitting nodes (nodes with more than one edge emanating from it).
- RG = Number of regions (areas bounded by edges with no edges crossing).

A16.3 Implementation. Using regions, or nodes and edges, a strongly connected graph of the module is required. A strongly connected graph is one in which a node is reachable from any other node. This is accomplished by adding an edge between the exit node and the entry node. Once the graph is constructed, the measure is computed as follows:

$$C = E - N + 1$$

The cyclomatic complexity is also equivalent to the number of regions (RG) or the number of splitting nodes plus one (SN+1). If a program contains an N-way predicate, such as a CASE statement with N cases, the N-way predicate contributes N-1 to the count of SN.

A16.4 Interpretation. For a typical module, ten represents a maximum ideal complexity. For a very complex system, the cyclomatic number (complexity) may be larger. If the calculated complexity number is too large, modularization of the code is required [A41].

A16.5 Considerations. Since the construction of the graph can be a tedious, error-prone process, automation of graph construction is desirable. The cyclomatic complexity method does not take into account the complexity of sequential program statements, a single program statement, or control flow caused by a multi-branching conditional statement.

The cyclomatic complexity can be used to limit intra-module complexity. However, to accomplish this one may increase the intermodule complexity by adding to the number of modules needed to accomplish a given function. The user should optimize both inter- and intra-module complexity, not one at the expense of the other.

A16.6 Training. If a tool is used, training in the use of a tool is required. If performed manually, training in graph construction is required.

A16.7 Example. Figure A16.7-1 illustrates a strongly connected graph. The nodes are labeled A (the entry node) through J (the exit node). Each node represents a block of code where control flow can only go from one statement to the next. There are 14 edges, 5 numbered regions, and 10 nodes. The complexity can be computed using either of the three methods:

C = complexity = number of regions = 5

The five regions are bounded by the paths:

A-B-C-E-G-J-A and J-A
A-B-C-E-F-I-J-A and A-B-C-E-G-J-A
A-B-C-E-F-H-J and A-B-C-E-F-I-J
A-B-C-D-J and A-B-C-E-F-H-J
D-D (this could be a DO statement)

Nodes and edges: complexity = $E - N + 1$
$= 14 - 10 + 1 = 5$

Splitting nodes: complexity = $SN + 1 = 4 + 1 = 5$

The four splitting nodes are: C, D, E and F

A16.8 Benefits. The cyclomatic number can be a good indicator of module complexity, and may be used to keep modules within an understandable and workable size. This measure also results in the computation of the number of distinct paths in a module without considering the complexity of an individual statement.

A16.9 Experience. There is empirical evidence [A41] that the cyclomatic complexity can reduce the difficulty encountered by programmers. There is some evidence that using the cyclomatic measure results in a module with fewer faults. Basili and Perricone [A40] provide a critical evaluation of this measure.

A16.10 References. See also Conte, Dunsmore, and Shen [A28] and McCabe [A39].

[A40] BASILI, V. R., and PERRICONE, B. T. Software Errors and Complexity: An Empirical Investigation. *Communications of the ACM*, Jan 1984.

[A41] McCABE, T. J. *Structured Testing: A Software Testing Methodology Using the Cyclomatic Complexity Metric.* National Bureau of Standards Special Publication 500-99, Dec 1982.

A17. Minimal Unit Test Case Determination

A17.1 Application. This measure determines the number of independent paths through a module so that a minimal number of covering test cases can be generated for unit test. It is applied during unit testing.

A17.2 Primitives

- N = number of nodes; a sequential group of program statements.
- E = number of edges; program flow between nodes.
- SN = number of splitting nodes; a node with more than one edge emanating from it.
- RG = number of regions; in a graph with no edges crossing, an area bounded by edges.

A17.3 Implementation. The cyclomatic complexity is first computed using the cyclomatic

Fig A16.7-1
Module Control Graph

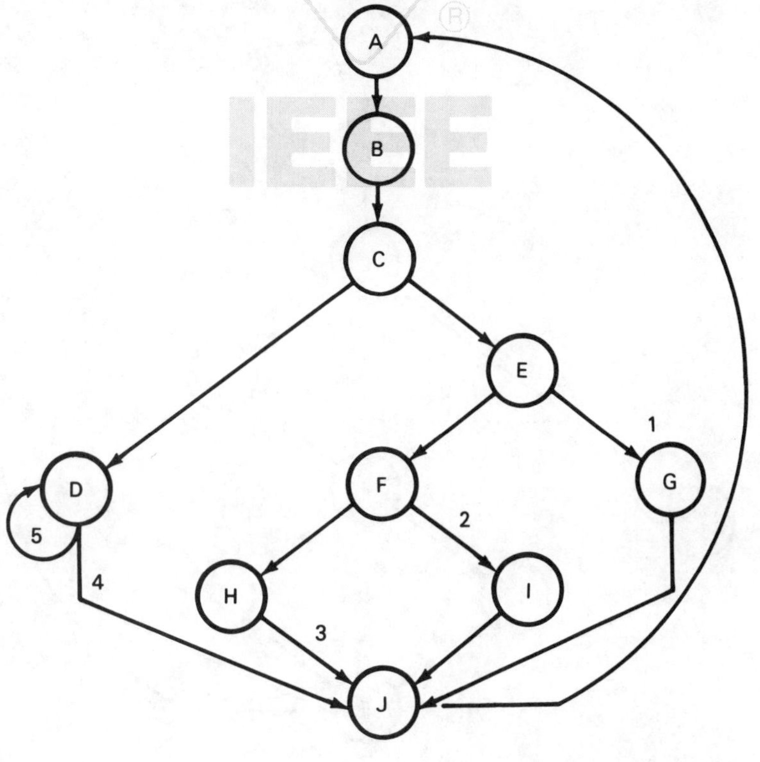

complexity measure described in A16. The complexity of the module establishes the number of distinct paths. The user constructs test cases along each path so all edges of the graph are traversed. This set of test cases forms a minimal set of cases that covers all paths through the module.

A17.4 Interpretation. The minimal set of test cases is the number of independent paths through the module. Execution of these test cases generally causes every statement and decision outcome to be executed at least once. Additional test cases may be added (eg, to test upper and lower bounds on variables).

A17.5 Considerations. The construction of the graph can be a tedious, error-prone process. Thus, automation of the graph construction is desirable. Once the graph is constructed, the generation of test cases is done by hand. Since the graph produces a minimal set of test cases, additional test cases should be generated to comprehensively test the module.

A17.6 Training. Training may be required in graph construction and interpretation in order to determine the minimal set of test cases.

A17.7 Example. Figure A17.7-1 illustrates a strongly connected graph. The nodes are labeled A (entry node) through J (exit node). Each node represents a block of code where control flow can only go from one statement to the next. Using the method for computing complexity (A16), the complexity of the module represented in Fig A17.7-1 is five. There are five distinct paths through the graph. They are:

A-B-C-E-G-J
A-B-C-E-F-I-J
A-B-C-E-F-H-J
A-B-C-D-J
A-B-C-D-D-J

The user selects five test cases causing the five distinct paths to be executed. The selection of minimal test case is demonstrated in McCabe [A41].

A17.8 Benefits. The minimal test case provides a rigorous method of determining minimal test coverage. This same set can be used, with appropriate modifications, during maintenance.

A17.9 Experience. There is empirical evidence [A41] that determining minimal test cases reduces

Fig A17.7-1
Module Control Graph

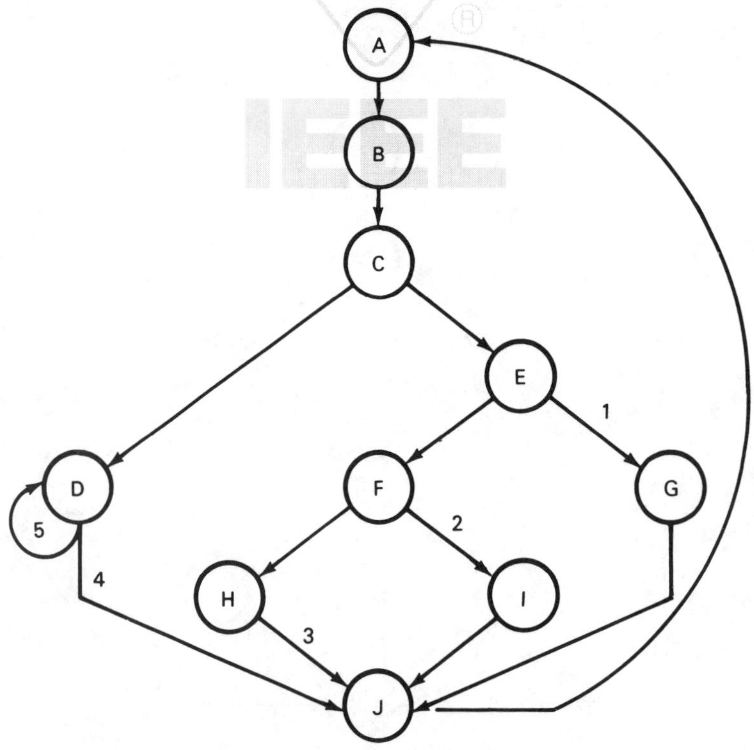

the difficulty encountered by programmers in testing every path in a module. The advantage of this approach is the completeness of the test of a module and the assurance that all segments of the module are tested.

A17.10 References. See Conte, Dunsmore, and Shen [A28] and McCabe [A39, A41].

A18. Run Reliability

Run reliability (R_k) is the probability that k randomly selected runs (corresponding to a specified period of time) will produce correct results.

A18.1 Application. The run reliability measure may be applied at any phase in the life cycle when the set of possible discrete input patterns and states can be identified. The sequence is randomly selected based on the probability assigned to selection of any one of them.

A18.2 Primitives

NR = Number of runs in a given test sample.

nc = Number of correct runs in a given test sample.

k = Number of runs for the specified period of time.

S = Sample space of possible input patterns and states. (S_i, i =1 ...) are elements in the sample space. For each input pattern and state there is a unique output pattern and state. Thus, S_i designates a given ((input, state), (output, state)) that constitutes a run.

P = Probability measure over the sample space.

P_i = Probability that the ith run is selected from the sample space.

A18.3 Implementation

A18.3.1 Sample Space (*S*). The sample space is viewed as the set of possible inputs into the program. In the early phases of the life cycle, the sample space consists of operational scenarios. For instance, in the early requirements phase the inputs and states are the listed requirements for the program. In the later phases of the life cycle, the sample space consists of all detailed input and state conditions of the program. For a given life cycle phase, a single sample space (S) is determined and a probability measure (P) is assigned. Runs are then generated by randomly choosing input patterns and states from the sample space according to the assigned probability P.

A18.3.2 Probability Measure (*P*). For each possible run i, a number p_i (between zero and one inclusive) must be assigned so that the sum of all the p_i's is 1. The simplest case is the assumption of a uniform probability distribution. However, in the operational environment some runs are more likely to occur than others, and should be weighted appropriately.

A18.3.3 Test *NR* Randomly Selected Runs. The accuracy of the measure R_k is determined by the number of runs *NR* used for estimation. The runs are randomly selected according to the probability distribution. The results of each run are examined for correctness. The number of correct runs is *nc*.

A18.3.4 Probability of a Successful Run (P_r). The probability of a randomly selected run being correct (P_r) is estimated by the sum of the probabilities for the correct runs, divided by the sum of the probabilities for all runs. In the case of a uniform distribution $P_r = nc/NR$.

A18.3.5 Run Reliability (R_k). Given k randomly selected runs during the specified period of time, the probability that all k runs give correct results is $R_k = P_r^k$.

A18.4 Interpretation. The reliability obtained using the number of runs for the specified period of time is the probability that the software will perform its intended function for the specified period of time under the stated conditions. Thus, it satisfies the standard definition for systems reliability [A42, A46] and may be combined with other components of the system, such as the hardware component, using the usual rules of probability.

A18.5 Considerations. The run reliability is not defined until the sample space and probability measure are defined for the specific application. These are not unique for the program. They must be carefully constructed by all parties with knowledge of the application environment, the program, and the test procedures, as well as the construction of probability spaces. Construction of the input sample space (A18.3.1) can be done in a number of different ways. There must be a unique output for each input. Thus attention must be given to the initialization of the variables. If more than one input channel is possible, an input pattern may be a vector over time. If a real time system is involved, the exact time of each input must be specified. When a hardware/software system is considered, there must be agreement on the accuracy of the input magnitude and timing.

During the specification or early design phase, a sample space might involve the variety of application scenarios using the various system functions in different ways. A run might be judged successful if all the functions needed in that scenario are appropriately specified.

Construction of the probability measure (P) is possibly the most difficult and potentially misleading error source. The uniform distribution on all possible inputs is the simplest and might be agreed on for test purposes, but may not be representative of the application environment. An inappropriate probability measure will not predict what happens in the field. Changes in the way in which the system is used constitute a change in the probability measure and may change the actual and predicted run reliability. A high reliability measure during one phase or period of time will be applicable to other stages only to the extent that the program remains constant and the sample space and probability measure is representative of the runs that will be made in that other phase.

A18.6 Training. Training should include the basic four chapters in Feller [A44], random sampling techniques, a beginning level of statistical knowledge, and an understanding of the application environment.

A18.7 Example

A18.7.1 Concept Phase. In order for the final system to work reliably, a list of necessary functions must be identified. Suppose a list of functions has been prepared which contains $NR = 20$ different scenarios. The list of functions and scenarios are given to a review team that traces each of the scenarios to check that all the functions required for mission success are available. Further, suppose the review team reports that in one of the scenarios a function necessary for the success of the mission was not in the list. The estimate of the system reliability at this point is .95. After adding the necessary function, one has a new system that works for these scenarios. In order to make a statement concerning the reliability of the new system, however, one would need to "randomly" select a new set of scenarios and test again. Suppose then, in this second test, that in all 20 scenarios the mission could have been performed successfully in the sense that all necessary functions were in the list. This does not mean, however, that following the next scenario through will necessarily find satisfactory results. Suppose the required reliability for the run is .9 and we wish to demonstrate that this requirement has been met with an accepted 5% risk of failing to reject an unreliable program. That is to say, we wish to test the null hypothesis that the probability of a successful run is less than .9 at the 5% significance level. The probability of making 30 successful runs when the probability of success is less than or equal to .9 is at most $.9^{30} = .047$. Thus, by obtaining success in 30 randomly selected test cases, one could conclude that the requirement of a run reliability of .9 had been met with less than a 5% chance of making an incorrect conclusion.

A18.7.2 Implementation Phase. Suppose the software program has nautical miles (nmi) as input and the range is broken up into the following categories: (0, 500 nmi), (500, 1000 nmi), (1000, 2000 nmi), and (above 2000 nmi). In addition, suppose the associated probabilities assigned by the user are ¼, ⅛, ⅛, and ½ respectively. The user believes that ¼ of the operational time ranges will come from the interval (0, 500), ⅛ of the time from (500, 1000), etc. A random selection of ranges are generated according to the distribution where, once an interval is chosen, a range is drawn uniformly from the chosen interval. Now suppose nr_i ranges were randomly selected from interval i with nc_i being run successfully, $i=1, 2, 3, 4$. The estimated reliability is then

$$R = \frac{nc_1}{4nr_1} + \frac{nc_2}{8nr_2} + \frac{nc_3}{8nr_3} + \frac{nc_4}{2nr_4}$$

Another example within the implementation phase is as follows:

Alphameric input patterns can be defined for use in code walk-through or computer runs. Consider a module with two input variables A and B. The range as viewed by the user for A is the alphameric characters A through Z and for B is all positive real numbers. Regardless of how the user views the ranges, an 8 bit computer will view each input as one of 2^8 possibilities. The two characters together will be one of 2^{16} possibilities, presuming here that timing is of no concern. For simplicity it might be agreed that each of the 2^{16}th possible inputs representing an input for which the algorithm was intended will have a constant probability p of being chosen, and the rest will have probability p'. One can easily develop a random number generator to randomly select among these possible inputs. One can either select from both intended and unintended inputs and weight the results, or one can develop a random number generator that will have an appropriate probability for selecting from the intended or unintended inputs. Numerical results for real numbers will not always be exactly correct, but are said to be "correct" if the difference is within some acceptable bounds of accuracy. The results computed by the computer operating on these inputs may then be compared to those calculated by hand or other "oracle", perhaps a program in double precision instead of single precision.

A18.8 Benefits. The technique is solidly based theoretically and very easy to interpret if one accepts the assumed sample space and probability measure. This measure can be integrated with a hardware reliability measure to form system reliability, maintainability, and availability estimates.

A18.9 Experience. The concepts and experiences with this measure are documented in [A43, A45, and A47-A49].

A18.10 References

[A42] ANSI/IEEE 729-1983, IEEE Standard Glossary of Software Engineering Terminology.

[A43] BROWN, J. R. and LIPOW, M. Testing for Software Reliability. Proceedings of the 1975 International Conference on Reliable Software, Apr 21-23, 1975, IEEE catalog no 75-CH0940-7CSR, pp 518-527.

[A44] FELLER, W. *An Introduction to Probability Theory and Its Applications.* New York: John Wiley and Sons, Inc, 1957, chaps I, V, VI, and IX.

[A45] LIPOW, M. *Measurement of Computer Software Reliability.* AFSC-TR-75-05, 1979.

[A46] MIL Std 721.

[A47] NELSON, E. C. *A Statistical Basis for Software Reliability Assessment.* TRW-SS-73-03, Redondo Beach, California: TRW, Mar 1973.

[A48] NELSON, E. C. *Software Reliability.* TRW-SS-75-05, Redondo Beach, California: TRW, Nov 1975.

[A49] THAYER, T. A., LIPOW, M and NELSON, E. C. *Software Reliability: A Study of Large Project Reality.* New York: North Holland Publishing Co, 1978.

A19. Design Structure

A19.1 Application. This measure is used to determine the simplicity of the detailed design of a software program. Also, the values determined for the associated primitives can be used to identify problem areas within the software design.

A19.2 Primitives

- *P*1 = total number of modules in the program
- *P*2 = number of modules dependent on the input or output
- *P*3 = number of modules dependent on prior processing (state)
- *P*4 = number of database elements
- *P*5 = number of non-unique database elements
- *P*6 = number of database segments (partition of the state)
- *P*7 = number of modules not single entrance/single exit.

A19.3 Implementation. The design structure measure is the weighted sum of six derivatives determined by using the primitives given above. The six derivatives are:

- D_1 = design organized top down (Boolean)
- D_2 = module dependence (*P*2/*P*1)
- D_3 = module dependent on prior processing (*P*3/*P*1)
- D_4 = database size (*P*5/*P*4)
- D_5 = database compartmentalization (*P*6/*P*4)
- D_6 = module single entrance single exit (*P*7/*P*1).

The design structure measure (*DSM*) can be expressed as:

$$DSM = \sum_{i=1}^{6} W_i D_i$$

The weights (W_i) are assigned by the user based on the priority of each associated derivative. Each W_i has a value between 0 and 1 ($\Sigma_i W_i = 1.0$).

A19.4 Interpretation. The value of the design structure measure is scaled between 0 and 1 by the appropriate weights. A score near 0 is considered better than a score near 1. Design structure measure values that are considered high could be traced to "offending" primitive(s) to highlight particular priority areas for change in the design. As changes are made to the design structure, the incremental design structure measure values can be plotted to show whether improvements are being made and how rapidly. Also, comparisons of design structure measures between different projects allows a relative scaling to be made for values determined.

A19.5 Considerations. Each primitive is calculated to help identify those characteristics in the design that promote simplicity in the construction of modules and databases.

A19.6 Training. Training would be necessary to understand the definitions of the primitives for the particular application. The use of a program design language (PDL) would enhance and standardize the definition procedure for primitives.

A19.7 Example. Previous to calculating the primitive (and associated derivative) values, the following steps should occur:

(1) The definitions of the primitives for the particular application must be determined. For example, if a program design language (PDL) were being used to develop the software design, then the primitives would be defined in association with the PDL constructs.

(2) Priorities should be determined for each derivative (D_i). These priorities should then be used to assign the associated weighting factors (W_i). If no priorities are established, the weight for each derivative would be one-sixth (1/6).

To arrive at a value for the design structure measure, assume that the primitives have the following values:

$P1 = 250 \quad P3 = 50 \quad P5 = 500 \quad P7 = 10$
$P2 = 125 \quad P4 = 2500 \quad P6 = 50$

The derivative values are calculated to be:

D_1 = 0 (assumed, top-down design)
D_2 = .5 ($P2/P1$)
D_3 = .2 ($P3/P1$)
D_4 = .2 ($P5/P4$)
D_5 = .02 ($P6/P4$)
D_6 = .04 ($P7/P1$)

Using a weight of one-sixth (1/6) for each W_i the design structure measure value is:

$$DSM = \sum_{i=1}^{6} W_i D_i$$

$$= \tfrac{1}{6}(0) + \tfrac{1}{6}(.5) + \tfrac{1}{6}(.2) + \tfrac{1}{6}(.2) + \tfrac{1}{6}(.02) + \tfrac{1}{6}(.04)$$

$$= .16$$

A19.8 Benefits. The design structure measure will give an indication of the simplicity (value near 0) or complexity (value near 1) of the software design.

A19.9 Experience. There is limited published experience with the use of the design structure measure. This measure is similar to the completeness measure [A35]. The experience consists of the determination of the proper definitions and measurements of primitives and calculation of associated derivatives. This technique worked successfully for the completeness measure, and similar results are expected for the design structure measure.

A19.10 References

[A50] FRANCIS, J. et al. *The Application of Software Quality Metrics to Mx Operational G&C Software.* Dynamics Research Corporation, Sept 1982.

[A51] McCALL, J., RICHARDS, P., and WALTERS, G. *Factors in Software Quality,* RADC-TR-77-369, 3 vols, Nov 1977.

[A52] McCALL, J., and MATSUMOTO, M. *Metrics Enhancements.* RADC-TR-80-109, 2 vols, Apr 1980.

[A53] MILLER, D. et al. *The Application of Software Quality Metrics to PCKR Operational Guidance and Control Software.* Dynamics Research Corporation, Sept 1983.

A20. Mean Time to Discover the Next *K* Faults

A20.1 Application. This measure can be used to project the average length of time until the next K faults are discovered. This can provide an indication of how much time would be required until a desired level of reliability is achieved.

A20.2 Primitives

f = number of failures found from the beginning of testing to the present

t_i = observed time between the $(i-1)$st and ith failure for a given severity level i=1,...

A20.3 Implementation. The mean time to failure (see A30) should be used to estimate the mean time to discover the next K faults in the software. This can then be expressed as:

$$\text{mean time to discover the next } K \text{ faults} = \sum_{i=f}^{f+K-1} \widehat{\text{MTTF}}_i$$

where $\widehat{\text{MTTF}}_i$ is an estimate of the mean time to failure between the ith and $(i+1)$st failure.

The estimate of the mean time to failure between the ith and $(i+1)$st failure can be calculated using any of the software models based upon time between failures [A56-A58]. Suppose that estimate is:

$$\widehat{\text{MTTF}}_i = \hat{E}\{\text{time between the } i\text{th and the } (i+1)\text{st failures}\} \; f \leq i \leq f+K-1$$

Notice that if $K=1$, then we simply have the estimate of the MTFF (see A30) between the fth and $(f+1)$st failure. Then the estimate is:

$$\begin{pmatrix}\text{mean time to}\\ \text{discover the}\\ \text{next } K \text{ faults}\end{pmatrix} = \sum_{i=f}^{f-K+1} \hat{E} \begin{Bmatrix}\text{time between}\\ \text{the } i\text{th and the}\\ (i+1)\text{st}\end{Bmatrix}$$

By estimating the mean time to failure, one can then estimate how much additional time will be required to discover all, or a subset, of the estimated remaining faults. One can judge how long it will take before the software achieves a desired level of reliability.

A20.4 Interpretation. Actual numerical calculations of the estimate depends on the form of the model chosen to represent the distribution of MTTF. Within the software life cycle, the estimate is useful when planning for time necessary to achieve stabilization.

A20.5 Considerations. To apply this measure, one must collect the times between failure and then fit the data to one of the software models. For better estimates, it is desirable to have time units with as much resolution as feasible, eg, CPU execution time is especially appropriate in a software development environment. Sometimes wall-clock time is the only time available, and in this situation estimates can be made, but with much less precision. For the situations where operational or application usage requires less resolution, estimates based on wall-clock time units would be appropriate.

During the software development life cycle, evaluation of model predictions versus actual time required to achieve a certain level of reliability should be used to construct realistic schedules.

A20.6 Training. The implementation requires knowledge of the application of software models that use the time between failure data.

A20.7 Example. In the fitting of the Jelinski and Moranda "de-eutrophication" model [A56], the estimate of the mean time to failure between the ith and $(i+1)$st error is

$$\text{MTTF}_i = \hat{E}\{\text{time between } i\text{th}, (i+1)\text{st})\} = \frac{1}{\hat{Q}(\hat{NF}-i)}$$

where $\hat{Q}$ is the estimate of the proportionality constant in that model and $\hat{NF}$ is the estimate of the total number of faults in the program. The estimate of the mean time to discover the next K faults is then:

$$\sum_{i=f}^{f+K-1} \frac{1}{\hat{Q}(\hat{NF}-i)}$$

For illustrative purposes suppose $f=20$ and $\hat{Q}$ and $\hat{NF}$ were calculated as .05 and 100 respectively. If one were interested in the mean time to discover the next $K=2$ failures then the estimate becomes:

$$\sum_{i=20}^{21} \frac{1}{(.05)(100-i)} = \frac{1}{(.05)(80)} + \frac{1}{(.05)(79)} = 0.50$$

A20.8 Benefits. This measure can be plotted against K ($K=1, 2, 3, \ldots NF$ remaining number of faults) to judge the integrity of the system at any point in time.

A20.9 Experience. Experience is a function of application of any of the given models in the references.

A20.10 References. See also Musa, Iannino, and Okumoto [A7].

[A54] GOEL, AMRIT L., and OKUMOTO, K. *A Time Dependent Error Detection Rate Model for Software Performance Assessment with Applications.* RADC #F3062-78-C-0351, Mar 1980, p 76.

[A55] LITTLEWOOD, B. A Stochastic Reliability Growth: A Model for Fault Removal in Computer Programs and Hardware Designs. *IEEE Transactions on Reliability*, vol R-30, no 4, Oct 1981, pp 313-320.

[A56] MORANDA, PAUL L., and JELINSKI, Z. *Final Report on Software Reliability Study.* McDonnell-Douglas Astronautics Company, MDC Report no 63921, 1972.

[A57] MUSA, J. D. A Theory of Software Reliability and Its Application. *IEEE Transactions on Software Engineering*, vol SE-1, no 3, 1975, pp 312-327.

[A58] SCHICK, GEORGE J., and WOLVERTON, RAY, W. An Analysis of Competing Software Reliability Models. *IEEE Transactions on Software Engineering*, vol SE-4, no 2, 1978, pp 104-120.

A21. Software Purity Level

A21.1 Application. The software purity level provides an estimate of the relative fault-freeness of a computer program at any specified point in time during the operational phase.

A21.2 Primitives

t_i = observed times between failures (eg, execution time) for a given severity level

f = total number of failures in a given time interval

A21.3 Implementation. Suppose f failures have occurred during the operational phase of the life cycle of the program. Suppose also the length of time in this phase when the fth failure is detected is t_f. Then the estimate of the purity level of the program at that point in time is

$$PL = \frac{\hat{Z}(t_0) - \hat{Z}(t_f)}{\hat{Z}(t_0)}$$

where t_0 is the start of the operations and maintenance phase and $\hat{Z}(t)$ is the estimated hazard (or failure) rate at time t. The hazard rate is defined as the conditional probability that a software failure happens in an interval of time $(t, t+\Delta t)$ given that the software has not failed up to time t. It is derived from any of the software reliability models that use time between failures data t_i. PL denotes the relative change in the hazard rate function from the beginning of the operations and maintenance phase to the time of the fth failure detection.

A21.4 Interpretation. The closer PL gets to 1 the greater the reliability of the program. Values close to 1 indicate that many of the initial faults in the program have been eliminated.

A21.5 Considerations. The application of this measure is especially applicable for those classes of models in which the total number of remaining faults in the program cannot be predicted (eg, Moranda's geometric model [A60 and A61]). Its use is restricted to those phases where significant test results can be obtained.

A21.6 Training. Familiarity with the various software reliability models employing time between failure data is essential.

A21.7 Example. For the Moranda geometric model (A60), the estimate of the hazard rate at any time t between the occurrence of the ith failure and the $(i+1)$st is:

$$\hat{Z}(t) = \hat{D}\hat{Q}^i$$

$\hat{D}$ is the estimate of the initial hazard rate at time t_o and $(0<Q<1)$ is the estimate of the proportionality constant in the model [A60]. Then the purity level using this model is

$$PL = \frac{\hat{Z}(t_0) - \hat{Z}(t_f)}{\hat{Z}(t_0)} = 1 - \hat{Q}^f$$

A21.8 Benefits. A plot of PL versus n (the number of failures) can be used to see the relative "fault-freeness" of the program as the number of detected faults increases.

A21.9 Experience. Limited experience is provided in the references.

A21.10 References. See also Musa, Iannino, and Okumoto [A7].

[A59] FARR, W. H. *A Survey of Software Reliability, Modeling and Estimation.* Dahlgren, Virginia: Naval Surface Weapons Center, NSWC TR 82-171, Sept 1983.

[A60] MORANDA, PAUL Predictions of Software Reliability During Debugging. *1975 Proceedings of the Annual Reliability and Maintainability Symposium*, 1975.

[A61] MORANDA, PAUL Event-Alerted Rate Models for General Reliability Analysis. *IEEE Transactions on Reliability*, vol R-28, no 5, 1979, pp 376-381.

A22. Estimated Number of Faults Remaining (by Seeding)

A22.1 Application. The estimated number of faults remaining in a program is related to the reliability of the program. There are many sampling techniques that estimate this number. This section describes a simple form of seeding that assumes a homogeneous distribution of a representative class of faults [A67].

This measure can be applied to any phase of the software life cycle. The search for faults continues for a determined period of time that may be less than that required to find all seeded faults. The measure is not computed unless some non-seeded faults are found.

A22.2 Primitives

N_s = the number of seeded faults

n_s = the number of seeded faults found

n_F = the number of faults found that were not intentionally seeded

A22.3 Implementation. A monitor is responsible for error seeding. The monitor inserts (seeds) N_s faults representative of the expected indigenous faults. The test team reports to the monitor the faults found during a test period of predetermined length.

Before seeding, a fault analysis is needed to determine the types of faults and their relative frequency of occurrence expected under a particular set of software development conditions [A49, A65]. Although an estimate of the number of faults remaining can be made on the basis of very few inserted faults, the accuracy of the estimate (and hence the confidence in it) increases as the number of seeded faults increases.

Faults should be inserted randomly throughout the software. Personnel inserting the faults should be different and independent of those persons later searching for the faults. The process of searching for the faults should be carried out without knowledge of the inserted faults. The search should be performed for a previously determined period of time (or effort) and each fault reported to the central monitor.

Each reported fault should be reviewed to determine whether it is in the class of faults being studied, and if so, whether it is a seeded or an indigenous fault. The maximum likelihood estimate of the number of indigenous (unseeded) faults in the specified class is:

$$\hat{NF} = \frac{n_F N_s}{n_s} \qquad \text{(eq A22-1)}$$

where $\hat{NF}$ is truncated to the integer value. The estimate of the remaining number of faults is then: $\hat{NF}_{rem} = \hat{NF} - n_F$.

The probability of finding n_F of NF indigenous faults and n_F of N_s seeded faults, given that there are $n_F + n_s$ faults found in the program is $C(N_s, n_s)\, C(NF, n_F) / C(NF + N_s, n_F + n_s)$ where the function $C(x,y) = x!/(x-y)!y!$ is the combination of "x" things taken "y" at a time. Using this relation one can calculate confidence intervals.

A22.4 Interpretation. The number of seeded and indigenous faults discovered enables the number of faults remaining to be estimated for the fault type being considered. The phrase "fault type being considered" means that if, for example, one was seeding typographical faults, one would not expect a good prediction of the number of omitted functions or algorithmic faults. If one were seeding faults of the type found in unit testing, one would not expect the estimate to apply to those interface faults found in integration testing.

A22.5 Considerations. This measure depends on the assumption that the seeded (inserted) faults are representative of existing (unseeded) faults. In general, not all faults are equally likely to be found in any given test procedure. To assure that the seeded faults are representative of a specific class of faults, and the result will have the desired accuracy, enough faults of the kind expected should be inserted to provide the desired accuracy.

Faults are corrected in the original software only after the fault has been determined to be unseeded by rerunning the test case on the original unseeded software. Good configuration management practices are needed to assure that the seeded version is not the version finally released and that indigenous faults discovered are corrected only in the unseeded version.

The correction of the indigenous faults in the original version raises the problem of whether the correction introduces further faults. At this time this must be left as an engineering judgment as to whether the new (corrected) program needs to be seeded to give an estimate of its reliability or whether the estimate of the faults remaining in the new (corrected) program is $NF - n_F$ where n_F is the number of indigenous faults found and corrected.

In lieu of actually seeding faults in a program, the number of "seeded" faults may sometimes be generated by examining the results of testing by two independent test teams [A71 and A63]. The seeded faults would be those faults identified by both test teams. The unseeded faults are those identified by either, but not both, of the test teams. An estimate of the number of remaining faults can then be calculated using Eq A22-1.

A22.6 Training. No additional training is required for the developers or the testers. Training in seeding the faults and monitoring the process is needed. Some general training and practice in classifying faults is also needed.

A22.7 Example. Suppose 100 were seeded. During the prescribed test period, 50 of the 100 seeded faults and 2 unseeded faults were found.

Then:

$$N_s = 100$$
$$n_s = 50$$
$$n_F = 2$$
$$\hat{NF} = \left[\frac{n_F N_s}{n_s}\right] = \left[\frac{2(100)}{50}\right] = 4$$

Thus, it is estimated that there are $\hat{NF}_{rem} = \hat{NF} - n_F = 2$ faults remaining.

A22.8 Benefits. This procedure encourages the reporting of faults and competition between developers and testers. Since faults are known to be there, the tester knows there is something to search for. The reporting of faults does not necessarily admit to an error on the part of the developers.

The procedure could be carried out by a customer monitor with little effort, high effectiveness, and minimal interference with the developer's normal patterns. For the cost of a second independent testing group, an estimate of the number of remaining faults can be obtained without seeding errors.

A22.9 Experience. Nippon Telephone and Telegraph reported [A73] good results applying their version of the seeding method to an operating system consisting of 150,000 lines of code. A mixture of seeding and a software reliability growth model at IBM Japan Ltd. for predicting the number of faults to be found during the operational phase is described. Techniques for seeding faults include: (1) deferring correction of actual faults by programmers; (2) mutants (eg, replacing "and" with "or") that are considered to be similar inherent defects due to misinterpretation of the specifications; and (3) transplanted defects (eg, adding or deleting a flow-control statement) simulating the design mistakes. In two experiments involving 3000 and 4000 lines of code for modules in an on-line terminal operating program, the authors claim to have predicted (to within $\pm 10\%$) the fraction of defects found during testing with those remaining to be found during operation. The authors claim that seeding is practical in their experience.

In the US, a number of published papers have developed the principles and techniques for seeding [A64, A65, A67, A70, A74, A75].

A22.10 References. See also Thayer, Lipow, and Nelson [A49].

[A62] BASIN, S. L. *Estimation of Software Error Rates Via Capture-Recapture Sampling.* Palo Alto: Science Applications Inc, Sept 1973.

[A63] BASIN, S. L. *Measuring the Error Content of Software.* Palo Alto: Science Applications Inc, Sept 1974.

[A64] BOWEN, J. B. and SAIB, S. H. *Association of Software Errors, Classifications to AED Language Elements.* Prepared under Contract Number NAS 2-10550 by Hughes Aircraft Company, Fullerton, and General Research Corporation, Santa Barbara, California, Nov 1980.

[A65] BOWEN, J. B. and SAIB, S. H. *Error Seeding Technique Specification.* Prepared under Contract Number NAS 2-10550 by Hughes Aircraft Company, Fullerton, and General Research Corporation, Santa Barbara, California, Dec 1980.

[A66] DACS. *Rudner Model, Seeding/Tagging.* Quantitative Software Models, DACS, SSR-1, Mar 1979, pp 3-56 to 3-58.

[A67] DURAN, J. W. and WIORKOWSKI, J. J. Capture-Recapture Sampling for Estimating Software Error Content. *IEEE Transactions on Software Engineering*, vol SE-7, Jan 1981.

[A68] FELLER, W. *An Introduction to Probability Theory and Its Applications.* New York: John Wiley and Sons, Inc, 1957, p 43.

[A69] *System Specification for Flexible Interconnect.* Specification Number SS078779400, May 15, 1980.

[A70] LIPOW, M. *Estimation of Software Package Residual Errors.* TRW Software Series SS-72-09, Redondo Beach: TRW E & D, 1972.

[A71] McCABE, THOMAS J. *Structural Testing.* Columbia, Maryland: McCabe & Associates, Inc, 1984.

[A72] MILLS, H. D. *On the Statistical Validation of Computer Programs.* FSC-72-6015, Gaithersburg, Maryland: Federal Systems Division, International Business Machines Corporation, 1972.

[A73] OHBA, M., et al. *S-Shape Reliability Control Curve: How Good Is It?* Proceedings COMPSAC82, IEEE Computer Society, 1982, pp 38-44.

[A74] RUDNER, B. Seeding/Tagging Estimation of Software Errors: Models and Estimates. RADC-TR-15, 1977.

[A75] SEBER, G. A. F. *Estimation of Animal Abundance and Related Parameters.* 2nd ed, New York: McMillan Publishing Co, 1982.

A23. Requirements Compliance

A23.1 Application. This analysis is used to verify requirements compliance by using system verification diagrams (SVDs), a logical interconnection of decomposition elements (eg, stimulus and response) that detect inconsistencies, incompleteness, and misinterpretations.

A23.2 Primitives

*DE*s = Decomposition elements

- Stimulus = External input
- Function = Defined input/output process
- Response = Result of the function
- Label = Numerical *DE* identifier
- Reference = Specification paragraph number

Requirement errors detected using SVDs:

N_1 = Number due to inconsistencies
N_2 = Number due to incompleteness
N_3 = Number due to misinterpretation.

A23.3 Implementation. The implementation of a SVD is composed of the following phases:

(1) The decomposition phase is initiated by mapping the system requirement specifications into stimulus/response elements (*DE*s). That is, all key words, phrases, functional or performance requirements or both, and expected output are documented on decomposition forms (see Fig A23.3-1).

(2) The graph phase uses the *DE*s from the decomposition phase and logically connects them to form the SVD graph.

(3) The analysis phase examines the SVD from the graph phase by using connectivity and reachability matrices. The various requirement error types are determined by experiencing the system verification diagram and identifying errors as follows:

inconsistencies. Decomposition elements that do not accurately reflect the system requirement specification.

incompleteness. Decomposition elements that do not completely reflect the system requirement specification.

misinterpretation. Decomposition elements that do not correctly reflect the system requirement specification. These errors may occur during translation of the requirements into decomposition elements, constructing the SVD graph, or interpreting the connectivity and reachability matrices.

Fig A23.3-1
Decomposition Form

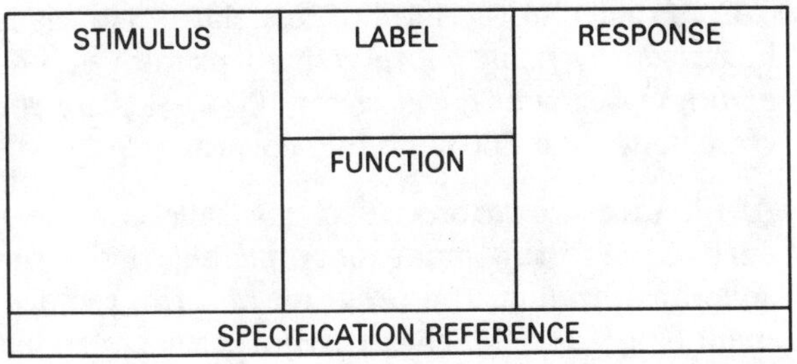

An analysis is also made of the percentages for the various requirement error types for the respective categories: inconsistencies, incompleteness, and misinterpretation.

Inconsistencies (%) $= N_1/(N_1+N_2+N_3) \times 100$
Incompleteness (%) $= N_2/(N_1+N_2+N_3) \times 100$
Misinterpretation (%) $= N_3/(N_1+N_2+N_3) \times 100$

This analysis can aid also in future software development efforts.

A23.4 Interpretation. The SVDs are analyzed by interpreting the connectivity and reachability matrices. The rules governing their use are as follows:

Connectivity Matrix. The rules governing the use of connectivity matrices are as follows:

Rule 1. The matrix size is $N \times N$ where N equals the number of decomposition elements in a given SVD.

Rule 2. Any (i, j) matrix element is equal to one, if DE_i transfers directly to DE_j. It is equal to zero otherwise.

Rule 3. Any matrix column of all zeros identifies a *DE* that is not transferred to or by any other *DE* and, therefore, must be an entry *DE*.

Rule 4. Any matrix row of all zeros identifies a *DE* that does not transfer to any other *DE* and, therefore, must be a terminal *DE*.

Rule 5. If there is a one along the diagonal, it indicates that a particular *DE* loops back to itself. Though possible, this is improbable at the requirement level and usually indicates a fault.

Rule 6. Any *DE* with an associated zero row and zero column indicates a stand alone system function. Though possible, they are rare and should be double checked for authenticity.

Reachability Matrix. The rules governing the use of reachability matrices include the rules 1–6 for connectivity matrices and the following reachability rule:

Rule 7. Any (i, j) matrix element is equal to one if DE_j can be reached (directly or indirectly) from DE_i. It is equal to zero otherwise.

An analysis of the percentages will aid requirements specifications and future code testing. The categories with the higher percentages should receive the most scrutiny for future requirement specifications and test case design.

A23.5 Considerations. SVDs can be implemented either manually or with the aid of automation. Automation is recommended for large SVDs. An SVD can be used during the system requirement definition phase and/or during the software requirement phase.

A23.6 Training. Training is required if automation is used. The manual approach requires a familiarization with logic methodology.

A23.7 Example. See Fig A23.7-1.

A23.8 Benefits. SVDs are good communication devices for internal and external reviews. The reachability matrix associated with SVDs can be used during the maintenance phase to assess modification impact and test direction. Requirements can be verified per life cycle phase.

A23.9 Experience. See also Fischer and Walker [A76].

A23.10 Reference

[A76] FISCHER, K. F. and WALKER, M. G. *Improved Software Reliability Through Requirement Verification.* IEEE Transactions on Reliability, vol R-28, no 3, Aug 1979, pp 233-239.

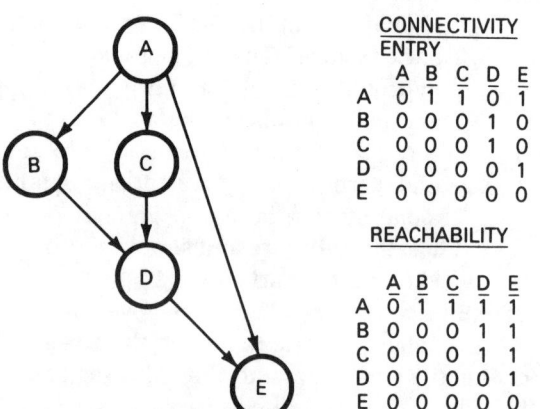

Fig A23.7-1

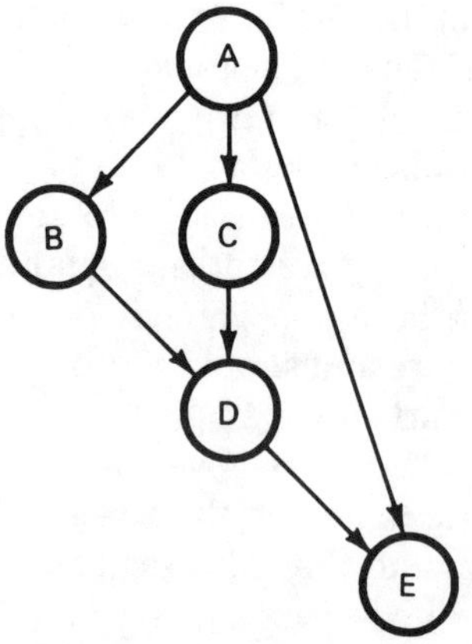

CONNECTIVITY
ENTRY

	A	B	C	D	E
A	0	1	1	0	1
B	0	0	0	1	0
C	0	0	0	1	0
D	0	0	0	0	1
E	0	0	0	0	0

REACHABILITY

	A	B	C	D	E
A	0	1	1	1	1
B	0	0	0	1	1
C	0	0	0	1	1
D	0	0	0	0	1
E	0	0	0	0	0

NOTE: Assume A, B, C, D, E are decomposition elements. Using the connectivity matrix rules 1-6 to identify the entry *DE* as A (Rule 3) B-to-A would not be allowed (it violates Rule 2). This results in column 1 having all zeros.

A24. Test Coverage

A24.1 Application. Test coverage is a measure of the completeness of the testing process from both a developer and a user perspective. The measure relates directly to the development, integration and operational test stages of product development: unit, system and acceptance tests. The measure can be applied by developers in unit tests to obtain a measure of thoroughness of structural tests. The developer can use the program class of primitives. The system tester can apply the measure in two ways: (1) focusing on requirement primitives, the system tester can gain a user-view of the thoroughness of functional tests, or (2) the program class of primitives can be used to measure the amount of implementation in the operational environment.

A24.2 Primitives. The primitives for test coverage are in two classes, program and requirement. For program, there are two types, functional and data. The program functional primitives are either modules, segments, statements, branches (nodes), or paths. Program data primitives are equivalence classes of data. Requirement primitives are either test cases or functional capabilities.

A24.3 Implementation. Test coverage (TC) is the percentage of requirement primitives implemented times the percentage of primitives executed during a set of tests. A simple interpretation of test coverage can be expressed by the following formula:

$$TC(\%) = \frac{\text{(Implemented capabilities)}}{\text{(Required capabilities)}} \times \frac{\text{(Program primitives tested)}}{\text{(Total program primitives)}} \times 100$$

A24.4 Interpretation. Test coverage is only an indication of the thoroughness of test. Due to the interplay of data with function, there are usually an infinite number of cases to test. This can be significantly reduced, if equivalence relations can be logically defined on the data and functions.

Confidence in the level of test thoroughness is increased by using more refined primitives. For example, segment coverage of 100% is a stronger statement than 100% module coverage.

A24.5 Considerations. Test coverage is a measure of the testing made on two categories of the software product, the program and the requirement (Fig A24.5-1). The program is a set of coded

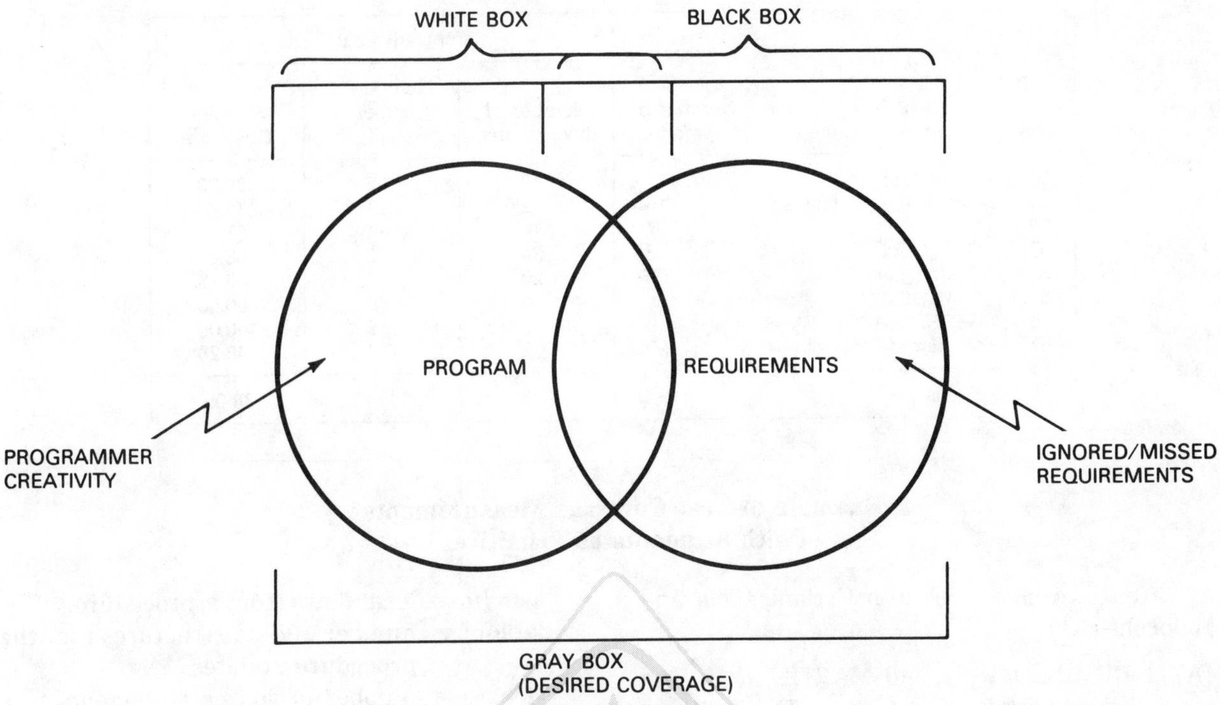

Fig A24.5-1
Test Coverage

instructions. The requirement is a set of user-intended capabilities. The intersection is the set of implemented user-intended capabilities. The left area represents either programmer creativity or those areas for which necessary implementation decisions were made due to the hardware, for example. The right area represents those user-intended capabilities that are missing in the implementation either unintentionally or intentionally due to other overriding factors such as storage. Corresponding to this model we can associate test activities and test coverage measures.

To the program, we associate a unit or functional test activity that is based on the premise that the structure of the programmed implementation is known. Hence the program primitives are known and available for a developer-oriented measure of test coverage. This is usually known as white box testing or clear box testing.

To the requirements, we associate a system test activity that in most cases assumes no knowledge of the programmed implementation. Test scenarios are designed to demonstrate correct operation from a user's view. The requirement primitives are known and can be used to give a user-oriented test coverage measure. This is usually known as black box testing.

A combination activity can be postulated. This is known as gray box testing. Test coverage in this activity is the product of the test coverage of program and requirement.

A24.6 Training. The user should understand basic testing theory.

A24.7 Example. Assuming all capabilities are implemented, Fig A24.7-1 gives the test coverage of a set of tests with segments as the primitives.

A24.8 Benefits. The test coverage measure is important in regulating effort expended to benefit achieved increasing the efficiency of the test process. Test cases can be developed to maximize the coverage measure.

A24.9 Experience. Test coverage is faciliated by code instrumented with probes to monitor usage. These, however, are programming language dependent. It is not a standard practice in program language specifications to provide this monitoring feature. Many projects are "tooling up" by customizing probes into language precompilers to automate this measure. DeMillo and Martin [A77] gives an assessment of test coverage usage in the DoD community.

No.	Module Name	Number of Segments:	(Archived) Past Tests		
			Number of Invocations	Number of Segments Hit	Percent Coverage
50:	do_one_to_one	Tio 177	12	52	29.38
51:	calculate_and_test_so	15	2	11	73.33
52:	a_to_r	7	14	4	57.14
53:	GET_CELL_FLG	3	34	2	66.67
54:	Put_txt_cell	54	20	18	33.33
55:	CUR_DOWN	5	5	3	60.00
56:	RESET_GRAPH_VARS	9	1	9	100.00
57:	set_target_loop_ctr	29	2	14	48.28
	Totals	1192	397	454	38.09

Fig A24.7-1
Example of Test Coverage Measurements*
(with Segments as Primitives)

A24.10 References. See also Ceriani, Cicu, and Maiocchi [A11].

[A77] DEMILLO, R. A. and MARTIN, R. J. *Software Test and Evaluation: Current Defense Practices Overview.* Georgia Institute of Technology, Jun 1983.

[A78] McCABE, T. *Tutorial Text: Structured Testing.* IEEE Computer Society Press, 1981.

[A79] MILLER, E. *Tutorial: Program Testing Techniques.* IEEE Computer Society Press, 1977.

A25. Data or Information Flow Complexity

A25.1 Application. This is a structural complexity or procedural complexity measure that can be used to evaluate the following:

(1) The information flow structure of large scale systems;
(2) The procedure and module information flow structure;
(3) The complexity of the interconnections between modules.

Moreover, this measure can also be used to indicate the degree of simplicity of relationships between subsystems and to correlate total observed failures and software reliability with data complexity.

A25.2 Primitives

lfi = local flows into a procedure.
datain = number of data structures from which the procedure retrieves data.
lfo = local flows from a procedure.
dataout = number of data structures that the procedure updates.
length = number of source statements in a procedure (excludes comments in a procedure.

A25.3 Implementation. Determine the flow of information between modules or subsystems or both by automated data flow techniques, HIPO charts, etc.

A local flow from module A to B exists if one of the following holds true:

(1) A calls B;
(2) B calls A and A returns a value to B that is used by B; or
(3) Both A and B are called by another module that passes a value from A to B.

Values of primitives are obtained by counting the data flow paths directed into and out of the modules.

$$\text{fanin} = lfi + \text{datain}$$
$$\text{fanout} = lfo + \text{dataout}.$$

The information flow complexity (*IFC*) is $IFC = (\text{fanin} \times \text{fanout})^2$.

$$\text{Weighted IFC} = \text{length} \times (\text{fanin} \times \text{fanout})^2.$$

A25.4 Interpretation. A module with a high information flow complexity is assumed to be more likely to have faults than a module with a low complexity value.

Measurements taken during integration testing show possible areas for redesign or restructuring of excessively complex subsystems/modules, or where maintenance of a system might be difficult.

Procedure complexities show the following:

*Coverage Analyzer, Version 1.8 (80 Column).

(1) Procedures that lack functionality (may have more than one function),
(2) Stress points in the system (high information traffic), or
(3) Excessive functional complexity of the subsystem/module.

A25.5 Considerations. Evaluation of procedural complexity is better suited for structured code. This measure generally is applied first during detailed design, and re-applied during integration to confirm the initial implementation. For large-scale systems, an automated procedure for determining data flow is essential.

A25.6 Training. Familiarity with data flow and complexity analysis and some experience in software design and development is required. A background in mathematics and statistics would aid in correlation studies.

A25.7 Example

Module *A*

Call Module *B*	1 fanout
Update global structure *X*	1 fanout
Read from file *Y*	1 fanin

End *A*

fanin = 1,
fanout = 2, therefore,
$IFC = (1*2)**2 = 4$

A25.8 Benefits. Designers can aim toward a lower information flow complexity for reliable systems.

The complexity can be verified early in the design and again in the testing cycle, enabling changes before extensive testing has been conducted.

High information flow complexity indicates candidate modules and procedures for extensive testing or redesign. For failure correlation studies, associate the failure with a particular procedure/module.

A25.9 Experience. Limited experience is currently available [A83]. The use of this measure is being evaluated by a NASA/Goodard software group.

A25.10 References

[A80] BIEMAN, J. W., and EDWARDS, W. R. *Measuring Software Complexity.* Technical Report 83-5-1, Computer Science Department, University of Southwestern Louisiana, Feb 1983.

[A81] BIEMAN, J. W., and EDWARDS, W. R. *Measuring Data Dependency Complexity.* Technical Report 83-5-3, Computer Science Department, University of Southwestern Louisiana, Jul 1983.

[A82] BIEMAN, J. W., BAKER, A., CLITES, P. GUSTAFSON, D., and MILTON, A. A Standard Representation of Imperative Language Program for Data Collection and Software Measures Specification. *Journal of Systems and Software,* Dec 1987.

[A83] HENRY, S., and KAFURA, D. Software Structure Metrics Base on Information Flow. *IEEE Transactions on Software Engineering,* vol SE-7 (5), Sept 1981.

A26. Reliability Growth Function

A26.1 Application. This measure provides an estimate (or prediction) of the time or stage of testing when a desired failure rate or fault density goal will be acheived. It is an indicator of the level of success of fault correction.

A26.2 Primitives

NR_k = Total number of test cases during the kth stage

NS = Total number of stages

nc_k = Total number of successful test cases during the kth stage

A26.3 Implementation. Good record keeping of failure occurrences is needed to accurately document at which stage the failure occurred. Detailed failure analysis is required to determine whether a fault was inserted by previous correction efforts. This will be used to calculate the reinsertion rate of faults (r), which is the ratio of the number of faults reinserted to the total number of faults found.

A test-sequence of software is conducted in N stages (periods between changes to the software being tested). The reliability for the kth stage is:

$$R(k) = R(u) - A/k \qquad \text{(eq A26-1)}$$

where:

$$\lim_{k \to \infty} R(k) = R(u)$$

The unknown parameter A represents the growth parameter of the model. An $A > 0$ indicates the reliability is increasing as a function of the testing stage; an $A < 0$ indicates it is decreasing. The estimation of $R(u)$ and A is done using least-square estimates. The two equations used to derive the estimates are:

$$\sum_{k=1}^{NS} \left(\frac{nc_k}{NR_k} - R(u) + \frac{A}{k} \right) = 0 \qquad \text{(eq A26-2)}$$

$$\sum_{k=1}^{NS} \left(\frac{nc_k}{NR_k} - R(u) + \frac{A}{k} \right) \frac{1}{k} = 0 \qquad \text{(eq A26-3)}$$

The simultaneous solution of these two equations provides the estimates. If failure analysis was performed to determine a fault reinsertion rate (r); a third equation can be used in conjunction with (A26-2), and (A26-3) to estimate the fault insertion rate, r.

$$\sum_{k=1}^{NS} \left(\frac{nc_k}{NR_k} - R(u) + \frac{A}{k(1-r)} \right) \frac{1}{k(1-r)} = 0$$

(eq A26-4)

A26.4 Interpretation. A positive number (A) or essentially monotonic increasing function indicates positive reliability growth as well as a successful fault correction program. A negative number (A) or a monotonic decreasing function indicates reliability degradation as well as an unsuccessful fault correction program.

A26.5 Considerations. Some testing and accumulation of failure experience is necessary before a first estimate of the growth function can be made. Projecting growth when moving from one testing phase to the next will generally not be applicable unless the level of testing is comparable. Those models that use the success of test cases to project growth to some reliability goal are very dependent on the randomness of testing done and the completeness of coverage.

Determination of a significant rate of growth can be a statistically difficult task. Some models circumvent this by determining the distribution function of the parameter whose growth is being estimated. This reduces the problem to hypothesis testing [A89]. However, these models are generally more difficult to implement.

A26.6 Training. Some knowledge of software development and testing is necessary if models using test cases or the reinsertion rate of faults, r, are desired. Some statistical knowledge would aid in the interpretation of results for most models. The calculation involved in some of the models will require implementation on a digital computer.

A26.7 Example. A number of practical examples can be found in LaPadula [A88].

A26.8 Benefits. Once some initial testing experience is accumulated, this metric can be used throughout the testing phase and re-estimated as needed. Some models will estimate the distribution function of the parameter whose growth is being tracked. This often simplifies hypothesis testing to determine whether a specific goal has been achieved. Additionally, in some cases the time necessary to achieve a specific reliability goal can be calculated.

A26.9 Experience. See LaPadula [A88].

A26.10 References. See also Musa, Iannino, and Okumoto [A7].

[A84] DOWNS, T. Extensions to an Approach to the Modeling of Software Testing with Some Performance Comparisons. *IEEE Transactions on Software Engineering*, vol SE-12, no 9, Sept 1986.

[A85] DOWNS, T. An Approach to the Modeling of Software Testing With Some Applications. *IEEE Transactions on Software Engineering*, vol SE-11, 1985, pp 375-386.

[A86] GOEL, A. L., and OKUMOTA, K. *Baysian Software Prediction Models.* RADCTR-78-155 (5 vols), Jul 1978.

[A87] HECHT, H. *Measurement, Estimation and Prediction of Software Reliability.* NASA-CR-145135, Aerospace Corporation, Jan 1977.

[A88] LAPADULA, L. J. *Engineering of Quality Software Systems, Volume VIII: Software Reliability Modeling and Measurement Techniques.* RADC-TR-74-325, MITRE Corporation, Jan 1975.

[A89] LARSON, H. J. *Introduction to Probability Theory and Statistical Inference.* John Wiley & Sons, Inc, 1969.

[A90] LIPOW, M. *Some Variations of a Model for Software Time-to-Failure.* TRW Systems Group, Correspondence ML-74-2260.1.9.-21, Aug 1974.

[A91] LITTLEWOOD, B., and VERRALL, J. L. A Bayesian Reliability Model with a Stochastically Monotone Failure Rate. *IEEE Transactions on Reliability*, vol R-23, no 2, Jun 1974, pp 108-114.

A27. Residual Fault Count

A27.1 Application. This measure provides an indication of software integrity.

A27.2 Primitives

t_i = observed time between the ith and $(i-1)$st failure of a given severity level

f_i = number of failures during the ith time interval of a given severity level.

A27.3 Implementation. The failure-rate class of models can be used to predict the remaining faults. This class of models is used to estimate the shape of a hypothesized hazard function from which an estimate of the number of remaining faults can be obtained [A96].

A27.4 Interpretation. Ideally, the software failure rate is constant between failures. Where inter-failure times are not independent, a non-homogeneous Poisson-type model for failure count data may be used to predict the number of remaining faults [A96]. This measure is the parameter of the Poisson distribution describing the number of failures if testing is continued.

A27.5 Considerations. Assumptions for this class of models should be verified in order to select an appropriate model to fit the data. The appropriateness of the measure depends upon the validity of the selected model. Among the most common assumptions are the following:

- Failure rate is generally decreasing.
- The numbers of failures in non-overlapping time intervals are independent and distributed exponentially with different failure rates. However, for the non-homogeneous Poisson type process, the model utilizing failure count data assumes that the number of errors has independent increments even though the times between failures are not independent.
- No two failures occur simultaneously.
- The instantaneous failure rate of software is proportional to the number of errors remaining, each of which is equally likely to cause the next failure.

A27.6 Training. The implementation of this measure requires an understanding of probability theory and numerical analysis techniques.

A27.7 Example. A numerical example using a set of failure times to compute the number of remaining faults with the Jelinski-Moranda "De-eutrophication" and non-homogeneous Poisson process type models are compared in [A96].

A27.8 Benefits. The conditional distribution of remaining faults, given a number of known faults, can be used for deciding whether the software is acceptable for release [A92].

A27.9 Experience. A case study showing an actual analysis of failure data from a Space Shuttle Software project using a non-homogeneous Poisson type process is shown in [A95]. The reference illustrates the number of failures during the mission and subsequent verification of these projections using this measure. Experience with this measure can be found also in [A97].

A27.10 References. See also Musa, Iannino, and Okumoto [A7].

[A92] GOEL, A. L., and OKUMOTO, K. Time-Dependent Error-Detection Rate Model for Software Performance Assessment with Applications. *Annual Technical Report*, Contract Number F30602-78-C-0351, Rome Air Development Center, Griffis Air Force Base, Mar 1980.

[A93] JEWELL, W. S. *Bayesian Estimation of Undetected Errors.* Oper Res Center, University of California at Berkeley, Rep ORC 83-11.

[A94] JEWELL, W. S. Bayesian Extension to a Basic Model of Software Reliability. *IEEE Transactions on Software Engineering*, vol SE-11, no 12, Dec 1985.

[A95] MISRA, P. N. Software Reliability Analysis. IBM Systems Journal, vol 22, no 3, 1983.

[A96] *Software Reliability Modelling and Estimation Technique.* RADC-TR-82-263 Final Technical Report, Oct 1982.

[A97] SRIVASTAVA, V. K., and FARR, W. The Use of Software Reliability Models in the Analysis of Operational Systems. *1986 Proceedings of the Institute of Environmental Sciences*, 32nd Annual Technical Meeting, Dallas/Fort Worth, 1986.

A28. Failure Analysis Using Elapsed Time

A28.1 Applications. This measure can be used to determine reliability growth based on the estimated number of remaining faults and software reliability. It can be used to:

- predict the total number of faults in the software
- predict the software reliability
- estimate required testing time for reliability goal
- estimate required resource allocation

A28.2 Primitives

t_i = Observed time between failures of a given severity level (eg, execution time).

A28.3 Implementation. Observed failures should be recorded and the associated faults identified. The time between failures (CPU or other unit which represents actual execution time of the software) should also be recorded.

Using the maximum likelihood estimation, the method of least squares, or the Newton-Raphson optimizing scheme, the parameters and normalizing constants of candidate models can be estimated. These can be interpreted as initial fault content (N_o), normalizing constants, and initial mean time to failure (M_o) based on the model selected. Once a model has been successfully fitted to the data using any of the well-known statistical tests (eg, goodness-of-fit), then the model can be used to estimate the remaining faults (N), MTTF (M), and reliability (R).

A28.4 Interpretation. Based on the confidence in the determination of total faults, MTTF, and reliability, decisions can be made on the need for additional testing. The testing time required to reach a specified reliability can be determined and evaluated in terms of resources required to reach the goal. Resources include testing personnel, debugging personnel and available computer time.

A28.5 Considerations. Failures must be observed and recorded to improve reliability and obtain statistically valid results. The test coverage must be random and comprehensive, and the goodness-of-fit tests should be applied to determine the validity of the selected model. Failure analysis is required to determine severity and class of failures.

A28.6 Training. A background in software testing procedures is needed to perform the necessary failure analysis. The model, including the assumptions and limitations, used to determine initial values and parameters must be understood. A program to perform parameters estimation must be developed, or obtained from the author of the model if it is available.

A28.7 Example. There are many examples available in the listed references [A99, A57].

A28.8 Benefits. This measure can be re-used throughout test and operation phases to provide continuing assessment of the quality of the software.

A28.9 Experience. Extensive experience has been accumulated on the applicaiton of the Musa Model [A102]. The performance of various models are reported in [A97].

A28.10 References. See also Musa, Iannino, and Okumoto [A7] and Farr [A59].

[A98] ANGUS, J. E. The Application of Software Reliability Models to a Major C3I System. *1984 Proceedings of the Annual Reliability and Maintainability Symposium*, Jan 1984, pp 268-274.

[A99] GOEL, A. L., and OKUMOTA, K. Time Dependent Error Detection Model for Software Reliability and Other Performance Measures. *IEEE Transactions on Reliability*, vol R-28, no 3, 1979, pp 206-211.

[A100] JELINSKI, Z. and MORANDA, P. B. Software Reliability Research. In *Statistical Computer Performance Evaluation*, W. Frieberger, ed, New York: Academic Press, 1972, pp 465-484.

[A101] MORANDA, P. B. An Error Detection Model for Application During Software Development. *IEEE Transactions on Reliability*, vol R-30, no 4, 1981, pp 309-312.

[A102] MUSA, J. D. The Measurement and Management of Software Reliability. *Proceedings of the IEEE*, vol 68, no 9, 1980, pp 1131-1143.

[A103] MUSA, J. D. and IANNINO, A. Software Reliability Modeling: Accounting for Program Size Variation Due to Integration or Design Changes. *ACM SIGMETRICS Performance Evaluation Review*, 10(2), 1981, pp 16-25.

[A104] ROSS, M. Software Reliability: The Stopping Rule. *IEEE Transactions on Software Engineering*, vol SE-11, no 12, Dec 1985, pp 1472-1476.

[A105] SUKERT, A. N. An Investigation of Software Reliability Models. *1977 Proceedings of the Annual Reliability and Maintainability Symposium*, Philidelphia, 1977.

A29. Testing Sufficiency

A29.1 Application. This measure assesses the sufficiency of software-to-software integration testing by comparing actual to predicted faults.

A29.2 Primitives

NF = Total number of faults predicted in the software

F_{it} = Total number of faults detected to date in software integration testing

F_{pit} = Number of faults detected prior to software integration testing

M_{it} = Number of modules integrated

M_{tot} = Total number of modules in final configuration

A29.3 Implementation. The fault density ($M1$) should be used to calculate the estimated total number of faults (NF) in the software. The number of faults remaining in the integrated portion of the software can then be estimated using the following equation:

$$NF_{rem} = (NF - F_{pit})\, M_{it}/M_{\text{tot}}$$

Maximum and minimum tolerance coefficients (l_1 and l_1) should be established based on user experience. Values of 0.5 and 1.5 are suggested for use as the default values.

The guidelines given in Table A29.3-1 assume that all scheduled integration tests have been run.

A29.4 Interpretation. The interpretation of testing sufficiency is given in Table A29.3-1 under "Recommended Action" and "Comments."

A29.5 Considerations. The total predicted faults (NF) should be calculated using either micro quantitative software reliability models [A108] based on path structure, or Halstead's software science measures [A106, A107] based on operators and operands. The usefulness of this measure hinges on the accuracy of the prediction of NF.

The measure assumes faults are evenly distributed between modules. Due to this assumption, caution should be exercised in applying it during early stages of integration testing (eg, less than 10% of modules integrated). Tolerance coefficients (l_1 and l_2) may be tailored to support the user's tolerance experience. Examples of experience factors are the degree of software reliability desired, and historical accuracy of the fault prediction measure used.

A29.6 Training. Some mathematical and software development background is necessary to predict total faults and to determine testing sufficiency tolerance coefficients.

A29.7 Example. Assume that 30 modules of a 100-module system are integrated for software-to-software testing. Prior to integration testing, 20 faults of a total predicted fault count of 150 were discovered. During the initial stage of integration testing, 27 more faults were discovered. The standard min/max tolerance coefficients of l_1 = 0.5 and l_2 = 1.5 were selected. Then:

$$\hat{NF}_{rem} = (150 - 20) \times (30)/100 = 39$$
$$l_1\hat{NF}_{rem} = 0.5(39) = 19.5$$
$$l_2\hat{NF}_{rem} = 1.5(39) = 58.5$$
$$F_{\text{it}} = 27$$

Therefore, the recommended action is to proceed with integration testing or the next stage of testing since $19.5 < 27 < 58.5$.

A.29.8 Benefits. The measure is relatively simple to apply, and provides an early indication of testing sufficiency.

A29.9 Experience. No published experience is available.

A29.10 References

[A106] HALSTEAD, M. H. *Elements of Software Science.* Operating and Programming Systems

Table A29.3-1
Testing Sufficiency

Measure Result	Interpretation	Recommended Action	Comments
$l_1 NS_{\text{rem}} < F_{it} < l_2 N_{\text{rem}}$	Testing sufficiency is adequate	Proceed	—
$F_{it} > l_2 NF_{\text{rem}}$	Detected more faults than expected	Proceed, but apply fault density measure for each integrated module. Re-calculate NF.	Error-ridden modules may exist that should be replaced by a redesigned module.
$F_{it} < l_1 NF_{\text{rem}}$	Detected fewer faults than expected	Apply test coverage measure (see A24) before proceeding	May not have designed adequate number or variety of tests

Series, P. J. Denning, ed, New York: Elsevier North Holland, 1977, pp 84-91.

[A107] NASA-GODDARD, *Fortran Static Source Code Analyzer Program (SAP) User Guide (Revision 1)*, Sept 1982, pp 3-31.

[A108] SHOOMAN, M. L. *Software Engineering Design/Reliability/Management*. New York: McGraw Hill, 1983, chap 5.

A30. Mean Time to Failure

A30.1 Application. This measure is used for hypothesis testing a specified MTTF requirement.

A30.2 Primitives. Mean time to failure is the basic parameter required by most software reliability modules. Computation is dependent on accurate recording of failure time (t_i), where t_i is the elapsed time between the ith and the ($i-1$)st failure. Time units used should be as precise as feasible. CPU execution time provides more resolution than wall-clock time. Thus, CPU cycles would be more appropriate for a software development environment. For an operational environment, which might require less resolution, an estimate based on wall-clock time could be used.

A30.3 Implementation. Detailed record keeping of failure occurrences that accurately track the time (calendar or execution) at which the faults manifest themselves is essential. If weighting or organizing the failures by complexity, severity or the reinsertion rate is desired, detailed failure analysis must be performed to determine the severity and complexity. Prior failure experience or model fitting analysis (eg, goodness-of-fit test) can be used to select a model representative of a failure process, and to determine a reinsertation rate of faults.

A30.4 Interpretation. This measure gives an estimate of the mean time to the next failure. A high value implies good reliability and availability of the software. This must be balanced against severity and complexity, if such weights are used.

A30.5 Considerations. The calculation of the mean of the time-to-failure distribution is dependent upon the analytical form of the failure distribution. This, in turn, is dependent upon the underlying assumptions of the failure process.

The number, description, and weights of the levels of severity and complexity should be established prior to data gathering if these factors are to be considered. Techniques for validating statements of complexity and severity should be established. Test planning must emulate operational experience.

A30.6 Training. Depending upon the number of assumptions placed on the failure process and the extent to which severity and complexity weighting is desired, the user's basic knowledge may range from little or no background in mathematics and software development to a need for extensive background in both. The simplest models are easy to implement and apply. Those that attempt to account for input space, human factors, or imperfect debugging or all three require detailed data gathering and rigorous analysis. The references (A30.10) describe various techniques, including the relevant assumptions regarding the failure processes, for some or the more sophisticated approaches.

Training requirements depend upon the type of model used. In data gathering, some background in software development would be necessary to maximize the information obtained from failure analysis. An elementary background in mathematics and reliability theory would promote better interpretation of the results, but is not essential unless assumptions require use of a complex model. The calculation for most models will require implementation on a digital computer.

A30.7 Example. A simple estimate of the MTTF is illustrated. Through prior test exerience and analysis, the user assumes a constant failure rate, with no further correction of faults to be performed. Three levels of severity failure classes are considered. Suppose the levels are labeled SF_1, SF_2, and SF_3 respectively. Every failure is then assigned to one of the classes with the respective time between failure recorded within that class. Suppose the following data is recorded:

SF_1: 180, 675, 315, 212, 278, 503, 431
SF_2: 477, 1048, 685, 396
SF_3: 894, 1422

Then a simple estimate of the mean time to failure is

$$\text{MTTF} = \sum_{k=1}^{i} \frac{t_k}{i} \quad \text{for each class,}$$

where

t_k = time between failures

and

i = number of failures in the respective severity class. The calculated estimates are:

$$MTTF_{SF_1} = \frac{2594}{7} = 370.57,$$

$$MTTF_{SF_2} = \frac{2606}{4} = 651.5,$$

$$MTTF_{SF_3} = \frac{2316}{2} = 1158$$

These values may be compared against some specified MTTF for each severity class, by any of a number of statistical techniques.

Since the data confirms the existence of a constant failure rate, the failure distribution can be assumed to be exponential; ie, $F(t) = 1\text{-exp}(-t/\text{MTTF})$, which is the probability of failure of the software within time t.

A30.8 Benefits. This measure can be used throughout the testing and operational phase of the software, as long as data gathering efforts are maintained. A number of hardware statistical techniques are based on this measure and, if the justification for similar failure processes in the software exists, extensive modeling is available.

A30.9 Experience. Significant experience with this measure has been documented in several reports [A57, A86, A111]. The reader is cautioned to utilize the assumptions required for the various models.

A30.10 References. See also Musa, Iannino, and Okumoto [A7]; Musa [A57]; Farr [A59]; and Goel and Okumoto [A86].

[A109] CURRIT, P. A., DYER, M., and MILLS, H. D. Certifying the Reliability of Software. *IEEE Transactions on Software Reliability*, vol SE-12, no 1, Jan 1986, pp 3-11.

[A110] MUSA, J. D., and OKUMOTO, K. A. Logarithmic Poisson Execution Time Model for Software Reliability Measurement. *Proceedings of the 7th International Conference on Software Engineering*, 1984, pp 230-238.

[A111] RUSHFORTH, C., STAFFANSON, F., and CRAWFORD, A. Software Reliability Estimation Under Conditions of Incomplete Information, University of Utah, RADC-TR-230, Oct 1979.

[A112] SHOOMAN, M. L., and TRIVEDI, A. K. A Many-State Markov Model for Computer Software Performance Parameters. *IEEE Transactions on Reliability*, vol R-25, no 2, Jun 1976, pp 66-68.

[A113] SUKERT, A. N., *A Software Reliability Modeling Study*. RADC-TR-76-247, Aug 1976.

[A114] WAGONER, W. L. *The Final Report on Software Reliability Measurement Study*. Aerospace Corporation, Report Number TOR-0074 (4112), Aug 1973.

A31. Failure Rate

A31.1 Application. This measure can be used to indicate the growth in the software reliability as a function of test time.

A31.2 Primitives

t_i = Observed times between failures (eg, execution time) for a given severity level, i=1,...

f_i = number of failures of a given severity level in the ith time interval

A31.3 Implementation. The failure rate $\lambda(t)$ at any point in time can be estimated from the reliability function, $R(t)$ which in turn can be obtained from the cumulative probability distribution, $F(t)$, of the time until the next failure using any of the software reliability growth models such as the non-homogeneous Poisson process (NHPP) [A99] or a Bayesian type model [A55, A115]. The failure rate is

$$\lambda(t) = -\frac{1}{R(t)}\left[\frac{dR(t)}{dt}\right] \qquad \text{(eq A31-1)}$$

where $R(t) = 1 - F(t)$.

A31.4 Interpretation. The failure rate $\lambda(t)$ obtained from NHPP depends only upon time t and decreases continuously. However, $\lambda(t)$ derived from Littlewood's reliability growth model depends both upon time t and the value growth function, $\psi(i)$ at the ith failure. By requiring the function $\psi(i)$ to be increasing, the condition

$$\lambda(t_i) \leq \lambda(t_{i-1})$$

is met in a probabilistic sense, ie, the programmer may introduce new errors while correcting an error.

A31.5 Considerations. The underlying assumptions for the NHPP model are the following:

(1) Equal probability of exposure of each fault.

(2) The fault count type NHPP Model assumes that the number of failures detected during the non-overlapping intervals, f_i, are independent.

(3) The time between failure type NHPP model assumes that the time between the $(i\text{-}1)$st and ith failures depends upon time to the $(i\text{-}1)$st failure.

The underlying assumptions for Bayesian reliability growth model are as follows:

(1) Successive execution time between failures with different failure rates are independently exponentially distributed

ie, $pdf(t_i|\lambda_i) = \lambda_i \exp(-\lambda_i t_i)$

(2) In the Littlewood-Verrall model [A115] the successive failure rate forms a sequence of independent random variables $\{\lambda_i\}$ with gamma distribution with parameters α and $\psi(i)$

ie, $$pdf(\lambda_i|\alpha,\psi(i)) = \frac{[\psi(i)]^{\alpha}\lambda_i^{\alpha-1}\exp(-\psi(i)\lambda_i)}{\Gamma(\alpha)}$$

(3) The failure rate is statistically decreasing.

(4) In the Littlewood stochastic reliability growth model [A55], the failure rate of the program after removal of i errors is:

$$\lambda = \lambda_1 + \lambda_2 + \ldots \lambda_{NF-i}$$

where

NF = total number of faults in the program prior to testing and $\lambda_1 \ldots \lambda_{NF-i}$ are *i.i.d.* (identically independently distributed) and each has a gamma *pdf.*

A31.6 Training. The development computer programs needed to compute this measure require an understanding of stochastic processes and familiarity with numerical analysis and optimization techniques.

A31.7 Examples. A practical application for both NHPP and Littlewood-Verrall reliability growth models for obtaining the measure of software failure rate is shown in the following examples.

In Misra [A95] a fitted mean value function is obtained for the data collected by testing space shuttle flight software consisting of over .5 million lines of source code. After 38 wk of testing (2454.7 cumulative hrs) the following estimate of the parameters of the NHPP model for the major error category were calculated:

"a" = 163.813 "b" = $0.28759 * 10^{-3}$

The failure rate decrease is described by

$$\lambda(t) = ab \exp\left\{-b\left(\sum_{i=1}^{n} t_i + t\right)\right\}$$

$$\text{for } \sum_{i=1}^{n} t_i < t \qquad \text{(eq A31-2)}$$

In [A115] the probability distribution function of the ith failure rate $\{\lambda_i\}$ is assumed to be gamma (g) with parameters α and $\psi(i)$, then

$$R(t) = \int_0^{\infty} e^{-\lambda_i t} g(\lambda_i|\alpha, \psi(i))d\lambda_i \qquad \text{(eq A31-3)}$$

and the failure rate after the ith failure is now obtained by using equation A31-1 and is given by

$$\lambda(t) = \frac{\alpha}{t + \psi(i)}, \; t_i \leq t \leq t_{i+1} \qquad \text{(eq A31-4)}$$

Littlewood has examined the data set of 136 execution times reported by Musa [A57] to predict the future times to failure using a linear form of $\psi(i)$:

$$\psi(i) = \beta_1 + \beta_2 i \qquad \text{(eq A31-5)}$$

The parameters α, β_1 and β_2 obtained using maximum likelihood methods [A115] based upon the first 35 observations are:

$\alpha = 1.51890$; $\beta_1 = -0.9956$ and $\beta_2 = 7.8342$

The failure rate after the ith failure can be computed by substituting the value of the parameters α and $\psi(i)$ in equation A31-4.

$$\hat{\lambda}(t) = \frac{1.5189}{t - .9956 + 7.8342i}, \qquad \text{(eq A31-6)}$$

$$t_i \leq t \leq t_{i+1} (i=1, \ldots 136)$$

A31.8 Benefits. The stepwise decrease in the failure rate at each incidence of a failure model can be used to show the improvement in software reliabiilty as a result of operational usage and can also be used to estimate the test time needed to reach target reliability.

A31.9 Experience. Experience with the use of this measure is provided by Misra [A95].

A31.10 References. See also Downs [A84, A85]; Goel and Okumoto [A54]; Littlewood [A55]; Misra [A95]; and Musa [A7, A57].

[A115] LITTLEWOOD, B. Theories of Software Reliability: How Good Are They and How Can

They Be Improved? *IEEE Transactions on Software Engineering*, vol 6, no 5, 1980, pp 489-500.

[A116] MILLER, D. R. Exponential Order Statistic Models of Software Reliability Growth. *IEEE Transactions on Software Engineering*, vol SE-12, no 1, Jan 1986.

[A117] OKUMOTO, K. A Statistical Method for Quality Control. *IEEE Transactions on Software Engineering*, vol SE-11, no 12, Dec 1985, pp 1424-1430.

[A118] SINGPURWALLA, N., and SOYER, R. Assessing (Software) Reliability Growth Using a Random Coefficient Autoregressive Process and Its Ramifications. *IEEE Transactions on Software Engineering*, vol SE-11, no 12, Dec 1985, pp 1456-1463.

[A119] YAMADA, S., and OSAKI, S. Software Reliability Growth Modeling: Models and Applications. *IEEE Transactions on Software Engineering*, vol SE-11, no 12, Dec 1985, pp 1431-1437.

A32. Software Documentation and Source Listings

A32.1 Application. The primary objective of this measure is to collect information to identify the parts of the software maintenance products that may be inadequate for use in a software maintenance environment. Two questionnaires are used to examine the format and content of the documentation and source code attributes from a maintainability perspective.

A32.2 Primitives. The questionnaires examine the following primitive product characteristics:

(1) modularity
(2) descriptiveness
(3) consistency
(4) simplicity
(5) expandability
(6) testability.

Sub-characteristics include format, interface, math models, and data/control.

A32.3 Implementation. Two questionnaires; Software Documentation Questionnaire and the Software Source Listing Questionnaire, are used to evaluate the software products in a desk audit. The questionnaires are contained in *Software Maintainability—Evaluation Guide* [A120].

For the software documentation evaluation, the resource documents should include those that contain program design specifications, program testing information and procedures, program maintenance information, and guidelines used in preparation of the documentation. These documents may have a variety of physical organizations depending upon the particular source, application, and documentation requirements. The documentation will, in general, consist of all documents that reveal the software design and implementation. A single evaluation of all the documents is done. Typical questions from the software Documentation Questionnaire include the following:

- The documentation indicates that data storage locations are not used for more than one type of data structure.
- Parameter inputs and outputs for each module are explained in the documentation.
- Programming conventions for *I/O* processing have been established and followed.
- The documentation indicates that resource (storage, timing, tape drives, disks, consoles, etc.) allocation is fixed throughout program execution.
- The documentation indicates that there is a reasonable time margin for each major time-critical program function (rate group, time slice, priority level, etc.).
- The documentation indicates that the program has been designed to accommodate software test probes to aid in identifying processing performance.

For the software source listings evaluation, the program source code is evaluated. The source code may be either a high order language or assembler. Multiple evaluations using the questionnaire are conducted for the unit (module) level of the program. The units (modules) selected should represent a sample size of at least 10% of the total source code. Typical questions from the Source Listing Questionnaire include the following:

- Each function of this module is an easily recognizable block of code.
- The quantity of comments does not detract from the legibility of the source listing.
- Mathematical models as described/derived in the documentation correspond to the mathematical equations used in the modules source listing.
- Esoteric (clever) programming is avoided in this module.
- The size of any data structure that affects the processing logic of this module is parameterized.

- Intermediate results within this module can be selectively collected for display without code modification.

A32.4 Interpretation. The average scores across evaluators, test factors, product categories, and programs are used to develop a relative degree of confidence in the software documentation and the source code.

A32.5 Considerations. The software source listings and documentation evaluation assumptions are as follows:

(1) Software source listing and documentation considerations are essentially independent of application and implementation language.
(2) The evaluators must be knowledgeable in software maintenance, but do not necessarily require detailed knowledge about the specific application software.
(3) At least five independent evaluators (with software maintenance experience) must be used to provide a 75% confidence that the resulting scores indicate the actural condition of the documentation and source listing.
(4) The software source listings selected for evaluation may be from any unit level of the program that would provide conclusions that hold for the general population of the program.

A32.6 Training. Prior to an evaluation, the evaluators must participate in a calibration exercise by completing each of the questionnaires on a sample software product. This exercise is to ensure a reliable evaluation through a clear understanding of the questions and their specific response guidelines on each questionnaire. The completed questionnaires are reviewed by the evaluator group to detect and resolve areas of misunderstanding.

A32.7 Example. Table A32.7-1 demonstrates the results of an evaluation. The questionnaires employ a six-point response scale where 6 is the highest possible score (completely agree), and 1 is the lowest subjective rating (completely disagree). The bracketed score indicates that for the documentation, the instrumentation test factor (how well the program has been designed to include test aids) scored below the minimum acceptable threshold criteria.

Table A32.7-1
Example Results of a Source Listing and Documentation Evaluation

Test Factor	Documentation	Source Listings
Modularity	4.3	5.3
Descriptiveness	3.9	4.5
Consistency	4.8	5.0
Simplicity	4.7	5.3
Expandability	4.5	5.1
Instrumentation	(3.0)	4.5
Weighted Score	4.3	5.0
Combined Score	4.7	

A32.8 Benefits. The application of the questionnaires provides an identification of potential problems in the software documentation and source listings that may affect the maintainability of the software.

A32.9 Experience. The evaluation is consistently used during operational test and evaluation for most Air Force systems.

A.32.10 References

[A120] *Software Maintainability Evaluators Guide.* AFOTEC Pamphlet 800-2, vol 3, no 2, Mar 1987.[4]

[A121] PEERCY, D. A Software Maintainability Evaluation Methodology. *IEEE Transactions on Software Engineering*, no 4, Jul 1981.

A33. RELY—Required Software Reliability

A33.1 Application. At the early planning phases of a project, RELY provides a measure that makes visible the tradeoffs of cost and degree of reliability. It is recognized that reliability may vary relative to the system purpose. Man-rated software in space applications, for example, has higher reliability requirements than game software. The development processes for high reliability software, especially integration and test, should correspondingly be greater than that of average software.

A33.2 Primitives. Required reliability ratings are as follows:[5]

[4] This guide can be obtained from the Air Force Operational Test and Evaluation Center (AFOTEC/DAP), Kirtland Air Force Base, NM 87117-7001.

[5] Definition of primitives and figures from Boehm [A122], reprinted by permission.

Very low. The effect of a software failure is simply the inconvenience incumbent on the developers to fix the fault. Typical examples are a demonstration prototype of a voice typewriter or an early feasibility phase software simulation model.

Low. The effect of a software failure is a low level, easily-recoverable loss to users. Typical examples are a long-range planning model or a climate forecasting model.

Nominal. The effect of a software failure is a modereate loss to users, but a situation from which one can recover without extreme penalty. Typical examples are management information systems or inventory control systems.

High. The effect of a software failure can be a major financial loss or a massive human inconvenience. Typical examples are banking systems and electric power distribution systems.

Very high. The effect of a software failure can be the loss of human life. Examples are military command and control systems or nuclear reactor control systems.

A33.3 Implementation. Depending on the required rating, the effort required for each phase of the development cycle can be adjusted to include the processes necessary to ensure that the product achieves the reliability goal. Figure A33.3-1 shows the effort factors relative to nominal necessary to achieve each of the required reliability ratings.

This technique can be used conversely to provide a reliability rating for a product through examination of the processes used to develop it (see Table A33.3-1).

A33.4 Interpretation. Differences in required reliability effort factors are relatively small for development phases prior to, and including, code unit test. The major factor difference is in the integration and test phases. The added requirements of operational and stress testing can make a 70% difference from the nominal.

A33.5 Considerations. These effort factors were developed empirically to reflect development processes used in the 1970 timeframe. They should be updated where the data exists to reflect local development processes including the productivity benefits of tools.

A33.6 Training Required. No special training is required.

Fig A33.3-1
Effort Multipliers by Phase: Required Software Reliability

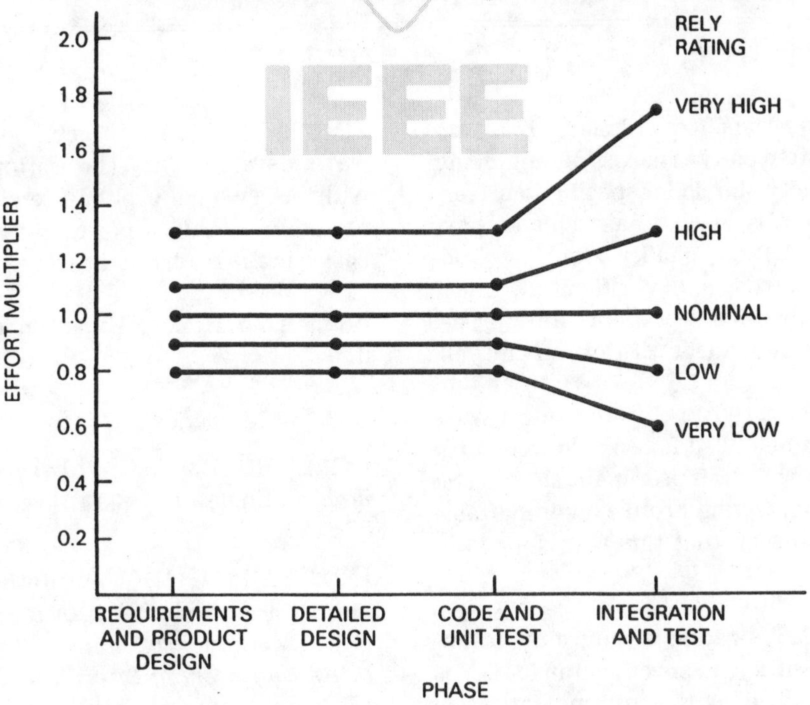

Table A33.3-1
Projected Activity Differences Due to Required Software Reliability

Rating	Requirements and Product Design	Detailed Design	Code and Unit Test	Integration and Test
Very low	Little detail Many TBDs Little verification Minimal quality assurance (QA), configuration management (CM) draft user manual, test plans Minimal program design review (PDR)	Basic design information Minimum QA, CM, draft user manual, test plans Informal design inspections	No test procedures Minimal path test, standards check Minimal QA, CM Minimal *I/O* and off-nominal tests Minimal user manual	No test procedures Many requirements untested Minimal QA, CM Minimal stress, off-nominal tests Minimal as-built documentation
Low	Basic information, verification Frequent TBDs Basic QA, CM, standards, draft user manual, test plans	Moderate detail Basic QA, CM, draft user manual, test plans	Minimal test procedures Partial path test, standards check Basic QA, CM, user manual Partial *I/O* and off-nominal tests	Minimal test procedures Frequent requirements untested Basic QA, CM, user manual Partial stress off-nominal tests
Nominal	Nominal project V & V	—	—	—
High	Detailed verification, QA, CM, standards, PDR, documentation Detailed test plans, procedures	Detailed verification, QA, CM, standards, CDR, documentation Detailed test plans, procedures	Detailed test procedures, QA, CM, documentation Extensive off-nominal tests	Detailed test procedures, QA, CM, documentation Extensive stress, off-nominal tests
Very high	Detailed verification, QA, CM, standards, PDR, documentation IV & V interface Very detailed test plans, procedures	Detailed verification, QA, CM, standards, CDR, documentation Very thorough design inspections Very detailed test plans, procedures IV & V interface	Detailed test procedures, QA, CM, documentation Very thorough code inspections Very extensive off-nominal tests IV & V interface	Very detailed test procedures, QA, CM, documentation Very extensive stress, off-nominal tests IV & V interface

A33.7 Examples. The effect of failures in an airplane control system can be the loss of human life. Hence the reliability should be specified as "Very High." To obtain this, each phase should have detailed documentation, quality assurance, adherence to standards, and verificaiton. There should be very detailed test plans and procedures, including independent verification and validation.

Suppose, however, that the Statement of Work and level of funding called for (or allowed) only basic verification, QA, draft user manuals and test plans with minimal testing. From examining Table A33.3-1, it can be seen that this corresponds to low reliability.

A33.8 Benefits. This rating is important to apply as soon as sufficient specificaiton detail is available, to justify using the intermediate level COCOMO Model for projecting costs for the software development. The ratings are consistent with a very high-level failure effects analysis and are an important input to costing and, therefore, cost-benefit tradeoffs at the earliest level.

A33.9 Experience. Experience is somewhat limited.

A33.10 References

[A122] BOEHM, B. *Software Engineering Economics*. Englewood Cliffs: Prentice-Hall, 1981, pp 374-376.

[A123] LIPOW, M. Quantitative Demonstration and Cost Consideration of a Software Fault Removal Methodology. *Journal Quality and Reliability Engineering International*, vol 1, 1985, pp 27-35.

A34. Software Release Readiness

A34.1 Application. This measure is used to quantify the user and support (consumer) risk of ownership, based on either quantitative or subjective assessments of user and support issues. Given a number of issues, one can combine them to obtain a composite risk assessment. Although the primitives described here are designed for the operation and maintenance phase, the risk assessment method is applicable during any phase of the lifecycle by the identification of appropriate issues and the selection or design of corresponding measures for assessment.

A34.2 Primitives. The measurements of effectiveness, $ME(i)$, $i=1, \ldots, I$, for issues relating to software risk assessment. Example issues are:

- Functional test coverage
- Software maturity
- Software source code listings quality factors
- Documentation quality factors
- Software operator-machine interface
- Software support resources assessments

A34.3 Implementation. This measure assumes that I issues can be combined to assess the readiness of software for release and the attendant consumer risk. For each issue i the measure $ME(i)$ is converted into an associated risk $RK(i)$ as it relates to the user and supporter. This risk is subjectively assigned by the evaluators and is defined to be in the range of 0 to 1.0, where zero denotes no risk and one denotes extreme risk. For the functional test coverage, maturity, and quality factor primitives, the associated risk is determined by:

$RK(i) = 1.0 - ME(i)$

Further, each of the primitives $ME(i)$ is assigned a subjective, relative weight that represents its importance to the user (supporter). For each $ME(i)$ value, there is a corresponding $RK(i)$ risk and a $W(i)$ relative importance weight. All the relative weights $W(i)$ for all user (supporter) measures sum to 1.0. Further, there is an influence matrix $[S]$ that provides a modification factor to the risk $RK(i)$ when a measure $ME(i)$ is influenced by another measure $ME(j)$. For example, consider the influence between software maturity (the fraction of software modified and added during a test [see A4.10]) and functional test coverage (the fraction of code demonstrated during a test [see A4.5]). It is clear that incomplete testing would reduce the confidence in the resulting maturity score because of incomplete demonstration of the software functions. The influence matrix $S(i,j)$ coefficients are assigned values that are representative of the dependence between $ME(i)$ and $ME(j)$.

The following steps are used in calculating this measure:

(1) Evaluate each primitive $ME(i)$.

(2) Assign a risk value $RK(i)$ to the $ME(i)$ measure such that $RK(i)$ is between zero and one (eg, $RK(i) = 1.0 - ME(i)$.)

Or, for subjective assessments, note the following:

low risk	=	0.0 to 33
medium risk	=	.34 to .66
high risk	=	.67 to 1.0

(3) For each measure $ME(i)$, determine the weighting $W(i)$ that reflects the importance of the measure to the total user (supporter). A suggested default value is $1/I$ giving equal weight to all issues.

(4) For each pair of measures $ME(i)$ and $ME(j)$, assign a value for the $S(i,j)$ influence coefficient that represents the subjective or quantified influence between the measures. The $S(i,j)$ coefficients vary between zero and one, with zero representing no influence (low correlation), and one representing high dependence (high correlation). Coefficient $S(i,j)$ is the measured or subjective value of measure $ME(i)$'s dependence on measure $ME(j)$. Usually matrix [S] is symmetric.

Let the apportioned risk $RK'(i)$ for measure i in relation to the other measures be:

$$RK'(i) = \frac{\sum_{j=1}^{I} RK(j) \times S(i,j)}{\sum_{j=1}^{I} S(i,j)}$$

Then combined user (supporter) risk is:

$$R_{(\text{User/Supporter})} = \sum_{i=1}^{I} RK'(i) \times W(i)$$

A34.4 Interpretation. The value R(user) or R(supporter) is a cumulative measure of either user or supporter risk that can be compared against a predefined rating scale for reporting.

A34.5 Considerations. The quantities for $W(i)$, $S(i,j)$, and some values of $ME(i)$ are subjectively determined. It is important that the acceptance criteria be kept firmly in mind when these values

Table A34.7-1
Primitive Scores and Weighting

	Measurement				Weighting $W(i)$	
Measure	Range	Score	$ME(i)$	$RK(i)$	User W(U)	Supporter W(S)
Test coverage: $ME(1)$	0-1	0.6	0.6	0.4	0.5	0.0
Maturity index: $ME(2)$	0-1	0.83	0.83	0.17	0.5	0.0
Source listings: $ME(3)$	0-6	5.0	0.83	0.17	0.0	0.5
Documentation: $ME(4)$	0-6	4.3	0.72	0.28	0.0	0.5

Table A34.7-2
Influence Matrix (S)

User Influence Matrix			Supporter Influence Matrix		
User Primitives: $ME(1)$, $ME(2)$			Supporter Primitives: $ME(3)$, $ME(4)$		
	$ME(1)$	$ME(2)$		$ME(3)$	$ME(4)$
$ME(1)$	1	0.6	$ME(3)$	1	1
$ME(2)$	0.6	1	$ME(4)$	1	1

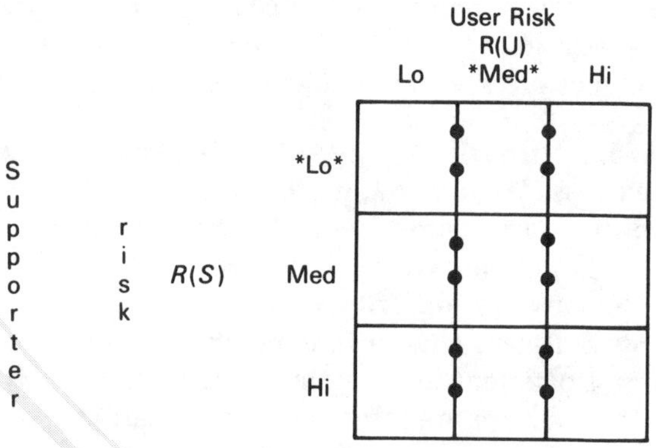

Fig A34.7-1

are established. The subjectively determined rating scale should be determined before the evaluation to avoid prejudicing the results.

A34.6 Training. Training in the evaluation/assessment of relative weights for different quality factors and for sensitivity coefficients is required, together with an understanding of the reciprocal influence of quality factors.

A34.7 Examples. Assume the primitive data values given in Table A34.7-1 are determined during testing:

Combining $ME(1)$ and $ME(2)$ for the user and $ME(3)$ and $ME(4)$ for the supporter, the influence matrices can be defined as shown in Table A34.7-2.

The above influence matrices result in the following confidence modifiers:

For the user combining $ME(1)$ and $ME(2)$,

$$RK'(1) = ((0.4*1.0) + (0.7*0.6))/1.6 = 0.31$$
$$RK'(2) = ((0.4*0.6) + (0.17*1.0))/1.6 = 0.25$$

For the supporter combining $ME(3)$ and $ME(4)$,

$$RK'(3) = ((0.17*1.0) + (0.28*1.0))/2.0 = 0.23$$
$$RK'(4) = ((0.17*1.0) + (0.28*5.0))/2.0 = 0.23$$

Calculating the user $R(U)$ and Supporter $R(S)$ risks,

$$R(U) = (0.31*0.5) + (0.25*0.5) = 0.28$$
$$R(S) = (0.23*0.5) + (0.23*0.5) = 0.23$$

The calculated $R(U)$ and $R(S)$ values represent a low-low risk respectively. The results may be presented in the combined format shown in Fig A34.7-1.

A34.8 Benefits. This approach provides a method to combine a number of measures. As such, it can be a viable approach to use in the decision process to release or buy software.

A34.9 Experience. Use of the risk assessment reporting and evaluation technique has been limited to methodology development investigations using data obtained from operational test and evaluation programs. Current efforts include a study to identify the contributing elements to the supporter risk.

A34.10 References

[A124] *Software Operator-Machine Interface Evaluators Guide.* AFOTEC Pamphlet 800-2, vol 4, Feb 1983.

[A125] *Software Support Resources Evaluation Users Guide.* AFOTEC Pamphlet 800-2, vol 5, Feb 1983.

[A126] FISK, F. B. and MURCH, W. G. *Computer Resources Risk Assessment During Operatonal Test and Evaluation.* Journal of Operational Test and Evaluation, International Test and Evaluation Association (ITEA), Jan 1985.

A35. Completeness

A35.1 Application. The purpose of this measure is to determine the completeness of the software specification during the requirements phase. Also, the values determined for the primitives associated with the completeness measure can be used to identify problem areas within the software specification.

A35.2 Primitives. The completeness measure consists of the following primitives:

B_1 = number of functions not satisfactorily defined
B_2 = number of functions
B_3 = number of data references not having an origin
B_4 = Number of data references
B_5 = number of defined functions not used
B_6 = number of defined functions
B_7 = number of referenced functions not defined
B_8 = number of referenced functions
B_9 = number of decision points not using all conditions or options or both
B_{10} = number of decision points
B_{11} = number of condition options without processing
B_{12} = number of condition options
B_{13} = number of calling routines with parameters not agreeing with defined parameters
B_{14} = number of calling routines
B_{15} = number of condition options not set
B_{16} = number of set condition options having no processing
B_{17} = number of set condition options
B_{18} = number of data references having no destination

A35.3 Implementation. The completeness measure (CM) is the weighted sum of ten derivatives expressed as:

$$CM = \sum_{i=1}^{10} w_i D_i$$

where for each $i=1,\ldots,10$ each weight, w_i has a value between 0 and 1, the sum of the weights is equal to 1, and each D_i is a derivative with a value between 1 and 0.

To calculate the completeness measure, the definitions of the primitives for the particular application must be determined, and the priority associated with the derivatives must also be determined. This prioritization would affect the weights used to calculate the completeness measure.

Each primitive value would then be determined by the number of occurrences related to the definition of the primitive.

Each derivative is determined as follows:

$D_1 = (B_2 - B_1)/B_2$ = functions satisfactorily defined
$D_2 = (B_4 - B_3)/B_4$ = data references having an origin
$D_3 = (B_6 - B_5)/B_6$ = defined functions used
$D_4 = (B_8 - B_7)/B_8$ = referenced functions defined
$D_5 = (B_{10} - B_9)/B_{10}$ = all condition options at decision poiints
$D_6 = (B_{12} - B_{11})/B_{12}$ = all condition options with processing at decision points are used
$D_7 = (B_{14} - B_{13})/B_{14}$ = calling routine parameters agree with the called routine's defined parameters
$D_8 = (B_{12} - B_{15})/B_{12}$ = all condition options that are set
$D_9 = (B_{17} - B_{16})/B_{17}$ = processing follows set condition options
$D_{10} = (B_4 - B_{18})/B_4$ = data references have a destination

A35.4 Interpretation. The value of the completeness measure is scaled between 0 and 1 by the appropriate weights. A score near 1 is considered better than a score near 0. Those values near zero should be traced to the suspect primitive(s) to highlight any need for change in the software specification. As changes are made to the specification, the incremental specification measure values can be plotted to show if improvements are being made and how rapidly. The comparison of specification measures among different projects permits relative evaluations to be accomplished for improved completeness.

A35.5 Considerations. Each derivative helps identify characteristics in the software specification that promote completeness during the construction of the software.

A35.6 Training. Training would be necessary to understand the definitions of the primitives (which are based on the use of a specification language, eg, PSL) for the particular application.

A35.7 Example. The following example is developed to show the numerical procedure associated with the calculation of the completeness measure.

To arrive at a value for the completeness measure, assume that the primitives have been determined to have the following values:

$B_1 = 10$	$B_7 = 8$	$B_{13} = 2$
$B_2 = 50$	$B_8 = 40$	$B_{14} = 10$
$B_3 = 50$	$B_9 = 2$	$B_{15} = 4$
$B_4 = 2500$	$B_{10} = 100$	$B_{16} = 2$
$B_5 = 2$	$B_{11} = 5$	$B_{17} = 20$
$B_6 = 50$	$B_{12} = 50$	$B_{18} = 100$

These primitives are then combined to determine the derivative values.

$D_1 = .8$	$D_5 = .98$	$D_9 = .9$
$D_2 = .98$	$D_6 = .9$	$D_{10} = .98$
$D_3 = .96$	$D_7 = .8$	
$D_4 = .8$	$D_8 = .92$	

Assuming each weight as one-tenth (1/10), the completeness measure would be calculated as follows:

$$\text{Since } CM = \sum_{i=1}^{10} w_i D_i = 0.9$$

This value could be used in comparison with other completness measures or could be recalculated following improvements made within the software specification (as additions or deletions are made to the specification).

A35.8 Benefits. The completeness measure will give an indication of the completeness (value near 1) or incompleteness (value near 0) of the software specification during the early development stages.

A35.9 Experience. Validation of the completeness measure [A50, A53] consists of determining the proper definitions and measurements of primitives and calculation of associated derivatives using PSL/PSA. Other measures of completeness are also given in Murine [A127].

A35.10 References. See also Francis [A50], and Miller et al [A53].

[A127] MURINE, G. E. On Validating Software Quality Metrics. *4th annual IEEE Conference on Software Quality*, Phoenix, Arizona, Mar 1985.

[A128] SAN ANTONIO, R, and JACKSON, K. Application of Software Metrics During Early program Phases. *Proceedings of the National Conference on Software Test and Evaluation, Feb 1982.*

A36. Test Accuracy

A36.1 Application. This measure can be used to determine the accuracy of the testing program in detecting faults. With a test coverage measure, it can be used to estimate the percentage of faults remaining.

A36.2 Primitives

N_s = Number of seeded faults

$\hat{N}_s$ = Estimated number of detectable seeded faults

A36.3 Implementation. The software to be tested is seeded with faults. The number of seeded faults detected in each testing time interval is recorded along with time to detect faults, and a mathematical model is selected to represent the cumulative seeded faults detected across the total testing period. The cumulative seeded faults detected at time infinity is then estimated and test accuracy is calculated:

$$\text{ALPHA} = \hat{N}_s / N_s$$

A36.4 Interpretation. Ideally, ALPHA is independent of test duration and approaches 100%. However, ALPHA can be used in conjunction with GAMMA, a test coverage measure [A129, A131], to estimate the percentage of inherent faults remaining at the end of test.

$$NF_{\text{rem}}(\%) = (1 - \text{ALPHA} \times \text{GAMMA}) \times 100$$

A36.5 Considerations. To meet the requirement that seeded faults reflect typical ones, a scheme for categorizing seeded faults according to difficulty of detection is required. A mathematical model must be selected that accurately describes the fault detection process. The model is likely to be complex with non-trivial estimation of its parameters, thereby requiring automation. A single model may not be appropriate for all processes.

A36.6 Training. The level of training required depends on the automated tool used. Training in mathematical model fitting and tool usage is required. Experience in software testing would be applicable as well.

A36.7 Example. A software module to be tested was seeded with 37 faults. Given the following observed fault detection profile, a model was fitted to describe the testing process.

Model estimated seeded faults detectable at time infinity = 32; ALPHA = 32/37 = .865.

A36.8 Benefits. The test accuracy measure is an indicator of a test's ability to accurately detect faults, which will identify problem areas in testing practices.

A36.9 Experience. Limited published experience is available.

A36.10 References

[A129] OHBA, M. Software Quality = Test Accuracy × Test Coverage. *IEEE International Symposium on Software Engineering*, Chicago, 1982, pp 287-293.

[A130] OHBA, M. *Software Quality = Test Coverage × Test Accuracy.* (In Japanese.) IPS-J, Proceedings WGSE Meeting, vol 21, 1981.

[A131] SHINODA, T., ISHIDA, T., and OHBA, M. *Control Defects and Test Accuracy.* (In Japanese.) IPS-J, Proceedings Spring conference, 5C-7, 1981.

Fig A36.7-1
Control Defect Removal Process

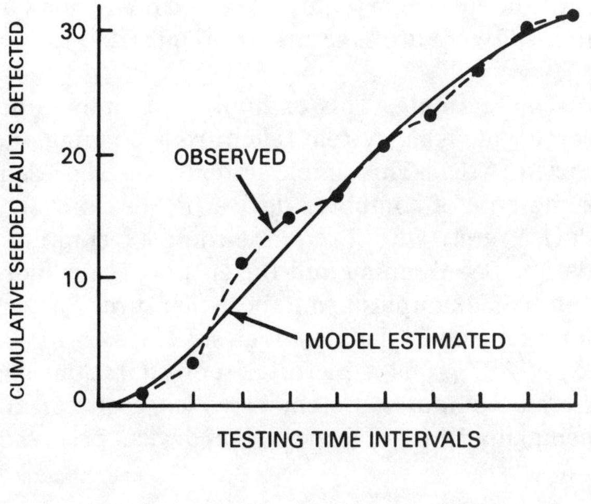

A37. System Performance Reliability

A37.1 Application. This measure assesses the system's performance reliability, the probability that the value of each performance requirement will be less than or equal to a predefined threshold value. The specific performance requirements addressed in this measure are:

U = Utilization
X = Throughput
Q = Queue length distribution
WT = Waiting time distribution
SE = Mean server's efficiency
RT = Response time distribution
ST = Service time distribution

The application of these derived measures will ensure that reliability planning functions are done by all inter- and intra-organizations, periodic reliability etimations during the software life cycle are done to track reliability development, and verificaiton and validation are done on the system capacity.

A37.2 Primitives. The following primitives quantify the basic performance attributes that are measured over a time period of length *T*.

A = The number of arrivals (functional jobs) during the time period *T*.
SB = The total amount of time "server" is busy.
J = The number of jobs completed during *T*.
VR = The number of requests (visits) per functional job for each server during time period *T*.
T = Time period over which measurements are made.

A37.3 Implementation. These measures are applicable to operating systems and networks. Based upon the measured primitives the derived quantifiable measures are:

Γ = A/T, the average arrival rate of jobs
X = J/T, the average throughput rate
U = SB/T, the average utilization
AS = SB/J, the average service time
WT = $f(\Gamma, U, AS, VR)$, the waiting time distribution (expressed as a function of arrival rate, utilization, service time, and visit rate)
SE = $A/(AS+W)$, the server's efficiency of each job

$R = \sum_{i=1}^{k} (VR \times S)_i + \sum_{i=1}^{k} (VR \times W)_i$, the total response time for each functional job over the k servers [see (5) below]

$AQ = W \times \Gamma$, the average queue length

Using any of these measures, one can derive the corresponding probability distribution of the measure under the stated assumptions of the system. The distribution can then be used to calculate the probability that the measure will achieve a desired level.

The following step by step process can be followed to calculate the probability of achieving the desired level.

(1) Determine the infrastructure of the performance model. This involves identifying the critical system resources and the system's underpinning connections in the form of a queueing network model (QNM). The basic idea of the model is that the "essential" part of the system's architecture is represented by a network of "servers" and queues that are connected by transition paths. Jobs circulate through the network, the flow being controlled by the transition probabilities.

(2) Define, qualify, and quantify the workload classes. This is to identify the resource demand characteristics of the different classes of jobs and their dynamic performance attribute matrix. This determines the apportionment of the utilization of each server by each work class.

(3) Measure the resource demands for each work class. The service time, arrival rate, and visit ratios of each system resource are measured for each class of job.

(4) Solve the QNM Model. The approximation algorithms in analytic queueing theory and operations research techniques are used to solve the model.

(5) Perform the reliability evaluation. For example, suppose the response time R must meet the goal of $R \leq R_o$ where R is given in A37.3. Calculate the system performance reliability as reliability = Probability ($R \leq R_o$) for stated assumptions during time period of length T. The system performance is not achieved if the desired reliability is not attained.

A37.4 Interpretation. In order to determine that the model did, in fact, represent the significant dynamic behavior of the system, the monitored measures from the real system need to be compared with that of the model. The validated and verified model can then be used to develop the planning strategy by answering the following questions:

(1) Where are the bottlenecks in the system and why do they exist?

(2) What actions are required to rectify the deficiencies?

(3) What performance improvement can be expected by upgrading the system level software efficiency for a given scheduling policy?

(4) How will the addition of a new application functionality affect the current performance?

(5) What are the single failure paths in the system configuration and their effects on downtime? The system downtime is qualified and quantified as the elapsed time during which a degradation or a cessation of system performance occurs.

A37.5 Considerations. There are two basic operational techniques to the deployment of the monitors for the primitives.

(1) The event trace mode records all state transition events that can be used for a complete "reconstruction" of the critical activities via a trace driven simulation program.

(2) The sampling mode involves the gathering and sampling states of the system at predetermined times. A "steady state" condition must be assumed. The performance model must be validated via measurements before the model can be used with a high degree of confidence.

A37.6 Training. Knowledge of probability, statistics, queuing theory, hardware and operating system software architecture are required.

A37.7 Example. This example is a simple one-server queueing system taken from Denning and Buzen [A137]. This simple system could represent some type of computer device (ie, disk unit, I/O device, etc.) within a more complex computer design. See Denning and Buzen [A137] for more complex examples using these measures for performance and reliability analysis.

Fig A37.7-1 is a pictorial representation of a simple computer system in which requests are being made to a device. The device processes

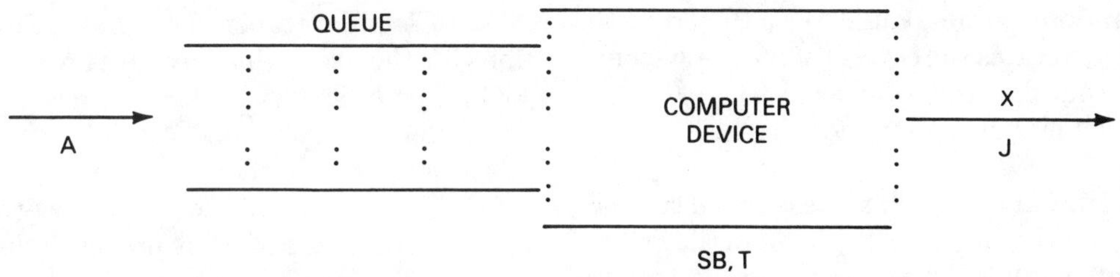

Fig A37.7-1
Single Server System

those requests immediately if it is free; otherwise it files the request in a queue to be processed when it becomes free.

Suppose the device is observed over a period of $T = 20$ sec. When the device is first observed there are two requests in the queue and a third has just entered processing. During this time period seven new requests are made of the device (ie, A = 7). It is also observed that the device was busy processing the requests for a period of 16 seconds and that during this time period all ten requests were completed. Hence B = 16 and C = 10.

The basic performance measures can then be calculated as:

$\Gamma = A/T = 7/20 = .35$ jobs per second

$X = J/T = 10/20 = .5$ jobs per second for throughput

$U = SB/T = 16/20 = .8$ utilization factor

$AS = SB/J = 16/10 = 1.6$ seconds for the average service time

See Denning and Buzen [A137] for the derivation of the remaining measures.

A37.8 Benefits. These measures can be used throughout the system life cycle to ensure an effective and resource-efficient design. These measures will provide the logical and economic framework for critical tradeoff decisions, (eg, performance vs functionality, cost vs performance, etc).

A37.9 Experience. Many examples can be found in the literature on queueing theory of this network analysis approach [A133, A135, A136, and A137].

A37.10 References

[A132] ALLEN, A. O. *Probability, Statistics and Queueing Theory.* Academic Press, 1978.

[A133] ALLEN, A. O. Queueing Models of Computer Systems. *Computer*, vol 13, no 4, Apr 1980.

[A134] BARD, Y. An Analytic Model of the VM/370 System. *IBM Journal of Research and Development*, vol 22, no 5, Sept 1978.

[A135] BASKETT, F., CHANDY, K. M., and PALACIOS, F. G. Open, Closed, and Mixed Networks of Queues with Different Classes of Customers. *Communications of the ACM*, vol 22, no 2, Apr 1975.

[A136] BUZEN, J. P., and DENNING, P. J. Measuring and Calculating Queue Length Distributions. *Computer*, vol 13, no 4, Apr 1980.

[A137] DENNING, P. J., and BUZEN, J. P., The Operational Analysis of Queueing Network Models. *Computing Surveys*, vol 10, no 3, Sept 1978.

[A138] GRAHAM, G. S. Queueing Network Models of Computer System Performance. *Computing Surveys*, vol 10, no 3, Sept 1978.

[A139] TRIVEDI, K. S. and KINICKI, R. E. A Model for Computer Configuration Design. *Computer*, vol 14, no 4, Apr 1980.

A38. Independent Process Reliability

A38.1. Application. This measure provides a direct method to compute reliability (R) of certain types of software systems such as telephone switching and business transaction systems in which the programs have no loops and no local dependencies exist. This is a measure of the reliability of service that a software system provides.

A38.2 Primitives

f_{ij} = frequency of execution of intermodule transfer from module i to j.

MD = number of modules

P_i = ith process which can be generated in a user environment.

q_i = probability that P_i will be generated in a user environment.

r_i = random variable equal to 1 if the process P_i generates the correct software system output and zero otherwise.

R_i = reliability of the ith module.

A38.3 Implementation. This measure assumes that a large program is composed of logically independent modules which can be designed, implemented and tested independently.

Let L = set of processes P_i that can be generated by the software system corresponding to different input values. Then the reliability R of the software system can be computed from

$$R = \sum_{\forall P_i \in L} q_i r_i$$

In large programs, it is infeasible to evaluate r_i and q_i for each process P_i because L could be large. To circumvent this difficulty, a simple Markov model is developed with intermodule probabilities, (f_{ij}), as the user profiles.

The reliability parameters of the program are expressed in terms of transitional probability parameters between states. The reliability R of the software system is defined as the probability of reaching the correct state [after module n] from the initial state [from module 1] of the Markov process, ie:

$$R = S(1, MD)\, R_n$$

where $S = [I - Q]^{-1}$;

Q is the state transition matrix spanning the entire Markov graph program; I is the identity matrix.

Elements of the matrix, $f_{ij}R_i$ represent the probability that execution of module i produces the correct result and transfers control to module j. R_i is determined from experimentation as the ratio of the number of output sets generated by module i to the number of input sets when the software system is tested by samples of representative valid input.

A38.4 Interpretation. The reliability measure provides the user with a direct estimate of the confidence in system software performance and indicates whether further testing and software updates are required for a given operational environment. In addition, this approach also indicates to the user how to improve the system reliability most effectively by evaluating the sensitivity of the system reliability with respect to that of a module [A142]. A high-sensitivity coefficient indicates a critical module that has greater impact on software reliability.

A38.5 Considerations. The underlying assumptions for the use of this measure are the following:

(1) The reliability of the modules are independent — ie, one module fault is not compensated by another.

(2) The transfer of control between program modules is a Markov process. (Next module to be executed depends probabilistically on the present module only and is independent of past history). When no modification is made on the modules, the transition probabilities are assumed constant. These characterize the user environment with respect to the reliability model.

A38.6 Training. The implementation of this methodology requires an understanding of stochastic processes.

A38.7 Examples. An example of the use of this measure is illustrated in Cheung [A142].

A38.8 Benefits. The measure gives a direct indication of the reliability of service to the user and determines whether further testing and improvement is required for the application. The sensitivity coefficient provides a scheme for correcting faults by providing priority updates to modules that have the greatest impact on software reliability.

A38.9 Experience. Limited published experience is available.

A38.10 References

[A140] CHEUNG, R. C. A Structural Theory for Improving SW Reliability. Ph.D. Dissertation, University of California at Berkeley, Dec 1974.

[A141] CHEUNG, R. C. and RAMAMOORTHY, C. V. Optimal Measurement of Program Path Frequencies and Its Applications. In Proc. 1975, *Int Fed Automat Contr Congr*, Aug 1975.

[A142] CHEUNG, R. C. A User Oriented Software Reliability Model. *IEEE Transactions on Software Engineering*, vol SE-6, no 2, Mar 1980.

A39. Combined Hardware and Software (System) Operational Availability

A39.1 Application. This measure provides a direct indication of system dependability, that is, whether it is operating or operable when required by the user.

A39.2 Primitives

λ = Observed software failure rate

β = Observed hardware failure rate

μ_i = Observed software fault correction rate with i faults in the software

γ = Observed hardware repair rate

NF = Estimated number of remaining software faults

P_s = Probability of correcting a software fault when detected $(0 \leq P_s \leq 1)$

P_h = Probability of correctly repairing a hardware failure $(0 \leq P_h \leq 1)$

A39.3 Implementation. The basic Markovian model is used for predicting combined hardware and software (system) availability as a function of operating time. System upstate probabilities $P_{NF,n}(t)$ with n remaining faults, given that there were NF software faults at the commissioning $(t=0)$ of the system, is computed for n = 0, 1, 2, ..., N.

$$\text{System availability } A(t) = \sum_{n=0}^{NF} P_{N,n}(t)$$

The expression for $P_{NF,n}(t)$, n=1, ..., NF is derived as follows [A96]:

$$P_{NF,n}(t) = G_{NF,n}(t) - \sum_{j=1}^{K} \frac{\prod_{i=n+1}^{NK} (P_s\lambda_i\mu_i)(-x_j+P_h\gamma)^{NF-n} A(-x_j)(1-e^{-x_jt})}{x_j \prod_{\substack{i=1\\i\neq j}}^{K} (-x_j+x_i)}$$

where

$G_{NF,n}(t)$ = Cumulative distribution function of the first passage time for operational state with NF faults to operational state with n faults and is expressed as:

$$\sum_{j=1}^{K} \frac{\prod_{i=n+1}^{NF} (P_s\lambda_i\mu_i)(-x_j+P_h\gamma)^{NF-n}}{\prod_{\substack{i=1\\i\neq j}}^{K} (-x_j+x_i)} \frac{1}{-x_j}(e^{-x_jt}-1)$$

$\lambda_i = i\lambda$

$\mu_i = i\mu$

$K = 3\,(NF-n)$

$x_1 = x_{1,(n+1)}$

$x_2 = x_{2,(n+1)}$

$x_3 = x_{3,(n+1)}$

$x_4 = x_{1,(n+2)}$

$x_5 = x_{2,(n+2)}$

$x_6 = x_{3,(n+2)}$

.

.

.

$x_{1(NF-n)} = x_{1,NF}$

$x_{2(NF-n)} = x_{2,NF}$

$x_{3(NF-n)} = x_{3,NF}$

$-x_{1,i}$, $-x_{2,i}$ and $-x_{3,i}$ $(i=n+1, \ldots, NF)$ are the roots of the polynomial

$$S^3 + S^2(\lambda + \mu + \beta + P\gamma) + S(P\lambda\mu + \beta\mu + \lambda P\gamma + \mu P_h\gamma) + P_s P_h \gamma \lambda_i \mu_i$$

Also,

$$A(-x_j) = (-x_j\beta)(-x_j + \mu_n) + \lambda_n(-x_j + P_s\mu_n)(-x_j + P_h\gamma)$$

A39.4 Interpretation. $A(t)$ will show a characteristic drop initially and then will rise, approaching a steady state value determined by the hardware availability.

A39.5 Considerations. The underlying assumptions for the use of this measure based on *Software Reliability Modelling and Estimation Technique* [A96] are as follows:

(1) The occurrence of software and hardware failures are independent.

(2) The probability of two or more software or hardware failures occurring simultaneously is negligible.

(3) Failures and repairs of the hardware are independent of both fault detection and correction of the software.

(4) The software failure rate and the hardware failure rate are constants.

(5) The time to repair hardware failures and the time to correct software failures follow exponential distributions, each with a fixed parameter.

A39.6 Training. The implementation of this methodology requires an understanding of stochastic processes and familiarity with programming analytical models.

A39.7 Example. See combined HW/SW Reliability Models, Section A2.4.2 [A143] for a specific example for system availability.

A39.8 Benefits. A sampling measure for the average availabiity $A_{av}(t)$ of an operational system can be developed and compared with the theoretically computed figure for availability $A(t)$.

A39.9 Experience. Few hardware/software models have been developed that can be applied to the measurement of system operational availability (see Software Reliability Modelling and Estimation Technique [A96]). These models have not yet been tested against actual system failure data. Yet, because it is judged to have great potential for addressing the problem of measuring combined hardware/software performance, their application to actual system failure data is encouraged. However, as other models become available, they too should be considered when system availability calculations/predictions need to be made [A144].

A39.10 References. See also *Software Reliability Modelling and Estimation Technique* [A96].

[A143] *Combined HW/SW Reliability Models*, RADC-TR-82-68, Final Technical Report, Apr 1982.

[A144] SUMITA, U., and MASUDA, Y. Analysis of Software Availability/Reliability Under the Influence of Hardware Failures. *IEEE Transactions on Software Reliability*, vol SE-12, no 1, Jan 1986.

ANSI/IEEE
Std 990-1987

An American National Standard

IEEE Recommended Practice for Ada* As a Program Design Language

Sponsor

Software Engineering Standards Subcommittee of the Technical Committee on Software Engineering of the IEEE Computer Society

Approved December 11, 1986
Reaffirmed September 17, 1992

IEEE Standards Board

Approved October 1, 1987

American National Standards Institute

*Ada is a registered trademark of the United States Government, Department of Defense (Ada Joint Program Office).

The Institute of Electrical and Electronics Engineers, Inc
345 East 47th Street, New York, NY 10017, USA

IEEE Standards documents are developed within the Technical Committees of the IEEE Societies and the Standards Coordinating Committees of the IEEE Standards Board. Members of the committees serve voluntarily and without compensation. They are not necessarily members of the Institute. The standards developed within IEEE represent a consensus of the broad expertise on the subject within the Institute as well as those activities outside of IEEE which have expressed an interest in participating in the development of the standard.

Use of an IEEE Standard is wholly voluntary. The existence of an IEEE Standard does not imply that there are no other ways to produce, test, measure, purchase, market, or provide other goods and services related to the scope of the IEEE Standard. Furthermore, the viewpoint expressed at the time a standard is approved and issued is subject to change brought about through developments in the state of the art and comments received from users of the standard. Every IEEE Standard is subjected to review at least once every five years for revision or reaffirmation. When a document is more than five years old, and has not been reaffirmed, it is reasonable to conclude that its contents, although still of some value, do not wholly reflect the present state of the art. Users are cautioned to check to determine that they have the latest edition of any IEEE Standard.

Comments for revision of IEEE Standards are welcome from any interested party, regardless of membership affiliation with IEEE. Suggestions for changes in documents should be in the form of a proposed change of text, together with appropriate supporting comments.

Interpretations: Occasionally questions may arise regarding the meaning of portions of standards as they relate to specific applications. When the need for interpretations is brought to the attention of IEEE, the Institute will initiate action to prepare appropriate responses. Since IEEE Standards represent a consensus of all concerned interests, it is important to ensure that any interpretation has also received the concurrence of a balance of interests. For this reason IEEE and the members of its technical committees are not able to provide an instant response to interpretation requests except in those cases where the matter has previously received formal consideration.

Comments on standards and requests for interpretations should be addressed to:

Secretary, IEEE Standards Board
345 East 47th Street
New York, NY 10017
USA

Foreword

(This Foreword is not a part of IEEE Std 990-1987, IEEE Recommended Practice for Ada As a Design Language.)

Software Engineering is an emerging field. As part of that process, the Department of Defense initiated, and ANSI approved, ANSI/MIL-STD-1815A-1983, which defines the Ada* Programming Language. In recent years, there has been a growing demand for the use of Ada as a Program Design Language (PDL). Recognizing that an adequate definition of an Ada PDL did not exist, a project was approved in March 1983 to provide that definition as part of a voluntary consensus process. This recommended practice is the result of that process.

This is one of an evolving set of integrated software engineering standards; for example,

ANSI/IEEE Std 729-1983, IEEE Standard Glossary of Software Engineering Terminology
ANSI/IEEE Std 730-1984, IEEE Standard for Software Quality Assurance Plans
ANSI/IEEE Std 828-1983, IEEE Standard for Software Configuration Management Plans
ANSI/IEEE Std 829-1983, IEEE Standard for Software Test Documentation
ANSI/IEEE Std 830-1983, IEEE Guide for Software Requirement Specifications
ANSI/IEEE Std 983-1986, IEEE Guide for Software Quality Assurance Planning
ANSI/IEEE Std 1008-1987, IEEE Standard for Software Unit Testing

This recommended practice may be used either in conjunction with those standards or separately.

As a recommended practice, this document should be helpful to PDL designers, PDL evaluators, software designers, and other members of the software engineering community concerned with the use of Ada as a PDL.

Members of the Executive Steering Committee were as follows:

Robert M. Blasewitz, *Chairman*
Mark S. Gerhardt, *Vice-Chairman*
Susan P. Mardinly, *Executive Chairman*
Dianna H. Peet, *Secretary*

Michael J. Devlin
Debbie Faith
Michael Gordon
Charlene Hayden
Thomas J. Walsh

*Ada is a registered trademark of the United States Government, Department of Defense, (Ada Joint Program Office).

The Ada as a PDL Working Group had the following members:

Robert M. Blasewitz, *Chairman*

George H. Alessi
Ed Amoroso
Christine M. Anderson
John A. Anderson
Peter G. Anderson
Grebenc Andrej
Barbara Ardary
Jeannine Arsenault
John Bailey
James Baldo, Jr
Richard W. Baldwin
Leo Beltracchi
Mordechai Ben Menachem
Yechiel Ben Naftali
John C. Bennett
Victor G. Berecz
Ed Bevard
Lee Blaine
William Bogdan
Roy Bollinger
Graham D. Boose
Robert Borland
Jack Boudreaux
Carol Brade
James Bradley
Eric J. Braude
Christine L. Braun
Alton L. Brintzenhoff
Dwight R. Brooks
Jerry R. Brookshire
Al Brown
Fletcher J. Buckley
Ruck Byrne
Jim Cain
Lorie J. Call
Robert Calland
Miguel A. Carrio
Virginia L. Castor
Phil Caverly
Ann Chase Charles
R. Childress
Antonio M. Cicu
James H. Cistone
Rita Coco
Gerald Cohen
Richard L. Conn
Jack W. Crenshaw
John J. Cupak, Jr
Patricia W. Daggett
B. K. Daniels
Adriam Davidoviciv
Theodore F. DeMuro
Phil A. J. DeVicci
Michael J. Devlin
C.J. DiPietro
Jack Dozier
Einar Dragstedt
Lawrence E. Druffel
Walter DuBlanica
Robert Eachus
Michael W. Evans
Richard E. Fairley
Debbie Faith
Jeffrey K. Farmer
Sal Fazzolari
Hal C. Ferguson
Kathy A. Fieldstad
Charles A. Finnell
Herman A. Fischer
Gerald Fisher
Larry Fishtahler
A.M. Foley
Alain Fontaine
Kevin Fosso
Helene Freedman
Jean Friedman
Bob Fritz
Sigrid Fritz
Vivian M. Gaetano
Michael J. Gagnon
Michel Galinier
Gary Garb
Forrest Karl Gardner
William Gardner
Anthony Gargaro
Dale Gaumer
Charles L. Gausche
William X. Gebele
David Gelperin
Mark S. Gerhardt
Larry D. Gilchrist
Shirley A. Gloss-Soler
Philip Goldstein
Michael Gordon
D.J. Gorman
Allain Griesemer
Thomas A. Grobicki
Howard Hamer
Richard M. Hanchett
Larry E. Hanlan
Ralph V. Harris
Michele Hartman
Charlene R. Hayden
Marlow Henne Herman
Ness Richard F. Hilliard
Warren Hoffnung
Michael Olin Hogan
Maretta T. Holden
Michael Horton
Mary Inglis
Jonathan James
Vicki Johnson
Lesa Kaitz
Gilbert H. Kemp
Robert Knapper
Martin Koenekamp
Shai Koenig
John F. Kramer, Jr
Bill Krueger
Arthur F. Krummenoeh
Joseph A. Krupinski
Mike Kuchinski
Joan Kundig
Carole J. Kuruma
Frank X. Laslo
Cony Lau
C. Crissman Laubach, III
Chris Laudbach
Carol LeDoux
Raymond C. Leber
Min Lee
Roger Lee
Larry Lindley
Steven Litvintchouk
Warren Loper
Michael E. Luken
Paul Maguire
Mark Maiocco
Allen Malberg
Sue Mardinly
D.H. Martin
Robert F. Mathis
Cathy Maxson
R.D. McCamy
Robert D. McClure
Ed McCronen
Gregory McFarland
Raymond J. McGlynn
George McPherson
Loren Meck
Mike Meirink
Louis Minham
James Moloney
David Moore
John I. Moore, Jr
William L. Morrison
A.J. Murfin
J.O. Neilson
Thomas Newsome
Edward Ng
Robert F. Owens
Eddie Paramore
Bruce R. Parker
Michael Patrick
Dianna H. Peet
George Petrovay
Larry Pochetti
Tim Portor
John Privitera
Thomas S. Radi
Stan F. Ralph
Salim Ramji
Kim T. Rawlinson
Ann Reedy
Alan Reiblein
Donald J. Reifer
Patrick J. Reilly
Herbert L. Resnick
Carol Righini
John W. Roberts
Kenneth Roberts
Mike Rockenhause
Paul Rogoway
Helen E. Romanowsky
Steven M. Rowan
R.C. Roy
David Rudd
Ruth Rudolph
Richard Rupolo
John L. Rymer
Mark Sadler
Sabina Saib
Arthur E. Salwin
Burnett H. Sams
Jack Schaefer
David F. Schick
Richard Schneider
Harvey E. Schock, Jr

Joann Schultz
William M. Scott
Alfred Seita
A.E. Severin
Rod Sheffield
Sylvia B. Sheppard
Tracy G. Shoor
Jeffrey E. Simon
Dave Sloyer
Joan D. Spalding
Robert D. Spray
Donald Squires
William Stafford
David Steinberg

Putnam Texel
R.C. Thomas
Terrence L. Tillmanns
William Stephen Turner, III
M.V. Underwood
Joseph E. Urban
David Usechak
A. Vandenakker
Ralph Wachter
Larry K. Walker
Fred L. Wallace
John R. Wallace
John P. Walsh
Thomas J. Walsh

Martin M. Waxman
Robert Weissensee
Walt Whipple
B.A. Wichmann
Herbert E. Willman, Jr
Daryl R. Winters
Martin I. Wolfe
Helen Wu
Fred E. Wuebker
Lawrence Yelowitz
Michael E. York
Janusz Zalewski
George L. Zenzerovich
Sandra Zucker

The following persons were on the balloting committee that approved this standard for submission to the IEEE Standards Board:

A. Frank Ackerman
William W. Agresti
Dock Allen
Dennis R. Allison
Charles J. Antwelli
Barbara Ardary
Wolf Arfuidson
Tom Armbruster
James Baldo
Geoff R. Baldwin
Karl G. Balke
Bryce M. Bardin
John G.P. Barnes
B.C. Bass
Richard E. Batty
August A. Bauer
Leo Beltracchi
Frank Belz
Mordechai Ben-Menachem
Victor G. Berecz
H. Ronald Berlack
Brett L. Binns
Michael A. Blackledge
Robert M. Blasewitz
John J. Blyskal
Barry W. Boehm
William Bogdan
William Boyden
Carl Brandon
Jerry R. Brookshire
Al Brown
Fletcher J. Buckley
Harry Carl
David J. Carlson
Ingemar Carlson
A.J. Carvalho III
Janice A. Chelini
John Chihorek
Nhan V. Chu
Won L. Chung
Antonio M. Cicu
James H. Cistone
Suzette N. Clafton
John R. Clark
Donald R. Clarson
Corey Clinger
Richard T. Close
Peter Coad, Jr
Norman Cohen
Benjamin J. Consilvio
Chrisopher M. Cooke
Bard S. Crawford
James A. Darling
Sid David
Thomas Davis
Phil A.J. DeVicci
Vincent P. De-vito
Robert J. Decker
Michael J. Devlin
David G. Doty
Einar Dragstedt
Walter Du-Blanica
Robert E. Dwyer
Theodore J. Dzik
John D. Earls
Lange Brian Eliot
Richard E. Fairly
Raouf H. Farag
John W. Fendrich
Hal C. Ferguson
Glenn S. Fields
Gerry Fisher
A.M. Foley
Julian Forster
Kenneth A. Foster
Deborah L. Franke
Craig D. Fuget
Alfred Ganz
Leonard B. Gardner
Anthony Gargaro
David Gelperin
Edward L. Gibbs
Luther E. Gifford
Shirley A. Gloss-Soler
Marty Goldberg
Michael Gordon
Jacob Vadim Gore
Robert M. Grahm
Benjamin W. Green
Thomas A. Grobicki
Robert S. Grossman
Lawrence M. Gunther
Virl E. Haas
Harry E. Hansen, Jr
Hal M. Hart
Clark M. Hay
Paul L. Hazan
Jeffrey M. Hickey
L.J. Hoffman
Robert Hofkin
C.F. Howard
Henry B. Hoyle
Wendy J. Hudson
Charles J. Huller
James H. Ingram
Garland M. Jett, Jr
David Johnson III
Owen K. Kato
Mansour Kavianpour
Judith S. Kerner
Glenn M. Kersnick
Robert A. Kessler
Duane E. Kiefer
Genevieve M. Knight
Joseph A. Krupinski
Joan Kundig
Thomas M. Kurihara
Robert G. Kurkjian
Robin B. Lake
Robert A.C. Lane
Gregory N. Larsen
Randal Leavitt
Raymond C. Leber
David H. Lee
John A.N. Lee
James M. Lepsch
Ear Leung
Ben Livson
Paul E. MacNeil
Kartic C. Majumdar
Armand Marchesin
Sue Mardinly
Borut Maricic
Uchida Mark-Rene
Gregory C. Marr
Thomas H. Maryanski
Paul A. Mauro
C. Mazza
Maurice B. McEoy
Gregory McFarland
Raymond J. Mc-glynn
James McKelvey
Philip N. Merritt
Ben W. Miller
Robert P. Miller
Siba N. Mohanty
James Moody
Charles S. Mooney
John I. Moore, Jr
Nancy Moore
Gene T. Morun
Stephen V. Mroczek
David G. Mullens
Jose L. Munoz
W.M. Murray
Myron L. Nack
Hironobu Nagano
Jainendra K. Navlakha
Geraldine Rajcul Neidhart
States L. Nelson
Thomas Newsome
Dennis E. Nickle
T.L. Norman
John C. Norrell
Tim O'Bannon
James E. O'Day
Bruce R. Parker
Judson F. Parker
Michael Patrick
Robert L. Patton, Jr
Dianna H. Peet
Paul Peterson
Ramona Pfau
Ronald N. Pipes
Tim Porter
Ian Pyle
Edward Purvis
James E. Quelle
Sandra J. Raddue
Jock A. Rader
Thomas S. Radi
Salim Ramji
John Reddan
Larry K. Reed
T.D. Regulinski
Donald J. Reifer
Helen E. Romanowsky
Steven M. Rowan
Daniel M. Roy
Ruth Rudolph
Frances A. Ruhlman
John L. Rymer
H. Saha
Paul J. Sakson
Arthur E. Salwin
Jean E. Sammet
Burnett H. Sams
Raymond E. Sandborgh
Julio Gonzalez Sanz
Stephen R. Schach
Franz P. Schauer
Peter E. Schilling
Lee O. Schmidt
Norman F. Schneidewind
Wolf A. Schnoege
Leonard W. Seagren
Devdoot D. Sen

Gerard P. Shabe
Lawrence H. Shafer
S. Wayne Sherer
David M. Siefert
Jeffrey E. Simon
J.G. Snodgrass
Charles Snyder
Werner Sohn
Robert D. Spray
V. Srinivas
Paul D. Stachour
Manfred P. Stadel
G. Wayne Staley
Marilyn J. Stewart
Captain Mark D. Stotzer
A.W. Strohmeier
William G. Sutcliffe
Mary A. Sutton

Kou Chung Tai
Alan E. Ternstrom
Helmut E. Thiess
Booker T. Thomas
Terrence L. Tillmanns
Valentin W. Tirman, Jr
Henry J. Trochesset
C.L. Troyanowski
Kevin J. Tully
Erwin A. Ulbrich, Jr
David Usechak
Kazuo Ushijima
Howard E. Verne
Thomas Vollman
Ralph Wachter
John P. Walsh
Thomas J. Walsh
William M. Walsh III

Roger D.H. Warburton
Douglas W. Waugh
Martin M. Waxman
Peter J.D. Weyman
Thomas J. Wheeler
Walter L. Whipple
W.A. Whitaker
Paul A. Willis
Herbert E. Willman, Jr
Andrew F. Wilson
Patric J. Wilson
Paul A.T. Wolfgang
S.Y. Wong
Paul R. Work
Tom Worthington
Yung-Koh Yin
Michael E. York
Don Zeleny

Special representatives to the Software Engineering Standards Subcommittee were:

F. Gracza, ADAPSO
William C. Perry, DPMA
H. Ronald Berlack, EIA
T. D. Regulinski, IEEE Reliability
S. I. Heisler, Z1 Committee

When the IEEE Standards Board approved this standard on December 11, 1986, it had the following membership:

John E. May, *Chairman*

Irving Kolodny, *Vice Chairman*

Sava I. Sherr, *Secretary*

James H. Beall
Fletcher J. Buckley
Paul G. Cummings
Donald C. Fleckenstein
Jay Forster
Daniel L. Goldberg
Kenneth D. Hendrix
Irvin N. Howell

Jack Kinn
Joseph L. Koepfinger*
Edward Lohse
Lawrence V. McCall
Donald T. Michael*
Marco W. Migliaro
Stanley Owens
John P. Riganati
Frank L. Rose

Robert E. Rountree
Martha Sloan
Oley Wanaselja
J. Richard Weger
William B. Wilkens
Helen M. Wood
Charles J. Wylie
Donald W. Zipse

*Member emeritus

IEEE

Contents

IEEE Recommended Practice for Ada As a Program Design Language

1. Introduction

1.1 Scope. This document provides recommendations reflecting the state of the art and alternate approaches to good practice for characteristics of Program Design Languages (PDLs) based on the syntax and semantics of the Ada Programming Language. In this recommended practice, these are referred to as Ada PDLs.

1.2 Scope Restrictions. This recommended practice addresses the characteristics of an Ada PDL and not the use of an Ada PDL. Although certain capabilities are recommended to be provided by an Ada PDL, this document does not state how a designer will design, nor how the design is to be documented, using an Ada PDL. While certain capabilities are recommended for an Ada PDL, specification of the ways to use those capabilities is beyond the scope of this document.

While it is widely recognized that graphic representations may enhance the design activity, there is no clear consensus concerning graphic representations at this time. As such, this document is principally concerned with the aspects of textual representations.

This recommended practice does not specify:

(1) A single PDL syntax

(2) The programming languages in which a design may be implemented

(3) A specific methodology to be used in conjunction with an Ada PDL

(4) The method by which a PDL text is represented, stored, or processed

This recommended practice does not provide:

(1) A tutorial on the use of:

(a) The Ada Programming Language, to include an exhaustive list of Ada constructs

(b) An Ada PDL

(2) A survey of PDLs or a history of their use

(3) A means for quantitatively determining the cost effectiveness of using an Ada PDL

1.3 Terminology. Where recommendations are made that represent the position of the IEEE, the verb *should* is used. Where alternate approaches are provided and no firm recommendations are made, the verb *may* is used.

1.4 Cautions. These are as follows:

(1) This document focuses on Ada PDLs. The use of a design language that is consistent with this recommended practice for other areas—for example, system requirements or hardware requirements—is not prohibited by this document. However, the reader is warned that there may very well be other substantial considerations in these uses, and that these considerations are beyond the scope of this recommended practice.

(2) An Ada PDL may be used to document a design when the implementation is projected to be in a Programming Language other than Ada. Users should be aware that an Ada PDL may not have the ability to represent such a design.

(3) Personnel associated with the use of a PDL should take special care to ensure that the designers do not become preoccupied with the details of the implementation when they should be designing. This may require special training, additional informal reviews, etc.

1.5 Examples. Examples are incorporated into the text of this recommended practice to enhance clarity and to promote understanding. All examples are explicitly identified. Examples should not be construed as recommended implementations.

2. Definitions and References

2.1 Definitions. The definitions listed in this section establish meaning in the context of this recommended practice. Other definitions can be found in: ANSI/IEEE Std 729-1983 [1][1] and ANSI/MIL-STD-1815A-1983 [2].

design element. A basic component or building block in a design.

design unit. A logically related collection of design elements. In an Ada PDL, a design unit is represented by an Ada compilation unit.

2.2 References. This standard shall be used in conjunction with the following publications:

[1] ANSI/IEEE Std 729-1983, IEEE Standard Glossary of Software Engineering Terminology.[2,3]

[2] ANSI/MIL-STD-1815A-1983 Reference Manual for the Ada Programming Language.[4]

3. Characteristics

3.1 General Methodology Support. A specific Ada PDL may support more than one design methodology. For example, both rapid prototyping and object-oriented design may be supported by the same Ada PDL. This is because no single development methodology is known to be superior for all applications and for all development organizations.

3.1.1 Abstraction. An Ada PDL should support the extraction of essential concepts while supporting the suppression of nonessential details.

3.1.2 Decomposition. An Ada PDL should support the division of a large software system into smaller, more manageable pieces while maintaining a fixed level of detail.

3.1.3 Information Hiding. An Ada PDL should support isolating and making inaccessible certain details that ought not to affect other parts of the software system.

3.1.4 Stepwise Refinement. An Ada PDL should support the progressive addition of detail to a software design.

3.1.5 Modularity. An Ada PDL should support the development of the design from standardized units.

3.2 Specific Design Support

3.2.1 Algorithm Design. An Ada PDL should support algorithm design. For example, depending on the intended usage, the PDL may support the use of structured control flow, computations, finite state machines, and Petri nets.

3.2.2 Data Structure Design. An Ada PDL should support data structure design. Specifically, an Ada PDL should support:

(1) Data structure definition

(2) Formalization of data structures

(3) Identification of constraints on acceptable values

(4) Identification of allowable operations on objects

(5) Location of points of access to data objects

(6) Modification of data objects

(7) Specification of data structure scope, duration, and storage methodology (for example, stored in shared memory, files, stack, etc) and constraints (for example, size limitations).

3.2.3 Connectivity. An Ada PDL should support the identification of explicit connections, including dependencies.

(1) The following should be formally described by the PDL:

(a) Ordering of component execution. As a part of this, the PDL should support the expression of:

(i) Sequential invocation of computational processes

(ii) Initiation and termination of parallel processes

(iii) Synchronization of parallel processes

(b) Data definition dependencies

[1] The numbers in brackets correspond to those of the references in 2.2 of this section.

[2] ANSI documents are available from the Sales Department, American National Standards Institute, 1430 Broadway, New York, NY 10018.

[3] See, specifically, Algorithm, Data Structure, Design, Design Language, Design Methodology, Life Cycle, Process, Program Design Language, and Software Life Cycle.

[4] See, specifically, Ada Programming Language, Compilation Unit, Generic Unit, Object, Package, Program Unit, Subprogram, Task, and Type.

(c) Data flow
(d) Possible error conditions and their associated consequences
(e) Interfaces between design units and between design elements
(f) Asynchronous interrupts

(2) The following may be formally describable by the Ada PDL:
(a) How the hardware works
(b) How interacting systems are expected to behave

3.2.4 Adaptability. The Ada PDL may have the capability to:

(1) Be adjusted under controlled forms to allow for national characters in a language other than English

(2) Implement restriction of certain syntax and semantics for particular applications (see 3.4.1.)

(3) Support graphic representations of the design being described

3.3 Other Support. The PDL may support the expression of Product and Management Information.

3.3.1 Product Information. Examples include:

(1) Performance. This may include critical timing, frequency, capacity, and other constraints.

(2) Fault Tolerance. This may include error detection/diagnosis and error handling, backup and recovery, reliability, and redundancy.

(3) Security. This may include multilevel security constraints, set/use access restrictions, breach detection and handling, and the identification of the security classification(s) of the material itself.

(4) Distribution. This may include geographic distribution of processing, data storage, and access.

(5) Adaptation. This may include accommodations to be made to support differing levels of user expertise.

(6) Assumptions. Description of a context within which an algorithm exists. For example, a function that does division may be built on the assumption that the denominator is not zero.

(7) History. This may include design decisions and alternate, rejected solutions to the chosen design, together with a rationale for the choice.

(8) Traceability. This may include traceability of:
(a) Detailed Design to Preliminary or Top-Level Design, and further to the Software Requirements specifications
(b) Preliminary, or Top-Level Design to Detailed Design
(c) Applicable standards

3.3.2 Management Information. Examples include:

(1) Organizational information, such as division of work and assignment of tasks to team members

(2) Planning information, such as milestone definitions, resource estimation, dependencies that affect the development process itself, and scheduling

(3) Status information, such as milestone completion

(4) Configuration Management information, to include Configuration Identification and Change Control restrictions

3.4 Ada Relationships. The PDL should be related to the Ada Programming Language in the following respects:

3.4.1 Conformance. An Ada PDL should conform syntactically and semantically to ANSI/MIL-STD-1815A-1983 [2]. Specifically, an Ada PDL should be processible by a validated Ada compiler without error.

(1) An Ada PDL may be processible by other tools: for example, a PDL Preprocessor. Preprocessing should not be required prior to error-free processing by a validated Ada compiler.

(2) There is no requirement that an Ada PDL provide the full capabilities of the Ada Programming Language. A conforming subset should be adequate for the application and is allowable, for example, to prevent the use of:
(a) Untranslatable Ada constructs when designing for a target language other than Ada
(b) Inefficient control structures when developing embedded computer systems software
(c) Excessively detailed design constructs during high-level design, for example, use of representation specifications

3.4.2 Extensions. Commentary text may be used to extend the expressive capability of an Ada PDL beyond the semantics of Ada.

Two forms of comments are available:
(1) Unstructured comments
(2) Structured comments

3.4.2.1 Unstructured Comments. Unstructured comments may be used for:

(1) Natural language explanation of statements made in Ada

(2) Any information required in the design process where formal structures are not required: for example, for humanto-human communication

The user of unstructured comments should be aware that tools can process unstructured comments only in very primitive ways (for example, storage, retrieval, and crossreferencing).

3.4.2.2 Structured Comments. Structured comments (also known as annotations):

(1) May be used to provide design information in additional design-oriented semantics.

(2) Should be consistent with the Ada language. For example, in compound constructs, the end of the construct should mirror the beginning:

```
--*High Level Design
--*
--*
--*End High Level Design
```

(3) Are identified by a sentinel character, word, or phrase immediately following the double dash that indicates a comment to an Ada complier, for example, "--keyword" or "--*".

(a) The sentinel has two functions:

(i) To highlight the comment as belonging to the formal structure of the PDL, alerting any reader that the information is of special significance

(ii) To direct PDL processing tools toward information upon which the tools may be required to act

(b) Associated with the sentinel are semantic rules that indicate:

(i) Whether the comment applies to the preceding or the following Ada construct

(ii) What constructs are allowed after the sentinel, based on the context in which the sentinel appears

3.4.2.3 Replication Constraints. All concepts that can be reasonably expressed in noncommentary Ada should be so expressed. Information that can be provided in the Ada portion of the PDL should not be replicated within the commentary text by Ada constructs or by any other means.

The following organizations supported working group members in the development of this recommended practice:

Ada Joint Program Office
AT&T Bell Laboratories
BDM Corporation
Bendix Corporation
Boeing-Vertol
Burroughs Corporation
Canadian Marconi Company
Comptek Research, Inc
Computer Sciences Corporation
Control Data Corporation
Convex Computer Corporation
Digital Equipment Corporation
Federal Aviation Administration
Federal Department of Transportation
Ford Aerospace & Communications Division
General Dynamics
General Electric Company
General Research Corporation
Grumman Aerospace Corporation
GTE Government Systems Division
GTE Sylvania
SSD Harris Corporation
Hughes Aircraft Company
IBM
I.C.L. Intermetrics
Johns Hopkins Applied Physics Lab
Kearfott Softech, Inc
Litton Data Systems
Lockheed Electronics Company
M/A Com—Linkabit
Magnavox
Martin Marietta Aerospace
MITRE
National Bureau of Standards
Naval Air Development Center
Naval Avionics Center
NBC
Norden Systems
Prior Data Sciences, Ltd
Raytheon Company
RCA SAI Comsystems
SDC
Singer
Sperry
SYSCON Corporation
Teledyne Brown Engineering
Texas Instruments
Transport Canada
U.S. Air Force
U.S. Army
U.S. Navy
Vitro Corporation

IEEE

ANSI / IEEE
Std 1002-1987

An American National Standard

IEEE Standard Taxonomy for Software Engineering Standards

Sponsor

Software Engineering Standards Subcommittee of the Technical Committee on Software Engineering of the IEEE Computer Society

Approved December 11, 1986
Reaffirmed December 3, 1992

IEEE Standards Board

Approved June 4, 1987

American National Standards Institute

The Institute of Electrical and Electronics Engineers, Inc
345 East 47th Street, New York, NY 10017, USA

Foreword

(This Foreword is not a part of ANSI / IEEE Std 1002-1987, IEEE Standard Taxonomy for Software Engineering Standards.)

Software Engineering is an emerging field. As part of that process a set of software engineering standards is being developed. They are used to:

(1) Improve communications between and among software engineers and others.

(2) Achieve economy of cost, human effort, and essential materials.

(3) Institutionalize practical solutions to recurring problems.

(4) Achieve predictability of cost and quality.

(5) Establish norms of acceptable professional practice.

To support the development, integration, and use of software engineering standards, a need for a taxonomy is recognized. A project was approved in June 1983 to define a taxonomy as part of a voluntary consensus process. This document is the result of that process.

This is one of an evolving set of integrated IEEE Software Engineering standards, recommended practices, and guides. The set currently includes:

ANSI/IEEE Std 729-1983, IEEE Standard Glossary of Software Engineering Terminology
ANSI/IEEE Std 730-1984, IEEE Standard for Software Quality Assurance Plans
ANSI/IEEE Std 828-1983, IEEE Standard for Software Configuration Management Plans
ANSI/IEEE Std 829-1983, IEEE Standard for Software Test Documentation
ANSI/IEEE Std 830-1984, IEEE Guide to Software Requirements Specifications
ANSI/IEEE Std 983-1986, IEEE Guide for Software Quality Assurance Planning
ANSI/IEEE Std 1008-1987, IEEE Standard for Software Unit Testing

This standard may be used in conjunction with this set of standards or separately.

The taxonomy can be applied, but is not limited to, project, program, organization, industrial, national, and international standards. As a document, this standard should be useful to those who develop, use, manage, and evaluate software engineering standards. The taxonomy provides a:

(1) Comprehensive scheme for classifying software engineering standards, recommended practices, and guides.

(2) Framework for identifying the need for new software engineering standards, recommended practices, and guides.

(3) Comprehensive scheme for analyzing a set of software engineering standards, recommended practices, and guides appropriate for a given industry, company, program, project, or particular work assignment.

(4) Framework for comparing sets of software engineering standards, recommended practices, and guides to support the selection of the most useful set for a particular software product.

The application of the taxonomy to achieve the above purposes is described in the appendix.

Keywords applicable to this standard are: nomenclature standard, notation standard, software engineering.

The sponsor for this standard was the Software Engineering Standards Subcommittee of the Software Engineering Technical Committee of the IEEE Computer Society, John W. Horch, Chairman.

Special representatives to the Software Engineering Standards Subcommittee were:

P.W. Abrahams
H.R. Berlack
A. Ferlan
S.R. Jarocki
R.R. Jones
J.A.N. Lee
J. Milandin
W.F. Mitchell
W.E. Perry
T.L. Regulinski
P.E. Schilling

The working group that developed this standard had the following membership:

Leonard L. Tripp, *Chairperson* **Perry R. Nuhn,** *Co-Chairperson*
Ralph G. Wachter, *Co-Chairperson*

A. Frank Ackerman
Eleanor Antreasian
Joan P. Bateman
H. Ronald Berlack
Richard L. Chilausky
Francois Coallier
Stewart Crawford
James Darling
John W. Fendrich
Mehmet Ficici
Craig D. Fuget
David Gelperin
Jeff van Gilder
Paul Howley
John Horch
Harry Kalmbach
Louis B. Kiersky
Thomas M. Kurihara
John B. Lane
F. C. Lim
Phillip C. Marriott
Virginia Marting
Dan G. McNicholl
Mordechai Ben-Menachim
Fred Mervine
Manijeh Moghis
Dennis E. Nickle
Robert C. Olsen
Sharon R. Cobb-Pierson
Robert B. Poston
Max J. Schindler
David Schultz
Leonard W. Seagren
John Selman
David M. Siefert
Dave Simkins
R. van Tilburg
William S. Turner, III
Clyde E. Willis
Paul A. Willis

When the IEEE Standards Board approved this standard on December 11, 1986, it had the following membership:

John E. May, *Chairman* **Irving Kolodny,** *Vice Chairman*
Sava I. Sherr, *Secretary*

James H. Beall
Fletcher J. Buckley
Paul G. Cummings
Donald C. Fleckenstein
Jay Forster
Daniel L. Goldberg
Kenneth D. Hendrix
Irvin N. Howell
Jack Kinn
Joseph L. Koepfinger*
Edward Lohse
Lawrence V. McCall
Donald T. Michael*
Marco W. Migliaro
Stanley Owens
John P. Riganati
Frank L. Rose
Robert E. Rountree
Martha Sloan
Oley Wanaselja
J. Richard Weger
William B. Wilkens
Helen M. Wood
Charles J. Wylie
Donald W. Zipse

*Member emeritus

The following persons were on the balloting committee that approved this document for submission to the IEEE Standards Board:

A. Frank Ackerman
Jagdish C. Agrawal
Richard L. Aurbach
K. Ramesh Babu
James Baldo, Jr
H. Jack Barnard
Roy W. Bass
Leo Beltracchi
Yechiel Ben-Naftali
Victor G. Berecz
H.R. Berlack
J. Emmett Black
Michael A. Blackledge
Ron Blair
Kevin W. Bowyer
Kathleen L. Briggs
Fletcher J. Buckley
Margaret Butler
Homer C. Carney
Ronald R. Carter
Robert N. Charette
Tsun S. Chow
Jung K. Chung
Peter Coad, Jr
Francois Coallier
Christopher M. Cooke
A.J. Cote, Jr
Stewart Crawford
George D. Darling
Taz Daughtrey
P.O. Denny
Harpal S. Dhama
Mike Dotson
William P. Dupros
Michael Dutton
Robert E. Dwyer
Mary Eads
John D. Earls
Michael Edward
L.G. Egan
Steven R. Eisen
Caroline L. Evans
David W. Favor
John W. Fendrich
Robert G. Ferreol
Glenn S. Fields
Gordon Force
J. Forster
Deborah L. Franke
C.R. Frederick
Carl Friedlander
Ismael Fuentes-Crespo
Micheel Galinier
Leonard B. Gardner
David Gelperin
James L. Gildersleeve
Shirley Gloss-Soler
Ole Golubjatnikov
J. Kaye Grau
Andrej Grebenc
Thomas Griest
Victor M. Guarnera
Lawrence M. Gunther
David A. Gustafson
Russell Gustin
Howard Hamer
Hans-Ludwig Hansen
George B. Hawthorne
Clark M. Hay
Terry L. Hengl
Charles P. Hollocker
John W. Horch
Cheng Hu
Shang-Sheng Jeng
David Johnson, III
Laurel V. Kaleda
Constantine Kaniklidis
Myron S. Karasik
Adi N. Kasad
Ron Kenett
R.A. Kessler
Joseph A. Krupinski
Hirayr M. Kudyan
Joan Kundig
T.M. Kurihara
Robin B. Lake
Lak-Ming Lam
John B. Lane
Robert A.C. Lane
William P. LaPlant, Jr
Greg Larsen
Jack A. Latimer
Jay Levenson
Leon S. Levy
Paul Lieberaz
F.C. Lim
Bertil Lindberg
David Linsson
William M. Lively
John M. Long
John Lowell
L.J. Mablack
Bill Macre
Andy Mahindru
Henry Malec
Paulo Cesar Marcondes
Stuart Marcotte
Philip C. Marriott
Nicholas L. Marselos
Roger J. Martin
Robert F. Martini
Ivano Mazza
J.A. McCall
John McKissick, Jr
Glen A. Meldrum
Belden Menkus
Ben W. Miller
Manijeh Moghis
Charles S. Mooney
Joyce E. Mortison
Gene T. Morun
Dale N. Murray
Myron L. Nack
Hironobu Nagano
Saied Najafi
Gerry Neidhart
Brian Nejmeh
Dennis E. Nickle
I.H. Obbink
Wilma Osborne
D.J. Ostrom
David G. Owens
Thomas D. Parrish
M.T. Perkins
Donald J. Pfeiffer
R.M. Poston
Peter Ron Prinzivalli
Thomas S. Radi
Meir Razy
John Reddan
Larry K. Reed
Matthias F. Reese, III
T.D. Regulinski
Donald J. Reifer
Steven M. Rowan
R. Waldo Roth
Hom Sack
Julio Gonzalez Sanz
Stephen R. Schach
Franz P. Schauer
Max Schindler
Norman Schneidewind
Nolf A. Schnoege
Robert G. Schueppert
David J. Schultz
Gregory D. Schumacher
Leonard W. Seagren
Devdoot Sen
Gerard P. Share
Robert W. Shillato
David M. Siefert
David J. Simkins
Jacob Slonim
Marion P. Smith
Harry M. Sneed
J.G. Snodgrass
Al R. Sorkowitz
Hugh B. Spillane
Lee Sprague
G. Wayne Staley
Alan N. Sukert
William G. Sutcliffe
Richard H. Thayer
Booker T. Thomas
Paul U. Thompson
E.O. Tilford
Terrence L. Tillmanns
Lawrence F. Tracey
Glendon R. Trebble
Robert Troy
C.L. Troyanowski
Dana L. Ulery
R.L. Van Tilburg
P.M. Vater
Osmo Vikman
R. Wachter
Dolores R. Wallace
Andrew H. Weigel
R.W. Werlwas
Walter L. Whipple
Paul A. Willis
Patrick J. Wilson
Paul Wolfgang
W. Martin Wong
Dennis L. Wood
Paul R. Work
Tom Worthington
Charles Wortz
Stephen D. Yaste
Natalie C. Yopconka
Michael E. York
Marvin Zelkowitz
Peter F. Zoll

IEEE

Contents

IEEE

An American National Standard

IEEE Standard Taxonomy for Software Engineering Standards

1. Introduction

1.1 Scope. This document describes the form and content of a software engineering standards taxonomy. Applicability is not restricted by software application, size, complexity, criticality, or hardware environment. This taxonomy applies to standards (from the related disciplines of engineering management, systems engineering, computer hardware engineering, computer science, and information science) with which a software engineer would be reasonably acquainted. This taxonomy is application independent. For example, an accounting test standard would be placed under test standards, but the qualifier, accounting, has no significance. The document explains the various types of software engineering standards, their functional and external relationships, and the role of various functions participating in the software life cycle. The taxonomy may be used as a method for planning the development or evaluation of standards for an organization. It could also serve as a basis for classifying a set of standards or for organizing a standards manual.

1.2 Terminology. The word *shall* identifies the mandatory material within this standard. The words *should* and *may* identify optional material.

1.3 References. This standard shall be used in conjunction with the following reference:

[1] ANSI/IEEE Std 729-1983, IEEE Standard Glossary of Software Engineering Terminology.[1]

[1] ANSI/IEEE publications can be obtained from the Sales Department, American National Standards Institute, 1430 Broadway, New York, NY 10018, or from the Service Center, The Institute of Electrical and Electronics Engineers, 445 Hoes Lane, P.O. Box 1331, Piscataway, NJ 08855-1331.

2. Definitions

The definitions listed below establish meaning in the context of this standard. Other definitions can be found in ANSI/IEEE Std 729-1983 [1].[2] **See specifically: audit, certification, configuration management, conversion, debugging, design, design phase, implementation phase, installation and checkout phase, integration, maintenance, operation and maintenance phase, quality assurance, requirements analysis, requirements phase, retirement phase, review, software engineering, software maintenance, test phase, and testing.** For the purpose of this standard, the term "software" includes the computer programs, data, and documentation portions of both software and firmware.

code of ethics standard. A standard that describes the characteristics of a set of moral principles dealing with accepted standards of conduct by, within, and among professions.

coding. The transforming of logic and data from design specifications into a programming language.

component standard. A standard that describes the characteristics of data or program components.

concept phase. The period of time in the software life cycle during which the user needs are described and evaluated through documentation (for example, statement of needs, advance planning report, project initiation memo, feasibility studies, system definition documentation, regulations, procedures or policies relevant to the project).

[2] The numbers in square brackets refer to those of the references listed in 1.3.

curriculum standard. A standard that describes the characteristics of a course of study on a body of knowledge that is offered by an educational institution.

description standard. A standard that describes the characteristics of product information or procedures provided to help understand, test, install, operate, or maintain the product.

design standard. A standard that describes the characteristics of a design or a design description of data or program components.

job function. A group of engineering processes that is identified as a unit for the purposes of work organization, assignment, or evaluation. Examples are design, testing, or configuration management.

language standard. A standard that describes the characteristics of a language used to describe a requirements specification, a design, or test data.

licensing standard. A standard that describes the characteristics of an authorization given by an official or a legal authority to an individual or organization to do or own a specified thing.

manufacturing phase. The period of time in the software life cycle during which the basic version of a software product is adapted to a specified set of operational environments and is distributed to a customer base.

measurement standard. A standard that describes the characteristics of evaluating a process or product.

method standard. A standard that describes the characteristics of the orderly process or procedure used in the engineering of a product or performing a service.

nomenclature standard. A standard that describes the characteristics of a system or set of names, or designations, or symbols.

notation standard. A standard that describes the characteristics of formal interchanges within a profession.

occupational title standard. A standard that describes the characteristics of the general area of work or profession.

plan standard. A standard that describes the characteristics of a scheme for accomplishing defined objectives or work within specified resources.

process management. The direction, control, and coordination of work performed to develop a product or perform a service. Example is quality assurance.

process standard. A standard that deals with the series of actions or operations used in making or achieving a product.

product analysis. The process of evaluating a product by manual or automated means to determine if the product has certain characteristics.

product engineering. The technical processes to define, design, and construct or assemble a product.

product management. The definition, coordination, and control of the characteristics of a product during its development cycle. Example is configuration management.

product standard. A standard that defines what constitutes completeness and acceptability of items that are used or produced, formally or informally, during the software engineering process.

product support. The providing of information, assistance, and training to install and make software operational in its intended environment and to distribute improved capabilities to users.

professional standard. A standard that identifies a profession as a discipline and distinguishes it from other professions.

report standard. A standard that describes the characteristics of describing results of engineering and management activities.

representation standard. A standard that describes the characteristics of portraying aspects of an engineering or management product.

requirement standard. A standard that describes the characteristics of a requirements specification.

resource management. The identification, estimation, allocation, and monitoring of the means used to develop a product or perform a service. Example is estimating.

software life cycle. The period of time that starts when a software product is conceived and ends when the product is no longer available for use. The software life cycle typically includes a concept phase, requirements phase, design phase, implementation phase, test phase, manufacturing phase, installation and checkout phase, operation and maintenance phase, and sometimes, retirement phase.

taxonomy. A scheme that partitions a body of knowledge and defines the relationships among the pieces. It is used for classifying and understanding the body of knowledge.

technical management. The application of technical and administrative resources to plan, organize, and control engineering functions.

technique standard. A standard that describes the characteristics of applying accumulated technical or management skills and methods in the creation of a product or performing a service.

verification and validation. The process of determining whether the requirements for a system or component are complete and correct, the products of each development phase fulfill the requirements or conditions imposed by the previous phase, and the final system or component complies with specified requirements.

3. Taxonomy of Software Engineering Standards

The taxonomy shall consist of a standards partition, software engineering partition, and a framework that relates the two partitions. Each partition results in the definition of a set of categories wherein each category has a name and a membership rule. The standards partition characterizes the roles of standards. The software engineering partition characterizes the aspects of software engineering with which a standard can be associated. The framework combines the two partitions into a two-dimensional scheme, which describes the set of possible software engineering standards. The taxonomy framework also describes how the categories are organized for classification purposes. Section 3.1 describes the standards partition, Section 3.2 describes the software engineering partition, and Section 3.3 describes the taxonomy framework and its relationships.

3.1 Standards Partition. The standards partition shall be organized by type of standard. The

Fig 1
Partition of Standards by Type

four types are process, product, professional, and notation standards. See Fig 1 for the complete partition.

Process standards deal with the series of actions or operations used in engineering a product or delivering a service. The actions or operations make use of methods, tools, and techniques. They give the "whos," "whats," "hows," "wheres," "whens," and levels of the work done in software engineering. Product standards are concerned with the format and content of things. The products are the documented results of the software development and maintenance activities and provide a baseline for future activities. Professional standards deal with all aspects of software engineering that identify it as a profession. An example is a curriculum for a Master of Software Engineering degree. Notation standards deal with the communication of common items among the software engineering professionals in a uniform manner. An example is a glossary. The output of a process is a product; the process is performed by people using tools and techniques within the profession.

3.2 Software Engineering Partition. The software engineering partition shall consist of two parts: job functions and software life cycle. These two parts or perspectives are used in order to compare, judge, evaluate, and determine the scope and content of software engineering standards. See Fig 2 for the software engineering

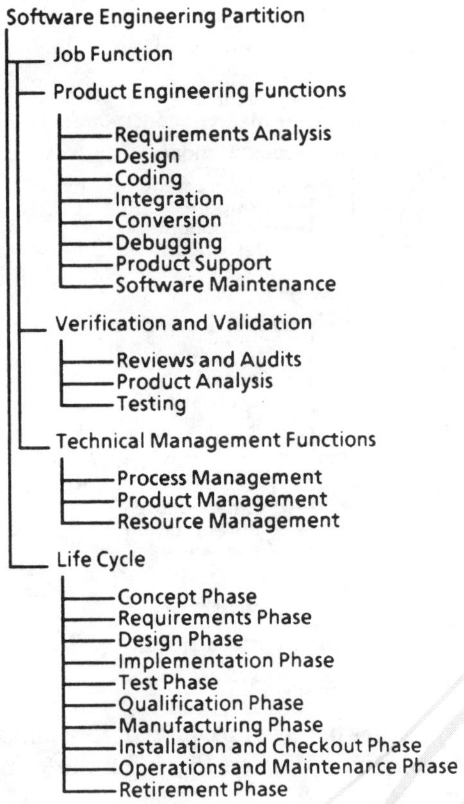

Fig 2
Partition of Software Engineering by Function and Life Cycle

partition. Job functions are the identifiable processes of software engineering. Job functions often occur in parallel. For example, designs are updated as software elements are developed. No strict temporal sequence exists among the job functions since planning, execution, or follow-up within a function will certainly overlap other job functions.

Job functions are divided into three parts: product engineering functions, verification and validation functions, and technical management functions. The three parts contain the major ongoing, parallel activities of producing, checking, and controlling that are not concentrated in a single life cycle phase. The product engineering functions includes those processes that are necessary to define, produce, and support the final software product. Verification and validation functions are the technical activities that check the quality of the product. Technical management functions are those processes that structure and control the engineering functions. Project management is viewed as being related to technical management in the following way: Typically, project management is the use, by one or more organizations, of the technical management functions of process management, product management, and resource management to develop a product within specified resources.

3.3 Taxonomy Framework. The taxonomy framework shall consist of:

(1) Names of the categories in the standards partition and the relationships among the names

(2) Names of the categories in the software engineering partition and the relationships among the names

(3) Rules for composing the framework

(4) Presentation format for the framework

The taxonomy may be presented in different ways, depending on how it can be used most effectively. The rows and columns may be reversed, higher or lower levels of classification can be shown, or only part of the table may be used.

This standard presents three versions of the taxonomy framework for use. The three versions are titled:

(a) Basic Taxonomy Framework (Version A)

(b) Basic Taxonomy Framework (Version B)

(c) Comprehensive Taxonomy Framework

The two Basic Taxonomy Frameworks have the same column labels with the row labels being somewhat different. The row labels for Version A are a selection from the job function portion of the software engineering partition that generally are present in all software life phases and the software life cycle phases. The column labels are the major categories of the standards partition. The row labels for Version B are the complete job function portion of the software engineering partition.

The two Basic Taxonomy Frameworks are illustrated in Figs 3 and 4. The frameworks are presented in the form of a two-dimensional table. An entry in one of the tables is defined by the names from the respective row label and column label of the entry. For example, in Fig 4, the most upper left table entry would be process standards for requirements analysis.

The Comprehensive Taxonomy Framework (see Fig 5) uses the full depth of both the standards partition and the software engineering partition. For presentation purposes, the framework is organized into two parts with the row labels from the standards partition and the column labels from the software engineering partition. For this framework, the entry name is defined by the names of the respective column label and row label of the entry.

The framework composition rules define the layout for the framework and how the entries in the table are composed. The rules are:

(1) The framework is displayed as a two-dimensional table with a set of labels for the rows and a set of labels for the columns.

(2) The names from either the standards partition or the software engineering partition are assigned as the source for the row labels. The remaining partition is the source for the column labels.

(3) A suitable set of names for the row and column labels is selected from the lists shown in Figs 1 and 2, starting at the left and proceeding to the desired level of detail.

(4) The scope of the framework is defined by eliminating those row-column pairs that are not feasible.

(5) An entry in the table is defined by names from the respective row and column of the entry.

Examples of how to classify standards using this taxonomy are contained in Appendix A.

			Type of Standard			
			Process Standard	Product Standard	Professional Standard	Notation Standard
Job Function	Ver & Val	Reviews & Audits				
		Product Analysis				
		Testing				
	Tech Mgmt	Process Management				
		Product Management				
		Resource Management				
S/W Life Cycle		Concept				
		Requirement				
		Design				
		Implementation				
		Test				
		Manufacturing				
		Operation and Maintenance				
		Retirement				

Fig 3
Basic Taxonomy Framework (Version A)

Job Function		Type of Standard			
		Process Standard	Product Standard	Professional Standard	Notation Standard
Product Engineering	Requirements Analysis				
	Design				
	Coding				
	Integration				
	Conversion				
	Debugging				
	Product Support				
	Software Maintenance				
Ver & Val	Reviews and Audits				
	Product Analysis				
	Testing				
Tech Mgmt	Process Management				
	Product Management				
	Resource Management				

Fig 4
Basic Taxonomy Framework (Version B)

Type of Standard		Job Function: Product Engineering								Job Function: Verification & Validation			Job Function: Technical Management		
		Requirements Analysis	Design	Coding	Integration	Conversion	Debugging	Product Support	Software Maintaince	Reviews and Audits	Product Analysis	Testing	Process Management	Product Management	Resource Management
Process	Method														
	Technique														
	Measurement														
Product	Requirements														
	Design														
	Component														
	Description														
	Plan														
	Report														
Professional	Occupational Title														
	Code of Ethics														
	Certification														
	Licensing														
	Curriculum														
Notation	Nomenclature														
	Representation														
	Language														

Fig 5
Comprehensive Taxonomy Framework
(Part 1)

Type Of Standard		Software Life Cycle								
		Concept	Requirements	Design	Implementation	Test	Manufacturing	Installation & Checkout	Operation & Maintenance	Retirement
Process	Method									
	Technique									
	Measurement									
Product	Requirements									
	Design									
	Component									
	Description									
	Plan									
	Report									
Profession	Occupational Title									
	Code of Ethics									
	Certification									
	Licensing									
	Curriculum									
Notation	Nomenclature									
	Representation									
	Language									

Fig 5 (Cont'd)
Comprehensive Taxonomy Framework
(Part 2)

Appendix
Taxonomy Usage Examples

(This Appendix is not a part of ANSI / IEEE Std 1002-1987, IEEE Standard Taxonomy for Software Engineering Standards, but is included for information only.)

This Appendix illustrates how the taxonomy can be used to:

(1) Classify a set of software engineering standards

(2) Annotate software engineering standards with keywords

(3) Characterize a software engineering standards program

(4) Correlate functions and software life cycle viewpoints

A1. Classification of Selected Standards

This section presents a selection of references on software engineering standards. The key for selection was that the reference is publicly available through a trade association, government agency, or national society other than IEEE. The references are listed below with their identifier. The identifiers are placed in the two tables (Figs A1 and A2). The selected standards were classified using the job function table of the Comprehensive Taxonomy Framework organized by software life cycle phase. In a complete example, there would be a job function table for each software life cycle phase. The example presented contains two tables. The first table (see Fig A1) depicts those standards that essentially have equal applicability over most software life cycle phases. The second table (see Fig A2) depicts those standards that are of special importance for the design phase of the software life cycle.

Identifier	*Title*
ICAM	Air Force Materials Laboratory, ICAM Documentation Standards, IDS 150120000A, December 28, 1981.
480	Department of Defense, Configuration Control-Engineering Changes, Deviations, and Waivers, DOD-STD-480A, 1978.[3]
483	Department of Defense, Configuration Management Practices for Systems, Equipment, Munitions, and Computer Programs, MIL-STD-483A, June 4, 1985.[4]
499	Department of Defense, Engineering Management, MIL-STD-499, May 1, 1974.
52779	Department of Defense, Software Quality Assurance Program Requirements, MIL-S-52779A, August 1, 1979.
490	Department of Defense, Specification Practices, MIL-STD-490, June 4, 1985.
RADC	Rome Air Development Center, RADC Computer Software Development Specification, CP 0787796100E, May 1979.
TADSTAD9	Department of Defense, Tactical Digital System Standard, Software Quality Assurance Testing Criteria, TADSTAD 9, 1978.[5]
1521	Department of Defense, Technical Reviews and Audits for Systems, Equipment, and Computer Software, MIL-STD-1521B, June 4, 1985.
2167	Department of Defense, Defense System Software Department, DOD-STD-2167, June 4, 1985.

[3] DOD and MIL publications are available from the Director, US Navy Publications and Printing Service, Eastern Division, 700 Robbins Avenue, Philadelphia, PA 19111.

[4] See footnote 3.

[5] Information on this publication can be obtained by writing to TAD, Chief of Materiel Command Headquarters, Washington, DC 20360.

Identifier	*Title*	
2167.1	Section 5.1	Requirements Analysis
2167.2	Sections 5.2, 5.3	Design
2167.3	Section 5.4	Coding
2167.4	Sections 5.5, 5.6	Integration and Testing
2167.5	Section 5.7	Configuration Management
2167.6	Section 5.8	Quality Evaluation
2167.7	Section 5.8.1.5	Installation and Checkout
2167.8	Sections 4.1, 4.2, 5.9	Project Management
FIPS 38	National Bureau of Standards, Guidelines for Documentation of Computer Programs and Automated Data Systems, Federal Information Processing Standards (FIPS) Publication (PUB) 38, February 15, 1976.[6]	
FIPS 64	National Bureau of Standards, Guidelines for Documentation of Computer Programs and Automated Data Systems for the Initiation Phase, FIPS PUB 64, August 1, 1979.	
FIPS 99	National Bureau of Standards, Guideline: A Framework for the Evaluation and Comparison of Software Development Tools, FIPS PUB 99, March 1983.	
FIPS 101	National Bureau of Standards, Guideline for Lifecycle Validation, Verification, and Testing of Computer Software, FIPS PUB 101, June 1983.	
FIPS 105	National Bureau of Standards, Guideline for Software Documentation Management, FIPS PUB 105, June 1984.	
FIPS 106	National Bureau of Standards, Guideline on Software Maintenance, FIPS PUB 106, July 1984.	
NSAC-39	Nuclear Safety Analysis Center, Verification and Validation for Safety Parameter Display Systems, NSAC-39, December 1981.	
178	Radio Technical Commission for Aeronautics, Software Considerations in Airborne Systems and Equipment Certification, RTCA/DO-178A, March 22, 1985.[7]	
178.1	Section 6	Development Verification and Validation
178.2	Sections 7.1, 7.2	Configuration Management
178.3	Sections 7.1, 7.3	Software Quality Assurance
9650	MITRE, Software Reporting Metrics, ESD-TR-85-145, MTR 9650, Revision 2, November 1985.	

[6] FIPS publications are available from the Standards Processing Coordinator, Institute for Computer Sciences and Technology, National Bureau of Standards, Gaithersburg, MD 20899.

[7] RTCA publications are available from the Radio Technical Commission for Aeronautics (RTCA), 1425 K Street, NW, Suite 500, Washington, DC 20005.

			Type of Standard			
			Process Standard	Product Standard	Professional Standard	Notation Standard
Job Functions	Product Engineering	Requirement Analysis	FIPS 99			
		Design	FIPS 99			
		Coding	FIPS 99			
		Integration	FIPS 99			
		Conversion	FIPS 99			
		Debugging	FIPS 99			
		Product Support	FIPS 99			
		Software Maintenance	FIPS 99			
	V&V	Reviews and Audits	1521,178.1, FIPS 101 NSAC-39			
		Product Analysis	178.1, FIPS 101 NSAC-39			
		Testing	TADSTAD 9, 178.1, FIPS 101, NSAC-39			
	Tech Mgmt	Process Management	52779, 2167.6, 1521, FIPS 105, RADC, 2167.8,178.3	2167		
		Product Management	480, 483, 178.2, 2167.5	483, 2167		
		Resource Management	2167.8, 9650			

Fig A1
Example of General Standard Classification (Phase Independent)

Job Functions			Type of Standard			
			Process Standard	Product Standard	Professional Standard	Notation Standard
Job Functions	Product Engineering	Requirement Analysis	499*, 2167.1*	2167.1*, FIPS 64*, ICAM*		
		Design	2167.2, RADC	2167.2, FIPS 38, ICAM, 490		
		Coding	2167.3*, RADC*	2167.3*, ICAM*		
		Integration	2167.4	2167.4		
		Conversion				
		Debugging				
		Product Support				
		Software Maintenance	FIPS 106*			
	V&V	Reviews and Audits	1521, 178.1, FIPS 101, NSAC-39			
		Product Analysis	178.1, FIPS 101 NSAC-39			
		Testing	TADSTAD 9, 178.1, FIPS 101, NSAC-39			
	Tech Mgmt	Process Management	52779, 2167.6, 1521, FIPS 105, RADC, 2167.8, 178.3	2167		
		Product Management	480, 483, 178.2, 2167.5	483, 2167		
		Resource Management	2167.8, 9650			

Legend *Examine for planning purposes

Fig A2
Example of General Standard Classification (Design Phase)

A2. An Approach to Annotating Software Engineering Standards with Keywords

The process of analysis, selection, and comparing of standards will benefit from a systematic means of keyword identification, which may then be incorporated into an organization's classification and retrieval procedures. An example set of keyword formation rules follows:

(1) Software engineering standards shall be classified with keywords. This shall be accomplished as part of a standard's development.

(2) Keywords shall be included in a standard's introduction. Keyword inclusion shall use the following format: "Keywords applicable to this standard are: Keyword 1, Keyword 2, . . ., Keyword n."

(3) Keywords shall be limited to words or phrases as contained in IEEE Std 1002-1987.

(4) Multiple keywords may be used in classifying a standard.

(5) Commas shall be used to separate keywords. The keyword shall will be terminated with a period.

(6) A standard shall be assigned at least one keyword from both the standards partition and software engineering partition. Within the categories of function and life cycle, multiple primary keywords may be selected.

The application of the keyword rules to some of the IEEE software engineering standards is illustrated in the following list:

Example #1. ANSI/IEEE Std 729-1983, IEEE Standard Glossary of Software Engineering Terminology. Keywords applicable to this standard are: nomenclature standard, notation standard, software engineering.

Example #2. ANSI/IEEE Std 730-1984, IEEE Standard for Software Quality Assurance Plans. Keywords applicable to this standard are: process management, product standard, software engineering, technical management.

Example #3. ANSI/IEEE Std 828-1983, IEEE Standard for Software Configuration Management Plans. Keywords applicable to this standard are: product management, product standard, technical management, software engineering.

Example #4. ANSI/IEEE Std 829-1983, IEEE Standard for Software Test Documentation. Keywords applicable to this standard are: product standard, software engineering, testing, verification and validation.

Example #5. ANSI/IEEE Std 830-1984, IEEE Guide to Software Requirements Specifications. Keywords applicable to this standard are: product engineering, product standard, requirements analysis, software engineering.

Example #6. ANSI/IEEE Std 983-1986, IEEE Guide to Software Quality Assurance Planning. Keywords applicable to this standard are: process standard, process management, technical management, software engineering.

Example #7. ANSI/IEEE Std 1008-1987, IEEE Standard for Software Unit Testing. Keywords applicable to this standard are: process standard, testing, verification and validation, software engineering.

A3. Application of Taxonomy to IEEE Software Engineering Standards (SES) Program

The IEEE Technical Committee on Software Engineering has an active program for software engineering standards. Listed below are the standards that are complete and those that are still in progress. The list of standards has been categorized by the taxonomy. To do that, three tables were created. The first table (see Fig A3) consists of the job function portion of the software engineering partition down the side and standards partition across the top. This orientation was chosen for presentation purposes.

Each entry on the standards list below was placed in the appropriate table entry. The S, R, and G refer to standard, recommended practice, and guide, respectively. The empty entries indicate possible areas for future standards.

The second and third tables use the standards partition down the side and functions across the top. The next lower level of detail was added for the standards partition. See Figs A4 and A5.

Approved Software Engineering Standards

Ref	*Description*
729	IEEE Standard Glossary or Software Engineering Terminology
730	IEEE Standard for Software Quality Assurance Plans
828	IEEE Standard for Software Configuration Management Plans

Ref	*Description*
829	IEEE Standard for Software Test Documentation
830	IEEE Guide to Software Requirements Specifications
983	IEEE Guide for Software Quality Assurance Planning
990	IEEE Guide for the Use of Ada* As a PDL
1002	IEEE Standard Taxonomy for Software Engineering Standards
1008	IEEE Standard for Software Unit Testing
1012	IEEE Standard for Software Verification and Validation Plans
1016	IEEE Recommended Practice for Software Design Descriptions

Approved Software Engineering Standards Projects

Ref	*Description*
P982	Standard for Software Reliability Measurement
P1028	Standard for Software Reviews and Audits
P1042	Guide for Software Configuration Management
P1044	Standard Classification of Software Errors, Faults, and Failures
P1045	Standard for Software Productivity Metrics
P1058	Standard for the Software Project Management Plan
P1059	Guide for Software Verification and Validation
P1060	Standard for Software Maintenance
P1061	Standard for Software Quality Metrics
P1062	Guide for Third Party Software Acquisition
P1063	Standard for User Documentation
P1074	Standard for the Software Life Cycle Processes

A4. Job Function to Software Life Cycle Correlation

In some sense, job functions and phases can be correlated to each other. The purpose of this section is to illustrate that relationship. See Fig A6.

Note that in the product engineering and verification and validation categories each row is filled in to indicate where

(1) the planning or monitoring activity takes place (empty square)

(2) the focus of the phase and job function partially coincide (shaded square)

(3) the focus of the phase and job function directly coincide (dark square)

For product engineering and verification and validation activities, this indicates the respective phases for which these activities build, reach and stay at peak effort, and then taper off. The maintenance phase is typically a repeat of the basic software life cycle, and this is denoted in the respective column by an asterisk.

Note that for the technical management functions, activities generally happen across all phases. This is indicated by dark squares for all phases for these job functions.

* Ada is a registered trademark of the U.S. Government, AJPO.

			Type of Standard			
			Process Standard	Product Standard	Professional Standard	Notation Standard
Job Functions	Product Engineering	Requirement Analysis	1074(S)	830(G)		729, 1002(S)
		Design	1074(S)	1016(R)		729(S), 990(R), 1002(S), 1016(R)
		Coding	1074(S)			729(S), 1002(S)
		Integration	1074(S)			729(S), 1002(S)
		Conversion	1074(S)			729(S), 1002(S)
		Debugging	1074(S)			729(S), 1002(S)
		Product Support	1074(S)	1063(S)		729(S), 1002(S)
		Software Maintenance	1060(S), 1074(S)			729(S), 1002(S)
	V & V	Review and Audits	1028(S), 1074(S)	1012(S)		729(S), 1002(S)
		Product Analysis	1059(G)			729(S), 1002(S)
		Testing	829(S), 1008(S), 1012(S), 1074(S), 1059(G)	829(S), 1012(S)		729(S), 1002(S)
	Tech Mgmt	Process Management	1028(S), 1062(S), 1074(S), 983(G), 1061(S)	730(S), 1058(S)		729(S), 1002(S)
		Product Management	982(S), 1028(S), 1042(G), 1044(S), 1074(S)	828(S), 1063(S)		729(S), 1002(S)
		Resource Management	1045(S)			729(S), 1002(S)

Fig A3
Classification of IEEE Software Engineering Standards (Gross Level)

Type of Standard		Job Function: Product Engineering — Requirements Analysis	Design	Coding	Integration	Conversion	Debugging	Software Maintenance	Product Support
Process	Method	1074	1074	1074	1074	1074	1074	1060, 1074	1074
Process	Technique								
Process	Measurement								
Product	Requirement	830							
Product	Design		1016						
Product	Component								
Product	Description								1063
Product	Plan								
Product	Report								
Profession	Occupational Title								
Profession	Code of Ethics								
Profession	Certification								
Profession	Licensing								
Profession	Curriculum								
Notat	Nomenclature	729,1002	729,1002	729,1002	729,1002	729,1002	729,1002	729,1002	729,1002
Notat	Representation		1016						
Notat	Language		990						

Fig A4
Classification of IEEE Software Engineering Standards (Refined Level—Part I)

Type of Standard		Job Function					
		Technical Management Functions			Verification & Validation		
		Process Management	Product Management	Resource Management	Review and Audits	Product Analysis	Testing
Process	Method	983,1028,1062,1074	1028,1042,1074	1074	1028, 1074	1074	829, 1008, 1074
	Technique						
	Measurement	1061	982, 1044	1045			
Product	Requirement						
	Design						
	Component						
	Description		1063				829
	Plan	730, 1058	828		1012	1012	829, 1012
	Report						829
Profession	Occupational						
	Code of Ethics						
	Certification						
	Licensing						
	Curriculum						
Notat	Nomenclature	729,1002	729,1002	729,1002	729,1002	729,1002	729,1002
	Representation						
	Language						

Fig A5
Classification of IEEE Software Engineering Standards (Refined Level—Part II)

Legend (symbols in table): P = Primary Role (solid box); S = Support Role (hatched box); M = Planning/Monitoring role (open box); * = Repeat of Life Cycle

Job Function		Concept	Requirements Definition	Design	Implementation	Test	Manufacturing	Installation & Checkout	Operation & Maintenance	Retirement
Product Engineering	Requirements Analysis	P	P	S	M	M	P	M	*	
	Design	S	S	P	S	M	S	M	*	
	Coding	M	M	S	P	S	S	M	*	
	Integration	M	S	S	S	P	P	M	*	
	Conversion	M	S	S	S	S	S	P	*	
	Debugging	M	M	S	P	P	S	S	*	
	Product Support	M	S	S	S	S	S	P	P	P
	Software Maintenance	M	M	M	M	M	S	S	P	S
V & V	Review and Audits	S	P	P	P	P	P	P	*	M
	Product Analysis	M	P	P	P	S	S	S	*	
	Testing	M	M	S	S	P	P	S	*	
Tech Mgmt	Process Management	P	P	P	P	P	P	P	P	M
	Product Management	S	P	P	P	P	P	P	P	M
	Resource Management	P	P	P	P	P	P	P	P	M

Legend:
- Primary Role
- Support Role
- Planning/Monitoring role
- * Repeat of Life Cycle

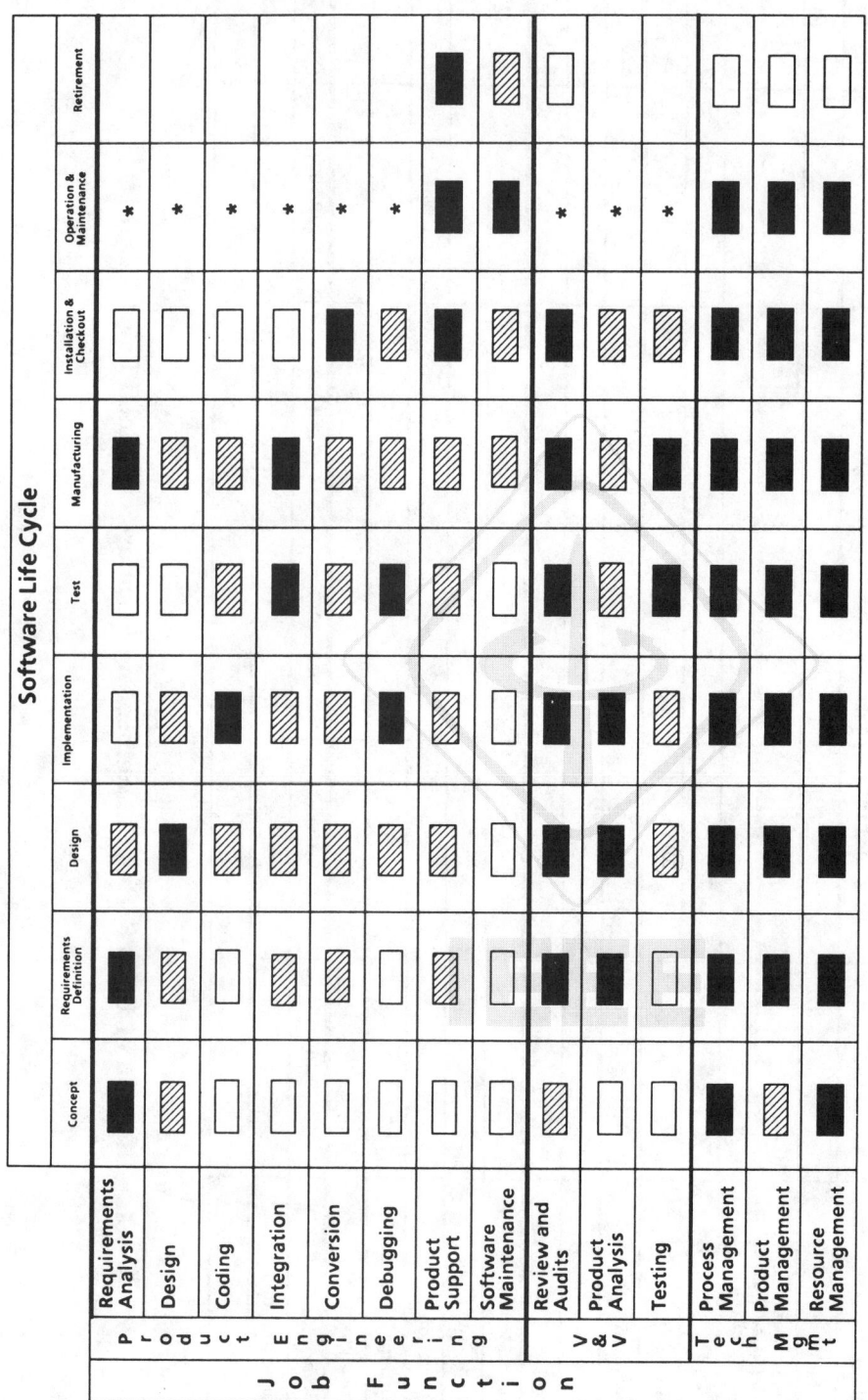

Fig A6
Job Function–Software Life Cycle Correlation

Acknowledgements

The following organizations provided support for the development of this standard:

AccuRay Corporation
Applied Physics Laboratory
AT&T Bell
Canada Bell
Northern Research
The Boeing Company
Bradley University
Computer Sciences Corporation
E-Systems
Edinboro University of Pennsylvania
Hewlett-Packard
Hughes
IBM
INCO, Inc.
ITT Corporation
McDonnell Douglas
Mervine and Pallesen
MIV-MEDA Ltd.
NCR Corporation
Northern Telecom
Pratt & Whitney Aircraft
Programming
Environments, Inc.
Sanders Associates Software
Engineering Associates Software
Quality Engineering
Teledyne Brown Engineering
Tennessee Valley Authority
The Algoma Steel Corporation, Ltd.
U.S. Department of Housing and Urban Development
U.S. Department of Transportation

This support does not constitute or imply approval or endorsement of this standard.

IEEE

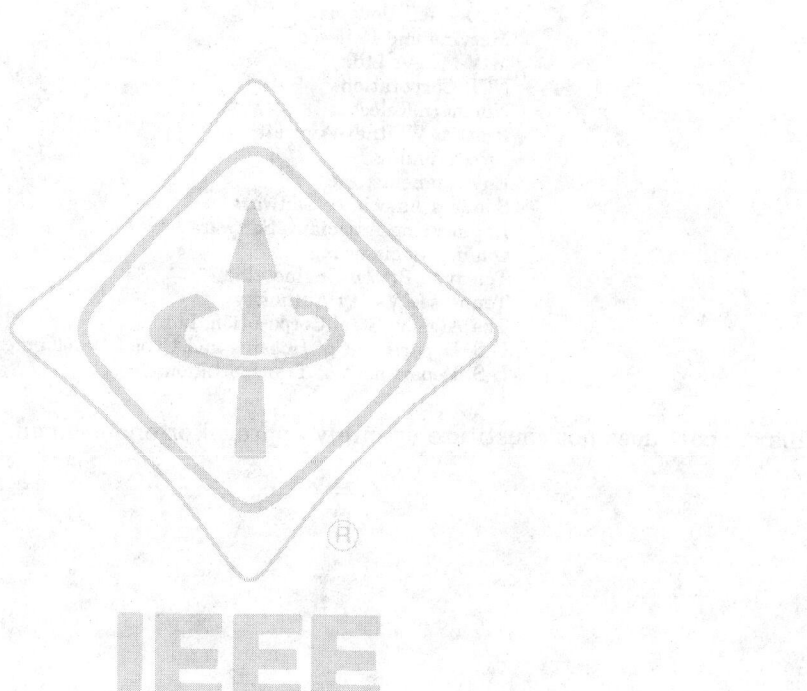

ANSI/IEEE
Std 1008-1987

An American National Standard

IEEE Standard for Software Unit Testing

Sponsor

Software Engineering Standards Subcommittee of the Technical Committee on Software Engineering of the IEEE Computer Society

Approved December 11, 1986

IEEE Standards Board

Approved July 28, 1986

American National Standards Institute

The Institute of Electrical and Electronics Engineers, Inc
345 East 47th Street, New York, NY 10017, USA

Secretary, IEEE Standards Board
345 East 47th Street
New York, NY 10017
USA

Foreword

(This Foreword is not a part of ANSI/IEEE Std 1008-1987, IEEE Standard for Software Unit Testing.)

Objectives

This standard's primary objective is to specify a standard approach to software unit testing that can be used as a basis for sound software engineering practice.

A second objective is to describe the software engineering concepts and testing assumptions on which this standard approach is based. This information is contained in Appendix B. Note that Appendix B is not a part of this standard.

A third objective is to provide guidance and resource information to assist with the implementation and usage of the standard unit testing approach. This information is contained in Appendixes A, C, and D. Note that these Appendixes are not a part of this standard.

Motivation

A consensus definition of sound unit testing provides a baseline for the evaluation of specific approaches. It also aids communication by providing a standard decomposition of the unit testing process.

Audience

The primary audience for this standard is unit testers and unit test supervisors. This standard was developed to assist those who provide input to, perform, supervise, monitor, and evaluate unit testing.

Relationship with Other Software Engineering Standards

ANSI/IEEE Std 829-1983, IEEE Standard for Software Test Documentation, describes the basic information needs and results of software testing. This unit testing standard requires the use of the test design specification and test summary report specified in ANSI/IEEE Std 829-1983.

This standard is one of a series aimed at establishing the norms of professional practice in software engineering. Any of the other software engineering standards in the series may be used in conjunction with it.

Terminology

Terminology in this standard is consistent with ANSI/IEEE Std 729-1983, IEEE Standard Glossary of Software Engineering Terminology. To avoid inconsistency when the glossary is revised, its definitions are not repeated in this standard.

The *test unit* referred to in this standard is a specific case of the *test item* referred to in ANSI/IEEE 829-1983. The term *test unit* is used because of this standard's narrower scope.

The use of the term *specification, description,* or *document* refers to data recorded on either an electronic or paper medium.

The word *must* and imperative verb forms identify mandatory material within the standard. The words *should* and *may* identify optional material.

Overview

The unit testing process is composed of three *phases* that are partitioned into a total of eight basic *activities* as follows:

(1) *Perform the test planning*
- (a) Plan the general approach, resources, and schedule
- (b) Determine features to be tested
- (c) Refine the general plan

(2) *Acquire the test set*
- (a) Design the set of tests
- (b) Implement the refined plan and design

(3) *Measure the test unit*
   (a) Execute the test procedures
   (b) Check for termination
   (c) Evaluate the test effort and unit

The major dataflows into and out of the phases are shown in Fig A.

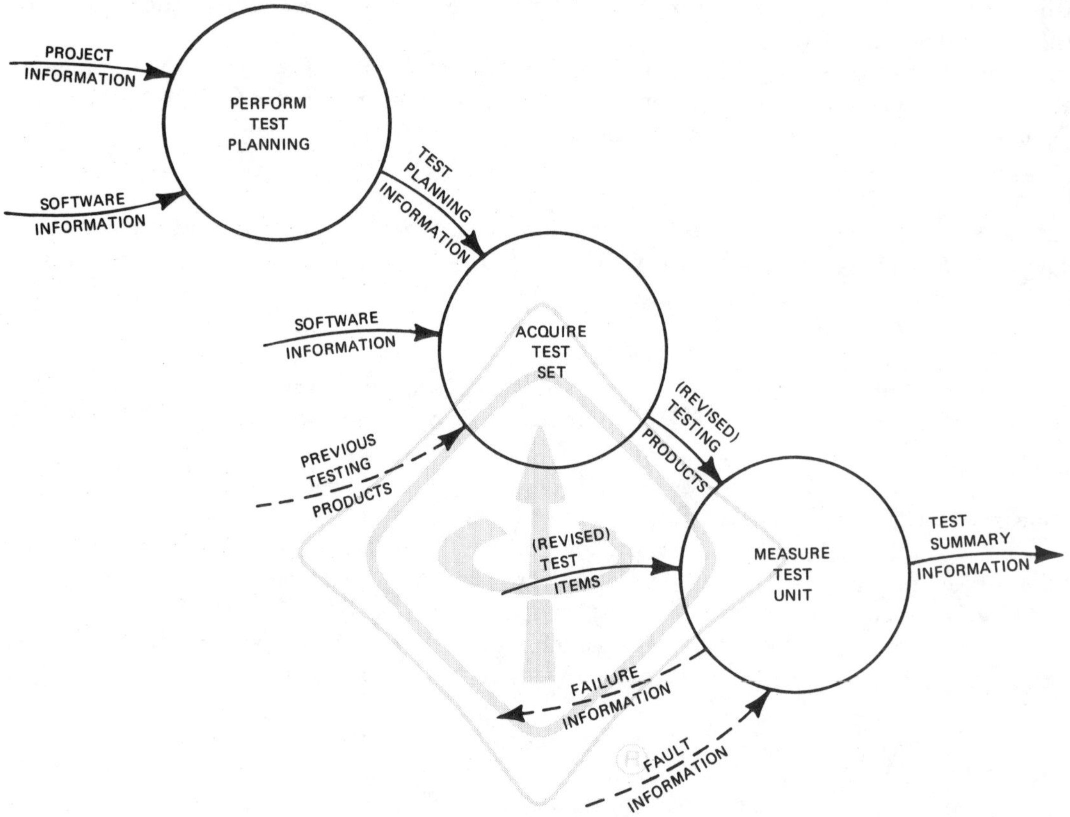

Fig A
Major Dataflows of the Software Unit Testing Phases

Within a phase, each basic activity is associated with its own set of inputs and outputs and is composed of a series of tasks. The inputs, tasks, and outputs for each activity are specified in the body of this standard.

The set of outputs from all activities must contain sufficient information for the creation of at least two documents—a test design specification and a test summary report. Both documents must conform to the specifications in ANSI/IEEE Std 829-1983.

History

Work on this standard began in February 1983, following announcement of the formation of the task group in the technical and commercial press in late 1982. The project authorization request was approved by the IEEE Standards Board on June 23, 1983 following the second meeting. A total of seven meetings held throughout the United States at three month intervals produced the draft submitted for ballot in March 1985. A total of over 90 persons contributed to the initial development of this standard. Contributors are those individuals who either attended a working-group meeting, submitted written comments on a draft, or both.

This standard was developed by a working group with the following members:

David Gelperin, *Chairperson*

Pat Wilburn, *Cochairperson*

A. Frank Ackerman
Craig Adams
David Adams
Jack Barnard
Wanda Beck
Boris Beizer
K. Mack Bishop
Jill E. Boogaard
Milt Boyd
Nathan B. Bradley
Martha Branstad
Fletcher Buckley
John W. Cain
Christopher Cooke
L. L. Doc Craddock
Palmer Craig
Michael Cramer
Dave Dahlinghaus
Noah Davids
Henry Davis
Bruce Dawson
Claudia Dencker
Michael Deutsch
Judie Divita
Jim Dobbins
David C. Doty
Bill Dupras
Jim Edwards
Karen Fairchild
Peter Farrell-Vinay
Thom Foote-Lennox
Ken Foster
John Fox
Roger Fujii
Ross Gagliano
Mark Gerhard
Ed Gibson
Therese Gilbertson
Gary Girard
Keith Gordon
Paul Grizenko
Jeff Grove
Ismet Gungor
Mark Heinrich
Rudolph Hodges
R. A. Kessler
Tom Kurihara
Costas Labovites
Frank LaMonica
F. C. Lim
Philip C. Marriott
Debra L. McCusker
Charlie McCutcheon
Rudolf van Megen
Denis Meredith
Edward Miller, Jr
William Milligan
Marcus Mullins
W. M. Murray
Bruce Nichols
Dennis Nickle
Larry Nitzsche
John Owens
William Perry
Gerald Peterson
Bob Poston
Patricia Powell
Samuel T. Redwine, Jr
Sanford Rosen
Hans Schaefer
Eric Schnellman
Harvey Schock
Al Sema, Jr
Harlan Seyfer
Victor Shtern
Rick Simkin
Wayne Smith
Harry Sneed
Hugh B. Spillane
Ben Sun
Murray Tabachnick
Barbara Taute
Leonard Tripp
William S. Turner III
John Vance
Guy Vogt
Dolores Wallace
John Walter
John C. Wang
Cheryl Webb
William Wilson
Ed Yasi
Natalie C. Yopconka

The following persons were on the balloting committee that approved this document for submission to the IEEE Standards Board:

Frank Ackerman
Leo Beltracchi
Ron Berlack
William Boll, Jr
F. Buckley
Douglas Burt
Homer Carney
Skip Carpenter, Jr
Jung Chung
Won Lyang Chung
Francois Coallier
Richard Coates
A.J. Cote, Jr
Patricia Daggett
Jim Darling
N.S. Davids
Henry Davis
Peter Denny
A. Dniestrowski
David Dobratz
David Doty
Walter DuBlanica
R.E. Dwyer
Mary Eads
John Earls
L.G. Egan
John Fendrich
Glenn Fields
Charles Finnell
Jim Flournoy
Violet Foldes
Julian Forster
Rick Fredrick
Lee Gagner
M. Galinier
David Gelperin
L.M. Gunther
David Gustafson
Russell Gustin
Virl Haas
William Hanrahan
Carolyn Harrison
G.B. Hawthorne
Clark Hay
Leslie Heselton, III
Mark Holthouse
John Horch
Frank Jay
Laurel Kaleda
Adi Kasad
Ron Kenett
Bob Kessler
Gary Kroc
Robert Lane
Greg Larsen
F.C. Lim
Bertil Lindberg
Gary Lindsay
Ben Livson
M. Malagarois
W.A. Mandeville
Stuart Marcotte
Philip C. Marriott
Roger Martin
Paul Mauro
Belden Menkus
Jerome Mersky
Gene Morun
Hironobu Nagano
Geraldine Neidhart
G.A. Niblack
Dennis Nickle
Larry Nitzsche
Peter Olsen
Wilma Osborne
Bill Perry
Poul Grav Peterson
Donald Pfeiffer
Sharon Cobb-Pierson
Robert Poston
Thomas Radi
Meir Razy
Larry Reed
R. Waldo Roth
Raymond Sandborgh
Hans Schaefer
Norm Schneidewind
Eric Schnellman
Wolf Schnoege
Robert Schueppert
David Schultz
Leonard Seagren
Gary Shea
Craig Shermer
Robert Shillato
David Siefert
David Simkins
Shirley Gloss-Soler
William Sutcliffe
K.C. Tai
Barbara Taute
Paul Thompson
Terrence Tillmanns
R.L. Van Tilburg
Dolores Wallace
M.L. Weisbein
Joseph Weiss
N.P. Wilburn
Paul Wolfgang
Charles Wortz
Edward Yasi
Zhou Zhi Ying
Natalie Yopconka

When the IEEE Standards Board approved this standard on December 11, 1986, it had the following membership:

John E. May, *Chairman*

Irving Kolodny, *Vice Chairman*

Sava I. Sherr, *Secretary*

James H. Beall
Fletcher J. Buckley
Paul G. Cummings
Donald C. Fleckenstein
Jay Forster
Daniel L. Goldberg
Kenneth D. Hendrix
Irvin N. Howell
Jack Kinn
Joseph L. Koepfinger*
Edward Lohse
Lawrence V. McCall
Donald T. Michael*
Marco W. Migliaro
Stanley Owens
John P. Riganati
Frank L. Rose
Robert E. Rountree
Martha Sloan
Oley Wanaselja
J. Richard Weger
William B. Wilkens
Charles J. Wylie
Donald W. Zipse

*Member emeritus

Contents

An American National Standard

IEEE Standard for Software Unit Testing

1. Scope and References

1.1 Inside the Scope. Software unit testing is a process that includes the performance of test planning, the acquisition of a test set, and the measurement of a test unit against its requirements. Measuring entails the use of sample data to exercise the unit and the comparison of the unit's actual behavior with its required behavior as specified in the unit's requirements documentation.

This standard defines an integrated approach to systematic and documented unit testing. The approach uses unit design and unit implementation information, in addition to unit requirements, to determine the completeness of the testing.

This standard describes a testing process composed of a hierarchy of phases, activities, and tasks and defines a minimum set of tasks for each activity. Additional tasks may be added to any activity.

This standard requires the performance of each activity. For each task within an activity, this standard requires either that the task be performed, or that previous results be available and be reverified. This standard also requires the preparation of two documents specified in ANSI/IEEE Std 829-1983 [2][1]. These documents are the Test Design Specification and the Test Summary Report.

General unit test planning should occur during overall test planning. This general unit test planning activity is covered by this standard, although the balance of the overall test planning process is outside the scope of this standard.

This standard may be applied to the unit testing of any digital computer software or firmware. However, this standard does *not* specify any class of software or firmware to which it must be applied, nor does it specify any class of software or firmware that must be unit tested. This standard applies to the testing of newly developed and modified units.

This standard is applicable whether or not the unit tester is also the developer.

1.2 Outside the Scope. The results of some overall test planning tasks apply to all testing levels (for example, identify security and privacy constraints). Such tasks are not considered a part of the unit testing process, although they directly affect it.

While the standard identifies a need for failure analysis information and software fault correction, it does not specify a software debugging process.

This standard does not address other components of a comprehensive unit verification and validation process, such as reviews (for example, walkthroughs, inspections), static analysis (for example, consistency checks, data flow analysis), or formal analysis (for example, proof of correctness, symbolic execution).

This standard does not require the use of specific test facilities or tools. This standard does not imply any particular methodology for documentation control, configuration management, quality assurance, or management of the testing process.

1.3 References. This standard shall be used in conjunction with the following publications.

[1] ANSI/IEEE Std 729-1983, IEEE Standard Glossary of Software Engineering Terminology.[2]

[2] ANSI/IEEE Std 829-1983, IEEE Standard for Software Test Documentation.

[1] The numbers in brackets correspond to the references listed in 1.3 of this standard.

[2] These publications are available from American National Standards Institute, Sales Department, 1430 Broadway, New York, NY 10018 and from IEEE Service Center, 445 Hoes Lane, Piscataway, NJ 08854.

2. Definitions

This section defines key terms used in this standard but not included in ANSI/IEEE Std 729-1983 [1] or ANSI/IEEE Std 829-1983 [2].

characteristic. *See:* **data characteristic** or **software characteristic.**

data characteristic. An inherent, possibly accidental, trait, quality, or property of data (for example, arrival rates, formats, value ranges, or relationships between field values).

feature. *See:* **software feature.**

incident. *See:* **software test incident.**

nonprocedural programming language. A computer programming language used to express the parameters of a problem rather than the steps in a solution (for example, report writer or sort specification languages). Contrast with **procedural programming language.**

procedural programming language. A computer programming language used to express the sequence of operations to be performed by a computer (for example, COBOL). Contrast with **nonprocedural programming language.**

software characteristic. An inherent, possibly accidental, trait, quality, or property of software (for example, functionality, performance, attributes, design constraints, number of states, lines of branches).

software feature. A software characteristic specified or implied by requirements documentation (for example, functionality, performance, attributes, or design constraints).

software test incident. Any event occuring during the execution of a software test that requires investigation.

state data. Data that defines an internal state of the test unit and is used to establish that state or compare with existing states.

test objective. An identified set of software features to be measured under specified conditions by comparing actual behavior with the required behavior described in the software documentation.

test set architecture. The nested relationships between sets of test cases that directly reflect the hierarchic decomposition of the test objectives.

test unit.[3] A set of one or more computer program modules together with associated control data, (for example, tables), usage procedures, and operating procedures that satisfy the following conditions:

(1) All modules are from a single computer program

(2) At least one of the new or changed modules in the set has not completed the unit test[4]

(3) The set of modules together with its associated data and procedures are the sole object of a testing process

unit. *See:* **test unit.**

unit requirements documentation. Documentation that sets forth the functional, interface, performance, and design constraint requirements for the test unit.

3. Unit Testing Activities

This section specifies the activities involved in the unit testing process and describes the associated input, tasks, and output. The activities described are as follows:

(1) Perform test planning phase
  (a) Plan the general approach, resources, and schedule
  (b) Determine features to be tested
  (c) Refine the general plan
(2) Acquire test set phase
  (a) Design the set of tests
  (b) Implement the refined plan and design
(3) Measure test unit phase
  (a) Execute the test procedures
  (b) Check for termination
  (c) Evaluate the test effort and unit

When more than one unit is to be unit tested (for example, all those associated with a software project), the Plan activity should address the total set of test units and should not be repeated for each test unit. The other activities must be performed at least once for each unit.

Under normal conditions, these activities are sequentially initiated except for the Execute and Check cycle as illustrated in Fig 1. When per-

[3] A test unit may occur at any level of the design hierarchy from a single module to a complete program. Therefore, a test unit may be a module, a few modules, or a complete computer program along with associated data and procedures.

[4] A test unit may contain one or more modules that have already been unit tested.

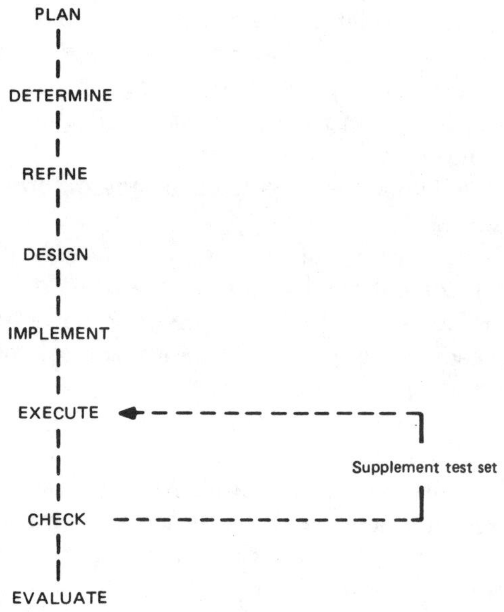

Fig 1
Unit Testing Activities

forming any of the activities except Plan, improper performance of a preceding activity or external events (for example, schedule, requirements, or design changes) may result in the need to redo one or more of the preceding activities and then return to the one being performed.

During the testing process, a test design specification and a test summary report must be developed. Other test documents may be developed. All test documents must conform to the ANSI/IEEE Std 829-1983 [2]. In addition, all test documents must have identified authors and be dated.

The test design specification will derive its information from the Determine, Refine, and Design activities. The test summary report will derive its information from all of the activities.

3.1 Plan the General Approach, Resources, and Schedule. General unit test planning should occur during overall test planning and be recorded in the corresponding planning document.

3.1.1 Plan Inputs

(1) Project plans

(2) Software requirements documentation

3.1.2 Plan Tasks

(1) *Specify a General Approach to Unit Testing.* Identify risk areas to be addressed by the testing. Specify constraints on characteristic determination (for example, features that must be tested), test design, or test implementation (for example, test sets that must be used).

Identify existing sources of input, output, and state data (for example, test files, production files, test data generators). Identify general techniques for data validation. Identify general techniques to be used for output recording, collection, reduction, and validation. Describe provisions for application software that directly interfaces with the units to be tested.

(2) *Specify Completeness Requirements.* Identify the areas (for example, features, procedures, states, functions, data characteristics, instructions) to be covered by the unit test set and the degree of coverage required for each area.

When testing a unit during software development, every software feature must be covered by a test case or an approved exception. The same should hold during software maintenance for any unit testing.

When testing a unit implemented with a procedural language (for example, COBOL) during software development, every instruction that can be reached and executed must be covered by a test case or an approved exception, except for instructions contained in modules that have been separately unit tested. The same should hold during software maintenance for the testing of a unit implemented with a procedural language.

(3) *Specify Termination Requirements.* Specify the requirements for normal termination of the unit testing process. Termination requirements must include satisfying the completeness requirements.

Identify any conditions that could cause abnormal termination of the unit testing process (for example, detecting a major design fault, reaching a schedule deadline) and any notification procedures that apply.

(4) *Determine Resource Requirements.* Estimate the resources required for test set acquisition, initial execution, and subsequent repetition of testing activities. Consider hardware, access time (for example, dedicated computer time), communications or system software, test tools, test files, and forms or other supplies. Also consider the need for unusually large volumes of forms and supplies.

Identify resources needing preparation and the parties responsible. Make arrangements for these resources, including requests for resources that require significant lead time (for example, customized test tools).

Identify the parties responsible for unit testing and unit debugging. Identify personnel requirements including skills, number, and duration.

(5) *Specify a General Schedule.* Specify a schedule constrained by resource and test unit availability for all unit testing activity.

3.1.3 Plan Outputs

(1) General unit test planning information (from 3.1.2(1) through (5) inclusive)

(2) Unit test general resource requests—if produced from 3.1.2(4)

3.2 Determine Features To Be Tested

3.2.1 Determine Inputs

(1) Unit requirements documentation

(2) Software architectural design documentation—if needed

3.2.2 Determine Tasks

(1) *Study the Functional Requirements.* Study each function described in the unit requirements documentation. Ensure that each function has a unique identifier. When necessary, request clarification of the requirements.

(2) *Identify Additional Requirements and Associated Procedures.* Identify requirements other than functions (for example, performance, attributes, or design constraints) associated with software characteristics that can be effectively tested at the unit level. Identify any usage or operating procedures associated only with the unit to be tested. Ensure that each additional requirement and procedure has a unique identifier. When necessary, request clarification of the requirements.

(3) *Identify States of the Unit.* If the unit requirements documentation specifies or implies multiple states (for example, inactive, ready to receive, processing) software, identify each state and each valid state transition. Ensure that each state and state transition has a unique identifier. When necessary, request clarification of the requirements.

(4) *Identify Input and Output Data Characteristics.* Identify the input and output data structures of the unit to be tested. For each structure, identify characteristics, such as arrival rates, formats, value ranges, and relationships between field values. For each characteristic, specify its valid ranges. Ensure that each characteristic has a unique identifier. When necessary, request clarification of the requirements.

(5) *Select Elements to be Included in the Testing.* Select the features to be tested. Select the associated procedures, associated states, associated state transitions, and associated data characteristics to be included in the testing. Invalid and valid input data must be selected. When complete testing is impractical, information regarding the expected use of the unit should be used to determine the selections. Identify the risk associated with unselected elements.

Enter the selected features, procedures, states, state transitions, and data characteristics in the *Features to be Tested* section of the unit's Test Design Specification.

3.2.3 Determine Outputs

(1) List of elements to be included in the testing (from 3.2.2(5))

(2) Unit requirements clarification requests—if produced from 3.2.2(1) through (4) inclusive

3.3 Refine the General Plan

3.3.1 Refine Inputs

(1) List of elements to be included in the testing (from 3.2.2(5))

(2) General unit test planning information (from 3.1.2(1) through (5) inclusive)

3.3.2 Refine Tasks

(1) *Refine the Approach.* Identify existing test cases and test procedures to be considered for use. Identify any special techniques to be used for data validation. Identify any special techniques to be used for output recording, collection, reduction, and validation.

Record the refined approach in the *Approach Refinements* section of the unit's test design specification.

(2) *Specify Special Resource Requirements.* Identify any special resources needed to test the unit (for example, software that directly interfaces with the unit). Make preparations for the identified resources.

Record the special resource requirements in the *Approach Refinements* section of the unit's test design specification.

(3) *Specify a Detailed Schedule.* Specify a schedule for the unit testing based on support software, special resource, and unit availability and integration schedules. Record the schedule in the *Approach Refinements* section of the unit's test design specification.

3.3.3 Refine Outputs

(1) Specific unit test planning information (from 3.3.2(1) through (3) inclusive)

(2) Unit test special resource requests—if produced from 3.3.2(2).

3.4 Design the Set of Tests

3.4.1 Design Inputs

(1) Unit requirements documentation

(2) List of elements to be included in the testing (from 3.2.2(5))

(3) Unit test planning information (from 3.1.2(1) and (2) and 3.3.2(1))

(4) Unit design documentation

(5) Test specifications from previous testing—if available

3.4.2 Design Tasks

(1) *Design the Architecture of the Test Set.* Based on the features to be tested and the conditions specified or implied by the selected associated elements (for example, procedures, state transitions, data characteristics), design a hierarchically decomposed set of test objectives so that each lowest-level objective can be directly tested by a few test cases. Select appropriate existing test cases. Associate groups of test-case identifiers with the lowest-level objectives. Record the hierarchy of objectives and associated test case identifiers in the *Test Identification* section of the unit's test design specification.

(2) *Obtain Explicit Test Procedures as Required.* A combination of the unit requirements documentation, test planning information, and test-case specifications may implicitly specify the unit test procedures and therefore minimize the need for explicit specification. Select existing test procedures that can be modified or used without modification.

Specify any additional procedures needed either in a supplementary section in the unit's test design specification or in a separate procedure specification document. Either choice must be in accordance with the information required by ANSI/IEEE Std 829-1983 [2]. When the correlation between test cases and procedures is not readily apparent, develop a table relating them and include it in the unit's test design specification.

(3) *Obtain the Test Case Specifications.* Specify the new test cases. Existing specifications may be referenced.

Record the specifications directly or by reference in either a supplementary section of the unit's test design specification or in a separate document. Either choice must be in accordance with the information required by ANSI/IEEE Std 829-1983 [2].

(4) *Augment, as Required, the Set of Test-Case Specifications Based on Design Information.* Based on information about the unit's design, update as required the test set architecture in accordance with 3.4.2(1). Consider the characteristics of selected algorithms and internal data structures.

Identify control flows and changes to internal data that must be recorded. Anticipate special recording difficulties that might arise, for example, from a need to trace control flow in complex algorithms or from a need to trace changes in internal data structures (for example, stacks or trees). When necessary, request enhancement of the unit design (for example, a formatted data structure dump capability) to increase the testability of the unit.

Based on information in the unit's design, specify any newly identified test cases and complete any partial test case specifications in accordance with 3.4.2(3).

(5) *Complete the Test Design Specification.* Complete the test design specification for the unit in accordance with ANSI/IEEE Std 829-1983 [2].

3.4.3 Design Outputs

(1) Unit test design specification (from 3.4.2(5))

(2) Separate test procedure specifications—if produced from 3.4.2(2)

(3) Separate test-case specifications—if produced from 3.4.2(3) or (4)

(4) Unit design enhancement requests—if produced from 3.4.2(4)

3.5 Implement the Refined Plan and Design

3.5.1 Implement Inputs

(1) Unit test planning information (from 3.1.2(1), (4), and (5) and 3.3.2(1) through (3) inclusive)

(2) Test-case specifications in the unit test design specification or separate documents (from 3.4.2(3) and (4)

(3) Software data structure descriptions

(4) Test support resources

(5) Test items

(6) Test data from previous testing activities—if available

(7) Test tools from previous testing activities—if available

3.5.2 Implement Tasks

(1) *Obtain and Verify Test Data.* Obtain a copy of existing test data to be modified or used without modification. Generate any new data required. Include additional data necessary to ensure data consistency and integrity. Verify all data (including those to be used as is) against

the software data structure specifications. When the correlation between test cases and data sets is not readily apparent, develop a table to record this correlation and include it in the unit's test design specification.

(2) *Obtain Special Resources.* Obtain the test support resources specified in 3.3.2(2).

(3) *Obtain Test Items.* Collect test items including available manuals, operating system procedures, control data (for example, tables), and computer programs. Obtain software identified during test planning that directly interfaces with the test unit.

When testing a unit implemented with a procedural language, ensure that execution trace information will be available to evaluate satisfaction of the code-based completeness requirements.

Record the identifier of each item in the *Summary* section of the unit's test summary report.

3.5.3 Implement Outputs

(1) Verified test data (from 3.5.2(1))

(2) Test support resources (from 3.5.2(2))

(3) Configuration of test items (from 3.5.2(3))

(4) Initial summary information (from 3.5.2(3))

3.6 Execute the Test Procedures

3.6.1 Execute Inputs

(1) Verified test data (from 3.5.2(1))

(2) Test support resources (from 3.5.2(2))

(3) Configuration of test items (from 3.5.2(3))

(4) Test-case specifications (from 3.4.2(3) and (4))

(5) Test procedure specifications (from 3.4.2 (2))—if produced

(6) Failure analysis results (from debugging process)—if produced

3.6.2 Execute Tasks

(1) *Run Tests.* Set up the test environment. Run the test set. Record all test incidents in the *Summary of Results* section of the unit's test summary report.

(2) *Determine Results.* For each test case, determine if the unit passed or failed based on required result specifications in the case descriptions. Record pass or fail results in the *Summary of Results* section of the unit's test summary report. Record resource consumption data in the *Summary of Activities* section of the report. When testing a unit implemented with a procedural language, collect execution trace summary information and attach it to the report.

For each failure, have the failure analyzed and record the fault information in the *Summary of Results* section of the test summary report. Then select the applicable case and perform the associated actions.

Case 1: *A Fault in a Test Specification or Test Data.* Correct the fault, record the fault correction in the *Summary of Activities* section of the test summary report, and rerun the tests that failed.

Case 2: *A Fault in Test Procedure Execution.* Rerun the incorrectly executed procedures.

Case 3: *A Fault in the Test Environment (for example, system software).* Either have the environment corrected, record the fault correction in the *Summary of Activities* section of the test summary report, and rerun the tests that failed OR prepare for abnormal termination by documenting the reason for not correcting the environment in the *Summary of Activities* section of the test summary report and proceed to check for termination (that is, proceed to activity 3.7).

Case 4: *A Fault in the Unit Implementation.* Either have the unit corrected, record the fault correction in the *Summary of Activities* section of the test summary report, and rerun all tests OR prepare for abnormal termination by documenting the reason for not correcting the unit in the *Summary of Activities* section of the test summary report and proceed to check for termination (that is, proceed to activity 3.7).

Case 5: *A Fault in the Unit Design.* Either have the design and unit corrected, modify the test specification and data as appropriate, record the fault correction in the *Summary of Activities* section of the test summary report, and rerun all tests OR prepare for abnormal termination by documenting the reason for not correcting the design in the *Summary of Activities* section of the test summary report and proceed to check for termination (that is, proceed to activity 3.7).

NOTE: The cycle of Execute and Check Tasks must be repeated until a termination condition defined in 3.1.2(3) is satisfied (See Fig 3). Control flow within the Execute activity itself is pictured in Fig 2).

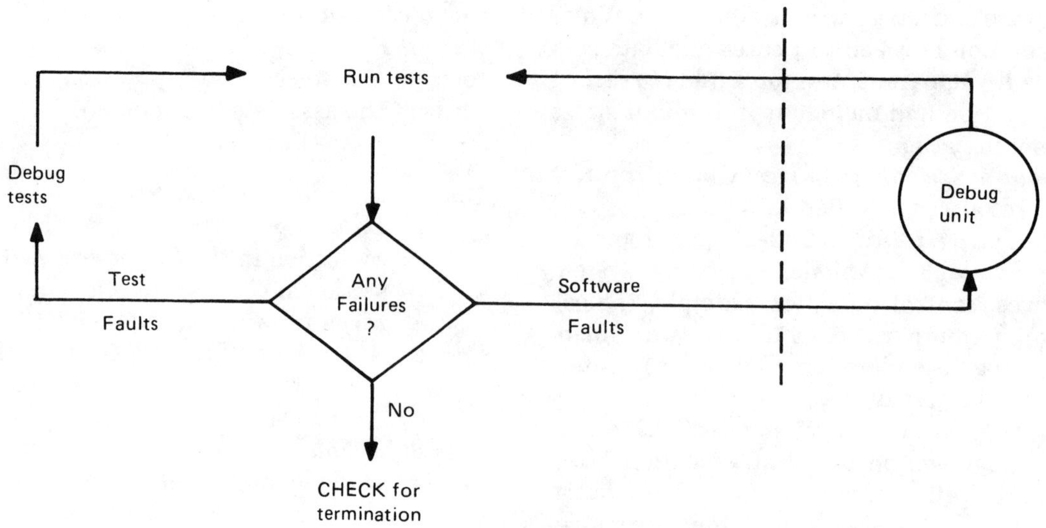

Fig 2
Control Flow Within the Execute Activity

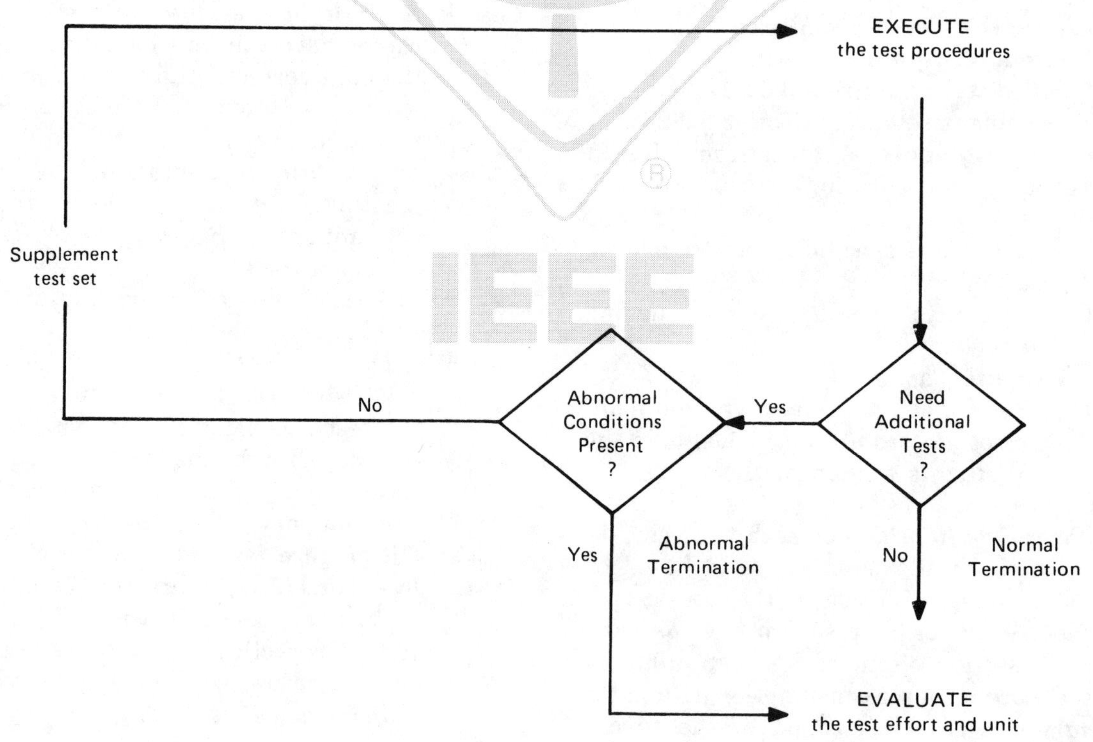

Fig 3
Control Flow Within the Check Activity

3.6.3 Execute Outputs

(1) Execution information logged in the test summary report including test outcomes, test incident descriptions, failure analysis results, fault correction activities, uncorrected fault reasons, resource consumption data and, for procedural language implementations, trace summary information (from 3.6.2(1) and (2))

(2) Revised test specifications—if produced from 3.6.2(2)

(3) Revised test data—if produced from 3.6.2(2)

3.7 Check for Termination

3.7.1 Check Inputs

(1) Completeness and termination requirements (from 3.1.2(2) and (3))

(2) Execution information (from 3.6.2(1) and (2))

(3) Test specifications (from 3.4.2(1) through (3) inclusive)—if required

(4) Software data structure descriptions—if required

3.7.2 Check Tasks

(1) *Check for Normal Termination of the Testing Process.* Determine the need for additional tests based on completeness requirements or concerns raised by the failure history. For procedural language implementations, analyze the execution trace summary information (for example, variable, flow).

If additional tests are *not* needed, then record normal termination in the *Summary of Activities* section of the test summary report and proceed to evaluate the test effort and unit (that is, proceed to activity 3.8).

(2) *Check for Abnormal Termination of the Testing Process.* If an abnormal termination condition is satisfied (for example, uncorrected major fault, out of time) then ensure that the specific situation causing termination is documented in the *Summary of Activities* section of the test summary report together with the unfinished testing and any uncorrected faults. Then proceed to evaluate the test effort and unit (that is, proceed to activity 3.8).

(3) *Supplement the Test Set.* When additional tests are needed and the abnormal termination conditions are not satisfied, supplement the test set by following steps (a) through (e).

(a) Update the test set architecture in accordance with 3.4.2(1) and obtain additional test-case specifications in accordance with 3.4.2(3).

(b) Modify the test procedure specifications in accordance with 3.4.2(2) as required.

(c) Obtain additional test data in accordance with 3.5.2(1).

(d) Record the addition in the *Summary of Activities* section of the test summary report.

(e) Execute the additional tests (that is, return to activity 3.6).

3.7.3 Check Outputs

(1) Check information logged in the test summary report including the termination conditions and any test case addition activities (from 3.7.2(1) through (3) inclusive)

(2) Additional or revised test specifications—if produced from 3.7.2(3)

(3) Additional test data—if produced from 3.7.2(3)

3.8 Evaluate the Test Effort and Unit

3.8.1 Evaluate Inputs

(1) Unit Test Design Specification (from 3.4.2(5)

(2) Execution information (from 3.6.2(1) and (2))

(3) Checking information (from 3.7.2(1) through (3) inclusive)

(4) Separate test-case specifications (from 3.4.2(3) and (4))—if produced

3.8.2 Evaluate Tasks

(1) *Describe Testing Status.* Record variances from test plans and test specifications in the *Variances* section of the test summary report. Specify the reason for each variance.

For abnormal termination, identify areas insufficiently covered by the testing and record reasons in the *Comprehensiveness Assessment* section of the test summary report.

Identify unresolved test incidents and the reasons for a lack of resolution in the *Summary of Results* section of the test summary report.

(2) *Describe Unit's Status.* Record differences revealed by testing between the unit and its requirements documentation in the *Variances* section of the test summary report.

Evaluate the unit design and implementation against requirements based on test results and detected fault information. Record evaluation information in the *Evaluation* section of the test summary report.

(3) *Complete the Test Summary Report.* Complete the test summary report for the unit in accordance with ANSI/IEEE Std 829-1983 [2].

(4) *Ensure Preservation of Testing Products.* Ensure that the testing products are collected,

organized, and stored for reference and reuse. These products include the test design specification, separate test-case specifications, separate test procedure specifications, test data, test data generation procedures, test drivers and stubs, and the test summary report.

3.8.3 Evaluate Outputs

(1) Complete test summary report (from 3.8.2(3))

(2) Complete, stored collection of testing products (from 3.8.2(4))

Appendixes

(These Appendixes are not a part of ANSI/IEEE Std 1008-1987, IEEE Standard for Software Unit Testing, but are included for information only.)

Appendix A

Implementation and Usage Guidelines

This section contains information intended to be of benefit when the standard is being considered for use. It is therefore recommended that this section be read in its entirety before any extensive planning is done.

A1. Use of the Standard

The standard can be used

(1) As a basis for comparison to confirm current practices

(2) As a source of ideas to modify current practices

(3) As a replacement for current practices

A2. Additional Testing Requirements

Requirements such as the amount of additional test documentation (for example, test logs), the level of detail to be included, and the number and types of approvals and reviews must be specified for each project. Factors, such as unit criticality, auditing needs, or contract specifications will often dictate these requirements. The standard leaves it to the user to specify these requirements either by individual project or as organizational standards. If the requirements are project specific, they should appear in the project plan, quality assurance plan, verification and validation plan, or overall test plan.

A3. Additional Test Documentation

The information contained in the test design specification and the test summary report is considered an absolute minimum for process visibility. In addition, it is assumed that any test information need can be satisfied by the set of test documents specified in ANSI/IEEE Std 829-1983 [2], either by requiring additional content in a required document or by requiring additional documents.

A4. Approvals and Reviews

If more control is desired, the following additional tasks should be considered:

(1) Approval of general approach at the end of Plan

(2) Approval of identified requirements at the end of Determine

(3) Approval of specific plans at the end of Refine

(4) Approval of test specifications at the end of Design

(5) Review of test readiness at the end of Implement

(6) Review of test summary report at the end of Evaluate

A5. Audit Trails

It is assumed that auditing needs are taken into account when specifying control requirements. Therefore, the set of test documents generated together with the reports from test reviews should be sufficient to supply all required audit information.

A6. Configuration Management

Configuration management should be the source of the software requirements, software architectual design, software data structure, and unit requirements documentation. These inputs must be managed to ensure confidence that we have current information and will be notified of any changes.

The final unit testing products should be provided to configuration management. These outputs must be managed to permit thorough and economical regression testing. See ANSI/IEEE Std 828-1983, IEEE Standard for Software Configuration Management Plans, for details.

A7. Determination of Requirements-Based Characteristics

Psychological factors (for example, self-confidence, a detailed knowledge of the unit design) can make it very difficult for the unit developer to determine an effective set of requirements-based elements (for example, features, procedures, state transitions, data characteristics) to be included in the testing. Often, this determination should be made by someone else.

There are several ways to organize this separation.

(1) Developers determine these elements for each other.

(2) Developers fully test each other's code. This has the added advantage that at least two developers will have a detailed knowledge of every unit.

(3) A separate test group should be available The size of the project or the criticality of the software may determine whether a separate group can be justified.

If developers determine requirements-based elements for their own software, they should perform this determination *before* software design begins.

A8. User Involvement

If the unit to be tested interacts with users (for example, menu displays), it can be very effective to involve those users in determining the requirements-based elements to be included in the testing. Asking users about their use of the software may bring to light valuable information to be considered during test planning. For example, questioning may identify the relative criticality of the unit's functions and thus determine the testing emphasis.

A9. Stronger Code-Based Coverage Requirements

Based on the criticality of the unit or a shortage of unit requirement and design information (for example, during maintenance of older software), the code-based coverage requirement specified in 3.1.2(2) could be strengthened. One option is to strengthen the requirement from instruction coverage to branch coverage (that is, the execution of every branch in the unit).

A10. Code Coverage Tools

An automated means of recording the coverage of source code during unit test execution is highly recommended. Automation is usually necessary because manual coverage analysis is unreliable and uneconomical. One automated approach uses a code instrumentation and reporting tool. Such a tool places software probes in the source code and following execution of the test cases provides a report summarizing data and control-flow information. The report identifies unexecuted instructions. Some tools also identify unexecuted branches. This capability is a feature in some compilers.

A11. Process Improvement

To evaluate and improve the effectiveness of unit testing, it is recommended that failure data be gathered from those processes that follow unit testing, such as integration test, system test, and production use. This data should then be analyzed to determine the nature of those faults that should have been detected by unit testing but were not.

A12. Adopting the Standard

Implementing a new technical process is itself a process that requires planning, implementation, and evaluation effort. To successfully implement a testing process based on this standard, one must develop an implementation strategy and tailor the standard. Both activities must reflect the culture and current abilities of the organization. Long-term success will require management commitment, supporting policies, tools, training, and start-up consulting. Management can demonstrate commitment by incorporating the new process into project tracking systems and performance evaluation criteria.

A13. Practicality of the Standard

This standard represents consensus on the definition of good software engineering practice. Some organizations use practices similar to the process specified here while others organize this work quite differently. In any case, it will involve considerable change for many organizations that choose to adopt it. That change involves new policies, new standards and procedures, new tools, and new training programs. If the differences between the standard and current practice are too great, then the changes will need to be phased in. The answer to the question of practicality is basically one of desire. How badly does an organization want to gain control of its unit testing?

Appendix B

Concepts and Assumptions

B1. Software Engineering Concepts

The standard unit testing process specified in this standard is based on several fundamental software engineering concepts which are described in B1.1 through B1.8 inclusive.

B1.1 Relationship of Testing to Verification and Validation. Testing is just one of several complementary verification and validation activities. Other activities include technical reviews (for example, code inspections), static analysis, and proof of correctness. Specification of a comprehensive verification and validation process is outside the scope of this standard.

B1.2 Testing As Product Development. Testing includes a product development process. It results in a *test set* composed of data, test support software, and procedures for its use. This product is documented by test specifications and reports. As with any product development process, test set development requires planning, requirements (test objectives), design, implementation, and evaluation.

B1.3 Composition of Debugging. The debugging process is made up of two major activities. The objective of the first activity, *failure analysis,* is to locate and identify all faults responsible for a failure. The objective of the second, *fault correction,* is to remove all identified faults while avoiding the introduction of new ones. Specification of the process of either failure analysis or fault correction is outside the scope of this standard.

B1.4 Relationship of Testing to Debugging. Testing entails attempts to cause failures in order to detect faults, while debugging entails both failure analysis to locate and identify the associated faults and subsequent fault correction. Testing may need the results of debugging's failure analysis to decide on a course of action. Those actions may include the termination of testing or a request for requirements changes or fault correction.

B1.5 Relationship Between Types of Units. A one-to-one relationship between design units, implementation units, and test units is not necessary. Several design units may make up an implementation unit (for example, a program) and several implementation units may make up a test unit.

B1.6 Need for Design and Implementation Information. Often, requirements information is not enough for effective testing, even though, fundamentally, testing measures actual behavior against required behavior. This is because its usually not feasible to test all possible situations and requirements often do not provide sufficient guidance in identifying situations that have high failure potential. Design and implementation information often are needed, since some of these high-potential situations result from the design and implementation choices that have been made.

B1.7 Incremental Specification of Elements To Be Considered in Testing. Progressively more detailed information about the nature of a test unit is found in the unit requirements documentation, the unit design documentation, and finally in the unit's implementation. As a result, the elements to be considered in testing may be built up incrementally during different periods of test activity.

For procedural language (for example, COBOL) implementations, element specification occurs in three increments. The first group is specified during the Determine activity and is based on the unit requirements documentation. The second group is specified during the Design activity and is based on the unit design (that is, algorithms and data structures) as stated in a software design description. The third group is specified during the Check activity and is based on the unit's code.

For nonprocedural language (for example, report writer or sort specification languages) implementations, specification occurs in two increments. The first is during the Determine activity and is based on requirements and the second is during Design and is based on the nonprocedural specification.

An incremental approach permits unit testing to begin as soon as unit requirements are available and minimizes the bias introduced by detailed knowledge of the unit design and code.

B1.8 Incremental Creation of a Test Design Specification. Information recorded in the test design specification is generated during the Determine, Refine, and Design activities. As each of these test activities progress, information is recorded in appropriate sections of the specification. The whole document must be complete at the end of the final iteration of the Design activity.

B1.9 Incremental Creation of the Test Summary Report. Information recorded in the test summary report is generated during all unit testing activities expect Plan. The report is initiated during Implement, updated during Execute and Check, and completed during Evaluate.

B2. Testing Assumptions

The approach to unit testing specified in this standard is based on a variety of economic, psychological, and technical assumptions. The significant assumptions are given in B2.1 through B2.7 inclusive.

B2.1 The objective of unit testing is to attempt to determine the correctness and completeness of an implementation with respect to unit requirements and design documentation by attempting to uncover faults in:

(1) The unit's required features in combination with their associated states (for example, inactive, active awaiting a message, active processing a message)

(2) The unit's handling of invalid input

(3) Any usage or operating procedures associated only with the unit

(4) The unit's algorithms or internal data structures, or both

(5) The decision boundaries of the unit's control logic

B2.2 Testing entails the measurement of behavior against requirements. Although one speaks informally of *interface testing, state testing,* or even *requirement testing,* what is meant is measuring actual behavior associated with an interface, state, or requirement, against the corresponding required behavior. Any verifiable unit testing process must have documented requirements for the test unit. This standard assumes that the documentation of unit requirements exists before testing begins.

B2.3 Unit requirements documentation must be thoroughly reviewed for completeness, testability, and traceability. This standard assumes the requirements have been reviewed either as a normal part of the documentation review process or in a special unit requirements review.

B2.4 There are significant economic benefits in the early detection of faults. This implies that test set development should start as soon as practical following availability of the unit requirements documentation because of the resulting requirements verification and validation. It also implies that as much as practical should be tested at the unit level.

B2.5 The levels of project testing (for example, acceptance, system, integration, unit) are specified in project plans, verification and validation plans, or overall test plans. Also included is the unit test planning information that is applicable to all units being tested (for example, completeness requirements, termination requirements, general resource requirements). Subsequently, based on an analysis of the software design, the test units will be identified and an integration sequence will be selected.

B2.6 The availability of inputs and resources to do a task is the major constraint on the sequencing of activities and on the sequencing of tasks within an activity. If the necessary resources are available, some of the activities and some of the tasks within an activity may be performed concurrently.

B2.7 This standard assumes that it is usually most cost-effective to delay the design of test cases based on source-code characteristics until the set of test cases based on requirements and design characteristics has been executed. This approach minimizes the code-based design task. If code-based design is started before test execution data is available, it should not start until the test cases based on unit requirements and design characteristics have been specified.

Appendix C

Sources for Techniques and Tools

C1. General

Software tools are computer programs and software techniques are detailed methods that aid in the specification, construction, testing, analysis, management, documentation, and maintenance of other computer programs. Software techniques and tools can be used and reused in a variety of development environments. Their effective use increases engineering productivity and software quality.

The references given in C2 of this Appendix contain information on most of the testing techniques and tools in use today. The set of references is not exhaustive, but provides a comprehensive collection of source material. To keep up to date, the reader is encouraged to obtain information on recent IEEE tutorials and recent documents in the Special Publications series of the National Bureau of Standards.[5] Current information on test tools can be obtained from the Federal Software Testing Center[6] and software tool data bases are accessible through the Data & Analysis Center for Software.[7]

A set of general references on software testing is listed in Appendix D.

C2. References

BEIZER, BORIS. *Software Testing Techniques*. New York: Van Nostrand Reinhold, 1983. This book presents a collection of experience-based test techniques. It describes several test design techniques together with their mathematical foundations. The book describes various techniques (decision tables and formal grammars) that provide a precise specification of the input and software. It also discusses a data-base-driven testing technique. Many techniques are based on the author's first-hand experience as director of testing and quality assurance for a telecommunications software producer. The inclusion of experiences and anecdotes makes this book enjoyable and informative.

HOUGHTON, Jr, RAYMOND C. Software Development Tools: A Profile. *IEEE Computer* vol

[5] The NBS publications and software tools survey may be obtained from Superintendent of Documents, US Government Printing Office, Washington, DC 20402.

[6] Information regarding test tools may be obtained by contacting Federal Software Testing Center, Office of Software Development, General Services Administration, 5203 Leesburg Pike, Suite 1100, Falls Church, VA 22041.

[7] Information regarding the tools data base may be obtained from Data & Analysis Center for Software (DACS), RADC/ISISI, Griffiss AFB NY 13441.

16, no 5, May 1983.[8] The Institute of Computer Science and Technology of the National Bureau of Standards studied the software tools available in the early 1980's. This article reports the results of that study and analyzes the information obtained. Various categorizations of the tools are presented, with tools listed by their characteristics. The lists incorporate percentage summaries based on the total number of tools for which information was available.

OSD/DDT & E Software Test and Evaluation Project, Phases I and II, Final Report, vol 2, *Software Test and Evaluation: State-of-the-Art Overview*. School of Information and Computer Science, Georgia Institute of Technology, June 1983, 350 pp.[9] This report contains a concise overview of most current testing techniques and tools. A set of references is provided for each one. A set of test tool data sheets containing implementation details and information contacts is also provided.

POWELL, PATRICIA B. (ed). *Software Validation, Verification, and Testing Technique and Tool Reference Guide*. National Bureau of Standards Special Publication 500–93, 1982. Order from GPO SN-003-003-02422-8.[5] Thirty techniques and tools for validation, verification, and testing are described. Each description includes the basic features of the technique or tool, its input, its output, and an example. Each description also contains an assessment of effectiveness and usability, applicability, an estimate of the learning time and training, an estimate of needed resources, and associated references.

PRESSON, EDWARD. *Software Test Handbook: Software Test Guidebook*. Rome Air Development Center RADC-TR-84-53, vol 2 (of two) March 1984. Order from NTIS A147-289. This guidebook contains guidelines and methodology for software testing including summary descriptions of testing techniques, typical paragraphs specifying testing techniques for a Statement of Work, a cross-reference to government and commercial catalogs listing automated test tools, and an extensive bibliography.

REIFER, DONALD J. *Software Quality Assurance Tools and Techniques*. John D. Cooper and Matthew J. Fisher (eds). Software Quality Management, New York: Petrocelli Books, 1979, pp. 209–234. This paper explains how modern tools and techniques support an assurance technology for computer programs. The author first develops categories for quality assurance tools and techniques (aids) and discusses example aids. Material on toolsmithing is presented next. Finally, an assessment is made of the state of the technology and recommendations for improving current practice are offered.

SOFTFAIR 83. *A Conference on Software Development Tools, Techniques, and Alternatives*. IEEE Computer Society Press, 1983.[8] This is the proceedings of the first of what is likely to be a series of conferences aimed at showing the most promising approaches within the field of software tools and environments. It is a collection of 42 papers covering a broad range of software engineering tools from research prototypes to commercial products.

Software Aids and Tools Survey. Federal Software Management Support Center, Office of Software Development, Report OIT/FSMC-86/002, 1985.[6] The purpose of this document is to support management in various government agencies in the identification and selection of software tools. The document identifies and categorizes tools available in the marketplace in mid 1985. Approximately 300 tools are presented with various data concerning each one's function, producer, source language, possible uses, cost, and product description. The survey is expected to be updated periodically.

---

[8] Information regarding IEEE Computer Society publications may be obtained from IEEE Computer Society Order Department, PO Box 80452, Worldway Postal Center, Los Angeles, CA 90080.

[9] The Georgia Technology report may be obtained from Documents Librarian, Software Test and Evaluation Project, School of Information and Computer Science, Georgia Institute of Technology, Atlanta, Georgia 30332.

Appendix D

General References

This section identifies a basic set of reference works on software testing. While the set is not exhaustive, it provides a comprehensive collection of source material. Additional references focusing specifically on testing techniques and tools are contained in Appendix C.

CHANDRASEKARAN, B. and RADICCHI, S., (ed) *Computer Program Testing,* North-Holland, 1981. The following description is from the editors Preface:

> "The articles in this volume, taken as a whole, provide a comprehensive, tutorial discussion of the current state of the art as well as research directions in the area of testing computer programs. They cover the spectrum from basic theoretical notions through practical issues in testing programs and large software systems to integrated environments and tools for performing a variety of tests. They are all written by active researchers and practitioners in the field."

DEUTSCH, MICHAEL S. *Software Verification and Validation.* ENGLEWOOD CLIFFS: Prentice-Hall, 1982. The following description is taken from the Preface.

> "The main thrust of this book is to describe verification and validation approaches that have been used successfully on contemporary large-scale software projects. Methodologies are explored that can be pragmatically applied to modern complex software developments and that take account of cost, schedule, and management realities in the actual production environment. This book is intended to be tutorial in nature with a 'This is how it's done in the real world' orientation. Contributing to this theme will be observations and recounts from actual software development project experiences in industry."

Guideline for Lifecycle Validation, Verification, and Testing of Computer Software. Federal Information Processing Standards (FIPS) Publication 101.[10] Order from NTIS FIPSPUB101 1983 (See Appendix C). This guideline presents an integrated approach to validation, verification, and testing that should be used throughout the software lifecycle. Also included is a glossary of technical terms and a list of supporting ICST publications. An Appendix provides an outline for formulating a VV & T plan.

HETZEL, WILLIAM, *The Complete Guide to Software Testing.* QED Information Sciences, 1984. This book covers many aspects of software verification and validation with a primary emphasis on testing. It contains an overview of test methods and tools including sample reports from several commercially available tools. The book is especially useful when used for viewing testing from a management perspective and discussing many of the associated management issues. An extensive bibliography is included.

McCABE, THOMAS J. (ed). *Structured Testing.* IEEE Computer Society Press, Cat no EHO 200–6, 1983.[8] This IEEE Tutorial is a collection of papers focusing on the relationship between testing and program complexity. The first two papers define cyclomatic complexity and describe an associated technique for developing program test cases. The third paper describes a systematic approach to the development of system test cases. The fourth paper provides general guidelines for program verification and testing. The balance of the papers deal with complexity and reliability.

MILLER, EDWARD and HOWDEN, WILLIAM E. (ed). Tutorial: *Software Testing & Validation Techniques* (2nd ed) IEEE Computer Society Press, Cat no EHO 180–0, 1981.[8] This IEEE Tutorial is a collection of some significant papers dealing with various aspects of software testing. These aspects include theoretical foundations, static analysis, dynamic analysis, effectiveness assessment, and software management. An extensive bibliography is included.

MYERS, GLENFORD J. *The Art of Software Testing.* New York: Wiley–Interscience, 1979. This book contains practical, *How To Do It* technical information on software testing. The main emphasis is on methodologies for the design of effective test cases. It also covers psychological and economic issues, managerial aspects of testing, test tools, debugging, and code inspections. Comprehensive examples and checklists support the presentation.

[10] The FIPS VV & T Guideline may be obtained from National Technical Information Service, 5285 Port Royal Road, Springfield, VA 22161.

POWELL, PATRICIA B. (ed). *Plan for Software Validation, Verification, and Testing.* National Bureau of Standards Special Publication 500–98, 1982.[5] Order from GPO SN-003-003-02449-0 (See Appendix C). This document is for those who direct and those who implement computer projects. It explains the selection and use of validation, verification, and testing (VV & T) tools and techniques. It explains how to develop a plan to meet specific software VV & T goals.

Acknowledgment

Appreciation is expressed to the following companies and organizations for contributing the time of their employees to make possible the development of this text:

Algoma Steel
Applied Information Development
AT & T Bell Labs
AT & T Information Systems
Automated Language Processing Systems
Bank of America
Bechtel Power
Bell Canada
Boeing Computer Services
Boston University
Burroughs, Scotland
CAP GEMINI DASD
Central Institute for Industrial Research, Norway
Communications Sciences
Conoco
Digital Equipment Corp
US Department of the Interior
US Department of Transportation
Data Systems Analysts
E-Systems
K.A. Foster, Inc
General Dynamics
Georgia Tech
General Services Administration
Honeywell
Hughes Aircraft
IBM
IBM Federal Systems Division
International Bureau of Software Test
Johns Hopkins University Applied Physics Laboratory
Lear Siegler
Logicon
Management and Computer Services
Martin Marietta Aerospace
McDonald-Douglas
Medtronic
Micom
Mitre
M. T. Scientific Consulting
NASA
National Bureau of Standards
NCR
Product Assurances Consulting
Professional Systems & Technology
Programming Environments
Quality Assurance Institute
RCA
Reynolds & Reynolds
Rolm Telecommunications
Rome Air Development Center
Sallie Mae
Seattle—First National Bank
SHAPE, BELGIUM
Software Engineering Service, Germany
Software Quality Engineering
Software Research Associates
Solo Systems
Sperry
SQS GmbH, Germany
Tandem Computers
Tektronix
Televideo
Tenn Valley Authority
Texas Instruments
Time
University of DC
University of Texas, Arlington
US Army Computer Systems Command
Warner Robins ALC
Westinghouse Hanford

An American National Standard

IEEE Standard for Software Verification and Validation Plans

Sponsor

Software Engineering Standards Subcommittee of the Technical Committee on Software Engineering of the IEEE Computer Society

Approved September 18, 1986
Reaffirmed September 17, 1992

IEEE Standards Board

Approved February 10, 1987

American National Standards Institute

This standard has been adopted for Federal Government use.

Details concerning its use within the Federal Government are contained in Federal Information Processing Standards Publication 132, Guideline for Software Verification and Validation Plans. For a complete list of the publications available in the Federal Information processing Standards Series, write to the Standards Processing Coordinator (ADP), Institute for Computer Sciences and Technology, National Bureau of Standards, Gaithersburg, MD 20899.

This standard has been adopted for Federal Government use.

Details concerning its use within the Federal Government are contained in Federal Information Processing Standards Publication 132, Guideline for Software Verification and Validation Plans. For a complete list of the publications available in the Federal Information processing Standards Series, write to the Standards Processing Coordinator (ADP), Institute for Computer Sciences and Technology, National Bureau of Standards, Gaithersburg, MD 20899.

Foreword

(This Foreword is not a part of IEEE Std 1012-1986, IEEE Standard for Software Verification and Validation Plans.)

This standard provides uniform and minimum requirements for the format and content of Software Verification and Validation Plans (SVVPs). Performing software verification and validation (V&V) as defined in this standard provides for a comprehensive evaluation throughout each phase of the software project to help ensure that:

(1) Errors are detected and corrected as early as possible in the software life cycle
(2) Project risk, cost, and schedule effects are lessened
(3) Software quality and reliability are enhanced
(4) Management visibility into the software process is improved
(5) Proposed changes and their consequences can be quickly assessed

This standard applies to both critical and noncritical software.

(1) For critical software, this standard:

(a) Requires that minimum V&V tasks, inputs, and outputs specified in this standard be included in SVVPs

(b) Permits the SVVP to be extended by selecting additional V&V tasks from the optional tasks described in this standard or new tasks identified by the V&V planner

(2) For noncritical software, this standard:

(a) Recommends the use of minimum V&V tasks

(b) Permits the SVVP to be tailored to V&V efforts by selecting any of the V&V tasks (minimum, optional, new)

This standard applies to all phases of the software life cycle from the Concept Phase to the Operation and Maintenance Phase. Maximum benefits are derived when V&V is started early in the software life cycle, preferably at project initiation during the Concept Phase. Benefits can be derived for software already in development or in the Operation and Maintenance Phase if the V&V requirements from this standard are invoked consistent with cost and schedule constraints. When V&V is invoked for software in development or in operation and maintenance, required V&V inputs may not exist. Under these conditions, this standard permits the V&V tasks to be tailored to adjust for missing V&V inputs. In some instances, this may require the generation of appropriate software documentation.

V&V is performed in parallel with software development. Each V&V life-cycle phase ends when the V&V tasks of that phase are completed and the software development products are determined to be adequate. V&V life-cycle phases may overlap as activities of the new life-cycle phase are beginning and activities of the previous life-cycle phase are completing.

V&V tasks are iterative: as changes are made to the software product, selected V&V tasks from the previous life-cycle phases are reperformed, or additional V&V tasks are performed to address the changes. V&V tasks are reperformed if errors are discovered in the V&V inputs or outputs. The complexity and scope of changes determine the level of detail covered by the iteration. The SVVP identifies the criteria for performing the iterative V&V tasks.

This standard defines a V&V reporting structure by identifying format and content of the Software Verification and Validation Report (SVVR). The standard for Software Quality Assurance Plans (SQAP, ANSI/IEEE Std-730-1984) requires the SVVR to include both V&V and other quality assurance results. The SVVR defined here is flexible enough to include both types of results. The interim phase reports, final summary report, and optional SQAP-related activity reports defined by the SVVP provide visibility into the development and V&V processes.

This standard considers both the software and its system or operating environment. It can be used where software is the system or where software is part of a larger system. V&V should have a total system scope (that is, including interfaces between software, hardware, and operators) during the product life cycle. Embedded software is strongly coupled to hardware and other subsystems, and requires a system-level SVVP.

This standard was written to provide direction to organizations responsible for preparing or assessing a Software Verification and Validation Plan. This standard may be used by project management, software developers, quality assurance organizations, purchasers, end users, maintainers, and verification and validation organizations. If V&V is performed by an independent group, then the SVVP should specify the criteria for maintaining the independence of the V&V effort from the software development and maintenance efforts.

Suggestions for the improvement of this standard will be welcomed. They should be sent to

Secretary
IEEE Standards Board
Institute of Electrical and Electronics Engineers, Inc
345 East 47th Street
New York, New York 10017

The working group that developed this standard consisted of the following members:

Roger U. Fujii, *Chairman*
Doug McMann, *Vice Chairman*
Dolores R. Wallace, *Secretary*

Stephen Benz
Julian O. Blosiu
Martha Branstad
Fletcher J. Buckley
François Coallier
James A. Darling
Taz Daughtrey
David C. Doty
Sam Dugdale
William Dupras
Michael Edwards
John Horch
Ralph A. Kubek
Joyce Lewis
Roger J. Martin
Jerome W. Mersky
Dennis E. Nickle
Larry E. Nitszche
A.E. Nountor
Jane W. Radatz
Don J. Robbins
J. A. Ronbeck
Hans Schaefer
David Schultz
David M. Siefert
Hugh Spillane
George Tice
Richard Thayer
David Turner
William S. Turner
Adam Valentine
Robert A. Walker
Jay W. Wiley
Andrea Williams
Laurence Wilson
Helen M. Wood

When the IEEE Standards Board approved this standard on September 18, 1986, it had the following membership:

The standard was approved by the Software Engineering Standards Subcommittee of the IEEE Computer Society. At the time it approved this standard, the Ballot Group had the following membership:

John W. Horch, *Chairman*

A. Frank Ackerman
Jagdish Agrawal
Tom Armbruster
Richard L. Aurbach
James Baldo, Jr
Geoff Baldwin
H. Jack Barnard
Roy W. Bass
Leo Beltracchi
Yechiel Ben-Naftau
H.R. Berlack
Matt Biewer
J. Emmett Black
Michael A. Blackledge
Ronald M. Blair
Walter DuBlanica
Kevin W. Bowyer
Ingar Brauti
Michael F. Brennter
Kathleen L. Briggs
William L. Bryan
Fletcher J. Buckley
Douglas Burt
Homer C. Carney
C.L. Carpenter, Jr
Ronald R. Carter
R.L. Chilavsky
Tsun S. Chow
Jung K. Chung
Peter Coad, Jr
François Coallier
Sharon R. Cobb
William J. Cody
Christopher M. Cooke
Gail A. Cordes
A.J. Cote
Patricia W. Daggett
James A. Darling
George D. Darling
Taz Daughtrey
P.A. Denny
James H. Dobbins
David C. Doty
Einar Dragstedt
Robert Dunn
William P. Dupras
Robert E. Dwyer
Mary Eads
John D. Earls
Michael Edwards
L.G. Egan
Wolfgang Ehrenberger
Steven R. Eisen
Caroline L. Evans
David W. Favor
John Fendrich
Robert G. Ferreol
Glenn S. Fields
Wayne Fischer
Gordon Force
Julian Forster
C.R. Frederick
Carl Friedlander
Richard C. Fries
Ismael Fuentes
Roger U. Fujii
Michel Galinier
Leonard B. Gardner
David Gelperin
J. Kaye Grau
Andres Grebenc
Thomas Griest
James L. Gildersleeve
Shirley A. Gloss-Soler
Victor M. Guarnera
Lawrence M. Gunther
David A. Gustafson
Russell Gustin
Howard Hamer
Harry E. Hansen
Allen L. Hankinson
Robert M. Haralick
Hans Ludwig Hausen
Clark M. Hay
Herb Hecht
Terry L. Hengl
Charles P. Hollocker
John W. Horch
James W. Howatt
Cheng Hu
Peter L. Hung
Don L. Jackson
Shang-Sheng Jeng
Laurel Kaleda
Constantine Kaniklidis
Myron S. Karasik
Adi Kasad
Ron Kenett
R.A. Kessler
John M. Kinn
Shaye Koenig
Edward E. Kopicky
Joseph A. Krupinski
Joan Kundig
Tom Kurihara
Lak Ming Lam
John B. Lane
Robert A. Lane
William P. LaPlant
Greg Larsen
John A. Latimer
Paul Lebertz
J.A.N. Lee
Leon S. Levy
F.C. Lim
Bertil Lindberg
Gary Lindsay
David P. Linssen
Steven Litvintchouk
John M. Long
Donald C. Loughry
John K. Lowell
Bill Macre
Harold T. Maguire
Andy Mahindru
Kartik C. Majumdar
Henry A. Malec
Paulo C. Marcondes
Stuart Marcotte
Philip C. Marriott
Nicholas L. Marselos
Roger J. Martin
Paul Mauro
L.J. Mazlack
Ivano Mazza
J.A. McCall
Paul E. McKenney
Jack McKissick
Stanley E. McQueen
Glen A. Meldrum
Mordechai Ben Menachen
Belden Menkus
Jerome W. Mersky
W.F. Mitchell
Celia Modell
Charles S. Mooney
Gary Moorhead
Gene T. Morun
David G. Mullens
Myron L. Nack
Hironobu Nagano
Saied Najafi
G.R. Neidhart
Dennis E. Nickle
Perry R. Nuhn
J.H. Obbink
Deene Ogden
Wilma Osborne
D.J. Ostrom
Thomas D. Parrish
William E. Perry
Donald J. Pfeiffer
Harpal S. Phama
Robert M. Poston
Peter Prinzivalli
I.C. Pyle
Jane W. Radatz
Thomas S. Radi
Jock Rader
Wendy Rauch-Hindein
Meir Razy
John Reddan
Larry K. Reed
Matthias F. Reese
T.D. Regulinski
Paul Renaud
John P. Riganati
Gary S. Robinson
Hom Sack
J. Gonzales Sanz
Lawrence R. Satz
Franz P. Schauer
Peter E. Schilling
Max J. Schindler
Norman Schneidewind
Wolf A. Schnoege
Robert Schueppert
David J. Schultz
Gregory D. Schumacher
Leonard W. Seagren
Craig L. Shermer
Robert W. Shillato
Victor Shtern
David M. Siefert
David J. Simkins
Jacob Slonim
Jean-Christopher Slucki
Marion P. Smith
Harry M. Sneed
Al Sorkowitz
Hugh B. Spillane
Lee Sprague
G. Wayne Staley
Robert G. Stewart
Vegard Stuan
Alan N. Sukert
William G. Sutcliffe
Robert A. Symes
Richard H. Thayer
Paul U. Thompson
Michael H. Thursby
George Tice
R.L. Van Tilburg
Terrence L. Tillmanns
Lawrence F. Tracey
Henry J. Trochesset
Robert Troy
C.L. Troyanowski
Dana L. Ulery
David Usechak
P.M. Vater
Osmo Vikman
R. Wachter
Dolores R. Wallace
Thomas J. Walsh
William M. Walsh
Roger Warburton
Robert Werlwas

(Continued on next page)

(Continued from preceding page)

Charles J. Wertz
N.P. Wilburn
Andrew F. Wilson
Patrick J. Wilson
Paul A. Willis
Walter L. Whipple
Theodore J. Wojcik
Paul Wolfgang
Tom Worthington
W. Martin Wong
Dennis L. Wood
Helen M. Wood
Charles Wortz
A.W. Yonda
Natalie C. Yopconka
Michael E. York
Janusz Zalewski
Donald J. Zeleny
Marvin Zelkowitz
Hugh Zettel
Peter F. Zoll

Contents

IEEE

IEEE Standard for Software Verification and Validation Plans

1. Scope and References

1.1 Scope. This standard has a threefold purpose:

(1) To provide, for both critical and noncritical software, uniform and minimum requirements for the format and content of Software Verification and Validation Plans (SVVPs)

(2) To define, for critical software, specific minimum verification and validation (V&V) tasks and their required inputs and outputs that shall be included in SVVPs

(3) To suggest optional V&V tasks to be used to tailor SVVPs as appropriate for the particular V&V effort

This standard requires that an SVVP be written for both critical and noncritical software. Critical software is software in which a failure could have an impact on safety or could cause large financial or social losses.

This SVVP shall include V&V tasks to:

(1) Verify that the products of each software life-cycle phase:

(a) Comply with previous life-cycle phase requirements and products (for example, for correctness, completeness, consistency, accuracy)

(b) Satisfy the standards, practices, and conventions of the phase

(c) Establish the proper basis for initiating the next life-cycle phase activities

(2) Validate that the completed end product complies with established software and system requirements.

For critical software, this standard requires that minimum V&V tasks and their inputs and outputs be included in all SVVPs. For noncritical software, this standard does not specify minimum required V&V tasks; however, all other requirements of this standard shall be satisfied. This standard does recommend that the minimum V&V tasks for critical software also be employed for noncritical software.

This standard defines optional V&V tasks that permit V&V planners to tailor an SVVP for a V&V effort. For critical software, the minimum tasks may be supplemented with tasks selected from the optional tasks. For noncritical software, tasks may be selected from the minimum and optional tasks. Additional tasks identified by the user of this standard may be included in the SVVP for critical and noncritical software.

The life cycle used in this standard serves as a model and consists of the following life-cycle phases:

(1) Concept
(2) Requirements
(3) Design
(4) Implementation
(5) Test
(6) Installation and checkout
(7) Operation and maintenance

Compliance with this standard does not require use of the life-cycle model presented here. If a different model is used, the SVVP shall include cross-references to this standard's life cycle and to the V&V tasks, inputs, and outputs specified here for each life-cycle phase.

This standard requires that the following be defined for each phase:

(1) Verification and validation tasks
(2) Methods and criteria
(3) Inputs and outputs
(4) Schedule
(5) Resources
(6) Risks and assumptions
(7) Roles and responsibilities

This standard requires a management effort that encompasses all life-cycle phases. The management section of the SVVP defines information necessary to manage and perform the V&V effort, and to coordinate V&V with other aspects of the project. The standard requires the SVVP to specify how the V&V results shall be documented in the Software Verification and Validation Report (SVVR).

When this standard is invoked for existing software, the SVVP shall describe how V&V will be performed when required inputs do not exist. The standard does not prohibit the incorporation of additional content into an SVVP.

The SVVP standard derives its scope from ANSI/IEEE Std 730-1984 [2].[1] The SVVP standard may be applied in conjunction with, or independent of, other IEEE software engineering standards. This standard uses the definitions of ANSI/IEEE Std 729-1983 [1]. This SVVP standard contains V&V configuration analysis tasks that, in part or in whole, are reflected in ANSI/IEEE Std 828-1983 [3]. Test documentation is compatible with that in ANSI/IEEE Std 829-1983 [4].

1.2 References. This standard shall be used in conjunction with the following publications:

[1] ANSI/IEEE Std 729-1983, IEEE Standard Glossary of Software Engineering Terminology.[2]

[2] ANSI/IEEE Std 730-1984, IEEE Standard for Software Quality Assurance Plans.

[3] ANSI/IEEE Std 828-1983, IEEE Standard for Software Configuration Management Plans.

[4] ANSI/IEEE Std 829-1983, IEEE Standard for Software Test Documentation.

[1] Numbers in brackets correspond to those of the references in 1.2 of this standard.

[2] ANSI documents are available from the Sales Department, American National Standards Institute, 1430 Broadway, New York, NY 10018.

2. Conventions, Definitions, and Acronyms

2.1 Conventions. The use of the term *documentation* rather than *document* indicates that the information may exist in several documents or may be embedded within a document addressing more than one subject.

2.2 Definitions. The following terms, including those defined in other standards, are used as indicated in this standard.

acceptance testing. Formal testing conducted to determine whether or not a system satisfies its acceptance criteria and to enable the customer to determine whether or not to accept the system. (See ANSI/IEEE Std 729-1983 [1].)

anomaly. Anything observed in the documentation or operation of software that deviates from expectations based on previously verified software products or reference documents. A critical anomaly is one that must be resolved before the V&V effort proceeds to the next life-cycle phase.

component testing. Testing conducted to verify the implementation of the design for one software element (for example, unit, module) or a collection of software elements.

concept phase. The initial phase of a software development project, in which user needs are described and evaluated through documentation (for example, statement of needs, advance planning report, project initiation memo, feasibility studies, system definition documentation, regulations, procedures, or policies relevant to the project).

critical software. Software whose failure could have an impact on safety, or could cause large financial or social loss.

design phase. The period of time in the software life cycle during which the designs for architecture, software components, interfaces, and data are created, documented, and verified to satisfy requirements. (See ANSI/IEEE Std 729-1983 [1].)

implementation phase. The period of time in the software life cycle during which a software product is created from design documentation and debugged. (See ANSI/IEEE Std 729-1983 [1].)

installation and checkout phase. The period of time in the software life cycle during which a software product is integrated into its operational environment and tested in this environment to ensure that it performs as required. (See ANSI/IEEE Std 729-1983 [1].)

integration testing. An orderly progression of testing in which software elements, hardware elements, or both are combined and tested until the entire system has been integrated. (See ANSI/IEEE Std 729-1983 [1].)

life-cycle phase. Any period of time during software development or operation that may be characterized by a primary type of activity (such as design or testing) that is being conducted. These phases may overlap one another; for V&V purposes, no phase is concluded until its development products are fully verified.

minimum tasks. Those V&V tasks applicable to all projects. V&V planning for critical software shall include all such tasks; these tasks are recommended for the V&V of noncritical software.

operation and maintenance phase. The period of time in the software life cycle during which a software product is employed in its operational environment, monitored for satisfactory performance, and modified as necessary to correct problems or to respond to changing requirements. (See ANSI/IEEE Std 729-1983 [1].)

optional tasks. Those V&V tasks that are applicable to some, but not all, software, or that may require the use of specific tools or techniques. These tasks should be performed when appropriate. The list of tasks provided in Table 2 is not exhaustive.

required inputs. The set of items necessary to perform the minimum V&V tasks mandated within any life-cycle phase.

required outputs. The set of items produced as a result of performing the minimum V&V tasks mandated within any life-cycle phase.

requirements phase. The period of time in the software life cycle during which the requirements, such as functional and performance capabilities for a software product, are defined and documented. (See ANSI/IEEE Std 729-1983 [1].)

software design description. A representation of software created to facilitate analysis, planning, implementation, and decision making. The software design description is used as a medium for communicating software design information, and may be thought of as a blueprint or model of the system.

software requirements specification. Documentation of the essential requirements (functions, performance, design constraints, and attributes) of the software and its external interfaces. (See ANSI/IEEE Std 730-1984 [2].)

software verification and validation plan. A plan for the conduct of software verification and validation.

software verification and validation report. Documentation of V&V results and appropriate software quality assurance results.

system testing. The process of testing an integrated hardware and software system to verify that the system meets its specified requirements. (See ANSI/IEEE Std 729-1983 [1].)

test case. Documentation specifying inputs, predicted results, and a set of execution conditions for a test item. (See ANSI/IEEE Std 829-1983 [4].)

test design. Documentation specifying the details of the test approach for a software feature or combination of software features and identifying the associated tests. (See ANSI/IEEE Std 829-1983 [4].)

test phase. The period of time in the software life cycle in which the components of a software product are evaluated and integrated, and the software product is evaluated to determine whether or not requirements have been satisfied. (See ANSI/IEEE Std 729-1983 [1].)

test plan. Documentation specifying the scope, approach, resources, and schedule of intended testing activities. (See ANSI/IEEE Std 829-1983 [4].)

test procedure. Documentation specifying a sequence of actions for the execution of a test. (See ANSI/IEEE Std 829-1983 [4].)

validation. The process of evaluating software at the end of the software development process to ensure compliance with software requirements. (See ANSI/IEEE Std 729-1983 [1].)

verification. The process of determining whether or not the products of a given phase of the software development cycle fulfill the requirements established during the previous phase. (See ANSI/IEEE Std 729-1983 [1].)

2.3 Acronyms. The following acronyms appear in this standard:

SDD	Software Design Description
SRS	Software Requirements Specification
SVVP	Software Verification and Validation Plan
SVVR	Software Verification and Validation Report
V&V	Verification and Validation

3. Software Verification and Validation Plan

The Software Verification and Validation Plan (also referred to as the Plan) shall include the sections shown below to be in compliance with this standard. If there is no information pertinent to a section or a required paragraph within a section, the following shall appear below the section or paragraph heading together with the appropriate reason for the exclusion: *This section/paragraph is not applicable to this plan.* Additional sections may be added at the end of the plan as required. Some of the material may appear in other documents. If so, reference to those documents shall be made in the body of the Plan.

Software Verification and Validation Plan Outline

1. Purpose
2. Referenced Documents
3. Definitions
4. Verification and Validation Overview
   - 4.1 Organization
   - 4.2 Master Schedule
   - 4.3 Resources Summary
   - 4.4 Responsibilities
   - 4.5 Tools, Techniques, and Methodologies
5. Life-Cycle Verification and Validation
   - 5.1 Management of V&V
   - 5.2 Concept Phase V&V
   - 5.3 Requirements Phase V&V
   - 5.4 Design Phase V&V
   - 5.5 Implementation Phase V&V
   - 5.6 Test Phase V&V
   - 5.7 Installation and Checkout Phase V&V
   - 5.8 Operation and Maintenance Phase V&V
6. Software Verification and Validation Reporting
7. Verification and Validation Administrative Procedures
   - 7.1 Anomaly Reporting and Resolution
   - 7.2 Task Iteration Policy
   - 7.3 Deviation Policy
   - 7.4 Control Procedures
   - 7.5 Standards, Practices, and Conventions

3.1 Purpose. (Section 1 of the Plan.) This section shall delineate the specific purpose and scope of the Software Verification and Validation Plan, including waivers from this standard. The software project for which the Plan is being written and the specific software product items covered by the Plan shall be identified. The goals of the verification and validation efforts shall be specified.

3.2 Referenced Documents. (Section 2 of the Plan.) This section shall identify the binding compliance documents, documents referenced by this Plan, and any supporting documents required to supplement or implement this Plan.

3.3 Definitions. (Section 3 of the Plan.) This section shall define or provide a reference to the definitions of all terms required to properly interpret the Plan. This section shall describe the acronyms and notations used in the Plan.

3.4 Verification and Validation Overview. (Section 4 of the Plan.) This section shall describe the organization, schedule, resources, responsibilities, and tools, techniques, and methodologies necessary to perform the software verification and validation.

3.4.1 Organization. (Section 4.1 of the Plan.) This section shall describe the organization of the V&V effort. It shall define the relationship of V&V to other efforts such as development, project management, quality assurance, configuration or data management, or end user. It shall define the lines of communication within the V&V effort, the authority for resolving issues raised by V&V tasks, and the authority for approving V&V products.

3.4.2 Master Schedule. (Section 4.2 of the Plan.) This section shall describe the project life cycle and milestones, including completion dates. It shall summarize the scheduling of V&V tasks and shall describe how V&V results provide feedback to the development process to support project management functions (for example, comments on design review material).

If the life cycle used in the Plan differs from the life-cycle model in the standard, this section shall show how all requirements of the standard are satisfied (for example, cross-reference for life-cycle phases, tasks, inputs, and outputs). When planning V&V tasks, it should be recognized that the V&V process is iterative. The summary of tasks may be in narrative, tabular, or graphic form (for example, Fig 1). The life-cycle model in Fig 1 is a sample model used for this standard.

3.4.3 Resources Summary. (Section 4.3 of the Plan.) This section shall summarize the resources needed to perform the V&V tasks, including staffing, facilities, tools, finances, and special procedural requirements such as security, access rights, or documentation control.

3.4.4 Responsibilities. (Section 4.4 of the Plan.) This section shall identify the organizational element(s) responsible for performing each V&V tasks. It shall identify the specific responsibility of each element for tasks assigned to more than one element. This section may be a summary of the roles and responsibilities defined in each of the life-cycle phases (see 3.5 of this standard).

3.4.5 Tools, Techniques, and Methodologies. (Section 4.5 of the Plan.) This section shall identify the special software tools, techniques, and methodologies employed by the V&V effort. The purpose and use of each shall be described. Plans for the acquisition, training, support, and qualification for each shall be included. This section may reference a V&V Tool Plan.

3.5 Life-Cycle Verification and Validation. (Section 5 of the Plan.) This section of the Plan shall provide the detailed plan for the V&V tasks throughout the life cycle. The detailed plan (Section 5.1—Management, and Sections 5.2 through 5.8—Life-Cycle Phases) shall address the following topics:

(1) Verification and Validation Tasks. Identify the V&V tasks for the phase. Describe how each task contributes to the accomplishment of the project V&V goals. For all critical software, the SVVP shall include all minimum V&V tasks for the management of V&V and for each life-cycle phase. Any or all of these minimum tasks may be used for noncritical software. These minimum V&V tasks are referenced in the management and life-cycle phases sections of the standard (3.5.1 through 3.5.8), and are described in Table 1. The minimum tasks are also consolidated in graphic form in Fig 1.

Optional V&V tasks may also be selected to tailor the V&V effort to project needs for critical or noncritical software. Optional V&V tasks are defined in the Appendix and a suggested application for the management of V&V and for each life-cycle phase is presented in Table 2. The optional V&V tasks identified in this standard may be applicable to some, but not all, critical software. These tasks may require the use of specific tools or techniques. The list in Table 2 is illustrative and not exhaustive. The standard allows for the optional V&V tasks and any others identified by the planner to be used as appropriate.

Testing requires advance planning that spans several life-cycle phases. Test documentation and its occurrence in specific life-cycle phases are shown in Fig 2 as a recommended approach. To be in compliance with this standard, the test documentation and test execution specified in Fig 2 shall be required. If the V&V planner uses different test documentation or test types (for example, component, integration, system, acceptance) from those in this standard, the SVVP shall contain a mapping of the proposed test documentation and execution to the items shown in Fig 2. Test planning criteria defined in Table 1 (Tasks 5.3 (4a), 5.3 (4b), 5.4 (4a), 5.4 (4b)) shall be implemented in the test plan, test design(s), test case(s), and test procedure(s) documentation, and shall be validated by test execution.

(2) Methods and Criteria. Identify the methods and criteria used in performing the V&V tasks. Describe the specific methods and procedures for each task. Define the detailed criteria for evaluating the task results.

(3) Inputs/Outputs. Identify the inputs re-

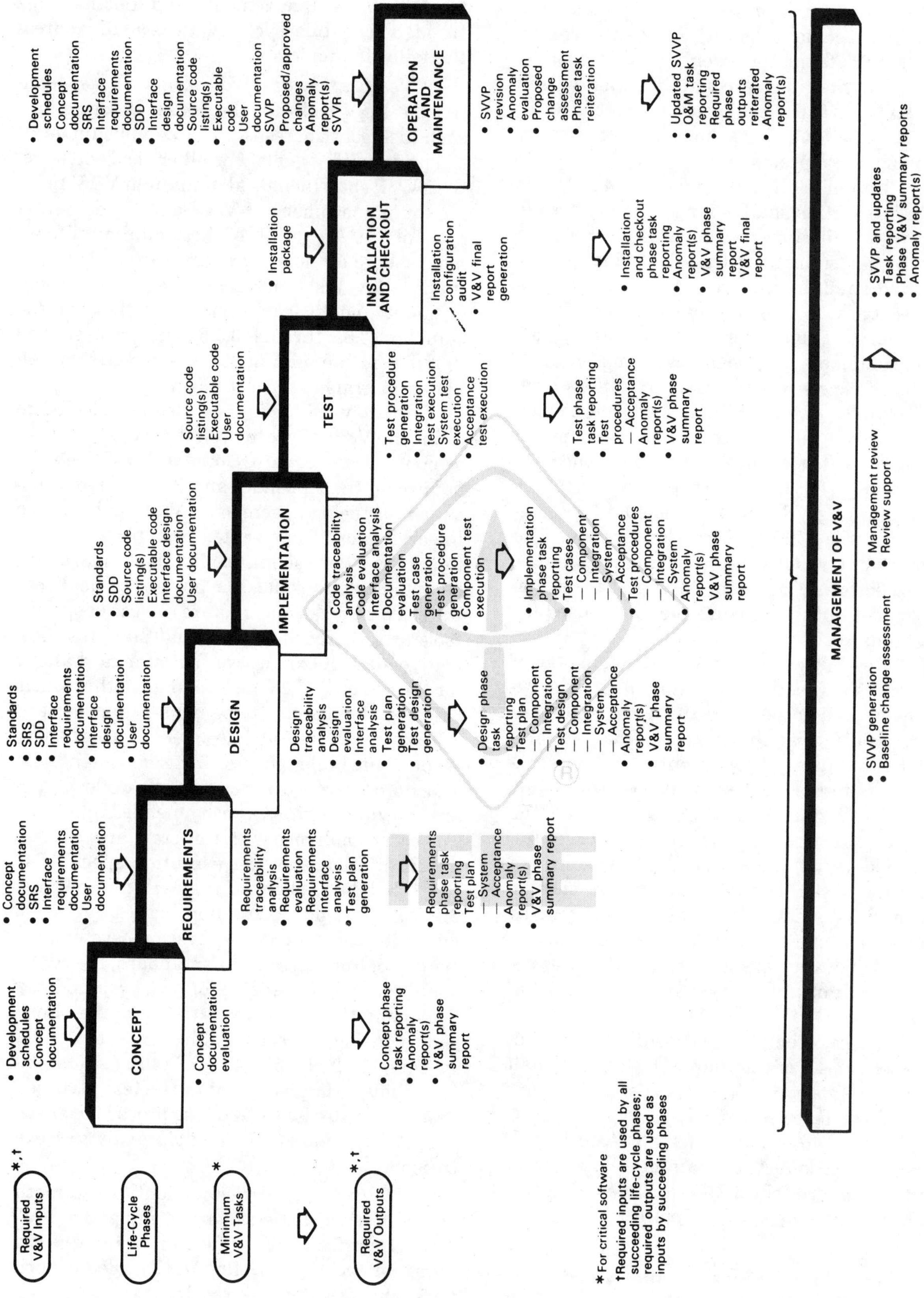

Fig 1
Software Verification and Validation Plan Overview

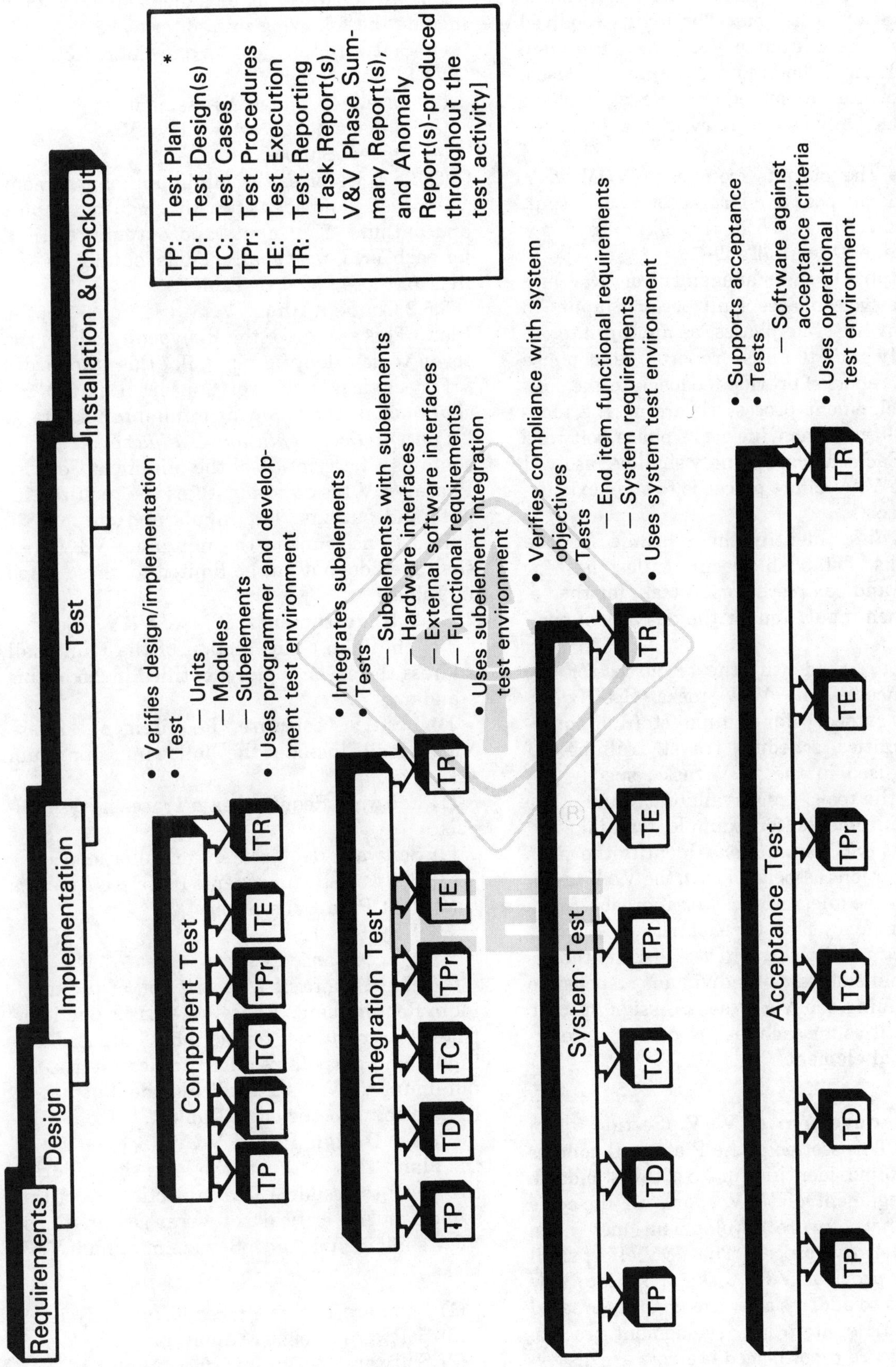

*This test planning documentation need not be individual documents. The placement of test outputs in specific life-cycle phases indicates a recommended approach.

Fig 2
V&V Test Tasks and Documentation

quired for each V&V task. Specify the source and format of each input. The inputs required for each of the minimum V&V tasks are identified in Table 1. The required inputs are used, as appropriate, by subsequent life-cycle phase V&V tasks. Only the primary inputs are listed in Table 1.

Identify the outputs from each V&V task. Specify the purpose and format for each output. The outputs from each of the minimum V&V tasks are identified in Table 1.

The outputs of the management of V&V and of the life-cycle phases shall become inputs to subsequent life-cycle phases, as appropriate.

Anomaly report(s), task report(s), and phase summary report(s) provide feedback to the software development process regarding the technical quality of each life-cycle phase software product. Each critical anomaly shall be resolved before the V&V effort proceeds to the next life-cycle phase.

(4) Schedule. Identify the schedule for the V&V tasks. Establish specific milestones for initiating and completing each task, for the receipt of each input, and for the delivery of each output.

(5) Resources. Identify the resources for the performance of the V&V tasks. Specify resources by category (for example, staffing, equipment, facilities, schedule, travel, training). If tools are used in the V&V tasks, specify the source of the tools, their availability, and other usage requirements (for example, training).

(6) Risks and Assumptions. Identify the risks and assumptions associated with the V&V tasks, including schedule, resources, or approach. Specify a contingency plan for each risk.

(7) Roles and Responsibilities. Identify the organizational elements or individuals responsible for performing the V&V tasks. Assign specific responsibilities for each task to one or more organizational element.

3.5.1 Management of V&V. (Section 5.1 of the Plan.) This section of the Plan shall address the seven topics identified in 3.5 of this standard. The management of V&V spans all life-cycle phases. The software development may be a cyclic or iterative process. The V&V effort shall reperform previous V&V tasks or initiate new V&V tasks to address software changes created by the cyclic or iterative development process. V&V tasks are reperformed if errors are discovered in the V&V inputs or outputs.

For all software, management of V&V shall include the following minimum tasks:

(1) Software Verification and Validation Plan (SVVP) Generation

(2) Baseline Change Assessment

(3) Management Review of V&V

(4) Review Support

Table 1 describes the minimum management V&V tasks and identifies the required inputs and outputs. The inputs and outputs required for each V&V task shall include, but not be limited to, those listed in Table 1.

3.5.2 Concept Phase V&V. (Section 5.2 of the Plan.) This section of the Plan shall address the seven topics identified in 3.5 of this standard.

For critical software, Concept Phase V&V shall include the following minimum V&V task: *Concept Documentation Evaluation.* Table 1 contains a description of the minimum Concept Phase V&V task and identifies the required inputs and outputs. The inputs and outputs required to accomplish the minimum V&V task shall include, but not be limited to, those listed in Table 1.

3.5.3 Requirements Phase V&V. (Section 5.3 of the Plan.) This section of the Plan shall address the seven topics identified in 3.5 of this standard.

For critical software, Requirements Phase V&V shall include the following minimum tasks:

(1) Software Requirements Traceability Analysis

(2) Software Requirements Evaluation

(3) Software Requirements Interface Analysis

(4) Test Plan Generation

(a) System Test

(b) Acceptance Test

Table 1 contains a description of the minimum Requirements Phase V&V tasks and identifies the required inputs and outputs. The inputs and outputs required to accomplish the minimum V&V tasks shall include, but not be limited to, those listed in Table 1.

3.5.4 Design Phase V&V. (Section 5.4 of the Plan.) This section of the Plan shall address the seven topics identified in Section 3.5 of this standard. For critical software, Design Phase V&V shall include the following minimum V&V tasks:

(1) Software Design Traceability Analysis

(2) Software Design Evaluation

(3) Software Design Interface Analysis

(4) Test Plan Generation

(a) Component Test
(b) Integration Test
(5) Test Design Generation
(a) Component Test
(b) Integration Test
(c) System Test
(d) Acceptance Test

Table 1 contains a description of the minimum Design Phase V&V tasks and identifies the required inputs and outputs. The inputs and outputs required to accomplish the minimum V&V tasks shall include, but not be limited to, those listed in Table 1.

3.5.5 Implementation Phase V&V. (Section 5.5 of the Plan.) This section of the Plan shall address the seven topics identified in 3.5 of this standard.

For critical software, Implementation Phase V&V shall include the following minimum V&V tasks:

(1) Source Code Traceability Analysis
(2) Source Code Evaluation
(3) Source Code Interface Analysis
(4) Source Code Documentation Evaluation
(5) Test Case Generation
(a) Component Test
(b) Integration Test
(c) System Test
(d) Acceptance Test
(6) Test Procedure Generation
(a) Component Test
(b) Integration Test
(c) System Test
(7) Component Test Execution

Table 1 contains a description of the minimum Implementation Phase V&V tasks and identifies the required inputs and outputs. The inputs and outputs required to accomplish the minimum V&V tasks shall include, but not be limited to, those listed in Table 1.

3.5.6 Test Phase V&V. (Section 5.6 of the Plan.) This section of the Plan shall address the seven topics identified in 3.5 of this standard.

Testing activities and their interrelationships with previous V&V phases are shown in Fig 2.

For critical software, Test Phase V&V shall include the following minimum V&V tasks:

(1) Acceptance Test Procedure Generation
(2) Test Execution
(a) Integration Test
(b) System Test
(c) Acceptance Test

Table 1 contains a description of the minimum Test Phase V&V tasks and identifies the required inputs and outputs. The inputs and outputs required to accomplish the minimum V&V tasks shall include, but not be limited to, those listed in Table 1.

3.5.7 Installation and Checkout Phase V&V. (Section 5.7 of the Plan.) This section of the Plan shall address the seven topics identified in Section 3.5 of this standard.

For critical software, Installation and Checkout Phase V&V shall include the following minimum V&V tasks:

(1) Installation Configuration Audit
(2) Final V&V Report Generation

Table 1 contains a description of the minimum Installation and Checkout Phase V&V tasks and identifies the required inputs and outputs. The inputs and outputs required to accomplish the minimum V&V tasks shall include, but not be limited to, those listed in Table 1.

3.5.8 Operation and Maintenance Phase V&V. (Section 5.8 of the Plan.) This section of the Plan shall address the seven topics identified in Section 3.5 of this standard.

Any modifications, enhancements, or additions to software during this phase shall be treated as development activities and shall be verified and validated as described in 3.5.1 through 3.5.7. These modifications may derive from requirements specified to correct software errors (that is, corrective), to adapt to a changed operating environment (that is, adaptive), or to respond to additional user requests (that is, perfective).

If the software was verified under this standard, the standard shall continue to be followed in the Operation and Maintenance Phase. If the software was not verified under this standard, the V&V effort may require documentation that is not available or adequate. If appropriate documentation is not available or adequate, the SVVP shall comply with this standard within cost and schedule constraints. The V&V effort may generate the missing documentation.

For critical software, Operation and Maintenance Phase V&V tasks shall include the following minimum V&V tasks:

(1) Software Verification and Validation Plan Revision
(2) Anomaly Evaluation
(3) Proposed Change Assessment
(4) Phase Task Iteration

Table 1 contains a description of the minimum Operation and Maintenance Phase V&V tasks. The inputs and outputs required to accomplish the minimum V&V tasks shall include, but not be limited to, those listed in Table 1.

3.6 Software Verification and Validation Reporting. (Section 6 of the Plan.) This section shall describe how the results of implementing the Plan will be documented. V&V reporting shall occur throughout the software life cycle. This section of the Plan shall specify the content, format, and timing of all V&V reports. These V&V reports shall constitute the Software Verification and Validation Report (SVVR).

3.6.1 Required Reports. The following reports shall be generated for each software V&V effort.

(1) Task Reporting. These shall report on the individual V&V phase tasks and shall be issued as necessary. They may document interim results and status. They may be in a format appropriate for technical disclosure (for example, technical reports or memos).

(2) V&V Phase Summary Report. A Phase Summary Report shall summarize the results of V&V tasks performed in each of the following life-cycle phases: Concept, Requirements, Design, Implementation, Test, and Installation and Checkout. For the Operation and Maintenance Phase, V&V phase summary reports may be either updates to previous V&V phase summary reports or separate documents. Each V&V Phase Summary Report shall contain the following:

(a) Description of V&V tasks performed
(b) Summary of task results
(c) Summary of anomalies and resolution
(d) Assessment of software quality
(e) Recommendations

(3) Anomaly Report. An Anomaly Report shall document each anomaly detected by the V&V effort. Each Anomaly Report shall contain the following:

(a) Description and location
(b) Impact
(c) Cause
(d) Criticality
(e) Recommendations

(4) V&V Final Report. The Verification and Validation Final Report shall be issued at the end of the Installation and Checkout phase or at the conclusion of the V&V effort. The Final Report shall include the following information:

(a) Summary of all life-cycle V&V tasks
(b) Summary of task results
(c) Summary of anomalies and resolutions
(d) Assessment of overall software quality
(e) Recommendations

3.6.2 Optional Reports

The following reports are optional.

(1) Special Studies Report. This report shall describe any special studies conducted during any life-cycle phase. The report shall document technical results and shall include, at a minimum, the following information:

(a) Purpose and objectives
(b) Approach
(c) Summary of results

(2) Other Reports. These reports shall describe the results of tasks not defined in the SVVP. These other activities and results may include quality assurance results, end user testing results, or configuration and data management status results.

3.7 Verification and Validation Administrative Procedures. (Section 7 of the Plan). This section of the Plan shall describe, at a minimum, the V&V administrative procedures described in 3.7.1 through 3.7.5.

3.7.1 Anomaly Reporting and Resolution. (Section 7.1 of the Plan.) This section shall describe the method of reporting and resolving anomalies, including the criteria for reporting an anomaly, the anomaly report distribution list, and the authority and time lines for resolving anomalies. The section shall define the anomaly criticality levels. Each critical anomaly shall be resolved satisfactorily before the V&V effort can formally proceed to the next life-cycle phase.

3.7.2 Task Iteration Policy. (Section 7.2 of the Plan.) This section shall describe the criteria used to determine the extent to which a V&V task shall be reperformed when its input is changed. These criteria may include assessments of change, criticality, and cost, schedule, or quality effects.

3.7.3 Deviation Policy. (Section 7.3 of the Plan.) This section shall describe the procedures and forms used to deviate from the Plan. The information required for deviations shall include task identification, deviation rationale, and effect on software quality. The section shall define the authorities responsible for approving deviations.

3.7.4 Control Procedures. (Section 7.4 of the Plan.) This section shall identify control procedures applied to the V&V effort. These procedures shall describe how software products and results of software V&V shall be configured, protected, and stored.

These procedures may describe quality assurance, configuration management, data management, or other activities if they are not addressed by other efforts. At a minimum, this section shall describe how SVVP materials shall comply with existing security provisions and how the validity of V&V results shall be protected from accidental or deliberate alteration.

3.7.5 Standards, Practices, and Conventions. (Section 7.5 of the Plan.) This section shall identify the standards, practices, and conventions that govern the performance of V&V tasks, including internal organizational standards, practices, and policies.

Table 1
Required V&V Tasks, Inputs, and Outputs for Life-Cycle Phases[3]

Minimum V&V Tasks	Required Inputs	Required Outputs*
5.1 MANAGEMENT OF V&V		
(1) **Software Verification and Validation Plan (SVVP) Generation.** Generate SVVP (during Concept Phase) for all life-cycle phases in accordance with this standard based upon available documentation. Include estimate of anticipated V&V activities for Operation and Maintenance Phase. Update SVVP for each life-cycle phase, particularly prior to Operation and Maintenance. Consider SVVP to be a *living document,* and make changes as necessary. A baseline SVVP should be established prior to the Requirements Phase.	Development Schedules Concept Documentation SRS Interface Requirements Documentation SDD Interface Design Documentation Source Code Listing(s) Executable Code User Documentation Proposed Changes	SVVP and Updates
(2) **Baseline Change Assessment.** Evaluate proposed software changes (for example, anomaly corrections, performance enhancements, requirement changes, clarifications) for effects on previously completed V&V tasks. When changes are made, plan iteration of affected tasks which includes reperforming previous V&V tasks or initiating new V&V tasks to address the software changes created by the cyclic or iterative development process.	Proposed Changes	Updated SVVP
(3) **Management Review.** Conduct periodic reviews of V&V effort, technical accomplishments, resource utilization, future planning, risk management. Support daily management of V&V phase activities, including technical quality of final and interim V&V reports and results. Review the task and V&V phase summary reports of each life-cycle phase. Evaluate V&V results and anomaly resolution to determine when to proceed to next life-cycle phase and to define changes to V&V tasks to improve the V&V effort.	Development Schedules V&V Outputs	Task Reporting V&V Phase Summary Reports
(4) **Review Support.** Correlate V&V task results to support management and technical reviews (for example, Software Requirements Review, Preliminary Design Review, Critical Design Review). Identify key review support milestones in SVVP. Schedule V&V tasks to meet milestones. Establish methods to exchange V&V data and results with development effort.	V&V Outputs	Task Reporting Anomaly Report(s)
5.2 CONCEPT PHASE V&V		
(1) **Concept Documentation Evaluation.** Evaluate concept documentation to determine if proposed concept satisfies user needs and project objectives (for example, performance goals). Identify major constraints of interfacing systems and constraints or limitations of proposed approach. Assess allocation of functions to hardware and software items, where appropriate. Assess criticality of each software item.	Concept Documentation (for example, Statement of Need, Advance Planning Report, Project Initiation Memo, Feasibility Studies, System Definition Documentation, Governing Regulations, Procedures, Policies, and customer acceptance criteria/requirements)	Task Reporting Anomaly Report(s)
5.3 REQUIREMENTS PHASE V&V		
(1) **Software Requirements Traceability Analysis.** Trace SRS requirements to system requirements in concept documentation. Analyze identified relationships for correctness, consistency, completeness, accuracy.	Concept Documentation SRS Interface Requirements Documents	Task Reporting Anomaly Report(s)
(2) **Software Requirements Evaluation.** Evaluate SRS requirements for correctness, consistency, completeness, accuracy, readability, and testability. Assess how well SRS satisfies software system objectives. Assess the criticality of requirements to identify key performance or critical areas of software.	Concept Documentation SRS Interface Requirements Documentation	Task Reporting Anomaly Report(s)

* Outputs from phase tasks are used to develop corresponding V&V phase summary reports and are ongoing inputs to the SVVR. Outputs of V&V tasks become inputs to subsequent life-cycle V&V tasks.

[3] The section numbers referred to in this Table refer to Section 5 of the Plan.

Table 1 *(Continued)*

Minimum V&V Tasks	Required Inputs	Required Outputs*
5.3 REQUIREMENTS PHASE V&V *(Continued)*		
(3) Software Requirements Interface Analysis. Evaluate SRS with hardware, user, operator, and software interface requirements documentation for correctness, consistency, completeness, accuracy, and readability.	SRS Interface Requirements Documentation	Task Reporting Anomaly Report(s)
(4a) System Test Plan Generation. Plan system testing to determine if software satisfies system objectives. Criteria for this determination are, at a minimum: (a) compliance with all functional requirements as complete software end item in system environment (b) performance at hardware, software, user, and operator interfaces (c) adequacy of user documentation (d) performance at boundaries (for example, data, interface) and under stress condtions. Plan tracing of system end-item requirements to test design, cases, procedures, and execution results. Plan documentation of test tasks and results.	Concept Documentation SRS Interface Requirements Documentation User Documentation	System Test Plan Anomaly Report(s)
(4b) Acceptance Test Plan Generation. Plan acceptance testing to determine if software correctly implements system and software requirements in an operational environment. Criteria for this determination are, at a minimum: (a) compliance with acceptance requirements in operational environment (b) adequacy of user documentation. Plan tracing of acceptance test requirements to test design, cases, procedures, and execution results. Plan documentation of test tasks and results.	Concept Documentation SRS Interface Requirements Documentation User Documentation	Acceptance Test Plan Anomaly Report(s)
5.4 DESIGN PHASE V&V		
(1) Design Traceability Analysis. Trace SDD to SRS and SRS to SDD. Analyze identified relationships for correctness, consistency, completeness, and accuracy.	SRS SDD Interface Requirements Documentation Interface Design Documentation	Task Reporting Anomaly Report(s)
(2) Design Evaluation. Evaluate SDD for correctness, consistency, completeness, accuracy, and testability. Evaluate design for compliance with established standards, practices, and conventions. Assess design quality.	SDD Interface Design Documentation Standards (standards, practices, conventions)	Task Reporting Anomaly Report(s)
(3) Design Interface Analysis. Evaluate SDD with hardware, operator, and software interface requirements for correctness, consistency, completeness, and accuracy. At a minimum, analyze data items at each interface.	SDD Interface Design Documentation	Task Reporting Anomaly Report(s)
(4a) Component Test Plan Generation. Plan component testing to determine if software elements (for example, units, modules) correctly implement component requirements. Criteria for this determination are, at a minimum: (a) compliance with design requirements (b) assessment of timing, sizing, and accuracy (c) performance at boundaries and interfaces and under stress and error conditions (d) measures of test coverage and software reliability and maintainability. Plan tracing of design requirements to test design, cases, procedures, and execution results. Plan documentation of test tasks and results.	SRS SDD Interface Requirements Documentation Interface Design Documentation	Component Test Plan Anomaly Report(s)
(4b) Integration Test Plan Generation. Plan integration testing to determine if software (for example, subelements, interfaces) correctly implements the software requirements and design. Criteria for this determination are, at a minimum: (a) compliance with increasingly larger set of functional requirements at each stage of integration (b) assessment of timing, sizing, and accuracy (c) performance at boundaries and under stress conditions (d) measures of functional test coverage and software reliability. Plan tracing of requirements to test design, cases, procedures, and execution results. Plan documentation of test tasks and results.	SRS SDD Interface Requirements Documentation Interface Design Documentation	Integration Test Plan Anomaly Report(s)

* Outputs from phase tasks are used to develop corresponding V&V phase summary reports and are ongoing inputs to the SVVR. Outputs of V&V tasks become inputs to subsequent life-cycle V&V tasks.

Table 1 ***(Continued)***

Minimum V&V Tasks	Required Inputs	Required Outputs*
5.4 DESIGN PHASE V&V ***(Continued)***		
(5) Test Design Generation. Design tests for: (a) component testing (b) integration testing (c) system testing (d) acceptance testing. Continue tracing required by the Test Plan.	SDD Interface Design Documentation User Documentation	Component Test Design(s) Integration Test Design(s) System Test Design(s) Acceptance Test Design(s) Anomaly Report(s)
5.5 IMPLEMENTATION PHASE V&V		
(1) Source Code Traceability Analysis. Trace source code to corresponding design specification(s) and design specification(s) to source code. Analyze identified relationships for correctness, consistency, completeness, and accuracy.	SDD Interface Design Documentation Source Code Listing(s)	Task Reporting Anomaly Report(s)
(2) Source Code Evaluation. Evaluate source code for correctness, consistency, completeness, accuracy, and testability. Evaluate source code for compliance with established standards, practices, and conventions. Assess source code quality.	Source Code Listing(s) Standards (standards, practices, conventions) SDD Interface Design Documentation User Documentation	Task Reporting Anomaly Report(s)
(3) Source Code Interface Analysis. Evaluate source code with hardware, operator, and software interface design documentation for correctness, consistency, completeness, and accuracy. At a minimum, analyze data items at each interface.	Source Code Listing(s) User Documentation	Task Reporting Anomaly Report(s)
(4) Source Code Documentation Evaluation. Evaluate draft code-related documents with source code to ensure completeness, correctness, and consistency.	Source Code Listing(s) User Documentation	Task Reporting Anomaly Report(s)
(5) Test Case Generation. Develop test cases for: (a) component testing (b) integration testing (c) system testing (d) acceptance testing. Continue tracing required by the Test Plan.	SDD Interface Design Documentation Source Code Listing(s)	Component Test Cases Integration Test Cases System Test Cases Acceptance Test Cases Anomaly Report(s)
(6) Test Procedure Generation. Develop test procedures for: (a) component testing (b) integration testing (c) system testing. Continue tracing required by the Test Plan.	SDD Interface Design Documentation Source Code Listing(s) User Documentation	Component Test Procedures Integration Test Procedures System Test Procedures Anomaly Report(s)
(7) Component Test Execution. Perform component testing as required by component test procedures. Analyze results to determine that software correctly implements design. Document and trace results as required by the Test Plan.	Source Code Listing(s) Executable Code SDD Interface Design Documentation	Task Reporting Anomaly Report(s)
5.6 TEST PHASE V&V		
(1) Test Procedure Generation. Develop test procedures for acceptance test. Continue tracing required by the Test Plan.	SDD Interface Design Documentation Source Code Listing(s) User Documentation	Acceptance Test Procedures Anomaly Report(s)

* Outputs from phase tasks are used to develop corresponding V&V phase summary reports and are ongoing inputs to the SVVR. Outputs of V&V tasks become inputs to subsequent life-cycle V&V tasks.

Table 1 *(Continued)*

Minimum V&V Tasks	Required Inputs	Required Outputs*
5.6 TEST PHASE V&V *(Continued)*		
(2a) Integration Test Execution. Perform integration testing in accordance with test procedures. Analyze results to determine if software implements software requirements and design and that software components function correctly together. Document and trace results as required by the Test Plan.	Source Code Listing(s) Executable Code	Task Reporting Anomaly Report(s)
(2b) System Test Execution. Perform system testing in accordance with test procedures. Analyze results to determine if software satisfies system objectives. Document and trace all testing results as required by the Test Plan.	Source Code Listing(s) Executable Code User Documentation	Task Reporting Anomaly Report(s)
(2c) Acceptance Test Execution. Perform acceptance testing in accordance with test procedures under formal configuration control. Analyze results to determine if software satisfies acceptance criteria. Document and trace all testing results as required by the Test Plan.	Source Code Listing(s) Executable Code User Documentation	Task Reporting Anomaly Report(s)
5.7 INSTALLATION AND CHECKOUT PHASE V&V		
(1) Installation Configuration Audit. Audit installation package to determine that all software products required to correctly install and operate the software are present, including operations documentation. Analyze all site-dependent parameters or conditions to determine that supplied values are correct. Conduct analyses or tests to demonstrate that installed software corresponds to software subjected to V&V.	Installation Package (for example, Source Code Listing(s), Executable Code, User Documentation, SDD, Interface Design Documentation, SRS, Concept Documentation, Installation Procedures, and Installation Tests)	Task Reporting Anomaly Report(s)
(2) V&V Final Report Generation. Summarize all V&V activities and results, including status and disposition of anomalies in the V&V final report (see 3.6.1 of this standard).	All V&V Phase Summary Report(s)	V&V Final Report
5.8 OPERATION AND MAINTENANCE PHASE V&V		
(1) Software V&V Plan Revision. For software verified and validated under this standard, revise SVVP to comply with new constraints based upon available documentation. For software not verified and validated under this standard, write new SVVP.	Development Schedules Concept Documentation SRS Interface Requirements Documentation SDD Interface Design Documentation Source Code Listing(s) User Documentation Installation Package Proposed Changes	Updated SVVP
(2) Anomaly Evaluation. Evaluate severity of anomalies in software operation. Analyze effect of anomalies on system.	Anomaly Report(s)	Task Reporting
(3) Proposed Change Assessment. Assess all proposed modifications, enhancements, or additions to determine effect each change would have on system. Determine extent to which V&V tasks would be iterated.	Proposed Changes	Task Reporting
(4) Phase Task Iteration. For approved software changes, perform V&V tasks necessary to ensure that: planned changes are implemented correctly; all documentation is complete and up to date; and no unacceptable changes have occurred in software performance.	Approved Changes	Task Reporting from Iterated Tasks Anomaly Report(s) Required Phases Outputs of Iterated Tasks

* Outputs from phase tasks are used to develop corresponding V&V phase summary reports and are ongoing inputs to the SVVR. Outputs of V&V tasks become inputs to subsequent life-cycle V&V tasks.

Table 2
Optional V&V Tasks and Suggested Applications

Optional V&V Tasks	Management	Life-Cycle Phases: Concept	Requirements	Design	Implementation	Test	Installation and Checkout	Operation and Maintenance
Algorithm Analysis			•	•	•	•		•
Audit Performance								
Configuration Control					•	•	•	•
Functional					•	•	•	•
In-Process			•	•	•	•	•	•
Physical						•	•	•
Audit Support								
Configuration Control					•	•	•	•
Functional					•	•	•	•
In-Process			•	•	•	•	•	•
Physical						•	•	•
Configuration Management	•	•	•	•	•	•	•	•
Control Flow Analysis			•	•	•			•
Database Analysis			•	•	•	•		•
Data Flow Analysis			•	•	•			•
Feasibility Study Evaluation		•						•
Installation and Checkout Testing*			•	•	•	•	•	•
Performance Monitoring								•
Qualification Testing*			•	•	•	•	•	•
Regression Analysis and Testing			•	•	•	•	•	•
Reviews Support								
Operational Readiness							•	•
Test Readiness					•	•	•	•
Simulation Analysis			•	•	•	•	•	•
Sizing and Timing Analysis				•	•	•		•
Test Certification						•	•	•
Test Evaluation			•	•	•	•	•	•
Test Witnessing						•	•	•
User Documentation Evaluation		•	•	•	•	•	•	•
V&V Tool Plan Generation	•							•
Walkthroughs								
Design				•				•
Requirements			•					•
Source Code					•			•
Test					•	•	•	•

* Test plan, test design, test cases, test procedures, and test execution.

Appendix

(This Appendix is not a part of IEEE Std 1012-1986, IEEE Standard for Software Verification and Validation Plans, but is included for information only.)

Description of Optional V&V Tasks

The descriptions of optional V&V tasks listed in Table 2 of this standard are defined in this Appendix. These V&V tasks are not mandatory for all V&V projects because they may apply to only selected software applications or may force the use of specific tools or techniques. These optional V&V tasks are appropriate for critical and noncritical software. By selecting V&V tasks from these optional V&V tasks, one can tailor the V&V effort to project needs and also achieve a more effective V&V effort.

algorithm analysis. Ensure that the algorithms selected are correct, appropriate, and stable, and meet all accuracy, timing, and sizing requirements.

audit performance. Conduct independent compliance assessment as detailed for configuration control audit, functional audit, in-process audit, or physical audit.

audit support. Provide documentation for, or participate in, any audits performed on the software development (for example, configuration control, functional, in-process, physical).

configuration control audit. Assess the configuration control procedures and the enforcement of these procedures.

configuration management. Control, document, and authenticate the status of items needed for, or produced by, activities throughout the software life cycle.

control flow analysis. Ensure that the proposed control flow is free of problems, such as design or code elements that are unreachable or incorrect.

database analysis. Ensure that the database structure and access methods are compatible with the logical design.

data flow analysis. Ensure that the input and output data and their formats are properly defined, and that the data flows are correct.

design walkthrough. Participate in walkthroughs of the preliminary design and updates of the design to ensure technical integrity and validity.

feasibility study evaluation. Evaluate any feasibility study performed during the concept phase for correctness, completeness, consistency, and accuracy. Trace back to the statement of need for the user requirements. Where appropriate, conduct an independent feasibility study as part of the V&V task.

functional audit. Prior to delivery, assess how well the software satisfies the requirements specified in the Software Requirements Specifications.

in-process audit. Assess consistency of the design by sampling the software development process (for example, audit source code for conformance to coding standards and conventions and for implementation of the design documentation).

installation and checkout testing. Generate the test plan, test design, test cases, and test procedures in preparation for software installation and checkout. Place the completed software product into its operational environment, and test it for adequate performance in that environment.

operational readiness review. Examine the installed software, its installation documentation, and results of acceptance testing to determine that the software is properly installed and ready to be placed in operation.

performance monitoring. Collect information on the performance of the software under operational conditions. Determine whether system and software performance requirements are satisfied.

physical audit. Assess the internal consistency of the software, its documentation, and its readiness for delivery.

qualification testing. Generate the test plan, test design, test cases, and test procedures in preparation for qualification testing. Perform formal testing to demonstrate to the customer that the software meets its specified requirements.

regression analysis and testing. Determine the extent of V&V analysis and testing that must be repeated when changes are made to any software products previously examined.

requirements walkthrough. Ensure that the software requirements are correct, consistent, complete, unambiguous, and testable by participating in a walkthrough of the requirements specification.

review support. Provide the results of applicable V&V tasks to support any formal reviews. The results may be provided in written form or in a presentation at the formal review meeting (for example, operational readiness, test readiness).

simulation analysis. Simulate critical aspects of the software or system environment to analyze logical or performance characteristics that would not be practical to analyze manually.

sizing and timing analysis. Obtain program sizing and execution timing information to determine if the program will satisfy processor size and performance requirements allocated to software.

source code walkthrough. Ensure that the code is free from logic errors and complies with coding standards and conventions by participating in a walkthrough of the source code.

test certification. Ensure that reported test results are the actual findings of the tests. Test-related tools, media, and documentation shall be certified to ensure maintainability and repeatability of tests.

test evaluation. Confirm the technical adequacy of test plans, test design, test cases, test procedures, and test results.

test readiness review. Evaluate the code, software documentation, test procedures, test reporting, error detection, and correction procedures to determine that formal testing may begin.

test walkthrough. Ensure that the planned testing is correct and complete and that the test results are properly interpreted by participating in walkthroughs of test documentation.

test witnessing. Observe testing to confirm that the tests are conducted in accordance with approved test plans and procedures.

user documentation evaluation. Examine draft documents during the development process to ensure correctness, understandability, and completeness. Documentation may include user manuals or guides, as appropriate for the project.

V&V tool plan generation. Produce plans for the acquisition, development, training, and quality assurance activities related to tools identified for support of V&V tasks (for example, test bed software used in validation).

walkthrough. Participate in the evaluation processes in which development personnel lead others through a structured examination of a product. See specific descriptions of requirements walkthrough, design walkthrough, source code walkthrough, and test walkthrough.

Acknowledgements

The following organizations supported employee participation in the development of this standard:

ACEx Technology
Army Computer Systems Command
AT&T Technologies
Babcock & Wilcox
Bechtel Power Corporation
Bell Canada
The Boeing Company
Booz Allen Hamilton
Central Institute For Industrial Research
Computer Science Corporation
Data Logic
E-Systems
Gemini
Hewlett Packard
Jet Propulsion Laboratory
Johns Hopkins University Applied Physics Laboratory
Logicon, Inc
Lucas Micro, Ltd
National Bureau of Standards
NCR Corporation
RCA
STC - Standard Telecommunications
Teledyne Brown Engineering
Televideo Systems
TRW
U.S. Department of Agriculture
U.S. Department of Transportation
Veatch, Rich, & Nadler
Walt Disney World
Worldwide Service Technologies, Ltd

IEEE

ANSI/IEEE
Std 1016-1987

An American National Standard

IEEE Recommended Practice for Software Design Descriptions

Sponsor

Software Engineering Standards Subcommittee of the Technical Committee on Software Engineering of the IEEE Computer Society

Approved March 12, 1987
IEEE Standards Board

Approved October 6, 1987
American National Standards Institute

The Institute of Electrical and Electronics Engineers, Inc
345 East 47th Street, New York, NY 10017, USA

Foreword

(This Foreword is not a part of IEEE Std 1016-1987, IEEE Recommended Practice for Software Design Descriptions.)

Purpose

This recommended practice specifies the necessary information content and recommends an organization for software design descriptions. This document does not explicitly support, nor is it limited to, any particular software design methodology or descriptive technology. It will guide the production of anything from paper design documents to an automated database of design information. For an organization in the process of developing a design description standard, use of this document will help the new standard meet the needs of all of its users. For an organization with a mature design description standard, it should prove useful in evaluating and modifying that standard in light of the informational and organizational needs of the design description user community.

This practice can be applied to commercial, scientific, and military software. Applicability is not restricted by size, complexity, or criticality of the software. This practice considers both the software and its system operational environment. It can be used where software is the system or where software is part of a larger system that is characterized by hardware and software components and their interfaces.

Overview

This document consists of six sections. Section 1 defines the scope of the recommended practice and Section 2 references other ANSI/IEEE standards that should be followed when applying this practice. Section 3 provides definitions of terms within the context of the practice. Section 4 places the Software Design Description into the framework of the software development life cycle. Section 5 describes the minimum information that shall be included in a software design description and Section 6 gives a recommended organization for software design descriptions. The Appendix shows a sample table of contents for a software design description.

Audience

This document is intended for those in technical and managerial positions who prepare and use software design descriptions. It will guide a designer in the selection, organization, and presentation of design information. It will help standards developers ensure that a design description is complete, concise, and well organized.

Software design descriptions play a pivotal role in the development and maintenance of software systems. During its lifetime, a given design description is used by project managers, quality assurance staff, configuration managers, software designers, programmers, testers, and maintainers. Each of these users has unique needs, both in terms of required design information and optimal organization of that information. Hence, a design description must contain all the design information needed by those users.

Terminology

This recommended practice follows the IEEE Guide to Standards Development. In particular, the word *shall* and the imperative form identify mandatory material within the recommended practice. The words *should*, *might*, and *may* identify advisory material.

History

The project authorization request for development of this recommended practice was approved by the IEEE Standards Board on September 22, 1983. Modification of the authorization request to change the title and scope was approved on March 13, 1986. A series of 10 meetings were held within the United States and internationally between March, 1983 and March, 1986. These meetings produced the draft submitted for balloting in April, 1986.

Suggestions for the improvement of this practice will be welcome. They should be sent to

Secretary
IEEE Standards Board
Institute of Electrical and Electronics Engineers, Inc
345 East 47th Street
New York, NY 10017

Contributors

This document was developed by the Software Design Description Working Group of the Software Engineering Standards Subcommittee of the IEEE Computer Society. The Software Design Description Working Group Steering Committee had the following members:

H. Jack Barnard, *Chairman*

James A. Darling, *Vice Chairman*

Robert F. Metz, *Secretary*

Chris Beall
Patricia Cox
Leo Endres
H. Gregory Frank
Manoochehr Ghiassi
Daniel E. Klingler
John McArdle
Arthur L. Price
Basil Sherlund

The Software Design Description Working Group had the following members:

A. Frank Ackerman
Jim Anderson
Sandro Bologna
Fletcher Buckley
Lori J. Call
Wan P. Chiang
Francois Coallier
Cliff Cockerham
Patricia W. Daggett
Jim DeLeo
Cammie Donaldson
Euiar Dragstedt
Laurence E. Fishtahler
David Gelperin
Yair Gershkovitch
Tom Gilb
Shirley A. Gloss-Soler
Larry J. Hardouin
Fredrick Ho
David M. Home
William S. Junk
Laurel Kaleda
Tom Kurihara
Jim Lemmon
F. C. Lim
Oyvind Lorentzen
Bert Martin
Lindsay McDermid
Glen Meldrum
Walter Merenda
Randy Peterson
Robert Poston
Ian C. Pyle
Ann S. Ping
Hans Schaefer
David Schultz
David Siefert
Peter Smith
Richard H. Thayer
T. H. Tse
David Weiss
Charles J. Wertz
G. Robert Zambs

The following persons were on the balloting committee that approved this document for submission to the IEEE Standards Board:

A. Frank Ackerman
Jagdish Agrawal
Richard L. Aurbach
James Baldo, Jr
H. Jack Barnard
Leo Beltracchi
Yechiel Ben-Naftali
H. R. Berlack
Michael A. Blackledge
Ron Blair
Kevin W. Bowyer
Kathleen L. Briggs
A. Winsor Brown
F. Buckley
Homer C. Carney
Ronald G. Carter
Richard L. Chilausky
Robert N. Chorette
T. S. Chow
Slucki Jean Christophe
Jung K. Chung
Peter Coad, Jr
François Coallier
Sharon R. Cobb-Pierson
Christopher M. Cooke
A. J. Cote, Jr
Ismael Fuentes Crespo
Patricia W. Daggett
George D. Darling
Taz Daughtry
Peter A. Denny
Harpal S. Dhama
Mike Dotson
David C. Doty
Einar Dragstedt
W. DuBlanica
William P. Dupres
Michael Dutton
Robert E. Dwyer
Mary L. Eads
John D. Earls
Mike Edwards
L. G. Egan
W. D. Ehrenberger
Steven R. Eisen
Caroline L. Evans
John W. Fendrich
Robert G. Ferreol
Glenn S. Fields
Gordon Force
Julian Forster
Deborah L. Franke
C. R. Frederick
Carl Friedlander
Richard Fries
Michael Galinier
Leonard B. Gardner
David Gelperin
Tom Gilb
James L. Gildersleeve
Shirley Gloss-Soler
Ole Golubjatnikov
J. Kaye Grau
Andrej Grebenc
Thomas Griest
Robert S. Grossman
Victor M. Guarnera
Lawrence M. Gunther
David A. Gustafson
Russell Gustin
Michael Haggerty
Howard Hamer
Harry E. Hansen, Jr
Robert M. Haralick
Haus-Ludis Hauser
Clark M. Hay
H. Hect
Terry L. Hengl
Maretta T. Holden
Charles P. Hollocker
Mark Holthouse
John Horch
Cheng Hu
Peter L. Hung
Sheng-Sheng Jeng
Laurel Kaleda
Charles F. Kaminski
Constantine Kaniklidis
Myron S. Karasik
Adi N. Kasad
Ron Kenett
R. A. Kessler
Shaye Koenig
Edward E. Kopicky
Joseph A. Krupinski
H. M. Kudyan
Joan Kundig
Lak-Ming Lam
John B. Lane
Robert Lane
William P. LaPlant
Greg Larsen
John A. Latimer
John A. N. Lee
Leon S. Levy
Paul Liebertz
F. C. Lim
Bertil Lindberg

David P. Linssen
Steven Lituintchouk
William Lively
John M. Long
John Lowell
Bill Macre
Andy Mahindru
Kartik C. Majumdar
Henry A. Malec
Paulo C. Marcondes
Stuart Marcotte
Gregory Mark
Phillip C. Mariott
Nicholas L. Marselos
Roger Martin
Paul A. Mauro
Jean I. Maxwell
L. J. Mazlack
Ivano Mazza
John McArdle
J. A. McCall
John McKissick, Jr
Glen A. Meldrum
Belden Menkus
Ben W. Miller
Charles S. Mooney
Gary D. Moorhead
Joyce E. Mortison
Gene T. Morun
David G. Mullens
Myron L. Nack
Hironobu Nagano
Saied Najafi
Gerry Neidhart
Brian A. Nejmeh
Dennis E. Nickle
J. T. L. Obbink
Wilma M. Osborne
D. J. Ostrom
Thomas D. Parrish
William Perry
Donald J. Pfeiffer
Robert M. Poston
Peter Ron Prinzivalli
James E. Quelle
Thomas S. Radi
Edward B. Rawson
Meir Razy
John Reddan
Larry K. Reed
Matthais F. Reese II
T. D. Regulinski
R. T. Reiner
Paul Renaud
Steven M. Rowan
John Rymer
Hom Sack
Julio Gonzalez Samz
Stephen R. Schach
Franz P. Schauer
Max Schindler
Norman Schneidewind
Wolf A. Schnoege
Robert G. Schueppert
David J. Schultz
Gregory D. Schumacher
Leonard W. Seagren
Gary T. Shea
Craig Shermer
Robert W. Shillato
Victor Shtern
David M. Siefert
David J. Simkins
William G. Singer
Jacob Slonim
H. Bennett Smith
Harry M. Sneed
J. G. Snodgrass
A. R. Sorkowitz
Hugh B. Spilhne
G. Wayne Staley
Mary Jane Stoughton
Alan N. Sukert
Robert A. Symes
Michael Taint
Richard H. Thayer
Paul U. Thompson
Michael H. Thursby
Terrence L. Tillmanns
Lawrence F. Tracey
Illeana Trandafir
Henry J. Trochesset
Robert Troy
C. L. Troyanowski
Dana L. Ulery
David Usechok
R. L. Vantilburg
P. M. Vatez
Osmo Vikman
R. Wachter
Dolores R. Wallace
William M. Walsh III
Thomas J. Walsh
Roger D. H. Warburton
Andrew H. Weigel
R. W. Werlwas
Charles J. Wertz
W. L. Whipple
Patrick J. Wilson
T. J. Wojcik
Paul Wolfgang
W. Martin Wong
Dennis L. Wood
Tom Worthington
Charles Wortz
Zhou Zhi Ying
A. W. Yonda
Natalie C. Yoptanka
Michael E. York
Don Zeleny
Marvin Zelkowitz
Hugh Zettel
Peter F. Zoll

When the IEEE Standards Board approved this standard on March 12, 1987, it had the following membership:

Donald C. Fleckenstein, *Chairman* **Marco W. Migliaro,** *Vice-Chairman*
Sava I. Sherr, *Secretary*

James H. Beall
Dennis Bodson
Marshall L. Cain
James M. Daly
Stephen R. Dillon
Eugene P. Fogarty
Jay Forster
Kenneth D. Hendrix
Irvin N. Howell
Leslie I. Kerr
Jack Kinn
Irving Kolodny
Joseph L. Koepfinger*
Edward Lohse
John May
Lawrence V. McCall
L. Bruce McClung
Donald T. Michael*
L. John Rankine
John P. Riganati
Gary S. Robinson
Frank L. Rose
Robert E. Rountree
William R. Tackaberry
William B. Wilkens
Helen M. Wood

* Member emeritus

Contents

IEEE Recommended Practice for Software Design Descriptions

1. Scope

This is a recommended practice for describing software designs. It specifies the necessary information content, and recommended organization for a software design description. A software design description is a representation of a software system that is used as a medium for communicating software design information.

The practice may be applied to commercial, scientific, or military software that runs on any digital computer. Applicability is not restricted by the size, complexity, or criticality of the software.

This practice is not limited to specific methodologies for design, configuration management, or quality assurance. It is assumed that the quality design information and changes to the design of description will be managed by other project activities. Finally, this document does not support nor is it limited to any particular descriptive technique. It may be applied to paper documents, automated databases, design description languages, or other means of description.

2. References

This standard shall be used in conjunction with the following publications:

[1] ANSI/IEEE Std 729-1983, IEEE Standard Glossary of Software Engineering Terminology.[1]

[2] ANSI/IEEE Std 730-1984, IEEE Standard for Software Quality Assurance Plans.

[3] ANSI/IEEE Std 828-1983, IEEE Standard for Software Configuration Management Plans.

[4] ANSI/IEEE Std 830-1984, IEEE Guide to Software Requirements Specifications

[5] Freeman, P. and A. I. Wasserman. *Tutorial on Software Design Techniques*. 4th Edition, IEEE Computer Society Press, Annotated Bibliography, pp 715-718, 1983.

3. Definitions

The definitions listed here establish meaning in the context of this recommended practice. Definitions of other terms used in this document can be found in ANSI/IEEE Std 729-1983 [1].[2]

design entity. An element (component) of a design that is structurally and functionally distinct from other elements and that is separately named and referenced.

design view. A subset of design entity attribute information that is specifically suited to the needs of a software project activity.

entity attribute. A named characteristic or property of a design entity. It provides a statement of fact about the entity.

software design description (SDD). A representation of a software system created to facilitate analysis, planning, implementation, and decision making. A blueprint or model of the software system. The SDD is used as the primary medium for communicating software design information.

4. Considerations for Producing a Software Design Description (SDD)

This section provides information to be considered before producing an SDD. How the SDD fits

[1] ANSI/IEEE publications can be obtained from the Sales Department, American National Standards Institute, 1430 Broadway, New York, NY 10018, or from the Service Center, The Institute of Electrical and Electronics Engineers, 445 Hoes Lane, Piscataway, NJ 08855-1331.

[2] Numbers in brackets correspond to those of the references in Section 2 of this standard.

into the software life cycle, where it fits, and why it is used are discussed.

4.1 Software Life Cycle. The life cycle of a software system is normally defined as the period of time that starts when a software product is conceived and ends when the product is no longer available for use. The life cycle approach is an effective engineering management tool and provides a model for a context within which to discuss the preparation and use of the SDD. While it is beyond the scope of this document to prescribe a particular standard life cycle, a typical cycle will be used to define such a context for the SDD. This cycle is based on ANSI/IEEE Std 729-1983 [1] and consists of a concept phase, requirements phase, design phase, implementation phase, test phase, installation and checkout phase, operation and maintenance phase, and retirement phase.

4.2 Software Design Description (SDD) within the Life Cycle. For both new software systems and existing systems under maintenance, it is important to ensure that the design and implementation used for a software system satisfy the requirements driving that system. The minimum documentation required to do this is defined in ANSI/IEEE Std 730-1984 [2]. The SDD is one of these required products. It records the result of the design processes that are carried out during the design phase.

4.3 Purpose of a Software Design Description (SDD). The SDD shows how the software system will be structured to satisfy the requirements identified in the software requirements specification ANSI/IEEE Std 830-1984 [4]. It is a translation of requirements into a description of the software structure, software components, interfaces, and data necessary for the implementation phase. In essence, the SDD becomes a detailed blueprint for the implementation activity. In a complete SDD, each requirement must be traceable to one or more design entities.

5. Design Description Information Content

5.1 Introduction. A software design description is a representation or model of the software system to be created. The model should provide the precise design information needed for planning, analysis, and implementation of the software system. It should represent a partitioning of the system into design entities and describe the important properties and relationships among those entities.

The design description model used to represent a software system can be expressed as a collection of design entities, each possessing properties and relationships.[3] To simplify the model, the properties and relationships of each design entity are described by a standard set of attributes. The design information needs of project members are satisfied through identification of the entities and their associated attributes. A design description is complete when the attributes have been specified for all the entities.

5.2 Design Entities. A *design entity* is an element (component) of a design that is structurally and functionally distinct from other elements and that is separately named and referenced.

Design entities result from a decomposition of the software system requirements. The objective is to divide the system into separate components that can be considered, implemented, changed, and tested with minimal effect on other entities.

Entities can exist as a system, subsystems, data stores, modules, programs, and processes; see ANSI/IEEE Std 729-1983 [1]. The number and type of entities required to partition a design are dependent on a number of factors, such as the complexity of the system, the design technique used, and the programming environment.

Although entities are different in nature, they possess common characteristics. Each design entity will have a name, purpose, and function. There are common relationships among entities such as interfaces or shared data. The common characteristics of entities are described by design entity attributes.

5.3 Design Entity Attributes. A *design entity attribute* is a named characteristic or property of a design entity. It provides a statement of fact about the entity.

Design entity attributes can be thought of as questions about design entities. The answers to those questions are the values of the attributes. All the questions can be answered, but the content of the answer will depend upon the nature of the entity. The collection of answers provides a complete description of an entity.

---

[3] The design description model is similar to an entity-relationship model, a common approach to information modeling.

The list of design entity attributes presented in this section is the minimum set required for all software design descriptions. The selection of these attributes is based on three criteria:

(1) The attribute is necessary for all software projects
(2) An incorrect specification of the attribute value could result in a fault in the software system to be developed
(3) The attribute describes intrinsic design information and not information related to the design process. Examples of attributes that do not meet the second and third criteria are designer names, design status, and revision history. This important process information is maintained by other software project activities as described in ANSI/IEEE Std 730-1984 [2] and ANSI/IEEE Std 828-1983 [3].

All attributes shall be specified for each entity. Attribute descriptions should include references and design considerations such as tradeoffs and assumptions when appropriate. In some cases, attribute descriptions may have the value *none*. When additional attributes are identified for a specific software project, they should be included in the design description. The attributes and associated information items are defined in 5.3.1 through 5.3.10.

5.3.1 Identification. *The name of the entity.* Two entities shall not have the same name. The names for the entities may be selected to characterize their nature. This will simplify referencing and tracking in addition to providing identification.

5.3.2 Type. *A description of the kind of entity.* The type attribute shall describe the nature of the entity. It may simply name the kind of entity, such as subprogram, module, procedure, process, or data store. Alternatively, design entities may be grouped into major classes to assist in locating an entity dealing with a particular type of information. For a given design description, the chosen entity types shall be applied consistently.

5.3.3 Purpose. *A description of why the entity exists.* The purpose attribute shall provide the rationale for the creation of the entity. Therefore, it shall designate the specific functional and performance requirements for which this entity was created; see ANSI/IEEE Std 830-1984 [4]. The purpose attribute shall also describe special requirements that must be met by the entity that are not included in the software requirements specification.

5.3.4 Function. *A statement of what the entity does.* The function attribute shall state the transformation applied by the entity to inputs to produce the desired output. In the case of a data entity, this attribute shall state the type of information stored or transmitted by the entity.

5.3.5 Subordinates. *The identification of all entities composing this entity.* The subordinates attribute shall identify the *composed of* relationship for an entity. This information is used to trace requirements to design entities and to identify parent/child structural relationships through a software system decomposition.

5.3.6 Dependencies. *A description of the relationships of this entity with other entities.* The dependencies attribute shall identify the *uses* or *requires the presence of* relationship for an entity. These relationships are often graphically depicted by structure charts, data flow diagrams, and transaction diagrams.

This attribute shall describe the nature of each interaction including such characteristics as timing and conditions for interaction. The interactions may involve the initiation, order of execution, data sharing, creation, duplicating, usage, storage, or destruction of entities.

5.3.7 Interface. *A description of how other entities interact with this entity.* The interface attribute shall describe the *methods* of interaction and the *rules* governing those interactions. The methods of interaction include the mechanisms for invoking or interrupting the entity, for communicating through parameters, common data areas or messages, and for direct access to internal data. The rules governing the interaction include the communications protocol, data format, acceptable values, and the meaning of each value.

This attribute shall provide a description of the input ranges, the meaning of inputs and outputs, the type and format of each input or output, and output error codes. For information systems, it should include inputs, screen formats, and a complete description of the interactive language.

5.3.8 Resources. *A description of the elements used by the entity that are external to the design.* The resources attribute shall identify and describe all of the resources *external* to the design that are needed by this entity to perform its function. The interaction rules and methods for using the resource shall be specified by this attribute.

This attribute provides information about items such as physical devices (printers, disc-partitions, memory banks), software services (math libraries, operating system services), and processing resources (CPU cycles, memory allocation, buffers).

The resources attribute shall describe usage characteristics such as the process time at which resources are to be acquired and sizing to include quantity, and physical sizes of buffer usage. It should also include the identification of potential race and deadlock conditions as well as resource management facilities.

5.3.9 Processing. *A description of the rules used by the entity to achieve its function.* The processing attribute shall describe the algorithm used by the entity to perform a specific task and shall include contingencies. This description is a refinement of the function attribute. It is the most detailed level of refinement for this entity.

This description should include timing, sequencing of events or processes, prerequisites for process initiation, priority of events, processing level, actual process steps, path conditions, and loop back or loop termination criteria. The handling of contingencies should describe the action to be taken in the case of overflow conditions or in the case of a validation check failure.

5.3.10 Data. *A description of data elements internal to the entity.* The data attribute shall describe the method of representation, initial values, use, semantics, format, and acceptable values of internal data.

The description of data may be in the form of a data dictionary that describes the content, structure, and use of all data elements. Data information shall describe everything pertaining to the use of data or internal data structures by this entity. It shall include data specifications such as formats, number of elements, and initial values. It shall also include the structures to be used for representing data such as file structures, arrays, stacks, queues, and memory partitions.

The meaning and use of data elements shall be specified. This description includes such things as static versus dynamic, whether it is to be shared by transactions, used as a control parameter, or used as a value, loop iteration count, pointer, or link field. In addition, data information shall include a description of data validation needed for the process.

6. Design Description Organization

6.1 Introduction. Each design description user may have a different view of what is considered the essential aspects of a software design. All other information is extraneous to that user. The proportion of useful information for a specific user will decrease with the size and complexity of a software project. The needed information then becomes difficult or impractical to extract from the description and impossible to assimilate. Hence, a practical organization of the necessary design information is essential to its use.

This section introduces the notion of *design views* to aid in organizing the design attribute information defined in Section 5. It does not supplement Section 5 by providing additional design information nor does it prescribe the format or documentation practice for design views.

A recommended organization of design entities and their associated attributes are presented in this section to facilitate the access of design information from various technical viewpoints. This recommended organization is flexible and can be implemented through different media such as paper documentation, design languages, or database management systems with automated report generation, and query language access. Since paper documentation is currently the primary design description medium, a sample table of contents is given in the Appendix.

6.2 Design Views. Entity attribute information can be organized in several ways to reveal all of the essential aspects of a design. In so doing, the user is able to focus on design details from a different perspective or viewpoint. A *design view* is a subset of design entity attribute information that is specifically suited to the needs of a software project activity.

Each design view represents a separate concern about a software system. Together, these views provide a comprehensive description of the design in a concise and usable form that simplifies information access and assimilation.

A recommended organization of the SDD into separate design views to facilitate information access and assimilation is given in Table 1. Each of these views, their use, and representation are discussed in detail.

6.2.1 Decomposition Description

6.2.1.1 Scope. The decomposition description records the division of the software system into design entities. It describes the way the system has been structured and the purpose and function of each entity. For each entity, it provides a reference to the detailed description via the identification attribute.

Table 1
Recommended Design Views

Design View	Scope	Entity Attributes	Example Representations
Decomposition Description	Partition of the system into design entities	Identification, type, purpose, function, subordinates	Hierarchical decomposition diagram, natural language
Dependency Description	Description of the relationships among entities and system resources	Identification, type, purpose, dependencies, resources	Structure charts, data flow diagrams, transaction diagrams
Interface Description	List of everything a designer, programmer, or tester needs to know to use the design entities that make up the system	Identification, function, interfaces	Interface files, parameter tables
Detail Description	Description of the internal design details of an entity	Identification, processing, data	Flowcharts, N-S charts, PDL

The attribute descriptions for identification, type, purpose, function, and subordinates should be included in this design view. This attribute information should be provided for all design entities.

6.2.1.2 Use. The decomposition description can be used by designers and maintainers to identify the major design entities of the system for purposes such as determining which entity is responsible for performing specific functions and tracing requirements to design entities. Design entities can be grouped into major classes to assist in locating a particular type of information and to assist in reviewing the decomposition for completeness. For example, a module decomposition may exist separately from a data decomposition.

The information in the decomposition description can be used by project management for planning, monitoring, and control of a software project. They can identify each software component, its purpose, and basic functionality. This design information together with other project information can be used in estimating cost, staff, and schedule for the development effort.

Configuration management may use the information to establish the organization, tracking, and change management of emerging work products; see ANSI/IEEE Std 828-1983 [3]. Metrics developers may also use this information for initial complexity, sizing, staffing, and development time parameters. The software quality assurance staff can use the decomposition description to construct a requirements traceability matrix.

6.2.1.3 Representation. The literature on software engineering describes a number of methods that provide consistent criteria for entity decomposition [5]. These methods provide for designing simple, independent entities and are based on such principles as structured design and information hiding. The primary graphical technique used to describe system decomposition is a hierarchical decomposition diagram. This diagram can be used together with natural language descriptions of purpose and function for each entity.

6.2.2 Dependency Description

6.2.2.1 Scope. The dependency description specifies the relationships among entities. It identifies the dependent entities, describes their coupling, and identifies the required resources.

This design view defines the strategies for interactions among design entities and provides the information needed to easily preceive how, why, where, and at what level system actions occur. It specifies the type of relationships that exist among the entities such as shared information, prescribed order of execution, or well defined parameter interfaces.

The attribute descriptions for identification, type, purpose, dependencies, and resources should be included in this design view. This attribute information should be provided for all design entities.

6.2.2.2 Use. The dependency description provides an overall picture of how the system works in order to assess the impact of requirements and design changes. It can help maintainers to isolate entities causing system failures or resource bottlenecks. It can aid in producing the system integration plan by identifying the entities that are needed by other entities and that must be developed first. This description can also be used by integration testing to aid in the production of integration test cases.

6.2.2.3 Representation. There are a number of methods that help minimize the relationships among entities by maximizing the relationship among elements in the same entity. These methods emphasize low module coupling and high module cohesion [5].

Formal specification languages provide for the specification of system functions and data, their interrelationships, the inputs and outputs, and other system aspects in a well-defined language. The relationship among design entities is also represented by data flow diagrams, structure charts, or transaction diagrams.

6.2.3 Interface Description

6.2.3.1 Scope. The entity interface description provides everything designers, programmers, and testers need to know to correctly use the functions provided by an entity. This description includes the details of external and internal interfaces not provided in the software requirements specification.

This design view consists of a set of interface specifications for each entity. The attribute descriptions for identification, function, and interfaces should be included in this design view. This attribute information should be provided for all design entities.

6.2.3.2 Use. The interface description serves as a binding contract among designers, programmers, customers, and testers. It provides them with an agreement needed before proceeding with the detailed design of entities. In addition, the interface description may be used by technical writers to produce customer documentation or may be used directly by customers. In the later case, the interface description could result in the production of a human interface view.

Designers, programmers, and testers may need to use design entities that they did not develop. These entities may be reused from earlier projects, contracted from an external source, or produced by other developers. The interface description settles the agreement among designers, programmers, and testers about how cooperating entities will interact. Each entity interface description should contain everything another designer or programmer needs to know to develop software that interacts with that entity. A clear description of entity interfaces is essential on a multiperson development for smooth integration and ease of maintenance.

6.2.3.3 Representation. The interface description should provide the language for communicating with each entity to include screen formats, valid inputs, and resulting outputs. For those entities that are data driven, a data dictionary should be used to describe the data characteristics. Those entities that are highly visible to a user and involve the details of how the customer should perceive the system should include a functional model, scenarios for use, detailed feature sets, and the interaction language.

6.2.4 Detailed Design Description

6.2.4.1 Scope. The detailed design description contains the internal details of each design entity. These details include the attribute descriptions for identification, processing, and data. This attribute information should be provided for all design entities.

6.2.4.2 Use. This description contains the details needed by programmers prior to implementation. The detailed design description can also be used to aid in producing unit test plans.

6.2.4.3 Representation. There are many tools used to describe the details of design entities. Program design languages can be used to describe inputs, outputs, local data and the algorithm for an entity. Other common techniques for describing design entity logic include using metacode or structured English, or graphical methods such as Nassi-Schneidermann charts or flowcharts.

Appendix

(This Appendix is not a part of IEEE Std 1016-1987, IEEE Recommended Practice for Software Design Descriptions, but is included for information only.)

The following example of a table of contents shows only one of many possible ways to organize and format the design views and associated information presented in Section 6 of this standard.

Table of Contents for an SDD

SECTION PAGE

The following organizations supported working group members in the development of this recommended practice:

AT&T Bell Laboratories
AT&T Information Systems
Atkinson System Technologies Co
Bell Canada
Bendix Field Engineering Corp
California State University, Sacramento
Center for Industrial Research (Norway)
Computer Sciences Corp
Computer Systems & Sciences
Douglas Aircraft Co
Digital Equipment Corp
Erisoft AB, Sweden
GEAC Computers International, Inc
General Electric Co
Grumman-CTEC, Inc
Harris Corp
Hewlett Packard
Hughes Aircraft
ITT-Chernow Communications, Inc
Jet Propulsion Laboratory
John Fluke Mfg Co
London School of Economics
McDonald Dettwiler & Associates
National Semiconductor
NCR
Northern Telecom
Ortho Pharmaceutical Corp
Programming Environments, Inc
Raytheon
RCA
Santa Clara University
Storage Technology Corp
Systems Designers
Unisyn Inc
University of Hong Kong
University of Idaho
U.S. Dept of Transportation
Zilog Corp

Recognized as an
American National Standard (ANSI)

IEEE
Std 1028-1988

IEEE Standard for Software Reviews and Audits

Corrected Edition
June 30, 1989

Corrections have been made on pages 5, 8, 10, 11, 12, 25, 26, 27, 29, and 35. A black bar has been added opposite each correction to aid in identifying the changes made to this printing.

Sponsor

Software Engineering Standards Subcommittee of the Technical Committee on Software Engineering of the IEEE Computer Society

Approved June 9, 1988

IEEE Standards Board

Approved June 29, 1989

American National Standards Institute

The Institute of Electrical and Electronics Engineers, Inc
345 East 47th Street, New York, NY 10017 USA

Foreword

(This Foreword is not a part of IEEE Std 1028-1988, IEEE Standard for Software Reviews and Audits.)

This Foreword provides the user with the rationale and background of the review and audit procedures outlined in this standard, and their relation to other IEEE standards.

Purpose. This standard defines the review and audit processes applicable to critical and noncritical software, and the specific procedures required for the execution of the reviews and audits described.Also, this standard supports ANSI/IEEE Std 730-1984 by defining review and audit procedures.

This standard does not establish measures or mechanisms for judging individual contributions to product development. Conformance to this standard may be claimed where reviews and audits are performed using procedures defined by this standard.

Additional documents that should be referenced for specific application of this standard are as follows:

(1) ANSI/IEEE Std 729-1983, IEEE Standard Glossary of Software Engineering Terminology.
(2) ANSI/IEEE Std 730-1984, IEEE Standard for Software Quality Assurance Plans.
(3) ANSI/IEEE Std 828-1983, IEEE Standard for Software Configuration Management Plans.
(4) ANSI/IEEE Std 983-1986, IEEE Guide for Software Quality Assurance.
(5) ANSI/IEEE Std 1012-1986 IEEE Standard for Software Verification and Validation Plans.

These standards address specific applications to this standard. Although only IEEE standards are referenced in this standard, this standard can be applied in concert with local standards requiring reviews and audits.

Moreover, to support the use of this standard by ensuring uniform classification and codes, use of IEEE Std 1044-1988, IEEE Standard Classification for Software Errors, Faults, and Failures, is suggested.

General Application Intent. This standard applies to all phases of typical software life cycles and provides a standard against which review and audit plans can be prepared and assessed. Maximum benefit can be derived from this standard by planning for its application early in the project life cycle.

This standard can be used with different life cycles provided its intent is followed. ANSI/IEEE Std 730-1984 identifies specific (and minimum) review and audit applications for critical software, while this standard defines the specific processes available to meet these application needs. Planning for reviews and audits, as part of an integrated verification and validation approach, can be aided by following ANSI/IEEE Std 1012-1986.

This standard for software reviews and audits was written in consideration of both the software and its system operating environment. It can be used where software is the total system entity or where it is part of a larger system. Care should be taken to integrate software review and audit activities into any total system development planning; they should exist in concert with hardware system reviews and audits to the benefits of the entire system. To broaden the application possibilities of this standard, simply replace *software element* with *system element* when reading.

This standard was written with the assumption that organizations are void of corruption. This may become an issue where, for example, during the course of an audit, theft or embezzlement is discovered. In such a case, although the audit may proceed, the applicability of this standard is removed.

Appendixes. Although not considered part of this standard, appendixes are provided to assist the reader in understanding:

(1) Specific process applications required by ANSI/IEEE Std 730-1984.
(2) How processes defined in this standard might be applied to meet those application needs.

Audience. This standard was written for those who are responsible for defining, planning, implementing, or supporting software reviews and audits.

Conformance. Conformance to this standard can be claimed when review and audit processes, wherever performed, are performed as defined in this standard.

The following persons were on the balloting committee that approved this document for submission to the IEEE Standards Board.

A. Frank Ackerman
Richard L. Aurbach
Motoei Azuma
H. Jack Barnard
James B. Behm
Leo Beltracchi
Michael A. Blackledge
Gilles R. Bracon
Kathleen L. Briggs
A. Winsor Brown
William Bryan
F. Buckley
Lorie J. Call
Ronald L. Cariola
Harry Carl
John Center
T. S. Chow
J. K. Chung
Won L. Chung
Antonio Cicu
Corey Clinger
Peter Coach
Francois Coallier
Carolyn Collins
Chris Cooke
Rudolph P. Corbett
Stewart Crawford
Taz Daughtrey
Peter A. Denny
Fred M. Discenzo
David A. Dobratz
Michael P. Dotson
David C. Doty
Einar Dragstedt
William P. Dupras
Michael Dutton
Mary L. Eads
Robert G. Ebenau
L. G. Egan
W. D. Ehrenberger
Walter Ellis
Caroline L. Evans
David W. Favor
John Fendrich
Glenn S. Fields
Violet Foldes
Thom Foote-Lennox
Joel Forman
Julian Forster
Richrad C. Fries
Ismael Fuentes
F. Karl Gardner
Leonard B. Gardner
David Gelperin
Anne K. Geraci
Jean A. Gilmore
Shirley A. Gloss-Soler
J. G. Glynn
Andrej Grebenc
Benjamin W. Green
Victor M. Guarnera
Lawrence M. Gunther
David A. Gustafson
Clark Hay
David A. Hill
William A. Hoberg
Charles P. Hollocker
John W. Horch
Laurel V. Kaleda
Harry Kalmbach
Myron S. Karasik
Timothy C. Kasse
George A. Klammer
George Konstantinow
Joseph A. Krvpinsh
Joan Kundig
Tom Kurihara
Lak-Ming Lam
John B. Lane
Robert A. Lane
Gregorie N. Larsen
F. C. Lim
Bertil Lindbert
Ben Livson
Austin J. Maher
Stanley A. Marash
Paulo Cesar Marcondes
Philip C. Marriott
Nicholas L. Marselos
Roger J. Martin
Paul A. Mauro
J. A. McCall
Russell McDowell
Stanley E. McQueen
Manijeh Moghis
Charles S. Mooney
Gary D. Moorhead
D. D. Morton
G. T. Morun
Hirouobu Nagano
Geraldine Neidhart
Dennis E. Nickle
E. J. Oertel
Wilma Osborne
M. T. Perkins
William E. Perry
John Petraglia
Ronald T. Pfaff
Donald J. Pfeiffer
I. C. Pyle
Thomas Steven Radi
Salim Ramji
Jean-Claude Rault
Meir Razy
Donald J. Reifer
R. San Roman
John C. Rowe
Margaret Rumley
Julio Gonzalez Sanz
Stephen R. Schach
Hans Schaefer
Norman Schneidewind
Wolf A. Schnoege
Robert G. Schueppert
David J. Schultz
Gregory D. Schumacher
Leonard W. Seagren
Tony Sgarlatti
Isaac-Shahab Shadman
Gerald P. Share
Robert W. Shillato
David M. Siefert
William G. Singer
Jacob Slonim
G. Wayne Staley
Nick Stewart
W. G. Sutcliffe
Richard H. Thayer
Bob Thibodeau
Paul U. Thompson
George D. Tice
Terrence L. Tillmanns
Valentin W. Tirman
L. F. Tracey
Glenn R. Trebble
Henry J. Trochesset
C. L. Troyanowski
William Stephen Turner, III
Robert B. Urling
David Usechak
Tom Vollman
Dolores R. Wallace
John P. Walter
John W. Walz
Charles J. Wertz
G. Allan Whittaker
Patrick J. Wilson
David L. Winningham
W. M. Wong
Dennis L. Wood
Marian A. Wysocki
Natalie C. Yopconka
Donald Zeleny
Kenneth M. Zemrowski
Peter F. Zoll

At the time this standard was approved, the Software Reviews and Audits Working Group of the Software Engineering Technical Committee of the IEEE Computer Society had the following members:

Charles P. Hollocker, Chairman **Tim Kasse, Cochairman**

William A. Hoberg, Secretary

A. Frank Ackerman
Jack Barnard
William Bryan
Ronald L. Cariola
Francois Coallier
Christopher M. Cooke
Rudy Corbett
Stewart Crawford
Vince Dowd
Robert G. Ebenau
Michael Fagan
Violet Foldes
Gordon Grunewald
Clark Hay
Peter Hung
David R. Janson
Harry Kalmbach
Myron Karasik
Adi Kasad
Robert A. Kessler
Tom Kurihara
Philip C. Marriot
Stan McQueen
Belden Menkus
William Perry
William N. Sabor
Isaac Shadman
David J. Schultz
Richard H. Thayer
William S. Turner, III
Marian Wysocki
Natalie C. Yopconka

When the IEEE Standards Board approved this standard on June 9, 1988, it had the following membership:

Donald C. Fleckenstein, *Chairman* **Marco W. Migliaro**, *Vice Chairman*

Andrew G. Salem, *Secretary*

Arthur A. Blaisdell
Fletcher J. Buckley
James M. Daly
Stephen R. Dillon
Eugene P. Fogarty
Jay Forster*
Thomas L. Hannan
Kenneth D. Hendrix
Theodore W. Hissey, Jr
John W. Horch
Jack M. Kinn
Frank D. Kirschner
Frank C. Kitzantides
Joseph L. Koepfinger*
Irving Kolodny
Edward Lohse
John E. May, Jr
Lawrence V. McCall
L. Bruce McClung
Donald T. Michael*
Richard E. Mosher
L. John Rankine
Gary S. Robinson
Frank L. Rose
Helen M. Wood
Karl H. Zaininger
Donald W. Zipse

*Members Emeriti

IEEE

Contents

IEEE Standard for Software Reviews and Audits

1. Scope and References

1.1 Scope. The purpose of this standard is to provide definitions and uniform requirements for review and audit processes. It does not establish the need to conduct specific reviews or audits; that need is defined by local policy. Where specific reviews and audits are required, standard procedures for their execution must be defined.

This standard provides such definition for review and audit processes that are applicable to products and processes throughout the software life cycle. Each organization shall specify where and when this standard applies and any intended deviations from this standard.

1.2 References. This standard shall be used in conjunction with the following publications:

[1] ANSI/IEEE Std 729-1983, IEEE Standard Glossary of Software Engineering Terminology.[1]

[2] ANSI/IEEE Std 829-1983, IEEE Standard for Software Test Documentation.

2. Definitions

audit. An independent evaluation of software products or processes to ascertain compliance to standards, guidelines, specifications, and procedures based on objective criteria that include documents that specify

(1) The form or content of the products to be produced
(2) The process by which the products shall be produced
(3) How compliance to standards or guidelines shall be measured

review. An evaluation of software element(s) or project status to ascertain discrepancies from planned results and to recommend improvement. This evaluation follows a formal process (for example, management review process, technical review process, software inspection process, or walkthrough process).

software element. A deliverable or in-process document produced or acquired during software development or maintenance. Specific examples include but are not limited to

(1) Project planning documents (for example, software development plans, and software verification and validation plans)
(2) Software requirements and design specifications
(3) Test effort documentation (ie, as described in ANSI/IEEE Std 829-1983 [2])[2]
(4) Customer-deliverable documentation
(5) Program source code
(6) Representation of software solutions implemented in firmware
(7) Reports (for example, review, audit, projectect status) and data (for example, defect detection, test)

For other definitions, including verification and validation, see ANSI/IEEE Std 729-1983 [1].

---

[1]ANSI/IEEE publications are available from IEEE Service Center, 445 Hoes Lane, PO Box 1331, Piscataway, NJ 08855-1331, or from the Sales Department, American National Standards Institute, 1430 Broadway, New York, NY 10018.

[2]The numbers in brackets correspond to those of the references in 1.2.

3. Introduction

Reviews and audits can be used in support of objectives associated with software quality assurance, project management, and configuration management, or similar control functions, as shown in Table 1. Those quality objectives, valid throughout software development and maintenance, include the need for evaluation, verification, validation, and compliance confirmation. For the sake of completeness, Test is identified in Table 1 as the principal process of validation. Testing, however, is outside the scope of this standard. Processes defined in this standard include

(1) Management review
(2) Technical review
(3) Software inspection
(4) Walkthrough
(5) Audit

To support compliance confirmation, auditing activities may include performing reviews and tests to determine product consistency with respect to established baselines (ie, software requirements specifications or design descriptions) or to witness the correctness of implementation.

Moreover, since quality assurance deals with products and processes, Fig 1 provides a view of how various quality assurance processes can be mapped to examine product and project issues.

The examination of project issues (both technical and managerial) occurs at various phases during the project life cycle. The results of such examinations are meant to permit improvement of the methods of ensuring software quality and the ability to meet time and cost constraints. The evaluation of software elements occurs during the production of the element(s) and on its completion. This ensures that the element(s) completely and correctly embodies its baseline specifications.

Any standard process has prerequisite conditions; those conditions necessary, though not in themselves sufficient for the process to reach completion. For reviews and audits, these conditions are identified in 3.1 and 3.2 respectively.

Table 1
Some Principal Processes for Achieving Quality Objectives

Objectives	Principal Processes Include
Evaluation	Management review, Technical review
Verification	Inspection, Walkthrough
Validation	Test
Compliance, Confirmation	Audit

Fig 1
Relation of Some Quality Assurance Processes to Products and Projects

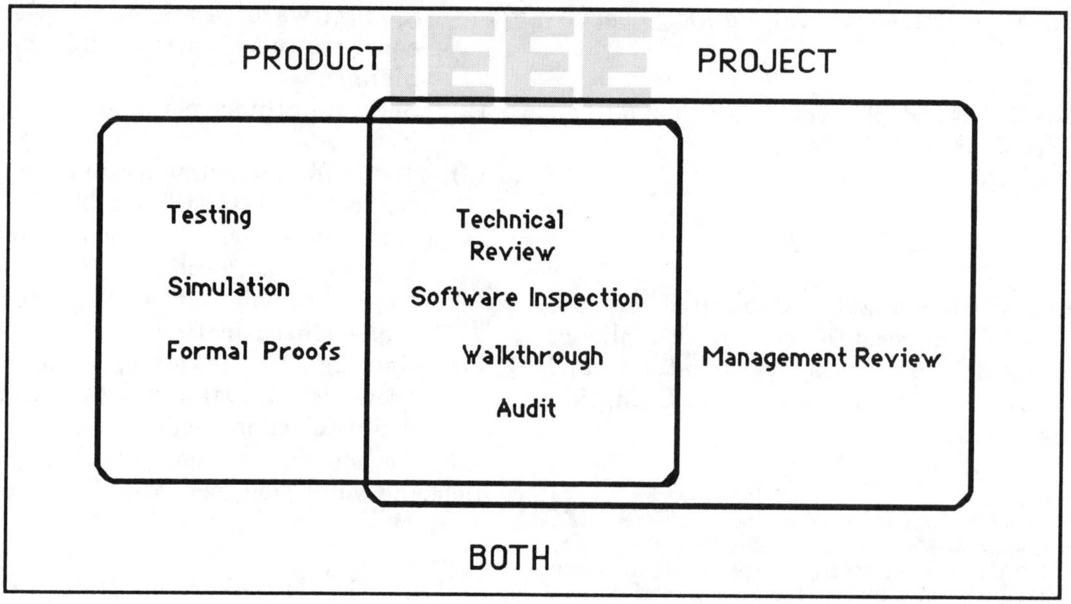

Section 3.3 presents the template used to define review and audit processes in the following sections.

3.1 Review Process Prerequisites. The objective of reviewing software elements is to evaluate software or project status to identify discrepancies from planned results and to recommend improvement where appropriate.

The following managerial offices are to achieve that objective:

3.1.1 Management

(1) Responsible for reviews, and the anticipated product rework

(2) Responsible for performance of reviews and reporting of review results against project milestone events

(3) Provides the necessary resources of time, personnel, budget, and facilities required to plan, define, execute, and manage the reviews

3.1.2 Development Staff

(1) The staff has a level of development expertise and product knowledge sufficient to comprehend the software under review.

(2) Training and orientation in the use of the review processes are provided to the staff.

3.1.3 Development Process Planning

(1) Standard entry and exit criteria have been defined for development phases.

(2) The product criteria (such as readability and modularity) are sufficiently defined by development standards.

(3) The product is partitioned into manageable, reviewable units.

(4) The software elements to be reviewed and the review process to be employed are identified in the project planning documents (for example, Software Quality Assurance Plan, Software Verification Plan, and Software Project Management Plan.

3.1.4 Review Process Planning

(1) Each type of review to be employed is fully specified.

(2) Administrative procedures are defined to enable the review to be initiated, executed, recorded, and acted on.

(3) The responsibility is assigned for the planning, specification, administration, and maintenance of the review process.

3.2 Audit Process Prerequisites. The objective of software auditing is to provide an objective evaluation of products and processes to confirm compliance to standards, guidelines, specifications, and procedures. The following requirements are prerequisite to achieve that objective:

(1) Objective audit criteria exist (for example, contracts, requirements, plans, specifications, standards) against which software elements and processes can be evaluated.

(2) Audit personnel are selected to promote team objectivity. They are usually independent of any direct responsibility for the products and processes examined and may be from an external organization.

(3) Audit personnel are given sufficient authority by appropriate management to perform the audit.

3.3 Procedural Description Template. The following descriptions establish the minimum template used to plan, prepare, and execute any review or audit. The review and audit process descriptions in this standard follow this common template:

().1 *Objective:* Process goals.

().2 *Abstract:* Process overview.

().3 *Special Responsibilities:* Roles unique to this specific process.

().4 *Input:* Products to which the process is applied, and supporting information.

().5 *Entry Criteria:* Conditions that must be satisfied before the process can begin.

().6 *Procedures:* Standard steps followed in performing the process.

().7 *Exit Criteria:* Conditions that must be satisfied before this process is considered complete.

().8 *Output:* The minimum set of deliverables resulting from process completion.

().9 *Auditability:* Description of evidence needed to determine at a later date that the process was followed.

Additional template sections have been added to these basic nine sections when needed.

Procedure descriptions in section "().6" will be presented as to include, but not be limited to, the following steps:

().6.1 Planning ().6.3 Preparation
().6.2 Overview ().6.4 Examination

Additional procedure subsections have been added where needed.

4. The Management Review Process

4.1 Objective. The objective of a management review is to provide recommendations for the following:

(1) Making activities progress according to plan, based on an evaluation of product development status;
(2) Changing project direction or to identify the need for alternative planning;
(3) Maintaining global control of the project through adequate allocation of resources.

The management review process can be applied to new development or to maintenance activities.

4.2 Abstract. A management review is a formal evaluation of a project level plan or project status relative to that plan by a designated review team.

During the review meeting the entire review team examines plans or progress against applicable plans, standards, and guidelines, or both. Each problem area identified by the review team is recorded. When critical data and information cannot be supplied, then an additional meeting shall be scheduled to complete the management review process.

4.3 Special Responsibilities. The review leader is responsible for the administrative tasks pertaining to the review, for assuring that the review is conducted in an orderly manner, and for issuing the management review report (see 4.8).

The individual(s) responsible for formally reporting the status of the project under review will ensure that the project status and all supporting documentation are available for distribution.

Each member of the review team is responsible for the following:

(1) Being adequately prepared for the meeting;
(2) Ensuring that the review meets its objectives.

4.4 Input. The minimum input to the management review process is as follows:

(1) A statement of objectives for the management review
(2) A list of issues to be addressed
(3) Current project schedule and cost data
(4) Reports (for example, managerial review reports, technical review reports, audit reports) from other reviews or audits, or both, already completed
(5) Reports of resources assigned to the project
(6) Data on the software elements completed or in progress

Additional applicable reference material can be supplied by project management or requested by the review leader.

4.5 Entry Criteria

4.5.1 Authorization. The need for conducting certain management reviews is initially established in the appropriate project planning documents (for example, Software Quality Assurance Plan, Software Development Plan, or Software Verification and Validation Plan). Under these plans, completion of a specific software element (for example, a Planning Document, a Requirements Specification, a Design Document, and Code Specification), or completion of a phase can trigger a management review.

In addition to those management reviews required by a specific plan, other management reviews may be formally announced and held at the request of software quality management, functional management, project management or the customer, according to local procedures.

4.5.2 Initiating Event. A management review is conducted when a selected review leader does the following:

(1) Establishes or confirms a statement of objectives for the meeting;
(2) Judges that the software element(s) and any other documentation or reports pertinent to the review are sufficiently complete and their status available to support the review objectives.

4.6 Procedures

4.6.1 Planning. During the planning step, the review leader, in conjunction with project management, does the following:

(1) Identifies the review team
(2) Schedules the meeting and identifies a meeting place
(3) Distributes input materials to the participants, allowing adequate time for preparation

4.6.2 Overview. A qualified person from the project under examination shall conduct an overview session for the review team when requested by the review leader. This overview can occur as a part of the examination meeting (see 4.6.4) or as a separate meeting.

4.6.3 Preparation. Each person on the review team individually studies the material and prepares for the review meeting. Any required presentations to the review team are prepared.

4.6.4 Examination. During the management review the review team holds one or more meetings to do the following:

(1) Examine project status and determine if it complies with the expected status according to a predefined plan;
(2) Examine project status and determine if it is overly constrained by external and internal factors not originally considered in the project plan;
(3) Record all deviations from the expected status accenting risks;
(4) Generate a list of issues and recommendations to be addressed by higher level management;
(5) Generate a list of issues and recommendations to be addressed by other responsible individuals, or organizations who affect the project;
(6) Recommend what course of action should be taken from this point on;
(7) Recommend authorization for additional reviews or audits;
(8) Identify other issues that must be addressed.

4.6.5 Rework. Any plan adjustments or product rework resulting from the management review is not considered as part of the management review process, except where needed as additional input to complete the examination process.

4.7 Exit Criteria. The management review is considered complete when

(1) All issues identified in the review Statement of Objectives have been addressed.
(2) The management review report has been issued (see 4.8).

4.8 Output. The output from the management review process is a Management Review Report that identifies the following:

(1) The project being reviewed;
(2) The review team;
(3) Inputs to the review;
(4) Review objectives;
(5) Action item ownership and status;
(6) A list of issues and recommendations identified by the review team that must be addressed for the project to meet its milestone;
(7) Recommendations regarding any further reviews and audits, and a list of additional information and data that must be obtained before they can be executed.

Although this standard sets minimum requirements for report content, it is left to local standards to prescribe any report format requirements.

4.9 Auditability. The management review report is an auditable item. It is recommended that this report be traceable to and from the appropriate project planning documents (for example, Software Development Plan, Software Quality Assurance Plan, or other applicable plans, or a combination of these).

5. The Technical Review Process

5.1 Objective. The objective of a technical review is to evaluate a specific software element(s) and provide management with evidence that

(1) The software element(s) conform to its specifications;
(2) The development (or maintenance) of the software element(s) is being done according to plans, standards, and guidelines applicable for the project;
(3) Changes to the software element(s) are properly implemented, and affect only those system areas identified by the change specification.

Moreover, to further tailor this review process for an individual software element, specific objectives are to be identified in a Statement of Objectives made available before the review meeting. The technical review concept can be applied to new development or to maintenance activities.

5.2 Abstract. A technical review is a formal team evaluation of a software element(s). It identifies any discrepancies from specifications and standards or provides recommendations after the examination of alternatives, or both. This examination may require more than one meeting.

5.3 Special Responsibilities. Roles for the technical review include:

5.3.1 Leader. The review leader is responsible for conducting a specific review. This includes administrative tasks pertaining to the review and ensuring that the review is conducted in an orderly manner. The review leader is also responsible for issuing the review report.

5.3.2 Recorder. The recorder is responsible for documenting findings (for example, defects, inconsistencies, omissions, and ambiguities), decisions, and recommendations made by the review team.

5.3.3 Team Member. Each team's members is responsible for their own preparation, and for ensuring that the review meets its objectives. Together, they are responsible for formulating recommendations in such a way that management can act on them promptly.

Management is responsible for acting on the review team recommendations in a timely manner.

5.4 Input. The minimum input to the technical review process is as follows:

(1) A statement of objectives for the technical review
(2) The software element(s) being examined
(3) Specifications for the software element(s) being examined
(4) Any plans, standards, or guidelines against which the software element(s) are to be examined

Additional applicable reference material can be made available by the individual(s) responsible for the software element, when requested by the review leader.

5.5 Entry Criteria

5.5.1 Authorization. The need for conducting technical reviews of specific software elements is defined by project planning documents.

Unscheduled technical reviews may be conducted at the request of functional management, project management, software quality management, or software engineers, according to local procedures.

5.5.2 Initiating Event. A technical review may not be conducted until

(1) A statement of objectives for the review is established;
(2) The responsible individual(s) for the software element(s) indicate readiness for review;
(3) The technical review leader is satisfied that the software element(s) are sufficiently complete for a technical review to be worthwhile

5.6 Procedures

5.6.1 Planning. A review leader is assigned responsibility for the following planning activities:

(1) Identify, with appropriate management support, the review team
(2) Schedule and announce the meeting place
(3) Distribute input materials to participants, allowing adequate time for their preparation

5.6.2 Overview. A technically qualified person shall conduct an overview session for the review team when requested by the review leader. This overview can occur as a part of the review meeting (see 5.6.4) or as a separate meeting.

5.6.3 Preparation. During the preparation step, each review team member individually examines the software element(s) and related materials in preparation for the review meeting.

5.6.4 Examination. At the review meeting the entire team reviews the software element, evaluating its condition relative to applicable guidelines, specifications and standards, or evaluating alternative problem solutions. Specifically, the review team performs the following tasks:

(1) Examines the software element(s) under review and verifies that it complies with the specifications and standards to which it must adhere. All deviations from the specifications and standards are recorded.
(2) Documents technical issues, related recommendations, and the individual responsible for getting the issues resolved.
(3) Identifies other issues that must be addressed.

After the software element(s) have been reviewed, a report is generated to document the meeting, list deficiencies found in the software element, and describe any recommendations for management.

When deficiencies are sufficiently critical or numerous, the review leader must recommend that an additional review process (that is, management review, technical review, or walkthrough) be applied to the reworked software element(s) after the deficiencies have been resolved. This, at a minimum, covers areas changed to resolve deficiencies.

5.7 Exit Criteria. A Technical Review is complete when

(1) All issues identified in the review Statement of Objectives have been addressed
(2) The technical review report (see 5.8) has been issued

5.8 Output. The output from the technical review process is a technical review report that identifies the following:

(1) The review team members
(2) The software element(s) reviewed
(3) Specific inputs to the review
(4) A list of unresolved software element(s) deficiencies
(5) A list of management issues
(6) Action item ownership and status
(7) Any recommendations made by the review team on how to dispose of unresolved issues and deficiencies

Although this standard sets minimum requirements for report content, it is left to local standards to prescribe any report format requirements.

5.9 Auditability. The technical review report is an auditable item. It is recommended that this report be traceable to/from the appropriate project planning documents (for example, Software Development Plan, Software Quality Assurance Plan).

6. The Software Inspection Process

6.1 Objective. The objective of a software inspection is to detect and identify software element defects. This is a rigorous, formal peer examination that does the following:

(1) Verifies that the software element(s) satisfy its specifications
(2) Verifies that the software element(s) conform to applicable standards
(3) Identifies deviation from standards and specifications
4) Collects software engineering data (for example, defect and effort data)
(5) Does not examine alternatives or stylistic issues

6.2 Abstract. Software inspections are conducted by peers, and typically comprise three to six participants. The process is led by a moderator impartial to the software element(s) under examination. The moderator is not the author. Defect resolution is mandatory, and rework is formally verified.

Defect data shall be systematically collected and stored in an inspection data base. Minimum requirements for data collection are presented in 6.10. When this data is analyzed, steps can be taken to improve both the product and the development process, and to assess the effectiveness of the inspection process.

6.3 Special Responsibilities. All team members, including those with special roles, are inspectors. Special roles required for the inspection process include

6.3.1 Moderator. The moderator is the chief planner and meeting manager for the inspection process, and is responsible for issuing the inspection reports (see 6.8). The moderator may also perform the role of recorder.

6.3.2 Reader. At the meeting(s), the reader leads the inspection team through the software element(s) in a comprehensive and logical fashion, generally paraphrasing sections of the work and by reading line-by-line where required by local standards.

6.3.3 Recorder. The recorder is charged with documenting defects detected at the meeting(s) and recording inspection data required for process analysis.

6.3.4 Inspector. The role of inspector is to identify and describe defects in the software element. Inspectors must be knowledgeable of the inspection process. They are chosen to represent different viewpoints at the meeting (for example, requirements, design, code, test, independent test, project management, quality management). Only those viewpoints pertinent to the inspection of the element are present.

6.3.5 Author. The author is responsible for the software element(s) meeting its inspection entry criteria, for contributing to the inspection based on special understanding of the software element, and for performing any rework required to make the software element(s) meet its inspection exit criteria. The author is not allowed to perform any other (that is, moderator, reader, or recorder) role.

6.4 Input. The necessary inputs to the inspection consist of the following:

(1) The software element(s) to be inspected; They must satisfy the inspection entry criteria;
(2) The approved software element(s) specification;
(3) The inspection checklist. See Appendix B for sample checklists;
(4) Any standards and guidelines against which the software element is to be inspected;
(5) All necessary inspection reporting forms.

For a reinspection, the previous inspection defect list is also required.

6.5 Entry Criteria

6.5.1 Authorization. Inspections are planned for, and documented in the appropriate project planning documents (for example, the overall project plan, software quality assurance plan, or software verification and validation plan).

6.5.2 Initiating Event. The software inspection process can be triggered by the following:

(1) Software element(s) availability
(2) Project plan compliance
(3) SQAP or SVVP schedule compliance
(4) Scheduled reinspection
(5) At the request of functional management, project management, software quality management, or software engineering

6.5.3 Minimum Entry Criteria Before Pannning Inspection. Before planning the inspection, the following minimum entry criteria must be met:

(1) The software element(s) conform to project standards of content, and format
(2) All prior milestones are satisfied, as identified in the the appropriate planning documents
(3) All required supporting documentation is available
(4) For a reinspection, all items noted on the defect list must be satisfied

6.6 Procedures

6.6.1 Planning. During the planning step, the author assembles the inspection package materials for the moderator.

The moderator is responsible for assuring that the materials meet the inspection entry criteria. The moderator is also responsible for assuring the selection of the inspection team and the assignment of their inspection meeting roles, for scheduling the inspection meetings, and for the distribution of the inspection materials.

6.6.2 Overview. If scheduled, an overview presentation of the software element(s)to be inspected is conducted by the moderator, and the author makes the presentation. This overview is used to educate the other inspectors concerning the software element(s) and may also be attended by other project personnel who could profit from the presentation.

6.6.3 Preparation. It is the individual responsibility of all inspectors to become thoroughly familiar with the software element, using the inspection checklist, the information provided in the overview, and the software specification.

6.6.4 Examination. The inspection meeting shall follow this agenda:

6.6.4.1 Introduce Meeting. To open the meeting, the moderator introduces the participants, and describes their roles. The moderator states the purpose of the inspection and directs the inspectors to focus their efforts toward defect detection, not solution-hunting.

The moderator reminds the inspectors to direct their remarks to the reader and to comment only on the product, not the author. It may also be useful to resolve any special procedural questions raised by the inspectors.

6.6.4.2 Establish Preparedness. The moderator asks for individual preparation times and records the total on the inspection report. It is the moderator's responsibility to reschedule the meeting if the inspectors are not adequately prepared.

6.6.4.3 Review the Inspection Checklist. The moderator reviews the inspection checklist with the team to ensure that the product has been adequately studied before the inspection meeting.

6.6.4.4 Read Software Elements and Record Defects. The reader presents the materials to the inspection team. The inspection team examines the software objectively, and the moderator focuses this part of the meeting on creating the defect list. The recorder enters each defect, location, description, and classification on the defect list. During this time, the author answers any specific questions and contributes to defect detection based on his/her special understanding of the software element.

6.6.4.5 Review the Defect List. At the end of the inspection meeting, the moderator must have the defect list reviewed with the team to ensure its completeness and accuracy.

6.6.4.6 Make Exit Decision. The purpose of the exit decision is to bring an unambiguous closure to the inspection meeting. The exit decision determines if the materials meet the inspection exit criteria and prescribes any appropriate rework verification. Specifically, the inspection team identifies the software element(s) disposition as one of the following:

(1) *Accept.* The software element is accepted *as is* or with only minor rework (for example, that would require no further verification)
(2) *Verify Rework.* The software element is to be accepted after the moderator verifies rework.
(3) *Reinspect.* Schedule a reinspection to verify rework after revision.

At a minimum, a reinspection examines the product areas changed to resolve defects identified in the last inspection.

6.6.5 Rework. During rework, the author revises the materials, addressing all items on the inspection defect list.

6.6.6 Follow-Up. The software inspection process provides follow-up on two levels:

(1) Verifying rework per inspection disposition
(2) Reporting inspection data

6.7 Exit Criteria. A single exit criterion applied to all inspections is that all of the defects that have been detected are resolved. Each project shall develop its own criteria to meet the needs of its specific products and development environment.

The moderator will ensure that the materials comply with the exit criteria and that the inspection results have been reported before certifying that the inspection is complete.

6.8 Output. For each software element(s), the reports produced by the inspection are:

(1) The defect list, containing the defect location, description, and categorization
(2) The inspection defect summary summarizing the number of defects identified by each defect category
(3) The inspection report, containing
 (a) The number of participants
 (b) The inspection meeting duration
 (c) The size of the materials inspected
 (d) The total preparation time of the inspection team
 (e) The disposition of the software element
 (f) An estimate of the rework effort and rework completion date

Information reports are retained for subsequent analysis as prescribed in the appropriate project planning documents. Although this standard sets minimum requirements for report content, it is left to local standards to prescribe any report format requirements.

6.9 Auditability. Auditability is provided by the following:

(1) Documented inspection procedures
(2) Retained inspection reports
(3) Retained inspection defect data

6.10 Data Collection Requirements. Software inspections provide data for the analysis of the quality of the software elements, the effectiveness of the development procedures, and the efficiency of the inspection process. To enable these analyses, defects that are identified at an inspection meeting are categorized by defect type, class, and severity.

6.10.1 The defect type identifies software element(s) attribute, and for example may be identified as affecting the software element's conformance to

(1) Standards compliance
(2) Capability
(3) Procedure
(4) Interface
(5) Description

6.10.2 Defect class characterizes evidence of nonconformance, and for example, may be categorized as

(1) Missing
(2) Wrong
(3) Extra

6.10.3 Additional defect classes used when inspecting documents could include

(1) Ambiguous
(2) Inconsistent

6.10.4 Defects are then ranked by severity, for example, as

(1) *Major*. Defects that would result in failure of the software element(s) or an observable departure from specification
(2) *Minor*. Defects that would affect only the nonfunctional aspects of the software element

In addition to counts of defects by type, class, and severity, retained inspection data shall contain the identification of the software element, the date and time of the inspection, the moderator, the preparation and inspection times, the volume of the materials inspected, and the disposition of the inspected software element. The recording of this information is required in setting local guidance for inspection effort and volume. Common practice would suggest up to 1.5 h preparation, up to 2 h meeting time, and whatever volume might be comfortably handled in that period of time.

The management of inspection data requires capabilities for the storage, entry, access, updating, and summarization and reporting of the categorized defects. The frequency and types of the inspection analysis reports, and their distribution, are left to the users of this standard.

7. The Walkthrough Process

7.1 Objective. The objective of a walkthrough is to evaluate a software element. Although long associated with code examinations, this process is also applicable to other software elements (for example, architectural design, detailed design, test plans/procedures, and change control procedures). The major objectives are to find defects, omissions, and contradictions; to improve the software element(s); and to consider alternative implementations.

Other important objectives of the walkthrough process include exchange of techniques and style variations, and education of the participants. A walkthrough may point out efficiency and readability problems in the code, modularity problems in design or untestable design specifications.

The walkthrough may be used in either new development or maintenance activities.

7.2 Abstract. During the walkthrough meeting, the author makes an overview presentation of the software element(s) under review. This is followed by a general discussion from the participants after which the presenter *"walks through"* the software element in detail. As the walkthrough progresses, errors, suggested changes, and improvements are noted and written. When the walkthrough is finished, the notes are consolidated into one report, which is distributed to the author and other appropriate personnel. A copy of the report is placed in the project file for auditability.

7.3 Special Responsibilities. The following roles are established for the walkthrough:

7.3.1 Moderator. The walkthrough moderator is responsible for conducting a specific walkthrough, handling the administrative tasks pertaining to the walkthrough, and ensuring that the walkthrough is conducted in an orderly manner. The moderator is also responsible for preparing the statement of objectives to guide the team through the walkthrough.

7.3.2 Recorder. The recorder is responsible for writing all comments made during the walkthrough that pertain to errors found, questions of style, omissions, contradictions, suggestions for improvement, or alternative approaches.

7.3.3 Author. The author is the person responsible for the software element(s) being examined, and presents the materials.

Each member of the walkthrough team is responsible for reviewing any input material prior to the walkthrough, and participating during the walkthrough to ensure that it meets its objective.

Roles may be shared among the walkthrough members. The author and walkthrough moderator may be the same person.

7.4 Input. The minimum input to the walkthrough process is as follows:

(1) A statement of objectives for the walkthrough
(2) The software element under examination
(3) Standards that are in effect for the development of the software element
(4) Specifications for the software element(s) under review

7.5 Entry Criteria

7.5.1 Authorization. The need for conducting walkthroughs shall be established in the appropriate planning documents, (for example, a software quality assurance plan (SQAP) or a software development plan). In addition, under either of these plans, completion of a specific software element(s) trigger the walkthrough for that element. Additional walkthroughs should be conducted during development of the software element(s) at the request of functional management, quality management, or the author, according to local procedures.

7.5.2 Initiating Event. A walkthrough is conducted when

(1) The author of the software element(s) to be reviewed indicates it is ready, and is prepared to present the materials.
(2) The moderator is appointed per local standards or practices and has concluded that the software element is sufficiently complete to conduct a walkthrough.

7.6 Procedures

7.6.1 Planning. During the planning phase, the walkthrough moderator does the following:

(1) Identifies the walkthrough team
(2) Schedules the meeting and selects the meeting place
(3) Distributes all necessary input materials to the participants, allowing for adequate preparation time

7.6.2 Overview. An overview presentation is made by the author as part of the walkthrough meeting. Before that meeting, however, individual preparation is still required.

7.6.3 Preparation. During the preparation phase participants shall review the input material that was distributed to them and prepare a list of questions and issues to be discussed during the walkthrough.

7.6.4 Examination. During the walkthrough meeting

(1) The presenter makes an overview presentation of the software element(s) under examination.
(2) The author walks through the specific software element(s) so that members of the walkthrough team may ask questions or raise issues regarding the software element, or document their concerns, or both.
(3) The recorder writes comments and decisions for inclusion in the walkthrough report.

At the completion of the walkthrough, the walkthrough team may recommend a follow-up walkthrough. This follow-up would follow the standard for walkthroughs, and would, at a minimum, cover areas changed by the author.

Within a reasonable time after the walkthrough, the walkthrough leader shall issue a walkthrough report detailing the walkthrough findings. Minimum content requirements are stated in 7.8.

7.7 Exit Criteria. The walkthrough process is complete when

(1) The entire software element(s) have been "*walked through*" in detail
(2) All deficiencies, omissions, efficiency issues, and suggestions for improvement have been noted
(3) The walkthrough report has been issued

7.8 Output. The output of the walkthrough process is a walkthrough report listing those deficiencies, omissions, efficiency issues, and suggestions for improvement that were recorded during the walkthrough.

The walkthrough report contains the following:

(1) Identification of the walkthrough team
(2) Identification of the software element(s) being examined
(3) The statement of objectives that were to be handled during this walkthrough meeting
(4) A list of the noted deficiencies, omissions, contradictions, and suggestions for improvement
(5) Any recommendations made by the walkthrough team on how to dispose of deficiencies and unresolved issues

If follow-up walkthroughs are suggested, this suggestion shall also be mentioned in the report.

Although this standard sets minimum requirements for report content, it is left to local standards to prescribe any report format requirements.

7.9 Auditability. The walkthrough report, meeting minutes, and other materials upon which conclusions are based shall be included in project documentation files. The walkthrough moderator files these documents.

8. The Audit Process

8.1 Objective. The objective of software auditing is to provide an objective compliance confirmation of products and processes to certify adherence to standards, guidelines, specifications, and procedures.

8.2 Abstract. Audits are performed in accordance with documented plans and procedures. The audit plan establishes a procedure to conduct the audit and for follow-up action on the audit findings.

In performing the audit, audit personnel evaluate software elements and the processes for producing them against objective audit criteria, such as contracts, requirements, plans, specifications, or procedures, guidelines, and standards.

The results of the audit are documented and are submitted to the management of the audited organization, to the entity initiating the audit, and to any external organizations identified in the audit plan. The report includes a list of the items in noncompliance or other issues for subsequent review and action. When stipulated by the audit plan, recommendations are reported in addition to the audit results.

8.3 Special Responsibilities. It is the responsibility of the audit team leader to organize and direct the audit and to coordinate the preparation and issuance of the audit report. The audit team leader shall ensure that the audit team is prepared to conduct the audit, and that audit procedures are performed and reports (see 8.8) issued in accordance with audit scope.

The entity initiating the audit is responsible for authorizing the audit. Management of the auditing organization assumes responsibility for the audit, and the allocation of the necessary resources to perform the audit.

Those whose products and processes are being audited provide all relevant materials and resources and correct or resolve deficiencies cited by the audit team.

8.4 Input. The following inputs are required to ensure the success of the audit:

(1) The purpose and scope of the audit.
(2) Objective audit criteria, such as contracts requirements, plans, specifications, procedures, guidelines, and standards.
(3) The software elements and processes to be audited and any pertinent histories.
(4) Background information regarding the organization responsible for the products and processes being audited (for example, organization charts).

8.5 Entry Criteria. The need for an audit is established by one of the following events:

(1) A special project milestone has been reached. The audit is initiated per earlier plans (for example, the software quality assurance plan, software development plan).
(2) External parties (for example, regulatory agencies, or end users) demand an audit at a specific calendar date or project milestone. This may be in fulfillment of a contract requirement, or as a prerequisite to contractual agreement.

(3) A local organizational element(s) (for example, project management, functional management, systems engineering, internal quality assurance/control) has requested the audit, establishing a clear and specific need.
(4) A special project milestone, calendar date, or other criterion has been met and, as part of the auditing organization's charter, it is to respond by initiating an audit.

8.6 Procedures

8.6.1 Planning. The auditing organization shall develop and document an audit plan for each audit. This plan shall, in addition to restating the audit scope, identify the following:
(1) Project processes to be examined (provided as input) and the time frame for audit team observation.
(2) Software required to be examined (provided as input) and their availability. Where sampling is used, a statistically valid sampling methodology shall be used to establish selection criteria and sample size.
(3) Reports shall be identified (that is, results report, and optionally, the recommendations report and their general format defined). Whether recommendations are required or excluded shall be explicitly stated.
(4) Report distribution
(5) Required follow-up activities
(6) Requirements: necessary activities, elements and procedures to meet the scope of the audit
(7) Objective audit criteria: provides the basis for determining compliance (provided as input)
(8) Audit procedures and checklists
(9) Audit personnel: required number, skills, experience, and responsibilities
(10) Organizations involved in the audit (for example, the organization whose products and processes are being audited)
(11) Date, time, place, agenda, and intended audience of *overview* session (optional)

The audit team leader shall ensure that the audit team is prepared and includes members with the necessary experience and expertise.

Notification of the audit shall be provided to the involved organizations at a reasonable amount of time before the audit is performed, except for unannounced audits. The notification shall be written and shall include the scope and the identification of processes and products to be audited, and to identify the auditors.

8.6.2 Overview. An optional overview meeting with the audited organization is recommended to *kick-off* the examination phase of the audit. The overview meeting, led by the audit team leader, provides the following:
(1) Overview of existing agreements (for example, audit scope, plan, related contracts);
(2) Overview of production and processes being audited;
(3) Overview of the audit process, its objectives, and outputs;
(4) Expected contributions of the audited organization to the audit process (that is, the number of people to be interviewed, meeting facilities, etc);
(5) Specific audit schedule.

8.6.3 Preparation

8.6.3.1 The following preparations are required by the audit team:
(1) Understand the organization: it is essential to identify functions and activities performed by the audited organization, and to identify functional responsibility.
(2) Understand the products and processes: it is a prerequisite for the team to learn about the products and processes being audited through readings and briefings.
(3) Understand the objective audit criteria: it is important that the audit team become familiar with the objective audit criteria to be used in the audit.
(4) Prepare for the audit report: it is important to choose the administrative reporting mechanism that will be used throughout the audit to develop the report that follows the layout identified in the audit plan.
(5) Detail the audit plan: choose appropriate methods for each step in the audit program.

8.6.3.2 In addition, the audit team leader shall make the necessary arrangements for
(1) Team orientation and training as needed

(2) Facilities for audit interviews
(3) Materials, documents, and tools required by the audit procedures
(4) The software elements to be audited (for example, documents, computer files, personnel to be interviewed)
(5) Scheduling interviews

8.6.4 Examination. Elements that have been selected for audit shall be evaluated against the objective audit criteria. Evidence shall be examined to the depth necessary to determine if these elements comply with specified criteria.

The audit shall, as appropriate to its scope:
(1) Review procedures and instructions
(2) Examine the work breakdown structures
(3) Examine evidence of implementation and balanced controls
(4) Interview personnel to ascertain the status and functioning of the processes and the status of the products
(5) Examine element documents
(6) Test the element(s)

8.6.5 Reporting. Subsequent to the audit examination, the audit team will issue a draft audit report to the audited organization for review and comments.

Audit team rework of the audit report occurs before formal results reporting. This rework is performed, in concert with the draft report review, resolve any misunderstandings or ambiguities while maintaining objectivity and correctness. It also serves to ensure report usability by adding consistency to the level of report details and by adding any freshly verified information. The recommended practice is to involve representatives of the audited organization in reviewing audit results, as
(1) An ongoing, periodic activity integrated into the overall examination schedule, or
(2) As a closure step to the examination period

Involving the audited organization contributes to report quality through interaction and the possible delivery of any further evidence.

The audit team shall conduct a post audit conference to review with audited organization staff the deficiencies, findings, and (if applicable) recommendations. Comments and issues raised by the audited organization must be resolved.

The final audit report shall then be prepared, approved, and issued by the audit team leader to the organizations specified by the audit plan.

8.7 Exit Criteria. An audit shall be considered complete when
(1) Each element(s) within the scope of the audit has been examined;
(2) Findings have been presented to the audited organization;
(3) Response to draft findings have been received and evaluated;
(4) Final findings have been formally presented to the audited organization and initiating entity;
(5) The audit report has been prepared and submitted to recipients designated in the audit plan;
(6) The recommendation report, if required by plan, has been prepared and submitted to recipients designated in the audit plan;
(7) All of the auditing organization's follow-up actions included in the scope (or contract) of the audit have been performed.

8.8 Output. As a standard framework for audit reports, the draft and final audit reports shall, as a minimum, contain the following:
(1) *Audit identification.* Report title, audited organization, auditing organization, date of the audit.
(2) *Scope.* Scope of the audit, including an enumeration of the standards, specifications, practices, and procedures constituting the objective audit criteria against which the audit was conducted of the software elements and processes audited.
(3) *Conclusions.* A summary and interpretation of the audit findings including the key items of nonconformance.
(4) *Synopsis.* A listing of all the audited software elements, processes, and associated findings.
(5) *Follow-up.* The type and timing of audit follow-up activities.

Additionally, when stipulated by the audit plan, recommendations shall be provided to the audited organization, or the entity that initiated the audit. Recommendations shall be reported separately from results.

8.9 Auditability. The materials documenting the audit process must be maintained by the audit organization for a stipulated period of time subsequent to the audit and include the following:

(1) All work programs, checklists, etc are fully annotated

(2) Team staffing

(3) Interview notes, observation notes

(4) Compliance test evidence

(5) Copies of examined items, annotated

(6) Report draft(s) with response by audited organization

(7) Follow-up memo(s) as necessary

IEEE

Appendixes

(These Appendixes are not a part of IEEE Std 1028-1988, IEEE Standard for Software Reviews and Audits, but are included here for information only.)

Appendix A

Guide to Process Applications for Critical Software

A1.

ANSI/IEEE Std 730-1984 [A1] has identified a minimum set of review and audit process applications for critical software (for example, where failure could impact safety, or cause large financial or social losses).

(1) Software requirements review (SRR)
(2) Preliminary design review (PDR)
(3) Critical design review (CDR)
(4) Software verification and validation plan review (SVVPR)
(5) Functional audit (FA)
(6) Physical audit (PA)
(7) In-process audit (IPA)
(8) Managerial review (MR)

A2.

A2.1 The goal of this Appendix is to provide one possible mapping of specific process application needs identified in that standard, to candidate processes for meeting those needs. Selection of a specific process should be made as local, contractual, or project specific conditions dictate.

For example:

(1) The software inspection process may be used to meet the software verification and validation plan review application need.
(2) The management review process may be used to meet the managerial review application need.

Table A1
Critical Software Examination

ANSI/IEEE Std 730-1984 Requirements	SRR	PDR	CDR	SVVPR	FCA	PCA	IPA	MR
Management review			X					X
Technical review	X	X	X	X				
Software inspection	X	X	X	X				
Walkthrough	*	*	*	*				
Audit					X	X	X	**

* As common practice in many companies, walkthroughs are allowed wherever software inspections might be applied. It is suggested however, that for critical software as presented in ANSI/IEEE Std 730-1984, only more formal/rigorous techniques be used. One significant difference is disallowing the author from presenting the work.

** The audit process may be tailored in its application or administration to meet the need for a managerial review.

A particular process need not be prescribed for all applications. For example, using the same process for all the SRR, PDR, and CDR might not be cost effective or might unwisely be biased toward either technical or business concerns.

A2.2 Similarly, a combination of distinct processes may be applied to meet the needs of a specific application. An example is providing adequate examination of an SRR for a very large and complex system. SRR concerns could be subdivided into three categories:

(1) Customer satisfaction with functionality and performance with consideration for technical and business feasibility
(2) Technical completeness and correctness of requirements
(3) Fitness-for-use of the specifications document(s) as viewed by development, test, and maintenance organizations

In this example, it may be appropriate to use a management review to examine the first category, a technical review for the second category, and a software inspection to verify fitness-for-use of the document itself.

Table A1 shows possible mappings of review and audit processes to the applications referenced in ANSI/IEEE Std 730-1984 [A1].

A3.

The following references apply to Appendixes A through C:

[A1] ANSI/IEEE Std 730-1984, IEEE Standard for Software Quality Assurance Plans.

[A2] ANSI/IEEE Std 1016-1987, IEEE Recommended Practice for Software Design Descriptions.

Appendix B

Guide to Specific Review Applications

This Appendix is added to guide in the application of review processes, and to delineate some specific applications.

Although review processes defined by this standard have distinct objectives, Table B1 is provided to further accent process distinctions.

In addition, the following review process applications are presented:

(1) Software requirements review (SRR)
(2) Preliminary design review (PDR)
(3) Critical design review (CDR)
(4) Software verification and validation plan review (SVVPR)
(5) Managerial reviews (MR)

B1. Software Requirements Review (SRR)

The SRR is held to ensure the adequacy of the requirements stated in the software requirements specification. See ANSI/IEEE Std 730-1984 [A1].

The SRR is an evaluation of the software requirements specification (SRS) to ensure adequacy, technical feasibility, and completeness. Moreover, the SRR is held with user participation to examine the SRS to verify that is is unambiguous, verifiable, consistent, modifiable, traceable, and usable during the operation and maintenance phase. All organizational elements (for example, software design, software test, software quality assurance, systems engineering, marketing, manufacturing, and field service) that are directly affected by the requirements should participate.

The review checklist for the software requirements review may include but is not limited to the following:

(1) Traceability and completeness of the requirement from the next higher level specification (such as a system specification or user requirements specification)
(2) Adequacy of rationale for any derived requirements
(3) Compatibility of external (hardware and software) interfaces
(4) Adequacy of requirements for the man-machine interface
(5) Availability of constants and tables for calculations
(6) Testability of the functional requirements
(7) Adequacy and completeness of the verification and acceptance requirements
(8) Conformance to requirements specification standards
(9) Adequacy and feasibility of performance requirements
(10) Adequacy of consideration for human factors

B2. Preliminary Design Review (PDR)

B2.1 The PDR is held to evaluate the technical adequacy of the preliminary design of the software as depicted in a preliminary version of the Software Design Description. See ANSI/IEEE Std 730-1984 [A1].

Specifically, the need is to apply a review process to assess the progress, consistency, and technical adequacy of the selected design approach.

All organizational elements (for example, software test, software quality assurance, systems engineering, marketing, manufacturing,and field service) that are directly affected by the software design description should participate.

The following items may be included in the review checklist for the preliminary design review (PDR):

(1) Compatibility of the interfaces between the software, hardware, and end users.
(2) Fulfillment of the requirements contained in the SRS.
(3) Conformance to design documentation standards.

B2.2 Concerns that may be addressed by the checklist for preliminary design review

Table B1

Category and Attributes	Management Review	Technical Review	Software Inspection	Walkthrough
Objective	Ensure progress. Recommend corrective action. Ensure proper allocation of resources.	Evaluate conformance to specifications and plans. Ensure change integrity.	Detect and identify defects. Verify resolution.	Detect defects. Examine alternatives. Forum for learning.
Delegated Controls				
Decision making	Management team charts course of action. Decisions are made at the meeting or as a result of recommendations.	Review team petitions. Management or technical leadership to act on recommendations.	Team chooses from predefined product dispositions. Defects must be removed.	All decisions made by producer. Change is the prerogative of the producer.
Change verification	Change verification left to other project controls.	Leader verifies as part of review report.	Moderator verifies rework.	Change verification left to other project controls.
Group Dynamics				
Recom-mended size	Two or more persons.	Three or more persons.	Three to six persons.	Two to seven persons.
Attendance	Management, technical leadership, and peer mix.	Technical leadership and peer mix.	College of peers meet with documented attendance.	Technical leader-ship and peer mix.
Leadership	Usually the responsible manager.	Usually the lead engineer.	Trained moderator.	Usually producer.
Procedures				
Matrial volume	Moderate to high, depending on the specific *statement of objectives* for the meeting.	Moderate to high, depending on the specific *statement of objectives* for the meeting.	Relatively low.	Relatively low.
Presenter	Project representative.	Software element representative.	Presentation by *reader* other than producer.	Usually the producer.
Data collection	As required by applicable policies, standards, or plans.	Not a formal project requirement. May be done locally.	Formally required.	Not a formal project requirement. May be done locally.
Outputs				
Reports	Management review report.	Technical review reports.	Defect list and summary. Inspection report.	Walkthrough report.
Data base entries	Any schedule changes must be entered into the project tracking database.	No formal data base required.	Defect counts, characteristics, severity, and meeting attributes are kept.	No formal data base requirement.

(PDR) include (but are not limited to):

(1) Software interfaces
(2) Hardware interfaces
(3) Baseline for configuration
(4) Functional overview
(5) Design alternative selection rationale
(6) Standard operating environments
(7) Human factors requirements
(8) Documentation requirements
(9) Testing considerations
(10) Manufacturability
(11) Maintainability
(12) Assumptions
(13) Risks

More information is available in ANSI/IEEE Std 1016-1987 [A2].

B3. Critical Design Review (CDR)

The CDR is held to determine the acceptability of the detailed software designs as depicted in the software design description in satisfying the requirements of the software requirements specification. See ANSI/IEEE Std 730-1984 [A1].

The CDR is an evaluation of the completed software design description (SDD) to evaluate its technical adequacy, completeness, and correctness. Other concerns include its compatibility with the other software and hardware (where the product is required to interact), and the technical, cost, and schedule risks of the product design.

All other organizational elements that impose requirements or are affected by the design should participate (for example, software design, software test, and systems engineering).

The following items may be included in the review checklist for the critical design review:

(1) The compatibility of the detailed design with the SRS
(2) Available data in the form of logic diagrams, algorithms, storage allocation charts, and detailed design representations (for example, flow chart, program design language) to establish design integrity
(3) Compatibility and completeness of interface design requirements
(4) Adequacy and completeness of algorithms and equations
(5) Correctness and suitability of logic descriptions that may be warranted
(6) Technical accuracy and currency of all available test documentation and its compatibility with the test requirements of the SRS
(7) The requirements for the support and test software and hardware to be used in the development of the product
(8) The inclusion in the final design of function flow, timing, sizing, storage requirements, memory maps, data base, and other performance factors

B4. Software Verification and Validation Plan Review (SVVPR)

The software verification and validation plan review is held to evaluate the adequacy and completeness of the verification and validation methods described in the SVVP. See ANSI/EEE Std 730-1984 [A1].

The SVVPR is an evaluation of the completed software verification and validation plan (SVVP). Since the SVVP may be developed incrementally, multiple reviews may be required. These reviews are held to ensure that the verification and validation methods described in the SVVP are adequate and will provide complete evaluation data.

All organizational elements that impose requirements or are impacted by the SVVP should participate. These groups may include system engineering, software marketing, software design, software test, software quality assurance, customers, and users.

The following items may be included as review requirements for the software verification and validation plan review:

(1) All verification and validation methods, along with completion criteria to assure traceability to, and compatibility with, the functional and performance requirements expressed in the SRS.
(2) The methods to be used to verify and validate that the product satisfies the requirements of the SRS; these should include review process applications (for example, technical review, inspection, or walkthrough), demonstration, analysis, and test.

(3) Reports that adequately document the results of all reviews, audits, and tests based on the requirements listed in the SVVP.

(4) Adequate descriptions of the software configuration to be tested including test support software and hardware.

(5) Test plans, test procedures, test cases, and test data to ensure that all specification requirements are tested and that test instructions are clear and concise.

(6) Test procedures and test cases to ensure that test inputs and success criteria are adequately defined.

(7) A test plan and test case schedule identifying tests to be done, when, and by whom.

(8) Conformance to test documentation standards.

B5. Managerial Reviews

These reviews are held periodically to assess the execution of (the SQA) plan. These reviews shall be held by an organizational element(s) independent of the unit being audited, or by a qualified third party. See ANSI/IEEE Std 730-1984 [A1].

The planned frequency and structure of the (SQA Plan) managerial reviews should be stated in the SQA Plan. They should be conducted at the direction of the program manager.

Although the application of the *Management Review Process* meets this review requirement, an alternative is to perform the *Quality Systems Audit* (as presented in Appendix C) to the extent possible given the particular degree of independence and authority.

Appendix C

A Guide to Specific Audit Applications

To guide in the application of the audit process, and to delineate some specific applications, this Appendix has been added. The following audit process applications are presented:

(1) Functional audit (FA)
(2) Physical audit (PA)
(3) In-process audit (IPA)
(4) Quality systems audit (QSA)

Where self-examination (that is, application of the audit process by an element(s) not organizationally independent of the area audited) is desired, the general audit process is applied, with the independence requirement waived.

C1. The Functional Audit (FA)

The objective of the functional audit (FA) is to provide an independent evaluation of software products, verifying that its configuration items' actual functionality and performance is consistent with the requirement specifications. Specifically, this audit is held prior to the software delivery to verify that all requirements specified in the Software Requirements Specification have been met. See ANSI/IEEE Std 730-1984 [A1].

C1.1 Central to the FA is the identification of software elements to be audited by:

1) Nomenclature
2) Specification identification number
3) Configuration item number

C1.2 In addition, materials to be provided by the audited organization include:

(1) The software requirements specification
(2) Object copy of code
(3) Current listing of waivers against specific configuration items
(4) When available, the status of test programs to test configured items with automatic test equipment
(5) The software verification and validation report
(6) All in-process audit reports for items under audit (see C3)
(7) Any other test documentation (for example, plans, specifications, procedures, and reports) for the configuration item
(8) Listing of all successfully accomplished functional testing
(9) Listing of all planned, yet unexecuted, functional testing

C1.3 The following activities are required to conduct a functional audit:

(1) An audit of the formal test documentation shall be performed against test data. Results shall be checked for completeness and accuracy, and all deficiencies documented.
(2) An audit of the software verification and validation report shall be made to validate that the reports are accurate and completely describe the testing effort. All approved changes (problem reporting and corrective action) shall be reviewed to ensure that they have been technically incorporated and verified.
(3) Updates to previously delivered documents shall be reviewed to ensure accuracy and consistency.
(4) Preliminary design review and critical design review outputs shall be sampled to ensure that all findings have been incorporated and completed.

The audit team shall compare the code with the documented software requirements as stated in the current specifications document, to determine that the code addresses all (and only) the documented requirements.

C1.4 This audit is concerned not only with functionality, but also with performance as follows: Testing accomplished with appropriate test documentation and validated data shall sufficiently establish configuration item performance. For performance parameters that can not be verified completely during testing, simulations or other analysis shall be accomplished to establish confidence that the configuration item does meet performance criteria when in operation as stated in its specifications.

The FA report should include an evaluation of each software element(s) examined, and provides this evaluation within the standard audit report framework. The evaluation shall take the form of

(1) *Approval.* If the software element(s) had been observed as having all required functions and shows evidence of meeting minimum performance standards.
(2) *Contingent Approval.* If the evaluation of the software element(s) would result in approval given successful completion of specific, well-defined (observable) corrective action.
(3) *Disapproval.* If the software element(s) were observed to be seriously inadequate.

C2. The Physical Audit (PA)

The objective of the physical sudit (PA) is to provide an independent evaluation of a software product configuration item to confirm that components in the *as-built version* map to its specifications. Specifically, this audit is held to verify that the software and its documentation are internally consistent and are ready for delivery. See ANSI/IEEE Std 730-1984 [A1].

C2.1 Central to the PA is the identification of software elements to be audited by

(1) Nomenclature
(2) Specification identification number
(3) Configuration item number

C2.2 In addition, materials to be provided by the audited organization include

(1) Current listing of waivers against specific configuration items
(2) Requirements and architectural and detailed design specifications
(3) Listing of approved changes against the configuration with outstanding changes identified
(4) Acceptance test documentation (for examplee, plans, specifications, procedures, and reports) for the configuration item
(5) Appropriate customer deliverable documentation (for example, operating manuals, and maintenance manuals)
(6) Approved nomenclature, markings, and nameplates
(7) Software version description document
(8) FA reports

In addition, the audited organization shall identify any differences between the configuration of the system in the development environment, and the specific configuration of the system under examination. Moreover, they shall certify or otherwise demonstrate that any differences do not degrade the functional or performance characteristics of the system.

C2.3 To provide evidence of adequate control of system content and consistency, the audit team should as a minimum, examine

(1) The system specification document(s) for format and completeness
(2) Functional (FA) reports for discrepancies and actions taken
(3) Design descriptions (at least on a sampling basis) for proper symbols, labels, references, and data descriptions
(4) Design descriptions at various levels of abstraction, cross-checking for consistency
(5) Manuals (for example, user's manuals, programmer's manuals, and operator's manuals,) for format completeness and conformance with data item descriptions. Formal verification or acceptance of these manuals shall be waived until all other system testing is completed to ensure that procedural contents are correct.
(6) The software element(s) delivery media (and media controls) to ensure proper transfer or transmittal.

The audit team shall examine the system for vendor-provided or supplier-developed software elements, and seek evidence that any such software elements were produced under reasonable and prudent quality controls.

C2.4 The audit team shall examine the engineering release and change control function (and associated documentation) for evidence that it can

(1) Identify the composition of any configuration in terms of its subordinate units
(2) Determine, given a unit identifier, the parent element

(3) Describe the composition of a configuration item or its identifier with respect to other configuration items or identifiers
(4) Identify specifications relating to a given configuration item
(5) Identify outstanding changes against a given configuration item
(6) Identify changes and retain records of earlier configurations

C2.5 The PA report should include an evaluation of all software elements as a whole, and shall provide this evaluation within the standard audit report framework. The evaluation shall take the form of

(1) Approval. When the system of software elements has been observed as having all deliverable components accounted for, and of compatible issue.
(2) Contingent Approval. When the evaluation of the system of software elements results in approval given successful completion of specific, well-defined (observable) corrective action.
(3) Disapproval. When the system of software elements was observed to be seriously inadequate.

C2.6 The audit team shall examine the engineering release and change control function (and associated documentation) for evidence that it can

(1) Identify the composition of any configuration in terms of its subordinate units
(2) Determine, given a unit identifier, the parent element
(3) Describe the composition of a configuration item or its identifier with respect to other configuration items' identifiers
(4) Identify specifications relating to a given configuration item

C3. In-Process Audits

In-process audits are held during the design and development phases prior to the functional audit to verify the consistency of the design.

The objective is to verify the consistency of the product as it evolves through the development process by determining, on a sampling basis, that

(1) Hardware and software interfaces are consistent with design requirements in the software requirements specification (SRS)
(2) The code is fully tested by the SVVP to ensure that the functional requirements of the SRS are satisfied
(3) The design of the product, as the software design description (SDD) is evolving, satisfies the functional requirements of the SRS
(4) The code is consistent with the SDD

Moreover, in-process audits can be applied to determine compliance with applicable process standards (for example, auditing of the inspection process, on a sampling basis, to determine if inspection process rules are being followed).

Input material should include formal process descriptions and a product sample evidencing process execution.

In-process audit procedures are unique to the process and product examined. Specific procedures should be established locally, using the general steps found in Section 8.

The results of all in-process audits shall be documented in in-process audit reports, which identify all discrepancies found, and provide an overall opinion accordingly. The opinion should take the form of approval, contingent approval, or disapproval. Significant compliance deviations are noted and must be followed up to ensure their correction or waiver. This occurs during or before the functional audit.

C4. The Quality Systems Audit (QSA)

The purpose of a quality systems audit, or quality program evaluation, is to provide an independent assessment of the compliance to a software quality assurance plan.

C4.1 Specifically, the QSA objective is to determine, based on observable (verifiable) evidence, that

(1) The software quality program documentation established by the development organization addresses as a minimum, the basic elements of ANSI/IEEE Std 730-1984 [A1], or other appropriate standards.

(2) The software development organization follows its documented software quality program.

The SQA plan must incorporate all objective organizational performance criteria; internal standards and procedures; process requirements mandated by law, contract, or other policy; and conform to the ANSI/IEEE 730-1984 [A1] or other appropriate standards for software quality assurance.

C4.2 Central to the QSA is the identification of quality program documentation, and its availability to the audit team.

The following activities are required:

(1) A preaudit conference with audited organization personnel is held to familiarize them with audit goals and procedures
(2) Examination of quality program documents and related items for completeness, traceability, and consistency
(3) Perform selective compliance testing to objectively ascertain that SQA procedures and standards are implemented correctly
(4) Interview staff
(5) Perform in-process audits as appropriate (for example, observing inspections and their documented evidence)
(6) Examine reports from any recent functional and physical configuration audits.

The QSA report should include an evaluation of the quality program as a whole, and should provide this evaluation within the standard audit report framework.

The evaluation (following the general format of Section 8) shall take the form of approval, contingent approval, or disapproval for each major program element(s) identified in the audit plan.

Acknowledgments

The following organizations supported the development of this standard:

A. Frank Ackerman Associates
AT&T Bell Laboratories
AT&T Information Systems
AT&T Technologies
Bell Canada
Bell Communications Research
Burroughs Corporation
C.S. Draper Laboratory
CAP GEMINI/DASD
Coldframe, Inc
Combustion Engineering
Computer Sciences Corporation
DP Auditing Report
Grumman-CTEC
IBM Corp
Intermetrics, Inc
Martin-Marietta
McDonnell Douglas Corporation
Motorola
Naval Weapons Center
NCR Corporation
Northern Telecom, Ltd
Northern Telecom, Inc
OASAS, Ltd
Pacific Gas and Electric
Pansophic Systems, Inc
Pinpoint Retail Systems, Inc
Quality Assurance Institute
RCA
RGE Software Methodologies, Inc
Sperry
US Department of Transportation
University of California, Sacramento
Worldwide Service Technologies, Inc

ANSI/IEEE
Std 1042-1987

An American National Standard

IEEE Guide to Software Configuration Management

Sponsor

Software Engineering Standards Subcommittee of the Technical Committee on Software Engineering of the IEEE Computer Society

Approved September 10, 1987

IEEE Standards Board

Approved March 10, 1988

American National Standards Institute

The Institute of Electrical and Electronics Engineers, Inc
345 East 47th Street, New York, NY 10017, USA

Foreword

(This Foreword is not a part of ANSI/IEEE Std 1042-1987, IEEE Guide for Software Configuration Management.)

The purpose of this guide is to provide guidance in planning software configuration management (SCM) practices that are compatible with ANSI/IEEE Std 828-1983, IEEE Standard for Software Configuration Management Plans. Three groups are served by this guide: developers of software, software management community, and those responsible for preparation of SCM Plans. The developers of software will be interested in the different ways SCM can be used to support the software engineering process. The management community will be interested in how the SCM Plan can be tailored to the needs and resources of a project. Those preparing plans for SCM will be interested in the suggestions and examples for preparation of a Plan.

The introduction of this guide presents a technical and philosophical overview of the SCM planning process. Subsequent paragraphs in the body of the guide contain general statements of principles, commentary on issues to consider, and *lessons learned* for the corresponding paragraph in the outline of the ANSI/IEEE Std 828-1983 Plan. Four Appendixes illustrate how the ANSI/IEEE Std 828-1983 can be used for a variety of different projects. A fifth Appendix lists current references that may be useful in planning SCM.

This guide was prepared by a working group chartered by the Software Engineering Subcommittee of the Technical Committee on Software Engineering of the Computer Society of IEEE. This guide represents a consensus of individual working-group participants with broad expertise in software engineering and configuration management, staffed with both members within the Institute and from other groups that have expertise and interest in participating.

The following individuals contributed to the writing of this guide by attendance to two or more working sessions, or by substantial written commentary, or both.

Richard L. Van Tilburg, *Chairman*

David Schwartz, *Cochairman*

Bakul Banerjee
H. Ronald Berlack
Grazyna Bielecka
Jack L. Cardiff
Larry Cummings
Michael A. Daniels
David Gelperin
Curtis F. Jagger
Allen T. L. Jin
Dwayne Knirk
Nancy Murachanian
Sarah H. Nash
Wilma Osborne
Brian F. Rospide
Margaret Rumley
Edward Showalter
Jean Stanford
William S. Turner, III
Albert T. Williams

When the IEEE Standards Board approved this standard on September 10, 1987, it had the following membership:

Donald C. Fleckenstein, *Chairman*

Marco W. Migliaro, *Vice Chairman*

Andrew G. Salem, *Secretary*

James H. Beall
Dennis Bodson
Marshall L. Cain
James M. Daly
Stephen R. Dillon
Eugene P. Fogarty
Jay Forster
Kenneth D. Hendrix
Irvin N. Howell
Leslie R. Kerr
Jack Kinn
Irving Kolodny
Joseph L. Koepfinger*
Edward Lohse
John May
Lawrence V. McCall
L. Bruce McClung
Donald T. Michael*
L. John Rankine
John P. Riganati
Gary S. Robinson
Frank L. Rose
Robert E. Rountree
William R. Tackaberry
William B. Wilkens
Helen M. Wood

*Member emeritus

The following person were on the balloting committee that approved this document for submission to the IEEE Standards Board:

A. Frank Ackerman
Richard L. Aurbach
Motoei Azuma
H. Jack Barnard
Roy Bass
James Behm
H. R. Berlack
Michael A. Blackledge
Gilles Bracon
Kathleen L. Briggs
A. Winsor Brown
William L. Bryan
Fletcher Buckley
Lorie J. Call
Harry Carl
John Center
T. S. Chow
J. K. Chung
Won L. Chung
Antonio M. Cicu
Francos Coallier
Peter Cond, Jr
Christopher Cook
Richard Cotter
Arthur N. Damask
Taz Daughtrey
Peter A. Denny
Fred M. Discenzo
William P. Dupras
Robert E. Dwyer
Mary L. Eads
W. D. Ehrenberger
L. G. Egan
Walter J. Ellis
Caroline L. Evans
David W. Favor
Joan Feld
John W. Fendrich
Glenn S. Fields
A. M. Foley
Joel J. Forman
Julian Foster
Crespo Fuentes
F. K. Gardner
Leonard B. Gardner
David Gelperin
Anne K. Geraci
Shirley Gloss-Soler
J. G. Glynn
Andrej Grebnec
Benjamin W. Green
Victor M. Guarnera
Lawrence M. Gunther
David A. Gustafson
G. B. Hawthorne
John W. Horch
Cheng Hu
Harry Kalmbach
Myron S. Karasik
Dwayne L. Knirk
Shaye Koenig
George Konstantinow
Joseph A. Krupinski
Joan Kundig
T. M. Kurihara
Lak Ming Lam
John B. Lane
Robert A. C. Lane
Gregory N. Larsen
Ming-Kin Leung
F. C. Lim
Bertil Lindberg
Austin J. Maher
Paulo Cesar Marcondes
C. D. Marsh
Roger J. Martin
John McArdle
Russell McDowell
W. F. Michell
Manijeh Mogh
Charles S. Mooney
George Morrone
D. D. Morton
G. T. Morum
Hironobu Nagano
Gerry Neidhart
Dennis Nickle
Wilma M. Osborne
Thomas D. Parish
David E. Peercy
Michael T. Perkins
John Petraglia
Donald J. Pfeiffer
I. C. Pyle
Thomas S. Radi
Salim Ramji
Jean-Claude Rault
Meir Razy
Donald Reifer
John C. Rowe
Julio Gonzalez Sanz
Stephen R. Schach
Lee O. Schmidt
N. Schneidewind
Wolf A. Schnoege
Robert Schueppert
David J. Schultz
Gregory D. Schumacher
Leonard W. Seagren
Robert W. Shillato
David M. Siefert
Jacob Slonim
Harry M. Sneed
V. Srinivas
Manfred P. Stael
Wayne G. Staley
Franklin M. Sterling
Mary Jane Stoughton
William G. Sutcliffe
Richard H. Thayer
Bob Thibodeau
Paul U. Thompson
Terrence L. Tillmanns
G. R. Treble
Henry J. Trochesset
C. L. Troyanowski
William S. Turner III
W. T. Valentin, Jr
R. I. Van Tilburg
Tom Vollman
Dolores R. Wallace
Martha G. Walsh
John P. Walter
Andrew H. Weigel
Peter J. Weyman
G. Allen Whittaker
Patrick J. Wilson
David L. Winningham
W. M. Wong
Dennis L. Wood
Nancy Yavne
William W. Young
Janusz Zalewski
Donald Zeleny
Hugh Zettel
Peter F. Zoll

Acknowledgment

Appreciation is expressed to the following companies and organizations for contributing the time of their employees to make possible the development of this text:

Boeing
Burroughs
General Dynamics
Hughes Aircraft Co
Intel Corporation
IBM
Goodyear Atomic Corporation
GTE
National Bureau of Standards
MITRE
Motorola
Programming Environments, Inc
RCA Astro Electronics
Sperry
Telos
Texas Instruments
ZTROW Software Inc

Contents

Contents

An American National Standard

IEEE Guide to Software Configuration Management

1. Introduction

1.1 Scope. This guide describes the application of configuration management (CM) disciplines to the management of software engineering projects. Software configuration management (SCM) consists of two major aspects: planning and implementation. For those planning SCM activities, this guide provides insight into the various factors that must be considered.

Users implementing SCM disciplines will find suggestions and detailed examples of plans in this guide. This guide also presents an interpretation of how ANSI/IEEE Std 828-1983 [2][1] can be used for planning the management of different kinds of computer program development and maintenance activities.

The guide is presented in two parts. The first part, the main body of the guide, presents issues to consider when planning software configuration management for a project or organization. The second part of the guide presents, for those preparing SCM Plans, a series of sample Plans illustrating different concepts discussed in the body of the guide.

The text of the guide introduces the essential concepts of SCM, particularly those of special significance (for example, libraries and tools) to software engineering. It then presents the planning for SCM in terms of documenting a Plan following the outline of ANSI/IEEE Std 828-1983 [2] so that a user who is unfamiliar with the disciplines of software configuration management can gain some insight into the issues. For those preparing SCM Plans, the second part of the guide provides sample plans for consideration.

The sample SCM Plans include a variety of software configuration management applications for different types of projects and organizations. Appendix A illustrates a software configuration management plan (SCMP) for a project developing a complex, critical computer system. It describes a Plan for managing a typical software development cycle where the development is contracted to an organization that does not have responsibility for its maintenance or use. Appendix B illustrates a SCMP for a small software development project. It describes a Plan for supporting a prototype development activity where the goal of the project is to demonstrate the feasibility of a concept. Appendix C illustrates a SCMP used by an organization where the emphasis is on maintaining programs developed by other activities or organizations. Appendix D illustrates a SCMP for an organization developing and maintaining computer programs embedded in a hardware product line. It describes a Plan for managing both software development and maintenance of a commercial product line. Some of the different characteristics illustrated are shown in Table 1.

[1] The numbers in brackets correspond with those of the references in 1.2.

Table 1
Characteristics of Appendixes*

Appendix Number	Emphasis of Control (Life Cycle Phase)	Type of Project	Relative Size (Dollar/Manhour)	SCM Tools Available	Life Span of Plan	Writing for Plan
1	Development	Critical	Medium	Advanced	Short	Highly structured
2	Concept	Prototype	Small	Basic	Short	Informal
3	Operations	Support sw	Large	On-line	Full life cycle	Structured
4	All	Commercial	Small	Integrated	Full life cycle	Organizational Informal

*NOTE: The purpose of the Appendixes is not to provide an illustration for every possible combination of project characteristics but rather to show that the ANSI/IEEE Std 828-1983 [2] can be applied to a wide variety of projects.

1.2 References. This guide shall be used in conjunction with the following publications:

[1] ANSI/IEEE Std 729-1983, IEEE Standard Glossary of Software Engineering Terminology.[2]

[2] ANSI/IEEE Std 828-1983, IEEE Standard for Software Configuration Management Plans.

Additional references useful in understanding software configuration management are given in Appendix E.

1.3 Mnemonics. The following acronyms are used in the text of this guide:

CCB	Configuration Control Board
CDR	Critical Design Review
CI	Configuration Item
CM	Configuration Management
CPC	Computer Program Component
CPCI	Computer Program Configuration Item
CSC	Computer Software Component
CSCI	Computer Software Configuration Item
[EP]ROM	[Electrically Programmable] Read Only Memory
FCA	Functional Configuration Audit
OEM	Original Equipment Manufacturer
PCA	Physical Configuration Audit
PDR	Preliminary Design Review
RAM	Random Access Memory
ROM	Read Only Memory
SCA	System/Software Change Authorization
SCCB	Software Configuration Control Board
SCM	Software Configuration Management
SCMP	Software Configuration Management Plan
SCR	System/Software Change Request
SQA	Software Quality Assurance
VDD	Version Description Document

1.4 Terms. Some terms used in SCM circles have restricted meanings or are not defined in the guide. General statements of the contextual meanings are given to aid in understanding the concepts in the guide. These are not formal definitions, subject to review and approval as in a standard, but contextual definitions serving to augment the understanding of configuration management activities as described within this guide.

As used here, the term **baseline**[3] represents the assignment of a documented identifier to each software product configuration item (CI) and associated entities. That is, the source code, relocatable code, executable code, files controlling the process of generating executable code from source code, documentation, and tools used to support development or maintenance of the software product should all be captured, labeled and somehow denoted or recorded as parts of the same baseline. As computer programs move from an initial idea to the maintenance phase, it is common for a series of developmental baselines of increasing complexity to be established during the various internal and external reviews conducted by management (and customers) to determine progress and technical suitability. The baseline concept is as useful to engineering during development as it is after release for use and maintenance.

The various SCM functions are dependent on the baseline concept. Several valuable uses of the baseline concept include

(1) To distinguish between different internal releases for delivery to a customer (that is, successive variants of the same product baseline)
(2) To help to ensure complete and up-to-date technical product documentation
(3) To enforce standards (SQA)
(4) To be used as a means of promoting (that is, internally releasing) each CI from one phase of development or test to another
(5) To identify customer involvement in internal (developmental) baselies

Since SCM disciplines are an integral part of the engineering process they guide the management of internal developmental baselines as well as the more formal functional, allocated, and product baselines. The SCM disciplines, as applied to developmental baselines, are used (implicitly or explicitly) to coordinate most engineering activities that occur within the context of each baseline. Varying levels of formality provide flexibility and responsiveness to the engineering process, yet maintain the benefits of recognizing SCM disciplines.

[2] ANSI/IEEE publications are available from IEEE Service Center, 445 Hoes Lane, Piscataway, NJ 08855-1331 and from the Sales Department, American National Standards Institute, 1430 Broadway, New York, NY 10018.

[3] A specification or product that has been formally reviewed and agreed to by responsible management, that thereafter serves as the basis for further development, and can be changed only through formal change control procedures.

The term **promotion** is used here to indicate a transition in the level of authority needed to approve changes to a controlled entity, such as a baseline CI.

Promotions typically signify a change in a CI's internal development state. The term **release** is used to designate certain promotions of CI that are distributed outside the development organization.

In general, as the development process continues, there are more constraints imposed on the change process (coordination with interfacing hardware, user's adaptations, etc) and correspondingly higher levels of authority are needed for approving the changes. When an entity is finally released as a formal baseline, a high level of authority is needed to approve changes. When internal or developmental baselines are created as a part of the engineering process and entitites are moved or released to another internal activity for additional work, integration, or testing the term **promotion** is used to distinguish this type of release from the more formal releases to users.

Promotion from one developmental baseline to another represents the visibility granted to some organizations for a given baseline. As developmental baselines are promoted within an organization, they tend to become more stable. The more stable a baseline is, the higher the level of visibility it is granted.

The term **version** is used here to indicate a software CI having a defined set of functional capabilities. As functional capabilities are added, modified, or deleted the CI is given a different version identifier. It is common and recommended practice to use a configuration identification scheme that permits easy and automatic identification of particular version labels.

The term **revision** is commonly associated with the notion of *bug fixing*, that is, making changes to a program that corrects only errors in the design logic but does not affect documented functional capabilities since none of the requirements have changed. The configuration identification scheme must provide for clear identification of revisions and versions of each specific promotion and release.

2. SCM Disciplines in Software Management

2.1 The Context of SCM. This guide discusses SCM as a set of management disciplines within the context of the software engineering process rather than as a set of specific activities performed, or as functions within an organization. The reason for this approach is that software CM, as contrasted with hardware CM, tends to be more deeply involved in the software engineering process and, while the same general CM functions are performed, the disciplines are extended to include the process of developing a baseline.

Software CM and release processing are performed within the context of several basic CM functions: configuration identification, baseline management, change control and library control, status accounting, reviews and audits, and release processing. In practice, the ways in which these functions are performed are different for the different kinds of programs being developed (commercial, embedded, OEM, etc), and may vary in the degree of formal documentation required within and across different life-cycle management phases (research phase, product development, operations, and maintenance).

Software CM also provides a common point of integration for all planning, oversight and implementation activities for a project or product line. These functions are performed within the context of a project—providing the framework (labeling and identification) for interfacing different activities and defining the mechanisms (change controls) necessary for coordinating parallel activities of different groups. SCM provides a framework for controlling computer program interfaces with their underlying support hardware, coordinating software changes when both hardware and software may be evolving during development or maintenance activities.

Finally, SCM is practiced within the context of management, providing management with the visibility (through status accounting and audits) of the evolving computer products that it needs to perform effectively.

2.1.1 SCM is a Service Function. Software CM is a support activity that makes technical and managerial activities more effective. Effectiveness of the SCM processes increases in proportion to the degree that its disciplines are an explicit part of the normal day-to-day activities of everyone involved in the development and maintenance efforts, (as opposed to a separate SCM organization or activity). This holds true whether SCM is administered by a separate SCM group, distributed among many projects, or a mixture of both.

2.1.2 SCM is a Part of the Engineering Process. The disciplines of SCM apply to the development of programmed logic, regardless of the form of packaging used for the application. Software engineering technology is effectively used in the generation of stored programmed logic when the complexity of the function is large. SCM disciplines assist in the identification and evolution of changes during the engineering process, even though the final package may be ROM, and managed as a hardware configuration item.

Configuration management is practiced in one form or another as a part of every software engineering activity where several individuals or organizations have to coordinate their activities. Although the basic disciplines of configuration management are common to both hardware and software engineering activities, there are some differences in emphasis due to the nature of the design activity. Software products (as compared to hardware products) are easy to change[4] (little if any lead time is needed for parts procurement and production setup).

Software CM is a discipline for managing the evolution of computer program products, both during the initial stages of development and during all stages of maintenance. The designs of programs are not easily partitioned into independent tasks due to their complexity. Therefore, configuration management disciplines are more valuable during the design (and redesign during maintenance) phases. This is when using techniques of multiple levels of baselines and internal releases (or promotions) to a larger degree than is typically practiced by hardware CM really pays off.

Whether software is released for general use as programs in RAM or embedded in ROM, it is a form of logic. Therefore, SCM disciplines can and should be extended to include development of the computer programs' component parts (for example, source code and executable code) whereas hardware CM focuses mainly on the management of documentation.

The differences between hardware and software CM, of importance to software CM, include

(1) Software CM disciplines are used to simultaneously coordinate configurations of many different representations of the software product (source code, relocatable code and executable code) rather than just their *documentation*. The nature of computer programs requires this extension and the SCM disciplines and related SCM support software adapt readily to this task.
(2) The use of interactive software development environments extends the concepts of software CM to managing evolutionary changes that occur during the routine generation of specifications, designs, and implementation of code, as well as to the more rigidly documented and controlled baselines defined during development and system maintenance.
(3) Software development environments are rapidly becoming automated with interactive tool sets. This modifies many of the traditional methods used in hardware CM but the fundamental concepts of CM still apply.

2.1.3 SCM Manages all Software Entities. Software CM extends the management disciplines of hardware CM to include all of the entities of the product as well as their various representations in documentation. Examples of entities managed in the software engineering process include

(1) Management plans
(2) Specifications (requirements, design)
(3) User documentation
(4) Test design, case and procedure specifications
(5) Test data and test generation procedures
(6) Support software
(7) Data dictionaries and various cross-references
(8) Source code (on machine-readable media)
(9) Executable code (the run-time system)
(10) Libraries
(11) Data bases:
 (a) Data which are processed,
 (b) Data which are part of a program
(12) Maintenance documentation (listings, detail design descriptions, etc)

All supporting software used in development, even though not a part of the product, should also be controlled by configuration management disciplines.

Not all entities are subject to the same SCM disciplines at the same time. When the software product is under development, the documentation entities (baselined specifications and user requirements) are the most important. When coding begins, the documentation representing the design is the most important entity to be

[4] Even what is traditionally thought of as *hard* software—that is, firmware, is becoming easier to modify. An example is card edge programming where the programs in a ROM are easily modified, though not under program control during execution.
NOTE: While the time to change a design may be the same for hardware engineering as for software engineering, implementation and installation time is greater and consequently more expensive for hardware configuration items.

managed. Finally, when the product is ready for general use, the source code is the most accurate representation of the real product and the documentation is related so that representation is most important. These transitions of disciplinary focus over time are common to all SCM disciplines and need to be recognized in planning systems for effectively supporting project management.

Firmware[5] raises some special considerations for configuration management. While being developed, the disciplines of software CM apply; but when made a part of the hardware (*burned* into [EP]ROM), the disciplines of hardware CM apply. Testing may vary but the SCM requirements are generally the same. The packaging of [EP]ROM versus RAM code also introduces and necessitates different identification procedures, which are noted in 3.3.1.

2.1.3.2 The issue of what entities are to be managed often arises in the practical context of what gets captured in each library, and when. Consideration need also be given to the hierarchy of entities managed during this process. There are several different ways of looking at this hierarchy of entities; one, for example, is a three-level hierarchy:

(1) Configuration item (CSCI, CPCI, System, System Segment, Program package, module)
(2) Component (CPC, CSC, Subsystem, Unit, Package, Program function)
(3) Unit (Procedure, function Routine, Module)

The configuration control boards (CCB) that are oriented to business type management decisions usually select one level in this hierarchy as the level at which they will control changes. Other CCB may focus on more technical issues and would each select other levels, the module for example, as the control level for reviewing changes. See 2.2.5 for further discussion of control levels.

[5]**Firmware.** Computer programs and data loaded in a class of memory that cannot by dynamically modified by the computer during processing. Used here to generically refer to any programmed code implemented in nonvolatile memory such as [EP]ROM, regardless of its function; contrasts with code designed to execute out of volatile memory, such as RAM. There are differences between software intensive firmware and hardware intensive firmware. The key is ease of adaptability or degree with which programmed instructions are used, and the size of the program. Software intensive firmware denotes an activity that has available a set of tools commonly used in software engineering. Hardware intensive firmware denotes a development activity that has available a minimum of tools necessary for creation (*burn in*) of the firmware.

Another way of looking at entities to be managed is in terms of the interrelationships between the computer programs being developed and the other software entities used during development and testing of that program. This hierarchy is illustrated in Table 2.

Table 2
Hierarchy of Controlled Entities

Entity	Layer
Released entities	Product layer
Promoted entities	Test layer
Modifiable unique entities and support software	Invocation layers
Product development environment	Support software layer
Operating system	Run-time software layer

The SCM process should support each of these layers.

2.1.3.3 Still another way of viewing the entities is in terms of the intermediate products generated in the process of building the computer program product. Each of these intermediate products may be viewed as:

(1) *Modifiable entities.* These items are the individually modifiable units that are required to produce the deliverable entities. They are the source code, control files, data descriptions, test data, documents, etc, that constitute the focus of SCM. The entities at this level are referenced as *units* or *components* in this guide.
(2) *The compilation or assembly entities, such as compilers.* These are needed to develop, test and maintain the program throughout the life cycle of the product. These entities are referenced as *support software* in this guide.
(3) *Application-specific entities.* These are the different representations that are created in the process of producing the deliverables. Examples are the results produced by the compilation and assembly entities, and link/load entities, such as a link editor/locator. These culminate in the product that is released for general use. These entities are referenced as *configuration items* (CI) in this guide.

2.2 The Process of SCM

2.2.1 Management Environment of SCM. Software engineering, and therefore SCM, takes place within an organizational business environment. To be effective, SCM must blend in with and reflect the organization. It must take into account the management style — entrepreneurial, very disciplined, etc. The technical skills of the implementing organization must be taken into account as well as available resources when specifying whether SCM is to be performed by a single organization or distributed among several. The organization must also be responsive to the kinds of controls needed by the organization that will ultimately be using the product.

SCM management provides support to the organization by working within it to define implement policies, techniques, standards, and tools that facilitate their control of the SCM process. These processes assist other managers (and customers as required) by supporting effective configuration identification, change controls, status accounting, audits, and reviews.

2.2.2 Dynamics of SCM. The cornerstone activity of SCM is managing the change process and tracking changes to ensure that the configuration of the computer program product is accurately known at any given time. The change management is accomplished by completely identifying each baseline and tracking all subsequent changes made to that baseline. This process is used whether the baseline represents preliminary documentation, such as requirements, or a fully documented program including source and object code. All entities (specifications, documents, text data, and source code) are subject to this change management discipline.

Effectively managing baseline changes requires that a scheme for identifying the *structure* of the software product must be established. This structure relates to the hierarchical organization of the computer program and is extended to include all entities or work-products associated with the program. This identification scheme must normally be maintained throughout the full life of the computer program product. Usually a numbering scheme or file name scheme is associated with the structure, and unique and appropriate labels are assigned to each entity of the product.

As new baselines are created in transition by a promotion or release, the aggregate of entities is reviewed or audited to verify consistency with the old baseline, and the identification labeling is modified to reflect the new baseline. Changes to the different versions and revisions of each baseline are maintained. The history of changes to baselined configurations is maintained and made available to engineering and management in status reports. Figure 1 illustrates a model of the SCM process.

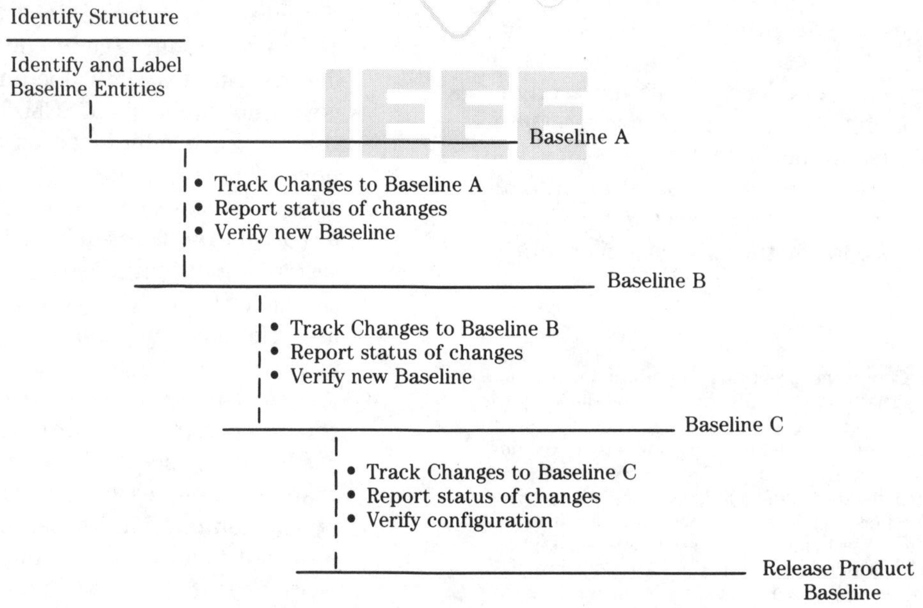

Fig 1
Model of Change Management

2.2.3 Role of Source Code in SCM. A key entity to be managed is the source code, since it is the basic representation in readable form of the product being controlled. Other forms of documentation and data are verified by comparison to this entity. At different phases in a development cycle, source code may not be available and different baselined entities may be defined as the basic representation. However, for most of the software life cycle, the source code provides the key entity for verification. The creation of executable code for the machine is directly derived (in the majority of computer systems) from the source code by various mechanized tools, such as assemblers, compilers, link/loaders, and interpreters. Recreation of source code (and object code) from design documentation can be costly. Therefore, to control only design documentation does not usually fully capture the implementation of the software. If the source code were to be lost because of improper, unreliable, or insufficient controls, the cost of recreating all of the source code would (in the majority of cases) be very expensive because of the typically incomplete state of the documentation.

Design documentation is verified against the product represented by the source code. The test entities (test design, text cases and procedures), test data (including data generation procedures) and test reports, are used to verify that the executable code (produced by the source code) matches the documentation. Documentation needed for maintenance (programming notebooks, etc) and user documentation are also verified against the source code.

Depending on the difficulty of rebuilding a complete set of executable code, the relocatable code may also be identified and considered an entity. However, the source code is generally considered to be the primary, if not sole source in establishing the product configuration.

Since source code can be interpreted differently by different compilers, it is necessary to control the versions of the support software used for a specific released product so as to have full control over the computer program product.

2.2.4 Different Levels of Control. Management delegates the authority for action downward to and including the work done by nonmanagement personnel. Management also selectively delegates aspects of control to nonmanagement personnel. In this guide, the term **levels of control** includes all control exercised by both management and nonmanagement. The term **authority** refers to control reserved by management for management decisions relative to allocation of resources: schedule, production cost, customer requirements for product cost, performance, delivery, etc. Nonmanagement provides technical data to support these evaluations. Since the SCM Plan must identify all software CI (or classes thereof) that will be covered by the Plan, it must also define the level of management needed to authorize changes to each entity. As the software product evolves, it may be wise or necessary to increase the management authorization level (that is, level of control) needed. This can be accomplished through the internal part promotion hierarchy.

A general-use facility, which has many released software CI as well as CI under development, will often require many separate levels of control, and possibly different levels of authority for approving changes. For example, software CI that are used by several organizations may require change approval by management that is in charge of all those organizations. Not only the CI that will be delivered by the development group but also the level of authority for all vendor-supplied or internally developed software tools, utilities, operating systems, etc, used in the development need to be identified. Software CI used within any intermediate organization may usually require change approval by that organization's management. These intermediate organizations may have unique design or analysis tools for their own use on the project and can have change control authority over these tools.

2.3 The Implementation of SCM

2.3.1 Using Software Libraries. The techniques and methods used for implementing control and status reporting in SCM generally center around the operation of software libraries. Software libraries provide the means for identifying and labeling baselined entities, and for capturing and tracking the status of changes to those entities.

Libraries have been historically composed of documentation on hard copy and software on machine readable media, but the trend today is towards all information being created and maintained on machine-readable media.[6] This trend, which encourages the increased use of automated tools, leads to higher productivity. The trend also

[6] There may still be valid *legal* needs for maintaining hard copy versions of all baselined materials. The ability to eliminate hard copy media should not be construed as a necessary or even wise thing for an organization to do.

means that the libraries are a part of the software engineering working environment. The SCM functions associated with the libraries have to become a part of the software engineering environment, making the process of configuration management more transparent to the software developers and maintainers.

The number and kind of libraries will vary from project to project according to variations in the access rights and needs of their users, which are directly related to levels of control. The entities maintained in the libraries may vary in physical form based on the level of technology of the software tooling. When the libraries are automated, the libraries that represent different levels of control may be functionally (logically) different even though they are physically the same. The insertion of entities and changes to entities in a controlled library should produce an auditable authorization trail.

The names of libraries may vary, but fundamentally three kinds should be considered, as outlined in Fig 2.

The **dynamic library**, sometimes called the *programmer's library*, is a library used for holding newly created or modified software entities (units/modules or data files and associated documentation). This is the library used by programmers in developing code. It is freely accessible to the programmer responsible for that unit at any time. It is the programmers' workspace and controlled by the programmers.

The **controlled library**, sometimes called the *master library*, is a library used for managing the current baseline(s) and for controlling changes made to them. This is the library where the units and components of a configuration item that have been promoted for integration are maintained. Entry is controlled, usually after verification. Copies may be freely made for use by programmers and others. Changes to units or components in this library must be authorized by the responsible authority (which could be a configuration control board or other body with delegated authority).

The **static library**, sometimes called the *software repository*, is a library used to archive various baselines released for general use. This is the library where the master copies plus authorized copies of computer program configuration items that have been released for operational use are maintained. Copies of these masters may be made available to requesting organizations.

2.3.2 Controlling Changes to Libraries. Several possible methods for controlling access to libraries are illustrated in the Appendixes. Appendix B prescribes formal change control of several configuration items at the component level within established baselines. Another approach is having rather informal methods for authorizing changes to configuration items. This method is used for fast integration of changes in a research type environment, as in Appendix B. For libraries having several configuration items including both external (third-party software) and internal (in-house developments) sources of supply, a mixture of formal methods for authorizing changes is applicable, as illustrated in Appendix C. Externally developed computer programs may be controlled at CI levels, whereas internally developed computer programs may be controlled at more discrete component levels. The procedures for authorizing changes may be integrated with the software tools in an integrated environment, as illustrated in Appendix D.

In summary, the levels of control described in each appendix are illustrated in Table 3.

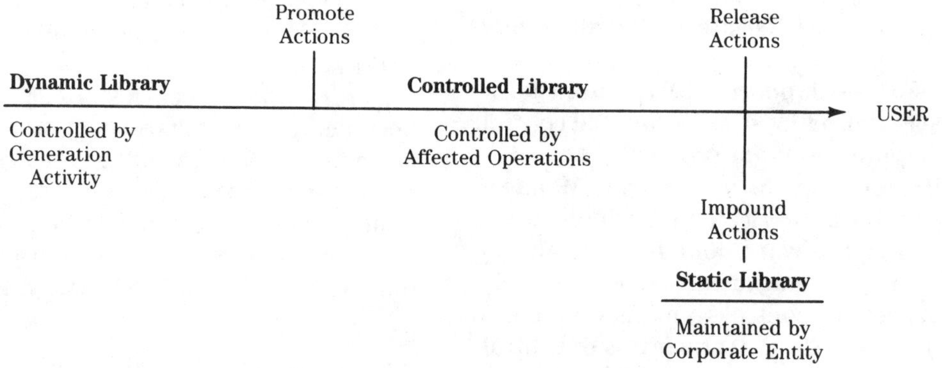

Fig 2
Three Types of Libraries

Table 3
Levels of Control in Sample Plans

	Appendix A	Appendix B	Appendix C	Appendix D
Number of CI	Several CI (internal)	3 CI (internal)	Internal CI External CI	2 CI (internal)
Components (CSC)	All components	NA	Internal components	Unit
Type of control	Formal	Informal	Formal	Formal (automated)

2.3.3 Using Configuration Control Boards. Another functional concept of SCM is the extended use of configuration control boards (CCB). This concept provides for implementing change controls at optimum levels of authority. Configuration control boards can exist in a hierarchical fashion (for example, at the program, system design, and program product level), or one such board may be constituted with authority over all levels of the change process. In most projects, the CCB is composed of senior level managers. They include representatives from the major software, hardware, test, engineering, and support organizations. The purpose of the CCB is to control major issues such as schedule, function, and configuration of the system as a whole.

The more technical issues that do not relate to performance, cost, schedule, etc, are often assigned to a software configuration control board (SCCB). The SCCB discusses issues related to specific schedules for partial functions, interim delivery dates, common data structures, design changes and the like. This is the place for decision-making concerning the items that must be coordinated across CI but which do not require the attention of high level management. The SCCB members should be technically well-versed in the details of their area; the CCB members are more concerned with broad management issues facing the project as a whole and with customer issues.

2.4 The Tools of SCM. The SCM software tools selected for use by a project and described in a Plan need to be compatible with the software engineering environment in which the development or maintenance is to take place.

SCM tools are beginning to proliferate and choices have to be made as to the tool set most useful for supporting engineering and management. There are many different ways of examining available SCM tools. One way is to categorize them according to characteristics of their products: a filing system, a data-base management system, and an independent knowledge-based system.[7] Another way is to examine the functions they perform: clerical support, testing and management support, and transformation support.[8] A third way of categorizing the SCM tools is by how they are integrated into the software engineering environment on the project. The current set of available SCM tools is classed in terms of the level of automation they provide to the programming environment on a project.

2.4.1 Basic Tool Set. This set includes:

(1) Basic data-base management systems
(2) Report generators
(3) Means for maintaining separate dynamic and controlled libraries
(4) File system for managing the check-in and check-out of units, for controlling compilations, and capturing the resulting products

This set is compatible with a programming environment that is relatively unsophisticated.

The tools control the information on hard copy regarding a program product. They assume a capability for maintaining machine processable libraries that distinguish between controlled and uncontrolled units or components. The tools simplify and minimize the complexity, time, and methods needed to generate a given baseline. Appendix B illustrates a project using such a tool set.

2.4.2 Advanced Tool Set. This set includes:

(1) Items in the basic tool set
(2) Source code control programs that will maintain version and revision history
(3) Compare programs for identifying (and helping verify) changes

[7] Reference: British Alvey Programme.

[8] Reference: *Life Cycle Support in the Ada*[9] *Environment* by Mc Dermid and Ripken.

[9] Ada is a registered trademark of the US Government, AJPO.

(4) Tools for building or generating executable code
(5) A documentation system (word processing) to enter and maintain the specifications and associated user documentation files
(6) A system/software change request/authorization (SCR/SCA) tracking system that makes requests for changes machine readable

This set provides a capability for a SCM group to perform more efficiently on larger, more complex software engineering efforts. It assumes a programming environment that has more computing resources available.

It provides the means of efficiently managing information about the units or components and associated data items. It also has rudimentary capabilities for managing the configurations of the product (building run-time programs from source code) and providing for more effective control of the libraries. Appendix A illustrates use of such a tool set.

2.4.3 On-Line Tool Set. This set includes:

(1) Generic tools of the advanced tool set integrated so they work from a common data base
(2) An SCR/SCA tracking and control system that brings generation, review, and approval of changes on-line
(3) Report generators working on-line with the common data base, and an SCR/SCA tracking system that enables the SCM group to generate responses to on-line queries of a general nature

This set of tools requires an interactive programming environment available to the project. It also provides an organization with the minimal state-of-the-art SCM capabilities needed to support the typical interactive programming environment currently available in industry. It assumes on-line access to the programming data base and the resources necessary for using the tools. Appendix C illustrates use of such a SCM tool set.

2.4.4 Integrated Tool Set. This set includes:

(1) On-line SCM tools covering all functions
(2) An integrated engineering data base with SCM commands built into the on-line engineering commands commonly used in designing and developing programs (most functions of CM are heavily used during design and development phases)
(3) The integration of the SCM commands with on-line management commands for building and promoting units and components

This set integrates the SCM functions with the software engineering environment so that the SCM functions are transparent to the engineer. The software engineer becomes aware of the SCM functions only when he/she attempts to perform a function or operation that has not been authorized (for example, changing a controlled entity when the engineer does not have the required level of authority or control). Appendix D illustrates a project having such an approach to SCM.

2.5 The Planning of SCM. Planning for SCM is essential to its success. Most of the routine activities associates with SCM are repetitious, clerical-type activities, which can be automated fairly easily. Effective SCM involves planning for how activities are to be performed, and performing these activities in accordance with the Plan. The more important disciplines of SCM, such as defining a scheme for identifying the configuration items, components, and units, or the systematic review of changes before authorizing their inclusion in a program, are management activities that require engineering judgment. Relating engineering judgment with management decisions, while also providing the necessary clerical support without slowing the decision-making process, is the critical role of SCM personnel and tools, or both.

SCM defines the interaction between a number of activities extending throughout the life cycle of the product. The SCM Plan functions as a centralized document for bringing together all these different points of view. The cover sheet of the Plan is usually approved by all of the persons with responsibilities identified in the Plan. This makes the Plan a living document, to be maintained by approved changes throughout the life of the computer programs.

Maintenance of the Plan throughout the life of the software is especially important as the disciplines of identification, status reporting, and record keeping apply throughout the maintenance part of the life cycle. Differences may be expected in how change processing is managed; and these need to be understood by all participants.

It should be clear from the information given above, but it is stated explicitly here, that the application (and thus the planning) of SCM is very sensitive to the context of the project and the organization being served. If SCM is applied as a corporate policy, it must not be done blindly, but rather it should be done in such a way that the details of a particular SCM application are reexamined for each project (or phase for very large projects). It must take into consideration the size, complexity, and criticality of the software system being managed; and the number of individuals, amount of personnel turnover, and organizational form and structure that have to interface during the life of the software system being managed.

This guide provides suggestions as to how ANSI/IEEE Std 828-1983 [2] can be interpreted for specific projects, and items to be considered in preparing a plan. The objective of the planner is to prepare a document that

(1) Clearly states the actions to be performed by software engineering and supporting activities that are required to maintain visibility of the evolving configuration of the computer program products
(2) Supports management in the process of evaluating and implementing changes to each configuration
(3) Assures that the changes have been properly and completely incorporated into each computer program product.

3. Software Configuration Management Plans

3.1 Introduction. Because SCM extends throughout the life cycle of the software product, the SCM Plan is the recommended focal point for integrating and maintaining the necessary details for software CM. Projects do differ in scope and complexity and a single format may not always be applicable. ANSI/IEEE Std 828-1983 [2] describes a minimum format for plans with a maximum amount of flexibility. If a section of the format is not applicable, the sentence *There is no pertinent information for this section* should be inserted to indicate that the section has not been overlooked.

It is desirable to provide a synopsis for users of the Software Configuration Management Plan and for the managers who must approve it. In each Appendix to this guide, a synopsis has been prepared to set the context surrounding the generation of the sample SCM Plan. For purposes of this guide, the viewpoint of each synopsis in the Appendixes is directed towards the user of the guide.

3.1.1 Purpose. The theme here is to inform the reader of the specific purpose of the SCM activity(ies) to be defined in the SCM Plan. It is sufficient to write a brief paragraph identifying the system to which the particular SCM Plan applies, noting any dependencies on other SCM or CM Plans. For example, Appendix A emphasizes thoroughness of audits and reviews to assure conformance to contractual requirements for a computer program product; the theme is rigorous control of the configuration during development. Appendix B is directed towards low cost, quick response to changes, and documentation of the as-built versions of the computer programs. In Appendix C the theme is maintaining configuration control of many computer program products after development and while they are in use. This is complicated by the necessity to manage third-party software and subcontracted software along with internally developed software. Appendix D is directed towards the complex process of generating computer programs, and includes third-party software and subcontracted software in an environment where changes to configurations are driven by marketing, engineering, vendor changes, and customer demands, as well as the normal iteration of engineering changes.

3.1.2 Scope. The scope of the Plan encompasses the tasks of SCM. The function of the subsection is to

(1) Identify the specific SCM concerns
(2) Define what the Plan will and will not address
(3) Identify the items to be managed.

3.1.2.1 It is also important to identify the

(1) Lowest entity in the hierarchy (the control element) that will be reviewed by the top level project or system management CCB
(2) Smallest useful entity that will be reviewed (a module, a unit, a line of code) by technical management (SCCB)
(3) Deliverable entities or configuration item(s) to be released for use as separate entities

The definition and scope of each entity of the configuration item and the kind of control to be considered for each type of entity is also needed. A short description of relationships among configuration items may be appropriate. The boundary of the SCM activities may be described here with the help of graphics (block diagrams, tables, engineering drawing) as necessary.

Issues to Consider in Planning Section 1.2—Scope

(1) What are the characteristics of the configuration items to be controlled?

(a) Only one application program[10]
(b) Many separate small application programs
(c) An integrated set of application and support programs embedded in a system
(d) Computer programs as an integral part of a hardware system

(2) What are the different high-level interfaces to be managed?
(a) People, organization interfaces
(b) Subcontractor interfaces
(c) Specification interfaces
(d) Contractor interfaces
(e) Hardware interfaces
(f) Life cycle phase interfaces
(g) Software interface

(3) What are the time frames of the project
(a) Life cycle phases
(b) Calendar time

(4) What resources will be available or required for the SCM activities?
(a) Machine resources
(b) Space resources
(c) People resources
(d) Schedule dependencies

(5) What are the software engineering entities to be controlled?
(a) Contractual documents
(b) Specifications
(c) Other documentation
(d) Test procedures, data, verification reports
(e) Source code
(f) Support software

3.1.3 Definitions. Subsection 1.3 of the Plan is used to capture all definitions needed for understanding the Plan or helpful for communication.

Issues to Consider in Planning Section 1.3 — Definitions

(1) Are the definitions easily understood?
(2) Is there a list of definitions that can be easily referenced?
(3) Do you really need to define a new term?
(4) Can a glossary of acronyms be used?

It is best to use standard definitions that are common to the industry. For example, terms defined in ANSI/IEEE Std 729-1983 [1] have been arrived at by a consensus of professionals in the industry; it is a good source to use. Numerous new definitions tend only to make understanding the Plan more difficult. Define only those new terms that have to be defined — usually specific to the computer program product. Also duplicating definitions used elsewhere leads to unnecessary work to maintain them current — another configuration management task.

3.1.4 References. Subsection 1.4 of the Plan lists the documents cited elsewhere in the Plan. References made here refer to existing documents and, when customers are involved, the contractual standards and directives cited in the Plan. Having all the references in one place eliminates duplication of citing different sources. This makes a Plan that is more readable and supports general standardization of work instructions.

Issues to Consider in Planning Section 1.4 — References

(1) Can policies, practices, and procedures that already exist within the organization be referenced?
(2) Is each reference necessary for the Plan?
(3) Are some references a part of the organization's directive system?

Large, critical software developments, such as illustrated in Appendix A, tend to rely on a set of standards that are shared with other projects. This makes for better communication among those using the same general system but at the cost of some flexibility. Smaller projects, such as cited in Appendix B do not need the cross-checks and redundancy of these generalized standards and tend to rely on fewer documented standards.

Referencing helps to reduce the bulk of the document that must be maintained. Care should be taken to reference only those documents that are directly applicable to the Plan. Excessive references will lessen the effectiveness of the more important references. A distinction should be made between references that are necessary for *execution* of the Plan and those documents that are included as *general or supplementary* information.

[10]Throughout the guide, when lists are added to questions in the *issues to consider* NOTES, the lists are to be considered as suggested items, not an exhaustive checklist as in a standard.

3.2 Management. Section 2 of the Plan has the theme of relating the elements of the SCM discipline to specific activities of the project's or company's management organization. It also provides an opportunity to specify budgetary, schedule, and resource requirements necessary to carry out the Plan.

3.2.1 Organization. In 2.1 of the Plan, functions are allocated to organizational entities. Interfaces between organizations are handled in a separate section (2.3). The functions of the SCM department itself (if it will exist) are defined in more detail in 2.2. It is not necessary or desirable in most cases to allocate all SCM functions to an SCM department; SCM is a part of the entire software engineering process and as such may best be accomplished by the various organizations actually performing the systems engineering or integration. Software Development, Systems Engineering, Test and Quality Assurance departments all may assume significant roles in carrying out SCM functions. The *Issues to Consider* listed below are designed to provide a starting point in looking at the project's work-flow in relation to the current management structure and to support consideration of how the SCM activities can be best allocated or coordinated.

Issues to Consider in Planning Section 2.1 — Organization

(1) What kind of product interfaces have to be supported within the project itself?
- (a) Software — hardware
- (b) Software — software
- (c) Software maintained at multiple sites
- (d) Software developed at different sites
- (e) Dependencies on support software
- (f) Maintenance changes generated from different sites

(2) What are the capabilities of the staff available to perform CM specific activities?

(3) What is the management style of the organization within which the software is being developed or maintained?

(4) Who will be responsible for maintaining the support software?

(5) What organizational responsibilities are likely to change during the life of the Plan?
- (a) Project management organization
- (b) Organizational interfaces
- (c) Configuration management organization

(6) Who has the authority to capture data and information and who has authority to direct implementation of changes?

(7) What are the plans for maintaining current organization charts(s)?

(8) What level of management support is needed forimplementing various portions of the SCM discipline?

(9) Will the project management be confined to a single organization or will it be distributed among several organizations?

(10) Are responsibilities for processing changes to baselines clearly indicated, including who
- (a) Originates changes
- (b) Reviews changes
- (c) Signs-off changes
- (d) Approves changes
- (e) Administers the process
- (f) Validates and checks for completion?

(11) Who has the authority to release any software, data, and associated documents?

(12) Who has the responsibility for various SCM activities?
- (a) Ensuring the integrity of the software system
- (b) Maintaining physical custody of the baselines
- (c) Performing product audits (versus quality audits)
- (d) Library management
- (e) Developing and maintaining specialized SCM tools

(13) How is authority vested for handling exceptional situations and waivers?

If the plan for maintaining organizational charts shows a certain organization or management group (such as the program office or the business management office) assuming this responsibility, it may be wise to reference those charts in the Plan rather than placing the actual chart in the document, which must then be maintained every time another group of charts is updated. Alternatively, the organizational chart may be shown in the initial version of the Plan with a footnote directing readers to the proper official source for updates. It is usually best to include organizational charts that refer only to functional names (such as department names) rather than to individuals responsible for managing them. This information is quite dynamic in most organizations, and it is probably not worth updating a Plan every time a department is assigned a new manager.

Consider advantages of alternative forms of organizing activities. Appendix A illustrates a complex, critical software development where there is a strong need for independence and centralization of SCM duties in a functional type organization. Appendix C also illustrates a functional type organization but for a different reason: in a software maintenance environment, SCM plays a stronger role in managing the change processing, even to the scheduling of work—more so than in a typical development environment.

Another point to consider is the management support for the various SCM disciplines. Note, for example, in Appendix B the management supported some concepts of SCM but wanted the process to be as *painless* as possible for the software developers and customers. The SCM administrator established a method of collecting information necessary to achieve the purpose without interfering with the flow of changes to the sites. Similarly, the other Appendixes illustrate SCM practices that are tailored to the reality of the situations in which they are found.

For ease of reading, organize the tasks and the owners in terms of the classical set of CM functions: identification, configuration control, status accounting, and audits and reviews. The matrix in Appendix A, Table 1 illustrates how this kind of information can easily be presented.

3.2.2 SCM Responsibilities. If a specific SCM department or group is identified in the management structure, this section provides a specific description of the role this organization will play in the overall SCM process.

Issues to Consider in Planning Section 2.2—SCM Responsibilities

(1) Are there any special considerations for this project that require the SCM department to change its standard method of doing business?

(2) What explicit assumptions is the SCM group making in planning their part of the project?

(3) Are there specific expectations on the part of the customer or client (such as contractual requirements) for an SCM group that need to be taken into account?

While the major considerations may center on responsibilities of the configuration control boards (CCB), there is the need to consider the responsibilities of other activities such as software quality assurance (SQA), users of the system, other system or hardware configuration control boards, and other management activities.

3.2.3 Interface Control. The theme of subsection 2.3 of the Plan is how SCM disciplines are coordinated and how they are used to manage interfaces throughout the project's life. This is the place to define the roles and composition of the various CCB, SCCB, and other activities and practices used for interface control. All types of interfaces should be considered.

The scope of the SCM Plan (1.2) specifies the boundaries of the CI and the jurisdiction of the Plan, but this boundary is often not as clear as it should be and the control mechanisms are even fuzzier. The definition of interfaces is one of the most important planning elements for ensuring a smooth operation. Every possible effort should be made to reach a common agreement regarding each organization's responsibility regarding the interface(s), and then document them in this subsection. The basic types of interfaces to consider here include organization, phase, software, and hardware.

Organizational interface elements include interfaces between various organizations involved with the product; for example, vendor to buyer, subcontractor to contractor, and co-developer to co-developer. It is typical that different organizations have different views of a product and will apply different expectations to it. Effective SCM disciplines can help minimize and resolve these differences whenever and wherever they may arise.

Phase interface elements include transition interfaces between those life cycle phases of the product that are included in the Plan. They are often coincident with a transition in control of the product between different organizations; for example, promotion from a development group to a formal testing group. Effective SCM disciplines can support these transitions with all the documentation, code, data, tools, and records that are needed for management to smoothly continue SCM on the product.

Software interface elements are the agreements shared between the computer program product and other software entities (for example, operating system, utilities, communication system). These agreements involve the structure and meanings assigned to data passing and operational coordination of the data and the results. The other software may already exist or may be concurrently developed. Effective SCM disciplines can make these agreements generally known and assist management in maintaining the integrity of the product(s).

Hardware interface elements are the agreements shared between the computer program product and characteristics of any hardware in the environment with which the program product interacts. These agreements involve capabilities provided by the hardware and operations defined by the computer programs. Effective SCM disciplines help make these agreements known and support their evaluation for consistency throughout the evolution of both hardware and software.

Issues to Consider in Planning Section 2.3 — Interface Control

(1) What are the organizational interfaces?
(2) What are the important interfaces between adjacent phases of the life cycle?
(3) What are the interfaces between different entities of the computer programs?
(4) What are the dependent hardware interfaces?
(5) Where are the documents defined and maintained that are used in interface control?
(6) What are the procedures for making changes to these interface documents?

Interface control should be extended to include more than just documentation. If the hardware configuration and its supporting software interfaces are complex, then the Plan must also include or reference controls for hardware drawings and equipment as well. The sample Plan in Appendix D illustrates the interface between multiple kinds of computer programs in a variable hardware configuration. In real-time system environments, the interface controls may involve tracking changes to configurations of external sensors, valves, etc. Typically, in a software modification and maintenance situation, human operator interface controls may play a significant role in this section. In some organizations, [EP]ROM are considered hardware, yet the programs residing in them must be explicitly dealt with in this section of the Plan. The guiding principle of SCM is that any proposed changes to the product or to its expected use be considered and evaluated in an open, documented, deliberate, and mutually acceptable fashion.

3.2.4 SCM Plan Implementation. Subsection 2.4 of the Plan has the theme of providing details concerning the implementation of the key SCM milestones identified in the Plan. These details include:

(1) Identification of prerequisites or required activities that affect the Plan and the sequencing of events in the Plan
(2) Schedules for accomplishing these items
(3) Resource requirements (for example, machine time, disk space, specialized tool availability, and staff support)

The implementation section's level of detail and complexity are dependent on the level of complexity of the system being controlled. Small software development activities, particularly those that focus primarily on software and are not currently tied to hardware systems development, may need relatively simple implementation schedules. SCM Plans that support more complex activities, such as software maintenance (Appendix C) or development and maintenance of product line software (Appendix D), will have more complex implementation schedules but will focus more on events such as release for use, new product baselines, audits, and reviews.

Issues to Consider in Planning Section 2.4 — SCM Plan Implementation

(1) Are the resources planned for SCM commensurate with the size and complexity of the system being controlled?
(2) How will the SCM activities be coordinated with other project activities?
(3) How will the different phases (development, maintenance) be managed throughout the software life cycle?

Resource requirements should be carefully considered and included here only when they are important factors in implementing the Plan. If there are any separate project documents that contain the necessary information (for example, department budgets, development laboratory implementation Plans), include them here by reference to avoid unnecessary document maintenance. Items to include are:

(1) People resources
(2) Computer and computer-related resources
(3) Library space
(4) Storage space (including electronic media)

It is usually impractical to put actual dates in the Plan for events. In general, it is better from the maintenance perspective to put actual dates in a schedule chart kept in an appendix or a separate document. In this section it is more appropriate to refer to significant events in terms of their relationships to other milestones (for example, a controlled library for source code will be established following the completion of the critical design review), or in terms of their relationship in time to other events (for example, the physical configuration audit will be held 90 days after the functional qualification test).

Requirements for implementation should be discussed in the same sequence in this section as they are discussed in the body of your Plan (for example, configuration identification is followed by product baselines). This should make correlating the Plan with the implementation considerations easier for the user.

Keep in mind that this section should be updated as the project continues. Consider reviewing this section and making any necessary additions or changes upon the achievement of each major milestone in the system development life cycle (for example, completion of functional design) or on a periodic basis (for example, once per quarter).

Project managers are often asked to provide a budget for SCM separate from the development budget. Little historical data are reported in the literature, primarily because every SCM activity has a slightly different organizational structure. In the example given in Appendix B, the project defined 0.5 full time equivalent man-months. Other types of projects, such as illustrated in Appendix A, will require a larger portion of dedicated SCM personnel. In general, however, as more effective automated tools are deployed and used, the need for dedicated personnel will diminish.

3.2.5 Applicable Policies, Directives, and Procedures. Subsection 2.5 of the Plan has the theme of identifying and defining the degree to which existing and future SCM policies and procedures apply to the Plan. The actual identification of referenced documents, and information on how to obtain them should be cited in Section 1.4 of the Plan. Subsection 2.5 provides the opportunity to *interpret the use* of reference document(s) and to describe any new document(s) that may be planned or are under development (which, obviously, cannot be cited in Section 1.4 of the Plan).

Issues to Consider in Planning Section 2.5—Applicable Policies, Directives and Procedures

(1) Are any standard identification procedures available?
  (a) Standard labels for products
  (b) Identification of the hierarchical structure of computer programs
  (c) Component and unit naming conventions and limitations
  (d) Numbering or version level designations
  (e) Media identification methods (including [EP]ROM)
  (f) Data-base identification methods
  (g) Documentation labeling and identification standards
(2) Are any specific procedures existing for interacting with the dynamic libraries?
  (a) Promoting from one type of library to another
  (b) Documentation releases
  (c) Releasing computer program products
  (d) Releasing firmware products
(3) Are there standard procedures for managing the change process?
  (a) Handling change or enhancement requests
  (b) Provisions for accepting changes into a controlled library
  (c) Processing problem reports
  (d) Membership in CCB
  (e) Operating CCB
  (f) Capturing the audit trail of changes
(4) Are any status accounting procedures available?
  (a) Reporting procedures for summarizing problem reports

   (b) Standard reports and other formatted management information
   (c) Distributing status data
(5) Are there procedures for audits?
   (a) Procedures for functional configuration audits
   (b) Procedures for physical configuration audits
(6) Are there procedures for other general SCM activities?
   (a) Standards for accessing and controlling libraries, including security provisions, change processing, backups and long-term storage
   (b) Forms or file definitions for problem reports, change requests, documentation change notices, etc

The set of procedures need not be developed at one time; but effort consistently applied over a period of time can generate an adequate set of policies and procedures that are effective. The kinds of policies, directives, and procedures that are part of an organization's general practices and procedures might also be considered a part of the Plan.

3.3 SCM Activities. The SCM organizational descriptions in Section 2 of the Plan describe who has what responsibilities for software configuration management. Section 3 of the Plan describes how these groups accomplish their responsibilities.

3.3.1 Configuration Identification. The theme of this subsection is to document an identification scheme that reflects the structure of the product. This is a critical task of SCM, a most difficult task but one that is necessary for a smoothly running SCM operation. It is critical because the flow of management control must follow the structure of the software being managed. It is important because the identification scheme carries forth through the life of the computer program(s). It is difficult because at the time the identification scheme is constructed, the structure of the product is rarely known to the level of detail required during the development process.

Relating the identification scheme to the structure of the computer programs is complicated because there are generally two levels of identification that SCM has historically kept separate. The first level, the identification of configuration items and components recognized by management and users, is identified traditionally by documentation. This is the level associated with released programs. The second level, the labeling of files (parts), is more unique to software and is constrained by the support software used in generating code. File nomenclature must support the structure of the product. Typically, these files are identified with mnemonics unique to a project and need to be correlated back to the identification scheme. This is the level associated with the parts of a released program. SCM not only must set identification schemes for both of these levels, but also must devise a method for relating the two different views of the same product.

Project management generally determines the criteria for identifying CI and subordinate control level items. SCM then devises the identification numbering or labeling structure for tracking those entities.

Other kinds of problems that should be considered include legal responsibilities. Some contracts require that all new code added to a program belongs legally to the owner of the original computer programs. Problems of third-party software acquisition must also be considered. The legal status of each program should be accurately identifiable before the computer programs are released for use. Usually some controls must be placed on the number of copies of third-party software *passed through* and delivered to customers as royalty payments might even be required.

Issues to Consider in Planning
Section 3.1 — Configuration Identification

(1) What scheme is to be used to relate the identification of files to the formal (document based) identification scheme?
(2) How does one relate the software identification scheme to the hardware identification scheme when the computer programs are deeply embedded in the system (for example, device controller firmware, code and data split between ROM firmware and loadable RAM image code)?
(3) How does one identify computer programs embedded in [EP]ROM?
(4) What specifications and management plans need to be identified and maintained under configuration management?
(5) What timing is involved in naming documents as CI?

(a) When does a document enter into controlled status (for example, when presented by author, when reviewed, when rework is verified, or when the document is formally distributed)?

(b) When and how does a document get removed from the CI status?

(6) Is a separate identification scheme needed to track third-party software?

(7) Is a special scheme needed to identify reusable/reused software as different from other software parts?

(8) Are there differences in identification across projects that have different fiscal accounting?

(9) How does one identify support software such as language translators, linkers, and cross-support tools?

(10) Is a special identification scheme needed to identify test data (transaction files, data-bases, etc) that must be kept for regression testing?

(11) Is there a need to identify tables and files for data driven systems?

One practice for identification of parts of a CI (as illustrated in Appendix A) is to use a version description document to relate the different files to the component or configuration item scheme. A suggested practice for embedding computer programs into hardware systems is illustrated in Appendix D where the system index type of project identification is used.

The management of firmware changes can become difficult when the package becomes a part of the hardware item. The problem remains to relate functional capabilities to physical part identifiers, especially when changes to the firmware are closely coupled to changes in the system or application software (for example, boot loaders, device controllers, and high-level ROM-resident system debuggers).

Third-party software needs to be tracked even though it is not changed in the same manner as other software. This is especially important if you, as a reseller, accept responsibility of collecting and dealing with problem reports generated by your customers for these products. It may be necessary too for compliance with legal restrictions on copies and distribution accounting. Appendix C describes this identification situation.

The successful reuse of pieces of software in a (controlled) production library requires a standardized identification scheme to retrieve packages or units and account for their use in different configurations. Appendix C, 3.1 references identification of reused software. It should be noted that it is important to control the test procedures and test cases needed for regression testing in an environment that maintains such software or has extensive dynamic libraries of reusable software.

The identification scheme needs to reference dependent supporting software. Therefore, provisions must be made for identifying the internal documentation, data, and programs used in the generation of the computer program product(s).

3.3.1.2 Identify Project Baselines. Baselines are an effective mechanism to allow many people to work together at the same time. They are a way of synchronizing people working on the same project. The SCM discipline, as in all CM, focuses its activity around the construction and maintenance of baselines. The modifiable units need an identifying mechanism, and a way of describing what is contained in their aggregates is needed. Even if the program is small, a baseline is used to let the other, nonprogramming people, know what is taking place.

Issues to Consider in Defining Baselines

(1) Are baselines other than, for example, the traditional three required[11] to support the project?

(2) Who is needed to authorize the creation of new baselines?

(3) Who approves a baseline for promotion?

(4) How and where are the baselines created and who is responsible for them?

(5) How will the numbering system account for different baselines?

[11] The traditional baselines used in CM (functional, allocated, product) are defined in ANSI/IEEE Std 828-1983 [2] along with the minimal requirements for identifying and establishing those baselines. Additional internal or developmental baselines can be defined and included in the Plan when necessary. For example, in making multiple builds, it is useful to define separate baselines for each build to keep the status of changes straight. The sample SCM Plan in Appendix B illustrates the use of multiple builds. These developmental baselines are very helpful for integrating and testing large software systems.

(a) Different versions (functional changes)
(b) Different revisions (something to make the existing functions work)

(6) How are baselines verified?
(a) Reviews
(b) Customer approval
(c) Developer test reports
(d) Independent verification and validation

(7) Are baselines tied to milestones?
(a) Developmental milestones
(b) New versions

Baselines tie documentation, labeling, and the program together. Developmental baselines define a state of the system at a specific point in time, usually relative to an integration level, and serve to synchronize the engineering activity and documentation that occurs at that time.

Promotions are basically a change in the informal authority required to effect changes in developmental baselines. The new authority commonly represents a higher level of engineering management. The programmer cannot change a unit that has been promoted and integrated with other programmer's units without notifying the others involved, and gaining their (explicit or implicit) approval by way of an SCCB (or CCB).

The more formal baselines (functional, allocated, and product) define a product capability associated with performance, cost, and other user interests. These baselines relate the product to contractual commitments.

3.3.1.3 Delineate Project Titling, Labeling, Numbering. This part of the Plan defines the procedures and labels for identifying the CI, components, and units. This is important for identifying and retrieving information, reporting status and for legal protection of data rights.

Issues to Consider in Labeling and Numbering

(1) Is there a (corporate) standard for labeling that must be used?

(2) Does the identification scheme provide for identification of versions and revisions for each release?

(3) How can or will the physical media be identified?

(4) Are specific naming conventions available for all modifiable entities?

(5) Does the identification scheme need to identify the hierarchy of links between modifiable entities?

(6) Are there constraints on unit and file names?
(a) Compiler and file system limitations on name length and composition
(b) Mnemonic requirements
(c) Names that cannot be used

It is often useful to have the identification label indicate the level (that is, release, version, and revision) of the product it identifies. Labeling the components or units of computer programs can be accomplished in several ways. Numbering schemes can be devised to identify the components. A hierarchy of names can be devised that organizes and identifies parts using mnemonic or English labels. Naming conventions that are associated with the compilation system and are significant for a project are most easily used.

[EP]ROM labeling has special problems and will require a different scheme than that used for RAM-based packages shipped on disk or tape. In developing embedded computer programs, there is the additional consideration of labeling the media ([EP]ROM) with the correct version of the programs. This means that the identification scheme of some computer program packages must somehow relate to the hardware identification scheme. One possible solution is to use the version description document (VDD) form for relating the computer program identification documents to the altered item drawings conventionally used for identifying the [EP]ROM parts.

3.3.2 Configuration Control. Subsection 3.2 of the Plan describes how the configuration control process is managed. The theme here deals with identifying the procedures used to process changes to known baselines. An appropriate level of authority for controlling changes must be identified or delegated for each baseline. The organizations assigned responsibilities for control in Section 2 of the Plan have to manage changes made to the entities identified as defined in Section 3.1 of the Plan. Procedures for processing the requests for changes and approvals must be defined.

3.3.2.1 Levels of Authority. The levels of authority required to make changes to configuration items under SCM control can vary. The system or contract may often dictate the level of authority needed. For example, internally controlled software tools may require less change controls than man-rated or critical software developed under contract. The levels of authority may vary throughout the life cycle. For example, changes to code in the development cycle usually require a lower level of control to be authorized than changes to the same code after it has been released for general use. The level of authority required can also depend on how broadly the change impacts the system. A change affecting specifications during the requirements analysis phase has less ramifications than a change affecting software in operational use. Likewise, changes to draft versions of documents are less controlled than changes to final versions. Changes to a product distributed to several sites and used by many different users requires a different level of authority than products with a very restricted or minimal user base.

The level of control needed to authorize changes to developmental baselines depends on the level of the element in relation to the system as a whole (for example, a change in logic affecting one or a few units usually has less impact on the system than an interface between CI, especially if the CI are developed by different organizations.

Issues to Consider in Defining Levels of Authority

(1) Is the level of authority consistent with the entities identified in subsection 3.1 of the Plan?

(2) When are levels of control assigned to the modifiable units (parts) of the computer programs during top level and detail design stages (technical engineering phase) for developmental baselines?

(3) Do control levels assigned for developmental baselines (for both components and configuration items) need to be reviewed by management?

(4) Are there significant increases in levels of control for transitions between developmental baselines?
  (a) During design
  (b) For promotion from design to implementation
  (c) For unit testing
  (d) For integration

(5) Does management need to know specifically who requested a change?

(6) Do changes originating from outside the organization, such as customers or general users, require different authority for approval than changes from a technical development group?

(7) Do changes that do not impact formal baselines require coordination and approval by a CCB or can they be authorized by a SCCB?

The Plan should clearly define the level of authority to be applied to the baselined entities throughout the life cycle of the system, and should distinguish between controls applied to processing technical changes that do not impact formal baselines and the authority needed to approve changes to formal baselines. For example, during maintenance or in the latter stages of preparing multiple builds for a project, authority for making changes to all entities at all levels is typically restricted. However, when beginning development of a new version or build, the controls on the dynamic library and testing with the controlled library can be relaxed.

Table 4 suggests some ideas for assigning different levels of change authority to different SCM elements during the life cycle.

3.3.2.2 Processing Changes. The theme of these paragraphs is to describe the methods to be used for processing change requests. Generally, no single procedure can meet the needs of all levels of change management and approval levels. These paragraphs must concentrate on

(1) Defining the information needed for approving a change
(2) Identifying the routing of this information

Table 4
Variable Levels of Control

Element	Internal Coordination	Developmental Baselines	Formal Baselines
Specifications	Supervision	CCB	CCB
Test data	Supervision	SCCB	CCB
Unit code	Supervision	SCCB	CCB
Configuration Item code	SCCB	CCB	CCB

(3) Describe the control of the library(ies) used in processing the changes
(4) Describe or refer to the procedure for implementing each change in the code, in the documentation, and in the released program (for example, field upgrades).

The change initiator should analyze the proposed change to assess its impact on all configuration items (documentation, software, and hardware) and the CCB should satisfy themselves that this has been done and interface with the CCB in the impacted areas (if any).

Another area that is often overlooked (and not specifically covered) is that of the maintenance of design documentation. The documentation hierarchy should be fully defined and a change to any level should be analyzed to ensure that the higher levels of documentation have been considered and that the change is *rippled through* the lower levels to implementation in the code.

Source code changes, and indeed hardware changes, should first be implemented in the highest level of documentation and the change implemented through the subsequent levels. Provisions for backing up of changes and maintaining their history need to be considered.

A more critical issue centers on managing controlled libraries. This configuration management concept grew out of the SCM experience with managing source code and has been expanded to include all of the baseline items (including associated documentation and reports) that relate to the computer programs. One can observe that as the interactive programming environments continue to evolve, most of the procedural controls associated with SCM will probably be integrated into the programming environment. The procedures for processing changes are the same, whether for approval by a designated management authority or approval by a control activity (SCCB) delegated by management. The procedure needs to distinguish the proper channels for making the decisions, defining the flow for changes made to an established formal baseline, and the flow for changes made to developmental baselines. Most of this capability is now available in SCM and software engineering tools in one form or another.

Issues to Consider in Processing Changes

(1) What is the information necessary for processing a software/system change request (SCR) or authorizing a change (SCA)?
(2) What kind of information will a CCB or SCCB need in order to make a decision?
(3) What is the overall processing cycle of changes?
(4) What SCM support is provided by automated tools available in the environment?
(5) Will changes in procedures be required to support different kinds of reviews during each of the phases of the life cycle?
(6) When there are multiple CCB in a hierarchy, what are the procedures for information exchange and approval chains?
(7) Is there a need for dynamic libraries and controlled library interfaces?
(8) Is there a need for controlling all access to a library or just controlling changes made to the information in the libraries?
(9) Does the library system provide an audit trail, such as change histories?
(10) Are back-up and disaster files taken into account?
(11) Are there provisions for archive procedures to provide the static library support to the full life cycle?
(12) How are source items (source code) associated with their derived object (executable code) programs?
(13) What are the provisions for *draw down* or *check out* to get units from the controlled library?
(14) What are the provisions for keeping the data files synchronized with the program(s) using them?
(15) How does the change process itself support or accommodate the development of new versions or revisions?

Some library tools maintain *deltas* to base units of source code. Procedures for maintaining version histories of units as well as derived configuration items need to be established along with archiving maintenance.

A CCB concerned with project management may need information regarding estimated cost and schedules for a change, as illustrated in Appendix B. Other CCB may be interested only in the technical interfaces affected by a change, as illustrated in the sample Plan in Appendix C. Still others may need, in addition, information on proprietary rights and copyrights affected, as illustrated in Appendix D.

Some CCB review a proposed change to validate it (approve it as a necessary change; to expend time and resources for investigating feasibility of the change) while others may simply want completed (programmed and documented) changes to be approved prior to inclusion in released computer programs. There are different functions of SCCB responsibility, extending from coordinating engineering technical changes to allocating the work to a work group. Some organizations design, code and test all proposed changes with preliminary CCB approval before submitting them for final CCB approval. This technique may reduce total time to produce a change. The process for granting change approvals must guarantee that unauthorized changes do not contaminate baselined software.

Some advanced tools provide capabilities for formatting change requests, routing to different sets of individuals for approvals, and authorizing work to be done; reviewing changes and tests while in a holding area; and releasing a baseline to a controlled library for operational use. Others provide only for the recording of change information and a history of past versions of source code.

If secure procedures are not in place or feasible for controlling a library system, the library may necessarily be divided into physical entities that control access.

3.3.2.3 The Configuration Control Board. The theme of these paragraphs is identifying the authorities needed for granting change approvals. Subsection 2.2 of the management section of the Plan identifies the general role(s) of each CCB. These paragraphs go into detail on the roles and authority. It should be remembered that the CCB has traditionally been concerned with managing changes to established baselines of documented configuration items and the components of those configuration items. There may be other change control bodies (SCCB) that authorize changes subordinate to the CCB described here. The CCB described in these paragraphs of the Plan have the role of authorizing changes to baselined configuration items and components from the point of view of entrepreneurial management. They reflect concerns over the costs, schedules, and resources available to implement changes in response to user desires for change.

Issues to Consider in Identifying Configuration Control Boards

(1) Can the limits of authority be defined?
  (a) Limited to contractual baselines as in Appendix A
  (b) Limited to developmental baselines (noncontractual) as in Appendix D
(2) Will the project mix computer programs that are controlled by other CCB?
(3) Is there a need to limit the CCB tabling actions by setting time limits?
(4) Are there contractual requirements imposed on a CCB that must be reflected in the Plan?
(5) How are the different levels of authority determined?
(6) How are different organizational bodies phased in when transitioning from one phase of the life cycle to another?
(7) How are changes to a baselined product to be batched together for release?
  (a) For a new version
  (b) For a revision
(8) Does the CCB membership reflect the management style of the organization?
  (a) For a functional organization
  (b) For a matrixed organization

Large, complex systems require ongoing configuration control authorities to coordinate the technical work involved in generating specifications and code, and in continuing the work of technical coordination required for maintaining interacting software systems (such as defined in Appendix C). Such projects use the same principles of configuration management and perform the same generic approval and scheduling functions as the CCB concerned with smaller-scale entrepreneurial management, particularly where automated SCM tools are used to support both types of activities.

Large software systems are frequently not completely new. They are often mixtures of software in public domain, vendor-supplied products, vendor supplied but modified by a contractor, subcontracted software, proprietary software, and software paid for on another project but reused or adapted. The procedures of how the CCB handles the special nature of proprietary software and reusable software are important and need to be specifically addressed in a Plan.

It may be noted that the CCB concept is another one of those functional concepts of SCM. On a small project, the CCB could be the *chief programmer* and the system will function quite adequately.

Any other change approval activities, such as the SCCB that supports the CCB, also needs to be identified and their roles defined. In some installations, the CCB may need to have the technical expertise to make the final decision on whether a requested change is technically feasible. Other CCB must be supported by technical experts or be prepared to delegate a level of change authorization to qualified subordinate bodies. *In general, decision making that affects the allocation and scheduling of development or maintenance resources should be separated from decision making motivated by various technical and marketing issues.*

3.3.2.4 Interface With Other CCB. Large or complex systems can have many hardware-software interfaces (as documented in the Interface Control [2.3] subsection of the Plan) that require continued ongoing change coordination. Sometimes these boards are called program change review boards (PCRB). The Plan needs to include a description of how these interfaces are handled and documented so all of the people on the projects know how to get the job done (this will probably involve both formal and informal organizational structures and interfaces).

Issues to Consider in Describing CCB Interfaces

(1) Are there a number of CCB that have to work together, as illustrated in Appendix C, or is there only one that has total responsibility for the software configuration items?

(2) Is there a hierarchy of CCB that have authority for making business-type management decisions such as illustrated in Appendixes A and D?

(3) Who has the responsibility and authority for maintaining communications with these CCB?

(4) What body or authority has been designated to arbitrate deadlocks when two parallel CCB are unable to resolve an issue?

(5) What are the procedures for resolving differences of opinion?

(6) What needs to be done to maintain responsive communication and time limits on decision making?

3.3.2.5 Support Software. The theme of these paragraphs has to do with managing all the other software needed to build and maintain the computer program products throughout their life cycle. Specifically, this focus is on describing the necessary controls used to manage support software. Support software, which may be user-furnished, developed in-house, leased from a vendor or purchased off-the-shelf, is the class of software which may or may not be delivered with a product, but yet is necessary for designing, enhancing, or testing the changes made during the life of a delivered computer program product. The developer or maintainer needs to ensure that the support software is available for use for as long as may be necessary. For example, compilers need to be archived for use later *as is* when implementing enhancements to prevent subtle compiler dependencies from turning simple enhancements into major upgrades. Host systems, when used, and utility programs and test drivers are also needed.

Issues to Consider in Planning SCM of Support Software

(1) What is the total set of support software used to design, develop, and test the software controlled under this Plan?

(2) Is this set of software archived and maintained for the full life cycle of the computer program products?

(3) What procedures are to be followed to introduce new versions of support software that impact the software within the scope of the Plan?

(4) How are problems resolved and changes made in the support software that impact the configurability or maintainability of the software within the scope of the Plan?

(5) How is the hardware configuration used to develop and maintain the software product identified and maintained for the full life cycle of the computer program product?

It is necessary to determine the appropriate level of software support needed for maintenance of the product throughout its full life cycle. What is sufficient and necessary for the job but not prohibitive in terms of support software costs for maintenance? In some situations, it can be very costly to actually maintain or enhance some of the support tools. For example, fixing bugs in a compiler may trigger unknown changes in production software after it is simply recompiled. *Whenever a production baseline is established, it is very important to archive all environment and support tools along with the production code.*

3.3.3 Configuration Status Accounting. The theme of this subsection is identifying what information is needed for various activities, obtaining the information and reporting it. The concern is with the acquisition of the right information at the right time so reports may be made when they are needed. In essence, this is a typical data management problem. Status accounting may be literally thought of as an accounting system; many of the concepts used to track the flow of funds through accounts may be used to track the flow of software through its evolution. Using this accounting analogy, separate accounts can be established for each CI. Individual transactions can then be tracked through each account as they occur. The configuration status accounting function, at a minimum, is basically reporting the transactions occurring between SCM-controlled entities.

The functional capabilities of the library system (or the software programming environment), in conjunction with the SCM tools, determine in a large way the capabilities of the status accounting function. As well as providing *live* information regarding the development process, the configuration of each released baseline needs to be documented, together with the exact configuration of the released system (that is, historical records). The definition of the *Build Standard* of systems is an important tool for maintenance teams. Because of its impact on maintaining operational software, support software must be addressed in status accounting.

Status accounting reports need to be addressed in detail in the Plan. The theme should be able to answer queries as to *What is the status of SCR 21, 37, 38, 39 and 50?* when one is not always sure of the query in advance. More sophisticated SCM tools that capture transaction data in the library data base can use data management systems and report generators to provide flexibility. Other systems need to anticipate common queries by capturing information in a form where it is easily accessible.

Issues to Consider in Planning Section 3.3 — Configuration Status Accounting

(1) What types of information needs to be reported?
(2) What is the degree of control required by the customer (typically management)?
(3) Who are the different audiences for each report?
(4) What is the formality required by the organization's standards and procedures for requesting or obtaining reports, or both?
(5) What kind of reports are needed to support integration of units and the tracing of error sources?
(6) What information is needed to produce reports?
  (a) Any problem report number included in a release or promotion
  (b) Units that have been delivered within a given time to integration and test activity
  (c) Changes made and released as a result of a particular problem report
  (d) Units that have been through various types of testing but have not been promoted or released
  (e) Units that have been promoted as a result of a design change
(7) For large systems, is there a need for handling rollover of identification sequences?

Many different types of reports can and do prove useful. The project's managers may, for example, make use of the status accounting data to keep track of the project's progress. Typically the report requests must evolve over a period of time. For some projects, status reporting can be extended to include the status of data items and reviews that are more strictly management scheduling information rather than just configuration management status.

The basic information needed by a CCB relates to transactions applied to the baseline(s), particularly the operational (product) baselines. The disciplines involved in controlling computer programs complement traditional CM for this process. Information needed for more detailed technical management between baseline events should also be collected somehow. Interfaces with available software engineering tools can provide much of this information.

The procedure for tracking the status of CI should be established early enough in the software development process to allow data gathering when it is most easily generated (that is, at the decision and response points) rather than after the fact. The desirable amount of automation depends in large part on the tools available, the size of the project and the maturity of the existing procedures.

Status accounting for multiple sites represents a more complex reporting procedure. The sample Plan in Appendix B describes this problem. Other general requirements for reporting must anticipate management needs for various combinations of information. An ad hoc query capability is often most useful.

3.3.4 Audits and Reviews. The theme of subsection 3.4 of the Plan involves the procedures used to verify that the software product (executable code) matches the configuration item descriptions in the specifications and documents, and that the package being reviewed is complete. It should be noted that, as a general division of labor, the organization performing quality assurance functions also usually performs the audits that address change processing functions, operation of the library(ies), and other activities associated with the processes of software configuration management. This constrasts with the reviews and audits performed within the scope of a SCM activity or organization that verify that a software or firmware product is a consistent, well-defined collection of parts.

Audits are one means by which an organization can ensure that the developers have done all their work in a way that will satisfy any external obligations. Audits vary in formality and rigor, depending on the legal liability of external obligations. They are a check on the completeness of a computer program product. Any anomalies found during audits should not only be corrected but the root cause of the problem should be identified and corrected to ensure that the problem does not resurface.

Generally, there should be a physical configuration audit (PCA) and a functional configuration audit (FCA) of configuration items prior to the release of a product baseline or an updated version of a product baseline. The PCA portion of the audit consists of determining that all items identified as being part of the configuration are present in the product baseline. The audit must also establish that the correct version and revision of each part are included in the product baseline and that they correspond to information contained in the baseline's configuration status report.

The FCA portion is similar, in that someone acknowledges having inspected or tested each item to determine that it satisfies the functions defined in the specifications or contract(s) for which it was developed. The objectives of a PCA/FCA are for the developers to provide notice that contractual obligations are nearing completion, and to provide sufficient evidence for the clients or user organization to accept the product and initiate the transition into operational usage.

This section of the Plan should define ways to ensure that established configuration management procedures are followed:

(1) Test specifications are maintained current
(2) Test reports are properly prepared
(3) Test procedures explicitly define tests to be conducted
(4) Test results comply with acceptance criteria in the test procedure
(5) Test data package contents are complete and comply with approved formats

Issues to Consider in Planning Section 3.4 — Audits and Reviews

(1) Are there needs or provisions for more than one audit of each product baseline?
(2) Is there a single, separate audit trail for each component and for the personnel working on them?
(3) How are subcontractors involved in an audit (if part of project)?
(4) Are provisions made for auditing the SCM process?
(5) Are periodic reviews held to determine the progress and technical quality of a computer program product?

Audits of a configuration as it evolves can prevent massive problems at the time of release for operational use.

A higher-level audit trail for business-type management that reflects the real-time relationships and status of CI changes, component changes and individuals responsible for development is often very useful. When addressing subcontractor audits, reference Section 5, Supplier Control, in the Plan.

When addressing internal audits, the Plan should identify who will be performing these audits and exactly what is to be audited. For example, the SQA group may audit the SCM group's adherence to change control procedures (assuming an SCM group exists—otherwise the general use of tools is audited).

Although SCM functions generally do not initiate or direct reviews, quite often the mechanisms used by SCM to process changes are used to organize and process items in a review conducted by other functions such as software quality assurance (SQA). The mechanisms of status reporting are often useful in maintaining detailed action items from reviews of complex systems. SCM supports reviews in this way as any other support provided to management.

There should always be an audit of the configuration items at the time a product is released. This will vary according to the baseline being released and the criteria for the audit stated in the Plan. At a minimum, when the product baseline is established and whenever it is subsequently changed due to the release of a new version of the computer program, the configuration should be audited. Again, the roles of the SCM organization and its participation in the audit should be established in the Plan.

3.3.5 Release Process. Major releases of software must be described so that the recipient understands what has just been delivered. Often the recipient will need installation instructions and other data concerning the use of the new system. The installation instructions should define the environment on which the software will run. This is to cover both hardware (for example, machine type, peripherals needed, and extra memory required) and software (for example, operating system version, and utilities not provided) environments. SCM verifies that the release package is complete and ready to be handed over to the user.

A short outline of the documentation (often referred to as the version description document, or VDD) typically associated with the release package is given in 3.3.5.1. It may be modified to suit the project. The more critical or the larger the application, the more complete the documentation needs to be.

3.3.5.1 Version Description Document. The version description document describes the tapes, diskettes, or other media used to provide the software.

(1) *Release Media.* List the labels on each tape, diskette or [EP]ROM and provide some guidance as to the contents of each volume. For example, *Tape FG301 contains the executable load unit library required to run FRED.*

When one has a more complex system with many CI and associated data files, it may be necessary to describe each file on the tape in this section.

(2) *Functional Description.* When the release contains any functions not previously released, describe them briefly to inform the users of new capabilities. This is not intended to be a user's manual—just the summation of the new capabilities.

(3) *User Considerations.* If there are any special actions the users must take in using the new release, describe them here. Examples may be changes in the use of a new function key, a special procedure needed to complete a certain action, hardware limitations, etc.

In this section, also list any open problem reports (SCR) against the system. Typically the open reports are listed by short title and number in this section. This is for user reference. It may prevent users from filing duplicate problem reports and will give them a better understanding of the system's status.

(4) *Closed Problem Reports.* List in this section all SCR closed out in this release.

(5) *Inventory.* If necessary, provide in this section an inventory of the source and executable load units and data objects (typically at the file level) that are contained in this release. This inventory is generally necessary for those systems that must be tightly controlled. The units are usually listed in alphabetical order by CI, with a designation of version, revision, and date changed. In some cases, the SCR initiating the change is listed against each unit.

(6) *Installation Instructions.* This section may be used when the installation is made at a remote site, at numerous sites or when there are special actions to be taken. The instructions should be specific for each site.

The most important aspect of writing installation instructions is to walk through each step that the installer will have to perform and ensure that he/she will have the information necessary to perform it.

3.4 Tools, Techniques and Methodologies. The theme of Section 4 of the Plan is making it all happen — the easy way. A well planned project typically takes advantage of planning tools such as PERT charts and Gantt charts.

The audit trail reports should reflect directly back to milestones and other activities on the planning charts, thus giving management a tool for tracking progress on a project. An automated system for software configuration management may include some way of integrating these classical planning tools with the SCM data base to provide all parties (management, designers, developers, testers, quality assurance, etc) with an on-line tool for creating products and observing their current development status dynamically in real-time, correlated automatically with a predefined Plan to yield a quantitative performance-against-schedule measures. The group that is responsible for specific tools should be identified.

The tools, techniques, and methods used to implement SCM are usually discussed in terms of a (set of) libraries and the methods and techniques used to capture, store, and promote or release the items of each type of library in a controlled manner. The concept of *software library* varies according to the level of technology available for generating software. The degree to which all entities of the product are machine accessible is a rough measure of the level of automation for a particular project.

Issues to Consider in Planning Section 4 — Tools, Techniques, and Methodologies

(1) What are the number and types of libraries to be established?
   (a) A dynamic library (or programmer's library)
   (b) A controlled library (or master library)
   (c) A static library (or software repository)
   (d) Other libraries
(2) What is the amount of change activity anticipated for the project?
(3) Can the SCM tools in the library be used to manage documentation and source code?
(4) What kinds and amounts of training (for example, orientation and learning time) are needed to make the tools and procedures an effective solution for the organization?

Definition and use of a minimal set of libraries are illustrated in Appendix C and in 2.3.1. These libraries can accomplish all of the necessary functions of baseline control but usually need to be supplemented with other kinds of libraries to provide the necessary flexibility for smooth operation on larger projects. The libraries have to be structured in such a way that the source code associated with a given executable unit is promoted at the same time that the executable unit is. The source and executable load unit libraries should **always** be kept in synchronization. There are numerous technical methods for achieving this, depending on the development environment and the tools available.

For run-time efficiency, it may be necessary to merge various CI executable units into an integrated run-time environment. When this is done, it is also advisable to maintain the source separately that created the load units.

Note that the corresponding data files are included in the various levels of libraries. When table driven software is used, it is critical to maintain that data at the same level as the corresponding code. This can be handled by carefully structuring the libraries and using appropriate naming conventions.

Manual SCM methods may be perfectly adequate for a small project. However, if the tools and equipment are already in place, they may well be cost effective. The characteristics of the project must guide tool selection. A small project may not need the detailed planning and overhead supported by a complex set of integrated SCM tools. Problems in turnover of software developers may make automation attractive even though its initial cost is high.

In the selection of SCM tools, one needs to consider the cost effectiveness of their use for the given project, product, or site. New SCM tools and methods may be good, but if the engineering staff does not trust them, understand them, or is unwilling to learn new ways of working, they may hinder rather than support the performing organizations in getting the job done.

Current commercially available SCM tools focus primarily on controlling source code. They are written by programmers and code is the important element in programming. Due consideration should be made to bring documentation under control of the same tools as the code. Good SCM systems work on files, and files can consist of paragraphs of a document as well as code.

The kinds of SCM tools recommended in a Plan should also be considered in relation to the probable availability of the tools for use within the project's environment. That is, one should not make the entire Plan dependent on a tool set that may never materialize.

3.5 Supplier Control. The theme of Section 5 of the Plan is how to place effective CM on the computer programs over which you have no direct CM control. Computer program suppliers are considered to fall into one of two classes:

(1) Subcontracted software, or those contractors that develop unique or dedicated software under contract to a developer
(2) Vendor software, or those contractors that provide privately developed and existing software, and bundled application software such as operating systems, compilers, word processing tools, software configuration management tools, and data-base management systems.

Issues to Consider in Planning Section 5 — Supplier Control

(1) Is the product being procured to be used internally, delivered as part of your organization's product, or both?
(2) What post-delivery defect correction requirements and procedures need to be established?
(3) What changes is the purchaser permitted to make after delivery without invalidating the warranty or violating legal constraints?
(4) When should audits be performed?
  (a) When subcontractor or vendor releases parts to the buyer
  (b) After successful integration in buyer's system
(5) Is there a need to *pass through* SCM tools to a supplier or a vendor?
(6) Consider the use of *software in escrow*[12] as a method of enforcing SCM and quality
(7) What periodic reviews of the subcontractor's work will be needed?

3.5.1 Subcontractor Software. If a portion of a software development project is to be subcontracted to another organization, the responsibility for SCM is generally passed to that organization. However, the subcontractor can only be responsible for the portion of the work that his organization is tasked to perform, not for the integration of the subcontracted work with the final product.

Possible methods for integrating subcontractor SCM include

(1) Specifying or providing a library management tool and monitoring its use
(2) Letting the subcontractor(s) promote code to your software generation system and controlling it in the same fashion as is done in-house.
(3) Obtaining the source for all subcontractor deliveries and recompiling and relinking it using the buyer's software generation tools

To ease integration and maintenance, the subcontractor should be required to implement a system of configuration management based on the buyer's requirements — one that is compatible with the buyer's configuration management system or a subset thereof. Identification schemes should be compatible. A system for effectively managing interfaces should be developed. The subcontractor should have an internal configuration control system that is equivalent to the systems and procedures described by the buyer. The format and frequency of status reports also should be agreed upon.

Not all contractor-subcontractor relationships are easily identifiable. Sometimes, the contractual relationship does not afford the buyers any control over the subcontractor SCM processes and the buyer has to bound the relationship of the subcontracted software by alternate identification and by accepting the configuration as given, verified by testing the delivered product (as illustrated in Appendix C). Generally, it is possible to tailor the SCM requirements passed on to the subcontractor, using specifications or statements of work.

---

[12] If the executable code is the only code obtained, it may be advisable to have the supplier place the source code in *escrow* as a warranty that the source will be available if the supplier goes out of business.

Issues to Consider in Defining Subcontractor Relationships

(1) What SCM concerns need to be added to or removed from the contract?
(2) Who is responsible for auditing versus enforcing SCM for contractual products?
(3) What audits and procedures need to be established where the subcontractor has no documented SCM practices or procedures?

If the buyer's organization is developing the computer programs for a customer, the contract should be reviewed for any specific legal requirements that need to be passed on to the subcontractor, or special actions that have to be taken by the buyer to ensure the performance of the subcontractors' product.

Integration of subcontractor software is very difficult unless communication is kept open. One way is to allow subcontractor representatives to attend SCCB meetings to ensure that they are aware of all important technical issues. It may also be useful to accept incremental versions of the code for integration and test with the rest of the code, rather than waiting until the end of the development cycle.

In specifying delivery, identify all items that are to be a part of the deliverable. Possibilities include

(1) Source code
(2) Executable code
(3) Load units
(4) Data files
(5) Test cases
(6) Any JCL or other procedures used in running or creating the software
(7) Compilation listings or link-edit maps (for debugging)
(8) Documentation

Another concern for SCM is the subcontractor's actual performance to an agreed-upon Plan or statement of work. A preselection or purchase audit of the potential subcontractor's configuration management policies and procedures can provide an indication of the potential for the organization to perform satisfactorily. If possible, the buyer's software configuration management group should perform an in-process SCM audit of all project subcontractors to ensure satisfactory compliance. As part of this audit, a specific approved change should be traced through the subcontractor's system to the point of verifying the implementation.

A critical role for SCM is in the inspection (FCA/PCA) of the product as it is prepared for delivery to the buyer. This is most important as it determines the effort and resources that may be needed to integrate and maintain the product once it has been incorporated in the buyer's system. There are still compatibility problems and problems of error correction, and updates that have to be provided for even if the program is a stand-alone product (as for a compiler). If the program received is not well identified and documented, then the task of maintenance is generally increased.

3.5.2 Vendor Software. Warranties contained in purchase orders may be difficult to enforce. The specific criterion is that the vendor should furnish the computer program *media* as specified by a purchase order or as specified by the supplier's documentation referenced in the purchase order. Test documentation confirming compliance is desirable but often unavailable.

Issues to Consider in Defining Vendor Interfaces

(1) How is the vendor software identified?
(2) How are license agreements and data rights protected and enforced? Are there limitations on
   (a) Duplication of documentation
   (b) Your customer making copies of the program
(3) How will vendor support be provided over the life cycle of the computer program product being purchased?
(4) How will copyright interests be protected?
(5) How will legal copies of leased software be controlled?

The handling of vendor software can be very complex, particularly in a maintenance environment, such as described in Appendix C, where the vendor software is intermixed with internally developed software. More importantly, if you release the vendor product as a part of your organization's product, your organization may be responsible for ensuring its maintenance as part of your released product. An organization embedding third party software in a product delivered to a customer can be open to financial and legal liabilities if a vendor fails to perform—that is, making required changes in a timely manner. One possible consideration is the use of an escrow account with a vendor agreement tied to performance of his product.

3.6 Records Collection and Retention. The theme of Section 6 of the Plan is to *keep the information necessary only for the time required.* This is another service aspect of configuration management. Good configuration management practices include maintaining copies of released material for backup and disaster protection. Also the liability and warranty provisions and responsibilities make considering the retention of test and approval records a necessity. If a master disaster recovery plan exists for the company, the Plan needs to disclose all information regarding the location of backups and records that are impounded in relation with that plan.

Records collection can also be a part of risk management. Part of the trade-off must consider whether personnel will be available to recover lost software. Trade-offs can be made concerning the cost of capturing and maintaining records versus the potential cost savings for

(1) Recovering programs in the event of a disaster for
  (a) Software developed for internal use
  (b) Delivered products for which warranty is still in effect
  (c) Support software necessary for maintaining computer program products under warranty
(2) Liability for not being able to certify the reliability of delivered products
(3) Information gathered that may lead to performance or productivity improvements in development or maintenance activities.

Record keeping begins in planning the capture of all data that needs to be maintained. In addition to all other considerations, archiving the software should be done in a manner acceptable to any legal contracts that may affect the computer programs. Static libraries, disaster planning, and storage should consider the legal status of the software involved (for example, whether it has trade secret status) and the impact on the provisions made for the care and storage of the software components. Special attention should be given to the retention of support software associated with software on target machines.

Issues to Consider in Planning Section 6—Records Collection and Retention

(1) What type of information needs to be retained?
(2) What data need to be maintained over a period of time for trend data analysis?
(3) Is all the information, support software, and equipment needed to recreate the product available from archives?
(4) Is media protected from disaster?
(5) Is there a need to maintain copies of software licensed for use and distribution?
(6) What activities need to be recorded (and data captured) for maintaining a product after the project is completed?
  (a) Copyright records
  (b) Distribution records
  (c) Benchmarks
  (d) Change history (CCB activity, SPR, etc)
  (e) Audits, reviews, status reports
(7) For whose use are the records being maintained?
  (a) Engineering
  (b) Management
  (c) Software Quality Assurance
  (d) Legal, customer
(8) How are the records to be kept?
  (a) On line versus off line
  (b) Media and format (hard copy document versus electronic media, deterioration rate versus time needed)
  (c) Location (preservation conditions, accessibility both off site and on site)
  (d) Tools used on the project that affect data capture
(9) How long will the data be kept?

The information collected need not mirror that collected for hardware bit for bit. For example, serial information on production that is kept to identify configurations in hardware may not be necessary for software. Plan to keep only the data that will be of use in maintenance, disaster recovery, or which has other justification. Is the deterioration rate of the storage medium sufficient for the needed time span? Media can deteriorate in storage; also, work in-progress should be backed-up at specific intervals to protect the investment for projects that have long development periods or are of high cost.

Appendixes

(The following Appendixes are not a part of ANSI/IEEE Std 1042-1987, IEEE Guide to Software Configuration Management, but are included for information only.)

Appendix A

Software Configuration Management Plan for Critical Software for Embedded Systems

Version 1.0

Approved

____
Mgr, SCM Dept

____
Project Mgr

____
Contracts

____
Customer

Date: ___/___/___

Synopsis

This example contains a discussion of a hypothetical contract to provide a medium-sized real-time control system for the management of advanced vehicles. Sensors are used for input of information to the system; displays are used to support a man-machine interface. The contract for the system consists of eight software configuration items being developed concurrently with five new and seven off-the-shelf hardware configuration items. The project is expected to have at most three hundred and fifty-six personnel, with an average of thirty-four and peak of fifty software development personnel over the estimated three and a half year development cycle.

Most of the development work is performed in the contractor's main facility with some work being performed at a nearby subsidiary. Testing and acceptance is performed at the mock-up in the contractor's facility. Some commercial software is procured from a vendor for the support software and the firmware for the vehicle is subcontracted to the builder of the vehicle. This is a turnkey contract. The customer takes over all maintenance of the software after delivery of the first system.

The customer's procurement organization has a large staff for monitoring the contract and is expected to perform frequent audits. The contractor's project office wishes to minimize friction with the customer and is willing to perform most, but not all, of the necessary record keeping and in-process inspections. The configuration management department of the contractor has a long history of involvement in projects with the customer and there is a general familiarity and comfortableness in *doing business* in this manner. The software configuration management activity is relatively new but is strongly supported by the old line configuration management department.

In this environment, the software configuration management activity will be a very disciplined operation, logging and maintaining accurate records of *all* transactions against established baselines.

Contents

ATTACHMENTS

Appendix A

Software Configuration Management Plan for Critical Software for Embedded Systems

1. Introduction

This document is the Software Configuration Management (SCM) Plan for the *Critical Software for Embedded Systems* (CSES). The CSES system performs functions critical to the life and safety of human beings. The configuration management of this software during development is essential to the delivery of error-free and reliable software configuration items.

1.1 Purpose. This plan provides information on the requirements and procedures necessary for the configuration management activities of the CSES project. It identifies the software configuration management requirements and establishes the methodology for generating configuration identifiers, controlling engineering changes, maintaining status accounting, and performing audits and reviews during the design and development of software configuration items.

1.2 Scope. This plan applies to all software and associated documentation used in the production of computer programs produced under the critical software for embedded systems contract including, but not limited to, source, object, and executable load images. Software configuration items referenced in the contract and controlled by this plan include

CSES Operational System
CSES Training Program
CSES Test Program
CSES Hardware Acceptance Programs
CSES Diagnostic Software
CSES Software Support System
CSES Simulation System
CSES Utilities

The organizations involved in this project are identified in Fig 1.

This plan applies to all phases of the software development life cycle, up to and including the time of delivery to the customer. Maintenance of the software after delivery is covered by another contract.

1.3 Definitions and Mnemonics

1.3.1 Definitions. The definitions used in this plan conform to the company standards as set forth in Vol II of the company *Configuration Practices Manual*. Other definitions will conform to those found in ANSI/IEEE Std 729-1983, IEEE Standard Glossary of Software Engineering Terminology. See specifically: baseline, configuration item, configuration management, configuration control, configuration control board, configuration audit, configuration identification, configuration status accounting, and software library. Unique definitions used in this document include:

interface control. The process of

(1) Identifying all functional and physical characteristics relevant to the interfacing of two or more configuration items provided by one or more organizations.
(2) Ensuring that proposed changes to these characteristics are evaluated and approved prior to implementation.

1.3.2 Mnemonics. The following mnemonics are referred to within the text of this standard:

Fig 1
Program Organization Chart

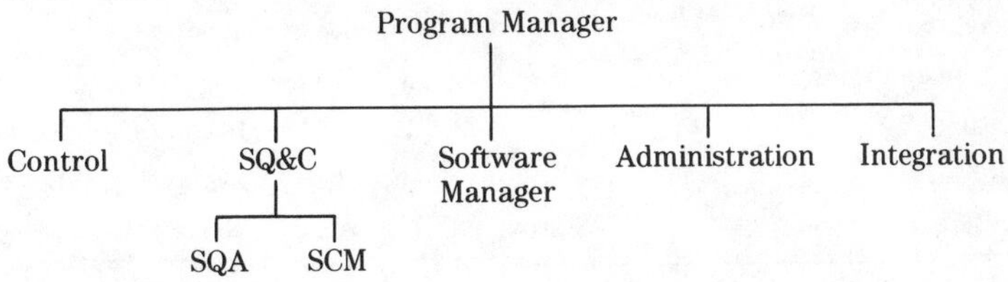

CCB	Configuration Control Board
CDR	Critical Design Review
CI	Configuration Item
CM	Configuration Management
CSES	Critical Software in Embedded System
ECN	Engineering Change Notice
FCA	Functional Configuration Audit
I&T	Integration and Test
PCA	Physical Configuration Audit
SCA	Software Change Authorization
SCM	Software Configuration Management
SCMP	Software Configuration Management Plan
SCR	Systems/Software Change Request
SQ&C	Software Quality and Control
SQA	Software Quality Assurance
SQAP	Software Quality Assurance Plan
SRR	System Requirements Review
SSR	Software Specifications Review

1.4 References. The standards listed here will be considered when applying this plan. The latest revisions apply:

[1] ANSI/IEEE Std 729-1983, IEEE Standard Glossary of Software Engineering Terminology.

[2] ANSI/IEEE Std 730-1984, IEEE Standard for Software Quality Assurance Plans.

[3] ANSI/IEEE Std 828-1983, IEEE Standard for Software Configuration Management Plans.

[4] ANSI/IEEE Std 829-1983, IEEE Standard for Software Test Documentation.

[5] Company Standard *Configuration Management Practices Manual*, Vol II.

[6] CSES Software Development Plan

Reference documents are available for use in the company library.

2. Management

2.1 Organization. The critical software for embedded systems program organization is designed to ensure clear lines of authority and to provide a framework within which administrative and technical control of software activities can be cost-effectively integrated into a quality product.

Primary responsibilities for various configuration management tasks are assigned as shown in Table 1. Within the CSES project organization, the program manager has total responsibility for the project. With this project, the program manager will have overall responsibility for configuration management of this project. The program manager serves as the project configuration control board (CCB) chairperson. The SCM project authority from the SCM organization cochairs the CCB. The SCM authority assists the program manager with planning and tailoring of the software configuration management plan (SCMP) and related CM procedures and is responsible for overseeing their implementation. The software configuration management authority reports functionally to the critical software for embedded systems program manager for the implementation of this plan. Administratively, the SCM authority reports to the SCM Department, which performs the necessary activities for the project.

Table 1
Responsibility Assignments

Responsibilities	Program Manager	Software Engineer	SCM Authority	SQA	Drafting
Configuration identification			Originate		
Approve/release tech documentation	Approve	Originate	Review	Review	
Change preparation		Originate			
Change control		Approve			
Change implementation		Approve	Review		Originate
Documentation maintenance		Approve			
Status accounting			Originate	Review	
Formal SCM audits		Approve	Originate	Review	
Baseline definition	Approve	Originate	Review	Review	Review

2.2 SCM Responsibilities. The software configuration management authority has the authority to require changes in practices and procedures that do not meet contract requirements. The general responsibilities of the software configuration management authority are outlined in Table 1. The software configuration management authority's functions include, but are not limited to the following tasks:

(1) Configuration control
(2) Status accounting
(3) Configuration identification
(4) Implementation and maintenance of the software configuration management plan
(5) Configuration control board cochairperson
(6) Establishment and maintenance of engineering baselines
(7) Cochairperson for formal audits
(8) Participation in reviews

2.2.1 Configuration Identification. Configuration identification is applied to all critical software for embedded software, both code and associated documentation. Associated documentation (that is, specifications, design documents, and program/procedure listings) along with the actual produced software makes up the configuration item. The software configuration management authority originates the identification scheme, with the approval of program management.

Configuration identification of computer programs and documentation during the development effort consists of established baselines and releases that are time-phased to the development schedules as described in the CSES software development plan.

2.2.1.1 Baselines. Baselines are established for the control of design, product, and engineering changes and are time-phased to the development effort. Baselines are established by the authority of the program manager. The software configuration management authority administers application of the baselines. Baselines defined for CSES include

(1) Functional baseline
(2) Allocated baseline
(3) Developmental baseline
(4) Product baseline

More details on baselines are presented in 2.4.2.

2.2.1.2 Releases. Throughout the development life cycle, at the discretion of the program manager, software manager, and SCM, baseline releases are performed. The releases fall into one of three categories

(1) Developer release (engineering release)
(2) Release to SCM (preliminary release)
(3) Final release (formal release to customer).

It is the responsibility of SCM to establish the release, version, and update number identifiers.

2.2.1.3 Documentation. All relevant specifications and documentation are given an identifier by SCM.

2.2.2 Configuration Control. All documentation and software entities are released to and maintained by software configuration management in a controlled library. SCM administers the change control process.

2.2.2.1 Systems/Software Change Request (SCR). The SCR is the mechanism by which change requests are presented to the CCB. This action allows a developer to check out software/documentation from SCM controlled libraries. The mechanism for requesting authorization is to present the SCR to the CCB and request approval for work to begin. The SCR form shown in Attachment A is used.

2.2.2.2 Software Change Authorization (SCA). The SCA is used to request SCM to place a new version of software/documentation into the controlled libraries. The approvals necessary are as follows: software manager, software quality assurance, and SCM. The SCA form shown in Attachment B is used.

2.2.3 Status Accounting. A software change authorization data base is used for generating reports that track changes to all of the controlled baselines. At project request, SCM generates reports that track the status of documentation and the software.

2.2.4 Audits. The SCM authority is responsible for cochairing, with the customer, all formal audits.

2.2.4.1 SQA Audits. It is the responsibility of SCM to assist SQA with their audit of the development effort. SCM maintains all documentation and software under strict controls to minimize the effort required by SQA to perform their function.

2.2.5 Configuration Control Board (CCB). The CSES project CCB is established by the program manager and SCM authority.

The program manager is the CCB chairperson and has the final responsibility for CCB actions relative to program SCM policies, plans, procedures, and interfaces. The software configuration management authority acts as cochair. In addition to the chairpersons and the CCB secretary, the CCB may include: development personnel; hardware representative; drafting representative; testing representative; customers; and always will include a representative from software quality assurance. CCB meetings are held on a regular basis determined by the CSES program manager, or when required at the call of the CCB chairperson. The system/software change request that is generated is reviewed by the CCB and one of the following actions taken: approved, disapproved, or tabled.

2.3 Interface Control. Interface control is handled in the same manner as other types of hardware, software, or documentation. Any differences between the SQAP and the SCMP must be resolved prior to the establishment of any baselines.

2.4 SCMP Implementation. The SCMP is implemented as soon as it is signed off by the CSES program manager but prior to holding any formal reviews with the customer. Any unresolved issues found once the SCMP is written must be resolved as soon as possible during the development period and prior to any baselines being established.

2.4.1 Configuration Control Board. The CCB is established at the time of SCMP approval but prior to the establishment of any baselines.

2.4.2 Configuration Baselines. Baselines are established by the following events:

2.4.2.1 Functional Baseline. The functional baselines are established by the acceptance, or customer approval of the CSES system/segment specification. Normally this occurs at the completion of the CSES system requirement review (SRR).

2.4.2.2 Allocated Baseline. The allocated baseline is established with the customer approval of the CSES software requirement specification. Normally this corresponds to the completion of the software specification review (SSR). The specification(s) and associated documentation define the allocated configuration identification.

2.4.2.3 Developmental Baseline. The developmental baseline is established by the approval of technical documentation that defines the top-level design and detailed design (including documentation of interfaces and data bases for the computer software). Normally, this corresponds to the time frame spanning the preliminary design review (PDR) and the critical design review (CDR).

2.4.2.4 Product Baseline. The product baseline is established upon customer approval of the product specification following completion of the last formal audit (FCA).

2.4.3 Schedules and Procedures for SCM Reviews and Audits. Reviews and audits are held as defined by CSES software development plan.

2.4.4 Configuration Management of Software Development Tools. The configurations of all support software used in development and test on the CSES project software is controlled in the same manner as the critical software. Nondeliverable support software baselines do not need customer approval.

2.5 Applicable Policies, Directives, and Procedures. The complete SCM policies, directives, and procedures that apply to this program are included as part of the procedures section of this document or are part of the referenced documents or one of the appendixes.

3. SCM Activities

3.1 Configuration Identification

3.1.1 Documentation. All supporting documentation generated for this project is identified by the use of the following convention: CSES, an abbreviation for the document nomenclature, a unique four digit number assigned by the CSES software configuration manager, and the product's version-revision-update number.
EXAMPLE: CSES-SDP-0024-1.2.1

Table 2
Baseline Objectives

Baseline	Purpose	Reviews & Audits
Functional	Functions established	SRR
Allocated	Requirement defined	SSR
Developmental	Top level design complete	PDR
Developmental	Detailed design complete	CDR
Product	Approval of product spec	FCA/PCA

Document Nomenclature	Mnemonic
Software Configuration Management Plan	SCMP
Software Detailed Design Document	SDD
Software Development Plan	SDP
Software Test Procedures	SPP
Software Product Specification	SPS
Software Quality Assurance Plan	SQAP
Software Requirements Specification	SRS
Software System Specification	SSS
Software Top-Level Design Document	STD
Software Test Plan	STP
Software Test Report	STR

3.1.2 Software Parts. The software configuration items, components, and units are identified by unique identification labels.

3.1.3 Configuration Identification of the Functional Baseline. The functional baseline is identified by the approval of the CSES system segment specification.

3.1.4 Configuration Identification of the Allocated Baseline. The allocated baseline is identified by the approval of the software requirement specification.

3.1.5 Configuration Identification of the Developmental Baselines. The developmental baselines are identified by the approved technical documentation that defines the top level design and detailed designs. The process by which the initial developmental baselines are established is shown in Attachment C, Create Initial Baseline.

3.1.6 Configuration Identification of the Product Baseline. The product baseline is identified by the approval of the CSES software product specification. This baseline specification is made up of the top level specification, detailed design specification, and the computer listings.

3.2 Configuration Control. Software configuration management and change control is applied to all documents and code, including CSES critical operational software and support software. Control is effected through the implementation of configuration identification, the CCB, change control, and status accounting functions.

3.2.1 Function of the Configuration Control Board. The configuration control board reviews proposed changes for assuring compliance with approved specifications and designs, and evaluates impacts on existing software. Each engineering change or problem report that is initiated against a formally identified configuration item is evaluated by the CCB to determine its necessity and impact. The CCB members electronically sign the document to indicate that they have reviewed the changes and provided their recommendations to the chairperson. The CCB approves, disapproves, or tables all changes. The mechanism for submitting changes to the software or documentation is the systems/software change request.

3.2.2 The System/Software Change Request. The SCR system is one of the major tools for identifying and coordinating changes to software and documentation. The SCR system is a minicomputer based tool used to track the status of a change from its proposal to its eventual disposition and assist in documenting important information about the change. The SCR form (Attachment A) contains a narrative description of the change or problem, information to identify the source of the report and some basic information to aid in evaluating the report. SCR is submitted only against baselined software or documentation. SCR may be submitted by anyone associated with the project effort or its products, but usually is submitted by a member of the software development team. SCM provides the single point for receiving and processing SCR. SCM, using the report writer feature of the SCR system, is capable of producing reports that provide change control tracking. A SCR is *closed* when

(1) Integration testing has shown that the changes have been correctly made
(2) No unexpected side-effects have resulted from making the change
(3) Documentation has been updated and reviewed

3.2.3 Software Change Authorization. The software change authorization form (Attachment B) is used to control changes to all documents and software under SCM control and for documents and software that have been released to SCM. The SCA is an on-line form that the software developers use to submit changes to software and documents to SCM for updating the master library. Approvals required for baselining or updating baselined software are as follows. The developer(s) first obtain the manager's signature, I&T signature, and an SCM signature. These approvals can either be written or added electronically. SCM signature testifies that the action has occurred. SQA signature signifies that they have verified that the change has been incorporated. SCM notifies the software developer through the electronic mail system that the change has occurred so the developer can delete extra copies of the changed parts. The SCA data base, along with the SCR data base, is used for status accounting needs.

The process by which changes are made is shown in Attachment D, change procedure.

3.2.4 Change Control Automated SCM Tools. The libraries of the CSES system are used to control all textual files containing the specifications, documentation, test plans and procedures, and source code. The support software (listed below) is also under configuration management by SCM. The library structure that is used is as follows:

(1) The CSES master library
(2) The program library
(3) The development library

3.2.4.1 For this mini-computer based development effort, the change control tools are as follows:

(1) *The Source Management System* The mechanism for creating and maintaining delta files (changes only) for the CSES master library. Only SCM has access to the CSES master libraries. The CSES master library data base is accessible by the SCM status accounting system.
(2) *The Package Management System* is used to automate the build process and is used to assist SCM with the generation of software.
(3) *SCM Get* is the function invoked by software developers to acquire software modules, or parts from the program libraries.
(4) *SCM Send* is the function invoked by software developers to impound a software module into the SCM program libraries. The use of this function implicitly and automatically generates an SCA.

3.3 Configuration Status Accounting. The status accounting system is capable of generating the following reports:

(1) *Report 1.* A list of all SCR with a status of *not closed* (that is, the same as *open*)
(2) *Report 2.* A cross-reference of SCA, engineering change notices (ECN), and drawings, per SCA
(3) *Report 3.* A monthly summary of the SCR and SCA data bases
(4) *Report 4.* A total of all SCR submitted per unit within a user-selected range of submittal dates
(5) *Report 5.* A list of all SCR which are *open*, *closed*, or *all* (selected by the user)
(6) *Report 6.* A summary of all SCR submitted by unit
(7) *Report 7.* A summary of the current approval status of all SCR with a status of *not closed*
(8) *Report 8.* A short summary of all SCR within a particular software component with a status of either open, closed, or all
(9) *Report 9.* A version description document
(10) *Report 10.* A report that gives the status of all documentation under SCM control
(11) *General Report.* Allows the user to define his/her own reports. The user must first specify which fields to include in the report.
(12) *On-Line Inquiry.* Allows the user to interactively view fields within the SCM data bases. The user specifies the fields that he/she wishes displayed and conditions for searching the data base

3.4 Audits and Reviews. The SCM authority co-chairs, with the customer, the formal CM audits: the functional configuration audit (FCA) and the physical configuration audit (PCA).

3.4.1 Functional Configuration Audit. The functional configuration audit is performed on the software configuration items when the acceptance tests have been completed. Both the functional baseline and the allocated baselines have previously been approved by the customer.

The audit is made on the formal test plans, descriptions, and procedures and compared against the official test data. The results are checked for completeness and accuracy. Deficiencies are documented and made a part of the FCA minutes.

Completion dates for all discrepancies are clearly established and documented. An audit of both draft and final test reports is performed to validate that the reports are accurate and completely describe the development tests.

Preliminary and critical design review minutes are examined to assure that all findings have been incorporated and completed.

3.4.2 Physical Configuration Audit. A physical examination is made of the CI to verify that the first article conforms *as-built* to its technical documentation. The SCM authority assembles and makes available to the PCA team at the time of the audit all data describing the item configuration. This includes a current set of listings and the final draft of the product baseline specifications. Customer acceptance or rejection of the CI and the CI product specification presented for the PCA is furnished to the project manager in writing by the responsible customer representative after completion of the PCA.

3.4.3 Reviews. The SCM authority participates in all formal reviews with the customer.

In addition, the SCM activity conducts two informal audits of the developing CI during the development cycle. The first informal audit is just prior to CDR. The second informal audit is performed at the discretion of the SCM authority midpoint between the CDR and final acceptance test.

4. Tools, Techniques, and Methodologies

4.1 Configuration Control Tools. An integrated set of SCM tools is used for configuration control and status accounting for this project. The particular tools are as follows:

(1) *Source Management System* (SMS). This tool is a file system for checking out vendor-supplied and internal software. A license agreement has been purchased from the vendor of this tool for use on this project.

(2) *Package Management System* (PMS). This tool is a vendor supplied data management tool used to automatically generate software. A license agreement has been secured from the vendor for use on this project.

(3) *Systems/Software Change Request Tool.* This is a proprietary piece of CSES software. This tool has two parts: the input form and its data base.

(4) *Software Change Authorization* (SCA) *Tool.* The SCA is a proprietary piece of CSES software. This tool has two parts: the input form and its data base.

(5) *Status Accounting Report Generator Tool.* This is a proprietary piece of CSES software. This is a report generation tool that gathers input from the following subsystems:

(a) Source management system

(b) Package management system

(c) System/software change request

(d) Software change authorization

5. Supplier Control

5.1 Vendor-Provided Software. Vendor-provided software that is to be used by this project must conform to *good business practice* SCM. The vendor provides to this project a copy of its SCM Plan for evaluation. This project must ensure that the vendor SCM system is adequate. If the vendor system is found to be inadequate, or if no vendor SCM Plan is available, then at the program manager's discretion, the vendor can be disqualified from providing software for this project.

5.2 Subcontracted Software. Any subcontractor wishing to do business with this project must provide a copy of its SCMP for evaluation by project SCM or agree to follow and abide by this SCMP. If the subcontractor SCMP is found inadequate, all other provisions of this SCMP apply. Any subcontractor not willing to abide by the above provision may be disqualified at the program manager's discretion.

5.3 Vendor and Subcontractor Software. All vendors and subcontractors are audited for compliance with *good business practice* SCM. The frequency and methods of audits are determined by the size, dollar value, and critical nature of the software.

6. Records Collection and Retention

All formal documentation produced for and by this project is retained and safeguarded for 20 years. A second copy of all software and documentation is stored in an off-site facility. This off-site facility is 21 mi from primary storage.

Attachment A
System/Software Change Request

SCR NUM.: ____________

1. Submitted by: ______________________________ DATE: ____/____/____

   Project Name: ______________________________

2. Software Program/Document Name: ______________________________

   Version/Revision ______________

3. SCR Type: (1-Development, 2-Problem, 3-Enhancement)

4. Short Task Description:

5. Detail Description:

6. Submitter's Priority [ ] 1=Critical 2=Very Important 3=Important 4=Inconvenient 5=Interesting

7. CCB Action: ______________ CCB Priority [ ]

8. Assigned to: ______________ Target Release Date ______________

9. Solution Comments:

10. Software Programs affected:

11. I&T Approval ______________________________ Date: ____/____/____

    SCM Approval ______________________________ Date: ____/____/____

12. Actual Release ______________________________ Date: ____/____/____

13. Closed by: ______________________________ Date: ____/____/____

    SCA Reference No: ______________

14. SQA Approval: ______________________________ Date: ____/____/____

Attachment B
Software Change Authorization

SCA Number: XXXXXX
Sheet Number: 1

Submitter: ______ System: ______ Date: ___/___/___ Time: ___/___/___ 00:00:00

Product Version ID: ______ Computer Name ______

Input Names	Release Names	Module Types	L N	A C	System/Software Change Request Numbers

Comments: ______

Approvals	I & T	SCM	SQA
Signature			
Date			

Attachment C

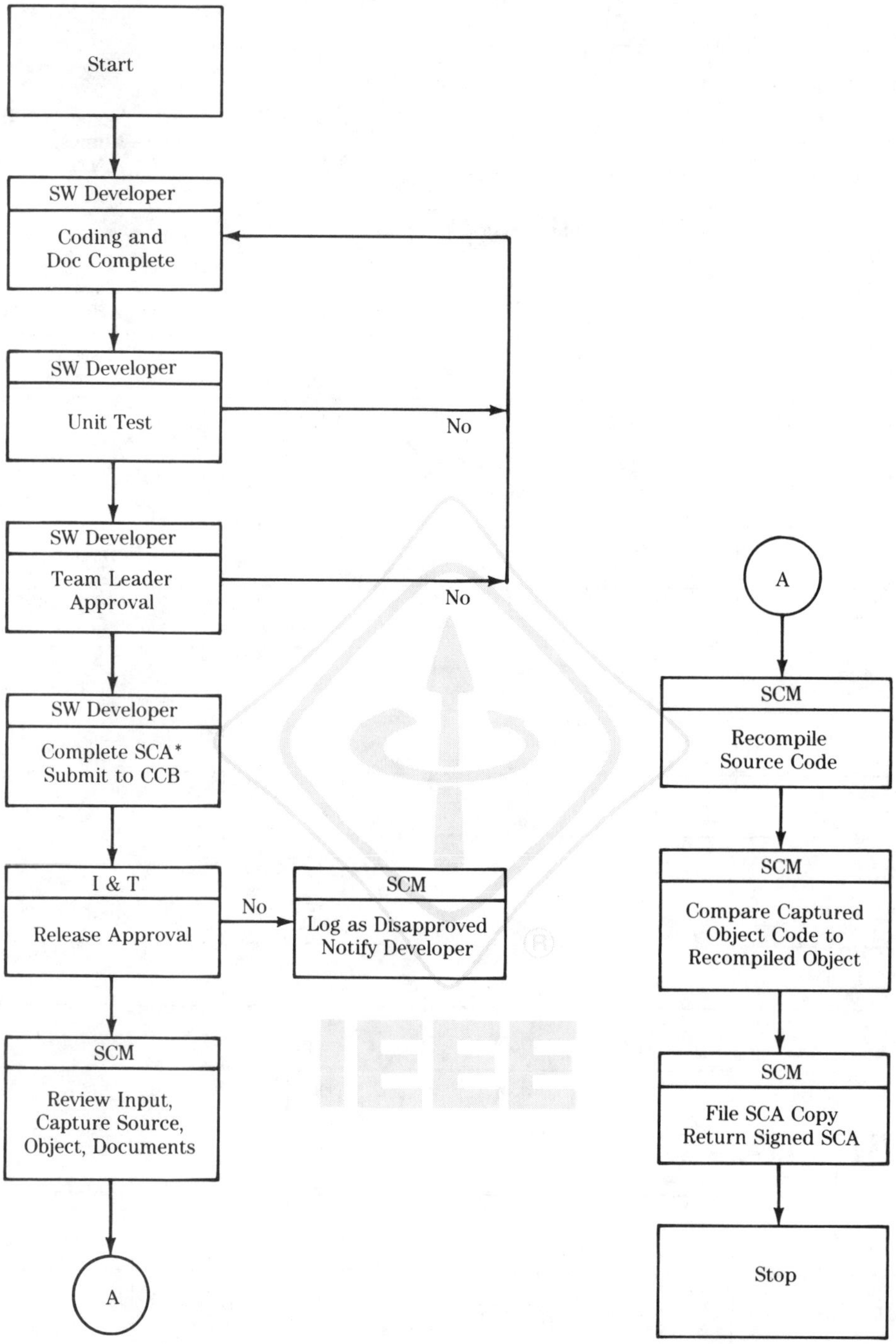

*NOTE: Developer's work files are retained until an approved SCA is received from SCM.

Fig 1
CSES Procedure for Creating Initial Baseline

Attachment D

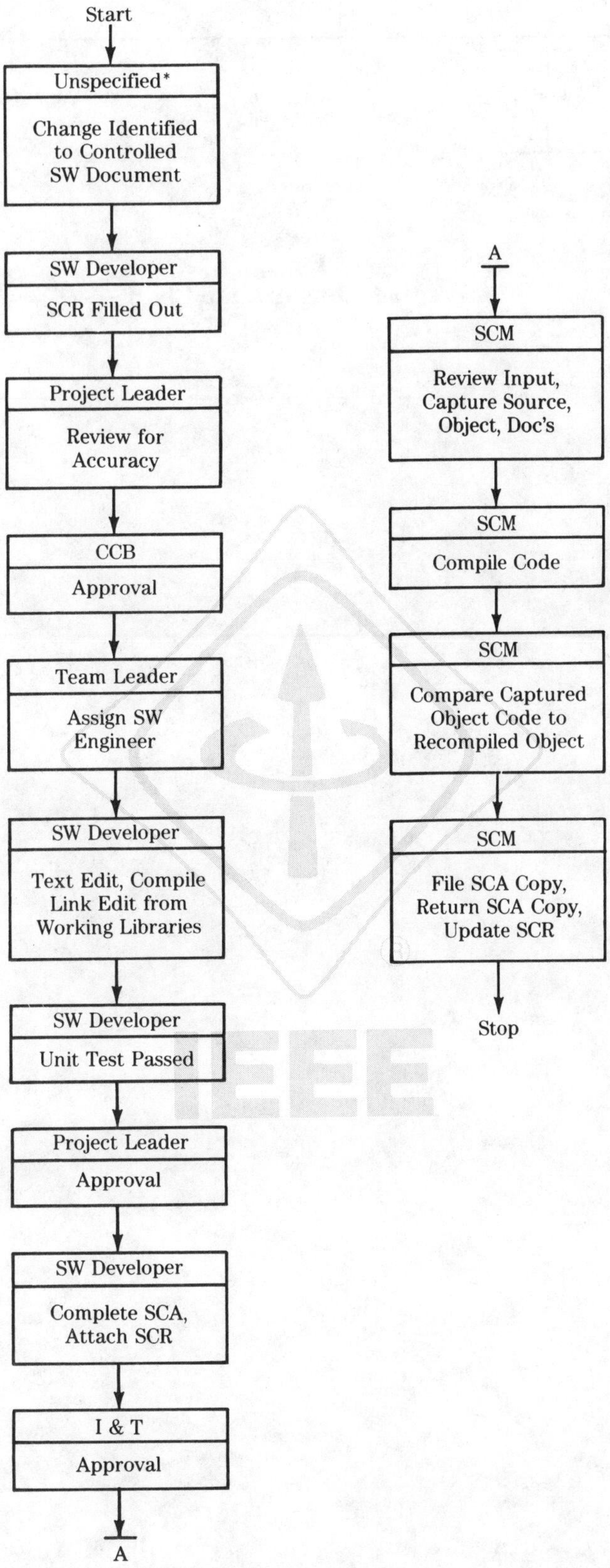

NOTE: If type of change is unspecified, submit SCR to SW Development.

Fig 1
CSES Procedures for Changes to Controlled Software/Documentation

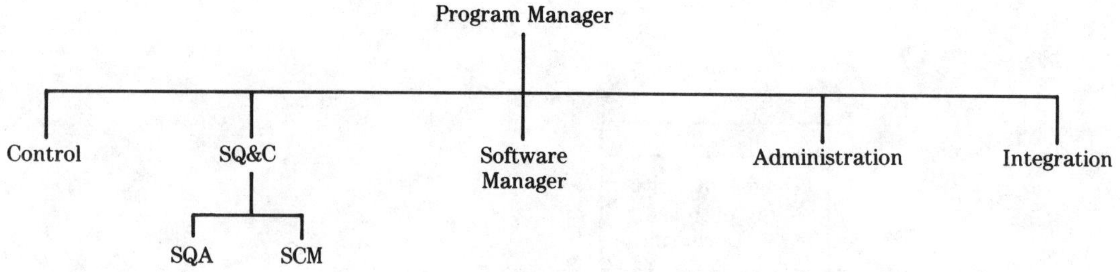

Fig 2
Program Organization Chart

Appendix B

Software Configuration Management Plan for Experimental Development Small System

Version 1.0

Approved

____
Project Manager

____
SCM Manager

____
Customer

Date: ___/___/___

Synopsis

This example contains a hypothetical contract to provide a prototype minicomputer-based system for a research-oriented customer. The system consists of three software programs, to be developed by a project team of twenty persons (of which ten are programmers) and is considered a prototype for installation in one field site. The software is written in COBOL. If the system is considered successful at that site, it will be expanded to an additional two sites for further evaluation. These sites may be supported by different hardware (for example, a transition may have to be made from hardware configuration A to hardware configuration B) or by different versions of the code (for example, one site may be a data input-processing installation and another a centralized data-gathering installation; each may use slightly different logic or data elements). The development time frame for the prototype system is two years. The expected life of the system is not known as the production system becomes part of a major procurement sometime in the future when the management of the first three sites agree on the requirements.

The contracting company and the customer are very end-user oriented, willing to sacrifice rigor in configuration management and specifications in the interest of speedy delivery of software to the sites and rapid response to changes. Because of this orientation, the configuration control board functions are administered by the project manager alone. All change requests are reviewed by the manager and an immediate ruling is made as to whether and when to implement them. The project manager meets with the customer technical representative regularly to review change requests that require consultation, making disposition of the requests quite rapid.

In this environment, the software configuration management (SCM) activity must be very supportive of the customer and manager or all SCM records will be lost. The SCM coordinator attends meetings between users and the project staff and prepares change requests on the spot. These are provided to the project manager and customer technical representative for resolution. The project emphasis is on intensive support to management in performing SCM—it is literally transparent to management since the SCM organization completes all of the required paperwork. The managers' and customers' responsibility is to review and authorize the resulting documentation.

Contents

Appendix B

Software Configuration Management Plan for Experimental Development Small System

1. Introduction

This document describes the software configuration management activities to be performed in support of the Experimental Development Small System (EDSS) Project. The EDSS project is charged with developing and demonstrating an advanced data processing concept, which, at a later date, may be converted to a fully functional system for processing special data. The project is considered to be a research/development program.

1.1 Purpose of the Plan. The software configuration management plan (SCMP) for the EDSS system describes how the software development activity supports EDSS management in the rapid iteration of software builds necessary for efficient development of the prototype demonstration software at site A. It also describes how this demonstration baseline is to be captured to provide for adaptation of the operational program to sites B and C and for subsequent up-grade of the software to full production quality for support of operational sites.

1.2 Scope. Three software configuration items (CI) are being developed as part of this contract:

(1) The Operational Program
(2) The Data Reduction Program
(3) The Test Generator Program

The development of these three CI is the responsibility of the contractor's software engineering organization. The internal build testing, the conduct of integration testing and demonstration of the prototype at site A is the responsibility of the contractor's test and control organization. The test and control organization is also responsible for demonstrations at sites B and C under this contract and possible subsequent upgrade testing of the software during later contracts.

The configuration of the operational program is managed at the unit level with all changes reviewed and approved as each unit comes under configuration management in the master library. The configuration of the data reduction program and test generator program is managed at the component level after being released for use with the operational program.

This SCMP specifically covers the configuration management support provided by the software configuration management department to the EDSS project office for

(1) The development of software used for different builds in test
(2) The prototype demonstration at site A
(3) The demonstrations at sites B and C.

1.3 Definitions and Mnemonics

1.3.1 Standard Definitions. Definitions used are found in ANSI/IEEE Std 729-1983, IEEE Standard Glossary of Software Engineering Terminology. Specifically, attention is called to definitions of

configuration item
configuration identification
configuration status accounting
master library
software library

1.3.2 Other Definitions

prototype system. The software developed for demonstrating the feasibility of the system concept.

1.3.3 Mnemonics. The following mnemonics are used within this document:

AXCESS	Vendor Software Company
CCB	Configuration Control Board
CI	Configuration Item
CM	Configuration Management
DRP	Data Reduction Program
EDSS	Experimental Development Software System
OP	Operational Program
SCA	Software Change Authorization
SCI	Software Configuration Item
SCM	Software Configuration Management
SCMP	Software Configuration Management Plan
SCR	System/Software Change Request
SDG	Software Development Group
SPR	Software Promotion Request
T & CG	Test and Control Group
TGP	Test Generation Program

1.4 References

[1] ANSI/IEEE Std 729-1983, IEEE Standard Glossary of Software Engineering Terminology.[13]

[2] ANSI/IEEE Std 828-1983, IEEE Standard for Software Configuration Management Plans.

[3] Contractor Software Engineering Organization Labeling Standards for EDSS System.

[4] Contractor Test and Control Malfunction Reports.[14]

[5] EDSS Software Development Plan

2. Management

2.1 Organizations. All authority for managing the EDSS system is vested in the EDSS project office. The software engineering organization and the test and control organization provide personnel on loan to the EDSS project office for the duration of the project. The configuration management department provides qualified personnel to the EDSS project office to perform the necessary SCM coordination. Figure 1 illustrates the major organizations.

The working organization is divided into two main groups

(1) EDSS software development group (SDG)

(2) EDSS test and control group (T & CG)

Both groups report to the EDSS project manager. The SCM coordinator is provided by the CM department to the EDSS project office to help support both the software development group and the test and control group.

The EDSS project office has full responsibility for program management functions, including configuration management, until the demonstrations at all three sites are concluded. The SDG has responsibility for preparing and maintaining requirements specifications, designing the software, and performing the unit testing needed for all builds. The T & CG is responsible for integration tests, field installations, and all demonstrations. The SCM coordinator is responsible for processing all changes affecting the documentation (including test data and test procedures) and programs after their release to the T & CG.

The EDSS project manager is responsible for approving/denying all changes to the program, whether originating from the T & CG or from the customer. The project manager functions as the configuration control board (CCB).

2.2 SCM Responsibilities. The general responsibilities of the SCM coordinator are to process the information needed to control changes in the prototype software as it develops and to capture the as-built documentation, test data and reports, and code that represent each successful site demonstration. The emphasis is placed on supporting the project change activities by independently handling all of the required paperwork —making the CM process transparent to management.

Specific organizational responsibilities of the SCM coordinator are as follows:

2.2.1 Identification. Naming conventions are established for

[13] IEEE publications are available in the company technical library.

[14] Organizational standards are available from the EDSS project office secretary.

Fig 1
Project Organization Chart

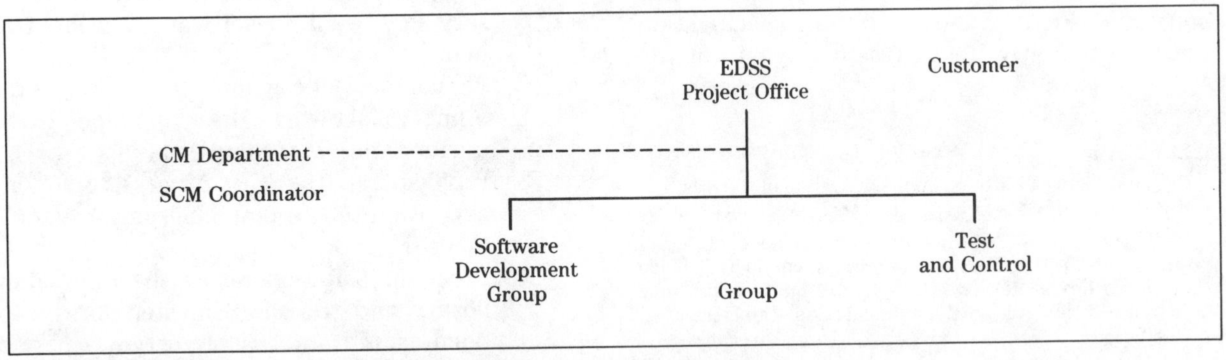

(1) *Unit Names.* These are designed so that unique identification of each item is possible. In addition, the unit naming conventions are structured so that it is possible to determine which SCI each unit belongs to by simply looking at the unit name.
(2) *File Names.* These are designed with the same mnemonic capability as the units.
(3) *Component Names.* These are given unique names so the source code can be matched to the supporting documentation.
(4) *Configuration Item Names.* These are defined in the same manner as in the contract statement of work.

2.2.2 Control. Control of all changes is maintained by

(1) Preparing and tracking approved system/software change requests (SCR), including all problem reports originatingfrom the customer, throughout implementation and testing
(2) Acting as software librarian, controlling the release of code to
    (a) The integration library for integration and testing by the T & CG at the contractor's development facility
    (b) The master library for installation and demonstrations at the site(s)

2.2.3 Status Accounting. The SCM coordinator provides the necessary status reports to the groups and project management. Typically, the reports cover

(1) SCR opened during period XXXX-XXXX[15]
(2) SCR closed for period XXXX
(3) Major SCR remaining open for three or more weeks
(4) SPR made during period XXXX
(5) SCR included in SPR, by date of promotion

2.2.4 Audits and Reviews. There is no pertinent information for this section.[16]

2.3 Interface Control. The EDSS system interfaces with the *AXCESS* software being developed by the *AXCESS Company.* The interface with this software is defined in an interface specification developed jointly by representatives from the software development activities of each company. The specification is approved by the responsible project managers of each company.

The EDSS interfaces with the hardware configurations found at customer sites are defined in a memorandum of agreement between the customer and EDSS project manager. Where agreement is not mutual, resolution is reached by contract negotiations. For changes to the EDSS system, the EDSS project manager initiates all change requests. For necessary changes to the *AXCESS* system, the *AXCESS* project manager initiates the change requests.

2.4 SCMP Implementation. The CM Department supports the EDSS project office with the services of a qualified SCM coordinator on the basis of 50% of one person's services per month.

One four-drawer file cabinet in the library is used for storage for the period of time specified in Section 6.

One workstation for execution of the data management system is used for the duration of the project.

Key events in the SCM planning phase are

(1) Establishing the integration library upon release of the first unit to T & CG for integration
(2) Establishing the EDSS master library upon release of the first software system configuration for demonstration at site A
(3) Impounding the master libraries from the three sites, along with the associated documentation and test data and reports, at the end of the final site demonstrations

2.5 Applicable Policies, Directives, and Procedures. The following standards and procedures apply for the duration of the contract:

(1) Labeling standards used for documentation, test data, and software media are in accordance with the standards in the software engineering organization's standards and procedures manual, modified as necessary in the EDSS software development plan.
(2) Version level designations are sequential numbers following a dash, appended to the documentation/media label.
(3) Problem report (SCR) processing is done according to the flow diagram in Attachment B.
(4) Procedures for operating the integration library and the EDSS master library are documented and distributed as a part of

[15]The period *XXXX* is left to the discretion of the program manager but is no less frequent than three-week intervals.

[16]No audits are performed as there is no contractual requirements. All reviews are informally conducted. Since there is no formal delivery, the software quality assurance activity is not involved in the configuration management of the software.

the EDSS software development plan prior to establishing the integration library

3. SCM Activities

3.1 Configuration Identification

3.1.1 EDSS Project Baselines. The requirements baseline (functional baseline) is established as the list of functional capabilities set forth in Addendum 2 of the statement of work in the contract.

The design baseline (allocated baseline) is established as the source code and associated design documentation, and all test procedures of the *as built* configuration items are successfully demonstrated to the customer at site A.

The prototype system baseline (product baseline) is established by the current design baseline of site A and versions of the configuration items for sites B and C at the end of the final demonstration.

Integration baselines are used to maintain successive builds during the development of the prototype demonstration at site A. A significant number of software builds at site A can be expected.

3.1.2 EDSS Project Labeling. The basis for labeling is by mnemonic labels assigned to each unit. In addition, each source unit shall have a prologue embedded in it. This prologue shall contain the following elements:

(1) Unit name
(2) Component name or identifier
(3) CI identifier
(4) Programmer name
(5) Brief description of the function of the module
(6) Change history
  (a) Date of each change
  (b) Reason for change (see SCR)
  (c) Change level (version being changed)

For example, the initial version of a unit is A-0, the second is A-1, etc. The change level is incremented each time the code is revised. The change level and the unit name are used to uniquely identify the version of the source code that incorporated a given problem correction, for example, ABC (3) for revision 3 of the unit ABC.

3.2 Configuration Control

3.2.1 Configuration Control Board. The EDSS project manager performs the functions of the change control board. The SCM coordinator supports the project manager by preparing SCR for the manager's review and processing the SCR subsequent to the manager's decision.

3.2.2 Processing SCR. The procedure for handling SCR is described in Attachment B.

3.2.3 CCB Interfaces. The EDSS project manager performs all of the coordination necessary with the customer in reviewing and in accepting, rejecting and negotiating changes. The manager also performs the liaison with the AXCESS vendor. Changes originating from the EDSS project are processed by the SCM coordinator. The two project managers provide coordination between projects and mutually resolve differences.

Changes to a system that result from these agreements are initiated by the responsible project manager.

3.3 Configuration Status Accounting.

Status accounting is accomplished by tracking the changes to units through the use of the SCR form. This manually generated form (reference Attachment C) is updated (upon release) with the version number of each release.

Status of each CI is reported periodically to the project manager or at the manager's request. The status of the revisions to the units and components is reported weekly to the managers of the SDG and T & CG. When a software system is released to a site, the release and version are recorded and the units contained in the system are listed, along with their current change level.

3.4 Audits and Reviews.

No audits are scheduled to be held for the EDSS system. Instead, the system is verified through the customer's functional testing. Parallel operation using the site's previous manual system and the new system is maintained until the users are confident that the system is producing accurate reports and displays. The SCM coordinator attends performance/functional reviews to record action items and change status.

Functional reviews are held periodically during the software development cycle. The principle document used is the *User Interface Guide*. This document contains the layouts of each of the displays and reports the users have available from the system. Each data element in each display or report is defined there, along with the method by which the element is derived (if any).

4. Tools, Techniques, and Methodologies

The primary technique for SCM is the manual processing of SCR, SCA, and SPR. The SCR form (see Attachment C) is used to record all customer requests for changes, their disposition, and eventual implementation. The same form is used to record enhancements or changes requested by the SDG. These forms later become the basis for updating the requirements specifications and for resolving questions concerning the origin of a change or the status of a requirement that arise during implementation, during integration, installation and checkout at site(s) and during the demonstrations.

A set of basic SCM tools is available for use. A data management system is used for recording and reporting status of the units, components, and CI.

The integration library uses a file system to check in and check out units for revision and test. The project master library uses the same system to impound master copies of the units and components.

Release of code to the integration library is made through software promotion requests (SPR) shown in Attachment A. The software is compiled and built into a protected integration package owned by the T & CG. Software successfully demonstrated at the sites is placed in the EDSS master library for future demonstrations and upgrades.

5. Supplier Control

There is no pertinent information for this section.

6. Records Collection and Retention

Copies of each status report are maintained as a historical record for the EDSS project until the project is terminated or the prototype demonstration system is replaced by the production system. These records are transferred to microfiche as they age over six months.

The prototype system baseline code, test data and reports, and documentation shall be maintained at the termination of the project for a period of two years or until replaced by a production system. The software media for retention of this baseline code is magnetic tape. The documentation for this is retained on microfiche.

Test procedures and test data resulting from the successful demonstrations shall be retained as a part of the data for use in defining the production system.

Attachment A

Software Promotion Requests

Table 1 defines the list of data elements included in the Transaction file for release of each unit.

Table 1
Data for Software Release

Element Name	Definition
CI number	Number assigned for CI identification
Sub-application	The name or number assigned to the unit or portion of the CI being released
Release request	Data release was requested
Action requested	The control action requested by the development activity (builds, move to test library)
Members	Names of modules, units to be included in the release
Change level	The change level or version number of the units being released
Justification	The number or the statement of justification concerning the reason for release
From library	The library location of the units before the release
Member type	The type of the unit being released (procedures, macros, test drivers)
Load module	The load module with which the units are linked
Time tag	The time tag for the version of the unit being promoted

Attachment B

IEEE Guide for Processing System Software Change Requests

System/Software Change Request (SCR) forms are used to document three types of situations:

(1) Requests for changes to the software by the customer (whether these requests result from tests, demonstrations, or from experience at the sites).

(2) Requests for changes by the designers or coders (generated within the company) that affect code already in use at the sites.

(3) Problems or errors in the code in test or at the sites that were clearly not requests for new or different functions—documented *bugs* in the released code

1.1 Processing steps are

(1) All SCR are logged in by the SCM coordinator and assigned a number on receipt. After logging, the SCR is forwarded to appropriate manager for action or resolution.

(2) When an SCR results in a software change (whether a correction or a new function), the software manager annotates the SCR form at the time of release of the new software to the sites and forwards the SCR to the SCM coordinator who then updates the master file.

1.2 SCM Coordinator. The SCM coordinator attends all customer/designer meetings and acts as the recorder of change requests. Signature approvals are obtained at that time.

When a release of software to sites is being prepared, the SCM coordinator meets with the project manager and review all outstanding SCR against the released software.

The SCR closed at that time are documented by the SCM coordinator.

Attachment C

System/Software Change Request Form

The following data elements are included on the SCR form.

Table 1
SCR Data Elements

Element	Values
CI	The name of the configuration item involved
Environment	The hardware site involved (may be more than one as project uses three different types of minicomputers)
Change type	Legal values: new function, error correction, design change
Date requested	DD/MM/YR
Narrative description	Description of the change desired in language as explicit as possible; description of the problem in the case of error reports
Disposition	Final disposition: fixed, accepted but delayed, rejected.
	If fixed, description of changes made are included here
Requester	Person making the request for the change
Requester site	Location of the person making the request
Release and version	The release and version number in which the problem existed
Implementation data	List of modules involved in the change on system/software change request form
Implementation release and version	Release and version number in which change appears
Implementation ship date	Date on which the change is shipped to the sites
Responsible manager signature	
Customer approval signature	(Used only for changes to software already released for field use)

Appendix C

Software Configuration Management Plan for a Software Maintenance Organization

Version 1.0

Approved

____
Mgr SPLIT Facility

____
Mgr SCM Dept

Date: ___/___/___

Synopsis

This example contains a discussion of a hypothetical programming facility that manages the support software systems used in the design, development, test and maintenance of the software systems for a large software engineering company. The company has approximately twenty-seven hundred employees of whom nine hundred are professional software engineers with degrees in computer science, computer systems or electrical engineering. The average experience of the professional engineers is five and one-half years. The software products they build and maintain are primarily real-time systems for many applications, some critical and some not. The company has an extensive investment in software engineering facilities. There are software engineering work stations for a third of the professional programming staff and terminals available for the support staff. The work stations are attached to a local area network that is integrated with a large number of mini-computers and two mainframes.

The programming facility, SPLIT, is staffed with one hundred and thirty-five people. Fifty are systems and maintenance programmers. There is a software configuration management department within the company that performs all of the configuration management activities for the facility and the software engineering groups. Special emphasis is placed on the management of the products in the SPLIT facility since the productivity and reputation of the company directly depends on the efficiency and reliability of the support software used by the engineering groups. A special software configuration management group is permanently assigned to the SPLIT facility with the responsibility for controlling the company's support software. The company management supports this focus — as long as the software engineering activities do not complain too loudly about the service they receive.

In this environment, the software configuration management group in the facility has a direct role in the control of the support software. This group processes all changes made to the support software by the system programmers, builds the run-time systems and performs all the other normal configuration management activities. The role of configuration management in maintenance makes this group a major part of the facility's management team.

Since the company has a considerable investment in the support software and data records, the disaster control practice requires that the support software in the production library have copies in the software archival repository. The company maintains the software repository in a protected shelter thirty-five miles from the main facility.

Contents

Appendix C

Software Configuration Management Plan for a Software Maintenance Organization

1. Introduction

This plan describes the standard operating procedures for managing the configuration of all the support software available to the users of the SPLIT facility. The SPLIT facility provides the supporting software used in the design, development and maintenance of software products produced by the company. All of the support software products available to the users of the SPLIT facility are maintained under configuration management to ensure that users have continual and reliable service from the software products in the run-time environment, and that errors in the support software and requests for enhancements are handled accurately, completely, and in a timely manner.

1.1 Purpose of the Plan. This operating plan specifies procedures whereby software configuration management supports the entire software change/enhancement process.

1.2 Scope. This plan defines the SCM activities necessary for maintaining all support software items being procured, tested, sustained and kept in the production environment in the facility. The list of the software configuration items will vary over time. The consolidated list of configuration items and their status is maintained by the SCM group within the SPLIT facility and published monthly in the SPLIT configuration summary.

1.3 Definitions and Mnemonics

1.3.1 Definitions. The terms used in this plan conform to the definitions found in ANSI/IEEE Std 729-1983, IEEE Standard Glossary of Software Engineering Terminology.

1.3.2 Mnemonics. The following mnemonics are used within this document:

CCB	Configuration Control Board
CCM	Configuration Change Management [system]
CI	Configuration Item
CM	Configuration Management
COMM	Communications Software
EWS	Engineering Work Stations
HW	Hardware
LAN	Local Area Network
SCA	Software Change Authorization
SCM	Software Configuration Management
SCMG	Software Configuration Management Group
SCMP	Software Configuration Management Plan
SSQAG	SPLIT Software Quality Assurance Group
SCR	System/Software Change Request
SQA	Software Quality Assurance
SQAG	Software Quality Assurance Group
STEG	SPLIT Test and Evaluation Group
SDT	Software Development Tools
TFR	Transfer File Request

1.4 References[17]

[1] ANSI/IEEE Std 729-1983, IEEE Standard Glossary of Software Engineering Terminology.

[2] ANSI/IEEE Std 828-1983, IEEE Standard for Software Configuration Management Plans.

[3] GP:25, Software Configuration Management.

[4] GP:26, Software Change Request Processing.

[5] SF:39, Vendor License Identification and Accountability.

[6] SF:27, Inspection and Test of Support Software Products.

[7] SF:15, Test and Evaluation Group Activities.

[8] CMP:13, Identification and Labeling of Software.

[9] CMP:25.3, Unit Naming Conventions.

[10] CMP:25.4, Version Level Designation.

[11] CMP:37, Computer Program Media Identification and Marking.

[12] CMP:12, Software Auditing.

[13] SP:17, Support Software Status Reporting.

[17] Referenced documents are available for use in the SPLIT software reference library.

[14] SP:12, Operation of SPLIT Configuration Control Board.

[15] SP:5, User Documentation Maintenance.

[16] SP:7, SPLIT Production Library Maintenance.

[17] SP:95, Work Station Request and Allocation.

[18] SCMG-WP:19, Data Retention—SCR/SCA.

[19] SCMG-WP:1, Software Release Procedures.

2. Management

2.1 Organization. The vice-president managing the SPLIT facility reports to the company president along with the vice-president in charge of the product effectiveness group and the vice-president in charge of the operations division (engineering). The configuration management (CM) department is part of the product effectiveness group. The software configuration management group (SCMG) is administratively a part of the CM department and their activities are responsive to the policies set by the CM department; but, functionally, they report to the manager of the SPLIT facility.

The organizational structure of the SPLIT facility is shown in Fig 1.

2.1.1 Operations Group. The operations group maintains the processing and communications systems, installs and reconfigures hardware installations, and performs the day-to-day operations of the processing environments.

2.1.2 Systems Software Programmers. The systems software programmers perform the maintenance on the support software developed in-house (generally by the engineering division) and subcontracted software acquired by the facility. Third party software acquired from vendors is not maintained by the SPLIT facility.

2.1.3 Test and Evaluation Group. The test and evaluation group performs the acceptance tests for vendor and subcontracted software and also all new releases for in-house support software maintained by the systems software programmers.

2.1.4 User Consultants. The user consultants provide training to that portion of the company that does not include Section 2.1.3 in the use of the support software systems, and consulting services to the software engineers as needed. They are the primary source of change requests for support software.

2.1.5 SPLIT Software Quality Assurance Group. The SSQAG is functionally a part of the product effectiveness group. They perform evaluations of new software as an incoming QA function, and periodic audits of the operations of the facility.

2.1.6 Multiple Configuration Control Boards. There are multiple configuration control boards (CCB) within the facility. The senior CCB, called the SPLIT CCB, has overall responsibility for managing the hardware and software configurations in the facility. This responsibility includes

(1) Allocating SPLIT resources for use on company projects
(2) Setting overall schedules for support software updates and new version releases
(3) Allocating resources to update configurations of mainframe processors, the minicomputer nodes, and the LAN/Hi-Speed data bus configurations.

Fig 1
SPLIT Facility Organization

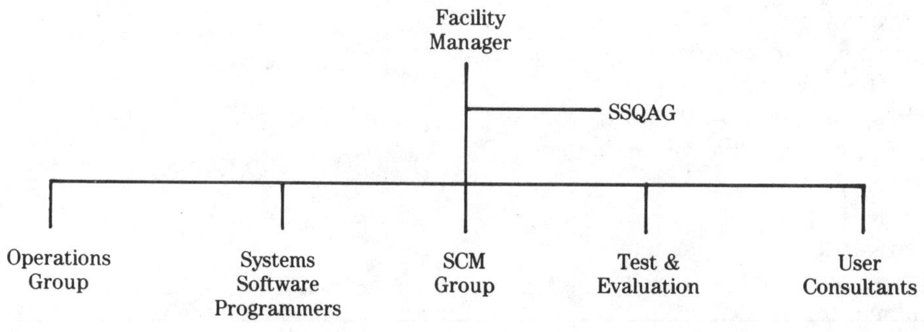

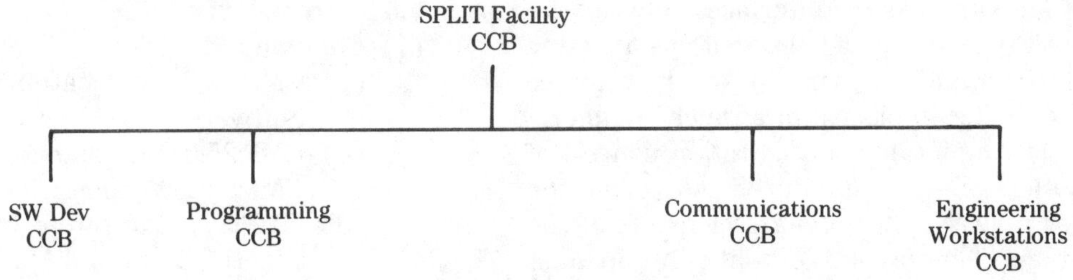

Fig 2
Structure of CCB

(4) Providing resources to subordinate CCB that manage software product lines

The manager of the SPLIT facility chairs the SPLIT CCB. The head of the SCMG is the alternate chairman and attends all meetings of the SPLIT CCB.

The in-house software is grouped by function into three separate CCB

(a) Software development (SWDEV) tools
(b) Programming environments (PROG)
(c) Communications (COMM) software

These subordinate CCB have configuration management responsibility for support software developed in-house, and managing the changes approved for software acquired from outside sources. Individual product line CCB are assigned to software products developed by the company, but their operation is independent of the SPLIT facility CCB. When these company software products are used in the SPLIT facility, they are controlled in the same way any product purchased from an outside vendor is controlled. The software used in the engineering work stations has a separate work station CCB for tracking the volatile hardware and software configuration.

Each SPLIT facility CCB is responsible for allocating resources needed for maintaining their assigned software products. Where changes affect interfaces with other hardware or software within the facility, or both, the issue must be brought before the SPLIT facility CCB. The head of the SCMG cochairs the SPLIT facility CCB and work station CCB with their respective managers.

Each project making use of a software product has representation on the CCB controlling that product.

2.2 SCM Responsibilities. The primary SCMG responsibilities involve supporting the change process as it affects existing software product baselines; maintaining an accounting of the status of *all* the software configuration items in the facility; and auditing physical configurations (CI) received from subcontractors, vendors of commercial software used in the facility, and support software from the company engineering division.

2.2.1 Identification. The SCMG is responsible for maintaining the identification (numbering, labeling, and integrity of documentation) for all the support software in the facility. Responsibility also extends to identifying the configuration items that are acquired from commercial vendors.

2.2.2 Configuration Control. The SCMG is responsible for supporting the change process for all of the support software used in the SPLIT facility.

2.2.3 Configuration Status Accounting. The SCMG maintains the data base used to prepare reports on the status of all support software products and hardware configurations used in the facility.

2.2.4 Audits and Reviews. Audits are performed by two groups

(1) The SCMG performs physical configuration audits of all support software acquired by the facility. Periodic inventory audits of the support software are also performed as directed by the SPLIT facility manager
(2) The SCMG supports SSQAG in performing functional configuration audits of incoming subcontracted and vendor-provided support software. The SCMG also provides SSQAG with summary data on probable causes of failure

The SCMG works directly with the STEG in evaluating software changes being released to the production library.

2.3 Interface Control. One of the most critical activities is controlling the interfaces between the different software systems in the facility and between the software and changing hardware configurations.

The SCMG supports the interfaces between the multiple CCB by recording action items affecting each interface and following up on them to see that they are accomplished in a timely manner.

The SCMG maintains configuration control of the specifications and standards controlling the interfaces between the software elements of the workstations. The workstation configuration must include both hardware and support software for each installation. This includes accounting for leased and licensed software used on personal computers and in workstations.

The SCMG maintains the operating system configuration used in the SPLIT facility as a means for enforcing control of the interfaces with the applications programs.

2.4 SCMP Implementation. The staff of the SCMG is composed of one group head, who acts as coordinator, and one qualified SCM administrator for each separate SPLIT facility CCB (one per CCB). One additional person has the function of tracking the EWS configuration(s).

Computer resources and work space are provided by the SPLIT facility manager for the SCMG.

Milestones for SCMG activity are set by the manager of the SPLIT facility and reflect the ongoing continuous support activities required for managing the various support software configurations.

2.5 Applicable Policies, Directives, and Procedures

2.5.1 Policies

(1) Company Policy
  (a) GP:25, Software Configuration Management
  (b) GP:26, Software Change Request Processing
(2) SPLIT Policies
  (a) SF:39, Vendor License Identification and Accountability
  (b) SF:27, Inspection and Test of Support Software Products
  (c) SF:15, Test and Evaluation Group Operations

2.5.2 Directives

(1) Company Bulletin, GB:87, *Use of Licensed Software*
(2) Company Directive, CD:34, *Copyright Protection*
(3) Company Bulletin(s), GB:(various), *CCB Membership*

2.5.3 Procedures

(1) Company Procedures
  (a) CMP:13, Identification and Labeling of Software
  (b) CMP:25.3, Unit Naming Conventions
  (c) CMP:25.4, Version Level Designations
  (d) CMP:37, Computer Program Media Identification and Marking
  (e) CMP:12, Software Auditing
(2) SPLIT Procedures
  (a) SP:17, Support Software Status Reporting
  (b) SP:12, Operation of SPLIT Configuration Control Board
  (c) SP:5, User Documentation Maintenance
  (d) SP:7, SPLIT Production Library Maintenance
  (e) SP:95, Work Station Request and Allocation
(3) SCMG Procedures
  (a) SCMG-WP:19, Data Retention — SCR/SCA
  (b) SCMG-WP:1, Software Release Procedure

3. SCM Activities

3.1 Configuration Identification. Each support software product in the facility is identified by configuration item title, specifications, user documentation, and media labels in accordance with established company procedures.

Since the software being managed has already had a product baseline established, the identification schema is already set. The SCMG uses the identification and labeling standards in the product baseline. In-house software identification follows company procedures CMP-13; 25.3; 25.4; and 37. Third-party software is labeled with company-defined labels for record-keeping purposes.

The elements of software (programs, documentation, test data, etc) in the production library (the library of software released for running on hardware in the facility) is organized as in Table 1.

Table 1
Hierarchy of Elements

Generic Term	Alternate Terms
Configuration item	Package, product
Component	Segment, program
Unit	Module, routine

The level of control applied by the SCMG will generally be to the component level. Components are considered to be the *controlled item* in managing the operation of the SPLIT facility. A given programming library used by systems programmers may have a system for managing configurations of software units previously used in the development and maintenance of other programs. Sometimes the units in these libraries are referred to as packages, following the concepts of *reusable software* being advocated.

3.1.1 Baseline Identification. Support software product baselines are established during incoming inspections of the product at the facility. New releases to a product baseline are labeled in accordance with 2.5.3(1)(c). New releases include changes or updates as necessary to the product package — specifications, user documentation, design documentation (listings), test procedures, and associated test and inspection reports. The procedure 2.5.3(1)(a) is followed for each new release of a support software product.

A new release of a support software product is made in accordance with 2.5.3(3)(b).

The scheduling of a new release is determined by the SPLIT CCB.

3.1.2 Product Baseline Cataloging. Labeling of product CI is in accordance with 2.5.3(1)(a). The SCMG reviews each request to be released for conformance to company procedures. The SCMG then checks the release package against the transfer file and the CCB authorization for completeness and STEG/SSQAG approvals.

3.2 Inspection and Receiving. New products entering into the facility for use are inspected for conformance to 2.5.3(1)(a) by the SCMG. Vendor software parts (configuration items) are given company CI part numbers in the 7000 series for maintaining separate accountability within the status accounting system.

3.3 Configuration Control

3.3.1 Levels of Authority for Approvals. All software is tested by the STEG prior to its promotion into the integration library or the production library. Both STEG approval and SCMG approval is required before the software is promoted to the integration library or production library.

The promotion of changes into the integration library is authorized by the SPLIT facility and work station CCB and approved by the SCMG after design checks by the STEG.

The release of changes to the production library is authorized by the SPLIT CCB. Prior to entering changes into the production library, each change is tested and verified as correct by the STEG, checked for conformance to packaging standards by SSQAG, and administratively approved by the head of the SCMG before being placed into the library.

3.3.2 Change Proposal Processing

3.3.2.1 SCR Processing. Software change requests are prepared using the form C-1049, software/system change request, or use of the SCR ENT command in the interactive configuration change management (CCM) system. Manually prepared forms (C-1049) are entered into the CCM system by the SCMG librarian. The same form used to initiate a problem report is used for requesting an enhancement to the system. All changes are concurrently routed to the SCMG files in the CCM system for administrative checks and to the appropriate product line manager for verification. Each SCR is reviewed by technical personnel and their evaluation is forwarded to the appropriate SPLIT CCB for action.

The SPLIT CCB can approve, reject, or table (with an action date) a request pending further information.

Action in response to a SCR is scheduled by the CCB in response to the severity of the problem reported or the need for enhancement. Problem reports are given priority over change requests not associated with an operating problem. Problem reports (as indicated on the SCR form) are processed on an expedited basis.

Problem reports that are determined to be valid errors in the performance of the system and given priority for solution with temporary fixes are incorporated into the subject system — along with publication of a bulletin notifying all users of the

Table 2
Problem Criteria

Category	Symptom
"C"	A software item cannot be executed by a user
"M"	Users have problems with a program but can work around with temporary fix
"S"	Minor irritation but users can still accomplish work

change in the system. Permanent modifications to correct the error are incorporated with the next upgrade released to all users.

Requests for system enhancements that are valid and within the scope and resources allocated to the software product are scheduled for incorporation in the next scheduled upgrade to that product.

Approvals are incorporated in the maintenance schedule and a release date tentatively identified for a scheduled upgrade or correction to the affected support software product(s). Status of these SCR is indicated as *approved*.

The SCR may be returned to the user when additional clarification is needed or when the results of the design review may necessitate additional design analysis or even modification to the change request. The SCR is held with the status *pending* until a course of action has been determined.

Testing for promotion to the integration library or release to the production library may result in additional design changes or recoding. In that event, the status of the SCR reflects *approved* and the status of the SCA reflects *in-work*. The status of the SCR/SCA action is changed to *implemented* only if the change has been completed, verified, and released into the production library.

3.3.2.2 SCA Processing. Approved SCR are forwarded by the CCM system to the appropriate programming activity for implementation. Similar changes that are grouped together for an upgrade are worked on at the same time. Emergency changes (needed to keep the system in operation) are expedited through the system. The programming activity extracts necessary files for work from the production library and makes the changes. When the supervisor is ready to integrate the file, the SCA and the code are completed and passed to the CCM_HLD/INT area for administrative checks by SCMG before being released to the integration library for integration and test.

STEG performs the integration and testing, requesting modifications from the programming activity as appropriate. When it has been demonstrated that the change package is correct and introduces no additional errors into the system, the SPLIT CCB is informed of the pending update whereby STEG initiates a transaction file request (TFR). Upon approval by the SPLIT CCB, the SCMG enters the change into the production library. The status of the SCR/SCA is then changed to *closed*.

The SCMG performs the systems generation of the run-time programs used in the facility, and loads, after verification by the STEG, into the necessary hardware configurations.

Failure of the users to accept the changes in the support software system may result in it being returned to a previous step or cancellation of the task.

3.3.2.3 Changes to EWS. The processing of changes to work station support software is the same as the above procedure except that the run-time software generation and allocation to HW configuration is controlled by the EWS CCB network manager.

3.3.2.4 Changes to Supplier Software. Change processing for subcontracted software is performed in the same manner described above when the source code is in-house and maintenance is being performed by the SPLIT systems software programmers. When the software product is under subcontractor warranty, the SCR is passed to the subcontractor and the new version is accepted into the production library in the usual manner. In the event where the subcontractor has a maintenance contract for the product, the SCR is passed on to them for processing.

3.3.2.5 Licensed Software. Licensed software is given a company label with a unique identifier to indicate limited use. Periodic audits are conducted by the SCMG to determine adherence to the license limitations by users.

3.3.2.6 Purchased Commercial Software. Purchased commercial software is relabeled with company identifying numbers and released for use and configuration management in the same manner as in-house developed software.

3.3.3 CCB Roles. The CCB evaluation takes into consideration, among other things, the staff resources available versus the estimated workload of the request; the estimated additional computing resources that are required for the design, test, debug, and operation of the modified system, and the time and cost of updating the documentation.

An essential function of each CCB is to coordinate the flow of information between the users of the software product and the maintenance organization supporting the product. This function is executed when the CCB representatives of the project use the products and monitor the evaluation of the significance of problem reports and requests for enhancements. The result of the CCB review is the assignment of a priority to each request.

3.3.4 Control of Interfaces. There is no pertinent information for this subsection.

3.4 Configuration Status Accounting. The SCMG supports the following reports:

(1) *SPLIT Software Configuration Report.* An accounting of the software and hardware configurations of all the systems within the SPLIT facility. This report is kept current at all times. Weekly reports are made to the SPLIT facility manager, including changes just completed and changes scheduled for the next week.

(2) *SPLIT Performance Summary.* A monthly summary of the up-time of all systems and an analysis of all problems causing unscheduled down-time.

(3) *SCR/SCA Summary.* For each configuration item, a summary of the current status of SCR/SCA activity is given on a weekly basis to the SPLIT facility manager. The SCR summary includes problem type and severity, priority given by the CCB, activity or programmer assigned, and target release date for either the fix or new release.

(4) *EWS Configuration Status.* This configuration status is maintained in a data base for general access. Status and configuration summaries are presented to the SPLIT facility manager on a weekly basis.

3.5 Audits and Reviews. The SCMG performs a physical configuration audit on all incoming third-party software.

The SCMG performs functional and physical configuration audits on each new release of software in the system.

The SCMG performs periodic audits of the software and hardware configurations in the facility to ascertain that no unauthorized changes have been made. Particular attention is paid to licensed software.

4. Tools, Techniques, and Methodologies

4.1 Use of the CCM System. The CCM system is used to manage and track all changes to the software in the SPLIT facility. The system provides for initiating changes, review and approval by management, assigning and monitoring work status, and the testing and releasing of all changes. Status reporting is provided as an output from the CCM data base. This configuration management tool is one of the set of software tools used in the SPLIT facility by all of the operating activities.

4.2 Inspections. Releases to the production library are inspected to confirm inclusion of scheduled SCR/SCA.

4.3 Library Management. The SCMG makes disciplined use of programming libraries to manage the changes to support software configuration items. The SCMG and the STEG cooperate in promoting software modifications from the development library into the integration library and from there releasing them to the production library.

4.3.1 Development Library. The development library is used by the systems software programmers as they develop their code. The units and components are controlled by the individual programmers. Criteria for allowing promotions into the integration library includes the successful completion of unit testing and approval by the group's supervisor.

4.3.2 Integration Library. The integration library is used by the SCMG to capture and build the code that is designated for promotion to the STEG for integration and test. This library contains the source code and executable load modules created as a result of a system build. The source code is placed in a special controlled library in preparation for a build. Then the code is recompiled and link edited before it is placed in the integration library. Criteria for releasing to the production library includes

(1) Submission of a software release request by the SPLIT CCB

(2) Completion of status accounting audits and resolution of issues by SCMG

(3) Acknowledgment of regression and integration test completion by the STEG and SQA

All test data and routines used to verify software released for use are also maintained under configuration control in the integration library.

4.3.3 Production Library. The production library contains the master copies of all the support software configuration items used in the SPLIT facility. Copies are made from the masters by the SCMG for use on other systems. The production library acts as backup for the run-time configurations used on the systems. Only current master copies of support software configuration items are maintained in the production library.

4.3.4 Software Repository. Current copies of all support software configuration items from the production library are maintained in the software repository. Historical copies of support software released for use outside the facility are maintained in the repository for a period of ten years after release.

5. Supplier Control

Since the SCMG does not have responsibility for supporting the development of subcontracted software, the SCMG has no interface with the support software developed in this way.

The SCMG does participate with the STEG in the receiving inspection of commercial software and subcontracted software to ascertain that

(1) All physical items are available as required by contract

(2) The proper labels are on the media to be placed in the integration library, and subsequently, in the production library

The SCMG is responsible for the physical configuration audit of subcontracted and vendor-supplied software. The SQA activity performs the functional configuration audit.

6. Records Collection and Retention

Records of SCR/SCA processing are retained for a period of five years to support fiscal standards of records. Status reports of the SPLIT facility configurations are also maintained for a period of five years.

Records defining the product baselines of all support software products released for use outside the facility (in conjunction with engineering division sales) are maintained for a period of twenty years to protect product warranties. The product baselines of all other support software products developed in-house but not released for use outside the facility are maintained for a period of ten years.

Records of licensed vendor software integrated, or otherwise used, with internal configurations are maintained for a period of five years after their removal from the system.

Biweekly backups of the systems are archived for a period of six months to protect the data files of the ongoing engineering division development activities. Backups of the systems processing company financial records are archived for a period of seven years, as required by law.

Attachment A

System/Software Change Request
(SPLIT Form C-1049)

Table 1
Definitions of Elements in SCR

Element	Values
Originator	Name of the person making the request
Product	Originator's subject support software product
Date	Date of change request (option: date of anomaly detection for the SCR
SCR number	Sequential number assigned for the product in question
SCR title	A concise descriptive title of the request
SCR type	One of the following types: AR—Anomaly Report SCN—Specification Change Notice ECR—Engineering Change Request ER—Enhancement Request IR—Impound Request
Program	Identification of the support software product for which the change is requested
System version	Version identifier of the system for which the change is requested
Description of change	Originator's description of the need for a change
Disposition	CCB indicates one of the following dispositions: Approved—Date approved and assigned for implementation _____ Deferred—Date deferred to _____ Rejected—Date rejected _____
User class	Indicates organization/activity using the software
Date needed	Indicates date the change is needed in the production system

For those SCR referencing anomalies detected in a product baseline, the CCB must verify that the problem exists and the following data should be added:

Optional Data for Anomaly Reports

Item	Data
1	System configuration on which the anomaly was detected.
2	Performance effect—The effect the anomaly has on the performance of the system [c] critical; [m] major; or [s] small

Attachment B

Software Change Authorization

Table 1 defines the list of data elements included in the SCA file for releasing each unit. The SPLIT facility CCB may add to the list of elements. Deletions are made only with explicit approval of the SPLIT CCB.

Table 1
Definitions of Elements in SCA

Element Name	Definition
CI number	Number assigned for CI identification
Date	(1) Date change was released to the integration library
	(2) Date change was released to the production library
SCR number	The SCR number of the request/authority for making the change
Subapplication	The name or number assigned to the unit or portion of the CI being released
Release request	Date release was requested
Action requested	The control action requested by the development activity (builds, move to integration library, etc)
Programmer(s)	The names of the programmer(s) making the changes
Members	Names of modules, units affected by the change in the release
Change level	The change level or version number of the units being released
Justification	The number or the statement of justification concerning the reason for release
From library	The library location of the units before the release
Member type	The type of the unit being released (procedures, macros, test drivers)
Load module	The load module with which the unit will be linked
Verified by	Name of the person approving the verification
Verified system name	Identification of system used for testing change
Time tag	The time tag for the version of the unit being released

Appendix D

Software Configuration Management Plan for a Product Line System

Version 1.0

Approved

____

Director, Engineering

____

PLAS Program Manager

Date: ___/___/___

Synopsis

This example Plan contains a discussion of a hypothetical project in a microelectronics company that makes microprocessors and microprocessor-based systems that are later embedded within other hi-tech electronic systems. The company has approximately nineteen hundred employees, of which one hundred and thirty-four are in the engineering division and the remainder are in the production division, marketing, and administration group. There is an extensive investment in hardware CAD/CAM to make the operation productive and a lesser investment in computer-aided engineering (CAE). Office automation is used to minimize the costly handling of paper; therefore, most of the communication within the company uses electronic media. Customers buy hardware or systems — receiving software products only as part of a system.

There is no independent software development activity. Software technology is considered a basic skill that electronic engineers and system designers use in their day-to-day work. The engineers design software for execution within their system's RAM or ROM with the same ease as they use the silicon compilers to design chips. There are two focal points where the different engineering design technologies interact with the configuration management discipline. The first focal point is in the system's computer aided engineering system where the engineering libraries (where functional logic and piece/part information is maintained) or data bases and VLSI design systems are maintained. The second focal point is in the production computer aided manufacturing system where the programmed logic is transformed from compiled into deliverable products. The two focal points are separate as the mode of implementation demands different interfaces — the production system interfaces directly with the hardware CAD/CAM systems in production; the engineering system with the software/firmware development stations and prototype-testing stations. The configuration management software to support management of these data bases is largely embedded within the program management system, which schedules work and manages the changes to baselines.

In this environment, the software configuration management disciplines are just another one of the tools used by engineering and production management for performing their daily tasks. The software configuration management plan focuses primarily on establishing unique project data base structures in the engineering systems, routing the change management materials to named organizational positions for approvals, and defining data-base baselines. Software configuration management is a service provided by the engineering, production, and management systems to help management more effectively perform their tasks.

Contents

Appendix D

Software Configuration Management Plan for a Product Line System

1. Introduction

This guide describes the plan for managing the configurations of stored program logic used in manufacturing the product line analysis system (PLAS) module. This module performs the computational, communications, and device-controller functions of a larger system — *The Quick Stretch*, which performs stress analysis for mechanical structures. This system is sold as a proprietary company product to customers and is maintained by field representatives of the company. The company intends that the PLAS module have functional flexibility through its use of computer programs to make the module adaptable to other company proprietary systems and possibly for sale to other systems manufacturers.

1.1 Purpose. This plan identifies the procedures for managing the configurations of the PLAS computer programs during their development and for maintenance of the programs throughout the time period the company sells and has warranty responsibility for the products that incorporate the PLAS as an embedded system.

1.2 Scope. This plan is applicable to the development and maintenance of all the computer programs embedded in ROM, loaded into EPROMS, or loaded into RAM for use in the PLAS module. Configuration management of the hardware associated with the PLAS module is covered in a PLAS hardware configuration management plan — PLAS-CMP. These computer programs, packaged in different media, are collectively managed under the single configuration item *PLAS software configuration item* regardless of their function. The computer programs packaged for ROM or EPROM are managed as hardware components, identified under their prime hardware configuration item identification. The support software used in production and test of the PLAS module components (both hardware and computer programs) is also controlled by this plan.

1.3 Definitions and Mnemonics

1.3.1 Definitions. The terms used in this plan conform to the definitions found in ANSI/IEEE Std 729-1983, *IEEE Standard Glossary of Software Engineering Terminology.*

hard logic. Programmed logic that is embedded as circuit logic in a chip. The logic is developed using the general software engineering tools and disciplines. Packaging of the logic uses silicon compilers for generating the geometry of the chip.

P-CAMS. The product computer aided manufacturing system (P-CAMS) environment that contains

(1) The engineering data bases of hard logic and stored-programmed logic defining the products in the production environment (the controlled libraries)
(2) The support software used in converting the controlled engineering data bases into instructions and data for
  (a) Production of chips, software and firmware
  (b) Test programs and data for verifying that the produced entities have been correctly implemented

User documentation is also produced using P-CAMS. Configuration management disciplines relating to product serialization, change labeling and tracking, and verification tests are a part of this environment.

project-management system (PMS). The PMS provides the capability for management to

(1) Define an identification schema for projects at start-up time and to make changes to the different schemes
(2) Authorize and control the release of project drawings and engineering data bases from the dynamic libraries in systems computer-aided engineering system (SCAES) to the controlled project libraries in P-CAMS

(3) Schedule the production and release of product changes, and coordinate the production schedules within the production division

In general, this system supports the configuration management change control board (CCB) and production scheduling activities.

stored program logic. Computer program instructions and data that are executed out of RAM, ROM, and EPROM in the PLAS module. The instructions and data are developed using general software engineering tools and disciplines. Packaging of the instructions and data uses technology appropriate for the media.

systems computer aided engineering system (SCAES). The SCAES environment is composed of

(1) A variety of engineering support software including different simulators, prototyping tools, modeling programs, engineering design aids, documentation tools, test generators, test simulators, utilities and compilers
(2) Engineering libraries (the **dynamic** libraries) that contain general algorithms that have widespread utility, reusable stored-programmed logic, reusable hard-logic functions, and access to selected product designs
(3) Design data bases representing the dynamic working libraries for product developments that are currently in progress (such as the PLAS module development)

The commands that are used in SCM disciplines for supporting identification of entities relating to a specific project and for tracking current versions of those entities are an integral part of SCAES.

1.3.2 Mnemonics. The following mnemonics are used within this document:

APM	Associate Program Manager
CAD/CAM	Computer-Aided Design/Computer-Aided Manufacturing
CAE	Computer-Aided Engineering
CAES	Computer-Aided Engineering Systems
CCB	Configuration Control Board
CI	Configuration Item
CM	Configuration Management
CMP	Configuration Management Plan
CMS	Change Management System
CSCI	Computer Software Configuration Item
DP&S	Data Processing and Support
EPROM	Erasable Programmable Read Only Memory
EWS	Engineering Work Stations
EWSW	Engineering Work Stations Environment
LSI	Large Scale Integration
MSI	Medium Scale Integration
P-CAM	Product Computer-Aided Manufacturing System
PLAS	Product Line Analysis System
PMS	Project Management System
QC	Quality Control
ROM	Read Only Memory
SCA	System Change Authorization
SCR	System Change Request
SCAES	Systems Computer-Aided Engineering System
TD	Technical Director
VDD	Version Description Document
VLSI	Very Large Scale Integration

1.4 References

[1] PLAS Functional Requirements.[18]

[2] Engineering Work Station and Environment User's Manual.

[3] Programming Standards Manual.

[4] Product Line Identification Numbering Standard.

[5] Software Quality Assurance Policy.

[6] Production Test Standards.

2. Management

2.1 Organization. The PLAS program manager of the product line has financial and administrative responsibility for all PLAS module engineering and production. He is part of the administration and reports directly to the general manager of the company. The company uses a matrix organization for managing projects.

The PLAS program manager has final responsibility for the business success of the program. The project staff consists of the financial staff, the technical director (TD), an associate program manager (APM), and a quality representative from the quality control (QC) department. The PLAS APM is functionally a part of the production division and attends all PLAS project meetings.

[18] All referenced documentation is available from the SCAES library.

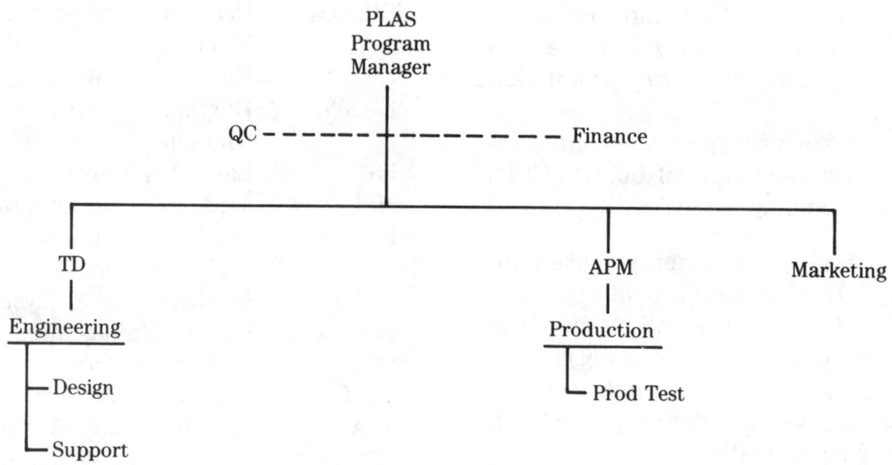

Fig 1
PLAS Organization Chart

The major elements in the administration, engineering division, and production division that support the PLAS product line include

(1) Marketing (administration) provides the sales and marketing support to
 (a) Perform market analyses and prepare functional requirements for the Quick Stretch System that indirectly determine the functional requirements for engineering the PLAS module
 (b) Maintain customer liaison for product maintenance and improvement and
 (c) Sell the Quick Stretch Systems

(2) The PLAS engineering design group (engineering division) is an ad hoc organization under the direction of the PLAS technical director, which provides engineering expertise to
 (a) Manage the overall system design activity
 (b) Develop the hard logic, the stored program logic, and drawings for PLAS assemblies
 (c) Review all proposed changes for feasibility, cost, and design integrity
 (d) Perform all necessary engineering design and logic changes

(3) The PLAS engineering support group (engineering division) provides the technicians and technical resources to
 (a) Maintain the SCAES_PLAS engineering data base
 (b) Perform product engineering based on design prototypes to be released for production
 (c) Support TD and PLAS program manager in verifying design changes prior to release to P-CAMS.

(4) The PLAS production group (production division) activity, under direction of the PLAS APM, provides the capability to
 (a) Manufacture hardware in accordance with PLAS drawings released for production
 (b) Compile, verify, and package programmed logic released as software for PLAS RAM
 (c) Compile, verify, and burn-in programmed logic released as firmware for PLAS EPROM
 (d) Compile, verify, and coordinate mask production or programmed logic released as firmware for PLAS ROM
 (e) Compile, verify, and coordinate production of hard logic released as VLSI chips
 (f) Test complete assemblies of PLAS modules
 (g) Maintain inventories
 (h) Ship PLAS modules to customers as directed by the PLAS program manager

The functions that are generally performed by a separate SCM activity and not supported by SCAES and PMS are shared between the quality control representative and the APM. This is possible because most of the detailed SCM processing activities and library interface management are accomplished by the PMS.

The PLAS technical director is the chairperson of the configuration control board (CCB). The PLAS identification scheme implemented in the SCAES control system is approved by the chairperson of the CCB. The responsibility for reviewing and approving all changes to established baselines and scheduling releases belongs to the CCB chairperson. Release of PLAS engineering data base(s) to P-CAMS and all changes to the P-CAMS data base for PLAS is authorized by the CCB chairperson.

2.2 SCM Responsibilities

(1) The PLAS program manager provides general direction to the TD for establishing the identification scheme, to the APM for production scheduling, and authorizes the establishment of baselines. The PLAS program manager also provides general direction to the TD for CCB actions and issues requests for QC to audit and review the integrity of the SCAES_PLAS engineering data base and the P-CAMS_PLAS production data base.

(2) The PLAS TD establishes the contract identification schema used by the PLAS project engineers and performs (or delegates to engineering support group) the duties of updating the P-CAMS_PLAS production data base when authorized by CCB actions. All changes to the P-CAMS_PLAS production data base are approved by the TD.

(3) The PLAS associate program manager (or a delegated assistant, such as a librarian) has overall responsibility for maintaining the P-CAM PLAS data base, PLAS unit and module tests, and production schedules.

(4) The production test group is responsible for testing the hardware assemblies, including the units containing the packages of programmed logic (ROM and EPROM), and verifying that the correct version of the logic is embedded in the device. The group also verifies that the diskettes containing the dynamically loadable software for the PLAS module is the correct version for shipment. Final assembly tests of these units along with VLSI chips are also conducted by this group.

(5) The PLAS quality control representative is responsible for reviewing the production test group's verification activities, and auditing the integrity and use of SCAES_PLAS engineering data base and P-CAMS_PLAS production data base. The QC representative verifies the physical configuration of the PLAS module, its associated user documentation, and its functional capabilities (review of module acceptance testing) as a part of the quality review prior to shipment.

(6) The engineering support group provides special extractions from the SCAES, P-CAMS and PMS systems data bases showing status of the various baselines when information other than that provided by general project status commands is required.

(7) The marketing organization provides the functional requirements for the system and is the major source of high-level system changes and improvements. In effect, this organization defines the functional baseline. Customers purchasing a PLAS module for their own use or for the PLAS module integration in the Quick Stretch System have no direct interface or review authority over PLAS baseline activities or product capabilities.

2.3 Interface Control. The data bases for the PLAS module are maintained in two different library systems: the SCAES_PLAS engineering data base and the P-CAMS_PLAS production data base. The interface between these two data bases is controlled by PLAS CCB authorizations.

The SCAES_PLAS engineering data base is made up of several parts representing

(1) Top-level drawing of the PLAS module

(2) Detail design representations of the programmed logic as it is to be packaged for implementation in ROM, EPROM, and RAM based software

(3) Detail designs for implementation in chips (LSI and VLSI designs)

(4) Electrical engineering drawings for cards and assemblies and

(5) Mechanical drawings for the module assemblies

The interfaces between these subdata bases are managed as developmental baselines during the engineering development phase of a PLAS module.

The interface with the Quick Stretch System, or with customer defined systems using the PLAS module, is defined by the top-drawing design data base. Changes in this interface are made only with the authority of the TD. In case of conflict, the PLAS program manager negotiates the changes with the appropriate system representative.

Interfaces with the P-CAMS_PLAS production data base and the computer-aided manufacturing software are managed by the APM in production division, as long as the changes do not affect the CAES_PLAS engineering data-base interface.

2.4 SCMP Implementation

2.4.1 PLAS Configuration Baselines. The functional baseline is established when the system level description for the PLAS module is approved by the general manager for prototype development. Marketing surveys and analyses of potential customer applications provide a description of the desired functional capabilities of the proposed system. The functional baseline is documented with the marketing analysis report, supplemented by a preliminary top-level drawing of a proposed system. This baseline is considered obsolete after acceptance of the preproduction baseline.

The allocated baseline is established upon approval of the top-level drawing and preliminary detailed designs, verified by simulation runs, by the PLAS program manager. This baseline is obsoleted after acceptance of the preproduction baseline.

The developmental baselines are established by the TD at his/her discretion as needed for coordinating the changing allocated baselines during development. The developmental baselines represent incremental software builds needed to develop the prototype system and to verify revisions to the production baseline or different models of the production baseline for various customer applications.

The preproduction baseline is established with the successful demonstration of a prototype system and an absence of any priority 1 (emergency) error reports or changes outstanding. The PLAS program manager authorizes development of the preproduction baseline when given the go-ahead by Marketing management.

The production baseline is established with the concurrence of the PLAS APM and PLAS TD that the design is functionally adequate and that the production facilities of the production division can produce the design in an economical way. The production baseline is a formal agreement between the PLAS program manager and the production division manager.

2.4.2 The Configuration Control Board. The PLAS technical director is the chairperson of the PLAS CCB. This review activity is established at the initiation of preproduction model development.

2.4.3 The Support Environment. The SCAES environment consists of a compatible set of engineering and software development tools that can work with the general engineering data base and special data bases set up for different projects, such as PLAS. The configuration of this support software environment is most carefully controlled by the company data processing and support (DP & S) organization. The support software that interfaces with the data-base management system is most rigidly controlled but there is latitude for engineers to develop special programs restricted to engineering work stations (EWS), that do not generate data for entry into the dynamic engineering data bases. Access keys for controlling entry to the SCAES_PLAS engineering data base are assigned to responsible engineers at the onset of allocated baseline development.

The P-CAMS environment interfaces with a wide variety of CAM and computer-aided test (CAT) systems. These interfaces are critical for the reliable management and administration of company operations. The company DP & S organization manages these interfaces. Any changes must be approved (among other approvals) by the PLAS APM. This review activity is initiated with the development of the preproduction baseline.

Vendor software is used extensively in the supporting software environments of CAES and P-CAMS. Vendor software is also used extensively in the EWS environment supporting SCAES. The management of the vendor software in the EWS environment that is not under the control of the company DP & S organization is initiated by the PLAS TD after the preproduction baseline is established.

2.4.4 SCM Resource Requirements. The resources required for providing configuration management of the PLAS module development and production are embedded in the requirements for training, management oversight, computer resources, administrative support from the engineering support group and DP & S maintenance.

(1) *Training requirements.* Approximately two days training is needed for a new hire engineer to become familiar with use of the data bases and control programs relative to managing configurations. This time is allocated as a part of the overall training program for new hires.

(2) *Management oversight.* Approximately two hours a week are spent on CCB reviews and six hours a week using the PMS control program to schedule analysis and imple-

mentation of system change requests (SCR).

(3) *Computer resources.* Storage requirements for configuration data are a small part of the engineering and production data bases for PLAS modules. The requirements for processor time varies from day to day, but generally does not exceed three minutes of CPU time per day for processing each SCR.

(4) *Support software maintenance.* DP & S is budgeted three man-years effort per year for maintaining the software used for PLAS module configuration management.

2.5 Applicable Policies, Directives, and Procedures

2.5.1 Existing Policies and Procedures. The following company policies are used for configuration management on the PLAS subsystem:

(1) Product Line Identification Numbering—Supplement 2
(2) Corporate Software Protection Policy (Rev 3)
(3) Quality Control Policy for Engineering Data Bases
(4) Production Test Standards
(5) Engineering Standards for Detail Design and Drawings
(6) User's Manual for SCAES
(7) User's Manual for EWS
(8) User's Manual for P-CAMS

2.5.2 New Policies and Procedures To Be Written. The following procedure(s) will be developed for the PLAS project:

(1) Managing of Third-Party Software: Proprietary Marking
(2) PLAS Project Naming Standards

3. SCM Activities

3.1 Configuration Identification. The identification scheme for the PLAS project is developed by the engineering support group and approved by the PLAS TD. The numbering and labeling standards are distributed for project use in the *PLAS Project Naming Standards document.*

3.1.1 Naming Conventions. All data in the SCAES_PLAS engineering data base is arranged and retrievable under the collective identifier PLAS-1800000.

All control level items (programmed logic components and hardware assemblies) are identified within a block of numbers beginning with 532000 and ending with 554000. The engineering support group allocates the numbers for the control level items.

Programmed-logic components have a version description document (VDD) associated with their assigned number. Each assigned number has a preceeding letter identifying the media in which the logic is embedded:

ROM = R
EPROM = E
Diskette[19] = S
Gate arrays = G
PLA = P
Programmable microcontrollers = M

Hardware drawing numbers are assigned to a control level drawing. Parts list for the drawing is made up of part numbers assigned from the 700000 series of numbers.

Reprogrammed logic components keep their basic 1000 number assigned to them in the general SCAES engineering data base. Dash numbers, referencing appropriate VDD, tracks embedded CI, and associated SCR.

3.1.2 Implementation. Identification is assigned to each component and unit defined in the top-level drawing. When an engineer defines a unit, he/she indicates to the program the type of component he/she is defining and the system assigns the appropriate number. Programmed login associated with a defined hardware component or unit is linked to that component's identifier in a *packaging list* associated with the top-level drawing.

Components and units are identified by form, fit, and function (data flow). The engineer defining a component or unit is automatically made *owner* of that component or unit. Changes in the form, fit, or function cannot be made without his/her consent and approval of change. The CAES design tools automatically flag conflicts and force resolution before another of the iterative development baselines can be created.

All system entities associated with the design (specifications, drawings, detail documentation, test data, test procedures, etc) are assigned the appropriate component or unit identifier with which they are associated.

The identifiers assigned in the SCAES_PLAS engineering data base are transferred to the P-CAMS_PLAS production data base at the time

[19]Used for shipping software that executes out of RAM. Software media characteristics may vary but the implementation designator is always *S*.

the preproduction baseline definition effort is initiated.

3.1.3 Ownership Notification Procedures. Filing of software copyright notices for proprietary programmed logic developed for the PLAS project will be performed by Marketing.

Notification to users of the PLAS module copyright will be included in the load module of the software released to the user on the PLAS module diskette. Visual indication of ownership and copyright registration will be displayed at the console when the system is booted, in accordance with Revision 3 (current) of the corporate software protection policy.

All documentation released to customers will be marked with a proprietary notice, vendor license number, or both.

3.2 Configuration Control. Authority for approving changes to baselines varies in accordance with the baseline being changed and the phase of the project.

(1) Authority for approving changes to the *functional baseline* is vested in the PLAS program manager. The PLAS program manager coordinates all changes with the production department manager and with the PLAS TD. This baseline is obsoleted with the initiation of the production baseline.

(2) Authority for approving changes to the *allocated baseline* is vested in the PLAS TD. The PLAS TD coordinates all changes in the allocated baseline with the PLAS program manager and PLAS APM for production. This baseline is shared by SCAES and P-CAMS during the period after the preproduction demonstration is accepted and the production baseline is formally defined.

(3) Authority for approving changes to *developmental baselines* is vested in the PLAS TD. The PLAS TD establishes the developmental baseline criteria, resolves conflicts in allocation and ownership of components or units, and sets schedules for iteration of these baselines.

(4) Authority for approving changes to the *preproduction baseline* is vested in the PLAS TD. The PLAS TD makes changes in allocation and detail design to fit the production facilities on the recommendation of the PLAS APM from production division. Conflicts are resolved by the PLAS program manager.

(5) Authority for approving changes to the *PLAS production baseline* is vested in the PLAS CCB, chaired by the PLAS TD. The PLAS APM and PLAS marketing representative are members of the PLAS CCB. Technical representation from PLAS engineering and PLAS production activities are made when necessary. The PLAS QC representative and production test group representative are permanent members of the PLAS CCB.

Technical review of the system change requests (SCR) is provided by members of the engineering support group who assemble engineering analyses as required, and by members of the PLAS production team who assemble information on the impact of a proposed SCR as required

3.2.1 Change Processing. Changes to the system may originate from the marketing organization (in response to customer desires), from the test group in the production division, or from within the engineering division. Requests for changes are submitted by way of electronic mail using the SCR format provided in the EWS environment. Changes originating from outside the company are entered into the program management system (PMS) by marketing representatives. Internally originated changes are submitted by way of local engineering work stations.

The PMS control system routes SCR to the originator's supervisor for verification when appropriate, and then queues it for review and disposition by the appropriate change authority for the affected baseline. When change requests require further analysis, the change authority routes the SCR (electronically) to the appropriate support group for gathering information. When the support group has assembled a complete analysis package, it is again queued to the appropriate review authority or CCB for disposition. This authority then disposes of the request by indicating approval (providing a schedule and effectivity date of change), deferring it for further analysis or allocation of resources, or disapproving it with reason(s) for disapproval noted.

Approved changes are electronically routed to the PLAS engineering group for implementation.

The tracking of changes is performed in the PMS control system, based on the SCR approval flow status and system change authorizations (SCA), or by extractions from the PLAS data bases in SCAES or P-CAMS to which it has access.

3.2.2 Production Baseline Changes. Changes to the production baseline are made only after changes have been verified in a test environment on a test model of the PLAS module, using simulated test drivers or mock-ups to test the system.

Table 1
Processing Approved Changes

Baseline	Entity	Implemented By	Verified By	Scheduled By
Functional	Document	Engineering	Eng check	Various
Allocated	Document	Engineering	Eng check	Various
Developmental	Document	Engineering	Eng check	TD
	Design data	Engineering	Simulation	TD
	Drawings	Engineering	Eng check	TD
Preproduction	Document	Eng or prod	Eng check	TD
	Design data	Engineering	Simulation	TD
	Drawings	Engineering	Eng check	TD
Production	Document	Production	Test Gp	APM
	Design data	Engineering	Test Gp	APM
	Drawings	Engineering	Eng check	APM

The production test group verifies the changes as operational and authorizes release of the change data from the SCAES_PLAS engineering data base to the P-CAMS_PLAS production data base. The transfer of data is performed by the engineering support group.

3.2.3 PLAS Module Release. Each PLAS module version is released for use in a Quick Stretch System or to individual customers for incorporation into their systems, along with a technical data kit containing the top-level drawings of the system, associated parts lists, and the VDD for control level programmed logic components.

Since PLAS software, released on diskettes, provides the most flexible means of adaptation, provisions exist to release the software VDD independently of the rest of the data packages. This way, revisions to the PLAS functions can be made to PLAS modules in systems released previously. This requires that the configuration of all released modules be maintained in an archive, along with an extraction from the P-CAMS configuration environment containing all support software used in the production and test of that delivery.

3.3 Configuration Status Accounting. The following PLAS configuration status reports are regularly available:

(1) *PLAS Module Development Status.* This is a listing of all configuration items, control level items, and units that are being designed or modified by engineering. The report identifies each unit/control-level-item/CI, status of technical work, outstanding SCR, SCA ready for release, and units or changes released since the last reporting period. This report is generated weekly for the PLAS management team.

(2) *PLAS Module Production Status.* This is a listing of all configuration items, control level items and units that are in production. The report identifies all units in production during the period, SCR/SCA incorporated, scheduled release date (by contract number), and schedule variance. The report is generated weekly for the PLAS management team.

(3) *SCR Status Summary.* This report lists all outstanding SCR that have not been resolved or incorporated into delivered modules. The report lists, for each SCR: CCB action date and disposition; group or department presently responsible for action; status of activity; and schedule for completion. The report is prepared weekly but is available any time the PLAS management team requests it.

(4) *Special Queries.* The report generator of the PMS program provides a query capability that allows anyone to extract the status of:

(a) Any one SCR
(b) All open SCR
(c) All SCR in engineering
(d) All SCR in production
(e) PLAS modules in production with associated SCR number

The general query capability for the data-management systems allow formulation of special queries in the PMS control program for interrogating the SCAES_PLAS engineering data base and the P-CAMS_PLAS production data base for information relative to any changes that are in process or that have been released to customers.

3.4 Audits and Reviews

3.4.1 Audits. The PLAS module configuration is audited each time a baseline is established.

(1) *Functional Baseline.* The PLAS program manager is responsible for ascertaining if the reports and design descriptions are complete enough to present to management.

(2) *Allocated Baselines.* The PLAS technical director is responsible for reviewing the designs to ascertain if the designs are complete enough to present to the PLAS program manager. The engineering support group assists the TD in this review.

(3) *Developmental Baselines.* The engineering support group uses the PMS control program to

(a) Generate set/use type analyses of the detailed designs to uncover outstanding discrepancies and

(b) Establish design activity cut-offs for a specific iteration.

This group also supports the changes by modifying access codes to the new baseline to restrict entry of changes. The TD reviews the summaries of design activities to estimate technical progress in the design.

(4) *Preproduction Baseline.* Prior to establishing the preproduction baseline, the configuration is again audited by the engineering support group to ascertain that the design of the demonstration meets all functional requirements established by the functional baseline and that all entities generated in the developmental baselines are present or accounted for in the demonstration. The QC representative assists in the review of entities for this baseline.

(5) *Production Baseline.* The QC representative reviews the entities in the P-CAMS_PLAS production data base to ascertain that all functional capabilities demonstrated for the preproduction model and all changes stemming from the review of the demonstration are present in the data base. The production test group reviews the entities to verify that all changes and modifications to the preproduction demonstration have been made to the production data base. The engineering support group performs a comparison of the engineering data base with the production data base to verify that the transfer of data is complete. The PLAS TD is responsible for preparing this audit.

(6) *Shipping Review.* The PLAS module and its associated documentation package is audited prior to shipment to a customer, either as a part of the Quick Stretch System or as an independent line item to a customer.

The functional audit is performed by the QC representative who reviews the PLAS module against the appropriate extracted data from the P-CAM_PLAS library for that item. A representative from the PLAS engineering support group reviews the product to ascertain that the physical configuration of the module and its associated documentation represents

(a) The specified configuration ordered by the customer

(b) The corresponding configuration in the P-CAMS_PLAS data base and

(c) Accurately reflects any changes that have been made to the data base by the PLAS CCB

Discrepancies or problems uncovered in reviews and audits are reported to the PLAS program manager for resolution.

4. Tools, Techniques, and Methodologies

The basic configuration management tool used for PLAS module is the change management program (CMP), which is a part of the PMS. This program supports change management by

(1) Providing the means to enter system/software change requests (SCR)

(2) Forcing reviews by appropriate supervision by way of the electronic mail system

(3) Deriving analytical data from each SCR

(4) Providing for supervision or CCB review and approval, as appropriate

(5) Directing authorized changes to engineering or production supervision

(6.) Providing for authorizing of changes to the P-CAMS_PLAS data base

(7) Providing for transfering data from the PLAS engineering data base to the production data base

The SCM tool for establishing the identification scheme for PLAS data bases is resident in the SCAES system. This information is transferred to the production data base during the preproduction phase. It is verified when the production baseline is established.

Order information from marketing is entered into the PLAS production schedule by way of the program management system. The detailed configuration is formatted by the configuration management program in CMS, passed on to the P-CAMS_PLAS data base upon approval of the PLAS program manager, and reviewed for schedule and resource consumption by the PLAS APM. Upon his/her approval, resources are committed to the production configuration. Extractions of this configuration are released for inspection and auditing at time of shipment.

5. Supplier Control

Subcontracted PLAS support software is placed under configuration management after inspection and acceptance by the QC representative.

6. Records Collection and Retention

6.1 Backup Data Base. The engineering data base from SCAES_PLAS is backed-up on a weekly basis and stored in Beskin's storage building during the engineering phase (up to the time the production baseline is established). Following establishment of the production baseline, the engineering data base is backed-up on a monthly basis.

The production data base from P-CAMS_PLAS is backed-up on a weekly basis.

6.2 Archive Data Base. Archive data is maintained for purposes of warranty protection, proprietary data production, and liability insurance. The following data are maintained in on-line optical storage media:

(1) Copies of each baseline data base extracted at the time the baseline is established
(2) Copies of order and configuration data passed from PMS to the production data base for each order and
(3) Copies of each configuration of the data base used for production of customer order
(4) Copies of reviews and audits performed on each production item

Appendix E

References Bibliography

Preface

This Appendix contains selected bibliography pertaining to the subject of software configuration management. The list of publications contains both government and private sector references so users may find material applicable to their situation. Because of the scarcity of literature pertaining to configuration management, and especially to software configuration management, the fullest possible list of references will be useful to the practitioner.

Most of the references contain some information regarding software configuration management. The topic of software configuration management plans is addressed in a subset of these references.

References Bibliography

E1. General Bibliography

[1] BERSOFF, E., HENDERSON, V., and SIEGEL, S. *Software Configuration Management, An Investment in Product Integrity.* Englewood, N.J.: Prentice-Hall, 1980.

[2] BERSOFF, E., HENDERSON, V., and SIEGEL, S. *Software Configuration Management: A Tutorial.* Computer, *IEEE Computer Society Magazine,* vol 12 no 1, Jan 1979.

[3] *Configuration Management Procedures (CMP),* Global Engineering Documents, 1984.

[4] *IEEE Transactions on Software Engineering,* IEEE Computer Society, vol SE-10, nr 1, Jan 1984.

[5] BUCKLE, J. K. *Software Configuration Management,* New York: The Macmillan Press Ltd, 1982.

[6] DANIELS, M. A. *Principles of Configuration Management,* Advanced Applications Consultants, Inc, 1987.

[7] BABICH, W. A. *Software Configuration Management*: Coordination for Team Productivity, New York: Addison-Wesley, 1986.

E2. Military Standards for SCM[20]

[8] MIL-STD-481A Configuration Control—Engineering Changes, Deviations, and Waivers (Short Form).

[9] MIL-STD-482A Configuration Status Accounting Data Elements and Related Features.

[10] MIL-STD-483A Configuration Management Practices for Systems Equipment, Munitions, and Computer Programs.

[11] MIL-STD-490A Specification Practices.

[12] MIL-STD-499A Engineering Management.

[13] MIL-STD-881A Work Breakdown Structure.

[14] MIL-STD-962A Outline of Forms and Instructions for the Preparation of Military Standards and Military Documents.

[15] MIL-STD-1456 Contractor Configuration Management Plan.

[20] Military Standards may be ordered from the Commanding Officer (Code 301) Naval Publications and Forms Center, 5801 Tabor Avenue, Philadelphia, PA 19120.

[16] MIL-STD-1521B Technical Reviews and Audits for Systems, Equipments, and Computer Programs.

E3. Department of Defense Standards

[17] DoD-STD-480 Configuration Control-Engineering Changes, Deviations and Waivers.

[18] DoD-STD-1467 Software Support Environment.

[19] DoD-STD-2167 Defense System Software Development.

[20] DoD-STD-2168 Software Quality Evaluation.

[21] DoD-STD-7935 Automated Data Systems Documentation.

E4. Military Specification

[22] MIL-D-1000B Drawings, Engineering, and Associated List.

[23] MIL-S-83490 Specifications, Types and Forms.

E5. Department of Defense Directives

[24] DoDD 4120.21 Specifications and Standards Applications.

[25] DoDD 5000.1 Major Systems Applications.

[26] DoDD 5000.19L Acquisition Management Systems and Data Requirements Control List.

[27] DoDD 5000.39 Acquisition and Management of Integrated Logistic Support for Systems and Equipment.

[28] DoDD 5010.19 Configuration Management.

[29] DoDD 7920.1 Life Cycle Management of Automated Information Systems (AIS).

E6. Department of Defense Instructions

[30] DoDI 5000.2 Major Systems Acquisition Process.

[31] DoDI 5000.38 Production Readiness Reviews.

[32] DoDI 7045.7 The Planning, Programming and Budgeting System.

[33] DoDI 7935.1 DoD Automated Data Systems Documentation Standards.

E7. US Government Publications[21]

[34] DoD Configuration Management Standardization Program, (CMAM) Plan.

[35] DoD Trusted Computer System Evaluation Criteria, CSC-STD-001-83, 15 Aug 1983.

[36] *NASA Handbook 8040.2.* System Engineering Management Guide, Defense System Management College, 1983. Configuration Management, Management Instruction, GMI8040.1A. NASA Goddard Space Flight Center.

[37] Federal Information Processing Standards (FIPS) *Publication 106.* Guideline on Software Maintenance, National Bureau of Standards. Institute for Computer Sciences and Technology, 1984.

[38] MARTIN, R. and OSBORNE, W. *Special Publication 500-106,* Guidance on Software Maintenance. National Bureau of Standards, Institute for Computer Sciences and Technology, 1983.

[39] McCALL, JIM, HERNDON, MARY, and OSBORNE, WILMA. *Special Publication 500-129,* Software Maintenance Management, National Bureau of Standards, Institute for Computer Sciences and Technology, 1985.

[21] Copies of these publications can be obtained from the Superintendent of Documents, US Governmental Printing Office, Washington, DC 20402.

E8. Electronic Industries Association Publications[22]

[40] EIA CMB 4-1a (Sept 1984), Configuration Management Definitions for Digital Computer Programs.

[41] EIA CMB 4-2 (June 1981), Configuration Identification for Digital Computer Programs.

[42] EIA CMB 4-3 (Feb 1981), Computer Software Libraries.

[43] EIA CMB 4-4 (May 1982), Configuration Change Control for Digital Computer Programs.

[44] EIA CMB 5 (April 1973), Subcontractor/Vendor Configuration Management and Technical Data Requirements.

[22] EIA publications can be obtained from the Standards Sales Department, Electronics Industries Association, 2001 Eye Street, NW, Washington DC 20006.

E9. American Defense Preparedness Association Publications[23]

[45] Proceedings of the 24th Annual Meeting, Technical Documentation Division, May 1982, Denver, Colorado.

[46] Proceedings of the 25th Annual Meeting, Technical Documentation Division, May 1983, Ft. Monroe, Virginia.

[47] Proceedings of the 26th Annual Meeting, Technical Documentation Division, May 1984, San Antonio, Texas.

[23] Copies of these publications can be obtained from the American Defense Preparedness Association, 1700 N. Monroe St, Suite 900, Arlington, VA 22209.

IEEE Standard for Software Productivity Metrics

Sponsor

Software Engineering Standards Subcommittee
of the
Technical Committee on Software Engineering
of the
IEEE Computer Society

Approved September 17, 1992

IEEE Standards Board

Abstract: A consistent way to measure the elements that go into computing software productivity is defined. Software productivity metrics terminology are given to ensure an understanding of measurement data for both source code and document production. Although this standard prescribes measurements to characterize the software process, it does not establish software productivity norms, nor does it recommend productivity measurements as a method to evaluate software projects or software developers. This standard does not measure the quality of software. This standard does not claim to improve productivity, only to measure it. The goal of this standard is for a better understanding of the software process, which may lend insight to improving it.
Keywords: attribute, primitive, productivity ratio, source statement, staff-hour

---

The Institute of Electrical and Electronics Engineers, Inc.
345 East 47th Street, New York, NY 10017-2394, USA

ISBN 1-55937-258-3

Introduction

(This introduction is not a part of IEEE Std 1045-1992, IEEE Standard for Software Productivity Metrics.)

This introduction is intended to provide the reader with some background into the rationale used to develop the standard. This information is being provided to aid in the understanding and usage of the standard. The introduction is nonbinding.

This standard defines a framework for measuring and reporting software productivity. It focuses on definitions of how to measure software productivity and what to report when giving productivity results. It is meant for those who want to measure the productivity of the software process in order to create code and documentation products.

Past software productivity metrics have not proven as useful as desired to provide insight into the software process. Although there is an accumulation of more than 20 years of data, consistent productivity indicators for software development have not emerged from this information. The problem is not as much the fault of the metrics being used as it is the inaccuracy and incompleteness of the data being collected.

The definition of productivity states that it is the ratio of a unit of output to a unit of input used to produce the output. For this relationship to be useful for software, the data used in it must be accurate and complete. For instance, reported software productivity of 5000 lines of source code per year leaves many questions unanswered, *What is a line of source code? How long, in work hours, was the year? What activities were included? Whose effort was counted?*

Interpreting productivity based on a single number leaves much unknown about the process being measured. Without knowing the scope and characteristics of the process measured, or the precision of the data used in the calculations, the resulting productivity values are inconclusive.

The goal of this standard is to build a foundation to accurately measure software productivity. This is done through a set of precisely defined units of measure. However, not all software processes lend themselves to precise measurement. Software development is a new and rapidly evolving field, and it is strongly influenced by the variability of the people who build the software. In those situations where precise measurement definitions are not possible, this standard requests that descriptions of the processes used and the measurements taken be done in a specified format.

The intention of the standard is to formalize the presentation of productivity data so that it is useful to anyone wishing to improve the software process. This standard is not an end in itself. Instead, it is the beginning of increased precision in collecting and reporting software productivity data. The hope is that this will lead to an improved understanding of the software development process and to improved productivity metrics.

Participants

At the time this standard was completed, the Software Productivity Metrics Working Group had the following membership:

Robert N. Sulgrove, *Chair*
Christine H. Smith, *Co-chair*
Eleanor Antreassian, *Past Chair*
Nicholas L. Marselos, *Editor*

Bakul Banerjee
Stephen E. Blake
Thomas P. Bowen
David N. Card
Thomas J. Carlton
Deborah Caswell
Mike Demshki
Sherman Eagles
Ruth S. Euler
Michael Evangelist
Al Freund
James T. Fritsch
John E. Gaffney, Jr.
Stuart Glickman
Lennor Gresham
Stuart Jeans
Robert W. Judge
Lawrence King
Thomas M. Kurihara
Arnold W. Kwong
Fred Lau
Chi Yun Lin
Denis C. Meredith
Lois J. Morton
Andrew Najberg
Jainendra K. Navlakha
Dennis E. Nickle
Richard Reese
Julian Roberts
Brian Sakai
Sylvia Shiroyama
Paul Stevens
Wolfgang B. Strigel
Leonard L. Tripp
Scott A. Whitmire
Ron Willis
Paul Wolfgang

Contributors

The following individuals also contributed to the development of the standard:

William W. Agresti
Lowell Jay Arthur
Jeff A. Aune
Victor R. Basili
Mordechai Ben-Menachem
Victor G. Berecz
Robert C. Birss
Bob Bisschoff
Barry Boehm
George Bozoki
Fred Burke
Neva Carlson
Sally Cheung
Rutherford Cooke
Charles D'Argenio
James B. Dolkas
Carl Einar Dragstedt
Christof Ebert
Violet Foldes
Andrew S. Fortunak
Robert Fraley
Jack Fried
Jean A. Gilmore
Clell Gladson
J. G. Glynn
Robert Grady
Dan Grigore
Amal Gupta
Nash Hair
H. D. Hall
Jack Harrington
Warren Harrison
Bruce Healton
Francis B. Herr
Herman Hess
Geoffrey W. Higgin
John W. Horch
David Hurst
Randall W. Jensen
Bud Jones
T. Capers Jones
Bill Junk
Motti Y. Klein
Phil Kolton
Steven E. Kreutzer
Walt Kutz
Robert L. Lanphar, Jr.
F. C. Lim
Michael Lyu
Andy Mahindru
Jukka Marijarvi
Phillip C. Marriott
Roger J. Martin
Robert F. Martini
Joseph F. Mathews
Bruce Millar
James Miller
Robert C. Natale
Stephen R. Neuendorf
Ken O'Brien
Randy Paddock
Bruce Parker
Bud W. Pezet
Wes Philp
Robert M. Poston
Lawrence H. Putnam
Donald J. Reifer
Niall Ross
Vince Rupolo
Norman F. Schneidewind
Roger Scholten
David J. Schultz
Suzanne E. Schwab
Carl Seddio
Al Serna
Jean Shaffer
Vincent Y. Shen
Josef Sherif
David M. Siefert
Vijaya K. Srivastava
Edwin J. Summers
David Swinney
Robert C. Tausworthe
C. L. Troyanowski
Dolores Wallace
Richard Werling
John Westergaard
Clyde E. Willis
William Wong
Weider Yu

Sponsoring Organizations

The following persons were on the balloting committee that approved this standard for submission to the IEEE Standards Board:

M. Amaya
B. Banerjee
L. Beltracchi
M. Ben-Menache
R. Birss
S. Blake
W. Boll
R. Both
F. Buckley
D. Card
N. Carlson
W. Chung
F. Coallier
P. Daggett
B. Derganc
C. Ebert
R. Euler
W. Eventoff
F. Frati
R. Fries
J. Gaffney, Jr.
Y. Gershkovitch
A. Godin
D. Gustafson
W. Harrison
W. Hefley
P. Hinds
J. Horch
C. Kemerer
R. Kessler
L. King
T. Kurihara
L. Lam
R. Lamb
J. Lane
J. Lawrence
F.C. Lim
B. Livson
D. Look
M. Lyu
J. Maayan
H. Mains
N. Marselos
R. Martin
T. Matsubara
I. Mazza
L. Miller
A. Najberg
J. Navlakha
D. Nickle
P. Petersen
S. Redwine
R. Reese
D. Reifer
B. Sakai
R. San Roman
J. Sanz
H. Schaefer
N. Schneidewind
G. Schumacher
C. Seddio
R. Shillato
S. Shiroyama
D. Siefert
C. Smith
V. Srivastava
W. Strigel
R. Sulgrove
W. Thetford
G. Trebble
L. Tripp
M. Updike
R. Van Scoy
D. Wallace
J. Walz
S. Whitmire
P. Work
A. Yonda
W. Yu
L. Heselton
C. Hu
W. Perry
I. Trandafir
A. Wainberg
P. Zoll

When the IEEE Standards Board approved this standard on Sept. 17, 1992, it had the following membership:

Marco W. Migliaro, *Chair* **Donald C. Loughry,** *Vice Chair*
Andrew G. Salem, *Secretary*

Dennis Bodson
Paul L. Borrill
Clyde Camp
Donald C. Fleckenstein
Jay Forster*
David F. Franklin
Ramiro Garcia
Thomas L. Hannan
Donald N. Heirman
Ben C. Johnson
Walter J. Karplus
Ivor N. Knight
Joseph Koepfinger*
Irving Kolodny
D. N. "Jim" Logothetis
Lawrence V. McCall
T. Don Michael*
John L. Rankine
Wallace S. Read
Ronald H. Reimer
Gary S. Robinson
Martin V. Schneider
Terrance R. Whittemore
Donald W. Zipse

*Member Emeritus

Also included are the following nonvoting IEEE Standards Board liaisons:

Satish K. Aggarwal
James Beall
Richard B. Engelman
David E. Soffrin
Stanley Warshaw

Rachel Auslander
IEEE Standards Project Editor

Contents

IEEE Standard for Software Productivity Metrics

1. Overview

This standard describes the data collection process and calculations for measuring software productivity. This standard is divided into eight clauses. Clause 1 provides the scope of this standard. Clause 2 lists references to other standards that are useful in applying this standard. Clause 3 provides an abbreviated set of definitions and acronyms defined more fully in the standard, but provided here as a quick reference. Clause 4 provides an introduction to the standard's measurement approach. Clause 5 describes data collection for measuring output. Clause 6 describes data collection for measuring input. Clause 7 describes productivity results represented by ratios of outputs to inputs. Clause 8 provides a method to capture the characteristics of the software process to better understand their effects on productivity results.

This standard also contains four annexes. These provide additional information for understanding and using this standard, but they are not part of the standard. Annex A is a data collection form for recording quantitative metrics data defined in this standard, and Annex B is a data collection form for recording the characteristics data defined in this standard. Annex C contains a bibliography of some of the many references used in developing this standard. Annex D describes a counting method for the relationships defined in the standard.

1.1 Scope

Measuring software productivity is similar to measuring other forms of productivity; that is, it is measured as the ratio of units of output divided by units of input. The inputs consist of the effort expended to produce a given output. For software, the tangible outputs are source code and documentation. Of course the product of software is a process, an algorithm that drives a computer to do work. Unfortunately, understanding of the functionality incorporated into a software product is still rudimentary. Only by understanding what can be measured will it be possible to understand the essence of the software process.

Toward this end, this document standardizes software productivity metrics terminology to ensure an understanding of measurement data for both code and documentation production. It defines a set of units to measure the output products and input effort.

The lowest level of measurement defined in this standard is called a *primitive*. The output primitives measured are software source statements, documentation pages, and, optionally, function points. The input primitives measure the efforts of those developing the software products. The capacity and capability of automated support tools are not directly measured by this standard, but are indirectly measured by the improvements in the productivity of the people who use them.

This standard prescribes measurements to characterize the software process, and in doing so gives insight for improving it. This standard does not establish software productivity norms, nor does it recommend productivity measurements as a method to evaluate software projects or software developers.

Although the overall value of a product cannot be separated from the quality of what is produced, this standard does not measure the quality of software. The issue of measuring quality is beyond the scope of this standard, because it covers a different aspect of the software process. Nevertheless, productivity metrics should be interpreted in the context of the overall quality of the product. It is left to the user of this standard to look to other standards covering quality metrics for that information.

The definition of productivity as the ratio of product to effort was selected in this standard because it is more stable than value relationships like product to monetary units or production to sales. The effects of inflation on the value of monetary units, or the caprice of the marketplace on sales, cause these measures to vary unpredictably. As a result, they do not offer a stable measure over time. However, the quantity of the product and the effort in hours expended to produce it are more consistent measures, and over time these measures will provide a better gauge of software productivity. Users may wish to translate productivity into monetary equivalents, but results shall be reported in the units specified in this standard.

The metrics in this standard apply equally well to new development and to the enhancement or maintenance of an existing software product. Subsequent releases or changes to a released or delivered software product should be viewed as a new product for the purpose of applying these metrics.

This standard defines a consistent way to measure the elements that go into computing software productivity. A consistent measurement process will lead to a better understanding of the software development process, and a better understanding will lead to improvement. This standard does not claim to improve productivity, only to measure it.

1.2 Terminology

The words *shall*, *must*, and words in the imperative form identify the mandatory (essential) material within this standard. The words *should* and *may* identify optional (conditional) material. As with other IEEE Software Engineering Standards, the terminology in this document is based on the IEEE Std 610.12-1990.[1] To avoid inconsistency when the glossary is revised, the definitions are not repeated in this document. New terms and modified definitions as applied in this standard are included in clause 3.

1.3 Audience

This standard should be of interest to software development managers, software productivity and process assessment personnel, quality assurance personnel, software engineering improvement personnel, and researchers.

2. References

This standard shall be used in conjunction with the following publications:

IEEE Std 610.12-1990, IEEE Standard Glossary of Software Engineering Terminology (ANSI).

IEEE Std 1074-1991, IEEE Standard for Developing Software Life Cycle Processes (ANSI).

[1]Information on references can be found in clause 2.

3. Definitions

This clause contains key terms as they are used in this standard.

3.1 activities: Events in the software life cycle for which effort data is collected and reported.

3.2 added source statements: The count of source statements that were created specifically for the software product.

3.3 attributes: Measurable characteristics of a primitive.

3.4 characteristics: Those inherent factors of software development that may have a significant impact on productivity.

3.5 comment source statements: Source statements that provide information to people reading the software source code and are ignored by the compiler.

3.6 compiler directive source statements: Source statements that define macros, or labels, or direct the compiler to insert external source statements (for example, an *include* statement), or direct conditional compilation, or are not described by one of the other type attributes.

3.7 data declaration source statements: Source statements that reserve or initialize memory at compilation time.

3.8 deleted source statements: Source statements that are removed or modified from an existing software product as a new product is constructed.

3.9 delivered source statements: Source statements that are incorporated into the product delivered to the customer.

3.10 developed source statements: Source statements that are newly created for, added to, or modified for a software product.

3.11 direct staff-hour: The amount of effort directly expended in creating a specific output product.

3.12 document page count: The total number of nonblank pages contained in a hard-copy document.

3.13 document screen count: The total number of page images for electronically displayed documents.

3.14 documents: Hard copy, screen images, text, and graphics used to convey information to people.

3.15 executable source statements: Source statements that direct the actions of the computer at run time.

3.16 function point: A measure of the delivered software functionality.

3.17 granularity: The depth or level of detail at which data is collected.

3.18 incremental productivity: The productivity computed periodically during development.

3.19 input primitive: The effort to develop software products, expressed in units of staff-hours.

3.20 logical source statements (LSS): Source statements that measure software instructions independently of the physical format in which they appear.

3.21 modified source statements: Original source statements that have been changed.

3.22 new source statements: The sum of the added and modified source statements.

3.23 nondelivered source statements: Source statements that are developed in support of the final product, but not delivered to the customer.

3.24 nondeveloped source statements: Existing source statements that are reused or deleted.

3.25 origin attribute: The classification of software as either developed or nondeveloped.

3.26 original source statements: Source statements that are obtained from an external product.

3.27 output primitives: Primitives that include source statements, function points, and documents.

3.28 page size: The edge-to-edge dimensions of hard-copy documents, or the average characters per line and the number of lines per screen for electronically displayed documents.

3.29 physical source statements (PSS): Source statements that measure the quantity of software in lines of code.

3.30 primitive: The lowest level for which data is collected.

3.31 productivity ratio: The relationship of an output primitive to its corresponding input primitive.

3.32 reused source statements: Unmodified source statements obtained for the product from an external source.

3.33 source statements (SS): The encoded logic of the software product.

3.34 staff-hour: An hour of effort expended by a member of the staff.

3.35 support staff-hour: An hour of effort expended by a member of the staff who does not directly define or create the software product, but acts to assist those who do.

3.36 tokens: The content of a document as characterized by words, ideograms, and graphics.

3.37 type attributes: The classification of each source statement as either executable, data declaration, compiler directive, or comment.

3.38 usage attributes: The classification of software as delivered to a user of the final product, or as nondelivered when created only to support the development process.

4. Software productivity metrics

This standard defines measurement primitives for computing software productivity. A primitive is the lowest level for which data is collected. The output primitives for software are source statements and, optionally, function points. For documentation, the output primitive is the page. The input primitive is the staff-hour.

Primitives are categorized by attributes. An attribute is a measurable characteristic of a primitive. This standard requires that all attributes be measured for each primitive. For example, the source statement primitive may be either new or reused, and it may also be either delivered or nondelivered. Each of these attributes is a different variation of the primitive. Thus, a new delivered source statement differs from a new nondelivered source statement. By using this scheme of primitives and attributes, the elements of productivity are consistently categorized.

Because productivity measurements are only as valid as the primitive data used to calculate them, accuracy and consistency of the data used are essential for the results to be meaningful. The degree of granularity, which is the depth or level of detail at which data is collected, is important in determining the precision and consistency of the data.

Data of fine granularity is obtained when collecting data by staff-hour for each hour worked. Tracking the effort expended at this level reduces the potential for large errors. Estimates, such as those made at the end of a project by best guess approximation of effort, are an example of very coarse granularity. In this situation, large errors may be introduced into the productivity results.

This standard requires the use of the finest degree of granularity obtainable in collecting software productivity data. For the results of this standard to be most useful, the measuring process used shall be both accurate and detailed. Therefore, recording input effort as it is expended is the only acceptable method for this standard.

5. Output primitives

Three categories of output primitives are defined in this standard: source statements, function points, and documents. Source statements are a fundamental part of software, representing the encoded logic of the software product. Function points are a measure of the functional content of software. Production of documents is a significant component of the effort expended in software development, and measuring productivity for it is important. This standard requires reporting productivity results for source statements and documents. The use of function points is optional but recommended.

5.1 Source statement output primitives

This clause defines methods for counting software statements, and methods for categorizing the nature, origin, and disposition of the software.

Two methods are used to count software source statements: the logical source statement (LSS) method, which counts instructions, and the physical source statement (PSS) method, which counts lines of code. Logical source statement counting is the preferred method for this standard. Physical source statement counting is included in this standard because it is commonly found in published data.

Software is categorized by a set of attributes that describe it. Each source statement primitive is defined by three attribute qualifiers. The first of these is the type attribute that classifies each source statement as either executable, data declaration, compiler directive, or comment. The second is the origin attribute that classifies software as either developed or nondeveloped. Developed software is created new, or modified from existing software, for this product. Nondeveloped software is reused or deleted from the existing software. The last attribute is the usage attribute that identifies whether the software was delivered to a user of the final product, or produced only to support the development process and not delivered to the user.

5.1.1 Source statement counting

Source statements in different programming languages shall be counted separately. The programming language used shall be identified for each count along with its software module name. If two languages are used in the development, for example Pascal and C, the quantity of source statements of each language shall be counted and reported separately. Combining counts of different languages into a single count shall not be permitted.

This standard requires that only those source statements written by people be counted. Other counting practices, such as counting compiler derived instructions, program generator output, reuse library output, or machine instructions may be counted in addition to the people-created source statements provided these counts are kept separate and clearly identified. Counts of object code, executable code, and code that is mechanically generated from source code are not required by this standard. It may be most useful to count source statements at the level that the source is maintained. As a minimum, counting shall be done at product completion, when the product is ready for delivery. In all cases, what is counted shall be specifically stated along with the quantity of software measured.

Source statements that are expanded within a software module, for example, macro expansions, or supplied to the program, for example, by an *include* statement, shall be counted only once for all modules being measured. Source statements that invoke, call, or direct inclusion of other source statements in the module shall be counted each time they are used.

Source statements are counted in one of two ways, as logical source statements (LSS) or as physical source statements (PSS):

a) *Logical source statements.* The LSS counting method measures the number of software instructions. When a source statement is the count of instructions irrespective of its relationship to lines, the count shall be stated as being in logical source statements.

   The LSS method is used to count software statements independently of the physical format in which they appear. For example, if two instructions appear on a single line, the LSS count would be two. If one instruction spans two lines, the LSS count would be one.

   An LSS count shall be accompanied by a description of the procedure for counting the source statements. This description shall define the algorithm used to determine the beginning and end of each source statement, and how embedded source statements are counted.

b) *Physical source statements.* The PSS counting method measures the number of software lines of code. When the end-of-line character or a line of code method is used to count source statements, the count shall be stated as being in physical source statements.

   A PSS measurement is line counting where a typical line format is 80 characters. Any deviation from the typical line format shall be noted. A PSS may consist of one LSS, more than one LSS, or part of an LSS.

   Blank lines shall be excluded from PSS counts. If desired, blank lines may be counted separately as the number of blank lines.

5.1.2 Source statement attributes

This standard partitions source statements into three attributes: type, origin, and usage. The type attribute consists of executable, data declaration, compiler directive, and comment source statements. The origin attribute consists of developed and nondeveloped source statements. The usage attribute consists of delivered and nondelivered source statements.

Separate counts for each combination of attribute values shall be stated when reporting productivity results. For example, separate counts shall be stated for executable source statements that are developed delivered and for executable source statements that are developed nondelivered.

5.1.2.1 Type attribute

The type attribute classifies all LSS into the categories of executable, data declaration, compiler directive, and comment source statements. Each LSS shall be counted as one of the following:

a) *Executable source statements.* Source statements that direct the actions of the computer at run time shall be counted as executable source statements.
b) *Data declaration source statements.* Source statements that reserve or initialize memory at compilation time; that are directives to the compiler to constrain or check data; or that define the structure of the data that will be reserved, allocated, or created at run time shall be counted as data declaration source statements.
c) *Compiler directive source statements.* Source statements that define macros; are labels; direct the compiler to insert external source statements, for example, *include* statement; direct conditional compilation; or are not described by one of the other type attributes shall be identified as compiler directive source statements.
d) *Comment source statements.* Source statements that provide information to people reading the software source code and are ignored by the compiler shall be counted separately from other source statements and reported as comment source statements.

Physical source statement counting is a count of the number of nonblank lines. This count is expressed as the number of PSS. Physical source statements are further subdivided as follows:

a) *Noncomment lines.* Lines of software that contain either executable, data declaration, or compiler directive source statements.
b) *Comment lines.* Lines that contain only comment source statements.

All counts of LSS and PSS shall be kept by source module, and identified by module name and software language. The counts may be combined for all modules when expressing aggregate results for the software product, but the combined count shall be only of those modules of the same software source language.

5.1.2.2 Origin attribute

Each source statement is designated by a second attribute called the origin attribute. Each source statement can have one of two possible origins:

a) *Developed source statements.* Source statements added or modified for the specific product being measured shall be counted as new source statements. Added source statements are those that did not previously exist and were created specifically for this product. Modified source statements are those taken from another software product to which any changes were made to make the software suitable for this application.
b) *Nondeveloped source statements.* Source statements that were not developed new for this product are counted in two categories: deleted source statements and reused source statements. Deleted source statements shall be the count of all source statements that have been removed or modified from an earlier version of this software product. Reused source statements are unmodified source statements obtained for the product from an external source of software. The size (LSS or PSS) of this external source would be counted as original source statements and could be a previous version of this product, a reuse library, or acquired software. Reused source statements shall be counted as a part of the software module count. Modifying a source statement is considered to be the process of removing one existing source statement and then adding one or more new source statements. When a single source statement is modified, and the result is two or more source statements, all but one source statement shall be counted in added source statements, and one shall be counted as a modified source statement.

The following computations shall be used for calculating the counts of new, reused, and deleted source statements:

Number of New SS = Number of Added SS + Number of Modified SS

Number of Deleted SS = Number of Modified SS + Number of Removed SS

Number of Reused SS = Number of Original SS – Number of Modified SS – Number of Removed SS

The modified source statement count is identical in each relationship above in which it is used.

Pictorially, these relationships can be represented as in figure 1.

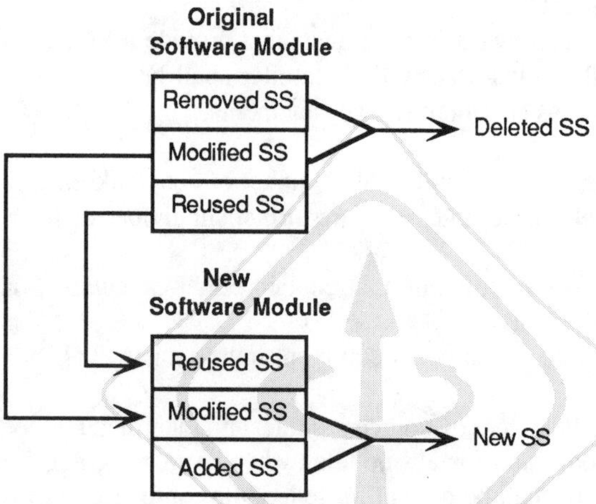

Figure 1—Source statements counts

5.1.2.3 Usage attribute

All source statements shall be divided into two categories based upon their usage:

a) *Delivered source statements.* All source statements incorporated into the final product delivered to the customer, shall be counted as delivered source statements. This includes all source statements that are used directly in the product's designed functions, and all source statements that support the product in its operating environment such as installation, diagnostic, and support utility software.
b) *Nondelivered source statements.* All software developed for the final product but not delivered to the customer shall be counted as nondelivered source statements. This includes all software not counted as delivered source statements that was produced to support development of the final product such as test software, tools, and aids to the developers.

5.2 Function point output primitive

The output primitive used to measure delivered software functionality is the function point. This standard uses the term *function point* to mean Albrecht's definition of function point (see [B1[2]]) or similar methods of measuring functionality.

Measuring function points is not required by this standard. However, those who do measure function points shall also accompany the measurements with source statement counts as defined in clause 5.1. This requirement is meant to enable a better understanding of the relationship between function point and source statement measures of productivity.

5.2.1 Function point counting

Function points are computed from an algorithm that uses various characteristics of the application's functionality expressed as a relationship of function types. Each function type is a variable that defines a characteristic of the application, and is set to a specific value for each application called the function value.

Productivity measurement given in function points shall be accompanied by the following:

a) The function point algorithm shall be stated explicitly. If the algorithm is proprietary, and cannot be stated, then the source and version of the algorithm shall be identified.
b) Each function type used in the function point algorithm shall be specified and defined. The function type definitions shall be complete (see 5.2.2).
c) A listing of the function values used for each function type shall be stated. This is the numeric quantity or factor supplied for each function type in the algorithm.

5.2.2 Function point attributes

The type attribute describes the function types. The origin and usage attributes are not generally used to describe function points since function points are computed only for delivered software.

Function types used in the function point algorithm shall be precisely defined. An example of how a function type definition might be stated is

> *External output type:* Any unique user data or control output type that leaves the boundary of the application being measured. An external output should be considered unique if it has a format different from other external outputs, or if the external (logical) design requires that processing logic be different from other external outputs with the same format. External outputs include reports and messages that leave the application directly for the user, and output files of reports and messages that leave the application boundary for other applications.

A definition is required for each function type used in the function point algorithm.

5.3 Document output primitives

This standard requires measurement of all documents that consume a nontrivial (as determined by the user of the standard) amount of project resources. Documents include hard copy, screen images, text, and graphics used to convey information to people. The effort associated with the preparation of each document measured shall be recorded separately.

---

[2]The numbers in brackets correspond to those of the bibliographical references in Annex C.

All documents that actively support the development or the usage of a software product shall be measured. Typical documents of this type are requirements statements, architectural and design specifications, data definitions, user manuals, reference manuals, tutorials, training guides, installation and maintenance manuals, and test plans.

Documents that are produced, but not preserved beyond the completion of the project should also be measured if they require a significant amount of effort to produce. These include such documents as proposals, schedules, budgets, project plans, and reports.

5.3.1 Document counting

The primitive unit of measure for a document is the page. This is a physical page for hard-copy documents, and a screen or page image for electronically displayed documents. The primary form of the output determines which measure is used.

The document measurement is augmented by reporting the page (or screen) size and the counts of three kinds of tokens: words, ideograms, and graphics. These auxiliary details help to distinguish between different document sizes and densities.

5.3.1.1 Document page count

The document page count is defined to be the total number of nonblank pages contained in a hard-copy document. For documents that are not printed, such as computer displays, a document screen count replaces the document page count.

The document page count is an integer value. Partially filled pages, such as at clause and chapter breaks, are counted as full pages. Blank pages are not counted.

5.3.1.2 Document page size

The page size for the document shall be specified. Both the width and the height dimensions of the document shall be measured in inches or equivalent units. This is the edge-to-edge dimensions, not the margin-to-margin dimensions.

For electronically displayed documents, the screen dimensions shall be specified. The screen width is measured by the average number of characters per line, and the screen height is measured by the number of lines per screen.

5.3.1.3 Document token count

The total number of tokens contained in each document are counted to characterize the document. Three kinds of token counts shall be made: words, ideograms, and graphics. The counting rules for each are as follows:

a) *Number of words*. When counting words in the text, these rules shall apply:
   - All simple words are counted as single words.
   - Contractions, such as *can't*, *won't*, *aren't*, are counted as single words.
   - Numeric values, such as *1234*, *12.34*, and *$1 234 567.89*, are counted as single words.
   - Acronyms, Roman numerals, abbreviations, and hyphenated words are counted as single words.
   - Punctuation marks are ignored.
b) *Number of ideograms*. These are symbols representing ideas rather than words, such as Kanji characters, or equations. When counting ideograms, each type of symbol is counted and reported separately, for example, the number of Kanji characters, and the number of equations.

c) *Number of graphics*. These are the number of graphs, tables, figures, charts, pictures, etc., that are included in the document. When counting graphics, the number of each type of graphic is reported separately, for example, the number of tables, the number of figures, the number of graphs, the number of pictures.

5.3.2 Document attributes

Document attributes define the type, origin, and usage of the documents measured.

5.3.2.1 Document type

Document type is reported with two values: the name of the document and its purpose. The name of the document is the name used by the development organization. The document purpose describes the intention of the document phrased in commonly used terminology.

5.3.2.2 Document origin

The amount of reuse of documents may be specified by the document's percentage reused. This value is computed by dividing the number of tokens in the document that are not modified or added by the total number of tokens in the document. The result is expressed as a percentage of the type of tokens measured. The type of tokens used for calculating the percentage shall be stated. For example, if a document contains 8000 word tokens from the original document that were not modified or added, and the final document size is 10 000 word tokens, then the document would be reported to have a value for the document percentage reused of 80% word tokens (8000/10 000).

5.3.2.3 Document usage

Each document shall be identified as to its usage, delivered or nondelivered. The document usage is delivered if it is provided to the user or to the user's facility. A nondelivered document is one that is not provided to the user.

6. Input primitive

In the productivity relationship for this standard, input represents the effort applied to develop the software product. The principal measure for effort in this standard is labor expressed in units of staff-hour.

6.1 Staff-hour input primitive

Effort shall be measured only in staff-hour units. A staff-hour is an hour of time expended by a member of the staff. The staff-hours collected shall include those directly expended in creating a specific output product for which productivity is calculated.

The accuracy of productivity results depends on how precisely the effort expended to produce an output product is recorded. Recording effort as it is expended is required by this standard.

The staff-hour measure shall include all effort expended on the product, including all overtime hours, both compensated and uncompensated.

Staff-hours are not counted in productivity calculations if they do not directly contribute to the software product. Any time away from the job, such as vacations, holidays, jury duty, and sick leave, are not counted. Also, time expended on something other than the specific product being measured, or time spent on other products or projects is not counted.

Staff-hours may be expressed as larger units for convenience. To express effort in larger units, such as staff-day, staff-month, or staff-year, a conversion factor shall be specified to translate the larger unit into staff-hours. For example, stating results in staff-months, the user would accompany it with a statement similar to "one staff-month = 152 staff-hours for this data."

6.2 Staff-hour attribute

The nature of the effort expended by personnel shall be measured in the following categories:

a) *Direct staff-hour.* The effort expended by those members of the development staff that directly contribute to defining or creating the software product is measured as direct staff-hours. This category should include, but not be limited to, first level supervisors and members of the staff that perform analysis, design, programming, testing, and documentation tasks.
   1) *Direct delivered staff-hour.* All direct staff-hours resulting in the production of output primitives (namely, source statements, function points, or documents) that are delivered to the customer shall be counted as direct delivered staff-hours.
   2) *Direct nondelivered staff-hour.* All direct staff-hours resulting in the production of output primitives (namely, source statements, function points, or documents) that are not delivered to the customer shall be counted as direct nondelivered staff-hours.

b) *Support staff-hour.* The effort expended by those members of the staff who do not directly define or create the software product, but act to assist those who do, shall be collected and recorded as support staff-hours. This category should include, but not be limited to, members of the staff who perform clerical functions or support activities, such as development computer operators or project coordinators. This category also includes those who contribute to the production process but whose efforts are too distributed to allocate their effort directly to a specific product, such as configuration managers and quality assurance personnel.

6.3 Activities

This standard does not specify a standard life cycle, nor does it imply the existence of a standard software life cycle. Users of this software standard shall specify activities of their own life cycle that directly contribute to producing specific output primitives in order to compute the productivity associated with those outputs (see IEEE Std 1074-1991 for life cycle activities). Staff-hours shall be collected and reported for each output primitive by staff-hour attribute.

7. Relationships

This clause describes several types of relationships, using the primitives defined in clauses 5 and 6. These relationships are presented as examples of the way that output and input primitives may be combined. It is left to the users to decide which combinations of primitives are most useful to them.

7.1 Productivity ratios

In this standard, productivity is defined as the ratio of the output product to the input effort that produced it. For a specific product output, such as the number of source statements or the number of document pages, productivity is computed by dividing that product quantity by the effort expended on it.

Productivity is computed using the ratio of output to input for each measured output primitive for which related input effort data is collected. The productivity for product *a*, which has the quantity of output primitive O_a and which required effort E_a to create, is defined by the relationship

$$\text{Productivity}_a = \frac{O_a}{E_a}$$

The ratio's units of measure are those from the dimensions of the primitives used, for example, source statements per staff-hour, or document page count per staff-hour.

All statements of productivity shall be accompanied by information about the characteristics (see clause 8) and about the activities included in the measurement (see IEEE Std 1074-1991).

The usefulness of productivity values depends on the accuracy of the data used to compute them. Here accuracy refers to the level of detail and precision of the data collection process; estimates are not acceptable. Only recording the input effort as it is worked and counting the output produced are acceptable methods for measuring the primitives.

Only the product quantity and the effort expended to build that product should be used in calculating productivity. Any degree of ambiguity introduced in measuring the output product or capturing the effort diminishes the usefulness of the productivity value. For example, consider computing the productivity of a software module when the effort is not specifically recorded for it. If the effort for writing source statements was not recorded separately, but included in the effort of creating documentation for it, the resulting productivity would be the output of source statements divided by the effort for source statements and documentation. This result would be difficult to interpret because the productivity would not be for source statements alone.

7.1.1 Incremental productivity ratios

Productivity shall be computed at the completion of an output product, that is, when the product is delivered to the user. At the point of delivery, the productivity is

$$\text{Final Productivity} = \frac{O_{\text{Final}}}{E_{\text{Final}}}$$

where O_{Final} is the total quantity of the output product being measured, and E_{Final} is the total effort expended in creating it.

This relationship might also be used during the development process prior to delivery to ascertain accumulated productivity results. In this case the output measured is the quantity of the product at that point in the process, and the input is the effort expended in producing that incremental quantity of output.

During development of a product, it may be useful to measure productivity at intervals to assess trends as it progresses toward final productivity. This periodic sampling of productivity is called the incremental productivity and computed by

$$\text{Incremental Productivity} = \frac{O_{tn} - O_{tn-1}}{E_{tn} - E_{tn-1}}$$

where O_{tn} is the output production and E_{tn} is the direct effort for that output expended through time t_n, and O_{tn-1} and E_{tn-1} are the output production and direct effort through some prior time t_{n-1}.

If the incremental productivity is computed at intervals throughout the development process, it may show productivity fluctuations. It is useful to chart the progress of productivity in order to show trends, or to estimate final productivity based on trend patterns from past projects.

7.1.2 Source statement productivity ratios

The source statement output primitives that may be useful in productivity calculations are:

Delivered New SS

Delivered Reused SS

Nondelivered New SS

Nondelivered Reused SS

Nondelivered Deleted SS

where SS stands for logical source statements or physical source statements.

The input primitives used in productivity relationships are:

Direct Delivered Staff-Hour

Direct Nondelivered Staff-Hour

Support Staff-Hour

Ratios of output primitives to input primitives will show various types of productivity results. For example, the productivity for direct delivered source statements may be computed for the output primitives:

Delivered New SS

Delivered Reused SS

by dividing each by the input primitive for

Direct Delivered Staff-Hours

The productivity for direct nondelivered source statements is computed by taking each of the output primitives:

Nondelivered New SS

Nondelivered Reused SS

Nondelivered Deleted SS

and dividing by the input primitive:

Direct Nondelivered Staff-Hours

The differences between software languages are sufficiently great to make cross-language comparisons of productivity difficult. This standard provides a foundation for collecting accurate productivity data. This may make cross-language comparisons possible in the future.

This standard supports only comparing source statement productivity of identical source languages. When attempting to compare the source statement productivity of two software developments, they shall be in the same software programming languages. This means that the productivity computed for a software product development in a third-generation language shall not be directly compared with the productivity for a software product developed in an assembler-level language, nor should it be compared with a different third-generation language.

7.1.3 Function point productivity ratios

The function point output primitive is the number of function points.

The input primitives used in productivity relationships are:

Direct Delivered Staff-Hour

Direct Nondelivered Staff-Hour

Support Staff-Hour

Dividing the number of function points by each of the above input primitives provides different productivity ratios.

7.1.4 Documentation productivity ratios

Documentation is another form of software output, and document outputs are treated similarly to source statement outputs.

The document output primitives are:

Document Page Count or Screen Count

Number of Words

Number of Ideograms

Number of Graphics

The input primitives used for document productivity are:

Direct Delivered Staff-Hour

Direct Nondelivered Staff-Hour

Support Staff-Hour

All of the productivity ratios described for source statements apply analogously for documents.

7.2 Output-to-output ratios

The following clauses describe some output-to-output ratios. Other combinations of output-to-output ratios will provide additional insights into the process being measured.

7.2.1 Source statement output-to-output ratios

Consider the matrix of the source statement origin to usage attributes in table 1.

Table 1—Source statement origin to usage attribute matrix

		USAGE	
		Delivered	Nondelivered
ORIGIN	Developed	New SS (1)	New SS (2)
	Nondeveloped	Reused SS (3)	Reused SS (4)
		Deleted SS* (5)	Deleted SS (6)

*Measurement data for this variable is not collected, since deleted software is not delivered to the user.

Output source statement primitives in the cells of the preceding table combine to form numerous relationships. Some of these are:

The total number of developed source statements:

Developed SS = (1) + (2)

The total number of delivered source statements:

Delivered SS = (1) + (3)

All source statements contributing to the total product:

Total SS = (1) + (2) + (3) + (4)

The total number of source statements not delivered to the user:

Nondelivered SS = (2) + (4) + (6)

The total number of reused source statements:

Reused SS = (3) + (4)

The total number of source statements deleted from the product prior to delivery to the user:

Deleted SS = (6)

The proportion of delivered source statements to the number of source statements in the total output:

$$\frac{\text{Delivered SS}}{\text{Total SS}} = \frac{(1) + (3)}{(1) + (2) + (3) + (4)}$$

The proportion of reuse in the total product:

$$\frac{\text{Reused SS}}{\text{Total SS}} = \frac{(3) + (4)}{(1) + (2) + (3) + (4)}$$

The proportion of delivered source statements that are new:

$$\frac{\text{New}_{\text{Delv}}\ \text{SS}}{\text{Delivered SS}} = \frac{(1)}{(1) + (3)}$$

The proportion of delivered source statements that are reused:

$$\frac{\text{Reused}_{\text{Delv}}\ \text{SS}}{\text{Delivered SS}} = \frac{(3)}{(1) + (3)}$$

The proportion of nondelivered source statements that are reused:

$$\frac{\text{Reused}_{\text{Nondelv}}\ \text{SS}}{\text{Nondelivered SS}} = \frac{(4)}{(2) + (4) + (6)}$$

Ratios of the type attribute values may prove to be useful. Consider the type attribute values for logical source statements:

Executable LSS	(7)
Data Declaration LSS	(8)
Compiler Directive LSS	(9)
Comment LSS	(10)

A ratio of interest might be the executable LSS to the total LSS for a module:

$$\frac{\text{Executable SS}}{\text{Module's Total LSS}} = \frac{(7)}{(7) + (8) + (9) + (10)}$$

Consider similar ratios for the values of the PSS type attribute:

Noncomment PSS	(11)
Comment PSS	(12)

Finally, consider the ratio of comments to the total number of PSS:

$$\frac{\text{Comment PSS}}{\text{Total PSS}} = \frac{(12)}{(11) + 12}$$

7.2.2 Function point output-to-output ratios

Output-to-output ratios are meaningless for the cases where the function point count is a single number. In other cases, ratios similar to those above can be constructed.

7.2.3 Documentation output-to-output ratios

Three document content ratios are computed to describe the density of a document. These ratios help to distinguish high density documents from low density ones:

Number of Words per Page

Number of Ideograms per Page

Number of Graphics per Page

Document usage ratios are equivalent to the source statement usage ratios. Measurement of delivered documents versus nondelivered documents is at the document level; either the document is delivered or it is nondelivered. Measurement of developed versus nondeveloped documents shall be made at the token level; the page level is inadequate due to page break realignments and changes made to tokens.

Document products are developed in tokens, but often are measured in pages or screens. The origin to usage matrix for document pages is shown in table 2. A similar matrix could be made for screens or for each of the individual tokens, namely, words, ideograms, or graphics.

Table 2—Document origin to usage attribute matrix

		USAGE	
		Delivered	Nondelivered
ORIGIN	Developed	New Pages (1)	New Pages (2)
	Nondeveloped	Reused Pages (3)	Reused Pages (4)
		Deleted Pages* (5)	Deleted Pages (6)

*Measurement data for this variable is not collected, since deleted pages are not delivered to the user.

The document output-to-output terminology and ratio definitions are applied at the token level, and are similar to the terminology and ratio definitions described for source statement output-to-output ratios.

7.2.4 Mixed output primitive ratios

Ratios comparing output primitives of different types may provide insight into the software development process. Two possible combinations are shown here for consideration:

$$\frac{\text{Function Points}}{\text{Total Source Statements}} \quad \text{or} \quad \frac{\text{Document Pages}}{\text{Total Source Statements}}$$

7.3 Input-to-input ratios

Ratios of input primitives to input effort primitives provide insights about the effort expended. The input primitives are

Direct Delivered Staff-Hours	(A)
Direct Nondelivered Staff-Hours	(B)
Support Staff-Hours	(C)

Some meaningful combinations with these primitives are

Total Effort = (A) + (B) + (C) and Total Direct Effort = (A) + (B)

The ratio of Direct Effort to Total Effort:

$$\frac{\text{Total Direct Effort}}{\text{Total Effort}} = \frac{(A) + (B)}{(A) + (B) + (C)}$$

The ratio of Support Effort to Total Direct Effort:

$$\frac{\text{Support Effort}}{\text{Total Direct Effort}} = \frac{(C)}{(A) + (B)}$$

The ratio of Direct Delivered to Direct Nondelivered Effort:

$$\frac{\text{Direct Delivered Effort}}{\text{Direct Nondelivered Effort}} = \frac{(A)}{(B)}$$

Many other meaningful combinations are possible. Users of this standard may wish to explore them.

8. Characteristics

Within the context of this document, characteristics are defined as those inherent factors of software development that may have a significant impact on productivity. The purpose of recording measures of characteristics is to ensure consistent comparisons between projects developing software products.

The characteristics are divided into three categories: project characteristics, management characteristics, and product characteristics. Project characteristics describe the people and processes involved in the development effort. Management characteristics describe how a project is managed. Product characteristics reflect the nature of the product itself.

Whenever data is collected to assess software productivity, the characteristics shall be recorded. Comparing productivity data between projects is applicable only if the characteristics are similar. This standard does not attempt to precisely quantify characteristics, but it does require that all characteristics be documented and reported along with productivity data.

Most of the required characteristics data shall be recorded in the early stages of the project. Some data, however, will not be available until the later stages. Characteristics shall be monitored throughout the project and recorded in the characteristics clause as new data is available.

The following is the minimum set of characteristics that shall be recorded.

8.1 Project characteristics

Project characteristics are factors involving the people and the working environment of the development effort. They represent factors that the developer may be able to control or alter. Project characteristic information is recorded in one of two main categories: personnel or software development environment (SDE).

8.1.1 Personnel

The personnel category includes most of the human elements that are involved in a software development project, such as education, experience, expert experience, training, size, and turnover. These personnel characteristics are explained below, and when possible, a metric is included for each characteristic.

8.1.1.1 Education

Education refers to the highest level of education beyond high school.

Level of education:

— No Degree
— Associate's Degree
— Bachelor's Degree
— Master's Degree
— Doctorate Degree

Classify each member of the project team according to the above list. Record this data as an educational profile expressed as a percentage of total team (for example, 10% Associate's, 50% Bachelor's, 30% Master's, 10% Doctorate degrees).

8.1.1.2 Experience

Experience refers to the number of years of relevant experience, and encompasses three aspects:

a) Years of work in software engineering
b) Years of work with specific software applications and technologies relevant to this project (for example, 4GL, graphics, real-time)
c) Years of experience in the organization

Record years of relevant experience as a profile in the three categories for the highest, lowest, and median years (for example, Experience in current job: Highest = 8 yrs, Lowest = <1 yr, Median = 2.5 yrs).

8.1.1.3 Expert assistance

Expert assistance refers to a person, or group of persons, external to the project team who has knowledge and experience in the application being developed by the project team.

Indicate if expert assistance was required on this project. Record expert assistance required as either yes or no.

Indicate if expert assistance was available as needed for this project. Record expert assistance availability as either yes or no.

8.1.1.4 Training

Training refers to all formal professional training. This includes external training courses, such as seminars, and in-house training courses, such as training on company coding standards, software development environment, testing techniques, etc.

Record the average number of days each project employee spends in training per year (for example, an employee receives an average of 6.5 days of training per year).

8.1.1.5 Size

Size refers to the number of direct and support staff involved in the project. Record the number of people on the project at peak and average staff levels.

8.1.1.6 Turnover

Turnover refers to a shift in personnel during a project. Record if turnover was a disruptive factor as either yes or no.

8.1.2 Software development environment

The software development environment (SDE) is the combination of tools, techniques, and administration used during the development. For recording this part of the project characteristics, below is a checklist of the items to be included:

a) On-line documentation with word processing
b) Configuration management techniques and tools
c) Project libraries
d) Formal design techniques
e) Coding standards
f) Format and content standards for documentation
g) Software cost estimation tools
h) Formal project management methods (for example, PERT charts, work breakdown structures, critical path analysis, etc.)
i) Reuse libraries
j) Walkthroughs, code inspections, design reviews, etc.
k) Automated test tools
l) Debugging tools
m) Defect tracking and resolution systems
n) Requirements traceability
o) Other

Record all letters that are used by this project.

8.2 Management characteristics

This clause provides some insight into how the project was managed. The data for this clause should be recorded after the project is completed.

8.2.1 User participation

User participation refers to the level of participation by the user or their representative on the project.

— *High* is user participation in all reviews, as well as commenting on all documentation.
— *Low* is user participation limited to just the start and end of the project.
— *Medium* is all user participation between the levels of *High* and *Low.*
— *N/A* is when user participation is not applicable.

Record the appropriate level of user participation.

8.2.2 Stability of product requirements

Stability of product requirements characterizes the extent that the requirements remained constant throughout development. Record whether instability of product requirements was a disruptive factor as either yes or no.

8.2.3 Constraining factors

Specify the factors that constrained the project. The following is a list of possible constraining factors:

— Fixed cost
— Fixed staff size
— Fixed functionality
— Fixed quality and/or reliability
— Fixed schedule
— Limited accessibility to development system
— Limited accessibility to target system

Record these and any other limiting factors as a checklist (for example, cost, schedule, access to target system).

8.3 Product characteristics

Product characteristics are those factors imposed upon the product. The specific product characteristics that shall be recorded are defined below.

8.3.1 Criticality

The following are product critical characteristics that directly impact productivity.

8.3.1.1 Timing critical

Certain products must work in environments where the real-time behavior, user response, or throughput is critical. Record timing critical as either yes or no.

8.3.1.2 Memory critical

Certain products must fit into a limited amount of memory. Record memory critical as either yes or no.

8.3.1.3 Quality/reliability critical

Certain products must meet very stringent quality or reliability criteria. Record quality/reliability critical as either yes or no.

8.3.2 Degree of innovation

This characteristic represents the technological risk of the project.

0 = Never done before

1 = Previously done by others

2 = Previously done by us

Record the degree of innovation as either 0, 1, or 2.

8.3.3 Complexity

This standard requires a rating for three types of complexities: programming, data, and organizational.

8.3.3.1 Programming complexity

Programming complexity addresses the program control flow of a software product.

— *Low* is straight line code, simple loops and branches, simple calculations.
— *Medium* is simple nesting, simple intermodule communications, moderately difficult calculations.
— *High* is re-entrant/recursive code, data structure control, complex calculations requiring accurate results.

Record programming complexity. Other formal complexity measures may be recorded as well. In this case, the complexity measurement methodology used shall be cited.

8.3.3.2 Data complexity

Data complexity refers to the arrangement, access, and retrieval of stored data.

— *Low* are simple arrays or files in main memory, few inputs/outputs, no restructuring of data.
— *Medium* are multiple inputs/outputs, data typing, restructuring of data, access to other storage media (for example, tape, hard disk, other machines).
— *High* are highly coupled and relational data structures, optimized search algorithms, background data consistency checks.

Record data complexity.

8.3.3.3 Organizational complexity

Organizational complexity refers to the difficulty in coordinating and communicating with all parties on the project team.

SP = Single Person

SD = Single Department/Division

MD = Multiple Departments/Divisions

MS = Multiple Sites

SC = Subcontracted development to third party

Record all levels of organizational complexity that apply (for example, MD, MS).

8.3.4 Development concurrency

Some products require concurrent, that is, parallel development of software (S), hardware (H), and firmware (F).

H-S: hardware and software concurrent

H-F: hardware and firmware concurrent

S-F: software and firmware concurrent

S-S: software and software concurrent

H-S-F: hardware, software, and firmware concurrent

Record which areas were being developed concurrently.

8.3.5 Product description

Provide a brief description of the software application, that is, a brief description of what the product does.

Annexes

(These informative annexes are not a part of IEEE Std 1045-1992, IEEE Standard for Software Productivity Metrics, but are included for information only.)

Annex A
Sample metrics data collection summary list

(informative)

The items listed here are required by the standard. Items inside brackets "[...]" are optional or may be required under special conditions. Numbers in parentheses "(...)" are the clause numbers of this standard that describe that measurement.

A.1 Descriptive fields

This information identifies the source of the measurements.

— Product Name
— Product Release and Version
— Development Organization
— Current Date
— Name of Data Collector

A.2 Software module information (5.1.1)

— Software Module Name
— Software Language

A.3 Type attribute primitives (5.1.2.1)

— Logical Source Statement (LSS) Count:
- Number of Executable LSS
- Number of Data Declarations
- Number of Compiler Directives
- Number of Comments

— Physical Source Statement (PSS) Count:
- Number of Noncomment Lines
- Number of Comment Lines
- Number of Characters per Line (if different from 80 characters per line)
- [Number of Blank Lines]

A.4 Origin attribute source statement primitives (5.1.2)

— Number of Developed Source Statements
— Number of Nondeveloped Source Statements
— Source Statement Counts:
  - Number of Original SS
  - Number of Added SS
  - Number of Modified SS
  - Number of Removed SS

A.5 Usage attribute source statement primitives (5.1.2.3)

— Number of Delivered Source Statements
— Number of Nondelivered Source Statements

A.6 Function point primitives (5.2.1)

— Number of Function Points
— Function Point Algorithm
— Function Types Description
— Function Type Values for Each Function Type

A.7 Documentation primitives (5.3)

— Document Name
— Document Purpose
— Document Usage (delivered or nondelivered)
— Document Medium (hard copy or screen)
— For Hard-Copy Documents:
  - Document Page Count (blank pages not counted)
  - Page Size (edge-to-edge in inches)
— For Electronically Displayed Documents:
  - Document Screen Count
  - Average Number of Screen Characters per Line
  - Lines per Screen
— Number of Words
— Number of Ideograms
— Number of Graphics (list each type separately)
— [Document Percentage Reused (name the token measured)]

A.8 Input primitives by activity category (6.0)

— Activity Name
— Direct Delivered Staff-Hours
— Direct Nondelivered Staff-Hours
— Support Staff-Hours

Annex B
Characteristics data collection form

(informative)

Project Characteristics (8.1)

Personnel

Education	Percent of Project Team Members
No Degree:	______%
Associate's Degree:	______%
Bachelor's Degree:	______%
Master's Degree:	______%
Doctorate Degree:	______%

Experience

1) Years in software engineering:	Highest____	Lowest____	Median____
2) Years in specific s/w technology:	Highest____	Lowest____	Median____
3) Years in organization:	Highest____	Lowest____	Median____

Expert Assistance	Required:	________ YES/NO
	Available:	________ YES/NO
Training	Average:	________ days per year
Size	Peak:	________ number of people
	Average:	________ number of people
Turnover	Disruptive:	________ YES/NO

Software Development Environment: ________, ________, ________, ________

Management Characteristics (8.2)

User Participation		________ H/M/L/NA
Product Requirements Stability	Disruptive:	________ YES/NO
Constraining Factors		________, ________, ________, ________

Product Characteristics (8.3)

Criticality

Timing Critical:	________ YES/NO
Memory Critical:	________ YES/NO
Quality/Reliability Critical:	________ YES/NO

Degree of Innovation: ________ 0/1/2

Complexity

Programming:		________ H/M/L
Data:		________ H/M/L
Organizational:	____, ____, ____	SP/SD/MD/MS/SC (Record all that apply.)

Development Concurrency: ________ H-S/H-F/S-F/S-S/H-S-F

Product Description:____

Annex C Bibliography

(informative)

The following references were used extensively in the development of this standard. Users of this standard may wish to become familiar with these and other software productivity literature to further their understanding of the subject.

[B1] Albrecht, Allan J., and Gaffney, John E., Jr., "Software function, source lines of code, and development effort prediction: a software science validation." *IEEE Transactions on Software Engineering*, vol. SE-9, no. 6, pp. 639–648, Nov. 1983.

[B2] Basili, Victor R., and Weiss, David M., "A methodology for collecting valid software engineering data." *IEEE Transactions on Software Engineering,* vol. SE-10, no. 6, pp. 728–738, Nov. 1984.

[B3] Boehm, Barry W., *Software Engineering Economics,* Prentice Hall, Inc., Englewood Cliffs, NJ, 1981.

[B4] Conte, S. D., Dunsmore, H. E., Shen, V. Y., *Software Engineering Metrics and Models,* Benjamin/Cummings Publishing, Menlo Park, CA, 1986.

[B5] Grady, Robert B., Caswell, Deborah L., *Software Metrics: Establishing a Company-Wide Program,* Prentice Hall, Inc., Englewood Cliffs, NJ, 1987.

[B6] Jones, T. Capers, *Programming Productivity,* McGraw–Hill Book Company, New York, 1986.

[B7] Putnam, Lawrence H., "A general empirical solution to the macro software sizing and estimation problem." *IEEE Transactions on Software Engineering,* vol. SE-4, no. 4, pp. 345–361, Jul. 1978.

Annex D
Software counting relationships

(informative)

Presented here is an example of several relationships among the various categories of source statements included in a software product or application system. Rules relating the counts of each of these categories are also provided.

A new software system may consist of code obtained from an existing one and of new code created specifically for it. The earlier system may be a member of the same family as the new one or may be a member of a different family. Formulas are provided here that relate the source statement counts for the several categories of statements involved in creating a new software system. The formulas and relationships presented apply to both logical and physical statements, with or without comments. However, in any given instance, they are to be applied to only one category of statement (for example, physical statements, without comments). The logical source statement (LSS) count measures the number of software instructions independent of their physical format. It is imperative that LSS counts be accompanied by a description of the way in which they were counted. The physical source statement (PSS) count measures the quantity of software in lines of code.

A system consists of two categories of code: *new* and *reused.* It is expected that the development labor costs for a new application system are to be assigned corresponding to these categories of code. The definitions of *new* and *reused* source statements are as follows:

new source statements: The number of LSS or PSS that were newly created or modified for the application or system.

reused source statements: The number of LSS or PSS incorporated unmodified into the application system. Code that is ported is considered to be reused under the definition here.

When a new system is created in part from an earlier one, some of the statements from the earlier one are deleted. Figure D1 is a Venn diagram that depicts the relationships between the three categories of statements, new, reused, and deleted.

The development of a new software system using some source statements from an existing one employs four types of operations: removal, addition, modification, and reuse of some of the original system's code. The counts of each of the four types of source statements correspond to those operations; removed (re), added (a), modified (m), and reused original (o); are elements of the counts for the more general categories, new (n), reused (r), and deleted (d), related as shown in figure D1.

a) new = added + modified or, $n = a + m$
b) deleted = modified + removed or, $d = m + re$
c) reused = original – deleted or, $r = o - m - re$

Note that *removed* means physically removed. If a source statement is changed in any way, it is called *modified.* Hence, the count of *new* statements is the sum of the *added* and the *modified* counts. Figure D2 is a Venn diagram that depicts the relationships between the sets of source statements of the different categories cited above. It shows the components of the new, reused, and deleted categories depicted in figure D1.

The formulas given above are for the special case of modifying one system to produce another. Note that the generalization works well, that is, incorporating code from several *original systems* into a *new* one. However, it is necessary to carefully define the quantities appropriately when doing so.

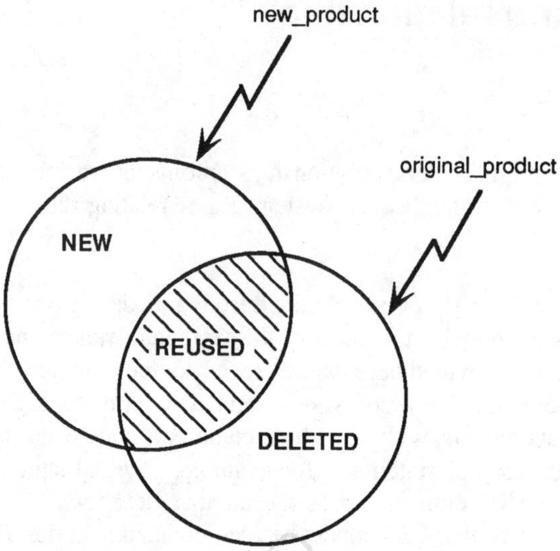

Figure D1—Statement relations

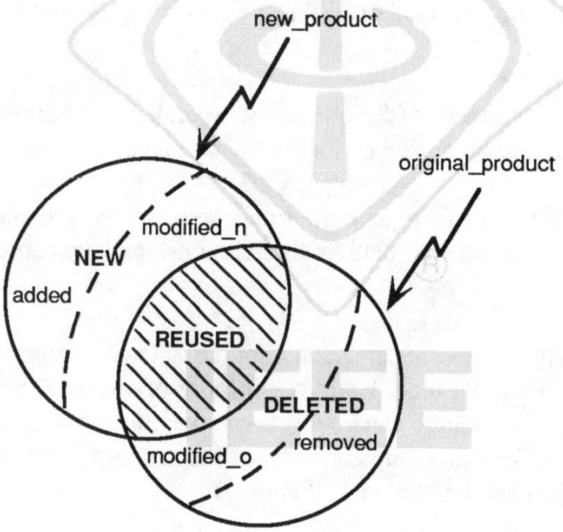

new_file = new ∪ reused

old_file = reused ∪ deleted

diff_file = new ∪ deleted

new = added ∪ modified_n

deleted = removed ∪ modified_o

NOTE—SS_count(modified_n) = SS_count(modified_o); that is both of these sets are the same size.

Figure D2—Detailed statement relations

Suppose there are three files of source corresponding to the original system (old_file), the new system (new_file), and the difference between the two (diff_file). The (diff_file) is the set of elements not found in both the (new_file) and the (old_file). The Venn diagram in figure D2 shows them to be the *new* and *deleted* elements. The counts indicated below show this. The counts of the reused source (r), the new source (n), and the deleted source (d), as defined above, can be obtained very simply from the counts of the three files. Let c() mean *count of*. Then the following relationships exist:

a) c(old_file) = reused + deleted = r + d.
   By the formulas given above,
   c(old_file) = (o – m – re) + (m + re) = o.

b) c(diff_file) = new + deleted = n + d.
   By the formulas given above,
   c(diff_file) = (a + m) + (m + re) = a + 2m + re

c) c(new_file) = reused + new = r + n.
   By the formulas given above,
   c(new_file) = (o – m – re) + (a + m) = a + o – re.

Observe that the diff_file count, c(diff_file), includes a factor 2m, twice the number of the modified source statements. The reason for this can be understood by considering the Venn diagram in figure D2. There are actually two sets of *modified* statements, both of size m. The first set is in the original system. The statements in that set are modified or transformed into a somewhat different set of statements in the new system. Note that the original or *old* system may have some statements in it that will be modified or changed and become *new* statements in the new system.

The counts for reused (r), new (n), and deleted (d) statements, as defined above, can be obtained from the counts for the old_file, the diff_file, and the new_file, as now shown. Verifications of the correctness of the formulas are also provided. The formulas are as follows:

a) ((c(old_file) + c(new_file)) – c(diff_file))/2 = r
   Verification; ((r + d + r + n) – (n + d))/2 = r,
   or, ((o + (a + o – re)) – (a + 2m + re))/2 = (2o – 2m – 2re)/2 = o – m – re = r,
   by definition.

b) c(new_file) – r = n
   Verification; (r + n) – r = n
   or, (a + o – re) – (o – m – re) = a + m = n,
   by definition.

c) c(old_file) – r = d
   Verification; (r + d) – r = d
   or, (o – (o – m – re)) = m + re = d,
   by definition.

An example is now provided for applying of the counting rules presented above. In it, a new module is created using some statements obtained from another module developed earlier. The counts for the various categories of statements involved are:

Statement Category	Statement Count
Original module size (o):	100
Statements modified (m):	7

Statements added (a): 3

Statements removed (re): 2

Therefore:

Statements reused = r = o – m – re = 100 – 7 – 2 = 91

Statements new = n = a + m = 3 + 7 = 10

Statements deleted = d = m + re = 7 + 2 = 9.

Consequently, the total product size, which is the sum of the new and the reused statements, is

10 + 91 = 101

The counts of the new (n), reused (r), and deleted statements (d), can be determined very simply using the relationships presented by the three equations in the text immediately preceding this example. Suppose the statement counts for the old_file, the new_file, and the diff_file were as follows:

a) c(old_file) = 100

b) c(new_file) = 101

c) c(diff_file) = 19

Then the desired counts can be determined as follows:

a) count of reused,
r = (c(old_file) + c(new_file) – c(diff_file))/2 = (100 + 101 – 19)/2 = 91.

b) count of new,
n = c(new_file) – r = 101 – 91 = 10.

c) count of deleted,
d = c(old_file) – r = 100 – 91 = 9.

These values are the same as those derived earlier in the example from the counts for modified, added, original, and removed, demonstrating the correctness of the calculations used to obtain them. The example illustrates the simplicity of calculating the number of new, reused, and deleted statements from the counts of the statements in the three files.

ANSI/IEEE
Std 1058.1-1987

An American National Standard

IEEE Standard for Software Project Management Plans

Sponsor

Software Engineering Standards Subcommittee of the Technical Committee on Software Engineering of the IEEE Computer Society

Approved December 10, 1987

IEEE Standards Board

Approved October 6, 1988

American National Standards Institute

The Institute of Electrical and Electronics Engineers, Inc
345 East 47th Street, New York, NY 10017, USA

IEEE Standards documents are developed within the Technical Committees of the IEEE Societies and the Standards Coordinating Committees of the IEEE Standards Board. Members of the committees serve voluntarily and without compensation. They are not necessarily members of the Institute. The standards developed within IEEE represent a consensus of the broad expertise on the subject within the Institute as well as those activities outside of IEEE which have expressed an interest in participating in the development of the standard.

Use of an IEEE Standard is wholly voluntary. The existence of an IEEE Standard does not imply that there are no other ways to produce, test, measure, purchase, market, or provide other goods and services related to the scope of the IEEE Standard. Furthermore, the viewpoint expressed at the time a standard is approved and issued is subject to change brought about through developments in the state of the art and comments received from users of the standard. Every IEEE Standard is subjected to review at least every five years for revision or reaffirmation. When a document is more than five years old, and has not been reaffirmed, it is reasonable to conclude that its contents, although still of some value, do not wholly reflect the present state of the art. Users are cautioned to check to determine that they have the latest edition of any IEEE Standard.

Comments for revision of IEEE Standards are welcome from any interested party, regardless of membership affiliation with IEEE. Suggestions for changes in documents should be in the form of a proposed change of text, together with appropriate supporting comments.

Interpretations: Occasionally questions may arise regarding the meaning of portions of standards as they relate to specific applications. When the need for interpretations is brought to the attention of IEEE, the Institute will initiate action to prepare appropriate responses. Since IEEE Standards represent a consensus of all concerned interests, it is important to ensure that any interpretation has also received the concurrence of a balance of interests. For this reason IEEE and the members of its technical committees are not able to provide an instant response to interpretation requests except in those cases where the matter has previously received formal consideration.

Comments on standards and requests for interpretations should be addressed to:

Secretary, IEEE Standards Board
345 East 47th Street
New York, NY 10017
USA

Foreword

(This Foreword is not a part of IEEE Std 1058.1-1987, IEEE Standard for Software Project Management Plans.)

Purpose

This standard specifies the format and contents of software project management plans. It does not specify the exact techniques to be used in developing project plans, nor does it provide examples of project management plans. Each organization that uses this standard should develop a set of practices and procedures to provide detailed guidance for preparing and updating software project management plans based on this standard. These detailed practices and procedures should take into account the environmental, organizational, and political factors that influence application of the standard.

Not all software projects are concerned with development of source code for a new software product. Some software projects consist of a feasibility study and definition of product requirements. Other projects terminate upon completion of product design, and some projects are concerned with major modifications to existing software products. This standard is applicable to all types of software projects; applicability is not limited to projects that develop operational versions of new products. Application of this standard is not limited by project size. Small projects may require less formality in planning than large projects, but all components of this standard should be addressed by every software project.

Software projects are sometimes component parts of larger projects. In these cases, the software project management plan may be a separate component of a larger plan or it may be merged into the system level project management plan.

Overview

This standard contains three sections. Section 1 defines the scope of the standard and provides references to other IEEE standards that should be followed when applying this standard. Section 2 provides definitions of terms that are used throughout the standard. Section 3 contains an overview and a detailed specification of the standard, including required components that must be included, and optional components that may be included in project plans based on this standard. The sequence of project plan elements presented in Section 3 does not imply that project plans should be developed in the order of presentation. In most instances, project plans based on this standard will be developed by repeated iteration and refinement of the various elements in the plan.

Audience

This standard is intended for use by software project managers and other personnel who prepare and update project plans and monitor adherence to those plans.

Evolution of Plans

Developing the initial version of the software project management plan should be one of the first activities to be completed on a software project. As the project evolves, the nature of the work to be done and the decomposition of work will be better understood. The project management plan must be updated periodically to reflect the evolving situation. Thus, each version of the plan should be placed under change control, and each version should contain a schedule for subsequent updates to the plan.

Terminology

This standard follows the IEEE Guide to Standards Development. In particular, the words shall, must, and the imperative form identify mandatory material within the standard. The words should, might, and may identify optional material.

History

The project authorization request for development of this standard was approved by the IEEE Standards Board on December 13, 1984. Modification of the authorization request was approved in September, 1986. Ten meetings were held within the United States and internationally between September, 1984, and September, 1986. These meetings produced the draft submitted for balloting in December, 1986.

Contributors

This standard was developed by the Software Project Management Plans Working Group of the Software Engineering Standards Subcommittee of the Computer Society of the IEEE. The following individuals contributed to the development of this standard:

Richard H. Thayer, *Chairman*
Richard E. Fairley, *Co-Chairman*
Gary L. Whitten, *Secretary*

Steering Committee

Ronald L. Atchley
H. Jack Barnard
François Coallier
Hosein Fallah
Richard Johansson
Kari Kansala
Robert F. Metz
Patrick A. Rich
Hans Schaefer

Working Group

Bakul Banerju
George J. Bozoki
V. Churchill
Peter Coad
P. I. Davis
Raymond Day
T. Debling
J. Deleo
Ake Dovstram
R. Ferreol
Galwin Ferwin
Cheng Hu
John A. King
Thomas M. Kurihara
F. C. Lim
Richard W. MacDonald
Roger Martin
Randy Paddock
Francoise Perrodeau
Robert Poston
David Schultz
Robert Shillato
Daniel Solis
George Spidel
Richard Van Tilburg
Delores Wallace
David Weiss
Lauri Werth
Janusz Zalweski

Supporting Organizations

The following organizations provided support for development of this standard:

AT&T Bell Laboratories
AT&T Information Systems
Bell Canada
California State University, Sacramento
Center for Industrial Research, Norway
Compagnie D'Informatique Militaire, France
Computer Sciences Corporation
Goodyear Atomic Corporation
Hughes Aircraft Company
Institute of Atomic Energy, Poland
Intercon Systems Corporation
Lockheed Missiles & Space Co.
Mirror Systems, Inc.
National Bureau of Standards
NCR Corporation
Programming Environments, Inc.
Standard Telecommunications Labs
System Development Corporation
Technical Research Centre of Finland
Teleindustrier AB, Sweden
U.S. Department of Commerce
U.S. Department of Transportation
U.S. Naval Research Laboratories
University of Nevada, Las Vegas
University of Texas, Austin
Wang Institute of Graduate Studies

The Software Engineering Standards Subcommittee comprised the balloting committee that approved this document for submission to the IEEE Standards Board, and at the time of balloting was composed of the following persons:

A. F. Ackerman
Richard L. Aurbach
Motoei Azuma
H. J. Barnard
J. Behm
H. Ronald Berlack
Michael A. Blackledge
Giles Bracon
J. Joseph Brandt
Kathleen L. Briggs
A. Winsor Brown
F. Buckley
L. J. Call
H. Carl
John W. Center
John Chihorek
T. S. Chow
J. K. Chung
Won L. Chung
Antonio M. Cicu
Judith Clapp
Peter Coad, Jr.
François Coallier
Christopher M. Cooke
Richard Cotter
T. Daughtrey
Peter Denny
F. M. Discenzo
David A. Dobraiz
David Doty
Einar Dragstedt
William Dupres
Albert D. DuRee
Mary Eads
L. E. Egan
W. D. Ehrenberger
Steven R. Eisen
Walter Ellis
Caroline Evans
Richard E. Fairley
David W. Favor
Joan Feld
John Fendrich
Glenn S. Fields
Violet Foldes
T. Foote-Lennox
Joel Forman
Julian Forster
Richard C. Fries
F. K. Gardner
L. B. Gardner
David Gilperin
Shirley Gloss-Soler
J. G. Glynn
Andrej Grebenc
Victor Guarnera
Lawrence M. Gunther
David A. Gustafson
J. A. Haksi
Jeffrey Hickey
John W. Horch
Cheng Hu
Laurel V. Kaleda
Harry Kalmbach
Daniel E. Klingler
Shaye Koenig
Joseph A. Krupinski
Joan Kundig
T. Kurihara
Lak Ming Lam
John B. Lane
Robert A. C. Lane
G. Larsen
F. C. Lim
Bertil Lindberg
B. Livson
Austin Maher
Paulo Cesar Marcondes
Nicholas Marselos
Roger Martin
John McArdle
J. A. McCall
R. McDowell
Manijeh Moghis
Charles S. Mooney
Gary D. Moorhead
D. D. Morton
G. T. Morun
Hiranobu Nagano
Geraldine Neidhart
Dennis Nickle
Wilma M. Osborne
Michael T. Perkins
W. E. Perry
John Petraglia
Donald J. Pfeiffer
I. C. Pyle
Thomas S. Radi
Salim Ramji
Jean-Claude Rault
Meir Razy
Donald Reifer
Patrick A. Rich
R. San Roman
John C. Rowe
Margaret Rumley
Julio G. Sanz
Steven Schach
Wolf A. Schnoege
Norman Schneidewind
David Schultz
Gregory D. Schumacker
Leonard W. Seagren
Gerard P. Shabe
Robert Shillato
David Siefert
William J. Singer
Jacob Slonim
H. M. Sneed
V. Srinivas
G. Wayne Staley
Franklin M. Sterling
Mary Jane Stoughton
W. G. Sutcliffe
Michael H. Taint
Richard H. Thayer
Paul U. Thompson
Terrence L. Tillmans
Valentin Tirman
G. R. Trebble
C. L. Troyanowski
William S. Turner, III
Robert Urling
David Usechak
Thomas E. Vollman
Dolores R. Wallace
John P. Walter
Dale R. Webdale
Charles J. Wertz
Peter J. Weyman
Allan Whitaker
Gary L. Whitten
Andrea S. Williams
Patrick J. Wilson
W. Martin Wong
Dennis L. Wood
Paul R. Work
Nancy Yavne
Natalie C. Yopronka
Leon Young
Donald Zelenu
Hugh Zettel
Peter Zoll

Contents

IEEE

IEEE Standard for Software Project Management Plans

1. Scope and References

1.1 Scope. This standard prescribes the format and content of software project management plans. A software project management plan is the controlling document for managing a software project; it defines the technical and managerial processes necessary to satisfy the project requirements.

This standard may be applied to all types of software projects. Use of this standard is not restricted by the size, complexity, or criticality of the software product. This standard is applicable to all forms of product delivery media, including firmware, embedded systems code, programmable logic arrays, and software-in-silicon. This standard can be applied to any and all segments of a software product lifecycle.

This standard identifies the minimal set of elements that shall appear in all software project management plans. In order to conform to this standard, software project management plans must adhere to the format and content for project plans specified in the standard. However, users of this standard may incorporate other elements by appending additional sections or subsections to their project management plans. In any case, the numbering scheme of the required sections and subsections must adhere to the format specified in this standard. Various sections and subsections of a software project management plan may be included in the plan by direct incorporation or by reference to other plans and documents.

This standard for software project management plans incorporates and subsumes the software development plans described in ANSI/IEEE Std 729-1983 [1][1] and ANSI/IEEE Std 730-1984 [2].

[1]The numbers in brackets correspond to those of the references in 1.2.

1.2 References. The standards listed here should be consulted when applying this standard. The latest revisions shall apply.

[1] ANSI/IEEE Std 729-1983, IEEE Standard Glossary of Software Engineering Terminology.[2]

[2] ANSI/IEEE Std 730-1984, IEEE Standard for Software Quality Assurance Plans.

[3] ANSI/IEEE Std 828-1983, IEEE Standard for Software Configuration Management Plans.

[4] ANSI/IEEE Std 829-1983, IEEE Standard for Software Test Documentation.

[5] ANSI/IEEE Std 983-1986, IEEE Guide for Software Quality Assurance Planning.

[6] ANSI/IEEE Std 1012-1986, IEEE Standard for Software Verification and Validation Plans.

2. Definitions

The definitions listed here establish meanings within the context of this standard. Definitions of other terms that may be appropriate within the context of this standard can be found in ANSI/IEEE Std 729-1983 [1].

activity. A major unit of work to be completed in achieving the objectives of a software project. An activity has precise starting and ending dates, incorporates a set of tasks to be completed, consumes resources, and results in work products. An activity may contain other activities in a hierarchical manner.

[2]ANSI/IEEE publications are available from the Sales Department, American National Standards Institute, 1430 Broadway, New York, NY 10018; or from the IEEE Service Center, 445 Hoes Lane, P.O. Box 1331, Piscataway, NJ 08855-1331.

baseline. A work product that has been formally reviewed and agreed upon, and that can be changed only through formal change control procedures. A baseline work product may form the basis for further work activity(s).

customer. The individual or organization that specifies and accepts the project deliverables. The customer may be internal or external to the parent organization of the project, and may or may not be the end user of the software product. A financial transaction between customer and developer is not necessarily implied.

project agreement. A document or set of documents agreed to by the designated authority for the project and the customer. Documents in a project agreement may include some or all of the following: a contract, a statement of work, system engineering specifications, user requirement specifications, functional specifications, the software project management plan, a business plan, or a project charter.

project deliverables. The work product(s) to be delivered to the customer. The quantities, delivery dates, and delivery locations are specified in the project agreement.

project function. An activity that spans the entire duration of a software project. Examples of project functions include project management, configuration management, quality assurance, and verification and validation.

review. A meeting at which a work product or a set of work products is presented to project personnel, managers, users, customers, or other interested parties for comment or approval.

software project. The set of all project functions, activities, and tasks, both technical and managerial, required to satisfy the terms and conditions of the project agreement. A software project may be self-contained or may be part of a larger project. A software project may span only a portion of the software product lifecycle.

software project management. The process of planning, organizing, staffing, monitoring, controlling, and leading a software project.

software project management plan. The controlling document for managing a software project. A software project management plan defines the technical and managerial project functions, activities, and tasks necessary to satisfy the requirements of a software project, as defined in the project agreement.

SPMP. Software project management plan.

task. The smallest unit of work subject to management accountability. A task is a well-defined work assignment for one or more project members. The specification of work to be accomplished in completing a task is documented in a work package. Related tasks are usually grouped to form activities.

work package. A specification for the work to be accomplished in completing an activity or task. A work package defines the work product(s), the staffing requirements, the expected duration, the resources to be used, the acceptance criteria for the work products, the name of the responsible individual, and any special considerations for the work.

work product. Any tangible item that results from a project function, activity, or task. Examples of work products include customer requirements, project plan, functional specifications, design documents, source and object code, users' manuals, installation instructions, test plans, maintenance procedures, meeting minutes, schedules, budgets, and problem reports. Some subset of the work products will form the set of project deliverables.

3. Software Project Management Plans

The individual or organization responsible for a software project shall also be responsible for the software project management plan (hereafter referred to as the SPMP). This section of the standard describes each of the essential elements of a SPMP. These elements shall be ordered in the sequence of sections and subsections prescribed in Table 1.

Table 1
Software Project Management Plan Format

Title Page
Revision Chart
Preface
Table of Contents
List of Figures
List of Tables

1. Introduction
   1.1 Project Overview
   1.2 Project Deliverables
   1.3 Evolution of the SPMP
   1.4 Reference Materials
   1.5 Definitions and Acronyms

2. Project Organization
   2.1 Process Model
   2.2 Organizational Structure
   2.3 Organizational Boundaries and Interfaces
   2.4 Project Responsibilities

3. Managerial Process
   3.1 Management Objectives and Priorities
   3.2 Assumptions, Dependencies, and Constraints
   3.3 Risk Management
   3.4 Monitoring and Controlling Mechanisms
   3.5 Staffing Plan

4. Technical Process
   4.1 Methods, Tools, and Techniques
   4.2 Software Documentation
   4.3 Project Support Functions

5. Work Packages, Schedule, and Budget
   5.1 Work Packages
   5.2 Dependencies
   5.3 Resource Requirements
   5.4 Budget and Resource Allocation
   5.5 Schedule

Additional Components

Index

Appendices

The ordering of SPMP elements presented in Table 1 is not meant to imply that the sections and subsections must be developed in that order. The order of presentation is intended for ease of use, not as a guide to the order of preparing the various elements of a SPMP. The sections and subsections of a SPMP may be included by direct incorporation or by reference to other plans and documents.

Detailed descriptions of each section and subsection in a SPMP are presented in sections 3.1 through 3.5 of this standard. Certain additional components may be included in a SPMP. Additional components are described in section 3.6.

Each version of a SPMP based on this standard shall contain a title and a revision notice sufficient to uniquely identify the document. Revision information may include the project name, version number of the plan, date of release, approval signature(s), a list of pages that have been changed in the current version of the plan, and a list of version numbers and dates of release of all previous versions of the plan.

The preface of a SPMP based on this standard shall describe the purpose, indicate the scope of activities, and identify the intended audience for the SPMP. A Table of Contents, and lists of the Figures and Tables in the SPMP shall be included in every SPMP, as indicated in Table 1.

3.1 Introduction (Section 1 of the SPMP). This section of the SPMP shall provide an overview of the project and the product, a list of project deliverables, the plan for development and evolution of the SPMP, reference materials for the SPMP, and definitions and acronyms used within the SPMP.

3.1.1 Project Overview (1.1 of the SPMP). This subsection of the SPMP shall provide a concise summary of the project objectives, the product to be delivered, major work activities, major work products, major milestones, required resources, and master schedule and budget. The project overview shall also describe the relationship of this project to other projects, as appropriate. This overview shall not be construed as an official statement of product requirements. Reference to the official statement of product requirements shall be provided in this subsection of the SPMP.

3.1.2 Project Deliverables (1.2 of the SPMP). This subsection of the SPMP shall list all of the items to be delivered to the customer, the delivery dates, delivery locations, and quantities required to satisfy the terms of the project agreement. This list of project deliverables shall not be construed as an official statement of project requirements.

3.1.3 Evolution of the SPMP (1.3 of the SPMP). This subsection of thc SPMP shall specify the plans for producing both scheduled and unscheduled updates to the SPMP. Methods of disseminating the updates shall be specified. This subsection shall also specify the mechanisms used to place the initial version of the SPMP under change control and to control subsequent changes to the SPMP.

3.1.4 Reference Materials (1.4 of the SPMP). This subsection of the SPMP shall provide a complete list of all documents and other sources of information referenced in the SPMP. Each document should be identified by title, report number, date, author, and publishing organization. Other sources of information, such as electronic files, shall be identified in an unambiguous manner using identifiers such as date and version number. Any deviations from referenced standards or policies shall be identified and justifications shall be provided.

3.1.5 Definitions and Acronyms (1.5 of the SPMP). This subsection of the SPMP shall define, or provide references to the definition of all terms and acronyms required to properly interpret the SPMP.

3.2 Project Organization (Section 2 of the SPMP). This section of the SPMP shall specify the process model for the project, describe the project organizational structure, identify organizational boundaries and interfaces, and define individual responsibilities for the various project elements.

3.2.1 Process Model (2.1 of the SPMP). This subsection of the SPMP shall define the relationships among major project functions and activities by specifying the timing of major milestones, baselines, reviews, work products, project deliverables, and sign-offs that span the project. The process model may be described using a combination of graphical and textual notations. The process model must include project initiation and project termination activities.

3.2.2 Organizational Structure (2.2 of the SPMP). This subsection of the SPMP shall describe the internal management structure of the project. Graphical devices such as hierarchical organization charts or matrix diagrams may be used to depict the lines of authority, responsibility, and communication within the project.

3.2.3 Organizational Boundaries and Interfaces (2.3 of the SPMP). This subsection of the SPMP shall describe the administrative and managerial boundaries between the project and each of the following entities: the parent organization, the customer organization, subcontracted organizations, or any other organizational entities that interact with the project. In addition, the administrative and managerial interfaces of the project support functions, such as configuration management, quality assurance, and verification and validation shall be specified in this subsection.

3.2.4 Project Responsibilities (2.4 of the SPMP). This subsection of the SPMP shall identify and state the nature of each major project function and activity, and identify the individuals who are responsible for those functions and activities. A matrix of functions and activities versus responsible individuals may be used to depict project responsibilities.

3.3 Managerial Process (Section 3 of the SPMP). This section of the SPMP shall specify management objectives and priorities; project assumptions, dependencies, and constraints; risk management techniques; monitoring and controlling mechanisms to be used; and the staffing plan.

3.3.1 Management Objectives and Priorities (3.1 of the SPMP). This subsection of the SPMP shall describe the philosophy, goals, and priorities for management activities during the project. Topics to be specified may include, but are not limited to, the frequency and mechanisms of reporting to be used; the relative priorities among requirements, schedule, and budget for this project; risk management procedures to be followed; and a statement of intent to acquire, modify, or use existing software.

3.3.2 Assumptions, Dependencies, and Constraints (3.2 of the SPMP). This subsection of the SPMP shall state the assumptions on which the project is based, the external events the project is dependent upon, and the constraints under which the project is to be conducted.

3.3.3 Risk Management (3.3 of the SPMP). This subsection of the SPMP shall identify and assess the risk factors associated with the project. This subsection shall also prescribe mechanisms for tracking the various risk factors and implementing contingency plans. Risk factors that should be considered include contractual risks, technological risks, risks due to size and complexity of the product, risks in personnel acquisition and retention, and risks in achieving customer acceptance of the product.

3.3.4 Monitoring and Controlling Mechanisms (3.4 of the SPMP). This subsection of the SPMP shall define the reporting mechanisms, report formats, information flows, review and audit mechanisms, and other tools and techniques to be used in monitoring and controlling adherence to the SPMP. Project monitoring should occur at the level of work packages. The relationship of monitoring and controlling mechanisms to the project support functions shall be delineated in this subsection of the SPMP (see 3.4.3).

3.3.5 Staffing Plan (3.5 of the SPMP). This subsection of the SPMP shall specify the numbers and types of personnel required to conduct the project. Required skill levels, start times, duration of need, and methods for obtaining, training, retaining, and phasing out of personnel shall be specified.

3.4 Technical Process (Section 4 of the SPMP). This section of the SPMP shall specify the technical methods, tools, and techniques to be used on the project. In addition, the plan for software documentation shall be specified, and plans for project support functions such as quality assurance, configuration management, and verification and validation may be specified.

3.4.1 Methods, Tools, and Techniques (4.1 of the SPMP). This subsection of the SPMP shall specify the computing system(s), development methodology(s), team structure(s), programming language(s), and other notations, tools, techniques, and methods to be used to specify, design, build, test, integrate, document, deliver, modify or maintain or both (as appropriate) the project deliverables. In addition, the technical standards, policies, and procedures governing development or modification or both of the work products and project deliverables shall be included, either directly or by reference to other documents.

3.4.2 Software Documentation (4.2 of the SPMP). This subsection of the SPMP shall contain either directly or by reference, the documentation plan for the software project. The documentation plan shall specify the documentation requirements, and the milestones, baselines, reviews, and sign-offs for software documentation. The documentation plan may also contain a style guide, naming conventions and documentation formats. The documentation plan shall provide a summary of the schedule and resource requirements for the documentation effort. ANSI/IEEE Std 829-1983 [4] provides a standard for software test documentation.

3.4.3 Project Support Functions (4.3 of the SPMP). This subsection of the SPMP shall contain, either directly or by reference, plans for the supporting functions for the software project. These functions may include, but are not limited to, configuration management [3]; software quality assurance [2] and [5]; and verification and validation [6]. Plans for project support functions shall be developed to a level of detail consistent with the other sections of the SPMP. In particular, the responsibilities, resource requirements, schedules, and budgets for each supporting function shall be specified. The nature and type of support functions required will vary from project to project; however, the absence of a software quality assurance, configuration management, or verification and validation plan shall be explicitly justified in project plans that do not include them.

3.5 Work Packages, Schedule, and Budget (Section 5 of the SPMP). This section of the SPMP shall specify the work packages, identify the dependency relationships among them, state the resource requirements, provide the allocation of budget and resources to work packages, and establish a project schedule.

3.5.1 Work Packages (5.1 of the SPMP). This subsection of the SPMP shall specify the work packages for the activities and tasks that must be completed in order to satisfy the project agreement. Each work package shall be uniquely identified; identification may be based on a numbering scheme and descriptive titles. A diagram depicting the breakdown of activities into subactivities and tasks (a work breakdown structure) may be used to depict hierarchical relationships among work packages.

3.5.2 Dependencies (5.2 of the SPMP). This subsection of the SPMP shall specify the ordering relations among work packages to account for interdependencies among them and dependencies on external events. Techniques such as dependency lists, activity networks, and the critical path method may be used to depict dependencies among work packages.

3.5.3 Resource Requirements (5.3 of the SPMP). This subsection of the SPMP shall provide, as a function of time, estimates of the total resources required to complete the project. Numbers and types of personnel, computer time, support software, computer hardware, office and laboratory facilities, travel, and maintenance requirements for the project resources are typical resources that should be specified.

3.5.4 Budget and Resource Allocation (5.4 of the SPMP). This subsection of the SPMP shall specify the allocation of budget and resources to the various project functions, activities, and tasks. An earned value scheme may be used to allocate budget and resources, and to track expenditures and resource utilization.

3.5.5 Schedule (5.5 of the SPMP). This subsection of the SPMP shall provide the schedule for the various project functions, activities, and tasks, taking into account the precedence relations and the required milestone dates. Schedules may be expressed in absolute calendar time or in increments relative to a key project milestone.

3.6 Additional Components. Certain additional components may be required. These may be included by appending additional sections or subsections to the SPMP. However, the numbering scheme for the required sections and subsections must adhere to the format specified in this standard. Additional items of importance on any particular project may include subcontractor management plans, security plans, independent verification and validation plans, training plans, hardware procurement plans, facilities plans, installation plans, data conversion plans, system transition plans, or the product maintenance plan. If present, additional components must be developed in a format and to a level of detail consistent with the required sections of the SPMP.

3.6.1 Index. An index to the key terms and acronyms used throughout the SPMP is optional, but recommended to improve usability of the SPMP.

3.6.2 Appendices. Appendices may be included, either directly or by reference, to provide supporting details that could detract from the SPMP if included in the body of the SPMP.

IEEE Standard for a Software Metrics Methodology

Sponsor

Software Engineering Standards Subcommittee of the Technical Committee on Software Engineering of the IEEE Computer Society

Approved December 3, 1992

IEEE Standards Board

The Institute of Electrical and Electronics Engineers, Inc.
345 East 47th Street, New York, NY 10017-2394, USA

P-1061/D24

Draft - May 1, 1992

Standard for a
Software Quality Metrics Methodology

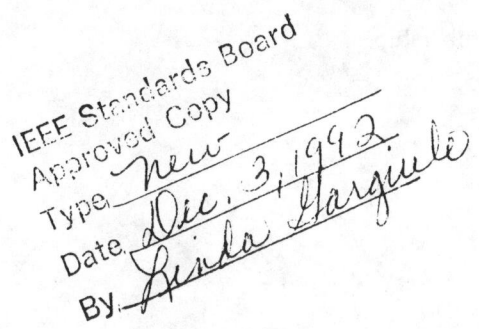

Sponsor
Software Engineering Standards Subcommittee
of the
IEEE Computer Society

The Working Group that developed this Standard had the following membership:

Chairman: Norman Schneidewind
Vice Chairman: George Klammer
Editors: Chris Baldwin, Elizabeth Banks
Secretaries: Ron Braun, Craig Fuget

Martha Amis
James Anderson
Nelson Andrews
John Bowen
Fletcher Buckley
S.C. Chang
David Classick
Taz Daughtrey
Raymond Day
Deborah De Toma
Rose Der
James Dinkey
Ruth Euler
Michael Evangelist
David Favor
Violet Foldes
Al Freund
Oscar Garcia
John Girard
Randy Greene
Warren Harrison
Clark Hay
Dan Hocking
Meinhard Hoffmann
Robert Holibaugh
John Horch
Bud Jones
William Junk
Maria Kaufmann
Thomas Kurihara
Hal Larson
Philip Marriott
Denis Meredith
Mary Mikhail
Celia Modell
Jai Navlakha
Wilma Osborne
Art Price
Horst Richter
Carl Seddio
Raghu Singh
Karen Snow
William Turner
John Walker
Gene Walters
Paul Wolfgang

Contents

Figures

Tables

1.0 Introduction

1.1 Scope

This standard provides a methodology for establishing quality requirements and identifying, implementing, analyzing and validating process and product software quality metrics. This methodology applies to all software at all phases of any software life cycle structure. Sections 1 through 4 provide scope, definitions and background information on which the standard is based; all portions of Section 5 are mandatory. Appendices A through D are included for illustrative and reference purposes only.

This standard does not prescribe specific metrics. However, the appendices include examples of metrics together with a complete example of the use of this standard.

1.2 Audience

This standard is intended for those associated with the acquisition, development, use, support, maintenance or audit of software. The standard is particularly aimed at those measuring or assessing the quality of software.

This standard can be used by:

- An acquisition/project manager to identify, define and prioritize the quality requirements for a system
- A system developer to identify specific traits that should be built into the software in order to meet the quality requirements
- A quality assurance/control/audit organization and a system developer to evaluate whether the quality requirements are being met
- A system maintainer to assist in change management during product evolution
- A user to assist in specifying the quality requirements for a system

2.0 Definitions

critical range metric values used to classify software into categories of acceptable, marginal and unacceptable

critical value metric value of a validated metric which is used to identify software which has unacceptable quality

direct metric a metric applied during development or during operations that represents a software quality factor (e.g., mean time to software failure for the factor reliability)

factor sample a set of factor values which is drawn from the metrics data base and used in metrics validation

factor value a value (see metric value) of the direct metric that represents a factor

measure to ascertain or appraise by comparing to a standard; to apply a metric

measurement

1. the act or process of measuring
2. a figure, extent, or amount obtained by measuring

metrics framework a tool used for organizing, selecting, communicating and evaluating the required quality attributes for a software system; a hierarchical breakdown of factors, sub-factors and metrics for a software system

metrics sample a set of metric values which is drawn from the metrics data base and used in metrics validation

metric validation the act or process of ensuring that a metric correctly predicts or assesses a quality factor

metric value an element from the range of a metric; a metric output

predictive assessment the process of using a predictive metric(s) to predict the value of another metric

predictive metric a metric applied during development and used to predict the values of a software quality factor

process step any task performed in the development, implementation or maintenance of software (e.g., identify the software components of a system as part of the design)

process metric metric used to measure characteristics of the methods, techniques, and tools employed in developing, implementing and maintaining the software system

product metric metric used to measure the characteristics of the documentation and code

quality attribute a characteristic of software; a generic term applying to factors, sub-factors, or metric values

quality factor[1] management oriented attribute of software that contributes to its quality

quality requirement a requirement that a software attribute be present in software to satisfy a contract, standard, specification, or other formally imposed document

quality sub-factor[1] a decomposition of a quality factor or quality sub-factor to its technical components

sample software software selected from a current or completed project from which data can be obtained for use in preliminary testing of data collection and metric computation procedures

software component general term used to refer to a software system or an element such as module, unit, data or document

software quality metric[1] a function whose inputs are software data and whose output is a single (numerical) value that can be interpreted as the degree to which software possesses a given attribute that affects its quality[2]

validated metric a metric whose values have been statistically associated with corresponding quality factor values

1 The terms factor, sub-factor, and metric are used throughout this standard to refer to quality factor, quality sub-factor, and software quality metric respectively. For the sake of brevity these terms are not used with the preceding adjective.

2 This definition differs from the definition of quality metric found in the IEEE Standard Glossary of Software Engineering Terminology, ANSI/IEEE Std 729-1983.

3.0 Purpose of Software Quality Metrics

Software quality is the degree to which software possesses a desired combination of attributes. This desired combination of attributes must be clearly defined; otherwise, assessment of quality is left to intuition. For the purposes of this standard, defining software quality for a system is equivalent to defining a list of software quality attributes required for that system. An appropriate set of software metrics must be identified in order to measure the software quality attributes.

The purpose of software metrics is to make assessments throughout the software life cycle as to whether the software quality requirements are being met. The use of software metrics reduces subjectivity in the assessment of software quality by providing a quantitative basis for making decisions about software quality. However, the use of software metrics does not eliminate the need for human judgement in software evaluations. The use of software metrics within an organization or project is expected to have a beneficial effect by making software quality more visible.

More specifically, the use of metrics within the methodology of this standard allows an organization to:

- Achieve quality goals
- Establish quality requirements for a system at its outset
- Establish acceptance criteria and standards
- Evaluate the level of quality achieved against the established requirements
- Detect anomalies or point to potential problems in the system
- Predict the level of quality which will be achieved in the future
- Monitor for changes of quality when software is modified
- Assess the ease of change to the system during product evolution
- Normalize, scale, calibrate, or validate a metric.

To accomplish these aims, both process and product metrics should be represented in the system metrics plan.

4.0 Software Quality Metrics Framework

The software quality metrics framework (See Figure 1 on page 6) begins with the establishment of quality requirements by the assignment of various quality attributes. All attributes defining the quality requirements must be agreed upon by the project team, and definitions established. Quality factors, which represent management and user oriented views are then assigned to the attributes, then sub-factors, if necessary, assigned to each factor. Associated with each factor is a direct metric, which serves as a quantitative representation of a quality factor. For example, a direct metric for the factor reliability could be mean time to failure. Each factor must have one or more associated direct metrics and target values, such as 1 hour of execution time, that is set by project management. Otherwise, there is no way to determine whether the factor has been achieved. Some examples of factors are listed in Appendix A.

At the second level of the hierarchy are the quality sub-factors, which represent software-oriented attributes that indicate quality. These are obtained by decomposing each factor into measurable software attributes. Sub-factors are independent attributes of software, and therefore may correspond to more than one factor (refer to Appendix A for further explanation). The sub-factors are concrete attributes of software that are more meaningful than factors to technical personnel, such as analysts, designers, programmers, testers, and maintainers. The decomposition of factors into sub-factors facilitates objective communication between the manager and the technical personnel regarding the quality objectives. Some examples of sub-factors are listed in Appendix A.

At the third level of the hierarchy the sub-factors are decomposed into metrics used to measure system products and processes during the development life cycle. Direct metric values (factor values) are typically unavailable or expensive to collect early in the software life cycle. Therefore, metrics on the third level, that are validated against direct metrics, are used to estimate factor values early in the software life cycle.

The framework, in a top-down fashion, facilitates:

- establishment of quality requirements in terms of factors by managers early in a system's life cycle
- communication of the established factors to the technical personnel in terms of quality sub-factors, and
- identification of metrics that are related to the established factors and sub-factors.

On the other hand, the framework, in a bottom-up fashion, enables the managerial and technical personnel to obtain feedback by:

- evaluating the software products and processes at the elementary metrics level, and
- analyzing the metrics values to estimate and assess the quality factors.

The framework is designed to be flexible. It permits additions, deletions, and modifications of factors, sub-factors, and metrics. Each level may be expanded to several sub-levels. The framework can thus be applied to all systems and can be adapted as appropriate without changing the basic concept.

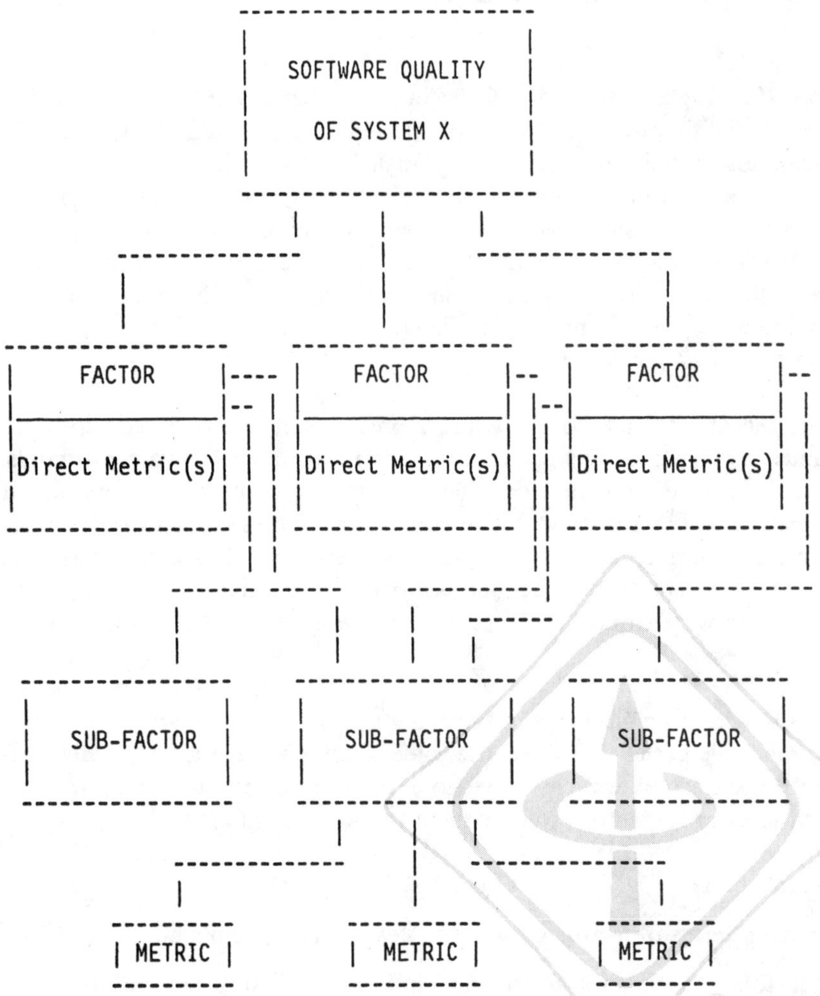

Figure 1. Software Quality Metrics Framework

5.0 The Software Quality Metrics Methodology

5.1 Introduction

The software quality metrics methodology is a systematic approach to establishing quality requirements and identifying, implementing, analyzing and validating process and product software quality metrics for a software system. It spans the entire software life cycle and comprises five steps.

These steps shall be applied iteratively because insights gained from applying a step may show the need for further evaluation of the results of prior steps.

- Establish Software Quality Requirements - A list of quality factors is selected, prioritized and quantified at the outset of system development or system change. These requirements shall be used to guide and control the development of the system and, on delivery of the system, to assess whether the system met the quality requirements specified in the contract.
- Identify Software Quality Metrics - The software quality metrics framework is applied in the selection of relevant metrics.
- Implement the Software Quality Metrics - Tools are procured or developed, data is collected, and metrics are applied at each phase of the software life cycle.
- Analyze the Software Quality Metrics Results - The metrics results are analyzed and reported to help control the development and assess the final product.
- Validate the Software Quality Metrics - Predictive metrics results are compared to the direct metrics results to determine whether the predictive metrics accurately "measure" their associated factors.

The documentation produced as a result of the preceding steps is shown in Table 1

Table 1. Outputs of Metrics Methodology Steps

METRIC METHODOLOGY STEP	OUTPUT
Establish Software Quality Requirements	• Quality Requirements
Identify Software Quality Metrics	• Approved Quality Metrics Framework • Metrics Set • Cost Benefit Analysis
Implement the Software Quality Metrics	• Description of Data Items • Metrics/Data Item • Traceability Matrix • Training Plan and Schedule
Analyze the Software Quality Metrics Results	• Organization and Development Process Changes
Validate the Software Quality Metrics	• Validation Results

5.2 Establish Software Quality Requirements

Quality requirements shall be represented in either of the following forms:

- direct metric value - a numerical target for a factor to be met in the final product. For example, mean time to failure (MTTF) is a direct metric of final system reliability.
- predictive metric value - a numerical target related to a factor to be met during system development. This is an intermediate requirement that is an early indicator of final system performance. For example, design or code errors may be early predictors of final system reliability.

5.2.1 Identify a List of Possible Quality Requirements

Identify quality requirements that may be applicable to the software system. Use organizational experience, and required standards, regulations, or laws to create this list. Appendix A contains sample lists of factors and sub-factors. In addition, list other system requirements that may affect the feasibility of the quality requirements. Consider acquisition concerns, such as cost or schedule constraints, warranties, and organizational self-interest. Do not rule out mutually exclusive requirements at this point. Focus on factor/direct metric combinations instead of predictive metrics.

All parties involved in the creation and use of the system shall participate in the quality requirements identification process.

5.2.2 Determine the Actual List of Quality Requirements

Rate each of the listed quality requirements by importance. Importance is a function of the system characteristics and the viewpoints of the people involved. To determine the actual list of the possible quality requirements, at a minimum, follow two steps:

- Survey all Involved Parties

  Discuss the relative priorities of the requirements with all involved parties. Have each group weigh the quality requirements against the other system requirements and constraints. Ensure that all viewpoints are considered.

- Create the Actual List of Quality Requirements

  Resolve the results of the survey into a single list of quality requirements.

  This shall involve a technical feasibility analysis of the quality requirements. The proposed factors for this list may have cooperative or conflicting relationships.

  Conflicts between requirements shall be resolved at this point. In addition, if the choice of quality requirements is in conflict with cost, schedule or system functionality, one or the other shall be altered. Care shall be exercised in choosing the desired list to ensure that the requirements are technically feasible, reasonable, complementary, achievable, and verifiable.

  All involved parties shall agree to this final list.

5.2.3 Quantify Each Factor

For each factor, assign one or more direct metrics to represent the factor, and direct metric values to serve as quantitative requirements for that factor. For example, if "high efficiency" was one of the quality requirements from the previous item, the direct metric "actual resource utilization/allocated resource utilization" with a value of 90% could represent that factor. This direct metric value is used to verify the achievement of the quality requirement. Without it, there is no way to tell whether or not the delivered system meets its quality requirements.

The quantified list of quality requirements and their definitions shall again be approved by all involved parties.

5.3 Identify Software Quality Metrics

5.3.1 Apply the Software Quality Metrics Framework

Create a chart of the quality requirements based on the hierarchical tree structure found in Figure 1 on page 6. At this point, only the factor level shall be complete. Now decompose each factor into sub-factors as indicated in Section 4.0. The decomposition into sub-factors shall continue for as many levels as needed until the sub-factor level is complete.

Using the software quality metric framework, decompose the sub-factors into measurable metrics. For each validated metric on the metric level, assign a target value and a critical value and range that should be achieved during development. The target values constitute additional quality requirements for the system.

The framework and the target values for the metrics shall be reviewed and approved by all involved parties.

To help ensure that metrics are used appropriately, only validated metrics (i.e., either direct metrics or metrics validated with respect to direct metrics) shall be used to assess current and future product and process quality (see Section 5.6 for a description of the validation methodology and Appendix C for examples of applying the validation methodology). Non-validated metrics may be included for future analysis, but shall not be included as a part of the system requirements. Furthermore, the metrics which are used shall be those which are associated with the quality requirements of the software project. However, given that the above conditions are satisfied, the selection of specific metrics as candidates for validation and the selection of specific validated metrics for application is at the discretion of the user of this standard. Examples of metrics and experiences with their use are given in Appendix B.

Document each metric using the format shown in Figure 2 on page 10.

TERM	DESCRIPTION
Name	Name of the Metric
Costs	The costs of using the metric (See Section 5.3.2.1)
Benefits	The benefits of using the metric (See Section 5.3.2.2)
Impact	An indication of whether a metric may be used to alter or halt the project (i.e., Can the metric be used to indicate deficient software quality ?).
Target Value	Numerical value of the metric that is to be achieved to meet quality requirements. Include the critical value and range of the metric.
Factors	Factors that are related to this metric
Tools	Software or hardware tools that are used to gather and store data, compute the metric and analyze the results
Application	A description of how the metric is used and what is its area of application
Data Items	The data items (i.e., input values) that are necessary for computing the metric values
Computation	An explanation of the computation of the metric (i.e., steps involved in the computation).
Interpretation	An interpretation of the results of the metrics computation (See Section 5.5.1)
Considerations	Metric assumptions, appropriateness (e.g., Can data be collected for this metric ? Is the metric appropriate for this application ?)
Training Required	Training required to implement or use the metric
Example	An example of applying the metric (See Appendix C)
Validation History	The names of projects that have used the metric and the validity criteria the metric has satisfied
References	References for further details on understanding or implementing the metric. List of projects, project details, etc.

Figure 2. METRICS SET

ITEM	DESCRIPTION
Name	Name of the data item
Metrics	The metrics that are associated with the data item
Definition	Unambiguous description of the data item
Source	Location where data originates
Collector	Entity responsible for collecting the data
Timing	Time(s) in life cycle at which data is to be collected (Some data items are collected more than once.)
Procedures	Methodology used to collect data (e.g., automated or manual)
Storage	Location where data is stored
Representation	The manner in which data is represented; its precision and format (e.g., Boolean, dimensionless, etc.)
Sample	The method used to select the data to be collected and the percentage of the available data that is to be collected
Verification	The manner in which the collected data is to be checked for errors
Alternatives	Methods that may be used to collect the data other than the preferred method
Integrity	Who is authorized to alter this data item and under what conditions

Figure 3. Description of a Data Item

5.3.2 Perform a Cost-Benefit Analysis

5.3.2.1 Identify the Costs of Implementing the Metrics

Identify and document (See Figure 2 on page 10) all the costs associated with the metrics in the metrics set. For each metric, estimate and document the following impacts and costs:

- Metrics Utilization Costs - Associated with each metric are the costs of collecting data, automating the metric value calculation (when possible), and analyzing, interpreting and reporting the results.
- Software Development Process Change Costs - The set of metrics may imply a change in the development process.
- Organizational Structure Change Costs - The set of metrics may imply a change in the organizational structure used to produce the software system.
- Special Equipment - Hardware or software tools may have to be located, purchased, adapted or developed to implement the metrics.
- Training - The quality assurance/control organization or the entire development team may need training in the use of the metrics and data collection procedures. If the introduction of metrics has caused changes in the development process, the development team may need to be educated about the changes.

5.3.2.2 Identify the Benefits of Applying the Metrics

Identify and document (see Figure 2 on page 10) the benefits that are associated with each metric in the metrics set.

Some benefits to be considered are:

- Identify quality goals and increase awareness of the goals in the software organization
- Provide timely feedback useful in developing higher quality software
- Increase customer satisfaction by quantifying the quality of the software before it is delivered to the customer
- Provide a quantitative basis for making decisions about software quality
- Reduce software life cycle costs by improving process efficiency based on metric data.

5.3.2.3 Adjust the Metrics Set

Weigh the benefits, tangible and intangible, against the costs of each metric. If the costs exceed the benefits of a given metric, alter or delete it from the metrics set. On the other hand, for metrics that remain, make plans for any necessary changes to the software development process, organizational structure, tools and training. In most cases it will not be feasible to quantify benefits. In these cases judgement shall be exercised in weighing qualitative benefits against quantitative costs.

5.3.3 Gain Commitment to the Metrics Set

All involved parties shall review the revised metrics set to which the cost/benefit analysis has been added. The metrics set shall be formally adopted and supported by this group.

5.4 Implement the Software Quality Metrics

5.4.1 Define the Data Collection Procedures

For each metric in the metric set, determine the data that will be collected and assumptions made about the data (e.g., random sample, subjective or objective measure). The flow of data shall be shown from point of collection to evaluation of metrics. Describe or reference when and how tools are to be used and data storage procedures. Also identify tools from which final selection will be made. Select tools for use with the prototyping process. A traceability matrix shall be established between metrics and data items.

Describe each data item thoroughly using the format shown in Figure 3 on page 11.

Identify the organizational entities that will directly participate in data collection including those responsible for monitoring data collection. Describe the training and experience required for data collection and the training process for personnel involved.

5.4.2 Prototype the Measurement Process

Test the data collection and metric computation procedures on selected software. If possible, samples selected should be similar to the project(s) on which the metrics will later be used. An analysis shall be made to determine if the data is collected uniformly and if instructions have always been interpreted in the same manner. In particular, data requiring subjective judgements shall be checked to determine if the descriptions and instructions are clear enough to ensure uniform results.

In addition, the cost of the measurement process for the prototype shall be examined to verify or improve the cost analysis.

Use the results to improve the metric descriptions (Figure 2 on page 10) and descriptions of data items (Figure 3 on page 11).

5.4.3 Collect the Data and Compute the Metrics Values

Following instructions in the metrics set and descriptions of data items, collect and store data at the appropriate time in the life cycle. The data shall be checked for accuracy and proper unit of measure.

Data collection shall be monitored. If a sample of data is used, requirements such as randomness, minimum size of sample and homogeneous sampling shall be verified. If more than one person is collecting the data, it shall be checked for uniformity.

Compute the metrics values from the collected data.

5.5 Analyze the Software Metrics Results

5.5.1 Interpret the Results

The results shall be interpreted and recorded against the broad context of the project as well as for a particular product or process of the project. The differences between the collected metric data and the target values for the metrics shall be analyzed against the quality requirements. Substantive differences shall be investigated.

5.5.2 Identify Software Quality

Quality metric values for software components shall be determined and reviewed. Quality metric values which are outside the anticipated tolerance intervals (low or high quality) shall be identified for further study. Unacceptable quality may be manifested as excessive complexity, inadequate documentation, lack of traceability, or other undesirable attributes. The existence of such conditions is an indication that the software may not satisfy quality requirements when it becomes operational. Since many of the direct metrics which are usually of interest (e.g., reliability metrics) cannot be measured during software development, validated metrics shall be used when direct metrics are not available. Direct or validated metrics shall be measured for software components and process steps. The measurements shall be compared with critical values of the metrics. Software components whose measurements deviate from the critical values shall be analyzed in detail. The fact that a measurement deviates from a critical value does not necessarily mean that the software component will exhibit unacceptable quality during operation. This may be the case because metrics are not infallible; they are only indicators of quality. What metrics indicate about quality during development may not be the quality achieved in operation. Depending on the results of the analysis, software components shall be redesigned (acceptable quality can be achieved by redesign), scrapped (quality is so poor that redesign is not feasible), or not changed (deviations for critical metric values are judged to be insignificant).

Unexpected high quality metric values shall cause a review of the software development process as the expected tolerance levels may need to be modified or the process for identifying quality metric values may need to be improved.

5.5.3 Make Software Quality Predictions

During development validated metrics shall be used to make predictions of direct metric values. Predicted values of direct metrics shall be compared with target values to determine whether to flag software components for detailed analysis. Predictions shall be made for software components and process steps. Software components and process steps whose predicted direct metric values deviate from the target values shall be analyzed in detail.

Potentially, prediction is very valuable because it estimates the metric of ultimate interest -- the direct metric. However, prediction is difficult because it involves using validated metrics from an early phase of the life cycle (e.g., development) to make prediction about a different but related metric (direct metric) in a much later phase (e.g., operations).

5.5.4 Ensure Compliance with Requirements

Direct metrics shall be used to ensure compliance of software products with quality requirements during system and acceptance testing (see Section 5.2). Direct metrics shall be measured for software components and process steps. These values shall be compared with target values of the direct metrics which represent quality requirements. Software components and process steps whose measurements deviate from the target values are noncompliant.

5.6 Validate the Software Quality Metrics

The reader who is unfamiliar with the statistical techniques used in this section can consult References 5 on page 97, 6 on page 97 and 8 on page 97 (Appendix D.2), or similar references.

5.6.1 Purpose of Metrics Validation

The purpose of metrics validation is to identify both product and process metrics that can predict specified quality factor values, which are quantitative representations of quality requirements. If metrics are to be useful, they shall indicate accurately whether quality requirements have been achieved or are likely to be achieved in the future. When it is possible to measure factor values at the desired point in the life cycle, these direct metrics are used to evaluate software quality. At some points in the life cycle, certain quality factor (e.g., reliability) values are not available; they are obtained after delivery or late in the project. In these cases, other metrics are used early in a project to predict quality factor values.

The history of the application of metrics indicates that predictive metrics were seldom validated (i.e., it was not demonstrated through statistical analysis that the metrics measured software characteristics that they purported to measure.) However, it is important that predictive metrics be validated before they are used to evaluate software quality. Otherwise, metrics might be misapplied (i.e., metrics might be used that have little or no relationship to the desired quality characteristics).

Although quality sub-factors are useful when identifying and establishing factors and metrics, they need not be used in metrics validation, because the focus in validation is on determining whether a statistically significant relationship exists between predictive metric values and factor values.

Quality factors may be affected by multiple variables. A single metric, therefore, may not sufficiently represent any one factor if it ignores these other variables.

5.6.2 Validity Criteria

To be considered valid, a predictive metric shall demonstrate a high degree of association with the quality factors it represents. This is equivalent to accurately portraying the quality condition(s) of a product or process. A metric may be valid with respect to certain validity criteria and invalid with respect to other criteria.

Someone in the organization who understands the consequence of the values selected shall designate threshold values for the following:

- V - square of the linear correlation coefficient
- B - rank correlation coefficient
- A - prediction error
- P - success rate

A short numerical example follows the definition of each validity criterion. Detailed examples of the application of metrics validation are contained in Appendix C.

- Correlation: The variation in the quality factor values explained by the variation in the metric values, which is given by the square of the linear correlation coefficient (R) between the metric and the corresponding factor, shall exceed V, where $R^2 > V$.

  This criterion assesses whether there is a sufficiently strong linear association between a factor and a metric to warrant using the metric as a substitute for the factor, when it is infeasible to use the latter.

  For example, the correlation coefficient between a complexity metric and the factor reliability may be .8. The square of this is .64. Only 64% of the variation in the factor is explained by the variation in the metric. If V has been established as .7, the conclusion would be drawn that the metric is invalid (i.e., there is insufficient association, or correlation between the metric and reliability). If this relationship is demonstrated over a representative sample of software components, the conclusion could be drawn that the metric is invalid.

- Tracking: If a metric M is directly related to a quality factor F, for a given product or process, then a change in a quality factor value from F_{T1} to F_{T2}, at times T1 and T2, shall be accompanied by a change in metric value from M_{T1} to M_{T2}, which is the same direction (e.g., if F increases, M increases). If M is inversely related to F, then a change in F shall be accompanied by a change in M in the opposite direction (e.g., if F increases, M decreases). To perform this test, compute the coefficient of rank correlation (r) from n paired values of the factor and the metric. Each of the factor/metric pairs is measured at the same point in time, and the n pairs of values are measured at n points in time. The absolute value of (r) shall exceed B.

This criterion assesses whether a metric is capable of tracking changes in product or process quality over the life cycle.

For example, if a complexity metric is claimed to be a measure of reliability, then it is reasonable to expect a change in the reliability of a software component to be accompanied by an appropriate change in metric value (e.g., if the product increases in reliability, the metric value should also change in a direction that indicates the product has improved). That is, if MTTF is used to measure reliability and is equal to 1000 hours during testing (T1) and 1500 hours during operation (T2), a complexity metric whose value is 8 in T1 and 6 in T2, where 6 is 'better' than 8 (i.e., complexity has decreased), is said to track reliability for this software component. If this relationship is demonstrated over a representative sample of software components, the conclusion could be drawn that the metric can track reliability (i.e., indicate changes in product reliability) over the software life cycle.

- Consistency: If factor values F1, F2, ..., Fn, corresponding to products or processes 1, 2, ..., n, have the relationship F1 > F2 > ..., Fn, the the corresponding metric values shall have the relationship M1 > M2 > ..., Mn. To perform this test, compute the coefficient of rank correlation (r) between paired values (from the same software components) of the factor and the metric; $|r|$ shall exceed B.

This criterion assesses whether there is consistency between the ranks of the factor values of a set of software components and the ranks of the metric values for the same set of software components. Thus this criterion is used to determine whether a metric can accurately rank, by quality, a set of products or processes.

For example, if the reliability of software components X, Y and Z, as measured by MTTF, is 1000, 1500 and 800 hours, respectively, and the corresponding complexity metric values are 5, 3 and 7, where low metric values are 'better' than high values, the ranks for reliability and metric values, with '1' representing the 'highest' rank, are as follows:

Software Component	Reliability Rank	Complexity Metric Rank
Y	1	1
X	2	2
Z	3	3

If this relationship is demonstrated over a representative sample of software components, the conclusion could be drawn that the metric is consistent and can be used to rank the quality of software components. For example, the ranks could be used to establish priority of testing and allocation of budget and effort to testing (i.e., the 'worst' software component would receive the most attention, largest budget and most staff).

- Predictability: If a metric is used at time T1 to predict a quality factor for a given product or process, it shall predict a related quality factor Fp_{T2} with an accuracy of:

$$\left| \frac{Fa_{T2} - Fp_{T2}}{Fa_{T2}} \right| < A$$

where Fa_{T2} is the actual value of F at time T2.

This criterion assesses whether a metric is capable of predicting a factor value with the required accuracy.

For example, if a complexity metric is used during development to predict the reliability of a software component during operation (T2) to be 1200 hours MTTF (Fp_{T2}) and the actual MTTF that is measured during operation is 1000 hours (Fa_{T2}), then the error in prediction is 200 hours, or 20%. If the acceptable prediction error (A) is 25%, prediction accuracy is acceptable. If the ability to predict is demonstrated over a representative sample of software components, the conclusion could be drawn that the metric can be used as a predictor of reliability. For example, prediction could be used during development to identify those software components that need to be improved.

- Discriminative Power: A metric shall be able to discriminate between high quality software components (e.g., high MTTF) and low quality software components (e.g., low MTTF). For example, the set of metric values associated with the former should be significantly higher (or lower) than those associated with the latter.

  This criterion assesses whether a metric is capable of separating a set of high quality software components from a set of low quality components. This capability identifies critical values for metrics which can be used to identify software components which may have unacceptable quality. The Mann-Whitney Test and the Chi-Square Test for Differences in Probabilities (Contingency Tables) can be used for this validation test.

  For example, if all software components with a complexity metric value of > 10 (critical value) have a MTTF of 1000 hours and all components with a complexity metric value equal to or less than 10 have a MTTF of 2000 hours, and this difference is sufficient to pass the statistical tests, then the metric separates low from high quality software components. If the ability to discriminate is demonstrated over a representative sample of software components, the conclusion could be drawn that the metric can discriminate between low and high reliability components for quality assurance and other quality functions.

- Reliability: A metric shall demonstrate the above correlation, tracking, consistency, predictability and discriminative power properties for P percent of the applications of the metric.

  This criterion is used to ensure that a metric has passed a validity test over a sufficient number or percentage of applications so that there will be confidence that the metric can perform its intended function consistently.

  For example, if the required 'success rate' (P) for validating a complexity metric against the Predictability criterion has been established as 80%, and there are 100 software components, the metric shall predict the factor with the required accuracy for at least 80 of the components.

5.6.3 Validation Procedure

Metrics validation shall include the following steps.

5.6.3.1 Identify the Quality Factors Sample

These factor values (e.g., measurements of reliability), which represent the quality requirements of a project, were previously identified (see Section 5.2.3) and collected and stored (see Section 5.4.4). For validation purposes, draw a sample from the metrics database.

5.6.3.2 Identify the Metrics Sample

These metrics (e.g., design structure) are used to predict or to represent quality factor values, when the factor values cannot be measured. The metrics were previously identified (see Section 5.3.1) and their data collected and stored, and values computed from the collected data (see Section 5.4.4). For validation purposes, draw a sample from the same domain (e.g., same software components) of the metrics data base as used in Section 5.6.3.1.

5.6.3.3 Perform a Statistical Analysis

The tests described under Validity Criteria shall be performed. (See Section 5.6.2)

Before a metric is used to evaluate the quality of a product or process, it shall be validated against the criteria described in Section 5.6.2.. If a metric does not pass all of the validity tests, it shall only be used according to the criteria prescribed by those tests (e.g., if it only passes the 'Tracking' validity test, it shall be used only for 'tracking' the quality of a product or process).

5.6.3.4 Document the Results

This shall include the direct metric, predictive metric, validation criteria and numerical results, as a minimum.

5.6.4 Additional Requirements

5.6.4.1 The Need for Re-Validation

It is important to re-validate a predictive metric before it is used for another environment or application. As the software engineering process changes, the validity of metrics changes. Cumulative metric validation values may be misleading because a metric that has been valid for several uses may become invalid. It is wise to compare the one-time validation of a metric with its validation history to avoid being misled. The following statements of caution should be noted:

- A validated metric may not necessarily be valid in other environments or future applications.
- A metric that has been invalidated may be valid in other environments or future applications.

5.6.4.2 Confidence in Analysis Results

Metrics validation is a continuous process. Confidence in metrics is increased over time and with a variety of projects as metrics are validated, the metrics data base increases and sample size increases. Confidence is not a static, one-time property. If a metric is valid, confidence will increase with increased use (i.e., the correlation coefficient will be significant at decreasing values of the significance level). Greatest confidence occurs when metrics have been tentatively validated based on data collected from previous projects. Even when this is the case, the validation analysis will continue into future projects as the metrics data base and sample size grow.

5.6.4.3 Stability of Environment

To the extent practicable, metrics validation shall be undertaken in a stable development environment (i.e., where the design language, implementation language or program development tools do not change over the life of the project in which validation is performed). In addition, there shall be at least one project in which metrics data have been collected and validated prior to application of the predictive metrics. This project shall be similar to the one in which the metrics are applied with respect to software engineering skills, application, size and software engineering environment.

Validation and application of metrics shall be performed during the same life cycle phases on different projects. Example: if metric X is collected during the development phase of project A and the saved values are later validated with respect to direct metric Y, whose values are collected during the operations phase of project A, the metric X shall be used during the development phase of project B to assess direct metric Y with respect to the operations phase of project B.

Appendix A. Examples of Factors, Sub-Factors and Metrics, and the Relationships Among Them

THIS APPENDIX IS NOT A PART OF IEEE STD 1061-1992, STANDARD FOR A SOFTWARE QUALITY METRICS METHODOLOGY, BUT IS INCLUDED FOR INFORMATION ONLY.

THE METRICS PRESENTED IN THIS APPENDIX ARE ONLY ILLUSTRATIVE OF CURRENT POPULAR METRICS. THEIR INCLUSION DOES NOT CONSTITUTE AN ENDORSEMENT OF THEIR USE NOR ARE THESE METRICS PART OF THIS STANDARD.

Tables A-1 and A-2 illustrate descriptions of factors and sub-factors, respectively. This selection was made to provide illustrative and usable definitions of factors and sub-factors. Figure A-1 illustrates a possible set of metrics for one of those factors and its associated sub-factors. The example of the mapping of a factor to sub-factors to metrics is for illustrative purposes only. Note that, in general, mappings between factors, sub-factors and metrics may be one-to-one, one-to-many, or many-to-one.

These tables are not exhaustive. There are many possible sets of factors, sub-factors and metrics that can be used. Consult Appendix D for additional sources of this information.

TABLE A-1: Sample Factors

Efficiency	An attribute that bears on the relationship of the level of performance to the amount of resources used under stated conditions.
Functionality	An attribute that bears on the existence of certain properties and functions that satisfy stated or implied needs of users.
Maintainability	An attribute that bears on the effort needed for specific modifications.
Portability	An attribute that bears on the ability of software to be transferred from one environment to another.
Reliability	An attribute that bears on the capability of software to maintain its level of performance under stated conditions for a stated period of time.
Usability	An attribute that bears on the effort needed for use (including preparation for use and evaluation of results) and on the individual assessment of such use by users.

TABLE A-2: Sample Sub-Factors

- Efficiency

Time Economy	Capability of software to perform specified functions under stated or implied conditions within appropriate time frames.
Resource Economy	Capability of software to perform specified functions under stated or implied conditions using appropriate amounts of resources.

- Functionality

Completeness	The degree to which software possesses necessary and sufficient functions to satisfy user needs.
Correctness	The degree to which all software functions are specified.

Security — The degree to which software can detect and prevent information leak, information loss, illegal use, and system resource destruction.

Compatibility — The degree to which new software can be installed without changing environments and conditions which were prepared for the replaced software.

Interoperability — The degree to which software can be connected easily with other systems and operated.

- Maintainability

Correctability — The degree of effort required to correct errors in software and cope with user complaints.

Expandability — The degree of effort required to improve or modify the efficiency or functions of software.

Testability — The effort required to test software.

- Portability

Hardware Independence — The degree to which software does not depend on specific hardware environments.

Software Independence — The degree to which software does not depend on specific software environments.

Installability — The effort required to adjust software to a new environment.

Reusability — The degree to which software can be reused in applications other than the original application.

- Reliability

Non-Deficiency — The degree to which software does not contain undetected errors.

Error Tolerance — The degree to which software will continue to work without a system failure that would cause damage to the users. Also, the degree to which software includes degraded operation and recovery functions.

Availability — The degree to which software remains operable in the presence of system failures.

- Usability

Understandability — The amount of user effort required to understand software.

Ease of Learning — The degree to which user effort required to understand software is minimized.

Operability — The degree to which the operation of software matches the purpose, environment, and physiological characteristics of users, including ergonomic factors such as color, shape, sound, etc.

Communicativeness — The degree to which software is designed in accordance with the psychological characteristics of users.

FIGURE A-1: Sample Diagram to Show the Relationships Between Factors, Sub-Factors, and Some Metrics

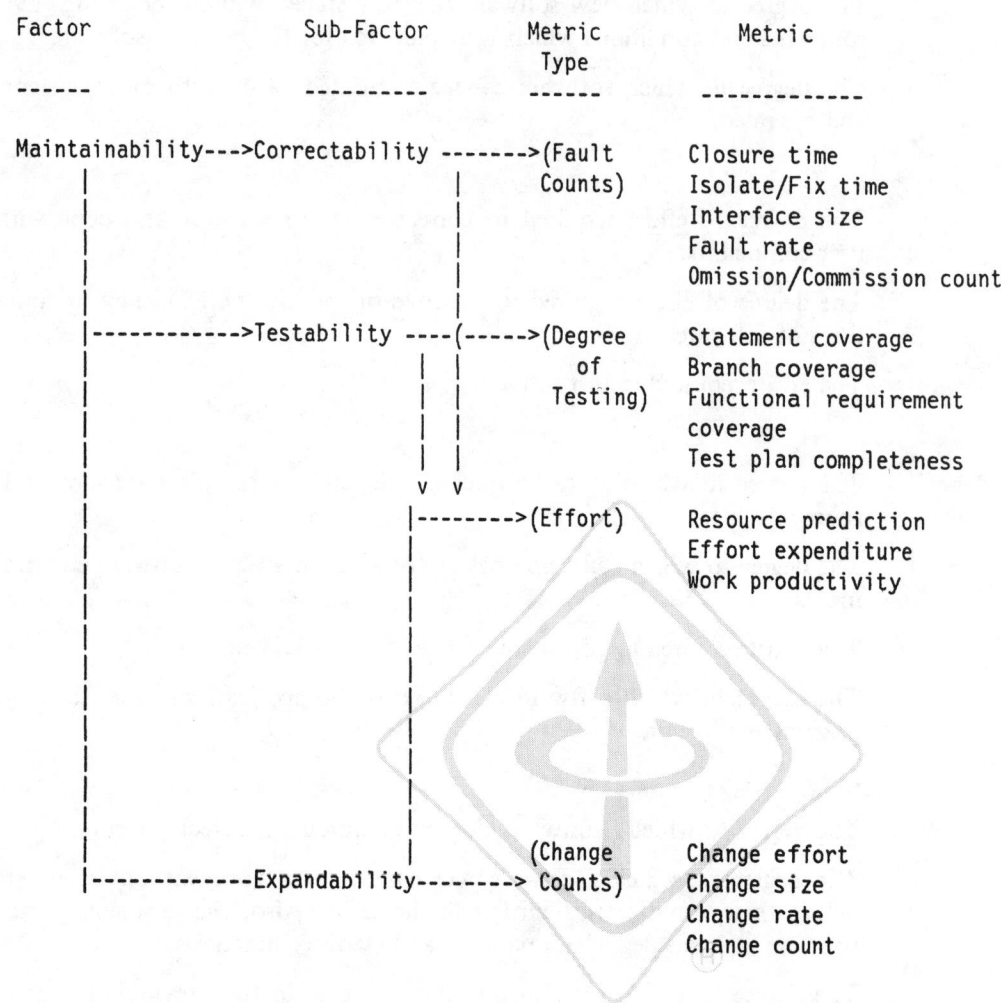

```
Factor                   Sub-Factor        Metric          Metric
                                            Type
------                   ----------        ------         ------------

Maintainability--->Correctability -------->(Fault        Closure time
      |                              |      Counts)      Isolate/Fix time
      |                              |                   Interface size
      |                              |                   Fault rate
      |                              |                   Omission/Commission count
      |                              |
      |------------>Testability ----(----->(Degree       Statement coverage
      |                           |  |        of         Branch coverage
      |                           |  |      Testing)     Functional requirement
      |                           |  |                   coverage
      |                           |  |                   Test plan completeness
      |                           v  v
      |                           |-------->(Effort)     Resource prediction
      |                           |                      Effort expenditure
      |                           |                      Work productivity
      |                           |
      |                           |
      |                           |
      |                           |
      |                           |
      |                           |
      |                           |
      |                           |
      |                           |        (Change       Change effort
      |-------------Expandability--------> Counts)       Change size
                                                         Change rate
                                                         Change count
```

Appendix B. Sample Metrics Descriptions

THIS APPENDIX IS NOT A PART OF IEEE STD 1061-1992, STANDARD FOR A SOFTWARE QUALITY METRICS METHODOLOGY, BUT IS INCLUDED FOR INFORMATION ONLY.

THE METRICS PRESENTED IN THIS APPENDIX ARE ONLY ILLUSTRATIVE OF CURRENT POPULAR METRICS. THEIR INCLUSION DOES NOT CONSTITUTE AN ENDORSEMENT OF THEIR USE NOR ARE THESE METRICS PART OF THIS STANDARD.

This section serves the following purposes:

1. Provide examples of how to compute software metrics.
2. Provide detailed descriptions of some major metrics.
3. Provide sample metric results.

The examples are not intended to be all inclusive. Additional examples exist but due to space limitations, all of them cannot be documented here.

List of Abbreviations:

R	Simple Linear Correlation Coefficient
r	Spearman Rank Order Correlation coefficient

B.1 Example Metrics Computations

Factor/Sub-factor	Computation
Completeness	Ratio of number of completed documents or software components to total number of documents or software components.
Consistency	Ratio of number of documents or software components which are free of contradictions to total number of documents or software components.
Correctness	Ratio of number of user mission objectives which have been correctly specified in the requirements specifications or correctly implemented in software components to total number of user mission objectives.
Interoperability	Ratio of number of interface specifications or software components whose interfaces are compatible to total number of interface specifications or software components.
Maintainability	Ratio of total error correction labor time to total number of corrections.
Reliability	Ratio of number of computer runs which produce correct outputs to total number of computer runs.
Testability	Identification of independent paths corresponding to McCabe metric for path testing.
Traceability	Ratio of number of documents or software components for this phase which can be traced to the previous phase to total number of documents or software components for this phase.

B.2 Detailed Metrics Descriptions

The following summarizes some major metrics. The references listed below should be consulted for a complete understanding of the metrics.

B.2.1 Halstead - Software Science

Purpose: Measures properties and structure of computer programs in order to predict the following for a computer program: 1)length, volume, difficulty and level; 2) number of errors; and 3) effort and time required for development.

Given variables:

η_1 = number of distinct operators in a program
η_2 = number of distinct operands in a program
N_1 = number of occurrences of operators in a program
N_2 = number of occurrences of operands in a program

Then compute results:

η	= Program Vocabulary	$= \eta_1 + \eta_2$
N	= Observed Program Length	$= N_1 + N_2$
$\hat{N}$	= Estimated Program Length	$= \eta_1(\log_2(\eta_1)) + \eta_2(\log_2(\eta_2))$
V	= Program Volume	$= N(\log_2(\eta))$
D	= Program Difficulty	$= (\eta_1/2)/(N_2/\eta_2)$
L	= Program Level	= 1/D
E	= Effort	= V/L
$\hat{B}$	= Number of Errors	$= (V)/E_0$ (E_0 is the programming error rate, $3{,}000 \leq E_0 \leq 3{,}200$)
$\hat{T}$	= Time (in seconds)	= E/S (S is the Stroud number, $5 \leq S \leq 20$)

Application considerations:

Correlation may be demonstrated between a high degree of difficulty and a high number of errors and increased maintenance effort. A similar correlation may be demonstrated with very large programs.

References: Appendix D.2, #7 on page 97 and Appendix D.1, #88 on page 94.

B.2.2 Boehm - Constructive Cost Model (COCOMO)

Purpose: Estimate "cost driver factors" and lines of code in order to predict project effort, cost and schedule.

For a project: Estimate KDSI _____ (Thousands of Delivered Source Instructions)

Choose Project Type (and its associated difficulty factor)

Calculate Reference value for Effort and Schedule (Reference Page 75, Appendix D.2, #4 on page 97)

Project Type	Effort (SM = Staff Months)	Schedule (TDEV = Time)
Stand-alone (Organic)	$SM = 2.4(KDSI)^{1.05}$	$TDEV = 2.5(SM)^{0.38}$
Mixed (Semi-detached)	$SM = 3.0(KDSI)^{1.12}$	$TDEV = 2.5(SM)^{0.35}$
Embedded	$SM = 3.6(KDSI)^{1.20}$	$TDEV = 2.5(SM)^{0.32}$

Choose values for cost driver factors:

Very Low	Low	* Nom	High	Very High	Value	
___	___	___	___	___	___	Required Development Schedule
___	___	___	___	___	___	Required Software Reliability
___	___	___	___	___	___	Data Base Size
___	___	___	___	___	___	Product Complexity
___	___	___	___	___	___	Execution Time Constraint
___	___	___	___	___	___	Main Storage Constraint
___	___	___	___	___	___	Virtual Machine Volatility
___	___	___	___	___	___	Analyst Capability
___	___	___	___	___	___	Applications Experience
___	___	___	___	___	___	Programmer Capability
___	___	___	___	___	___	Virtual Machine Experience
___	___	___	___	___	___	Programming Language Experience
___	___	___	___	___	___	Computer Turnaround Time
___	___	___	___	___	___	Use of Modern Programming Practices
___	___	___	___	___	___	Use of Software Tools

* Nom (Nominal) = 1 indicating no change.

Note: These factors must be calibrated for a software development organization before the factors are applied (Reference Part IV B, Chapters 23-27 of Appendix D.2, #4 on page 97).

Distribute reference estimates to life cycle phase (by percentages).

Apply Cost driver factors (Phase Sensitive and Product Sensitive).

Apply Factors for Maintained- code verses new-code.

Sum up the estimates by phase and product level.

Application considerations:

Use of the COCOMO model may provide more accurate cost and schedule estimates when used on a consistent basis with training.

References: See Appendix D.2, #4 on page 97.

B.2.3 Albrecht - Function Points

Purpose: Measures the "functions the software is to perform" from requirements information in order to estimate the effort required to develop the software.

Count the following "functions":

EI = External Inputs
EO = External Outputs
LF = Logical Internal Files
EF = External Interface Files
IQ = External Inquiries

Assign weights to the functions as follows and total:

Type	Complexity			Total
	Simple	Average	Complex	
EI	__x3=__	__x 4=__	__x 6=__	____
EO	__x4=__	__x 5=__	__x 7=__	____
LF	__x7=__	__x10=__	__x15=__	____
EF	__x5=__	__x 7=__	__x10=__	____
IQ	__x3=__	__x 4=__	__x 6=__	____

FC = Total Unadjusted Function Points = ____

Given the following values for Degrees of Influence:

DI	Description
0	Not present, or no influence if present
1	Insignificant influence
2	Moderate influence
3	Average influence
4	Significant influence
5	Strong influence throughout

Assign Degree of Influence values to the following characteristics:

DI	Characteristic
__	Data Communications
__	Distributed Functions
__	Performance
__	Heavily Used Configuration
__	Transaction Rate
__	On-line Entry
__	End-User Efficiency
__	On-line Update
__	Complex Processing
__	Reusability
__	Installation Ease
__	Operational Ease

__ Multiple Sites
__ Facilitate Changes

__ Total Degree of Influence (PC)

Compute the following results:

PCA = Processing Complexity Adjustment = 0.65 + (0.01 x PC)
FP = Function Points Measure = FC x PCA

Application considerations:

Albrecht's Function Points may be measured earlier in the life cycle than some of the other metrics. The number of Function Points may be correlated with the lines of code and effort required for development.

References: See Appendix D.2, #1 on page 97 and #2 on page 97 .

B.2.4 McCabe - Cyclomatic Complexity

Purpose: Measures the control flow structure in order to predict the following about a program: 1) difficulty of understanding; and 2) extent to which it it likely to contain defects.

Count the following values

P = number of control paths into the program
E = number of edges (transfers of control)
N = number of nodes (sequential group of statements containing only one transfer of control)

Then compute the result:

$$\text{Cyclomatic Complexity} = E - N + 2P$$

Application considerations:

Use of McCabe's Cyclomatic Complexity metric may help to ensure developers are sensitive to which programs are likely to be difficult to understand and contain defects. The results may be correlated to lines of code as well as number of defects.

References: See Appendix D.2, #3 on page 97 and #9 on page 97 .

B.3 Sample Metrics Results

The following lists were obtained in using metrics on various projects in terms of advantages, limitations, accuracy/precision, effectiveness of the measurements and comments.

B.3.1 Halstead Effort

Definition: See Section B.2.1

Advantages: Fairly easy to compute. Can automate. Tools exist.

Limitations: Cannot be computed until software is designed. Controversy about validity. Does not represent all aspects of complexity.

Project	Accuracy/Precision	Effectiveness	Comments
NASA Goddard Software Engineering Laboratory (SEL)	R = .65 with programming time. r = .488 with observed programming effort.	No significant relationship was observed	
Naval Air Dev. Center	R = .51 with known errors R = .46 with total changes	Same as NASA	
Purdue Univ.	R = .98 with number of errors	High association with number of errors.	
General Electric Co.	R = .76 with number of delivered errors. R = .20 with median debug time. R = .78 with mean number of errors in debugging. R = -.68 with understanding of program based on quiz.		

B.3.2 Halstead Difficulty

Definition: See Section B.2.1.

Advantages: Same as Halstead Effort.

Limitations: Same as Halstead Effort.

Project	Accuracy/Precision	Effectiveness	Comments
NASA Goddard SEL	R = .417 with observed programming effort.	Same as Halstead Effort.	

B.3.3 McCabe Complexity V(G)

Definition: See Section B.2.4

Advantages: Easy to compute. Tools exist. Can apply to both code and preliminary design.

Limitations: Must have some idea of design structure before it can be applied. Controversy about validity. Does not represent all aspects of complexity.

Project	Accuracy/Precision	Effectiveness	Comments
NASA Goddard SEL	As module size varied between 50 and > 200 LOC, McCabe metric varied between 6.2 and 77.5, and errors/1000 LOC varied between 65.0 and 9.7. r = .467 with observed programming effort. R = .65 with time to locate and correct bugs.	No significant relationship was observed.	
Naval P. G. School	R = .78 with number of errors. R = .67 with time to find errors. R = .72 with time to correct errors. Ratio of V(G) for error modules/v(G) for zero error modules = 2.79. Ratio of avg. error finding time for high v(G) modules/avg. error finding time for low v(G) modules = 1.94. Ratio of avg. error correction time for high v(G) modules/avg. error correction time for low v(G) modules = 1.72.	Good association when data partitioned between high/low v(G) and high/low error counts.	Obtaining correct understanding and interpretation of directed graphs. Easy to automate
Naval Air Dev. Center	R = .46 with known errors. R = .43 with total changes.	Same as Naval P. G. School.	Same as Naval P. G. School.

B.3.4 Source of Software Error

Definition: Count of errors by type (e.g., related to error in or misunderstanding of functional specification).

Advantages: Relates problem to source of error so problem can be fixed.

Limitations: Not easy to automate. Not easy to identify source of error.

Project	Accuracy/Precision	Effectiveness	Comments
NASA Goddard SEL	44% of errors related to functional specs. 39% of errors were interface errors.	Provided good insight into sources of major errors.	

B.3.5 Number of Changes Which Affect Module

Definition: Count of changes to a module.

Advantages: Easy to compute. Can automate. Tools exist.

Limitations: Cannot use until software exists.

Project	Accuracy/Precision	Effectiveness	Comments
NASA Goddard SEL	r = .469 with observed programming effort.	No significant relationship was observed.	

B.3.6 Defect Metrics

Definition: Error count, time between errors, error rate, error correction count, time to correct error.

Advantages: Evaluate reliability and design approach.

Limitations: Data may be difficult to collect.

Project	Accuracy/Precision	Effectiveness	Comments
Schneidewind reliability model applied to Naval Tactical Data System and Naval Surface Weapons Center error data.	Error prediction within + or - 10% of actual errors for 40 week prediction period.	Effective for indicating what to test and how long to test and ranking reliability of modules.	Difficult to get projects to collect the kind of data needed to feed the model. Data collection must be automated to capture error data in real time. Model must be automated.

B.3.7 Traceability

Definition: See Table B-1.

Advantages: Excellent for assessing whether software and documentation is fully integrated.

Limitations: Subject to various interpretations. Difficult to define quantitatively. Difficult to automate.

Project	Accuracy/Precision	Effectiveness	Comments
Naval Trident Command And Control System Maint. Agency.	Traceability was able to pinpoint where certain Navy software specifications and standards (e.g. 1679) were not adequate for doing software maintenance.	Demonstrated the infeasibility of using development standards for maintenance.	Tedious to do traceability manually. Need automated tool.

B.3.8 Number of Program Paths (Np)

Definition: Number of distinct execution sequences from entry node to exit node.

Advantages: Representative of execution sequences in a program.

Limitations: Can be difficult to compute because number of paths may be large. Computer time may be excessive.

Project	Accuracy/Precision	Effectiveness	Comments
Naval P. G. School	R = .76 with number of errors. R = .90 with time to find errors. R = .65 with time to correct errors. Ratio of avg. Np for modules with errors/ avg. Np for modules with no errors = 13.05.	Same as McCabe metric for Naval P. G. School.	Number of paths can be very large and even infinite. Difficult to automate.

Appendix C. Examples of Use of the Methodology

THIS APPENDIX IS NOT A PART OF IEEE STD 1061-1992, STANDARD FOR A SOFTWARE QUALITY METRICS METHODOLOGY, BUT IS INCLUDED FOR INFORMATION ONLY.

THE METRICS PRESENTED IN THIS APPENDIX ARE ONLY ILLUSTRATIVE OF CURRENT POPULAR METRICS. THEIR INCLUSION DOES NOT CONSTITUTE AN ENDORSEMENT OF THEIR USE NOR ARE THESE METRICS PART OF THIS STANDARD.

Note: Numerical values used in the two examples in this appendix are for illustrative purposes only. These values would not necessarily apply in other situations.

This section presents two examples of the use of the methodology in Section 5.0 of the standard. One example is a mission critical example from the military sector and the other is an "off the shelf" software application from the commercial sector. There are two primary differences between the examples:

1. Emphasis in the mission critical example is on development process quality requirements, while the emphasis in the commercial example is on end-user quality requirements.
2. The quality factors and sub-factors used in the commercial example differ significantly from those used by the mission critical example. This is due to differing environments. Neither application of the standard is "better" than the other.

C.1.0 Mission Critical Example

C.1.1 Introduction

A command and control system example is used to illustrate some of the steps outlined in Section 5: The Software Quality Metrics Methodology. The command and control system used in this example is adapted from RADC-TR-85-37, Volume II, Final Technical Report, February, 1985. The system is described by the following characteristics and functions:

SYSTEM:	Airborne Radar System
LIFE CYCLE:	15-20 years
COMPUTING SYSTEM:	Centralized, Redundant Processors

SYSTEM FUNCTIONS:

- Surveillance and Identification
- Threat Evaluation
- Weapons Assignment/Control
- Battlestaff Management
- Communications

The Software Quality Metrics Methodology should be applied to each system function individually; however, for the purposes of this example it will be applied only to the Surveillance and Identification function.

C.1.2 Establish Software Quality Requirements

C.1.2.1 Identify a List of Possible Requirements

The Surveillance and Identification can be decomposed into a number of smaller system functions. These functions are listed in the first column of Figure 4. Figure 4 is a tabulation of the quality factors that are associated with these individual system functions. The process used to identify these functions will not be discussed in this example.

SOFTWARE QUALITY FACTOR / SYSTEM FUNCTION	EFFICIENCY	INTEGRITY	RELIABILITY	SURVIVABILITY	USABILITY	CORRECTNESS	MAINTAINABILITY	VERIFIABILITY	EXPANDABILITY	FLEXIBILITY	INTEROPERABILITY	PORTABILITY	REUSABILITY
SURVEILLANCE AND IDENTIFICATION													
-DATA COLLECTION/REDUCTION	X		X	X						X	X		
-DYNAMIC GRAPHIC DISPLAY	X		X		X								
-TARGET RECOGNITION	X		X										
-THREAT DETECTION/ IDENTIFICATION	X		X										
-THREAT DISPLAY	X		X		X	X	X			X			
-THREAT RESPONSE AIDS	X	X	X		X	X	X	X		X			X

Figure 4. Important Software Quality Factors for Surveillance and Identification

It is also helpful to consider the application and/or environmental characteristics of the system insofar as these characteristics have implications for particular quality factors. See Table 2 on page 40.

Table 2. Examples of Application/Environment Characteristics and Software Quality Factors	
APPLICATION/ENVIRONMENT CHARACTERISTICS	**SOFTWARE QUALITY FACTORS**
Human lives affected	Integrity Reliability Correctness Verifiability Survivability
Long life cycle	Maintainability Expandability
Experimental system or high rate of change	Flexibility
Many Changes over life cycle	Flexibility Reusability Expandability
Real time application	Efficiency Reliability Correctness
On-board computer application	Efficiency Reliability Correctness Survivability
Processing of classified information	Integrity
Interrelated systems	Interoperability

For example, the long life-cycle of Airborne Radar System dictates specific quality factors, maintainability and expandability, be considered.

Finally, system-level requirements should be examined to determine if they have any software requirements implications. Figure 5 on page 42 is an example of the relationship between a system quality factor and software quality factors. The availability of a system, defined as the portion of total operational time that the system performs or supports critical functions, requires that the software be reliable, survivable, and maintainable.

C.1.2.2 Order the Quality Requirements

Techniques that facilitate this step include conducting a quality requirements survey and analyzing the interrelationships among quality factors and life-cycle costs.

C.1.2.2.1 Survey All Involved Parties

The thirteen software quality factors listed in Figure 4 on page 39 represent aspects of software quality that are recognized as being important for certain software products. A survey is used to identify and rate the quality factors for each software function.

Each participant in the survey is given a copy of Table 3 on page 43 defining the software quality factors and asked to indicate whether they consider the factor to be: very important (Excellent (E) quality), important (Good (G) quality), somewhat important (Average (A) quality), or either not important (blank) or not applicable (NA). Figure 6 on page 44 is the consensus view of the importance of each quality factor as it pertains to the Surveillance and Identification Function.

C.1.2.2.2 Determine the Actual List of Quality Requirements

Analyzing interrelationships among factors is important in order to assess the impact of either low or high quality levels of some factors on other factors. For example, in the Surveillance and Identification function, a high (E) quality level was specified for reliability and a 'good' quality level for verifiability. However, if the software is difficult to verify, then even though metric scores for reliability might be high, the actual reliability could be low. A complete specification for reliability would require that if reliability is given a high quality level, then verifiability should also be high. Thus the 'G'(Figure 6 on page 44) for verifiability is changed to 'E' (Figure 8 on page 46).

Further analysis on the interrelationships among factors explores the fact that factors may have cooperative or conflicting relationships. These relationships are presented in Figure 7 on page 45.

In order to arrive at a prioritized set of factors and associated metrics, one must assess the potential costs and benefits for performing any additional quality-related activities. A detailed cost analysis of this type is not easy and will initially rest on judgement rather than data. This analysis might show that in the initial stage in which requirements are examined and allocated, costs for all factors increase, because quality requirements may be difficult to determine for a given function. During full scale development, the costs for reliability, for example, may include cost additions due to additional verification effort. However, cost savings may be realized through fewer errors and through emphasis on error handling and error avoidance. Actual cost savings and cost additions will be known via the data.

The main conflict in the requirements initially assigned to the Surveillance and Identification function is between efficiency and the factors assigned an excellent goal: integrity, reliability, survivability, maintainability and verifiability.

A solution is to lower the requirement for efficiency to G and to require efficient processing hardware as a means of relaxing the requirement for highly efficient software. Also, a further analysis of Figure 7 on page 45 indicates that survivability conflicts with other factors and usability is relatively supportive of other factors. As a consequence, survivability and usability are changed from 'E' and 'G' respectively in Figure 6 on page 44 to 'G' and 'E' in Figure 8 on page 46. The revised quality requirements for Surveillance and Identification are in Figure 8.

ACQUISITION CONCERN	PERFORMANCE					DESIGN			ADAPTATION				
SOFTWARE QUALITY FACTOR / SYSTEM QUALITY FACTOR	EFFICIENCY	INTEGRITY	RELIABILITY	SURVIVABILITY	USABILITY	CORRECTNESS	MAINTAINABILITY	VERIFIABILITY	EXPANDABILITY	FLEXIBILITY	INTEROPERABILITY	PORTABILITY	REUSABILITY
AVAILABILITY			X	X			X						

Figure 5. System/Software Quality Factor Correlation

Table 3. Software Quality Requirements Survey		
ACQUISITION CONCERN	**QUALITY FACTOR**	**DEFINITION**
PERFORMANCE	EFFICIENCY	Relative extent to which a resource is utilized (i.e. storage space, processing time, communication time)
	INTEGRITY	Extent to which the software will perform without failures due to unauthorized access to the code or data within a specified time period.
	RELIABILITY	Extent to which the software will perform without any failures within a specified time period.
	SURVIVABILITY	Extent to which the software will perform and support critical functions without failures within specified time period when a portion of the system is inoperable.
	USABILITY	Relative effort for training or software operation (e.g. familiarization, input preparation, execution, output interpretation)
DESIGN	CORRECTNESS	Extent to which the software conforms to its specifications and standards.
	MAINTAIN-ABILITY	Ease of effort for locating and fixing a software failure within a time period.
	VERIFIABILITY	Relative effort to verify the specified software operation and performance
ADAPTATION	EXPANDABILITY	Relative effort to increase the software capability or performance by enhancing current functions or by adding new functions or data.
	FLEXIBILITY	Ease of effort for changing the software missions, functions or data to satisfy other requirements.
	INTEROPERABI-LITY	Relative effort to couple the software of one system to the software of another system.
	PORTABILITY	Relative effort to transport the software for use in another environment (hardware configuration and/or software system environment).
	REUSABILITY	Relative effort to convert a software component for use in another application.

ACQUISITION CONCERN	PERFORMANCE					DESIGN			ADAPTATION				
SOFTWARE QUALITY FACTOR / SYSTEM FUNCTION	EFFICIENCY	INTEGRITY	RELIABILITY	SURVIVABILITY	USABILITY	CORRECTNESS	MAINTAINABILITY	VERIFIABILITY	EXPANDABILITY	FLEXIBILITY	INTEROPERABILITY	PORTABILITY	REUSABILITY
SURVEILLANCE AND IDENTIFICATION	E	E	E	E	G	E	E	G	G	G	G	NA	G

Figure 6. Software Quality Factor Identification Form - Survey Results

QUALITY FACTORS	EFFICIENCY	FLEXIBILITY	INTEGRITY	INTEROPERABILITY	MAINTAINABILITY	PORTABILITY	RELIABILITY	SURVIVABILITY	CORRECTNESS	REUSABILITY	VERIFIABILITY	USABILITY	EXPANDABILITY
EFFICIENCY													
FLEXIBILITY	X												
INTEGRITY	X												
INTEROPERABILITY	X	0	X										
MAINTAINABILITY	X	0											
PORTABILITY	X			0									
RELIABILITY	X				0								
SURVIVABILITY	X	X	X										
CORRECTNESS		0											
REUSABILITY	X		X		0	0	0	X	0				
VERIFIABILITY	X				0	0	0		0	0			
USABILITY	X	0			0		0	0			X		
EXPANDABILITY	X		X		0			X	0				

X	FACTORS CONFLICT
0	FACTORS SUPPORT ONE ANOTHER
BLANK	NO RELATIONSHIP

Figure 7. Quality Factor Relationships

ACQUISITION CONCERN	PERFORMANCE					DESIGN			ADAPTATION				
SOFTWARE FACTOR / SYSTEM FUNCTION	EFFICIENCY	INTEGRITY	RELIABILITY	SURVIVABILITY	USABILITY	CORRECTNESS	MAINTAINABILITY	VERIFIABILITY	EXPANDABILITY	FLEXIBILITY	INTEROPERABILITY	PORTABILITY	REUSABILITY
SURVEILLANCE AND IDENTIFICATION	G**	E	E	G**	E**	E	E	E**	G	G	G	NA	G

Note: ** indicates a change from a previous step

Figure 8. Software Quality Factor Identification Form - Revised Requirements

C.1.2.3 Quantify Each Factor

A direct metric was assigned to each quality factor and a direct metric value was chosen as the requirement for that factor. The following are the direct metrics and the direct metric values used for Reliability:

Factor	Direct Metric	Acceptance Value
Reliability	Errors per HOL Statement	< .05
Reliability	Errors per HOL Procedure	< .60

C.1.3 Identify Software Quality Metrics

C.1.3.1 Apply the Software Quality Metrics Framework

Once the quality factors have been selected, it is necessary to select the sub-factors for the quality factors chosen.

Since the quality factors integrity, reliability, usability, correctness, maintainability, and verifiability are considered most important, sub-factors from these must certainly be considered. Sub-factors related to the most important quality factors are:

FACTORS	SUB-FACTORS
Integrity	System Accessibility
Reliability	Accuracy
	Anomaly management
	Simplicity
Usability	Operability
	Training
Correctness	Completeness
	Consistency
	Traceability
Maintainability	Consistency
	Visibility
	Modularity
	Self-descriptiveness
	Simplicity
Verifiability	Visibility
	Modularity
	Self-descriptiveness
	Simplicity

Simplicity is related to three quality factors and modularity, self-descriptiveness, visibility and consistency are related to two quality factors. This might be a consideration in choice of metrics if trade-offs become necessary.

For each sub-factor, one or more metrics may be required. These metrics will vary in different phases of the life cycle. As an example, metrics will be considered for modularity and simplicity in the various phases of the life cycle. This is not a complete set of metrics. The phases of the life cycle considered will be (1) software requirements analysis, (2) preliminary design, (3) detailed design, and (4) coding and testing. Example metrics are described below.

- Requirements Analysis Phase
  - Modularity
    - Modular Implementation M1: Are all software functions and computer software systems developed according to structured design techniques?
    - Modular Design M2: What is the average cohesive value of all software functions in this software system?
  - Simplicity
    - Design Structure S1: Are there diagrams identifying all functions in a structured fashion?
    - Design Structure S2: Has a programming standard been established?
- Preliminary Design

- Modularity
  - Modular Implementation M1: Are all software functions and software components developed according to structured design techniques?
  - Modular Design M2: What is the average cohesive value of all top level software components in this system?
- Simplicity
  - Design Structure S2: Has a programming standard been established?

- Detailed Design
  - Modularity
    - Modular Design M2: What is the cohesive value of each software component?
    - Design Structure M3: Is control always returned to the calling software component when execution is completed?
  - Simplicity
    - Coding Simplicity S3: Is the flow of control simple?
    - Cyclomatic Number S4: What is the cyclomatic number (complexity) of each software component
    - Size S5: How large is each software component (e.g., HOL procedure)?
- Code
  - Modularity
    - Modular Design M2: What is the cohesive value of each software component?
    - Design Structure M3: Is control always returned to the calling software component when execution is completed?
  - Simplicity
    - Coding Simplicity S3: Is the flow of control simple?
    - Cyclomatic Number S4: What is the Cyclomatic number (complexity) of each component?
    - Size S5: How large is each software component (e.g., HOL procedure)?

C.1.3.1.1 Metric Documentation

For each of the sample metrics given above, an example of the metric description is given using Figure 2 on page 10.

Metrics Set -- Metric Description #1

Item	Description
Name	Modular Implementation M1
Costs	Two labor weeks plus training
Benefits	This metric serves as a check to assure proper design techniques are used.
Impact	Software which does not satisfy these metrics should be examined and possibly corrected.
Target Value	The target value should be 1.
Factors	Maintainability and verifiability
Tools	No specific tools required.
Application	This metric is used to check proper design technique.
Data Items	List of structured design techniques together with evaluation of functions and software systems.
Computation	Metric requires yes or no answer based on subjective evaluation of whether all software development has been done according to structured design techniques.
Interpretation	This metric will be factored in with other metrics to derive an estimate of modularity. It is important that this metric be evaluated as a problem indicator,, but statistical regression analysis would not be appropriate.
Considerations	Value of the metric is subjective.
Training Required	To properly use this metric would require substantial knowledge of structured design techniques.
Example	N/A
Validation History	None for this application
References	RADC-TR-85-37

Metrics Set -- Metric Description #2

Item	Description
Name	Modular Design M2
Cost	4-6 man weeks.
Benefits	If used to enforce high value of cohesion, should provide improved modularity.
Impact	If value is less than .4, further examination is required.
Target Value	The target value is an average equal to.4 or higher.
Factors	Maintainability and verifiability
Tools	No specific tools required.
Applications	Used to determine modular strength of the appropriate portion of software (phase dependent).
Data Items	Cohesion values of appropriate portion of software (e.g., software component)
Computation	Cohesion values of appropriate software are determined (see reference below as well as RADC-TR-85-37) and an average is calculated.
Interpretation	Since the metric is subjective, the results will depend on the ability and judgement of persons performing the measurements. However, a low score would certainly indicate problems.
Considerations	Somewhat hard to implement. Determination of metric values somewhat subjective.
Training Required	Due to the subjective nature of metric values, substantial knowledge of the subject is required.
Example	

Module	Cohesion value
A	.5
B	.6
C	.5
D	.7
E	.7
Sum	3.0
Average	.6

Validation History	None on this application
References	Appendix D.2, #10 on page 97.

Metrics Set -- Metric Description #3

Item	Description
Name	Design Structure M3
Cost	4-6 man weeks.
Benefits	The metric checks that one aspect of software development is done properly.
Impact	If answer is 0, the programming characteristics of other software components should be checked.
Target Value	Target value is 1.
Factors	Reliability, maintainability and verifiability
Tools	No tools are required.
Application	The metric is used to check that control is always returned to the calling software component thus retaining the proper control structure.
Data Items	Representation of the control structure of appropriate software segments in usable form.
Computation	Metric requires yes or no answer based on whether proper call returns have been used for all control structures.
Interpretation	If the answer to the metric is "no" then there is an indication of poor software design.
Considerations	Appropriate as a flag to indicate problems.
Training Required	Need to be able to read appropriate description of control structures.
Example	N/A
Validation History	None on this application
References	RADC-TR-85-37

Metrics Set -- Metric Description #4

Item	Description
Name	Design Structure S1
Costs	1-2 man weeks
Benefits	By using the metric to enforce use of diagrams representing functions in a structured manner, the diagrams produced form a useful tool for use in proper development of the software system.
Impact	Low impact. This metric alone would probably not affect development.
Target Value	The target value is 1.
Factors	Reliability, maintainability and verifiability
Tools	No specific tools are required.
Application	Check on quality (or existence) of diagram representation of functions.
Data Items	Diagrams of functions of the system.
Computation	Metric requires yes or no answer based on subjective examination of all diagrams to determine whether all functions have been identified in a structured fashion.
Interpretation	Since the metric is subjective, the results will depend on the ability and judgement of persons performing the measurements.
Considerations	Although hard to apply objectively, this metric is a useful check that necessary work is done properly.
Training Required	Application of this metric requires use of experienced personnel.
Example	N/A
Validation History	None on this application
References	RADC-TR-85-37

Metrics Set -- Metric Description #5

Item	Description
Name	Design Structure S2
Costs	One man day.
Benefits	Simply a reminder.
Impact	High if used early in the software project.
Target Value	Target value is 1.
Factors	Reliability, maintainability and verifiability
Tools	No tools are required.
Application	The metric is simply used as a reminder that standards need to be used.
Data Items	N/A
Computation	Simple yes or no answer about whether standards have been applied.
Interpretation	Standards are certainly desirable but any mathematical treatment of this metric would be difficult.
Considerations	This metric does not take into account the quality of the programming standard being used.
Training Required	Only knowledge of what constitutes a standard.
Example	N/A
Validation History	None on this application
References	RADC-TR-85-37

Metrics Set -- Metric Description #6

Item	Description
Name	Coding Simplicity S3
Costs	4-6 man weeks.
Benefits	The metric checks that an important aspect of proper software development is done correctly.
Impact	If the answer is 0, faulty software components will be corrected.
Target Value	The target value is 1.
Factors	Reliability, maintainability and verifiability
Tools	No tools are required.
Application	Checks that control flow is from top to bottom in proper hierarchical decomposition.
Data Items	Representation of the control structure of appropriate software segments in a usable form.
Computation	Metric requires yes or no answer based on whether there is proper hierarchical control in all control structures.
Interpretation	If answer is "no", there is an indication of poor software design.
Considerations	Appropriate as a flag to indicate a problem.
Training Required	Minimal. Need to be able to read appropriate description of control structure.
Example	N/A
Validation History	None on this application
References	RADC-TR-85-37

Metrics Set -- Metric Description #7

Item	Description
Name	Cyclomatic Number S4
Costs	3 man weeks plus cost of software.
Benefits	Gives a measure of complexity of the software which may be used to flag low quality software, develop priorities for testing and allocate resources to testing.
Impact	If the value of the metric is exceedingly high, software components will be further divided.
Target Value	Not to exceed 3.
Factors	Reliability and maintainability
Tools	Metric data collection and processing software.
Application	Used to estimate complexity of the software.
Data Items	Number of edges E and number of nodes N in directed graph representation of software component (e.g., HOL procedure)
Computation	E - N + 2
Interpretation	A high value on a software component indicates that the software component is too long or too complex.
Considerations	This metric is one of several complexity metrics and may or may not be the best choice. The correlation of this metric with actual "complexity" of the software is a controversial issue.
Training Required	Minimal. Work can be computerized.
Example	E = 12 N = 10 metric value = 12 - 10 + 2 = 4
Validation History	See C.1.6
References	See Appendix D.2, #9 on page 97

Metrics Set -- Metrics Description #8

Item	Description
Name	Size (Number of statements in High Order Language (HOL) procedure) S5
Costs	1 man week plus cost of software.
Benefits	Gives a measure of size and complexity (e.g., excessive size of the software which may be used to flag low quality software and to estimate programmer effort.
Impact	If the value of the metric is exceedingly high, software components will be further divided.
Target Value	Not to exceed 13 for HOL procedures.
Factors	Reliability and maintainability.
Tools	Metric data collection and processing software.
Application	Used to estimate size and complexity of the software.
Data Items	Identification of syntactical elements that comprise the statements of the language (e.g., IF, WHILE, assignment)
Computation	Count of statements in HOL procedure, excluding comments
Interpretation	A high value on a software component indicates that the software component is too long or too complex.
Considerations	This metric is one of several size metrics and may or may not be the best choice. The correlation of this metric with actual "size" and "complexity" of the software is a controversial issue.
Training Required	Minimal. Work can be computerized.
Example	Count statements by computer
Validation History	See C.1.6

C.1.3.2 Perform a Cost Benefit Analysis

C.1.3.2.1 Identify the Costs of Implementing the Metrics

Metric Utilization Costs - Detailed work breakdown structures will be used to allocate cost of collecting analyzing, interpreting and reporting metric results.

Software Development Process Change Cost - It is not anticipated at this time that there will be software development process change cost.

Organizational Structure Change Costs - Organizational structure change costs will be distributed equally among the metrics for cost analysis purposes.

Special Equipment - Only new hardware and software specifically obtained for collecting data and implementing metrics for this project will be included in the cost. Cost for equipment used for implementing more than one metric will be prorated among the metrics.

Training - If training for implementing metrics will be used for more than one project, cost will be distributed among the projects and the metrics within the projects.

C.1.3.2.2 Identify the Benefits of Applying the Metrics

Identify and document benefits which it is estimated will result from implementation of each metric in the metrics set and specify the appropriate action which will be taken based on metric results. Where possible assign cash values to these benefits. Identify costs other than metric costs necessary to realize these benefits.

C.1.3.2.3 Adjust the Metrics Set

Based on a cost benefit analysis using information obtained above for each metric, add, alter, or delete metrics in the metrics set. Reallocation of costs for other metrics may be necessary if metrics are added or dropped.

C.1.3.3 Gain Commitment to the Metrics Set

Benefits of the use of metrics will be presented to management in a series of seminars. When management is committed to the plan, similar seminars will be presented for others involved in implementing the plan.

C.1.4 Implement the Software Quality Metrics

C.1.4.1 Define the Data Collection Procedures

Data collection will follow the Software Quality Metrics Methodology. Data item descriptions are provided for each data item. An example of a data item description is given below:

Item	Description
Name	Cohesive (module strength) value of module.
Metrics	Modular Design M2
Definition	Cohesion is the measure of the strength of functional association of elements within a module (See Appendix D.2, #11 on page 97). The following cohesive values are assigned to module types: Type / Value Functional 1.0 Informational 0.7 Communicational 0.5 Procedural 0.3 Classical 0.1 Logical 0:1 Coincidental 0.0 For definition of module types see Appendix D.2, #10 on page 97.
Source	Detailed Design Documentation
Collector	Specifically trained personnel from Quality Assurance.
Timing	At end of preliminary design phase
Procedures	Values determined manually by examination of each module.
Storage	Information stored on data base file on microcomputer disk.
Representation	Fixed point notation with significant digits correct to nearest tenth.
Sample	Ten percent of available data selected randomly is to be collected.
Verification	Modules are to be examined and evaluated by two independent persons or teams.
Alternatives	None
Integrity	The supervisor for data collection may authorize altering data if an error is determined or if the modules being evaluated are altered.

C.1.4.2 Prototype the Measurement Process

A small similar project has been selected for testing data collection and metric implementation procedures. All procedures will be performed twice using different personnel to check for uniformity.

Results of the prototype testing will be used to evaluate cost analysis for the metric set and to evaluate clarity of instructions and descriptions used for collection of data and implementation of metrics.

C.1.4.3 Select Tools to Apply to Metrics

When possible, tools will be purchased off the shelf. Remaining tools will be custom made by outside sources.

C.1.4.4 Collect the Data and Compute the Metrics Values

A statistical analysis will be made to determine that the samples are appropriately selected. When more than one person is collecting the data, an analysis will be made to determine that the data collection is uniform.

C.1.5 Analyze the Software Metrics Results

For each metric, results will be interpreted. The system will be evaluated with regard to the metric and the results will be reported. An example is given below for the metrics Cyclomatic Number, S4, and Size, S5, evaluated during the preliminary design phase.

C.1.5.1 Interpret the Results

Identify all CSCs (Computer Software Components) for which the value of S4 exceeds 3 or the value of S5 exceeds 13.

C.1.5.2 Identify Software Quality

CSCs with values that exceed target values are examined and, if possible, redesigned to reduce complexity or reduce size, as appropriate. If this cannot be done, then the reasons should be documented. Exceptions to the target value requirement can only be given by the supervisor of the project.

C.1.5.3 Make Software Quality Predictions

Although the ability to make mathematical predictions about software reliability failed the validity test, the ability to discriminate between quality levels (e.g., procedures with errors vs, procedures with no errors) was validated. Therefore, it is 'predicted' that errors in the software will occur if complexity and software component size exceed critical values of approximately 3 for Cyclomatic number and 13 statements, per HOL procedure, respectively (see C.1.6).

C.1.5.4 Ensure Compliance With Requirements

The direct metrics Errors/Statement and Errors/Procedure, listed in C.1.2.3 are used to ensure that the target values are achieved. The target values given in C.1.2.3 are .05 Errors/Statement and .60 Errors/Procedure. From the data presented in C.1.6, number of errors is 64, number of statements is 1600, and number of procedures is 112, giving Errors/Statement and Errors/Procedure of .04 and .57, respectively; these are less than the target values.

C.1.6 Validate the Software Quality Metrics

The following example is provided to show how to make metric validation tests (See References #5 on page 97, #6 on page 97 and #8 on page 97 in Appendix D.2). No inferences should be drawn from this example regarding the validity of these metrics for other applications. These metrics are used for illustrative purposes only. The results of the validation tests could be different for other applications. The data used in the validation tests were collected from actual software projects. For the purpose of this example, these projects will be assumed to be similar to the Surveillance and Identification application. Characteristics of the data, such as sample size, format, and data categories, are illustrative and could be different for other applications.

C.1.6.1 Purpose of Metrics Validation

The purpose of the validation is to determine whether the complexity (cyclomatic number) and size (number of source statements) metrics, either singly or in combination, could be used to predict and assess the factor reliability, as represented by the direct metric error count, for the Surveillance and Identification application.

C.1.6.2 Validity Criteria

Select values of V, B, A, and P. The values of V, B, A, and P (See Section 5.6.2), used in the example are .7, .7, 20%, and 80%, respectively. The criterion used for selecting these values is reasonableness (i.e., judgement must be exercised in selecting values to strike a balance between the one extreme of causing a metric which has a high degree of association with a factor to fail validation and the other extreme of allowing a metric of questionable validity to pass validation). It is not possible for validation to be completely mechanistic. Judgement must be exercised in any statistical analysis.

Apply the validity criteria of Section 5.6.2 in the validation procedure which follows.

C.1.6.3 Validation Procedure

Perform the following validation steps:

C.1.6.3.1 Identify the Quality Factors Sample

Draw a sample of procedures (i.e., software component) from the metrics data base of the quality factor reliability, which is represented by the direct metric error count (Errors). This sample is shown for procedures with no errors (Table 4 on page 61) and for procedures with errors (Table 5 on page 63) for four software projects.

C.1.6.3.2 Identify the Metrics Sample

Using the same procedures as in C.1.6.3.1, identify the metrics samples for cyclomatic number (Complexity) and size (Statements). The samples are listed in Table 4 on page 61 and Table 5 on page 63.

Table 4 (Page 1 of 2). Procedures with No Errors

Complexity	Statements	Errors	Project
2	6	0	1
1	8	0	1
1	11	0	1
1	4	0	1
3	18	0	1
3	15	0	1
1	3	0	2
1	3	0	2
1	3	0	2
1	3	0	2
1	3	0	2
1	3	0	2
1	3	0	2
1	3	0	2
1	5	0	2
1	5	0	2
1	5	0	2
1	13	0	2
1	3	0	2
1	3	0	2
1	3	0	2
1	3	0	2
1	3	0	2
1	3	0	2
1	3	0	2
1	2	0	4
1	2	0	4
1	7	0	4
1	5	0	4
1	7	0	4
1	5	0	4
1	5	0	4
1	5	0	4
1	5	0	4
1	4	0	4
1	3	0	4
1	3	0	4
1	3	0	4
1	3	0	4
1	3	0	4
1	3	0	4
1	3	0	4
1	3	0	4
1	5	0	4
1	5	0	4
1	6	0	4
1	9	0	4
1	6	0	4
1	8	0	4
1	9	0	4
1	9	0	4
2	4	0	4

Table 4 (Page 2 of 2). Procedures with No Errors

Complexity	Statements	Errors	Project
2	7	0	4
2	9	0	4
4	56	0	4
1	24	0	4
2	13	0	4
2	13	0	4
2	10	0	4
2	9	0	4
2	12	0	4
5	21	0	4
5	49	0	4
3	19	0	4
4	20	0	4
2	6	0	4
2	12	0	4
2	9	0	4
2	10	0	4
1	21	0	4
4	21	0	4
3	11	0	4
2	13	0	4
3	14	0	4
7	19	0	4
2	15	0	4
2	10	0	4
2	17	0	4
3	19	0	4
3	15	0	4
2	15	0	4

Table 5. Procedures with Errors

Complexity	Statements	Errors	Project
2	14	1	1
6	26	5	1
5	7	2	1
5	21	1	1
2	6	1	1
1	3	1	2
1	11	1	2
1	8	1	2
2	15	3	2
8	45	3	2
4	18	1	2
6	54	3	2
2	34	2	2
4	19	1	2
5	30	2	2
4	26	1	2
16	94	8	2
2	13	1	3
6	83	1	4
5	28	1	4
8	37	5	4
3	13	2	4
3	16	1	4
7	34	1	4
5	24	1	4
4	18	3	4
5	35	2	4
13	49	5	4
4	19	1	4
4	27	1	4
4	17	2	4

C.1.6.3.3 Perform a Statistical Analysis

Perform the tests described under Validity Criteria in Section 5.6.2. Significance level and sample size are denoted by α and N, respectively; when it is necessary to specify a critical level of α in hypothesis tests, .05 is used. Statistical formulas are not given; these can be found in the references. Only results are shown.

C.1.6.3.4 Document the Results

C.1.6.3.4.1 Correlation

Note: See Appendix D.2, #8 on page 97

Test 1: Linear Correlation

Compute the sample linear correlation coefficient (R) for Errors (E) and Complexity (C) and for Errors (E) and Statements (S) and compare each R^2 with V = .7 .

Table 6. Sample Correlations of Procedures with Errors		
	Complexity	**Statements**
Errors with	R = .7834	R = .5880
Confidence Level	100.0% (α = .0000)	99.95% (α = .0005)
Number of Observations(N)	31	31

Table 7. Sample Correlations of All Procedures (Errors and No Errors)		
	Complexity	**Statements**
Errors with	R = .8010	R = .6596
Confidence Level	100.0% (α = .0000)	100.0% (α = .0000)
Number of Observations(N)	112	112

RESULT: $R^2 < V = .7$ in all cases. Fails test; thus neither complexity nor statements correlate with errors.

Test 2: Null Hypothesis

Perform a null hypothesis test H_o: $\rho = 0$ for E and C. This test is usually a part of Test 1.

RESULT: Reject H_o with $\alpha = .0000$ and N = 31 (Table 6, Procedures with Errors).

Test 3: Null Hypothesis

Perform a null hypothesis test H_o: $\rho > \sqrt{V} = .836$ for E and C, since we want $R^2 > V = .7$.

RESULT: Accept H_o with $\alpha = .01$ and N = 31 (Procedures with Errors).

Test 4: Partial Correlations

Compute the partial correlation coefficients for E, C, and S. These coefficients give the strength of the linear relationship between two variables while controlling for the effects of the remaining variables.

Table 8. Sample Partial Correlations of Procedures with Errors	
Correlations	**R Values**
Errors with Complexity	.6430
Errors with Statements	-.0816
Complexity with Statements	.6557
Note: with 31 observations (N)	

RESULT: From the low R for E and S, it can be seen that Statements contributes essentially no additional information about Errors, once Complexity has been used as a predictor of Errors.

Test 5: Confidence Interval

Compute a confidence interval of ρ for E and C.

RESULT: $.593 < \rho < .891$ with $\alpha = .05$ and N = 31 (Procedures with Errors).

CONCLUSION: The results are mixed. Complexity failed mandatory Test1 but had favorable results for Tests 2, 3 and 5. Statements failed Test 1 and did not have as favorable results in the other tests as Complexity. Neither Complexity nor Statements correlate with errors.

C.1.6.3.4.2 Tracking

Note: See Appendix D.2, #5 on page 97 and #6 on page 97

Test 1: Rank Correlation

Compute the Spearman Coefficient of Rank Correlation (r) for E with C for Projects 1, 2, and 4 separately (Project 3 is not used because it has only one error). Correlation is lower for E with S than for E with C and is not shown. Compare r with B = .7 and α with .05. Procedures with errors are used rather than all procedures because the latter has too many ties in the sample. Rank correlation should not be used when there is a large number of ties. A moderate number of ties is tolerable.

Table 9. Spearman Rank Correlations of Procedures with Errors

	Complexity	Confidence Level	Remarks
Errors, Project 1, with (N = 5)	r = .8250	90.10%(α = .0990) α > .05	r > .7 Small sample size
Errors, Project 2, with (N = 12)	r = .6723	97.42%(α = .0258) α < .05	r < .7
Errors, Project 4, with (N = 13)	r = .2522	61.78%(α = .3824) α > .05	r < .7

RESULT: The desired result is r > .7 and α < .05 (i.e. indication of non-zero correlation) for each project. Complexity does not track with changes in Errors sufficiently for any of the projects. Therefore, neither changes in Complexity nor changes in Statements "track" with the observed changes in Errors.

C.1.6.3.4.3 Consistency

Note: See Appendix D.2, #5 on page 97 and #6 on page 97

Test 1: Rank Correlation

Compute the Spearman Coefficient of Rank Correlation (r) for E and C over all procedures with errors. Correlation is lower for E and S than for E and C and is not shown. Compare r with B = .7 and α with .05

Table 10. Spearman Rank Correlations of Procedures with Errors

	Complexity	Confidence Level	Remarks
Errors with (N = 31)	r = .5119	99.49%(α = .0051) α < .05	r < .7

RESULT: The desired result is r > .7 and α < .05. Complexity does not change consistently with changes in Errors across all procedures with errors. Therefore neither Complexity nor Statements are consistent with Errors.

C.1.6.3.4.4 Predictability

Note: See Appendix D.2, #8 on page 97

Test 1: Scatter Plot

Make a scatter plot of E and C for procedures with errors to obtain a rough analysis of linearity.

RESULT: The dots on Figure 9 show the relationship.

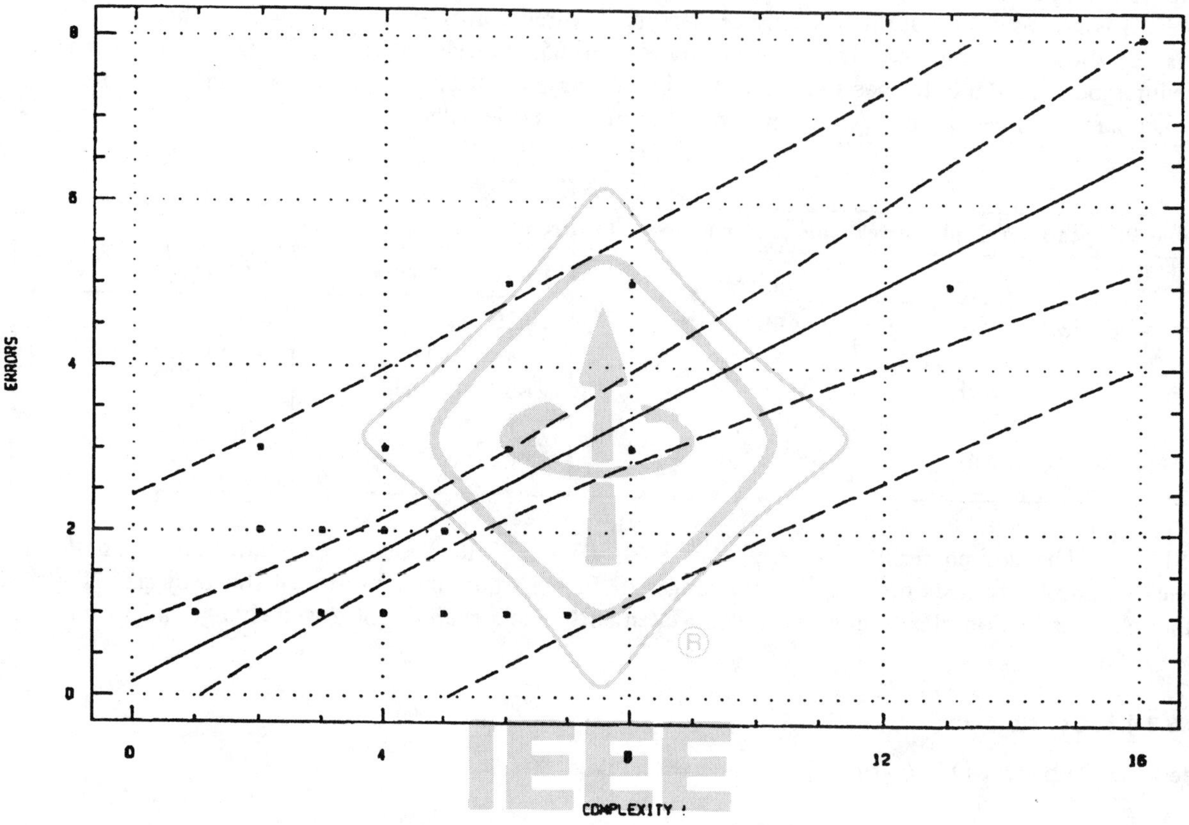

Figure 9. Regression of Errors on Complexity - Procedures with Errors

Test 2: Linear Regression

Perform a linear regression analysis of E on C for procedures with errors.

(a) Test whether the assumptions of linear regression analysis hold for these data. Two of the important assumptions are: (1) E is normally distributed for given values of C and (2) the variances of E are equal for given values of C.

RESULT: For cases of C = 1 and 2, where there was an adequate sample size, tests were conducted and it was found that neither assumption holds. In addition, E was not normally distributed when all 112 procedures were used in the analysis. The best fit for E is a negative binomial distribution.

(b) Examine the residuals of E (difference between observed and predicted as a function of C).

RESULT: Residuals increase with increasing C. This indicates that prediction error increases with increasing C. This is an undesirable result since we want prediction error to be independent of C.

The same results were obtained in a. and b. when all procedures were used.

Test 3: Regression Model

Plot the regression model in Figure 9 on page 66 for E on C for procedures with errors. The equation is: $E = .151 + .404C$. The inner band is the 95% confidence interval for average E (i.e., 95% chance that, for a given C, the estimate of average E will fall within the band) and the outer band is the 95% prediction interval of E (i.e., 95% chance that, for a given C, the estimate of E will fall within the band). The fit is worse for regression of E on S (not shown).

Test 4: Observed vs. Predicted Errors

Compare Observed Errors with Predicted Errors (obtained from regression model) and note whether Predictability $< A = 20\%$, for $P \geq 80\%$ of the predictions.

RESULT: Table 11 on page 68 indicates that Predictability < 20% for only 11 out of 31 cases, or only 35%; the result is 16% when all procedures are used (not shown). The test fails.

Table 11. Procedures with Errors

Observed Errors	Predicted Errors	Prediction Error	Predictability (%)	Project
1	0.957831	0.04217	4.21686	1
5	2.572289	2.42771	48.55421	1
2	2.168674	-0.16868	8.43373	1
1	2.168674	-1.16867	116.86747	1
1	0.957831	0.04217	4.21686	1
1	0.554216	0.44578	44.57831	2
1	0.554216	0.44578	44.57831	2
1	0.554216	0.44578	44.57831	2
3	0.957831	2.04217	68.07228	2
3	3.379518	-0.37952	12.65060	2
1	1.765060	-0.76506	76.50602	2
3	2.572289	0.42771	14.25702	2
2	0.957831	1.04217	52.10843	2
1	1.765060	-0.76506	76.50602	2
2	2.168674	-0.16868	8.43373	2
1	1.765060	-0.76506	76.50602	2
8	6.608433	1.39157	17.39457	2
1	0.957831	0.04217	4.21686	3
1	2.572289	-1.57229	157.22891	4
1	2.168674	-1.16867	116.86747	4
5	3.379518	1.62048	32.40963	4
2	1.361445	0.63855	31.92771	4
1	1.361445	-0.36145	36.14457	4
1	2.975903	-1.97590	197.59036	4
1	2.168674	-1.16867	116.86747	4
3	1.76506	1.23494	41.16465	4
2	2.168674	-0.16868	8.43373	4
5	5.397590	-0.39759	7.95180	4
1	1.765060	-0.76506	76.50602	4
1	1.765060	-0.76506	76.50602	4
2	1.765060	0.23494	11.74698	4

Test 5: Non-linear Regression

Try non-linear single independent variable regression models.

RESULT: Several non-linear (e.g., exponential) regressions of E on C for procedures with errors had lower correlation and worse fit (not shown) than the linear model.

Test 6: Multiple Linear Regression

Perform multiple linear regression analysis, using E as dependent variable and C and S as independent variables'.

(a) Test whether the assumptions of the multiple regression model hold. An important assumption of this method is that the 'independent variables' are actually independent.

RESULT: The significant R between C and S of .833 for all procedures indicates dependence.

(b) Examine the residuals of E for all procedures.

RESULT: Residuals increase with increasing C and S indicating that prediction error would increase with increasing C and S - an undesirable result.

(c) Plot the multiple regression model and compare with results of Test 3.

RESULT: The plots were made but are not shown because the fit is worse than in Test 3. For procedures with errors the regression equation is: E = .174 + .437C - .00672S. Statements contributes little to the relationship. The comparison between simple and multiple regression is summarized in Table 12, where F-Ratio is a measure of goodness of fit (generally, high value signifies good fit) and P is the percentage of predictions that are within the prediction error tolerance (A = 20%).

Table 12. Regression Comparison

	E vs. C Procedures with Errors	**E. vs. C All Procedures**	**E vs. C & S Procedures with Errors**	**E vs. C & S All Procedures**
R	.783	.801	.785	.801
F-Ratio	46.1	196.9	22.5	97.6
P for A < 20%	35%	16%	35%	22%

CONCLUSION: Neither C nor S meets the Predictability criterion, either singly or in combination, for predicting E. Multiple regression has no advantage over single variable regression for these data. Also, the assumptions of both models are not satisfied. Therefore, neither Complexity nor Statements are valid predictors of Errors

C.1.6.3.4.5 Discriminative Power

Note: See Appendix D.2, #5 on page 97 and #6 on page 97

Test 1: Mann-Whitney Test

Divide the data into two sets: procedures with errors and procedures with no errors. Rank these sets according to their C and S values (statistical programs will do the ranking automatically) and perform the Mann-Whitney test to see whether C and S can discriminate between the two sets of procedures.

RESULT: The results of the Mann-Whitney test for C and S are shown in Table 13 on page 70 The average ranks of C and S for procedures with errors are much higher than the average ranks for procedures with no errors, respectively. We can conclude from the low probabilities of higher statistics that C and S for procedures with errors have significantly higher medians. Passes tests. Caution: a large number of ties weakens this test. There are a large number of ties in C but not in S.

Table 13. Mann-Whitney Test: Comparison of Two Samples					
Sample	**Average Rank**	**Number of Values**	**Large Sample Test Statistic**	**Two-tailed probability ≥ Z**	**Observations**
Complexity Procedures with errors	85.9032	31	Z= -6.30181	2.95465E-10	112
Complexity Procedures with no errors	45.2469	81			
Statements Procedures with errors	85.2419	31	Z= -5.82408	5.76106E-9	112
Statements Procedures with no errors	45.5	81			

Test 2a: Chi-Square Test (Complexity)

Divide the data into four categories, as shown in Table 14 according to a critical value of Complexity, C_c, so that a Chi-square test can be performed to determine whether C_c can discriminate between procedures with errors and those with no errors. C_c is chosen to provide at least five observations for each cell in the table in order to ensure the validity of the test. This may involve trial and error.

Table 14. Contingency Table			
Procedures with	**Complexity ≤ 3**	**Complexity > 3**	**Row Total**
No Errors	75	6	81
Errors	10	21	31
ALL	85	27	112

RESULT: The result of the Chi-square test is shown in Table 15. The high value of Chi-square and the very small significance level indicate that C_c can discriminate between procedures with errors and those without errors. Passes test.

Table 15. Summary Statistics for Contingency Tables. $C_c = 3$		
Chi-Square	**D. F.**	**Significance**
44.6081	1	2.40692E-11

Test 2b: Chi-Square Test (Statements)

Do Test 2a. for Statements. The Contingency Table is shown in Table 16 on page 71.

Table 16. Contingency Table

Procedures with	Statements ≤ 13	Statements > 13	Row Total
No Errors	64	17	81
Errors	7	24	31
All	71	41	112

Table 17. Summary Statistics for Contingency Tables. $S_c = 13$

Chi-Square	D. F.	Significance
30.7658	1	2.91118E-81

RESULT: The same comments made in Test 2a. apply to S_c. Passes test.

CONCLUSION: Complexity and Statements are valid with respect to the Discriminative Power criterion and both can be used to distinguish between acceptable ($C \leq 3$, $S \leq 13$) and unacceptable ($C > 3$, $S > 13$) quality for the Surveillance and Identification application during life cycle phases when this data can be collected. It should be noted that it is less expensive to collect Statement counts than to compute Complexity.

C.1.6.4 Additional Requirements

C.1.6.4.1 The Need For Re-validation

Repeat all validation tests for C and S on future projects, keeping track of P, the Reliability requirement (i.e., percentage of applications for which a metric must pass validity tests to be certified as valid).

C.1.6.4.2 Confidence in Analysis Results

Confidence in analysis results will be achieved if C and S, when used on this and future projects, are able to flag poor quality software during development so that it can be corrected before being delivered to the customer.

C.1.6.4.3 Stability of Environment

To the extent practical, perform future validity tests for applications and environments that are similar to this one so that validation results can be compared and aggregated across projects.

C.2.0 Example From a Commercial Environment

C.2.1 Introduction

This section describes how a company in the commercial sector might apply the steps in Section 5.0 of the standard. It presents a portion of the company's quality framework and discusses some of the methods used to implement the methodology.

There are two primary differences between this example and the mission critical example, Section C.1:

1. Emphasis in the mission critical example is on development process quality requirements, while the emphasis in this example is on end-user quality requirements.
2. All software in this example is sold off the shelf. A result of this difference is the fact that the choice of factors and sub-factors used by this company directly conflict with the factor and sub-factor definitions used by the mission critical example; this contradiction is to be expected from the differing environments, and in no way indicates that one application of the standard is "better" than the other.

C.2.2 Establish Software Quality Requirements

C.2.2.1 Identify a list of Possible Quality Requirements

While the quality factors listed in military handbooks such as RADC-TR-85-37 ("Boeing Report") are of interest as possible examples, companies pursuing an "off the shelf" software marketing strategy may need to add functionality to the list of quality requirements. (e.g. Does our product provide all of the functionality that the target market wants? needs? Does it beat the competition's functionality?) In this example, the requirements have been expressed in terms of: Functionality, Usability, Reliability, Performance, and Supportability (FURPS). Table 3 on page 43 provides examples of how environmental characteristics may affect the software quality requirements identification process.

C.2.2.2 Order the Quality Requirements

Techniques that facilitate this step include a quality requirement survey and performing an analysis on the interrelationships among quality factors and life-cycle costs.

C.2.2.2.1 Survey all Involved Parties

A Business Team composed of, but not limited to Marketing, R&D, QA, Technical Support, and Publications is formed to determine the relative importance of the quality requirements. Other organizational entities that may be involved could be Sales, Legal, Internal Standards or Metrics Administration. There may be significant differences between the involved survey parties about the relative importance of different quality requirements. For example, developers may desire more importance for some factors than end users, and vice-versa.

C.2.2.2.2 Determine the Actual List of Quality Requirements

Discussions (and additional analysis, if necessary) are held until such time that consensus is reached on a single ordered list of requirements. It is very important that an agreement is reached for the final ordering of the list, because it may directly affect cost as well as other characteristics. In this example, the company creates real time software so Performance and Reliability are very important and require an excellent quality level. Functionality and Supportability are important and require a good quality level, and Usability is least important. At this point, wherever conflicts arise between the various quality factors, the developers have clear instructions on how the conflicts are to be resolved.

C.2.2.3 Quantify each Factor

Now that each quality factor has been identified and ordered relative to importance, and to cost and schedule constraints, the involved organizations need to assign a set of direct metrics to represent each quality factor. More importantly, quantitative values must be assigned to each direct metric as a way of determining if the delivered system meets its quality requirements.

C.2.3 Identify Software Quality Metrics

C.2.3.1 Apply the Software Quality Metrics Framework

Once the quality factors relevant to the project are identified, it is time to fill in the rest of the metrics framework (the sub-factors) referred to in Figure 1 on page 6 of the standard.

There are several ways to choose sub-factors. One would be to apply a pre-existing hierarchy such as a corporate metrics standard or the RADC Report (RADC-TR-85-37). In this case one would simply refer to the pages documenting the desired factors and gather a list of the related sub-factors. The list could then be prioritized based on the rank order of the factors.

A second way would be to form a committee to select technical attributes which are related to the factors. This is more time consuming than the prior method, but has the advantage of being optimized for the local environment. The actual selections made are archived so that subsequent projects can benefit from the committee's work. (Corporate metrics standards often start this way).

Finally, it may be decided that one or more of the quality factors chosen have technical significance. In this example, the company could define usability as its own sub-factors. Examples of sub-factors associated with each quality factor are shown in Appendix A. Once a set of sub-factors has been selected, the list is circulated and agreed upon (especially if it is based on original work). In the case of our example, sub-factors were chosen from Table 18 on page 74. (For example, speed, efficiency, resource needs, throughput and response time are the high priority sub-factors associated with the high priority factor Performance.)

Table 18. Factors and Sub-Factors	
FACTORS	**SUB-FACTORS**
Functionality	Feature Set Applicability Capabilities Generality Compatibility Security
Usability	Usability
Reliability	Failure Rate Recoverability Predictability Accuracy MTTF
Performance	Speed Efficiency Resources Needs Throughput Response Time
Supportability	Testability Extensibility Adaptability Maintainability Configurability Serviceability Installability Integratability Localizability

Having chosen sub-factors, actual metrics must be chosen using a similar process: if validated metrics are already available, they are used; if not, those metrics which are reasonable and are accepted by all of those involved are applied. Appendix D.1, Annotated Bibliography, lists several references which contain metric suggestions. It may be useful to include non-validated metrics at this point in order to validate them in the future; however, these metrics must not be used as predictors. In our example, the company has decided that the "speed" of its operating systems (a high priority characteristic related to performance, see Table 18) may be considered a function of millions of user instructions executed per second (MIPS) and the percentage of CPU time spent in the operating system (system overhead). It has also been decided that "efficiency" is characterized by both system overhead and memory utilization. A partial hierarchy based on these decisions is shown in Figure 10 on page 75.

```
                 +----------------+
                 | Performance    |
                 +----------------+
                         |
        +----------+--+-----------------------------------+
        |             |                                   |
     +-------+     +------------+                   +---------------+
     | Speed |     | Efficiency |     . . .         | Response Time |
     +-------+     +------------+                   +---------------+
        |             |
  +-------------+   +--------------+
  |             |   |              |
+------+     +------------+     +-------------+
|      |     |   System   |     |   Memory    |
| MIPS |     |  Overhead  |     | Utilization |
+------+     +------------+     +-------------+
```

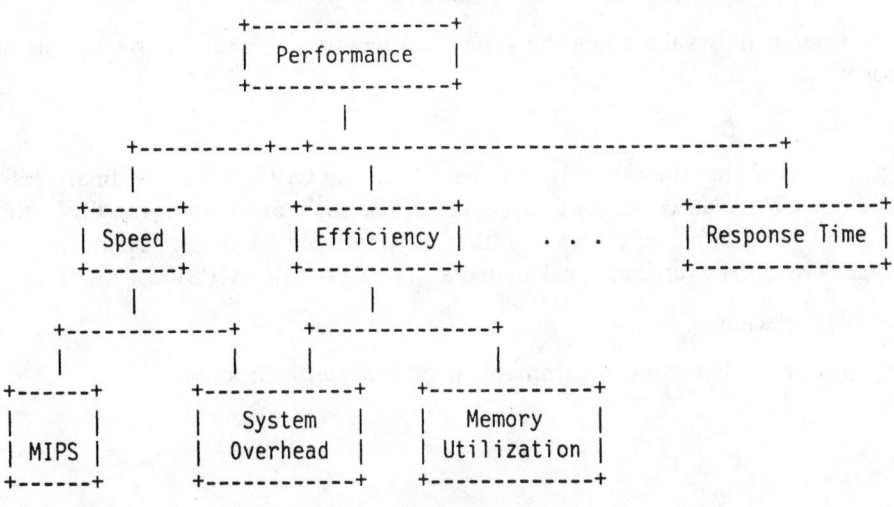

Figure 10. A partial Hierarchy from the Metrics Framework

Metrics Set -- Metric Description #1

Item	Description
Name	System Overhead
Metric	Number of cycles divided by MIPS (during test time)
Costs	1. Logic analyzers must be purchased and attached to the test system - $5K per system. User training for one person week. 2. Parts of the operating system must be instrumented - 2 person weeks. 3. Technician must be assigned to run equipment - 5 person weeks.
Benefits	Useful for characterizing cost of our software to the customers. Will flag an alert when the operating system is no longer "true realtime".
Impact	If system overhead exceeds target value plus 2%, the project must undergo management review.
Target Value	The goal is to keep system overhead to less than 5% of the CPU time.
Factors	Performance
Tools	Logic analyzer, database, and plotting software.
Application	This metric is required during system test to verify that the operating system meets its performance requirements. It is also required at the end of the development phase to verify that the system is ready for third party testing.
Data Items	Fraction of CPU time.
Computation	The metric value is the fraction of the total CPU cycles spent executing operating system instructions (privileged bit enabled). The measurement is to be taken while the machine is executing the standard regression test suite (see the project test plan for further details).

Interpretation The metric value is the reciprocal of the available CPU power.

Considerations The metric value is only valid when the system is executing a representative sample of application code.

Training Required Logic analyzer training.

Example Project X has a goal that the OS only requires 5% of the CPU cycles. At final verification, the test technician connects the programmable logic analyzer to the CPU and sets it to count the number of cycles in which the privileged bit is set. Then, the full test package is run, the overhead is calculated as: (# of cycles)/(MIPS)(test time).

Validation History None for this application

References Refer to project test plan and programmable logic analyzer instructions.

Metrics Set -- Metric Description #2

Item	Description
Name	Defect Rate
Metric	Defects reported divided by number of work weeks. See Computation.
Costs	1. Defect database must be maintained - 4 person hours per week. 2. All defects discovered must be logged - 1 hour per tester per week. 3. Periodic reports must be generated - 2 hours per week. 4. Labor for developers and testers to attend the defect database class.
Benefits	Useful for predicting post-release Mean Time To Failure (MTTF). Also useful for tracking progress of the test phase.
Impact	If the defect rate differs from an historical average for this type of project by more than one standard deviation, then review the testing procedures.
Target Value	There is no target value for the defect finding rate per se. The goal is to find all of the defects prior to system release.
Factors	Reliability
Tools	Defect database and report generation software.
Application	This metric is required during all defect finding activities including design and code review, functional and system test, and (for validation purposes) post system release.
Data Items	Defect descriptions including date found, date fixed, type of defect (real error or tester misunderstanding), and severity.
Computation	The defect rate is calculated by dividing the number of defects reported by the number of work weeks. The defect rate may be calculated for all reported defects, all defects that actually have to be fixed and all defects of high severity.
Interpretation	The defect rate is to be plotted on a chart vs. the average defect rate for this type of project. If the rate is far higher than average, then the software may be exceptionally poor; extra investigation of the software is required. If the rate is far lower than average, then the test procedures may not be stringent enough; a review of the test is required. The MTTF is to be predicted using the non-homogeneous Poisson model.
Considerations	The metric is only to be used as a sanity check and potential predictor. Do not base software release decision on it.
Training Required	All developers and testers must take the defect database class (4 hours).
Example	For the 5 weeks of testing, the number of defects reported against a software package is: 20, 20, 14, 35, and 44. The rate is out of the bounds allowable for that type of package - it is reaching a peak at the wrong time (too soon). The software under test is sent back for additional code inspections, and the data is not used for prediction of MTTF - it will not converge.
Validation History	None for this application
References	See Appendix D.2, #13 on page 98

C.2.3.2 Perform a Cost-Benefit Analysis

C.2.3.2.1 Identify the Costs of Implementing the Metrics

At this time, each proposed metric must be examined to consider how much it would cost to implement. For example, what is the overhead involved in tracking every defect? What is the (anticipated) gain in knowing this information? For each metric that it uses, the example company considers:

- What tools exist to use this metric, and, if necessary, how much would it cost to acquire them?
- How much staffing and training is required, by each organization, in order to effectively use each tool? Use of a tool may also require a change in the overall development process.
- How much time and associated cost will it take development team to collect, analyze, interpret and report each metric?
- How much of the data collection process can be automated? The cost of the hardware and software used for this purpose must be included.

C.2.3.2.2 Identify the Benefits of Applying the Metrics

For each proposed metric, consider:

- Who (developer, management, marketing) benefits from the information?
- How much will the final software product benefit, in quality terms, by having this metric data?
- How much, if anything, will be saved over the software life cycle by using this information? For example, will having defect information early shorten regression testing time?

C.2.3.2.3 Adjust the Metrics Set

Based on the cost-benefit analysis performed in sections C.2.3.2.1 and C.2.3.2.2, decisions must be made to either use, alter, or delete each proposed metric. It would be helpful, for future projects, to note the rationale for altering or deleting a metric from the metrics set.

C.2.3.3 Gain Commitment to the Metrics Set

The final metrics set including the cost/benefit analysis must be presented to management, understood, and accepted before implementation. This may be done by a combination of circulating review copies of the metrics set, having inspections, or holding meetings.

C.2.4 Implement the Software Quality Metrics

C.2.4.1 Define the Data Collection Procedures

At this point, explicit information must be recorded regarding who will collect what metrics data and when. These procedures should be recorded according to the format stated in the standard (Figure 3 on page 11).

An illustration of the data item, Defect Description, used by the Defect Rate metric (see Section C.2.3.1) follows.

<u>Metrics Set -- Description of a Data Item</u>

Item	**Description**
Name	Defect Description (Test Phase)
Metrics	Defect Rate, Defect Locality, Unresolved Defects.
Definition	The Defect Description is a set of data stored at the time a tester discovers an anomaly in the software. The description must contain, but is not limited to the following data items: 1. Tester name 2. Suspect Software 3. Date Found 4. General Description 5. Defect Type 6. Resolution (includes tester error) 7. Date Resolved 8. Modules fixed (if appropriate) 9. Related defects.
Source	The primary source is the test procedure(s). However, any person associated with the project that finds a defect, regardless of how, must report it.
Collector	See Source
Timing	This type of defect description is valid after the software has passed inspections through its release.
Procedure	The descriptions are to be entered manually using the relational database access programs.
Storage	The defect database
Representation	ASCII text, with keyed fields
Sample	All defects during testing shall be recorded and entered into the database.
Verification	All defect resolutions must have the approval of the originator or the project management team.
Alternatives	Software Problem Report form.
Integrity	Any member of the project may submit a defect description at any time. However, only the database administrator may remove one from the system.

C.2.4.2 Prototype the Measurement Process

The company has decided to test the metrics program on a small project. In this case, they have decided to apply as many of the metrics as possible to already released software, and to compare them to the direct measures they received from the field (this is particularly useful with predictive measures on defect rates). The company has also decided to apply the metrics to a minor upgrade of the product. This has the advantages of being a small enough project to manage, and of providing a base line for cost benefits analysis. (How much longer/shorter did it take to release this version of the product?)

C.2.4.3 Select Tools to Apply the Metrics

In order to save time and money, our company has decided to use a third party defect data base and defect tracking system from a previous project, and will develop its own data entry procedures.

C.2.4.4 Collect the Data and Compute the Metrics Values

As the project life-cycle progresses, the responsible parties are collecting and storing defect rate data into the newly acquired database. An organization must be elected to monitor and analyze the data collection process and metric computations for accuracy, uniformity and validity.

C.2.5 Analyze the Software Metrics Results

The organization responsible for archiving, analyzing, and reporting the software quality metrics for the example company is quality assurance. Their job includes making occasional sanity checks on the metrics data base, seeing to it that the data is accumulated (whether automatically or manually), interpreting the documented metrics set and reporting (ideally, in tabular or graphical form) to the appropriate project personnel. On the prototype project, close attention is paid to how much QA time is taken by this activity, and how much use is made of the metrics. This information is used for future cost benefit-analysis.

C.2.5.1 Interpret the Results

In accordance with Metric Description #2, the Defect Rate is calculated three ways: 1) for all reported defects; 2) for those defects that result in fixes; and 3) for those defects of high severity. Meetings are held with the proper project personnel to determine the cause of unusually high or low defect rates.

C.2.5.2 Identify Software Quality

The accuracy and timeliness of the non-predictive metrics are evaluated as the project progresses.

Before the software becomes operational, all predictive values not satisfying the agreed upon quality requirement direct metric target values need detailed analysis. It is important to note, if a metric falls outside its target value, it does not always result in unacceptable software quality during operation.

Based on the example metrics set, the following should be considered: Are all defects being reported ?; Are the system overhead figures reproducible ?; and What is the cost of gathering, storing and correlating the data? After delivery of the system, the predictive metrics are re-examined.

C.2.5.3 Make Software Quality Predictions

After project delivery, a metrics report is published complete with an updated metrics analysis where actual cost data replaces the original estimates and predictive figures are published using the formulas in the metrics set. This information becomes part of the project history, which is archived for future reference.

For the System Overhead metric, data has been gathered regarding what percentage of CPU cycles is used by the Operating System (OS). Since the overhead changes are based on what the OS is doing, the data was gathered during the execution of a set of standard benchmark programs. The metrics set indicates how to normalize this data in order to predict post release Efficiency.

C.2.5.4 Ensure Compliance with Requirements

All Quality requirements and factors, metrics and associated direct metric target values measured are compared to actual metric results. Each measurement which does not meet the specified target value(s) are non-compliant. It is up to Project Management, QA and Marketing to:

1. have the quality requirement met before shipment
2. waive the quality requirement, or
3. schedule the rework of the design in the future to improve the quality of the product.

C.2.6 Validate the Software Quality Metrics

The methodology used to validate the metrics described in this commercial example was similar to the methodology described in Section D.1.6 of the Mission Critical Example. The methodology is not presented here both to save space and to prevent unnecessary duplication of information.

Appendix D. Annotated Bibliography, References, and Standards

THIS APPENDIX IS NOT A PART OF IEEE STD 1061-1992, STANDARD FOR A SOFTWARE QUALITY METRICS METHODOLOGY, BUT IS INCLUDED FOR INFORMATION ONLY.

Appendix D.1 Annotated Bibliography

1. Adamov, R., Lutz, R.; "A Proposal for Measuring the Structural Complexity of Programs", *The Journal of Systems Software*, Volume 12, 1990, pp. 55-70.

   This article presents the basic ideas behind a proposed structural complexity metric.

2. Bailey, C.T., Dingee, W.L.; "A Software Study Using Halstead Metrics", *Performance Evaluation Review*, Volume 10, March 1981, pp. 189- 197.

   This paper examines two of Halstead's premises: that software errors can be correlated with effort or volume, and that language level is a constant over all algorithms in a given language. The authors results did not agree with these premises.

3. Baker, A., Bieman, J ., Fenton, N., Gustafson, D., Melton, A., Whitty, R.; "A Philosophy for Software Measurement"; *The Journal of Systems and Software*, Volume 12, Number 3, July 1990, pp. 277-281.

   This paper presents a discussion on validation of software measurement and discusses uses for structural measures.

4. Baker, A.L., Zweben, S.H.; "A Comparison of Measures of Control Flow Complexity", *IEEE Transactions on Software Engineering*, Volume SE- 6, November 1980, pp. 506-512.

   The authors analytically examine the strengths and weakness of three measures, namely software efforts (Halstead), program knots (Woodard, Henner, and Hedley), and cyclomatic complexity (McCabe), with respect to three control flow issues. They come to the conclusion that McCabe's cyclomatic complexity measure is the best measure of program control flow complexity as it is based on firm analytical ground and unlike, the knots measure, it does not suffer from the disadvantage of language dependency. They also conclude that it would be worthwhile to develop a metric which is a combination of software effort and cyclomatic complexity since their respective strengths and weakness complement each other.

5. Basili, V.R.; *Tutorial on Models and Metrics for Software Management and Engineering*, Computer Society Press, 1980.

   This tutorial collects several papers on different topics of software metrics. Some of the papers listed in this bibliography are included in this tutorial.

6. Basili, V.R., Phillips, T.; "Evaluating and Comparing the Software Metrics in the Software Engineering Laboratory", *ACM Sigmetrics*, 1981 ACM Workshop and Symposium on Measurement and Evaluation of Software Quality, Vol. 10, March 1981, pp. 95-106.

This paper presents results of a statistical regression carried out on data to find a relationship between Halstead's effort metric and various stages of the software development process. It also examines whether other measures such as lines of source code and executable statements, provide a better relationship with the effort metric and whether factors such as size, complexity, and testing level affect the correlations.

7. Basili, V.R., Selby, R.W., Phillips, T.Y.; "Metric Analysis and Data Validation Across FORTRAN Projects", *IEEE Transactions on Software Engineering*, Volume SE-9, Number 6, November 1983, pp. 652-663.

   As a step towards validating some of the available quality metrics, the authors have analyzed the software science metrics, cyclomatic complexity and various standard program measures for their relation to effort, development errors, and one another. The data investigated are collected from a production FORTRAN environment and examined across several project at once, within individual projects, and by individual programmers across projects.

8. Bastani, F.G.; "An Approach to Measuring Program Complexity", *Proceedings of COMPSAC 83*, Chicago, IL, 1983, pp. 90-94.

   The author proposes a measure of program complexity based on the program dependency graph and on the simulation of the program understanding process. The model uses two parameters, induction ability and a good memory ability to determine complexity.

9. Beizer, B.; *Software Testing Techniques (second edition)*, Van Nostrand Reinhold, New York, New York, 1990.

   This book has a chapter devoted to metrics that includes a summary of the strengths, weaknesses, and criticism of McCabe's metrics; Halstead's metrics; and various structural, linguistic and hybrid metrics in addition to extensive bibliographical references to the metrics literature.

10. Berns, G.M.; "Assessing Software Maintainability", *Communications of the ACM*, Volume 27, Number 1, January 1984, pp. 15-23.

    This paper suggests that how easy it is to maintain a program depends on how difficult the program is to understand and presents a technique to measure program difficulty by quantifying carefully selected weights and factors. This technique is implemented in the Maintainability Analysis Tool (MAT), a superset of FORTRAN 77, for the VAX computer.

11. Berry, R.E., Meekings, B.A.E., "A Style Analysis of C Programs", *Communications of the ACM*, Volume 28, Number 1, January 1985, pp. 80-88.

    This paper presents a metric for measuring the "style" of C programs.

12. Bowen, T., Wigle, G., Tsai, J.; "Specification of Software Quality Attributes", *RADC-TR-85-37*, 3 Volumes, February 1985.

    This document is a three volume set which was produced to provide methods, procedures, techniques, and guidance to Rome Air Development Center Air Force software acquisition managers who specify the requirements for software quality.

13. Card, D, Glass, R.L.; *Measuring Software Design Quality*; Prentice Hall, Englewood Cliffs, New Jersey, 1990.

This book proposes a set of metrics relating to software design complexity, describes a software complexity model, and validates this model using data from actual projects.

14. Cheung, R.C.; "A User-Oriented Software Reliability Model", *IEEE Transactions on Software Engineering*, Volume SE-6, Number 2, March 1980, pp. 118-125.

This paper gives some calculations of program reliability based on how reliable its modules are. The effect of module change on the whole program and ways of estimating probability measures of module reliability are presented.

15. Christensen, K., Fitsos, G.P., Smith, C.P.; "A Perspective on Software Science", *IBM Systems Journal*, Volume 20, Number 4, April 1981, pp. 372-387.

This paper provides an overview of an approach to the measurement of software based on the count of operators and operands contained in a program and is consistent across programming language barriers. This paper is critical of software science as a practical engineering tool but praises it as a step.

16. Conte, S., Dunsmore, H., Shen, V.; *Software Engineering Metrics and Models*, Benjamin Cummings Publishing Co., 1986.

A textbook describing the topic of software metrics.

17. Cook, M.L.; "Software Metrics: An Introduction and Annotated Bibliography", *Software Engineering Notes*, Volume 7, Number 2, April 1982, pp. 41-60.

The author introduces and presents an annotated bibliography on software metrics. As well as program complexity metrics he discusses resource measurement, system measurement, and overviews of software engineering and software metrics in general.

18. Cote, V., Bourque, P., Oligny, S., Rivard, N.; "Software Metrics: An Overview of Recent Results", *The Journal of Systems and Software*, Volume 8, 1988.

This paper classifies and compares 124 articles on software metrics.

19. Coulter, N.S., Cooper, R.B., Solomon, M.K.; "Information-Theoretic Complexity of Program Specifications", *The Computer Journal*, Volume 30, Number 3, June 1987, pp. 223-227.

This paper proposes an entropy metric for measuring the complexity of a program specification.

20. Crawford, S.G., McIntosh, A.A., Pregibon, D.; "An Analysis of Metrics and Faults in C Software"; *The Journal of Systems and Software*, Volume 5, Number 1, February 1985, pp. 37-48.

This paper evaluates the extent to which a set of software measures (including McCabe's and Halstead's) correlate with the number of faults and total estimated repair effort for a large software system.

21. Currans, N.; "A Comparison of Counting Methods for Software Science and Cyclomatic Complexity", *Pacific Northwest Software Quality Conference*, 1986.

Counting methods for Halstead's metrics, McCabe's metric, lines of code, and bugs are correlated and compared. This article is based on a study of 30 "C" modules (no module size is given) and presents a correlation between alternative ways of counting McCabe's complexity.

22. Curtis, B.; "Measurement and Experimentation in Software Engineering", *Proceedings of the IEEE*, Volume 68, Number 9, September 1980, pp. 1144-1157.

The contributions of measurement and experimentation to the state of the art in software engineering are reviewed. The role of measurement in developing theoretical models is discussed, and concerns for reliability and validity are stressed.

23. Davcev, D.; "Some New Observations about Software Science Indicators for Estimating Software Quality", *Empirical Foundations of Information and Software Science, Proceedings of the First Symposium*, Atlanta GA., November 1982, pp. 245-248.

In this paper the author points out the drawbacks of Halstead's and Mccabe's metrics in estimating implementation time and proposes an estimator for computing the total number of mental comparisons for implementing a program in a given language and estimating implementation time taking into account the level of nesting in a program. Experiments on FORTRAN programs showed a high degree of agreement between observed times and predicted times.

24. Davis, J.S.; "Chunks: A Basis for Complexity Measurement", *Empirical Foundations of Information and Software Science, Proceedings of the First Symposium*, Atlanta, GA, November 1982, pp. 119-128.

The author contends that chunks play an important role in cognitive process and are thus a more convincing basis for complexity measurement than existing direct measures such as operators and operands. Chunks are loosely defined as statements that are related functionally and conceptually. Any complexity measure must account for the complexity of the chunks themselves and their interconnections, to determine overall program complexity.

25. DeMarco, T.; *Controlling Software Project, Management, Measurements, and Estimation*, Yourdon Press, New York, 1982.

This book provides various methods to estimate the costs of software development and to determine the validity of the estimation as the software is developed. The metrics suggested in this book are based on the methods provided in the author's earlier book, "Structured Analysis and System Specifications."

26. Deutsch, M.S., Willis, R.R.; *Software Quality Engineering* , Prentice Hall, Englewood Cliffs, New Jersey, 1988.

This book contains a section which describes an approach to specifying software quality, achieving quality and mapping the quality framework into a set of activities.

27. Dunsmore, H.E.; "Software Metrics: An Overview of an Evolving Methodology", *Empirical Foundations of Information and Software Science, Proceedings of the First Symposium*, , Atlanta, GA, November 1982, pp. 183-192.

This paper describes (with examples) lines of code, cyclomatic complexity, average nesting depth, and the software science length, effort, and time metrics. Software metrics that are to be used for time, cost, or reliability estimates should be validated statistically via data analyses that take into consideration the application, size, implementation language, and programming techniques employed. The critical need is for software metrics that can be calculated early in the software development cycle to estimate the time and cost involved in software construction.

28. Ejiogu, L.O.; "The Critical Issues of Software Metrics", *ACM SIGPLAN Notices*, March 1987, pp. 59-63.

This paper defines Software Metrics as the science of measurements of software productivity for the purposes of comparison, cost estimation and forecasting and discusses four techniques of measurement: Enumeration, estimation, dimensionalization and parameterization and when it is appropriate to use each technique.

29. Elshoff, J.L.; "Characteristic Program Complexity Measures", *Seventh International Conference on Software Engineering*, Orlando, March 26-29, 1984.

Twenty metrics (including Halstead's Software Science) are applied to 585 PL/I procedures and the results are correlated.

30. Evangelist, M .; "Program Complexity and Programming Style", *Proceedings of the International Conference on Data Engineering (COMPDEC), IEEE*, 1984, pp. 534-541.

Shows that popular software complexity metrics are not consistently sensitive to the application of programming style rules.

31. Evans, M., Marciniak, J.; *Software Quality Assurance & Management*, John Wiley & Sons, 1987.

This book discusses the importance of measurement to software quality and outlines a software quality framework.

32. Evans, W.E., Marciniak, J.J.; "Software Quality Metrics" in *Software Quality Assurance and Management*, John Wiley and Sons, 1987, pp. 157-186.

This chapter states that to achieve a true indication of quality software must be subjected to measurement, that is the attributes of quality must be related to specific product requirements and quantified.

33. Fagan, M; "Advances in Software Inspections", *IEEE Transactions on Software Engineering*, Volume SE-12, Number 7, July 1986.

This paper contains a description of the Fagan inspection technique.

34. Fitsos, G.P.; "Vocabulary Effects in Software Science", *Seventh International Conference on Software Engineering*, Orlando, March 26-29, 1984.

This paper states that the unique operators for a set of programs tends to be a constant number for PL/S and possibly for PL/I (and postulates that this may hold true for other high level languages). It proposes a methodology to provide a quantitative measure of difficulty against which an individual programmer can measure themselves.

35. Gaffney, J.E.; "Estimating the Number of Faults in Code", *IEEE Transactions on Software Engineering*, Volume SE-10, Number 4, July 1984, pp. 459-465.

This paper provides formulas relating the number of faults to the number of lines of code and to the number of conditional jumps and determines that there are, on the average, about 21 bugs per KSLOC discoverable after successful compilation. It shows that the number of bugs appears not to be a function of the "level" of the coding language employed and knowledge of items such as the size of the vocabulary (operator and operand) used appears to be of little consequence to the estimate of bug content beyond that based on SLOC count.

36. Gong, H.S., Schmidt, M.; "A Complexity Metric Based on Selection and Nesting", *ACM Sigmetrics -- Performance Evaluation Review* 13-1 ,1985, pp. 14-19.

These authors present a structural metric which augments Cyclomatic complexity to include nesting depth.

37. Grady, R., Caswell, D.; *Software Metrics: Establishing a Company- Wide Program*, Prentice-Hall, 1987.

Contains a discussion of how Hewlett-Packard recognized a need for a measurable, controllable software process and describes the method they used to meet that need by putting a software metrics program into place. Lessons and examples can be transferred to other companies.

38. Hall, W.E., Zweben, S.H.; "The Cloze Procedure and Software Comprehensibility Measurement", *IEEE Transactions on Software Engineering*, Volume SE-12, Number 5, May 1986, pp. 608-623.

Cloze tests seem to offer software engineers several theoretical and practical advantages over multiple-choice comprehension quizzes, the most common software comprehension measurement tool. A model of software cloze tests was developed to identify a software characteristic that may produce invalid results. The developed model was shown to be consistent with software cloze test results of another researcher and led to suggestions for improving software cloze testing.

39. Hamer, P.G., Frewin, G.D.; "M.H. Halstead's Software Science - A Critical Examination", *Proceedings of the Sixth International Conference on Software Engineering*, Tokyo, 1982, pp. 197-206.

Halstead's Software Science is examined and critiqued.

40. Harrison, W.A., Magel, K.; "A Topological Analysis of the Complexity of Computer Programs with Less than Three Binary Branches", ;cit.ACM SIGPLAN Notices, Volume 16, 1981, pp. 51-63.

This paper proposes complexity measures called "Scope Number" and "Scope Ratio" which are based on the topological analysis of the software's flow of control. The scope number recognizes the fact that the complexity at each node may not be equal, and assigns a complexity to it depending on the complexity of the statements within the node with the scope number being the aggregate of the complexities of the nodes and giving the complexity of the program as a whole. The authors also introduce the concept of "scope ratio" which is a ratio of the number of nodes in the program to the scope number.

41. Harrison, W.K., Kluczny, M.R., DeKock, A.; "Applying Software Complexity Metrics to Program Maintenance", *IEEE Computer*, September 1982, pp. 65-79.

This paper describes many of the popular complexity metrics in each of four categories: control flow, size, data, and hybrid. The conclusion offers a table of metrics surveyed and a qualitative evaluation of their scope of usefulness and the effectiveness for discriminating program text based on complexity.

42. Harrison, W., Cook, C.R.; "A Note on the Berry-Meekings Style Metrics", *Communications of the ACM*, Volume 29, Number 2, February 1986, pp. 123-125.

Testing C Language programs against a variant of the Berry-Meekings style metrics based on how closely a program conforms to a given set of rules reveals little relationship between style scores and error proneness.

43. Harrison, W.; "How Complex is Your Software?", *Computer Language*, January 1988, pp. 73-75.

Contains an explanation of complexity measures using PASCAL programs as an example and explains why software complexity is important to the programmer.

44. Henry, S., Selig, C., "Predicting Source-Code Complexity at the Design Stage", *IEEE Software*, Volume 7, Number 2, March 1990, pp. 36-44.

This paper states that the use of design metrics allow for determination of the quality of source code by evaluating design specifications before coding causing a shortened development life cycle.

45. Henry, S.M., Kafura, D., Harris, K.; "On the Relationships among Three Software Metrics", *Proceedings of ACM SIGMETRICS*, 1981, pp. 81-89.

This paper reports the results of correlation studies made among three complexity metrics which were applied to the same software system. The primary result of this study is that Halstead's and McCabe's metrics are highly correlated while the information flow metric appears to be an independent measure of complexity.

46. Henry, S.M., Kafura, D.; "Software Structure Metrics Based on Information Flow", *IEEE Transactions on Software Engineering*, Volume 7, Number 5, May 1981, pp. 510-518.

This paper defines the basic notions of the information flow technique and analyzes the UNIX operating system to demonstrate the application of the technique and proposes a structural complexity measure which is used to evaluate the procedure and module structure of UNIX. The authors validate this metric by demonstrating that its correlation to the occurrence of system changes is as high as 0.98.

47. Hess, J.A.; "Measuring Software for Its Reuse Potential", *1988 Proceedings Annual Reliability and Maintainability Symposium*, January 1988, pp. 202-206.

Examines a variety of measures for software and shows why the physical properties of software are important for determining reuse potential, and provides design guidelines for the structuring and analysis of software to enhance its reusability.

48. Humphrey, W.S., Sweet, W.L., Edwards, R.K., LaCroix, G.R., Owens, M.F., Schulz, H.P.; *A Method for Assessing the Software Engineering Capability of Contractors*, CMU/SEI-87-TR-23, Software Engineering Institute, Carnegie Mellon University, Pittsburgh, Pennsylvania.

This document provides guidelines and procedures for assessing the ability of potential DoD contractors to develop software in accordance with modern software engineering methods. It includes specific questions and a method for evaluating the results.

49. Ince, D.; "Software Metrics: Introduction", *Information and Software Technology*, Volume 32, Number 4, May 1990, pp. 297-303.

This paper outlines the nature of software quality metrics, places them in historical context, and describes how they might be used.

50. Iyengar, S.S., Parameswaran, N., Fuller, J.W.; "A Measure of Logical Complexity of Programs", *Journal of Computer Languages*, Volume 7, 1982, pp. 147-160.

The authors point out the shortcomings of Halstead's, McCabe's and the knots measure in quantifying complexity of programs and propose a measure based on the dependency of values of variables upon the past computations in the program, the inductive effort involved in writing the loops, and the data structure complexity.

51. Jensen, H.A., Vairavan, K.; "An Experimental Study of Software Metrics for Real-time Software", *IEEE Transactions on Software Engineering*, Volume SE-11, Number 2, February 1985, pp. 231-234.

The authors have introduced a new expression, empirically derived, for the program length estimator which predicts program length more accurately for the data gathered than Halstead's length estimator. The relationship between various software metrics were determined by computing Pearson's correlation coefficient's for every pair of metrics.

52. Johnston, D.B., Lister, A.M.; *An Experiment in Software Science*, Language Design and Programming Methodology, Jeffrey M. Tobias, editor, Springer-Verlag, 1980, pp. 195-215.

Several hundred student Pascal programs were studied. The results do not support Halstead's equations. This may be because of poor program construction and many impurities in student programs, or may indeed show that Halstead's metrics are not good in practice. This is one of the few papers showing poor results using Halstead's theory.

53. Jorgensen, A.H.; "A Methodology for Measuring the Readability and Modifiability of Computer Programs", *BIT*, Volume 20, 1980, pp. 394-405.

Various measures of the readability of programs and what program features may be important are discussed. The amount of comments, number of blank lines, average length of variable names, average number of arithmetics operators, and average number of goto's per label were studied.

54. Kafura, D., Redy, G.R.; "The Use of Software Complexity in Software Maintenance", *IEEE Transactions on Software Engineering*, Volume SE-13, Number 3, March 1987, pp 335-343.

This paper reports on a study which relates seven different software complexity metrics to the experience of maintenance activities performed on a medium size software system. Three different versions of the system including a major revision which occurred during design that evolved over a period of three years were analyzed in this study.

55. Kearney, J.K., Sedlmeyer, R.L., Thompson, W.B., Gray, M.A., Adler, M.A., "Software Complexity Measurement", *Communications of the ACM*, Volume 29, Number 11, November 1986, pp. 1044-1050.

The authors contend that the reason why software metrics have not realized their full potential for the reduction and management of software costs has been a lack of a unified approach to the development, testing, and use of these measures. Complexity measures have been developed without any particular use in mind. The authors suggested approach for the creation of complexity measures is that a clear specification of what is being measured and why it is to be measured must be formulated.

56. Khoshgoftaar, T.M., Munson, J.C., "Predicting Software Development Errors Using Software Complexity Metrics", *IEEE Journal on Selected Areas in Communications*, Volume 8, Number 2, February 1990, pp. 253- 261.

This paper develops predictive models that incorporate a functional relationship of program error measures with software complexity metrics and metrics based on factor analysis of empirical data. Specific techniques for assessing regression models are presented.

57. Kitchenham, B.A.; "Measures of Programming Complexity", *ICL Technical Journal*, Volume 2, Number 3, 1981, pp. 298-316.

This paper reports on an attempt to assess the ability of the measures of complexity proposed to provide objective indicators of the effort involved in software production when applied to selection subsystems of an operating system.

58. Kitchenham, B.A.; "Towards a Constructive Quality Model", *Software Engineering Journal*, July 1987.

This paper proposes a quality model (COQUAMO) whose goal is to identify a predictive model of product quality based on quality drivers.

59. Kitchenham , B.A., Linkman, S.J.; "Design Metrics: in Practice", *Information and Software Technology*, Volume 32, Number 4, May 1990, pp. 304-310.

This paper describes a method of software quality control based on the use of software metrics and applies this method to software design metrics.

60. Kitchenham, B.A., Walker, J.G.; "The Meaning of Quality", *Software Engineering 86*, D. Barnes and P. Brown (eds), Peter Peregrinus Ltd, pp. 393-406.

This discusses some of the problems relating to the use of quality factors and associated criteria.

61. Konstam, A.H., Wood, D.E.; "Software Science Applied to APL", *IEEE Transactions on Software Engineering*, Volume SE-11, Number 10, October 1985.

This paper contains an investigation into the application of software metrics to APL to try to resolve some of the inconsistency and counter-intuitive results found in previous studies. Evidence is presented that verifies that APL has a higher language level than any other common programming language previously studied.

62. Koss, W.E.; "Software Reliability Metrics for Military Systems", *1988 Proceedings Annual Reliability and Maintainability Symposium*, January 1988, pp. 190-194.

Discusses the statistics of software reliability and why reliability is critical.

63. Levitin, A.V.; "How to Measure Software Size, and How Not To", *Tenth International Computer Software and Applications Conference*, Chicago, Illinois, October 8-10, 1986.

Includes critique of such metrics as: Lines of code, statement counts, and Halstead's Software Science. This article suggests the use of token counts.

64. Li, H.F.; Chung, W.K.; "An Empirical Study of Software Metrics", *IEEE Transactions on Software Engineering*, Volume 13, Number 6, June 1987, pp. 697-708.

Comparison and correlation of 31 different software metrics applied to 250 small programs by students.

65. Lind, R.K., Vairavan, K.; "An Experimental Investigation of Software Metrics and Their Relation to Software Development Effort", *IEEE Transactions on Software Engineering*, Volume 15, Number 5, May 1989, pp. 649-653.

This paper reports the results of a study of software metrics for a large software system used in a real-time application.

66. Lister, A.M.; "Software Science - The Emperor's New Clothes", *Technical Report No 21, Department of Computer Science*, University of Queensland, October 1980.

Halstead's Software Science is examined and critiqued.

67. McCall, J.A.; "An Assessment of Current Software Metric Research", *EASCON'80*, 1980, pp. 323-333.

This paper surveys work in software metrics and covers how metrics may be used, classes of metrics, validation of metrics, applications of metrics, theoretical approaches to metrics, and the role of metrics in quality assurance and meeting the customer's needs.

68. Melton, A., Gustafson, D., Bieman, J., Baker, A.; "A Mathematical Perspective for Software Measures Research"; *Software Engineering Journal*, September, 1990.

This paper identifies and analyzes the basic principles which underlie software measures research. It also discusses the difference between structure complexity and psychological complexity and the importance of not equating them.

69. Mizuno, Y.; "Software Quality Improvement", *COMPUTER*, IEEE Computer Society, Volume 16, Number 3, March 1983, pp. 66-72.

This article stresses that teamwork is the key to improved software quality at Nippon Electric Company. The 'metrics' which drive their productivity are: specific to volatility, user complexity, generality of the product, requested quality type of contract and human factor, with the last item being the most important.

70. Munson, J.C., Khoshgoftaar, T.M., "The Dimensionality of Program Complexity", :cit,Proceedings of the 11th International Conference on Software Engineering, IEEE Computer Society Press, May 15-18, 1989, pp. 245-251.

This paper examines some recent investigations in the area of software complexity using factor analysis to begin an exploration of the actual dimensionality of the complexity metrics. Some correlation coefficients from recent empirical studies on software metrics were factor analyzed, showing the probable existence of five complexity dimensions within thirty five different complexity measures.

71. Musa, J.D.; "Software Reliability Measurement", *The Journal of Systems and Software*, Volume 1, Number 3, 1980, pp. 223-241.

A model of software reliability based on the execution time of programs is developed which relates execution (CPU) time to calendar time. This information is useful for scheduling projects and monitoring of program testing. These estimated can be changed as the project proceeds.

72. Musa, J.D.; "The Measurement and Management of Software Reliability", *Proceedings of the IEEE*, Volume 68, Number 9, September 1980, pp. 1131-1143.

The author discusses what software reliability is and why it is a useful study and includes comparisons between software and hardware reliability, the detail's of Musa's and Littlewood's reliability theories, and research needs. A lengthy bibliography of related works is included.

73. Navlakha, J.K.; "A Survey of System Complexity Metrics", *The Computer Journal*, Volume 30, Number 3, 1987, pp. 233-238.

A survey of available complexity metrics for software.

74. Perlis, A., Sayward, F., Shaw, M.; *Software Metrics: An Analysis and Evaluation*, MIT Press, Cambridge, Massachusetts, 1981.

These authors present a survey of metrics literature and research including a large bibliography of metrics articles.

75. Perry, W.E.; *Effective Methods of EDP Quality Assurance*, QED Information Sciences Inc., 1981, Chapter 11: Metrics-A Tool for Defining and Measuring Quality.

This chapter presents procedures and guidelines for introducing and utilizing current quality measurement techniques in a quality assurance program associated with large-scale system developments. These procedures and guidelines explain how to identify and specify software quality requirements.

76. Pierce, P., Hartley, R., Worrells, S.; *Software Quality Measurement Demonstration Project II*, RADC-TR-87-164, October 1987.

This document provides an evaluation of an implementation of the guidelines for specifying software quality attributes presented in RADC- TR-85-37 by Bowen, Wigle, and Tsai. Also see Demonstration Project I report RADC-TR-87-247 by Warthman.

77. Piwowarski, P.; "A Nesting Level Complexity Measure", *ACM SIGPLAN Notices*, Volume 17, 1980, pp. 44-50.

The author proposes a new complexity measure to overcome the difficulty of ranking structured versus unstructured, sequential versus nested control structure, and the reduced complexity of Case statements. He shows that while metrics based on McCabe's cyclomatic complexity do not necessarily rank structured programs better than unstructured ones or sequential predicates less complex than nested predicates, the proposed measure succeeds in ranking programs so that it penalizes unstructuredness and the nesting of predicates and rewards the use of case statements.

78. Pollock, G.M., Sheppard, S.; "A Design Methodology for the Utilization of Metrics within Various Phases of the Software Lifecycle Model", *Eleventh International Computer Software and Applications Conference*, Tokyo, Japan, October 7-9, 1987.

This paper includes a survey of metrics and a description of a general purpose metrics tool.

79. Porter, A.A., Selby, R.W., "Empirically Guided Software Development Using Metric-Based Classification Trees", *IEEE Software*, Volume 7, Number 2, March 1990, pp. 46-54.

This paper develops a method of generating measurement-based models of high-risk components automatically and a methodology for its application to large software projects. This method, automatic generation of metric-based classification trees, uses metrics from previous releases or projects to identify components that are likely to have some high-risk property based on historical data.

80. Putnam, L.H.; The Real Metrics of Software Development", *EASCON'80*, 1980, pp. 310-322.

A set of equations related to Shannon's Information Theory describing the software development process are given and discussed. Proper use of life-cycle equations can yield optimal solutions and trade-offs in planning the development process.

81. Rama Rao, K.V.S., Iyengar, S.; "A General Measure for Program Complexity", *Software Engineering Workshop*, Nice, France, June 1984.

The authors have introduced a general measure which deals with the overall program complexity and can also be extended to encompass all aspects of a program control structure, data structure and operating sequence. The measure is shown to be more powerful than the cyclomatic measure, as it reflects the structuredness better and unlike cyclomatic complexity which is applicable only to flow graphs, the proposed logical effort measure can be applied to programs in any language as well as flow graphs.

82. Ramamoorthy, C.V., Tsai, W.T., Yamaura, T., Bhide, A.; "Metrics Guided Methodology", *Ninth International Computer Software and Applications Conference*, Chicago, Illinois, October 9-11, 1985.

This paper presents a discussion of metric taxonomy and properties; various program models and associated metrics; and the role of metrics in design and test.

83. Redish, K.A., Smyth, W.F.; "Evaluating Measures of Program Quality", *The Computer Journal*, Volume 30, Number 3, 1987, p p. 228-232.

This paper examines available software quality metrics.

84. Rodriguez, V, Tsai, W.T.; "Software Metrics Interpretation through Experimentation", *Tenth International Computer Software and Applications Conference*, Chicago, Illinois, 1986.

Statistical comparison of Halstead's, Cyclomatic complexity, lines-of-code, data flow, and other metrics for bug prediction and maintenance effort.

85. Rodriguez, V, Tsai, W.T.; "Evaluation of Software Metrics Using Discriminate Analysis", *Eleventh International Computer Software and Applications Conference*, Tokyo, Japan, October 7-9,1987.

Statistical investigation of the ability of seven metrics to distinguish between simple and complicated software.

86. Roman, D.; "A Measure of Programming", *Computer Decisions*, January 1987, pp. 32-33.

In this article, the author talks about the superiority of the function points technique as a method of measuring programmer productivity. He presents results obtained by various applications of this technique.

87. Schneidewind, N.F., "Methodology for Validating Software Metrics", *IEEE Transactions on Software Engineering*, Volume 18, Number 5, May 1992, pp. 410-421.

This paper proposes a comprehensive metrics validation methodology that has six validation criteria, each of which supports certain quality functions. New criteria are defined and illustrated, including consistency, discriminative power, tracking and repeatability.

88. Shen, V.Y., Conte, S.D., Dunsmore, H.E.; "Software Science Revisited: A Critical Analysis of the Theory and Its Empirical Support", *IEEE Transaction on Software Engineering*, Volume SE-9, Number 2, March 1983, pp. 155-165.

Halstead Difficulty (D) has some validity as indicator of error proneness. Halstead Effort (E) is as good as any other metric for indicating programming effort. Other Halstead metrics are suspect.

89. Shen, V.Y., Yu, T.J., Thebaut, S.M., Paulsen, L.R.; "Identifying Error-Prone Software -- an Empirical Study", *IEEE Transactions on Software Engineering*, Volume 11, Number 4, April 1985, pp. 317-324.

Empirical study of 1423 modules averaging 420 LINEs of code relating Halstead's and McCabe's metrics to bug density.

90. Shepperd, M.; " A Critique of Cyclomatic Complexity as a Software Metric", *Software Engineering Journal*, March 1988, pp. 30-36.

This paper critiques McCabe s Cyclomatic Complexity. It states that it is based upon poor theoretical foundations and an inadequate model of software development.

91. Shepperd, M.; "Early Life-Cycle Metrics and Software Quality Models", *Information and Software Technology*, Volume 32, Number 4, May 1990, pp. 311-316.

This paper describes an mechanism for integrating early metrics into the software development environment to improve software quality.

92. Sheppard, S.B., Milliman, P., Curtis, B.; "Experimental Evaluation of On-Line Program Construction", *COMPSAC 80*, October 1980, pp. 505-510.

Halstead's effort and volume metrics and McCabe's v(G) were better estimators of programming time than the number of lines of code. Documentation for the problems did not seem to affect performance.

93. Sikaczowski, R.O.; "Measuring Customer satisfaction and Software Productivity through Quality Metrics", *Quality Data Processing*, January 1988, pp. 37-44.

Software quality metrics can be used to provide data for cost/benefit analysis while measuring customer satisfaction, evaluating the effects of new tools or methodologies, and helping manage/enhance quality processed during the software life cycle. Metrics of interest to three levels of management (executive, middle, and first line) are presented.

94. Singh, R., Schneidewind, N.F.; "Concept of a Software Quality Metrics Standard", *Digest of Papers, Spring COMPCON 86*, IEEE Computer Society, March 3-6, 1986, A.G. Bell (ed), pp. 362-368.

A concept of software quality is presented which provides the framework for the development of the IEEE Standard for Software Quality Metrics Methodology (P1061). This paper provides the basis for future development of the standard.

95. Sunohara, T., Takano, A., Uehara, K., Ohkawa, R.; "Program Complexity Measure for Software Development Management", *Fifth International Conference on Software Engineering*, San Diego, California, March 9-12, 1981.

McCabe's, Halstead's, lines of code, and other metrics are compared and correlated to productivity and bug rate for 137 modules.

96. Symons, C.R.; "Function Point Analysis: Difficulties and Improvements",*IEEE Transactions on Software Engineering*, Volume 14, Number 1, January 1988, pp. 2-11.

This article contains a critique and suggested enhancements for the function point metric.

97. Tse, T.H.; "Towards a Single Criterion for Identifying Program Unstructuredness", *The Computer Journal*, Volume 30, Number 4, August 1987, pp. 378-380.

This paper defines the concept of fully embedded skeletons and partially overlapping skeletons in program flowgraphs. A program is determined unstructured if it contains partially overlapping skeletons.

98. Trachtenberg, M.; "Validating Halstead's Theory with System 3 Data",*IEEE Transactions on Software Engineering*, Volume 12, Number 4, April 1986, pp. 584.

This letter disagrees with Thayre s software reliability data being used to validate Halstead's Software Science.

99. Tsai, W.T., Lopez, M .A., Rodriguez, V., Volovik, D.; "An Approach to Measuring Data Structure Complexity", *Tenth International Computer Software and Applications Conference*, Chicago, Illinois, October 8-10, 1986.

This paper proposes a topological complexity metric for data structures.

100. Van Verth, P.B.; "A Program Complexity Model that Includes Procedures", *Eleventh International Computer Software and Application Conference*, Tokyo, Japan, October 7-9, 1987.

This paper proposes a hybrid data-flow/control-flow structural metric.

101. Waguespack, L.J, Badlani, S.; "Software Complexity Assessment: An Introduction and Annotated Bibliography", *ACM SIGSOFT Software Engineering Notes*, Volume 12, Number 4, October 1987, pp. 52-71.

This article includes an introduction to software complexity, an index of 19 topics, and an annotated bibliography.

102. Walker, J.G., Kitchenham, B.A.; "The Architecture of an Automated Quality Management System", *ICL Technical Journal*, Volume 6, Issue 1, May 1988, pp. 156-170.

This article shows general support for the draft version of this standard and how it can fit into a wider framework of Quality Management.

103. Wang, A.S., Dunsmore, H.D.; "Back to Front Programming Effort Prediction", *Empirical Foundations of Information and Software Science, Proceedings of the First Symposium*, November 1982, pp. 139-150.

This paper discusses metrics for estimating the total software development effort: designing, coding, testing, and documenting. The main obstacle for the proper functioning of prediction models is the lack of availability of reliable estimates of the values of the parameters used in the models and the authors suggest that this could be overcome by trying to estimate the values only at a later point in the development process, when the estimate should be more reliable. They propose a family of metrics that will explain effort after the completion of a project and predict remaining effort when applied at some milestone prior to completion.

104. Warthman, J.; *Software Quality Measurement Demonstration Project I*, RADC-TR-87-247, December 1987.

This document provides an evaluation of an implementation of the guidelines for specifying software quality attributes presented in RADC- TR-85-37 by Bowen, Wigle, and Tsai. Also see Demonstration Project II report RADC-TR-87-164 by Pierce, Hartley, and Worrells.

105. Weiser, M.D., Gannon, J.D., McMullin, P.R.; "Comparison of Structural Test Coverage Metrics", *IEEE Software*, Volume 2, March, 1985, pp. 80-85.

This paper contains comparisons of data definition-use (du-path), statement, and branch coverage metrics and variations.

106. Weyuker, E.J.; "Evaluating Software Complexity Measures",*IEEE Transactions on Software Engineering*, Volume 14, Number 9, 1988, pp. 1357-1365.

This paper contains a formal analysis of axioms for complexity metrics and evaluations of several popular metrics and their problems.

107. Woodfield, S.N., Shen, V.Y., Dunsmore, H.E.; "A Study of Several Metrics for Programming Efforts", *J. System Software*, volume 2, December 1981, pp. 97-103.

This paper reports on an empirical study designed to compare three measures of complexity: lines of code measure; McCabe's cyclomatic complexity; and Halstead's effort measure. It also introduces and evaluates a fourth measure proposed by the authors based on a module of programming. The new measure which estimates time based on the logical module was found to have better correlation coefficients with actual time taken, than the other three metrics.

108. Yau, S.S., Colofello, S.; "Some Stability Measures for Software Maintenance", *IEEE Transactions on Software Engineering*, Volume SE-6, Number 6, November 1980, pp. 545-552.

Proposes logical stability metrics for software maintenance. Measured by variables affected by modification and modules and module interfaces affected by change in variable which results in propagation of change within module and across module boundaries.

109. Yau, S.E., Collofello, J.S.; "Design Stability Measures for Software Maintenance", *IEEE Transactions on Software Engineering*, Volume SE-11, Number 9, September 1985, pp. 849-856.

The high cost of software during its life cycle can be attributed largely to software maintenance activities and a major portion of these activities is to deal with the modifications of the software. In this paper, design stability measures which indicate the potential ripple effect characteristics due to modifications of the program at the design level are presented.

Appendix D.2 References

1. Albrecht, A.J.; "Measuring Application Development Productivity", *Proceedings, IBM Application Development Symposium*, Monterey, CA, October 14-17, 1979, GUIDE Int and SHARE, Inc., IBM Corp.

2. Albrecht, A.J. and Gaffney, J.E.; "Software Function, Source Lines of Code and Development Effort Prediction: "A Software Science Validation", *IEEE Software Engineering Transactions*, Volume 9, Number 6, November 1983.

3. Basili, V.R. and Perricone, B.T.; "Software Errors and Complexity: An Empirical Investigation", *Communications of the ACM*, January 1984.

4. Boehm, B.W.; *Software Engineering Economics*, Prentice-Hall, 1981.

5. Conover, W.J.; *Practical Nonparametric Statistics*, John Wiley & Sons, Inc., 1971.

6. Gibbons, J.D.; *Nonparametric Statistical Inference*, McGraw-Hill Book Company, 1971.

7. Halstead, H.M.; *Elements of Software Science*, North-Holland, 1977.

8. Kleinbaum, David G. and Kupper, Lawrence L.,; *Applied Regression Analysis and Other Multivariable Methods*, Duxbury Press, 1978.

9. McCabe, T.J.; "Complexity Measure", *IEEE Transactions on Software Engineering*, SE-2, Number 4, December 1976, pp. 308-320.

10. Myers, G.J.; *Reliable Software Through Composite Design*, Petrocelli/Charter, 1975.

11. Page-Jones, M.; *The Practical Guide to Structured Systems Design*, Yourdon Press, 1980.

12. Shen, V.Y., Conte, S.D., and Dunsmore, H.E.; "Software Science Revisited: A Critical Analysis of the Theory and Its Empirical Support", *IEEE Transaction on Software Engineering*, Volume 9, Number 2, March 1983.

13. Sukert, A. and Goel, A.; "A Guidebook for Software Reliability Assessment", *1980 Proceedings Annual Reliability and Maintainability Symposium* , pages 186 through 190;

Appendix D.3 Standards

1. AFSCP 800-14, *Air Force Systems Command Software Quality Indicators*, 20 January 1987.

2. AFSCP 800-43,*Air Force Systems Command Software Management Indicators*, 31 January 1986.

3. DoD STARS,*Guidebook for the STARS Measurement Program*, draft, version 1, September 30, 1985.

4. DOD-STD-2167A, *Defense System Software Development*, 29 February 1988.

5. DOD-STD-2168,*Defense System Software Quality Program*, 29 April 1988.

6. ISO/TC97/SC07/WG3 -- Document N-102,*Definition of 2nd Quality Characteristics*, March 1987.

7. ISO/TC97/SC07/WG3 -- Document N-106,*Software Quality Characteristics*, June 1987.

8. ISO/IEC JTC1/SC7/WG3 -- Document N-120, *Evaluation of Software Product - Software Quality Characteristics & Guidelines For Their Use (DP-9126)*, October 1988.

ANSI/IEEE Std 1063-1987

An American National Standard

IEEE Standard for Software User Documentation

Sponsor

Software Engineering Standards Subcommittee of the Technical Committee on Software Engineering of the IEEE Computer Society

Approved December 10, 1987

IEEE Standards Board

Approved February 2, 1989

American National Standards Institute

The Institute of Electrical and Electronics Engineers, Inc
345 East 47th Street, New York, NY 10017, USA

IEEE Standards documents are developed within the Technical Committees of the IEEE Societies and the Standards Coordinating Committees of the IEEE Standards Board. Members of the committees serve voluntarily and without compensation. They are not necessarily members of the Institute. The standards developed within IEEE represent a consensus of the broad expertise on the subject within the Institute as well as those activities outside of IEEE which have expressed an interest in participating in the development of the standard.

Use of an IEEE Standard is wholly voluntary. The existence of an IEEE Standard does not imply that there are no other ways to produce, test, measure, purchase, market, or provide other goods and services related to the scope of the IEEE Standard. Furthermore, the viewpoint expressed at the time a standard is approved and issued is subject to change brought about through developments in the state of the art and comments received from users of the standard. Every IEEE Standard is subjected to review at least once every five years for revision or reaffirmation. When a document is more than five years old, and has not been reaffirmed, it is reasonable to conclude that its contents, although still of some value, do not wholly reflect the present state of the art. Users are cautioned to check to determine that they have the latest edition of any IEEE Standard.

Comments for revision of IEEE Standards are welcome from any interested party, regardless of membership affiliation with IEEE. Suggestions for changes in documents should be in the form of a proposed change of text, together with appropriate supporting comments.

Interpretations: Occasionally questions may arise regarding the meaning of portions of standards as they relate to specific applications. When the need for interpretations is brought to the attention of IEEE, the Institute will initiate action to prepare appropriate responses. Since IEEE Standards represent a consensus of all concerned interests, it is important to ensure that any interpretation has also received the concurrence of a balance of interests. For this reason IEEE and the members of its technical committees are not able to provide an instant response to interpretation requests except in those cases where the matter has previously received formal consideration.

Comments on standards and requests for interpretations should be addressed to:

Secretary, IEEE Standards Board
345 East 47th Street
New York, NY 10017
USA

Foreword

(This Foreword is not a part of IEEE Std 1063-1987, IEEE Standard for Software User Documentation.)

Two factors motivated the development of this standard: The concern of the software user communities over the poor quality of much user documentation, and a need for requirements expressed by producers of documentation.

This standard applies only to traditional documentation, either printed on paper or stored in some other medium in the format of a printed document and used in a manner analogous to the way a printed document is used. On-line documentation is not addressed (documentation designed for interactive access via computer) because such information is processed and used differently from printed documents.

This standard does not cover the actual writers and publishers of user documentation. The responsibility for ensuring that satisfactory software user documentation is produced rests with the organization that generates the software. Responsibility for ensuring that software user documentation is satisfactorily updated rests with the organization that repairs or modifies the software. Configuration management of the documentation is outside the scope of this standard.

Sections 4 and 5 are written as directions. An audit checklist for compliance with this standard can be compiled by identifying each direction and setting up a "yes/no/nonapplicable" condition for the direction. For example, this standard states "identify and describe all data required for the correct processing of each function," in 5.7.2.4. A checklist entry for this condition would then be as follows:

All data is identified and described:
yes   no   nonapplicable

A successful user document is the result of proper audience determination, careful document planning, and good writing style, in addition to the contents requirement addressed by this standard. However, the ultimate test of any software document is that it is easily usable by its intended audience for its intended purpose.

At the time of approval, the Working Group on Software User Documentation which prepared this standard, had the following membership:

Christopher M. Cooke, *Chairman*   **Ruth L. Oldfield**, *Vice-Chairman & Editor*

A. Frank Ackerman
George W. Barton, Jr
Mordechai Ben-Menachem
Jill Boogaard
Ingar Brauti
Fletcher Buckley
Lorie J. Call
François Coallier
Elizabeth Connolly
Margaret Daniel
J. T. Deignan
Claudia Dencker
Mary Jane Dodgen
Henry H. Fong
Yair Gershkovitch
John W. Horch
Ed Humphries
Tim Kalisz
Tom Kurihara
Joel Lang
Richard Alan Lee
F. C. Lim
William Lyon
Borut Maričić
Phillip C. Marriott
Roger J. Martin
Alicia McCurdy
Sandra L. Merscher
Carolyn J. Mullins
Sarah H. Nash
Frank Nellis
Françoise Perrodeau
William E. Perry
Polly Perryman
Sherwood F. Prescott, Jr
Ian C. Pyle
Annette D. Reilly
Luke J. Rheaume
Horst P. Richter
Richard A. Ries
Lois K. Rosstedt
Julio Gonzalez Sanz
Hans Schaefer
Mitzi Sokol
Peter Stein
William Sutcliffe
Jan Tanzer
Peter Thorp
William S. Turner III
Clifford Way
Andrew H. Weigel
Edmond H. Weiss
Timothy Whalen

The following persons were on the balloting committee that approved this document for submission to the IEEE Standards Board:

A. Frank Ackerman
Richard L. Aurbach
Motoei Azuma
H. Jack Barnard
Jim Behm
Leo Beltracchi
Mordechai Ben-Menachem
H. R. Berlack
Michael A. Blackledge
Kathleen L. Briggs
A. Winsor Brown
Fletcher Buckley
Lorie J. Call
Harry Carl
John W. Center
T. S. Chow
Won L. Chung
Antonio M. Cicu
Peter Cord
F. Coallier
Elizabeth Connolly
Christopher Cooke
Gail A. Cordes
Taz Daughtrey
J. T. Deignan
Claudia Dencker
Boštjan K. Derganc
Harpal Dhama
Fred M. Discenzo
David A. Dobratz
David C. Doty
William P. DuPras
Albert D. Duree
Robert E. Dwyer
Mary L. Eads
L. G. Egan
W. D. Ehrenberger
Walter Ellis
Caroline L. Evans
David W. Favor
John W. Fendrich
Glen S. Fields
Julian Forster
Richard Fries
Ismael Fuentes-Cresto
L. B. Gardner
Shirley A. Gloss-Soler
J. G. Glynn
Andrej Grebenc
Victor M. Guarnera
Lawrence M. Gunther
David A. Gustafson
G. B. Hawthorn, Jr
John W. Horch
David Johnson III
L. V. Kaleda
Timothy Kalisz
Harry Kalmbach
Owen K. Kato
Joseph A. Krupinski
Joan Kundig
Tom Kurihara
Lak-Ming Lam
John B. Lane
Robert Lane
Greg Larsen
Richard Alan Lee
F. C. Lim
Bertil Lindberg
John D. Lithe
Ben Livson
Nicholas L. Marselos
Roger J. Martin
J. A. McCall
Alicia L. McCurdy
Russ McDowell
Manijeh Moghis
Charles S. Mooney
Paulo Cesar Morcondes
D. D. Morton
Gene T. Morun
Carolyn J. Mullins
Hironobu Nagano
Geraldine R. Neidhart
Dennis E. Nickle
Ruth L. Oldfield
Wilma M. Osborne
Michael T. Perkins
John Petraglia
Donald J. Pfeiffer
William E. Perry
I. C. Pyle
Thomas S. Radi
Salim Ramji
Jean-Claude Rault
Meir Razy
Donald J. Reifer
Annette D. Reilly
Luke J. Rheaume
Margaret Rumley
Julio Gonzalez Sanz
Steven R. Schach
Hans Schaefer
Lee O. Schmidt
Norman Schneidewind
Wolf A. Schnoege
Robert G. Schueppert
David J. Schultz
Greg Schumacher
Leonard W. Seagren
Gerard P. Shabe
Robert W. Shillato
David M. Siefert
Randall W. Simons
Jacob Slonim
Lee Sprague
V. Srinivas
G. Wayne Stanley
William G. Sutcliffe
Richard H. Thayer
Paul U. Thompson
Peter M. Thorp
Terrence L. Tillmann
Valentin W. Tirman, Jr
G. R. Trebble
C. L. Troyanowski
William Stephen Turner III
Mark-René Uchida
Robert Urling
Tom Vollman
Dolores R. Wallace
John P. Walter
Stephen F. Webb
Andrew H. Weigel
G. Allan Whittaker
Andrew F. Wilson
Patrick J. Wilson
W. M. Wong
Dennis L. Wood
Natalie C. Yopconka
Peter F. Zoll

When the IEEE Standards Board approved this standard on December 10, 1987, it had the following membership:

Donald C. Fleckenstein, *Chairman* **Marco W. Migliaro,** *Vice Chairman*
Andrew G. Salem, *Secretary*

James H. Beall
Dennis Bodson
Marshall L. Cain
James M. Daly
Stephen R. Dillon
Eugene P. Fogarty
Jay Forster
Kenneth D. Hendrix
Irvin N. Howell
Leslie R. Kerr
Jack Kinn
Irving Kolodny
Joseph L. Koepfinger*
Edward Lohse
John May
Lawrence V. McCall
L. Bruce McClung
Donald T. Michael*
L. John Rankine
John P. Riganati
Gary S. Robinson
Frank L. Rose
Robert E. Rountree
William R. Tackaberry
William B. Wilkens
Helen M. Wood

* Member emeritus

Contents

IEEE Standard for Software User Documentation

1. Scope

This standard provides minimum requirements on the structure and information content of user documentation. It addresses editorial and stylistic considerations only when they impact structure and content. It applies primarily to technical substance rather than to style. Users of this standard may want to develop a style manual for use within their own organizations to complement the guidance provided in the standard. They may also select an industry-recognized style manual such as the *Chicago Manual of Style* [2][1] or the *GPO Style Manual* [3].

Adherence to the standard does not preclude the application of additional, more stringent requirements or standards, or the inclusion of additional topics or materials not required by this standard.

1.1 Applicability. This standard applies to documentation that guides users in installing, operating, and managing software of any size, and conducting those aspects of software maintenance that do not involve modification of the software source code.

This standard does not apply to the following:

(1) Requirements, design, development, and manufacturing specifications

(2) Marketing materials

(3) Specialized course materials intended primarily for use in formal training programs

(4) User materials to be presented interactively via terminals, and other nontraditional media, such as videotape or slide presentations with recorded narration

(5) Instructions needed to install hardware or prepare it for operation

(6) Configuration management of software user documentation

(7) Verification of software user documentation

[1] The numbers in brackets correspond to those of the bibliography in Section 7.

1.2 Organization. The six sections in this standard cover the following topics:

Section 1 describes the scope of this standard, including its applicability.

Section 2 defines terms used in this standard.

Section 3 covers how to determine required document sets by defining product and audience, and describes how to determine usage modes.

Section 4 gives the requirements for information inclusion.

Section 5 covers what shall be contained in each document, including topics such as placement of title page, list of illustrations, etc.

Section 6 covers how to present material in document sets so that user documents are easy to read and understand.

2. Definitions

Certain key terms used in this standard are defined in this section. Other key terms used this standard are defined generally in ANSI/IEEE Std 729-1983 [1], or in *Webster's Third New International Dictionary of the English Language (unabridged)* [4].

action. Step a user takes to complete a task; a step that cannot be subdivided further. A single user action may invoke one or more functions but need not invoke any.

audience. Persons who are expected to need a given software user document.

caution. Advisory in a software user document that performing some action may lead to consequences that are unwanted or undefined. Compare ***warning.***

document set. Document or group of documents that offers an audience the information it needs about a software product.

function. A specific purpose of an entity, or its characteristic action.

illustration. Material that is labeled, numbered, set apart from the main body of text, and, normally, cited within the main text. In this standard, the term *illustration* is used as the generic term for table, figure, drawing, exhibit, and equivalent terms.

note. Helpful hint(s) and other material that may assist the user.

procedure. Ordered series of instructions that a user follows to do one or more tasks.

software user document. Body of material that provides information to users; typically printed or stored on some medium in the format of a printed document.

style. Set of editorial conventions covering grammar, terminology, punctuation, capitalization, etc, of a software user document.

task. Piece of work that a user does, following a given procedure, to achieve a specific goal. A task may include one or more actions.

usage mode. Primary manner in which the document issuer expects that document to be used. This standard recognizes two usage modes, instructional and reference, described in Section 3.

user. Person who uses software to perform some task.

warning. Advisory in a software user document that performing some action will lead to serious or dangerous consequences. Compare ***caution.***

3. Identifying Required User Documents

To identify the required user documents; the software product, its applications, and the audiences that will use the product must first be identified. The document set for the audiences, and the usage mode for each document, can then be determined.

3.1 Identifying the Software. The software, its user interfaces, and the tasks that users perform with the software, shall be identified at the start of documentation planning.

3.2 Determining the Document Audience. A software user document shall be keyed to its audience. The different ways that users interact with software shall be considered when preparing user documents: for example, amount of interaction, level of interaction, direct or indirect interaction. Users can form different audiences. Each intended audience shall be identified before the document (or set of documents) is planned and written. The identified audience will dictate the document presentation style and level of detail. Audience determination is especially important in instructional mode documents.

3.3 Determining the Document Set. A document set may consist of one or more documents, depending on the amount of information to be presented and the needs of the intended audience. Each document of a document set may be one or more volumes depending upon the amount of information to be presented. For example, a command manual might have one volume covering half the commands and a second volume covering the other half of the commands. When a document contains both instructional and reference material, the two shall be clearly separated.

A document set shall contain the information needed by each audience. Depending on the nature of the software and hardware, the software user documentation set may need to be integrated with system-level documentation. The presentation style and level of detail shall be tailored for the intended audience. When a document set must be prepared for audiences with widely differing needs, at least one of the following approaches shall be used:

(1) Separate materials devoted to the needs of specific audiences. The audiences and their needs shall be covered specifically in the introduction, allowing each user to pick out the sections of interest.

(2) Separate documents or document sets for each specific audience.

3.4 Determining Document Usage Modes. Users of software need documents either to learn about the software (instructional mode) or to refresh their memory about it (reference mode). Instructional mode documents may be either information- or task-oriented. Information-oriented documents give the reader information needed to understand the computer software and its functions; task-oriented documents show the reader how to complete a task or reach a goal.

3.4.1 Instructional Mode. An instructional mode document shall

(1) Provide the background and information needed to understand the system.

(2) Provide the information needed to learn what can be done with the software and how to use it (for example, what goals it supports).

(3) Provide examples to reinforce the learning process.

Information-oriented instructional documents provide the user with background or technical information (for example, models and algorithms) needed to use the software properly. Examples of typical information-oriented instructional mode documents include

(1) overview
(2) theory of operation manual
(3) tutorial

Task-oriented instructional mode documents provide the user with procedures to achieve specific goals. Examples of task-oriented instructional mode documents include

(1) diagnostic procedures manual
(2) operations manual
(3) software installation manual

3.4.2 Reference Mode. A reference mode document shall

(1) Organize and provide necessary information
(2) Facilitate random access to information

Examples of typical reference mode documents include

(1) command manual
(2) error message manual
(3) program calls manual
(4) quick reference guide
(5) software tools manual
(6) utilities manual

4. User Document Inclusion Requirements

This section summarizes the information required in user documents. The mandatory information described in this section shall be included in all documents, unless it is not applicable. The sequence, location grouping, and labeling of this information are left to the judgment of the document preparer. (For example, information suggested for the introduction could go in a section labeled "Preface.")

Table 1 specifies 12 basic components of a software user document. Additional information may be added as required.

Table 2 is a matrix of inclusion requirements for specific components of a document. If a component listed as mandatory contains information not applicable to a specific document, that component may be omitted (for example, a description of conventions may not be applicable in an overview document).

Table 1
Software User Document Components

User Document Components	See Paragraph:
Title page	5.1
Restrictions	5.2
Warranties	5.3
Table of contents	5.4
List of illustrations	5.5
Introduction	5.6
Body of document	5.7
Error conditions	5.8
Appendixes	5.9
Bibliography	5.10
Glossary	5.11
Index	5.12

5. User Document Content Requirements

This section describes the required content of user documents. Specific information and the level of detail for each document are determined by the audience and the usage mode of the document. The information specified in this section shall be included in a user document, unless it is not applicable or otherwise noted.

For convenience, this standard uses generic titles or labels to identify parts of a user document. As noted in Section 4, the user document itself need not use these labels. For example, in an introduction the audience description and applicability statement need not be specifically labelled "Audience Description" and "Applicability Statement."

5.1 Title Page. On the title page of a user document include at least the following information:

(1) Document name
(2) Document version and date
(3) Software covered
(4) Issuing organization

The design and arrangement of these items on the title page are at the discretion of the organization preparing the document. The identification of the document and the software shall be consistent with the configuration management system of the issuing organization.

5.2 Restrictions. When restrictions apply to using or copying the document or software product, describe these on the title page or immediately following the title page. Ensure that any proprietary markings, such as trademarks, meet appropriate accepted practices and legal conventions.

Table 2
Inclusion Requirements

	Single-Volume Document		Multi-Volume Document	
Component	8 Pages or Less	More Than 8 Pages	First Volume	Other Volume
Title page	M	M	M	M
Restrictions	M	M	M	M
Warranties	R	R	R	R
Table of contents	O	M	M	M
List of illustrations	O	O	O	O
Introduction				
Audience description	R	M	M	R
Applicability	M	M	M	M
Purpose	R	M	M	R
Document usage	R	M	M	R
Related documents	R	R	R*	R
Conventions	M	M	M	R
Problem reporting	R	M	M	R
Body				
Instruction mode	1	1	1	1
Reference mode	1	1	1	1
Error conditions	R	R	R	R
Appendixes	O	O	O	O
Bibliography	M	M	M**	M**
Glossary	M	M	M**	M**
Index	2	2	M**	M**

Key:

M Mandatory—Shall be included when information exists.

O Optional

R Reference—Either include the section or a reference to where the information can be found within the document set.

* Shall address relationship to other volumes.

** Mandatory in at least one volume in the document set, with references to information in other volumes.

1 Every document has a body; each document set shall address the instructional and reference needs of the audience. Required content is in 5.7.1 and 5.7.2.

2 An index is manditory for documents of 40 pages or more and optional when under 40 pages.

5.3 Warranties and Contractual Obligations. Specify any warranties and contractual obligations or disclaimers.

5.4 Table of Contents. Include a table of contents in every document over eight pages long. For single-volume documents, this requirement shall be met in one of two ways:

(1) A comprehensive table of contents for the whole document

(2) A simplified table of contents, with a comprehensive section table of contents preceding each section

For multi-volume documents (a single document in multiple volumes), meet this requirement by including a simple table of contents for the entire document in the first volume. In addition each subsequent volume shall contain either

(1) A comprehensive table of contents for the volume, or

(2) A simplified table of contents for the volume, with a comprehensive table of contents preceding each section.

5.4.1 Comprehensive Table of Contents. Construct a comprehensive table of contents, for a complete document or for a section, as follows:

(1) Carry entries to at least the third level of the document structure hierarchy
(2) Give page numbers for every entry
(3) Choose a method to assist the reader in matching entries with their corresponding page numbers, such as
(a) Leader strings (strings of dots in the form "...") or equivalent, connecting entries and corresponding page numbers
(b) Double-spacing between entries

5.4.2 Simple Table of Contents. In a simple table of contents include at least the first level of the document structure hierarchy with the corresponding page numbers.

5.5 List of Illustrations. Optionally, include one or more lists of the titles and locations of all illustrations in the document. Use separate lists for figures, tables, and exhibits, or merge all types of illustrations into a single list. In each list, include
(1) Number and title of each illustration
(2) Page numbers for each illustration
(3) A method to assist the user in matching entries with their corresponding page numbers, such as
(a) Leader strings (strings of dots in the form "...") or equivalent, connecting entries and corresponding page numbers
(b) Double-spacing between entries

5.6 Introduction. Include the following information in the introduction:
(1) Audience description
(2) Applicability statement
(3) Purpose statement
(4) Document usage description
(5) Related documents list or information
(6) Conventions description
(7) Problem reporting instructions

5.6.1 through 5.6.7 describe the topics further.

5.6.1 Audience Description. Describe the intended audience. If different sections of a document (or a document set) are for different audiences, indicate the intended audience for each section. In the audience section, specify the
(1) Experience level expected of the user
(2) Previous training expected of the user

5.6.2 Applicability Statement. State the software version covered by the document the document version number, and the environment (hardware and software) in which this software runs.

5.6.3 Purpose Statement. Explain why the document was written and summarize the purpose of the software. Include typical intended applications of the software.

5.6.4 Document Usage Description. Describe what each section of the document contains, its intended use, and the relationship between sections. Also provide any other directions necessary for using the document.

5.6.5 Related Documents. List related documents and give the relationship of the document to the others. In document sets comprised of may volumes, this information may be provided in a separate "roadmap" or guide to the document set.

5.6.6 Conventions. Summarize symbols, stylistic conventions, and command syntax conventions used in the document.

5.6.6.1 Symbols. Describe symbols and their usage in the document, illustrating each.

5.6.6.2 Stylistic Conventions. Describe conventions unfamiliar to the intended audience that allow users to understand text or illustrations, such as highlighting or use of boldface or italic type.

5.6.6.3 Command Syntax Conventions. Explain the conventions used for command syntax. Include examples showing options, variable parameters, and required parameters.

5.6.7 Problem Reporting Instructions. Tell the users how to report documentation or software problems. Also describe how users can suggest changes in the software or documentation. List the name and contact information for the organization responsible for responding to the problem reports or suggestions for improvements.

5.7 Body of Document. Determine the content, organization, and presentation of the body of the document after determining whether the document is an instructional mode or reference mode document. In either mode, use a consistent organizational structure based on the expected use of the document, providing examples as necessary.

5.7.1 Body of Instructional Mode Documents. Information-oriented instructional documents give the reader background information or theory needed to understand the software. Include a scope as described in 5.7.1.1 before giving the information forming the major portion of the document. Use topics to organize an information-oriented instructional document; for example, organize the document by
(1) Theory
(2) Software features
(3) Software architecture

Task-oriented instructional documents give the reader the necessary information to carry out a specific task or attain a specific goal. Include the information described in 5.7.1.1 through 5.7.1.7. Use task relations to organize a task-oriented document or section; for example, organize by

(1) Task groups
(2) Task sequence

5.7.1.1 Scope. Begin this section by indicating to the user the scope of the material to be discussed.

5.7.1.2 Materials. Describe any materials the user will need to complete the task (for example, input manuals, passwords, computers, peripherals, cabling, software drivers, interfaces, and protocols). Optionally, describe separately materials common to all or many functions and refer to that description.

5.7.1.3 Preparations. Describe any actions, technical or administrative, that must be done before starting the task (for example, obtain system passwords, access authorization, disk space). Optionally, describe in a separate section preparations common to all or many functions and refer to that section.

5.7.1.4 Cautions and Warnings. Describe general cautions and warnings that apply to the task. Place specific cautions and warnings on the same page and immediately before the action that requires the caution or warning. (See Section 2 for definitions of *caution* and *warning.*)

5.7.1.5 Method. Describe each task, including

(1) What the user must do.

(2) What function, if any is invoked (including how to invoke the function and how to recognize normal termination).

(3) Possible errors, how to avoid them, and how to resolve them.

(4) What results to expect.

5.7.1.6 Related Information. Provide other useful information about the task, such as

(1) Tasks frequently performed together and their relationship.

(2) Other tasks customarily performed by users of this document that could be supported by the methods described in this section. Describe this support.

(3) Notes, limitations, or constraints (notes may also be placed in the specific area to which they apply).

5.7.2 Body of Reference Mode Documents. Organize a reference mode document the way a user accesses a software function. Examples of the ways users access functions include

(1) By command
(2) By menu
(3) By system calls

Within this organization, arrange the functions for easy access and random user access (for example, alphabetical order or a menu-tree hierarchy). For each function, include in the body of a reference mode document the information described in 5.7.2.1 through 5.7.2.11.

5.7.2.1 Purpose. Describe the purpose of the function.

5.7.2.2 Materials. Describe materials needed to use the function or command (for example, input manuals, passwords, computers, peripherals, cabling, software drivers, interfaces, and protocols). Optionally, describe separately materials common to all or many functions and refer to that description.

5.7.2.3 Preparations. Describe any actions, technical or administrative, that must be completed before using the function or command (for example, obtain system passwords, access authorization, disk space). Optionally, describe separately preparations common to all or many functions and refer to that description.

5.7.2.4 Input(s). Identify and describe all data required for the correct processing of each function. Use one of the following methods:

(1) Describe inputs used only by a single function in the section devoted to that function.

(2) Describe in a single section or in an appendix inputs used by multiple functions. Refer to that section or appendix when describing these functions.

5.7.2.5 Cautions and Warnings. Describe general cautions and warnings that apply to each function. Place specific cautions and warnings on the same page and immediately before the action that requires a caution or warning.

5.7.2.6 Invocation. Provide all information needed to use and control the function. Describe all parameters. Include:

(1) Required parameters
(2) Optional parameters
(3) Default options
(4) Order and syntax

5.7.2.7 Suspension of Operations. Describe how to interrupt the function during execution and how to restart it.

5.7.2.8 Termination of Operations. Describe how to recognize function terminations, including abnormal terminations.

5.7.2.9 Output(s). Describe the results of executing the function, such as

(1) Screen display

(2) Effect on files or data

(3) Completion status vaues or output parameters

(4) Outputs that trigger other actions (such as mechanical actions in process control applications).

Provide a complete results description for each function. If several results are possible, explain the situations that produce each.

5.7.2.10 Error Conditions. Describe common error conditions that could occur as a result of executing the function, and describe how to detect that the error has occurred. For example, list any error messages that the system displays. (Error recovery instructions need not be provided here if they are covered in the "Error Messages, Known Problems, and Error Recovery" listing described in 5.8.)

5.7.2.11 Related Information. Provide other useful information about the function that does not readily fit under any of the sections previously described. Such information might include

(1) Limitations and constraints

(2) Notes

(3) Related functions

Notes may also be placed in the specific area to which they apply.

5.8 Error Messages, Known Problems, and Error Recovery. Describe error messages in an easily accessed location (for example, in a separate section, chapter, appendix, or a separate document). For each error message, describe in detail the error that caused it, the procedures needed to recover from it, and the action(s) required to clear it. Describe known software problems here or in a separate document and provide alternative methods or recovery procedures.

5.9 Appendixes. Include in the appendixes any supporting material, arranged for ease of access. For example, the appendixes might include

(1) Detailed input and output data or formats used in common by multiple functions

(2) "Codes" used in input or output (for example, country codes or stock number codes)

(3) Interactions between tasks or functions

(4) Global processing limitations

(5) Description of data formats and file structures

(6) Sample files, reports, or programs

5.10 Bibliography. List all publications specifically mentioned in the text. Other publications containing related information may also be listed.

5.11 Glossary. List alphabetically in the glossary definitions of

(1) All terms, acronyms, and abbreviations used in the document that may be unfamiliar to the audience

(2) All terms, acronyms, and abbreviations used in a manner that may be unfamiliar to the audience

If desired, the acronyms and abbreviations may be listed in a separate section.

5.12 Index. Develop an index, based on key words or concepts, for user documents over eight pages. Construct this index as follows:

(1) Indicate importance of information; place minor key words under major ones.

(2) Give location references for each entry, to the right of the entry.

(3) List location references in one of the following ways:

(a) By page number

(b) By section or paragraph number

(c) By illustration number

(d) By another index entry

(4) Use only one level of index reference. (For example, if an entry points to a second index entry, the second entry shall give a page number, section or paragraph number, or illustration number. The second entry shall not point to a third index entry.)

6. User Document Presentation Requirements

This section discusses the required presentation methods for user documents. The information in this section shall be included unless it is not applicable.

The method of presenting material, in addition to the style of writing and the level of detail, contributes to making a user document easy to read and understand. Presentation considerations include highlighting, consistency, terminology, and references to other material.

6.1 Highlighting. For every user document or set of documents, find a method to highlight selected material of special importance, especially cautions and warnings. Select highlighting methods that provide prominence and segregation to the material being emphasized. Describe the highlighting method in the introduction.

Choice of a specific highlighting method is left to the users of this standard, consistent with the practices or their organizations. Common highlighting methods include the use of bold and italic typefonts, the enclosure of material within lines or boxes, or the use of color.

6.2 Consistency. Use terminology and typographic and stylistic conventions consistently throughout a user document or set of documents. Identify any deviations from the conventions the first time they appear.

6.3 Terminology. Define all terms requiring a glossary entry, acronyms, and abbreviations when first used in the document.

6.4 Referencing Related Material. If related material is placed in separate parts of a document or in separate documents of a document set, repetition of the information can be avoided by providing specific references to the related information.

7. Bibliography

[1] ANSI/IEEE Std 729-1983, IEEE Standard Glossary of Software Engineering Terminology.[2]

[2] The Chicago Manual of Style, 13th ed, The University of Chicago Press, 1982.

[3] Government Printing Office (GPO) Style Manual, Government Printing Office, Washington, DC, 1984.

[4] Webster's Third New International Dictionary of the English Language (unabridged), Springfield, MA: Merriam-Webster, Inc, 1986.

[2] ANSI/IEEE publications are available from IEEE Service Center, 445 Hoes Lane, PO Box 1331, Piscataway, NJ 08855-1331, or from the Sales Department, American National Standards Institute, 1430 Broadway, New York, NY 10018.

Index

L

M

N

O

P

R

S

T

U

V

W

Acknowledgements

Working group members were individually supported by their organizations with travel expenses and working days to attend meetings. This support does not constitute or imply approval or endorsement of this standard. These organizations were:

Apollo Computer
Army Materials Technology Laboratory
AT&T Bell Laboratories
Bell Canada (Canada)
Bell Communications Research
Boeing Computer Services
Burroughs Corp.
International Bureau of Software Testing
Martin Marietta Aero and Naval Systems
3M
Mitre Corp
NCR Systems Engineering b.v.
PDA Engineering
Pratt & Whitney, Inc
Ross Laboratories
SAGE Federal Systems, Inc
Texas Instruments, Inc
US Department of Transportation
Virginia Polytechnic Institute & State University

Recognized as an
American National Standard (ANSI)

IEEE
Std 1074-1991

IEEE Standard for Developing Software Life Cycle Processes

Sponsor

Software Engineering Standards Subcommittee of the Technical Committee on Software Engineering of the IEEE Computer Society

Approved September 26, 1991

IEEE Standards Board

Approved April 20, 1992

American National Standards Institute

Abstract: The set of activities that constitute the processes that are mandatory for the development and maintenance of software, whether stand-alone or part of a system, is set forth. The management and support processes that continue throughout the entire life cycle, as well as all aspects of the software life cycle from concept exploration through retirement, are covered. Associated input and output information is also provided. Utilization of the processes and their component activities maximizes the benefits to the user when the use of this standard is initiated early in the software life cycle. This standard requires definition of a user's software life cycle and shows its mapping into typical software life cycles; it is not intended to define or imply a software life cycle of its own.

Keywords: project management process, project monitoring and control process, software development process, software implementation process, software installation process, software life cycle, software life cycle model process, software life cycle process, software maintenance process, software operation and support process, software post-development process, software pre-development process, software quality management process, software requirements process, software retirement process, software system allocation process

The Institute of Electrical and Electronics Engineers, Inc.
345 East 47th Street, New York, NY 10017-2394, USA

Library of Congress Cataloging in Publication information will be found on the following page.

IEEE Standards documents are developed within the Technical Committees of the IEEE Societies and the Standards Coordinating Committees of the IEEE Standards Board. Members of the committees serve voluntarily and without compensation. They are not necessarily members of the Institute. The standards developed within IEEE represent a consensus of the broad expertise on the subject within the Institute as well as those activities outside of IEEE which have expressed an interest in participating in the development of the standard.

Use of an IEEE Standard is wholly voluntary. The existence of an IEEE Standard does not imply that there are no other ways to produce, test, measure, purchase, market, or provide other goods and services related to the scope of the IEEE Standard. Furthermore, the viewpoint expressed at the time a standard is approved and issued is subject to change brought about through developments in the state of the art and comments received from users of the standard. Every IEEE Standard is subjected to review at least every five years for revision or reaffirmation. When a document is more than five years old, and has not been reaffirmed, it is reasonable to conclude that its contents, although still of some value, do not wholly reflect the present state of the art. Users are cautioned to check to determine that they have the latest edition of any IEEE Standard.

Comments for revision of IEEE Standards are welcome from any interested party, regardless of membership affiliation with IEEE. Suggestions for changes in documents should be in the form of a proposed change of text, together with appropriate supporting comments.

Interpretations: Occasionally questions may arise regarding the meaning of portions of standards as they relate to specific applications. When the need for interpretations is brought to the attention of IEEE, the Institute will initiate action to prepare appropriate responses. Since IEEE Standards represent a consensus of all concerned interests, it is important to ensure that any interpretation has also received the concurrence of a balance of interests. For this reason IEEE and the members of its technical committees are not able to provide an instant response to interpretation requests except in those cases where the matter has previously received formal consideration.

Comments on standards and requests for interpretations should be addressed to:

Secretary, IEEE Standards Board
445 Hoes Lane
P.O. Box 1331
Piscataway, NJ 08555-1331
USA

IEEE Standards documents are adopted by the Institute of Electrical and Electronics Engineers without regard to whether their adoption may involve patents on articles, materials, or processes. Such adoption does not assume any liability to any patent owner, nor does it assume any obligation whatever to parties adopting the standards documents.

Library of Congress Cataloging in Publication Data

Institute of Electrical and Electronics Engineers, Inc., the.
IEEE standard for developing software life cycle processes / sponsor, Software Engineering Standards Subcommittee of the Technical Committee on Software Engineering of the IEEE Computer Society.
p. cm.
"Approved September 26, 1991, IEEE Standards Board."
"IEEE Std 1074-1991."
Includes index.
ISBN 1-55937-170-6
1. Computer software—Development—Standards—United States. 2. Software maintenance—Standards—United States. I. IEEE Computer Society. Software Engineering Standards Subcommittee. II. IEEE Standards Board. III. Title
QA76.76.D47I545 1992
005.1'021873—dc20 91-41510
CIP

Foreword

(This Foreword is not a part of IEEE Std 1074-1991, IEEE Standard for Developing Software Life Cycle Processes.)

This Foreword is intended to provide the reader with some background into the rationale used to develop this standard. This information is being provided to aid in the understanding and usage of the standard. The Foreword is nonbinding.

Purpose

This is a standard for the Processes of software development and maintenance. This standard requires definition of a user's software life cycle and shows mapping into typical software life cycles, but it is not intended to define or imply a software life cycle of its own. This standard applies to the management and support Processes that continue throughout the entire life cycle, as well as all aspects of the software life cycle from concept exploration through retirement. Utilization of these Processes, and their component Activities, maximizes the benefits to the user when the use of this standard is initiated early in the software life cycle.

Software that has proceeded past the initialization phase when this standard is invoked should gradually comply with the standard.

This standard was written for any organization responsible for managing and developing software. It will be useful to project managers, software developers, quality assurance organizations, purchasers, users, and maintainers. Since it was written to consider both software and its operating environment, it can be used where software is the total system or where software is embedded in a larger system.

Terminology

The words *shall, must,* and the imperative form identify the mandatory (essential) material within this standard. The words *should* and *may* identify optional (conditional) material. As with other IEEE Software Engineering Standards, the terminology in this document is based on IEEE Std 610.12-1990, IEEE Standard Glossary of Software Engineering Terminology (ANSI). To avoid inconsistency when the Glossary is revised, the definitions are not repeated in this document. New terms and modified definitions are included, however.

History

Work on this standard began in August 1984. A total of 15 meetings produced the draft submitted for ballot in January 1990. Two additional meetings were held to resolve comments and negative ballots, and the document was resubmitted for recirculation in February 1991.

Participants

This standard was developed by a working group consisting of the following members who attended two or more meetings, provided text, or submitted comments on more than two drafts of the standard:

David J. Schultz, *Chair*
John W. Horch, *Vice Chair*
Dennis E. Nickle, *Secretary*

Jean A. Gilmore, *Group Leader*
Art Godin, *Group Leader*
Lynn D. Ihlenfeldt, *Group Leader*
Robert W. Shillato, *Group Leader*

Joseph J. Guidos,* David W. Burnett, *Configuration Managers*
Michael Buckley, *Editor*

Joe Albano
Tom Antczak
Susan Burgess
David Burrows
Dan Chang
Paul Christensen
Raymond Day
Marvin Doran
Mike Ellwood
Arden Forrey
John Graham
Daniel Gray
Rob Harker
Carolyn Harrison
Peter Harvey
Eric Hensel
Denise Holmes
George Jackelen
Linell Jones
Laurel Kaleda
Phil Keys
Tom Kurihara
Bill Mar
Darrell Marsh
Leroy May
Denis Meredith
Manijeh Moghis
Richard Morton
Gerry Neidhart
Brian Nejmeh
Hans Schaefer
Isaac Shadman
Kelley Stalder
David Taylor
Leonard Tripp
George Tucker
Odo Wang
Richard Werling

*Deceased

Contributors

The following individuals also contributed to the development of the standard by attending one meeting or providing comments on one or two drafts:

Scott Allen
Kathleen Alley
Robert Baris
Dwight Bellinger
H. Ronald Berlack
William Blum
Robert Both
Fletcher Buckley
John Chihorek
Geoff Crellin
M. A. Daniels
Geoffrey Darnton
Leonard DeBaets
Ingrid deBuda
Kristin Dittmann
Gary Driver
Susan East
Leo Egan
Violet Foldes
Roger Fujii
Michael Garrard
Yair Gershkovitch
Ole Golubjatnikov
Jim Harkins
James Heil
Cheng Hu
Jim Hughes
Suzana Hutz
Ron Hysom
Phyllis Illyefalvi
Corbin Ingram
Ramon Izbinsky
Tom Jepson
Jia Yaoliang
Allen Jin
David Johnson
Richard Karcich
E. Klamm
Rick Kuhn
Stephan Lacasse
F. C. Lim
Ben Livson
Theresa Mack
Karen Mackey
Stan Magee
John Marciniak
Richard McClellan
Neal Mengel
Rocco Novak
George O'Connell
John Patchen
Jeff Pattee
Virgil Polinski
P. A. Rhodes
Bill Romstadt
Benson Scheff
Richard Schmidt
David Schwartz
Carl Seddio
Paul Sevcik
Randy Shipley
Kimberly Steele
Karen Steelman
Jim Stoner
Wayne Sue
Ann Sullivan
Daniel Teichroew
Russell Theisen
Donna Thomas
George Tice
R. Van Tilburg
Graham Tritt
Dolores Wallace
Valerie Winkler
Grady Wright
Fred Yonda
Lin Zucconi

Balloting Committee

The following persons were on the balloting committee that approved this document for submission to the IEEE Standards Board:

Joseph Albano, Jr.
Eleanor Antreassian
Au Man Kit
Emanuel R. Baker
David Barber
H. Jack Barnard
Dwight Bellinger
M. Ben-Menachem
H. Ronald Berlack
Michael Blackledge
William J. Boll
Ronald Braun
Bruce Brocka
Winsor A. Brown
Fletcher Buckley
Susan Burgess
David Burnett
David Burrows
Kay Bydalek
Clyde Camp
James L. Cartwright
John Chihorek
S. V. Chiyyarath
Won L. Chung
François Coallier
Christopher Cooke
Michael A. Daniels
Geoffrey Darnton
Taz Daughtrey
Bostjan K. Derganc
Audrey Dorofee
Carl E. Dragstedt
Mary L. Eads
Vera D. Edelstein
L. G. Egan
Caroline L. Evans
John W. Fendrich
A. L. Fleetwood
Roger G. Fordham
Joel J. Forman
Julian Forster
Kirby Fortenberry
Thomas J. Fouser
Clairmont Fraser
Roger Fujii
Casey K. Fung
Yair Gershkovitch
Jean Gilmore
Shirley A. Gloss-Soler
Arthur Godin
Richard Goldsmith
Ole Golubjatnikov
Steven Grady
J. Kaye Grau
Thomas A. Grobicki
Victor M. Guarnera
Cynthia Hardenbrook
Lina Hardenburg
R. T. Harley
George B. Hawthorne
Clark Hay
William E. Hefley
Manfred Hein
John W. Horch
Richard Horner
Pei Hsia
James R. Hughes
Lynn Ihlenfeldt
S. C. Jain
Debra Jasinski
Shang-Sheng Jeng
J. O. Jenkins
Jia Yaoliang
Todd Jochim
David Johnson
Donna C. Johnson
Laurel V. Kaleda
Eiichi Kaneko
Myron S. Karasik
Peter Klopfenstein
Shaye Koenig
Richard Kuhn
Joan Kundig
Tom Kurihara
Renee Lamb
John B. Lane
Robert A. C. Lane
J. Dennis Lawrence
Cheryl Leventhal
F. C. Lim
Bertil Lindberg
Carlo Lipizzi
William M. Lively
Ben Livson
Dieter Look
Harold Mains
Kartik C. Majumdar
John H. Manley
Philip C. Marriott
Roger J. Martin
Tomoo Matsubara
Ann Miller
Edward Miller
Manijeh Moghis
Richard Morton
Gene T. Morun
Hironobu Nagano
Saied Najafi
Gerry Neidhart
Dennis E. Nickle
James O'Day
Tuncer I. Oren
Martin F. Owens
Thomas Parrish
Betty Paul
William Perry
Donald J. Pfeiffer
John G. Phippen
John Pope
Salim Ramji
Jean-Claude Rault
Meir Razy
Larry K. Reed
Donald J. Reifer
James R. Roberts
R. Waldo Roth
Rafael San Roman
Julio Sanz
Stephen R. Schach
Hans Schaefer
Benson H. Scheff
Max J. Schindler
Norman Schneidewind
Wolf A. Schnoege
David J. Schultz
Gregory D. Schumacher
Leonard Seagren
Carl S. Seddio
Tony Sgarlatti
Isaac Shadman
Lawrence H. Shafer
Robert Shillato
David M. Siefert
Harry M. Sneed
A. R. Sorkowitz
Kelley Stalder
David Szombatfaluy
William Theiford
Russell E. Theisen
Glendon R. Trebble
Leonard Tripp
Mark-Rene Uchida
Margaret Updike
Spyrpos Villios
Thomas E. Vollman
Dolores R. Wallace
John W. Walz
Andrew H. Weigel
Richard Werling
Paul Wolfgang
Paul R. Work
Natalie C. Yopconka
Peter F. Zoll

When the IEEE Standards Board approved this standard on September 26, 1991, it had the following membership:

Marco W. Migliaro, *Chairman*
Donald C. Loughry, *Vice Chairman*
Andrew G. Salem, *Secretary*

Dennis Bodson
Paul L. Borrill
Clyde Camp
James M. Daly
Donald C. Fleckenstein
Jay Forster*
David F. Franklin
Ingrid Fromm
Thomas L. Hannan
Donald N. Heirman
Kenneth D. Hendrix
John W. Horch
Ben C. Johnson
Ivor N. Knight
Joseph L. Koepfinger*
Irving Kolodny
Michael A. Lawler
John E. May, Jr.
Lawrence V. McCall
Donald T. Michael*
Stig L. Nilsson
John L. Rankine
Ronald H. Reimer
Gary S. Robinson
Terrance R. Whittemore

*Member Emeritus

Kristin M. Dittmann
IEEE Standards Project Editor

Acknowledgments

Participants in the working group were individually supported by their employers with travel expenses and working days. This support does not constitute or imply approval or endorsement of this standard. These organizations were:

Abbott Critical Care
ARINC, Inc.
Apollo Computer Inc.
AT&T Bell Laboratories
AT&T Technologies
Bell Canada
Bellcore
Bell Northern Research, Inc.
Boeing Computer Services
Burnett Associates
Computer Sciences Corp.
Digital Switch Corporation
E. I. Dupont de Nemours & Co.
E-Systems, Inc.
Eastman Kodak Co.
Hewlett Packard
Honeywell, Inc.
IBM
Institute for Defense Analyses
Jet Propulsion Laboratory
Litton Aero Products
Lockheed Aircraft Service Co.
Martin Marietta
MUMPS Development Committee
NCR Corp.
Naval Air Development Center
Northern Telecom Canada Ltd.
Northrop Electronics Div.
Northrop Aircraft Div.
Perkin-Elmer
Quality Assurance Institute
Singer Link
Tandem Telecommunications Systems, Inc.
Tektronix
Teledyne Brown Engineering
Teledyne Controls
Texas Instruments
The Horch Company
U. S. Air Force
U. S. Dept. of Transportation
Unisys
3M

The following organizations hosted working group meetings in their respective cities:

AT&T Bell Laboratories, Columbus, OH
Bellcore, Piscataway, NJ
Boeing Computer Services, Seattle, WA
Computer Sciences Corp., Silver Spring, MD
E-Systems, Inc., Salt Lake City, UT
Eastman Kodak Company, Rochester, NY
Hewlett Packard, San Jose, CA
Honeywell, Inc., Phoenix, AZ
IEEE Computer Society, Dallas, TX
Martin Marietta, Orlando, FL
NCR Corp, San Diego, CA
Northrop Electronics, Hawthorne, CA
Northern Telecom, Ottawa, Ont.
Tektronix, Beaverton, OR
Teledyne Brown Engineering, Huntsville, AL
Travelers Companies, Hartford, CT
Unisys, Eagan, MN

AT&T Bell Laboratories provided word processing support. Bellcore and Computer Sciences Corporation assisted with mailings. The X3K1 Logical Flow Project provided technical coordination.

Suggestions for the improvement of this standard will be welcome. They should be sent to the Secretary, IEEE Standards Board, Institute of Electrical and Electronics Engineers, P. O. Box 1331, Piscataway, NJ 08855-1331.

Contents

FIGURES PAGE

TABLES

APPENDIXES

APPENDIX TABLES

APPENDIX FIGURE

IEEE Standard for Developing Software Life Cycle Processes

1. Introduction

1.1 Scope. This standard provides the set of Activities that constitute the Processes that are mandatory for the development and maintenance of software, whether stand-alone or part of a system. (Non-software Activities, such as hardware development and purchasing, are outside of the scope of this standard.) This standard also provides associated Input and Output Information.

For convenience, Activities are listed and described under specific Processes. In practice, the Activities may be performed by persons whose organizational titles or job descriptions do not clearly convey that a Process is part of their job. The Process under which an Activity is listed in this standard may be transparent in practice.

This standard does not prescribe a specific software life cycle model (SLCM). Each using organization must map the activities specified in the standard into its own software life cycle (SLC). If an organization has not yet defined an SLC, it will be necessary for them to select or define one before attempting to follow this standard. Further, this standard does not presume the use of any specific software development methodology nor the creation of specific documents.

For software already developed, it is recommended that these requirements, or a subset thereof, be applied. The existence of this standard should not be construed to prohibit the imposition of additional or more stringent requirements where the need exists, e.g., critical software.

Compliance with this standard is defined in 1.5.1.

1.2 References. No other publications are required for use of this standard. However, a list of other IEEE standards, which may be consulted for additional guidance, is given in the Bibliography in Section 8. Although this standard does not require adherence to any other IEEE standard, knowledge of principles and concepts described in the standards listed in the Bibliography would be helpful.

1.3 Definitions and Acronyms

1.3.1 Definitions. The definitions listed here establish meanings within the context of this standard. Definitions of other terms used in this document can be found in IEEE Std 610.12-1990 [1].[1]

Activity. A constituent task of a Process. *See:* **task.**

analysis. Examination for the purpose of understanding.

anomaly. Any deviation from requirements, expected or desired behavior, or performance of the software.

contractual requirements. Customer-imposed performance, logistics, and other requirements and commitments governing the scope of software development, delivery, or support.

customer. The person, or persons, who pay for the product and usually (but not necessarily) decide the requirements. In the context of this document the customer and the supplier may be members of the same organization. [5]

data base. A collection of data fundamental to a system. [22]

[1] The numbers in brackets correspond to those of the bibliographic references listed in Section 8.

evaluation. Determination of fitness for use.

external. An Input Information source or Output Information destination that is outside the control of this standard, and therefore may or may not exist.

function. A specific purpose of an entity or its characteristic action. [22]

installation. The period of time in the software life cycle during which a software product is integrated into its operational environment and tested in this environment to ensure that it performs as required. [1]

Mapping. Establishing a chronological relationship of the Activities in this standard according to a selected SLCM.

methodology. A body of methods, rules, and postulates employed by a discipline.

owner. A single point of contact, identified by organization position.

problem. The inability of a system or component to perform its required functions within specified performance requirements. [1]

Process. A function that must be performed in the software life cycle. A Process is composed of Activities.

product. Any output of the software development Activities; e.g., document, code, model.

quality management. That aspect of the overall management function that determines and implements the quality policy. (ISO 9000)

quality policy. The overall quality intentions and direction of an organization as regards quality, as formally expressed by top management. (ISO 9000)

revision. A controlled item with the same functional capabilities as the original plus changes, error resolution, or enhancements.

software life cycle (SLC). A project-specific, sequenced mapping of Activities.

software life cycle model (SLCM). The skeleton framework selected by each using organization on which to map the Activities of this standard to produce the software life cycle.

software quality management. That aspect of the overall software management function that determines and implements the software quality policy.

software quality policy. The overall quality intentions and direction of an organization as regards software quality, as expressed by top management.

software system. Software that is the subject of a single software project.

supplier. The person, or persons, who produce a product for a customer. In the context of this document, the customer and the supplier may be members of the same organization. [5]

task. The smallest unit of work subject to management accountability. A task is a well-defined work assignment for one or more project members. Related tasks are usually grouped to form Activities. [17]

unit. A logically separable part of a program. [1]

user. The person, or persons, who operate or interact directly with the system. [5]

1.3.2 Acronyms. The following acronyms appear within the text of this standard:

CASE	Computer-Aided Software Engineering
I/O	Input/Output
PR&RP	Problem Report and Resolution Planned Information
SCMP	Software Configuration Management Planned Information
SDD	Software Design Description
SLC	Software Life Cycle
SLCM	Software Life Cycle Model
SPMP	Software Project Management Planned Information
SQA	Software Quality Assurance
SRS	Software Requirements
SVVP	Software Verification and Validation Planned Information

1.4 Organization of This Document. The organization of this standard provides a logical approach to the development, operation, and maintenance of software. The detailed requirements of this document are organized into 17 Processes, which are comprised of a total of 65 Activities. The Processes and their Activities are described in six major sections. Table 1 depicts this organization.

Table 1
Organization of the Standard

Section	Title	Processes
2	Software Life Cycle Model Process	Software Life Cycle Model
3	Project Management Processes	Project Initiation Project Monitoring and Control Software Quality Management
4	Pre-Development Processes	Concept Exploration System Allocation
5	Development Processes	Requirements Design Implementation
6	Post-Development Processes	Installation Operation and Support Maintenance Retirement
7	Integral Processes	Verification and Validation Software Configuration Management Documentation Development Training

All of a Process' required actions are specified in its constituent Activities. Each Activity discussion has three parts:

(1) Input Information, which lists information that is to be used by the Activity, and its source.
(2) Description, which details the actions to be performed.
(3) Output Information, which lists the information that is generated by the Activity, and its destination.

Where information flows between Activities, it can be traced from its original Activity to the receiving Activity through the Input and Output Information tables.

As mentioned above, all Processes are mandatory. Activities, however, are categorized as mandatory[2] or "If Applicable."[3] "If Applicable" Activities are marked "If Applicable" in the Activity title. All other Activities are mandatory. Each "If Applicable" Activity contains an explanation of the cases to which it will apply (e.g., 5.2.4, Design Data Base, applies when the software product contains a data base).

1.5 Use of This Standard. To facilitate the understanding and use of a standard of this magnitude, this section provides additional information.

1.5.1 Applicability. This standard applies to software development and maintenance projects.

This standard can be applied to commercial, scientific, and military software. Applicability is not restricted by size, complexity, or criticality of the software. This standard considers both the software and its context.

It is recognized that a project may be too small, in terms of schedule, budget, risk, nature, or use of software to be developed, used, and maintained, to warrant total application of the standard. In such cases, selected Activities may be applied even though compliance with this standard may not be claimed. This may also apply when only purchased software is involved.

A large project may be subdivided into smaller manageable projects, and this standard applied to each of the smaller projects and then to the whole. Similarly, some projects may be of long duration, and may be delivered in multiple versions or releases; it may be helpful in some cases to treat the development of each successive version as a separate project with its own life cycle.

1.5.2 Compliance. Compliance with this standard is defined as the performance of all mandatory Activities. Some mandatory Activities may occur in different instances (e.g., performing tests at various levels); compliance with this standard means the complete performance of each instance of the mandatory Activity. The standard does not specify instances of any Activity.

The performance of an Activity or an instance thereof is complete when all Input Information has been processed, and all Output Information has been generated. This may require several iterations of an Activity or instance.

All Input and Output Information are not required for a given occurrence of an iterative Activity. The presence of sufficient Input Information to permit processing by the Activity to begin constitutes the entry criterion, and the creation of any Output Information is a sufficient exit criterion.

This standard does not impose the order in which Activities must be performed. However, an order must be established by executing the Activities defined in Section 2 and the Activity in 3.1.3.

In some cases, certain Input and Output Information may not be required for completion of an Activity. These are indicated as "External" to the SLC and may not exist. To the extent that they exist, they must be processed by affected Activities.

This standard prescribes the *processes* of the software life cycle, not the *products* of that life cycle. Therefore, the standard does not require the completion of specific documents. The information generated by Activities, listed in the Output Information tables, may be collected into documents in any manner consistent with the selected SLCM.

In the event that this standard is contractually imposed, and one or more subcontractors are involved in the project, it is recommended that the requirements of this standard be imposed on the subcontractors.

---

[2]The term "mandatory" as used in this standard is synonymous with the term "essential."

[3]The term "if applicable" as used in this standard is synonymous with the terms "conditional" and "optional."

1.5.3 Intended Audience. This standard cannot be implemented by a single functional group within a development organization. Mapping this standard's Activities into an organization's SLCM, and coordinating these Activities with existing development and support methodologies and standards, require specific expertise and authority within the organization.

After mapping is complete, the Activities in Sections 3–7 are ready for execution. These Activity descriptions are directed to the functional specialist most likely to be performing them (e.g., the Requirements and Analysis Activities assume a basic familiarity with analysis techniques).

1.5.4 Process and Activity Relationships

1.5.4.1 Project Management Processes. There are three Processes in this section: the Project Initiation Process, the Project Monitoring and Control Process, and the Software Quality Management Process. The Project Initiation Process consists of those Activities that create and maintain the project framework. The Activities within the Project Monitoring and Control Process and the Software Quality Management Process are performed throughout the life of the project to ensure the appropriate level of project management and compliance with the mandated Activities.

1.5.4.2 Development-Oriented Processes. These are the Processes that must be performed before, during, and after the development of the software. The Pre-Development Processes are Concept Exploration and System Allocation. Development Processes include Requirements, Design, and Implementation. Finally, the Post-Development Processes include Installation, Operation and Support, Maintenance, and Retirement.

1.5.4.3 Integral Processes. This section includes those Processes that are necessary to ensure the successful completion of a project, but are not Development Processes. The Integral Processes are Verification and Validation, Software Configuration Management, Documentation Development, and Training. All of these Processes contain two types of Activities:

(1) Those that are performed discretely and are therefore mapped into an SLCM.
(2) Those that are performed in the course of completing another Activity. These are invoked Activities and will not be mapped into the SLCM in every instance.

Many Activities invoke, or call like a subroutine, appropriate Integral Process(es). This is an intuitive method of getting a task, such as the evaluation or production of a document, done without specifying an exact control flow within this standard.

To track the flow of a product into, through, and back from an Integral Process, there are generic sources and destinations listed in the Input and Output Information tables called "Creating Process." Within the Integral Process that is invoked, the Activity that first receives the product has a generic Input Information whose source is Creating Process. This product passes through one or more Activities of that Integral Process, then is returned to the invoking Activity through an Activity's Output Information, whose destination is Creating Process. An example of this flow is shown in Fig 1, which illustrates how one Activity within the Design Process invokes the Integral Processes. This figure will be easier to follow if it is compared directly with 5.2.7, "Perform Detailed Design." The order of Invoked Processes in the figure differs from that in 5.2.7.

The invoked Process is specified in the text by the name of the Process and the number of the first Activity to be performed within that Process [e.g., Verification and Validation (7.1.4)].

1.5.4.4 Use of I/O Tables. The Input Information to and Output Information from each Activity are listed in tables that accompany the Activity descriptions. As a convention of this document, Input and Output Information names are always capitalized in the text.

The I/O tables show the flow of Information through the Activities. The pertinent Information is listed in the left-hand column. The source or destination of the Information (both Process and Activity) is shown in the right-hand columns. The Information names were chosen, where possible, to suggest the titles of documents commonly used in the software industry. The Information names also frequently relate to the documents described in the standards listed in Section 8. Some of these Information items are represented in the text by acronyms that were deliberately chosen to suggest the commonly used names of the corresponding documents.

External Input Information sources and External Output Information destinations are outside the scope of this standard. External Input Information may or may not exist, and if it does not exist, it is not required. When an External Input does exist and is therefore used, it is presumed to include any associated documentation. External output destinations also may or may not exist. External sources and destinations are not necessarily Processes, and no corresponding Activities are shown in the I/O tables.

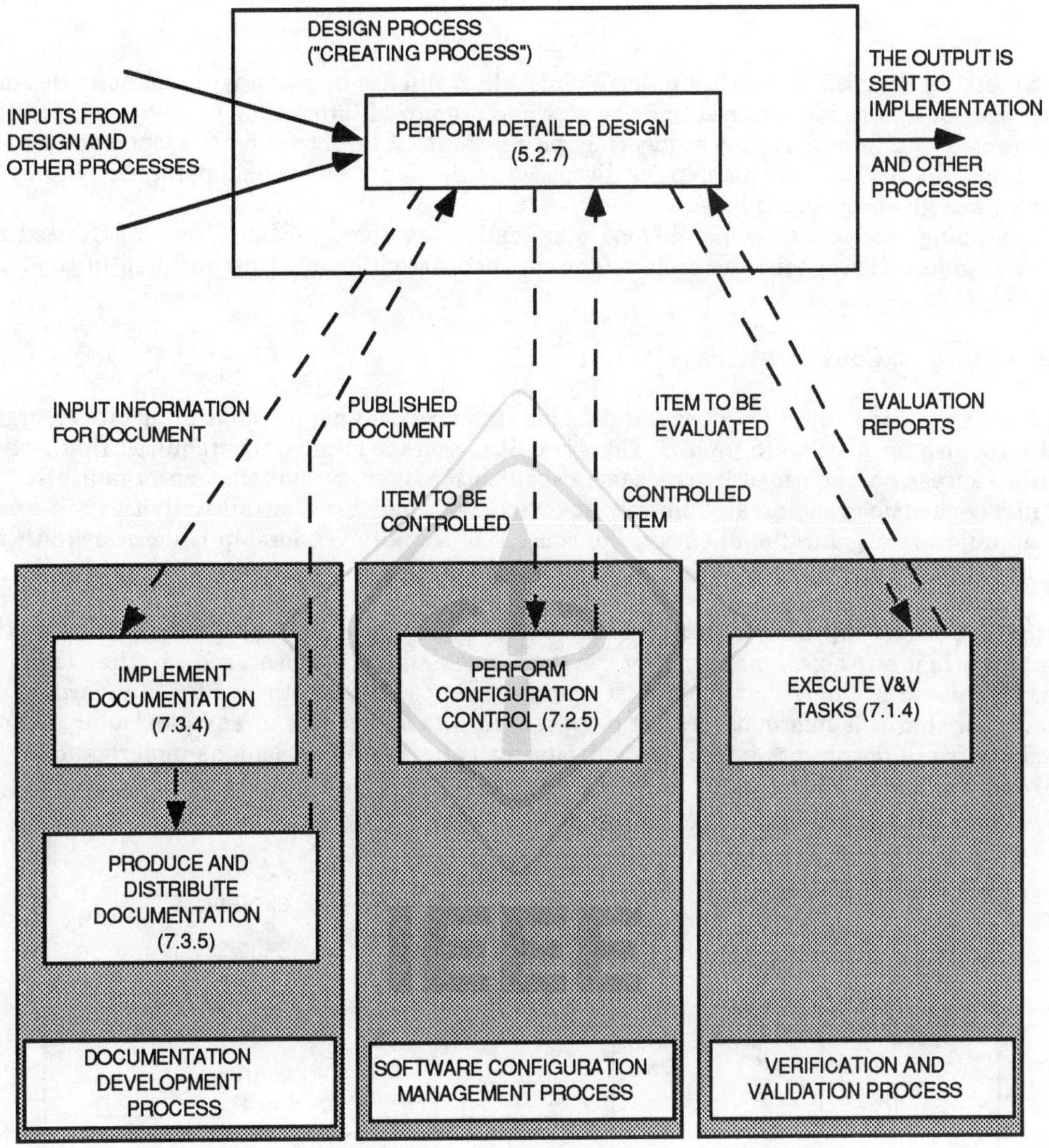

Fig 1
Example of Invoked Processes

In most cases, the Input Information and Output Information columns of the tables designate the specific information that enters or exits the Activity. However, since many Activities have Output Information whose destination is Retain Records (3.2.6), the various Input Information to Retain Records is collected under the term "Original Records." The corresponding Process and Activity columns refer simply to Originating Process and Originating Activity. Figure 2 depicts the conceptual flow of Input Information and Output Information into and out from an Activity, respectively.

1.5.5 Getting Started. Before beginning a project that will use this standard, the Activities need to be reviewed for applicability to a specific project and organized into a time sequence appropriate to that project. To perform that time sequencing, an SLCM must be chosen or developed and Activities mapped into the SLCM. This mapping is discussed in Section 2 and the mapping Activity in 3.1.3. Examples are given in Appendix A.

This mapping produces a temporal "road map" called the Software Life Cycle (SLC) used to follow this standard throughout the project. The mapped Activities must be initiated in their designated sequence.

1.5.6 Additional Considerations

1.5.6.1 Organizational Independence. This standard does not presume or dictate an organizational structure for a software project. Therefore, it is neither implied nor required that Activities within a Process be performed by the same organizational entity, nor that an organizational entity's involvement be concentrated in only one Process. To ensure that all Activities are assigned to an appropriate organizational entity, the concept of Activity Ownership is described in the Activity in 3.1.3.

1.5.6.2 Combining Documents. The Information developed in this standard, as shown in the Output Information tables, may carry generic names similar to those used in other IEEE standards. This does not imply that the format and content specified in other IEEE standards must be followed, nor that this information must be packaged into documents in any particular manner.

Combination of documents into a single document is acceptable as long as understanding is not compromised.

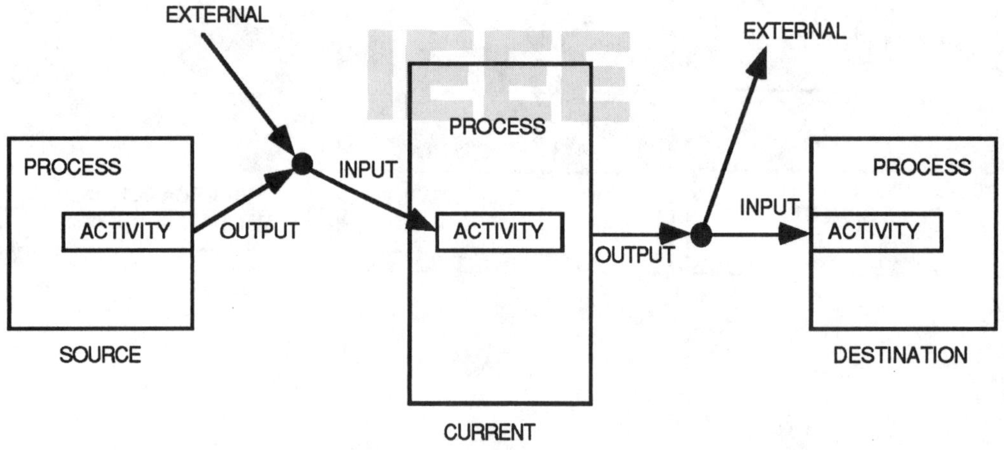

Fig 2
Information Flow

2. Software Life Cycle Model Process

2.1 Overview. Many variables affect an organization's selection of a software life cycle model (SLCM). While this standard neither dictates nor defines a specific software life cycle (SLC) or its underlying methodologies, it does require that an SLCM be chosen and used.

This Process provides the Activities required to identify candidate SLCMs and select the SLCM to be used by other Activities in the standard.

This standard includes the specification of the non-time-ordered set of "Mandatory" Activities that must be incorporated into an SLCM. An SLCM (e.g., Rapid Prototyping) defines a specific approach to producing software. It specifies a time-ordered set of Activities (including all of the "Mandatory" Activities identified in this standard), which is to be used as the basis for mapping the Activities of this standard. An SLCM may also propose standards for the performance of the Activities or the deliverables produced during the project.

The SLC (defined for a project by the Activity in 3.1.3) is the time-ordered set of Activities or instances of Activities to be performed. This set is to be mapped into a selected SLCM. The SLC also identifies specific responsibilities for each Activity. While the same SLCM may be valid for several projects, each project must define its own SLC.

Once an SLCM is selected, there are two additional required actions:

(1) Mapping the Activities described in this standard into the chosen life cycle (3.1.3).
(2) Identifying and documenting the standards and controls that govern the SLC (3.1.5).

Figure 3 illustrates this progression from this standard to a project-specific SLC.

Section 1.5, "Use of This Standard," provides background information necessary for the successful understanding and application of this material. It should be read prior to proceeding further in this section.

2.2 Activities List

(1) Identify Candidate Software Life Cycle Models
(2) Select Project Model

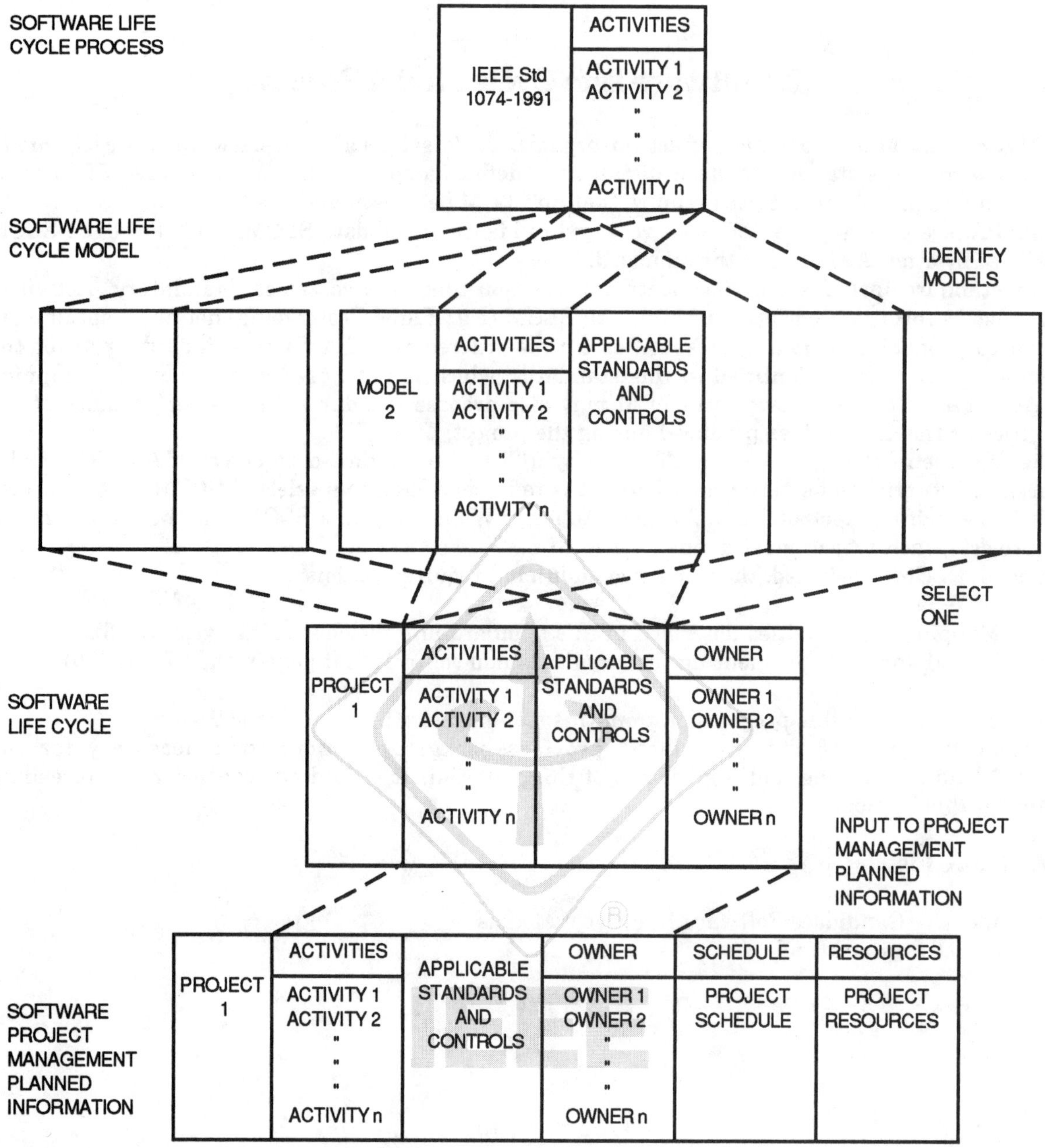

Fig 3
Software Life Cycle Relationships

2.3 Identify Candidate Software Life Cycle Models

2.3.1 Input Information

Input Information	Source	
	Process	Activity
Available Software Life Cycle Models)	External	
Constraints	External	

2.3.2 Description. In this Activity, the set of Available SLCMs and applicable Constraints shall be considered and Candidate SLCMs identified. A new model may be constructed by combining elements of other SLCMs.

Maintenance is an iteration of the Software Life Cycle, and the SLCM must support this iteration.

2.3.3 Output Information

Output Information	Destination	
	Process	Activity
Candidate Software Life Cycle Model(s)	Software Life Cycle Model	Select Project Model (2.4)

2.4 Select Project Model

2.4.1 Input Information

Input Information	Source	
	Process	Activity
Historical Project Records	External	
Constraints	External	
Candidate Software Life Cycle Model(s)	Software Life Cycle Model	Identify Candidate Software Life Cycle Models (2.3)

2.4.2 Description. In this Activity, one of the candidate SLCMs from 2.3.2 is selected for use.

Based on the type of product (interactive, batch, transaction processing, etc.), Constraints, and Historical Project Records, an SLCM analysis shall be conducted, and a decision made as to which model will best support the management of the project.

It is possible for an organization to have more than one SLCM, but only one model may be selected for a project. It is not necessary to have a single, organization-wide SLCM.

The SLCM shall provide the necessary framework for software projects to map the Activities to produce the SLC (as shown in Fig 3). The mapping effort is specified in the Project Initiation Process, Map Activities to Software Life Cycle Model (3.1.3).

2.4.3 Output Information

Output Information	Destination	
	Process	Activity
Selected Software Life Cycle Model	Project Initiation	Map Activities to Software Life Cycle Model (3.1.3)

3. Project Management Processes

These are the Processes that initiate, monitor, and control software projects throughout the software life cycle (SLC).

3.1 Project Initiation Process

3.1.1 Overview. This Process contains those Activities that create the framework for the project. During this Process, the SLC is created for this project, and plans for managing the project are established. Standards, methodologies, and tools needed to manage and execute the project are identified and a plan prepared for their timely implementation.

Section 1.5, "Use of This Standard," provides background information necessary for the successful understanding and application of this material. It should be read prior to proceeding further in this section.

3.1.2 Activities List

(1) Map Activities to Software Life Cycle Model
(2) Allocate Project Resources
(3) Establish Project Environment
(4) Plan Project Management

3.1.3 Map Activities to Software Life Cycle Model

3.1.3.1 Input Information

Input Information	Source	
	Process	Activity
Contractual Requirements	External	
Selected Software Life Cycle Model	Software Life Cycle Model	Select Project Model (2.4)
Statement of Need	Concept Exploration	Refine and Finalize the Idea or Need (4.1.7)

3.1.3.2 Description. The Activities identified in this standard shall be mapped into the selected SLC Model (SLCM). Mapping involves establishing the chronological relationship of the Activities in this standard according to the selected SLCM. It may be necessary to use the Contractual Requirements and the Statement of Need to accomplish this mapping. Appendix A provides several examples of such mappings. Appendix B is a template for adding additional project-specific information, such as document titles and applicable standards, to the mapped Activities.

The use of certain software development methods defines the execution of some Activities to be automated. Compliance with this standard must be demonstrated by mapping those automated Activities into the appropriate points within the SLCM.

Each Activity shall be assigned a single "owner." An owner is a single point of contact, and is identified by organizational position. Ownership is assumed by the person currently filling that position. Each owner has the responsibility and authority to control and complete the Activity within the planned schedule and budget. In addition, each owner is accountable for the quality of the Activity outputs. If Activities are to be performed by multiple organizations, the owning organization and position of the owner shall be identified. In the case of multiple instances of an Activity, an owner for each instance shall be identified.

The resulting map of the Activities to be performed, with their corresponding owners, is the SLC for this project. All "If Applicable" Activities that do not apply to this project shall be identified and explained in the List of Activities Not Used.

3.1.3.3 Output Information

Output Information	Destination	
	Process	Activity
Software Life Cycle	Project Initiation	Allocate Project Resources (3.1.4)
		Establish Project Environment (3.1.5)
		Plan Project Management (3.1.6)
List of Activities Not Used	Project Monitoring and Control	Retain Records (3.2.6)

3.1.4 Allocate Project Resources

3.1.4.1 Input Information

Input Information	Source	
	Process	Activity
Historical Project Records	External	
Resources	External	
Statement of Need	Concept Exploration	Refine and Finalize the Idea or Need (4.1.7)
Software Life Cycle	Project Initiation	Map Activities to Software Life Cycle Model (3.1.3)
System Functional Software Requirements	System Allocation	Decompose System Requirements (4.2.5)

3.1.4.2 Description. Resource Allocations shall be identified at the Software Life Cycle's Activity level. Resources to be allocated include personnel, equipment, space, etc. Available Historical Project Records and the Statement of Need may provide valuable insight into Resource Allocation.

3.1.4.3 Output Information

Output Information	Destination	
	Process	Activity
Resource Allocations	Project Initiation	Establish Project Environment (3.1.5)
		Plan Project Management (3.1.6)
	Project Management and Control	Analyze Risks (3.2.3)

3.1.5 Establish Project Environment

3.1.5.1 Input Information

Input Information	Source	
	Process	Activity
Methodologies	External	
Standards	External	
Tools	External	
Software Library	External	
Purchased Software	External	
Contractual Requirements	External	
Analysis of Risks	Project Monitoring and Control	Analyze Risks (3.2.3)
Software Life Cycle	Project Initiation	Map Activities to Software Life Cycle Model (3.1.3)
Defined Metrics	Software Quality Management	Define Metrics (3.3.4)
Collection and Analysis Methods	Software Quality Management	Define Metrics (3.3.4)
Resource Allocations	Project Initiation	Allocate Project Resources (3.1.4)
Statement of Need	Concept Exploration	Refine and Finalize the Idea or Need (4.1.7)

3.1.5.2 Description. The needs of the project for procedural and technological Tools, Methodologies, and Standards shall be defined. Approaches to these needs shall be identified and evaluated. These approaches could include automated and nonautomated tools, modeling and prototyping methodologies, environment simulators, test beds, and software libraries. Selection criteria for Tools and Methodologies should include resource, schedule, safety, and security considerations, and the project requirements defined in the Statement of Need and Analysis of Risks. The project standards shall include requirements, design, coding, test, and documentation standards.

After evaluating the approaches, a set of Tools, Methodologies, Standards, and reusable or Purchased Software shall be selected to provide the Project Environment, considering the Input Information.

The selected tools shall be acquired or developed and installed for use in project Activities. The owner of this Activity shall ensure that applicable personnel are familiar with the Tools, Methodologies, and Standards selected for the project.

For assistance in identifying applicable standards, [9] should be consulted.

Prior to distribution of the Project Environment, the Training Process (7.4.4) shall be invoked.

3.1.5.3 Output Information

Output Information	Destination	
	Process	Activity
Project Environment	Project Initiation	Plan Project Management (3.1.6)

3.1.6 Plan Project Management

3.1.6.1 Input Information

Input Information	Source	
	Process	Activity
Contractual Requirements	External	
Software Life Cycle	Project Initiation	Map Activities to Software Life Cycle Model (3.1.3)
Resource Allocations	Project Initiation	Allocate Project Resources (3.1.4)
Project Environment	Project Initiation	Establish Project Environment (3.1.5)
Contingency Planned Information	Project Monitoring and Control	Perform Contingency Planning (3.2.4)
Project Management Reported Information	Project Monitoring and Control	Manage the Project (3.2.5)
Preliminary Statement of Need	Concept Exploration	Identify Ideas or Needs (4.1.3)
Recommendations	Concept Exploration	Conduct Feasibility Studies (4.1.5)
Statement of Need	Concept Exploration	Refine and Finalize the Idea or Need (4.1.7)

3.1.6.2 Description. Project management planning requires collection and synthesis of a great deal of information into a coherent and organized Software Project Management Planned Information (SPMP) based on the SLC. This Activity shall initially define and subsequently update the SPMP using the Input Information. This Activity shall detail the project organization and assign responsibilities. Standards, methodologies, and tools for configuration management, quality assurance, verification and validation, training, documentation, and development shall be specified. This Activity shall apportion the project budget and staffing, and define schedules, using the applicable Input Information. It also shall define procedures for scheduling, tracking, and reporting, and shall address considerations such as regulatory approvals, required certifications, user involvement, subcontracting, and security.

This Activity shall include planning for support, problem reporting, and retirement. Support planning shall include methods for supporting the software in the operational environment. Problem Reporting and Resolution Planning Information shall include, at a minimum, defining a method for logging, routing, and handling problem reports; categories of severity; and the method for verifying problem resolution. Retirement Planned Information shall address issues such as probable retirement date, archiving, replacement, and residual support issues.

As new or revised Input Information is received in this Activity, project plans shall be updated and further project planning shall be based upon these updated plans.

Additional guidance for SPMPs can be found in [17].

Prior to distribution of the SPMP, the following Processes shall be invoked:

(1) Verification and Validation (7.1.4)
(2) Software Configuration Management (7.2.5)
(3) Documentation Development (7.3.4)

3.1.6.3 Output Information

Output Information	Destination	
	Process	Activity
Problem Reporting and Resolution Planned Information	Project Monitoring and Control	Manage the Project (3.2.5)
		Analyze Risks (3.2.3)
		Implement Problem Reporting Method (3.2.7)
Retirement Planned Information	Project Monitoring and Control	Manage the Project (3.2.5)
	Retirement	Notify User (6.4.3)
		Conduct Parallel Operations (If Applicable) (6.4.4)
		Retire System (6.4.5)
Software Project Management Planned Information	Most Processes	Most Activities
Support Planned Information	Project Monitoring and Control	Analyze Risks (3.2.3)
		Manage the Project (3.2.5)
	Operation and Support	Maintain Support Request Log (6.2.5)
		Operate the System (6.2.3)
		Provide Technical Assistance and Consulting (6.2.4)

3.2 Project Monitoring and Control Process

3.2.1 Overview. Monitoring and control is an iterative Process of tracking, reporting, and managing costs, schedules, problems, and performance of a project throughout its life cycle. The progress of a project is reviewed and measured against project milestones established in the Software Project Management Planned Information (SPMP).

Section 1.5, "Use of This Standard," provides background information necessary for the successful understanding and application of this material. It should be read prior to proceeding further in this section.

3.2.2 Activities List

(1) Analyze Risks
(2) Perform Contingency Planning
(3) Manage the Project
(4) Retain Records
(5) Implement Problem Reporting Method

3.2.3 Analyze Risks

3.2.3.1 Input Information

Input Information	Source	
	Process	Activity
Procurement/Lease Data	External	
System Constraints	External	
Historical Project Records	External	
Support Planned Information	Project Initiation	Plan Project Management (3.1.6)
Resource Allocations	Project Initiation	Allocate Project Resources (3.1.4)
Software Project Management Planned Information	Project Initiation	Plan Project Management (3.1.6)
Problem Reporting and Resolution Planned Information	Project Initiation	Plan Project Management (3.1.6)
Transition Impact Statement (If Applicable)	Concept Exploration	Plan System Transition (If Applicable) (4.1.6)
Statement of Need	Concept Exploration	Refine and Finalize the Idea or Need (4.1.7)
Software Interface Requirements	Requirements	Define Interface Requirements (5.1.4)
Software Requirements	Requirements	Prioritize and Integrate Software Requirements (5.1.5)
Software Design Description	Design	Perform Detailed Design (5.2.7)
Integration Planned Information	Implementation	Plan Integration (5.3.7)
Analysis Reported Information	Verification and Validation	Collect and Analyze Metric Data (7.1.5)
Test Planned Information(s)	Verification and Validation	Plan Testing (7.1.6)
Test Summary Reported Information	Verification and Validation	Execute the Tests (7.1.8)

3.2.3.2 Description. Because risk management often involves trade-offs between many factors, risk analysis is an iterative Activity performed throughout a project's life. This analysis shall consider project risks, including technical, economic, operational support, and schedule risks.

Factors that may impair, prevent, or require technical trade-offs for accomplishing the technical objectives of the project or product shall be identified and analyzed. Technical factors may include such items as real-time performance, safety considerations, security considerations, implementation considerations, testability, and maintainability. Analytical approaches for technical risk assessment may include static and dynamic modeling and simulation, prototyping, independent reviews, and audits.

Cost, resource factors, earnings, liabilities, or other economic measures involved in the project shall be identified and analyzed. The objective of this analysis is to identify potential economic opportunities, losses, and trade-offs. Analytical approaches for economic risk assessment may include financial analysis, such as return on investment and possible incentive and penalty contract clauses.

Operational and support risk analysis shall determine the probability that the delivered software will meet the user's requirements. Operational and support requirements such as interoperability, security, performance, installability, and maintainability shall be considered. Both completeness of, and conformance to, these requirements shall be analyzed.

Cost, resource, technical, and other requirements shall be evaluated for their impact on project schedule. This analysis should consider project interdependence and the effect of schedule adjustments. Analytical approaches for schedule risk assessment may include critical path analysis and resource leveling techniques.

3.2.3.3 Output Information

Output Information	Destination	
	Process	Activity
Analysis of Risks	Project Initiation	Establish Project Environment (3.1.5)
	Project Monitoring and Control	Perform Contingency Planning (3.2.4)
	Requirements	Define and Develop Software Requirements (5.1.3)
	Verification and Validation	Plan Verification and Validation (7.1.3)

3.2.4 Perform Contingency Planning

3.2.4.1 Input Information

Input Information	Source	
	Process	Activity
Analysis of Risks	Project Monitoring and Control	Analyze Risks (3.2.3)
Analysis Reported Information	Verification and Validation	Collect and Analyze Metric Data (7.1.5)

3.2.4.2 Description. This Activity shall define alternative actions in the event that a given risk materializes, using the Input Information. Contingency Planned Information shall include resource planning and the establishment of trigger conditions that would invoke a contingency action. Contingency actions may include consideration of revised requirements, delay, or cancellation of the project.

3.2.4.3 Output Information

Output Information	Destination	
	Process	Activity
Contingency Planned Information	Project Initiation	Plan Project Management (3.1.6)
	Project Monitoring and Control	Manage the Project (3.2.5)

3.2.5 Manage the Project

3.2.5.1 Input Information

Input Information	Source	
	Process	Activity
Problem Reporting and Resolution Planned Information	Project Initiation	Plan Project Management (3.1.6)
Retirement Planned Information	Project Initiation	Plan Project Management (3.1.6)
Software Project Management Planned Information	Project Initiation	Plan Project Management (3.1.6)
Support Planned Information	Project Initiation	Plan Project Management (3.1.6)
Contingency Planned Information	Project Monitoring and Control	Perform Contingency Planning (3.2.4)
Software Quality Management Planned Information	Software Quality Management	Plan Software Quality Management (3.3.3)
Quality Improvement Recommendations	Software Quality Management	Identify Quality Improvement Needs (3.3.6)
Integration Planned Information	Implementation	Plan Integration (5.3.7)
Installation Reported Information	Installation	Install Software (6.1.5)
Evaluation Reported Information	Verification and Validation	Execute Verification and Validation Tasks (7.1.4)
Analysis Reported Information	Verification and Validation	Collect and Analyze Metric Data (7.1.5)
Test Planned Information(s)	Verification and Validation	Plan Testing (7.1.6)
Test Summary Reported Information	Verification and Validation	Execute the Tests (7.1.8)
Status Reported Information	Software Configuration Management	Perform Status Accounting (7.2.6)
Feedback Data	Operation and Support	Operate the System (6.2.3)

3.2.5.2 Description. Throughout the life cycle, the progress of the project shall be reviewed and measured against the established milestones and budget in the plan(s) (i.e., predicted and planned progress versus actual progress, and budgeted versus actual expenditures). Project tracking and reporting includes analyzing the Input Information, collecting other pertinent data, and monitoring project Activities. Anomalies may result. Risk management procedures must be implemented to control risk.

This Activity also encompasses the day-to-day management of the project needed to ensure successful project completion. Information collected within this Activity is used to improve the performance of the project.

Prior to distributing the Project Management Reported Information, the Verification and Validation Process (7.1.4) should be invoked.

3.2.5.3 Output Information

Output Information	Destination	
	Process	Activity
Project Management Reported Information	Project Initiation	Plan Project Management (3.1.6)
	Project Monitoring and Control	Retain Records (3.2.6)
	External	
Anomalies	Project Monitoring and Control	Implement Problem Reporting Method (3.2.7)

3.2.6 Retain Records

3.2.6.1 Input Information

Input Information	Source	
	Process	Activity
Documentation Retention Standards	External	
Original Records	Originating Process	Originating Activity
Software Project Management Planned Information	Project Initiation	Plan Project Management (3.1.6)
Software Configuration Management Planned Information	Software Configuration Management	Plan Configuration Management (7.2.3)
Documentation Planned Information	Documentation Development	Plan Documentation (7.3.3)
Published Document	Documentation Development	Produce and Distribute Documentation (7.3.5)

3.2.6.2 Description. This Activity accepts the original project documentation and records from each originating Process. The records shall be retained in accordance with the SPMP, Software Configuration Management Planned Information, and any external document retention standards. Input Information documentation becomes part of the Historical Project Records of the organization. Uses for these records may include project audits, future project planning, and corporate accounting.

3.2.6.3 Output Information

Output Information	Destination	
	Process	Activity
Historical Project Records	External	

3.2.7 Implement Problem Reporting Method

3.2.7.1 Input Information

Input Information	Source	
	Process	Activity
Anomalies	External	
	Creating Process	
Controlled Item	Software Configuration Management	Perform Configuration Control (7.2.5)
Problem Reporting and Resolution Planned Information	Project Initiation	Plan Project Management (3.1.6)

3.2.7.2 Description. This Activity accepts Anomalies from any source and prepares a problem report. The problem report shall contain information as specified in the Problem Reporting and Resolution Planned Information (PR&RP). Possible problem solutions may be suggested by the problem reporter. Problems may be resolved through corrections or enhancements (as defined in the PR&RP). Corrections are documented in the Correction Problem Reported Information for further consideration. Enhancements may be documented in the Enhancement Problem Reported Information and are possible candidates for new projects. A Report Log shall be maintained to assure that all problems are tracked until they are resolved and the resolution has been approved.

This Activity shall also analyze the problem including the Controlled Item, the problem report, and the Report Log to make the following determinations:

(1) What the anomalies are.
(2) Source and cause of product or process problem.
(3) Product(s) or process(es) presumed to contain the error, including documentation.
(4) Problem severity.
(5) Course of corrective action.

Problem reports that originate from an Activity not included in this standard are noted as resolved within this Activity and forwarded for appropriate action to the responsible authority.

This Activity shall monitor the problem correction efforts performed by the responsible Process, shall determine (according to the PR&RD) that the implementation of the solution by the responsible Process has been completed, and shall then record the resolution of the problem in the Resolved Problem Reported Information. The Resolved Problem Reported Information shall be distributed as specified in the Problem Reporting and Resolution Planned Information.

Further information related to this Activity may be found in [15].

The Resolved Problem Reported Information should be made available to the Process or external source that reported the problem.

Prior to distribution of a Problem Reported Information or the Report Log, the Software Configuration Management Process (7.2.5) should be invoked.

3.2.7.3 Output Information

Output Information	Destination	
	Process	Activity
Resolved Problem Reported Information	External	
	Creating Process	
	Software Quality Management	Manage Software Quality (3.3.5)
	Verification and Validation	Execute Verification and Validation Tasks (7.1.4)
		Collect and Analyze Metric Data (7.1.5)
Report Log	Software Quality Management	Manage Software Quality (3.3.5)
	Verification and Validation	Collect and Analyze Metric Data (7.1.5)
Enhancement Problem Reported Information	Concept Exploration	Identify Ideas or Needs (4.1.3)
	Verification and Validation	Collect and Analyze Metric Data (7.1.5)
Correction Problem Reported Information	Maintenance	Reapply Software Life Cycle (6.3.3)
	Verification and Validation	Collect and Analyze Metric Data (7.1.5)

3.3 Software Quality Management Process

3.3.1 Overview. An important role of Software Quality Management is to address the planning and administration of the Software Quality Assurance (SQA) program. It further addresses such concerns as client satisfaction (which transcends adherence only to established technical requirements), and internal quality improvement programs. The responsibilities, functions, obligations, and duties of an SQA program are properly a constituent part of all Activities in the Software Life Cycle, and thus are interspersed into each Activity as appropriate. Software Quality Management is the methodology used in this standard for tying the SQA responsibilities together with other Quality concerns. The Activities of this Process span the entire Software Life Cycle (SLC).

Section 1.5, "Use of This Standard," provides background information necessary for the successful understanding and application of this material. It should be read prior to proceeding further in this section.

3.3.2 Activities List

(1) Plan Software Quality Management
(2) Define Metrics
(3) Manage Software Quality
(4) Identify Quality Improvement Needs

3.3.3 Plan Software Quality Management

3.3.3.1 Input Information

Input Information	Source	
	Process	Activity
Software Project Management Planned Information	Project Initiation	Plan Project Management (3.1.6)
Defined Metrics	Software Quality Management	Define Metrics (3.3.4)
Collection and Analysis Methods	Software Quality Management	Define Metrics (3.3.4)

3.3.3.2 Description. A Software Quality Management program shall be initiated and documented.

It shall include a Software Quality Assurance program, which may be documented separately.

The goals of the Software Quality Management program are to identify SQA actions, describe supplier quality requirements, address client satisfaction, and provide for the identification of quality improvement needs.

Overall quality objectives are derived using the organizational guidelines and contractual requirements from the Software Project Management Planned Information.

The program information shall include the Software Quality Management organization and responsibilities, and the tools, techniques, and methodologies to implement the program.

The goals and standards to be applied to the project shall also be identified.

The goals are further expanded into quality objectives and milestones in the Software Quality Management Planned Information.

Further information related to this Activity may be found in [2] and [8].

Prior to distribution of the Software Quality Management Planned Information, the following Processes shall be invoked:

(1) Verification and Validation (7.1.4)
(2) Software Configuration Management (7.2.5)
(3) Documentation Development (7.3.4)

3.3.3.3 Output Information

Output Information	Destination	
	Process	Activity
Software Quality Management Planned Information	Project Monitoring and Control	Manage the Project (3.2.5)
	Software Quality Management	Define Metrics (3.3.4)
		Manage Software Quality (3.3.5)
		Identify Quality Improvement Needs (3.3.6)
	Verification and Validation	Plan Verification and Validation (7.1.3)
		Collect and Analyze Metric Data (7.1.5)

3.3.4 Define Metrics

3.3.4.1 Input Information

Input Information	Source	
	Process	Activity
Software Quality Management Planned Information	Software Quality Management	Plan Software Quality Management (3.3.3)
Software Project Management Planned Information	Project Initiation	Plan Project Management (3.1.6)

3.3.4.2 Description. The metrics required for the project, based on the Software Project Management Planned Information, shall be defined. Metrics should be applied to the products of the project and to the processes that affect the project. The metrics shall be used throughout the SLC. For each Defined Metric, Collection and Analysis Methods shall be specified.

Further information related to this Activity may be found in [6], [7], [16], and [19].

Prior to the distribution of Defined Metrics, the Verification and Validation Process (7.1.4) shall be invoked.

3.3.4.3 Output Information

Output Information	Destination	
	Process	Activity
Defined Metrics	Software Quality Management	Manage Software Quality (3.3.5)
		Plan Software Quality Management (3.3.3)
	Project Initiation	Establish Project Environm't (3.1.5)
	Verification and Validation	Collect and Analyze Metric Data (7.1.5)
Collection and Analysis Methods	Software Quality Management	Plan Software Quality Management (3.3.3)
		Manage Software Quality (3.3.5)
	Verification and Validation	Collect and Analyze Metric Data (7.1.5)
	Project Initiation	Establish Project Environm't (3.1.5)

3.3.5 Manage Software Quality

3.3.5.1 Input Information

Input Information	Source	
	Process	Activity
Report Log	Project Monitoring and Control	Implement Problem Reporting Method (3.2.7)
Resolved Problem Reported Information	Project Monitoring and Control	Implement Problem Reporting Method (3.2.7)
Software Quality Management Planned Information	Software Quality Management	Plan Software Quality Management (3.3.3)
Defined Metrics	Software Quality Management	Define Metrics (3.3.4)
Collection and Analysis Methods	Software Quality Management	Define Metrics (3.3.4)
Quality Improvement Recommendations	Software Quality Management	Identify Quality Improvement Needs (3.3.6)
Analysis Reported Information	Verification and Validation	Collect and Analyze Metric Data (7.1.5)
Post-Operation Review Reported Information	Retirement	Retire System (6.4.5)

3.3.5.2 Description. Using the listed Input Information, this Activity implements the provisions of the Software Quality Management Planned Information. Based on the Software Quality Management Planned Information quality objectives and milestones, progress shall be measured and reported in Project Quality Assessments.

3.3.5.3 Output Information

Output Information	Destination	
	Process	Activity
Project Quality Assessments	Verification and Validation	Execute Verification and Validation Tasks (7.1.4)

3.3.6 Identify Quality Improvement Needs

3.3.6.1 Input Information

Input Information	Source	
	Process	Activity
Software Project Management Planned Information	Project Initiation	Plan Project Management (3.1.6)
Software Quality Management Planned Information	Software Quality Management	Plan Software Quality Management (3.3.3)
Software Verification and Validation Planned Information	Verification and Validation	Plan Verification and Validation (7.1.3)
Evaluation Reported Information	Verification and Validation	Execute Verification and Validation Tasks (7.1.4)
Analysis Reported Information	Verification and Validation	Collect and Analyze Metric Data (7.1.5)
Test Planned Information(s)	Verification and Validation	Plan Testing (7.1.6)
Training Planned Information(s)	Training	Plan Training Program (7.4.3)

3.3.6.2 Description. This Activity identifies needs for quality improvements and outputs the Quality Improvement Recommendations in accordance with the Software Quality Management Planned Information. This is accomplished by using the Input Information. These recommendations shall include their impact on the quality of the software delivered. In addition, applicable tools, techniques, and methods for implementation of these recommendations should be identified.

3.3.6.3 Output Information

Output Information	Destination	
	Process	Activity
Quality Improvement Recommendations	Project Monitoring and Control	Manage the Project (3.2.5)
	Software Quality Management	Manage Software Quality (3.3.5)
	External	

4. Pre-Development Processes

These are the Processes that must be performed before software development can begin.

4.1 Concept Exploration Process

4.1.1 Overview. A development effort is initiated with the identification of an idea or need for a system to be developed, whether it is a new effort or a change to all or part of an existing application. The Concept Exploration Process examines the requirements at the system level, producing a Statement of Need that initiates the System Allocation or Requirements Process. The Concept Exploration Process includes the identification of an idea or need, its evaluation and refinement, and, once boundaries are placed around it, generation of a Statement of Need for developing a system.

Section 1.5, "Use of This Standard," provides background information necessary for the successful understanding and application of this material. It should be read prior to proceeding further in this section.

4.1.2 Activities List

(1) Identify Ideas or Needs
(2) Formulate Potential Approaches
(3) Conduct Feasibility Studies
(4) Plan System Transition (If Applicable)
(5) Refine and Finalize the Idea or Need

4.1.3 Identify Ideas or Needs

4.1.3.1 Input Information

Input Information	Source	
	Process	Activity
Changing Software Requirements	External	
Customer Requests	External	
Ideas from Within the Development Organization	External	
Marketing Information Sources	External	
User Requests	External	
Enhancement Problem Reported Information	Project Monitoring and Control	Implement Problem Reporting Method (3.2.7)
Maintenance Recommendations	Maintenance	Reapply Software Life Cycle (6.3.3)
Feedback Data	Operation and Support	Operate the System (6.2.3)

4.1.3.2 Description. An idea or a need for a new or modified system is generated from one or more of the sources identified in the table above. Input Information to the Preliminary Statement of Need shall be documented, outlining function and performance needs. Changing Software Requirements may come from legislation, regulations, national and international standards, maintenance, etc.

Prior to distribution of the Preliminary Statement of Need to other Activities, the Verification and Validation Process (7.1.4) may be invoked.

4.1.3.3 Output Information

Output Information	Destination	
	Process	Activity
Preliminary Statement of Need	Project Initiation	Plan Project Management (3.1.6)
	Concept Exploration	Formulate Potential Approaches (4.1.4)
		Conduct Feasibility Studies (4.1.5)
		Plan System Transition (If Applicable) (4.1.6)
		Refine and Finalize the Idea or Need (4.1.7)

4.1.4 Formulate Potential Approaches

4.1.4.1 Input Information

Input Information	Source	
	Process	Activity
Development Resources and Budget	External	
Market Availability Data	External	
Resource Information	External	
Preliminary Statement of Need	Concept Exploration	Identify Ideas or Needs (4.1.3)

4.1.4.2 Description. Using Resource Information, budget data, and availability of third party software products, Potential Approaches shall be developed based upon the Preliminary Statement of Need and any data pertinent to the decision to develop or acquire the system. The Formulate Potential Approaches Activity shall also produce the constraints and benefits with regard to development of the software. The Constraints and Benefits should include all aspects of the life cycle.

Prior to release of Constraints and Benefits and Potential Approaches, the following Processes may be invoked:

(1) Verification and Validation (7.1.4)
(2) Software Configuration Management (7.2.5)

4.1.4.3 Output Information

Output Information	Destination	
	Process	Activity
Constraints and Benefits	Concept Exploration	Conduct Feasibility Studies (4.1.5)
		Refine and Finalize the Idea or Need (4.1.7)
Potential Approaches	Concept Exploration	Conduct Feasibility Studies (4.1.5)
		Refine and Finalize the Idea or Need (4.1.7)

4.1.5 Conduct Feasibility Studies

4.1.5.1 Input Information

Input Information	Source	
	Process	Activity
Preliminary Statement of Need	Concept Exploration	Identify Ideas or Needs (4.1.3)
Constraints and Benefits	Concept Exploration	Formulate Potential Approaches (4.1.4)
Potential Approaches	Concept Exploration	Formulate Potential Approaches (4.1.4)

4.1.5.2 Description. The feasibility study shall include the analysis of the idea or need, Potential Approaches, and all life cycle Constraints and Benefits. Modeling and prototyping techniques may be considered. In conducting the feasibility study, there may be a need to decide whether to make or buy the system, in part or in total. Justification for each Recommendation shall be fully documented and formally approved by all concerned organizations (including the user and the developer).

Prior to the distribution of the Recommendations, the Verification and Validation Process (7.1.4) may be invoked.

4.1.5.3 Output Information

Output Information	Destination	
	Process	Activity
Recommendations	Project Initiation	Plan Project Management (3.1.6)
	Concept Exploration	Plan System Transition (If Applicable) (4.1.6)
		Refine and Finalize the Idea or Need (4.1.7)
	System Allocation	Analyze Functions (4.2.3)

4.1.6 Plan System Transition (If Applicable)

4.1.6.1 Input Information

Input Information	Source	
	Process	Activity
Retirement Planned Information	External	
Preliminary Statement of Need	Concept Exploration	Identify Ideas or Needs (4.1.3)
Recommendations	Concept Exploration	Conduct Feasibility Studies (4.1.5)

4.1.6.2 Description. This Activity is applicable only when an existing system (automated or manual) is being replaced with a new system. The transition shall be planned and documented in accordance with the Retirement Planned Information of the system being replaced, Preliminary Statement of Need, and recommended solutions. Transition strategies and tools shall be part of the Transition Planned Information. A Transition Impact Statement shall also be produced.

Prior to distribution of the Transition Planned Information, the following Processes may be invoked:

(1) Verification and Validation (7.1.4)
(2) Software Configuration Management (7.2.5)
(3) Documentation Development (7.3.4)

4.1.6.3 Output Information

Output Information	Destination	
	Process	Activity
Transition Impact Statement	Project Monitoring and Control	Analyze Risks (3.2.3)
Transition Planned Information	Concept Exploration	Refine and Finalize the Idea or Need (4.1.7)
	Installation	Plan Installation (6.1.3)

4.1.7 Refine and Finalize the Idea or Need

4.1.7.1 Input Information

Input Information	Source	
	Process	Activity
Preliminary Statement of Need	Concept Exploration	Identify Ideas or Needs (4.1.3)
Constraints and Benefits	Concept Exploration	Formulate Potential Approaches (4.1.4)
Potential Approaches	Concept Exploration	Formulate Potential Approaches (4.1.4)
Recommendations	Concept Exploration	Conduct Feasibility Studies (4.1.5)
Transition Planned Information (If Applicable)	Concept Exploration	Plan System Transition (If Applicable) (4.1.6)

4.1.7.2 Description. The idea or need shall be refined by analyzing the Preliminary Statement of Need, the Potential Approaches, Recommendations, and Transition Planned Information (If Applicable). An approach shall be selected and documented that refines the initial idea or need.

Based upon the refined ideas or needs, a Statement of Need shall be generated that identifies the software idea, need, or desire, the recommended approach for its implementation, and any data pertinent to a management decision concerning the initiation of the described development effort.

Prior to distribution of the Statement of Need, the following Processes may be invoked:

(1) Verification and Validation (7.1.4)
(2) Documentation Development (7.3.4)

4.1.7.3 Output Information

Output Information	Destination	
	Process	Activity
Statement of Need	Project Initiation	Map Activitieso Software Life Cycle Model (3.1.3)
		Allocate Project Resources (3.1.4)
		Establish Project Environment (3.1.5)
		Plan Project Management (3.1.6)
	Project Monitoring and Control	Analyze Risks (3.2.3)
	System Allocation	Analyze Functions (4.2.3)
		Develop System Architecture (4.2.4)

4.2 System Allocation Process

4.2.1 Overview. The System Allocation Process is the bridge between Concept Exploration and the definition of software requirements. This Process maps the required functions to software and hardware.

The Statement of Need forms the basis for the analysis of the system, resulting in system requirements. This definition determines the inputs to the system, the processing to be applied to the inputs, and the required outputs. The software and hardware operational functions are also identified in these definitions.

The architecture of the system must be developed during the System Allocation Process. The system functions are derived from system requirements, and the hardware, software, and operational requirements are identified. These requirements are analyzed to produce System Functional Software Requirements and System Functional Hardware Requirements. The hardware, software, and operational interfaces must be defined and closely monitored. The hardware requirements analysis is not discussed in this document since it is beyond the scope of this standard.

Section 1.5, "Use of This Standard," provides background information necessary for the successful understanding and application of this material. It should be read prior to proceeding further in this section.

4.2.2 Activities List

(1) Analyze Functions
(2) Develop System Architecture
(3) Decompose System Requirements

4.2.3 Analyze Functions

4.2.3.1 Input Information

Input Information	Source	
	Process	Activity
Recommendations	Concept Exploration	Conduct Feasibility Studies (4.1.5)
Statement of Need	Concept Exploration	Refine and Finalize the Idea or Need (4.1.7)

4.2.3.2 Description. The Statement of Need and Recommendations for solution shall be analyzed to identify the functions of the total system. Once the functions have been defined, they are delineated in the Functional Description of the System and used to develop the system architecture and identify the hardware and software functions.

Prior to the distribution of the Functional Description of the System, the following Processes shall be invoked:

(1) Verification and Validation (7.1.4)
(2) Software Configuration Management (7.2.5)

4.2.3.3 Output Information

Output Information	Destination	
	Process	Activity
Functional Description of the System	System Allocation	Develop System Architecture (4.2.4)
		Decompose System Requirements (4.2.5)
	Requirements	Define Interface Requirements (5.1.4)

4.2.4 Develop System Architecture

4.2.4.1 Input Information

Input Information	Source	
	Process	Activity
Project Environment	Project Initiation	Establish Project Environment (3.1.5)
Statement of Need	Concept Exploration	Refine and Finalize the Idea or Need (4.1.7)
Functional Description of the System	System Allocation	Analyze Functions (4.2.3)

4.2.4.2 Description. The Statement of Need and the Functional Description of the System shall be transformed into the System Architecture, using the methodology, standards, and tools established by the organization. The System Architecture becomes the basis for the Design Process and the determination of the hardware and software functions.

4.2.4.3 Output Information

Output Information	Destination	
	Process	Activity
System Architecture	System Allocation	Decompose System Requirements (4.2.5)
	Design	Perform Architectural Design (5.2.3)

4.2.5 Decompose System Requirements

4.2.5.1 Input Information

Input Information	Source	
	Process	Activity
Functional Description of the System	System Allocation	Analyze Functions (4.2.3)
System Architecture	System Allocation	Develop System Architecture (4.2.4)

4.2.5.2 Description. The system functions documented in the Functional Description of the System shall be divided according to the System Architecture to form software requirements, hardware requirements, and the system interfaces. The System Interface Requirements define the interfaces that are external to the system and the interfaces between configuration items that comprise the system. Note that the hardware requirements go to an external destination since they are beyond the scope of this standard. The decomposition of the system may result in requirements for more than one project. Each software project shall be managed individually.

Prior to distribution of the requirements produced by this Activity, the following Processes shall be invoked:

(1) Verification and Validation (7.1.4)
(2) Software Configuration Management (7.2.5)
(3) Documentation Development (7.3.4)
(4) Training (7.4.4)

4.2.5.3 Output Information

Output Information	Destination	
	Process	Activity
System Functional Hardware Requirements	External	
System Functional Software Requirements	Project Initiation	Allocate Resources (3.1.4)
	Requirements	Define and Develop Software Requirements (5.1.3)
		Define Interface Requirements (5.1.4)
System Interface Requirements (If Applicable)	Requirements	Define and Develop Software Requirements (5.1.3)
		Define Interface Requirements (5.1.4)
	External	

5. Development Processes

These are the Processes that must be performed during the development of a software product.

5.1 Requirements Process

5.1.1 Overview. This Process includes those Activities directed toward the development of software requirements. In the development of a system containing both hardware and software components, the Requirements Process follows the development of total system requirements, and the functional allocation of those system requirements to hardware and software. For a system involving only software development, this effort begins once the Statement of Need is completed.

Section 1.5, "Use of This Standard," provides background information necessary for the successful understanding and application of this material. It should be read prior to proceeding further in this section.

5.1.2 Activities List

(1) Define and Develop Software Requirements
(2) Define Interface Requirements
(3) Prioritize and Integrate Software Requirements

5.1.3 Define and Develop Software Requirements

5.1.3.1 Input Information

Input Information	Source	
	Process	Activity
Installation Support Requirements	External	
System Constraints	External	
Project Environment	Project Initiation	Establish Project Environment (3.1.5)
Software Project Management Planned Information	Project Initiation	Plan Project Management (3.1.6)
Analysis of Risks	Project Monitoring and Control	Analyze Risks (3.2.3)
System Functional Software Requirements (If Applicable)	System Allocation	Decompose System Requirements (4.2.5)
System Interface Requirements (If Applicable)	System Allocation	Decompose System Requirements (4.2.5)

5.1.3.2 Description. The first Activity in this Process, defining the software requirements, is iterative in nature. Whether the software development constitutes the entire project or is part of a system (hardware and software), software requirements, including constraints, shall be generated from Input Information documents and the results of modeling, prototyping, or other techniques.

Using the above Input Information, the developer shall analyze the software requirements to determine traceability, clarity, validity, testability, safety, and any other project-specific characteristics. The use of a comprehensive methodology is recommended to ensure that requirements are complete and consistent. Techniques such as structured analysis, modeling, prototyping, or transaction analysis are helpful in this Activity. When needed, the requirements for a data base shall be included in the requirements.

The Preliminary Software Requirements shall include consideration of System Constraints such as timing, sizing, language, marketing restrictions, and technology.

Further information related to this Activity may be found in [5].

Prior to the distribution of the Preliminary Software Requirements and Installation Requirements, the following Processes shall be invoked:

(1) Verification and Validation (7.1.4)
(2) Software Configuration Management (7.2.5)
(3) Documentation Development (7.3.4)

5.1.3.3 Output Information

Output Information	Destination	
	Process	Activity
Preliminary Software Requirements	Requirements	Prioritize and Integrate Software Requirements (5.1.5)
		Define Interface Requirements (5.1.4)
	Verification and Validation	Plan Testing (7.1.6)
Installation Requirements	Installation	Plan Installation (6.1.3)

5.1.4 Define Interface Requirements

5.1.4.1 Input Information

Input Information	Source	
	Process	Activity
System Constraints	External	
Software Project Management Planned Information	Project Initiation	Plan Project Management (3.1.6)
Preliminary Software Requirements	Requirements	Define and Develop Software Requirements (5.1.3)
Functional Description of the System (If Applicable)	System Allocation	Analyze Functions (4.2.3)
System Functional Software Requirements (If Applicable)	System Allocation	Decompose System Requirements (4.2.5)
System Interface Requirements (If Applicable)	System Allocation	Decompose System Requirements (4.2.5)

5.1.4.2 Description. All user, software, and hardware interfaces shall be defined using the applicable Input Information. These interfaces shall be defined either as requirements or as constraints and shall be reviewed by all involved parties.

The user interface is critical in determining the usability of the system. The user interface definition shall specify not only the information flow between the user and the system but also how a user goes about using the system. For a complex interactive system, user interface definition may be a separate document.

The Software Interface Requirements shall specify all software interfaces required to support the development and execution of the software system. Software interfaces may be affected by System Constraints including operating system, data base management system, language compiler, tools, utilities, network protocol drivers, and hardware interfaces.

Prior to the distribution of the Output Information, the following Processes shall be invoked:

(1) Verification and Validation (7.1.4)
(2) Documentation Development (7.3.4)
(3) Software Configuration Management (7.2.5)

5.1.4.3 Output Information

Output Information	Destination	
	Process	Activity
Software Interface Requirements	Project Monitoring and Control	Analyze Risks (3.2.3)
	Requirements	Prioritize and Integrate Software Requirements (5.1.5)
	Design	Design Interfaces (5.2.5)
	Implementation	Create Operating Documentation (5.3.6)

5.1.5 Prioritize and Integrate Software Requirements

5.1.5.1 Input Information

Input Information	Source	
	Process	Activity
Preliminary Software Requirements	Requirements	Define and Develop Software Requirements (5.1.3)
Software Interface Requirements	Requirements	Define Interface Requirements (5.1.4)

5.1.5.2 Description. The functional and performance requirements shall be reviewed and a prioritized list of requirements shall be produced, addressing any tradeoffs that may be needed. The organization of the emerging Software Requirements shall be reviewed and revised as necessary. While completing the requirements, a particular design shall not be imposed (i.e., design decisions are made in the Design Process). The Software Requirements shall describe the functional, interface, and performance requirements. It shall also define the required operational and support environments.

Further information related to this Activity may be found in [5].

Prior to distribution of the Software Requirements, the following Processes shall be invoked:

(1) Verification and Validation (7.1.4)
(2) Software Configuration Management (7.2.5)
(3) Documentation Development (7.3.4)

5.1.5.3 Output Information

Output Information	Destination	
	Process	Activity
Software Requirements	Project Monitoring and Control	Analyze Risks (3.2.3)
	Design	All Activities (5.2)
	Implementation	Create Test Data (5.3.3)
		Plan Integration (5.3.7)
	Verification and Validation	Plan Testing (7.1.6)
		Develop Test Specification(s) (7.1.7)
	Training	Plan Training Program (7.4.3)

5.2 Design Process

5.2.1 Overview. During the Design Process, major decisions are made that determine the structure of the system. The objective of the Design Process is to develop a coherent, well-organized representation of the software system that meets the Software Requirements.

The Design Process maps the "what to do" of requirements specifications into the "how to do it" of design specifications. At the architectural design level, the focus is on the functions and structure of the software components that comprise the software system. At the detailed design level, the emphasis is on the data structures and algorithms that are used within each software component.

The Perform Architectural Design and Perform Detailed Design Activities are usually carried out in sequence because detailed design is derived from the architectural design. They differ from each other in the level of design detail. Other Design Process Activities may be carried out in parallel with these Activities.

Section 1.5, "Use of This Standard," provides background information necessary for the successful understanding and application of this material. It should be read prior to proceeding further in this section.

5.2.2 Activities List

(1) Perform Architectural Design
(2) Design Data Base (If Applicable)
(3) Design Interfaces
(4) Select or Develop Algorithms (If Applicable)
(5) Perform Detailed Design

5.2.3 Perform Architectural Design

5.2.3.1 Input Information

Input Information	Source	
	Process	Activity
Software Project Management Planned Information	Project Initiation	Plan Project Management (3.1.6)
System Architecture	System Allocation	Develop System Architecture (4.2.4)
Software Requirements	Requirements	Prioritize and Integrate Software Requirements (5.1.5)

5.2.3.2 Description. The Perform Architectural Design Activity transforms the Software Requirements and the System Architecture into high-level design concepts. During this Activity the software components constituting the software system and their structures are identified. Purchased software and the contents of the software libraries (as referenced in the SPMP) may influence the architectural design. Techniques such as modeling and prototyping may be used to evaluate alternative designs if called for in the SPMP.

By the end of the Perform Architectural Design Activity, the design description of each of the software components shall have been completed. The data, relationships, and constraints shall be specified. In addition, all internal interfaces (among components) shall be defined. This Activity shall create the Software Architectural Design Description.

Prior to distribution of the Software Architectural Design Description, the following Processes shall be invoked:

(1) Verification and Validation (7.1.4)
(2) Software Configuration Management (7.2.5)
(3) Documentation Development (7.3.4)

5.2.3.3 Output Information

Output Information	Destination	
	Process	Activity
Software Architectural Design Description	Design	Perform Detailed Design (5.2.7)

5.2.4 Design Data Base (If Applicable)

5.2.4.1 Input Information

Input Information	Source	
	Process	Activity
Project Environment	Project Initiation	Establish Project Environment (3.1.5)
Software Requirements	Requirements	Prioritize and Integrate Software Requirements (5.1.5)

5.2.4.2 Description. The Design Data Base Activity applies when a data base is to be created as a part of the project. This Activity shall specify the information structure outlined in the Software Requirements and its characteristics within the software system. The Design Data Base Activity involves three separate but dependent steps: conceptual data base design, logical data base design, and physical data base design. Techniques such as data dictionary, data base optimization, and data modeling may be considered. Requirements are molded into an external schema that describes data entities, attributes, relationships, and constraints. The various external schemas are integrated into a single conceptual schema. The conceptual schema is then mapped into an implementation-dependent logical schema. Finally, the physical data structures and access paths are defined. The result of this Activity is to generate the Data Base Description.

Prior to distribution of the Data Base Description, the following Processes shall be invoked:

(1) Verification and Validation (7.1.4)
(2) Software Configuration Management (7.2.5)
(3) Documentation Development (7.3.4)

5.2.4.3 Output Information

Output Information	Destination	
	Process	Activity
Data Base Description	Design	Perform Detailed Design (5.2.7)

5.2.5 Design Interfaces

5.2.5.1 Input Information

Input Information	Source	
	Process	Activity
Software Interface Requirements	Requirements	Define Interface Requirements (5.1.4)
Software Requirements	Requirements	Prioritize and Integrate Software Requirements (5.1.5)

5.2.5.2 Description. The Design Interfaces Activity shall be concerned with the interfaces of the software system contained in the Software Requirements and Software Interface Requirements. This Activity shall consolidate these interface descriptions into a single Interface Description of the software system.

5.2.5.3 Output Information

Output Information	Destination	
	Process	Activity
Interface Description	Design	Perform Detailed Design (5.2.7)

5.2.6 Select or Develop Algorithms

5.2.6.1 Input Information

Input Information	Source	
	Process	Activity
Software Requirements	Requirements	Prioritize and Integrate Software Requirements (5.1.5)

5.2.6.2 Description. This Activity is concerned with selecting or developing a procedural representation of the functions specified in the Software Requirements for each software component and data structure. The algorithms shall completely satisfy the applicable functional and/or mathematical specifications. To the extent possible, the use of existing algorithms should be considered.

Prior to distribution of the Algorithm Descriptions, the following Processes shall be invoked:

(1) Verification and Validation (7.1.4)
(2) Software Configuration Management (7.2.5)

5.2.6.3 Output Information

Output Information	Destination	
	Process	Activity
Algorithm Descriptions	Design	Perform Detailed Design (5.2.7)

5.2.7 Perform Detailed Design

5.2.7.1 Input Information

Input Information	Source	
	Process	Activity
Software Project Management Planned Information	Project Initiation	Plan Project Management (3.1.6)
Software Requirements	Requirements	Prioritize and Integrate Software Requirements (5.1.5)
Software Architectural Design Description	Design	Perform Architectural Design (5.2.3)
Data Base Description (If Applicable)	Design	Design Data Base (If Applicable) (5.2.4)
Interface Description	Design	Design Interfaces (5.2.5)
Algorithm Descriptions	Design	Select or Develop Algorithms (5.2.6)

5.2.7.2 Description. In the Perform Detailed Design Activity, design alternatives shall be chosen for implementing the functions specified for each software component. By the end of this Activity, the data structure, algorithm, and control information of each software component shall be specified. The Software Design Description (SDD) contains the consolidated data for all of the above Input Information. The details of the interfaces shall be identified within the SDD.

For further information on this topic, see [12].

Prior to distribution of the SDD, the following Processes shall be invoked:

(1) Verification and Validation (7.1.4)
(2) Software Configuration Management (7.2.5)
(3) Documentation Development (7.3.4)

5.2.7.3 Output Information

Output Information	Destination	
	Process	Activity
Software Design Description	Project Monitoring and Control	Analyze Risks (3.2.3)
	Implementation	Create Test Data (5.3.3)
		Create Source (5.3.4)
		Create Operating Documentation (5.3.6)
		Plan Integration (5.3.7)
	Verification and Validation	Plan Testing (7.1.6)
		Develop Test Specification(s) (7.1.7)
	Training	Develop Training Materials (7.4.4)

5.3 Implementation Process

5.3.1 Overview. The Activities completed during the Implementation Process result in the transformation of the Detailed Design representation of a software product into a programming language realization. This Process produces the source code, data base (if applicable), and the documentation constituting the physical manifestation of the design. In addition, the code and data base are integrated. Care must also be taken during the Implementation Process to apply the appropriate coding standards.

The output of this Process must be the subject of all subsequent testing and validation. The code and data base, along with documentation produced during previous Processes, are the first complete representation of the software product.

Section 1.5, "Use of This Standard," provides background information necessary for the successful understanding and application of this material. It should be read prior to proceeding further in this section.

5.3.2 Activities List

(1) Create Test Data
(2) Create Source
(3) Generate Object Code
(4) Create Operating Documentation
(5) Plan Integration
(6) Perform Integration

5.3.3 Create Test Data

5.3.3.1 Input Information

Input Information	Source	
	Process	Activity
Software Requirements	Requirements	Prioritize and Integrate Software Requirements (5.1.5)
Software Design Description	Design	Perform Detailed Design (5.2.7)
Source Code (If Applicable)	Implementation	Create Source (5.3.4)
Data Base (If Applicable)	Implementation	Create Source (5.3.4)
Test Planned Information(s)	Verification and Validation	Plan Testing (7.1.6)
Test Requirements	Verification and Validation	Develop Test Requirements (7.1.7)

5.3.3.2 Description. Using the Software Requirements, the Software Design Description (SDD), and the Source Code (when required), Test Data shall be generated. The Test Planned Information(s) describe the test environment. Test Requirements define the type of test data to be used. To support the testing effort, test Stubs and Drivers may be generated at this time for each item to be tested. The test drivers allow the execution of software tests on an individual or integrated basis. Test Data may be loaded for use in testing the data base.

Further information may be found in [10].

5.3.3.3 Output Information

Output Information	Destination	
	Process	Activity
Stubs and Drivers (If Applicable)	Implementation	Perform Integration (5.3.8)
Test Data	Verification and Validation	Execute the Tests (7.1.8)

5.3.4 Create Source

5.3.4.1 Input Information

Input Information	Source	
	Process	Activity
Software Project Management Planned Information	Project Initiation	Plan Project Management (3.1.6)
Software Design Description	Design	Perform Detailed Design (5.2.7)

5.3.4.2 Description. The Source Code, including suitable comments, shall be generated using the project environment, as found in the Software Project Management Planned Information (SPMP) and the Software Design Description. If the software requires a Data Base, then the Data Base utilities may need to be coded. If Source Code is going to be used to create test data, the Source Code shall be made available to the Create Test Data Activity (5.3.3).

5.3.4.3 Output Information

Output Information	Destination	
	Process	Activity
Data Base (If Applicable)	Implementation	Create Test Data (5.3.3)
		Generate Object Code (5.3.5)
Source Code (If Applicable)	Implementation	Create Test Data (5.3.3)
Source Code	Implementation	Generate Object Code (5.3.5)

5.3.5 Generate Object Code

5.3.5.1 Input Information

Input Information	Source	
	Process	Activity
Data Base (If Applicable)	Implementation	Create Source (5.3.4)
Source Code	Implementation	Create Source (5.3.4)

5.3.5.2 Description. The code shall be grouped into processable units. (This will be dictated by selected language and design information.) All assembly language units shall be assembled and all high-level language units compiled into Object Code. Syntactically incorrect code, identified by the assembler or compiler output, shall be reworked until the source code can be processed free of syntactical errors. These units shall be debugged. If a Data Base is coded, it too shall be debugged.

Prior to distribution of the software, the following Processes shall be invoked:

(1) Verification and Validation (7.1.4)
(2) Software Configuration Management (7.2.5)

5.3.5.3 Output Information

Output Information	Destination	
	Process	Activity
Corrected Data Base (If Applicable)	Implementation	Perform Integration (5.3.8)
Corrected Source Code	Implementation	Perform Integration (5.3.8)
Object Code	Implementation	Perform Integration (5.3.8)

5.3.6 Create Operating Documentation

5.3.6.1 Input Information

Input Information	Source	
	Process	Activity
Software Design Description	Design	Perform Detailed Design (5.2.7)
Software Interface Requirements	Requirements	Define Interface Requirements (5.1.4)
Documentation Planned Information(s)	Documentation Development	Plan Documentation (7.3.3)

5.3.6.2 Description. This Activity shall produce the software project's operating documentation from the SDD and the Software Interface Requirements in accordance with the Documentation Planned Information. The Operating Documentation is required for installing, operating, and supporting the system throughout the life cycle.

For further information, [21] may be used.

Prior to distribution of the documents listed below, the following Processes shall be invoked:

(1) Verification and Validation (7.1.4)
(2) Software Configuration Management (7.2.5)
(3) Documentation Development (7.3.4)

5.3.6.3 Output Information

Output Information	Destination	
	Process	Activity
Operating Documentation	Installation	Distribute Software (6.1.4)

5.3.7 Plan Integration

5.3.7.1 Input Information

Input Information	Source	
	Process	Activity
Software Project Management Planned Information	Project Initiation	Plan Project Management (3.1.6)
Software Requirements	Requirements	Prioritize and Integrate Software Requirements (5.1.5)
Software Design Description	Design	Perform Detailed Design (5.2.7)
Test Planned Information(s)	Verification and Validation	Plan Testing (7.1.6)

5.3.7.2 Description. During the Plan Integration Activity, the Software Requirements and the SDD are analyzed to determine the order of combining software components into an overall system. The project environment, as defined in the SPMP, shall be considered when planning integration. The integration methods shall be documented in the Integration Planned Information. The Integration Planned Information shall be coordinated with the Test Planned Information(s) and they may be combined.

Prior to distribution of the Integration Planned Information, the following Processes shall be invoked:

(1) Verification and Validation (7.1.4)
(2) Software Configuration Management (7.2.5)
(3) Documentation Development (7.3.4)

5.3.7.3 Output Information

Output Information	Destination	
	Process	Activity
Integration Planned Information	Project Monitoring and Control	Analyze Risks (3.2.3)
		Manage the Project (3.2.5)
	Implementation	Perform Integration (5.3.8)
	Verification and Validation	Plan Testing (7.1.6)

5.3.8 Perform Integration

5.3.8.1 Input Information

Input Information	Source	
	Process	Activity
Stubs and Drivers (If Applicable)	Implementation	Create Test Data (5.3.3)
Corrected Data Base (If Applicable)	Implementation	Generate Object Code (5.3.5)
Corrected Source Code	Implementation	Generate Object Code (5.3.5)
Integration Planned Information	Implementation	Plan Integration (5.3.7)
System Components	External	
Software Project Management Planned Information	Project Initiation	Plan Project Management (3.1.6)
Object Code	Implementation	Generate Object Code (5.3.5)
Tested Software	Verification and Validation	Execute the Tests (7.1.8)

5.3.8.2 Description. This Activity shall execute the Integration Planned Information. This is accomplished by appropriately combining the Corrected Data Base, Corrected Source Code, Object Code, and Stubs and Drivers, as specified, into Integrated Software. Other necessary Object Code, from the project environment as defined in the SPMP, shall also be integrated. If a system includes both hardware and software components, the system integration may be included as part of this Activity.

Prior to software integration and the distribution of the Integrated Software, the following Processes shall be invoked:

(1) Verification and Validation (7.1.4)
(2) Software Configuration Management (7.2.5)

5.3.8.3 Output Information

Output Information	Destination	
	Process	Activity
Integrated Software	Verification and Validation	Execute the Tests (7.1.8)

6. Post-Development Processes

These are the Processes that must be performed to install, operate, support, maintain, and retire a software product.

6.1 Installation Process

6.1.1 Overview. Installation consists of the transportation and installation of a software system from the development environment to the target environment. It includes the necessary software modifications, checkout in the target environment, and customer acceptance. If a problem arises, it must be identified and reported; if necessary and possible, a temporary "work-around" may be applied.

During the Installation Process, the software to be delivered is installed, operationally checked out, and monitored. This effort culminates in formal customer acceptance. The scheduling of turnover and customer acceptance is defined in the Software Project Management Planned Information (SPMP).

Section 1.5, "Use of This Standard," provides background information necessary for the successful understanding and application of this material. It should be read prior to proceeding further in this section.

6.1.2 Activities List

(1) Plan Installation
(2) Distribute Software
(3) Install Software
(4) Accept Software in Operational Environment

6.1.3 Plan Installation

6.1.3.1 Input Information

Input Information	Source	
	Process	Activity
Software Project Management Planned Information	Project Initiation	Plan Project Management (3.1.6)
Installation Requirements	Requirements	Define and Develop Software Requirements (5.1.3)
Transition Planned Information (if applicable)	Concept Exploration	Plan System Transition (4.1.6)
Operating Documentation	Implementation	Create Operating Documentation (5.3.6)

6.1.3.2 Description. The tasks to be performed during installation shall be described in Software Installation Planned Information. The Installation Requirements and the other Input Information shall be analyzed to guide the development of the Software Installation Planned Information. This Planned Information, the associated documentation, and the developed software shall be used to install the software product.

Prior to distribution of the Software Installation Planned Information, the following Processes shall be invoked:

(1) Verification and Validation (7.1.4)
(2) Software Configuration Management (7.2.5)
(3) Documentation Development (7.3.4)
(4) Training (7.4.4)

6.1.3.3 Output Information

Output Information	Destination	
	Process	Activity
Software Installation Planned Information	Installation	Distribute Software (6.1.4)

6.1.4 Distribute Software

6.1.4.1 Input Information

Input Information	Source	
	Process	Activity
Operating Documentation	Implementation	Create Operating Documentation (5.3.6)
Software Installation Planned Information	Installation	Plan Installation (6.1.3)
Data Base Data	External	
Tested Software	Verification and Validation	Execute the Tests (7.1.8)
Software Project Management Planned Information	Project Initiation	Plan Project Management (3.1.6)

6.1.4.2 Description. During this Activity, the Tested Software with necessary Data Base Data, Operating Documentation, and Installation Planned Information shall be packaged onto their respective media as designated in the SPMP. The Packaged Software is distributed to the appropriate site(s) for installation. The Installation Planned Information is distributed as appropriate to the site(s) to facilitate the installation efforts. The Packaged Operating Documentation shall be available for operation of the system.

Prior to distribution of the Output Information, the following Processes shall be invoked:

(1) Software Configuration Management (7.2.5)
(2) Verification and Validation (7.1.4)
(3) Documentation Development (7.3.4)

6.1.4.3 Output Information

Output Information	Destination	
	Process	Activity
Packaged Operating Documentation	Operation and Support	Operate the System (6.2.3)
Packaged Installation Planned Information	Installation	Install Software (6.1.5)
Packaged Software	Installation	Install Software (6.1.5)

6.1.5 Install Software

6.1.5.1 Input Information

Input Information	Source	
	Process	Activity
Packaged Installation Planned Information	Installation	Distribute Software (6.1.4)
Packaged Operating Documentation	Installation	Distribute Software (6.1.4)
Packaged Software Installation	Installation	Distribute Software (6.1.4)
Data Base Data	External	

6.1.5.2 Description. The packaged software and any required Data Base Data shall be installed in the target environment according to the procedures in the Software Installation Planned Information. This may include tailoring by the customer. The Installation Reported Information shall document the installation and any problems encountered.

6.1.5.3 Output Information

Output Information	Destination	
	Process	Activity
Installation Reported Information	Project Monitoring and Control	Manage the Project (3.2.5)
Installed Software	Installation	Accept Software in Operational Environment (6.1.6)

6.1.6 Accept Software in Operational Environment

6.1.6.1 Input Information

Input Information	Source	
	Process	Activity
User Acceptance Planned Information	External	
Test Summary Reported Information	Verification and Validation	Execute the Tests (7.1.8)
Installed Software	Installation	Install Software (6.1.5)

6.1.6.2 Description. The software acceptance shall consist of analysis of the Test Summary Reported Information(s) according to the User Acceptance Planned Information to assure that the Installed Software performs as expected. When the results of the analysis satisfy the requirements of the User Acceptance Planned Information, the Installed Software System is accepted by the User.

Prior to completion of accepting software in the operational environment, the following Processes should be invoked:

(1) Verification and Validation (7.1.4)
(2) Software Configuration Management (7.2.5)

6.1.6.3 Output Information

Output Information	Destination	
	Process	Activity
Customer Acceptance	External	
Installed Software System	Operation and Support	Operate the System (6.2.3)
	Retirement	Conduct Parallel Operations (If Applicable) (6.4.4)

6.2 Operation and Support Process

6.2.1 Overview. The Operation and Support Process involves user operation of the system and ongoing support. Support includes providing technical assistance, consulting with the user, and recording user support requests by maintaining a Support Request Log. Thus the Operation and Support Process may trigger Maintenance Activities via the ongoing Project Monitoring and Control Process, which will provide information re-entering the software life cycle (SLC).

Section 1.5, "Use of This Standard," provides background information necessary for the successful understanding and application of this material. It should be read prior to proceeding further in this section.

6.2.2 Activities List

(1) Operate the System
(2) Provide Technical Assistance and Consulting
(3) Maintain Support Request Log

6.2.3 Operate the System

6.2.3.1 Input Information

Input Information	Source	
	Process	Activity
Packaged Operating Documentation	Installation	Distribute Software (6.1.4)
Support Planned Information	Project Initiation	Plan Project Management (3.1.6)
Installed Software System	Installation	Accept Software in Operational Environment (6.1.6)

6.2.3.2 Description. During this Activity, the Installed Software System shall be utilized in the intended environment and in accordance with the operating instructions. Feedback Data are collected for product and documentation improvement and system tuning. The user shall analyze the Feedback Data and identify System Anomalies (which include desired enhancements). System Anomalies are reported.

Prior to the distribution of the Output Information, the following Processes shall be invoked:

(1) Verification and Validation (7.1.4)
(2) Software Configuration Management (7.2.5)

6.2.3.3 Output Information

Output Information	Destination	
	Process	Activity
System Anomalies	Project Monitoring and Control	Implement Problem Reporting Method (3.2.7)
Operation Logs	External	
Feedback Data	Project Monitoring and Control	Manage the Project (3.2.5)
	Concept Exploration	Identify Ideas or Needs (4.1.3)

6.2.4 Provide Technical Assistance and Consulting

6.2.4.1 Input Information

Input Information	Source	
	Process	Activity
Request for Support	External	
Support Planned Information	Project Initiation	Plan Project Management (3.1.6)

6.2.4.2 Description. This Activity applies after the user has accepted the software. The support function shall include providing responses to the user's technical questions or problems. A Support Response is sent to the Maintain Support Request Log Activity so that feedback can be provided to other Processes.

6.2.4.3 Output Information

Output Information	Destination	
	Process	Activity
Support Response	Operation and Support	Maintain Support Request Log (6.2.5)
	External	

6.2.5 Maintain Support Request Log

6.2.5.1 Input Information

Input Information	Source	
	Process	Activity
Support Planned Information	Project Initiation	Plan Project Management (3.1.6)
Support Response	Operation and Support	Provide Technical Assistance and Consulting (6.2.4)

6.2.5.2 Description. This Activity shall record support requests in the Support Request Log. Methodology regarding management of this Activity shall be identified in the Support Planned Information. Anomalies that are reported shall be reported also to the Project Monitoring and Control Process. Prior to release of the Support Request Log, the Verification and Validation Process (7.1.4) shall be invoked.

6.2.5.3 Output Information

Output Information	Destination	
	Process	Activity
Anomalies	Project Monitoring and Control	Implement Problem Reporting Method (3.2.7)
Support Request Log	Verification and Validation	Execute Verification and Validation Tasks (7.1.4)

6.3 Maintenance Process

6.3.1 Overview. The Maintenance Process is concerned with the resolution of software errors, faults, and failures. The requirement for software maintenance initiates software life cycle (SLC) changes. The SLC is remapped and executed, thereby treating the Maintenance Process as iterations of development.

Section 1.5, "Use of This Standard," provides background information necessary for the successful understanding and application of this material. It should be read prior to proceeding further in this section.

6.3.2 Activities List

(1) Reapply Software Life Cycle

6.3.3 Reapply Software Life Cycle

6.3.3.1 Input Information

Input Information	Source	
	Process	Activity
Software Project Management Planned Information	Project Initiation	Plan Project Management (3.1.6)
Correction Problem Reported Information	Project Monitoring and Control	Implement Problem Reporting Method (3.2.7)

6.3.3.2 Description. The information provided by the Correction Problem Reported Information and the current Software Project Management Planned Information (SPMP) shall result in the generation of Maintenance Recommendations. These Maintenance Recommendations will then enter the SLC at the Concept Exploration Process to improve the quality of the software system.

6.3.3.3 Output Information

Output Information	Destination	
	Process	Activity
Maintenance Recommendations	Concept Exploration	Identify Ideas or Needs (4.1.3)

6.4 Retirement Process

6.4.1 Overview. The Retirement Process involves the removal of an existing system from its active support or use either by ceasing its operation or support, or by replacing it with a new system or an upgraded version of the existing system.

Section 1.5, "Use of This Standard," provides background information necessary for the successful understanding and application of this material. It should be read prior to proceeding further in this section.

6.4.2 Activities List

(1) Notify User
(2) Conduct Parallel Operations (If Applicable)
(3) Retire System

6.4.3 Notify User

6.4.3.1 Input Information

Input Information	Source	
	Process	Activity
Retirement Planned Information	Project Initiation	Plan Project Management (3.1.6)

6.4.3.2 Description. This Activity shall be the formal notification to any user (both internal and external customers) of an operating software system that is to be removed from active support or use. This notification can take any of several forms as appropriate for the individual environment. It is important that all users of the outgoing system be made aware that it will become unsupported. The actual dates of the removal of support are to be clearly specified and must allow time for current users to make whatever arrangements are necessary to respond to this notification. Included in the user notification should be one or more of the following:

(1) Description of the replacement system including its date of availability.
(2) Statement as to why the system is not being supported.
(3) Description of possible other support.

Prior to the distribution of the Official Notification, the Documentation Development Process (7.3.4) shall be invoked.

6.4.3.3 Output Information

Output Information	Destination	
	Process	Activity
Official Notification	Project Monitoring and Control	Retain Records (3.2.6)
	External	

6.4.4 Conduct Parallel Operations (If Applicable)

6.4.4.1 Input Information

Input Information	Source	
	Process	Activity
Transition Planned Information (for the replacing system)	External	
Retirement Planned Information	Project Initiation	Plan Project Management (3.1.6)
Installed Software System	Installation	Accept Software in Operational Environment (6.1.6)

6.4.4.2 Description. If the outgoing system is being replaced by a new system, this Activity may apply. This Activity shall involve a period of dual operation utilizing the retiring system for official results, while completing the preparation of the new system for formal operation. It is a period of user training on the new system and validation of the new system. The Retirement Planned Information, as well as the Transition Planned Information, may be used to provide information to conduct parallel operations for the replacing system.

While conducting this Activity, the following Processes shall be invoked:

(1) Verification and Validation (7.1.4)
(2) Software Configuration Management (7.2.5)
(3) Training (7.4.4)

6.4.4.3 Output Information

Output Information	Destination	
	Process	Activity
Parallel Operations Log	Project Monitoring and Control	Retain Records (3.2.6)

6.4.5 Retire System

6.4.5.1 Input Information

Input Information	Source	
	Process	Activity
Retirement Planned Information	Project Initiation	Plan Project Management (3.1.6)

6.4.5.2 Description. This Activity shall consist of the actual removal and archiving of the retiring system from regular usage according to the Retirement Planned Information. It may be spread over a period of time and take the form of a phased removal, or it may be the simple removal of the entire system from the active software library. Prior to the retirement, users must have been notified of the event. Any preparations for the use of a replacement system should have been completed. The Post-Operation Review Reported Information is generated at this time. The Retire System Activity must be documented in Archive Reported Information.

Prior to the final distribution of the Post-Operation Review Reported Information and Archive Reported Information, the following Processes shall be invoked:

(1) Verification and Validation (7.1.4)
(2) Software Configuration Management (7.2.5)
(3) Documentation Development (7.3.4)

6.4.5.3 Output Information

Output Information	Destination	
	Process	Activity
Post-Operation Review Reported Information	Project Monitoring and Control	Retain Records (3.2.6)
	Software Quality Management	Manage Software Quality (3.3.5)
Archive Reported Information	External	

7. Integral Processes

These are the Processes needed to successfully complete project Activities. These Processes are utilized to ensure the completion and quality of project functions.

7.1 Verification and Validation Process

7.1.1 Overview. The Verification and Validation Process includes planning and performing both Verification and Validation tasks. Verification tasks include reviews, configuration audits, and quality audits. Validation tasks include all phases of testing. These Verification and Validation tasks are conducted throughout the software life cycle (SLC) to ensure that all requirements are satisfied. This Process addresses each life cycle Process and product.

Section 1.5, "Use of This Standard," provides background information necessary for the successful understanding and application of this material. It should be read prior to proceeding further in this section.

7.1.2 Activities List

(1) Plan Verification and Validation
(2) Execute Verification and Validation Tasks
(3) Collect and Analyze Metric Data
(4) Plan Testing
(5) Develop Test Requirements
(6) Execute the Tests

7.1.3 Plan Verification and Validation

7.1.3.1 Input Information

Input Information	Source	
	Process	Activity
Software Project Management Planned Information	Project Initiation	Plan Project Management (3.1.6)
Analysis of Risks	Project Monitoring and Control	Analyze Risks (3.2.3)
Software Quality Management Planned Information	Software Quality Management	Plan Software Quality Management (3.3.3)

7.1.3.2 Description. This Activity shall be responsive to the Software Project Management Planned Information and the Software Quality Assurance (SQA) Planned Information by identifying Processes and Process Output Information to be verified and validated. The purpose and scope of the verification and validation task shall be defined for each Process and all Process Output Information. The planning shall include developing schedules, estimating resources, identifying special resources, staffing, and establishing exit or acceptance criteria. Verification and validation methods to be considered in this planning Activity include audits (e.g., functional and physical configuration, compliance), reviews (e.g., design, code, document), prototyping, inspection, formal proof, analysis, and demonstration. Special attention should be given to minimizing technical risks and verifying requirements traceability. This planning shall be documented in the Software Verification and Validation Planned Information (SVVP).

Because of the importance of testing in the Verification and Validation Process, this standard addresses testing Activities separately. Test planning and execution may be included in the Verification and Validation Planning and Execution Activities.

Further information on verification and validation planning may be found in [2], [3], [4], [6], [7], [8], [12], [13], [14], [15], and [16].

Prior to distribution of the SVVP, the following Processes shall be invoked:

(1) Verification and Validation (7.1.4)
(2) Documentation Development (7.3.4)
(3) Software Configuration Management (7.2.5)

7.1.3.3 Output Information

Output Information	Destination	
	Process	Activity
Software Verification and Validation Planned Information	Software Quality Management	Identify Quality Improvement Needs (3.3.6)
	Verification and Validation	Execute Verification and Validation Tasks (7.1.4)
		Plan Testing (7.1.6)

7.1.4 Execute Verification and Validation Tasks

7.1.4.1 Input Information

Input Information	Source	
	Process	Activity
Item(s) to Be Evaluated	Creating Process	
Resolved Problem Reported Information	Project Monitoring and Control	Implement Problem Reporting Method (3.2.7)
Project Quality Assessments	Software Quality Management	Manage Software Quality (3.3.5)
Support Request Log	Operation and Support	Maintain Support Request Log (6.2.5)
Software Verification and Validation Planned Information	Verification and Validation	Plan Verification and Validation (7.1.3)
Basis or Bases for Evaluation	External	
	Creating Process	

7.1.4.2 Description. This Activity shall include performing the tasks specified in the SVVP using the Input Information. Results shall be provided in Evaluation Reported Information. Anomalies identified during the performance of these tasks shall be reported.

Further information related to this Activity may be found in [2], [3], [8], [12], [13], and [14].

Prior to distribution of Evaluation Reported Information, the following Processes shall be invoked:

(1) Documentation Development (7.3.4)
(2) Software Configuration Management (7.2.5)

7.1.4.3 Output Information

Output Information	Destination	
	Process	Activity
Evaluation Reported Information	Project Monitoring and Control	Manage the Project (3.2.5)
	Software Quality Management	Identify Quality Improvement Needs (3.3.6)
	Verification and Validation	Collect and Analyze Metric Data (7.1.5)
	Creating Process	
Anomalies	Project Monitoring and Control	Implement Problem Reporting Method (3.2.7)

7.1.5 Collect and Analyze Metric Data

7.1.5.1 Input Information

Input Information	Source	
	Process	Activity
Support Personnel Reported Information	External	
User Input Information	External	
Metric Data	Originating Process	Originating Activity
Correction Problem Reported Information	Project Monitoring and Control	Implement Problem Reporting Method (3.2.7)
Enhancement Problem Reported Information	Project Monitoring and Control	Implement Problem Reporting Method (3.2.7)
Report Log	Project Monitoring and Control	Implement Problem Reporting Method (3.2.7)
Resolved Problem Reported Information	Project Monitoring and Control	Implement Problem Reporting Method (3.2.7)
Software Quality Management Planned Information	Software Quality Management	Plan Software Quality Management (3.3.3)
Defined Metrics	Software Quality Management	Define Metrics (3.3.4)
Collection and Analysis Methods	Software Quality Management	Define Metrics (3.3.4)
Evaluation Reported Information	Verification and Validation	Execute Verification and Validation Tasks (7.1.4)

7.1.5.2 Description. This Activity collects Evaluation Reported Information, Problem Reported Information, and project-generated Metric Data, as stated in the Software Quality Management Planned Information. The data shall be analyzed using defined methodologies. This Activity shall identify improvements in both quality and requirements as a result of Support Personnel and User Input Information. Analysis Reported Information shall be generated describing the results of metrics validation and analysis, defect trend analysis, and the user's view analysis.

Further information related to this Activity may be found in [6], [7], [15], and [16].

Prior to distribution of the Analysis Reported Information, the following Processes should be invoked:

(1) Verification and Validation (7.1.4)
(2) Software Configuration Management (7.2.5)
(3) Documentation Development (7.3.4)

7.1.5.3 Output Information

Output Information	Destination	
	Process	Activity
Analysis Reported Information	Project Monitoring and Control	Analyze Risks (3.2.3)
		Perform Contingency Planning (3.2.4)
		Manage the Project (3.2.5)
	Software Quality Management	Manage Software Quality (3.3.5)
		Identify Quality Improvement Needs (3.3.6)

7.1.6 Plan Testing

7.1.6.1 Input Information

Input Information	Source	
	Process	Activity
Software Project Management Planned Information	Project Initiation	Plan Project Management (3.1.6)
Preliminary Software Requirements	Requirements	Define and Develop Software Requirements (5.1.3)
Software Requirements	Requirements	Prioritize and Integrate Software Requirements (5.1.5)
Software Design Description	Design	Perform Detailed Design (5.2.7)
Integration Planned Information	Implementation	Plan Integration (5.3.7)
Software Verification and Validation Planned Information	Verification and Validation	Plan Verification and Validation (7.1.3)

7.1.6.2 Description. This Activity shall identify the overall scope, approach, resources, and schedule of the testing tasks over the entire SLC and document them in Test Planned Information(s). The Test Planned Information(s) shall define the generic levels of testing and the basic test environment and structure needed to support required levels of testing. Each Test Planned Information shall identify the items to be tested, the requirements to be tested, and the test pass-or-fail criteria based on the Software Requirements and the Software Design Description (SDD) (as soon as available). The Test Planned Information(s) shall identify test coverage criteria, the tools and approaches being applied, the environmental needs, the testing tasks to be performed, the organizational structure, the management controls and reporting procedures, and the risks and contingencies.

The Test Planned Information(s) shall be coordinated with, and may be combined with, the Integration Planned Information and SVVP.

Further information related to this Activity may be found in [4], [10], [12], and [18].

Prior to distribution of the Test Planned Information(s), the following Processes shall be invoked:

(1) Verification and Validation (7.1.4)
(2) Software Configuration Management (7.2.5)
(3) Documentation Development (7.3.4)

7.1.6.3 Output Information

Output Information	Destination	
	Process	Activity
Test Planned Information(s)	Project Monitoring and Control	Analyze Risks (3.2.3)
		Manage the Project (3.2.5)
	Software Quality Management	Identify Quality Improvement Needs (3.3.6)
	Implementation	Create Test Data (5.3.3)
		Plan Integration (5.3.7)
	Verification and Validation	Develop Test Requirements (7.1.7)
		Execute the Tests (7.1.8)

7.1.7 Develop Test Requirements

7.1.7.1 Input Information

Input Information	Source	
	Process	Activity
Software Requirements	Requirements	Prioritize and Integrate Software Requirements (5.1.5)
Software Design Description	Design	Perform Detailed Design (5.2.7)
Test Planned Information(s)	Verification and Validation	Plan Testing (7.1.6)

7.1.7.2 Description. Test Requirements for each generic level of testing shall be developed to refine the test approach from the Test Planned Information(s) to item-specific test procedures used for test execution. The Test Requirements shall define what is to be tested, the data to be used in testing, expected results, the test environment components, and the procedures to be followed in testing. Information from the SRS, the SDD, and the Test Planned Information(s) is used to generate the Test Requirements.

Further information related to this Activity may be found in [4] and [10].

Prior to distribution of the Test Requirements, the following Processes shall be invoked:

(1) Verification and Validation (7.1.4)
(2) Software Configuration Management (7.2.5)
(3) Documentation Development (7.3.4)

7.1.7.3 Output Information

Output Information	Destination	
	Process	Activity
Test Requirements	Implementation	Create Test Data (5.3.3)
	Verification and Validation	Execute the Tests (7.1.8)

7.1.8 Execute the Tests

7.1.8.1 Input Information

Input Information	Source	
	Process	Activity
Test Environment Components	External	
Test Data	Implementation	Create Test Data (5.3.3)
Integrated Software	Implementation	Perform Integration (5.3.8)
Test Planned Information(s)	Verification and Validation	Plan Testing (7.1.6)
Test Requirements	Verification and Validation	Develop Test Requirements (7.1.7)

7.1.8.2 Description. This Activity shall configure the Test Environment Components as required by the Test Requirements. Each test shall be conducted on the Integrated Software using Test Data as defined in its associated Test Requirements and in accordance with the Test Planned Information(s).

This Activity could be iterative, with several instances performed during the software's life. Not all Input Information and Output Information are required for a given iteration; the presence of any Input Information is sufficient as an entry criterion, and the creation of any Output Information is a sufficient exit criterion.

Based on comparison of actual results with expected results, according to the pass-fail criteria, a pass-fail determination shall be made and recorded in a test log. Each anomalous event that occurs during execution which requires further investigation shall be reported. The impact on the validity of the test should also be noted.

Test Summary Reported Information shall summarize the results of a test based on its Test Requirements and test log. Tested Software is that software which has successfully passed all tests at the appropriate level and met the specified criteria and requirements. Tested Software may then be further integrated with other software or sent for installation.

Further information related to this Activity may be found in [4] and [10].

Prior to distribution of the Output Information from this Activity, the following Processes shall be invoked:

(1) Verification and Validation (7.1.4)
(2) Software Configuration Management (7.2.5)
(3) Documentation Development (7.3.4)

7.1.8.3 Output Information

Output Information	Destination	
	Process	Activity
Test Summary Reported Information	Project Monitoring and Control	Analyze Risks (3.2.3)
		Manage the Project (3.2.5)
	External	
Tested Software	Implementation	Perform Integration (5.3.8)
	Installation	Distribute Software (6.1.4)
Anomalies	Project Monitoring and Control	Implement Problem Reporting Method (3.2.7)

7.2 Software Configuration Management Process

7.2.1 Overview. Software Configuration Management the items in a software development project and provides both for control of the identified items and for the generation of Status Reported Information for management visibility and accountability throughout the software life cycle (SLC). Items to be managed are those defined in Software Configuration Management Planned Information (SCMP). Examples to be considered for inclusion in the SCMP are code, documentation, plans, and specifications. Configuration audits, if required by the Project, should be addressed in the Verification and Validation Process. The Software Configuration Management approach for a given project should be compatible with the Configuration Management approach being used on associated systems.

Section 1.5, "Use of This Standard," provides background information necessary for the successful understanding and application of this material. It should be read prior to proceeding further in this section.

7.2.2 Activities List

(1) Plan Configuration Management
(2) Develop Configuration Identification
(3) Perform Configuration Control
(4) Perform Status Accounting

7.2.3 Plan Configuration Management

7.2.3.1 Input Information

Input Information	Source	
	Process	Activity
Contract Deliverable List	External	
Software Project Management Planned Information	Project Initiation	Plan Project Management (3.1.6)
Configuration Identification	Software Configuration Management	Develop Configuration Identification (7.2.4)

7.2.3.2 Description. This Activity shall plan and document specific software configuration management organizations and responsibilities, procedures, tools, techniques, and methodologies in an SCMP. The SCMP shall also describe how and when such procedures are to be performed.

Overall software configuration management objectives are derived using internal guidelines as well as contractual requirements from the Software Project Management Planned Information (SPMP).

Further information related to this Activity may be found in [3] and [14].

Prior to distribution of the Planned Information, the following Processes shall be invoked:

(1) Verification and Validation (7.1.4)
(2) Documentation Development (7.3.4)

7.2.3.3 Output Information

Output Information	Destination	
	Process	Activity
Software Configuration Management Planned Information	Project Monitoring and Control	Retain Records (3.2.6)
	Software Configuration Management	Develop Configuration Identification (7.2.4)
		Perform Configuration Control (7.2.5)
		Perform Status Accounting (7.2.6)

7.2.4 Develop Configuration Identification

7.2.4.1 Input Information

Input Information	Source	
	Process	Activity
Software Project Management Planned Information	Project Initiation	Plan Project Management (3.1.6)
Software Configuration Management Planned Information	Software Configuration Management	Plan Configuration Management (7.2.3)

7.2.4.2 Description. This Activity shall define a Configuration Identification that includes project baseline definition, titling, labeling, and numbering to reflect the structure of the product for tracking. The SCMP identifies those configuration items to be addressed by the Configuration Identification. The identification shall support the software throughout the SLC, and shall be documented in the SCMP. The Configuration Identification shall also define the documentation required to record the functional and physical characteristics of each Configuration Item.

A series of baselines shall be established as the product moves from initial idea to the maintenance phase as required by the SPMP.

Further information related to this Activity may be found in [3] and [14].

7.2.4.3 Output Information

Output Information	Destination	
	Process	Activity
Configuration Identification	Software Configuration Management	Plan Configuration Management (7.2.3)

7.2.5 Perform Configuration Control

7.2.5.1 Input Information

Input Information	Source	
	Process	Activity
Items to Be Controlled	Creating Process	
Software Configuration Management Planned Information	Software Configuration Management	Plan Configuration Management (7.2.3)

7.2.5.2 Description. This Activity controls the configuration of products. Changes to controlled products shall be tracked to assure that the configuration of the product is known at all times. Each baseline shall be established and all subsequent changes tracked relative to it. All items specified in the SCMP are subject to this change management discipline. The history of changes to each configuration item shall be maintained throughout the SLC for status accounting.

Changes to Controlled Items shall be allowed only with approval of the responsible authority. This may result in establishment of a formal software configuration control board. Controlled Items shall be maintained in a software library.

Further information related to this Activity may be found in [3] and [14].

7.2.5.3 Output Information

Output Information	Destination	
	Process	Activity
Change Status	Software Configuration Management	Perform Status Accounting (7.2.6)
Controlled Item	Creating Process	
	Project Monitoring and Control	Implement Problem Reporting Method (3.2.7)

7.2.6 Perform Status Accounting

7.2.6.1 Input Information

Input Information	Source	
	Process	Activity
Software Configuration Management Planned Information	Software Configuration Management	Plan Configuration Management (7.2.3)
Change Status	Software Configuration Management	Perform Configuration Control (7.2.5)

7.2.6.2 Description. This Activity shall include the receipt of Change Status from the Perform Configuration Control Activity and the preparation of Status Reported Information that reflects the status and history of controlled items. Status Reported Information may include such data as number of changes to date for the project, number of releases, and the latest version and revision identifiers.

Further information related to this Activity may be found in [3] and [14].

Prior to the distribution of the Status Reported Information, the following Processes shall be invoked:

(1) Verification and Validation (7.1.4)
(2) Documentation Development (7.3.4)

7.2.6.3 Output Information

Output Information	Destination	
	Process	Activity
Status Reported Information	Project Monitoring and Control	Manage the Project (3.2.5)
	External	

7.3 Documentation Development Process

7.3.1 Overview. The Documentation Development Process for software development and usage is the set of Activities that plan, design, implement, edit, produce, distribute, and maintain those documents needed by developers and users. The purpose of the Documentation Development Process is to provide timely software documentation to those who need it, based on Input Information from the invoking Processes.

This Process covers both product- and procedure-oriented documentation for internal and external users. Examples of internal users include those who plan, design, implement, or test software. External users may include those who install, operate, apply, or maintain the software.

The Documentation Development Process occurs over various phases of the software life cycle (SLC) depending on the individual document and the timing of its development. Typically there will be multiple documents, each at different stages of development.

The Documentation Development Process has Activities that must be performed concurrently with the software development or usage. Since the software is seldom stable during development or testing, this requires effective communication and timely response between the software personnel and documentation personnel.

7.3.2 Activities List

(1) Plan Documentation
(2) Implement Documentation
(3) Produce and Distribute Documentation

7.3.3 Plan Documentation

7.3.3.1 Input Information

Input Information	Source	
	Process	Activity
Contractual Requirements	External	
Project Standards	Project Initiation	Establish Project Environment (3.1.5)
Software Project Management Planned Information	Project Initiation	Plan Project Management (3.1.6)

7.3.3.2 Description. In this Activity, information such as the Software Project Management Planned Information (SPMP) product descriptions, schedules, and resource constraints shall be assimilated to create a consistent and disciplined approach to achieving the required documentation. The approach shall identify required documents, document production schedules and delivery schedules, and documentation standards. Responsible organizations, information sources, and intended audiences shall be defined for each document. The approach shall be documented in the Documentation Planning Information. The Documentation Planning Information shall include resource allocations for this Activity.

Additional guidance for the development of user documentation can be found in [21].

Prior to distribution of the Documentation Planning Information, the following Processes shall be invoked:

(1) Verification and Validation (7.1.4)
(2) Documentation Development (7.3.4)

The Software Configuration Management Process (7.2.5) should also be invoked.

7.3.3.3 Output Information

Output Information	Destination	
	Process	Activity
Documentation Planned Information	Project Monitoring and Control	Retain Records (3.2.6)
	Implementation	Create Operating Documentation (5.3.6)
	Documentation Development	All Activities (7.3)

7.3.4 Implement Documentation

7.3.4.1 Input Information

Input Information	Source	
	Process	Activity
Input Information for Document	Creating Process	
Project Environment	Project Initiation	Establish Project Environment (3.1.5)
Documentation Planned Information	Documentation Development	Plan Documentation (7.3.3)

7.3.4.2 Description. This Activity includes the design, preparation, and maintenance of documentation. Those documents identified in the Documentation Planned Information shall be defined in terms of audience, approach, content, structure, and graphics. Arrangements may be made with word or text processing and graphics facilities for their support of implementation.

Input Information shall be used to produce the document, including related graphics. This involves extensive use of information sources, close communication with the responsible subject matter experts, and utilization of word or text processing and graphics tools.

Following a documentation review, any changes shall be incorporated to produce a technically correct document. Format, style, and production rules shall be applied to produce a final document.

Prior to distribution of the Document, the following Processes should be invoked:

(1) Verification and Validation (7.1.4)
(2) Software Configuration Management (7.2.5)

7.3.4.3 Output Information

Output Information	Destination	
	Process	Activity
Document	Documentation Development	Produce and Distribute Documentation (7.3.5)

7.3.5 Produce and Distribute Documentation

7.3.5.1 Input Information

Input Information	Source	
	Process	Activity
Documentation Planned Information	Documentation Development	Plan Documentation (7.3.3)
Document	Documentation Development	Implement Documentation (7.3.4)

7.3.5.2 Description. This Activity shall provide the intended audience with the needed information collected in the document, as specified in the Documentation Planned Information. Document production and distribution may involve electronic file management, paper document reproduction and distribution, or other media handling techniques.

7.3.5.3 Output Information

Output Information	Destination	
	Process	Activity
Published Document	Project Monitoring and Control	Retain Records (3.2.6)
	Creating Process	
	External	

7.4 Training Process

7.4.1 Overview. The development of quality software products is largely dependent upon knowledgeable and skilled people. These include the developer's technical staff and management. Customer personnel may also have to be qualified to install, operate, and maintain the software. Training is therefore essential for developers, technical support staff, and customers. It is essential that Training Planned Information be completed early in the software life cycle, prior to the time when personnel would be expected to apply required expertise to the project. Plans for customer training should be prepared and reviewed with the customer.

Section 1.5, "Use of This Standard," provides background information necessary for the successful understanding and application of this material. It should be read prior to proceeding further in this section.

7.4.2 Activities List

(1) Plan the Training Program
(2) Develop Training Materials
(3) Validate the Training Program
(4) Implement the Training Program

7.4.3 Plan the Training Program

7.4.3.1 Input Information

Input Information	Source	
	Process	Activity
Applicable Information	External	
Skills Inventory	External	
Project Environment	Project Initiation	Establish Project Environment (3.1.5)
Software Project Management Planned Information	Project Initiation	Plan Project Management (3.1.6)
Software Requirements	Requirements	Prioritize and Integrate Software Requirements (5.1.5)
Training Feedback	Training	Implement the Training Program (7.4.6)
		Validate the Training Program (7.4.5)

7.4.3.2 Description. This Activity shall identify the needs for different types of training and the categories of people requiring training for each need. Customer and project documents shall be reviewed along with existing personnel inventories. This information is used to produce documented Training Planned Information. Implementation schedules shall also be generated and resources allocated to the training program. Implementation schedules, resource allocations, and training needs shall be specified in the Training Planned Information.

Prior to distribution of the Training Planned Information, the following Processes shall be invoked:

(1) Verification and Validation (7.1.4)
(2) Software Configuration Management (7.2.5)
(3) Documentation Development (7.3.4)

7.4.3.3 Output Information

Output Information	Destination	
	Process	Activity
Training Planned Information	Software Quality Management	Identify Quality Improvement Needs (3.3.6)
	Training	All Activities (7.4)

7.4.4 Develop Training Materials

7.4.4.1 Input Information

Input Information	Source	
	Process	Activity
Applicable Documentation	External	
	Creating Process	
Project Environment	Project Initiation	Establish Project Environment (3.1.5)
Software Design Description	Design	Perform Detailed Design (5.2.7)
Training Planned Information	Training	Plan Training Program(7.4.3)

7.4.4.2 Description. This Activity shall consist of identification and review of all available materials that appear pertinent to the training objectives. Included in the Develop Training Materials Activity shall be the development of the substance of the training, training manual, and materials to be used in presenting the training, such as outlines, text, exercises, case studies, visuals, and models.

Prior to distribution of the Training Manual and Training Materials, the following Processes shall be invoked:

(1) Verification and Validation (7.1.4)
(2) Documentation Development (7.3.4)

The Software Configuration Management Process (7.2.5) should also be invoked.

7.4.4.3 Output Information

Output Information	Destination	
	Process	Activity
Training Manual	Training	Validate Training Program (7.4.5)
Training Materials	Training	Validate Training Program (7.4.5)

7.4.5 Validate the Training Program

7.4.5.1 Input Information

Input Information	Source	
	Process	Activity
Training Planned Information	Training	Plan Training Program7.4.3)
Training Manual	Training	Develop Training Materials (7.4.4)
Training Materials	Training	Develop Training Materials (7.4.4)

7.4.5.2 Description. This Activity shall consist of presenting the training to a class of evaluators using the preliminary training manual and materials. The evaluators shall assess the training presentation and materials in detail. The purpose is to evaluate the effectiveness of the delivery and the validity of the material presented. Lessons learned in the test of the training program shall be incorporated into the material prior to a general offering. All training manuals and materials shall be evaluated and, if necessary, updated at this time.

Prior to distribution of Updated Training Manuals and Materials, the following Processes shall be invoked:

(1) Verification and Validation (7.1.4)
(2) Documentation Development (7.3.4)

The Software Configuration Management Process (7.2.5) should be invoked.

7.4.5.3 Output Information

Output Information	Destination	
	Process	Activity
Updated Training Manual	Training	Implement Training Program (7.4.6)
Updated Training Materials	Training	Implement Training Program (7.4.6)
Training Feedback	Training	Plan Training Program (7.4.3)

7.4.6 Implement the Training Program

7.4.6.1 Input Information

Input Information	Source	
	Process	Activity
Staff Participants	External	
Students	External	
Training Planned Information	Training	Plan Training Program(7.4.3)
Updated Training Manual	Training	Validate Training Program (7.4.5)
Updated Training Materials	Training	Validate Training Program (7.4.5)

7.4.6.2 Description. This Activity shall ensure the provision of all necessary materials, arrange the locations and facilities for training, assign instructors and, if necessary, train them. Included in this Activity shall be the enrolling of students and monitoring of the course effectiveness.

Lessons learned and information needed for updating the materials for the next training cycle shall be fed back into the beginning of the Training Process.

7.4.6.3 Output Information

Output Information	Destination	
	Process	Activity
Trained Personnel	Creating Process	
Training Feedback	Training	Plan Training Program (7.4.3)
Updated Skills Inventory	External	

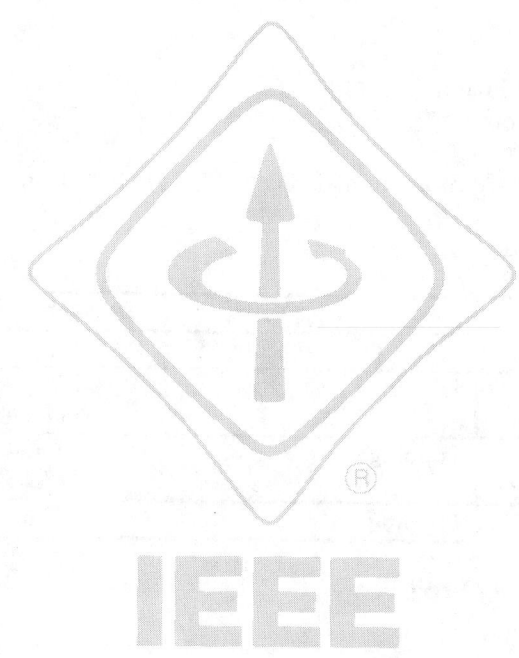

8. Bibliography

The IEEE standards listed below and other subsequent standards should be consulted when using this document. However, compliance with this standard neither requires nor implies compliance with the listed standards. Table 2 provides a cross reference of specific Activities to other IEEE standards.

[1] IEEE Std 610.12-1990, IEEE Standard Glossary of Software Engineering Terminology (ANSI).[4]

[2] IEEE Std 730-1989, IEEE Standard for Software Quality Assurance Plans (ANSI).

[3] IEEE Std 828-1990, IEEE Standard for Software Configuration Management Plans (ANSI).

[4] IEEE Std 829-1983, IEEE Standard for Software Test Documentation (ANSI).

[5] IEEE Std 830-1984, IEEE Guide to Software Requirements Specifications (ANSI).

[6] IEEE Std 982.1-1988, IEEE Standard Dictionary of Measures to Produce Reliable Software (ANSI).

[7] IEEE Std 982.2-1988, IEEE Guide for the Use of IEEE Standard Dictionary of Measures to Produce Reliable Software (ANSI).

[8] IEEE Std 983-1986, IEEE Guide for Software Quality Assurance Planning (ANSI).

[9] IEEE Std 1002-1987, IEEE Standard Taxonomy for Software Engineering Standards (ANSI).

[10] IEEE Std 1008-1987, IEEE Standard for Software Unit Testing (ANSI).

[11] IEEE Std 1012-1986, IEEE Standard for Software Verification and Validation Plans (ANSI).

[12] IEEE Std 1016-1987, IEEE Recommended Practice for Software Design Descriptions (ANSI).

[13] IEEE Std 1028-1988, IEEE Standard for Software Reviews and Audits (ANSI).

[14] IEEE Std 1042-1987, IEEE Guide to Software Configuration Management Planning (ANSI).

[15] P1044, Standard for Classification of Software Errors, Faults, and Failures.[5]

[16] P1045, Standard for Software Productivity Metrics.

[17] IEEE Std 1058.1-1987, IEEE Standard for Software Project Management Plans (ANSI).

[18] P1059, Guide for Software Verification and Validation.

[4]IEEE publications are available from the Institute of Electrical and Electronics Engineers, Service Center, 445 Hoes Lane, P.O. Box 1331, Piscataway, NJ 08855-1331, USA.

[5]References [15], [16], [18], [19], and [20] are authorized standards projects that were not approved by the IEEE Standards Board at the time this document went to press. The latest drafts of the documents are available from the IEEE Service Center.

[19] P1061, Standard for a Software Quality Metrics Methodology.

[20] P1062, Recommended Practice for Software Acquisition.

[21] IEEE Std 1063-1987, IEEE Standard for Software User Documentation (ANSI).

[22] ANSI Technical Report, American National Dictionary for Information Processing, X3/TR-1-77, September 1977.

Table 2
Cross Reference of IEEE Standards and Authorized Standards Projects

	Applicability of Standards								
Activities (Paragraph Numbers) / Referenced IEEE Standards and Authorized Standards Projects	1.3.1	3.1.5	3.1.6	3.2.7	3.3.3	3.3.4	5.1.3 5.1.5	5.2.7	5.3.3 5.3.5
[1] 610.12-1990	X								
[2] 730-1989					X				
[3] 828-1990									
[4] 829-1983									
[5] 830-1984	X						X		
[6] 982.1-1988						X			
[7] 982.2-1988						X			
[8] 983-1986					X				
[9] 1002-1987		X							
[10] 1008-1987									
[11] 1012-1986									
[12] 1016-1987									
[13] 1028-1988									
[14] 1042-1987									
[15] P1044				X					
[16] 1045						X			
[17] 1058.1-1987	X		X						
[18] P1059									
[19] P1061						X			
[20] P1062									
[21] 1063-1987									

Table 2
Cross Reference of IEEE Standards and Authorized Standards Projects *(Continued)*

	Applicability of Standards								
Activities (Paragraph Numbers)	5.3.3 5.3.5	5.3.6	7.1.3	7.1.4	7.1.5	7.1.6	7.1.7 7.1.8	7.2.3 7.2.4 7.2.5 7.2.6	7.3.3
Referenced IEEE Standards									
[1] 610.12-1990									
[2] 730-1989			X	X					
[3] 828-1990			X	X				X	
[4] 829-1983			X			X	X		
[5] 830-1984									
[6] 982.1-1988			X		X				
[7] 982.2-1988			X		X				
[8] 983-1986			X	X					
[9] 1002-1987									
[10] 1008-1987	X					X			
[11] 1012-1986			X	X		X	X		
[12] 1016-1987									
[13] 1028-1988			X	X					
[14] 1042-1987			X	X				X	
[15] P1044			X		X				
[16] P1045			X		X				
[17] 1058.1-1987									
[18] P1059						X			
[19] P1061									
[20] P1062									
[21] 1063-1987		X							X

Appendixes

(These Appendixes are not a part of IEEE Std 1074-1991, IEEE Standard for Developing Life Cycle Processes, but are included for information only.)

Appendix A
Mapping Software Life Cycle Processes to Various Examples of Software Life Cycles

This Appendix demonstrates the mappings of the Activities in this standard to four different software life cycles (SLCs). This Appendix is not intended to be comprehensive. Many other SLCs are possible, for example, small development, quick reaction, and the spiral model. The SLCs presented here are examples only, and the user of this document is not required to select any of these SLCs.

Table A1 demonstrates a mapping of Activities to an eight-phase SLC.

Table A2 demonstrates a mapping of Activities to a five-phase SLC.

Table A3 demonstrates a mapping of Activities to an SLC that uses prototyping to establish requirements and design.

Table A4 demonstrates a mapping of Activities to an SLC that includes a theoretical, highly automated software development mode.

Section 1.5, "Use of This Standard," provides background information necessary for the successful understanding and application of this material. It should be read prior to proceeding further in these Appendixes.

Table A1
Software Life Cycle Example Based on Eight Phases

Concept Exploration (CE)
Requirements (RQ)
Design (DE)
Implementation (IM)
Test (TE)
Installation and Checkout (IN)
Operation and Maintenance (OM)
Retirement (RT)

Activities	CE	RQ	DE	IM	TE	IN	OM	RT
SOFTWARE LIFE CYCLE PROCESS								
Identify Candidate SLC Models	X							
Select Project Model	X							
PROJECT MANAGEMENT PROCESSES								
Project Initiation Process								
Map Activities to SLC Model	X							
Allocate Project Resources	X	X	X	X	X	X	X	X
Establish Project Environment	X	X	X					
Plan Project Management	X	X						
Project Monitoring and Control Process								
Analyze Risks	X	X	X	X	X	X		
Perform Contingency Planning		X	X	X	X	X		
Manage the Project	X	X	X	X	X	X	X	X
Retain Records	X	X	X	X	X	X	X	X
Implement Problem Reporting System		X	X	X	X	X	X	X
Software Quality Management Process								
Plan Software Quality Management	X	X	X					
Define Metrics		X	X					
Manage Software Quality	X	X	X	X	X	X	X	X
Identify Quality Improvement Needs	X	X	X	X	X	X	X	X
PRE-DEVELOPMENT PROCESSES								
Concept Exploration Process								
Identify Ideas or Needs	X							
Formulate Potential Approaches	X	X						
Conduct Feasibility Studies	X	X	X	X	X	X	X	X
Plan System Transition (If Applicable)	X	X						X
Refine and Finalize the Idea or Need		X						
System Allocation Process								
Analyze Functions		X	X					
Develop System Architecture		X	X					
Decompose System Requirements		X						

Table A1
Software Life Cycle Example Based on Eight Phases *(Continued)*

Activities	CE	RQ	DE	IM	TE	IN	OM	RT
DEVELOPMENT PROCESSES								
Requirements Process								
Define and Develop Software Requirements		X	X					
Define Interface Requirements		X	X					
Prioritize and Integrate Software Requirements		X	X					
Design Process								
Perform Architectural Design			X					
Design Data Base (If Applicable)			X					
Design Interfaces			X					
Select or Develop Algorithms		X	X					
Perform Detailed Design			X					
Implementation Process								
Create Test Data			X	X				
Create Source			X	X				
Generate Object Code			X	X				
Create Operating Documentation			X	X				
Plan Integration			X					
Perform Integration				X	X			
POST-DEVELOPMENT PROCESSES								
Installation Process								
Plan Installation					X			
Distribute Software						X		
Install Software						X		
Accept Software in Operational Environment						X		
Operation and Support Process								
Operate the System							X	
Provide Tech. Asst. & Consult.							X	
Maintain Support Request Log							X	
Maintenance Process								
Reapply Software Life Cycle							X	
Retirement Process								
Notify User							X	X
Conduct Parallel Operations (If Applicable)								X
Retire System								X

Table A1
Software Life Cycle Example Based on Eight Phases *(Continued)*

Activities	CE	RQ	DE	IM	TE	IN	OM	RT
INTEGRAL PROCESSES								
Verification and Validation Process								
Plan Verification and Validation	X	X	X					
Execute V&V Tasks	X	X	X	X	X	X	X	X
Collect and Analyze Metric Data		X	X	X	X	X	X	X
Plan Testing		X	X	X				
Develop Test Requirements			X	X				
Execute the Tests				X	X	X		
Software Configuration Management Process								
Plan Configuration Management		X	X					
Perform Configuration Identification		X	X	X	X			
Perform Configuration Control			X	X	X	X	X	X
Perform Status Accounting			X	X	X	X	X	X
Documentation Development Process								
Plan Documentation		X	X					
Implement Documentation		X	X					
Produce and Distribute Documentation				X	X			
Training Process								
Plan the Training Program		X	X					
Develop Training Materials			X	X	X			
Validate the Training Program					X	X		
Implement the Training Program						X		

Table A2
Software Life Cycle Example Based on Five Phases

Project Initiation (PI)
Concept Development (CD)
Definition and Design (DD)
System Development (SD)
Installation and Operation (IO)

Activities	PI	CD	DD	SD	IO
SOFTWARE LIFE CYCLE PROCESS					
Identify Candidate SLC Models	X				
Select Project Model	X				
PROJECT MANAGEMENT PROCESSES					
Project Initiation Process					
Map Activities to SLC Model	X				
Allocate Project Resources	X	X	X	X	X
Establish Project Environment	X	X	X		
Plan Project Management	X	X			
Project Monitoring and Control Process					
Analyze Risks	X	X	X	X	X
Perform Contingency Planning		X	X	X	X
Manage the Project	X	X	X	X	X
Retain Records	X	X	X	X	X
Implement Problem Reporting System		X	X	X	X
Software Quality Management Process					
Plan Software Quality Management	X	X	X		
Define Metrics		X	X		
Manage Software Quality	X	X	X	X	X
Identify Quality Improvement Needs	X	X	X	X	X
PRE-DEVELOPMENT PROCESSES					
Concept Exploration Process					
Identify Ideas or Needs	X				
Formulate Potential Approaches	X	X			
Conduct Feasibility Studies	X	X			
Plan System Transition (If Applicable)	X	X			
Refine and Finalize the Idea or Need		X			
System Allocation Process					
Analyze Functions		X	X		
Develop System Architecture		X	X		
Decompose System Requirements		X			

Table A2
Software Life Cycle Example Based on Five Phases *(Continued)*

Activities	PI	CD	DD	SD	IO
DEVELOPMENT PROCESSES					
Requirements Process					
Define and Develop Software Requirements		X	X		
Define Interface Requirements		X	X		
Prioritize and Integrate Software Requirements		X	X		
Design Process					
Perform Architectural Design			X		
Design Data Base (If Applicable)			X		
Design Interfaces			X		
Select or Develop Algorithms		X	X		
Perform Detailed Design			X		
Implementation Process					
Create Test Data			X	X	
Create Source			X	X	
Generate Object Code			X	X	
Create Operating Documentation			X	X	
Plan Integration			X		
Perform Integration				X	
POST-DEVELOPMENT PROCESSES					
Installation Process					
Plan Installation				X	
Distribute Software					X
Install Software					X
Accept Software in Operational Environment					X
Operation and Support Process					
Operate the System					X
Provide Tech. Asst. & Consult.					X
Maintain Support Request Log					X
Maintenance Process					
Reapply Software Life Cycle					X
Retirement Process					
Notify User					X
Conduct Parallel Operations (If Applicable)					X
Retire System					X

Table A2
Software Life Cycle Example Based on Five Phases *(Continued)*

Activities	PI	CD	DD	SD	IO
INTEGRAL PROCESSES					
Verification and Validation Process					
Plan Verification and Validation	X	X	X		
Execute V&V Tasks		X	X	X	X
Collect and Analyze Metric Data		X	X	X	X
Plan Testing			X	X	
Develop Test Requirements			X	X	
Execute the Tests			X	X	X
Software Configuration Management Process					
Plan Configuration Management		X	X		
Perform Configuration Identification		X	X	X	
Perform Configuration Control			X	X	X
Perform Status Accounting			X	X	X
Documentation Development Process					
Plan Documentation		X	X		
Implement Documentation			X	X	
Produce and Distribute Documentation				X	X
Training Process					
Plan the Training Program		X	X		
Develop Training Materials			X	X	
Validate the Training Program				X	X
Implement the Training Program					X

Table A3
Software Life Cycle Example Based on Prototyping

Concept Exploration (CE)
Implementation (IM)
Installation and Checkout (IN)
Retirement (RT)
Prototyping (PT)
Test (TE)
Operation and Maintenance (OM)

Activities	CE	PT	IM	TE	IN	OM	RT
SOFTWARE LIFE CYCLE PROCESS							
Identify Candidate SLC Models	X						
Select Project Model	X						
PROJECT MANAGEMENT PROCESSES							
Project Initiation Process							
Map Activities to SLC Model	X						
Allocate Project Resources	X	X	X	X	X	X	X
Establish Project Environment	X	X					
Plan Project Management	X	X					
Project Monitoring and Control Process							
Analyze Risks	X	X	X	X	X		
Perform Contingency Planning		X	X	X	X		
Manage the Project	X	X	X	X	X	X	X
Retain Records	X	X	X	X	X	X	X
Implement Problem Reporting System		X	X	X	X	X	X
Software Quality Management Process							
Plan Software Quality Management		X					
Define Metrics		X					
Manage Software Quality	X	X	X	X	X	X	X
Identify Quality Improvement Needs	X	X	X	X	X	X	X
PRE-DEVELOPMENT PROCESSES							
Concept Exploration Process							
Identify Ideas or Needs	X						
Formulate Potential Approaches	X	X					
Conduct Feasibility Studies	X	X					
Plan System Transition (If Applicable)	X	X					X
Refine and Finalize the Idea or Need		X					
System Allocation Process							
Analyze Functions		X					
Develop System Architecture		X					
Decompose System Requirements		X					

Table A3
Software Life Cycle Example Based on Prototyping *(Continued)*

Activities	CE	PT	IM	TE	IN	OM	RT
DEVELOPMENT PROCESSES							
Requirements Process							
Define and Develop Software Requirements		X					
Define Interface Requirements		X					
Prioritize and Integrate Software Rqmts.		X					
Design Process							
Perform Architectural Design		X					
Design Data Base (If Applicable)		X					
Design Interfaces		X					
Select or Develop Algorithms		X					
Perform Detailed Design		X					
Implementation Process							
Create Test Data		X	X				
Create Source		X	X				
Generate Object Code		X	X	X			
Create Operating Documentation		X	X				
Plan Integration		X					
Perform Integration			X	X			
POST-DEVELOPMENT PROCESSES							
Installation Process							
Plan Installation				X			
Distribute Software					X		
Install Software					X		
Check out Software in Operational Envnmt.					X		
Operation and Support Process							
Operate the System						X	
Provide Tech. Asst. & Consult.						X	
Maintain Support Request Log						X	
Maintenance Process							
Reapply Software Life Cycle						X	

Table A3
Software Life Cycle Example Based on Prototyping *(Continued)*

Activities	CE	PT	IM	TE	IN	OM	RT
Retirement Process							
Notify User						X	X
Conduct Parallel Operations (If Applicable)							X
Retire System							X
INTEGRAL PROCESSES							
Verification and Validation Process							
Plan Verification and Validation		X					
Execute V&V Tasks		X	X	X	X	X	X
Collect and Analyze Metric Data		X	X	X	X	X	X
Plan Testing		X	X				
Develop Test Specifications		X	X				
Execute the Tests			X	X	X		
Software Configuration Management Process							
Plan Configuration Management		X					
Perform Configuration Identification		X	X	X			
Perform Configuration Control		X	X	X	X	X	X
Perform Status Accounting		X	X	X	X	X	X
Documentation Development Process							
Plan Documentation		X					
Implement Documentation		X	X				
Produce and Distribute Documentation				X	X		
Training Process							
Plan the Training Program		X					
Develop Training Materials		X	X	X			
Validate the Training Program				X	X		
Implement the Training Program					X		

Table A4
Software Life Cycle Example Based on an Operational Specification*

System Requirements (SR) Operational Specification (OS)
Transformed Specification (TS) Delivered System (DS)

Activities	SR	OS	TS	DS
SOFTWARE LIFE CYCLE PROCESS				
Identify Candidate SLC Models	X			
Select Project Model	X			
PROJECT MANAGEMENT PROCESSES				
Project Initiation Process				
Map Activities to SLC Model	X			
Allocate Project Resources	X	X	X	X
Establish Project Environment	X	X		
Plan Project Management	X			
Project Monitoring and Control Process				
Analyze Risks	X	X	X	X
Perform Contingency Planning	X	X	X	X
Manage the Project	X	X	X	X
Retain Records	X	X	X	X
Implement Problem Reporting System		X	X	X
Software Quality Management Process				
Plan Software Quality Management	X	X		
Define Metrics	X	X		
Manage Software Quality	X	X	X	X
Identify Quality Improvement Needs	X	X	X	X
PRE-DEVELOPMENT PROCESSES				
Concept Exploration Process				
Identify Ideas or Needs	X			
Formulate Potential Approaches	X			
Conduct Feasibility Studies	X	X		
Plan System Transition (If Applicable)	X			X
Refine and Finalize the Idea or Need	X			
System Allocation Process				
Analyze Functions	X	X		
Develop System Architecture	X	X		
Decompose System Requirements	X			

* As defined in the IEEE Tutorial, "New Paradigms for Software Development," by William W. Agresti.

Table A4
Software Life Cycle Example Based on an Operational Specification *(Continued)*

Activities	SR	OS	TS	DS
DEVELOPMENT PROCESSES				
Requirements Process				
Define and Develop Software Requirements	X	X		
Define Interface Requirements	X	X		
Prioritize and Integrate Software Requirements	X	X		
Design Process				
Perform Architectural Design		X		
Design Data Base (If Applicable)		X		
Design Interfaces		X		
Select or Develop Algorithms	X	X		
Perform Detailed Design		X		
Implementation Process				
Create Test Data		X	X	
Create Source		X	X	
Generate Object Code		X	X	
Create Operating Documentation		X	X	
Plan Integration		X		
Perform Integration			X	
POST-DEVELOPMENT PROCESSES				
Installation Process				
Plan Installation			X	
Distribute Software				X
Install Software				X
Check out Software in Operational Environment				X
Operation and Support Process				
Operate the System				X
Provide Tech. Asst. & Consult.				X
Maintain Support Request Log				X
Maintenance Process				
Reapply Software Life Cycle				X
Retirement Process				
Notify User				X
Conduct Parallel Operations (If Applicable)				X
Retire System				X

Table A4
Software Life Cycle Example Based on an Operational Specification *(Continued)*

Activities	SR	OS	TS	DS
INTEGRAL PROCESSES				
Verification and Validation Process				
Plan Verification and Validation	X	X		
Execute V&V Tasks	X	X	X	X
Collect and Analyze Metric Data	X	X	X	X
Plan Testing		X	X	
Develop Test Specifications		X	X	
Execute the Tests			X	X
Software Configuration Management Process				
Plan Configuration Management	X	X		
Perform Configuration Identification	X	X	X	
Perform Configuration Control		X	X	X
Perform Status Accounting		X	X	X
Documentation Development Process				
Plan Documentation	X	X		
Implement Documentation		X	X	
Produce and Distribute Documentation			X	X
Training Process				
Plan the Training Program	X	X		
Develop Training Materials		X	X	
Validate the Training Program			X	X
Implement the Training Program				X

Appendix B
Software Project Management Tailoring Template

The Software Project Management Tailoring Template is designed to assist project managers in identifying project-critical deliverables and assuring their completion as needed.

This template may be used to assist in the project-specific mapping of information into the required project documentation.

Table B1
Software Project Management Tailoring Template

SOFTWARE PROJECT MANAGEMENT TAILORING TEMPLATE			
Process or Activity Name	Section	Output Information	Mapped Deliverables or Activities
PROCESS GROUP **Process** Activity		Required Output Information	
SOFTWARE LIFE CYCLE PROCESS	2		
Identify Candidate SLC Models	2.3	Candidate SLC Model(s)	
Select Project Model	2.4	Selected SLC Model	
PROJECT MANAGEMENT PROCESSES	3		
Project Initiation	3.1		
Map Activities to SLC Model	3.1.3	Software Life Cycle	
		List of Activities Not Used	
Allocate Project Information	3.1.4	Resource Allocations	
Establish Project Environment	3.1.5	Project Environment	
Plan Project Management	3.1.6	Problem Reporting & Resolution Planned Info.	
		Retirement Planned Info.	
		Software Project Management Planned Info.	
		Support Planned Info.	
Project Monitoring and Control	3.2		
Analyze Risks	3.2.3	Analysis of Risks	
Perform Contingency Planning	3.2.4	Contingency Planned Info.	
Manage the Project	3.2.5	Project Management Reported Info.	
		Anomalies	
Retain Records	3.2.6	Historical Project Records	
Implement Problem Reporting Method	3.2.7	Resolved Problem Reported Info.	
		Report Log	
		Enhancement Problem Reported Info.	
		Corrections Problem Reported Info.	

Table B1
Software Project Management Tailoring Template
(Continued)

SOFTWARE PROJECT MANAGEMENT TAILORING TEMPLATE			
Process or Activity Name	Section	Output Information	Mapped Deliverables or Activities
Software Quality Management	3.3		
Plan Software Quality Management	3.3.3	Software Quality Management Planned Info.	
Define Metrics	3.3.4	Defined Metrics	
		Collection and Analysis Methods	
Manage Software Quality	3.3.5	Project Quality Assessments	
Identify Quality Improvement Needs	3.3.6	Quality Improvement Recommendations	
PRE-DEVELOPMENT PROCESSES	4		
Concept Exploration	4.1		
Identify Ideas or Needs	4.1.3	Prelim. Statement of Need	
Formulate Potential Approaches	4.1.4	Constraints and Benefits	
		Potential Approaches	
Conduct Feasibility Studies	4.1.5	Recommendations	
Plan System Transition (If Applicable)	4.1.6	Transition Impact Statement	
		Transition Planned Info.	
Refine and Finalize the Idea or Need	4.1.7	Statement of Need	
System Allocation	4.2		
Analyze Functions	4.2.3	Funct'l Description of System	
Develop System Architecture	4.2.4	System Architecture	
Decompose System Requirements	4.2.5	Funct'l Hardware Rqmts.	
		Funct'l Software Rqmts.	
		System Interface Requirements (If Applicable)	
DEVELOPMENT PROCESSES	5		
Requirements	5.1		
Define and Develop Software Rqmts.	5.1.3	Prelim. Software Rqmts.	
		Installation Rqmts.	
Define Interface Requirements	5.1.4	Software Interface Rqmts.	
Prioritize and Integrate Software Rqmts.	5.1.5	Software Rqmts.	

Table B1
Software Project Management Tailoring Template
(Continued)

SOFTWARE PROJECT MANAGEMENT TAILORING TEMPLATE			
Process or Activity Name	Section	Output Information	Mapped Deliverables or Activities
Design	**5.2**		
Perform Architectural Design	5.2.3	Software Architectural Design Description	
Design Data Base (If Applicable)	5.2.4	Data Base Description	
Design Interfaces	5.2.5	Interface Description	
Select or Develop Algorithms	5.2.6	Algorithm Descriptions	
Perform Detailed Design	5.2.7	Software Design Description	
Implementation	**5.3**		
Create Test Data	5.3.3	Stubs and Drivers (If Applicable)	
		Test Data	
Create Source	5.3.4	Data Base (If Applicable)	
		Source Code	
Generate Object Code	5.3.5	Corrected Data Base (If Applicable)	
		Corrected Source Code	
		Object Code	
Create Operating Documentation	5.3.6	Operating Documentation	
Plan Integration	5.3.7	Integration Planned Info.	
Perform Integration	5.3.8	Integrated Software	
POST-DEVELOPMENT PROCESSES	**6**		
Installation	**6.1**		
Plan Installation	6.1.3	Software Installation Planned Info.	
Distribute Software	6.1.4	Packaged Operating Docs.	
		Packaged Software	
		Packaged Installation Planned Info.	
Install Software	6.1.5	Installation Reported Info.	
		Installed Software	
Accept Software in Operational Envrmt.	6.1.6	Installed Software System	
		Customer Acceptance	

Table B1
Software Project Management Tailoring Template
(Continued)

SOFTWARE PROJECT MANAGEMENT TAILORING TEMPLATE			
Process or Activity Name	Section	Output Information	Mapped Deliverables or Activities
Operation and Support	**6.2**		
Operate the System	6.2.3	System Anomalies	
		Operation Logs	
		Feedback Data	
Provide Tech. Asst. & Consult.	6.2.4	Support Response	
Maintain Support Request Log	6.2.5	Anomalies	
		Support Request Log	
Maintenance	**6.3**		
Reapply Software Life Cycle	6.3.3	Maintenance Recommendations	
Retirement	**6.4**		
Notify User	6.4.3	Official Notification	
Conduct Parallel Operations	6.4.4	Parallel Operations Log	
Retire System	6.4.5	Post-Operation Review Reported Information	
		Archive Reported Info.	
INTEGRAL PROCESSES	**7**		
Verification and Validation	**7.1**		
Plan V&V	7.1.3	Software V&V Planned Info.	
Execute V&V Tasks	7.1.4	Evaluation Reported Info.	
		Anomalies	
Collect and Analyze Metric Data	7.1.5	Analysis Reported Info.	
Plan Testing	7.1.6	Test Planned Info.	
Develop Test Requirements	7.1.7	Test Requirements	
Execute the Tests	7.1.8	Test Summary Reported Info.	
		Tested Software	
		Anomalies	

Table B1
Software Project Management Tailoring Template
(Continued)

SOFTWARE PROJECT MANAGEMENT TAILORING TEMPLATE			
Process or Activity Name	Section	Output Information	Mapped Deliverables or Activities
Software Configuration Management	**7.2**		
Plan Configuration Management	7.2.3	Software Config. Management Planned Info.	
Develop Configuration Identification	7.2.4	Config. Identification	
Perform Configuration Control	7.2.5	Change Status Controlled Item	
Perform Status Accounting	7.2.6	Status Reported Info.	
Documentation Development	**7.3**		
Plan Documentation	7.3.3	Documentation Planned Info.	
Implement Documentation	7.3.4	Document	
Produce and Distribute Documentation	7.3.5	Published Document	
Training	**7.4**		
Plan the Training Program	7.4.3	Training Planned Info.	
Develop Training Materials	7.4.4	Training Manual	
		Training Materials	
Validate the Training Program	7.4.5	Updated Training Manual	
		Updated Training Materials	
		Training Feedback	
Implement the Training Program	7.4.6	Trained Personnel	
		Training Feedback	
		Updated Skills Inventory	

Appendix C
Process Interrelationships

Figure C1 in this Appendix shows the interrelationships between the Processes. The boxes in Fig C1 are Processes; the directed lines show the flow of input and output information between Processes. The Management Processes are grouped in the center of the figure, with the Development-Oriented Processes arranged around them.

This figure does not attempt to show Process invocations. All the directed lines to and from the Invoked Processes represent explicit information passed between those Processes.

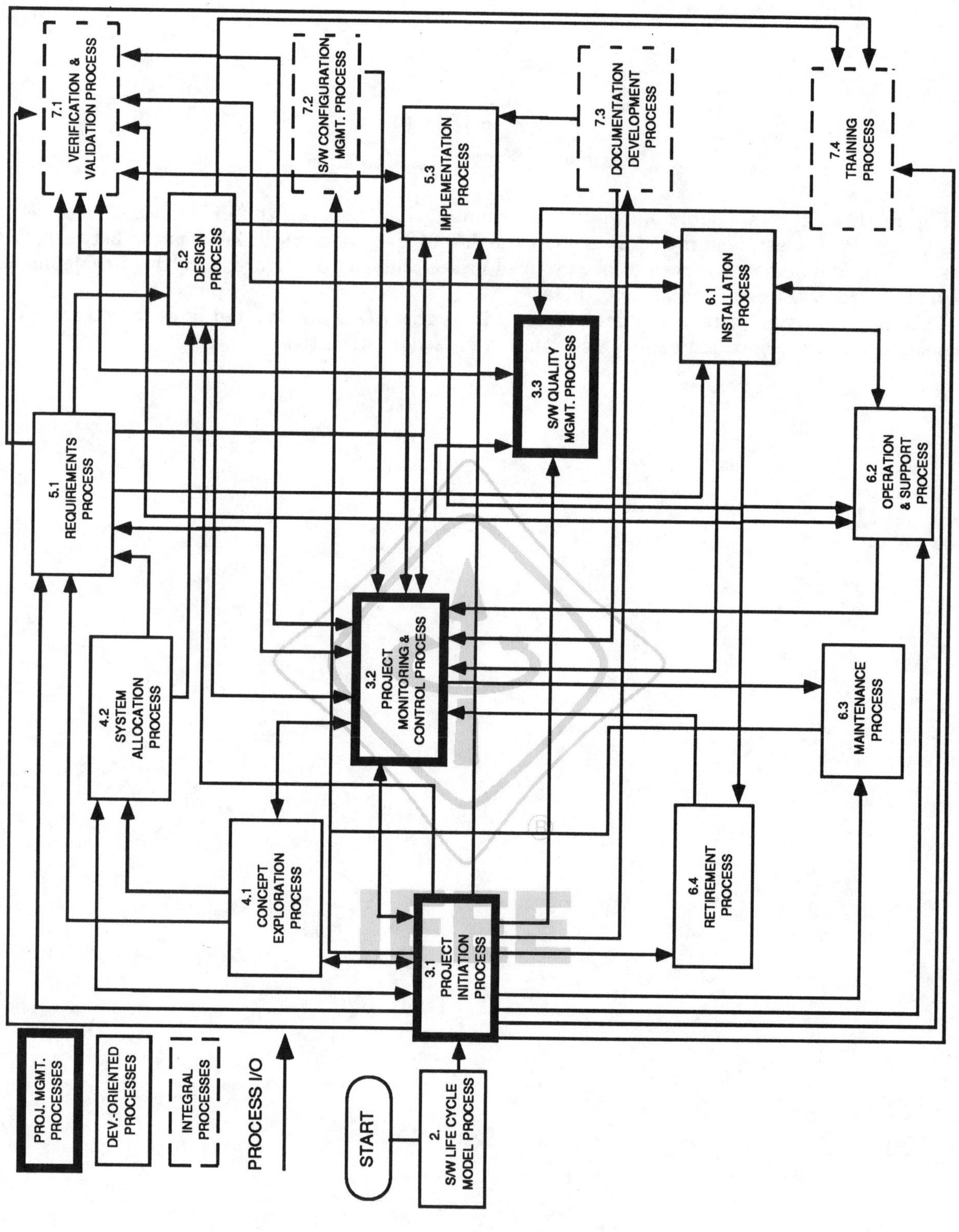

Fig C1
Process Interrelationships

Index

IEEE

IEEE Recommended Practice for the Evaluation and Selection of Case Tools

Sponsor

Software Engineering Standards Subcommittee of the Technical Committee on Software Engineering of the IEEE Computer Society

Approved December 3, 1992

IEEE Standards Board

The Institute of Electrical and Electronics Engineers, Inc.
345 East 47th Street, New York, NY 10017-2394, USA

DRAFT

Recommended Practice for the Evaluation and Selection of CASE Tools

Prepared by the
IEEE P1209 Working Group
of the
Software Engineering Standards Subcommittee
of the
Technical Committee on Software Engineering
of the
IEEE Computer Society

Foreword

(This Foreword is not part of IEEE P1209, IEEE Standard Practice for the Evaluation and Selection of CASE Tools.)

Overview

This standard provides a recommended practice for the evaluation and selection of CASE tools. The focus of this standard does not intend to minimize the complexity and challenge of a successful introduction and deployment of CASE tools within an organization. In that respect, it should be emphasized that:

- CASE tools are support mechanisms of techniques and methods and, as such, represent only the automation components of software engineering technology improvement strategies.
- Evaluation and selection of CASE tools needs to be understood in the context of a global technology implementation process which includes activities such as assessment of needs, technology awareness, deployment, and usage.

This standard was primarily developed to provide guidance for the evaluation and selection of tools used to support software engineering activities, as opposed to general purpose tools (e.g., word processors, spreadsheets) which may incidentally be used in support of software engineering activities.

Developers

This standard was developed by a working group consisting of the following members who attended two or more meetings, provided text, or submitted comments on two or more drafts of the standard.

Thomas Vollman, Chair
Michael Lackner, Secretary

Syed Ali	Thomas Kurihara	Ian C. Pyle
Fletcher Buckley	Patricia Lawliss	Carol Rieping
John P. Chihorek	Tomoo Matsubara	Marilyn Sander
Mehmet Ficici	Jacques Meekel	Leonard L. Tripp
John Grotzky	Sandra Mulholland	Jim Van Buren
Bob Hanrahan		

Contributors

The following individuals also contributed to the development of the standard by attending one meeting or providing comments on one draft of the standard.

Tarek Abdel-Hamid
Glen Baker
Frederick Bennett
Gordon Berkley
Ron Berlack
Christopher Byrnes
Francois Collier
Ivan R. Corey
Stewart Craig
Sanjay Dewal
H. Stephen Hutchinson
Lindsay Jones
Jyh-Sheng Ke
Alaisdair Kemp
Jaime Lau
Michel Lissandre
George Lee
Brian McEvoy
Denis Meredith
Celia Modell
Phil Mullen
Dennis Nickle
James M. Perry
Carolyn Peterson
Mohan Prabandham
Benson Scheff
Howard Seeger
Saul Serben
Basil Sherlund
David Shewmake
Billie Stevens
Raymond Szymanski
Harold Tamburro
Dawn Timberlake
Susan Wong
William Wong
Gordon Wright
Mariana Yaegle

Sponsoring Organization

At the time this standard was approved, the balloting group had the following membership:

Tom Armbruster
Ron Berlack
Susan Bontly
Fletcher Buckley
Kay Bydalek
Hu Cheng
R.A. Clinkenbeard
Geoff Cozens
Scott Duncan
John Fendrich
Glenn Fields
Kirby Fortenberry
Juan Garbajosa-Sopena
Yair Gershkovitch
Gregg Giesler
Julio Gonzalez-Sanz
David Gustafson
Robert Hanrahan
John Harauz
Mark Heinrich
John Horch
Jo Jenkins
Jim Keller
Roy Ko
Robert Kozinski
Thomas Kurihara
Ben Livson
Joseph Maayan
Jukka Marijarvi
Roger Martin
Tomoo Matsubara
Ivano Mazza
Brian McEvoy
Jacques Meekel
Dennis Nickel
Robert Poston
Stephen Schach
Gregory Schumacher
Robert Shillato
D.M. Siefert
Harry Sneed
Ole Solberg
V. Srinivas
Vijaya Srivastava
Richard Thayer
Booker Thomas
George Tice
Leonard Tripp
Van Sandwyk
Thomas Vollman
Dolores Wallace
C.J. Wertz
Paul Work
Natalie Yopconka
Janusz Zalewski
Peter Zoll

The P1209 representative to the Software Engineering Standards Subcommittee was Tom Vollman.

TABLE OF CONTENTS

1. Introduction

1.1 Purpose. The purpose of this document is to provide guidance to individuals and organizations engaged in the evaluation and selection of computer-aided software engineering (CASE) tools. To this end, the following recommended practice provides organized and comprehensive evaluation and selection processes.

1.2 Scope. This document addresses the evaluation and selection of tools supporting software engineering processes including: project management processes, pre-development processes, development processes, post-development processes, and integral processes (See IEEE Std. 1074). It is not intended to address systems engineering, integrated software engineering environments, or general purpose tools such as spreadsheets or word processors.

This recommended practice assumes that evaluation/selection activities are initiated by a person or group with the authority to commit the resources necessary to perform the activities. It assumes that recommendations resulting from these activities are provided to the initiator and/or to some other decision maker external to the process. It does not address activities leading up to the evaluation/selection process initiation, nor activities following a decision recommendation, such as acquisition related activities, or qualification activities such as use in pilot projects.

This recommended practice assumes that its user understands the job the CASE tool is to perform and the environmental constraints that would affect the use of the CASE tool. It does not address process maturity, technological readiness, or implementation of tools.

The evaluation and selection processes recommended in this document are based upon a CASE tool user's perspective. Thus the evaluation and selection criteria address only program characteristics visible to the user, such as program inputs and outputs, program function, user interfaces, and documented external program interfaces. Not addressed are the internals of the tool's programs or the process by which they were developed.

This document neither dictates nor advocates particular or specific development standards, design methods, methodologies, techniques, programming languages, or life cycle paradigms.

The existence of this document should not be construed to prohibit additional efforts in the evaluation and selection processes.

1.3 Definitions.

ANSI/IEEE 610.12-1990, IEEE Standard Glossary of Software Engineering Terminology is a part of this standard. Additional definitions are provided below.

Assumptions: Conditions and/or resource requirements which are mandatory for process completion.

CASE: Computer-aided software engineering

CASE tool: A software tool to aid in software engineering activities, including but not limited to requirements analysis and tracing, software design, code production, testing, document generation, quality assurance, configuration management and project management.

CASE tool evaluation: A process wherein various aspects of a CASE tool are measured against defined criteria and the results are recorded for future use.

CASE tool selection: A process wherein the data from one or more CASE tool evaluations are weighted and compared against defined criteria to determine whether one or more of the CASE tools can be recommended for selection.

Constraints: Conditions and/or resource requirement limitations affecting the process.

Criteria: Parameters against which the CASE tool is evaluated, and upon which selection decisions are made.

Evaluators: Those who execute the evaluation portion of the process described in this standard. They may also act in other roles (e.g., selector).

Objectives: The desired goals and results of the evaluation/ selection process in terms relevant to the organization(s) involved.

Selectors: Those who execute the selection process described in this standard. They may also act in other roles (e.g., users).

Software engineering: The application of a systematic, disciplined, quantifiable approach to the development, operation, and maintenance of software, that is, the application of engineering to software (from ANSI/IEEE 610.12-1990).

Suppliers: Those who build and/or sell the tools, or intermediate distributors of the tools.

Users: Those who use the tools. They are not necessarily those who will execute this evaluation and selection process.

User needs: The user's set of qualitative and quantitative requirements in a particular problem domain.

1.4 Introduction to the rest of the document. Section 2 of the standard provides a list of references. In Section 3, the overall approach recommended in this standard is described. A process model is given which shows the evaluation and selection processes as individual processes. A statement of user needs is required to define the scope of the evaluation and/or selection effort. A set of criteria provides the basis upon which the evaluation and/or selection is made. Several possible relationships between evaluation and selection are discussed. Tailoring of criteria and the process is discussed and the various participants in the process are identified.

In Section 4, the recommended practice for evaluation of CASE tools is given. The process begins with the development of an evaluation task definition and continues through to the development of an evaluation report. Section 5 defines the recommended practice for selection in similar terms. In Section 6, the criteria to be used in the evaluation and selection processes are discussed. The criteria themselves are defined.

2. References

The standards listed below of the exact date of issue are a part of this standard to the extent specified elsewhere in this document.

ANSI/IEEE Std 610.12-1990, IEEE Standard Glossary of Software Engineering Terminology.

IS 9126: 1991, Information technology - Software product evaluation - Quality characteristics and guidelines for their use.

IEEE Std 1074, IEEE Standard for Developing Software Lifecycle Processes.

3. Approach

The process model discussed in this section describes the most general evaluation and selection case, and illustrates the relationship between the evaluation and the selection of CASE tools. As can be seen, the evaluation and selection processes can either stand alone or work together, and each requires the application of criteria. All or any branches of these processes may need to be repeated as the needs of the user of this standard change or as additional information is obtained.

3.1 Process model. The overall process may be performed to satisfy several purposes, including:

1. The evaluation of several CASE tools and the selection of

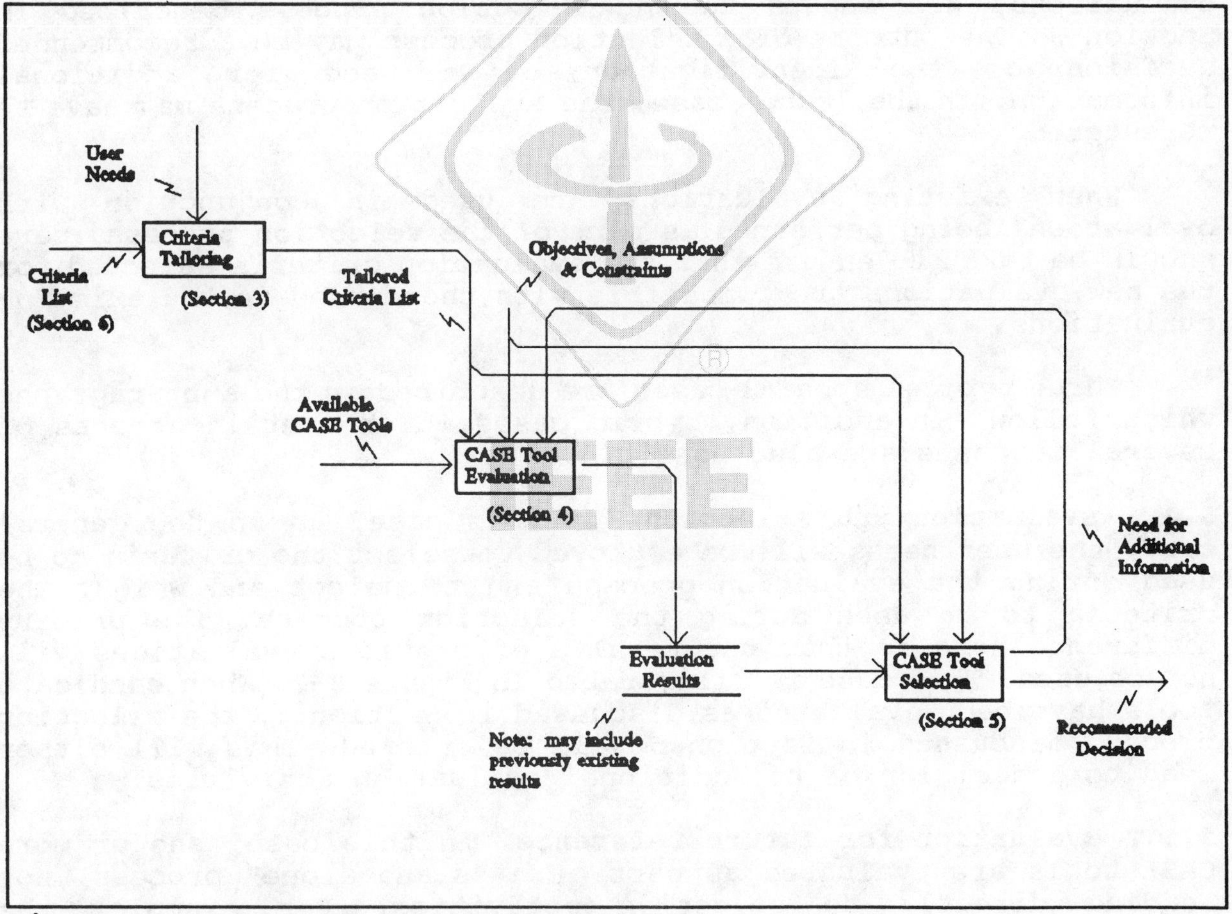

Figure 3-1: General Process Model

one or more,

2. The evaluation of one or more CASE tools with the resulting data maintained for future reference, or

3. The selection of one or more CASE tools using data from previous evaluations.

This overall process is illustrated in Figure 3-1. (Note: the figures in this section do not adhere to any specific methodology. The lines are intended to show process inputs and outputs, and illustrate the flow of information and control.) The user needs and the criteria of Section 6 are used to create a Tailored Criteria List. Based upon the tailored criteria and the other parameters, available CASE tools are evaluated using the evaluation process discussed in Section 4, leading to a set of evaluation results. These results, perhaps used along with the results of previous evaluations, are inputs to the selection process described in Section 5. The outcome of a selection process may be a recommended decision or the identification of a need for additional information. In the latter case, the evaluation process may have to re-entered.

When existing evaluations are used in conjunction with evaluations being performed as part of the selection process, care should be taken to ensure that the evaluation criteria selected for the new evaluations are compatible with those used in the existing evaluations.

Three typical special cases are described in the subparagraphs which follow. In addition, hybrid cases which contain aspects of several subcases are also possible.

3.1.1 Evaluation and selection. In this case, as in the general case, the user needs will be employed to select the criteria to be used during the evaluation process and to select and weight the criteria to be used during the selection process. The primary difference here is that the results of previous evaluations will not be used. This case is illustrated in Figure 3-2. When candidate tools have been evaluated as discussed in Section 4, the selection process discussed in Section 5 will be entered. This will either lead to a decision or to additional evaluation activities.

3.1.2 Evaluation for future reference. In this case, one or more CASE tools are evaluated as part of a "stand-alone" process, not leading directly to selection activities. For example, the evaluation(s) may be performed as a self-evaluation by a CASE tool

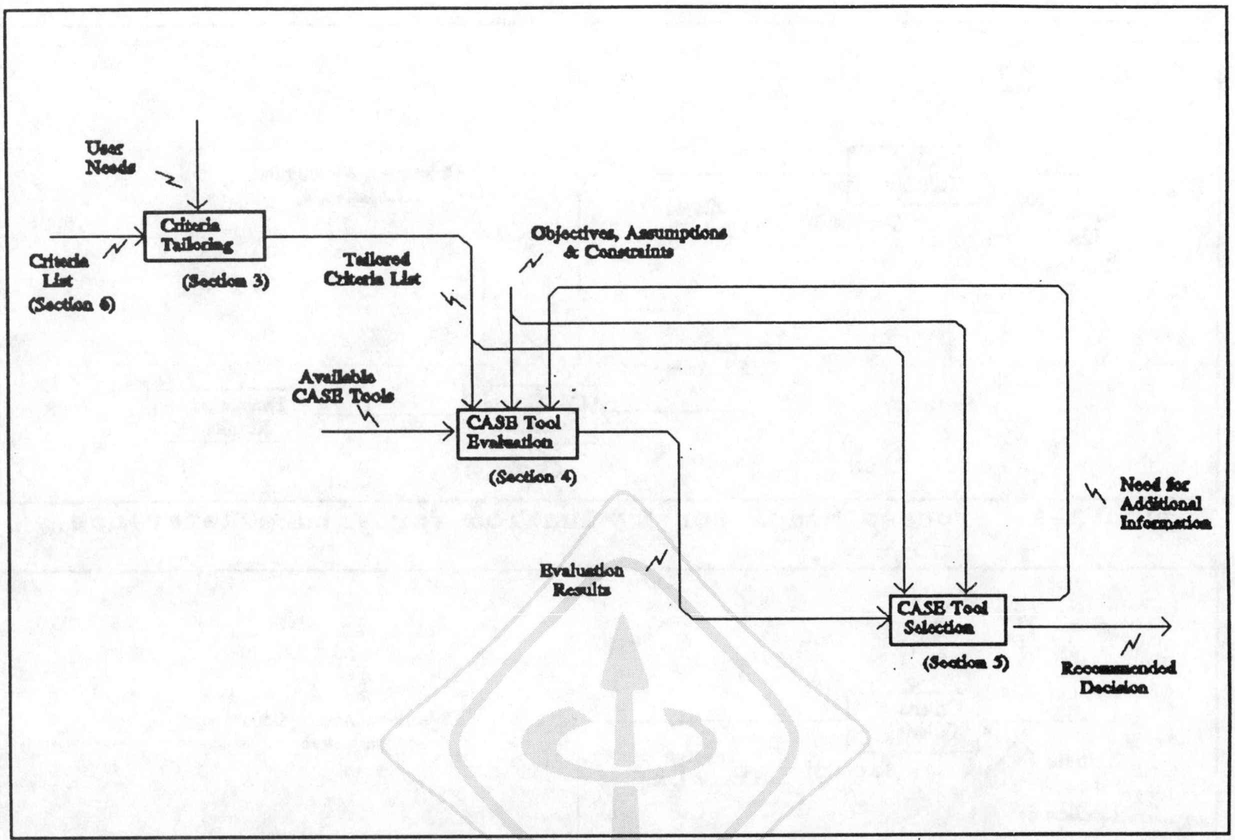

Figure 3-2: Process Model for Evaluation and Selection

supplier, for entry into a data repository by a tool evaluation organization, or for publication by a trade magazine. In this case, the evaluations should be performed against all relevant criteria, in as much as the criteria of interest to future selectors cannot be determined. This case is illustrated in Figure 3-3.

3.1.3 Selection based on previous evaluations. In this case, existing evaluations are used as the sole basis for selection. The evaluation criteria used for the various evaluations should be compared, and consideration given to the expertise, motivation, and possible biases of the organization(s) which originally performed the evaluation. This case is illustrated in Figure 3-4.

3.2 Process Elements. The elements which comprise the process include:

1. Objectives, assumptions, and constraints
2. User needs
3. Criteria

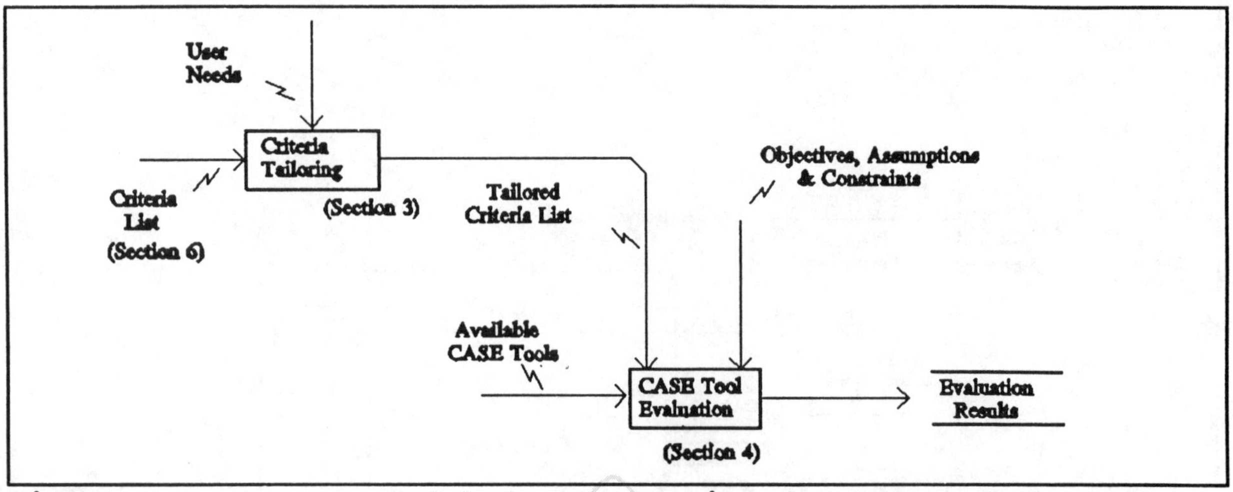

Figure 3-3: Process Model for Evaluation for Future Reference

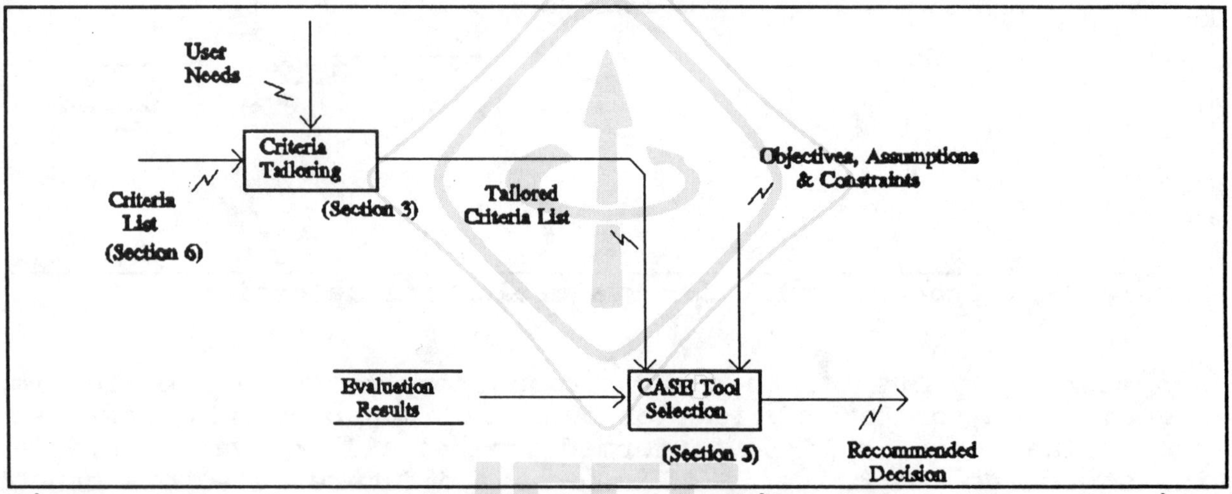

Figure 3-4: Process Model for Selection Based Upon Previous Evaluations

4. Evaluation results
5. Recommended decision

3.2.1 Objectives, assumptions, and constraints. These elements are provided as inputs to the evaluation/selection process upon its initiation. They may be further developed as part of the process.

3.2.2 User needs. The user needs are provided as an input to the evaluation/selection process upon its initiation. They reflect the user's qualitative and quantitative requirements for the CASE tool.

3.2.3 Criteria. The parameters against which the CASE tool is evaluated, and upon which selection decisions are made. Criteria may be used in evaluations, selections, or both.

3.2.4 Evaluation results. The results of evaluation activities performed on one or more CASE tools. The results are recorded formally for subsequent use in a selection process.

3.2.5 Recommended decision. The results of a selection process, usually either a recommended selection decision or a recommendation for further evaluation activities.

3.3 Process roles. The roles involved in the process include:

1. Users.
2. Suppliers.
3. Evaluators.
4. Selectors.

3.4 Tailoring. The purpose of tailoring is to adapt the contents of this document to fit the specific needs of the user of this standard.

3.4.1 Statement of user needs. Evaluation and/or selection activities can begin only when an individual, group, or organization becomes aware of specific user needs. Users of this standard should express these needs in a formal statement which reflects the user's set of qualitative and quantitative requirements in a particular problem domain. Throughout this document, the term "user needs" is understood to refer to this formal statement.

3.4.2 Tailoring of the process. The user of this standard will determine the intended sequence of activities and decisions, including the order in which selection and evaluation activities are performed, with any iteration that is necessary. For example, the process might be tailored as a decision tree, with progressive screening to select subsets of candidates for deeper evaluation. The description of the sequence of activities should identify the flow of data between the activities. This tailoring defines the context of the process as described in 3.1 (i.e., evaluation leading to selection, evaluation only, selection only).

3.4.3 Tailoring of the criteria. This standard provides evaluation/selection criteria (see Section 6) that may or may not be applicable for use in specific cases. Tailoring of the criteria is based upon user needs and will normally include:

- selection of criteria from Section 6 for use,
- identification of additional criteria (not found in Section 6) for use,
- determination of the use of each criterion for evaluation, selection, or both,
- definition of one or more metrics for each criterion to be used in evaluation, and
- weighting of each criterion to be used in selection.

4. Evaluation Process

The purpose of the evaluation process is to determine a CASE tool's functionality and quality for use in a subsequent selection process.

4.1 Introduction. During the evaluation process, tools are assessed with respect to specific criteria. The results of this assessment include both objective and subjective information, as well as the identifying characteristics of each tool. These results should be recorded in an appropriate manner so they may be useful in a subsequent selection process.

To distinguish between evaluation and selection: evaluation is a process of measurement while selection is a process of applying thresholds and weights to evaluation results and arriving at decisions. The evaluation process consists of the following steps, each of which is discussed below:

- prepare an evaluation task definition statement,
- identify criteria,
- identify candidate CASE tools,
- evaluate candidate CASE tools, and
- report results.

In cases where evaluation activities are followed by selection activities, the selection process might generate a need for additional evaluation data. In such cases, one or more of the steps described below will have to be re-entered. Evaluation documentation may require revision.

4.2 Prepare an evaluation task definition statement. A task definition statement should be prepared following the steps described in the subparagraphs below. If the evaluation is being performed as part of a selection process, the evaluation task definition statement and the selection task definition statement (see 5.2) may in some cases be a single document. Alternatively, a selection task definition statement may be provided as input to the evaluation process, and if this is so, it should be used to guide the development of the evaluation task definition statement(s).

The evaluation task definition statement should be checked for consistency with the selection task definition statement and/or the statement of user needs. It should be distributed, reviewed, and agreed upon prior to performing subsequent evaluation activities.

4.2.1 Define the purpose of the evaluation. The purpose of the evaluation should be defined in terms of the objectives stated upon process initiation. The goals and desired results should be clearly stated. If the evaluation is to be performed in conjunction with a selection process, its purpose should be related to that of the selection process.

4.2.2 Define the scope of the evaluation. The scope of the evaluation should establish the desired level of detail, necessary resources, and the extent to which the results are to be applied. For example, is the intent to evaluate:

- a set of one or more specific CASE tools,
- CASE tools to support one or more specific software engineering functions, or
- CASE tools to support one or more projects or types of projects?

4.2.3 Identify assumptions and constraints. Any assumptions and constraints understood to apply to the evaluation process should be explicitly stated. Examples of assumptions and constraints include:

- Installation and training support will be available.
- The CASE tool can be evaluated on existing hardware.
- A maximum of "X" hours of computer time will be available for evaluation activities.
- A maximum of "X" hours of personnel time will be available for evaluation activities.

4.2.4 Define evaluation activities. The activities to be performed in order to complete the evaluation are defined. These will include activities necessary to tailor the criteria, identify and evaluate candidate tools, and report the results.

4.3 Identify and select evaluation criteria. Based upon the evaluation task definition statement and the user needs, the evaluation criteria to be used should be selected and defined.

Given the extensive set of potential evaluation criteria and the fact that any evaluation effort will have a finite set of resources, the criteria in Section 6 should be tailored to establish an appropriate set for application in a specific evaluation. In some cases, the user may identify additional criteria not contained in Section 6, based on the user's need.

When the final set of criteria has been identified, they should be reviewed to ensure consistency with the task definition statement.

4.4 Identify candidate CASE tools. The first step in the identification of candidate software is to create a list of possible candidates from various sources such as market surveys, CASE vendors, CASE tool digests, and other similar publications. This list of possible candidates should be consistent with the task definition statement from 4.2.

The next step in this identification process is to obtain information about the software, or obtain the tool itself, or both. This information may consist of evaluations done by independent evaluators, write-ups by CASE tool vendors, a demonstration of the software capabilities by the CASE tool vendors, and information obtained directly from actual users. Access to the CASE tool may be obtained through purchase, through an evaluation copy, or by other means.

4.5 Evaluate candidate CASE tools. The software is evaluated in comparison with each of the chosen criteria. Data can be collected in a number of ways, including, but not limited to, the following:

- examining the software and the vendor-supplied documentation,
- interviewing actual users of the software,
- examining sample output from projects that have used the software,
- viewing demonstrations and interviewing demonstrators,
- executing test cases,
- applying in pilot projects, and
- examining any available results of previous evaluations.

There are objective and subjective criteria. The results of evaluation with respect to a criterion may be binary, fall within a numeric range, be a simple numeric value, or take some other form.

For the objective criteria, the evaluation should be made by a repeatable procedure so that another evaluator should be able to produce the same results. If test cases are used, a uniform, predefined, and documented set of cases should be used.

For the subjective criteria, a CASE tool should be evaluated by more than one person or group using the same criteria. The breadth and depth of experience of the persons or groups should be documented.

The evaluation results should be recorded in a quantified manner, where possible, together with justification, where applicable. The recording of the evaluation should be done in a uniform format for ease of use in any follow-on selection process.

4.6 Report results. When an evaluation has been completed, a report should be developed containing, at a minimum, the information described in the paragraphs which follow. An evaluation report may describe the evaluation of a single tool, or may report on the evaluations of several tools, to facilitate comparison.

4.6.1 Executive summary. A summary of the evaluation activities should be provided which contains an overview of the evaluation process and a listing of major results.

4.6.2 Evaluation background. The background of the evaluation should be described, including purpose of the evaluation and desired results, the timeframe during which the evaluation was carried out, and an identification of the roles and relevant experience of the evaluators.

4.6.3 Evaluation approach. The general approach taken should be identified, including tools obtained, supporting data, and other information establishing the context and scope of evaluation effort(s). Any assumptions and constraints should be identified. The approach should be related to the task definition statement and criteria, as appropriate.

4.6.4 Tool information. Information to be provided should include:

- CASE tool name.
- CASE tool version.
- Vendor.
- Point of contact.
- Host configuration.
- Cost elements.
- Background, as appropriate.
- Description of CASE tool.

A general description of the CASE tool which might include the following:

- Software engineering processes for which the CASE tool is intended.
- Tool software environment (e.g., programming language(s) supported, operating systems, database compatibility).
- Relevant tool functions.
- Input/output structure.
- Application domain.

4.6.5 Evaluation steps. The specific steps executed in the evaluation process should be described in the detail necessary to allow the reader both to understand the scope and depth of the evaluation and to repeat the evaluation, if desired.

4.6.6 Specific results. Evaluation results should be provided in terms of the evaluation criteria. In cases where the report covers multiple tools, or where the results of this evaluation will be compared to those of other evaluations, care should be taken to ensure the results are provided in a format which facilitates comparison. Subjective results should be provided apart from objective results and supported by text describing the specific reasons for the conclusions drawn.

4.6.7 Summary and conclusions. The results should be summarized and general conclusions offered as required by the task definition statement.

4.6.8 Appendices. The final report should contain as appendices the evaluation task definition statement and the tailored criteria list.

5. Selection Process

5.1 Introduction. During the selection process, the purpose is defined and selection criteria identified and weighted. Based upon the evaluation results and the application of selection criteria, a decision is made. Beginning with user needs, this may be arrived at in three ways.

1. An evaluation is performed, and then the selection process is entered.

2. The selection process is entered, and based upon existing evaluation results the selection process is completed.

3. The selection process is entered. Required evaluation results are not available, causing the evaluation process to be entered and one or more evaluations performed. The selection process is then re-entered.

The selection and evaluation processes interact with one another. An initial screening of available tools may be performed to provide focus for a subsequent evaluation process. On the basis of the evaluation results obtained, the goals of the selection process and/or the selection criteria and their weights may require modification. In such cases, the evaluation process may have to be re-entered. When the final evaluation results have been analyzed and selection criteria applied, a recommendation may be made to acquire a tool or set of tools. Alternately, it may be found that no adequate tool exists, in which case the user of the standard can choose between recommending: developing a new tool, modifying an existing tool, or abandoning the process.

5.2 Prepare a selection task definition statement. Following the steps described in the paragraph below, a selection task definition statement should be prepared based upon the statement of user needs. It should provide necessary guidance for the development of the evaluation task definition statements if evaluations are to be performed as part of a combined evaluation/selection process.

5.2.1 Define the purpose of the selection. The purpose of the selection should be defined in terms of the objectives stated upon process initiation. Any relationship between this selection process and previous evaluations should be clearly defined.

5.2.2 Define the scope of the selection. The scope should establish the desired level of detail, resource requirements, schedule, and expected results. There are a number of parameters that may be used to establish the scope, including:

- Use of pre-screening - for example, only look at CASE tools which run on some specific platform
- Use evaluation results obtained from evaluation processes which preceded this selection process
- Use evaluation results from external sources
- Use hybrid evaluation results which are a combination of external sources and results from evaluation processes which preceded the selection process.
- Iteration, if any, of the activities described in 5.3.

5.2.3 Identify the assumptions and constraints. Any assumptions and constraints understood to apply should be explicitly stated. Examples of assumptions and constraints to the selection process include:

- Acceptable evaluations are available for all candidate tools.
- Personnel performing selection activities can devote no more than "X"% time to these activities.
- The selection process will be completed with a specified timeframe.
- The lowest cost, acceptable tool will be selected.

5.2.4 Define selection activities. The activities to be performed in order to complete the selection are defined. These will include activities necessary to identify and weight selection criteria, identify and get evaluations of candidate CASE tools, and apply the selection criteria to obtain a recommendation.

5.3 Core selection activities. The activities described in 5.3.1 through 5.3.4 form the core of the selection process. As previously described, these activities may be iterated to the extent necessary to complete the selection process. In any specific iteration, the identification and weighting of selection criteria and the identification of candidate software may be performed in either order or concurrently.

5.3.1 Identify and weight selection criteria. Based upon the selection task definition statement and user needs, criteria to be used should be selected, weighted, and their intended use defined.

If a selection is to be made based upon evaluations to be performed, the selection criteria will be chosen and this choice will have an impact on the subsequent selection of evaluation criteria. If a selection is to be made only based upon existing evaluations, the choice of the selection criteria may be constrained by the available evaluation data.

As the selection process proceeds, the additional knowledge gained may indicate the need to modify the selection criteria. Criteria may be added, deleted or modified and/or weights changed. The selection approach itself may require modification. All such changes should be clearly documented (as notes in a revised tailored criteria list) and justified to provide for traceability of the process.

5.3.2 Identify candidate CASE tools. The identification and screening of the candidate software depends on whether any previous identifications or evaluations of CASE tools have been conducted. For the case when prior identifications and evaluations have been performed, no further identification of candidate software may be necessary, and previously obtained results from 4.4 can be utilized. When the user plans to use existing evaluations as a basis for selection, use the process described in 3.1.3. When the user plans to perform subsequent identifications of CASE tools, use the process described in 4.4. In any case, the user of this standard should note that software offerings change rapidly, and should ensure that the products considered are the latest appropriate versions, and that recent offerings are included.

5.3.3 Get evaluation results. After the initial screening process, the user should record the evaluation results for the identified software. If evaluation data are available from other evaluation sources, then all the data should be put in the same format for comparison purposes. If at this time, the available evaluation data are not sufficient to allow the selection process to proceed, the evaluation process may have to be re-entered to obtain the necessary data.

5.3.4 Apply weighted selection criteria to evaluation results. At this point in a selection process, one or more evaluations will have been performed and their results will be available. In each case, the results will include each CASE tool's measurement on each criterion. In the case that evaluations were performed using different sets of criteria, or using specific criteria in somewhat different ways, the evaluation data should be put into compatible form. When this step is complete, each candidate tool will be measured via a common set of criteria which are directly comparable.

A selection algorithm is now applied. The user of this standard will define such an algorithm based upon the specific aspects of the selection process. Algorithms commonly in use include scale-based algorithms, rank-based algorithms, and cost-based algorithms:

1. Scale-based algorithms calculate a single value for each tool by multiplying the weight given each criterion by its score (on a scale) and adding all such products. The CASE tool with the highest score is ranked first.
2. Rank-based algorithms use the rankings of the candidate tools on individual criteria or groups of criteria in place of the score on a scale. As above, the ranks of the CASE tools are then combined and an overall ranking is generated.
3. Cost-based algorithms identify some minimal acceptable level of capability (based upon the criteria) and identify all tools providing that capability. The acceptable tools are then ranked according to cost.

5.3.5 Selection assessment. At this point, the selection process may be considered complete. An algorithm has been applied, a highest-ranked tool has been identified and its use can be recommended. However, it may be appropriate to perform a sensitivity analysis to determine whether the difference in the scores of candidate tools are sensitive to specific key criteria. Such an analysis will determine whether tool rankings are affected by arbitrary weighting of criteria. It also can be used to identify where significant differences lie between candidate CASE tools with very close overall scores or rankings.

If no candidate tool meets minimum criteria, the core selection activities, possibly including evaluation activities, may be repeated with different candidate tools.

If there is no significant difference between leading candidates, additional information can be obtained by repeating core selection activities, possibly including evaluation activities, using additional or different criteria.

5.4 Recommend selection. The selection recommendation should clearly specify the reasons for the recommendation. It may be found that no adequate CASE tool exists, in which case alternatives such as modifying existing software, developing a new CASE tool, or abandoning the process may need to be considered.

6. Criteria

6.1 Introduction. Criteria form the basis for the evaluation and selection processes. Criteria, as discussed in this standard, take many forms: measures over a broad range, such as the amount of memory required for tool use; measures over a restricted range of values, such as ease of learning on a scale of 1 to 5; measures which are either true/false or yes/no, such as the capability to generate Postscript® output; and measures which can take on one or more of a finite set of values, such as platforms for which the tool is supported. A typical evaluation and/or selection process would make use of a set of criteria of various types.

Each criterion will be selected and tailored by the evaluator/selector based upon the characteristics of the specific process being performed as described in 3.4.3, 4.3, 5.3, and elsewhere in this standard. In most cases, only some of the many criteria described in this section will be appropriate for use, and additional criteria not found here will be added.

6.2 Use of criteria. A critical step in an evaluation and/or selection process is the selection and definitization of a set of criteria which will be used. Criteria are the means whereby the characteristics of the CASE tool are quantified and measured.

6.2.1 Criteria Definitization. When one of the criteria in 6.4 is selected for use in an evaluation or selection, the user of this standard should definitize the scope of the criterion. Many criteria are "checklist" type; they are essentially lists of closely related capabilities that a tool may or may not provide (e.g., languages supported). The user of this standard should identify the list elements of interest (e.g., C, Ada, and Pascal). Other criteria require additional definition in order to be applicable to a specific evaluation or selection activity. Criteria identified for use which are not contained in 6.4 should also be definitized as above.

6.2.2 Use of Criteria for Evaluation. When a criterion has been fully defined, its use in the evaluation process should be specified. The metric by which the criterion will be measured should be identified and the means whereby the metric value will be obtained should be defined. The value of a metric may be binary (e.g., capability is present or absent), may fall within a numeric range (e.g. ease of use on a scale of 1 to 10), may be a simple numeric value (e.g., "X" Mbytes required for execution) or

Postscript® is a registered trademark of Adobe Systems Inc

may take some other form. For "checklist" type criteria, the metric should identify the presence or absence of items of interest, and the quality of the items present, where appropriate.

6.2.3 Use of Criteria for Selection. In many cases, selection criteria are also evaluation criteria and have the same meaning in both processes. In cases where the usage is different in selection, the difference should be clearly defined.

In addition, in the selection process the weight (relative or absolute) of each criterion should be defined, and the method by which the criterion will be used in conjunction with other criteria in the selection algorithm should be specified.

6.3 Criteria granularity. The level of detail at which each of the criteria are evaluated will depend upon the relative importance of individual criteria with respect to the user's needs, and the particular version of the process model being followed. In particular, in the case of:

Evaluation only:

The user should estimate the greatest level of detail for each criterion required by future selectors and document that level of detail.

Evaluation then selection:

a. If the evaluation will be used as a part of future selection processes, proceed the same as above.

b. If the evaluation results will be used one time only, use the greatest level of detail necessary for the single project.

Selection from previous evaluation:

The level of detail is already established. If it is not satisfactory, the user should determine the necessary level of detail and re-enter the evaluation process.

6.4 Evaluation and selection criteria. The criteria defined in this section are intended to serve as the basic set of criteria for the evaluation and selection of CASE tools. The criteria are organized in accordance with ISO/IEC 9126: 1991, Information technology - Software product evaluation - Quality characteristics and guidelines for their use, with an additional section added to

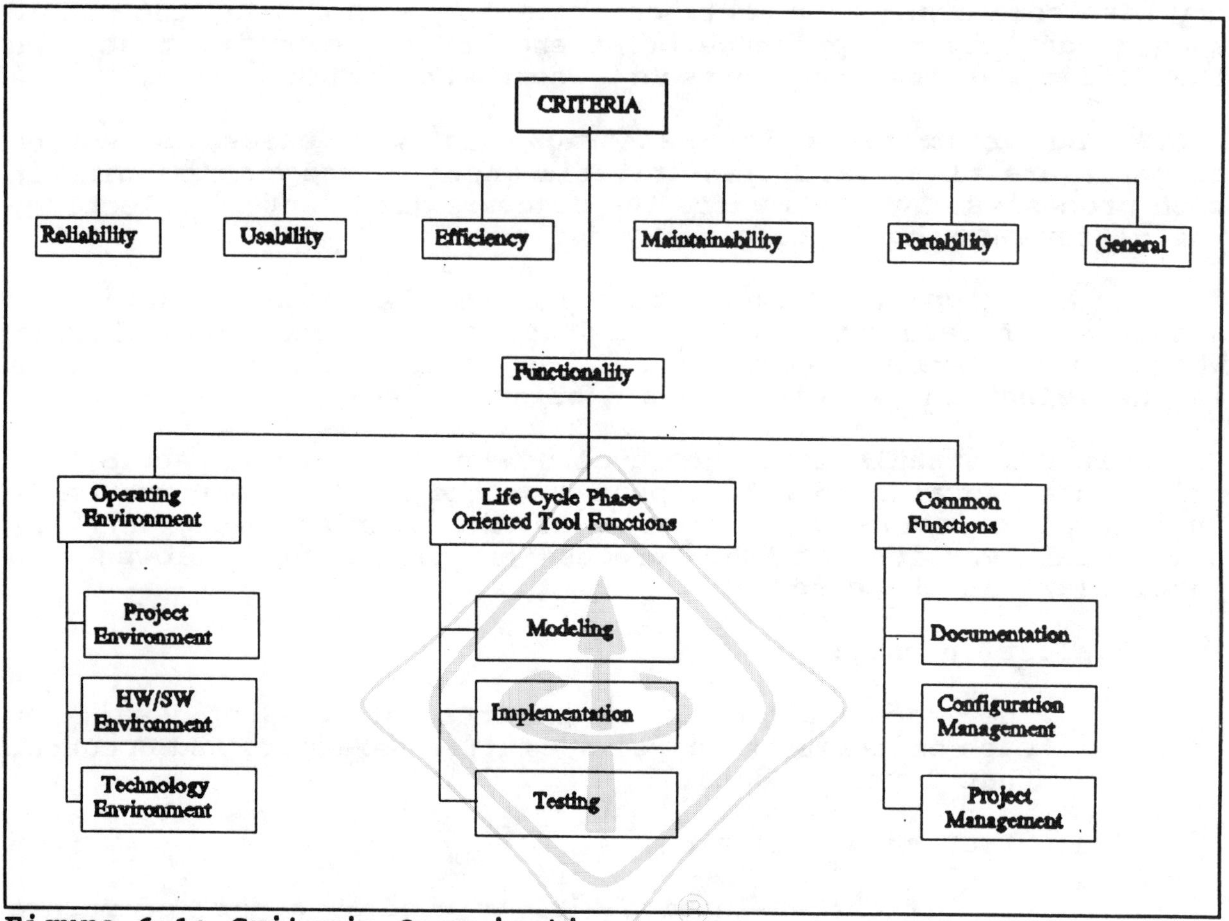

Figure 6-1: Criteria Organization

include general information not addressed in ISO/IEC 9126. The organization is depicted in Figure 6-1. For clarity, the *Functionality* group is further subdivided into criteria subsets which describe the tool's operating environment, its support for specific life cycle activities, and its support for functions common across several life cycle phases.

6.4.1 Functionality. The first class of criteria are intended to define the functionality of the tool. Functional criteria are subdivided into those which are specific to the operating environment, to a life cycle phase, or which are applicable across life cycle phases.

6.4.1.1 Operating environment. The criteria defining the operating environment are grouped into project environment, hardware/software environment, and technology environment.

6.4.1.1.1 Project Environment. The following criteria define the project-related aspects of the tool.

Life Cycle Process Support: the set of life cycle activities which the CASE tool supports. Examples of activities include requirements analysis, design, implementation, test and evaluation, maintenance, quality assurance, configuration management and project management, and are dependent upon the life cycle model adopted by the user of this standard.

Domain of Application: the application domains which the CASE tool is designed to support. Examples of application domains include transaction processing, real-time, information management, and safety critical, among others.

Size of Application Supported: the identification of size limitations of the tool which would limit its applicability. Such limitations might involve lines of code, levels of nesting, size of data base, number of data elements, and number of configuration items, among others.

6.4.1.1.2 Hardware/software environment. The following criteria relate the tool to the hardware/software environment in which it will be operated.

Hardware Required: the hardware required for operating the CASE tool, including choices of host processors, memory and disk storage requirements, among others.

Hardware Supported: the hardware items that can be used with the CASE tool. An example is input/output devices.

Software Required: the software required for operating the CASE tool, including choices of operating systems and windowing environments, among others.

Software Supported: the software packages that can be used with the CASE tool.

6.4.1.1.3 Technology environment. The following criteria define the technological breadth of the tool.

Conformance to Environmental Standards: a listing of all of the environmentally-oriented standards supported by the CASE tool. Such standards address language, data base, repository, communication, graphical user interface, documentation, development, configuration management, security, information interchange standards, and data, control or user-interface integration, among others.

Compatibility with Other Tools: a definition of the CASE tool's capability to interoperate with and/or directly exchange data with other software tools. Examples of other software tools include word processors and other documentation tools, data bases, repositories, and other CASE tools, among others.

Methodology Support: the set of methods and techniques which the CASE tool supports. Examples include Object Oriented Analysis, Object Oriented Design, and Top Down Design, among others.

Language Support: all languages in the operational domain of the CASE tool. Examples of such languages include programming languages (e.g. COBOL, Ada, C), data and query languages (e.g. Data Definition Language (DDL), Structured Query Language (SQL)), graphics languages (e.g. Postscript, Hewlett-Packard Graphics Language (HPGL), requirement and design languages, and operating system interfaces such as job control languages.

6.4.1.2 Life cycle phase-oriented tool functions. The following criteria define tool functions which are specific to life cycle phase-oriented groups: modeling, implementation, and test and evaluation.

6.4.1.2.1 Modeling. Modeling criteria are those which help define a CASE tool's capability to support the functions necessary to identify software requirements, to express software design, and to transform requirements into design. Modeling criteria include:

Diagramming: the capability of entering and editing diagram types which are of interest to the user. Typical diagram types include: Bachman, Block, Chen, Control Flow, Data Flow, Decomposition, Entity-Relationship, HIPO, Jackson, Nassi-Schneiderman, Object Oriented, Petri Net, State Transition, Structure Charts, and Warnier-Orr diagrams, among others.

Graphic Analysis: the capability of analyzing graphical figures input to the CASE tool and extracting and storing requirements and/or design information. Graphic analyzers are, in many cases, integrated with diagramming tools.

Requirement Specification Entry & Editing: the capability of entering and editing requirements definition and specification data. Classes of requirements information which may be considered include: function, data, interface, quality, performance, hardware, environment, cost, and schedule requirements, among others.

Requirement Specification Language: the capability of the tool to import, export, or edit requirements information using a formal language.

Design Specification Entry & Editing: the capability of entering and editing design description and/or specification data. Classes of design information which may be considered include: function, data, interface, structure, quality, performance, hardware, among others.

Design Specification Language: the capability of the tool to import, export, or edit design information using a formal language.

Data Modeling: the capability of entering and editing information describing the data elements of a system and their relationships.

Process Modeling: the capability of entering and editing information describing the process elements of a system and their relationships.

Simulation: the capability of simulating aspects of a system's potential operation based upon requirements and/or design data available to the CASE tool, including system effectiveness (operational utility), operator interface, and architectural performance (response time, utilization, throughput).

Prototyping: the capability of designing and generating a preliminary version of all or portions of a system based upon requirements and/or design data available to the CASE tool.

Screen Generation: the capability of generating display screens based upon requirements and/or design data available to the CASE tool.

Traceability: the capability to perform a traceability analysis relating system requirements specifications to software requirements specifications to design data to source code to test specifications, and to provide the results of the analysis to the user.

Specification Consistency and Completeness Checking: the capability to perform an analysis of the specification data available to the tool in order to identify any cases of inconsistent specifications or cases where entities are referenced but not specified, and to provide the results of the analysis to the user.

Other Analysis: the capability to perform analyses of the existing requirements and design data available to the tool and provide the results to the user. Specific additional types of analyses might include: algorithm, control flow, data flow, data normalization, data use, interface, man-machine interface, range bound, and structure, among others.

Report Designing: the capability to automate the design of reports to be produced by the system under development.

6.4.1.2.2 Implementation. Implementation refers to functions performed to produce operational (e.g., executable) elements of the final system to be fielded, or to modify an existing system. Many of the criteria in this paragraph are dependent upon a specific language or languages. Examples of such languages include programming languages (e.g., COBOL, Ada, C), data and query languages (e.g., DDL, SQL), graphics languages (e.g., Postscript), and operating system interfaces such as job control languages. The user of this standard should identify those languages relevant to the specific effort. Implementation criteria include:

Syntax Directed Editing: the capability of entering source code in one or more specific languages with syntax support provided by the editor.

Code Generation: the capability of generating code in one or more specific languages based upon design data available to the CASE tool. Types of code generated may include general purpose code, data base, query, screen display/menu, and graphics, among others.

Data Base Schema Generation: the capability of generating data base schema based upon user-supplied information.

Compilation: the capability of compiling code in one or more specific languages.

Source Code Conversion: the capability of inputting existing source code in one or more specific languages, translating it into a different language, and outputting the resulting code.

Reliability Analysis: the capability to analyze the measures of software reliability, such as cyclomatic complexity, software science attributes, test coverage, and the number of remaining errors, among others.

Reverse Engineering: the capability of inputting existing source code in one or more specific languages, extracting design data, and providing the results to the user. Examples of typical outputs include design language code, and direct entry of design data into the CASE tool's data base.

Source Code Restructuring: the capability of inputting existing source code in one or more specific languages, modifying its format and/or structure, and outputting a source code file in the same language. Examples of typical capabilities are pretty printers and source-level optimizers.

Source Code Analysis: the capability of inputting existing source code in one or more specific languages, performing analyses, and providing the results to the user. Examples of such analyses include the measurements of size, calculation of complexity metrics, generation of cross-references, and review for conformance to standard usages, among others.

Debugging: the capability to support the identification and isolation of errors in a program. Typical capabilities include tracing program execution, providing tracebacks, traps, identifying fault location and frequently executed code segments in terms of source code, among others.

6.4.1.2.3 Testing. Testing criteria are those which help define a CASE tool's capability to support the test functions necessary to develop, deliver and maintain software; they include:

Test Definition: the capability of the CASE tool to support user definition of testing. Typical capabilities include test case entry, test case generation, test data generation, expected result entry, and expected result generation, among others.

Operator Input Capture and Replay: the extent to which the CASE tool can capture operator inputs (keyboard, mouse, etc.) and the extent to which such data can be edited and replayed in subsequent test cases.

Test Driving: the extent to which the CASE tool can automatically execute test cases.

Regression Testing: the extent to which the CASE tool supports regression testing. For example, the capability to re-run previous tests; the capability to modify previous tests to account for system and/or environmental differences (e.g. date, time), among others.

Test Result Analysis: the capability of the CASE tool to automatically analyze test results. Typical capabilities include comparison of expected and actual results, file comparison, and statistical analysis of results, among others.

Test Coverage Analysis: the capabilities provided by the CASE tool for the instrumentation of source code and the analysis and reporting of test coverage. For example, statements which were/were not executed, procedures which were/were not called, and variables which were/were not accessed, among others.

Performance Analysis: the capability of analyzing the performance of a program as it executes. Performance parameters analyzed may include cpu utilization, memory utilization, accesses to specified data elements and/or code segments, and timing characteristics, among others.

Run-Time Assertion Verification: the capability of the CASE tool to verify and report on assertions (or exceptions) during test execution.

Environment Simulation: the extent of simulation capabilities provided by the CASE tool in support of the test process. For example, the capability to automatically generate simulated systems inputs based upon received system outputs.

Scaffolding: the extent to which the CASE tool supports the scaffolding process. For example, the automatic generation of body stubs for top-down testing or the automatic generation of driver procedures for bottoms-up testing.

6.4.1.3 Common functions. The following criteria define tool functions which span multiple life cycle phases. The three common areas of functionality are: documentation, configuration management, and project management. Supporting all of these areas, and other areas as well is a data repository.

Data Repository: the existence of a repository which houses all relevant data input to and output from the tool.

6.4.1.3.1 Documentation. Criteria which define a tool's capability to support documentation development include:

Text Editing: the text editing capabilities of the CASE tool.

Graphical Editing: the capability of the CASE tool to enter and edit data in graphical format.

Forms-Based Editing: the capability of the CASE tool to support user definition of forms and subsequent forms-based editing.

Publishing: the desktop publishing capabilities provided by the CASE tool.

Hypertext Support: the capability of the CASE tool to support hypertext formats and functions.

Conformance to Documentation Standards: the documentation standards in accordance with which the CASE tool can produce output.

Automatic Data Extraction and Document Generation: the extent to which the CASE tool can extract textual and graphical data and generate a document as specified by the user.

6.4.1.3.2 Configuration Management. Criteria which define a tool's capability to support configuration management activities include:

Access and Change Control: the capability provided by the CASE tool to control physical access to data elements and to provide for change control. Access control includes the capability to specify components to be read only access, no access, etc., based upon work groups, or other similar identifier, as well as the capability to check-out data elements for modification and restrict access to them (locking) until they have been updated and checked back in (unlocking).

Tracking of Modifications: the capability of the CASE tool to maintain a record of all modifications made to the system under development or maintenance.

Version Management: the capability of the CASE tool to maintain records and perform management functions on multiple versions of a system which may share common components.

Configuration Status Accounting: the capability of the CASE tool to provide the user with reports defining the history, contents and status of the various configuration items being managed.

Release Generation: the capability of the CASE tool to support user definition of steps required to create a version (build) of the software for release, and to automatically execute those steps.

Archival Capability: the capability of the CASE tool to automatically archive data elements for subsequent retrieval.

6.4.1.3.3 Project Management. Criteria which define a tool's capability to support project management activities include:

Estimation: the capability of the CASE tool to estimate cost, schedule and other project parameters based upon user inputs. For example, various implementations of COCOMO.

Activity & Resource Management: the capability of supporting user entry of project planning data, actual activity data, and the analysis of the data. Typical data elements include schedule, computer resources, personnel allocations, and budget, among others. Also included is the capability of defining the project environment (management-oriented) including calendar, working hours, and holidays, among others.

Test Procedure Management: the extent to which the CASE tool supports management of test activities and a test program. For example, the capability to maintain a schedule of planned activities, capture and record the results of test activities, and generate status reports, among others.

Quality Management: the capability of the CASE tool to: support user entry of quality data, analyze quality data, and generate quality management reports.

Corrective Action: the capability of the CASE tool to support the management of corrective action activities, including support for problem report handling.

6.4.2 Reliability. The following criteria provide indicators of the tool's reliability:

Data Integrity: the capability of the tool to correctly store and retrieve information with a high degree of confidence.

Automatic Backup: the capability of the CASE tool to automatically initiate a backup routine to save the current state of the process. Typically backups are scheduled at a predetermined interval by the vendor or are scheduled by the user.

Security: the capability of the tool to prevent unauthorized use or misuse of itself.

Error Handling Capability: the capability of the tool to detect abnormal behavior, notify the user that a problem has occurred, and properly exit or save the work to the point of interruption. This may include error messages displayed to the screen and a screen directed means of either exiting or saving.

Hazard Analysis: the capability of the tool to support hazard analysis in critical applications.

6.4.3 Usability. The following criteria provide indicators of the tool's usability:

Consistency of User Interface: the consistency of various elements of the user interface, including: the locations and representations of commonly appearing display elements, and user input methods, among others.

Internationalization: the degree to which the CASE tool satisfies any legal and/or cultural requirements specific to the location of the user.

Ease of Learning: the amount of time and effort required for a user to understand normal CASE tool operations and to become productive.

Customizability: the capability of the CASE tool to be adapted by the user to meet user-specific needs, including different character sets, character and graphic presentation modes (left-right, top-bottom), different date formats, input and output methods (macros, screen displays and formats), and changes of methodology, among others.

Tool Documentation Quality: the overall quality of the documentation provided with the tool; factors include: completeness, clarity, readability, and usefulness, among others.

Availability and Quality of Training Materials: training materials to be considered include on-line materials (e.g., tutorials), training manuals, training courses, and visual materials such as video tapes. Both the availability of materials and their quality are to be considered.

Knowledge Requirements: the background, and levels of experience and expertise required for effective tool use.

Ease of Operations: the extent to which the tool is easy to operate, both for beginning and experienced users.

User Interface Commonality: the commonality of user interface between the CASE tool and other tools in the target environment.

On-Line Help: the completeness and quality of any on-line help function provided by the tool.

Clarity of Diagnostics: the understandability and usefulness of diagnostic messages received by the user.

Acceptable Response Time: acceptability of the time required for the CASE tool to respond to a user input with the appropriate response in the expected operational environment.

Ease of Installation: The extent to which the tool is easy to install, both initially and for subsequent updates.

6.4.4 Efficiency. The following criteria provide indicators of the tool's efficiency. In evaluating a CASE tool against these criteria, consideration should be given to jobs of both typical and maximal size.

Optimal Data Storage Requirements: the amount of mass storage required (e.g. disk, tape) to accommodate the tool and any data required and/or generated by the tool at an acceptable level of performance.

Optimal Memory Requirements: the amount of cpu addressable memory required to load and operate the tool at an acceptable level of performance.

Optimal Processor Requirements: the processor (type and speed) required to operate the CASE tool at an acceptable level of performance.

Workload Efficiency: the efficiency of the tool in providing user services as a function of the required user inputs. For example, the number of keystrokes or clicks required to perform certain functions.

Performance: the performance of the tool in performing specific tasks (e.g., query response time, time to analyze 100,000 lines of code). In some cases, performance benchmark data are available from external sources.

6.4.5 Maintainability. The following criteria provide indicators of the tool's maintainability which are visible to the user:

Responsiveness: the capability of the vendor to provide updates addressing recognized and notified problems, new versions, and/or provide additional capabilities in a timely fashion.

Update Traceability: the capability of the vendor to provide updates whose differences from previous versions are easy to understand.

Update Compatibility: the capability of the vendor to provide updates compatible with previous versions of the tool. Examples of compatibility include data (input or output) compatibility.

Delivered Product Maintainability: the ease with which the delivered product can be updated by the user in the field, including the ease of updating documentation (e.g., via change pages inserted into a binder).

6.4.6 Portability. The following criteria provide indicators of the tool's portability:

Compatibility With Versions of OS: the capability of a CASE tool to run on various versions of the same operating system, and the ease with which it can be modified to run on updates to the operating system.

Ability to Move Data Between Versions of the Tool: the capability of one version of the tool to use data generated by a different version of the tool, and the extent of data manipulation required for reuse.

Conformance to Portability Standards: the extent to which the tool conforms to standards which are relevant to portability.

Such standards include documentation standards, communication and user interface standards, windowing systems, and programming and query language standards, among others.

6.4.7 General. The following criteria are general in nature, and do not fall within the set of quality indicators provided in IS 9126. The user of this standard wish to organize these criteria into subcategories for clarity and to appropriately emphasize areas of interest and/or concern to the organization.

Cost of Tool Implementation: includes purchase price, installation, initial maintenance, and training. Price data on all relevant configurations should be considered, including single copy, multiple copies, site license, corporate license, and network license.

Estimated Tool Affect: the expected affect of the tool on the user organization, including level of productivity, quality, cycle time, among others. This may require a cost/benefit analysis.

Development/Delivery Constraints: any schedule constraints involving further product development and/or delivery.

Supplier Profile: a general indication of the supplier's overall capability. Such a profile might include the supplier's size, number of years in business, a financial statement, listing of any complementary products, identification of relevant business relationships (e.g., other tool suppliers), and the company's planned direction for future development.

Vendor Certification: the certification of a professionally recognized software engineering evaluation organization (e.g., the Software Engineering Institute, the ISO) that the software engineering practices of the vendor meet some minimum level, or are at some defined level. Certification may be informal, for example by reviewing vendor-supplied quality/defect data.

Licensing Policies: the available license options, the right to copy (media and documentation), and any restrictions and/or fees for secondary usage (i.e., the tool user sells products which include some element or aspect of a tool used to develop the product).

Export Restrictions: restrictions on the export of the product, or on any secondary usage of the product.

Product Profile: general information including: product age, number of paid installations, existence, size and level of activity of a user's group, formal problem reporting system, product development program, body of applications, freedom from error, and availability (commercial, government, public domain, in-house, or under development).

Vendor Support: the availability, responsiveness, and quality of services provided by the vendor to tool users. Such support services might include telephone support, local technical support, and on-site support.

Availability and Quality of Training: Training may be provided at the vendor's site, the user's site, elsewhere, or may be self-administered. Both the availability and quality are to be considered.

Workarounds Required for User Organization: workarounds which would be required to implement the CASE tool in the user's environment. An example of such a workaround is finding a way to use a centralized tool (single common data base) in a distributed environment.

IEEE

IEEE Std 1219-1992

IEEE Standard for Software Maintenance

Sponsor

Software Engineering Standards Subcommittee of the Technical Committee on Software Engineering of the IEEE Computer Society

Approved December 3, 1992

IEEE Standards Board

The Institute of Electrical and Electronics Engineers, Inc.
345 East 47th Street, New York, NY 10017-2394, USA

STANDARD FOR SOFTWARE MAINTENANCE

SPONSOR

Software Engineering Standard Subcommittee
of the
IEEE Computer Society

PREPARED BY

Software Maintenance Working Group

IEEE Standards Department
Copyright and Permissions
445 Hoes Lane, P. O. Box 1331
Piscataway, NJ 08855-1331, USA

Foreword

(This Foreword is not part of IEEE P1219, IEEE Standard for Software Maintenance.)

Overview

This standard describes the process for managing and executing software maintenance activities. Section 1 lists references to other standards useful in applying this standard. Section 2 provides a set of definitions and acronyms that either are not found in other standards, or have been modified for use with this standard. Section 3 contains required information pertaining to the Software Maintenance process. In order to be in compliance with this standard, Section 3 must be adhered to.

Appendix A, Maintenance Guidelines, contains additional information that is not required for compliance. Topics in this Appendix include: the source of Maintenance forms discussed in the standard, Validation and Verification (V&V), Software Quality Assurance, Risk Assessment, Safety, Security, Software Configuration Management (SCM), Metrics, Software Replacement Policy, and the Maintenance Process. Appendix B, Supporting Maintenance Technology, includes the topics Reengineering, Reverse Engineering, Reuse, Maintenance Planning, Impact Analysis, and Software Tools.

Audience

The audience of this standard is: software development managers, maintainers, Software Quality Assurance personnel, SCM personnel, programmers, and researchers.

Participants

This standard was developed by a working group consisting of the following members who attended two or more meetings, provided text, or submitted comments on more than two drafts of the standards.

D. Vera Edelstein
Chair

Salvatore Mamone
Secretary

Shawn A. Bohner
Robert Dufresne
Gregory Haines
Moisey Lerner
Rita Costello
Frank Douglas
Alan Huguley
Julio Gonzalez Sanz

Ben Scheff
Carl Seddio
Ahlam Shalhout
Malcolm Slovin
Edwin Summers
Richard Weiss
Ralph Wootton

Contributors

The following individuals also contributed to the development of the standard by attending one meeting or providing comments on one or two drafts.

Ray Abraham
Joseph Barrett
James E. Cardow
Neva Carlson
Sharon Cobb
Sandra Falcone
Mari Georges
Meinhard Hoffman
T. S. Katsoulakos
Thomas Kurihura
Robert Leif
Suzanne Leif
K.C. Leung
Yuan Liu
John Lord
Kenneth Mauer
Basil Sherlund
Harry Sneed
Harry Trivedi
Bob Walsh

The following persons were on the Ballot Group that approved this document for submission to the IEEE Standards Board:

Ron Berlack
William Boll
Fletccher Buckley
Kay Bydalek
Evelyn Dow
Einar Dragstedt
Vera Edelstein
Caroline Evans
John Fendrich
Kirby Fortenberry
Yar Gershkovitch
David Gustafson
John Harauz
John Horch
Roy Ko
Robert Kosinski
Thomas Kurihara
Robert Lane
Boniface Lau
Moisey Lerner
Ben Livson
Joseph Maayan
Kukka Marijarvi
Roger Martin
Ivano Mazza
James Perry
Andrew Sage
Julio Gonzalez Sanz
Stephen Schach
Hans Schaefer
David Schultz
Gregory Schumacher

D.M. Siefert
Al Sorkowitz
Richard Thayer
Leonard Tripp
William Walsh
Natalie Yopconka

Malcom Slovin
Vijaya Srivastava
George Tice
Dolores Wallace
Robert Wells
Janusz Zalewski

Acknowledgments

Participants in the working group were individually supported by their employers with travel expenses and working days. This support does not constitute or imply approval or endorsement of this standard. These organizations were:

Computer Sciences Corporation
Eastman Kodak Company
FISERV - CBS Division
Naval Undersea Warfare Center
NYNEX Corp.
Scheff Associates
Softran Corp.
Software Management Technologies
Sanford Process Corp.
Tomin Corp.
United States Marine Corps
Weiss Associates

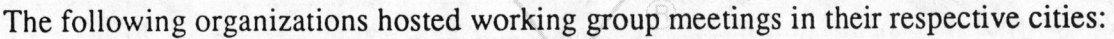

The following organizations hosted working group meetings in their respective cities:

Computer Sciences Corporation
Naval Undersea Warfare Center
NYNEX Corporation

NYNEX provided word processing support as well as assistance with mailings.

Contents

List of Figures

List of Tables

IEEE Standard for Software Maintenance

1. Scope and References

1.1 Scope. This standard describes an iterative process for managing and executing software maintenance activities. Use of this standard is not restricted by size, complexity, criticality, or application of the software product. This standard uses the process model, depicted in Figure 3, to discuss and depict each phase of software maintenance. The criteria established apply to both the planning of maintenance for software while under development, as well as the planning and execution of software maintenance activities for existing software products. Ideally, maintenance planning should begin during the planning for software development (See Appendix A3 for guidance).

This standard prescribes requirements for process, control, and management of the planning, execution, and documentation of the software maintenance activities. In totality, the requirements constitute a minimal set of criteria that are necessary and sufficient conditions for conformance to this standard. Users of this standard may incorporate other items by reference or as text to meet their specific needs.

The basic process model includes input, process, output, and control for software maintenance. Metrics/measures captured for maintenance should enable the manager to manage the process and the implementor to implement the process. (see Figure 4) This standard does not presuppose the use of any particular development model (e.g., waterfall, spiral, etc).

This standard provides additional software maintenance guidance on associated topics in Appendix A, "Maintenance Guidelines"; and tools/technology assistance in Appendix B, "Supporting Maintenance Technology".

1.2 References. The following standards are directly referenced in this standard. Figure 2 provides a cross-reference of IEEE standards which address various topics related to software maintenance. These standards are binding to the extent specified within the text of this standard and are referenced to avoid duplication of requirements.

[1] IEEE Std 610.12-1990, IEEE Glossary of Software Engineering Terminology (ANSI)
[2] IEEE Std 730-1989, Software Quality Assurance Plans (ANSI)
[3] IEEE Std 828-1990, Standard for Software Configuration Management Plans (ANSI)
[4] IEEE Std 829-1983, Standard for Software Test Documentation
[5] IEEE Std 982.1-1988, Standard Dictionary of Measures to Produce Reliable Software (ANSI)
[6] IEEE Std 982.2-1988, Guide for the Use of IEEE Standard Dictionary of Measures to Produce Reliable Software (ANSI)
[7] IEEE Std 983-1986, Guide for Software Quality Assurance Planning (ANSI)
[8] IEEE Std 1012-1986, Standard Software Verification and Validation Plans (ANSI)
[9] IEEE Std 1028-1988, Standard for Software Reviews and Audits (ANSI)
[10] IEEE Std 1042-1987, Guide to Software Configuration Management (ANSI)

[11] IEEE Std 1058.1-1987, Standard for Software Project Management Plans (ANSI)
[12] IEEE Std 1074-1992, Standard for Software Life Cycle Processes

1.3 Terminology. The words *shall* and *must* identify the mandatory (essential) material within this standard. The words *should* and *may* identify optional (conditional) material. The terminology in this standard is based on the Glossary of Software Engineering Terminology (IEEE Std 610.12-1990 [1]). New terms and modified definitions as applied in this standard are included in Section 2.

1.4 Conventions. The following explains the conventions used in each figure depicting a maintenance phase.

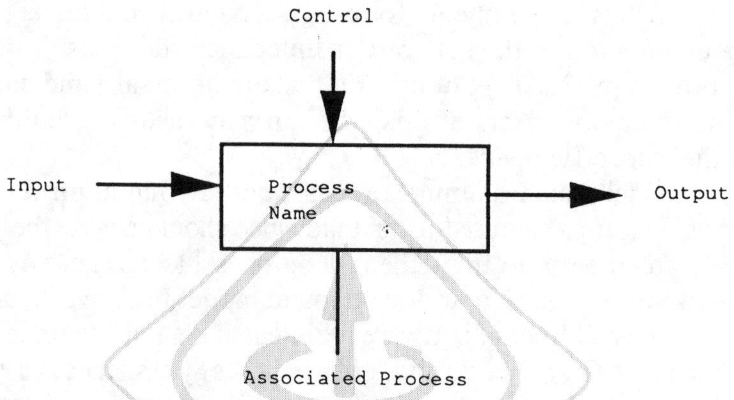

Figure 1 Conventions

Associated processes refer to such external processes that are defined in other standards, i.e., Software Quality Assurance, Software Configuration Management, V & V. Associated processes also refer to the metrics process illustrated within this document.

	IEEE STANDARD							
PROCESS								
Problem Id/Classification								
Analysis	830-1984	1074-1991						
Design	830-1984	1016-1987	1074-1991					
Implementation	1008-1987	1074-1991						
System Testing	829-1983	1074-1991	1028-1988	1012-1986				
Acceptance Testing	1074-1991	1012-1986						
Delivery								
CONTROL								
Problem Id/Classification								
Analysis	830-1984							
Design	830-1984	1016-1987						
Implementation	829-1983	1008-1987						
System Testing	829-1983	1028-1988	1012-1986					
Acceptance Testing	829-1983	1028-1988	1012-1986					
Delivery	1063-1987							
MANAGEMENT								
Configuration Management	828-1990	1042-1987						
Measurement/Metrics	982.1-1988	982.2-1988						
Planing	829-1983	1012-1986	1058.1-1987					
Tools/Techniques								
QA	730-1989	983-1986						
Risk Assessment	730-1989	982.2-1988						
Safety								
Security								

FIGURE 2 IEEE Standards and Their Relationship to P1219

2. Definitions and Acronyms

2.1 Definitions. The definitions listed below establish meaning in the context of this standard. These are contextual definitions serving to augment the understanding of software maintenance activities as described within this standard. Other definitions can be found in IEEE Std 610.12-1990 [1].

adaptive maintenance. Modification of a software product performed after delivery to make a computer program usable in a changed environment.

corrective maintenance. Reactive modification of a software product performed after delivery to correct discovered faults.

customer. The person, or persons, for which the product is intended and usually (but not necessarily) decides the requirements.

emergency maintenance. Unscheduled corrective maintenance performed to keep a system operational.

interoperability testing. Testing conducted to ensure that the modified system retains the capability to exchange, and use information between multiple systems.

modification request (MR). A generic term that includes the forms associated with the various trouble/problem reporting documents (e.g., incident report, trouble report) and the configuration change control documents (e.g., Software Change Request (SCR), IEEE Std 1042-1987) [10]

perfective maintenance. Modification of a software product after delivery to improve performance or maintainability.

project. A subsystem that is subject to maintenance activity.

regression test. Retesting to detect faults introduced by modification.

repository. 1) collection of all software-related artifacts (e.g., software engineering environment) belonging to a system 2) location/format in which such a collection is stored.

reverse engineering. The process of extracting software system information (including documentation) from source code.

software maintenance. Modification of a software product after delivery to correct faults, to improve performance or other attributes, or to adapt the product to a modified environment.

system. A set of interlinked units organized to accomplish one or several specific functions.

user. The person, or persons, who operate or interact directly with the system.

2.2 Acronyms. The following acronyms are referred to in the standard:

SCM - Software Configuration Management
CSA - Configuration Status Accounting
FCA - Functional Configuration Audit
PCA - Physical Configuration Audit
PDL - Program Design Language
SQA - Software Quality Assurance
SCR - System/Software Change Request
V&V - Verification and Validation
VDD - Version Description Document

	PROBLEM IDENTIFICATION	ANALYSIS	DESIGN	IMPLEMENTATION	SYSTEM TEST	ACCEPTANCE TEST	DELIVERY
INPUT	MR	Project/System Doc. Repository Inf. Validated MR	Project/System Doc Source code Databases Analysis Phase output	Source code Project/System Doc. Results of Design phase	Updated software documentation Test Readiness Review Report Updated system	Test Readiness Review Report Fully integrated system Acceptenance test - plans - cases - procedures	Tested/accepted system
PROCESS	Assign change no. Classify Accept or reject chg Preliminary magnitude estimate Prioritize	Feasibility analysis Detailed analysis Redocument if needed	Create test cases Revise -requirements -implementation plan	Code Unit test Test readiness review	Functional test Interface testing regression testing Test readiness review	Acceptenance test Interoperability test	PCA Install Training
CONTROL	Uniquely identify MR Enter MR into repository	Conduct technical review Verify -test strategy - documentation is updated Identify safety & security issues	Software inspection/ review Verify design	Software inspection/ review Verify -CM control of software -traceability of design	CM control of -code -listings -MR -test documentation	Acceptenance test Functional audit Establish baseline	PCA VDD
OUTPUT	Validated MR Process determinations	Feasibility Report Detailed Analysis Rpt. Updated req. Preliminary modification list Implementation Plan Test Strategy	Revised -modification list -detail analysis -implementation plan Updated -design baseline -test plans	Updated -software -design doc. -test docs. -user documents -training material Test Readiness Review Report	Tested system Test reports	New system baseline Acceptance Test Rpt. FCA Report	PCA Report VDD
METRICS	See Figure 4						

FIGURE 3 Process Model For Software Maintenance

	PROBLEM IDENTIFICATION	ANALYSIS	DESIGN	IMPLEMENTATION	SYSTEM TEST	ACCEPTANCE TEST	DELIVERY
FACTORS	CORRECTNESS MAINTAINABILITY	FLEXIBILITY TRACEABILITY REUSABILITY USABILITY MAINTAINABILITY COMPREHENSIBILITY	FLEXIBILITY TRACEABILITY REUSABILITY TESTABILITY MAINTAINABILITY COMPREHENSIBILITY RELIABILITY	FLEXIBILITY TRACEABILITY MAINTAINABILITY COMPREHENSIBILITY RELIABILITY	FLEXIBILITY TRACEABILITY VERIFIABILITY TESTABILITY INTEROPERABILITY COMPREHENSIBILITY RELIABILITY	FLEXIBILITY TRACEABILITY INTEROPERABILITY TESTABILITY COMPREHENSIBILITY RELIABILITY	COMPLETENESS RELIABILITY
METRICS	# OMMISSIONS ON MR # OF MR SUBMITTALS # OF DUPLICAT MR'S TIME EXPENDED FOR PROBLEM VALIDATION	REQUIREMENTS CHANGES DOCUMENTATION ERROR RATES EFFORT PER FUNCTION AREA (SQA, SE, ETC.) ELAPSED TIME (SCHEDULE) ERROR RATES GENERATED BY PRIORITY & TYPE	S/W COMPLEXITY DESIGN CHANGES EFFORT PER FUNCTION AREA ELAPSED TIME TEST PLANS AND PROCEDURE CHANGES ERROR RATES GENERATED BY PRIORITY & TYPE NUMBER OF LINES OF CODE, ADDED, DELETED, MODIFIED, TESTED NUMBER OF APPLICATIONS	VOLUME/FUNCTION-ALITY (FUNCTION POINTS OR SLOC) ERROR RATES GENERATED BY PRIORITY & TYPE	ERROR RATES BY PRIORITY & TYPE - GENERATED - CORRECTED	ERROR RATES BY PRIORITY & TYPE - GENERATED - CORRECTED	DOCUMENTATION CHANGES (I.E. VERSION DESCRIPTION DOCUMENTS, TRAINING MANUALS, OPERATION GUIDELINES)

Figure 4 Process Model Metrics for Software Maintenance

3. Software Maintenance

This standard defines changes to software process through a defined maintenance process which includes the following phases:

(1) Problem/Modification Identification and Classification
(2) Analysis
(3) Design
(4) Implementation
(5) Regression/System Testing
(6) Acceptance Testing
(7) Delivery

These phases are graphically depicted in Figure 3. Software maintenance factors in Figure 4 are the entities qualified by the associated metrics/measures identified for each phase.

3.1 Problem/Modification Identification and Classification. In this phase, software modifications are identified, classified, and assigned an initial priority ranking. Each Modification Request (MR) shall be evaluated to determine its classification and handling priority. Classification shall be identified from the following maintenance types: corrective, adaptive, perfective, and emergency. Metrics/measures and associated factors identified for this phase should be collected and reviewed at appropriate intervals (see Figure 4 and IEEE Stds 982.1 [5] and 982.2 [6]).

Figure 5 summarizes the inputs, process, control and output for the Problem/Modification Identification and Classification phase of maintenance. For additional information see also A4.1.

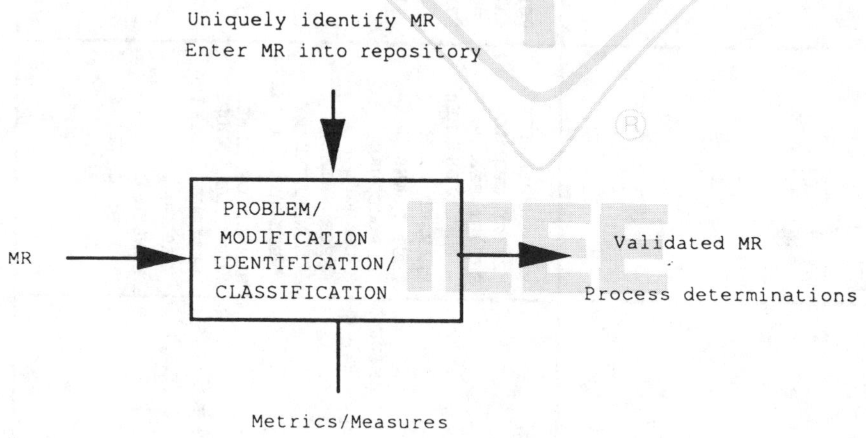

FIGURE 5 **Problem/Modification Identification and Classification Phase**

3.1.1 Input. Input for the Problem/Modification Identification and Classification phase shall be an MR.

3.1.2 Process. If a modification to the software is required, the following determinative activities must occur within the maintenance process:

(1) Assign an identification number
(2) Classify the type of maintenance
(3) Analyze the modification to determine whether to accept, reject or further evaluate
(4) Make a preliminary estimate of the modification size/magnitude
(5) Prioritize the modification
(6) Assign MR to a block of modifications scheduled for implementation.

3.1.3 Control. MR and process determinations shall be uniquely identified and entered into a repository. See also A11.1 for guidance.

3.1.4 Output. The output of this process shall be the validated MR and the process determinations that were stored in a repository. The repository shall contain the following items:

(1) a statement of the problem or new requirement
(2) a problem or requirement evaluation,
(3) classification of the type of maintenance required,
(4) initial priority,
(5) verification data (for corrective modifications),
(6) initial estimate of resources required to modify the existing system.

3.2 Analysis. The analysis phase shall use the repository information and the MR validated in the modification identification and classification phase, along with system and project documentation, to study the feasibility and scope of the modification and to devise a preliminary plan for design, implementation, test, and delivery. Metrics/measures and associated factors identified for this phase should be collected and reviewed at appropriate intervals (see Figure 4 and IEEE Stds 982.1 [5] and 982.2 [6]).

Figure 6 summarizes the inputs, process, control and output for the Analysis phase of maintenance. For additional guidance see A4.2.

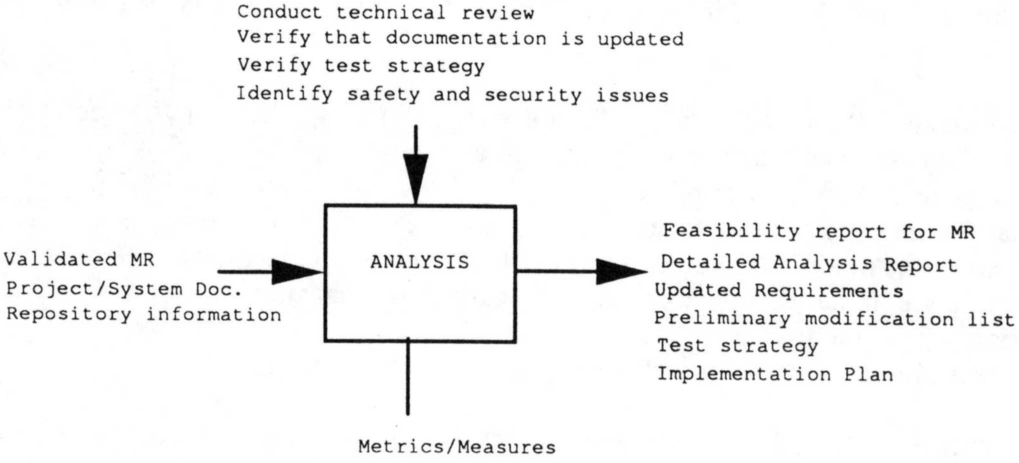

FIGURE 6 Analysis Phase

3.2.1 Input. The input to the analysis phase of the maintenance process shall include the following :

(1) Validated MR
(2) Initial resource estimate and other repository information
(3) Project and system documentation, if available

3.2.2 Process. Analysis is an iterative process having at least two components, (1) a feasibility analysis and (2) a detailed analysis. If the documentation is not available or is insufficient and the source code is the only reliable representation of the software system, reverse engineering is recommended. (See Appendix B for guidance)

3.2.2.1 Feasibility Analysis. A feasibility analysis shall be performed for MR and a Feasibility Report (FR) shall be prepared. This FR should contain the following:

(1) Impact of the modification
(2) Alternate solutions, including protyping
(3) Analysis of conversion requirements
(4) Safety and security implications
(5) Human factors
(6) Short term and long term costs
(7) Value of the benefit of making the modification

3.2.2.2 Detailed Analysis. Detailed analysis shall

(1) Define firm requirements for the modification,
(2) Identify the elements of modification,
(3) Identify safety and security issues (See also A9 and A10 for guidance)
(4) Devise a test strategy, and

(5) Develop an implementation plan.

In identifying the elements of modification, (creating the preliminary modification list) analysts examines all products (e.g., software, specifications, databases, documentation) which are affected. Each of these products shall be identified, generated if necessary, specifying the portions of the product to be modified, the interfaces affected, the user-noticeable changes expected, the relative degree and kind of experience required to make changes, and the estimated time to complete the modification.

The test strategy is based on input from the previous activity identifying the elements of modification. Requirements for at least three levels of test, including individual element tests, integration tests, and user-oriented functional acceptance tests shall be defined. Regression test requirements associated with each of these levels of test shall be identified as well. The test cases to be used for testing to establish the test baseline shall be revalidated.

A preliminary implementation plan shall state how the design, implementation, testing, and delivery of the modification is to be accomplished with a minimal impact to current users.

3.2.3 Control. Control of analysis shall include the following :

(1) Retrieval of the relevant version of project and system documentation from the configuration control function of the organization.
(2) Conducting a review of the proposed changes and engineering analysis to assess technical and economic feasibility, and assess correctness.
(3) Identifying safety and security issues.
(4) Consideration of the integration of the proposed change within the existing software.
(5) Verification that all appropriate analysis and project documentation is updated and properly controlled.
(6) Verification that the test function of the organization is providing a strategy for testing the change(s), and that the change schedule can support the proposed test strategy.
(7) Review of the resource estimates and schedules and verification of their accuracy.
(8) Conducting a technical review to select the problem reports and proposed enhancements to be implemented in the new release. The list of changes shall be documented.

Consult A6, A7 and A11.2 for guidance on Verification and Validation, Software Quality Assurance, and Software Configuration Management related activities.

At the end of the analysis phase, a risk analysis shall be performed. (See also A8 for guidance) Using the output of the analysis phase, the preliminary resource estimate shall be revised, and a decision, that includes the customer, is made on whether to proceed to the design phase.

3.2.4 Output. The output of the maintenance process analysis phase shall include the following :

(1) Feasibility Report for MRs
(2) Detailed analysis report
(3) Updated requirements (including traceability list)

(4) Preliminary modification list
(5) Test strategy
(6) Implementation plan

3.3 Design. In the design phase, all current system and project documentation, existing software and databases, and the output of the analysis phase (including detailed analysis, statements of requirements, identification of elements affected, test strategy, and implementation plan) shall be used to design the modification to the system. Metrics/measures and associated factors identified for this phase should be collected and reviewed at appropriate intervals (see Figure 4 and IEEE Stds 982.1 [5] and 982.2 [6]).

Figure 7 summarizes the inputs, process, control and output for the design phase of maintenance. For additional guidance see also A4.3.

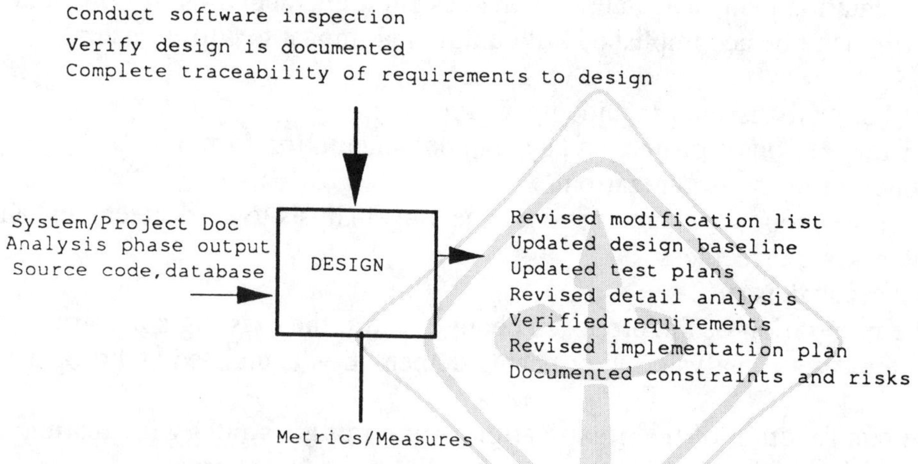

FIGURE 7 DESIGN PHASE

3.3.1 Input. Input to the design phase of the maintenance process shall include:
(1) Analysis phase output including:
  (a) Detailed analysis
  (b) Updated statement of requirements
  (c) Preliminary modification list
  (d) Test strategy
  (e) Implementation plan
(2) System and project documentation
(3) Existing source code, comments and databases

3.3.2 Process. The process steps for design shall include:
(1) Identify affected software modules
(2) Modify software module documentation (e.g., data and control flow diagrams, schematics, PDL, etc.)

(3) Create test cases for new design, including safety and security issues (for guidance see also A9 and A10)
(4) Identify/create regression tests
(5) Identify documentation (system/user) update requirements
(6) Update modification list

3.3.3 Control. The following control mechanism shall be used during the design phase of a change:
(1) Conduct software inspection of the design in compliance with IEEE Std 1028-1988 [9]
(2) Verify that the new design/requirement are documented as an Software Change Authorization (SCA) per IEEE Std 1042-1987 [10]
(3) Verify the inclusion of new design material, including safety and security issues
(4) Verify that the appropriate test documentation has been updated
(5) Complete the traceability of the requirements to the design.

Consult A6, A7 and A11.2 for guidance on Verification and Validation, Software Quality Assurance, and Software Configuration Management related activities.

3.3.4 Output. The output of the design phase of the maintenance process shall include the following :
(1) Revised modification list
(2) Updated design baseline
(3) Updated test plans
(4) Revised detailed analysis
(5) Verified requirements
(6) Revised implementation plan
(7) A list of documented constraints and risks (for guidance see A8).

3.4 Implementation. In the implementation phase, the results of the design phase, the current source code, and project and system documentation (i.e., the entire system as updated by the analysis and design phases) shall be used to drive the implementation effort. Metrics/measures and associated factors identified for this phase should be collected and reviewed at appropriate intervals (see Figure 4 and IEEE Stds 982.1 [5] and 982.2 [6]).

Figure 8 summarizes the inputs, process, control and output for the Implementation phase of maintenance. For additional guidance see also A4.4.

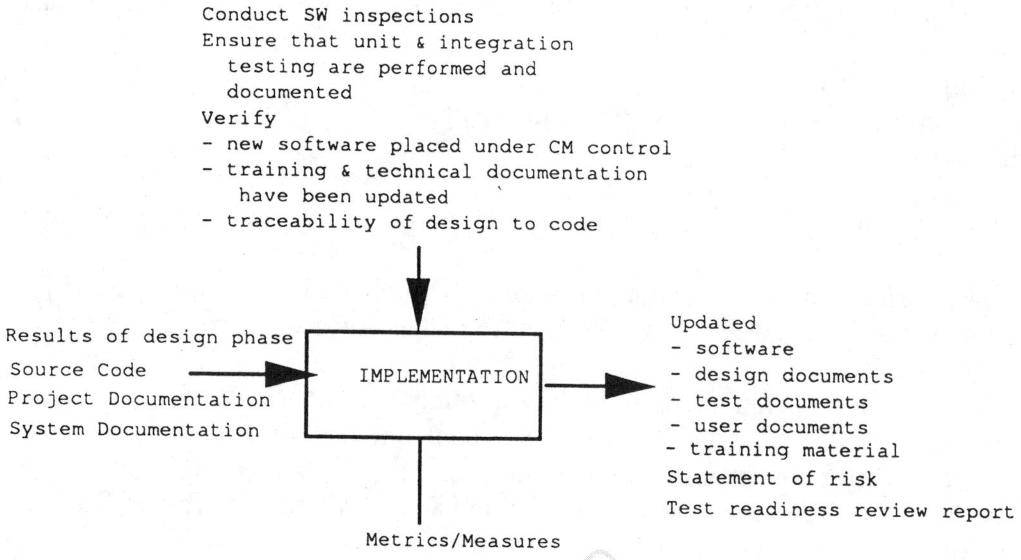

FIGURE 8 Implementation Phase

3.4.1 Input. The input to the implementation phase shall include the following :
(1) Results of the design phase
(2) Current source code, comments and databases
(3) Project and system documentation

3.4.2 Process. The implementation phase shall include the following four subprocesses, which may be repeated in an incremental, iterative approach:
(1) Coding and unit testing
(2) Integration
(3) Risk analysis
(4) Test readiness review

Metrics/measures and associated factors identified for this phase should be collected and reviewed at appropriate intervals (see Figure 4 and IEEE Stds 982.1 [5] and 982.2 [6]).

3.4.2.1 Coding and Unit Testing. Implement the change into the code and perform unit testing and other appropriate SQA and V&V processes.

3.4.2.2 Integration. After the modifications are coded and unit tested, or at appropriate intervals during coding, the modified software shall be integrated with the system and integration and regression tests shall be refined and performed. All effects (e.g. functional, performance, usability, safety) , of the modification on the existing system shall be assessed.

Any unacceptable impacts shall be noted. A return to the coding and unit testing subprocess shall be made to remedy these.

3.4.2.3 Risk Analysis and Review. In the implementation phase, risk analysis and review shall be performed periodically during the phase rather than at its end, as in the design and analysis phases. Metrics/measurement data should be used to quantify risk analysis. For additional guidance see A8.

3.4.2.4 Test Readiness Review. To assess preparedness for system test, a test readiness review shall be held in accordance with IEEE Std 1028-1988 [9].

3.4.3 Control. The control of implementation shall include :
(1) Conduct software inspections of the code in compliance with IEEE Std 1028-1988 [9].
(2) Ensure that unit and integration testing are performed and documented in a software development folder
(3) Ensure that test documentation (e.g., test plan, test cases and test procedures) are either updated or created
(4) Identify, document and resolve any risks exposed during software and test readiness reviews
(5) Verify that the new software is placed under Software Configuration Management control
(6) Verify the training and technical documentation have been updated
(7) Verify the traceability of the design to the code.

Consult A6, A7 and A11.2 for guidance on Verification and Validation, Software Quality Assurance, and Software Configuration Management related activities.

3.4.4 Output. The output of the implementation phase shall include:
(1) Updated software
(2) Updated design documentation
(3) Updated test documentation
(4) Updated user documentation
(5) Updated training material
(6) A statement of risk and impact to users
(7) Test readiness review report (IEEE Std 1028-1988) [9]

3.5 System Test. System testing, as defined in IEEE Std 610.12-1990 [1], shall be performed on the modified system. Regression testing is a part of system testing and shall be performed to validate that the modified code does not introduce faults that did not exist prior to the maintenance activity. Metrics/measures and associated factors identified for this phase should be collected and reviewed at appropriate intervals (see Figure 4 and IEEE Stds 982.1 [5] and 982.2 [6]).

Figure 9 summarizes the inputs, process, control and output for the System test phase of maintenance. For additional guidance see also A4.5.

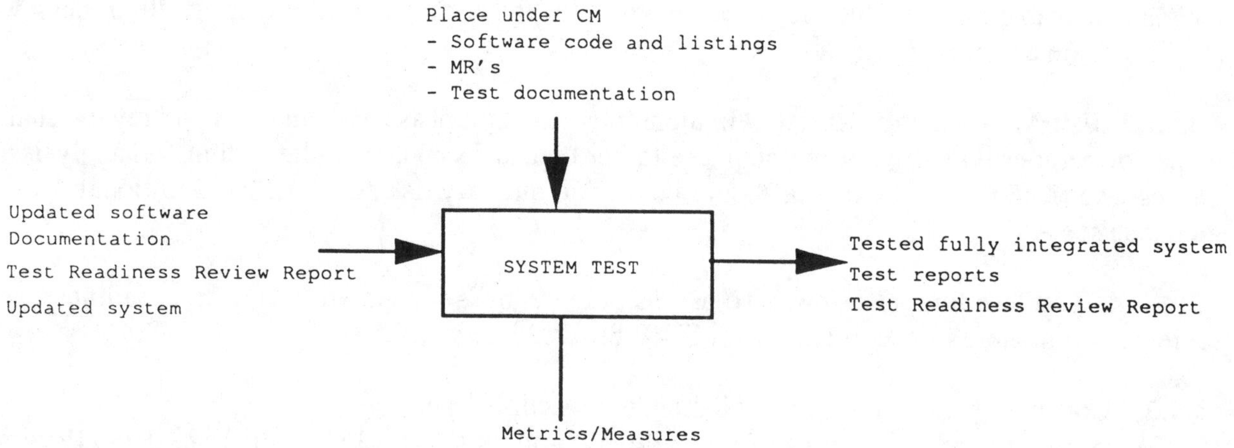

FIGURE 9 System Test Phase

3.5.1 Input. Input to the System test phase of maintenance shall include :
(1) Test Readiness Review Report
(2) Documentation, which includes:
  (a) System Test Plans (IEEE 829-1983) [4]
  (b) System Test Cases (IEEE 829-1983) [4]
  (c) System Test Procedures (IEEE 829-1983) [4]
  (d) User manuals
  (e) Design
(3) Updated system

3.5.2 Process. System tests shall be conducted on a fully integrated system. Testing shall include the performance of:
(1) System functional test
(2) Interface testing
(3) Regression testing
(4) Test readiness review to assess preparedness for acceptance testing.

Note: Results of tests conducted prior to the Test Readiness Review should not be used as part of the System Test Report to substantiate requirements at the system level. This is necessary to ensure that the test organization does not consider that testing all parts (one at a time) of the system constitutes a "system test."

3.5.3 Control. System tests shall be conducted by an independent test function, or by the Software Quality Assurance function. Prior to the completion of System Testing, the test function shall be responsible for reporting the status of the criteria that had been established in the test plan for satisfactory completion of System Testing. The status shall be reported to the appropriate review committee prior to proceeding to Acceptance Testing. Software code listings, MRs and test documentation shall be placed under SCM. The customer shall participate in the review to ascertain that the maintenance release is ready to begin Acceptance Testing.

Consult A6, A7 and A11.2 for guidance on Verification and Validation, Software Quality Assurance, and SCM related activities.

3.5.4 Output. The output for this phase of maintenance shall include the following :
(1) Tested and fully integrated system
(2) Test report
(3) Test Readiness Review Report

3.6 Acceptance Test. Acceptance tests shall be conducted on a fully integrated system. Acceptance Tests shall be performed by either the customer, the user of the modification package, or a third party designated by the customer. Acceptance Test is conducted with software that is under SCM in accordance with the provisions of IEEE Std 828-1990 [3], and in accordance with the IEEE Std 730-1989 [2]. Acceptance testing, as defined in IEEE Std 610.12-1990 [1], shall be performed on the modified system. Metrics/measures and associated factors identified for this phase should be collected and reviewed at appropriate intervals (see Figure 4 and IEEE Stds 982.1 [5] and 982.2 [6]).

Figure 10 summarizes the inputs, process, control and output for the Acceptance test phase of maintenance. For additional guidance see also A4.6.

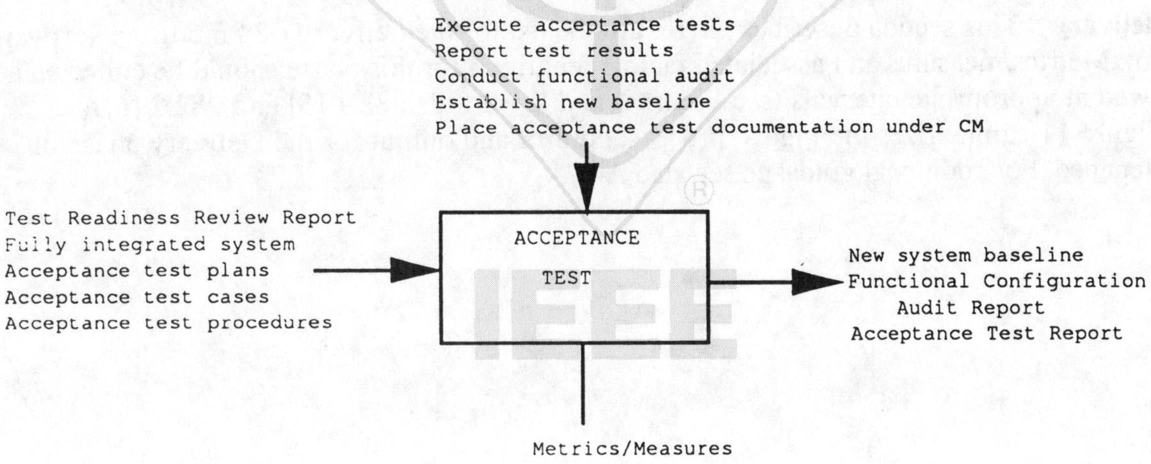

FIGURE 10 Acceptance Test Phase

3.6.1 Input. The input for acceptance testing shall include the following :
(1) Test Readiness Review Report
(2) Fully integrated system
(3) Acceptance test plans

(4) Acceptance test cases
(5) Acceptance test procedures

3.6.2 Process. The following are the process steps for acceptance testing:
(1) Perform acceptance tests at the functional level
(2) Perform interoperability testing
(3) Perform regression testing

3.6.3 Control. Control of acceptance test shall include the following :
(1) Execute acceptance tests
(2) Report test results for the Functional Configuration Audit (FCA)
(3) Conduct functional audit
(4) Establish the new system baseline
(5) Place the acceptance test documentation under SCM control

Consult A6, A7 and A11.2 for guidance on Verification and Validation, Software Quality Assurance, and SCM related activities.

3.6.4 Output. The output for the acceptance phase shall include the following :
(1) New system baseline
(2) Functional Configuration Audit Report (IEEE Std 1028-1988) [9]
(3) Acceptance Test Report (IEEE Std 1042-1987) [10]
Note: The customer shall be responsible for the acceptance test report.

3.7 Delivery. This section describes the requirements for the delivery of a modified software system. Metrics/measures and associated factors identified for this phase should be collected and reviewed at appropriate intervals (see Figure 4 and IEEE Stds 982.1 [5] and 982.2 [6]).

Figure 11 summarizes the inputs, process, control and output for the Delivery phase of maintenance. For additional guidance see also A4.7.

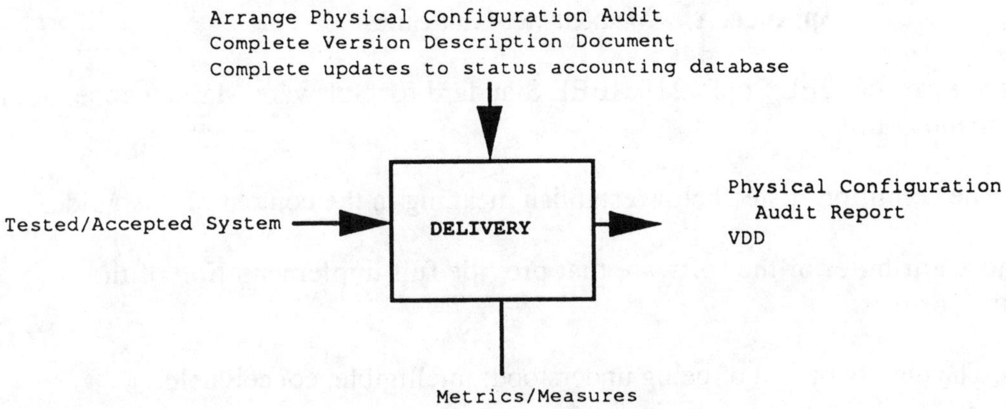

FIGURE 11 Delivery Phase

3.7.1 Input. The input to this phase of the maintenance process shall be the fully tested version of the system as represented in the new baseline.

3.7.2 Process. The process steps for delivery of a modified product shall include the following :
(1) Conduct a Physical Configuration Audit
(2) Notify the user community
(3) Develop an archival version of the system for backup
(4) Perform installation and training at the customer facility

3.7.3 Control. Control for delivery shall include the following :
(1) Arrange and document a Physical Configuration Audit
(2) Provide system materials for access to users, including replication and distribution
(3) Complete the Version Description Document (IEEE Std 1042-1987) [10]
(4) Complete updates to Status Accounting database
(5) Place under SCM control.

Consult A6, A7 and A11.2 for guidance on Verification and Validation, Software Quality Assurance, and SCM related activities.

3.7.4 Output. Output for delivery shall include the following:
(1) PCA Report (IEEE Std. 1028-1988 [9])
(2) Version Description Document (VDD)

Appendix A Maintenance Guidelines

This Appendix is not part of IEEE Std P1219, IEEE Standard for Software Maintenance, but is included for information only.

A1 Definitions. The definitions listed below establish meaning in the context of this guide.

completeness. Those attributes of the software that provide full implementation of the functions required.

comprehensibility. The quality or fact of being understood; intelligible, conceivable.

consistency. Those attributes of the software that provide uniform design and implementation techniques and notation.

correctness. Those attributes of the software that provide traceability, consistency, and completeness.

instrumentation. Those attributes of the software that provide for the measurement of usage or identification of errors.

modularity. Those attributes of the software that provide a structure of highly independent modules.

preventive maintenance. Maintenance performed for the purpose of preventing problems before they occur.

self-descriptiveness. Those attributes of the software that provide explanation of the implementation of a function.

simplicity. Those attributes of the software that provide implementation of functions in the most understandable manner (usually avoidance of practices which increase complexity).

testability. Those attributes of the software that provide simplicity, modularity, instrumentation, and self-descriptiveness.

traceability. Those attributes of the software that provide a thread from the requirements to the implementation with respect to the specific development and operational environment.

verifiability. Capable of being verified, proved or confirmed by examination or investigation.

A2 References. The following standards are directly referenced in this standard. Figure 2 provides a cross-reference of IEEE standards which address various topics related to software maintenance. These standards are binding to the extent specified within the text of this standard and are referenced to avoid duplication of requirements.

[1] IEEE Std 730-1989, Software Quality Assurance Plans (ANSI)
[2] IEEE Std 828-1990, Standard for Software Configuration Management Plans (ANSI)
[3] IEEE Std 829-1983, Standard for Software Test Documentation
[4] IEEE Std 982.1-1988, Standard Dictionary of Measures to Produce Reliable Software (ANSI)
[5] IEEE Std 982.2-1988, Guide for the Use of IEEE Standard Dictionary of Measures to Produce Reliable Software (ANSI)
[6] IEEE Std 983-1986, Guide for Software Quality Assurance Planning (ANSI)
[7] IEEE Std 1012-1986, Standard Software Verification and Validation Plans (ANSI)
[8] IEEE Std 1028-1988, Standard for Software Reviews and Audits (ANSI)
[9] IEEE Std 1042-1987, Guide to Software Configuration Management (ANSI)
[10] IEEE Std 1058.1-1987, Standard for Software Project Management Plans (ANSI)
[11] IEEE Std P1045-1990, Standard for Software Productivity Metrics (ANSI)
[12] IEEE Std P1061, Standard for a Software Quality Metrics Methodology (ANSI)
[13] IEEE Std P1228, Software Safety Plans (ANSI)
[14] NBS Special Publication 500-106, Guidance on Software Maintenance

A3 Maintenance Planning. Planning for maintenance may include: determining the maintenance effort, determining the current maintenance process, quantifying the maintenance effort, projecting maintenance requirements, and developing a Maintenance Plan. IEEE Std 1058.1-1987 [10] may also be used for guidance in maintenance planning.

A3.1 Determine Maintenance Effort. The first step in the maintenance planning process is an analysis of current service levels and capabilities. This includes an analysis of the existing maintenance portfolio and the "state" of each system within that portfolio. At the system level each system should be examined to determine:

(1) age since placed in production
(2) number and type of changes during life
(3) usefulness of the system
(4) the types and number of requests received for changes
(5) quality and timeliness of documentation
(6) any existing performance statistics (CPU, disk I/O, etc.)

Descriptions at the portfolio level can assist in describing the overall effort and needs of the maintenance area. This includes the amount and kinds of functional system overlap and gaps within the portfolio architecture.

The reviews of the maintenance staff and the maintenance procedures are also necessary to determine the overall maintenance effort. The analysis at this stage is to simply gather those measures needed to determine:

(1) the number of maintainers, their job descriptions, and their actual jobs
(2) the experience level of the maintenance staff both industry-wide and for the particular application
(3) the rate of turnover and possible reasons for leaving
(4) current written maintenance methods at the systems and program level
(5) actual methods used by programming staff
(6) tools used to support the maintenance process and how they are used

Information at this stage is used to define the baseline for the maintenance organization and provide a means of assessing the necessary changes.

A3.2 Determine Current Maintenance Process. The maintenance process is a natural outgrowth of many of the baseline measures. Once those measures have been collected the actual process needs to be determined. In some organizations the process is tailored to the type of maintenance being performed and can be divided in several different ways. This can include different processes for corrections vs. enhancements, small changes vs. large changes, etc. It is helpful to classify the maintenance approaches used before defining the processes.

Each process will then be described by a series of events. In general the flow of work is described from receipt of a request to its implementation and delivery.

A3.3 Quantify Maintenance Effort . Each step in the process needs to be described numerically in terms of volumes or time. These numbers can then be used as a basis to determine actual performance of the maintenance organization.

A3.4 Project Maintenance Requirements. At this stage the maintenance process needs to be coupled to the business environment. A review of future expectations should be completed and may include:
(1) Expected external or regulatory changes to the system
(2) Expected internal changes to support new requirements
(3) Wish-list of new functions and features
(4) Expected upgrades for performance, adaptability, connectivity, etc.
(5) New lines of business that need to be supported
(6) New technologies that need to be incorporated

These need to be quantified (or "sized") to determine the future maintenance load for the organization.

A3.5 Develop Maintenance Plan. The information collected will provide a basis for a new maintenance plan. The plan should cover four main areas:
(1) The maintenance process
(2) The organization
(3) Resource allocations
(4) Performance tracking

Each of these issues are addressed and imbedded in the final maintenance plan. The actual process should be described in terms of its scope, the sequence of the process, and the control of the process.

A3.5.1 Process Scope. The plan needs to define the boundaries of the maintenance process. The process begins at some point (receipt of the request) and will end with some action (delivery and sign off). In addition, the difference between maintenance and development should be addressed at this point. Is an enhancement considered new development or maintenance? At what point does a newly developed system enter the maintenance process?

Another issue that should be defined within the scope is whether and how the maintenance process will be categorized. Will there be differences between reporting and other types of maintenance? Will adaptations and enhancements be considered within the same process or will they be handled differently?

A3.5.2 Process Sequence. The overall flow of work (and paper) needs to be described. This should include the following:
(1) Entry into automated SCM and project management systems
(2) Descriptions of each process step and their interfaces
(3) The data flow between processes

The sequence should use the process described in this standard as a guideline.

A3.5.3 Process Control. Each step in the process should be controlled and measured. Expected levels of performance should be defined. The control mechanisms should be automated if possible. The control process should follow the standards set forth in this document.

A3.5.4 Organization. Staff size can be estimated from the current work load and estimates of future needs. This estimate may also be based on the expected productivity of each step in the process.

A3.5.5 Resource Allocation. An important part of the maintenance plan is an analysis of the hardware and software most appropriate to support the organization's needs. The development, maintenance, and target platforms should be defined and differences between the environments described. Tool sets that enhance productivity should be identified and provided. The tools should be accessible by all who need them and sufficient training should be provided so that their use is well understood.

A3.5.6 Tracking. Once the process is in place it should be tracked and evaluated to judge its effectiveness. If each step in the process has measurement criteria it should be a straightforward process to collect and evaluate performance over time.

A3.5.7 Implementation of Plan. Implementing a maintenance plan is accomplished in the same way that any organizational change is performed. It is important to have as much technical, professional, and management input as possible when the plan is being developed.

A4 Maintenance Process. The phases presented herein mirror those in the standard.

A4.1 Problem/Modification Identification and Classification. Each System/Software and Modification Request should be evaluated to determine its classification and handling priority and assignment for implementation as a block of modifications that will be released to the user. A suggested method for this is to hold a periodic review of all submitted items. This provides a regular, focused forum and helps prevent the review/analyze/design/implement/test process (which may be iterative) from stalling due to lack of direction. It also increases awareness of the most requested and most critical items. An agenda should be distributed prior to the meeting listing the items to be classified and prioritized.

The frequency and duration for modification classification review meetings should be project-dependent. A guideline might be to consider them as status reviews rather than as technical reviews. Using this guideline, if, after the first few sessions, the reviews take more than an hour or so, their frequency should be increased to as often as weekly. If review time still seems insufficient, determine whether one of the following cases applies and handle accordingly:

(1) Discussion is focused on major system enhancements (perfective maintenance). This may require analysis/review cycles of a development magnitude, rather than at a sustaining maintenance level.

(2) The system is new and design/implementation problems require a significant maintenance effort immediately following delivery. A suggested strategy, to be used where the impact to operations is acceptable, is to classify the MRs as corrective/ adaptive/ perfective/ preventive and integrate them into sets that share the same design areas. Then, rather than prioritizing by individual MR, prioritize by set. This minimizes repetition of design, code, test and delivery tasks for the same code modules. In this case, review meetings may be longer and more frequent until the system is stabilized. A long- term plan should have a goal of gradually reducing the review meeting overhead.

(3) The system is aging and system replacement or reverse engineering and redesign are under consideration.

These are not the only possible cases. They are described to highlight the importance of understanding the goals for classifying modifications as they apply to a particular system.

Modification Requests should be assigned a priority from:

(1) the MR author or a designated representative

(2) a knowledgeable user

(3) a domain expert

(4) software engineers (depending on the project, this may include representatives of system analysis and design, development, integration, test, and maintenance, quality control, SCM), or

(5) project management.
The following criteria should be considered :
(1) Rough resource estimate, which may be derived from;
  (a) Relative ease/difficulty of implementation;
  (b) Approximate time to implement given available human and system resources;
(2) Expected impact to current and future users:
  (a) General statement of benefits;
  (b) General statement of drawbacks
(3) Assignment to an implementation of a block of modifications that are scheduled to minimize the impact on the user.

Thorough, low-level cost and impact studies should be performed in the analysis phase, but general cost estimates and statements of impact are desirable for initial classification. Since this is an iterative process, it is likely that handling priority may change during the phases that follow.

A4.2 Analysis. A Modification Request may generate several system-level functional, performance, usability, reliability, and maintainability requirements. Each of these may be further decomposed into several software, database, interface, documentation, and hardware requirements. Involvement of requesters, implementers, and users is necessary to ensure that requirement(s) are unambiguous statements of the request.

Software change impact analysis should:
(1) Identify potential ripple effects
(2) Allow trade-offs between suggested software change approaches to be considered
(3) Be done with the help of documentation abstracted from the source code
(4) Consider the history of prior changes, both successful, and unsuccessful

A detailed analysis should consider the following:
(1) Determine if additional problem analysis/identification is required.
(2) Record acceptance or rejection of the proposed change(s).
(3) Develop an agreed upon project plan .
(4) Evaluate any software or hardware constraints that may result from the changes and which need consideration during the design phase.
(5) Document any project or software risks resulting from the analysis to be considered for subsequent phases of the change life cycle.
(6) Recommend the use of existing designs, if applicable.

A4.3 Design. Actual implementation should begin during this phase while keeping in mind the continued feasibility of the proposed change. For example, the engineering staff may not fully understand the impact and magnitude of a change until the design is complete, or the design of a specific change may be too complex to implement.

The vehicles for communicating the updated design are project / organization-dependent and may include portions of a current design specification, software development files, and entries in software engineering case tool databases. Other items that may be generated during this phase include a revised analysis, revised statements of requirements, a revised list of elements affected, a revised plan for implementation, and a revised risk analysis.

The specifics of the design process may vary from one project to the next and are dependent on such variables as tool use, size of modification, size of existing system, availability of a development system, and accessibility to users and requesting organizations. Product characteristics should also be evaluated when developing the design so that decisions on how modules of software will be changed consider the reliability and future maintainability of the total system, rather than focusing on expediency.

A4.4 Implementation. The primary inputs to this phase are the results of the design phase. Other inputs required for successful control of this phase are:
(1) Approved and controlled requirements and design documentation
(2) Agreed upon set of coding standards to be used by the maintenance staff
(3) Any design metrics/measurement that may be applicable to the implementation phase. These metrics/measures may provide insight into code that may either complex to develop or maintain.
(4) A detailed implementation schedule noting how many code reviews will take place and at what level.
(5) A set of responses to the defined risks from the previous phase that are applicable to the testing phase.

Risk analysis and review should be performed periodically during the phase rather than at its end, as in the design and analysis phases. This is recommended because a high percentage of design, cost, and performance problems and risks are exposed while modifying the system. Careful measurement of this process is necessary, and becomes especially important if the number of iterations of the coding and unit testing and integration subprocesses is out of scope with the modification. If this is found true, the feasibility of the design and/or modification request may need reassessment, and a return to the design, analysis, or even the modification identification and classification phase may be warranted.

Prior to a review, the following information may be prepared and provided to attendees:
(1) Entry criteria for system test
(2) Resource allocation and need schedule
(3) Detailed test schedule
(4) Test documentation forms
(5) Anomaly resolution procedures
(6) SCM procedures
(7) Exit criteria for system test
(8) Lower-level test results

Attendees may include the following :
(1) The MR author, a designated representative, or a knowledgeable user
(2) A domain expert
(3) Software engineers (depending on the project, this may include representatives of system analysis and design, development, integration, test, and maintenance, quality control, SCM)
(4) Project management

A4.5 System Test. It is essential to maintain management controls over the execution of system tests to ensure that the non-technical issues concerning budget and schedule are given the proper attention. This function also ensures that the proper controls are in place to evaluate the product during testing for completeness and accuracy.

System Tests should be performed by an independent test organization, and may be witnessed by the customer and the end-user. System Test is performed on software that is under SCM in accordance with the provisions of IEEE Std 828-1990 [2]. Software Quality Assurance is conducted in accordance with the provisions of IEEE Std 730-1989 [1]. The System Test is performed with as complete a system as is possible, using simulation/stimulation to the smallest degree possible. Functions are tested "end-to-end", from input to output.

For maintenance releases it is possible that other testing may have to be done to satisfy requirements to interact with other systems, or sub-systems. It may also be necessary to conduct testing to validate that faults are not introduced as a result oi changes.

System tests should be conducted on a fully integrated system. Simulation / stimulation may be used in cases where it is not possible to have the completely integrated system in the test facility. However, its use should be minimized. If utilized, it should be identified and evaluated/justified.

The organization that is responsible for system test should be independent of the software developers and designers, but these organizations may be used as a resource of test personnel. Control of software builds, and all pertinent files (source, object, libraries, etc.) during system test should be done by the SCM function. Controls to ensure product integrity are executed by the Software Quality Assurance function. They should ensure that the changes to the products that are submitted are in fact authorized and technically correct.

If changes have been made to the software, or test cases, since the software has been delivered, then it may be necessary to run regression and unit tests during the analysis phase in order to establish the product baseline.

A4.6 Acceptance Test. The Acceptance Test is performed to ensure that the products of the modification are satisfactory to the customer. The products include the software system and the documentation necessary to support it. The culmination of the Acceptance Test is usually the completion of a Functional Audit and a Physical Audit (see IEEE Std 1028-1988) [8].

For maintenance releases it is possible that other testing may have to be done to satisfy requirements to interact with other systems, or sub-systems. It may also be necessary to conduct testing to validate that faults are not introduced as a result of changes.

Acceptance tests should be conducted on a fully integrated system. Simulation and/or Stimulation may be used in cases where it is not possible to have the completely integrated system in the test facility. However, its use should be minimized. This requirement may be modified to include the case where lower level testing is performed. The customer, or her representative, is responsible for determining the facility requirements that are necessary. These requirements are documented by the developer in the Modification Plan. Acceptance Test facilities may be either provided by the developer or customer, or a combination of both.

Results of tests conducted prior to the Acceptance Test Readiness Review may be used by the customer to reduce the scope of Acceptance Tests. If this is done, the customer should document in the Acceptance Test Report which results were taken from previous tests.

Prior to the completion of Acceptance Testing, the test organization should be responsible for reporting the status of the criteria that had been established in the test plan for satisfactory completion of Acceptance Testing. The status should be reported to the appropriate review committee. The customer, or his representative, should chair the review group and evaluate the exit criteria to ensure that the maintenance release is ready for delivery to the end-user.

A4.7 Delivery. Based on how the users access the system, the delivery may entail replacing the existing system with the new version, duplication of the configuration controlled master for delivery to remote users, or digital transmission.

To reduce the risks associated with installation of the new version of a software system, project management should plan for and document alternative installation procedures that may insure minimal impact on the system users due to unforeseen software failures not detected during testing. The planning should address time critical factors (e.g., date/times available for installation, critical milestones of the users, etc.) and restoration/recovery procedures.

When a system modification affects user interfaces or is a significant modification of functionally, user training may be necessary. This can include formal (classroom) and non-formal methods. When the modifications result in significant documentation changes, user training should be considered.

SCM is responsible for backing up the system. To ensure recovery, the backup should consist of the existing system version as well as the new version. To facilitate disaster recovery, complete copies of the system backup should be archived at an off-site location. The backup should consist of source code, requirements documentation, design documentation, test documentation (including test case data), and the support environment (i.e., operating system, compiler, assembler, test driver(s), and other tools).

A5 Maintenance Forms. Recording, tracking, and implementing software maintenance, requires that various forms be completed and managed. What follows is a list of forms that may be used to perform maintenance, and the IEEE standard that explains their format and usage.

(1) Test Log - IEEE Std 829-1983 [3]
(2) Test Incident Report - IEEE Std 829-1983 [3]
(3) Test Summary Report - IEEE Std 829-1983 [3]
(4) Test Design Specification - IEEE Std 829-1983 Documentation [3]
(5) System/Software Change Request - IEEE Std 1042-1987 [9]
(6) Software Change Authorization - IEEE Std 1042-1987 [9]

A6 Verification and Validation (V&V). IEEE Std 1012-1986 [7] should be used to verify and validate that all maintenance requirements are met.

A7 Software Quality Assurance. Software Quality Assurance should be considered when any modifications are made to an existing system. A modification to one segment of the system can cause errors to appear somewhere else. Other concerns can include: version control, new documentation release, etc. To ensure that quality is maintained for all modifications, standards as stated in IEEE Std 730-1989 [1], and IEEE Std 983-1986 [6] should be adhered to.

Continuing product quality assurance includes the following :

(1) Adherence to the Maintenance Plan and approach
(2) Testing (including regression testing)
(3) Revalidation activities
(4) Recertification activities

The same types and levels of assurance (e.g., inspections, reviews, audits, verification and validation, evaluation of metric data, records) should be conducted as were performed during development; the degree and conduct of these activities is specified in the Software Maintenance Plan. Special care should be given to ensuring that the original system documentation continues to describe the actual product; during operational use the time criticality of effecting a repair to the product often results in the lack of related changes to the documentation with concomitant loss of configuration control. Similarly, the operational facility should be able to maintain the distinction between proposed fixes to the software product needed to provide an immediate resolution of a critical problem, adopted fixes which due to time criticality should be utilized prior to having been authorized, and those corrections which through testing, revalidation and recertification have been officially authorized.

A8 Risk Assessment. Software maintenance activities consume considerable resources to implement software changes in existing systems. Traditionally, systems are tested to detect defects in the software. Since defects in various software workproducts cause failures with different consequences, the significance (or risk) of each failure/defect varies.

Software risk is defined as the potential loss due to the failure during a specific time period. Risk is measured as a product of the frequency or likelihood of loss and the magnitude or level of exposure. Risk assessment begins with an analysis of external exposure -- determination of the magnitude of loss that can result from invalid actions. The external exposure is mapped onto the system to determine the magnitude of loss caused by faults in individual software workproducts. The likelihood of failure for each workproduct is based on its use, verification, validation, adaptability, and size characteristics.

In the context of maintenance, the failure can be product or process oriented. That is, the failure of the product (i.e., errors in function and performance) and process (i.e., inaccurate estimates) have the potential of increasing costs of the product and are therefore considered risks. Risk abatement techniques for product risks include testing and maintainability measurement. Risk abatement for the process includes software change impact analysis.

To measure software risk several functions should be performed: external exposure identification, structural exposure analysis, and software failure likelihood estimation. The following is an outline of these functions as they pertain to software maintenance risk assessment.

A8.1 External Exposure Identification. The external exposure identification function has two primary objectives. The first is to determine what actions in the environment outside of the software can contribute to loss. The second objective is to assess the significance of the loss. To this end, the procedure involves the following steps:

(1) Definition of environmental hazards: determine how the organization intends to use the software system and potential hazards such as financial, explosions, incorrect patient treatment, misinformation, loss of life, and like accidents.

(2) Identification of accident sequences: investigate how accidents can occur and record them in event trees, scenarios, or annotated event sequence diagrams.

(3) Failure mode analysis: identify failure modes from accident sequences and record them in fault trees. Key failure areas are identified by working backwards in the fault tree.

(4) Consequence analysis: determine the consequence of the faults by weighting the loss estimated for each accident scenario. Since this has a wide range of factors and conditions, care should be taken to focus on the key failures.

A8.2 Structural Exposure Analysis. Structural exposure analysis is performed to discover how and where software faults can contribute to losses identified in the external exposure assessment. The objective of this function is to assign exposure levels to individual workproducts based on their capability to cause failures, The procedure includes the following activities:

(1) Identify software failure modes: indicate where erroneous information can contribute to loss and investigate how the software can fail as a result.

(2) Determine workproduct fault potential: locate the potential faults related to the fault modes and identify associated relationships between faults and losses.

(3) Analyze mode use: locate where potentially faulty workproducts are used.

(4) Compute workproduct exposure: estimate the module exposure by summing its potential loss for all accident scenarios to which it is related.

A8.3 Software Failure Likelihood. The objective of the software failure likelihood function is to predict failure likelihood from workproduct and maintenance process characteristics. As software testing proceeds, information about the testing process is used to update or confirm our initial estimates of failure likelihood. The likelihood of software failure depends on the number of faults in a workproduct and the probability that the fault will be encountered in the operation of the system. That is, failure likelihood depends on the number of faults and the probability that the faults will cause failures. Risks for each workproduct is determined by the probability of each type of failure times the costs of that failure.

A9 Safety. Safety is the ability of a system to avoid catastrophic behavior. Safety requirements may identify critical functions whose failure may be hazardous to people or property. The results of the procedure described in A8.1 may also be applicable. IEEE Standard P1228 [13] contains information that may be used to create and maintain systems.

A10 Security. The degree to which the system and information access needs to be protected can have an effect on the manner in which the system is maintained. A system is secure if unauthorized personnel cannot get at protected information and to the system itself.

Security during the maintenance process should ensure the following:
(1) The integrity of the system is preserved by ensuring only authorized personnel have access to the system and only authorized changes are implemented. This is accomplished in cooperation with SCM and SQA.
(2) Security features implemented during system development are not compromised, either by inadvertent action or failure to comply with the existing security requirements.
(3) New functions added to the system are compatible with the existing security features.

A11 Software Configuration Management (SCM). Software Configuration Management (SCM) is a critical element of the software maintenance process. Conformance to IEEE Stds 828 [2] and 1042 [9] should be adhered to. SCM, a procedure driven process, depends on sound, workable and repeatable procedures to implement the software engineering release function. The procedures should provide for the verification, validation, and certification of each step required to identify, authorize, implement, and release the software product. These procedures should also define the methods used to track the change throughout the maintenance process, to provide the required traceability, to ensure the integrity of the product, to keep project management informed with periodic reports, and to document all the activities involved. During the implementation of the software engineering release process, SCM has responsibilities in each of the major categories of SCM; i.e., configuration identification, configuration audits, change control, and status accounting.

SCM of documentation during system test should be done by the SCM function. The documents to be managed are:
(1) System Documentation
(2) Software code and listings
(3) MRs
(4) Test documentation

Although SCM is not very involved during the initial phases of traditional software development, SCM should be actively pursued throughout the entire software maintenance process. Failure to provide rigorous SCM can result in chaos during the maintenance process. The following items address the SCM requirements that should prevail during each phase of the maintenance process as defined in the Standard.

A11.1 Problem Identification. The SCM process is the principal element of the problem identification phase of software maintenance. SCM is responsible for receiving and logging the problem (corrective, adaptive, corrective) into the Configuration Status Accounting (CSA) system (IEEE Std 1042-1987) [9]. SCM personnel are responsible for routing the problem to the proper personnel (e.g., system/software engineering, test) for validation and evaluation of the problem. SCM provides tracking and coordination of the problem documentation during this phase.

A11.2 Analysis. During the analysis phase, it is a SCM responsibility to provide up-to-date documentation to the personnel performing the analysis (e.g., systems/software engineering). SCM should also provide up-to- date listings of the source code and accurate CSA reports showing the current status of the problem.

At the completion of the analysis phase, it is a SCM responsibility to ensure the analysis results are presented to a review board (a SCM activity). The review board provides visibility and tracking into the problem resolution since it is responsible for authorizing further analysis or implementation. The review board assigns the problems approved for implementation to a software engineering release (block change) package. Although each problem is implemented independently, control is done on a block of problems associated via the software engineering release. SCM is responsible for documenting the proceedings of the review board and updating the CSA records associated with the problem.

A11.3 Design. During the design phase, SCM is responsible for ensuring that the design personnel have up-to-date documentation from the system library. It is crucial that design personnel receive any changes to documentation as soon as possible after receipt. It is a SCM responsibility to archive and safeguard software inspection/review results and other design data provided by the design personnel. In an automated design environment (e.g., CASE), SCM may be required to provide assistance to the design personnel in maintaining version control. SCM is expected to provide assistance and guidance to design personnel in the selection and usage of consistent naming conventions.

At the completion of the design phase, it is a configuration management responsibility to ensure that design documentation is placed in safe keeping and receives SCM control to protect the integrity of the design product. In automated systems, configuration management is responsible for ensuring rigorous version control.

A11.4 Implementation. During implementation, SCM is responsible for providing the programmers with copies of the modules to be changed and ensuring rigorous version control. In situations where multiple changes are made to a single module, SCM is responsible to ensure proper staging to prevent losing changes. This requires complete cooperation and coordination between SCM and the maintenance team. SCM should notify the maintenance team when updated requirement or design data becomes available.

SCM is responsible for maintaining configuration control over all the support tools used in the software maintenance process. Control of the tools (i.e., compilers, assemblers, operating systems, link editors) is crucial to avoid major impacts to the maintenance schedule and preventing unnecessary re-work.

At the completion of the implementation phase, SCM is responsible for collecting all the modules that have been changed and placing them in secure library facilities. If a software development folder concept is used, SCM should ensure that each is placed under configuration control. SCM is often responsible for regenerating the system (compile, link, etc.) and making it available for the test personnel. This is a good practice that ensures consistent results and products for the test group. The librarian of a chief programmer team may perform this SCM task.

SCM is responsible for ensuring all the scheduled changes are included in the release package and made available for systems testing. The entire release package is subjected to a physical audit by Software SCM and validated by Software Quality Assurance. The audit verifies and validates that all the items (e.g., document updates, test plans/procedures, version descriptions, etc.) are complete. After the successful completion of the audit, the release package is presented to a review board for approval to proceed with systems testing. This approval process helps reduce wasting system resources for testing when a product is not ready, and provides a substantial cost/schedule benefit.

SCM is responsible for updating the CSA data base with the results of the review board decisions. Updated status reports are produced for management and the maintenance team. The results and reports generated by the audit are archived and become a permanent part of the release package documentation.

A11.5 System Testing. During the system testing phase, SCM is responsible for ensuring the integrity of :
(1) test case data
(2) the software product on suitable media
(3) other test material.

SCM provides the test group with up-to-date test material as requested. In test environments that are automated, SCM is responsible for maintaining version control over the test material (e.g., test case drivers, regression test case data, etc.).

When system testing is complete, SCM is responsible for archiving test material for the test group. SCM adds the test report data to the archived release package documentation. Problems encountered during testing are documented and entered into the CSA data base by SCM.

A11.6 Acceptance Testing. SCM provides total control of all the material made available to support acceptance testing. This material is returned to SCM at the completion of acceptance testing. SCM adds the acceptance test report data to the archived release package documentation. Problems encountered during testing are documented and entered into the CSA data base by SCM.

The review board is presented with all the test results along with recommendations from each group in the maintenance team to allow an informed decision on the suitability of the system for delivery to the user community. SCM updates the CSA data base with the results of the review board decision and provides management with current status reports.

A11.7 Delivery. After approval by the review board and concurrence by project management, SCM is responsible for delivery of the system to the user community. Based on how the users access the system, the delivery may entail replacing the existing system with the new version, duplication from a master for delivery to remote users, or digital transmission to the users. Irrespective of the method, SCM is responsible for preparing and disseminating the system.

In addition to the physical delivery of the system, SCM is responsible for updating the configuration index records to reflect the new version and archiving the complete system including all release package data. SCM should provide copies of the entire system for disaster recovery storage.

A12 Metrics/Measures. Establishing and implementing a metrics plan is critical for providing insight regarding an organization's level of productivity as well as the quality of the software maintained by that organization. Additional guidance in the form of definitions, methodologies and rationale for implementing a metrics plan is provided in IEEE Standards 982.1 [4], 982.2 [5], and will be provided in P1045 [11] and P1061 [12], when they become available. Metrics/measures captured for maintenance should enable the manager to manage the process and the implementor to implement the process. (Figure 2)

A12.1 The Use Of Metrics/Measures. To initialize a metrics process, management needs to identify technical factors which reflect the technical quality as well as management quality (i.e. effective use of schedule and resources) of the software being maintained. Once these factors are identified as indicators, then measures should be developed which correspond to the technical factors and quantify those technical factors. It is suggested that the selection of the technical factors and their corresponding metrics/measures be optimized such that only the factors that are most pertinent to the specific phase of the maintenance process are addressed during that respective phase of the maintenance process. Figure 2 illustrates some examples of technical factors and metrics/measures which may be used depending on the phase of the process.

Once these are identified, a cost-benefit analysis should be performed to determine the best value that can be achieved by the organization (in terms of increased productivity and overall better management of the process) in exchange for the effort expended to collect and analyze the metrics/measurement data. At the very minimum, effort in terms of work hours should be collected and converted to cost using the organization's internal labor rate. Additionally, some measure of functionality as well as the error rates generated and classified by priority and type should be collected.

Some common measures of functionality are source lines of code (SLOC), function points and feature points. Whatever method chosen, it should be well defined and agreed upon within the organization. Tools used for metrics/measurement collection, analysis and assessment should be validated, calibrated, and used consistently throughout the organization.

In the world of software maintenance there are three major cost drivers which dominate the effort expended during the software maintenance process. These are documentation, communication and coordination, and testing. Therefore, any software maintenance metrics plan should include metrics/measures which accurately track performance based on these cost drivers such as documentation change pages, effort to negotiate the scope of the work to be included in the change package and the error rates classified by priority and type. Furthermore, any measure of functionality used should be tied to the complexity of the software as well as the application type (i.e. enhancement, repair, etc.).

A complexity profile of each program may be comprised of but not limited to the following:

(1) Size of program (# statements or instructions)
(2) Number of modules in programs
(3) Number of variables in programs
(4) Number of global variables in programs
(5) Average module size (in statements)
(6) Average number of compares per module
(7) Average number of modules accessing a global variable .
(8) List of common modules
(9) List of modules that access more than the average number of global variables
(10) List of modules that exceed the module size limit of 50 statements or exceed the module compare limit of 10 compares

The primary data source for the initial metrics/measurement input to the application profile is the software configuration library. Once the initial data are captured, an on-going maintenance metrics repository should be established. This repository should be directly interfaced with the organization's modification control system. The modification control system is a primary data source for the continuing update of the applications inventory profiles.

A13 Software Replacement Policy. Planning for maintenance should be considered for all systems, even those under initial development. Although all systems eventually need maintenance, there comes a time when maintenance to an existing system is not technically or fiscally possible. Trade-offs as to resources, funds, priorities, etc., may dictate that a system should be replaced rather than changed. The management policy that can help in making a correct decision include determination of the following:

(1) System outages or failure rate
(2) Code > n years old
(3) Complex system structure or logic
(4) New hardware
(5) Excessive resource requirements
(6) Missing or deficient documentation or design specifications.

Additional information can be found in NBS Publication 500-106, Guidance on Software Maintenance [14].

Appendix B Supporting Maintenance Technology

This Appendix is not part of IEEE Std P1219, IEEE Standard for Software Maintenance, but is included for information only.

B1 Definitions The definitions listed below establish meaning in the context of this Appendix.

adaptive maintenance. Reactive modification of a software product performed after delivery to make a computer program usable in a changed environment.

emergency maintenance. Unscheduled corrective maintenance performed to keep a system operational.

formal unit. In reverse engineering, a unit of a system identified only by its links with other units.

functional unit. In reverse engineering, a unit of a system defined by its function; functional unit may include one or several formal units, or be a part of a formal unit.

re-engineering. A system changing activity which results in creating a new system that either retains or does not retain the individuality of the initial system.

restructuring. The translation of an unstructured program into a functionally and semantically equivalent structured program. Restructuring transforms unstructured code into structured code to make the code more understandable, and thus more maintainable.

schematic. In reverse engineering, a description of links between system units; links are represented by "jumps" - transfers of control.

B2 Re-engineering. Software Maintenance is a significant part of the software engineering process. New code inevitably requires change: new regulations, changes to functions or the rules that compose functions, corrections to problems, extensions to functions, etc. These changes are typically treated as a minor part of the development process and delegated to "less experienced" programmers. It was generally assumed that these newly developed systems would have a short life span and be rebuilt once the mass of changes needed by the system became too costly to undertake. However, these systems have continued to be of significant value to the organization and hence the revitalization of these aging systems has become a practical option. As a subset of software maintenance, re-engineering has received a significant amount of recent attention. Re-development of key systems has become extremely costly in both dollars and disruption. A critical analysis of the software portfolio and selective re-engineering is a more evolutionary way of bringing old systems up to current standards and supporting newer technologies. A sound approach to re-engineering can not only revitalize a system but also provide reusable material for future systems and form the functional framework for an object oriented environment. The techniques to do this have always been available within other engineering disciplines. However, their application to software is a recent trend and consequently the tools to support software re-engineering are just now emerging.

Re-engineering as an approach is generally composed of two components: reverse engineering, and forward engineering. Reverse engineering does not change the system. It provides an alternate view of the system at a different level of abstraction. This generally means "redocumenting" code as schematics, structure charts or flow diagrams to assist in understanding the logic of the code. Additionally, the process offers opportunities for measurement, and problem identification, and the formulation of corrective procedures. Forward engineering is the process of system building. This process begins with an existing system structure which is the framework for changes and enhancements.

Toolsets to support re-engineering are available and are evolving along the lines of CASE tools; single function tools have begun to evolve to component toolsets that will evolve to integrated sets. These Computer Assisted Re-engineering (CAREs) environments will provide seamless reverse and forward engineering tools that are repository-based. In addition, measurement will play an increasingly important role in problem identification and resolution.

B3 Reverse Engineering. Many systems have the source code as the only reliable representation. This is true for a large long-lived system which underwent many changes during its life time. These systems have substantially overgrown the initial base system, and have poorly updated documentation.

This is where reverse engineering is a recommended technique for redocumenting the system.

The first document that is needed to easily navigate in a system and to find the location of a problem at the analysis stage of system maintenance is program schematics. A program schematic is the analog of an electrical schematic which is the first document required for maintaining an electrical system.

Parallel definitions of schematic documentation are cited in Table B1.

The process of reverse engineering evolves through the following 6 steps:

<u>"in-the-small" - for local analysis on a unit level</u>
(1) dissecting source code into formal units;
(2) semantic description of formal units and declaration of functional units;
(3) creating input/output schematics of units;

<u>"in-the-large" - for global analysis on a system level</u>
(4) declaration and semantic description of linear circuits;
(5) declaration and semantic description of system applications;
(6) creating anatomy of the system.

Steps and products of reverse engineering a computer program are cited in Table B2.

B4 Holistic Reusing. A functioning reliable system during its life-time can give birth to a new, "stand-alone" system, having its own individuality. The functioning system then becomes a "parent" system. The new-born system is as reliable as the parent system (at least at the time of birth). The parent and the offspring systems concurrently exist and evolve. The process of "delivery" of a new system from the parent one is called "Holistic Reusing". This differs from system maintenance activity, which occurs within the bounds of one system.

Holistic Reusing is also a powerful tool for maintaining a system which can not be interrupted except for a quick corrective emergency maintenance (to take the bugs out) while the work-load is low. Perfective or adaptive maintenance may need a lot of system time which may not be available in the real world of a running business.

B5 Software Tools.. Typical methods and tools which can be used during the maintenance process are listed in Table B3. Information on the tools listed can be found in technical and vendor literature.

Table B1

Parallel Definitions for Schematic Documentation

<u>Electrical Engineering</u>	<u>Software Engineering</u>
electrical schematic. Description of links between units of a device (links are represented by wires).	**program schematic.** Description of links between units of a program (links are represented by "jumps" - transfer of control).
Schematics "in-the-small" - for local analysis on a unit level	
I/O electrical schematic. Description of all wires connecting an individual electrical unit to other units.	**I/O program schematic.** Description of all transfers of control to and from an individual program unit.
Schematics "in-the-large" - for global analysis on a system level	
linear electrical circuit. Succession of consecutively connected electrical units.	**linear program circuit.** Succession of consecutively connected program units.
electrical application.	**program application**
A family of linear circuits executing a specific task of an electrical device.	A family of linear circuits executing a specific task of a program.
electrical system anatomy	**program system anatomy**
A list of all applications with relevant electrical circuits.	A list of all applications with relevant program circuits.

Table B2

Process and Products of Reverse Engineering Program Schematics

Process Steps	Products
1. Formally describe all links (transfer of control) in the program.	Formal units *unit entrance*. Statement to which control is transferred from another unit, or the first program line. *unit output*. (exit) Statement from which control is transferred to another unit. *unit end*. Statement preceding the entrance of another unit. *subroutine unit*. Unit which ends with a RETURN-like command. *non-subroutine units:* *transiting*. One to one unit. *branching*. One to many unit. *rooting*. Many to one unit. *starting*. None to one unit. *ending*. One to none unit. *unit number*. Number assigned to a unit from two sets of consecutive numbers: one set for subroutine units, another - for non-subroutine units.
2. Semantically describe function for each formal unit, and create functional units.	Functional unit consisting of one or several formal units or being a part of a formal unit.
3. Describe links for each unit.	Input/Output (I/O) schematic which is combined with a segment of code belonging to a unit.
4. Create a map of all units.	Program Linear Circuits (LC). *FIRST* unit. Unit, from which LC starts. *LAST* unit. Unit, at which LC ends.
5. Create a map of all First and LAST units.	Program applications.
6. Create a list of all applications with relevant linear circuits.	Program Anatomy

Table B3

Methods and Tools for Maintenance

ACTIVITIES/METHODS	TOOLS	Manual	Auto
I. PROBLEM/MODIFICATION IDENTIFICATION			
1. Modification/problem reproduction	Automatic test equipment		X
II. ANALYSIS			
1. Code beautifying	Beautifiers		X
2. Reverse engineering program schematic			
"in the small"			
2.1 Declaring formal units	Diagrammer	X	X
2.2 Declaring functional units via dissecting/ combining formal units.	Expert system	X	X
2.3 Mapping input/output schematic for each functional unit	Mapper		X
'in the large"			
2.4 Mapping functional units, and declaring program linear circuits	Mapper	X	X
2.5 Mapping program linear circuits, and declaring program applications (families of linear circuits)	Mapper	X	X
2.6 Creating anatomy of program		X	
2.7 System metrics/measures	Metric analyzer	X	X
3. Code restructuring	Structure analyzer	X	X

Table B3

Methods and Tools for Maintenance (continued)

ACTIVITIES/METHODS	TOOLS	Manual	Auto
III DESIGN			
1. Reverse engineering design documentation			
1.1 Flow-charting	Diagrammer	X	X
1.2 Data-flow diagramming	Diagrammer	X	X
2. Visualizing	Visualizers	X	X
3. Documenting chgs(large)	Documenter	X	X
4. Documenting chgs(small)	Documenter	X	X
IV. IMPLEMENTATION			
1. Code generation	Code generator		X
2. Code analyzing	Code analyzer	X	X
3. Simulation/emulation	Simulators & Emulators	X	X
4. Test analyzing	Test analyzers	X	X
5. Test data generation	Test data generators		X
6. Profiling	Profilers	X	X
VI. SYSTEM/ACCEPTANCE TESTING			
1. Stress Testing		X	X
2. Performance Testing	Performance monitors	X	X
3. Function Testing		X	X
VII. DELIVERY			
1. Media duplication/ verification	Media duplicators/ verifers	X	X

IEEE Std 1298-1992
AS 3563.1—1991

IEEE Standard

Software Quality Management System

Part 1: Requirements

Adopted from Standards Australia

Sponsor

Software Engineering Standards Subcommittee of the Software Engineering Technical Committee of the IEEE Computer Society

Approved December 3, 1992

IEEE Standards Board

Abstract: Requirements for a software developer's quality management system are established. Each of the elements of a quality management system to be designed, developed, and maintained by the developer are identified, with the objective of ensuring that the software will meet the requirements of a contract, purchase order, or other agreement (collectively referred to as a "contract").
Keywords: software development, software quality, software quality management

---

This standard was originally developed and published by Standards Australia AS 3563.1—1991, Software Quality Management System, Part 1: Requirements. Standards Australia has granted the IEEE permission to adopt, reprint, and vend the Australian Standard. Standards Australia remains the owner of all property rights in, and custodian of the Australian Standard and is responsible for its future development and revisions. For information on the current status of this standard or for permission to reprint, please contact Standards Australia, P. O. Box 1055, Strathfield, NSW 2138.

ISBN 1-55937-289-3

IEEE Standards documents are developed within the Technical Committees of the IEEE Societies and the Standards Coordinating Committees of the IEEE Standards Board. Members of the committees serve voluntarily and without compensation. They are not necessarily members of the Institute. The standards developed within IEEE represent a consensus of the broad expertise on the subject within the Institute as well as those activities outside of IEEE that have expressed an interest in participating in the development of the standard.

Use of an IEEE Standard is wholly voluntary. The existence of an IEEE Standard does not imply that there are no other ways to produce, test, measure, purchase, market, or provide other goods and services related to the scope of the IEEE Standard. Furthermore, the viewpoint expressed at the time a standard is approved and issued is subject to change brought about through developments in the state of the art and comments received from users of the standard. Every IEEE Standard is subjected to review at least every five years for revision or reaffirmation. When a document is more than five years old and has not been reaffirmed, it is reasonable to conclude that its contents, although still of some value, do not wholly reflect the present state of the art. Users are cautioned to check to determine that they have the latest edition of any IEEE Standard.

Comments for revision of IEEE Standards are welcome from any interested party, regardless of membership affiliation with IEEE. Suggestions for changes in documents should be in the form of a proposed change of text, together with appropriate supporting comments.

Interpretations: Occasionally questions may arise regarding the meaning of portions of standards as they relate to specific applications. When the need for interpretations is brought to the attention of IEEE, the Institute will initiate action to prepare appropriate responses. Since IEEE Standards represent a consensus of all concerned interests, it is important to ensure that any interpretation has also received the concurrence of a balance of interests. For this reason IEEE and the members of its technical committees are not able to provide an instant response to interpretation requests except in those cases where the matter has previously received formal consideration.

Comments on standards and requests for interpretations should be addressed to:

Secretary, IEEE Standards Board
445 Hoes Lane
P.O. Box 1331
Piscataway, NJ 08855-1331
USA

Introduction

(This introduction is not a part of IEEE Std 1298-1992 [AS 3563.1-1991], Software Quality Management System, Part 1: Requirements.)

IEEE Std 1298-1992 (AS 3563.1-1991) is a comprehensive standard for the software development process. The level of detail is constrained by the size of the document. This standard, supplemented by standards in the topic areas of project management, software requirements, programming, testing, software configuration management, and quality assurance, provides an effective framework for achieving quality goals for a software development project.

Suggested references or clarifications for IEEE Std 1298-1992 (AS 3563.1-1991) paragraphs:

Clause 2:

For AS 1057, Quality Assurance and Quality Control—Glossary of Terms, use ISO 2382-1 : 1984, Data Processing—Vocabulary—Part 01: Fundamental Terms; ISO 8402 : 1988, Quality—Vocabulary; and IEEE Std 610.12-1990, IEEE Standard Glossary of Software Engineering Terminology.

For AS 3901, Quality Systems for Design/Development, Production, Installation, and Servicing, use ISO 9001 : 1987, Quality Systems—Model for Quality Assurance in Design/Development, Production, Installation and Servicing.

Clause 4:

4.1 For verification and validation, see IEEE Std 1012-1986, IEEE Standard for Software Verification and Validation Plans.

4.2 For quality management, see IEEE Std 730-1989, IEEE Standard for Software Quality Assurance Plans.

4.3 For project planning, see IEEE Std 1058.1-1987, IEEE Standard for Software Project Management Plans.

For software product requirements, see IEEE Std 830-1984, IEEE Guide for Software Requirements Specifications.

For software configuration management, see IEEE Std 828-1990, IEEE Standard for Software Configuration Management Plans, and IEEE Std 1042-1987, IEEE Guide to Software Configuration Management.

4.4 For software configuration management, see IEEE Std 828-1990, IEEE Standard for Software Configuration Management Plans, and IEEE Std 1042-1987, IEEE Guide to Software Configuration Management.

For reviews and audits, see IEEE Std 1028-1988, IEEE Standard for Reviews and Audits.

For design document, see IEEE Std 1016-1987, IEEE Recommended Practice for Software Design Descriptions.

For user documentation, see IEEE Std 1063-1987, IEEE Standard for Software User Documentation.

For program testing, see IEEE Std 829-1983, IEEE Standard for Software Test Documentation, and IEEE Std 1008-1987, IEEE Standard for Software Unit Testing.

4.5 For document configuration management, see IEEE Std 828-1990, IEEE Standard for Software Configuration Management Plans, and IEEE Std 1042-1987, IEEE Guide to Software Configuration Management.

4.8 For software configuration management, see IEEE Std 828-1990, IEEE Standard for Software Configuration Management Plans, and IEEE Std 1042-1987, IEEE Guide to Software Configuration Management.

4.10 For test procedures, see IEEE Std 829-1983, IEEE Standard for Software Test Documentation, and IEEE Std 1008-1987, IEEE Standard for Software Unit Testing.

4.15 For software configuration management, see IEEE Std 828-1990, IEEE Standard for Software Configuration Management Plans, and IEEE Std 1042-1987, IEEE Guide to Software Configuration Management.

4.16 For quality records, see IEEE Std 730-1989, IEEE Standard for Software Quality Assurance Plans.

4.17 For quality audits, see IEEE Std 730-1989, IEEE Standard for Software Quality Assurance Plans.

4.18 The Training Guarantee Act is an Australian law that requires most firms to set aside a percentage of the gross sales for employee training.

4.21 For software development environment configuration management, see IEEE Std 828-1990, IEEE Standard for Software Configuration Management Plans, and IEEE Std 1042-1987, IEEE Guide to Software Configuration Management.

The following persons were on the balloting committee that approved this standard for submission to the IEEE Standards Board:

Mark Amaya
Eleanor Antreassian
Wolf Arfvidson
Theodore K. Atchinson
Phillip S. Babel
Bakul Banerjee
David Barber
Boris Beizer
Mordechai Ben-Menachem
H.R. Berlack
Robert V. Binder
Stephen E. Blake
Thomas G. Bogart
William J. Boll
Sandro Bologna
Juergen Braendle
Thomas E. Braudt
Damien P. Brignell
Fletcher Buckley
Michael Buckley
Susan Marie Burgess
David W. Burnett
Neva M. Carlson
John Chihorek
T.J. Chung
François Coallier
Christopher Cooke
Stewart Crawford
Bjorn Cronhjort
Patricia W. Daggett
Michael A. Daniels
Taz Daughtrey
Paul I. Davis
Kent de Jong
Bostjan K. Derganc
Audrey Dorofee
Einar Dragstedt
Scott P. Duncan
Julian Edelman
D. Vera Edelstein
Michael Edward
Dr. Leo G. Egan
Lise Enstrom
Caroline L. Evans
William Eventoff
Richard Fairley
John W. Fendrich
Antonietta L. Fleetwood
Roger G. Fordham
Jay Forster
Kirby Fortenberry
Eugene P. Friedman
Barry L. Garner
Leanne Gasson
Yair Gershkovitch
Jean Gilmore
Shirley A. Gloss-Soler
John Garth Glynn
Arthur Godin
Victor M. Guarnera
P. Michael Guba
Praveen Gupta
David A. Gustafson
Jane R. Guttman
Thomas L. Hannan
William Hefley
Manfred Hein
Charles P. Hollocker
John W. Horch
Jody Howard
Peter L. Hung
Lynn Ihlenfeldt
Debra Jasinski
Shang-Sheng Jeng
J.O. Jenkins
Richard Johansson
L. Katherine Jones
Linell M. Jones
Ron S. Kenett
Dolores Kent
R.A. Kisaler
Dwayne L. Knirk
Roy W. Ko
Shaye Koenig
Robert E. Koles
Robert Kosinski
Joseph Krupinski
Edwared Kujawski
Rebecca Ann Lamb
Renee Lamb
John B. Lane
Robert A.C. Lane
J. Dennis Lawrence
Lawrence Lee
Raymond W. Lee
F.C. Lim
Bev Littlewood
Ben Livson
Hakan Ljungkvist
Dieter Look
Joseph Maayan
Harold Mains
Henry A. Malec
Roger Martin
Tomoo Matsubara
Ivano Mazza
Russell McDowell
G.A. Meldrum
Michael F. Merriman
Jerome W. Mersky
Louis E. Miller
Celia H. Modell
Nancy Morton
John Musa
Geraldine R. Neidhart
Jan-Willem Neurdenburg
Dennis E. Nickle
Robert Parys
Brian Peavey
Donald J. Pfeiffer
John D. Pope
Robert M. Poston
Jane Radatz
Samuel T. Redwine, Jr.
Larry K. Reed
Matthias F. Reese
James R. Roberts
Steven Rood-Ojalvo
Julio Sanz
Stephen R. Schach
Hans Schaefer
Benson H. Scheff
Norman Schneidewind
Wolf A. Schnoege
Roger W. Scholten
Gregory D. Schumacher
Carl S. Seddio
John Sheehan
Robert W. Shillato
David M. Siefert
Al Sorkowitz
Timothy E. Splitt
Vijaya Krishna Srivastava
Richard Staunton
Robert N. Sulgrove
William Thetford
Henry C. Thoelke
George D. Tice, Jr.
Glendon R. Trebble
Leonard L. Tripp
Margaret C. Updike
Roger Van Scoy
Udo Voges
Anneliese von Mayrhauser
Dolores Wallace
William M. Walsh
Carl Warren
Scott A. Whitmire
G.Allan Whittaker
James Wiektenstein
Andrew Wilson
Paul A. Wolfgang
Stephen Wong
Dennis L. Wood
Paul R. Work
Tom Worthington
Weider Yu
Janusz Zalewski
Lin Zocconi

When the IEEE Standards Board approved this standard on December 3, 1992, it had the following membership:

Marco W. Migliaro, *Chair* **Donald C. Loughry,** *Vice Chair*
Andrew G. Salem, *Secretary*

Dennis Bodson
Paul L. Borrill
Clyde Camp
Donald C. Fleckenstein
Jay Forster*
David F. Franklin
Ramiro Garcia
Thomas L. Hannan
Donald N. Heirman
Ben C. Johnson
Walter J. Karplus
Ivor N. Knight
Joseph Koepfinger*
Irving Kolodny
D. N. "Jim" Logothetis
Lawrence V. McCall
T. Don Michael*
John L. Rankine
Wallace S. Read
Ronald H. Reimer
Gary S. Robinson
Martin V. Schneider
Terrance R. Whittemore
Donald W. Zipse

*Member Emeritus

Also included are the following nonvoting IEEE Standards Board liaisons:

Satish K. Aggarwal
James Beall
Richard B. Engelman
David E. Soffrin
Stanley Warshaw

Australian Standard®

Software quality management system

Part 1: Requirements

First published as AS 3563—1988.
Revised and redesignated AS 3563.1—1991.

PUBLISHED BY STANDARDS AUSTRALIA
(STANDARDS ASSOCIATION OF AUSTRALIA)
STANDARDS HOUSE, 80 ARTHUR ST, NORTH SYDNEY NSW
ISBN 0 7262 7103 9

PREFACE

This Standard was prepared by the Standards Australia Committee on Software Quality Assurance to supersede AS 3563—1988, *Software quality management system*.

It is recognized that the principles contained within this Standard are representative of sound management practice and hence are recommended for use when either invoked as a contractual requirement or for the purpose of providing a quality management system within an organization.

It is intended to provide a common means for establishing an effective quality management system when related to software, which, together with procedures for the specification, design, implementation and evaluation, allow development of software in a controlled manner. This should result in creation of software in the most cost effective way, having due regard to the whole life cycle of the product, and should instil a high degree of confidence that the software will meet the operational requirements.

It is believed that integration of these principles, together with the ability to demonstrate their effectiveness, will also lead to greater confidence in potential purchasing organizations when evaluating a developer's capability.

In format, this Standard closely follows that of AS 3901/NZS 9001/ISO 9001, *Quality systems for design/development, production, installation and servicing*, and thus is suitable for adoption in parallel with hardware requirements under that Standard. This Standard bears a similar relationship to AS 3900 and AS 3904.1 as does AS 3901 to those Standards.

This Standard is presented so as to make obvious the correspondence with AS 3901/NZS 9001/ISO 9001 and adds to that Standard those areas of particular relevance to the software development process. This manner of presentation will enable it to coexist with AS 3901/NZS 9001/ISO 9001 and will also allow updating of this edition in conjunction with the planned upgradings of the International Standard. This reformatting also reflects the view of the Committee that AS 3563.1 places greater emphasis on the design activities whereas AS 3901/NZS 9001/ISO 9001 emphasizes production and quality of conformance aspects. For this reason, some of the clauses in this Standard are identified as not applicable to the software development process.

To assist users who are new to the concepts of quality assurance, interpretive guidance was given for many of the clauses of the Standard in AS 3563—1988. This proved very popular and the concept has been retained for this edition of the Standard, notwithstanding the interpretive guidance given in the forthcoming ISO Standard which is anticipated for publication in 1992: ISO 9000-2, *Guide for the implementation of ISO 9001, ISO 9002, ISO 9003*, and ISO 9000-3, *Guidelines for the application of ISO 9001 to the development, supply and maintenance of software*, published in June 1991.

AS 3563.2, *Software quality management system*, Part 2: *Implementation*, will provide information as a guide to users for implementing the requirements of Part 1 of this Standard.

In preparing this Standard, cognizance was taken of Australian Standards AS 3900/NZS 9000/ISO 9000, *Quality systems—Guide to selection and use*, AS 3901/NZS 9001/ISO 9001, *Quality systems for design/development, production, installation and servicing*, AS 3904.1/NZS 9004.1/ISO 9004, *Quality management and quality system elements—Guidelines*, ISO 9000-3, *Quality management and quality assurance standards*—Part 3: *Guidelines for the application of ISO 9001 to the development, supply and maintenance of software* and ISO 8402, *Quality—Vocabulary*.

CONTENTS

FOREWORD

The development and acquisition of computerized systems may be characterized by a recognized combination of two major components: hardware and software. The successful integration of these two major components is essential for compliance with overall user requirements. Essential to this successful integration is the application of a disciplined approach to management provided by a quality system.

This Standard is presented as a statement of requirements which may be nominated by individual customers, as a condition of contract or agreement, when seeking to obtain software for which they have need for assurance of quality prior to acceptance. The Standard is also recommended to developers whose software is distributed for general sale, as a guide to identifying the requirements of effective and economical management systems to control and assure the quality of their software.

It should be noted that the Standard only defines the essential features of the system and does not attempt to prescribe how the system will be implemented. Guidance is given after each clause identified as requiring such guidance. It is for developers to establish procedures appropriate to their own scale, methodologies and organization to achieve the requirements of the Standard. In the case of a potential customer, the developer's means of implementing the required system should be agreed on when signing a contract.

Where applicable in this Standard, the word 'software' includes installation and operator documentation, user and maintenance documentation, user procedures and training materials. Care should be taken by the developer and the customer to clarify their intentions in this regard when using this Standard.

This Standard may be used as a replacement for AS 3901/NZS 9001/ISO 9001, *Quality systems for design/development, production, installation and servicing*, in specifying a software quality management system or may be used as a supplement to the application of AS 3901/NZS 9001/ISO 9001 for the development of software.

STANDARDS AUSTRALIA

Australian Standard
Software quality management system

Part 1: Requirements

1 SCOPE AND FIELD OF APPLICATION

1.1 Scope This Standard establishes requirements for a software developer's quality management system. It identifies each of the elements of a quality management system to be designed, developed and maintained by the developer with the objective of ensuring that the software will meet the requirements of a contract, purchase order or other agreement (collectively referred to as a 'contract').

1.2 Application This Standard is applicable in contractual situations when the contract specifically requires design effort and the product requirements are stated principally in performance terms or require to be established.

When referenced in a contract, this Standard shall apply to the development of software whether the contract is for software alone or for software as a portion of a system. This Standard may also be applied to 'in-house' software development where the 'customer' can be taken to be that part of the organization requesting the development.

This Standard shall also apply to non-deliverable software developed under the contract, which affects the quality of the deliverable product, unless specifically exempted.

If an inconsistency exists between the contract requirements and this document, the contract requirements shall prevail.

2 REFERENCED DOCUMENTS The following documents are referred to in this Standard:

AS	
1057	Quality assurance and quality control—Glossary of terms
3901/NZS 9001/ISO 9001	Quality systems for design/development, production, installation and servicing

NOTE: Throughout this Standard reference to AS 3901 is to be taken as reference to AS 3901/NZS 9001/ISO 9001.

3 DEFINITIONS For the purpose of this Standard, the definitions given in AS 1057 and those below apply.

3.1 Baseline The agreed specification, or software item, which has been uniquely identified and becomes the focus for further development, and which can only be altered under strict control procedures.

3.2 Development All activities that are carried out to create a software product.

3.3 Software product requirements document The document that describes the full requirements for the software product that is to be developed.

NOTE: Equivalent names used in the software industry are—

(a) user requirements;

(b) segment specification;

(c) software product requirements specification; and

(d) technical requirements section of the contract.

3.4 Test specification Describes the test criteria and the methods to be used in a specific test to assure that the performance and design specifications have been satisfied. The test specification identifies the capabilities or program functions to be tested, and identifies the test environment.

4 QUALITY SYSTEM REQUIREMENTS

4.1 Management responsibility

4.1.1 *Quality policy* The developer's management shall define and document its policy and objectives for, and commitment to, quality. The developer shall ensure that this policy is understood, implemented and maintained at all levels in the organization.

4.1.2 *Organization*

4.1.2.1 *Responsibility and authority* The responsibility, authority and the interrelation of all personnel who manage, perform and verify work affecting quality shall be defined; particularly for personnel who need the organizational freedom and authority to—

(a) initiate action to prevent the occurrence of non-conformity;

(b) identify and record any quality problems;

(c) initiate, recommend or provide solutions through designated channels;

(d) verify the implementation of solutions; and

(e) limit further development or delivery of non-conforming software until the deficiency or unsatisfactory condition has been corrected.

4.1.2.2 *Verification and validation* The developer shall identify in-house verification and validation requirements, provide adequate resources and assign trained personnel for verification activities (see Clause 4.18).

4.1.2.3 *Management representative* The developer shall appoint a management representative who shall have defined authority and responsibility for ensuring that the requirements of this Standard are implemented and maintained, irrespective of other responsibilities.

Guidance *To establish a software quality system which meets the requirements of this Standard, developers should identify and document the functions and activities that directly affect quality and assign specific responsibilities and authority for their fulfilment and, further, fix specific accountability for decisions. Such documentation of the developer's quality management arrangements is often presented as a quality manual.*

The statements made in this requirement alone are not to be construed to mean that the developer's management must assign responsibility for the fulfilment of these requirements to a single division, department or person.

Although developers should have quality assurance, quality control and inspection functions, these alone cannot satisfy all of the requirements of the customer. Other functions of a developer's organization will contribute significantly to overall quality effectiveness.

In every organization, anybody having anything to do with developing the software, contributes to the quality. All responsibilities and authorities, which include those for quality, should therefore be clearly established and understood. Working relationships between sub-groups of the organization require clear understanding and coordination between managers, supervisors and employees.

The primary responsibility of a 'management representative' is to ensure that the requirements of the Standard are implemented and maintained. A further purpose is to establish an official channel of communication on quality matters between the customer and developer; this is particularly relevant in medium-sized and large organizations. The 'management representative' should also act as a focal point for coordination and resolution of quality matters.

Although the developer may select any competent member of staff to fulfil this role, the management representative (often referred to as the 'quality manager') should possess authority consistent with responsibility for the quality system extending throughout the company. If the management representative has other responsibilities, the responsibility for maintaining the integrity of the quality system and its effective use is as important and should not be subordinated to these other concerns. To provide freedom of action and independence necessary for effective execution of these duties, the management representative should report directly to senior executive management.

4.1.3 *Management review* The quality system adopted to satisfy the requirements of this Standard shall be reviewed at appropriate intervals by the developer's management to ensure its continuing suitability and effectiveness. Records of such reviews shall be maintained (see Clause 4.16).

NOTE: Management reviews normally include assessment of the results of internal quality audits, but are carried out by, or on behalf of, the supplier's management, i.e. management personnel having direct responsibility for the system. (See Clause 4.17.)

Guidance *It is important that the quality system be subject to continual review and assessment of its appropriateness and effectiveness. In this context, quality is a developer's management responsibility. To attain required quality, management has to specify its objectives, establish plans and procedures to accomplish them, assign duties, delegate authority, set up adequate methods and standards of performance, and evaluate results objectively. In order to ensure that these requirements for quality continue to be met, the developer's management should periodically and systematically conduct formal reviews.*

It is emphasized that such reviews need to be systematic and not merely casual or superficial inquiries. The findings of the quality system reviews should be analysed to determine the actions necessary to maintain the system's effectiveness.

The developer should utilize the management review as a means of identifying and recording observations, conclusions and recommendations reached, and evaluation should be submitted in documentary form to management for necessary action in establishing a program for quality improvement.

The developer should also establish and maintain appropriate measures for software quality improvement to ensure the ongoing effectiveness of the software quality management system.

The developer should establish and maintain procedures for the review of quality costs as a means of identifying opportunities to be adopted for their optimization.

4.2 Quality system

4.2.1 *General* The developer shall maintain an effective system for quality management, planned and developed in conjunction with other functions, which shall be documented. Requirements shall be met by the establishment and implementation of procedures which have the specific purpose of ensuring that only software conforming to contractual requirements is delivered. In pursuance of these requirements the system shall—

(a) demonstrate both recognition of the factors which may affect quality, and an organized approach to control these factors;

(b) ensure that quality requirements are determined and that standards and procedures are established to satisfy such requirements, including development, acquisition, inspection and testing, packaging, shipping, storage, installation and maintenance;

(c) provide for the early and prompt detection of actual or potential deficiencies, trends or conditions which could result in non-compliance with requirements and for timely and effective corrective action; and

(d) make available evidence that the quality system is effective.

Guidance *As noted in the Foreword, the Standard only defines the essential features of the system and does not attempt to prescribe how the system should be implemented. It is for developers to establish procedures appropriate to their own scale, methodologies and organization to achieve the requirements of the Standard. In the case of a potential customer, the developer's means of implementing the required system should be agreed on before signing a contract.*

4.2.2 *Development standards and procedures* The developer shall identify, adopt or develop and maintain clear and complete documented standards and procedures that prescribe the performance of development tasks. These standards and procedures shall be consistent with achievement of quality objectives and, where appropriate, shall describe the characteristics of the intermediate and deliverable products and services.

The standards and procedures shall be available for use by personnel at all locations where development tasks are performed.

Guidance *All standards and procedures (referred to in some organizations as codes of practice) to be used in the development of software should be well documented and readily accessible. They should detail standards of code and documentation, including planned content and format, and procedures to be executed in the testing and implementation of the software, and should cover the following additional subjects:*

(a) Project management—including milestones, resource allocation, sub-contractor control, significant timing and reporting structure.

(b) Design techniques—covering methodology selection and reference to other manuals where necessary.

(c) Review procedures—defining the method of review, responsibilities and corrective action, where appropriate.

To ensure that quality software is developed, all standards and procedures should be adhered to, and appropriate evidence of adherence through reporting and reviewing should be available at all times.

Periodic reviews of applicability and effectiveness of the standards and procedures should be conducted, to ensure that maximum benefit is gained from their implementation.

4.3 Contract review, planning and requirements control

4.3.1 *Contract review* The developer shall establish and maintain procedures for contract review and for the coordination of these activities.

Each contract shall be reviewed by the developer to ensure that—

(a) the requirements are adequately defined and documented;

(b) any requirements differing from those in the tender 'if applicable' are resolved;

(c) the developer has the capability to meet contractual requirements; and

(d) the responsibilities of the customer are defined.

Records of such contract review shall be maintained (see Clause 4.16).

NOTE: The contract review activities, interfaces and communication within the developer's organization should be coordinated with the customer's organization, as appropriate.

4.3.2 *Planning* The developer shall conduct planning activities, during the earliest practical phase of contract performance, to address the requirements for—

(a) adequate and documented control of development phases, including adequacy of inspection, validation, verification, testing and review and the appropriate use and development of tools and techniques;

(b) timely identification of, and establishment or acquisition of, controls, inspection and testing tools, facilities, computer aids and skills that may be needed to ensure compliance of the software with its contractual requirements, including quality; and

(c) the provision of a quality plan which identifies standards and procedures to be used to achieve the software quality objectives specific to the contract. Plans when produced shall be updated as development progresses.

Guidance *Planning is essential to ensure the control of quality. Planning should encompass all significant activities to be undertaken during the software development, particularly special or unusual requirements. All deliverables and project dependencies should be documented in plans. The contract may require the plcns to be subject to customer approval.*

The planning activity continues through the development process, and has to be timely and provide for review and assessment of all development processes, schedules and activities.

The developer should be able to demonstrate that software quality activities are planned as part of the overall plan for a project, and that these activities cover all of the quality requirements of the contract.

4.3.3 *Control of software product requirements* The developer shall adopt, establish and maintain procedures to exercise control over software product requirements, during the development cycle. These procedures shall include the following:

(a) A means to establish consultation between the developer and customer to resolve ambiguities, errors and omissions.

(b) A means to ensure that the software product requirements document with any resultant amendments specifies the requirements and that it is accepted by the customer.

(c) An analysis of the requirements to assure feasibility and testability.

Guidance *A prerequisite to developing quality software is the necessity to ensure that software product requirements for that software are clearly defined and agreed on between the developer and customer. It is the customer's responsibility to ensure that the software product requirements reflect the real needs of the user.*

It is important that control of requirements, once established and approved, be maintained. The impact of changes resulting from amendments, ambiguities or omissions in the requirements, and errors as a result of testing, should be fully measured, assessed and approved prior to implementation.

4.4 Design, programming and user documentation control

4.4.1 *Design control*

4.4.1.1 *Methods of control* The developer shall establish and maintain procedures for the control of design, wherever performed. The procedures shall including the following:

(a) Identification, documentation and review of design input.

(b) Use of defined methodologies, techniques and procedures.

(c) Task assignment to trained personnel.

(d) Establishment of design review and approval procedures.

(e) Identification of organizational and technical interfaces between different groups and the documentation, transmittal and review of information needed for control.

(f) Provision and use of feedback from previous developments, where appropriate.

(g) Consideration of safety, reliability and maintainability.

4.4.1.2 *Design reviews* The developer shall reference or document the procedures to be used for the control of such reviews to ensure that the software design is consistent with the contractual requirements. These reviews shall be carried out independently of the control of the designer of the particular part under review. The review procedures shall include the following:

(a) Descriptions of the objectives of each review.

(b) Identification of review points.

(c) Methods for specifying non-scheduled reviews.

(d) Identification of the functions of the personnel involved.

(e) Provision for the recording of analyses and recommendations of reviews.

(f) Methods to ensure that the recommendations arising from reviews are monitored to ensure that timely corrective action is taken.

4.4.1.3 *Design changes* After a design has been approved, any subsequent change shall require approval by the authority which approved the original design, or as otherwise designated in the contract.

All changes shall be fully documented and, after approval, transmitted to all functions involved in implementing the design.

All design changes shall be subject to the same controls as the original design.

Guidance *It is not the intention of this Standard to limit in any way the choice of a design methodology by a developer. Unless a methodology is prescribed by contract, developers should choose a methodology appropriate to the following:*

(a) The type of software being developed.

(b) The development environment being used.

Procedures and methods of design, including conduct of reviews and approvals, should be established and documented. This is necessary to ensure that the software design complies with organizational or project specific standards, and is consistent with the software product requirements.

One of the major problem areas in developing quality software is the controlling of changes. Design changes may result from problems in testing that require the design to be re-addressed, or from changes made to approved requirements.

The effect of such changes can be far reaching—they affect resources, schedules, costs, documentation, testing, and the code itself.

The total impact should be measured and documented in order to seek approval prior to implementation of the change. That approval should be gained from the authority responsible for approving the original design.

It is essential to have such procedures in place, and the approving authorities identified, to allow for smooth implementation of change.

4.4.2 *Programming and user documentation controls*

4.4.2.1 *Methods of control* The developer shall adopt, establish and maintain procedures to exercise control over all programming and user documentation activities.

The procedures shall include the following:

(a) Programming and user documentation standards.

(b) Means by which compliance to the programming and user documentation standards may be evaluated.

(c) Mechanisms for review of code and documents to assure their compliance with design criteria.

4.4.2.2 *Programming and user documentation standards* Programming standards shall describe approved programming practices, and list any prohibited practices appropriate to the programming language used. Such standards shall cover all appropriate areas, such as program design, coding, program testing, integration and documentation.

Standards for program testing shall include practices or criteria for all testing and inspection of programs, prior to release for subsequent integration.

Standards for user documentation shall include requirements for program documentation, to ensure that the programs are comprehensible, testable and maintainable.

NOTE: There are a further two classes of documentation referred to in this Standard, namely—

(a) *Quality system documentation*—Documents which form part of the quality system but not those detailing the content of particular products.

(b) *Design requirements documentation*—Documents describing the content of particular products.

Guidance To ensure development of quality software that is reliable and maintainable, accepted programming and user documentation standards should be adhered to. The employment of such standards should also aid in the reduction of errors in code.

Means of confirming adherence to standards could include code inspections and walk-throughs or automatic code analysis. The results of these should be recorded.

The appropriate programming and user documentation standards and methodologies should be chosen either from those which are externally published and documented, or from those which are internal or project specific. Due regard should be given to the developer's scale of operations, the contract requirements, the application, implementation, and run-time environments.

4.5 Quality system document control

4.5.1 *Document approval and issue* The developer shall establish and maintain procedures to control all documents and data that relate to the requirements of this Standard. These documents shall be reviewed and approved for adequacy by authorized personnel prior to issue.

4.5.2 *Control of standards and procedures* The developer shall implement a procedure to ensure the preparation, issue, application and maintenance of standards and procedures.

4.5.3 *Change procedure* All changes to the developer's standards and procedures shall be authorized, dated and processed in a manner which shall ensure prompt action at the specified effective date. The developer shall maintain a record of changes as they are made. Provision shall be made for the prompt removal of obsolete documents from all points of issue and use. Where contractually required, or where such changes significantly affect the quality, the customer shall be advised.

4.5.4 *Retention of documents* A copy of superseded standards and procedures shall be retained, as necessary, to satisfy contractual or mutually agreed requirements.

4.6 Purchasing

4.6.1 *Sub-contracted software development* The developer shall be responsible for ensuring that sub-contracted software conforms to the requirements of the main contract. The developer shall identify the methods and procedures for ensuring that the sub-contractors comply with these requirements. The developer shall establish and maintain records of acceptable sub-contractors.

Guidance The significance of this requirement is that the developer should either—

(a) ensure that the sub-contractors already have acceptable quality control systems and that these systems are working; or

(b) impose a quality system on the sub-contractor.

In any case, the developer has to ensure that there is appropriate coordination with the sub-contractors, and that objective evidence is produced and maintained for achievement of required quality. The developer should also have procedures which detail the system of review and audit to be employed in respect of the sub-contractor's activities.

By prior agreement between the developer and the sub-contractors, the customer's quality assurance representative should always have right of access to the sub-contractor's premises where activities on the project are taking place.

4.6.2 *Procurement*

4.6.2.1 *General* The developer shall be responsible for ensuring that all purchased software, hardware, and services conform to contractual requirements, and that all applicable requirements are included or referenced in all purchase orders for goods and services which are ultimately to apply to the contract.

4.6.2.2 *Customer confirmation* Where specified in the contract, the customer's quality assurance representative shall have the right to confirm at source, or after receipt, that purchased software, hardware and services conform to requirements. All arrangements for such activities, and all reporting of resulting actions, shall be made through the developer.

Guidance The developer is responsible for ensuring that all items purchased conform to the contract requirements. This does not necessarily mean that all purchased software has to be developed according to this Standard. For example, commercial software bought to support development, or even for inclusion as part of the deliverable software, may have been developed to a different or unspecified standard. The contract should specify the circumstances under which such software is acceptable.

4.7 Customer-supplied information and material The developer shall assess customer-supplied information and material for suitability. Any such information and material which is unsuitable for use shall be promptly reported to the customer. The developer shall establish and maintain procedures for the incorporation only of suitable information and material into the software development process. The developer shall provide for the safe custody of all such information and material, and shall retain a register of all customer-supplied information and material, as appropriate.

4.8 Configuration management (including product identification and traceability) The developer shall establish procedures for identifying and controlling software components, including changes, and for maintaining the integrity and traceability of the configuration at all stages of contract performance. These procedures shall also apply to deliverable documentation. The procedures shall include methods for—

(a) version identification, issue and control;

(b) obtaining approval to implement a modification;

(c) ensuring that modifications are properly integrated through formal change control procedures;

(d) controlling the identification of development status; and

(e) ensuring that non-conforming software is identified and controlled.

Guidance Configuration management procedures should be established at the beginning of the software development cycle. Procedures include identification, control and change of software configuration items.

Configuration items include specifications, design documents, test documentation and all modules whether purchased or developed.

Software is subject to constant change during the development cycle, due to defects discovered in code or changes in user requirements. It is critically important that appropriate controls be established to ensure that all affected configuration items be corrected according to established, approved change-control procedures.

One of the most vital decisions that a developer should take is the time at which code is to be brought under configuration control. General consensus seems to be that items of tested code should be brought under control immediately they are signed-off as completed, tested and documented, or released for further use.

In the case of documentation, it is suggested that once the customer has visibility of a document, or it ceases to be a draft, it should be placed under formal configuration control.

4.9 Process control This quality system element (described in AS 3901 as control of the manufacturing process) has no direct equivalent in a software development quality management system. Analogous activities are described in Clauses 4.4, 4.14 and 4.19 of this Standard.

4.10 Inspection and testing Either the developer or customer shall be responsible for providing test data, facilities and documentation needed to demonstrate conformance with the software product requirements, to the extent stated in the contract.

It is essential that test documentation, e.g. test plans, specifications and procedures, shall be produced and implemented so that satisfactory control of the quality of testing is achieved.

The developer shall identify all relevant quality assurance procedures related to inspection and testing. These procedures shall address the following:

(a) Test planning and its review.

(b) Test specifications and their review.

(c) Control of changes to software test plans and procedures.

(d) Conduct of testing and recording of results.

(e) Review and certification of test results.

(f) Appropriate inspection during all phases.

Guidance *Inspection and testing involves documentation and operation.*

The significant documentation items to be considered are test plans, specifications and procedures, which deal with test strategies and methods, as well as the design of test cases.

Test plans, specifications and procedures which allow for the adequate demonstration of contractual requirements have to be generated. The documentation of testing should be done in such a manner that results are at all times reproducible.

Errors in design and coding found during testing should be documented in software problem reports, and appropriate corrective action should be taken.

4.11 Inspection, measuring and test equipment This quality system element (described in AS 3901 as inspection, measuring and test equipment in a manufacturing environment) has no direct equivalent in a software development quality management system.

Analogous activities are described in Clauses 4.10, 4.19 and 4.21 of this Standard.

4.12 Inspection and test status This quality system element (described in AS 3901 as inspection and test status in a manufacturing environment) has no direct equivalent in a software development quality management system.

Analogous activities are described in Clauses 4.8, 4.10, 4.14 and 4.15 of this Standard.

4.13 Control of non-conforming product This quality system element (described in AS 3901 as physical control of non-conforming product in a manufacturing environment) has no direct equivalent in a software development quality management system.

Analogous activities are described in Clauses 4.8, 4.10, 4.14 and 4.15 of this Standard.

4.14 Corrective action The developer shall reference and document procedures for corrective action, including the following:

(a) Adoption of a system to report problems and deficiencies to the appropriate management level.

(b) Examination of problem and deficiency reports to determine their causes, and to propose corrective measures.

(c) Analysis of deficiency trends, to prevent the development of non-conforming software.

(d) Review of corrective measures, to determine their effectiveness.

(e) Provision for defining all necessary repetition of testing and reviews to determine the effectiveness of modifications to any item of software.

(f) Provision for ensuring that timely corrective action is taken by reviewing deficiencies and tracking their clearance.

Guidance *This Clause calls for the need to detect and correct not only non-conforming software, but also the faults in the development procedures and quality system that allowed this to occur. It is recognized that there are inherent limitations in software development that can result in non-conformance even under controlled conditions. However, the developer must have an effective system to detect, analyse and correct non-conforming software.*

The procedures to be applied in the detection, recording, tracking and correction of problems should be identified. The developer should apply procedures for the acceptance where necessary and control of software which does not conform to requirements.

The methods of reporting and analysing problems, and implementing corrective action, should be attended to. Additional procedures for tracking problems, trend analysis and reviews of the effectiveness of the corrective action program should be implemented.

4.15 Handling, storage, packaging and delivery

4.15.1 *General* The developer shall identify the procedures for protecting the integrity of the software to be delivered.

4.15.2 *Configuration status* The developer shall develop, adopt and maintain procedures to ensure the following:

(a) Correct identification and certification of the deliverable configuration.

(b) Assembly of the configuration on the appropriate medium.

4.15.3 *Packaging* The developer shall arrange for the packaging of software in order to ensure safe arrival at the destination.

4.15.4 *Marking* The developer shall arrange for the software to be marked for ready identification, to the extent required by the contract.

4.15.5 *Installation and other contractual services* Where installation and contractual services after delivery are involved, the developer shall provide procedures for the conduct of these activities.

Guidance *Procedures should include an independent check to ensure the right software modules at the correct issue status are included, and are authenticated by correlation with a listing from configuration control.*

Each physical software entity should be marked with its volume, name and issue together with any copyright restrictions.

Marking of external packing should include warning signs covering requirements against physical abuse, any scanning restrictions, the effects of stray radiation, and any special markings required to meet customs regulations.

4.16 Quality records The developer shall establish and maintain a system for identification, collection, cataloguing, filing, storage, maintenance and disposition of records.

The system shall require sufficient records to be maintained to demonstrate compliance with the requirements of, and effective operation of, the quality system. Pertinent sub-contractor records shall be an element of this data. All records shall be readable and identifiable with the product involved.

Records shall be stored and maintained in such a way that they are readily retrievable in facilities that provide a suitable environment to minimize deterioration or damage and to prevent loss.

The period of time for which records shall be retained will be determined by legislation, the contract, or developer policy.

Records shall be made available, when agreed on contractually, for evaluation by the customer or the customer's representative, for an agreed period.

Guidance *The developer should maintain records as objective evidence to substantiate that the system conforms to the requirements of the Standard and that the customer's quality requirements are being met.*

In order to provide objective evidence that quality has been achieved, it is necessary that all records produced in the attainment of quality be properly maintained and catalogued for future reference. These records should include minutes of reviews, quality system audit reports, test reports and change control documentation.

4.17 Internal quality audits The developer shall carry out a comprehensive system of planned and documented internal quality audits to verify whether quality activities comply with planned arrangements and to determine the effectiveness of the quality system.

Audits shall be scheduled on the basis of the status and importance of the activity.

The audits and follow-up actions shall be carried out in accordance with documented procedures.

The results of the audits shall be documented and brought to the attention of the personnel having responsibility in the area audited. The management personnel responsible for the area shall take timely corrective action on the deficiencies found by the audit (see Clause 4.1.3).

Guidance *The quality system should be subject to continued improvement and assessment of its effectiveness. In order to ensure this, the supplier's management should periodically and systematically conduct management reviews (see Clause 4.1.3) and internal quality audits.*

It is emphasized that such audits need to be systematic and not merely casual or superficial inquiries. The findings of the internal quality audits should be analysed to determine the actions necessary to maintain the system's effectiveness.

The internal quality audit should be a planned, purposeful and comprehensive examination of management objectives, assignment of duties, delegation of responsibilities and methods of operation.

Such audits are conducted by, or on behalf of, management to check that these objectives, delegations and methods are being complied with and are achieving the required results, to reveal defects or irregularities in any of the elements examined, to indicate possible improvements, and to identify discrepancies between actual practice and the quality system provisions described in the developer's quality manual.

Audits also serve as a check on management controls at all levels. They are also designed to uncover potential problems and to eliminate waste or unnecessary loss.

The audit should assess the actual operation of the system by reviewing work in progress, by checking documentation and records, and by evaluating the understanding of, and compliance with, the quality requirements by the management and the workforce. Records of the audit then provide objective evidence of the effectiveness of the quality system.

The requirement for management to conduct audits should not be interpreted to mean that top management has to conduct the audit personally. Although this may be the case in a small organization, in general this task will be delegated. It is important that the audit personnel are independent from the work being audited. In some cases delegation to an outside professional and unbiased agency, not subject to internal pressure, could be a more suitable arrangement.

To carry out an audit adequately, it is necessary to prepare procedures which define the conduct of the audit, who will perform the audit, what will be examined, how and where the audit will be done, to whom the results of the audit will be reported, and how any necessary corrective actions will be instituted. Audits should be conducted at intervals, depending on their demonstrated need. Some elements of the system will undoubtedly require more frequent auditing than others.

The developer should establish a schedule for audits and adjust it on the basis of previous results. Additional or unscheduled audits should be considered when significant changes have been made to the quality system, when major deficiencies are suspected, or when corrective actions require monitoring.

Audit personnel should be trained in the techniques of arranging and conducting audits. Wherever possible auditors should seek intended corrective actions for deficiencies detected, and note such intentions in the audit report, rather than simply reporting the deficiencies and highlighting the inadequacies of the area concerned.

4.18 Training The developer shall establish and maintain procedures for identifying the training needs of all staff performing activities affecting quality.

Staff shall have appropriate education, training and experience as are required for performing the specific assigned tasks. Training procedures should ensure that a suitable level of proficiency is achieved, maintained and recorded.

Guidance *Training needs of staff should encompass all environmental requirements (such as operating systems and languages), and techniques and procedures to be used both in the development of quality software, and in the application of quality management techniques. The training programs should include means of determining the effectiveness of the training. Developers should take note of the Training Guarantee Act.*

4.19 Software maintenance If software maintenance is specified in the contract, the developer shall establish and maintain post-commissioning support procedures for the identification of maintenance and enhancement methods. Such methods shall ensure the rectification of design errors as well as addressing the implementation of enhancements due to changes in documented requirements. Standards and procedures applied during software maintenance shall be consistent with the standards and procedures applied by the developer during software development.

Guidance *Software is subject to continual change throughout its life, both to rectify problems (referred to as 'maintenance') and to provide additional features or capabilities (referred to as 'enhancements'). These changes to a delivered system may be requested by a customer or may arise from reviews of this or other systems by the developer. In any case, it is important that appropriate quality management procedures are applied throughout the change process and that such procedures are not of a lesser standard than those that would be applied during the development process.*

When the testing system changes, the original system test cases should also be applied as necessary to ensure conformance to the originally accepted system.

4.20 Statistical techniques Where the developer chooses to use statistical techniques for verifying the acceptability of software characteristics, procedures used shall be documented appropriately.

4.21 Control of development environment The developer shall adopt, or develop and maintain, procedures for the control of the software development environment. These procedures shall include methods for—

(a) secure maintenance of libraries containing software under configuration control and the implementation of all changes;

(b) provision of authorized back-ups;

(c) proper identification, storage and handling of software media; and

(d) control of software support tools, techniques, and methodologies to be used. The extent and depth of testing for support software shall be defined.

Guidance *It is necessary to identify the environment that could be subject to change and where such changes could affect quality. Items that could constitute the development environment include the following:*

(i) Compilers.

(ii) Linkers.

(iii) Editors.

(iv) Development and target hardware.

(v) System software and support tools.

(vi) Communications hardware and software.

(vii) Test equipment.

To ensure the control of the software development environment, all operational and data centre procedures have to be documented and in place.